Literature
and
Ourselves

Literature
and
Ourselves

A Thematic Introduction
for Readers and Writers

FOURTH EDITION

GLORIA MASON HENDERSON
Gordon College

BILL DAY
Gordon College

SANDRA STEVENSON WALLER
Georgia Perimeter College

Longman

New York Boston San Francisco
London Toronto Sydney Tokyo Singapore Madrid
Mexico City Munich Paris Cape Town Hong Kong Montreal

Vice President and Editor-in-Chief: Joseph Terry
Acquisitions Editor: Erika Berg
Development Manager: Janet Lamphier
Development Editor: Katharine Glynn
Senior Marketing Manager: Melanie Craig
Senior Supplements Editor: Donna Campion
Production Manager: Ellen MacElree
Project Coordination, Text Design, and Electronic Page Makeup: Electronic
    Publishing Services Inc., NYC
Cover Design Manager: Wendy Ann Fredericks
Cover Designer: Kay Petronio
Cover Art: Monet, Claude (1840–1926). Waterlillies: Green Reflections. Detail of far
    left side. Room I, East wall. Musée de l'Orangerie, Paris, France. Reunion de
    Musées Nationaux/Art Resource, NY.
Photo Researcher: Photosearch, Inc.
Manufacturing Buyer: Lucy Hebard
Printer and Binder: R.R. Donnelley & Sons
Cover Printer: Coral Graphic Services

Library of Congress Cataloging-in-Publication Data
Literature and ourselves : a thematic introduction for readers and writers/Gloria
Mason Henderson, Bill Day, Sandra Stevenson Waller.—4th ed.
        p. cm.
    Includes index.
    ISBN 0-321-10216-9
        1. Literature—Collections. I. Henderson, Gloria Mason II. Day, William,
            Waller, Sandra Stevenson.
    PN6014.L5562 L58 2003
808.8—dc21   2002067899

Please visit our website at http://www.ablongman.com

ISBN 0-321-10216-9

3 4 5 6 7 8 9 10—DOC—05 04 03

Contents

THEMATIC ANTHOLOGY

FAMILY   46

MEN AND WOMEN   252

GRIEF AND LOSS   496

Writing about Grief and Loss 497

FREEDOM AND RESPONSIBILITY   816

IMAGINATION AND DISCOVERY   1024

QUEST   1278

Alternate Contents
by Genre

Essays

Fiction

Poetry

Drama

Preface

L *iterature and Ourselves: A Thematic Introduction for Readers and Writers* was written to speak to students' experiences, hopes, and ideas through a variety of selections representing a diversified panorama of authors and nationalities. Suitable for both freshman composition courses and introduction to literature courses, the new edition continues its dual emphasis on excellence and diversity. *Literature and Ourselves* treats literature as a continually expanding commentary on people's infinitely varied lives, helping students make the connection between literature and their own unique life stories. Each of the six themes—Family, Men and Women, Grief and Loss, Freedom and Responsibility, Imagination and Discovery, and Quest—progresses from the self outward. The Introduction overviews text-, author-, and reader-oriented approaches to literature, discusses elements of the four genres, and provides expanded guidance on writing about literature and the research paper. The expanded anthology, organized thematically, gives students a rich array of literature drawn from the finest writers of fiction, poetry, drama, and the essay.

New To This Edition

New Selections—Both Classic and Contemporary. Additions from the traditional canon include works such as Sophocles's *Antigone,* Shakespeare's *The Tempest,* Chaucer's "The Wife of Bath's Tale," Nathaniel Hawthorne's "The Birth-Mark," Abraham Lincoln's Gettysburg Address, Rudyard Kipling's "If," and F. Scott Fitzgerald's "Winter Dreams." The authors have also sought to strengthen the selection of essays by adding works of greater weight and seriousness for those instructors who want to assign more challenging readings for their students. New essays include a powerful essay by Czech playwright, dissident, and former president Vaclav Havel and thought-provoking essays by Paul Theroux and V.S. Naipaul. New fiction includes stories by highly regarded science fiction writers such as Isaac Asimov, Zenna Henderson, Ray Bradbury, Margaret Atwood, and Mark Bourne as well as a disturbingly grotesque satire, "A Story for Children" by Svava Jakobsdóttir.

New Casebooks. Three new casebooks have been added. Each casebook offers both original works by a noted author and critical analyses of these works. These readings give students a way to write documented literary analysis essays before they have progressed to longer papers using library and Internet research.

- **Casebook on Amy Tan: Writing about Vulnerability** offers students a chance to read and write about the lives and relationships between mothers and their daughters.
- **Casebook on Tim O'Brien: Writing about War** is a longer casebook that includes some of the most provocative, heartfelt war stories ever written. These stories explore the question of how to determine the truth between reality and perception.
- **Casebook on Joyce Carol Oates: Writing about Illusion and Reality** includes a longtime favorite story, " Where Are You Going, Where Have You Been," along with a very new story, "Valentine." These stories examine Oates's dreamlike—sometimes nightmarish—accounts of the experiences of two young girls.

The three new casebooks join the three casebooks kept from the third edition which include Casebook on August Wilson's play *Fences:* Writing about Relationships; Casebook on Emily Dickinson, Robert Frost, and Langston Hughes: Writing about Love and Gender; and Casebook on Flannery O'Connor: Writing about Faith. All six casebooks provide both original works and essays on eight major writers and cover the genres of drama, poetry, and short stories.

New Thematic Units. The thematic introductions have been strengthened by making more connections between the selections and by more specifically framing the theme's topics for students. A new unit on Grief and Loss replaces Human Vulnerability with a new casebook on Amy Tan and new anthology selections from John McCrae, Shirley Geok-lin Lim, and Adam Zagajewski. A new theme, Imagination and Discovery, replaces the Art and Language unit to better showcase the expanded focus of the unit. While the unit still stresses the use of language in creation, it now includes other forms of imaginative literature. The major additions are stories from science fiction; Shakespeare's *The Tempest,* one of the most significant works of imagination in the history of literature; and the Casebook on Joyce Carol Oates.

Improved Questions and Writing Assignments. Questions and writing assignments have been thoroughly revised to mirror the book's organization of moving from exploration of the self outward. These questions and writing assignments help students build confidence and think critically.

New Focus on Film. As a growing number of instructors use film in their classroom, we have added a section at the end of each theme, titled Writing about Film, which asks students to apply the knowledge gained from studying literature to the study of film. Students are asked to make connections between films they have seen and the literature they have read. Appendix B, Writing about Film, gives helpful support to instructors and students as they explore this new related genre.

The Organization

The themes were chosen to engage students in exploring their own lives through literature. Each thematic section includes literature from all four genres—fiction, poetry, drama, and the essay—and balances classic with contemporary selections. Casebooks on selected authors provide a context for writing short research papers about literature and build toward full-length research papers for instructors who cover the research paper in their course. Additional writing suggestions for each section further emphasize the link between reading and writing about literature. An appendix briefly discusses some of the major approaches to literature; another appendix includes the MLA Documentation Guidelines. A glossary defines all literary terms mentioned in both the introductions and the questions.

The six thematic units are arranged so that they progress outward from the self to concerns beyond the self. Since they also move from the concrete to the abstract, they become progressively more challenging. The sections are designed to form a coherent whole with selections that constitute a rich and varied commentary on the theme. Themes help support first-year students to build confidence in their study of literature. End-of-selection questions are written to reflect this same progression.

Each section begins with a brief introduction and a discussion about writing about that theme. Within thematic sections, selections are ordered by genre; within genres, selections are ordered chronologically. An instructor may choose to concentrate on one or two themes or assign the entire book in a semester-long course in introduction to literature or in a second-semester composition course.

We think we have packed an extraordinary variety of works into a relatively small anthology. The traditional works allow instructors to assign what they are familiar with, and new works allow them to share with their students the joy of discovery. The selections also represent a variety of cultures, including works by authors from around the world. Our text is unusually rich in questions both in number and in variety for discussion and suggestions for writing. Questions follow every work, and suggestions for exploration and writing follow nearly all, with some works having as many as six or seven of each. The questions and suggestions promote critical thinking not only about literature but also about students' own experiences. Our approach, then, is inductive, encouraging students to learn and develop their own ideas as they read.

Unlike many freshman literature anthologies which emphasize text over author and reader, *Literature and Ourselves* includes many author-oriented and reader-oriented questions as well as text-oriented ones. Students are encouraged to see the works as commentaries on their own lives and to bring their own experience to bear on what they read and write. They also are encouraged to analyze and evaluate their own experience based on what they read. We hope that, as a result, students will develop a lifelong appreciation of literature and come to view it as intimately connected to their lives.

Resources for Students and Instructors

Instructor's Manual (0-321-10775-6). An Instructor's Manual with detailed comments and suggestions for teaching each selection is available. Written by the authors, this important resource also contains references to critical articles and books that we have found helpful.

Literature and Ourselves **Website** <www.ablongman.com/henderson> The Companion Website offers a wealth of resources for students and instructors. Students can access resources for authors and in-depth information on casebook authors, as well as helpful links to literature and research sites.

Coursecompass Generic Site. Longman English Resources for Introduction to Literature, Fiction, Creative Writing, and Drama Access Code Card, Second Edition (0-321-14311-6) (Blackboard Content: 0-321-14313-2). This course provides a number of guides that will help students analyze literature, evaluate plays, critique and write about literature, and conduct research on-line. This course also includes a journal for writing about literature as well as a journal for creative writing. Instructors will find various additional resources, such as guides to teaching literature on-line and teaching multicultural literature. Available FREE when value-packed with *Literature and Ourselves.*

MLA Documentation Style: A Concise Guide for Students (0-321-10337-8). Replete with examples and clear explanations, this straightforward and accessible manual helps students understand and properly use the basic principles of MLA documentation. This brief guide includes information students need to properly cite works, avoid plagiarism, and format their papers. Available FREE when value-packed with *Literature and Ourselves.*

Glossary of Literary and Critical Terms (0-321-12691-2). A quick, reliable, and portable resource, this easy-to-use glossary includes definitions, explanations, and examples for over 100 Literary and Critical terms which students commonly encounter in their readings or hear in their lectures and class discussions. Available FREE when value-packed with *Literature and Ourselves.*

Literature Timeline (0-321-14315-9). This accessible and visually appealing timeline provides students with a chronological overview of the major literary works that have been written throughout history. In addition, the timeline also lists the major sociocultural and political events that had occurred contemporaneously with these major works of literature. Available FREE when value-packed with *Literature and Ourselves.*

Responding to Literature: A Writer's Journal (0-321-09542-1). This free journal provides students with their own personal space for writing. Helpful writing prompts for responding to fiction, poetry, and drama are also included. Available FREE when value-packed with *Literature and Ourselves.*

Evaluating a Performance (0-321-09541-3). Perfect for the student assigned to review a local production, this free supplement offers students a convenient place to record their evaluation. Useful tips and suggestions of things to consider when evaluating a production are included. Available FREE when value-packed with *Literature and Ourselves.*

Analyzing Literature, Second Edition (0-321-09338-0). This brief supplement provides critical reading strategies, writing advice, and sample student papers to help students interpret and discuss literary works in a variety of genres. Suggestions for collaborative activities and on-line research on literary topics are also featured, as well as numerous exercises and writing assignments. Available FREE when value-packed with *Literature and Ourselves.*

iSearch Guide for English (0-321-12411-1). A guide to online research. Featuring the Longman Internet Guide and access to the ContentSelect Research Database, each iSearch guide gives students and instructors instant access to thousands of academic journals and periodicals any time from any computer with an Internet connection. With helpful tips on the writing process, on-line research, and finding and citing valid sources, starting the research process has never been easier! Available FREE when value-packed with *Literature and Ourselves.*

Merriam-Webster Collegiate Dictionary (0-87779-709-9). This hardcover comprehensive dictionary is available at a significant discount when packaged with any Longman text.

The English Pages Website (http://www.ablongman.com/englishpages). This website provides professors and students with resources for reading, writing, and research practice in four areas: composition, literature, technical writing, and basic skills. Features include simulated searches; first-person essays that show students how everyday men and women have applied what they have learned in composition to a wide variety of situations; and annotated links that provide the best information on the widest variety of writing issues and research topics.

Penguin Discount Novel Program. In cooperation with Penguin Putnam, Inc., one of our sibling companies, Longman is proud to offer a variety of Penguin paperbacks at a significant discount when packaged with any Longman title. Excellent additions to any literature course, Penguin titles give students the opportunity to explore contemporary and classical fiction and drama. The available titles include works by authors as diverse as Toni Morrison, Julia Alvarez, Mary Shelley, and Shakespeare. To review the complete list of titles available, visit the Longman-Penguin-Putnam website: **http://www.ablongman.com/penguin.**

The Longman Printed Testbank for Literature   (0-321-14312-4). This printed testbank features various objective questions on the major works of Fiction, Short Fiction, Poetry, and Drama. A versatile and handy resource, this easy-to-use Testbank can be used for all quizzing and testing needs. (Electronic version also available—see CDs).

Teaching Literature On-line, Second Edition   (0-321-10618-0). Concise and practical, Teaching Literature On-line provides instructors with strategies and advice for incorporating elements of computer technology into the literature classroom.

Video Program. For qualified adopters, an impressive selection of videotapes is available to enrich students' experience of literature. Contact your Longman sales representative.

Acknowledgments

Our preparation of this text would not have been possible without the invaluable help of a number of people. Our Acquisitions Editor, Erika Berg, shared with us her enthusiasm for the book and encouraged us to make the contents even better. We are again deeply indebted to our Development Editor, Katharine Glynn, for sharing her wonderful ideas and keeping us organized and on task. Jennifer Mazurkie, our Production Editor, was both efficient and unfailingly cheerful in working with us.

We are also deeply indebted to many colleagues at Gordon College and Georgia Perimeter College. We want to thank Dr. Mary Alice Money, Chair of the Division of Humanities at Gordon College, Dr. Sherman Day, Interim President of Gordon College from June 2001 through March 2002, and Dr. Laurence V. Weill, President of Gordon College, for their encouragement and support. We also thank our colleagues on the English faculties at both colleges for their ideas and suggestions. At Gordon College, Drs. Anna Dunlap Higgins, Jason Horn, David Janssen, Greg McNamara, Steve Rainey, Ed Whitelock, and Rhonda Wilcox shared with us their enthusiasm about the book and suggested works that added both diversity and excellence. Beth Pye, Reference Librarian at Gordon, and Brett Cox, English Professor at Norwich University, shared their love of science fiction and made invaluable suggestions about science fiction stories to add to the contents.

At Georgia Perimeter College, we would like to thank Dr. Dennis Harkins, the provost of Clarkston campus, and Virginia Carson, former academic dean of the Clarkston campus and now Vice President of Academic Affairs at Floyd College, for their encouragement. The English faculty at Georgia Perimeter was especially helpful in making suggestions for works to include in the six units. In particular, we thank Drs. Tim Tarkington, Ellen Barker, Mike Hall, and Mark Nunes. Adrienne Scott and Jason Grant, part of the office staff, were especially helpful in making copies of new works being considered for the book.

We also wish to thank Dr. Michael Montgomery of Life College in Atlanta for suggesting works that we have added in each edition. A special thanks to Patrick McCord for writing the questions on film at the end of each thematic unit and the appendix on Writing about Film.

Finally we wish to thank our reviewers for their astute observations, constructive criticism, and valuable suggestions: Kirk D. Adams, Tarrant City Junior College; Carolyn Baker, San Antonio College; Edith Blicksilver, Georgia Tech; John Clark, Bowling Green University; Carolyn Baker, San Antonio College; Corla Dawson, Missouri Western State College; Jason De Polo, North Carolina Agriculture and Technical State University; Thomas Dukes, University of Akron; Lauri Fitzgerald, Madison Area Technical College; Elinor Flewellen, Santa Barbara City College; Jim Hauser, William Patterson University; Kristi Larkin Havens, University of Tennessee-Knoxville; Carol Haviland, California State University at San Bernardino; Katherine Griffin, Tuskegee University; Dr. Gwendolyn Jones, Tuskegee University; Lew Kamm, University of Massachusetts, Dartmouth; Brian Keener, New York Technical College; Martha Kendall, San Jose City College; Mary Klayder, University of Kansas; Lois Marchino, University of Texas-El Paso; John Marino, St. Charles County Community College; Ann V. Miller, Baylor University; B. Keith Murphy, Fort Valley State University; John O'Connor, George Mason University; Esther Panitz, William Patterson College of New Jersey; Linda Peevy, Louisiana College; Elaine Razzano, Lyndon State College; Peggy Richards, University of Akron; Glenn Sadler, Bloomsburg State University; Al Sawyer, Richard J. Daly College; Walter Shear, Pittsburgh State University; Kay Smith, Valencia Community College West; Rita Sturm, Santa Fe Community College; Marcy L. Tanter, Tarleton State University; Jim Wallace, University of Akron; and Gladys Willis, Lincoln University.

Gloria Mason Henderson
Bill Day
Sandra Stevenson Waller

Literature
and
Ourselves

Introduction

Literature

Literature is an art form whose medium is language, oral and written. It differs from ordinary spoken or written language primarily in three ways: (1) it is concentrated and meaningful (even when it sometimes denies meaning); (2) its purpose is not simply to explain, argue, or make a point but rather to give a sense of pleasure in the discovery of a new experience; (3) it demands intense concentration from readers. Literature, as defined and included in this text, falls into four large classes or **genres: essays, fiction, poetry,** and **drama.**

Literature is not only about ideas but also about experiences. It communicates what it feels like to undergo an experience, whether physical or emotional. A psychiatrist, in writing a case study of a patient, concentrates strictly on the facts. Though the doctor may give readers an understanding of the patient, he or she does not attempt to make readers feel what it is like to be that patient. In fact, the psychiatrist must strive to remain strictly objective, as should the readers. Writers of essays, fiction, drama, and poetry, however, may try to put their readers inside the mind of such a character, making readers intimately share the patient's experience and feel what it is like to be the patient. In interpreting literature, readers may adopt one or more of three basic approaches: text-oriented approaches, artist-oriented approaches, and reader-oriented approaches.

Text-Oriented Approaches

Adopting a text-oriented approach, a reader may analyze a work of literature as complete in itself without relating it to the outside world. This approach, which was fashionable from about 1920 to 1950, dominates many freshman literature anthologies. It finds expression in the line "a poem should not mean but be" from Archibald MacLeish's poem "Ars poetica." In its extreme form, this approach insists that the author's life and time as well as readers' responses to his or her work are not only unnecessary, but irrelevant. The kind of close analysis and attention to words and their contexts that this method requires can be very useful, both in illuminating a literary work and in teaching students to read carefully and critically. Consequently, this book emphasizes a text-oriented approach in the introductions to the four genres and in many of the questions for discussion and suggestions for exploration and writing that follow anthologized works.

Writing suggestions that require analysis of **tone, theme, plot,** or **character** are text-oriented. For example, one question about Patricia Grace's "It Used to Be Green Once" asks, "What is the speaker's attitude toward the poverty she endured as a child?" In asking about character, the question requires only an analysis of various passages in the story. A text-oriented question about Wilfred Owen's "Dulce et Decorum Est" requires the reader to contrast the patriotic last line to the first stanza. This question requires only a close examination of the poem itself.

Author-Oriented Approaches

Adopting an author-oriented approach, a reader may study an author's life, time, and culture to better understand the author's work. This approach requires research. A reader might, for example, in studying *Othello,* research the roles of women in Renaissance Venice and Elizabethan England in order to understand Othello's expectations of Desdemona. In addition to historical and biographical research, research on other literature, myths, rituals, and art forms can illuminate a work. Other works by the author being studied, including letters, statements of artistic purpose, and reviews, can also enhance a reader's understanding of a work. Many of the questions and suggestions in the casebooks require an author-oriented approach. Chinua Achebe's essay "Africa and Her Writers" applies a variation of an author-oriented approach in an especially interesting way to the Yoruban art festival called *mbari.*

Reader-Oriented Approaches

Each reader brings a unique set of experiences and expectations to literature. In its extreme form, the reader-oriented approach argues that a work of literature is recreated each time it is read; that it is produced by the reading, perceiving, imagining mind of the reader; and that, consequently, any reading of a work is valid. Certainly a range of interpretation, some of it conditioned by the reader's particular expectations, is not only valid, but desirable. Men and women, for example, are likely to react differently to such works as *Othello* and Bobby Ann Mason's "Shiloh." Similarly, atheists, Jews, evangelical Christians, and persons of other religious perspectives will react differently to the stories of Flannery O'Connor; the poems of Judith Ortiz Cofer, Gerard Manley Hopkins, and William Butler Yeats; and the plays of August Wilson and Terrence McNally. Quite fashionable today, reader-oriented interpretation is far from new. The writers of the New Testament, for example, read and reinterpreted Old Testament scripture in the light of Jesus' life and ministry.

Some of the questions for discussion and suggestions for exploration and writing in this text require a reader-oriented approach in conjunction with a text-oriented approach. For example, a text-oriented question on Ursula LeGuin's "The Ones Who Walk Away from Omelas," which asks about the details that make Omelas a Utopia, is immediately followed by the reader-oriented question "How does LeGuin involve the reader in making her description of Omelas believable?" The latter question requires readers to examine their own response, then return to the text to analyze the sources of that response.

Since one function of literature is to expose us to other people's experience, we should be open to others' interpretations as well as our own. This is not to say, however, that all interpretations are equal in value or even that all are valid. The most satisfying readings of literature may incorporate all three approaches, and all three apply equally to the four genres of literature included in this anthology.

Essays

The word **essay** as used in this text refers to a short, unified work of nonfiction prose. Included in this anthology are many kinds of essays, such as **expository essays, argumentative essays, sermons, epistolary essays, biographical essays, critical essays, personal essays,** and even essays excerpted from books. These categories are not mutually exclusive, and a single essay may fit more than one category. The most common are expository essays, argumentative essays, and personal essays. The primary purpose of an **expository essay** is to inform or explain; examples of such essays include Stephen Hawking's "Conclusion" to *A Brief History of Time* and Mark Mathabane's "The Road to Alexandra," both excerpts from books. In an **argumentative essay,** the writer tries to convince an audience to agree with his or her position on an issue; the Declaration of Independence and Martin Luther King Jr.'s "Letter from Birmingham City Jail" are argumentative essays. The vast majority of essays in this anthology are **personal essays,** which, as their name implies, reveal much about their authors. Examples of personal essays include Joan Didion's "On Going Home," Faye Moskowitz's "Jewish Christmas," and Annie Dillard's "Heaven and Earth in Jest."

Perhaps because they do not present fictional, imagined worlds but explore facts and ideas, essays are often neglected in literature textbooks. Unlike stories and plays, essays do not ordinarily develop characters or plots. They may contain well-developed portraits of actual human beings and may even tell stories, but these portraits and stories usually develop and are subordinate to an idea.

Theme

The reader of an essay must understand its **theme,** or main idea, and the various subpoints and examples that develop the theme. In expository and argumentative essays, the theme is usually quite clear. There is little question about the main idea of the Declaration of Independence or of King's "Letter from Birmingham City Jail." In personal essays like most of the ones in this anthology, the theme may be more subtly and obliquely stated, hence more difficult to comprehend. Often, a reader can find no **thesis,** no single sentence or group of sentences that fairly summarize the author's theme.

In addition to understanding an essayist's theme, a reader must understand how an essay is **unified,** how every part of the essay develops its theme. Chinua Achebe, for example, in "Africa and Her Writers" describes *mbari,* a festival practiced by the Igbo people of Nigeria in which selected members of the tribe work with skilled artists to fill a house with art. Achebe uses *mbari* to exemplify the interdependence of art and the people who produce it. In the Declaration of Independence, Thomas Jefferson lists the colonists' many grievances against the English king. This list has a purpose in Jefferson's argument: to demonstrate that the king has violated the unwritten contract between governments and the people they govern. In "Heaven and Earth in Jest," Annie Dillard's many precisely observed details illustrate her point: that nature is governed by a powerful unseen spirit, one that violently "pummels us," but that also delights us with moments of extraordinary grace and beauty. Thus, a good essay is unified; all its details and ideas develop its theme.

Tone

Tone may be defined as an author's attitude toward his or her subject. In some essays, the tone may be so personal that readers come to feel they know the author intimately. Among the essays on home and family included in this text, Frances Mayes's *"Bramare"* brims with enthusiasm over buying a new home, an eighteenth-century villa in Tuscany, whereas Didion's "On Going Home" is regretful over lost intimacy with her family. Even in Martin Luther King Jr.'s "Letter from Birmingham City Jail," the carefully measured, calmly reasoning tone becomes an integral part of the argument.

In reading or writing about an essay, then, a reader must consider not only the author's main idea but also his or her distinctive tone. Is he or she gently humorous or bitingly satiric, nostalgic or regretful, angry or forgiving, calmly controlled or awestruck? Like theme, tone helps to unify an essay. A reader should see how particular details form a pattern, thereby developing the theme and creating a tone appropriate to it.

Imagery

Essayists frequently use **images,** combinations of words that create pictures. In "Heaven and Earth in Jest," Annie Dillard's gruesome image of a frog, its body sucked dry by a giant water bug, its "skin formless as a pricked balloon," develops her idea of the extraordinary violence of nature and suggests her wonder at that violence.

Diction

A good essayist chooses words very carefully, paying particular attention to their **connotations,** their suggested or implied meanings, as opposed to their **denotations,** or explicit meanings. Consider, for example, the word *delicate* in the following passage from Annie Dillard's "Heaven and Earth in Jest": "When I cross again the bridge [. . .], the wind has thinned to the delicate air of twilight." The word *delicate* refers to something very fine and pleasing, fragile, or sensitive; none of these denotations seems to cover Dillard's meaning. As Dillard uses it, the word seems to connote air more than usually transparent, a breeze whose touch is so soft and gentle as to be barely felt.

An essayist's **level of diction,** his or her choice of words that are slangy or formal, unfamiliar or common, should also be appropriate to his or her theme and tone. The elevated diction of the Declaration of Independence and of Martin Luther King's "Letter from Birmingham City Jail" reinforces the seriousness of those documents.

Syntax

Finally, **syntax,** the patterns of an author's sentences, may develop his or her theme and tone. An author's sentences may be predominantly short and simple, even abrupt; or they may be predominantly long, ornate, and complex. The long, complex sentences of the Declaration of Independence suggest the logical relationships between ideas in a serious and carefully reasoned document. The long opening sentence is an example:

> When in the course of human events, it becomes necessary for one people to dissolve the political bands which have connected them with another, and to assume among the powers of the earth, the separate and equal station to which the Laws of Nature and Nature's God entitle them, a decent respect to the opinions of mankind requires that they should declare the causes which impel them to the separation.

Here the many subordinate clauses and phrases, including the long opening clause beginning with *when,* precisely define the logical dependence of one idea on another. Every part of the very long sentence is logically related to every other part.

Tone, imagery, diction, and syntax, then, develop the theme of an essay. In the following passage from Martin Luther King's "Letter from Birmingham Jail," all four work together:

> I guess it is easy for those who have never felt the stinging darts of segregation to say "Wait." But when you have seen vicious mobs lynch your mothers and fathers at will and drown your sisters and brothers at whim; when you have seen hate-filled policemen curse, kick, brutalize and even kill your black brothers and sisters with impunity; when you see the vast majority of your twenty million Negro brothers smothering in an airtight cage of poverty in the midst of an affluent society; when you suddenly find your tongue twisted and your speech stammering as you seek to explain to your six-year-old daughter why she can't go to the public amusement park that has just been advertised on television, and see tears welling up in her little eyes when she is told that Funtown is closed to colored children, and see the depressing clouds of inferiority begin to form in her little mental sky [. . .]; then you will know why we cannot wait.

Here the brutal images of oppression, the very formal diction, and the long parallel clauses all work together to create a tone of great weight, of intensely dignified seriousness.

REVIEW: READING AND ANALYZING ESSAYS

Theme
1. What is the author's theme? Is it simple enough to summarize in a sentence, or will it require several sentences?
2. How do the author's subpoints and examples develop his or her theme?

Tone
1. How would you describe the essay's tone?
2. How does the essay's tone help develop its theme?

Imagery
1. How does the writer's use of imagery contribute to the theme and tone of the essay?
2. What kinds of images does the essay contain? Are there images of animals? of violence? of religion?
3. How do the various images relate to one another?

Diction
1. What highly connotative words does the writer choose?
2. Is the essay's diction elevated, vulgar, simple, obscure?
3. How does the writer's diction contribute to the theme and tone of the essay?

Syntax
1. Is the writer's syntax complex and elaborate, simple, precise?
2. How does the writer's syntax contribute to the theme and tone of the essay?

Fiction

The short story is a relatively new form, although short fiction has long been a source of enjoyment and instruction in such forms as **parables, fables,** and **anecdotes** or **jokes. Fiction** is often thought of as the opposite of fact, but it may be based on facts and certainly can include factual material. A work described as fiction should be a **narrative;** that is, it should tell about a sequence of events. In addition, calling a work fiction denotes that it has **unity,** that all of its parts cohere. Short stories differ from other forms of short fiction in purpose. Parables and fables teach a lesson or a moral; anecdotes generally illustrate a point; and jokes entertain through humor. Furthermore, anecdotes and jokes, and even parables and fables, usually lack the complicated plots or the structure of most short stories. The longest form of fiction, the **novel,** is not included in this text precisely because of its prohibitive length, but most novels are made up of the same elements as short stories. The primary difference is length. In fact, readers sometimes disagree about whether a piece of fiction is a long short story, a **novella** or **novelette** (both terms used for short novels), or a novel. Because of the brevity of the short story, the writer should make every word and every scene an integral part of the creation.

Reading short stories with real understanding and appreciation is demanding. This kind of appreciation often requires at least three readings: a first reading of the story to enjoy the plot; a second reading to analyze its individual elements; and a third reading to see how those elements work together to create a cohesive, integrated whole. These elements include **point of view, setting, style, character, plot,** and **theme.**

Point of View
Point of view, the focus from which the story is told, is a crucial element; for it determines what we know about the characters and the action. The **omniscient,** all-knowing, point of view allows the author, writing in third person, to tell readers what any or all of the characters think or do.

The **first-person** point of view allows readers to see the action through the eyes of one character and to know only that character's thoughts. That character may be the main character or a minor character. When the author uses first person point of view, readers must decide whether the narrator is reliable or unreliable, whether the reader can trust him or her to tell the truth or even to understand the truth. An unreliable narrator may be too young or too slow-witted to perceive the truth, or he or she may select or alter details in order to present a biased account. For example, by using a biased and unreliable narrator, an author may effectively create irony or humor, as in Tim O'Brien's "The Man I Killed." One very popular first-person point of view in modern literature is that of a child whose innocence and lack of knowledge allow readers to draw their own conclusions or that of an adult remembering his or her childhood experiences and drawing adult conclusions, as in Truman Capote's "A Christmas Memory."

In the **third-person-limited** point of view, the author tells readers the thoughts of only one character and follows that character throughout the action. Carson McCullers uses this point of view when she follows Martin throughout "A Domestic Dilemma," telling only his thoughts and his theories about the causes of Emily's behavior rather than letting readers into her mind. When using third-person-limited point of view, as in first person, authors select the character who can reveal the information they want told in the story but who will not know the information they want withheld from readers. Finally, the author may write from the **objective** point of view. He may simply describe observable events.

Setting

The **setting** of a story—the time, place, and culture in which the action occurs—may be extremely significant. Time, place, and culture are integral elements in James Baldwin's "Sonny's Blues," for neither the music nor the racial relationships would be the same in another setting. Kurt Vonnegut's "Harrison Bergeron" takes place in the United States in 2081, a setting that is essential because the story depicts the ultimate fulfillment of the constitutional guarantee of equality. Ursula LeGuin's "The Ones Who Walk Away from Omelas" gains universality by taking place in some unknown mythic time and place.

Style

Style—the selection of words (**diction**); sentence structure (**syntax**); figurative devices, such as **simile** and **metaphor;** and **symbolism**—sets the **tone** and reflects the individuality of each author. Some writers use fairly simple, straightforward sentences, especially if they are using a first-person narrator who is unsophisticated. In "A Christmas Memory," Capote's adult narrator, remembering his childhood friendship and writing in present tense as if he were still a child, uses simple sentences like "Imagine a morning in late November" and "Queenie [the dog] tries to eat an angel." However, he combines childhood delight with adult perception and style when he vividly describes shelling pecans: "A cheery crunch, scraps of miniature thunder sound as the shells collapse and the golden mound of sweet oily ivory meat mounts in the milk-glass bowl." Some writers, like William Faulkner, use styles that are extremely complex and often almost poetic. They employ many of the metaphorical devices and sometimes even the rhythmical effects that readers expect from poetry.

The author's selection of descriptive details or his or her inclusion of a scene in a story may seem casual but seldom is. For example, in "A Good Man Is Hard to Find," Flannery O'Connor's vivid description of the grandmother's apparel as the family leaves home subtly reveals character and foreshadows the end of the story. While the other members of the family dress comfortably, the grandmother wears a "navy blue straw sailor hat with a bunch of white violets on the brim and a navy blue dress with a small white dot in the print," believing that "anyone seeing her dead on the highway would know at once that she was a lady." Similarly, the scene at Red Sammy's Barbecue, which at first glance may seem unimportant, further reveals the grandmother's character as she describes the cheating Red Sammy as a "good man." The scene also prepares readers for her reaction to the Misfit in the conclusion.

Similes, metaphors, and **personification** are elements of style that can make description more vivid and aid in interpretation. In Philip Roth's "The Conversion of the Jews," to Ozzie, who is standing on the roof,

> it looked as though Rabbi Binder was trying to tug the fireman's head out of his body, like a cork from a bottle. He had to giggle at the picture they made: it was a family portrait—rabbi in black

skullcap, fireman in red fire hat, and the little yellow hydrant squatting beside like a kid brother, bareheaded.

In O'Connor's "A Good Man Is Hard to Find," the simile describing the forest "like a dark open mouth" foreshadows the death of the family in the woods.

A **symbol** stands for both the thing it names and something else. Some symbols are almost universal: light is often used to symbolize a growth in knowledge, a realization, or enlightenment. Other elements are symbolic only in the particular context of the story and may be interpreted differently by different readers. For example, the tiny hand on Georgiana's cheek in Nathaniel Hawthorne's "The Birthmark" may symbolize her humanity or, as it does to Aylmer, her one imperfection.

All elements of style help the author create the tone of the story, the author's attitude toward the work, or the mood. The ominous and foreboding atmosphere of Charlotte Perkins Gilman's "The Yellow Wallpaper," for example, is emphasized by the unusual alliterative sounds with which the narrator describes her perceptions: "The color is repellent, almost revolting: a smouldering unclean yellow, strangely faded by the slow-turning sunlight. It is a dull yet lurid orange in some places, a sickly sulphur tint in others." The description seems to be hissing at the reader. Similarly, the short, choppy paragraphs reflect the narrator's thought patterns as she approaches insanity.

Character

Character refers to the people authors create to inhabit their stories. Characters should be believable and consistent. Being believable means not that all characters be like people we have known but that they be believable in the context of the story. Consistency requires not that the characters remain exactly the same, but that any changes in character be sufficiently motivated by what happens to them in the story. Authors may reveal characters in a variety of ways: by telling about them directly, by letting their actions and speech reveal their personalities, or by having other characters tell about them.

The major characters are usually **round characters;** that is, their personalities are well developed and believable. These characters frequently change as the story progresses; if they do, they are also described as **dynamic.** Minor characters often are **flat characters:** we see only one aspect of their personalities, presumably because the author does not need to reveal more about them for the purposes of the story. Flat characters are usually **static** characters; that is, they do not change. In F. Scott Fitzgerald's "Winter Dreams," Irene is a flat and static character; Dexter, the main character, is both round and dynamic.

Plot

The most apparent element of most short stories is the **plot,** the pattern of the action. A story has a beginning, a middle, and an end. The beginning of the story may not be the beginning of the action, for the story may begin at some high point in the action and use **flashback** or some other technique to fill in the information necessary for an understanding of the situation. If readers are to comprehend the plot of a story, the beginning must include **exposition,** information about the setting and the characters. The middle of the story presents a complication or conflict—within the main character, between the character and some force in nature, or between characters. This conflict builds until the story reaches a **climax,** a peak of action or suspense. The end presents the **resolution,** a solution or unraveling of the conflict, sometimes called the **denouement.** In modern stories, the ending seldom resolves all of the problems faced by the characters; however, the ending should include a sense of completion and an increase in the characters' or at least the readers' knowledge. In James Baldwin's "Sonny's Blues," the exposition begins simultaneously with the complication when the narrator reads in a newspaper article that his brother Sonny has been arrested on a drug charge. This shock triggers a flashback: the narrator's memory of the first time Sonny tried heroin. The complication continues with Sonny's release and return to Harlem and with further flashbacks describing their mother's advice and her account of a parallel situation faced by their father and uncle. The death of the narrator's little girl marks a turning point in the narrator's understanding of human suffering. The climax and resolution occur at the nightclub when the narrator sees Sonny in his element and, for the first time, really listens to Sonny's music.

Theme
Perhaps surprisingly, theme may be the most difficult aspect of a short story to identify. The **theme** is the major idea of the story. Readers often disagree about a story's theme. One reader may believe the theme of Carson McCullers's "A Domestic Dilemma" is the ways in which the complexities of love can serve as traps; another reader may say that the theme is that modern mobility may cause insecurity; a third reader might say that the theme is the conflict between love for a spouse and love for one's children.

While we may disagree about themes, a story without a theme usually seems trivial. We expect the author of a short story to use style, plot, and character to offer us insight into human behavior, to leave us feeling as if we have learned something about our world and about ourselves. This new insight may be repugnant or inspirational, sad or delightful; it may make us aware of human bestiality or nobility, of the wonders of friendship, or of the complexities of love. Whatever it says to readers and however they respond, the theme is the heart of the short story, its reason for being.

The following questions provide a general guide to reading and writing about short stories. Specific guidance follows each short story in the anthology.

Review: Reading and Writing about Short Stories

Point of View
1. What is the point of view in the story?
2. If it is first person or third person limited, through which character do readers see the story? Is the character a reliable or an unreliable narrator? How does his or her personality affect the perception of other characters and of the action?
3. Could the story be written just as effectively or more effectively from another point of view? If so, how and why? If not, why not?

Setting
1. Where and when does the story take place?
2. How does the author let readers know the time and place?
3. Could the story take place in any other time or place?

Style
1. What kind of sentence structure does the author seem to prefer in this story? Could the sentences be described as simple or complex? Are the language and sentence structure dictated by the point of view? By the subject? If so, how?
2. What kind of imagery does the author use? Does the language seem poetic? Examine any examples of similes, metaphors, or personification to see if they give clues about characters or foreshadow later actions or events.
3. Look for any symbols in the story, both symbols that are universally accepted and symbols that are particular to the story. What do they represent in the story, and how do they enrich its meaning?
4. What is the tone of the story? How is it reflected in the attitudes expressed or the connotations of words?

Character
1. Are the characters in the story believable? Why or why not?
2. How are the characters revealed: through what the author says about them, through what the other characters say about them, and/or through what they say and do?
3. Which characters are round characters?
4. Which characters are flat characters? Does their lack of development affect the success of the story? If so, in what way?
5. Do any of the characters develop or change in the story? Is this change one of the major points of the story?

Plot
1. What is the conflict in the story? When does the reader first realize there is a conflict?
2. List the steps in the development of the conflict. If possible, identify them as exposition, complication, crisis, climax, and resolution.

3. Where does the conflict reach a climax?
4. What is the resolution of the conflict?

Theme

1. What is the theme of the story? If possible, state it in one sentence.
2. How do the elements of the story work together to convey the theme?
3. Does the main character reach an epiphany or make a significant decision?
4. Did the theme provide an insight or understanding that is new to you? Does the theme relate to insights you have had?
5. Could the author have conveyed the same idea just as effectively in an essay? Why or why not?

Poetry

Unlike essays and short stories, poems are written in verse. Their primary units are lines and stanzas rather than sentences and paragraphs. Lyric poems, the main kind included in this anthology, differ from narrative poems, which tell a story, and epic poems, which are very long and heroic narrative poems. Usually short and often songlike in their rhythms, lyric poems lack plots. They focus not on a sequence of related events leading from conflict to climax but on a speaker's response to a single event, object, situation, or person.

Speaker and Situation

In most poems, the **speaker** is a character created by the author. For example, in T. S. Eliot's "The Love Song of J. Alfred Prufrock," Prufrock speaks; and in Robert Browning's "My Last Duchess," the Duke of Ferrara speaks. In Eliot's poem, Prufrock reveals himself to be a very timid man who has "measured out [his] life with coffee spoons" and who cannot generate enough assertiveness even to ask a question. Browning's Ferrara, on the other hand, shows himself to be a callous and egotistical murderer. Neither Prufrock nor Ferrara bears a clear resemblance to his creator.

Occasionally, if they have compelling reasons for doing so, readers may identify the speaker of a poem with the author. Sylvia Plath's "Daddy," for example, is clearly autobiographical. Like the speaker, Plath lost her father when she was quite young and had difficulty coping with his death. Also like her speaker, Plath had tried to kill herself. It is reasonable, then, to identify the speaker of "Daddy" with Plath.

Some poems, too, seem to arise out of a clearly defined **situation** in which the speaker is addressing a particular person for a particular purpose. In "My Last Duchess," for example, the Duke of Ferrara addresses the agent of a count in order to arrange a marriage to the count's daughter. Plath in "Daddy" clearly is addressing her dead father, hoping through the ritual of the poem to exorcise from her memory his oppressive presence. In Andrew Marvell's "To His Coy Mistress," the speaker addresses a woman he loves, trying to get her to realize their mortality and enjoy her youth and beauty while they can. Finally, in Dwight Okita's "In Response to Executive Order 9066," a teenage girl addresses the impersonal U.S. government that has consigned her to an internment camp. In each of these cases, understanding the speaker and the speaker's situation is essential to understanding the poem.

Theme

Though not all poems have a recognizable and paraphrasable **theme,** or major idea, many do. William Shakespeare's Sonnet 116, for example, clearly states that the beloved is "more lovely" than a beautiful day in summer and that the sonnet itself will ensure her immortality. Similarly, Mary TallMountain's "There Is No Word for Goodbye" clearly states the theme in its title, and Dylan Thomas's "Do Not Go Gentle into That Good Night" insistently repeats its theme that we should fight death with every ounce of will and energy we can muster. Other poems seem to have no readily paraphrasable theme, so subtle and complex is their meaning. For example, though we may understand them, it would be difficult to state the theme of Li-Young Lee's "Persimmons," T. S. Eliot's "The Love Song of J. Alfred Prufrock," or Sylvia Plath's "Daddy."

Tone

Whatever its apparent subject, the true subject of a lyric is a state of mind or attitude, known by the technical term **tone.** Tone may be defined as a complex of interrelated attitudes, those of the speaker, writer, and reader, toward the poem's situation. A lyric, then, communicates a tone or attitude, the essence of what it feels like to be in a particular situation. Li-Young Lee's poem "Persimmons," for example, is not simply about persimmons. Rather, it is about a whole of intense and complex emotions, attitudes, and relationships associated with persimmons in the speaker's and the author's minds.

The tone of a poem may be quite complex, expressing feeling that cannot even be suggested by such general words as *love, joy,* and *pain.* Anne Sexton's apparently simple poem "Ringing the Bells," for example, not only communicates the mind-numbing boredom of therapy in a mental institution but simultaneously communicates the speaker's mounting hysteria:

> And this is the way they ring
> the bells in Bedlam
> and this is the bell-lady
> who comes each Tuesday morning
> to give us a music lesson
> and because the attendants make you go

and because we mind by instinct
like bees caught in the wrong hive,
we are the circle of the crazy ladies
who sit in the lounge of the mental house.

As a poem's situation changes, its tone may change as well. In Wilfred Owen's "Dulce et Decorum Est," the first stanza graphically communicates the pain and exhaustion of World War I soldiers moving from trenches on the front lines to a place of rest behind the lines:

Men marched asleep. Many had lost their boots
But limped on, bloodshod. All went lame; all blind.

In the second stanza, as gas bombs drop among the soldiers and one soldier, unable to don his gas mask in time, dies a gruesome death, the tone changes to panic and horror:

Gas! Gas! Quick boys!—An ecstasy of fumbling,
Fitting the clumsy helmets just in time;
But someone still was yelling out and stumbling
And flound'ring like a man in fire or lime . . .

Though "Dulce et Decorum Est" is charged with overwhelming emotion which the speaker seems unable to control, in many poems the emotion seems much more subdued. The speaker in Mary TallMountain's "There Is No Word for Goodbye," for example, adopts a very controlled, accepting, reassuring tone, reinforced by the lines' relaxed, conversational rhythm:

We always think you're coming back,
    But if you don't
    We'll see you someplace else.
    You understand.
    There is no word for goodbye.

Similarly, the urbane speaker of Andrew Marvell's "To His Coy Mistress" declares his love in a carefully measured, precise, and witty compliment:

Had we but world enough, and time,
This coyness, lady, were no crime.
We would sit down, and think which way
To walk, and pass our long love's day.

Various elements of a poem work together to create its tone. The main elements are diction, syntax, imagery, and sound.

Diction

In creating tone, a poet uses language that communicates emotion. Curses, groans, and common adjectives such as *beautiful, wonderful,* and *marvelous* express emotion, but they do not often communicate so that the listener shares the speaker's feeling. Successful poets use language not merely to express but also to communicate emotion precisely. Their choice of words is called **diction.**

The **level of diction** in a poem may range from the very polite, complex, and formal to the very simple, slangy, even vulgar or profane. In Anne Sexton's "Ringing the Bells," for example, the very simple, ordinary, flat diction suggests the boredom of the music therapy session in which the speaker is trapped. In Robert Browning's "My Last Duchess," the Duke of Ferrara is speaking to a count's agent about marrying the count's daughter. As the Duke subtly recalls how he had his first duchess murdered, his precise, formal diction reveals his extraordinary self-control and frightening callousness:

> That's my last Duchess painted on the wall,
> Looking as if she were alive. I call
> That piece a wonder, now; Fra Pandolf's hands
> Worked busily a day, and there she stands.

A poet may choose to use many verbs to emphasize action, as in the following lines from John Donne's "Holy Sonnet 14":

> Batter my heart, three-person'd God; for, you
> As yet but knocke, breathe, shine, and seeke to mend.

A poet's **diction,** his or her choice of words, may create **paradox** or **verbal irony.** A **paradox** is an apparent contradiction. For example, in "Batter My Heart," John Donne addresses God with the paradoxes:

> Except You enthrall mee, never shall be free,
> Nor ever chast, except you ravish mee.

Since *enthrall* literally means to enslave or imprison, *chaste* means sexually pure, and *ravish* means rape, the two statements appear contradictory. For Donne, however, the ultimate freedom is service to God, and being overpowered by God is the ultimate purity. **Verbal irony** is simply saying the opposite of what one means. Owen's title "Dulce et Decorum Est," meaning "It is sweet and proper," is bitterly ironic since the entire poem emphatically demonstrates that dying in war is neither sweet nor proper.

Syntax

A poem's **syntax**—the structure of its phrases, clauses, and sentences—may also contribute to its tone. For example, though it is one very long sentence throughout most of its length, Sexton's "Ringing the Bells" is syntactically simple. The long sentence is almost childlike in its compounding of clauses, not complex like most adult writing and speech. Coordinating conjunctions like *and,* used frequently in Sexton's poem, merely connect phrases and clauses without emphasizing one over the other:

> And this is the way they ring
> the bells in Bedlam

and this is the bell-lady
[.......................]
and this is the gray dress next to me
[.....................................]
and this is the small hunched squirrel-girl
[...]
and this is how the bells really sound

Like the poem's very ordinary diction, the dull, repetitious compounding of clauses contributes to the sense of stifling boredom in the mental
institution.

On the other hand, in Browning's "My Last Duchess," the sentences are
long, formal, and complex, with many subordinate clauses. The speaker
uses perfect parallelism, similar forms in phrases and clauses joined by
and. This parallelism, followed by a brutally short, blunt, and unemotional
recounting of his command to have his wife murdered, contributes to a
reader's sense of the Duke's self-control and monstrous callousness:

Who'd stoop to blame
This sort of trifling? Even had you skill
In speech—(which I have not)—to make your will
Quite clear to such a one, and say, "Just this
Or that in you disgusts me; here you miss,
Or there exceed the mark"—and if she let
Herself be lessoned so, nor plainly set
Her wits to yours, forsooth, and made excuse
—E'en then would be some stooping; and I choose
Never to stoop. Oh sir, she smiled, no doubt,
Whene'er I passed her; but who passed without
Much the same smile? This grew; I gave commands;
Then all smiles stopped together. . . .

Who among us could speak so well in recalling a murder we had ordered?
The perfect and precise control of the long second sentence and the
short, matter-of-fact, almost smirking last sentence seem to reveal a mind
incapable of guilt.

Imagery

Probably a poet's most powerful tool for creating tone is **imagery.** An
image is a word picture; the phrase "neatly trimmed lawn," for example,
is an image. In analyzing images in a poem, readers should look for patterns,
for the kinds of images that predominate. In stanza 3 of Owen's "Dulce
et Decorum Est," images such as the following powerfully convey the horror of war:

If in some smothering dreams you too could pace
Behind the wagon that we flung him in,

And watch the white eyes writhing in his face
[..]
If you could hear, at every jolt, the blood
Come gargling from the froth-corrupted lungs.

Similes, explicit comparisons between unlike things using such indicators of comparison as *like* and *as,* and **metaphors,** implicit comparisons between unlike things lacking such indicators, create images. In Sexton's "Ringing the Bells," there are several images of animals; the simile "like bees caught in the wrong hive" and the metaphor "the small hunched squirrel-girl" suggest that the institution in which the speaker finds herself reduces its inmates to a subhuman state.

A **symbol** is an image used in such a way that it comes to mean more than it ordinarily would. A symbol, however, must be distinguished from a sign. A sign is a word or image that exactly corresponds to a particular meaning beyond itself. The meaning of a symbol is far less definite. For example, a stop sign signifies a particular command universally agreed upon throughout our culture. On the other hand, a stop sign removed from its normal setting, mangled into a heap of barely recognizable metal, and placed in an art museum may symbolize far more: perhaps the brutality of our culture, perhaps the degree to which machines dominate and even destroy lives, perhaps our sheer wastefulness and carelessness. Similarly, the word *bell* signifies a kind of musical instrument. In Sexton's "Ringing the Bells," however, bells take on far more meaning: they symbolize the dull, mechanical lives of the women in the mental hospital.

Sound

Finally, in poetry, as in music, **sound** is important. Poems create patterns in sound as they do in diction, imagery, and syntax. **Onomatopoeia** is the use of words that imitate the sounds they stand for, such as the word *buzz.* Words need not be onomatopoeic, however, for their sounds to affect a poem. At the most basic level, the sounds of words themselves may have emotional overtones apart from the meanings of those words. Such nonsense syllables as *hey diddle diddle* and *heigh ho* suggest joy, while *ugh* suggests pain or disgust. In the first stanza of Wilfred Owen's "Dulce et Decorum Est," such words as *trudge, sludge,* and *hags* have harsh, unpleasant sounds appropriate to the tone of the stanza. The smooth vowels and soft consonants in Marvell's "To His Coy Mistress" are pleasantly mellifluous:

Had we but world enough, and time,
This coyness, lady, were no crime.
We would sit down, and think which way
To walk, and pass our long love's day.

The movement or flow of a poem's sound may be fast or slow, smooth or rough, steady or broken and disjointed. For example, in the lines quoted above from the first stanza of "To His Coy Mistress," the movement is very smooth, stately, and unhurried. The frequent commas slow the passage to the pace of pleasant conversation and prevent the lines from becoming monotonous. On the other hand, the first stanza of Owen's "Dulce et Decorum Est" moves slowly and unsteadily, with frequent stops and starts:

> Bent double, like old beggars under sacks,
> Knock-kneed, coughing like hags, we cursed through sludge.

Here the frequent commas and the difficulty of pronouncing hard consonants slow down the line so that it moves in fits and starts, seeming to imitate the movement of the soldiers as they stagger forward, hurting and exhausted.

Meter, an important element in a poem's sound, refers to the regular pattern of accented and unaccented syllables in a poetic line. There are five basic metrical patterns in English: **iambic, trochaic, anapestic, dactylic,** and **spondaic.** An **iambic foot,** or metrical unit, consists of an unaccented syllable followed by an accented one. In the following line from Marvell's "To His Coy Mistress," accented syllables have been marked by ´, unaccented ones by ˘, and metrical feet separated by /:

> Nŏr wóuld/Ĭ lóve/ăt lów/ĕr ráte.

A **trochaic foot** consists of an accented foot followed by an unaccented foot. An **anapestic foot,** consisting of three syllables, accents the third syllable, and a **dactylic foot,** also containing three syllables, accents the first. A **spondaic foot** consists of two consecutive accented syllables.

Trimeter, tetrameter, pentameter, and **hexameter** refer to the number of feet in a line. Thus, **iambic trimeter** refers to a poetic line of three iambic feet; **trochaic tetrameter** to a line of four trochaic feet; **pentameter** to a line of five feet; and **hexameter** to a line of six feet.

Iambic is by far the most natural and common metrical pattern in English. In fact, the rhythms of English prose are often iambic. Departures from the natural **iambs** of English often call attention to themselves. John Donne uses a strong trochaic foot to emphasize the word *batter* in the opening of "Holy Sonnet 14":

> Báttĕr/m̆y heárt,/thr̆ee-pér/sŏned Gód.

In the following lines from the second stanza of "To His Coy Mistress," the fourth line begins with a strong trochaic foot:

> Bŭt át/m̆y báck/Ĭ ál/wăys heár,
> Timé's wíng/ĕd chár/iŏt húr/rўing néar.
> Ănd yónd/ĕr áll/bĕfóre/ŭs líe
> Désĕrts/ŏf vást/ĕtér/nĭtý.

The inverted accent emphasizes the word *deserts.* This accent and the metaphor "deserts of vast eternity" increase the poem's urgency.

In spite of such departures from the basic meter, "To His Coy Mistress" is a very regular poem, using one of the most regular, tightly controlled verse forms in English poetry, the **couplet,** a pair of metrically regular, rhymed lines. This regularity of meter suggests that the speaker is very much in control of his emotion. Often, regularity suggests control, as it does in Marvell's poem. In Browning's "My Last Duchess," also written in couplets, the regularity suggests the wife-murdering Duke of Ferrara's inappropriate, even pathological control. Sometimes metrical regularity may be comic, as in nursery rhymes. Lack of regularity, on the other hand, may suggest a speaker's lack of emotional control, as in Sexton's "Ringing the Bells" and Owen's "Dulce et Decorum Est." Poetry is so rich and diverse, however, that it is dangerous to generalize.

Alliteration and **rhyme** repeat certain sounds, thereby emphasizing them and helping to unify the poem. Alliteration, the repetition of consonants at the beginning of words or syllables, may enhance the effect of the repeated sounds. In the following lines from John Donne's "Holy Sonnet 14," the hard, alliterative *b*'s reinforce the violence of the strong verbs:

> That I may rise, and stand, o'erthrow mee, and bend
> Your force, to breake, blowe, burn, and make me new.

When words rhyme, their final accented syllables sound alike, as in *bestow* and *below* or *career* and *fear*. Rhymes usually occur at the end of poetic lines and are designated by letters so that the first sound is designated *a* and each new sound gets the next letter in the alphabet. In the following example from John Donne's "A Valediction: Forbidding Mourning," the rhyme scheme is *abab:*

As virtuous men pass mildly away	*a*
And whisper to their souls to go	*b*
Whilst some of their sad friends do say	*a*
The breath goes now, and some say no	*b*

Common rhyme patterns in English poetry include *abab, abba, abcb,* and couplets, in which successive lines rhyme.

Together, meter and rhyme define the stanza patterns of poems. The most common patterns in English include the quatrain, the couplet, and the sonnet. The **quatrain,** a stanza of four lines using any one of various rhyme schemes and metrical patterns, is the most often used stanza in English poetry. William Blake's "The Lamb" and "The Tyger" are written in quatrains. Quatrains are the loosest and most flexible of the three stanza forms defined here. A **couplet** is simply a pair of metrically regular, rhymed lines. Couplets are tightly controlled and challenging to write because of the difficulty of finding rhymes in English. A **sonnet** is a tightly controlled poem of fourteen lines written in iambic pentameter. The **Italian sonnet** consists of two parts, an eight-line octave rhyming *abbaabba* and a six-line sestet often rhyming *cdecde* or *cdcdcd*. The **English** or **Shakespearean sonnet** consists of three quatrains followed by a couplet. The most common rhyme scheme is *abab cdcd efef gg*. Because of its precise rhyme scheme and meter, the sonnet is a demanding form. William Shakespeare, John Donne,

William Wordsworth, Edna St. Vincent Millay, and Gerard Manley Hopkins are among the writers of sonnets included in this text.

REVIEW: READING AND WRITING ABOUT POEMS

Speaker, Situation, and Theme
1. What kind of person is speaking in the poem?
2. Is there reason to equate the speaker with the poet?
3. To whom is the poem addressed?
4. What is the situation of the poem?
5. Does the poem have a paraphrasable theme? If so, what is it?
6. Do tone, diction, syntax, imagery, and sound develop the theme of the poem?

Tone
1. How would you describe the tone of the poem?
2. Does the tone change over the course of the poem?
3. Do diction, syntax, imagery, and sound develop the tone of the poem?

Diction
1. What is the level of the poem's diction? Is it formal, informal, colloquial? Is it simple, difficult, elegant, profane, coarse?
2. Does the poem use paradox or verbal irony?

Syntax
1. How difficult are the sentences? Are they short and simple, or are they long and complex?
2. Are there any departures from standard grammar or syntax such as fragmented elliptical passages (incomplete due to words left out)?
3. Does the syntax change over the course of the poem?

Imagery
1. What patterns does the imagery suggest?
2. What colors predominate?
3. To what senses does the imagery appeal?
4. What similes, metaphors, and symbols does the poet use?
5. Are there contrasting images?
6. Does the imagery change over the course of the poem?

Sound
1. What effects are created by the sounds and location of particular words?
2. Does the poem move quickly or slowly? Does it flow smoothly, or does it contain abrupt shifts, stops, and starts?
3. How regular is the meter of the poem? If the poem uses a regular metrical pattern, what is that pattern? What meter does it use?
4. Does the poem use rhyme or alliteration? If so, what effects are created?
5. Does the sound of the poem change?

Drama

When people first looked at the sunset or the mating games of animals and birds, they saw drama unfolding. Imitating nature became an inevitable step. Whereas nature's dramas are not orchestrated for human entertainment, on a stage actors can orchestrate nature's rituals and embellish scenes for human amusement and diversion. People can change the locales, shift words in the mouths of participants, add or subtract colorful costumes, and tell the story realistically, abstractly, surrealistically, or absurdly. The playwright can also combine creation's dramas with critical or sometimes solemn discussions of issues pertinent to his or her agenda; thus, the playwright blends the uncomplicated with the complicated.

Performance versus Reading: Stage Directions

A play is meant to be performed and to be watched; therefore, the substance of a play can best be conveyed before an audience. Spectators are able to notice the actor's body language, to inspect the set, and to scrutinize the interplay between the people on the stage. The playwright may give elaborate instructions, such as descriptions of the characters, staging, entrances and exits, to the stage manager, the director, the actors, and all others involved in the production. These instructions are called **stage directions.**

Included in the stage directions are references to the set and props, which, along with the curtain, may be among the first items the audience sees. In some plays, the stage directions may be vague or unspecified, leaving the set, movement, and gestures entirely or partially dependent upon the director. In other plays, the stage directions may allow the actors and actresses to improvise. The opening and closing of a curtain and the dimming of lights in some productions indicate changes in dramatic time, while **props** and **set** help to define the **setting,** the cultural and physical environment as well as the time when the action takes place.

Another element of a play, technically known as blocking, is readily apparent only in performance. **Blocking** includes the gestures and body language of characters as well as their interactions and movements on stage. Again, many times the stage directions may be explicit; at other times they may be implied and, therefore, open to interpretation. Blocking enhances performance. Even Shakespeare's great play *Othello* would be dull if the actors simply stood on stage and mechanically recited their lines. Iago's facial expressions and movement can reveal much about him, and an actor portraying Iago has much room for interpretation. In his soliloquy in act I, scene 3, ll. 366–377, beginning "Thus do I ever make my fool my purse," one actor may portray Iago with a snarling smile; another may assume a dark and deadly serious facial expression.

Unfortunately, not everyone can see a particular play. The written words of the play then become the primary vehicle by which the playwright offers readers his or her version of truth. Nor does the playwright have the option, as does the fiction writer, of using **narrative point of view** to reveal necessary background information or a character's innermost thoughts. Rather, the playwright must rely almost exclusively on **dialogue,** the conversations the characters have with each other, to develop character and to handle **exposition,** background information necessary to the readers' understanding.

Setting

Setting encompasses both the physical location and the cultural environment, as well as the background and locale. For example, in Henrik Ibsen's *A Doll's House,* set in 1870s Norway, the Victorian attitude toward women is crucial to our understanding of the play. Similarly, the bare stage outside Thebes in Sophocles's Antigone is important to the understanding of Creon's position on the burial of a nephew he considers a traitor and Antigone's desire to follow the gods' law for her brother's burial. This stage, with very few, if any, props, enhances the audience's ability to imagine the rotting body and the cave where Antigone is eventually left to die. In *Andre's Mother,* the setting of Central Park in New York is also bare except for the balloons that are used as props to signify letting go of Andre. The cultural environment of the African American family struggling with racial problems clarifies family relationships and deepens the understanding of August Wilson's *Fences.*

Style

Style, the manner in which the playwright expresses himself or herself, also encompasses imagery, symbolism, diction, and sentence structure. When a playwright must reveal to the audience information about a character but wants to conceal the details from other characters, he or she relies on the **soliloquy,** a stylistic technique in which a character voices thoughts aloud to the audience. In Shakespeare's *Othello,* for example, Iago reveals to the audience through soliloquies motives he wants to conceal from other characters. Iago's deception is revealed in part by his variations in style. To those around him he appears the blunt, direct military man unable to embellish a compliment to women. But the complexity of imagery in his soliloquies and in some of his dialogues with Othello reveals a far more facile and manipulative command of language. His use of coarse sexual and animal imagery, too, helps to reveal his malignity.

Another stylistic device used to impart characters' thoughts is the **aside,** a passage or remark the characters speak to the audience or to themselves, giving the illusion that, while the audience hears them, other characters on stage do not. Some playwrights embellish their plays with a blend of music, dialogue, and action or depend on a choreographer to incorporate dance. A chorus, such as the one used by the Greek dramatist Sophocles in *Antigone,* created for the ancient Greeks the illusion of the townspeople's commentaries, an integral part of the structure. Unlike modern playwrights, the early playwrights did not use acts or scenes to establish breaks in the action.

Finally, playwrights may use their unique style to reveal much about a character's concealed attitudes and motivation by having him or her voice opposing opinions in different scenes with different characters present. As a simple hypothetical example, the playwright might imagine two consecutive scenes in a comedy: in the first, a woman laughingly rejects her would-be lover's advances; in the next, she tells her friend how much she loves that would-be lover. A series of scenes that effectively reveal concealed motives occur in the first act of *Othello*. In one scene, Iago promises loyalty to Roderigo in the latter's efforts to destroy Othello; then, in the next scene, Iago appears loyal to Othello.

Character

The term **character** refers, of course, to the people created by the playwright and actors and imagined by the readers or spectators. The main character in a play is the **protagonist;** his or her opponent or opposing force is the **antagonist.** Minor characters can also play a role in establishing meaning in any given situation. Christine Linde does not appear on stage often in Ibsen's *A Doll's House,* yet she acts as a foil for Nora.

Another element of character is **motivation,** the driving force or incentive for an action or actions. Sometimes the motivation is determined by a character flaw or defect, called **hamartia** by the ancient Greek philosopher Aristotle. In classical Greek tragedy, this hamartia often leads to the downfall of the **protagonist.** Thus, in Sophocles's *Antigone,* readers and spectators are acutely aware of how Creon's quick temper and his rush to judgment, qualities he has accused Oedipus of having, contribute to his devastating losses at the end. In *Fences,* Troy Maxson, a responsible worker who gives his paycheck to his wife every Friday night, minus his "allowance" for the week, is driven to act irresponsibly by the fences that restrict his life and by his desire to escape the boundaries of his marriage. These acts seem contradictory in nature but reflect the complexity of reality.

Another element of characterization is the protagonist's or antagonist's **anagnorisis,** Aristotle's term for recognition or discovery of some important truth. This discovery leads to the protagonist's self-awareness, a very important part of character development. For example, anagnorisis or, to use a modern term, **epiphany,** a manifestation or revelation, occurs in *Antigone.* Creon, in discovering the truth about his son's love for Antigone and the townspeople's desire to spare her, gains an understanding that the rule of law sometimes should be tempered with mercy. This epiphany is emphasized when his son, his wife, and his niece all commit suicide. In *A Doll's House,* Nora comes to realize that Helmer, her husband, has responded to the threat of exposure only as a father or authoritarian figure, demanding and controlling her life. This epiphany or anagnorisis leads to her bold decision at the end. Whether or not a character comprehends or discovers truth is a distinguishing trait in his or her temperament.

Dramatic characters may be classified as dynamic or static. If a character changes or grows during the course of the play, he or she is **dynamic.**

If, on the other hand, the character is stereotyped and simplified and fails to change or grow, he or she is **static.** In Carson McCullers's *The Member of the Wedding,* Frankie is a dynamic character; a series of experiences causes her to change as she learns more about her own identity. In *The Tempest,* Prospero, the main character, is dynamic, but Caliban is a minor character who is static.

Plot

In his *Poetics,* Aristotle claims that the most important element of a play is its **plot.** Most dramatists rely on **plot** as a framework, using a pattern of exposition, conflict, complication, climax, and resolution. As in fiction, a playwright may also use the **flashback** technique to convey missing information; he or she breaks into the chronology of the play to return to a previous time. Sometimes flashbacks allow readers to connect past events with present situations in order to understand personalities, the playwright's purpose, and/or theme. As a plot approaches its **climax,** the high point of the action, **dramatic tension,** the audience's desire to see the conflict resolved, increases. In Sophocles's *Antigone,* for instance, attentive readers and spectators learn immediately that Creon and Antigone are at odds because of Creon's decree. This tension builds when the chorus, his son, and the blind Teiresias tell Creon that his stubbornness may cause suffering. As Creon proceeds to ignore everyone in pursuit of his own agenda, the dramatic tension builds until he realizes his obstinacy has caused damage to his own family; tension decreases as he comes to accept his lonely fate.

    Dramatic irony, which may increase the dramatic tension of the plot, occurs when an important character, lacking information the audience knows, behaves in a way that is diametrically opposed to his or her own best interest or unknowingly says something that has a double meaning. Like Sophocles's *Antigone, Oedipus the King* is a famous example of dramatic irony. The audience knows that in *Oedipus* the tragic hero has killed his father, married his mother, and fathered four children by her. Accepting his fate of banishment and the subsequent curse on the family, Oedipus has left Thebes. However, the audience knows that the curse will follow the family in the battle between Creon and Antigone, two obstinate people whose growing arrogance and failure to listen to anyone will eventually lead to their doom.

    Though most of the plays in this anthology follow traditional patterns of plot, some modern and contemporary playwrights have experimented with plot, sometimes eliminating one or more of its traditional parts, sometimes deliberately avoiding a chronological sequence, and sometimes obscuring altogether any sense that one event necessarily follows or causes another. **Theater of the absurd,** in which both the form and the content of the play reflect the playwright's view of the absurdity of the human condition, exemplifies this experimentation with plot.

Theme

Theme refers to the major ideas or moral precepts that the play embodies. Sometimes it is impossible for any two people to agree upon the wording of the theme or themes because moral positions and abstract principles are, naturally, more difficult to express than concrete facts. Even when theme is expressed, often the tendency is to simplify a sometimes complex idea. In many cases, themes can also be related to social problems. For instance, in *Andre's Mother,* when Cal confronts Andre's mother about her son's death from AIDS, his last speech about being "fugitives from our parents' scorn or heartbreak" and his quotation from *Hamlet* ("Good night, sweet prince, and flights of angels sing thee to thy rest!") help the audience to arrive at a statement of theme.

Though drama may elucidate problems, it seldom advocates solutions to them. Sophocles' *Antigone,* for example, raises questions about laws and religious convictions as well as the inflexibility of lawmakers who refuse to grant mercy with justice. Tragic as *Antigone* is, however, it also affirms the dignity of suffering humanity. To understand the theme of the play, an audience or reader must consider all of these questions and ideas.

The following questions are intended as a general guide to reading and writing about a play. Specific guidance is provided by the questions following each of the plays in this anthology.

REVIEW: READING AND WRITING ABOUT PLAYS

Stage Directions

1. Have the stage directions helped you to envision the play? If so, how? Have the directions transmitted any of the author's meaning? If so, how?
2. What are some of the explicit descriptions of the set? How does the set help develop character, plot, theme, and setting?
3. What objects or props have contributed the most to the understanding of the story? How?

Setting

1. How does the playwright use the setting to convey character traits, theme, conflict, or irony?
2. How or why is the cultural or physical environment important to the readers' understanding of the play?
3. How important is the setting to the play as a whole?

Style

1. Are characters distinguished from each other by their speaking style—their use of imagery, diction, and sentence structure?
2. How does the playwright use language to develop characters or to convey information about them?
3. Does the playwright use structural devices to convey meaning? How?

Character
1. What types of characters are presented on the stage? Are they stereo-types or individuals?
2. Are the characters dynamic or static? If dynamic, how do they change or grow? How does the author reveal their depth and complexity?
3. How does the playwright develop character? What does the dialogue tell about characters? Does the playwright also use stage movements, gestures, or facial expressions to develop characters?
4. How does the playwright impart to the audience the thoughts, feel-ings, and ideas a character wants to conceal from other characters?
5. What motivates the protagonist, antagonist, and/or minor characters?
6. Does the protagonist experience anagnorisis? If so, precisely when does it occur and what does the character discover?
7. Does the protagonist have a tragic flaw (hamartia)? If so, how does this defect in character or mistake in deduction lead to his or her downfall?
8. What actions and/or words reveal qualities of character or personality?

Plot
1. Is the plot the traditional Aristotelian plot of beginning, middle, and end? If it is not traditional, what structure does the playwright use? How do the acts and/or scenes contribute to the overall understand-ing of the play?
2. What is the basic conflict in the play? Is it between two characters, within a character, or between a character and some large force such as fate, the environment, or an institution?
3. How does the author reveal the conflict? How does he or she create and sustain dramatic tension?
4. Is dramatic irony used to reinforce dramatic tension? If so, how does the playwright overcome the problem of revealing to the audience what he or she does not want a character to know?

Theme
1. What, in your opinion, is the main idea or theme in the play? Is there more than one theme?
2. What questions does the play raise or illuminate? Does it attempt to answer the questions or to solve a problem?
3. How do the plot, character, setting, style, and conflict develop the play's theme or central issue?

The Writing Process

Writing a paper is a process like building a house or baking bread; you should not try doing everything at once. A competent builder will not lay a foundation without blueprints or frame the walls before laying a foundation and floor. Similarly, in writing you should not try to plan, write, edit, and proofread all at the same time. Rather, you should write one step at a time.

Some papers may require more steps than others. A short, timed, in-class writing assignment may allow for only three steps: planning, writing, and proofreading. A simple plan for such an assignment need answer only two questions: "What am I going to say?" and "How am I going to develop my idea convincingly?" Suppose, for example, you have thirty minutes to answer the question. "Is the narrator of Bell's 'Customs of the Country' simply an evil person, or does she have redeeming qualities?" You might decide to answer "though she admits to having broken her son Davey's leg, the narrartor of Bell's 'Customs of the Country' is an extraordinarily honest woman who cares deeply about her son." You might go on to develop this response by citing examples from the story.

A longer out-of-class paper allows for more time to plan and organize your material and write more than one draft. You may also consider ways of developing your response, such as description, exemplification, enumeration, analysis, classification, comparison-contrast, and cause-effect. This section addresses the different aspects and steps of the writing process and some of the different essay models you can use when developing your essay.

Developing Ideas

Even seasoned writers sometimes have difficulty getting started on their writing. Common problems you may face include focusing your ideas, not knowing where to begin, having too little to say, having too much to say, and not knowing where exactly you stand on an issue. Whatever your particular "writer's block" may be, there are development strategies that can help get you started. Brainstorming, freewriting, clustering, and journaling all help you through the development process. You may find that you prefer only one or a combination of methods to help get your creative juices flowing.

Brainstorming

Brainstorming is a way of generating observations and ideas. You simply list your ideas as they come to mind without paying attention to sentence structure, spelling, order, or even relevance. The purpose is to produce ideas, not to criticize or edit them. Brainstorming can be done alone or in class groups; your teacher may even have the entire class brainstorm together. You may devote as few as five or as many as thirty minutes to the brainstorming process and try to keep listing ideas as they pop into your head. Don't worry about whether the ideas are good or bad. Even a "dumb" idea can trigger a brilliant one.

Jodi Deeter decided to write her paper on Ibsen's concern for women's rights as shown in Torvald's treatment of Nora in *A Doll's House*. Brainstorming for a few minutes, she produced the following list:

Ibsen—concern for women's rights

Analyze Torvald—"a man of his time," egotystical, worried

about reputation, He's selfish, and imature.

concerned w/society

morals

Nora trinket

Selfish Nora is there for him

Treating her as a child (she'll never make it w/o him)

Notice that this list has no apparent order or consistent form and that it contains spelling and grammatical errors. Even such a random list of ideas can help you focus and organize your paper. You should brainstorm until you have a wealth of specific ideas about your topic.

Freewriting

Freewriting works much the same way as brainstorming does—on hunches, impressions, and quick reactions. The important thing to remember when freewriting is to keep writing without consciously thinking about what you are saying. Set aside about ten minutes and make yourself write without pausing for the whole ten minutes. As with brainstorming, don't worry about mistakes, grammar, or spelling.

When you freewrite with a focus, write down the focus point at the top of your paper to help you stick with it as you write. This way you will have a visual reminder to keep you from straying too far away from the topic. Again, remember the rule of freewriting: *don't stop writing,* even if all you write is gibberish.

Clustering

Clustering, also called "mind mapping," "ballooning," or "grouping," is a visually presented variation of brainstorming popular in the corporate world. Clustering is best done with a large sheet of paper. In the middle of the page, write the main topic and draw a circle around it. Think of subtopics related to the main topic and write them down around the main topic circle. Then, draw a box around each of them (to differentiate them from the main idea) and then draw lines to connect the boxes back to the center circle. Try to express these subtopics in one or two key words. Repeat this process around the subcategories. This technique not only helps you to develop your ideas but enables you to see the connections between them.

Keeping a Journal

Keeping a journal gives you a reservoir of ideas to draw from in developing essays. Most great writers, including Nathaniel Hawthorne, F. Scott Fitzgerald, and Virginia Woolf, kept idea journals. Journaling helps you store away ideas, review them for further consideration, and develop them more fully over time.

A reader-response journal records your reaction to works you have read. Such a journal works best if you write down your first impressions immediately after you finish reading. Jot down any questions, ideas, or thoughts you had concerning the work. Include any emotional reactions you had (anger, pity, joy) and your impressions of the characters, theme, and plot. Later, reread your initial impressions and develop them more fully in the journal.

In addition to helping you develop ideas, a journal allows you to improve your writing without the fear of correction. It involves you more deeply with the material you read in class. By writing about your initial impressions of a story or poem, you may find yourself developing ideas that would not have otherwise occurred to you—ideas from which you can later draw for future essay assignments.

Narrowing the Topic

Once you have a general concept of what your topic will be, you need to narrow it down to a manageable idea. Some writers have trouble narrowing their topic because they like several ideas developed during brainstorming and they are not sure which one to choose, or they are afraid of committing to only one concept. This step does involve an element of risk, but remember that you can always backtrack to another idea if you find that you simply can't get your first choice off the ground. If your essay involves outside research, you may wish to locate your sources before committing to the final topic. The sources that you find can help determine the focus of your essay. Once you have narrowed your topic, you need to focus your paper and to develop a thesis statement for it.

Developing a Thesis Statement

When developing your thesis statement, think about what you want to say about the topic. A thesis statement makes an assertion; it indicates exactly what the writer intends to say about a subject. You might think of your paper as a kind of contract in which you make a commitment to discuss an idea. The first paragraph of your paper should provide a brief statement of the main point. The rest of the paper develops this point. If it is properly organized, it will first create an expectation in its thesis, a brief statement of the main point contained in the introduction to the paper. It will then fulfill that expectation in the body that follows. A thesis like "Henrik Ibsen's <u>A Doll's House</u> is about men and women" or "Ibsen's <u>A Doll's House</u> shows ideas of Ibsen's time" creates no clear expectation. A better thesis might be "Torvald Helmer consistently treats his wife Nora as a piece of property to be used for his own selfish ends." This thesis constitutes an informal contract with the reader that what follows, the body of the paper, will discuss Ibsen's play, showing Torvald's selfish possessiveness. It is perfectly normal for the thesis statement to change as you write your paper, becoming clearer and more precise as the paper evolves.

As she talked to her teacher and to other students in the class, Jodi came to realize what she wanted to emphasize in her paper: that while he had many faults and often treated Nora abysmally, Torvald loved Nora deeply. She began to rework her plan to emphasize Torvald's love:

1. show he's egotistical—selfish

2. show his concern for his reputation—how he uses Nora

3. show shallowness when he explodes (disowns Nora)

4. show he is like most men of his day—both victims of

    society's expectations

5. show that he <u>loves</u> Nora

Focusing Your Paper

Taking the time to define your focus is especially helpful if you have many fragmented ideas. The key to focusing your paper effectively is to answer the question "What is my paper about?" and to proceed from there. This is also an excellent way to develop your thesis statement. Try to keep your answer to only one sentence. This forces you to identify the main idea of the paper.

After you have identified exactly what your paper is about, you can then begin organizing the ideas that connect to the main point. This may involve answering another question, "How will I support my point?" which should prompt you to list the ways you intend to present and prove your idea. After you have provided the answers to this question, arrange your list in a logical order.

Defining the Purpose

The purpose of your paper is the reason you are writing it. Your objective may be to persuade your audience to your view or opinion, to inform them about new information or ideas, or to describe an experience or event so that they may understand it better. Your audience should be able to indentify your paper's objective and then realize what you need to do to accomplish this objective.

When preparing a persuasive paper, you should organize your material by first determining what you are trying to prove. Then list the support you will provide to prove your idea. Review your supporting evidence list and figure out how you should order this support to present a convincing discussion. From this simple organization, you should be able to begin writing your paper.

If your objective is to inform your readers, you first need to anticipate the questions your audience may have regarding the topic and how much background they will need to understand it. Once you have developed a list of questions about your topic that you will address in your paper, determine what order will best present the information.

A descriptive paper also involves answering several questions. First, you must identify what is important or relevant about the subject you intend to describe. To demonstrate its importance to your reader, you should determine what images, details, scenes, characters, and themes are vital to communicating this importance. List these elements and order them so that they present the reader with a clear view of the experience or topic that you are trying to present.

Researching

Once you have a strong thesis and a good list of supporting ideas, the next step is to research the topic. Research helps you to support the points you want to make in your paper. Research can involve a few or many steps, depending on the type and length of the paper you are writing. For lengthy critical papers that require outside sources, you will probably need to tap into library resources or even find information online.

Many students think that researching their paper means a trip to the library. While this is often the case, you should start by rereading the work about which you are writing, marking passages that relate to your ideas. You may find it helpful to copy onto three-by-five cards the passages from the stories that you want to quote in order to draft your paper without repeatedly referring to the textbook. As you read, write down any questions you have about the work. You may wish to discuss these questions with your teacher or peers. Discussion is an effective way to focus your ideas and find out how other people react to your topic.

Finding Sources

Researching a paper about a literary topic can be a daunting prospect. If you are unfamiliar with library research, the librarian should be the first person you speak to. Don't be afraid to ask librarians for assistance; they are there to help get you started.

Most libraries now use computerized card catalogues. These systems allow you to look up books by author, title, and subject. Remember that books are dated—that is, they are usually at least a year old by the time they reach the shelves and may not contain the most up-to-date information. However, having the latest information is usually not an issue when writing about literature.

The library also contains many journals and periodicals on a wide variety of subjects. Literary journals can be a good source of information on your topic, allowing you to see what other people have written about the work. Frequently, English professors and graduate students write the contributions to these journals, so don't be discouraged if the articles seem very academic and even hard to understand. They can still be excellent resources to help support your ideas.

The Internet is a relatively new way to research your topic. Many college-level English classes have webpages, on which students post their work and interact with each other. You may even find a literary newsgroup discussing your story or poem online! Some of these newsgroups are open to enrolled students only, but you can still read the groups' postings.

You should surf the web with the careful eye of a critic. Remember that other users can post anything they wish on the Internet, and some online material may be inaccurate or undocumented. Whenever possible, verify what you find on the web with its paper source. A few of the reputable Internet resources for literary research include:

www.ipl.org/ref/litcrit/ The Internet Public Library's Online Literary Criticism Collection contains over 1000 critical and biographical websites about authors and works that can be referenced by author, title, or literary period.

www.promo.net/pg/ Project Gutenberg provides a huge library of electronically stored books that can be downloaded for free and viewed offline.

humanitas.ucsb.edu/shuttle/english.html The University of California, Santa Barbara, maintains a website on general English literature resources, as well as categories for time period and genre.

www.poets.org/ The Academy of American Poets' website features an online poet database and critical essays about poetry.

Selecting Material

Once you have found a source that you think will be helpful, write it down immediately. Many students bemoan the loss of a valuable resource because they forgot to write down the title of the book or Internet address. Make a bibliography card for each source you find; a bibliography card is simply a three-by-five card listing information you will need in your Works Cited page (see the appendix on MLA documentation). For example:

Melton, Quimby IV. "Greenleaf's Destructive Bull and the Paean to the Common Man." <u>Literature and Ourselves.</u> 4th ed. Ed. Gloria Henderson, Bill Day, and Sandra Waller, New York: Longman, 2003. 1472-76.

Richardson, William. "Over There: Remembering
Flannery O'Conner." <u>Southern Humanities Review</u>
36.1 (Winter 2002):1. [here put the date that you
found the article, e.g., 6 Jan 2002]
<http://www.poets.org/LIT/poet/ehirfst2.htm>.

If you write each card carefully, being sure to use the correct MLA form, you will not have to waste time later hunting for details that you forgot to copy. (See the appendix on MLA documentation for correct form.) These cards allow you to add sources and arrange them alphabetically without having to rewrite as you would with a list. Ultimately, using bibliography cards will make the process of documenting your sources much easier.

You may also use three-by-five cards to take notes, listing author, page, and topic at the top and writing only one piece of information, either quoted or carefully paraphrased, on each. For example:

Cochran 402
"Torvald insinuates throughout the play that he
will be there to protect Nora; however, he fails
miserably."
Torvald repeatedly tells Nora how he will keep
her out of danger, but his actions are quite
opposite of his words.

You may also find it helpful to copy onto cards passages from the stories that you want to quote in order to draft the paper without repeatedly referring to the book.

Documenting Sources

Remember that you use sources to support your ideas and emphasize your points. It is important to document these sources whether you quote or paraphrase the material. You must let your reader know where the information you borrowed came from. Documenting your sources gives credit to the person who did the work and helps your readers locate information for further reading.

Even if you rewrite information in your own words, you still must document the source. Failure to document original information is called plagiarism—presenting someone else's work as your own—and it is considered by academic institutions as a form of theft. While it is not necessary to document common knowledge, such as dates, facts, or ideas that are generally known, the following checklist should help you determine when to document your sources:

- Quoting someone's exact words
- Citing someone else's opinion
- Summarizing someone else's ideas, although not directly quoting them
- Using specific information from a study
- Citing statistical data
- Reporting the results of someone else's research
- Paraphrasing someone else's ideas, even if it is in your own words

See the appendix on MLA documentation for information on how to cite your sources properly both in the body of your paper and in the Works Cited section at the end of your paper.

Organizing

Many students think organizing their paper means writing a structured and detailed outline, complete with Roman numerals and indented sub-points. While this is an effective way to organize your paper, it is not the only way to plan your essay. Organizing includes defining your focus, planning how to make your paper flow smoothly from point to point, and determining the order of your material. Quite often, organizing involves answering for yourself a series of questions designed to help you identify and keep to the points you want to cover.

Blocking and Planning

Although your teacher may require an outline, you may find other, less formal methods of organization helpful. One such method is called blocking, the arranging and rearranging of ideas in groups or blocks. Blocking produces not a finished order but a series of starting points from which to work. You might begin simply by blocking information by characters, listing together ideas related to each. Then you might rearrange the blocks until you arrive at a pattern that seems promising.

Identifying Your Audience

Identifying your audience is essential. Anticipating what your audience needs to know will help you compose a convincing, effective paper. Start by answering a few simple questions:

- Who is my audience?
- How much does my audience already know about my topic?
- How might my audience feel about this topic?
- What questions might my audience have about my topic or my conclusions?

- What does my audience need to know to understand my points?
- What is the best order to present the necessary information?
- Why are people in my audience reading my paper?

After you answer these questions, you should be able to organize your material to satisfy the needs of your audience while presenting your points and achieving your objective—writing a thoughtful essay.

These informal organization techniques can be the last step before you write your paper. If you feel more comfortable with an extensive and detailed outline, you will find that applying the above techniques before you construct your formal outline will make your task much easier. Once you have organized your material and composed your writing plan, you are ready to begin writing the actual paper.

Drafting

In drafting a paper, you should not think of your draft as a finished product. At this stage, neither neatness nor correctness is important. Your primary goal in drafting should be to get your ideas down in a reasonable order. If you stop to concern yourself with spelling, sentence structure, grammar, and neatness, you may lose your train of thought. If you find that you cannot continue with one paragraph, begin another and return later to the difficult one. You may want to leave gaps or write marginal notes in your manuscript to indicate omissions or changes you want to make later. Note the mark-outs and inattention to spelling in Jodi's rough draft on *A Doll's House:*

1 maybe 2 par

Set in the late nineteen-century, Henrick Ibsen's <u>A Doll's House</u> is justly viewed as an obvious fight for women's rights. Although Ibsen denied ever being directly involved in the fight for women's rights, he publicly displayed his position by submitting two recommendations to the Scandinavian Club in Rome in the spring before he wrote <u>A Doll's House</u>. Both of his suggestion were benifical to women and Ibsen made a lengthy, outspoken commentary trying ~~to to get~~ persuade members to—let women—become librarians and allow them to vote in club meetings (Templeton 399). Contrary to Ibsen's denials, it is apparent he was very much in favor of support of the fight for women's rights. /Many women can relate to Ibsen's <u>A Doll's House</u>. The Confusion of a love-hate relationship with a man who refuses to let go of his (the) "I am the man and you are the women" attitude. ~~Torvald and Nora.~~ Taking on individual roles set by society, Torvald and Nora spend eight years of marriage playing games with one another instead of growing together. However, Torvald's position concerning women is typical seemingly of men throughout the nineteenth-century (Cochran 401). Cochran also ~~see~~ understands the psychological implication so of a socieities views as a whole by sying "He (Torvald) is not intentionally abusing Nora but is acting as society dictates. He simply behaves like most men of his time." (Cochran 403). Torvald loves Nora in the best way he knows how. ~~His age is large~~ Being overly concerned with what society will think of him Torvald's has a large ego ~~ego is quite large~~. He continually makes reference to how beautiful Nora ~~looks~~ adding to his ~~own appeal~~ or outside appearance. ~~His~~ Torvald's moralistic views are also questioned throughout the play.

As this example indicates, when you draft a paper, you are likely to begin one way, change your mind, and then begin another way. While Jodi's introduction is neither well organized nor economically written, it is a promising start. Sometimes half the battle is just getting something on paper that you can go back and revise.

Getting Started, Writing Your Introduction

Many students find that the most challenging and daunting part of writing an essay is writing the very first paragraph. Of course, many writers experience that age-old malady, "writer's block." In *Shoptalk*, his biography of humor writer James Thurber, Donald Murray quotes Thurber as saying "Don't get it right, get it written." What he means is simply to start writing, regardless of whether you think what you are writing is good or not. Some students fear that if their first paragraph isn't perfect, the rest of their paper will go downhill from there. You may wish to use your thesis statement as a starting point. Remember, a good thesis statement is worth the time and effort because you can frame your paragraph around your thesis. After you have written the first paragraph, you can revise it immediately or continue writing and return to it later.

Developing Paragraphs and Making Transitions

A paragraph is a group of sentences that support and develop a central idea. The central idea serves as the core point of the paragraph, and the surrounding sentences support it. There are three primary types of sentences in a paragraph: the topic sentence, supporting sentences, and transitional sentences.

The core point, or the topic sentence, usually appears as the first or second sentence in the paragraph. It is the controlling idea of the paragraph. Featuring the topic sentence first lets the reader know immediately what the paragraph is about. However, sometimes you may need to provide a transition sentence or some supporting material before stating the topic sentence, in which case it may appear as the second or third sentence in the paragraph. Think of the topic sentence as a mini thesis statement; it should connect logically to the topic sentences in the paragraphs before and after it.

Supporting sentences do just that: support the topic sentence. This support may be from outside sources in the form of quotes or paraphrased material, or may be from your own ideas. Think of the support sentences as "proving" the validity of your topic sentence.

Transition sentences link paragraphs together, connecting the paper as a cohesive unit and promoting the essay's readability. Transition sentences usually appear as the first and last sentence of the paragraph. When they appear at the end of the paragraph, they foreshadow the topic that will come next. Words such as *in addition, yet, moreover, furthermore, meanwhile, likewise, also, since, before, hence, on the other hand, as well,* and *thus* are often used in transition sentences. Another natural and effective way to create transition is to repeat key words and phrases. All of these transition devices act as road signs for your readers, helping them to identify connections between your ideas and to know what to expect next.

Paragraphs have no required length. You should remember, however, that an essay composed of long, detailed paragraphs might prove tiresome and confusing to the reader. Likewise, short, choppy paragraphs may sacrifice clarity and leave the reader with unanswered questions. Remember that a paragraph presents a single unified idea. It should be just long enough to support its subject effectively. Begin a new paragraph when your subject changes.

Use this list to help keep your paragraphs organized and coherent:

- Organize material logically—present your core idea early in the paragraph.
- Include a topic sentence that expresses the core point of the paragraph.
- Support and explain the core point.
- Use transitional sentences and phrases to indicate where you are going and where you have been.

Concluding Well

Your **conclusion** should pull together the points made in your paper while also reiterating your final point. You may also use your conclusion as an opportunity to provoke a final thought you wish your audience to consider. Try to frame your conclusion to mirror your introduction—in other words, be consistent in your style. You may wish to repeat the point of the paper, revisit its key points, and then leave your reader with a final idea or thought on your topic.

Conclusions are your opportunity to explain to your reader how all your material fits together. Avoid the temptation simply to summarize your material; try to give your conclusions a little punch. However, it is equally important not to be overly dramatic either. Rather, conclusions should sound confident and reflective.

Revising and Editing

Once you have drafted a paper and, if possible, spent several hours or even a day away from it, you should begin revising and editing it. First, reread the essay to determine whether the organizational pattern you have selected is the best possible way to present your ideas. Rearranging or adding paragraphs or sections may create a clearer, more convincing essay; if you move or add sections, however, you may need to revise your thesis to reflect the new order.

To edit your paper, read it closely, marking the words, phrases, and sections you want to change. Have your grammar handbook nearby to check any grammar questions that may arise. Look for ideas that seem out of place or sound awkward, passages that lack adequate support and detail, and sentences that seem wordy or unclear. Many students find that reading the essay aloud helps them to recognize awkward sentences and ambiguous wording. This technique may also reveal missing words.

As you read, think about the voice and style you are using to present your material. Is your style smooth and confident? How much of yourself is in the essay, and is this level appropriate for the type of paper you are writing? Watch out for passive sentence construction. Employing the active voice in your sentences keeps the paper vibrant and engaging.

Using Active Voice

Although grammatically correct, passive voice can slow down the flow of a paper, or distance the reader from your material. In active voice, you make your agent "actively" perform an action. Consider the following examples:

Passive: In "the Yellow Wallpaper," John's wife is locked away

in a room to give her the "rest cure."

Active: In "the Yellow Wallpaper," John locks his wife away

    in a room to give her the "rest cure."

Passive: Torvald is baited by Nora.

Active: Nora baits Torvald.

Passive: In the poem "Daddy," Plath's perception of her father

    and childhood is described.

Active: Plath describes her perception of her father and

    childhood in her poem "Daddy."

The first example presents a very different impression of John from that in the second sentence, which makes clear that he imprisons his wife. In each case, the second sentences, using the active voice, are more concise and emphatic.

Grammar and Punctuation

You probably already have a grammar handbook; most first-year composition courses require students to purchase these invaluable books. If you don't have a grammar handbook, get one. You will use it throughout your college—and probably your professional—career. Grammar handbooks can help you identify problems with phrases and clauses, parallel structure, verb tense, agreement, and punctuation. Most have useful sections on common mistakes in diction, such as when to use "further" and "farther" and "effect" and "affect." While "grammar checkers" on word processors may be helpful in identifying agreement problems and even passive constructions, they are not infallible. Frequently, they highlight compound sentences as "too long" or claim that a sentence is incorrect when it is, in fact, correct. Remember that you are the best grammar checker for your writing.

Proofreading Effectively

The final step in preparing a paper is proofreading, the process of reading your paper to correct errors. You will probably be more successful if you wait until you are fresh to start: proofreading a paper at 3:00 A.M. immediately after finishing it is not a good idea. With the use of word-processing programs, proofreading usually involves three steps: spellchecking, reading, and correcting.

If you are writing your paper using a word-processing system, you probably have been using the spellchecker throughout the composition process. Most word-processing systems highlight misspelled words as you type them into the computer. Remember to run the spellchecker every time you change or revise your paper. Many students make last-minute changes to their papers and neglect to run the spellchecker one last time before printing it, only to discover a misspelled word as they turn in their paper or when it is returned to them. Keep in mind that spellcheckers can fix only words that are misspelled—not words that are mistyped but are still real words. Common typing errors in which letters are transposed, such as "from" and "form" and "won" and "own," will not be caught by a spellchecker because all are real words. Other common errors not caught by spellcheckers include words incompletely typed, such as leaving off the "t" in "the" or the second "e" in "here." Reading your paper carefully will catch these errors.

To proofread effectively, you must read slowly and critically. Try to distance yourself from the material. One careful, slow, attentive proofreading is better than six careless reads. Look for and mark the following: errors in spelling and usage, sentence fragments and comma splices, inconsistencies in number between nouns and pronouns and between subjects and verbs, faulty parallelism, other grammar errors, unintentional repetitions, and omissions.

After you have proofread and identified the errors, go back and correct them. When you have finished, proofread the paper one last time to make sure you caught everything. If you wrote your paper by hand and your errors are few, you may be able to correct them directly on the paper. Correct the errors *even if doing so will detract from the neatness of your paper.* Most teachers prefer a *slightly* messy but correct paper to a neat, incorrect one.

After editing and revising her paper, Jodi produced a final paper whose introduction and first two paragraphs read as follows:

Many women can relate to the confusion of a love-hate relationship with a man who refuses to let go of his "I am the man, you are the woman" attitude. That is the relationship between Torvald and Nora in Henrik Ibsen's A Doll's House. Taking on individual roles set by society, Torvald and Nora spend the eight years of their marriage playing games with one another. Torvald's position concerning women is typical of men throughout the nineteenth century (Cochran 401). Cochran understands the psychological implications of a society's view when she says, "He [Torvald] is not intentionally abusing Nora but is acting as society dictates. He simply behaves like most men of his time" (Cochran 403). Overly concerned with what society will think, Torvald often uses Nora as a pawn to enhance his own appearance. Torvald's moralistic views are also in question throughout the play. In addition, Torvald shows excessive selfishness in dealing with Nora. However, Torvald has loved Nora in the best way he knew how, by providing her with a stable home, money, security, and companionship.

Despite the surface appearance of Torvald's actions toward Nora, we soon come to realize the love and depth of emotion that he actually feels for her. Torvald's initial reaction to Krogstad's letter emerges as a selfish concern for himself. Understanding exactly what Nora has done, Torvald shouts:

> this thing must be hushed up at any price. As
> regards our relationship—we must appear to
> be living together just as before. Only appear,
> of course. You will therefore continue to reside
> here. That is understood. But the children
> shall be taken out of your hands. I dare no
> longer entrust them to you. Oh, to have to say
> this to the woman I once loved so dearly—and
> who I still—! (Ibsen 383)

Listening to what is not said, we are able to hear a lot more than Torvald would like to reveal. In the very last part of his reprimand, Torvald clearly admits that he loves Nora. The first part of his reprimand is said out of anger and fear. When Nora feels the impact of Torvald's words, without listening to their meaning, she mistakenly feels that Torvald doesn't love her. In fact, Nora never told Torvald how she felt about his treatment of her. She simply played out the role just as Torvald did.

In all fairness to Torvald, he was completely ignorant of the cruelty of his behavior; that does not mean he did not truly love Nora. Unfortunately, he learns too late of the profound effect his behavior has caused his marriage. His demeanor completely changes from anger to sadness realizing Nora's intent to leave. He says calmly, "I see it, I see it. A gulf has indeed opened between us. Oh, but Nora— couldn't it be bridged?" (Ibsen 398) In the last act we are able to see the true Torvald. He shows his weaknesses, bares his soul, and literally begs Nora not to leave. Torvald does need Nora, a fact that she should have been able to pick up on when he said, "Nora, Nora, not now! Wait till tomorrow!" (Ibsen 390) He repeatedly asks Nora how to mend what is wrong. Nora says that only the "miracle of miracles" can save their marriage, and after she is gone Torvald says to himself: "Nora! Nora! Empty! She's gone! (a hope strikes him) The miracle of miracles?—" (Ibsen 391)

Ways to Write About Literature

The Literary Response Essay

Response essays allow you to make connections between the literary work and your impressions of it. Did the work remind you of something in your childhood? Did you find it uplifting and affirming, or tragic? Perhaps you see a similarity between a particular character and someone you know. How did the work affect you? The literary response essay conveys to the audience your feelings and impressions of the work.

The response essay often applies a type of literary theory known as reader response criticism. Reader response is based on the idea that each reader brings a different history, personal outlook, and set of values and experiences to the work. Therefore, readers respond to literary works differently based on these variations in background. This way of approaching literature assumes that there is no "correct" reading of a text but that meaning is created when the reader interacts with the text. Thus, reactions will vary depending on factors such as the gender, socioeconomic background, occupation, and age of the reader. Think of the literary response essay as an opportunity to express your particular point of view and reaction to the work.

For example, Darren found the story "The Ones Who Walk Away from Omelas" by Ursula LeGuin particularly disturbing. In his opinion, the child in the closet in the story represents children in third-world countries who work in squalid factories in wretched conditions manufacturing American products such as sneakers and designer clothing. Such children are "locked away" from American consciousness because their labor and suffering produces goods that make American life luxurious and comfortable. Darren chose to write about his impressions of the story and connect them to this real-life circumstance.

The Comparison/Contrast Essay

The comparison essay usually compares two literary works to each other. More than simply listing the similarities and differences of two works, comparison/contrast essays make connections and provide thoughtful literary analysis. Start by critically reading the works to be compared, noting any parallel themes or ideas. Themes can include love and hate, innocence and experience, life, death and rebirth, progress and tradition, gender, family issues, freedom and responsibility, human nature, searches for identity, etc.

You may find after reading two works that you notice certain themes or similarities that approach the same issue from different perspectives. Likewise, two works may address the same issue and come to the same conclusions but approach the subject differently. You may be asked to compare one type of literature, such as a play, to another type, such as a poem, or even to another art form, such as a painting or piece of music.

When given the assignment to compare how two poems approach the same subject, Rose decided to write about the theme of love. She chose William Shakespeare's Sonnet 116, "Let me not to the marriage of true minds," and Elizabeth Barrett Browning's Sonnet 43, "How do I love thee?" While the poems are similar in theme, partially because the authors are of different genders and time periods, they express different attitudes toward love.

The Critical Analysis Essay

When you write a critical analysis essay, you examine how a part or parts of a literary work connect to the whole work. In other words, you evaluate how a particular part of a work contributes to the understanding of the whole. Analyzing a piece of literature requires that you look carefully at its parts, to see how these parts contribute to the meaning of the entire work. For example, you might examine how a particular character in a story influences the outcome of the tale, or you could evaluate how a play turns on a particularly critical scene. You could also address how the language of a poem contributes to its overall meaning or message.

Analysis often focuses on an element (or elements) of literature. It may center on structure, language, characters, sound, plot development, and even irony. It demonstrates how the particular elements analyzed contribute to the whole meaning of the work. Remember that an analysis is not a paraphrasing of the work (your impression in your own words) but an explanation on how the work communicates its idea—how its parts convey the meaning.

William decided to address the way that the language in Robert Browning's poem "My Last Duchess" contributes to the overall message of the poem. His essay specifically addressed the Duke's use of language and how it reveals the Duke's true message to the court ambassador. To write his essay, William needed to read through the poem many times to extract all the subtleties of the Duke's language. He then highlighted each of these conversational distinctions and explained how they connected to the overall point of the poem.

The Evaluative Essay

When you evaluate a literary work, you identify the values and beliefs expressed in the work and assess the validity of these elements. You may opt to support the values and beliefs expressed in the work or to refute or question them. Evaluative essays judge a work based on criteria set by what you have learned, experienced, and observed. In an evaluative essay, you could address whether you agree with the set of values expressed in an essay. You could also prove why the conclusions in a literary work are faulty or why you feel a particular play is unrealistic.

Evaluative essays are more than simply your opinion of a work. You must support your perspective by drawing from both the work and the value and belief system you use to evaluate it. In her essay on *A Doll's House*, Jodi evaluated Ibsen's play by placing it in social and historical context. She came to the conclusion, after initially believing otherwise, that Torvald loved Nora the best way he knew how. In her essay, Jodi proved her thesis using examples from the work and historical analysis.

The Research Paper

Literary research papers allow you to explore in depth a particular aspect of a work, using resources such as books, journals, Internet sources, and interviews to support your ideas. Research papers may employ the techniques of any of the essay forms described earlier in this section or may address a specific question you have about the work.

Juan wondered if the poem "Daddy" by Sylvia Plath reflected the reality of the author's life. Had she really tried to kill herself? What relationship did she have with her father? He decided to find out about the life of the author first and, depending on what he discovered, write a research paper on how "Daddy" is or is not an autobiographical poem.

Juan began his research at the library, where he found several biographies on Plath. He also located some literary criticism on Plath's work and her personal connection to her writings. With the help of a biography, he discovered that Plath was the daughter of German immigrants, that her father had died when she was eight years old of a gangrenous leg, and that she had indeed attempted suicide as a teenager—all events she describes in the poem "Daddy."

Although his research did seem to connect the real Plath with the voice of "Daddy," Juan read something in a literary journal that made him pause. A critic named Elizabeth Hardwick wrote that Plath's internal self-constructed chaos contributed much to this particular poem and that Plath wrote it shortly before committing suicide. Juan decided that rather than portraying a real-life description of her father, Plath's poem relayed her psychological state of mind. Her father became representative of her internal struggles—her scapegoat. Thus, the father in "Daddy" was a generalized perception rather than an accurate description of a particular person in Plath's life.

Juan continued his research on the Internet, locating a website maintained by the University of Alberta in Canada devoted entirely to the work of Sylvia Plath. The site answered some remaining questions he had regarding the author and gave him different literary perspectives on her work. The site also provided him with some supporting material he could use in his research paper. Although his topic deviated from his original idea of proving Plath's poem to be strictly autobiographical, Juan felt he had a solid and interesting topic to research and develop.

Family

Carmen L. Garza, "Tamalda," 1987. Courtesy of the Artist.

The earliest and usually the strongest influence on each of us is the family. Throughout history, people from every walk of life have accused or thanked, bemoaned or celebrated members of their own families. As a result, family relationships have provided the subject matter for a wide variety of themes. Some of the families may seem destructive while others are loving and supportive. As readers, we can sympathize with, perhaps even identify with, authors as they share their own family experiences and as they cope with problems involving parents, siblings, and other family members.

Through the characters in the stories or poems or the real people in the essays, we can vicariously experience family life in a variety of times, on different economic levels, and through diverse cultures. We can laugh at Grace's story of a family car or recoil at the mutilation of the mother in Svava Jakobsdóttir's "A Story for Children." We can also understand the joys and sorrows of a mother-daughter relationship as we read Didion, Ostriker, or Walker; with TallMountain we can share the beauty and wisdom of the Athabaskan language. Further, we can gain insight into the dynamics of a father-son relationship by reading Luke, Dorris, Salinas, and Li-Young Lee. Just as Yeats writes of a prayer for a daughter, Weaver wishes aloud for a son's security as he goes out into a hostile world. With the help of writers like Grace, we can compare our experiences of growing up with those of children from other cultural backgrounds. Writers as diverse as these share with us what it is like to be within or outside of their communities. By allowing us to participate in the hardships and confusion of modern dysfunctional families such as those portrayed by McCullers and Plath, literature helps us to understand that the "immense complexity of love" sometimes causes problems that have no easy solutions.

Authors teach us the value of learning to laugh at our problems within our families. They also share with us the realization that even the most disparate family members can work through problems to reach solutions and an even greater depth of love. August Wilson, in *Fences*, reveals a family in crisis. Li-Young Lee portrays two generations who will benefit from the father's "gift." Terrence McNally portrays a mother's and a partner's love.

Similarly, we can compare our experiences within the family unit with those of others. James Baldwin lets us share in the stories of two brothers and participate in their reconciliation. Truman Capote, drawing from his real-life experiences, tells us of the beautiful friendship between a little boy and an older woman in "A Christmas Memory." Michael Dorris reminds us of the tenderness between parents who try to deal with the loss of a child. Most important, through the enjoyment of this literature—the tears, the curses, the prayers, and the laughter— we can deepen our own understanding of others and ourselves.

Writing about Family

The essays you write about the works in the Family unit will be diverse. As you plan your essays, you should refer to the questions at the end of each genre section on writing about literature as well as to the questions after individual works and at the end of the thematic unit. Then consider which genre you want to write about and which work or works you prefer. You might select an essay or a poem that is rich in metaphorical devices and focus your essay on the ways that the metaphors expand, clarify, or enrich the work. For example, you could examine the way in which Frances Mayes, in "*Bramare*," uses both metaphors and a variety of sound devices to create the feelings and sounds of a peaceful time that lives in the narrator's memory. If you wanted to write about a poem, you might write an essay explaining how W. B. Yeats uses the images of the horn of plenty and the laurel tree to convey the kind of life he wishes for his daughter. If you prefer to write about fiction, you might write about point of view in James Baldwin's "Sonny's Blues" or examine the symbolism in Truman Capote's "A Christmas Memory." An essay on one of the plays might combine a researched study of the setting—time, place, and culture—with illustrations of the effect of that setting on the actions and opinions of the characters or on the theme. If your teacher asks you to write a personal essay as a reaction to one of the works, you might reread Joan Didion's description of her return home and write an essay on your home, or you might use Alicia Ostriker's poem as a basis for a description of your empathy with your child.

Fences, the play by August Wilson included in the casebook, provides a variety of topics for a documented essay using critical essays as well as your own ideas. When he was assigned an essay using the casebook, Jim Fowler first carefully read the play. Then, in order to get an overall picture of the assignment, he read the articles about the author and the play. Because of his personal interest in baseball and because baseball is so relevant to the main character, he chose for his subject the effect of baseball on Troy. Before deciding on a more specific subject and a thesis, Jim used his computer to list the many references to baseball and his interpretations of them in random order. He also listed any supporting references from the critical articles that he thought might be helpful. After examining the lists for ideas, Jim decided to cut and paste them into three categories: language, lifestyle, and character. His preliminary thesis statement was "The reader can easily conclude that Troy's baseball experience has a very significant effect upon his language, his lifestyle, and even his moral character." Jim was now ready to write his first draft, and he chose to write it by hand, using the ideas he had listed by category as the building blocks and tying them together coherently.

From this rough draft, Jim typed the essay into the computer so that he could easily make corrections and write revisions. At this point, he checked with his professor to see if he was on the right track with his essay. The professor made a few suggestions and corrections but felt that the essay really needed little work other than polishing, correcting, and documenting. For example, in a few places the essay included past tense when talking about the events in the play, and these were changed to present tense. Back on his computer, Jim made the necessary changes and added his documentation, double-checking his quotations and paraphrases to ensure that he had not plagiarized any material. He decided that the conclusion could also be improved; therefore, he rewrote the concluding paragraph. Finally, he selected a title for his essay. He was now ready to print the final copy of his essay, "Baseball Metaphors in *Fences*," which is included at the end of the casebook in this unit.

ESSAYS

Joan Didion (b. 1934)

Didion, an American novelist and journalist who grew up in California, writes both fiction and nonfiction. Her recent novel, The Last Thing He Wanted *(1996), is a tightly plotted story about an American journalist who investigated the sale of arms in Central America. She has also collaborated with her husband, John Gregory Dunn, on screenplays. In elegant essays such as those collected in* Slouching Toward Bethlehem *(1967), from which "On Going Home" comes, she examines contemporary Americans' loss of communal values and direction.*

ON GOING HOME   (1967)

1   I am home for my daughter's first birthday. By "home" I do not mean the house in Los Angeles where my husband and I and the baby live, but the place where my family is, in the Central Valley of California. It is a vital although troublesome distinction. My husband likes my family but is uneasy in their house, because once there I fall into their ways, which are difficult, oblique, deliberately inarticulate, not my husband's ways. We live in dusty houses ("D-U-S-T," he once wrote with his finger on surfaces all over the house, but no one noticed it) filled with mementos quite without value to him (what could the Canton dessert plates mean to him? how could he have known about the assay scales, why should he care if he did know?), and we appear to talk exclusively about people we know who have been committed to mental hospitals, about people we know who have been booked on drunk-driving charges, and about property, particularly about property, land, price per acre and C-2 zoning and assessments and freeway access. My brother does not understand my husband's inability to perceive the advantage in the rather common real-estate transaction known as "sale-leaseback," and my husband in turn does not understand why so many of the people he hears about in my father's house have recently been committed to mental hospitals or booked on drunk-driving charges. Nor does he understand that when we talk about sale-leasebacks and right-of-way condemnations we are talking in code about things we like best, the yellow fields and the cottonwoods and the rivers rising and falling and the mountain roads closing when the heavy snow comes in. We miss each other's points, have another drink and regard the fire. My brother refers to my husband, in his presence, as "Joan's husband." Marriage is the classic betrayal.

2   Or perhaps it is not any more. Sometimes, I think that those of us who are now in our thirties were born into the last generation to carry the burden of "home," to find in family life the source of all tension and drama. I had by all objective accounts a "normal" and a "happy" family situation, and yet I was almost thirty years old before I could talk to my family on the

telephone without crying after I had hung up. We did not fight. Nothing was wrong. And yet some nameless anxiety colored the emotional charges between me and the place that I came from. The question of whether or not you could go home again was a very real part of the sentimental and largely literary baggage with which we left home in the fifties; I suspect that it is irrelevant to the children born of the fragmentation after World War II. A few weeks ago in a San Francisco bar I saw a pretty young girl on crystal take off her clothes and dance for the cash prize in an "amateur-topless" contest. There was no particular sense of moment about this, none of the effect of romantic degradation, of "dark journey," for which my generation strived so assiduously. What sense could that girl possibly make of, say, *Long Day's Journey into Night?* Who is beside the point?

3   That I am trapped in this particular irrelevancy is never more apparent to me than when I am home. Paralyzed by the neurotic lassitude engendered by meeting one's past at every turn, around every corner, inside every cupboard, I go aimlessly from room to room. I decide to meet it head-on and clear out a drawer, and I spread the contents on the bed. A bathing suit I wore the summer I was seventeen. A letter of rejection from *The Nation,* an aerial photograph of the site for a shopping center my father did not build in 1954. Three teacups handpainted with cabbage roses and signed "E.M.," my grandmother's initials. There is no final solution for letters of rejection from *The Nation* and teacups handpainted in 1900. Nor is there any answer to snapshots of one's grandfather as a young man on skis, surveying around Donner Pass in the year 1910. I smooth out the snapshot and look into his face, and do and do not see my own. I close the drawer, and have another cup of coffee with my mother. We get along very well, veterans of a guerilla war we never understood.

4   Days pass. I see no one. I come to dread my husband's evening call, not only because he is full of news of what by now seems to me our remote life in Los Angeles, people he has seen, letters which require attention, but because he asks what I have been doing, suggests uneasily that I get out, drive to San Francisco or Berkeley. Instead I drive across the river to a family graveyard. It has been vandalized since my last visit and the monuments are broken, overturned in the dry grass. Because I once saw a rattlesnake in the grass I stay in the car and listen to a country-and-Western station. Later I drive with my father to a ranch he has in the foothills. The man who runs his cattle on it asks us to the round-up, a week from Sunday, and although I know that I will be in Los Angeles I say, in the oblique way my family talks, that I will come. Once home I mention the broken monuments in the graveyard. My mother shrugs.

5   I go to visit my great-aunts. A few of them think now that I am my cousin, or their daughter who died young. We recall an anecdote about a relative last seen in 1948, and they ask if I still like living in New York City. I have lived in Los Angeles for three years, but I say that I do. The baby is offered a horehound drop, and I am slipped a dollar bill "to buy

a treat." Questions trail off, answers are abandoned, the baby plays with the dust motes in a shaft of the afternoon sun.

6   It is time for the baby's birthday party: a white cake, strawberry-marshmallow ice cream, a bottle of champagne saved from another party. In the evening, after she has gone to sleep, I kneel beside the crib and touch her face, where it is pressed against the slats, with mine. She is an open and trusting child, unprepared for and unaccustomed to the ambushes of family life, and perhaps it is just as well that I can offer her little of that life. I would like to give her more. I would like to promise her that she will grow up with a sense of her cousins and of rivers and her great-grandmother's teacups, would like to pledge her a picnic on a river with fried chicken and her hair uncombed, would like to give her *home* for her birthday, but we live differently now and I can promise her nothing like that. I give her a xylophone and a sundress from Madeira, and promise to tell her a funny story.

Questions for Discussion

1. What does Didion mean when she says, "Marriage is the classic betrayal"? What is the source of tension between Didion's family and her husband?

2. Didion says that until she was "almost thirty," she would cry after calling her family. Why do you think she cried?

3. What is Didion's definition of home? What does she mean when she says, "I would like to give her [her daughter] *home*, [. . .] but we live differently now"? How does the **symbolism** of the graveyard develop Didion's feeling of rootlessness?

4. Why, in an essay about going home, does Didion begin and end with her daughter's first birthday?

5. Why does Didion say that she and her mother are "veterans of a guerilla war we never understood"?

Suggestions for Exploration and Writing

1. Discuss in detail how your relationship to your family has changed since you began college. How does your experience compare with Didion's?

2. In an essay, explain how you and other members of your family are "veterans of a guerilla war."

3. Nuclear families often develop private rituals, in-jokes, and special word usages that only they understand. Such rituals, jokes, and usages are one source of conflict between the writer's family and her husband. Write an essay in which you examine the private rituals and language of your own family.

4. Write an essay responding to Didion's belief that today's generation is unlikely to know the kind of home she describes.

Faye Moskowitz

As a child of immigrants, Moskowitz grew up in Michigan, where she was a Jew in a predominantly Christian community. Her experiences are chronicled in her collections of essays and memoirs A Leak in the Heart: Personal Essays and Life Stories *(1985) and And the* Bridge Is Love *(1991) and in her collection of stories,* Whoever Finds This: I Love You *(1991).* Her Face in the Mirror *(1994), an anthology edited by Moskowitz, showcases Jewish women's writings. After attending Wayne State University, she attended and now teaches creative writing at George Washington University.*

JEWISH CHRISTMAS   (1991)

1   "Jewish Christmas"—that's what my gentile friends called Chanukah when I was growing up in Michigan in the thirties and forties. Anachronistic, yes, but they had a point. Observing the dietary laws of separating milk and meat dishes was far easier for the handful of Jewish families in our little town than getting through December without mixing the two holidays.

2   Christmas was a miserable time for Jewish children in those days, nothing short of quarantine could have kept us from catching the Christmas fever. My parents were no help. Immigrants who had fled pogroms in Russia and Poland, they were world-class outsiders. If tee shirts with mottos had been in fashion then, our shirts would surely have read Keep a Low Profile. My mother would never have considered going to my school to complain about the Christmas tree in the lobby or the creche in our principal's office or the three life-size wise men, complete with camels, that we cut out of construction paper in Art and hung on our classroom walls.

3   If I still wasn't convinced Christmas was coming after all those reminders, I had only to look at the advent calendar hanging behind my teacher's desk or walk downtown, where carols blared out over loudspeakers and built to a crescendo in front of the six-foot neon cross decorating our largest department store. And as for keeping a low profile, try it when yours is the only neighborhood house in work clothes while every other is dressed for a party.

4   By the time we moved to the Jewish section of Detroit, I was old enough to accept Christmas as a holiday other people celebrated. Chanukah was our winter holiday, not a substitute at all, but a minor-league festival that paled before Passover, Rosh Hashanah, and Yom Kippur. All the cousins gathered at our grandparents' house where we lined up to get Chanukah gelt from the uncles: quarters and half dollars, and dollar bills, perhaps, for the older children. Mostly we ran around a lot, got very flushed, and ate latkes, plenty of them.

5   My own children were raised in a diverse neighborhood in Washington, D.C. The Ghost of Christmas Past clanked its chains for a while, and my husband and I learned to make a few concessions. Still, we never sunk to the Chanukah bush or an actual Christmas tree, though we knew Jews who did, we lit the menorah, bought presents for each of the eight nights, decorated our house with blue and white paper chains, and played with dreidels. In spite of that, our kids were pretty disgruntled for most of December, although even their non-Jewish friends had to concede we had something with those latkes.

6   For the past few years, with our children grown, my husband and I have cut off the Chanukah/Christmas debate entirely. We distribute the Chanukah gelt early and then leave the country. That's going to a lot of trouble to avoid office parties and the egg nog and pfeffernuss for which we never did develop a taste, but at least we don't have to get caught up in the general depression that afflicts not only the people who celebrate Christmas but all the rest who don't and wish they did.

7   Several years ago, we found ourselves in Venice during the holidays. In spite of all our rationalizations, we missed being home with our children, missed the ritual of lighting the menorah, the tacky paper chains, the dreidel game we play, gambling for raisins or nuts, and at that moment we would have traded any pasta dish, no matter how delectable, for potato latkes like the ones we ate at Chanukah as far back as we both could remember.

8   So maybe that's why, with the help of guidebooks and our faltering Italian, we threaded our way through the city's bewildering twists and turns until we suddenly emerged into a spacious square that marks the old Jewish ghetto of Venice. The clip-clop of our heels on cobblestones and the flutter of pigeons punctuated a silence that might have existed for centuries or only on that particular rest day, we didn't know. "There's an old synagogue at the other end of the square," my husband said. "Let's go see if maybe it's open for visitors." We pulled at the heavy brass-studded wooden door, and far down a long corridor I heard the sound of many voices chattering in Italian. "I'm probably hallucinating," I whispered to my husband, "but I swear I smell latkes."

9   In that musty, crumbling building, the memories flooded back as clear as the icicles we licked in those nose-numbing December days of my Michigan childhood. Bundled against the stunning cold, we walked hand in hand, my mother and father, my brothers and I, along darkened streets where orange candles in brass menorahs bravely illuminated each front window we passed.

10   In my grandparents' vestibule, we shed our snowy boots. The welcoming warmth of the coal furnace promised more coziness deep inside, there my aunts sucked in their bellies as they elbowed past one another in and out of Bobbe's tiny kitchen, from which they pulled a seemingly endless array of delicious dishes as if from a magician's opera hat: platters of bagels slathered with cream cheese, smoked fish with skins of iridescent gold, pickled herring, thick slices of Bermuda onion strong

enough to prompt a double-dare, boiled potatoes with their red jackets on, wallowing in butter. Best of all were the crisp potato latkes, hot from Bobbe's frying pan, to eat swaddled in cool sour cream, the contrasting textures and temperatures indelibly printing themselves on our memory.

11   Though our mothers' cooking styles were virtually interchangeable, my husband and I used to quarrel every year about whose family made the better latkes. My mother's potato pancakes were thin and lacy, delicate enough to float in their hot cooking oil. His mother's latkes, I pointed out at every opportunity, utterly lacked refinement: colossal, digestion-defying pancakes the size of hockey pucks, they were each a meal in themselves. "Just the way I like them," my husband would tell me as he wolfed yet another one.

12   I never learned to make my mother's latkes. She died just before my husband and I were married, and when we came to Washington we brought my mother-in-law with us, so her potato latkes won by default and became part of our children's Chanukah tradition. Which is not to say I ever accepted them graciously, and as we moved into our middle years, and cholesterol moved into our lexicon, my husband, too, scorned the latkes of his childhood. "The Israeli secret weapon," he called them when his mother wasn't listening. "Eat two, and you're on sick call for at least a week."

13   But friends came each Chanukah and brought their children to celebrate with ours. We exchanged small gifts: boxes of crayons, pretty bars of soap, cellophane bags of sour candies for Grandma, who, of course, supplied the latkes. Early in the afternoon, she would begin grating potatoes on a vicious four-sided grater, the invention of some fiendish anti-Semite who must have seen the opportunity to maim half the Jewish population each December.

14   The trick was to finish grating just before the guests arrived so the potatoes would not blacken, as they have a discouraging tendency to do. Meanwhile, as she mixed in eggs, matzo meal, salt, and baking powder, Grandma heated a frying pan with enough oil to light the Chanukah lamps into the next century. The finished latkes were drained on supermarket paper bags that promptly turned translucent with fat. Still, we ate them: great, golden, greasy, dolloped-with-sour-cream latkes, and our complaints became part of our Chanukah tradition, too.

15   The Venetian latkes didn't taste very much like Grandma's, but there was enough resemblance to quell our homesickness. Well, that was a while ago. Today, though November leaves, red and brown and gold, still hang on stubbornly, the Christmas drumming has already begun. My morning's *Washington Post* bursts with ads like a ripe pomegranate spewing seeds. Overnight, green wreaths have sprouted on our neighbors' doors, and the Salvation Army kettle, come out of storage, stands on its tripod in front of the Giant food store once again. I remember how little I cared for this time. For a moment, the buried stones of jealousy and of shame and not belonging work themselves to the surface with a speed that surprises me.

16   But this year something is different, suddenly, finally, *I* am the grandma who makes the latkes. Two little grandchildren, both named for my mother-in-law (may she rest in peace), will come to our house to watch us light the menorah. Baby Helen at two and a half can already say the Hebrew blessing over the candles, and if my joy in that could translate to Chanukah gelt, all the banks in America would be forced to close.

17   I close my eyes and think of Grandma tasting a bit of her childhood each Chanukah when she prepared the latkes as her mother had made them before her. My mother, my aunts, my own grandmothers float back to me, young and vibrant once more, making days holy in the sanctuaries of their kitchens, feeding me, cradling me, connecting me to the intricately plaited braid of their past, and even at this moment, looking down the corridor of what's to come, I see myself join them as they open their arms wide to enfold my children and grandchildren in their embrace.

Questions for Discussion

1. Historically, why would "Keep a Low Profile" be appropriate for Jews of the 1930s and 1940s in America?

2. What is the significance of Chanukah? What does it celebrate? Why does Moskowitz refer to it as a "minor-league festival"?

3. Explain why Moskowitz and her husband might find it easier to leave the country at Christmas.

4. What particular traditions and rituals associated with Chanukah does the speaker remember fondly, even after seeking escape from them?

5. What effect did all the sales pitches associated with Christmas have on the speaker's celebration of Chanukah?

6. Define the following words: creche, advent, gelt, latke, menorah, and dreidels. What is the significance of the discussion of potato latkes?

7. How does Moskowitz's Jewish humor enrich her short memoir?

Suggestion for Exploration and Writing

1. If you are Jewish and living or working in a non-Jewish community, write an expository essay about your Christmas experiences and Chanukah.

2. Moskowitz says that her female ancestors through her memories "[connect her] to the intricately plaited braid of their past [. . .]." Write an essay explaining how some of your memories have braided you to your past.

3. In an essay, discuss the degree to which traditional religious festivals such as Christmas and Chanukah are threatened by their commercialization and secularization.

4. Whether you are or are not Jewish, write a description of the traditions of Chanukah and an explanation of their meaning.

Frances Mayes (b. 1940)

A native of Fitzgerald, Georgia, Frances Mayes is a gourmet cook and the author of numerous articles on food and cooking as well as five books of poetry. Mayes became famous nationwide with the publication of Under the Tuscan Sun *(1996) which, along with the later volume,* Bella Tuscany *(1999), celebrates with passion and gusto not only the centuries-old villa Mayes bought near Cortona, Italy, but also the centuries-old traditions and culture of the surrounding Tuscan hill country. Formerly chair of the creative writing program at San Francisco State University, Mayes recently retired to devote full time to writing. With her second husband, Ed Kleinschmidt, who adopted her name when they married, Mayes lives alternately in San Francisco and in her villa near Cortona.*

BRAMARE: (ARCHAIC) TO YEARN FOR   (1996)

1   I am about to buy a house in a foreign country. A house with the beautiful name of Bramasole. It is tall, square, and apricot-colored with faded green shutters, ancient tile roof, and an iron balcony on the second level, where ladies might have sat with their fans to watch some spectacle below. But below, overgrown briars, tangles of roses, and knee-high weeds run rampant. The balcony faces southeast, looking into a deep valley, then into the Tuscan Apennines. When it rains or when the light changes, the facade of the house turns gold, sienna, ocher; a previous scarlet paint job seeps through in rosy spots like a box of crayons left to melt in the sun. In places where the stucco has fallen away, rugged stone shows what the exterior once was. The house rises above a *strada bianca*, a road white with pebbles, on a terraced slab of hillside covered with fruit and olive trees. Bramasole: from *bramare*, to yearn for, and *sole*, sun: something that yearns for the sun, and yes, I do.

2   The family wisdom runs strongly against this decision. My mother has said "Ridiculous," with her certain and forceful stress on the second syllable, "RiDICulous," and my sisters, although excited, fear I am eighteen, about to run off with a sailor in the family car. I quietly have my own doubts. The upright seats in the *notaio*'s outer office don't help. Through my thin white linen dress, spiky horsehairs pierce me every time I shift, which is often in the hundred-degree waiting room. I look over to see what Ed is writing on the back of a receipt: Parmesan, salami, coffee, bread. How can he? Finally, the signora opens her door and her torrential Italian flows over us.

3   The *notaio* is nothing like a notary; she's the legal person who conducts real-estate transactions in Italy. Ours, Signora Mantucci, is a small, fierce Sicilian woman with thick tinted glasses that enlarge her green eyes. She talks faster than any human I have ever heard. She reads long laws aloud. I thought all Italian was mellifluous; she makes it sound like rocks crashing down a chute. Ed looks at her raptly; I know he's in thrall to the sound of her voice. The owner, Dr. Carta, suddenly thinks he has asked too little; he *must* have, since we have agreed to buy it. We think his price is exorbitant. We *know* his price is exorbitant. The Sicilian doesn't pause; she will not be interrupted by anyone except by Giuseppe from the bar downstairs, who suddenly swings open the dark doors, tray aloft, and seems surprised to see his *Americani* customers sitting there almost cross-eyed in confusion. He brings the signora her midmorning thimble of espresso, which she downs in a gulp, hardly pausing. The owner expects to claim that the house cost one amount while it really cost much more. "That is just the way it's done," he insists. "No one is fool enough to declare the real value." He proposes we bring one check to the *notaio*'s office, then pass him ten smaller checks literally under the table.

4   Anselmo Martini, our agent, shrugs.

5   Ian, the English estate agent we hired to help with translation, shrugs also.

6   Dr. Carta concludes, "You Americans! You take things so seriously. And, *per favore,* date the checks at one-week intervals so the bank isn't alerted to large sums."

7   Was that the same bank I know, whose sloe-eyed teller languidly conducts a transaction every fifteen minutes, between smokes and telephone calls? The signora comes to an abrupt halt, scrambles the papers into a folder and stands up. We are to come back when the money and papers are ready.

8   A window in our hotel room opens onto an expansive view over the ancient roofs of Cortona, down to the dark expanse of the Val di Chiana. A hot and wild wind—the *scirocco*—is driving normal people a little crazy. For me, it seems to reflect my state of mind. I can't sleep. In the United States, I've bought and sold a few houses before—loaded up the car with my mother's Spode, the cat, and the ficus for the five- or five-thousand-mile drive to the next doorway where a new key would fit. You *have* to churn somewhat when the roof covering your head is at stake, since to sell is to walk away from a cluster of memories and to buy is to choose where the future will take place. And the place, never neutral of course, will cast its influence. Beyond that, legal complications and contingencies must be worked out. But here, absolutely everything conspires to keep me staring into the dark.

9   Italy always has had a magnetic north pull on my psyche. Houses have been on my mind for four summers of renting farmhouses all over Tuscany. In the first place Ed and I rented with friends, we started calculating on the first night, trying to figure out if our four pooled savings would buy the

tumbled stone farm we could see from the terrace. Ed immediately fell for farm life and roamed over our neighbors' land looking at the work in progress. The Antolinis grew tobacco, a beautiful if hated crop. We could hear workers shout *"Vipera!"* to warn the others of a poisonous snake. At evening, a violet blue haze rose from the dark leaves. The well-ordered farm looked peaceful from the vantage point of our terrace. Our friends never came back, but for the next three vacations, the circuitous search for a summer home became a quest for us—whether we ever found a place or not, we were happening on places that made pure green olive oil, discovering sweet country Romanesque churches in villages, meandering the back roads of vineyards, and stopping to taste the softest Brunello and the blackest Vino Nobile. Looking for a house gives an intense focus. We visited weekly markets not just with the purchase of picnic peaches in mind; we looked carefully at all the produce's quality and variety, mentally forecasting birthday dinners, new holidays, and breakfasts for weekend guests. We spent hours sitting in piazzas or sipping lemonade in local bars, secretly getting a sense of the place's ambiance. I soaked many a heel blister in a hotel bidet, rubbed bottles of lotion on my feet, which had covered miles of stony streets. We hauled histories and guides and wildflower books and novels in and out of rented houses and hotels. Always we asked local people where they liked to eat and headed to restaurants our many guidebooks never mentioned. We both have an insatiable curiosity about each jagged castle ruin on the hillsides. My idea of heaven still is to drive the gravel farm roads of Umbria and Tuscany, very pleasantly lost.

10   Cortona was the first town we ever stayed in and we always came back to it during the summers we rented near Volterra, Florence, Montisi, Rignano, Vicchio, Quercegrossa, all those fascinating, quirky houses. One had a kitchen two people could not pass in, but there was a slice of a view of the Arno. Another kitchen had no hot water and no knives, but the house was built into medieval ramparts overlooking vineyards. One had several sets of china for forty, countless glasses and silverware, but the refrigerator iced over every day and by four the door swung open, revealing a new igloo. When the weather was damp, I got a tingling shock if I touched anything in the kitchen. On the property, Cimabue, legend says, discovered the young Giotto drawing a sheep in the dirt. One house had beds with back-crunching dips in the middles. Bats flew down the chimney and buzzed us, while worms in the beams sent down a steady sifting of sawdust onto the pillows. The fireplace was so big we could sit in it while grilling our veal chops and peppers.

11   We drove hundreds of dusty miles looking at houses that turned out to be in the flood plain of the Tiber or overlooking strip mines. The Siena agent blithely promised that the view would be wonderful again in twenty years; replanting stripped areas was a law. A glorious medieval village house was wildly expensive. The saw-toothed peasant we met in a bar tried to sell us his childhood home, a windowless stone chicken house joined to

another house, with snarling dogs lunging at us from their ropes. We fell hard for a farm outside Montisi; the *contessa* who owned it led us on for days, then decided she needed a sign from God before she could sell it. We had to leave before the sign arrived.

12   As I think back over those places, they suddenly seem preposterously alien and Cortona does, too. Ed doesn't think so. He's in the piazza every afternoon, gazing at the young couple trying to wheel their new baby down the street. They're halted every few steps. Everyone circles the carriage. They're leaning into the baby's face, making noises, praising the baby. "In my next life," Ed tells me, "I want to come back as an Italian baby." He steeps in the piazza life: the sultry and buffed man pushing up his sleeve so his muscles show when he languidly props his chin in his hand; the pure flute notes of Vivaldi drifting from an upstairs window; the flower seller's fan of bright flowers against the stone shop; a man with no neck at all unloading lambs from his truck. He slings them like flour sacks over his shoulder and the lambs' eyeballs bulge out. Every few minutes, Ed looks up at the big clock that has kept time for so long over this piazza. Finally, he takes a stroll, memorizing the stones in the street.

13   Across the hotel courtyard a visiting Arab chants his prayers toward dawn, just when I finally can fall asleep. He sounds as though he is gargling with salt water. For hours, he rings the voice's changes over a small register, over and over. I want to lean out and shout, "Shut up!" Now and then I have to laugh. I look out, see him nodding in the window, a sweet smile on his face. He reminds me so much of tobacco auctioneers I heard in hot warehouses in the South as a child. I am seven thousand miles from home, plunking down my life savings on a whim. Is it a whim? It feels very close to falling in love and that's never really whimsical but comes from some deep source. Or does it?

14   Each time we step out of the cool, high rooms of the hotel and into the sharp-edged sun, we walk around town and like it more and more. The outdoor tables at Bar Sport face the Piazza Signorelli. A few farmers sell produce on the steps of the nineteenth-century *teatro* every morning. As we drink espresso, we watch them holding up rusty hand scales to weigh the tomatoes. The rest of the piazza is lined with perfectly intact medieval or Renaissance *palazzi*. Easily, someone might step out any second and break into *La Traviata*. Every day we visit each keystoned medieval gate in the Etruscan walls, explore the Fiat-wide stone streets lined with Renaissance and older houses and the even narrower *vicoli*, mysterious pedestrian passageways, often steeply stepped. The bricked-up fourteenth-century "doors of the dead" are still visible. These ghosts of doors beside the main entrance were designed, some say, to take out the plague victims—bad luck for them to exit by the main entrance. I notice in the regular doors, people often leave their keys in the lock.

15   Guidebooks describe Cortona as "somber" and "austere." They misjudge. The hilltop position, the walls and upright, massive stone build-

ings give a distinctly vertical feel to the architecture. Walking across the piazza, I feel the abrupt, angular shadows fall with Euclidean purity. I want to stand up straight—the upright posture of the buildings seems to carry over to the inhabitants. They walk slowly, with very fine, I want to say, *carriage*. I keep saying, "Isn't she beautiful?" "Isn't he gorgeous?" "Look at *that* face—pure Raphael." By late afternoon, we're sitting again with our espressi, this time facing the other piazza. A woman of about sixty with her daughter and the teenage granddaughter pass by us, strolling, their arms linked, sun on their vibrant faces. We don't know why light has such a luminous quality. Perhaps the sunflower crops radiate gold from the surrounding fields. The three women look peaceful, proud, impressively pleased. There should be a gold coin with their faces on it.

16   Meanwhile, as we sip, the dollar is falling fast. We rouse ourselves from the piazza every morning to run around to all the banks, checking their posted exchange rates. When you're cashing traveler's checks for a last-minute spree at the leather market, the rate doesn't matter that much, but this is a house with five acres and every lira counts. A slight drop at those multiples makes the stomach drop also. Every hundred lire it falls, we calculate how much more expensive the house becomes. Irrationally, I also calculate how many pairs of shoes that could buy. Shoes, before, have been my major purchase in Italy, a secret sin. Sometimes I'd go home with nine new pairs: red snake-skin flats, sandals, navy suede boots, and several pairs of black pumps of varying heels.

17   Typically, the banks vary in how much commission they bite when they receive a large transfer from overseas. We want a break. It looks like a significant chunk of interest they'll collect, since clearing a check in Italy can take weeks.

18   Finally, we have a lesson in the way things work. Dr. Carta, anxious to close, calls his bank—the bank his father and his father-in-law use—in Arezzo, a half hour away. Then he calls us. "Go there," he says. "They won't take a commission for receiving the money at all, and they'll give you whatever the posted rate is when it arrives."

19   His savvy doesn't surprise me, though he has seemed spectacularly uninterested in money the entire time we have negotiated—just named his high price and stuck to it. He bought the property from the five old sisters of an landowning family in Perugia the year before, thinking, he said, to make it a summer place for his family. However, he and his wife inherited property on the coast and decided to use that instead. Was that the case, or had he scooped up a bargain from ladies in their nineties and now is making a bundle, possibly buying coast property with our money? Not that I begrudge him. He's smart.

20   Dr. Carta, perhaps fearing we might back out, calls and asks to meet us at the house. He roars up in his Alfa 164, Armani from stem to stern. "There is something more," he says, as though continuing a conversation. "If you follow me, I will show you something." A few hundred feet down the road, he leads us up a stone path through fragrant yellow broom.

Odd, the stone path continues up the hill, curving along a ridge. Soon we come to a two-hundred-degree view of the valley, with the cypress-lined road below us and a mellow landscape dotted with tended vineyards and olive groves. In the distance lies a blue daub, which is Lake Trasimeno; off to the right, we see the red-roofed silhouette of Cortona cleanly outlined against the sky, Dr. Carta turns to us triumphantly. The flat paving stones widen here. "The Romans—this road was built by the Romans—it goes straight into Cortona." The sun is broiling. He goes on and on about the large church at the top of the hill. He points out where the rest of the road might have run, right through Bramasole's property.

21   Back at the house he turns on an outside faucet and splashes his face. "You'll enjoy the finest water, truly your own abundant *acqua minerale,* excellent for the liver. *Eccellente!*" He manages to be at once enthusiastic and a little bored, friendly and slightly condescending. I am afraid we have spoken too bluntly about money. Or maybe he has interpreted our law-abiding American expectations about the transaction as incredibly naive. He lets the faucet run, cupping his hand under the water, somehow leaning over for a drink without dislodging the well-cut linen coat tossed over his shoulders. "Enough water for a swimming pool," he insists, "which would be perfect out on the point where you can see the lake, overlooking right where Hannibal defeated the Romans."

22   We're dazzled by the remains of a Roman road over the hill covered with wildflowers. We will follow the stone road into town for a coffee late in the afternoons. He shows us the old cistern. Water is precious in Tuscany and was collected drop by drop. By shining a flashlight into the opening, we've already noticed that the underground cistern has a stone archway, obviously some kind of passageway. Up the hill in the Medici fortress, we saw the same arch in the cistern there and the caretaker told us that a secret underground escape route goes downhill to the valley, then to Lake Trasimeno. Italians take such remains casually. That one is allowed to own such ancient things seems impossible to me.

23   When I first saw Bramasole, I immediately wanted to hang my summer clothes in an *armadio* and arrange my books under one of those windows looking out over the valley. We'd spent four days with Signor Martini, who had a dark little office on Via Sacco e Vanzetti down in the lower town. Above his desk hung a photo of him as a soldier, I assumed for Mussolini. He listened to us as though we spoke perfect Italian. When we finished describing what we thought we wanted, he rose, put on his Borsolino, and said one word, *"Andiamo,"* let's go. Although he'd recently had a foot operation, he drove us over nonexistent roads and pushed through jungles of thorns to show us places only he knew about. Some were farmhouses with roofs collapsed onto the floor, miles from town and costing the earth. One had a tower built by the Crusaders, but the *contessa* who owned it cried and doubled the price on the spot when she saw that we really were interested. Another was attached to other farmhouses where

chickens were truly free range—they ran in and out of the houses. The yard was full of rusted farm equipment and hogs. Several felt airless or sat hard by the road. One would have required putting in a road—it was hidden in blackberry brambles and we could only peer in one window because a coiled black snake refused to budge from the threshold.

24   We took Signor Martini flowers, thanked him and said goodbye. He seemed genuinely sorry to see us go.

25   The next morning we ran into him in the piazza after coffee. He said, "I just saw a doctor from Arezzo. He might be interested in selling a house. *Una bella villa*," he added emphatically. The house was within walking distance of Cortona.

26   "How much?" we asked, although we knew by then he cringes at being asked that direct question.

27   "Let's just go take a look," was all he said. Out of Cortona, he took the road that climbs and winds to the other side of the hill. He turned onto the *strada bianca* and, after a couple of kilometers, pulled into a long, sloping driveway. I caught a glimpse of a shrine, then looked up at the three-story house with a curly iron fanlight above the front door and two tall, exotic palm trees on either side. On that fresh morning, the facade seemed radiant, glazed with layers of lemon, rouge, and terra-cotta. We both became silent as we got out of the car. After all the turns into unknown roads, the house seemed just to have been waiting all along.

28   "Perfect, we'll take it," I joked as we stepped through the weeds. Just as he had at other houses, Signor Martini made no sales pitch; he simply looked with us. We walked up to the house under a rusted pergola leaning under the weight of climbing roses. The double front door squawked like something alive when we pushed it open. The house's walls, thick as my arm is long, radiated coolness. The glass in the windows wavered. I scuffed through silty dust and saw below it smooth brick floors in perfect condition. In each room, Ed opened the inside window and pushed open the shutters to one glorious view after another of cypresses, rippling green hills, distant villas, a valley. There were even two bathrooms that functioned. They were not beautiful, but *bathrooms*, after all the houses we'd seen with no floors, much less plumbing. No one had lived there in thirty years and the grounds seemed like an enchanted garden, overgrown and tumbling with blackberries and vines. I could see Signor Martini regarding the grounds with a countryman's practiced eye. Ivy twisted into the trees and ran over fallen terrace walls. *"Molto lavoro,"* much work, was all he said.

29   During several years of looking, sometimes casually, sometimes to the point of exhaustion, I never heard a house say *yes* so completely. However, we were leaving the next day, and when we learned the price, we sadly said no and went home.

30   During the next months, I mentioned Bramasole now and then. I stuck a photo on my mirror and often wandered the grounds or rooms in my mind. The house is a metaphor for the self, of course, but it also is totally real. And a *foreign* house exaggerates all the associations houses carry.

Because I had ended a long marriage that was not supposed to end and was establishing a new relationship, this house quest felt tied to whatever new identity I would manage to forge. When the flying fur from the divorce settled, I had found myself with a grown daughter, a full-time university job (after years of part-time teaching), a modest securities portfolio, and an entire future to invent. Although divorce was harder than a death, still I felt oddly returned to myself after many years in a close family. I had the urge to examine my life in another culture and move beyond what I knew. I wanted something of a *physical* dimension that would occupy the mental volume the years of my former life had. Ed shares my passion for Italy completely and also shares the boon of three-month summer breaks from university teaching. There we would have long days for exploring and for our writing and research projects. When he is at the wheel, he'll *always* take the turn down the intriguing little road. The language, history, art, places in Italy are endless—two lifetimes wouldn't be enough. And, ah, the foreign self. The new life might shape itself to the contours of the house, which already is at home in the landscape, and to the rhythms around it.

31   In the spring, I called a California woman who was starting a real-estate development business in Tuscany. I asked her to check on Bramasole; perhaps if it had not sold, the price had come down. A week later, she called from a bar after meeting with the owner. "Yes, it's still for sale, but with that particular brand of Italian logic, the price has been raised. The dollar," she reminded me, "has fallen. And that house needs a lot of work."

32   Now we've returned. By this time, with equally peculiar logic, I've become fixed on buying Bramasole. After all, the only thing wrong is the expense. We both love the setting, the town, the house and land. If only one little thing is wrong, I tell myself, go ahead.

33   Still, this costs a *sacco di soldi*. It will be an enormous hassle to recover the house and land from neglect. Leaks, mold, tumbling stone terraces, crumbling plaster, one funky bathroom, another with an adorable metal hip bathtub and a cracked toilet.

34   Why does the prospect seem fun, when I found remodeling my kitchen in San Francisco a deep shock to my equilibrium? At home, we can't even hang a picture without knocking out a fistful of plaster. When we plunge the stopped-up sink, forgetting once again that the disposal doesn't like artichoke petals, sludge seems to rise from San Francisco Bay.

35   On the other hand, a dignified house near a Roman road, an Etruscan (Etruscan!) wall looming at the top of the hillside, a Medici fortress in sight, a view toward Monte Amiata, a passageway underground, one hundred and seventeen olive trees, twenty plums, and still uncounted apricot, almond, apple, and pear trees. Several figs seem to thrive near the well. Beside the front steps there's a large hazelnut. Then, proximity to one of the most superb towns I've ever seen. Wouldn't we be crazy not to buy this lovely house called Bramasole?

36   What if one of us is hit by a potato chip truck and can't work? I run through a litany of diseases we could get. An aunt died of a heart attack

at forty-two, my grandmother went blind, all the ugly illnesses. . . . What if an earthquake shakes down the universities where we teach? The Humanities Building is on a list of state structures most likely to fall in a moderately severe quake. What if the stock market spirals down?

37   I leap out of bed at three A.M. and step in the shower, letting my whole face take the cold water. Coming back to bed in the dark, feeling my way, I jam my toe on the iron bed frame. Pain jags all the way up my backbone. "Ed, wake up. I think I've broken my toe. How can you sleep?"

38   He sits up. "I was just dreaming of cutting herbs in the garden. Sage and lemon balm. Sage is *salvia* in Italian." He has never wavered from his belief that this is a brilliant idea, that this is heaven on earth. He clicks on the bedside lamp. He's smiling.

39   My half-on toenail is hanging half off, ugly purple spreading underneath. I can't bear to leave it or to pull it off. "I want to go home," I say.

40   He puts a Band-Aid around my toe. "You mean Bramasole, don't you?" he asks.

41   This sack of money in question has been wired from California but has not arrived. How can that be, I ask at the bank, money is wired, it arrives instantaneously. More shrugs. Perhaps the main bank in Florence is holding it. Days pass. I call Steve, my broker in California, from a bar. I'm shouting over the noise of a soccer match on the TV. "You'll have to check from that end;" he shouts back, "it's long gone from here and did you know the government there has changed forty-seven times since World War II? This money was well invested in tax-free bonds and the best growth funds. Those Australian bonds of yours earned seventeen percent. Oh well, *la dolce vita*."

42   The mosquitoes (*zanzare* they're called, just like they sound) invade the hotel with the desert wind. I spin in the sheets until my skin burns. I get up in the middle of the night and lean out the shuttered window, imagining all the sleeping guests, blisters on their feet from the stony streets, their guidebooks still in their hands. We could still back out. Just throw our bags in the rented Fiat and say *arrivederci*. Go hang out on the Amalfi coast for a month and head home, tanned and relaxed. Buy lots of sandals. I can hear my grandfather when I was twenty: "Be realistic. Come down out of the clouds." He was furious that I was studying poetry and Latin etymology, something utterly useless. Now, what am I thinking of? Buying an abandoned house in a place where I hardly can speak the language. He probably has worn out his shroud turning over in his grave. We don't have a mountain of reserves to bale us out in case that mysterious something goes wrong.

43   What is this thrall for houses? I come from a long line of women who open their handbags and take out swatches of upholstery material, colored squares of bathroom tile, seven shades of yellow paint samples, and strips of flowered wallpaper. We love the concept of four walls. "What is her house like?" my sister asks, and we both know she means what is *she*

like. I pick up the free real-estate guide outside the grocery store when I go somewhere for the weekend, even if it's close to home. One June, two friends and I rented a house on Majorca; another summer I stayed in a little *casa* in San Miguel de Allende in which I developed a serious love for fountained courtyards and bedrooms with bougainvillea cascading down the balcony, the austere Sierra Madre. One summer in Santa Fe, I started looking at adobes there, imagining I would become a Southwesterner, cook with chilies, wear squash blossom turquoise jewelry—a different life, the chance to be extant in another version. At the end of a month I left and never have wanted to return.

44   I love the islands off the Georgia coast, where I spent summers when I was growing up. Why not a weathered gray house there, made of wood that looks as though it washed up on the beach? Cotton rugs, peach iced tea, a watermelon cooling in the creek, sleeping with waves churning and rolling outside the window. A place where my sisters, friends, and their families could visit easily. But I keep remembering that anytime I've stepped in my own footprints again, I haven't felt renewed. Though I'm susceptible to the pull to the known, I'm just slightly more susceptible to surprise. Italy seems endlessly alluring to me—why not, at this point, consider the opening of *The Divine Comedy:* What must one do in order to grow? Better to remember my father, the son of my very literal-minded, penny-pinching grandfather. "The family motto," he'd say, "is 'Packing and Unpacking.'" And also, "If you can't go first class, don't go at all."

45   Lying awake, I feel the familiar sense of The Answer arriving. Like answers on the bottom of the black fortune-telling eight ball that I loved when I was ten, often I can feel an idea or the solution to a dilemma floating up through murky liquid, then it is as if I see the suddenly clear white writing. I like the charged zone of waiting, a mental and physical sensation of the bends as something mysterious zigzags to the surface of consciousness.

46   What if you did *not* feel uncertainty, the white writing says. Are you exempt from doubt? Why not rename it excitement? I lean over the wide sill just as the first gilded mauve light of sunrise begins. The Arab is still sleeping. The undulant landscape looks serene in every direction. Honey-colored farmhouses, gently placed in hollows, rise like thick loaves of bread set out to cool. I know some Jurassic upheaval violently tossed up the hills, but they appear rounded as though by a big hand. As the sun brightens, the land spreads out a soft spectrum: the green of a dollar bill gone through the wash, old cream, blue sky like a blind person's eye. The Renaissance painters had it just right. I never thought of Perugino, Giotto, Signorelli, et al., as realists, but their background views are still here, as most tourists discover, with dark cypress trees brushed in to emphasize each composition the eye falls on. Now I see why the red boot on a gold and blond angel in the Cortona museum has such a glow, why the Madonna's cobalt dress looks intense and deep. Against this land-

scape and light, everything takes on a primary outline. Even a red towel drying on a line below becomes totally saturated with its own redness.

47 Think: What if the sky doesn't fall? What if it's glorious? What if the house is transformed in three years? There will be by then hand-printed labels for the house's olive oil, thin linen curtains pulled across the shutters for siesta, jars of plum jam on the shelves, a long table for feasts under the linden trees, baskets piled by the door for picking tomatoes, arugula, wild fennel, roses, and rosemary. And who are we in that strange new life?

48 Finally the money arrives, the account is open. However, they have no checks. This enormous bank, the seat of dozens of branches in the gold center of Italy, has no checks to give us. "Maybe next week," Signora Raguzzi explains. "Right now, nothing." We sputter. Two days later, she calls. "I have ten checks for you." What is the big deal with checks? I get boxes of them at home. Signora Raguzzi parcels them out to us. Signora Raguzzi in tight skirt, tight T-shirt, has lips that are perpetually wet and pouting. Her skin glistens. She is astonishingly gorgeous. She wears a magnificent square gold necklace and bracelets on both wrists that jangle as she stamps our account number on each check.

49 "What great jewelry. I love those bracelets," I say.

50 "All we have here is gold," she replies glumly. She is bored with Arezzo's tombs and piazzas. California sounds good to her. She brightens every time she sees us. "Ah, California," she says as greeting. The bank begins to seem surreal. We're in the back room. A man wheels in a cart stacked with gold ingots—actual small bricks of gold. No one seems to be on guard. Another man loads two into dingy manila folders. He's plainly dressed, like a workman. He walks out into the street, taking the ingots somewhere. So much for Brinks delivery—but what a clever plainclothes disguise. We turn back to the checks. There will be no insignia of boats or palm trees or pony express riders, there will be no name, address, driver's license, Social Security number. Only these pale green checks that look as though they were printed in the twenties. We're enormously pleased. That's close to citizenship—a bank account.

51 Finally we are gathered in the *notaio*'s office for the final reckoning. It's quick. Everyone talks at once and no one listens. The baroque legal terms leave us way behind. A jackhammer outside drills into my brain cells. There's something about two oxen and two days. Ian, who's translating, stops to explain this archaic spiral of language as an eighteenth-century legal description of the amount of land, measured by how long it would take two oxen to plow it. We have, it seems, two plowing days worth of property.

52 I write checks, my fingers cramping over all the times I write *milione*. I think of all the nice dependable bonds and utility stocks and blue chips from the years of my marriage magically turning into a terraced hillside and a big empty house. The glass house in California where I lived for a

decade, surrounded by kumquat, lemon, mock orange, and guava, its bright pool and covered patio with wicker and flowered cushions—all seem to recede, as though seen through the long focus in binoculars. *Million* is such a big word in English it's hard to treat it casually. Ed carefully monitors the zeros, not wanting me to unwittingly write *miliardo,* billion, instead. He pays Signor Martini in cash. He never has mentioned a fee; we have found out the normal percentage from the owner. Signor Martini seems pleased, as though we've given him a gift. For me this is a confusing but delightful way to conduct business. Handshakes all around. Is that a little cat smile on the mouth of the owner's wife? We're expecting a parchment deed, lettered in ancient script, but no, the *notaio* is going on vacation and she'll try to get to the paperwork before she leaves. *"Normale,"* Signor Martini says. I've noticed all along that someone's word is still taken for that. Endless contracts and stipulations and contingencies simply have not come up. We walk out into the brutally hot afternoon with nothing but two heavy iron keys longer than my hand, one to a rusted iron gate, the other to the front door. They look nothing like the keys to anything I've ever owned. There is no hope for spare copies.

53   Giuseppe waves from the door of the bar and we tell him we have bought a house. "Where is it?" he wants to know.

54   "Bramasole," Ed begins, about to say where it is.

55   "Ah, Bramasole, *una bella villa!*" He has picked cherries there as a boy. Although it is only afternoon, he pulls us in and pours a *grappa* for us. "Mama!" he shouts. His mother and her sister come in from the back and everyone toasts us. They're all talking at once, speaking of us as the *stranieri,* foreigners. The *grappa* is blindingly strong. We drink ours as fast as Signora Mantucci nips her espresso and wander out in the sun. The car is as hot as a pizza oven. We sit there with the doors open, suddenly laughing and laughing.

56   We'd arranged for two women to clean and for a bed to be delivered while we signed the final papers. In town we picked up a bottle of cold *prosecco,* then stopped at the *rosticceria* for marinated zucchini, olives, roast chicken, and potatoes.

57   We arrive at the house dazed by the events and the *grappa.* Anna and Lucia have washed the windows and exorcised layers of dust, as well as many spiders' webs. The second-floor bedroom that opens onto a brick terrace gleams. They've made the bed with the new blue sheets and left the terrace door open to the sound of cuckoos and wild canaries in the linden trees. We pick the last of the pink roses on the front terrace and fill two old Chianti bottles with them. The shuttered room with its white-washed walls, just-waxed floors, pristine bed with new sheets, and sweet roses on the windowsill, all lit with a dangling forty-watt bulb, seems as pure as a Franciscan cell. As soon as I walk in, I think it is the most perfect room in the world.

58   We shower and dress in fresh clothes. In the quiet twilight, we sit on the stone wall of the terrace and toast each other and the house with

tumblers of the spicy *prosecco,* which seems like a liquid form of the air. We toast the cypress trees along the road and the white horse in the neighbor's field, the villa in the distance that was built for the visit of a pope. The olive pits we toss over the wall, hoping they will spring from the ground next year. Dinner is delicious. As the darkness comes, a barn owl flies over so close that we hear the whir of wings and, when it settles in the black locust, a strange cry that we take for a greeting. The Big Dipper hangs over the house, about to pour on the roof. The constellations pop out, clear as a star chart. When it finally is dark, we see that the Milky Way sweeps right over the house. I forget the stars, living in the ambient light of a city. Here they are, all along, spangling and dense, falling and pulsating. We stare up until our necks ache. The Milky Way looks like a flung bolt of lace unfurling. Ed, because he likes to whisper, leans to my ear. "Still want to go home," he asks, "or can this be home?"

Questions for Discussion

1. What attracts Mayes to the home in Italy? What is her family's opinion of her choice?

2. What part does "an insatiable curiosity" play in traveling or moving from one part of the country or world to another?

3. Mayes says of moving, "to sell is to walk away from a cluster of memories and to buy is choose where the future will take place." What are your impressions of moving? To what extent is her move affected by her divorce?

4. Explain Mayes's comment that "anytime I've stepped in my own footprints again, I haven't felt renewed."

5. Mayes says, "the circuitous search for a summer house became a quest for us." In what ways is the search for a place to live a kind of quest?

6. Although Mayes says little about Ed, their shared interests are apparent. What adjectives would you use to describe their relationship?

7. What difficulties do Mayes and Ed encounter in purchasing and renovating Bramasole? What do these difficulties suggest about methods of conducting business in Italy?

8. Why, in spite of the difficulties and the alien culture, do Mayes and Ed buy Bramasole?

9. How does the author build to the climax of buying Bramasole?

10. At what point does Mayes decide that Bramasole is "home"?

Suggestions for Exploration and Writing

1. In an essay, apply to yourself Mayes's statement, "The house is a metaphor for the self."

2. Write a description of what you would consider an ideal home.

3. Write an analysis of the various emotions associated with a move your family made while you were growing up.

4. Discuss in detail the reasons for Mayes's fascination with houses in general and Bramasole in particular, or discuss your own fascination with houses or with one particular house.

5. Using this essay and Frost's definitions of *home* in "The Death of the Hired Man" in the next unit as a basis for your discussion, define what home means to you.

6. Research the Tuscan area of Italy and write an essay explaining how Mayes's description does or does not portray it accurately.

7. Examine the techniques Mayes uses to make her description vivid and moving. Then write an essay using similar techniques to describe your home environment.

FICTION

Luke

Although few facts about the life of Luke are positively known, scholars believe that Luke, "the beloved physician," wrote the New Testament books Luke and Acts. They believe that Luke was a Gentile from Antioch in Syria and that he was a close companion of Paul. Although the exact date is unknown, the book of Luke was probably written between 59 and 80 AD. The following is from the King James version.

THE PARABLE OF THE PRODIGAL SON

LUKE 15:11–32

11 And he said, A certain man had two sons:

12 And the younger of them said to *his* father, Father, give me the portion of goods that falleth to *me*. And he divided unto them *his* living.

13 And not many days after the younger son gathered all together, and took his journey into a far country, and there wasted his substance with riotous living.

14 And when he had spent all, there arose a mighty famine in that land; and he began to be in want.

15 And he went and joined himself to a citizen of that country; and he sent him into his fields to feed swine.

16 And he would fain have filled his belly with the husks that the swine did eat: and no man gave unto him.

17 And when he came to himself, he said, How many hired servants of my father's have bread enough and to spare, and I perish with hunger!

18 I will arise and go to my father, and will say unto him, Father, I have sinned against heaven, and before thee.

19And am no more worthy to be called thy son: make me as one of thy hired servants.

20 And he arose, and came to his father. But when he was yet a great way off, his father saw him, and had compassion, and ran, and fell on his neck, and kissed him.

21 And the son said unto him, Father, I have sinned against heaven, and in thy sight, and am no more worthy to be called thy son.

22 But the father said to his servants, Bring forth the best robe, and put *it* on him; and put a ring on his hand, and shoes on *his* feet:

23 And bring hither the fatted calf, and kill *it;* and let us eat, and be merry:

24 For this my son was dead, and is alive again; he was lost, and is found. And they began to be merry.

25 Now his elder son was in the field: and as he came and drew nigh to the house, he heard musick and dancing.

26 And he called one of the servants, and asked what these things meant.

27 And he said unto him, Thy brother is come; and thy father hath killed the fatted calf, because he hath received him safe and sound.

28 And he was angry, and would not go in: therefore came his father out, and intreated him.

29 And he answering said to *his* father, Lo, these many years do I serve thee, neither transgressed I at any time thy commandment: and yet thou never gavest me a kid, that I might make merry with my friends:

30 But as soon as this thy son was come, which hath devoured thy living with harlots, thou hast killed for him the fatted calf.

31 And he said unto him, Son, thou art ever with me, and all that I have is thine.

32 It was meet that we should make merry, and be glad: for this thy brother was dead, and is alive again; and was lost, and is found.

Questions for Discussion

1. What is a parable? How does this form differ from the form of the modern short story?

2. Why would the son choose to give up the security of home and family for "riotous living" in a "far country"? Is it realistic for him to do so?

3. The father, upon seeing his son's return, prepares a rich feast and gives the returning son the "best robe" and a ring. Is such behavior fair or just? Why does the father greet the wasteful son so warmly? Why is the oldest son so angry? Is his reaction an expected one? Explain.

4. What does the father mean by the following words to the oldest son: "Son, thou art ever with me, and all that I have is thine"?

Suggestions for Exploration and Writing

1. Examine an act of unconditional love from several points of view.

2. Write an essay discussing a modern-day conflict between two siblings and discuss ways in which they might solve this conflict. For example, one brother might have fought in a war while the other marched for peace, or one sister might support abortion while the other opposes it.

3. Using the format of Luke, write a modern-day parable.

Carson McCullers (1917–1967)

*Born in Columbus, Georgia, Carson Smith McCullers is famous for her portrayal of lonely and insecure people. Some of her short stories and novels are described as modern **Gothic**. Her most famous novels include* The Heart Is a Lonely Hunter *(1940),* The Ballad of the Sad Cafe *(1951), and* The Member of the Wedding *(1946), which was made into an award-winning play and into a movie starring Julie Harris and Ethel Waters. McCullers learned about suffering firsthand: her health began to deteriorate because of a misdiagnosis of rheumatic fever while she was still in high school, and her marriage to Reeves McCullers was marked by many separations.*

A Domestic Dilemma   (1951)

1   On Thursday Martin Meadows left the office early enough to make the first express bus home. It was the hour when the evening lilac glow was fading in the slushy streets, but by the time the bus had left the Mid-town terminal the bright city night had come. On Thursdays the maid had a half-day off and Martin liked to get home as soon as possible, since for the past year his wife had not been—well. This Thursday he was very tired and, hoping that no regular commuter would single him out for conversation, he fastened his attention to the newspaper until the bus had crossed the George Washington Bridge. Once on 9-W Highway Martin always felt that the trip was halfway done, he breathed deeply, even in cold weather when only ribbons of draught cut through the smoky air of the bus, confident that he was breathing country air. It used to be that at this point he would relax and begin to think with pleasure of his home. But in this last year nearness brought only a sense of tension and he did not anticipate the journey's end. This evening Martin kept his face close to the window and watched the barren fields and lonely lights of passing townships. There was a moon, pale on the dark earth and areas of late, porous snow; to

Martin the countryside seemed vast and somehow desolate that evening. He took his hat from the rack and put his folded newspaper in the pocket of his overcoat a few minutes before time to pull the cord.

2   The cottage was a block from the bus stop, near the river but not directly on the shore; from the living-room window you could look across the street and opposite yard and see the Hudson. The cottage was modern, almost too white and new on the narrow plot of yard. In summer the grass was soft and bright and Martin carefully tended a flower border and a rose trellis. But during the cold, fallow months the yard was bleak and the cottage seemed naked. Lights were on that evening in all the rooms in the little house and Martin hurried up the front walk. Before the steps he stopped to move a wagon out of the way.

3   The children were in the living room, so intent on play that the opening of the front door was at first unnoticed. Martin stood looking at his safe, lovely children. They had opened the bottom drawer of the secretary and taken out the Christmas decorations. Andy had managed to plug in the Christmas tree lights and the green and red bulbs glowed with out-of-season festivity on the rug of the living room. At the moment he was trying to trail the bright cord over Marianne's rocking horse. Marianne sat on the floor pulling off an angel's wings. The children wailed a startling welcome. Martin swung the fat little baby girl up to his shoulder and Andy threw himself against his father's legs.

4   "Daddy, Daddy, Daddy!"

5   Martin set down the little girl carefully and swung Andy a few times like a pendulum. Then he picked up the Christmas tree cord.

6   "What's all this stuff doing out? Help me put it back in the drawer. You're not to fool with the light socket. Remember I told you that before. I mean it, Andy."

7   The six-year-old child nodded and shut the secretary drawer. Martin stroked his fair soft hair and his hand lingered tenderly on the nape of the child's frail neck.

8   "Had supper yet, Bumpkin?"

9   "It hurt. The toast was hot."

10   The baby girl stumbled on the rug and, after the first surprise of the fall, began to cry; Martin picked her up and carried her in his arms back to the kitchen.

11   "See, Daddy," said Andy. "The toast—"

12   Emily had laid the children's supper on the uncovered porcelain table. There were two plates with the remains of cream-of-wheat and eggs and silver mugs that had held milk. There was also a platter of cinnamon toast, untouched except for one tooth-marked bite. Martin sniffed the bitten piece and nibbled gingerly. Then he put the toast into the garbage pail.

13   "Hoo—phui—What on earth!"

14   Emily had mistaken the tin of cayenne for the cinnamon.

15   "I like to have burnt up," Andy said. "Drank water and ran outdoors and opened my mouth. Marianne didn't eat none."

16   "Any," corrected Martin. He stood helpless, looking around the walls of the kitchen. "Well, that's that, I guess," he said finally. "Where is your mother now?"

17   "She's up in you alls' room."

18   Martin left the children in the kitchen and went up to his wife. Outside the door he waited for a moment to still his anger. He did not knock and once inside the room he closed the door behind him.

19   Emily sat in the rocking chair by the window of the pleasant room. She had been drinking something from a tumbler and as he entered she put the glass hurriedly on the floor behind the chair. In her attitude there was confusion and guilt which she tried to hide by a show of spurious vivacity.

20   "Oh, Marty! You home already? The time slipped up on me. I was just going down—" She lurched to him and her kiss was strong with sherry. When he stood unresponsive she stepped back a pace and giggled nervously.

21   "What's the matter with you? Standing there like a barber pole. Is anything wrong with you?"

22   "Wrong with *me*?" Martin bent over the rocking chair and picked up the tumbler from the floor. "If you could only realize how sick I am—how bad it is for all of us."

23   Emily spoke in a false, airy voice that had become too familiar to him. Often at such times she affected a slight English accent, copying perhaps some actress she admired. "I haven't the vaguest idea what you mean. Unless you are referring to the glass I used for a spot of sherry. I had a finger of sherry—maybe two. But what is the crime in that, pray tell me? I'm quite all right. Quite all right."

24   "So anyone can see."

25   As she went into the bathroom Emily walked with careful gravity. She turned on the cold water and dashed some on her face with her cupped hands, then patted herself dry with the corner of a bath towel. Her face was delicately featured and young, unblemished.

26   "I was just going down to make dinner." She tottered and balanced herself by holding to the door frame.

27   "I'll take care of dinner. You stay up here. I'll bring it up."

28   "I'll do nothing of the sort. Why, whoever heard of such a thing?"

29   "Please," Martin said.

30   "Leave me alone. I'm quite all right. I was just on the way down—"

31   "Mind what I say."

32   "Mind your grandmother."

33   She lurched toward the door, but Martin caught her by the arm. "I don't want the children to see you in this condition. Be reasonable."

34   "Condition!" Emily jerked her arm. Her voice rose angrily. "Why, because I drink a couple of sherries in the afternoon you're trying to make me out a drunkard. Condition! Why, I don't even touch whiskey. As well you know. *I* don't swill liquor at bars. And that's more than you can say. I don't even have a cocktail at dinnertime. I only sometimes have a glass of sherry. What, I ask you, is the disgrace of that? Condition!"

35   Martin sought words to calm his wife. "We'll have a quiet supper by ourselves up here. That's a good girl." Emily sat on the side of the bed and he opened the door for a quick departure.

36   "I'll be back in a jiffy."

37   As he busied himself with the dinner downstairs he was lost in the familiar question as to how this problem had come upon his home. He himself had always enjoyed a good drink. When they were still in Alabama they had served long drinks or cocktails as a matter of course. For years they had drunk one or two—possibly three drinks before dinner, and at bedtime a long nightcap. Evenings before holidays they might get a buzz on, might even become a little tight. But alcohol had never seemed a problem to him, only a bothersome expense that with the increase in the family they could scarcely afford. It was only after his company had transferred him to New York that Martin was aware that certainly his wife was drinking too much. She was tippling, he noticed, during the day.

38   The problem acknowledged, he tried to analyze the source. The change from Alabama to New York had somehow disturbed her; accustomed to the idle warmth of a small Southern town, the matrix of the family and cousinship and childhood friends, she had failed to accommodate herself to the stricter, lonelier mores of the North. The duties of motherhood and housekeeping were onerous to her. Homesick for Paris City, she had made no friends in the suburban town. She read only magazines and murder books. Her interior life was insufficient without the artifice of alcohol.

39   The revelations of incontinence insidiously undermined his previous conceptions of his wife. There were times of unexplainable malevolence, times when the alcoholic fuse caused an explosion of unseemly anger. He encountered a latent coarseness in Emily, inconsistent with her natural simplicity. She lied about drinking and deceived him with unsuspected strategems.

40   Then there was an accident. Coming home from work one evening about a year ago, he was greeted with screams from the children's room. He found Emily holding the baby, wet and naked from her bath. The baby had been dropped, her frail, frail skull striking the table edge, so that a thread of blood was soaking into the gossamer hair. Emily was sobbing and intoxicated. As Martin cradled the hurt child, so infinitely precious at that moment, he had an affrighted vision of the future.

41   The next day Marianne was all right. Emily vowed that never again would she touch liquor, and for a few weeks she was sober, cold and downcast. Then gradually she began—not whiskey or gin—but quantities of beer, or sherry, or outlandish liqueurs; once he had come across a hatbox of empty crème de menthe bottles. Martin found a dependable maid who managed the household competently. Virgie was also from Alabama and Martin had never dared tell Emily the wage scale customary in New York. Emily's drinking was entirely secret now, done before he reached

the house. Usually the effects were almost imperceptible—a looseness of movement or the heavy-lidded eyes. The times of irresponsibilities, such as the cayenne-pepper toast were rare, and Martin could dismiss his worries when Virgie was at the house. But, nevertheless, anxiety was always latent, a threat of undefined disaster that underlaid his days.

42   "Marianne!" Martin called, for even the recollection of that time brought the need for reassurance. The baby girl, no longer hurt, but no less precious to her father, came into the kitchen with her brother. Martin went on with the preparations for the meal. He opened a can of soup and put two chops in the frying pan. Then he sat down by the table and took his Marianne on his knees for a pony ride. Andy watched them, his fingers wobbling the tooth that had been loose all that week.

43   "Andy-the-candyman!" Martin said. "Is that old critter still in your mouth? Come closer, let Daddy have a look."

44   "I got a string to pull it with." The child brought from his pocket a tangled thread. "Virgie said to tie it to the tooth and tie the other end to the doorknob and shut the door real suddenly."

45   Martin took out a clean handkerchief and felt the loose tooth carefully. "That tooth is coming out of my Andy's mouth tonight. Otherwise I'm awfully afraid we'll have a tooth tree in the family."

46   "A what?"

47   "A tooth tree," Martin said. "You'll bite into something and swallow that tooth. And the tooth will take root in poor Andy's stomach and grow into a tooth tree with sharp little teeth instead of leaves."

48   "Shoo, Daddy," Andy said. But he held the tooth firmly between his grimy little thumb and forefinger. "There ain't any tree like that. I never seen one."

49   "There *isn't* any tree like that and I never *saw* one."

50   Martin tensed suddenly. Emily was coming down the stairs. He listened to her fumbling footsteps, his arm embracing the little boy with dread. When Emily came into the room he saw from her movements and her sullen face that she had again been at the sherry bottle. She began to yank open drawers and set the table.

51   "Condition!" she said in a furry voice. "You talk to me like that. Don't think I'll forget. I remember every dirty lie you say to me. Don't you think for a minute that I forget."

52   "Emily!" he begged. "The children—"

53   "The children—yes! Don't think I don't see through your dirty plots and schemes. Down here trying to turn my own children against me. Don't think I don't see and understand."

54   "Emily! I beg you—please go upstairs."

55   "So you can turn my children—my very own children—" Two large tears coursed rapidly down her cheeks. "Trying to turn my little boy, my Andy, against his own mother."

56   With drunken impulsiveness Emily knelt on the floor before the startled child. Her hands on his shoulders balanced her. "Listen, my Andy— you wouldn't listen to any lies your father tells you? You wouldn't believe

what he says? Listen, Andy, what was your father telling you before I came downstairs?" Uncertain, the child sought his father's face. "Tell me. Mama wants to know."

57   "About the tooth tree."

58   "What?"

59   The child repeated the words and she echoed them with unbelieving terror. "The tooth tree!" She swayed and renewed her grasp on the child's shoulder. "I don't know what you're talking about. But listen, Andy, Mama is all right, isn't she?" The tears were spilling down her face and Andy drew back from her, for he was afraid. Grasping the table edge, Emily stood up.

60   "See! You have turned my child against me."

61   Marianne began to cry, and Martin took her in his arms.

62   "That's all right, you can take *your* child. You have always shown partiality from the very first. I don't mind, but at least you can leave me my little boy."

63   Andy edged close to his father and touched his leg. "Daddy," he wailed.

64   Martin took the children to the foot of the stairs. "Andy, you take up Marianne and Daddy will follow you in a minute."

65   "But Mama?" the child asked, whispering.

66   "Mama will be all right. Don't worry."

67   Emily was sobbing at the kitchen table, her face buried in the crook of her arm. Martin poured a cup of soup and set it before her. Her rasping sobs unnerved him; the vehemence of her emotion, irrespective of the source, touched in him a strain of tenderness. Unwillingly he laid his hand on her dark hair. "Sit up and drink the soup." Her face as she looked up at him was chastened and imploring. The boy's withdrawal or the touch of Martin's hand had turned the tenor of her mood.

68   "Ma-Martin," she sobbed. "I'm so ashamed."

69   "Drink the soup."

70   Obeying him, she drank between gasping breaths. After a second cup she allowed him to lead her up to their room. She was docile now and more restrained. He laid her nightgown on the bed and was about to leave when a fresh round of grief, the alcoholic tumult, came again.

71   "He turned away. My Andy looked at me and turned away."

72   Impatience and fatigue hardened his voice, but he spoke warily. "You forget that Andy is still a little child—he can't comprehend the meaning of such scenes."

73   "Did I make a scene? Oh, Martin, did I make a scene before the children?"

74   Her horrified face touched and amused him against his will. "Forget it. Put on your nightgown and go to sleep."

75   "My child turned away from me. Andy looked at his mother and turned away. The children—"

76   She was caught in the rhythmic sorrow of alcohol. Martin withdrew from the room saying: "For God's sake go to sleep. The children will forget by tomorrow."

77   As he said this he wondered if it was true. Would the scene glide so easily from memory—or would it root in the unconscious to fester in the

after-years? Martin did not know, and the last alternative sickened him. He thought of Emily, foresaw the morning-after humiliation: the shards of memory, the lucidities that glared from the obliterating darkness of shame. She would call the New York office twice—possibly three or four times. Martin anticipated his own embarrassment, wondering if the others at the office could possibly suspect. He felt that his secretary had divined the trouble long ago and that she pitied him. He suffered a moment of rebellion against his fate; he hated his wife.

78   Once in the children's room he closed the door and felt secure for the first time that evening. Marianne fell down on the floor, picked herself up and calling: "Daddy, watch me," fell again, got up, and continued the falling-calling routine. Andy sat in the child's low chair, wobbling the tooth. Martin ran the water in the tub, washed his own hands in the lavatory, and called the boy into the bathroom.

79   "Let's have another look at that tooth." Martin sat on the toilet, holding Andy between his knees. The child's mouth gaped and Martin grasped the tooth. A wobble, a quick twist and the nacreous milk tooth was free. Andy's face was for the first moment split between terror, astonishment, and delight. He mouthed a swallow of water and spat into the lavatory.

80   "Look, Daddy! It's blood. Marianne!"

81   Martin loved to bathe his children, loved inexpressibly the tender, naked bodies as they stood in the water so exposed. It was not fair of Emily to say that he showed partiality. As Martin soaped the delicate boy-body of his son he felt that further love would be impossible. Yet he admitted the difference in the quality of his emotions for the two children. His love for his daughter was graver, touched with a strain of melancholy, a gentleness that was akin to pain. His pet names for the little boy were the absurdities of daily inspiration—he called the little girl always Marianne, and his voice as he spoke it was a caress. Martin patted dry the fat baby stomach and the sweet little genital fold. The washed child faces were radiant as flower petals, equally loved.

82   "I'm putting the tooth under my pillow. I'm supposed to get a quarter."

83   "What for?"

84   "*You* know, Daddy. Johnny got a quarter for his tooth."

85   "Who puts the quarter there?" asked Martin. "I used to think the fairies left it in the night. It was a dime in my day, though."

86   "That's what they say in kindergarden."

87   "Who does put it there?"

88   "Your parents," Andy said. "You!"

89   Martin was pinning the cover on Marianne's bed. His daughter was already asleep. Scarcely breathing, Martin bent over and kissed her forehead, kissed again the tiny hand that lay palm-upward, flung in slumber beside her head.

90   "Good night, Andy-man."

91   The answer was only a drowsy murmur. After a minute Martin took out his change and slid a quarter underneath the pillow. He left a night light in the room.

92   As Martin prowled about the kitchen making a late meal, it occurred to him that the children had not once mentioned their mother or the scene that must have seemed to them incomprehensible. Absorbed in the instant—the tooth, the bath, the quarter—the fluid passage of child-time had borne these weightless episodes like leaves in the swift current of a shallow stream while the adult enigma was beached and forgotten on the shore. Martin thanked the Lord for that.

93   But his own anger, repressed and lurking, arose again. His youth was being frittered by a drunkard's waste, his very manhood subtly undermined. And the children, once the immunity of incomprehension passed—what would it be like in a year or so? With his elbows on the table he ate his food brutishly, untasting. There was no hiding the truth—soon there would be gossip in the office and in the town; his wife was a dissolute woman. Dissolute. And he and his children were bound to a future of degradation and slow ruin.

94   Martin pushed away from the table and stalked into the living room. He followed the lines of a book with his eyes but his mind conjured miserable images: he saw his children drowned in the river, his wife a disgrace on the public street. By bedtime the dull, hard anger was like a weight upon his chest and his feet dragged as he climbed the stairs.

95   The room was dark except for the shafting light from the half-opened bathroom door. Martin undressed quietly. Little by little, mysteriously, there came in him a change. His wife was asleep, her peaceful respiration sounding gently in the room. Her high-heeled shoes with the carelessly dropped stockings made to him a mute appeal. Her underclothes were flung in disorder on the chair. Martin picked up the girdle and the soft, silk brassière and stood for a moment with them in his hands. For the first time that evening he looked at his wife. His eyes rested on the sweet forehead, the arch of the fine brow. The brow had descended to Marianne, and the tilt at the end of the delicate nose. In his son he could trace the high cheekbones and pointed chin. Her body was full-bosomed, slender and undulant. As Martin watched the tranquil slumber of his wife the ghost of the old anger vanished. All thoughts of blame or blemish were distant from him now. Martin put out the bathroom light and raised the window. Careful not to awaken Emily he slid into the bed. By moonlight he watched his wife for the last time. His hand sought the adjacent flesh and sorrow paralleled desire in the immense complexity of love.

Questions for Discussion

1. What clues does McCullers give early in the story that **foreshadow** the problem in this family?

2. If you were in Martin's position, how would you react to the scene that greets him when he returns home?

3. What particular scenes and actions affect your judgment of Martin as a father? How does he show tenderness toward his children?

4. Martin feels anger at Emily's drunkenness and fear for the children under her care. Yet only a few minutes later, Martin feels tenderness and love for Emily. How can his feelings change so drastically in a few minutes? How is the **theme** of the story summed up in the phrase "the immense complexity of love"?

5. Explain what you think Martin should do in this situation. Justify your position.

Suggestions for Exploration and Writing

1. Examine a disturbing problem in your life that you refused to confront. Why did you fail to confront the problem? What were the consequences of this failure?

2. Families today must often cope with the stress of moving. Write either a personal narrative about a relocation of your family or a cause-and-effect essay about moving and its effect on family members.

3. Write a character sketch of either Martin or Emily.

4. Explain in detail your theories about what the situation in this family will be ten years in the future.

James Baldwin (1924–1987)

James Baldwin knew firsthand the rigors of poverty in Harlem, for he grew up there along with eight half-brothers and -sisters. His mother worked as a domestic; his stepfather, a laborer and part-time preacher, seemed to resent his small, unattractive stepson. Thus Baldwin learned early the importance of family and the need for love, themes that appear in "Sonny's Blues" and in his other works. Baldwin's novels, essays, and stories reveal both his talent as a writer and his intolerance of bigotry. To escape American racial prejudice, he spent much of his life in France. His most famous novels are Go Tell It on the Mountain *(1953) and* Giovanni's Room *(1956). Baldwin's essays, collected in* Notes of a Native Son *(1955),* Nobody Knows My Name *(1961), and* The Fire Next Time *(1963), strongly influenced his contemporaries.*

SONNY'S BLUES   (1957)

1   I heard about it in the paper, in the subway, on my way to work. I read it, and I couldn't believe it, and I read it again. Then perhaps I just stared at it, at the newsprint spelling out his name, spelling out the story. I stared at it in the swinging lights of the subway car, and in the faces and bodies of the people, and in my own face, trapped in the darkness which roared outside.

2   It was not to be believed and I kept telling myself that, as I walked from the subway station to the high school. And at the same time I couldn't doubt it. I was scared, scared for Sonny. He became real to me again. A great block of ice got settled in my belly and kept melting there slowly all day long, while I taught my classes algebra. It was a special kind of ice. It kept melting, sending trickles of ice water all up and down my veins, but it never got less. Sometimes it hardened and seemed to expand until I felt my guts were going to come spilling out or that I was going to choke or scream. This would always be at a moment when I was remembering some specific thing Sonny had once said or done.

3   When he was about as old as the boys in my classes his face had been bright and open, there was a lot of copper in it; and he'd had wonderfully direct brown eyes, and great gentleness and privacy. I wondered what he looked like now. He had been picked up, the evening before, in a raid on an apartment downtown, for peddling and using heroin.

4   I couldn't believe it: but what I mean by that is that I couldn't find any room for it anywhere inside me. I had kept it outside me for a long time. I hadn't wanted to know. I had had suspicions, but I didn't name them, I kept putting them away. I told myself that Sonny was wild, but he wasn't crazy. And he'd always been a good boy, he hadn't ever turned hard or evil or disrespectful, the way kids can, so quick, so quick, especially in Harlem, I didn't want to believe that I'd ever see my brother going down, coming to nothing, all that light in his face gone out, in the condition I'd already seen so many others. Yet it had happened and here I was, talking about algebra to a lot of boys who might, every one of them for all I knew, be popping off needles every time they went to the head. Maybe it did more for them than algebra could.

5   I was sure that the first time Sonny had ever had horse, he couldn't have been much older than these boys were now. These boys, now, were living as we'd been living then, they were growing up with a rush and their heads bumped abruptly against the low ceiling of their actual possibilities. They were filled with rage. All they really knew were two darknesses, the darkness of their lives, which was now closing in on them and the darkness of the movies, which had blinded them to that other darkness, and in which they now, vindictively, dreamed, at once more together than they were at any other time, and more alone.

6   When the last bell rang, the class ended, I let out my breath. It seemed I'd been holding it for all that time. My clothes were wet—I may have looked as though I'd been sitting in a steam bath, all dressed up, all afternoon. I sat alone in the classroom a long time. I listened to the boys outside, downstairs, shouting and cursing and laughing. Their laughter struck me for perhaps the first time. It was not the joyous laughter which—God knows why—one associates with children. It was mocking and insular, its intent was to denigrate. It was disenchanted, and in this, also, lay the authority of their curses. Perhaps I was listening to them because I was thinking about my brother and in them I heard my brother. And myself.

7   One boy was whistling a tune, at once very complicated and very simple, it seemed to be pouring out of him as though he were a bird, and it sounded very cool and moving through all that harsh, bright air, only just holding its own through all those other sounds.

8   I stood up and walked over to the window and looked down into the courtyard. It was the beginning of the spring and the sap was rising in the boys. A teacher passed through them every now and again, quickly, as though he or she couldn't wait to get out of that courtyard, to get those boys out of their sight and off their minds. I started collecting my stuff. I thought I'd better get home and talk to Isabel.

9   The courtyard was almost deserted by the time I got downstairs. I saw this boy standing in the shadow of a doorway, looking just like Sonny. I almost called his name. Then I saw that it wasn't Sonny, but somebody we used to know, a boy from around our block. He'd been Sonny's friend. He'd never been mine, having been too young for me, and anyway, I'd never liked him. And now, even though he was a grown-up man, he still hung around that block, still spent hours on the street corners, was always high and raggy. I used to run into him from time to time and he'd often work around to asking me for a quarter or fifty cents. He always had some real good excuse, too, and I always gave it to him. I don't know why.

10   But now, abruptly, I hated him. I couldn't stand the way he looked at me, partly like a dog, partly like a cunning child. I wanted to ask him what the hell he was doing in the school courtyard.

11   He sort of shuffled over to me, and he said, "I see you got the papers. So you already know about it."

12   "You mean about Sonny? Yes, I already know about it. How come they didn't get you?"

13   He grinned. It made him repulsive and it also brought to mind what he'd looked like as a kid. "I wasn't there. I stay away from them people."

14   "Good for you." I offered him a cigarette and I watched him through the smoke. "You come all the way down here just to tell me about Sonny?"

15   "That's right." He was sort of shaking his head and his eyes looked strange, as though they were about to cross. The bright sun deadened his damp dark brown skin and it made his eyes look yellow and showed up the dirt in his kinked hair. He smelled funky. I moved a little away from him and I said, "Well, thanks. But I already know about it and I got to get home."

16   "I'll walk you a little ways," he said. We started walking. There were a couple of kids still loitering in the courtyard and one of them said good-night to me and looked strangely at the boy beside me.

17   "What're you going to do?" he asked me. "I mean, about Sonny?"

18   "Look. I haven't seen Sonny for over a year, I'm not sure I'm going to do anything. Anyway, what the hell *can* I do?"

19   "That's right," he said quickly, "ain't nothing you can do. Can't much help old Sonny no more, I guess."

20   It was what I was thinking and so it seemed to me he had no right to say it.

21   "I'm surprised at Sonny, though," he went on—he had a funny way of talking, he looked straight ahead as though he were talking to himself—"I thought Sonny was a smart boy, I thought he was too smart to get hung."

22   "I guess he thought so too," I said sharply, "and that's how he got hung. And how about you? You're pretty goddamn smart, I bet."

23   Then he looked directly at me, just for a minute. "I ain't smart," he said. "If I was smart, I'd have reached for a pistol a long time ago."

24   "Look. Don't tell *me* your sad story, if it was up to me, I'd give you one." Then I felt guilty—guilty, probably, for never having supposed that the poor bastard *had* a story of his own, much less a sad one, and I asked, quickly, "What's going to happen to him now?"

25   He didn't answer this. He was off by himself some place. "Funny thing," he said, and from his tone we might have been discussing the quickest way to get to Brooklyn, "when I saw the papers this morning, the first thing I asked myself was if I had anything to do with it. I felt sort of responsible."

26   I began to listen more carefully. The subway station was on the corner, just before us, and I stopped. He stopped, too. We were in front of a bar and he ducked slightly, peering in, but whoever he was looking for didn't seem to be there. The juke box was blasting away with something black and bouncy and I half watched the barmaid as she danced her way from the juke box to her place behind the bar. And I watched her face as she laughingly responded to something someone said to her, still keeping time to the music. When she smiled one saw the little girl, one sensed the doomed, still-struggling woman beneath the battered face of the semiwhore.

27   "I never *give* Sonny nothing," the boy said finally, "but a long time ago I come to school high and Sonny asked me how it felt." He paused, I couldn't bear to watch him, I watched the barmaid, and I listened to the music which seemed to be causing the pavement to shake. "I told him it felt great." The music stopped, the barmaid paused and watched the juke box until the music began again. "It did."

28   All this was carrying me some place I didn't want to go. I certainly didn't want to know how it felt. It filled everything, the people, the houses, the music, the dark, quicksilver barmaid, with menace; and this menace was their reality.

29   "What's going to happen to him now?" I asked again.

30   "They'll send him away some place and they'll try to cure him." He shook his head. "Maybe he'll even think he's kicked the habit. Then they'll let him loose"—he gestured, throwing his cigarette into the gutter. "That's all."

31   "What do you mean, that's *all*?"

32   But I knew what he meant.

33   "I *mean*, that's *all*." He turned his head and looked at me, pulling down the corners of his mouth. "Don't you know what I mean?" he asked, softly.

34   "How the hell *would* I know what you mean?" I almost whispered it, I don't know why.

35 "That's right," he said to the air, "how would *he* know what I mean?" He turned toward me again, patient and calm, and yet I somehow felt him shaking, shaking as though he were going to fall apart. I felt that ice in my guts again, the dread I'd felt all afternoon; and again I watched the barmaid, moving about the bar, washing glasses, and singing. "Listen. They'll let him out and then it'll just start all over again. That's what I mean."

36 "You mean—they'll let him out. And then he'll just start working his way back in again. You mean he'll never kick the habit. Is that what you mean?"

37 "That's right," he said, cheerfully. "*You* see what I mean."

38 "Tell me," I said at last, "why does he want to die? He must want to die, he's killing himself, why does he want to die?"

39 He looked at me in surprise. He licked his lips. "He don't want to die. He wants to live. Don't nobody want to die, ever."

40 Then I wanted to ask him—too many things. He could not have answered, or if he had, I could not have borne the answers. I started walking. "Well, I guess it's none of my business."

41 "It's going to be rough on old Sonny," he said. We reached the subway station. "This is your station?" he asked. I nodded. I took one step down. "Damn!" he said, suddenly. I looked up at him. He grinned again. "Damn it if I didn't leave all my money home. You ain't got a dollar on you, have you? Just for a couple of days, is all."

42 All at once something inside gave and threatened to come pouring out of me. I didn't hate him any more. I felt that in another moment I'd start crying like a child.

43 "Sure," I said, "Don't sweat." I looked in my wallet and didn't have a dollar, I only had a five. "Here," I said. "That hold you?"

44 He didn't look at it—he didn't want to look at it. A terrible, closed look come over his face, as though he were keeping the number on the bill a secret from him and me. "Thanks," he said, and now he was dying to see me go. "Don't worry about Sonny. Maybe I'll write him or something."

45 "Sure," I said. "You do that. So long."

46 "Be seeing you," he said. I went on down the steps.

47 And I didn't write Sonny or send him anything for a long time. When I finally did, it was just after my little girl died, he wrote me back a letter which made me feel like a bastard.

48 Here's what he said:

49 Dear brother,

50 You don't know how much I needed to hear from you. I wanted to write you many a time but I dug how much I must have hurt you and so I didn't write. But now I feel like a man who's been trying to climb up out of some deep, real deep and funky hole and just saw the sun up there, outside. I got to get outside.

51 I can't tell you much about how I got here. I mean I don't know how to tell you. I guess I was afraid of something or I was trying to escape from something and you know I have never been very strong

in the head (smile). I'm glad Mama and Daddy are dead and can't see what's happened to their son and I swear if I'd known what I was doing I would never have hurt you so, you and a lot of other fine people who were nice to me and who believed in me.

52   I don't want you to think it had anything to do with me being a musician. It's more than that. Or maybe less than that. I can't get anything straight in my head down here and I try not to think about what's going to happen to me when I get outside again. Sometime I think I'm going to flip and *never* get outside and sometime I think I'll come straight back. I tell you one thing, though, I'd rather blow my brains out than go through this again. But that's what they all say, so they tell me. If I tell you when I'm coming to New York and if you could meet me, I sure would appreciate it. Give my love to Isabel and the kids and I was sure sorry to hear about little Gracie. I wish I could be like Mama and say the Lord's will be done, but I don't know it seems to me that trouble is the one thing that never does get stopped and I don't know what good it does to blame it on the Lord. But maybe it does some good if you believe it.

53   Your brother,

54   Sonny

55   Then I kept in constant touch with him and I sent him whatever I could and I went to meet him when he came back to New York. When I saw him many things I thought I had forgotten came flooding back to me. This was because I had begun, finally, to wonder about Sonny, about the life that Sonny lived inside. This life, whatever it was, had made him older and thinner and it had deepened the distant stillness in which he had always moved. He looked very unlike my baby brother. Yet, when he smiled, when we shook hands, the baby brother I'd never known looked out from the depths of his private life, like an animal waiting to be coaxed into the light.

56   "How you been keeping?" he asked me.

57   "All right. And you?"

58   "Just fine." He was smiling all over his face. "It's good to see you again."

59   "It's good to see you."

60   The seven years' difference in our ages lay between us like a chasm: I wondered if these years would ever operate between us as a bridge. I was remembering, and it made it hard to catch my breath, that I had been there when he was born; and I had heard the first words he had ever spoken. When he started to walk, he walked from our mother straight to me. I caught him just before he fell when he took the first steps he ever took in this world.

61   "How's Isabel?"

62   "Just fine. She's dying to see you."

63   "And the boys?"

64   "They're fine, too. They're anxious to see their uncle."

65   "Oh, come on. You know they don't remember me."

66   "Are you kidding? Of course they remember you."

67   He grinned again. We got into a taxi. We had a lot to say to each other, far too much to know how to begin.

68   As the taxi began to move, I asked, "You still want to go to India?"

69   He laughed. "You still remember that. Hell, no. This place is Indian enough to me."

70   "It used to belong to them," I said.

71   And he laughed again. "They damn sure knew what they were doing when they got rid of it."

72   Years ago, when he was around fourteen, he'd been all hipped up on the idea of going to India. He read books about people sitting on rocks, naked, in all kinds of weather, but mostly bad, naturally, and walking barefoot through hot coals and arriving at wisdom. I used to say that it sounded to me as though they were getting away from wisdom as fast as they could. I think he sort of looked down on me for that.

73   "Do you mind," he asked "if we have the driver drive alongside the park? On the west side—I haven't seen the city in so long."

74   "Of course not," I said. I was afraid that I might sound as though I were humoring him, but I hoped he wouldn't take it that way.

75   So we drove along, between the green of the park and the stony, lifeless elegance of hotels and apartment buildings, toward the vivid, killing streets of our childhood. These streets hadn't changed, though housing projects jutted up out of them now like rocks in the middle of a boiling sea. Most of the houses in which we had grown up had vanished, as had the stores from which we had stolen, the basements in which we had first tried sex, the rooftops from which we had hurled tin cans and bricks. But houses exactly like the houses of our past yet dominated the landscape, boys exactly like the boys we once had been found themselves smothering in these houses, came down into the streets for light and air and found themselves encircled by disaster. Some escaped the trap, most didn't. Those who got out always left something of themselves behind, as some animals amputate a leg and leave it in the trap. It might be said, perhaps, that I had escaped, after all, I was a school teacher; or that Sonny had, he hadn't lived in Harlem for years. Yet, as the cab moved uptown through streets which seemed, with a rush, to darken with dark people, and as I covertly studied Sonny's face, it came to me that what we both were seeking through our separate cab windows was that part of ourselves which had been left behind. It's always at the hour of trouble and confrontation that the missing member aches.

76   We hit 110th Street and started rolling up Lenox Avenue. And I'd known this avenue all my life, but it seemed to me again, as it had seemed on the day I'd first heard about Sonny's trouble, filled with a hidden menace which was its very breath of life.

77   "We almost there," said Sonny,

78   "Almost." We were both too nervous to say anything more.

79   We live in a housing project. It hasn't been up long. A few days after it was up it seemed uninhabitably new, now, of course, it's already rundown. It looks like a parody of the good, clean, faceless life—God knows the people

who live in it do their best to make it a parody. The beat-looking grass lying around isn't enough to make their lives green, the hedges will never hold out the streets, and they know it. The big windows fool no one, they aren't big enough to make space out of no space. They don't bother with the windows, they watch the TV screen instead. The playground is most popular with the children who don't play at jacks, or skip rope, or roller skate, or swing, and they can be found in it after dark. We moved in partly because it's not too far from where I teach, and partly for the kids; but it's really just like the houses in which Sonny and I grew up. The same things happen, they'll have the same things to remember. The moment Sonny and I started into the house I had the feeling that I was simply bringing him back into the danger he had almost died trying to escape.

80   Sonny has never been talkative. So I don't know why I was sure he'd be dying to talk to me when supper was over the first night. Everything went fine, the oldest boy remembered him, and the youngest boy liked him, and Sonny had remembered to bring something for each of them; and Isabel, who is really much nicer than I am, more open and giving, had gone to a lot of trouble about dinner and was genuinely glad to see him. And she's always been able to tease Sonny in a way that I haven't. It was nice to see her face so vivid again and to hear her laugh and watch her make Sonny laugh. She wasn't, or, anyway, she didn't seem to be, at all uneasy or embarrassed. She chatted as though there were no subject which had to be avoided and she got Sonny past his first, faint stiffness. And thank God she was there, for I was filled with that icy dread again. Everything I did seemed awkward to me, and everything I said sounded freighted with hidden meaning. I was trying to remember everything I'd heard about dope addiction and I couldn't help watching Sonny for signs. I wasn't doing it out of malice. I was trying to find out something about my brother. I was dying to hear him tell me he was safe.

81   "Safe!" my father grunted, whenever Mama suggested trying to move to a neighborhood which might be safer for children. "Safe, hell! Ain't no place safe for kids, nor nobody."

82   He always went on like this, but he wasn't, ever, really as bad as he sounded, not even on weekends, when he got drunk. As a matter of fact, he was always on the lookout for "something a little better," but he died before he found it. He died suddenly, during a drunken weekend in the middle of the war, when Sonny was fifteen. He and Sonny hadn't ever got on too well. And this was partly because Sonny was the apple of his father's eye. It was because he loved Sonny so much and was frightened for him, that he was always fighting with him. It doesn't do any good to fight with Sonny. Sonny just moves back, inside himself, where he can't be reached. But the principal reason that they never hit it off is that they were so much alike. Daddy was big and rough and loud-talking, just the opposite of Sonny, but they both had—that same privacy.

83   Mama tried to tell me something about this, just after Daddy died. I was home on leave from the army.

84   This was the last time I ever saw my mother alive. Just the same, this
picture gets all mixed up in my mind with pictures I had of her when she
was younger. The way I always see her is the way she used to be on Sunday afternoon, say, when the old folks were talking after the big Sunday
dinner. I always see her wearing pale blue. She'd be sitting on the sofa.
And my father would be sitting in the easy chair, not far from her. And
the living room would be full of church folks and relatives. There they sit,
on chairs all around the living room, and the night is creeping up outside, but nobody knows it yet. You can see the darkness growing against
the windowpanes and you hear the street noises every now and again, or
maybe the jangling beat of a tambourine from one of the churches close
by, but it's real quiet in the room. For a moment nobody's talking, but
every face looks darkening, like the sky outside. And my mother rocks a
little from the waist, and my father's eyes are closed. Everyone is looking
at something a child can't see. For a minute they've forgotten the children.
Maybe a kid is lying on the rug, half asleep. Maybe somebody's got a kid
in his lap and is absent-mindedly stroking the kid's head. Maybe there's a
kid, quiet and big-eyed, curled up in a big chair in the corner. The silence,
the darkness coming, and the darkness in the faces frightens the child
obscurely. He hopes that the hand which strokes his forehead will never
stop—will never die. He hopes that there will never come a time when the
old folks won't be sitting around the living room, talking about where
they've come from, and what they've seen, and what's happened to them
and their kinfolk.

85   But something deep and watchful in the child knows that this is bound
to end, is already ending. In a moment someone will get up and turn on
the light. Then the old folks will remember the children and they won't
talk any more that day. And when light fills the room, the child is filled
with darkness. He knows that every time this happens he's moved just a
little closer to that darkness outside. The darkness outside is what the old
folks have been talking about. It's what they've come from. It's what they
endure. The child knows that they won't talk any more because if he
knows too much about what's happened to *them*, he'll know too much too
soon, about what's going to happen to *him*.

86   The last time I talked to my mother, I remember I was restless. I wanted
to get out and see Isabel. We weren't married then and we had a lot to
straighten out between us.

87   There Mama sat, in black, by the window. She was humming an old
church song, *Lord, you brought me from a long ways off.* Sonny was out somewhere. Mama kept watching the streets.

88   "I don't know," she said, "if I'll ever see you again, after you go off from
here. But I hope you'll remember the things I tried to teach you."

89   "Don't talk like that," I said, and smiled. "You'll be here a long time yet."

90   She smiled, too, but she said nothing. She was quiet for a long time.
And I said, "Mama, don't you worry about nothing. I'll be writing all the
time, and you be getting the checks. . . ."

91   "I want to talk to you about your brother," she said, suddenly. "If anything happens to me he ain't going to have nobody to look out for him."

92   "Mama," I said, "ain't nothing going to happen to you *or* Sonny. Sonny's all right. He's a good boy and he's got good sense."

93   "It ain't a question of his being a good boy," Mama said, "nor of his having good sense. It ain't only the bad ones, nor yet the dumb ones that gets sucked under." She stopped, looking at me. "Your Daddy once had a brother," she said, and she smiled, in a way that made me feel she was in pain. "You didn't never know that, did you?"

94   "No," I said, "I never knew that," and I watched her face.

95   "Oh, yes," she said, "your Daddy had a brother." She looked out of the window again. "I know you never saw your Daddy cry. But I did—many a time, through all these years."

96   I asked her, "What happened to his brother? How come nobody's ever talked about him?"

97   This was the first time I ever saw my mother look old.

98   "His brother got killed," she said, "when he was just a little younger than you are now. I knew him. He was a fine boy. He was maybe a little full of the devil, but he didn't mean nobody no harm."

99   Then she stopped and the room was silent, exactly as it had sometimes been on those Sunday afternoons. Mama kept looking out into the streets.

100   "He used to have a job in the mill," she said, "and, like all young folks, he just liked to perform on Saturday nights. Saturday nights, him and your father would drift around to different places, go to dances and things like that, or just sit around with people they knew, and your father's brother would sing, he had a fine voice, and play along with himself on his guitar. Well, this particular Saturday night him and your father was coming home from some place, and they were both a little drunk and there was a moon that night, it was bright like day. Your father's brother was feeling kind of good, and he was whistling to himself, and he had his guitar slung over his shoulder. They was coming down a hill and beneath them was a road that turned off from the highway. Well, your father's brother, being always kind of frisky, decided to run down this hill, and he did, with that guitar banging and clanging behind him, and he ran across the road, and he was making water behind a tree. And your father was sort of amused at him and he was still coming down the hill, kind of slow. Then he heard a car motor and that same minute his brother stepped from behind the tree, into the road, in the moonlight. And he started to cross the road. And your father started to run down the hill, he says he don't know why. This car was full of white men. They was all drunk, and when they seen your father's brother they let out a great whoop and holler and they aimed the car straight at him. They was having fun, they just wanted to scare him, the way they do sometimes, you know. But they was drunk. And I guess the boy, being drunk, too, and scared, kind of lost his head. By the time he jumped it was too late. Your father says he heard his brother scream when the car rolled over him, and he heard the wood

of that guitar when it give, and he heard them strings go flying, and he heard them white men shouting and the car kept on a-going and it ain't stopped till this day. And, time your father got down the hill, his brother weren't nothing but blood and pulp."

101   Tears were gleaming on my mother's face. There wasn't anything I could say.

102   "He never mentioned it," she said, "because I never let him mention it before you children. Your Daddy was like a crazy man that night and for many a night thereafter. He says he never in his life seen anything as dark as that road after the lights of that car had gone away. Weren't nothing, weren't nobody on that road, just your Daddy and his brother and that busted guitar. Oh, yes. Your Daddy never did really get right again. Till the day he died he weren't sure but that every white man he saw was the man that killed his brother."

103   She stopped and took out her handkerchief and dried her eyes and looked at me.

104   "I ain't telling you all this," she said, "to make you scared or bitter or to make you hate nobody. I'm telling you this because you got a brother. And the world ain't changed."

105   I guess I didn't want to believe this. I guess she saw this in my face. She turned away from me, toward the window again, searching those streets.

106   "But I praise my Redeemer," she said at last, "that He called your Daddy home before me. I ain't saying it to throw no flowers at myself, but, I declare, it keeps me from feeling too cast down to know I helped your father get safely through this world. Your father always acted like he was the roughest, strongest man on earth. And everybody took him to be like that. But if he hadn't had *me* there—to see his tears!"

107   She was crying again. Still I couldn't move. I said, "Lord, Lord, Mama, I didn't know it was like that."

108   "Oh, honey," she said, "there's a lot that you don't know. But you are going to find it out." She stood up from the window and came over to me. "You got to hold on to your brother," she said, "and don't let him fall, no matter what it looks like is happening to him and no matter how evil you gets with him. You going to be evil with him many a time. But don't you forget what I told you, you hear?"

109   "I won't forget," I said. "Don't you worry, I won't forget. I won't let nothing happen to Sonny."

110   My mother smiled as though she were amused at something she saw in my face. Then, "You may not be able to stop nothing from happening. But you got to let him know you's *there*."

111   Two days later I was married, and then I was gone. And I had a lot of things on my mind and I pretty well forgot my promise to Mama until I got shipped home on a special furlough for her funeral.

112   And, after the funeral, with just Sonny and me alone in the empty kitchen, I tried to find out something about him.

113   "What do you want to do?" I asked him.

114   "I'm going to be a musician," he said.

115   For he had graduated, in the time I had been away, from dancing to the juke box to finding out who was playing what, and what they were doing with it, and he had bought himself a set of drums.

116   "You mean, you want to be a drummer?" I somehow had the feeling that being a drummer might be all right for other people but not for my brother Sonny.

117   "I don't think," he said, looking at me very gravely, "that I'll ever be a good drummer. But I think I can play a piano."

118   I frowned. I'd never played the role of the older brother quite so seriously before, had scarcely ever, in fact, *asked* Sonny a damn thing. I sensed myself in the presence of something I didn't really know how to handle, didn't understand. So I made my frown a little deeper as I asked: "What kind of musician do you want to be?"

119   He grinned. "How many kinds do you think there are?"

120   "Be *serious*," I said.

121   He laughed, throwing his head back, and then looked at me. "I *am* serious."

122   "Well, then, for Christ's sake, stop kidding around and answer a serious question. I mean, do you want to be a concert pianist, you want to play classical music and all that, or—or what?" Long before I finished he was laughing again. "For Christ's *sake*, Sonny!"

123   He sobered, but with difficulty. "I'm sorry. But you sound so—*scared!*" and he was off again.

124   "Well, you may think it's funny now, baby, but it's not going to be so funny when you have to make your living at it, let me tell you *that*." I was furious because I knew he was laughing at me and I didn't know why.

125   "No," he said, very sober now, and afraid, perhaps, that he'd hurt me, "I don't want to be a classical pianist. That isn't what interests me. I mean"—he paused, looking hard at me, as though his eyes would help me to understand, and then gestured helplessly, as though perhaps his hand would help—"I mean, I'll have a lot of studying to do, and I'll have to study *everything*, but, I mean, I want to play *with*—jazz musicians." He stopped. "I want to play jazz," he said.

126   Well, the word had never before sounded as heavy, as real, as it sounded that afternoon in Sonny's mouth. I just looked at him and I was probably frowning a real frown by this time. I simply couldn't see why on earth he'd want to spend his time hanging around nightclubs, clowning around on bandstands, while people pushed each other around a dance floor. It seemed—beneath him, somehow. I had never thought about it before, had never been forced to, but I suppose I had always put jazz musicians in a class with what Daddy called "good-time people."

127   "Are you *serious*?"

128   "Hell, *yes*, I'm serious."

129   He looked more helpless than ever, and annoyed, and deeply hurt.

130   I suggested, helpfully: "You mean—like Louis Armstrong?"

131   His face closed as though I'd struck him. "No. I'm not talking about none of that old-time, down home crap."

132   "Well, look, Sonny, I'm sorry, don't get mad. I just don't altogether get it, that's all. Name somebody—you know a jazz musician you admire."

133   "Bird."

134   "Who?"

135   "Bird! Charlie Parker! Don't they teach you nothing in the goddamn army?"

136   I lit a cigarette. I was surprised and then a little amused to discover that I was trembling. "I've been out of touch," I said. "You'll have to be patient with me. Now. Who's this Parker character?"

137   "He's just one of the greatest jazz musicians alive," said Sonny, sullenly, his hands in his pockets, his back to me. "Maybe *the* greatest," he added, bitterly, "that's probably why *you* never heard of him."

138   "All right," I said, "I'm ignorant. I'm sorry. I'll go out and buy all the cat's records right away, all right?"

139   "It don't" said Sonny, with dignity, "make any difference to me. I don't care what you listen to. Don't do me no favors."

140   I was beginning to realize that I'd never seen him so upset before. With another part of my mind I was thinking that this would probably turn out to be one of those things kids go through and that I shouldn't make it seem important by pushing it too hard. Still, I didn't think it would do any harm to ask: "Doesn't all this take a lot of time? Can you make a living at it?"

141   He turned back to me and half leaned, half sat, on the kitchen table. "Everything takes time," he said, "and—well, yes, sure, I can make a living at it. But what I don't seem to be able to make you understand is that it's the only thing I want to do."

142   "Well, Sonny," I said, gently, "you know people can't always do exactly what they *want* to do—"

143   "*No,* I don't know that," said Sonny, surprising me. "I think people *ought* to do what they want to do, what else are they alive for?"

144   "You getting to be a big boy," I said desperately, "it's time you started thinking about your future."

145   "I'm thinking about my future," said Sonny, grimly. "I think about it all the time."

146   I gave up. I decided, if he didn't change his mind, that we could always talk about it later. "In the meantime," I said, "you got to finish school." We had already decided that he'd have to move in with Isabel and her folks. I knew this wasn't the ideal arrangement because Isabel's folks are inclined to be dicty and they hadn't especially wanted Isabel to marry me. But I didn't know what else to do. "And we have to get you fixed up at Isabel's."

147   There was a long silence. He moved from the kitchen table to the window. "That's a terrible idea. You know it yourself."

148   "Do you have a *better* idea?"

149   He just walked up and down the kitchen for a minute. He was as tall as I was. He had started to shave. I suddenly had the feeling that I didn't know him at all.

150   He stopped at the kitchen table and picked up my cigarettes. Looking at me with a kind of mocking, amused defiance, he put one between his lips. "You mind?"

151   "You smoking already?"

152   He lit the cigarette and nodded, watching me through the smoke. "I just wanted to see if I'd have the courage to smoke in front of you." He grinned and blew a great cloud of smoke to the ceiling. "It was easy." He looked at my face. "Come on, now. I bet you was smoking at my age, tell the truth."

153   I didn't say anything but the truth was on my face, and he laughed. But now there was something very strained in his laugh. "Sure. And I bet that ain't all you was doing."

154   He was frightening me a little. "Cut the crap," I said. "We already decided that you was going to go and live at Isabel's. Now what's got into you all of a sudden?"

155   "*You* decided it," he pointed out. "*I* didn't decide nothing." He stopped in front of me, leaning against the stove, arms loosely folded. "Look, brother. I don't want to stay in Harlem no more, I really don't." He was very earnest. He looked at me, then over toward the kitchen window. There was something in his eyes I'd never seen before, some thoughtfulness, some worry all his own. He rubbed the muscle of one arm. "It's time I was getting out of here."

156   "Where do you want to go, Sonny?"

157   "I want to join the army. Or the navy, I don't care. If I say I'm old enough, they'll believe me."

158   Then I got mad. It was because I was so scared. "You must be crazy. You goddamn fool, what the hell do you want to go and join the *army* for?"

159   "I just told you. To get out of Harlem."

160   "Sonny, you haven't even finished *school*. And if you really want to be a musician, how do you expect to study if you're in the *army*?"

161   He looked at me, trapped, and in anguish. "There's ways. I might be able to work out some kind of deal. Anyway, I'll have the G.I. Bill when I come out."

162   "*If* you come out." We stared at each other. "Sonny, please. Be reasonable. I know the setup is far from perfect. But we got to do the best we can."

163   "I ain't learning nothing in school," he said. "Even when I go." He turned away from me and opened the window and threw his cigarette out into the narrow alley. I watched his back. "At least, I ain't learning nothing you'd want me to learn." He slammed the window so hard I thought the glass would fly out, and turned back to me. "And I'm sick of the stink of these garbage cans!"

164   "Sonny," I said, "I know how you feel. But if you don't finish school now, you're going to be sorry later that you didn't." I grabbed him by the shoulders. "And you only got another year. It ain't so bad. And I'll come

back and I swear I'll help you do *whatever* you want to do. Just try to put up with it till I come back. Will you please do that? For me?"

165   He didn't answer and he wouldn't look at me.

166   "Sonny. You hear me?"

167   He pulled away. "I hear you. But you never hear anything I say."

168   I didn't know what to say to that. He looked out of the window and then back at me. "OK," he said, and sighed. "I'll try."

169   Then I said, trying to cheer him up a little, "They got a piano at Isabel's. You can practice on it."

170   And as a matter of fact, it did cheer him up for a minute. "That's right," he said to himself. "I forgot that." His face relaxed a little. But the worry, the thoughtfulness, played on it still, the way shadows play on a face which is staring into the fire.

171   But I thought I'd never hear the end of that piano. At first, Isabel would write me, saying how nice it was that Sonny was so serious about his music and how, as soon as he came in from school, or wherever he had been when he was supposed to be at school, he went straight to that piano and stayed there until suppertime. And, after supper, he went back to that piano and stayed there until everybody went to bed. He was at the piano all day Saturday and all day Sunday. Then he bought a record player and started playing records. He'd play one record over and over again, all day long sometimes, and he'd improvise along with it on the piano. Or he'd play one section of the record, one chord, one change, one progression, then he'd do it on the piano. Then back to the record. Then back to the piano.

172   Well, I really don't know how they stood it. Isabel finally confessed that it wasn't like living with a person at all, it was like living with sound. And the sound didn't make any sense to her, didn't make any sense to any of them—naturally. They began, in a way, to be afflicted by this presence that was living in their home. It was as though Sonny were some sort of god, or monster. He moved in an atmosphere which wasn't like theirs at all. They fed him and he ate, he washed himself, he walked in and out of their door; he certainly wasn't nasty or unpleasant or rude, Sonny isn't any of those things; but it was as though he were all wrapped up in some cloud, some fire, some vision all his own; and there wasn't any way to reach him.

173   At the same time, he wasn't really a man yet, he was still a child, and they had to watch out for him in all kinds of ways. They certainly couldn't throw him out. Neither did they dare to make a great scene about that piano because even they dimly sensed, as I sensed, from so many thousands of miles away, that Sonny was at that piano playing for his life.

174   But he hadn't been going to school. One day a letter came from the school board and Isabel's mother got it—there had apparently, been other letters but Sonny had torn them up. This day, when Sonny came in, Isabel's mother showed him the letter and asked where he'd been spending his time. And she finally got it out of him that he'd been down in Greenwich Village, with musicians and other characters, in a white girl's apartment.

And this scared her and she started to scream at him and what came up, once she began—though she denies it to this day—was what sacrifices they were making to give Sonny a decent home and how little he appreciated it.

175   Sonny didn't play the piano that day. By evening, Isabel's mother had calmed down but then there was the old man to deal with, and Isabel herself. Isabel says she did her best to be calm but she broke down and started crying. She says she just watched Sonny's face. She could tell, by watching him, what was happening with him. And what was happening was that they penetrated his cloud, they had reached him. Even if their fingers had been a thousand times more gentle than human fingers ever are, he could hardly help feeling that they had stripped him naked and were spitting on that nakedness. For he also had to see that his presence, that music, which was life or death to him, had been torture for them, and that they had endured it, not at all for his sake, but only for mine. And Sonny couldn't take that. He can take it a little better today than he could then but he's still not very good at it and, frankly, I don't know anybody who is.

176   The silence of the next few days must have been louder than the sound of all the music ever played since time began. One morning, before she went to work, Isabel was in his room for something and she suddenly realized that all of his records were gone. And she knew for certain that he was gone. And he was. He went as far as the navy would carry him. He finally sent me a postcard from some place in Greece and that was the first I knew that Sonny was still alive. I didn't see him any more until we were both back in New York and the war had long been over.

177   He was a man by then, of course, but I wasn't willing to see it. He came by the house from time to time, but we fought almost every time we met. I didn't like the way he carried himself, loose and dreamlike all the time, and I didn't like his friends, and his music seemed to be merely an excuse for the life he led. It sounded just that weird and disordered.

178   Then we had a fight, a pretty awful fight, and I didn't see him for months. By and by I looked him up, where he was living, in a furnished room in the Village, and I tried to make it up. But there were lots of other people in the room and Sonny just lay on his bed, and he wouldn't come downstairs with me, and he treated these other people as though they were his family and I weren't. So I got mad and then he got mad, and then I told him that he might just as well be dead as live the way he was living. Then he stood up and he told me not to worry about him any more in life, that he *was* dead as far as I was concerned. Then he pushed me to the door and the other people looked on as though nothing were happening, and he slammed the door behind me. I stood in the hallway, staring at the door. I heard somebody laugh in the room and then the tears came to my eyes. I started down the steps, whistling to keep from crying, I kept whistling to myself, *You going to need me, baby, one of these cold, rainy days.*

179   I read about Sonny's trouble in the spring. Little Grace died in the fall. She was a beautiful little girl. But she only lived a little over two years. She

died of polio and she suffered. She had a slight fever for a couple of days, but it didn't seem like anything and we just kept her in bed. And we would certainly have called the doctor, but the fever dropped, she seemed to be all right. So we thought it had just been a cold. Then, one day, she was up, playing, Isabel was in the kitchen fixing lunch for the two boys when they'd come in from school, and she heard Grace fall down in the living room. When you have a lot of children you don't always start running when one of them falls, unless they start screaming or something. And, this time, Grace was quiet. Yet, Isabel says that when she heard that *thump* and then that silence, something happened in her to make her afraid. And she ran to the living room and there was little Grace on the floor, all twisted up, and the reason she hadn't screamed was that she couldn't get her breath. And when she did scream, it was the worst sound, Isabel says, that she'd ever heard in all her life, and she still hears it sometimes in her dreams. Isabel will sometimes wake me up with a low, moaning, strangled sound and I have to be quick to awaken her and hold her to me and where Isabel is weeping against me seems a mortal wound.

180   I think I may have written Sonny the very day that little Grace was buried. I was sitting in the living room in the dark, by myself, and I suddenly thought of Sonny. My trouble made his real.

181   One Saturday afternoon, when Sonny had been living with us, or, anyway, been in our house, for nearly two weeks, I found myself wandering aimlessly about the living room, drinking from a can of beer, and trying to work up the courage to search Sonny's room. He was out, he was usually out whenever I was home, and Isabel had taken the children to see their grandparents. Suddenly I was standing still in front of the living room window, watching Seventh Avenue. The idea of searching Sonny's room made me still. I scarcely dared to admit to myself what I'd be searching for. I didn't know what I'd do if I found it. Or if I didn't.

182   On the sidewalk across from me, near the entrance to a barbecue joint, some people were holding an old-fashioned revival meeting. The barbecue cook, wearing a dirty white apron, his conked hair reddish and metallic in the pale sun, and a cigarette between his lips, stood in the doorway, watching them. Kids and older people paused in their errands and stood there, along with some older men and a couple of very tough-looking women who watched everything that happened on the avenue, as though they owned it, or were maybe owned by it. Well, they were watching this, too. The revival was being carried on by three sisters in black, and a brother. All they had were their voices and their Bibles and a tambourine. The brother was testifying and while he testified two of the sisters stood together, seeming to say, amen, and the third sister walked around with the tambourine outstretched and a couple of people dropped coins into it. Then the brother's testimony ended and the sister who had been taking up the collection dumped the coins into her palm and transferred them to the pocket of her long black robe. Then she raised both hands, striking the tambourine against the

air, and then against one hand, and she started to sing. And the two other sisters and the brother joined in.

183   It was strange, suddenly, to watch, though I had been seeing these street meetings all my life. So, of course, had everybody else down there. Yet, they paused and watched and listened and I stood still at the window. *"Tis the old ship of Zion,"* they sang and the sister with the tambourine kept a steady, jangling beat, *"it has rescued many a thousand!"* Not a soul under the sound of their voices was hearing this song for the first time, not one of them had been rescued. Nor had they seen much in the way of rescue work being done around them. Neither did they especially believe in the holiness of the three sisters and the brother, they knew too much about them, knew where they lived, and how. The woman with the tambourine, whose voice dominated the air, whose face was bright with joy, was divided by very little from the woman who stood watching her, a cigarette between her heavy, chapped lips, her hair a cuckoo's nest, her face scarred and swollen from many beatings, and her black eyes glittering like coal. Perhaps they both knew this, which was why, when, as rarely, they addressed each other, they addressed each other as Sister. As the singing filled the air the watching, listening faces underwent a change, the eyes focusing on something within; the music seemed to soothe a poison out of them; and time seemed, nearly, to fall away from the sullen, belligerent, battered faces, as though they were fleeing back to their first condition, while dreaming of their last. The barbecue cook half shook his head and smiled, and dropped his cigarette and disappeared into his joint. A man fumbled in his pockets for change and stood holding it in his hand impatiently, as though he had just remembered a pressing appointment further up the avenue. He looked furious. Then I saw Sonny, standing on the edge of the crowd. He was carrying a wide, flat notebook with a green cover, and it made him look, from where I was standing, almost like a school-boy. The coppery sun brought out the copper in his skin, he was very faintly smiling, standing very still. Then the singing stopped, the tambourine turned into a collection plate again. The furious man dropped in his coins and vanished, so did a couple of the women, and Sonny dropped some change in the plate, looking directly at the woman with a little smile. He started across the avenue, toward the house. He has a slow, loping walk, something like the way Harlem hipsters walk, only he's imposed on this his own half-beat. I had never really noticed it before.

184   I stayed at the window, both relieved and apprehensive. As Sonny disappeared from my sight, they began singing again. And they were still singing when his key turned in the lock.

185   "Hey," he said.

186   "Hey, yourself. You want some beer?"

187   "No. Well, maybe." But he came up to the window and stood beside me, looking out. "What a warm voice," he said.

188   They were singing *If I could only hear my mother pray again!*

189   "Yes," I said, "and she can sure beat that tambourine."

190   "But what a terrible song," he said, and laughed. He dropped his note-book on the sofa and disappeared into the kitchen. "Where's Isabel and the kids?"

191   "I think they went to see their grandparents. You hungry?"

192   "No." He came back into the living room with his can of beer. "You want to come some place with me tonight?"

193   I sensed, I don't know how, that I couldn't possibly say no. "Sure. Where?"

194   He sat down on the sofa and picked up his notebook and started leafing through it. "I'm going to sit in with some fellows in a joint in the Village."

195   "You mean, you're going to play, tonight?"

196   "That's right." He took a swallow of his beer and moved back to the window. He gave me a sidelong look. "If you can stand it."

197   "I'll try," I said.

198   He smiled to himself and we both watched as the meeting across the way broke up. The three sisters and their brother, heads bowed, were singing *God be with you till we meet again.* The faces around them were very quiet. Then the song ended. The small crowd dispersed. We watched the three women and the lone man walk slowly up the avenue.

199   "When she was singing before," said Sonny, abruptly, "her voice reminded me for a minute of what heroin feels like sometimes—when it's in your veins. It makes you feel sort of warm and cool at the same time. And distant. And—and sure." He sipped his beer, very deliberately not looking at me. I watched his face. "It makes you feel—in control. Some-times you've got to have that feeling."

200   "Do you?" I sat down slowly in the easy chair.

201   "Sometimes." He went to the sofa and picked up his notebook again. "Some people do."

202   "In order," I asked, "to play?" And my voice was very ugly, full of con-tempt and anger.

203   "Well"—he looked at me with great, troubled eyes, as though, in fact, he hoped his eyes would tell me things he could never otherwise say—"they *think* so. And *if* they think so—!"

204   "And what do *you* think?" I asked.

205   He sat on the sofa and put his can of beer on the floor. "I don't know," he said, and I couldn't be sure if he was answering my question or pur-suing his thoughts. His face didn't tell me. "It's not so much to *play*. It's to *stand* it, to be able to make it at all. On any level." He frowned and smiled: "In order to keep from shaking to pieces."

206   "But these friends of yours," I said, "they seem to shake themselves to pieces pretty goddamn fast."

207   "Maybe." He played with the notebook. And something told me that I should curb my tongue, that Sonny was doing his best to talk, that I should listen. "But of course you only know the ones that've gone to pieces. Some don't—or at least they haven't *yet* and that's just about all any of us can say."

He paused. "And then there are some who just live, really, in hell, and they know it and they see what's happening and they go right on. I don't know." He sighed, dropped the notebook, folded his arms. "Some guys, you can tell from the way they play, they on something *all* the time. And you can see that, well, it makes something real for them. But of course," he picked up his beer from the floor and sipped it and put the can down again, "they *want* to, too, you've got to see that. Even some of them that say they don't—*some,* not all."

208   "And what about you?" I asked—I couldn't help it. "What about you? Do *you* want to?"

209   He stood up and walked to the window and remained silent for a long time. Then he sighed. "Me," he said. Then: "While I was downstairs before, on my way here, listening to that woman sing, it struck me all of a sudden how much suffering she must have had to go through—to sing like that. It's *repulsive* to think you have to suffer that much."

210   I said: "But there's no way not to suffer—is there, Sonny?"

211   "I believe not," he said and smiled, "but that's never stopped anyone from trying." He looked at me. "Has it?" I realized, with this mocking look, that there stood between us, forever, beyond the power of time or forgiveness, the fact that I had held silence—so long!—when he needed human speech to help him. He turned back to the window. "No, there's no way not to suffer. But you try all kinds of ways to keep from drowning in it, to keep on top of it, and to make it seem—well, like *you.* Like you did something, all right, and now you're suffering for it. You know?" I said nothing. "Well you know," he said, impatiently, "why *do* people suffer? Maybe it's better to do something to give it a reason, *any* reason."

212   "But we just agreed," I said, "that there's no way not to suffer. Isn't it better, then, just to—take it?"

213   "But nobody just takes it," Sonny cried, "that's what I'm telling you! *Everybody* tries not to. You're just hung up on the *way* some people try—it's not *your* way!"

214   The hair on my face began to itch, my face felt wet. "That's not true," I said, "that's not true. I don't give a damn what other people do, I don't even care how they suffer. I just care how *you* suffer." And he looked at me. "Please believe me," I said, "I don't want to see you—die—trying not to suffer."

215   "I won't," he said, flatly, "die trying not to suffer. At least, not any faster than anybody else."

216   "But there's no need," I said, trying to laugh, "is there? in killing yourself."

217   I wanted to say more, but I couldn't. I wanted to talk about will power and how life could be—well, beautiful. I wanted to say that it was all within; but was it? or, rather, wasn't that exactly the trouble? And I wanted to promise that I would never fail him again. But it would all have sounded—empty words and lies.

218   So I made the promise to myself and prayed that I would keep it.

219   "It's terrible sometimes, inside," he said, "that's what's the trouble. You walk these streets, black and funky and cold, and there's not really a living ass to talk to, and there's nothing shaking, and there's no way of getting it out—that storm inside. You can't talk it and you can't make love with it, and when you finally try to get with it and play it, you realize *nobody's* listening. So *you've* got to listen. You got to find a way to listen."

220   And then he walked away from the window and sat on the sofa again, as though all the wind had suddenly been knocked out of him. "Sometimes you'll do *anything* to play, even cut your mother's throat." He laughed and looked at me. "Or your brother's." Then he sobered. "Or your own." Then: "Don't worry. I'm all right now and I think I'll *be* all right. But I can't forget—where I've been. I don't mean just the physical place I've been, I mean where I've *been*. And *what* I've been."

221   "What have you been, Sonny?" I asked.

222   He smiled—but sat sideways on the sofa, his elbow resting on the back, his fingers playing with his mouth and chin, not looking at me. "I've been something I didn't recognize, didn't know I could be. Didn't know anybody could be." He stopped, looking inward, looking helplessly young, looking old. "I'm not talking about it now because I feel *guilty* or anything like that—maybe it would be better if I did, I don't know. Anyway, I can't really talk about it. Not to you, not to anybody," and now he turned and faced me. "Sometimes, you know, and it was actually when I was most *out* of the world, I felt that I was in it, that I was *with* it, really, and I could play or I didn't really have to *play*, it just came out of me, it was there. And I don't know how I played, thinking about it now, but I know I did awful things, those times, sometimes, to people. Or it wasn't that I *did* anything to them—it was that they weren't real." He picked up the beer can; it was empty; he rolled it between his palms: "And other times—well, I needed a fix, I needed to find a place to lean, I needed to clear a space to *listen*— and I couldn't find it, and I—went crazy, I did terrible things to *me*, I was terrible *for* me." He began pressing the beer can between his hands, I watched the metal begin to give. It glittered, as he played with it, like a knife, and I was afraid he would cut himself, but I said nothing. "Oh well. I can never tell you. I was all by myself at the bottom of something, stinking and sweating and crying and shaking, and I smelled it, you know? *my* stink, and I thought I'd die if I couldn't get away from it and yet, all the same, I knew that everything I was doing was just locking me in with it. And I didn't know," he paused, still flattening the beer can, "I didn't know, I still *don't* know, something kept telling me that maybe it was good to smell your own stink, but I didn't think that *that* was what I'd been trying to do—and—who can stand it?" and he abruptly dropped the ruined beer can, looking at me with a small, still smile, and then rose, walking to the window as though it were the lodestone rock. I watched his face, he watched the avenue. "I couldn't tell you when Mama died—but the reason I wanted to leave Harlem so bad was to get away from drugs. And then, when I ran away, that's what I was running from—really. When I

came back, nothing had changed, *I* hadn't changed, I was just—older."
And he stopped, drumming with his fingers on the windowpane. The sun
had vanished, soon darkness would fall. I watched his face. "It can come
again," he said, almost as though speaking to himself. Then he turned to
me. "It can come again," he repeated. "I just want you to know that."

223   "All right," I said, at last. "So it can come again. All right."

224   He smiled, but the smile was sorrowful. "I had to try to tell you," he said.

225   "Yes," I said. "I understand that."

226   "You're my brother," he said, looking straight at me, and not smiling
at all.

227   "Yes," I repeated, "yes. I understand that."

228   He turned back to the window, looking out. "All that hatred down
there," he said, "all that hatred and misery and love. It's a wonder it doesn't
blow the avenue apart."

229   We went to the only nightclub on a short, dark street, downtown. We
squeezed through the narrow, chattering, jam-packed bar to the entrance
of the big room, where the bandstand was. And we stood there for a
moment, for the lights were very dim in this room and we couldn't see.
Then, "Hello, boy," said a voice and an enormous black man, much older
than Sonny or myself, erupted out of all that atmospheric lighting and
put an arm around Sonny's shoulder. "I been sitting right here," he said,
"waiting for you."

230   He had a big voice, too, and heads in the darkness turned toward us.

231   Sonny grinned and pulled a little away, and-said, "Creole, this is my
brother. I told you about him."

232   Creole shook my hand. "I'm glad to meet you, son," he said, and it
was clear that he was glad to meet me *there,* for Sonny's sake. And he
smiled, "You got a real musician in *your* family," and he took his arm
from Sonny's shoulder and slapped him, lightly, affectionately, with the
back of his hand.

233   "Well. Now I've heard it all," said a voice behind us. This was another
musician, a friend of Sonny's, a coal-black, cheerful-looking man, built
close to the ground. He immediately began confiding to me, at the top of
his lungs, the most terrible things about Sonny, his teeth gleaming like a
lighthouse and his laugh coming up out of him like the beginning of an
earthquake. And it turned out that everyone at the bar knew Sonny, or
almost everyone; some were musicians, working there, or nearby, or not
working, some were simply hangers-on, and some were there to hear
Sonny play. I was introduced to all of them and they were all very polite to
me. Yet, it was clear that, for them, I was only Sonny's brother. Here, I was
in Sonny's world. Or, rather: his kingdom. Here, it was not even a question that his veins bore royal blood.

234   They were going to play soon and Creole installed me, by myself, at a
table in a dark corner. Then I watched them, Creole, and the little black
man, and Sonny, and the others, while they horsed around, standing just

below the bandstand. The light from the bandstand spilled just a little short of them and, watching them laughing and gesturing and moving about, I had the feeling that they, nevertheless, were being most careful not to step into that circle of light too suddenly: that if they moved into the light too suddenly, without thinking, they would perish in flame. Then, while I watched, one of them, the small, black man, moved into the light and crossed the bandstand and started fooling around with his drums. Then—being funny and being, also, extremely ceremonious— Creole took Sonny by the arm and led him to the piano. A woman's voice called Sonny's name and a few hands started clapping. And Sonny, also being funny and being ceremonious, and so touched, I think, that he could have cried, but neither hiding it nor showing it, riding it like a man, grinned, and put both hands to his heart and bowed from the waist.

235   Creole then went to the bass fiddle and a lean, very bright-skinned brown man jumped up on the bandstand and picked up his horn. So there they were, and the atmosphere on the bandstand and in the room began to change and tighten. Someone stepped up to the microphone and announced them. Then there were all kinds of murmurs. Some people at the bar shushed others. The waitress ran around, frantically getting in the last orders, guys and chicks got closer to each other, and the lights on the bandstand, on the quartet, turned to a kind of indigo. Then they all looked different there. Creole looked about him for the last time, as though he were making certain that all his chickens were in the coop, and then he—jumped and struck the fiddle. And there they were.

236   All I know about music is that not many people ever really hear it. And even then, on the rare occasions when something opens within, and the music enters, what we mainly hear, or hear corroborated, are personal, private, vanishing evocations. But the man who creates the music is hearing something else, is dealing with the roar rising from the void and imposing order on it as it hits the air. What is evoked in him, then, is of another order, more terrible because it has no words, and triumphant, too, for that same reason. And his triumph, when he triumphs, is ours. I just watched Sonny's face. His face was troubled, he was working hard, but he wasn't with it. And I had the feeling that, in a way, everyone on the bandstand was waiting for him, both waiting for him and pushing him along. But as I began to watch Creole, I realized that it was Creole who held them all back. He had them on a short rein. Up there, keeping the beat with his whole body, wailing on the fiddle, with his eyes half closed, he was listening to everything, but he was listening to Sonny. He was having a dialogue with Sonny. He wanted Sonny to leave the shoreline and strike out for the deep water. He was Sonny's witness that deep water and drowning were not the same thing—he had been there, and he knew. And he wanted Sonny to know. He was waiting for Sonny to do the thing on the keys which would let Creole know that Sonny was in the water.

237   And, while Creole listened, Sonny moved, deep within, exactly like someone in torment. I had never before thought of how awful the relationship must be between the musician and his instrument. He has to fill it, this instrument, with the breath of life, his own. He has to make it do what he wants it to do. And a piano is just a piano. It's made out of so much wood and wires and little hammers and big ones, and ivory. While there's only so much you can do with it, the only way to find this out is to try; to try and make it do everything.

238   And Sonny hadn't been near a piano for over a year. And he wasn't on much better terms with his life, not the life that stretched before him now. He and the piano stammered, started one way, got scared, stopped; started another way, panicked, marked time, started again; then seemed to have found a direction, panicked again, got stuck. And the face I saw on Sonny I'd never seen before. Everything had been burned out of it, and, at the same time, things usually hidden were being burned in, by the fire and fury of the battle which was occurring in him up there.

239   Yet, watching Creole's face as they neared the end of the first set, I had the feeling that something had happened, something I hadn't heard. Then they finished, there was scattered applause, and then, without an instant's warning, Creole started into something else, it was almost sardonic, it was *Am I Blue*. And, as though he commanded, Sonny began to play. Something began to happen. And Creole let out the reins. The dry, low, black man said something awful on the drums, Creole answered, and the drums talked back. Then the horn insisted, sweet and high, slightly detached perhaps, and Creole listened, commenting now and then, dry, and driving, beautiful and calm and old. Then they all came together again, and Sonny was part of the family again. I could tell this from his face. He seemed to have found, right there beneath his fingers, a damn brand-new piano. It seemed that he couldn't get over it. Then, for awhile, just being happy with Sonny, they seemed to be agreeing with him that brand-new pianos certainly were a gas.

240   Then Creole stepped forward to remind them that what they were playing was the blues. He hit something in all of them, he hit something in me, myself, and the music tightened and deepened, apprehension began to beat the air. Creole began to tell us what the blues were all about. They were not about anything very new. He and his boys up there were keeping it new, at the risk of ruin, destruction, madness, and death, in order to find new ways to make us listen. For, while the tale of how we suffer, and how we are delighted, and how we may triumph is never new, it always must be heard. There isn't any other tale to tell, it's the only light we've got in all this darkness.

241   And this tale, according to that face, that body, those strong hands on those strings, has another aspect in every country, and a new depth in every generation. Listen, Creole seemed to be saying listen. Now these are Sonny's blues. He made the little black man on the drums know it, and the bright, brown man on the horn. Creole wasn't trying any longer to get Sonny in

the water. He was wishing him Godspeed. Then he stepped back, very slowly, filling the air with the immense suggestion that Sonny speak for himself.

242   Then they all gathered around Sonny and Sonny played. Every now and again one of them seemed to say, amen. Sonny's fingers filled the air with life, his life. But that life contained so many others. And Sonny went all the way back, he really began with the spare, flat statement of the opening phrase of the song. Then he began to make it his. It was very beautiful because it wasn't hurried and it was no longer a lament. I seemed to hear with what burning he had made it his, with what burning we had yet to make it ours, how we could cease lamenting. Freedom lurked around us and I understood, at last, that he could help us to be free if we would listen, that he would never be free until we did. Yet, there was no battle in his face now. I heard what he had gone through, and would continue to go through until he came to rest in earth. He had made it his: that long line, of which we knew only Mama and Daddy. And he was giving it back, as everything must be given back, so that, passing through death, it can live forever. I saw my mother's face again, and felt, for the first time, how the stones of the road she had walked on must have bruised her feet. I saw the moonlit road where my father's brother died. And it brought something else back to me, and carried me past it, I saw my little girl again and felt Isabel's tears again, and I felt my own tears begin to rise. And I was yet aware that this was only a moment, that the world waited outside, as hungry as a tiger, and that trouble stretched above us, longer than the sky.

243   Then it was over. Creole and Sonny let out their breath, both soaking wet, and grinning. There was a lot of applause and some of it was real. In the dark, the girl came by and I asked her to take drinks to the bandstand. There was a long pause, while they talked up there in the indigo light and after awhile I saw the girl put a Scotch and milk on top of the piano for Sonny. He didn't seem to notice it, but just before they started playing again, he sipped from it and looked toward me, and nodded. Then he put it back on top of the piano. For me, then, as they began to play again, it glowed and shook above my brother's head like the very cup of trembling.

Questions for Discussion

1. Why do you think the **narrator,** after his daughter dies, chooses to write to Sonny, whom he has ignored for years?

2. Why does Sonny's letter make the narrator feel guilty?

3. Why do Isabel and her family seem to disapprove of Sonny? Does the narrator also disapprove of his brother? Why would Sonny give up his "future" for music?

4. What does the narrator mean when he says of his students, "All they really knew were two darknesses, the darkness of their lives [. . .] and the darkness of the movies"? What is suggested by these and other references to darkness?

5. "Sonny's Blues" contains a story within a story, the mother's tale of the narrator's father and his brother. What is the significance of this story?

6. Explain the importance of the sidewalk revival and of the location from which each brother views it.

7. In the last scene, the narrator enters Sonny's world for the first time. Explain the symbolism of the location, the jazz, and the drink.

Suggestions for Exploration and Writing

1. A key to an understanding of this story is an understanding of the character of the **narrator,** since we see Sonny only through his eyes. How does the narrator perceive himself? How does this perception affect his opinion of Sonny?

2. Baldwin's **symbolism** enriches "Sonny's Blues." Write an essay exploring the use of one or more of these **symbols:** light and darkness, windows, music.

3. Compare and contrast the story of the father and his brother with the story of Sonny and the narrator. Explain what the story within the story adds to the understanding of both the narrator and the reader.

4. What special claims does this story make for music as an art form? How can the blues played on instruments in a nightclub bring to mind for the narrator not only his own past but that of his whole family?

5. Write an essay illustrating the ways in which the narrator changes in the story and the causes for these changes.

6. In an essay, explain the influence of Harlem on each of the brothers.

7. One of the major **themes** in literature is that we learn wisdom through suffering. Discuss the wisdom that the brothers learn through suffering.

Truman Capote (1924–1984)

Truman Capote, born Truman Streckfus Persons in New Orleans, spent much of his childhood in Alabama, the background for "A Christmas Memory." He took the surname of his stepfather and during his adolescence lived in Greenwich, Connecticut, and New York City. Capote began to write as a copy boy for The New Yorker. *His first short story, "Miriam," was published in 1946;* Other Voices, Other Rooms, *a novel, was published in 1948. From that point he became what he called a media presence; moving to Hollywood, he wrote the script for* Breakfast at Tiffany's. *The publication of* In Cold Blood: A True Account of a Multiple Murder and Its Consequences *in 1965 marked the beginning of a new genre called the nonfiction novel. A collection of short essays,* Music for Chameleon, *was published in 1980. His unfinished novel,* Answered Prayers, *was published after his death.*

A CHRISTMAS MEMORY   (1956)

1   Imagine a morning in late November. A coming of winter morning more than twenty years ago. Consider the kitchen of a spreading old house in a country town. A great black stove is its main feature; but there is also a big round table and a fireplace with two rocking chairs placed in front of it. Just today the fireplace commenced its seasonal roar.

2   A woman with shorn white hair is standing at the kitchen window. She is wearing tennis shoes and a shapeless gray sweater over a summery calico dress. She is small and sprightly, like a bantam hen; but, due to a long youthful illness, her shoulders are pitifully hunched. Her face is remarkable—not unlike Lincoln's, craggy like that, and tinted by sun and wind; but it is delicate too, finely boned, and her eyes are sherry-colored and timid. "Oh my," she exclaims, her breath smoking the windowpane, "it's fruitcake weather!"

3   The person to whom she is speaking is myself. I am seven; she is sixty-something. We are cousins, very distant ones, and we have lived together—well, as long as I can remember. Other people inhabit the house, relatives; and though they have power over us, and frequently make us cry, we are not, on the whole, too much aware of them. We are each other's best friend. She calls me Buddy, in memory of a boy who was formerly her best friend. The other Buddy died in the 1880's, when she was still a child. She is still a child.

4   "I knew it before I got out of bed," she says, turning away from the window with a purposeful excitement in her eyes. "The courthouse bell sounded so cold and clear. And there were no birds singing; they've gone to warmer country, yes indeed. Oh, Buddy, stop stuffing biscuit and fetch our buggy. Help me find my hat. We've thirty cakes to bake."

5   It's always the same: a morning arrives in November, and my friend, as though officially inaugurating the Christmas time of year that exhilarates her imagination and fuels the blaze of her heart, announces: "It's fruitcake weather! Fetch our buggy. Help me find my hat."

6   The hat is found, a straw cartwheel corsaged with velvet roses out-of-doors has faded: it once belonged to a more fashionable relative. Together, we guide our buggy, a dilapidated baby carriage, out to the garden and into a grove of pecan trees. The buggy is mine; that is, it was bought for me when I was born. It is made of wicker, rather unraveled, and the wheels wobble like a drunkard's legs. But it is a faithful object; spring-times, we take it to the woods and fill it with flowers, herbs, wild fern for our porch pots; in the summer we pile it with picnic paraphernalia and sugar-cane fishing poles and roll it down to the edge of a creek; it has its winter uses, too: as a truck for hauling firewood from the yard to the kitchen, as a warm bed for Queenie, our tough little orange and white rat terrier who has survived distemper and two rattlesnake bites. Queenie is trotting beside it now.

7   Three hours later we are back in the kitchen hulling a heaping buggy-load of windfall pecans. Our backs hurt from gathering them: how hard

they were to find (the main crop having been shaken off the trees and sold by the orchard's owners, who are not us) among the concealing leaves, the frosted, deceiving grass. Caarackle! A cheery crunch, scraps of miniature thunder sound as the shells collapse and the golden mound of sweet oily ivory meat mounts in the milk-glass bowl. Queenie begs to taste, and now and again my friend sneaks her a mite, though insisting we deprive ourselves. "We mustn't, Buddy. If we start, we won't stop. And there's scarcely enough as there is. For thirty cakes." The kitchen is growing dark. Dusk turns the window into a mirror: our reflections mingle with the rising moon as we work by the fireside in the firelight. At last, when the moon is quite high, we toss the final hull into the fire and, with joined sighs, watch it catch flame. The buggy is empty, the bowl is brimful.

8   We eat our supper (cold biscuits, bacon, blackberry jam) and discuss tomorrow. Tomorrow the kind of work I like best begins: buying. Cherries and citron, ginger and vanilla and canned Hawaiian pineapple, rinds and raisins and walnuts and whiskey and oh, so much flour, butter, so many eggs, spices, flavorings: why, we'll need a pony to pull the buggy home.

9   But before these purchases can be made, there is the question of money. Neither of us has any. Except for skinflint sums persons in the house occasionally provide (a dime is considered very big money); or what we earn ourselves from various activities: holding rummage sales, selling buckets of hand-picked blackberries, jars of homemade jam and apple jelly and peach preserves, rounding up flowers for funerals and weddings. Once we won seventy-ninth prize, five dollars, in a national football contest. Not that we know a fool thing about football. It's just that we enter any contest we hear about: at the moment our hopes are centered on the fifty-thousand-dollar Grand Prize being offered to name a new brand of coffee (we suggested "A.M."; and, after some hesitation, for my friend thought it perhaps sacrilegious, the slogan "A.M.! Amen!"). To tell the truth, our only *really* profitable enterprise was the Fun and Freak Museum we conducted in a back-yard woodshed two summers ago. The Fun was a stereopticon with slide views of Washington and New York lent us by a relative who had been to those places (she was furious when she discovered why we'd borrowed it); the Freak was a three-legged biddy chicken hatched by one of our own hens. Everybody hereabouts wanted to see that biddy: we charged grownups a nickel, kids two cents. And took in a good twenty dollars before the museum shut down due to the decease of the main attraction.

10   But one way and another we do each year accumulate Christmas savings, a Fruitcake Fund. These moneys we keep hidden in an ancient bead purse under a loose board under the floor under a chamber pot under my friend's bed. The purse is seldom removed from this safe location except to make a deposit, or, as happens every Saturday, a withdrawal; for on Saturdays I am allowed ten cents to go to the picture show. My friend has never been to a picture show, nor does she intend to: "I'd rather hear you tell the story, Buddy. That way I can imagine it more. Besides, a person my age shouldn't squander their eyes. When the Lord comes, let me

see Him clear." In addition to never having seen a movie, she has never: eaten in a restaurant, traveled more than five miles from home, received or sent a telegram, read anything except funny papers and the Bible, worn cosmetics, cursed, wished someone harm, told a lie on purpose, let a hungry dog go hungry. Here are the few things she has done, does do: killed with a hoe the biggest rattlesnake ever seen in this county (sixteen rattles), dip snuff (secretly), tame hummingbirds (just try it) till they balance on her finger, tell ghost stories (we both believe in ghosts) so tingling they chill you in July, talk to herself, take walks in the rain, grow the prettiest japonicas in town, know the recipe for every sort of old-time Indian cure, including a magical wart-remover.

11   Now, with supper finished, we retire to the room in a faraway part of the house where my friend sleeps in a scrap-quilt-covered iron bed painted rose pink, her favorite color. Silently, wallowing in the pleasures of conspiracy, we take the bead purse from its secret place and spill its contents on the scrap quilt. Dollar bills, tightly rolled and green as May buds. Somber fifty-cent pieces, heavy enough to weight a dead man's eyes. Lovely dimes, the liveliest coin, the one that really jingles. Nickels and quarters, worn smooth as creek pebbles. But mostly a hateful heap of bitter-odored pennies. Last summer others in the house contracted to pay us a penny for every twenty-five flies we killed. Oh, the carnage of August: the flies that flew to heaven! Yet it was not work in which we took pride. And, as we sit counting pennies, it is as though we were back tabulating dead flies. Neither of us has a head for figures; we count slowly, lose track, start again. According to her calculations, we have $12.73. According to mine, exactly $13. "I do hope you're wrong, Buddy. We can't mess around with thirteen. The cakes will fall. Or put somebody in the cemetery. Why, I wouldn't dream of getting out of bed on the thirteenth." This is true: she always spends thirteenths in bed. So, to be on the safe side, we subtract a penny and toss it out the window.

12   Of the ingredients that go into our fruitcakes, whiskey is the most expensive, as well as the hardest to obtain: State laws forbid its sale. But everybody knows you can buy a bottle from Mr. Haha Jones. And the next day, having completed our more prosaic shopping, we set out for Mr. Haha's business address, a "sinful" (to quote public opinion) fish-fry and dancing café down by the river. We've been there before, and on the same errand; but in previous years our dealings have been with Haha's wife, an iodine-dark Indian woman with brassy peroxided hair and a dead-tired disposition. Actually, we've never laid eyes on her husband, though we've heard that he's an Indian too. A giant with razor scars across his cheeks. They call him Haha because he's so gloomy, a man who never laughs. As we approach his café (a large log cabin festooned inside and out with chains of garish-gay naked light bulbs and standing by the river's muddy edge under the shade of river trees where moss drifts through the branches like gray mist) our steps slow down. Even Queenie stops prancing and sticks close by. People have been murdered in Haha's café. Cut

to pieces. Hit on the head. There's a case coming up in court next month. Naturally these goings-on happen at night when the colored lights cast crazy patterns and the victrola wails. In the daytime Haha's is shabby and deserted. I knock at the door, Queenie barks, my friend calls: "Mrs. Haha, ma'am? Anyone to home?"

13   Footsteps. The door opens. Our hearts overturn. It's Mr. Haha Jones himself! And he *is* a giant; he *does* have scars; he *doesn't* smile. No, he glowers at us through Satan-tilted eyes and demands to know: "What you want with Haha?"

14   For a moment we are too paralyzed to tell. Presently my friend half-finds her voice, a whispery voice at best: "If you please, Mr. Haha, we'd like a quart of your finest whiskey."

15   His eyes tilt more. Would you believe it? Haha is smiling! Laughing, too. "Which one of you is a drinkin' man?"

16   "It's for making fruitcakes, Mr. Haha. Cooking."

17   This sobers him. He frowns. "That's no way to waste good whiskey." Nevertheless, he retreats into the shadowed café and seconds later appears carrying a bottle of daisy-yellow unlabeled liquor. He demonstrates its sparkle in the sunlight and says: "Two dollars."

18   We pay him with nickels and dimes and pennies. Suddenly, as he jangles the coins in his hand like a fistful of dice, his face softens. "Tell you what," he proposed, pouring the money back into our bead purse, "just send me one of them fruitcakes instead."

19   "Well," my friend remarks on our way home, "there's a lovely man. We'll put an extra cup of raisins in *his* cake."

20   The black stove, stoked with coal and firewood, glows like a lighted pumpkin. Eggbeaters whirl, spoons spin round in bowls of butter and sugar, vanilla sweetens the air, ginger spices it; melting, nose-tingling odors saturate the kitchen, suffuse the house, drift out to the world on puffs of chimney smoke. In four days our work is done. Thirty-one cakes, dampened with whiskey, bask on window sills and shelves.

21   Who are they for?

22   Friends. Not necessarily neighbor friends: indeed, the larger share is intended for persons we've met maybe once, perhaps not at all. People who've struck our fancy. Like President Roosevelt. Like the Reverend and Mrs. J. C. Lucey, Baptist missionaries to Borneo who lectured here last winter. Or the little knife grinder who comes through town twice a year. Or Abner Packer, the driver of the six o'clock bus from Mobile, who exchanges waves with us every day as he passes in a dust-cloud whoosh. Or the young Wistons, a California couple whose car one afternoon broke down outside the house and who spent a pleasant hour chatting with us on the porch (young Mr. Wiston snapped our picture, the only one we've ever had taken). Is it because my friend is shy with everyone *except* strangers that these strangers, and merest acquaintances, seem to us our truest friends? I think yes. Also the scrapbooks we keep of thank-you's on White House stationery,

time-to-time communications from California and Borneo, the knife grinder's penny post cards, make us feel connected to eventful worlds beyond the kitchen with its view of a sky that stops.

23   Now a nude December fig branch grates against the window. The kitchen is empty, the cakes are gone; yesterday we carted the last of them to the post office, where the cost of stamps turned our purse inside out. We're broke. That rather depresses me, but my friend insists on celebrating—with two inches of whiskey left in Haha's bottle. Queenie has a spoonful in a bowl of coffee (she likes her coffee chicory-flavored and strong). The rest we divide between a pair of jelly glasses. We're both quite awed at the prospect of drinking straight whiskey; the taste of it brings screwed-up expressions and sour shudders. But by and by we begin to sing, the two of us singing different songs simultaneously. I don't know the words to mine, just: *Come on along, come on along, to the dark-town strutters' ball.* But I can dance: that's what I mean to be, a tap-dancer in the movies. My dancing shadow rollicks on the walls; our voices rock the chinaware; we giggle: as if unseen hands were tickling us. Queenie rolls on her back, her paws plow the air, something like a grin stretches her black lips. Inside myself, I feel warm and sparky as those crumbling logs, carefree as the wind in the chimney. My friend waltzes round the stove, the hem of her poor calico skirt pinched between her fingers as though it were a party dress: *Show me the way to go home,* she sings, her tennis shoes squeaking on the floor. *Show me the way to go home.*

24   Enter: two relatives. Very angry. Potent with eyes that scold, tongues that scald. Listen to what they have to say, the words tumbling together into a wrathful tune: "A child of seven! whiskey on his breath! are you out of your mind? feeding a child of seven! must be loony! road to ruination! remember Cousin Kate? Uncle Charlie? Uncle Charlie's brother-in-law? shame! scandal! humiliation! kneel, pray, beg the Lord!"

25   Queenie sneaks under the stove. My friend gazes at her shoes, her chin quivers, she lifts her skirt and blows her nose and runs to her room. Long after the town has gone to sleep and the house is silent except for the chimings of clocks and the sputter of fading fires, she is weeping into a pillow already as wet as a widow's handkerchief.

26   "Don't cry," I say, sitting at the bottom of her bed and shivering despite my flannel nightgown that smells of last winter's cough syrup, "don't cry," I beg, teasing her toes, tickling her feet, "you're too old for that."

27   "It's because," she hiccups, "I *am* too old. Old and funny."

28   "Not funny. Fun. More fun than anybody. Listen. If you don't stop crying you'll be so tired tomorrow we can't go cut a tree."

29   She straightens up. Queenie jumps on the bed (where Queenie is not allowed) to lick her cheeks. "I know where we'll find real pretty trees, Buddy. And holly, too. With berries big as your eyes. It's way off in the woods. Farther than we've ever been. Papa used to bring us Christmas trees from there: carry them on his shoulder. That's fifty years ago. Well, now: I can't wait for morning."

30   Morning. Frozen rime lusters the grass; the sun, round as an orange and orange as hot-weather moons, balances on the horizon, burnishes the silvered winter woods. A wild turkey calls. A renegade hog grunts in the undergrowth. Soon, by the edge of knee-deep, rapid-running water we have to abandon the buggy. Queenie wades the stream first, paddles across barking complaints at the swiftness of the current, the pneumonia-making coldness of it. We follow, holding our shoes and equipment (a hatchet, a burlap sack) above our heads. A mile more: of chastising thorns, burs and briers that catch at our clothes; of rusty pine needles brilliant with gaudy fungus and molted feathers. Here, there, a flash, a flutter, an ecstasy of shrillings remind us that not all the birds have flown south. Always, the path unwinds through lemony sun pools and pitch-black vine tunnels. Another creek to cross: a disturbed armada of speckled trout froths the water round us, and frogs the size of plates practice belly flops; beaver workmen are building a dam. On the farther shore, Queenie shakes herself and trembles. My friend shivers, too: not with cold but enthusiasm. One of her hat's ragged roses sheds a petal as she lifts her head and inhales the pine-heavy air. "We're almost there; can you smell it, Buddy?" she says, as though we were approaching an ocean.

31   And, indeed, it is a kind of ocean. Scented acres of holiday trees, prickly-leafed holly. Red berries shiny as Chinese bells: black crows swoop upon them screaming. Having stuffed our burlap sacks with enough greenery and crimson to garland a dozen windows, we set about choosing a tree. "It should be," muses my friend, "twice as tall as a boy. So a boy can't steal the star." The one we pick is twice as tall as me. A brave handsome brute that survives thirty hatchet strokes before it keels with a creaking rending cry. Lugging it like a kill, we commence the long trek out. Every few yards we abandon the struggle, sit down and pant. But we have the strength of triumphant huntsmen; that and the tree's virile, icy perfume revive us, goad us on. Many compliments accompany our sunset return along the red clay road to town; but my friend is sly and noncommittal when passersby praise the treasure perched in our buggy: what a fine tree and where did it come from? "Yonderways," she murmurs vaguely. Once a car stops and the rich mill owner's lazy wife leans out and whines: "Giveya two-bits cash for that ol tree." Ordinarily my friend is afraid of saying no; but on this occasion she promptly shakes her head: "We wouldn't take a dollar." The mill owner's wife persists. "A dollar, my foot! Fifty cents. That's my last offer. Goodness, woman, you can get another one." In answer, my friend gently reflects: "I doubt it. There's never two of anything."

32   Home: Queenie slumps by the fire and sleeps till tomorrow, snoring loud as a human.

33   A trunk in the attic contains: a shoebox of ermine tails (off the opera cape of a curious lady who once rented a room in the house), coils of frazzled tinsel gone gold with age, one silver star, a brief rope of dilapidated, undoubtedly dangerous candy-like light bulbs. Excellent decorations, as far as they go, which isn't far enough: my friend wants our tree to blaze

"like a Baptist window," droop with weighty snows of ornament. But we can't afford the made-in-Japan splendors at the five-and-dime. So we do what we've always done: sit for days at the kitchen table with scissors and crayons and stacks of colored paper. I make sketches and my friend cuts them out: lots of cats, fish too (because they're easy to draw), some apples, some watermelons, a few winged angels devised from saved-up sheets of Hershey-bar tin foil. We use safety pins to attach these creations to the tree; as a final touch, we sprinkle the branches with shredded cotton (picked in August for this purpose). My friend, surveying the effect, clasps her hands together. "Now honest, Buddy. Doesn't it look good enough to eat?" Queenie tries to eat an angel.

34   After weaving and ribboning holly wreaths for all the front windows, our next project is the fashioning of family gifts. Tie-dye scarves for the ladies, for the men a home-brewed lemon and licorice and aspirin syrup to be taken "at the first Symptoms of a Cold and after Hunting." But when it comes time for making each other's gift, my friend and I separate to work secretly. I would like to buy her a pearl-handled knife, a radio, a whole pound of chocolate-covered cherries (we tasted some once, and she always swears: "I could live on them, Buddy, Lord yes I could—and that's not taking His name in vain"). Instead, I am building her a kite. She would like to give me a bicycle (she's said so on several million occasions: "If only I could, Buddy. It's bad enough in life to do without something *you* want; but confound it, what gets my goat is not being able to give somebody something you want *them* to have. Only one of these days I will, Buddy. Locate you a bike. Don't ask how. Steal it, maybe"). Instead, I'm fairly certain that she is building me a kite—the same as last year, and the year before: the year before that we exchanged slingshots. All of which is fine by me. For we are champion kite-fliers who study the wind like sailors; my friend, more accomplished than I, can get a kite aloft when there isn't enough breeze to carry clouds.

35   Christmas Eve afternoon we scrape together a nickel and go to the butcher's to buy Queenie's traditional gift, a good gnawable beef bone. The bone, wrapped in funny paper, is placed high in the tree near the silver star. Queenie knows it's there. She squats at the foot of the tree staring up in a trance of greed: when bedtime arrives she refuses to budge. Her excitement is equaled by my own. I kick the covers and turn my pillow as though it were a scorching summer's night. Somewhere a rooster crows: falsely, for the sun is still on the other side of the world.

36   "Buddy, are you awake?" It is my friend, calling from her room, which is next to mine; and an instant later she is sitting on my bed holding a candle. "Well, I can't sleep a hoot," she declares. "My mind's jumping like a jack rabbit. Buddy, do you think Mrs. Roosevelt will serve our cake at dinner?" We huddle in the bed, and she squeezes my hand I-love-you. "Seems like your hand used to be so much smaller, I guess I hate to see you grow up. When you're grown up, will we still be friends?" I say always. "But I feel so bad, Buddy. I wanted so bad to give you a bike. I tried to sell my cameo

Papa gave me. Buddy"—she hesitates, as though embarrassed—"I made you another kite." Then I confess that I made her one, too; and we laugh. The candle burns too short to hold. Out it goes, exposing the starlight, the stars spinning at the window like a visible caroling that slowly, slowly daybreak silences. Possibly we doze; but the beginnings of dawn splash us like cold water: we're up, wide-eyed and wandering while we wait for others to waken. Quite deliberately my friend drops a kettle on the kitchen floor. I tap-dance in front of closed doors. One by one the household emerges, looking as though they'd like to kill us both; but it's Christmas so they can't. First, a gorgeous breakfast: just everything you can imagine— from flapjacks and fried squirrel to hominy grits and honey-in-the-comb. Which puts everyone in a good humor except my friend and me. Frankly, we're so impatient to get at the presents we can't eat a mouthful.

37   Well, I'm disappointed. Who wouldn't be? With socks, a Sunday school shirt, some handkerchiefs, a hand-me-down sweater and a year's subscription to a religious magazine for children. *The Little Shepherd.* It makes me boil. It really does.

38   My friend has a better haul. A sack of Satsumas, that's her best present. She is proudest, however, of a white wool shawl knitted by her married sister. But she *says* her favorite gift is the kite I built her. And it *is* very beautiful; though not as beautiful as the one she made me, which is blue and scattered with gold and green Good Conduct stars; moreover, my name is painted on it, "Buddy."

39   "Buddy, the wind is blowing."

40   The wind is blowing, and nothing will do till we've run to a pasture below the house where Queenie has scooted to bury her bone (and where, a winter hence, Queenie will be buried, too). There, plunging through the healthy waist-high grass we unreel our kites, feel them twitching at the string like sky fish as they swim into the wind. Satisfied, sun-warmed, we sprawl in the grass and peel Satsumas and watch our kites cavort. Soon I forget the socks and hand-me-down sweater. I'm as happy as if we'd already won the fifty-thousand-dollar Grand Prize in the coffee-naming contest.

41   "My, how foolish I am!" my friend cries, suddenly alert, like a woman remembering too late she has biscuits in the oven. "You know what I've always thought?" she asks in a tone of discovery, and not smiling at me but a point beyond. "I've always thought a body would have to be sick and dying before they saw the Lord. And I imagined that when He came it would be like looking at the Baptist window: pretty as colored glass with the sun pouring through, such a shine you don't know it's getting dark. And it's been a comfort: to think of that shine taking away all the spooky feeling. But I'll wager it never happens. I'll wager at the very end a body realizes the Lord has already shown Himself. That things as they are"— her hand circles in a gesture that gathers clouds and kites and grass and Queenie pawing earth over her bone—"just what they've always seen, was seeing Him. As for me, I could leave the world with today in my eyes."

42   This is our last Christmas together.

43   Life separates us. Those who Know Best decide that I belong in a military school. And so follows a miserable succession of bugle-blowing prisons, grim reveille-ridden summer camps. I have a new home too. But it doesn't count. Home is where my friend is, and there I never go.

44   And there she remains, puttering around the kitchen. Alone with Queeie. Then alone. ("Buddy dear," she writes in her wild hard-to-read script, "yesterday Jim Macy's horse kicked Queenie bad. Be thankful she didn't feel much. I wrapped her in a Fine Linen sheet and rode her in the buggy down to Simpson's pasture where she can be with all her Bones . . ."). For a few Novembers she continues to bake her fruitcakes single-handed; not as many, but some: and, of course, she always sends me "the best of the batch." Also, in every letter she encloses a dime wadded in toilet paper: "See a picture show and write me the story." But gradually in her letters she tends to confuse me with her other friend, the Buddy who died in the 1880's; more and more thirteenths are not the only days she stays in bed: a morning arrives in November, a leafless birdless coming of winter morning, when she cannot rouse herself to exclaim: "Oh my, it's fruitcake weather!"

45   And when that happens, I know it. A message saying so merely confirms a piece of news some secret vein had already received, severing from me an irreplaceable part of myself, letting loose like a kite on a broken string. That is why, walking across a school campus on this particular December morning, I keep searching the sky. As if I expected to see, rather like hearts, a lost pair of kites hurrying toward heaven.

Questions for Discussion

1. The boy says of his friend, "She is still a child." Is this statement a compliment or an insult? What are her childlike qualities? In what ways are the boy and the woman alike?

2. What does "she" mean by "'As for me, I could leave the world with today in my eyes'"?

3. How would you describe the rest of the family's relationship to Buddy and his friend? Discuss the pattern of nurturing in which someone who is not a member of the immediate family nurtures the child.

4. In this story the **point of view** is that of an adult remembering his childhood. Why is this point of view essential to the creation of the story? Why is it written in present tense?

5. Why do the two friends go to the great trouble and expense of making and mailing fruitcakes every Christmas?

6. Explain the **symbolism** of the kites.

Suggestions for Exploration and Writing

1. Write an essay describing your most memorable holiday.

2. One of the strengths of the story is the vivid sensory detail given in the descriptions. Discuss Capote's use of such details, concentrating on at least three senses.

3. Write an essay explaining the relationship Buddy and his friend have with other people, both nearby and far away.

4. In an age of dysfunctional families, discuss how this short story exemplifies a truly functional family.

Patricia Grace (b. 1937)

Patricia Grace, a Maori from New Zealand, is a short story writer, a children's writer, and a novelist who was instrumental in popularizing Maori fiction in the 1970s. As a teacher, she began reading New Zealand authors, and at twenty-five began writing in addition to teaching and raising seven children. She published the first collection of short stories by a Maori woman, Waiariki, *in 1975. Other short story collections include* The Dream Sleepers *(1980),* Electric City and Other Stories *(1987), and* The Sky People *(1994). In the early 1980s, Grace began writing stories for Maori children. In collaboration with illustrator Robyn Kahukiwa, she has published several award-winning books for children. Her novels include* Mutuwhenua: The Moon Sleeps *(1978);* Potiki *(1986), her most successful novel;* Cousins *(1992);* Baby No-eyes *(1998); and* Dogside Story *(2001), winner of the 2001 Kiriyama Pacific Rim Book Prize.*

IT USED TO BE GREEN ONCE   (1987)

1   We were all ashamed of our mother. Our mother always did things to shame us. Like putting red darns in our clothes, and cutting up old swimming togs and making two—girl's togs from the top half for my sister, and boy's togs from the bottom half for my brother. Peti and Raana both cried when Mum made them take the togs to school. Peti sat down on the road by our gate and yelled out she wasn't going to school. She wasn't going swimming. I didn't blame my sister because the togs were thirty-eight chest and Peti was only ten.

2   But Mum knew how to get her up off the road. She yelled loudly, "Get up off that road, my girl. There's nothing wrong with those togs. I didn't have any togs when I was a kid and I had to swim in my nothings. Get up off your backside and get to school." Mum's got a loud voice and she knew how to shame us. We all dragged Peti up off the road before our mates came along and heard Mum. We pushed Peti into the school bus so Mum wouldn't come yelling up the drive.

3   We never minded our holey fruit at first. Dad used to pick up the cases of over-ripe apples or pears from town that he got cheap. Mum would dig out the rotten bits, and then give them to us to take for play-lunch. We didn't notice much at first, not until Reweti from down the road yelled

out to us one morning, "Hey you fullas. Who shot your pears?" We didn't have anywhere to hide our lunch because we weren't allowed schoolbags until we got to high school. Mum said she wasn't buying fourteen school-bags. When we went to high school we could have shoes too. The whole lot of us gave Reweti a good hiding after school.

4   However, this story is mainly about the car, and about Mum and how she shamed us all the time. The shame of rainbow darns and cut-up togs and holey fruit was nothing to what we suffered because of the car. Uncle Raz gave us the car because he couldn't fix it up any more, and he'd been fined because he lived in Auckland. He gave the car to Dad so we could drive our cream cans up to the road instead of pushing them up by wheelbarrow.

5   It didn't matter about the car not having brakes, because the drive from our cowshed goes down in a dip then up to the gate. Put the car in its first gear, run it down from the shed, pick up a bit of speed, up the other side, turn it round by the cream stand so that it's pointing down the drive again, foot off the accelerator and slam on the handbrake. Dad pegged a board there to make sure it stopped. Then when we'd lifted the cans out onto the stand, he'd back up a little and slide off down the drive—with all of us throwing ourselves in over the sides as if it were a dinghy that had just been pushed out into the sea.

6   The car had been red once, because you could still see some patches of red paint here and there. And it used to have a top too, that you could put down or up. Our uncle told us that when he gave it to Dad. We were all proud about the car having a top once. Some of the younger kids skited to their mates about our convertible and its top that went up and down. But that was before our mother started shaming us by driving the car to the shop.

7   We growled at Mum and we cried but it made no difference. "You kids always howl when I tell you to get our shopping," she said.

8   "We'll get it, Mum. We won't cry."

9   "We won't cry, Mum. We'll carry the sack of potatoes."

10   "And the flour."

11   "And the bag of sugar."

12   "And the tin of treacle."

13   "We'll do the shopping, Mum."

14   But Mum would say, "Never mind. I'll do it myself." And after that she wouldn't listen any more.

15   How we hated Wednesdays. We always tried to be sick on Wednesdays, or to miss the bus. But Mum would be up early yelling at us to get out of bed. If we didn't get up when we were told she'd drag us out and pull down our pyjama pants and set our bums on the cold lino. Mum was cruel to us.

16   Whoever was helping with the milking had to be back quickly from the shed for breakfast, and we'd all have to rush through our kai and get to school. Wednesday was Mum's day for shopping.

17   As soon as she had everything tidy she'd change into her good purple dress that she'd made from a Japanese bedspread, pull on her floppy, brimmed blue sunhat and her slippers and galoshes, and go out and start up the car.

18   We tried everything to stop her shaming us all.

19   "You've got no licence, Mum."

20   "What do I want a licence for? I can drive, can't I? I don't need the proof."

21   "You got no warrant."

22   "Warrant? What's warrant?"

23   "The traffic man'll get you, Mum."

24   "That rat. He won't come near me after what he did to my niece. I'll hit him right over his smart head with a bag of riwais and I'll hit him somewhere else as well."

25   We never could win an argument with Mum.

26   Off she'd go on a Wednesday morning, and once out on the road she'd start tooting the horn. This didn't sound like a horn at all but more like a flock of ducks coming in for a feed. The reason for the horn was to let all her mates and relations along the way know she was coming. And as she passed each one's house, if they wanted anything they'd have to run out and call it out loud. Mum couldn't stop because of not having brakes. "E Kiri," each would call. "Mauria mai he riwai," if they wanted spuds; "Mauria mai he paraoa," if they wanted bread. "Mauria mai he tarau, penei te kaita," hand spread to show the size of the pants they wanted Mum to get. She would call out to each one and wave to them to show she'd understood. And when she neared the store she'd switch the motor off, run into the kerbing and pull on the handbrake. I don't know how she remembered all the things she had to buy—I only know that by the time she'd finished, every space in that car was filled and it was a squeeze for her to get into the driver's seat. But she had everything there, all ready to throw out on the way back.

27   As soon as she'd left the store she'd begin hooting again, to let the whole district know she was on her way. Everybody would be out on the road to get their shopping thrown at them, or just to watch our mother go chuffing past. We always hid if we heard her coming.

28   The first time Mum's car and the school bus met was when they were both approaching a one-way bridge from opposite directions. We had to ask the driver to stop and give way to Mum because she had no brakes. We were all ashamed. But everyone soon got to know Mum and her car and they always stopped whenever they saw her coming. And you know, Mum never ever had an accident in her car, except for once when she threw a side of mutton out to Uncle Peta and it knocked him over and broke his leg.

29   After a while we started walking home from school on Wednesdays to give Mum a good chance of getting home before us, and so we wouldn't be in the bus when it had to stop and let her past. The boys didn't like

having to walk home, but we girls didn't mind because Mr. Hadly walked home too. He was a new teacher at our school and he stayed not far from where we lived. We girls thought he was really neat.

30   But one day, it had to happen. When I heard the honking and tooting behind me I wished that a hole would appear in the ground and that I would fall in it and disappear for ever. As Mum came near she started smiling and waving and yelling her head off. "Anyone wants a ride," she yelled, "they'll have to run and jump in."

31   We all turned our heads the other way and hoped Mr. Hadly wouldn't notice the car with our mother in it, and her yelling and tooting, and the brim of her hat jumping up and down. But instead, Mr. Hadley took off after the car and leapt in over the back seat on top of the shopping. Oh, the shame.

32   But then one day something happened that changed everything. We arrived home to find Dad in his best clothes, walking round and grinning, and not doing anything like getting the cows in, or mending a gate, or digging a drain. We said, "What are you laughing at, Dad? What are you dressed up for? Hey Mum, what's the matter with Dad?"

33   "Your dad's a rich man," she said. "Your dad, he's just won ten thousand pounds in a lottery."

34   At first we couldn't believe it. We couldn't believe it. Then we all began running round and laughing and yelling and hugging Dad and Mum. "We can have shoes and bags," we said. "New clothes and swimming togs, and proper apples and pears." Then do you know what Dad said? Dad said, "Mum can have a new car." This really astounded and amazed us. We went numb with excitement for five minutes then began hooting and shouting again, and knocking Mum over.

35   "A new car!"

36   "A new car?"

37   "Get us a Packard, Mum."

38   "Or a De Soto. Yes, yes."

39   Get this, get that . . .

40   Well, Mum bought a shiny green Chevrolet, and Dad got a new cowshed with everything modernised and water gushing everywhere. We all got our new clothes—shoes, bags, togs—and we even started taking posh lunches to school. Sandwiches cut in triangle, bottles of cordial, crisp apples and pears, and yellow bananas.

41   And somehow all of us kids changed. We started acting like we were somebody instead of ordinary like before. We used to whine to Dad for money to spend, and he'd always give it to us. Every week we'd nag Mum into taking us to the pictures, or if she was tired we'd go ourselves by taxi. We got flash bedspreads and a piano and we really thought we were neat.

42   As for the old car—we made Dad take it to the dump. We never wanted to see it again. We all cheered when he took it away, except for Mum. Mum stayed inside where she couldn't watch, but we all stood outside and cheered.

43   We all changed, as though we were really somebody, but there was one thing I noticed. Mum didn't change at all, and neither did Dad. Mum had a new car all right, and a couple of new dresses, and a new pair of galoshes to put over her slippers. And Dad had a new modern milking shed and a tractor, and some other gadgets for the farm. But Mum and Dad didn't change. They were the same as always.

44   Mum still went shopping every Wednesday. But instead of having to do all the shopping herself, she was able to take all her friends and relations with her. She had to start out earlier so she'd have time to pick everyone up on the way. How angry we used to be when Mum went past with her same old sunhat and her heap of friends and relations, and them all waving and calling out to us.

45   Mum sometimes forgot that the new car had brakes, especially when she was approaching the old bridge and we were coming the opposite way in the school bus. She would start tooting and the bus would have to pull over and let her through. That's when all our aunties and uncles and friends would start waving and calling out. But some of them couldn't wave because they were too squashed by people and shopping, they'd just yell. How shaming.

46   There were always ropes everywhere over Mum's new car holding bags of things and shovel handles to the roof and sides. The boot was always hanging open because it was too full to close—things used to drop out on to the road all the time. And the new car—it used to be green once, because if you look closely you can still see some patches of green paint here and there.

Questions for Discussion

1. Explain how the opening sentence sets the tone for the story.
2. Why are the children ashamed of their mother? What does their mother do that shames them?
3. Why are the children ashamed of the car? What would be your reaction to this car?
4. How do the children change after the father wins the lottery? What does the parents' refusal to change reveal about their character?
5. What is the speaker's attitude toward the poverty she endured as a child?
6. What elements of the story create humor?
7. What is the role of Mr. Hadly, the teacher, in the story?
8. Explain the double reference and irony of the title.

Suggestions for Exploration and Writing

1. Write a narrative essay in which you tell a tale of how a family member shamed you.

2. Discuss the emotional effects of poverty on a family you know.

3. Discuss in detail: why are people ashamed of poverty?

4. Using the clues given in the story, write a character sketch of the mother, contrasting her attitude toward life with her children's attitudes.

Alice Walker (b. 1944)

Alice Walker, writer of novels, short stories, poems, and essays, is perhaps best known for her popular novel The Color Purple *(1982), which was made into a movie. Many of her earlier works, including* The Color Purple *and the story included here, draw on her rural Southern upbringing and celebrate the complex, rich art of rural Southern African American women. However,* Possessing the Secret of Joy *(1992) is set in Africa. Her 1998 novel,* By the Light of My Father's Smile, *uses multiple narrators to examine father-daughter relationships. Her recent works frequently blend autobiography with fiction.*

EVERYDAY USE   (1973)

FOR YOUR GRANDMAMA

1   I will wait for her in the yard that Maggie and I made so clean and wavy yesterday afternoon. A yard like this is more comfortable than most people know. It is not just a yard. It is like an extended living room. When the hard clay is swept clean as a floor and the fine sand around the edges lined with tiny, irregular grooves, anyone can come and sit and look up into the elm tree and wait for the breezes that never come inside the house.

2   Maggie will be nervous until after her sister goes: she will stand hopelessly in corners, homely and ashamed of the burn scars down her arms and legs, eying her sister with a mixture of envy and awe. She thinks her sister has held life always in the palm of one hand, that "no" is a word the world never learned to say to her.

3   You've no doubt seen those TV shows where the child who has "made it" is confronted, as a surprise, by her own mother and father, tottering in weakly from backstage. (A pleasant surprise, of course: What would they do if parent and child came on the show only to curse out and insult each other?) On TV mother and child embrace and smile into each other's faces. Sometimes the mother and father weep, the child wraps them in her arms and leans across the table to tell how she would not have made it without their help. I have seen these programs.

4   Sometimes I dream a dream in which Dee and I are suddenly brought together on a TV program of this sort. Out of a dark and soft-seated limousine I am ushered into a bright room filled with many people. There I meet a smiling, gray, sporty man like Johnny Carson who shakes my hand and tells me what a fine girl I have. Then we are on the stage and Dee is embracing

me with tears in her eyes. She pins on my dress a large orchid, even though she has told me once that she thinks orchids are tacky flowers.

5   In real life I am a large, big-boned woman with rough, man-working hands. In the winter I wear flannel nightgowns to bed and overalls during the day. I can kill and clean a hog as mercilessly as a man. My fat keeps me hot in zero weather. I can work outside all day, breaking ice to get water for washing; I can eat pork liver cooked over the open fire minutes after it comes steaming from the hog. One winter I knocked a bull calf straight in the brain between the eyes with a sledge hammer and had the meat hung up to chill before nightfall. But of course all this does not show on television. I am the way my daughter would want me to be: a hundred pounds lighter, my skin like an uncooked barley pancake. My hair glistens in the hot bright lights. Johnny Carson has much to do to keep up with my quick and witty tongue.

6   But that is a mistake. I know even before I wake up. Who ever knew a Johnson with a quick tongue? Who can even imagine me looking a strange white man in the eye? It seems to me I have talked to them always with one foot raised in flight, with my head turned in whichever way is farthest from them. Dee, though. She would always look anyone in the eye. Hesitation was no part of her nature.

7   "How do I look, Mama?" Maggie says, showing just enough of her thin body enveloped in pink skirt and red blouse for me to know she's there, almost hidden by the door.

8   "Come out into the yard," I say.

9   Have you ever seen a lame animal, perhaps a dog run over by some careless person rich enough to own a car, sidle up to someone who is ignorant enough to be kind to him? That is the way my Maggie walks. She has been like this, chin on chest, eyes on ground, feet in shuffle, ever since the fire that burned the other house to the ground.

10   Dee is lighter than Maggie, with nicer hair and a fuller figure. She's a woman now, though sometimes I forget. How long ago was it that the other house burned? Ten, twelve years? Sometimes I can still hear the flame and feel Maggie's arms sticking to me, her hair smoking and her dress falling off her in little black papery flakes. Her eyes seemed stretched open, blazed open by the flames reflected in them. And Dee. I see her standing off under the sweet gum tree she used to dig gum out of; a look of concentration on her face as she watched the last dingy gray board of the house fall in toward the red-hot brick chimney. Why don't you do a dance around the ashes? I'd wanted to ask her. She had hated the house that much.

11   I used to think she hated Maggie, too. But that was before we raised the money, the church and me, to send her to Augusta to school. She used to read to us without pity; forcing words, lies, other folks' habits, whole lives upon us two, sitting trapped and ignorant underneath her voice. She washed us in a river of make-believe, burned us with a lot of knowledge we didn't necessarily need to know. Pressed us to her with the

serious way she read, to shove us away at just the moment, like dimwits, we seemed about to understand.

12   Dee wanted nice things. A yellow organdy dress to wear to her graduation from high school; black pumps to match a green suit she'd made from an old suit somebody gave me. She was determined to stare down any disaster in her efforts. Her eyelids would not flicker for minutes at a time. Often I fought off the temptation to shake her. At sixteen she had a style of her own: and knew what style was.

13   I never had an education myself. After second grade the school was closed down. Don't ask me why: in 1927 colored asked fewer questions than they do now. Sometimes Maggie reads to me. She stumbles along good-naturedly but can't see well. She knows she is not bright. Like good looks and money, quickness passed her by. She will marry John Thomas (who has mossy teeth in an earnest face) and then I'll be free to sit here and I guess just sing church songs to myself. Although I never was a good singer. Never could carry a tune. I was always better at a man's job. I used to love to milk till I was hooked in the side in '49. Cows are soothing and slow and don't bother you, unless you try to milk them the wrong way.

14   I have deliberately turned my back on the house. It is three rooms, just like the one that burned, except the roof is tin; they don't make shingle roofs any more. There are no real windows, just some holes cut in the sides, like the portholes in a ship, but not round and not square, with rawhide holding the shutters up on the outside. This house is in a pasture too, like the other one. No doubt when Dee sees it she will want to tear it down. She wrote me once that no matter where we "choose" to live, she will manage to come see us. But she will never bring her friends. Maggie and I thought about this and Maggie asked me, "Mama, when did Dee ever *have* any friends?"

15   She had a few. Furtive boys in pink shirts hanging about on washday after school. Nervous girls who never laughed. Impressed with her they worshiped the well-turned phrase, the cute shape, the scalding humor that erupted like bubbles in lye. She read to them.

16   When she was courting Jimmy T she didn't have much time to pay to us, but turned all her faultfinding power on him. He *flew* to marry a cheap city girl from a family of ignorant flashy people. She hardly had time to recompose herself.

17   When she comes I will meet—but there they are!

18   Maggie attempts to make a dash for the house, in her shuffling way, but I stay her with my hand. "Come back here," I say. And she stops and tries to dig a well in the sand with her toe.

19   It is hard to see them clearly through the strong sun. But even the first glimpse of leg out of the car tells me it is Dee. Her feet were always neat-looking, as if God himself had shaped them with a certain style. From the other side of the car comes a short, stocky man. Hair is all over his

head a foot long and hanging from his chin like a kinky mule tail. I hear Maggie suck in her breath. "Uhnnnh," is what it sounds like. Like when you see the wriggling end of a snake just in front of your foot on the road. "Uhnnnh."

20 Dee next. A dress down to the ground, in this hot weather. A dress so loud it hurts my eyes. There are yellows and oranges enough to throw back the light of the sun. I feel my whole face warming from the heat waves it throws out. Earrings gold, too, and hanging down to her shoulders. Bracelets dangling and making noises when she moves her arm up to shake the folds of the dress out of her armpits. The dress is loose and flows, and as she walks closer, I like it. I hear Maggie go "Uhnnnh" again. It is her sister's hair. It stands straight up like the wool on a sheep. It is black as night and around the edges are two long pigtails that rope about like small lizards disappearing behind her ears.

21 "Wa-su-zo-Tean-o!" she says, coming on in that gliding way the dress makes her move. The short stocky fellow with the hair to his navel is all grinning and he follows up with "Asalamalakim, my mother and sister!" He moves to hug Maggie but she falls back, right up against the back of my chair. I feel her trembling there and when I look up I see the perspiration falling off her chin.

22 "Don't get up," says Dee. Since I am stout it takes something of a push. You can see me trying to move a second or two before I make it. She turns, showing white heels through her sandals, and goes back to the car. Out she peeks next with a Polaroid. She stoops down quickly and lines up picture after picture of me sitting there in front of the house with Maggie cowering behind me. She never takes a shot without making sure the house is included. When a cow comes nibbling around the edge of the yard she snaps it and me and Maggie *and* the house. Then she puts the Polaroid in the back seat of the car, and comes up and kisses me on the forehead.

23 Meanwhile Asalamalakim is going through motions with Maggie's hand. Maggie's hand is as limp as a fish, and probably as cold, despite the sweat, and she keeps trying to pull it back. It looks like Asalamalakim wants to shake hands but wants to do it fancy. Or maybe he don't know how people shake hands. Anyhow, he soon gives up on Maggie.

24 "Well," I say. "Dee."

25 "No, Mama," she says. "Not 'Dee,' Wangero Leewanika Kemanjo!"

26 "What happened to 'Dee'?" I wanted to know.

27 "She's dead," Wangero said. "I couldn't bear it any longer, being named after the people who oppress me."

28 "You know as well as me you was named after your aunt Dicie," I said. Dicie is my sister. She named Dee. We called her "Big Dee" after Dee was born.

29 "But who was *she* named after?" asked Wangero.

30 "I guess after Grandma Dee," I said.

31 "And who was she named after?" asked Wangero.

32   "Her mother," I said, and saw Wangero was getting tired. "That's about as far back as I can trace it," I said. Though, in fact, I probably could have carried it back beyond the Civil War through the branches.

33   "Well," said Asalamalakim, "there you are."

34   "Uhnnnh," I heard Maggie say.

35   "There I was not," I said, "before 'Dicie' cropped up in our family, so why should I try to trace it that far back?"

36   He just stood there grinning, looking down on me like somebody inspecting a Model A car. Every once in a while he and Wangero sent eye signals over my head.

37   "How do you pronounce this name?" I asked.

38   "You don't have to call me by it if you don't want to," said Wangero.

39   "Why shouldn't I?" I asked. "If that's what you want us to call you, we'll call you."

40   "I know it might sound awkward at first," said Wangero.

41   "I'll get used to it," I said. "Ream it out again."

42   Well, soon we got the name out of the way. Asalamalakim had a name twice as long and three times as hard. After I tripped over it two or three times he told me to just call him Hakim-a-barber. I wanted to ask him was he a barber, but I didn't really think he was, so I didn't ask.

43   "You must belong to those beef-cattle peoples down the road," I said. They said "Asalamalakim" when they met you, too, but they didn't shake hands. Always too busy: feeding the cattle, fixing the fences, putting up salt-lick shelters, throwing down hay. When the white folks poisoned some of the herd the men stayed up all night with rifles in their hands. I walked a mile and a half just to see the sight.

44   Hakim-a-barber said, "I accept some of their doctrines, but farming and raising cattle is not my style." (They didn't tell me, and I didn't ask, whether Wangero (Dee) had really gone and married him.)

45   We sat down to eat and right away he said he didn't eat collards and pork was unclean. Wangero, though, went on through the chitlins and corn bread, the greens and everything else. She talked a blue streak over the sweet potatoes. Everything delighted her. Even the fact that we still used the benches her daddy made for the table when we couldn't afford to buy chairs.

46   "Oh, Mama!" she cried. Then turned to Hakim-a-barber. "I never knew how lovely these benches are. You can feel the rump prints," she said, running her hands underneath her and along the bench. Then she gave a sigh and her hand closed over Grandma Dee's butter dish. "That's it!" she said. "I knew there was something I wanted to ask you if I could have." She jumped up from the table and went over in the corner where the churn stood, the milk in it clabber by now. She looked at the churn and looked at it.

47   "This churn top is what I need," she said. "Didn't Uncle Buddy whittle it out of a tree you all used to have?"

48   "Yes," I said.

49   "Uh huh," she said happily. "And I want the dasher, too."

50   "Uncle Buddy whittle that, too?" asked the barber.

51   Dee (Wangero) looked up at me.

52   "Aunt Dee's first husband whittled the dash," said Maggie so low you almost couldn't hear her. "His name was Henry, but they called him Stash."

53   "Maggie's brain is like an elephant's," Wangero said, laughing. "I can use the churn top as a centerpiece for the alcove table," she said, sliding a plate over the churn, "and I'll think of something artistic to do with the dasher."

54   When she finished wrapping the dasher the handle stuck out. I took it for a moment in my hands. You didn't even have to look close to see where hands pushing the dasher up and down to make butter had left a kind of sink in the wood. In fact, there were a lot of small sinks; you could see where thumbs and fingers had sunk into the wood. It was a beautiful light yellow wood, from a tree that grew in the yard where Big Dee and Stash had lived.

55   After dinner Dee (Wangero) went to the trunk at the foot of my bed and started rifling through it. Maggie hung back in the kitchen over the dishpan. Out came Wangero with two quilts. They had been pieced by Grandma Dee and then Big Dee and me had hung them on the quilt frames on the front porch and quilted them. One was in the Lone Star pattern. The other was Walk Around the Mountain. In both of them were scraps of dresses Grandma Dee had worn fifty and more years ago. Bits and pieces of Grandpa Jarrell's Paisley shirts. And one teeny faded blue piece, about the size of a penny matchbox, that was from Great Grandpa Ezra's uniform that he wore in the Civil War.

56   "Mama," Wangero said sweet as a bird. "Can I have these old quilts?"

57   I heard something fall in the kitchen, and a minute later the kitchen door slammed.

58   "Why don't you take one or two of the others?" I asked. "These old things was just done by me and Big Dee from some tops your grandma pieced before she died."

59   "No," said Wangero. "I don't want those. They are stitched around the borders by machine."

60   "That'll make them last better," I said.

61   "That's not the point," said Wangero. "These are all pieces of dresses Grandma used to wear. She did all this stitching by hand. Imagine!" She held the quilts securely in her arms, stroking them.

62   "Some of the pieces, like those lavender ones, come from old clothes her mother handed down to her," I said, moving up to touch the quilts. Dee (Wangero) moved back just enough so that I couldn't reach the quilts. They already belonged to her.

63   "Imagine!" she breathed again, clutching them closely to her bosom.

64   "The truth is," I said, "I promised to give them quilts to Maggie, for when she marries John Thomas."

65   She gasped like a bee had stung her.

66   "Maggie can't appreciate these quilts!" she said. "She'd probably be backward enough to put them to everyday use."

67   "I reckon she would," I said. "God knows I been saving 'em for long enough with nobody using 'em. I hope she will!" I didn't want to bring up how I had offered Dee (Wangero) a quilt when she went away to college. Then she had told me they were old-fashioned, out of style.

68   "But they're *priceless!*" she was saying now, furiously; for she has a temper. "Maggie would put them on the bed and in five years they'd be in rags. Less than that!"

69   "She can always make some more," I said. "Maggie knows how to quilt."

70   Dee (Wangero) looked at me with hatred. "You just will not understand. The point is these quilts, *these* quilts!"

71   "Well," I said, stumped. "What would *you* do with them? "

72   "Hang them," she said. As if that was the only thing you *could* do with quilts.

73   Maggie by now was standing in the door. I could almost hear the sound her feet made as they scraped over each other.

74   "She can have them, Mama," she said, like somebody used to never winning anything, or having anything reserved for her. "I can 'member Grandma Dee without the quilts."

75   I looked at her hard. She had filled her bottom lip with checkerberry snuff and it gave her face a kind of dopey, hangdog look. It was Grandma Dee and Big Dee who taught her how to quilt herself. She stood there with her scarred hands hidden in the folds of her skirt. She looked at her sister with something like fear but she wasn't mad at her. This was Maggie's portion. This was the way she knew God to work.

76   When I looked at her like that something hit me in the top of my head and ran down to the soles of my feet. Just like when I'm in church and the spirit of God touches me and I get happy and shout. I did something I never had done before: hugged Maggie to me, then dragged her on into the room, snatched the quilts out of Miss Wangero's hands and dumped them into Maggie's lap. Maggie just sat there on my bed with her mouth open.

77   "Take one or two of the others," I said to Dee.

78   But she turned without a word and went out to Hakim-a-barber.

79   "You just don't understand," she said, as Maggie and I came out to the car.

80   "What don't I understand?" I wanted to know.

81   "Your heritage," she said. And then she turned to Maggie, kissed her, and said, "You ought to try to make something of yourself, too, Maggie. It's really a new day for us. But from the way you and Mama still live you'd never know it."

82   She put on some sunglasses that hid everything above the tip of her nose and her chin.

83   Maggie smiled; maybe at the sunglasses. But a real smile, not scared. After we watched the car dust settle I asked Maggie to bring me a dip of snuff. And then the two of us sat there just enjoying, until it was time to go in the house and go to bed.

Questions for Discussion

1. What does the narrating mother's opening description of the yard tell you about her and Maggie?

2. What does the mother's recurring dream and her response to it reveal about her relationship to Dee?

3. The narrator says of Dee, "She used to read to us without pity: forcing words, lies, other folks' habits, whole lives upon us two, sitting trapped and ignorant underneath her voice." Why does the narrator feel trapped by, rather than appreciative of, Dee's reading? Is the narrator merely ignorant and insensitive? Why does she regard what she hears as lies?

4. Why do Dee and her male friend use a strange language, and why has Dee changed her name?

5. Note that after the arrival of Dee, the narrator's style changes, becoming less formal and more colloquial. Why might Walker have chosen to change the style here?

6. What is the distinction between the mother's use of the churn and Dee's proposed use of it?

7. What is the significance of Maggie's saying, "'I can 'member Grandma Dee without the quilts'"?

Suggestions for Exploration and Writing

1. In a documented essay, contrast the distinctively different lifestyles of the intruders, Dee and her companion, with those of their hosts, Mama and Maggie, and explain how these lifestyles affect the intruders' attitudes toward art.

2. Walker is adept at using gestures to reveal her characters. In an essay on "Everyday Use," analyze Walker's use of such gestures to create her characters.

3. In a researched essay, contrast the conception of "heritage" exemplified by Dee with that exemplified by Maggie. Explain whether a heritage is best preserved by protecting it or by living it.

4. In an essay, show how Alice Walker's concept of art compares with that of Achebe in "Africa and Her Writers" in the Imagination and Discovery unit.

Michael Dorris (1945–1997)

Michael Dorris and his former wife, Louise Erdrich, are both noted for their works about Native Americans. In fact, Dorris founded the Native American Studies Program at Dartmouth. Dorris wrote historical novels for young readers as well as novels for adults. His nonfiction book

The Broken Cord (1989) is a tender and moving account of the life of his adopted son, who suffered from fetal alcohol symdrome. "The Benchmark," taken from the short story collection entitled Working Men *(1993), exhibits his compassionate and empathetic portrayal of complex relationships.*

THE BENCHMARK   (1993)

1   The naked eye deceives, that's the first lesson of making a pond. Sea level doesn't matter, is the second. Seek a constant or else you'll misjudge altitude.

2   To start a job, you drive a nail into a peak of ledge, pound it deep, make it your benchmark, your one-hundred scale. The transit measures from that arbitrary point as you compute all distance in links and chains. Weather patterns can alter, crops grow, houses get built and collapse, but you can return in fifty years and position a tripod, rotate the dials of the spirit until the air bubble precisely crosses the hairline, then aim an alidade at that solitary, centering nail and be in business.

3   I design a pond to order, I tell property owners as I set up, no two the same. You get more from me than a hole in the earth. There lacks a T square in nature's plan, and I don't pack one in my back pocket either.

4   If there's a boy handy, I have him hoist the end of the tape high above his head or fix him in my sight while he balances my seven-foot vernier. He stares back at me, his eyes to mine, and that stick can't help but adjust to vertical. For reward, I focus on, say, a birch protruding from a ridge of mountain miles away. Count the leaves, I dare him. He squints, peers through, glances at me, peers through again. He can't believe it, how close the branches of that white tree glisten. Sometimes a younger boy will extend his hand, nervous fingers reaching out as if to touch, but I don't laugh. I respect what he hasn't learned to hide.

5   My dad taught me the trade, and more often than not I use his words when I work because they still apply. He instructed my eye. One morning the year I became his journeyman, we were driving to a job in his Chevy. I was twenty, twenty-one at the time, still a kid, and thinking God knows what, when he called my attention to an abandoned field on the right.

6   What do you see, Frank, he asked me, and stopped the car.

7   There was nothing special. A pasture left fallow more than a few years—you could tell from the alder and maple saplings that had come back here and there—a loom of exposed ledge off to one side, a muddy rut where a culvert used to cut under the road.

8   Dad idled the truck to give me time. There was a depression in the weeds where once there had been a barnyard or a structure of some type. The grass all around had that yellow, wild color that appears when it hasn't been sowed fresh for too many seasons. Unbroken, the ground had turned tough, dense enough to seal a levee.

9   I'd sink a test at about thirty feet, I told Dad. Another halfway to the bank. We could conduct the overflow through a four-inch, and gravity would power it. With any luck we could go down six feet.

10   Five, he corrected, but he stepped on the gas, satisfied that my imagination would now fill any empty space with water.

11   He worked up to the week before he died, then left me his name and his equipment: A solid mahogany clipboard. A plane table. The glass with Swiss-ground lenses. It rests each night cushioned in its original case, in carved pockets lined with red velvet. The forged iron hammer. I've replaced the wooden handle, shattered once when anger got the better of me, but the head is as black and unmarred as if it never met a stake, never knew the flat of a nail.

12   I have his tape as well, that century-foot line of oiled cloth, mended with thread wherever ripped by sharp stones or roots. There've been some inches lost in the process, but it's still accurate enough. I used it until the printed numbers faded beyond recognition, then I wrapped it like a cast around my hand for the last time and stored it in the bottom drawer of my chest.

13   It bothers me, when I let it, that I've apprenticed no successor. My surviving children, Sam and Gloria, have moved with their families to other states. They work indoors, as was their ambition all along—he manages for Sears and she teaches school. They sleep in stone buildings with "interior windows" and "eternal fountains" in the lobbies. The seasons pass them by, blurred at the edges, of notice only on weekends. They never get so cold that they have to rub their toes, one at a time, or so warm that they fan the air with their hands. They never rise in the dark of the morning, never go to bed when it's still light. They heed clocks, my grown children, leave the world as they find it. They're content, but for their guilt over me since their mother passed away. I'm the loose board in their floor.

14   There's no right or wrong season for digging. You go in whenever the backhoe's free, and you're sure to fight something—hard crust in winter, swamp in spring, drought like as not the rest of the year. When I dam a pond site in late summer I forecast that the worst flood in a decade will sweep over the dusty rim. The runoff must have an escape, a waterfall if the contour of the bank will accommodate it. I sand the bottom, install a hydrant for fire protection. I insist on a minimum depth of eight feet. That way you can give up two for ice, allow another three for snow, and yet there'll remain sufficient oxygen in the water to keep trout alive.

15   Trout are the treasure of a healthy pond. They eat algae, you eat them. In summer, they can be lured to the surface to take food, and there's something fine about the way the light plays on those silver scales, crossing and reflecting like a handful of coins tossed in the air.

16   Sometimes, when we were courting and after we were new married, Martha would accompany me on an inspection. I bought her good boots, wool socks. Can't beat them. I explained each step of procedure and she nodded her head, interested, a quick study. She got so she could spot a bowl as well as I, foresaw the incline of slope, knew where to clear brush to make a view. It does her memory no disrespect to recall the use we put to certain warm afternoons, alone on what would become the bed of the pond, the deepest pitch.

17   That first time, Martha surprised me. She blushed when I realized why she had brought the blanket from the foot of her bed, then she laughed at the look on my face. If you could see yourself, Frank, she said.

18   She was strong, tall as me, a year older. Her hair was straight and brown, the shade of river clay, and afterwards I would comb the straw from its tangle while she lay watching clouds, identifying their silhouettes. Sam was an April baby, full-size though two months premature as everyone consented to agree, but Martha and I knew for a fact he came from one of those excursions. Ben was two years later, a June after a late fall, so we suspected that origin of him as well.

19   We had thirty-eight years, Martha and I, and I was never with another woman, she was never with another man. That's the way it should be, I admonished Sam when he divorced Suzanne and married a second time. Not anymore, Dad, he answered me. You and Mom had no options. You played by the book and didn't question the rules.

20   Read your birth certificate and learn to count, I was tempted to say, but I held my tongue. The truth would sound like bragging. I let him believe what he needed, but his accusation brought Ben to my mind.

21   They say the second born gets lost by his parents, that the middle child, being neither first nor last, becomes the independent one. Yet Ben was equal parts Martha and me, in spirit as well as in form, as different from Sam as fire from wood. He always had a question, awoke with one in his mind, the leftover from his dream, and he listened when you answered, he remembered what you said. He was good with his hands, fixed things that were broken, located what was invisible to everyone else. By the time he was seven he was my number one. He had the eye, no question. He could sense the vibration of water where it moved under layers of dry ground, could calculate on a sunny day the route a rain spill might follow.

22   When my business settled into the black, I saved enough to downpay twelve acres, then traded ponds for the labor and materials it took to construct a house. Our land had a southern exposure, a wooded knoll, but not the trickle of a stream.

23   Where on the property do you want it situated? I asked Martha before the frame was fully sided. There's two choices, behind the house or beyond the hill for privacy.

24   She stood in what would be her kitchen and faced the space at hand through the bars of pine.

25   I don't see water in so close, she said. Too cramped a pocket for my taste. Martha paused, caught my eye. And I always valued privacy in a pond.

26   I smiled, recalled, approved her choice. The next day I burned two meadow acres and used the far side of our hill as the near embankment. When the depression filled, we could smell the water, hear it lap, only not behold it from our door.

27   The first summer was paradise. Gloria was two then, unsteady on her feet. She waded to her ankles and dropped pebbles to see the bubbles swell, while Martha and I watched the boys cannonball off a weighted

plank. Some muggy nights, whispering on the stairs, Sam and Ben shut the door just so to keep from waking us, and stole outdoors to skinny-dip in the moonlight. Once I felt Martha's body stiffen as she prepared to call them back. They're good boys, I whispered, and stroked her arm the way she liked until instead she turned to me.

28   Ben, though younger, was the leader, and he was impatient with time. Clocks and calendars moved too slow for his ambition. Every day he was gone before breakfast, out of breath and home from school ten minutes when Sam walked through the front door. When the winter came, he couldn't wait for center ice to thicken to try his skates.

29   We shook our heads. He was late to dinner, the third time that week. We called the neighbor boy, his schoolmate, at seven, and he was missing also. By the time we thought where to search, the temperature had dropped, mending the hole, leaving as evidence only a glare in the shape of an explosion. I grabbed a pick, slammed it down and a pool broke through, then I dove into the darkness, calling his name until my mouth was filled. I touched the bottom with my palms—it was but ten feet—and encountered only silt, grainy as powder. But when I ascended, Ben blocked my entrance. Obedient and sorry, he had floated to the sound of our voices. Martha had already dragged his head and shoulders onto the cradle of her lap. His legs moved in the gentle waves, the steel of his skates clicking together in an undecipherable code.

30   I ran with him in my arms. Martha shouted a story of a boy who lived underwater in a frozen lake for close to an hour and was revived by immersion in a warm tub. She opened the tap while I lay Ben on the floor and pumped his lungs, pushing his back and raising his arms, bent like chicken wings. His body was cold to the touch, so logged it chafed as our skin rubbed together. The water overflowed and splashed the floor when Ben displaced it.

31   Later, men came, dragged the pond, and found the neighbor boy. The two were buried side by side. No word of blame was hurled. None was needed. Everyone knew which man had dug the hole. Martha and I did the bare minimum for Sam and Gloria, and had nothing left. For weeks after the service, we hardly saw each other. I for one was fearful of what might erupt if we spoke.

32   *You* had to have the pond so far away, I might easily have unleashed, and then that accusation could never again be caged. *Privacy* was a word we struck from our vocabularies, and thereafter, when it was uttered by another, we averted our eyes from any connection.

33   I sat by the parlor stove, kept the coals red, the drapes drawn, and did not answer the knocks of those who came when I failed to walk their land. Martha spent her hours elsewhere. I was not curious, but at meals I saw she wore the same dress as on that night, its torn hem still unrepaired. One morning, I brought out my father's level, set the case before me on the table. I lifted the hammer, brought it down with such force that the

handle split, but the metal box was made to last, and the Swiss glass did not shatter.

34   Ben was taken November twelfth. On December twelfth Martha opened the door, parted the curtains. She had changed her clothes and mashed her hair into a tight bun.

35   A month is all the mourning we shall indulge, she said. We have two remaining to us who will want their Christmas, and we're out of money. She grasped my hands, hauled me to my feet, and kept her hold as we faced each other, her breath beating on my cheek. She felt the tremble that started in my legs and worked its way up my body, but with a hard squeeze of her fingers, she dammed it, cinching it off the way you save a well by crimping a severed feeder pipe uncovered by a careless hoe.

36   We lived an ordinary life thereafter. Martha joined clubs of women and I worked steady. Even in hard times, and the county went through many, there were no lack of orders, no slack as people moved from cities and were willing to go into debt for their ideal. Those locals who knew my story never aired it, and if the new ones heard, they couldn't risk a question that might lose me. There was none other for a hundred miles trained to do my job, no other job I was trained to do. Necessity dictated amnesia and I stayed busy twenty years, every hour occupied, and I did quality work. First Sam and later Gloria showed no aptitude to follow me, the slant of their minds unpredictable and remote from my own. So I hired temporary assistants. I became less my father's son and more a man known for himself, in my own eyes as well as in the estimate of others.

37   I took for granted the patterns, the pathways worn by repetition. Divert a stream and eventually the shape of rocks will alter. Veins appear, then channels carved so deep they seem the natural order. I trusted in the warm wall of my wife beside me in sleep, in the last cup of evening coffee saved for breakfast and in the appearance of supper at five-thirty each night. My half of labor met and fit with Martha's. I depended on her sensible gifts—long johns and caps and heavy gloves—and gave her the same. We maintained our truce without ever declaring the war. And if something was missing, it was replaced by this reliability. We spared each other surprise, and each was grateful.

38   I expected I would go first. Men at sixty dropped all the time, survived by robust widows who improved their card playing, who became the backbone of the church. I had no fear. Death was not a polite topic. So when we went to the clinic for Martha's appointment I lacked premonition, was unprepared for the doctor's verdict. He had discovered a weakness in her circulation, an artery so tried that it might not long endure the pump of her heart. The condition was inoperable, he said. The weakness threaded into her brain beyond reach of the knife. The prognosis was unclear. It could burst at any time or last forever. She should avoid stress, take the pills he would prescribe, forget all worry if she could. She must not drive a car.

39   We walked to the parking lot in silence, embarrassed at this news. It was beyond our bounds. I turned the key, gripped the wheel.

40   Martha rested her hand on one of mine. Stop by the store on the way, she said. I have a list in my purse.

41   We didn't alert the children, adopted few changes in our routine. Any acknowledgment or compromise would make it real. We sold my Ford, because mine was older than hers. I tramped the ground each day, drew my geometric diagrams, satisfied my customers. On the surface, the nights with Martha were the same. We reported the news we had heard, we watched television after supper. We were careful of each other, but not so much we had to notice it.

42   We made a weir of habit that lasted almost a year, and gave the idea of death the time to settle, buried it from conscious thought the same as we had with Ben, or so I presumed. Martha saved her complaints for swollen ankles, for fingers that ached at the approach of rain. I lost my temper at chores. Railed when the sink was piled night after night with the caked pots Martha used for cooking, then left for me to scrub.

43   One evening, while she slept covered with an afghan on the couch, I had a craving and went to the freezer-box in the cellar for ice cream. I lifted the lid, propped it against the wall, and there before me were a month of meals, each neatly wrapped in dull foil and labeled with masking tape—stews, casseroles, succotash—and I understood the pots. I stared into that lighted chest, let the cold wash my face, until above me I heard the tread of Martha's steps.

44   The lights flickered, I called. I'm down here to check the fuse. I never mentioned what I'd seen, but after that it got so we could talk in cautious ways, discuss arrangements, agree on plans. Martha took the lead and I listened, became the sounding board for her memory as she compiled albums of photographs for Sam and Gloria. She'd pass the snapshots to me, and I held them the length of my arm for sharper focus.

45   The message from the hospital found me in a fenced quadrant, looking east through my sight. The day was overcast, warm. The soil was cracked and tan below the brown grass. It was a challenge, this property, for there were no natural outcrops in any direction. Either this pond would have to be much longer than was requested, or I'd have to force an artificial hollow into the land. I had paced for half an hour seeking some slight incline, some fixed basset where I could anchor a nail, but in the end I had no choice but to employ the door of Martha's car.

46   I parked at the terminus where the access road stopped, then measured eighty feet and set up my plane table. I sighted on the chrome knob of the handle, made it my hundred, stretched my chains. The perspective worked. I could see the completed pond in my mind, smaller than I had guessed, the water running before the breeze. Now the trick would be to locate again the exact same benchmark, to distinguish that precise point of origin from all the other impossible places, when I came back to dig.

Questions for Discussion

1. In your own words, explain what a benchmark is. Explain why the story starts and ends with a benchmark.

2. Define the words the narrator uses to describe the tools and techniques of his profession. He chooses not to use a T-square. Why?

3. Why, if the story is about the deaths of his wife and son, does the narrator give so much detail about his work?

4. Explain the narrator's statements that after his son's death, "I took for granted the patterns, the pathways worn by repetition" and that he and Martha "maintained our truce without ever declaring war." What war is he referring to? Would it have been healthier for them to talk? Why or why not?

5. What does the narrator realize when he sees that Martha has frozen "a month of meals"? What does he now understand about the dirty pots? Why, after that sight, can they "talk in cautious ways, discuss arrangements, agree on plans"?

6. After the death of the son, Ben, what are the implications of the narrator's statement that "we lived an ordinary life thereafter"?

7. The narrator never mentions his own grief or sadness at either death. Why? Does his reticence indicate lack of feeling? What does it reveal about him?

Suggestions for Exploration and Writing

1. Write about the effects of death on a family, or analyze the various ways people cope with grief.

2. Discuss the father-son relationships between Frank and his father and Frank and his son.

3. Analyze in detail the marriage described in this story. What does the narrator's way of describing his job reveal about his marriage? Explain.

4. Read Robert Frost's "Home Burial" in the next unit. Then write an essay explaining why the two couples' behavior after the death of a son differs so radically.

Svava Jakobsdóttir (b. 1930)

Although a native of Iceland, Jakobsdóttir lived as a child in Canada and studied at Smith College, Oxford University, and Uppsala University in Sweden. She also served in the Icelandic Parliament and was a delegate to the United Nations. She abandoned these careers to become a full-time writer. Jakobsdóttir's writing career includes radio scripts, plays, and collections of short stories, including her first,

Twelve Women (1965). Most of her writing focuses on equality for women, gender roles, and relationships of mothers to their children. The Saga of Gunnlod (1987), nominated for the Nordic Council Literary Prize, blends harsh realism with poetic mythology.

A Story for Children   <small>(1975)</small>

Translated by Dennis Auburn Hill

1   For as long as she could remember she had resolved to be true to her nature and devote all her energies to her home and her children. There were several children now and from morning till night she was swamped with work, doing the household chores and caring for the children. She was now preparing supper and waiting for the potatoes to boil. A Danish women's magazine lay on the kitchen bench as if it had been tossed there accidentally; in fact, she kept it there on purpose and sneaked a look at it whenever she got a chance. Without letting the pot of potatoes out of her mind she picked up the magazine and skimmed over Fru Ensom's advice column. This was by no means the column that seemed most interesting to her, but it was usually short. It was possible that it would last just long enough so that the potatoes would be boiling when she finished reading it. The first letter in the column was short: Dear Fru Ensom, I have never lived for anything other than my children and have done everything for them. Now I am left alone and they never visit me. What should I do? Fru Ensom answered: Do more for them.

2   This was the logical answer, of course. It was perfectly clear that nothing else was possible. She hoped that she wouldn't start writing to the magazines about such obvious things when the time came. No, these columns where people moaned and groaned were not to her liking. The columns which discussed child-rearing and the role of the mother—or rather, *the* column, since both subjects were discussed in one and the same column—were much more positive. The fundamental aspects of child-rearing had of course been familiar to her for quite some time now, but it did happen that she felt weak and fatigued at times. At that point she would leaf through the columns on child-rearing seeking courage and confirmation that she was on the right track in life. She only regretted having less and less time to read.

3   The uncleaned fish awaited her in the sink and she withstood the temptation to read the child-rearing column this time. She closed the magazine and stood up. She limped a little bit ever since the children had cut off the big toe on her right foot. They had wanted to find out what happened if someone had only nine toes. Within herself she was proud of her limp and of her children's eagerness to learn, and sometimes she limped even more than was necessary. She now turned the heat down under the potatoes and began cleaning the fish. The kitchen door opened and her little son, who was six years old and had blue eyes and light curly hair, came up to her.

4   "Mama," he said, and stuck a pin in her arm. She started and almost cut herself with the knife.

5   "Yes, dear," she said, and reached out her other arm so the child could stick it, too.

6   "Mama, tell me a story."

7   She put the knife down, dried her hands and sat down with the child in her lap to tell him a story. She was just about halfway through the story when it occurred to her that one of the other children might suffer psychological harm from not getting supper on time. In the boy's face she tried to see how he would take it if she stopped telling the story. She felt the old indecisiveness taking hold of her and she became distracted from the story. This inability of hers to make decisions had increased with the number of children and the ever-increasing chores. She had begun to fear those moments which interrupted her usual rush from morning to night. More and more often she lost her poise if she stopped to make a decision. The child-rearing columns gave little or no help at such moments, though she tried to call them to mind. They only discussed one problem and one child at a time. Other problems always had to wait until next week.

8   This time she was spared making a decision. The door opened and all the children crowded into the kitchen. Stjáni, the oldest, was in the lead. At an early age he had shown an admirable interest in both human and animal biology. The boy who had been listening to the story now slid out of her lap and took up a position among his brothers and sisters. They formed a semicircle around her and she looked over each of them one after the other.

9   "Mama, we want to see what a person's brain looks like."

10   She looked at the clock.

11   "Right now?" she asked.

12   Stjáni didn't answer his mother's question. With a nod of his head and a sharp glance he gave his younger brother a sign, and the younger brother went and got a rope, while Stjáni fastened the saw blade to the handle. The rope was then wrapped around the mother. She felt how the little hands fumbled at her back while the knot was tied. The rope was loose and it wouldn't take much effort to get free. But she was careful not to let it be noticed. He had always been sensitive about how clumsy he was with his hands. Just as Stjáni raised the saw up to her head the image of the children's father came into her mind. She saw him in front of her just as he would appear in a little while: on the threshold of the front door with his briefcase in one hand and his hat in the other. She never saw him except in the front doorway, either on his way out or on his way in. She had once been able to imagine him outside the house among other people or at the office, but now, after the children had been born, they had moved into a new house and he into a new office, and she had lost her bearings. He would come home soon and she still hadn't started frying the fish. The blood had now begun to flow down her head. Stjáni had gotten through with the saw. It seemed to be going well, and fairly quickly.

Now and then he stopped as if he were measuring with his eyes just how big the hole had to be. Blood spurted into his face and a curse crossed his lips. He nodded his head and the young brother went immediately and got the mop bucket. They placed it under the hole and soon it was half full. The procedure was over at the exact moment the father appeared in the doorway. He stood motionless for a while and pondered the sight which presented itself to him: his wife tied up, with a hole in her head, the eldest son holding a gray brain in his hand, the curious group of children huddled together, and only one pot on the stove.

13   "Kids! How can you think of doing this when it's already suppertime?"

14   He picked up the piece of his wife's skull and snapped it back in just as she was about to bleed to death. Then he took over and soon the children were busy tidying up after themselves. He wiped most of the blood stains off the walls himself before he checked on the pot on the stove. There was a suspicious sound coming from it. The water had boiled away and he took the pot off the stove and set it on the metal counter next to the sink. When he saw the half-cleaned fish in the sink he realized that his wife had still not gotten up from the chair. Puzzled, he knit his brow. It wasn't usual for her to be sitting down when there was so much to do. He went over to her and looked at her attentively. He noticed then that they had forgotten to untie her.

15   When he had freed her they looked into each other's eyes and smiled. Never was their harmony more deeply felt than when their eyes met in mutual pride over the children.

16   "Silly urchins," he said, and his voice was filled with the concern and affection that he felt for his family.

17   Soon afterward they sat down at the table. Everyone except Stjáni. He was in his room studying the brain under a microscope. Meanwhile, his mother kept his supper warm for him in the kitchen. They were all hungry and took to their food briskly; this was an unusually late supper. There was no change to be seen in the mother. She had washed her hair and combed it over the cut before she sat down. Her mild expression displayed the patience and self-denial usual at mealtimes. This expression had first appeared during those years when she served her children first and kept only the smallest and most meager piece for herself. Now the children were big enough so that they could take the best pieces themselves and the expression was actually unnecessary, but it had become an inseparable part of the meal. Before the meal was over Stjáni came in and sat down. The mother went to get his supper. In the kitchen she boned the fish thoroughly before putting it on the plate. When she picked up the garbage pail to throw the bones away she let out a scream. The brain was right on top of the pail.

18   The rest of the family rushed out as soon as her scream reached the dining room. The father was in the lead and was quick to discover what was wrong when he saw his wife staring down into the garbage pail. Her scream had died out, but it could still be seen in the contours of her face.

19   "You think it's a shame to throw it out, don't you, dear?" he asked.

20   "I don't know," she said and looked at him apologetically. "I didn't think."

21   "Mama didn't think, mama didn't think, mama didn't think," chanted one of the children who had an especially keen sense of humor.

22   They all burst out laughing and the laughter seemed to solve the problem. The father said he had an idea; they didn't have to throw the brain out, they could keep it in alcohol.

23   With that, he put the brain into a clear jar and poured alcohol over it. They brought the jar into the living room and found a place for it on a shelf of knick-knacks. They all agreed it fit well there. Then they finished eating.

24   There were no noticeable changes in the household routine due to the brain loss. At first a lot of people came to visit. They came to see the brain, and those who had prided themselves on their grandmother's old spinning wheel in the corner of their living room now looked with envy upon the brain upon the shelf. She felt no changes in herself either at first. It hadn't become a bit more difficult for her to do housework or to understand the Danish magazines. Many things even turned out to be easier than before, and situations that earlier had caused her to rack her brain no longer did so. But gradually she began to feel a heaviness in her chest. It seemed as if her lungs no longer had room enough to function and after a year had passed she went to the doctor. A thorough examination revealed that her heart had grown larger *usus innaturalis et adsidui causa*. She asked the doctor to excuse her for having forgotten all the Latin she had learned in school, and patiently he explained to her how the loss of one organ could result in changes in another. Just as a man who loses his sight will acquire a more acute sense of hearing, her heart had increased its activity a good deal when her brain was no longer available. This was a natural development, *lex vitae*, if one may say so—and at that, the doctor laughed—there was no need to fear that such a law could be anything but just. Therefore she didn't have to be afraid. She was in the best of health.

25   She felt relieved at these words. Lately she had even been afraid that she had only a short time to live, and this fear had become an increasingly loud voice within her breast which said: What will become of them if I die? But now she realized that this voice, whose strength and clarity grew steadily, was no prophecy, but rather the voice of her heart. This knowledge made her happy because the voice of one's heart could be trusted.

26   The years passed and her heart's voice showed her the way: from the children's rooms and her husband's study to the kitchen and the bedroom. This route was dear to her, and no gust of wind that blew through the front door was ever strong enough to sweep away her tracks. Only one thing aroused fear in her: unexpected changes in the world. The year they changed counter girls at the milk store five times she was never quite all right. But the children grew up. She awoke with a bad dream when her oldest child, Stjáni, began to pack his suitcase to go out into the world. With uncontrollable vehemence she threw herself over the threshold to block his exit. A sucking sound could be heard as the boy stepped on her on

his way out. He thought she was moaning and paused a moment and said that she herself was to blame. No one had asked her to lie down there. She smiled as she got up because what he had said wasn't quite right. Her heart had told her to lie there. She had heard the voice clearly and now, as she watched him walk down the street, the voice spoke to her again and said that she could still be glad that she had softened his first steps out into the world. Later on they all left one after the other and she was left alone. She no longer had anything to do in the children's rooms and she would often sit in the easy chair in the living room now. If she looked up, the jar on the shelf came into view, where the brain had stood all these years and, in fact, was almost completely forgotten. Custom had made it commonplace. Sometimes she pondered over it. As far as she could see, it had kept well. But she got less and less pleasure out of looking at it. It reminded her of her children. And gradually she felt that a change was again taking place within herself, but she couldn't bring herself to mention it to her husband. She saw him so seldom lately, and whenever he appeared at home she got up from the chair in a hurry, as if a guest had arrived. One day he brought up the question himself of whether she wasn't feeling well. Pleased, she looked up, but when she saw that he was figuring the accounts at the same time, she became confused in answering (she had never been particularly good in figuring). In her confusion she said she didn't have enough to do. He looked at her amazed and said there were enough things to be done if people only used their brain. Of course he said this without thinking. He knew very well that she didn't have a brain, but she nevertheless took him literally. She took the jar down from the shelf, brought it to the doctor and asked if he thought the brain was still useable. The doctor didn't exclude the possibility of its being of some use, but on the other hand, all organs atrophied after being preserved in alcohol for a long time. Therefore it would be debatable whether it would pay to move it at all; in addition, the *nervi cerebrales* had been left in rather poor shape, and the doctor asked whether some clumsy dolt had actually done the surgery.

27   "He was so little then, the poor thing," the woman said.

28   "By the way," said the doctor, "I recall that you had a highly developed heart."

29   The woman avoided the doctor's inquiring look and a faint pang of conscience gripped her. And she whispered to the doctor what she hadn't dared hint of to her husband:

30   "My heart's voice has fallen silent."

31   As she said this she realized why she had come. She unbuttoned her blouse, took it off and laid it neatly on the back of the chair. Her bra went the same way. Then she stood ready in front of the doctor, naked from the waist up. He picked up a scalpel and cut, and a moment later he handed her the gleaming, red heart. Carefully he placed it in her palm and her hands closed around it. Its hesitant beat resembled the fluttering of a bird in a cage. She offered to pay the doctor, but he shook his head and, seeing that she was having difficulty, helped her get dressed. He then offered

to call her a taxi since she had so much to carry. She refused, stuffed the brain jar into her shopping bag and slipped the bag over her arm. Then she left with the heart in her hands.

32   Now began the long march from one child to the next. She first went to see her sons, but found none of them at home. They had all gotten a berth on the ship of state and it was impossible to tell when they would return. Furthermore, they never stayed in home port long enough for there to be time for anything other than begetting children. She withdrew from the bitterness of her daughters-in-law and went to see her oldest daughter, who opened the door herself. A look of astonishment and revulsion came over her face when she saw the slimy, red heart pulsating in her mother's palm, and in her consternation, she slammed the door. This was of course an involuntary reaction and she quickly opened the door again, but she made it clear to her mother that she didn't care at all about her heart; and she wasn't sure it would go with the new furniture in the living room. The mother then realized that it was pointless to continue the march, because her younger daughters had even newer furniture. So she went home. There she filled a jar with alcohol and dropped the heart into it. A deep sucking sound, like a gasp within a human breast, could be heard as the heart sank to the bottom. And now they each stood on the shelf in their own jars, her brain and her heart. But no one came to view them. And the children never came to visit. Their excuse always was that they were too busy. But the truth was that they didn't like the sterile smell that clung to everything in the house.

Questions for Discussion

1. The story begins "she had resolved to be true to her nature and devote all of her energies to her home and her children." In this case, what does "true to her nature" appear to mean?

2. Why and how is this "a story for children"?

3. What role do the women's magazines and Fru Ensom's advice column play in the story?

4. Why were decisions difficult for her? What is the significance of not knowing her husband in any other situation other than leaving home or returning home? Why do they have such pride in their children?

5. What is symbolically represented by the various mutilations of the mother—first the big toe, then the brain, then the heart?

6. List the metaphorical references to the role of mother and wife, and beside each one explain the meaning of the metaphor.

7. What is the effect of the father's reaction to Stjáni's surgery to remove the mother's brain: "'Kids! How can you think of doing this when it's almost supper time'"?

8. What is suggested by Stjáni's stepping on his mother as he goes into the real world and his comment that "she herself was to blame"?

9. What does the ending suggest about the way children treat their parents?

Suggestions for Exploration and Writing

1. Discuss in detail a family you know in which one member has sacrificed for others.

2. Write a persuasive essay in which you argue the degree to which Jakobsdóttir's portrayal of women in the home is accurate.

3. In an essay, discuss how 'patience and self-denial' can lead to symbolic self-mutilation.

4. Write a detailed analysis of the various mutilations inflicted on the mother in this story.

5. Using the list from question 6 above, write an essay exploring the meaning of the metaphors and giving your interpretation of why Jakobsdóttir tells the story in allegorical form rather than realistically.

POETRY

William Butler Yeats (1865–1939)

An Irish poet and playwright, William Butler Yeats is regarded by many as one of the greatest twentieth-century poets. Yeats's first poems were published in 1885. Active in the Irish National Theatre, he became a leader in the Irish literary revival. His Collected Poems *(1933), spanning fifty years, shows his extraordinary range and his growth as a poet. Much of Yeats's poetry is powerfully and elaborately symbolic, referring to his vision of a spiritual world and his cyclical theory of history.*

A PRAYER FOR MY DAUGHTER (1924)

Once more the storm is howling, and half hid
Under this cradle-hood and coverlid
My child sleeps on. There is no obstacle
But Gregory's wood and one bare hill
5 Whereby the haystack- and roof-levelling wind,
Bred on the Atlantic, can be stayed;
And for an hour I have walked and prayed
Because of the great gloom that is in my mind.

I have walked and prayed for this young child an hour
10   And heard the sea-wind scream upon the tower,
And under the arches of the bridge, and scream
In the elms above the flooded stream;
Imagining in excited reverie
That the future years had come,
15   Dancing to a frenzied drum,
Out of the murderous innocence of the sea.

May she be granted beauty and yet not
Beauty to make a stranger's eye distraught,
Or hers before a looking-glass, for such,
20   Being made beautiful overmuch,
Consider beauty a sufficient end,
Lose natural kindness and maybe
The heart-revealing intimacy
That chooses right, and never find a friend.

25   Helen being chosen found life flat and dull
And later had much trouble from a fool,
While that great Queen, that rose out of the spray,
Being fatherless could have her way
Yet chose a bandy-leggèd smith for man.
30   It's certain that fine women eat
A crazy salad with their meat
Whereby the Horn of Plenty is undone.

In courtesy I'd have her chiefly learned;
Hearts are not had as a gift but hearts are earned
35   By those that are not entirely beautiful;
Yet many, that have played the fool
For beauty's very self, has charm made wise,
And many a poor man that has roved,
Loved and thought himself beloved,
40   From a glad kindness cannot take his eyes.

May she become a flourishing hidden tree
That all her thoughts may like the linnet be,
And have no business but dispensing round
Their magnanimities of sound,
45   Nor but in merriment begin a chase,
Nor but in merriment a quarrel.
O may she live like some green laurel
Rooted in one dear perpetual place.

My mind, because the minds that I have loved,
50   The sort of beauty that I have approved,
Prosper but little, has dried up of late,

Yet knows that to be choked with hate
May well be of all evil chances chief.
If there's no hatred in a mind
55 Assault and battery of the wind
Can never tear the linnet from the leaf.

An intellectual hatred is the worst,
So let her think opinions are accursed.
Have I not seen the loveliest woman born
60 Out of the mouth of Plenty's horn,
Because of her opinionated mind
Barter that horn and every good
By quiet natures understood
For an old bellows full of angry wind?

65 Considering that, all hatred driven hence,
The soul recovers radical innocence
And learns at last that it is self-delighting,
Self-appeasing, self-affrighting,
And that its own sweet will is Heaven's will;
70 She can, though every face should scowl
And every windy quarter howl
Or every bellows burst, be happy still.

And may her bridegroom bring her to a house
Where all's accustomed, ceremonious;
75 For arrogance and hatred are the wares
Peddled in the thoroughfares.
How but in custom and in ceremony
Are innocence and beauty born?
Ceremony's a name for the rich horn,
80 And custom for the spreading laurel tree.

Questions for Discussion

1. The speaker of the poem has been praying silently for an entire hour. What is he so concerned about that he prays at such length? Why does he pray that his daughter not be "beautiful overmuch"?

2. Why does Yeats declare "opinions accursed"?

3. Throughout the poem Yeats uses the **images** of the Horn of Plenty and "a flourishing hidden" laurel tree, and he returns to these in the last two lines of the poem. What do these images suggest that the narrator wants for his daughter as a result of his own experiences?

4. In light of the women's movement, do you think any of Yeats's comments are sexist? If so, which ones and why?

Suggestions for Exploration and Writing

1. If you have children, explain how you combine control with loving encouragement in raising them.

2. Yeats does not pray for control of his daughter; rather he prays that she may grow into a resilient, joyous woman who can protect herself psychologically from the perils of a hostile world. To what degree have your parents tried to control you and to what degree have they encouraged you to grow?

3. Yeats clearly regards custom and ceremony as important elements in a family's life. Discuss the importance of custom and ceremony in your own family or in two or more works in this section.

4. Choosing one of Yeats's abstract words such as *innocence, kindness,* or *beauty,* write an essay explaining why you think this quality is or is not important.

Theodore Roethke (1908–1963)

Theodore Roethke was both an acclaimed poet and an exuberant and popular professor of poetry. Partly because he threw himself wholeheartedly into both professions, he often suffered from exhaustion and mental breakdowns. Roethke's relationship with his own father, a German-American who combined authoritarianism with sensitivity, seems to have been ambivalent. His father died when Roethke was fourteen. Roethke received many awards during his long literary career, including two Guggenheim Fellowships, two Ford Foundation Grants, and a Pulitzer Prize in poetry in 1954 for The Waking: Poems *1933–53.*

My Papa's Waltz   (1942)

The whiskey on your breath
Could make a small boy dizzy;
But I hung on like death:
Such waltzing was not easy.

5   We romped until the pans
Slid from the kitchen shelf;
My mother's countenance
Could not unfrown itself.

The hand that held my wrist
10   Was battered on one knuckle;
At every step you missed
My right ear scraped a buckle.

You beat time on my head
With a palm caked hard by dirt,

15 Then waltzed me off to bed
    Still clinging to your shirt.

Questions for Discussion

1. What evidence in the poem indicates that there is a deep love within the family?
2. To what does the word *waltz* in the title refer? As he is "waltzed" to bed, the boy is "still clinging" to his father. What does this reaction indicate about the boy's feelings for his father?
3. What details does Roethke use to describe the father? What do these details indicate?
4. Roethke uses the three-beat line, which reflects the three beats of the waltz. Does the total effect of the poem reflect the smooth gliding motion of the dance? Why or why not?
5. What does the mother's behavior reveal about her?

Suggestions for Exploration or Writing

1. Using your imagination and the details given in the poem, describe this family.
2. Write an essay analyzing why memories that may be negative to some adults are not so to children. Also see Nikki Giovanni's "Nikki-Rosa."

Mary TallMountain (1918–1994)

Mary TallMountain, a native Alaskan, was born along the Yukon River to a Koyukon/Athabaskan mother, but after her mother's death, she was adopted by a non-native couple and moved to California. During most of her adult life, she lived in the Tenderloin district of San Francisco, where she was poet-in-residence at the Tenderloin Reflection and Education Center (TREC), a community-based program for writers and artists. TREC established the TallMountain Circle, which distributes and promotes the works of Mary TallMountain and selects the recipients of the TallMountain Award to be given to Tenderloin district or Native American writers. TallMountain reclaims her ancestry and homeland in her stories and poems. Among her books of poems are Nine Poems *(1979) and* There Is No Word for Goodbye *(1981). She celebrates in this poem a unique feature of her Native American language and culture.*

THERE IS NO WORD FOR GOODBYE (1981)

Sokoya, I said, looking through
  the net of wrinkles into

wise black pools
of her eyes.

5   What do you say in Athabaskan
when you leave each other?
What is the word
for goodbye?

A shade of feeling rippled
10   the wind-tanned skin.
Ah, nothing, she said,
watching the river flash.

She looked at me close.
We just say, Tlaa. That means,
15   See you.
We never leave each other.
When does your mouth
say goodbye to your heart?

She touched me light
20   as a bluebell.
You forget when you leave us;
you're so small then.
We don't use that word.

We always think you're coming back,
25   but if you don't,
we'll see you someplace else.
You understand.
There is no word for goodbye.

Questions for Discussion

1. The speaker's *sokoya,* or aunt, is described with natural **images,** particularly water. What do these images suggest about her character? What do they say about the sources of her wisdom?

2. Why is there no Athabaskan word for goodbye? What does the absence of such a word suggest about Athabaskans?

3. Explain the meaning of the question "When does your mouth say goodbye to your heart?" What does this question reveal about the relationship between the speaker and her aunt?

4. The speaker says, "we'll see you someplace else." Where might they see each other? Does the poem's imagery give any clue?

Suggestion for Exploration and Writing

1. Write an essay about a word you think should not exist in your native language.

Maxine Kumin (b. 1925)

*Pulitzer Prize–winning writer Maxine Kumin is an extremely versa-
tile writer who has won awards for her poetry, essays, and fiction. Her
works include four novels, a short story collection, many children's
books, three books of essays, and eleven books of poetry. Kumin often
expresses in her poetry a fascination with nature—with its rhythms
and its survival in the face of brutal human manipulation.*

NURTURE   (1987)

From a documentary on marsupials I learn
that a pillowcase makes a fine
substitute pouch for an orphaned kangaroo.

I am drawn to such dramas of animal rescue.
5 They are warm in the throat. I suffer, the critic proclaims,
from an overabundance of maternal genes.

Bring me your fallen fledgling, your bummer lamb,
lead the abused, the starvelings, into my barn.
Advise the hunted deer to leap into my corn.

10 And had there been a wild child—
filthy and fierce as a ferret, he is called
in one nineteenth-century account—

a wild child to love, it is safe to assume,
given my fireside inked with paw prints,
15 there would have been room.

Think of the language we two, same, and not-same,
might have constructed from sign,
scratch, grimace, grunt, vowel:

Laughter our first noun, and our long verb, howl.

Questions for Discussion

1. How does the opening reference to "a documentary on marsupials"
   relate to the speaker's "maternal genes"?

2. In what ways do the speaker and the "wild child" she imagines taking
   in constitute a family?

3. What does the "fireside inked with paw prints" reveal about the speaker?

4. Why might the speaker and the "wild child" she imagines construct a
   language from gestures and inarticulate sounds? How does the speaker
   feel about creating such a language? What does she mean by "Laughter our first noun, and our long verb, howl"?

Suggestions for Exploration and Writing

1. Write an essay discussing how your pet or pets are a part of your family. How do they communicate with you and the rest of the family? How do you communicate with them?

2. Develop a lexicon of noises, idioms, and signs that the narrator and her wild child might use to communicate.

Sylvia Plath (1932–1963)

Sylvia Plath is often admired for her powerful, intensely personal poetry. Her father, Otto Plath, died when she was only eight years old. In 1956 she married Ted Hughes, who later became poet laureate of England. After writing about her emotional turmoil and her suicidal tendencies in The Bell Jar, *Plath killed herself shortly after its publication in 1963. In her posthumously published* Ariel, *she reveals an inner turmoil and a fascination with death that to some readers are almost unbearable.*

DADDY   (1963)

You do not do, you do not do
Any more, black shoe
In which I have lived like a foot
For thirty years, poor and white,
5   Barely daring to breathe or Achoo.

Daddy, I have had to kill you.
You died before I had time—
Marble-heavy, a bag full of God,
Ghastly statue with one grey toe
10   Big as a Frisco seal

And a head in the freakish Atlantic
Where it pours bean green over blue
In the waters off beautiful Nauset.
I used to pray to recover you.
15   Ach, du.

In the German tongue, in the Polish town
Scraped flat by the roller
Of wars, wars, wars.
But the name of the town is common.
20   My Polack friend

Says there are a dozen or two.
So I never could tell where you
Put your foot, your root,

I never could talk to you.
25   The tongue stuck in my jaw.

It stuck in a barb wire snare.
Ich, ich, ich, ich,
I could hardly speak.
I thought every German was you.
30   And the language obscene

An engine, an engine
Chuffing me off like a Jew.
A Jew to Dachau, Auschwitz, Belsen.
I began to talk like a Jew.
35   I think I may well be a Jew.

The snows of the Tyrol, the clear beer of Vienna
Are not very pure or true.
With my gypsy ancestress and my weird luck
And my Taroc pack and my Taroc pack
40   I may be a bit of a Jew.

I have always been scared of *you*,
With your Luftwaffe, your gobbledygoo.
And your neat moustache
And your Aryan eye, bright blue.
45   Panzer-man, panzer-man, O You—

Not God but a swastika
So black no sky could squeak through.
Every woman adores a Fascist,
The boot in the face, the brute
50   Brute heart of a brute like you.

You stand at the blackboard, daddy,
In the picture I have of you,
A cleft in your chin instead of your foot
But no less a devil for that, no not
55   Any less the black man who

Bit my pretty red heart in two.
I was ten when they buried you.
At twenty I tried to die
And get back, back, back to you.
60   I thought even the bones would do.

But they pulled me out of the sack.
And they stuck me together with glue.
And then I knew what to do.
I made a model of you,
65   A man in black with a Meinkampf look

And a love of the rack and the screw.
And I said I do, I do.
So daddy, I'm finally through.
The black telephone's off at the root,
70   The voices just can't worm through.

If I've killed one man, I've killed two—
The vampire who said he was you
And drank my blood for a year,
Seven years, if you want to know.
75   Daddy, you can lie back now.

There's a stake in your fat black heart
And the villagers never liked you.
They are dancing and stamping on you.
They always *knew* it was you.
80   Daddy, daddy, you bastard, I'm through.

Questions for Discussion

1. The speaker remembers her father as a "black shoe," "a bag full of God," a huge and ghastly statue, a devil, a Nazi, and a vampire. Collectively, what do these **images** suggest to you about the father?

2. List and examine the various references to death and to killing in the poem. If the father is dead, how can he be such a threat to his daughter that she fears his "chuffing [her] off like a Jew [. . .] to Dachau, Auschwitz, Belsen"? In what sense must the speaker kill her father? Why?

3. If the speaker still feels love for her father, why does she repeatedly refer to destroying him and her memory of him?

4. Why do you think the speaker and her father have never been able to communicate? Is the speaker necessarily Plath? Explain.

Suggestions for Exploration and Writing

1. Write a character sketch of Daddy as he is depicted by Plath, using quotations from the poem to support your characterizations.

2. Many readers find this poem powerful and disturbing, even frightening. Write an essay describing the elements that contribute to its fearsome power.

Luis Omar Salinas (b. 1938)

Salinas, born in Robstown, Texas, later moved to Monterrey, Mexico. After his mother's death the family moved back to Robstown, where he was adopted by his mother's brother. They lived in several towns in California, where Salinas's exposure to the majority white culture and

- *the lack of overt racism such as he had experienced in Texas influenced his feelings of loneliness and alienation, themes often examined in his poems. Salinas has written several volumes of poetry and won the General Electric Foundation Award for Young Writers in 1985. He has suffered several nervous breakdowns and was institutionalized numerous times during the 1960s. Salinas is known for his portrayal of characters and his sensitivity toward people and the conditions that affect them.*

MY FATHER IS A SIMPLE MAN   (1987)

I walk to town with my father
to buy a newspaper. He walks slower
than I do so I must slow up.
The street is filled with children.
5   We argue about the price
of pomegranates, I convince
him it is the fruit of scholars.
He has taken me on this journey
and it's been lifelong.
10   He's sure I'll be healthy
so long as I eat more oranges,
and tells me the orange
has seeds and so is perpetual;
and we too will come back
15   like the orange trees.
I ask him what he thinks
about death and he says
he will gladly face it when
it comes but won't jump
20   out in front of a car.
I'd gladly give my life
for this man with a sixth
grade education, whose kindness
and patience are true . . .
25   The truth of it is, he's the scholar,
and when the bitter-hard reality
comes at me like a punishing
evil stranger, I can always
remember that here was a man
30   who was a worker and provider,
who learned the simple facts
in life and lived by them,
who held no pretense.
And when he leaves without
35   benefit of fanfare or applause
I shall have learned what little
there is about greatness.

Questions for Discussion

1. What does the argument over pomegranates versus oranges tell about the character of the father and son?

2. What is the lifelong journey on which the father has taken the narrator? What is its destination?

3. How is the father's sense of humor shown?

4. List the father's character traits as shown in this short poem.

Suggestions for Exploration and Writing

1. Write an essay or a poem about your relationship with either your father or your mother.

2. Write an essay in which you show the character of a parent or a guardian as revealed through a simple act such as walking to the store for a newspaper.

3. Using quotations from the poem, write an essay describing the relationship between the narrator and his father.

4. Write an essay in which you compare Salinas's father with Plath's father or with Li-Young Lee's father.

Alicia Ostriker (b. 1937)

Alicia Ostriker is a contemporary American poet who is especially noted for her ability to portray the wide range of emotions shared by women of all ages. A professor of English at Rutgers University, mother of two daughters and a son, and wife of an astrophysicist, she lives in Princeton, New Jersey. She is the author of eight books of poetry, most recently The Little Space: Poems Selected and New, *which was a finalist for the 1998 National Book Awards. In 1999 she published* Dancing at the Devil's Party: Essays on Poetry, Politics, and the Erotic. *As a critic, Ostriker is the author of books on poetry and on the Bible.*

FIRST LOVE (1989)

When the child begins to suffer, the mother
Finds in her mouth those burning coals
You can neither spit out nor swallow—

It tells you about this in Zen, you know
5   You're illuminated when
The coals dissolve and your mouth is cool—

The child's lost boyfriend permeates the home
Like hyacinth perfume,
Nothing can escape it, it is too much,

10 It is maddening, like the insane yellow
Of the first blooming forsythia, like a missing
Limb that goes on hurting the survivor.

Whatever doesn't suffer isn't alive,
You know your daughter's pain is perfectly normal.
15 Nevertheless you imagine

Rinsing all grief from the child's tender face
The way a sculptor might peel the damp dropcloths
Off the clay figure she's been working on

So she can add fresh clay, play
20 With some details, pat it, bring it closer
To completion, and so people can see
How good and beautiful it already is.

Questions for Discussion

1. Why does the speaker use the Zen image of burning coals in her mouth?
2. Why is a fragrance appropriate to describe the way "the child's lost boyfriend permeates the house"?
3. Explain the double meaning of the poem's title.
4. In describing her empathy for her daughter, the mother uses a series of **similes** and **metaphors.** Identify each of these devices. Why do you think the mother uses metaphors rather than direct statements? What is particularly appropriate about the simile of the sculpture to describe the child?

Suggestions for Exploration and Writing

1. Write an essay about a first in your family: perhaps the first to graduate from high school or to go to college, the first grandchild, the first date, or the first born.
2. Using two of the following works, explain how the mother or father conveys a daughter's specialness: Yeats, "A Prayer for My Daughter"; McCullers, "A Domestic Dilemma"; Ostriker, "First Love."

Raymond Carver (1939–1988)

A highly regarded contemporary writer of short stories and poems, Raymond Carver won many awards, including the National Book Award, the National Book Critics Circle Award, and the Pulitzer Prize. Carver writes in a plain, very spare style about blue-collar Americans. He is admired for his unadorned style and moving portraits of plain, inarticulate, suffering people.

PHOTOGRAPH OF MY FATHER
IN HIS TWENTY-SECOND YEAR   *(1983)*

October. Here in this dank, unfamiliar kitchen
I study my father's embarrassed young man's face.
Sheepish grin, he holds in one hand a string
of spiny yellow perch, in the other
5   a bottle of Carlsbad beer.

In jeans and denim shirt, he leans
against the front fender of a 1934 Ford.
He would like to pose bluff and hearty for his posterity,
wear his old hat cocked over his ear.
10   All his life my father wanted to be bold.

But the eyes give him away, and the hands
that limply offer the string of dead perch
and the bottle of beer. Father, I love you,
yet how can I say thank you, I who can't hold my liquor either,
15   and don't even know the places to fish?

Questions for Discussion

1. What is significant about the time of year and the setting of the poem?

2. The father has obviously posed for the picture. What impression has he tried to give by his manner of posing? What does the speaker mean by "the eyes give him away, and the hands"? What do they give away?

3. Although both Carver and Plath write from the **point of view** of an adult remembering the past, the **tone** of Carver's poem contrasts sharply with that of Plath's "Daddy." What is the **tone** of Carver's poem?

4. What does Carver say about the power of memory? the power of heredity?

Suggestion for Exploration and Writing

1. Write a comparison-contrast essay using at least two of the poems about fathers. As you write, consider such elements as **point of view, tone,** and use of specific detail.

Nikki Giovanni (b. 1943)

Yolande Cornelia Giovanni Jr., was born in Knoxville, Tennessee. She received her BA from Fisk University in 1967 and attended both the University of Pennsylvania and Columbia University. Since 1987 Giovanni has been a professor of English at Virginia Tech. Giovanni has published many poems and articles, notably Black Feeling Black Talk *(1968);* Spin a Soft Black Song: Poems for Children *(1971);* My House: Poems *(1972), a collection of poems about being Black in America; and* Grand Mothers: A Multicultural Anthology of Poems, Reminiscences, and Short Stories about the Keepers of Our Traditions. *In 1996 she published both* Selected Poems of Nikki Giovanni *and* The Genie in the Jar. James Baldwin and Nikki Giovanni: A Dialogue *was published in 1973 and* Cotton Candy on a Rainy Day *in 1980. Known as a militant African American poet, Giovanni also writes very personal poetry.*

NIKKI-ROSA   (1968)

childhood remembrances are always a drag
if you're Black
you always remember things like living in Woodlawn
with no inside toilet
5   and if you become famous or something
they never talk about how happy you were to have your mother
all to yourself and
how good the water felt when you got your bath from one of those
big tubs that folk in chicago barbecue in
10   and somehow when you talk about home
it never gets across how much you
understood their feelings
as the whole family attended meetings about Hollydale
and even though you remember
15   your biographers never understand
your father's pain as he sells his stock
and another dream goes
and though you're poor it isn't poverty that
concerns you
20   and though they fought a lot
it isn't your father's drinking that makes any difference
but only that everybody is together and you
and your sister have happy birthdays and very good christmasses
and I really hope no white person ever has cause to write about me
25   because they never understand Black love is Black wealth and they'll
probably talk about my hard childhood and never understand that
all the while I was quite happy

Questions for Discussion

1. What stereotype does Giovanni attack in this poem? Why does Giovanni not want a white biographer?

2. What attitude does this poem take toward poverty? What matters most to Giovanni about her childhood?

3. What does Giovanni mean by "Black love is Black wealth"? What are the qualities of "Black love" that Giovanni speaks of?

4. Why, in the opening line, does Giovanni say that "childhood remembrances"—not childhood—"are always a drag"?

Suggestions for Exploration and Writing

1. Discuss ways in which outsiders may misunderstand events, relationships, or traditions that occur within your family.

2. Discuss some differences between private, ordinary families and public, famous families.

Rita Dove (b. 1952)

*Rita Dove has the distinction of being both the first African American and the youngest poet laureate of the United States. Born in Akron, Ohio, Dove graduated summa cum laude with a BA from Miami University in 1973. In 1977 she received an MFA from the University of Iowa. Her works include books of poetry—*The Yellow House on the Corner *(1980),* Museum *(1983), and* Grace Notes *(1989); a collection of short stories—*Fifth Sunday *(1985); and a novel—* Through the Ivory Gate *(1992). Dove won the Pulitzer Prize in poetry in 1987 for her biographical poems about her maternal grandparents,* Thomas and Beulah *(1986). Her other honors include a Guggenheim Fellowship, a Fulbright, and grants from the National Endowment for the Arts and the National Endowment for the Humanities. Currently she is Commonwealth Professor of English at the University of Virginia.*

VARIATION ON GUILT (1986)

Count it anyway he wants—
by the waiting room clock,
by a lengthening hangnail,
by his buttons, the cigars crackling
5   in cellophane—

no explosion. No latch clangs
home. Perfect bystander, high
and dry with a scream caught
in his throat, he looks down

10   the row of faces coddled
in anxious pride. Wretched
little difference, he thinks,
between enduring pain and
waiting for pain
15   to work on others.

The doors fly apart—no,
he wouldn't run away!
It's a girl, he can tell
by that smirk, that strut of a mountebank!

20   But he doesn't feel a thing.
Weak with rage,
Thomas deals the cigars,
spits out the bitter tip in tears.

Questions for Discussion

1. What is the setting of this poem?

2. Why does Thomas refer to himself as a "perfect bystander"?

3. Thomas expresses a view of pain that many would disagree with. Explain why you would agree or disagree with his view of pain.

4. Discuss why Thomas is enraged by the birth of his daughter. Does his rage echo the common response of his era?

Suggestions for Exploration and Writing

1. Historically, husbands have wanted boy babies, yet girls are often daddy's girls. Explain the reasons for this apparent contradiction.

2. What does this poem say about society's attitudes toward male and female? Discuss.

3. Write an essay comparing the attitudes toward male or female children in two different cultures or two different time periods.

Li-Young Lee (b. 1957)

Born of Chinese parents in Jakarta, Indonesia, Lee has written three highly regarded books of poems, including Rose *(1986), which contains "The Gift," and* City in Which I Love You, *which won the Lamont Poetry Award of the Academy of American Poets for 1990. In 1995 Lee published a memoir,* The Winged Seed: A Remembrance, *and* Book of My Nights *was published in 2001. Lee has been strongly influenced by his father, a physician, philosopher, writer, and minister who spent a year as a political prisoner in an Indonesian prison.*

THE GIFT   (1986)

To pull the metal splinter from my palm
my father recited a story in a low voice.
I watched his lovely face and not the blade.
Before the story ended he'd removed

5 the iron sliver I thought I'd die from.
I can't remember the tale
but hear his voice still, a well
of dark water, a prayer.
And I recall his hands,
10 two measures of tenderness
he laid against my face,
the flames of discipline
he raised above my head.

Had you entered that afternoon
15 you would have thought you saw a man
planting something in a boy's palm,
a silver tear, a tiny flame.
Had you followed that boy
you would have arrived here,
20 where I bend over my wife's right hand.

Look how I shave her thumbnail down
so carefully she feels no pain.
Watch as I lift the splinter out.
I was seven when my father
25 took my hand like this,
and I did not hold that shard
between my fingers and think,
Metal that will bury me,
christen it Little Assassin,
30 Ore Going Deep for My Heart.
And I did not lift up my wound and cry,

Death visited here!
I did what a child does
when he's given something to keep.
35 I kissed my father.

Questions for Discussion

1. Explain the gift that the poet receives and gives to his family.

2. What is meant by *"Metal that will bury me,"* "Little Assassin," and *"Death visited here!"*? Why does the speaker use these words in this gentle poem?

3. Explain Lee's meaning in these lines:
   two measures of tenderness
   he laid against my face,
   the flames of discipline
   he raised above my head.

Suggestions for Exploration and Writing

1. Using one incident from your childhood, show how one of your parents, a grandparent, or some other relative gave you a lifelong "gift."

2. Using specific examples from the poem, write an essay describing the relationship between the narrator and his father.

3. Write an essay classifying and interpreting the metaphors in this poem.

Virginia Cerenio (b. 1955)

Cerenio, who is a Filipino American, grew up in the San Francisco area. Her writings reflect the condition of women in families and in communities.

[WE WHO CARRY THE ENDLESS SEASONS]   (1989)

we who carry the endless seasons
    of tropical rain in our blood
still weep our mother's tears
feel the pain of their birth
5   their growing
        as women in america

we wear guilt for their minor sins
        singing lullabies
        in foreign tongue
10   " . . . o ilaw sa gabing madilim
          wangis mo'y bituin sa langit . . ."
    their desires
        wanting us
        their daughters
15   to marry only
          " . . . a boy from the islands . . .
          ang guapo lalake . . . and
          from a good family too. . . ."
    like shadows
20   attached to our feet
    we cannot walk away

though we are oceans and dreams apart
waves carry the constant clicking of their rosary beads
        like heartbeats
25   in our every breathing

Questions for Discussion

1. Who are the narrators (we) in the poem?
2. Why do they feel pulled between two different countries and cultures?
3. What are the wishes of their mothers? Do they coincide with those of the narrators?
4. Explain the images of the shadow and the rosary beads.

Suggestion for Exploration and Writing

1. Describe a family whose members are "oceans and dreams apart" and yet share the same "heartbeats."

Afaa M. Weaver (b. 1951)

Born in Baltimore, Maryland, Weaver, formerly known as Michael S. Weaver, received fellowships from the Pennsylvania Council of the Arts and the National Endowment of the Arts. He has written several volumes of poetry, including Water Song *(1985),* My Father's Geography *(1992),* Timber and Prayer *(1995),* Talisman *(1998),* The Lights of God *(1999), and* Multitudes: Poems Selected and New *(2000). In addition, Weaver is a freelance journalist, a playwright, and a novelist. Currently he is Alumni Professor of English at Simmons College in Boston.*

IMPROVISATION FOR PIANO   (1985)

AFTER *MOOD INDIGO*

Freshly lit cigarette in his mouth,
his collar turned up in the cold,
his face turned wry, and the question,
the awful question hidden beneath.
5   It is so difficult to see the baby
I sent scooting over to my mother,
laughing out, "He can walk, see."
It is difficult to look in my arms and
remember how he once fit there, how
10   I could keep the world away from him
if it threatened to hurt him, to rob him.
When I admit that he has been hurt,
that he has been robbed and that I was helpless,
I wonder what register there is for pain.
15   He is leaving home, and I am sending
another black man into life's teeth and jaws.
All that I know about being black
is some kind of totem knotted with the prints
of my fists beating out a syncopated pain.

20   I can't begin to tell him how to carve.
I can cry. I can counsel other black men,
but love is its own resistance in
the eye a father shares with his son.

The storm window glass sticks to me
25   with its cold, and I watch him go under
the big tree up the street and away.
The night is some slow rendition of
Mood Indigo, and the blues takes me
away to some place and frightens the shit
30   out of me, as I think of how my son will live.
What life will he have without proper
attire, I wonder. I think to run after him,
catch him, and say, "Here, another sweater."
And I know the other sweater is the first time
35   I saw "nigger" in a white man's eyes.
I know he needs gloves, too, for his hands,
when they stiffen, as he wonders how
blackness colors his life. I close the door.
There is a silence like dead flesh
40   in the bedroom. My son has left home,
a big, black manchild. I pull my cold feet
under the comforter and swallow sleep medicine.

I slip away hoping there are angels.

Questions for Discussion

1. What is "the awful question hidden beneath"?

2. What are the fears of the father for his son? How are his fears intensified by his race?

3. Why does the father, who counsels others, feel unable to counsel his son?

4. What does "the proper attire" mean to the father? What does he wish it could do?

5. Explain the simile "silence like dead flesh."

6. What does the father mean by "love is its own resistance in / the eye a father shares with his son"?

7. Explain the last line: "I slip away hoping there are angels."

Suggestions for Exploration and Writing

1. Write an essay comparing what your parents want for you in your future and what you want for yourself.

2. Write an essay contrasting the father's mental image of his son with the way the son probably sees himself.

3. Write a letter home from the son explaining why he left home and how he coped with the world as a black man.

4. Compare the hopes, fears, and prayers of the father for his son in this poem with the hopes, fears, and prayers of the father for his daughter in Yeats's "A Prayer for My Daughter."

Marilyn Nelson (b. 1946)

Marilyn Nelson has published six books of poems, two of which, The Homeplace *in 1991 and* The Fields of Praise *in 1997, were finalists for the National Book Award in poetry. With Pamela Espeland, she has also published two collections of verse for children:* The Cat Walked through the Casserole and Other Poems for Children *(1984) and* Halfdan Rasmussen's Hundreds of Hens and Other Poems for Children *(1982), translated from Danish. Nelson has a PhD from the University of Minnesota and has served on the faculty of the University of Connecticut since 1978.*

THE HOUSE ON MOSCOW STREET   (1990)

It's the ragged source of memory,
a tarpaper-shingled bungalow
whose floors tilt toward the porch,
whose back yard ends abruptly
5   in a weedy ravine. Nothing special:
a chain of three bedrooms
and a long side porch turned parlor
where my great-grandfather, Pomp, smoked
every evening over the news,
10   a long sunny kitchen
where Annie, his wife,
measured cornmeal
dreaming through the window
across the ravine and up to Shelby Hill
15   where she had borne their spirited,
high-yellow brood.
In the middle bedroom's hard,
high antique double bed
the ghost of Aunt Jane,
20   the laundress
who bought the house in 1872,
though I call with all my voices,
does not appear.
Nor does Pomp's ghost,
25   with whom one of my cousins believes
she once had a long and intimate

unspoken midnight talk.
He told her, though they'd never met,
that he loved her; promised
30   her raw widowhood would heal
without leaving a scar.

The conveniences in an enclosed corner
of the slant-floored back side porch
were the first indoor plumbing in town.
35   Aunt Jane put them in,
incurring the wrath of the woman
who lived in the big house next door.
Aunt Jane left the house
to Annie, whose mother she had known
40   as a slave on the plantation,
so Annie and Pomp could move their children
into town, down off Shelby Hill.
My grandmother, her brother, and five sisters
watched their faces change slowly
45   in the oval mirror on the wall outside the door
into teachers' faces, golden with respect.
Here Geneva, the randy sister,
damned their colleges,
daubing her quicksilver breasts
50   with gifts of perfume.

As much as love,
as much as a visit
to the grave of a known ancestor,
the homeplace moves me not to silence
55   but to righteous, praise Jesus song:
Oh, catfish and turnip greens,
hot-water cornbread and grits.
Oh, musty, much-underlined Bibles;
generations lost to be found,
60   to be found.

Questions for Discussion

1. What gives this rather ramshackle, ordinary house its special
   significance?
2. Why does Nelson use the term "ragged" to refer to memory?
3. What kind of ghosts are said to inhabit this house? What does the narrator mean by "the ghost of Aunt Jane, [. . .] though I call with all my
   voices, / does not appear"?
4. How did Aunt Jane anger "the woman / who lived in the big house"?
5. How did the narrator's family acquire the house?

6. Explain the phrase "generations lost to be found."

7. What does the narrator mean by "righteous, praise Jesus song"? Why does the "homeplace" cause her to sing? Whom and what does she celebrate in her song?

Suggestions for Exploration and Writing

1. Write an essay about a place or heirloom that has been very important in your family's history. Describe in detail the place or heirloom and examine in detail the history that gives it special significance.

2. In an essay, compare the narrator's memories of this house with Nikki Giovanni's memories of her home in "Nikki-Rosa."

3. Compare or contrast the return home of Didion and Nelson.

DRAMA

Terrence McNally (b. 1939)

Terrence McNally was born in Florida but grew up in Texas. His talents in the theater are many and varied: he has been stage manager and film critic as well as author of a wide variety of plays, musicals, and television scripts. His awards include three Tony Awards—one for the book for the musical adaptation of Kiss of the Spider Woman—*and an Emmy Award for the television script of* Andre's Mother.

ANDRE'S MOTHER   (1988)

List of Characters

CAL:	a young man
ARTHUR:	his father
PENNY:	his sister
ANDRE'S MOTHER	

Time: Now
Place: New York City, Central Park

(Four people—Cal, Arthur, Penny, and Andre's Mother—enter. They are nicely dressed and each carries a white helium-filled balloon on a string.)

CAL: You know what's really terrible? I can't think of anything terrific to say. Goodbye. I love you. I'll miss you. And I'm supposed to be so great with words!
PENNY: What's that over there?
ARTHUR: Ask your brother.

CAL: It's a theatre. An outdoor theatre. They do plays there in the summer. Shakespeare's plays. (*To Andre's Mother.*) God, how much he wanted to play Hamlet again. He would have gone to Timbuktu to have another go at that part. The summer he did it in Boston, he was
10   so happy!

PENNY: Cal. I don't think she . . . ! It's not the time. Later.

ARTHUR: Your son was a . . . the Jews have a word for it . . .

PENNY (*quietly appalled*): Oh my God!

ARTHUR: Mensch, I believe it is, and I think I'm using it right. It means warm, solid, the real thing. Correct me if I'm wrong.

PENNY: Fine, Dad, fine. Just quit while you're ahead.

ARTHUR: I won't say he was like a son to me. Even my son isn't always like a son to me. I mean . . . ! In my clumsy way, I'm trying to say how much I liked Andre. And how much he helped me to know my own
20   boy. Cal was always two handsful but Andre and I could talk about anything under the sun. My wife was very fond of him, too.

PENNY: Cal, I don't understand about the balloons.

CAL: They represent the soul. When you let go, it means you're letting his soul ascend to Heaven. That you're willing to let go. Breaking the last earthly ties.

PENNY: Does the Pope know about this?

ARTHUR: Penny!

PENNY: Andre loved my sense of humor. Listen, you can hear him laughing. (*She lets go of her white balloon.*) So long, you glorious, won-
30   derful, I-know-what-Cal-means-about-words . . . *man!* God forgive me for wishing you were straight every time I laid eyes on you. But if any man was going to have you, I'm glad it was my brother! Look how fast it went up. I bet that means something. Something terrific.

ARTHUR (*lets his balloon go*): Goodbye. God speed.

PENNY: Cal?

CAL: I'm not ready yet.

PENNY: Okay. We'll be over there. Come on, Pop, you can buy your little girl a Good Humor.

ARTHUR: They still make Good Humor?

40   PENNY: Only now they're called Dove Bars and they cost twelve dollars.

(Penny takes Arthur off. Cal and Andre's Mother stand with their balloons.)

CAL: I wish I knew what you were thinking. I think it would help me. You know almost nothing about me and I only know what Andre told me about you. I'd always had it in my mind that one day we would be friends, you and me. But if you didn't know about Andre and me . . . If this hadn't happened. I wonder if he would have ever told you. When he was sick, if I asked him once I asked him a thousand times, tell her. She's your mother. She won't mind. But he was so afraid of hurting you and of your disapproval. I don't know which was worse. (*No response. He sighs.*) God, how many of us live in this city because
50   we don't want to hurt our mothers and live in mortal terror of their

disapproval. We lose ourselves here. Our lives aren't furtive, just our feelings toward people like you are! A city of fugitives from our parents' scorn or heartbreak. Sometimes he'd seem a little down and I'd say, "What's the matter, babe?" and this funny sweet, sad smile would cross his face and he'd say, "Just a little homesick, Cal, just a little bit." I always accused him of being a country boy just playing at being a hotshot, sophisticated New Yorker. (*He sighs.*)

It's bullshit. It's all bullshit. (*Still no response.*)

Do you remember the comic strip *Little Lulu*? Her mother had no name, she was so remote, so formidable to all the children. She was just Lulu's mother. "Hello, Lulu's Mother," Lulu's friends would say. She was almost anonymous in her remoteness. You remind me of her. Andre's mother. Let me answer the questions you can't ask and then I'll leave you alone and you won't ever have to see me again. Andre died of AIDS. I don't know how he got it. I tested negative. He died bravely. You would have been proud of him. The only thing that frightened him was you. I'll have everything that was his sent to you. I'll pay for it. There isn't much. You should have come up the summer he played Hamlet. He was magnificent. Yes, I'm bitter. I'm bitter I've lost him. I'm bitter what's happening. I'm bitter even now, after all this, I can't reach you. I'm beginning to feel your disapproval and it's making me ill. (*He looks at his balloon.*) Sorry, old friend. I blew it. (*He lets go of the balloon.*)

Good night, sweet prince, and flights of angels sing thee to thy rest! (*Beat.*)

Goodbye, Andre's mother.

(*He goes. Andre's Mother stands alone holding her white balloon. Her lips tremble. She looks on the verge of breaking down. She is about to let go of the balloon when she pulls it down to her. She looks at it awhile before she gently kisses it. She lets go of the balloon. She follows it with her eyes as it rises and rises. The lights are beginning to fade. Andre's Mother's eyes are still on the balloon. The lights fade.*)

Questions for Discussion

1. Cal's family has never before met Andre's mother. Why, then, do they assume that they understand her? How might their assumptions make her feel?

2. Why is it appropriate for this situation that Good Humor bars have been renamed Dove Bars?

3. What do the balloons symbolize?

4. Does Cal make things better or worse for the mother by what he tells her? Explain.

5. Explain the appropriateness of the quotation from Hamlet with which Cal says goodbye to his balloon.

6. Why did Andre fail to tell his mother the truth about his life and his death? What did his failure to do so deprive her of?

7. Why is Andre's mother silent?

8. Explain the significance of Andre's mother's releasing the balloon at the end. Why does she alone of all the characters keep watching it?

Suggestions for Exploration and Writing

1. What do the other characters' comments reveal about Andre?

2. Analyze what the release of the balloons reveals about each of the characters.

3. Discuss in an essay the following quotation from McNally's play: "God, how many of us live in this city because we don't want to hurt our mothers and live in mortal terror of their disapproval."

4. Discuss in an essay the causes and/or effects of one person's silence on another person who cares about him or her.

5. In an essay, discuss the failure of parents and children to communicate clearly.

Casebook
on August Wilson

WRITING ABOUT RELATIONSHIPS

This casebook on August Wilson's play *Fences* provides a glimpse into the joys and sorrows of a complex family at a time in United States' history when opportunities for blacks were limited. After you have carefully read the play and formed your own ideas about elements such as the themes, characters, and symbols, you can use the essays about *Fences* to expand your knowledge of the writer and the play. The essays included here also allow you to write a brief documented essay using the play as your primary source and the essays as secondary sources.

August Wilson (b. 1945)

August Wilson grew up in a Pittsburgh, Pennsylvania, ghetto probably much like the one in which Fences *is set. Able to read by age four, Wilson dropped out of high school at age fifteen, bought a typewriter, and began writing poetry. Still searching for his distinctive voice as poet and dramatist, Wilson in 1967 founded the Black Horizons Theater Company. Besides his Pulitzer Prize–winning* Fences, *first produced by the Yale Repertory Theater in 1985, Wilson's plays include* Ma Rainey's Black Bottom *(1984);* Joe Turner's Come and Gone *(1986), which was voted Broadway play of the 1987–1988 season by the New York Drama Critics' Circle;* The Piano Lesson *(1986), which in 1990 won Wilson a second Pulitzer Prize;* Two Trains Running *(1990);* Seven Guitars *(1995); and* King Hedley II *(2001).*

FENCES

(1985)

List of Characters

TROY MAXSON
JIM BONO: Troy's friend
ROSE: Troy's wife
LYONS: Troy's oldest son by previous marriage
GABRIEL: Troy's brother
CORY: Troy and Rose's son
RAYNELL: Troy's daughter

Setting

The setting is the yard which fronts the only entrance to the Maxson household, an ancient two-story brick house set back off a small alley in a big-city neighborhood. The entrance to the house is gained by two or three steps leading to a wooden porch badly in need of paint.

A relatively recent addition to the house and running its full width, the porch lacks congruence. It is a sturdy porch with a flat roof. One or two chairs of dubious value sit at one end where the kitchen window opens onto the porch. An old-fashioned icebox stands silent guard at the opposite end.

The yard is a small dirt yard, partially fenced, except for the last scene, with a wooden sawhorse, a pile of lumber, and other fencebuilding equipment set off to the side. Opposite is a tree from which hangs a ball made of rags. A baseball bat leans against the tree. Two oil drums serve as garbage receptacles and sit near the house at right to complete the setting.

The Play

Near the turn of the century, the destitute of Europe sprang on the city with tenacious claws and an honest and solid dream. The city devoured them. They swelled its belly until it burst into a thousand furnaces and sewing machines, a thousand butcher shops and bakers' ovens, a thousand churches and hospitals and funeral parlors and moneylenders. The city grew. It nourished itself and offered each man a partnership limited only by his talent, his guile, and his willingness and capacity for hard work. For the immigrants of Europe, a dream dared and won true.

The descendants of African slaves were offered no such welcome or participation. They came from places called the Carolinas and the Virginias, Georgia, Alabama, Mississippi, and Tennessee. They came strong, eager, searching. The city rejected them and they fled and settled along the riverbanks and under bridges in shallow, ramshackle houses made of sticks and tarpaper. They collected rags and wood. They sold the use of their muscles and their bodies. They cleaned houses and washed clothes, they shined shoes, and in quiet desperation and vengeful pride, they stole, and lived in pursuit of their own dream so that they could breathe free, finally, and stand to meet life with the force of dignity and whatever eloquence the heart could call upon.

By 1957, the hard-won victories of the European immigrants had solidi-
fied the industrial might of America. War had been confronted and won with
new energies that used loyalty and patriotism as its fuel. Life was rich, full,
and flourishing. The Milwaukee Braves won the World Series, and the hot
winds of change that would make the sixties a turbulent, racing, dangerous,
and provocative decade had not yet begun to blow full.

ACT 1

SCENE 1

It is 1957. Troy and Bono enter the yard, engaged in conversation. Troy is
fifty-three years old, a large man with thick, heavy hands; it is this largeness
that he strives to fill out and make an accommodation with. Together with
his blackness, his largeness informs his sensibilities and the choices he has
made in his life.

Of the two men, Bono is obviously the follower. His commitment to their
friendship of thirty-odd years is rooted in his admiration of Troy's honesty,
capacity for hard work, and his strength, which Bono seeks to emulate.

It is Friday night, payday, and the one night of the week the two men engage
in a ritual of talk and drink. Troy is usually the most talkative and at times he
can be crude and almost vulgar, though he is capable of rising to profound
heights of expression. The men carry lunch buckets and wear or carry burlap
aprons and are dressed in clothes suitable to their jobs as garbage collectors.

BONO: Troy, you ought to stop that lying!

TROY: I ain't lying! The nigger had a watermelon this big. *(He indicates*
with his hands.) Talking about . . . "What watermelon, Mr. Rand?"
I liked to fell out! "What watermelon, Mr. Rand?" . . . And it sitting
there big as life.

BONO: What did Mr. Rand say?

TROY: Ain't said nothing. Figure if the nigger too dumb to know he
carrying a watermelon, he wasn't gonna get much sense out of him.
Trying to hide that great big old watermelon under his coat. Afraid
to let the white man see him carry it home.

BONO: I'm like you . . . I ain't got no time for them kind of people.

TROY: Now what he look like getting mad cause he see the man from
the union talking to Mr. Rand?

BONO: He come to me talking about . . . "Maxson gonna get us fired."
I told him to get away from me with that. He walked away from me
calling you a trouble maker. What Mr. Rand say?

TROY: Ain't said nothing. He told me to go down the Commissioner's
office next Friday. They called me down there to see them.

BONO: Well, as long as you got your complaint filed, they can't fire you.
That's what one of them white fellows tell me.

TROY: I ain't worried about them firing me. They gonna fire me cause
I asked a question? That's all I did. I went to Mr. Rand and asked
him, "Why? Why you got the white mens driving and the colored

lifting?" Told him, "what's the matter, don't I count? You think
only white fellows got sense enough to drive a truck. That ain't no
paper job! Hell, anybody can drive a truck. How come you got all
white driving and the colored lifting?" He told me "take it to the
union." Well, hell that's what I done! Now they wanna come up with
this pack of lies.

30   BONO: I told Brownie if the man come and ask him any questions . . .
just tell the truth! It ain't nothing but something they done trumped
up on you cause you filed a complaint on them.

TROY: Brownie don't understand nothing. All I want them to do is
change the job description. Give everybody a chance to drive the
truck. Brownie can't see that. He ain't got that much sense.

BONO: How you figure he be making out with that gal be up at Taylors'
all the time . . . that Alberta gal?

TROY: Same as you and me. Getting just as much as we is. Which is to
say nothing.

40   BONO: It is, huh? I figure you doing a little better than me . . . and I
ain't saying what I'm doing.

TROY: Aw, nigger, look here . . . I know you. If you had got anywhere
near that gal, twenty minutes later you be looking to tell somebody.
And the first one you gonna tell . . . that you gonna want to brag
to . . . is gonna be me.

BONO: I ain't saying that. I see where you be eyeing her.

TROY: I eye all the women. I don't miss nothing. Don't never let nobody
tell you Troy Maxson don't eye the women.

BONO: You been doing more than eyeing her. You done bought her a
50   drink or two.

TROY: Hell yeah, I bought her a drink! What that mean? I bought you one,
too. What that mean cause I buy her a drink? I'm just being polite.

BONO: It's all right to buy her one drink. That's what you call being
polite. But when you wanna be buying two or three . . . that's what
you call eyeing her.

TROY: Look here, as long as you known me . . . you ever known me to
chase after women?

BONO: Hell yeah! Long as I done known you. You forgetting I knew you
when.

60   TROY: Naw, I'm talking about since I been married to Rose?

BONO: Oh, not since you been married to Rose. Now, that's the truth,
there. I can say that.

TROY: All right then! Case closed.

BONO: I see you be walking up around Alberta's house. You supposed to
be at Taylors' and you be walking up around there.

TROY: What you watching where I'm walking for? I ain't watching after
you.

BONO: I seen you walking around there more than once.

TROY: Hell, you liable to see me walking anywhere! That don't mean
70   nothing cause you see me walking around there.

BONO: Where she come from anyway? She just kinda showed up one day.

TROY: Tallahassee. You can look at her and tell she one of them Florida gals. They got some big healthy women down there. Grow them right up out the ground. Got a little bit of Indian in her. Most of them niggers down in Florida got some Indian in them.

BONO: I don't know about that Indian part. But she damn sure big and healthy. Woman wear some big stockings. Got them great big old legs and hips as wide as the Mississippi River.

TROY: Legs don't mean nothing. You don't do nothing but push them out of the way. But them hips cushion the ride!

BONO: Troy, you ain't got no sense.

TROY: It's the truth! Like you riding on Goodyears!

(Rose enters from the house. She is ten years younger than Troy, her devotion to him stems from her recognition of the possibilities of her life without him: a succession of abusive men and their babies, a life of partying and running the streets, the Church, or aloneness with its attendant pain and frustration. She recognizes Troy's spirit as a fine and illuminating one and she either ignores or forgives his faults, only some of which she recognizes. Though she doesn't drink, her presence is an integral part of the Friday night rituals. She alternates between the porch and the kitchen, where supper preparations are under way.)

ROSE: What you all out here getting into?

TROY: What you worried about what we getting into for? This is men talk, woman.

ROSE: What I care what you all talking about? Bono, you gonna stay for supper?

BONO: No, I thank you, Rose. But Lucille say she cooking up a pot of pigfeet.

TROY: Pigfeet! Hell, I'm going home with you! Might even stay the night if you got some pigfeet. You got something in there to top them pigfeet, Rose?

ROSE: I'm cooking up some chicken. I got some chicken and collard greens.

TROY: Well, go on back in the house and let me and Bono finish what we was talking about. This is men talk. I got some talk for you later. You know what kind of talk I mean. You go on and powder it up.

ROSE: Troy Maxson, don't you start that now!

TROY *(puts his arm around her):* Aw, woman . . . come here. Look here, Bono . . . when I met this woman . . . I got out that place, say, "Hitch up my pony, saddle up my mare . . . there's a woman out there for me somewhere. I looked here. Looked there. Saw Rose and latched on to her." I latched on to her and told her—I'm gonna tell you the truth—I told her, "Baby, I don't wanna marry, I just wanna be your man." Rose told me . . . tell him what you told me, Rose.

ROSE: I told him if he wasn't the marrying kind, then move out the way so the marrying kind could find me.

TROY: That's what she told me. "Nigger, you in my way. You blocking the view! Move out the way so I can find me a husband." I thought it

110   over two or three days. Come back—

ROSE: Ain't no two or three days nothing. You was back the same night.

TROY: Come back, told her . . . "Okay, baby . . . but I'm gonna buy me a banty rooster and put him out there in the backyard . . . and when he sees a stranger come, he'll flap his wings and crow . . ." Look here, Bono, I could watch the front door by myself . . . it was that back door I was worried about.

ROSE: Troy, you ought not talk like that. Troy ain't doing nothing but telling a lie.

TROY: Only thing is . . . when we first got married . . . forget the

120   rooster . . . we ain't had no yard!

BONO: I hear you tell it. Me and Lucille was staying down there on Logan Street. Had two rooms with the outhouse in the back. I ain't mind the outhouse none. But when the goddamn wind blow through there in the winter . . . that's what I'm talking about! To this day I wonder why in the hell I ever stayed down there for six long years. But see, I didn't know I could do no better. I thought only white folks had inside toilets and things.

Black is White (margin note)

ROSE: There's a lot of people don't know they can do no better than they doing now. That's just something you got to learn. A lot of folks

130   still shop at Bella's.

TROY: Ain't nothing wrong with shopping at Bella's. She got fresh food.

ROSE: I ain't said nothing about if she got fresh food. I'm talking about what she charge. She charge ten cents more than the A&P.

TROY: The A&P ain't never done nothing for me. I spends my money where I'm treated right. I go down to Bella, say, "I need a loaf of bread, I'll pay you Friday." She give it to me. What sense that make when I got money to go and spend it somewhere else and ignore the person who done right by me? That ain't in the Bible.

ROSE: We ain't talking about what's in the Bible. What sense it make to

140   shop there when she overcharge?

TROY: You shop where you want to. I'll do my shopping where the people been good to me.

ROSE: Well, I don't think it's right for her to overcharge. That's all I was saying.

BONO: Look here . . . I got to get on. Lucille going be raising all kind of hell.

TROY: Where you going, nigger? We ain't finished this pint. Come here, finish this pint.

BONO: Well, hell, I am . . . if you ever turn the bottle loose.

TROY *(hands him the bottle):* The only thing I say about the A&P is I'm

150   glad Cory got that job down there. Help him take care of his school clothes and things. Gabe done moved out and things getting tight around here. He got that job. . . . He can start to look out for himself.

ROSE: Cory done went and got recruited by a college football team.

TROY: I told that boy about that football stuff. The white man ain't gonna let him get nowhere with that football. I told him when he first come to me with it. Now you come telling me he done went and got more tied up in it. He ought to go and get recruited in how to fix cars or something where he can make a living.

160 ROSE: He ain't talking about making no living playing football. It's just something the boys in school do. They gonna send a recruiter by to talk to you. He'll tell you he ain't talking about making no living playing football. It's a honor to be recruited.

TROY: It ain't gonna get him nowhere. Bono'll tell you that.

BONO: If he be like you in the sports . . . he's gonna be all right. Ain't but two men ever played baseball as good as you. That's Babe Ruth and Josh Gibson. Them's the only two men ever hit more home runs than you.

TROY: What it ever get me? Ain't got a pot to piss in or a window to throw it out of.

170 ROSE: Times have changed since you was playing baseball, Troy. That was before the war. Times have changed a lot since then.

TROY: How in hell they done changed?

ROSE: They got lots of colored boys playing ball now. Baseball and football.

BONO: You right about that, Rose. Times have changed, Troy. You just come along too early.

TROY: There ought not never have been no time called too early! Now you take that fellow . . . what's that fellow they had playing right field for the Yankees back then? You know who I'm talking about Bono.
180 Used to play right field for the Yankees.

ROSE: Selkirk?

TROY: Selkirk! That's it! Man batting .269, understand? .269. What kind of sense that make? I was hitting .432 with thirty-seven home runs! Man batting .269 and playing right field for the Yankees! I saw Josh Gibson's daughter yesterday. She walking around with raggedy shoes on her feet. Now I bet you Selkirk's daughter ain't walking around with raggedy shoes on her feet! I bet you that!

ROSE: They got a lot of colored baseball players now. Jackie Robinson was the first. Folks had to wait for Jackie Robinson.

190 TROY: I done seen a hundred niggers play baseball better than Jackie Robinson. Hell, I know some teams Jackie Robinson couldn't even make! What you talking about Jackie Robinson. Jackie Robinson wasn't nobody. I'm talking about if you could play ball then they ought to have let you play. Don't care what color you were. Come telling me I come along too early. If you could play . . . then they ought to have let you play.

(Troy takes a long drink from the bottle.)

ROSE: You gonna drink yourself to death. You don't need to be drinking like that.

TROY: Death ain't nothing. I done seen him. Done wrassled with him. You
200   can't tell me nothing about death. Death ain't nothing but a fastball on
the outside corner. And you know what I'll do to that! Lookee here,
Bono . . . am I lying? You get one of them fastballs, about waist high,
over the outside corner of the plate where you can get the meat of the
bat on it . . . and good god! You can kiss it good-bye. Now, am I lying?

BONO: Naw, you telling the truth there. I seen you do it.

TROY: If I'm lying . . . that 450 feet worth of lying! *(Pause.)* That's all
death is to me. A fastball on the outside corner.

ROSE: I don't know why you want to get on talking about death.

TROY: Ain't nothing wrong with talking about death. That's part of life.
210   Everybody gonna die. You gonna die, I'm gonna die. Bono's gonna
die. Hell, we all gonna die.

ROSE: But you ain't got to talk about it. I don't like to talk about it.

TROY: You the one brought it up. Me and Bono was talking about baseball . . . you tell me I'm gonna drink myself to death. Ain't that right,
Bono? You know I don't drink this but one night out of the week.
That's Friday night. I'm gonna drink just enough to where I can handle it. Then I cuts it loose. I leave it alone. So don't you worry about
me drinking myself to death. 'Cause I ain't worried about Death.
I done seen him. I done wrestled with him.

220   Look here, Bono . . . I looked up one day and Death was marching
straight at me. Like Soldiers on Parade! The Army of Death was
marching straight at me. The middle of July, 1941. It got real cold
just like it be winter. It seem like Death himself reached out and
touched me on the shoulder. He touch me just like I touch you. I got
cold as ice and Death standing there grinning at me.

ROSE: Troy, why don't you hush that talk.

TROY: I say . . . What you want, Mr. Death? You be wanting me? You done
brought your army to be getting me? I looked him dead in the eye.
I wasn't fearing nothing. I was ready to tangle. Just like I'm ready to
230   tangle now. The Bible say be ever vigilant. That's why I don't get but
so drunk. I got to keep watch.

ROSE: Troy was right down there in Mercy Hospital. You remember he had
pneumonia? Laying there with a fever talking plumb out of his head.

TROY: Death standing there staring at me . . . carrying that sickle in his
hand. Finally he say, "You want bound over for another year?" See,
just like that . . . "You want bound over for another year?" I told him,
"Bound over hell! Let's settle this now!"

It seem like he kinda fell back when I said that, and all the cold
went out of me. I reached down and grabbed that sickle and threw
240   it just as far as I could throw it . . . and me and him commenced to
wrestling.

We wrestled for three days and three nights. I can't say where
I found the strength from. Every time it seemed like he was gonna
get the best of me, I'd reach way down deep inside myself and find
the strength to do him one better.

ROSE: Every time Troy tell the story he find different ways to tell it. Different things to make up about it.

TROY: I ain't making up nothing. I'm telling you the facts of what happened. I wrestled with Death for three days and three nights and I'm standing here to tell you about it. *(Pause.)* All right. At the end of the third night we done weakened each other to where we can't hardly move. Death stood up, throwed on his robe . . . had him a white robe with a hood on it. He throwed on that robe and went off to look for his sickle. Say, "I'll be back." Just like that. "I'll be back." I told him, say, "Yeah, but . . . you gonna have to find me!" I wasn't no fool. I wasn't going looking for him. Death ain't nothing to play with. And I know he's gonna get me. I know I got to join his army . . . his camp followers. But as long as I keep my strength and see him coming . . . as long as I keep up my vigilance . . . he's gonna have to fight to get me. I ain't going easy.

BONO: Well, look here, since you got to keep up your vigilance . . . let me have the bottle.

TROY: Aw hell, I shouldn't have told you that part. I should have left out that part.

ROSE: Troy be talking that stuff and half the time don't even know what he be talking about.

TROY: Bono know me better than that.

BONO: That's right, I know you. I know you got some Uncle Remus in your blood. You got more stories than the devil got sinners.

TROY: Aw hell, I done seen him too! Done talked with the devil.

ROSE: Troy, don't nobody wanna be hearing all that stuff.

(Lyons enters the yard from the street. Thirty-four years old, Troy's son by a previous marriage, he sports a neatly trimmed goatee, sport coat, white shirt, tieless and buttoned at the collar. Though he fancies himself a musician, he is more caught up in the rituals and "idea" of being a musician than in the actual practice of the music. He has come to borrow money from Troy, and while he knows he will be successful, he is uncertain as to what extent his lifestyle will be held up to scrutiny and ridicule.)

LYONS: Hey, Pop.

TROY: What you come "Hey, Popping" me for?

LYONS: How you doing, Rose? *(He kisses her.)* Mr. Bono. How you doing?

BONO: Hey, Lyons . . . how you been?

TROY: He must have been doing all right. I ain't seen him around here last week.

ROSE: Troy, leave your boy alone. He come by to see you and you wanna start all that nonsense.

TROY: I ain't bothering Lyons. *(Offers him the bottle.)* Here . . . get you a drink. We got an understanding. I know why he come by to see me and he know I know.

LYONS: Come on, Pop . . . I just stopped by to say hi . . . see how you was doing.

TROY: You ain't stopped by yesterday.

ROSE: You gonna stay for supper, Lyons? I got some chicken cooking in the oven.

LYONS: No, Rose . . . thanks. I was just in the neighborhood and thought I'd stop by for a minute.

290 TROY: You was in the neighborhood alright, nigger. You telling the truth there. You was in the neighborhood cause it's my payday.

LYONS: Well, hell, since you mentioned it . . . let me have ten dollars.

TROY: I'll be damned! I'll die and go to hell and play blackjack with the devil before I give you ten dollars.

BONO: That's what I wanna know about . . . that devil you done seen.

LYONS: What . . . Pop done seen the devil? You too much, Pops.

TROY: Yeah, I done seen him. Talked to him too!

ROSE: You ain't seen no devil. I done told you that man ain't had nothing to do with the devil. Anything you can't understand, you want to
300 call it the devil.

TROY: Look here, Bono . . . I went down to see Hertzberger about some furniture. Got three rooms for two-ninety-eight. That what it say on the radio. "Three rooms . . . two-ninety-eight." Even made up a little song about it. Go down there . . . man tell me I can't get no credit. I'm working every day and can't get no credit. What to do? I got an empty house with some raggedy furniture in it. Cory ain't got no bed. He's sleeping on a pile of rags on the floor. Working every day and can't get no credit. Come back here—Rose'll tell you—madder than hell. Sit down . . . try to figure what
310 I'm gonna do. Come a knock on the door. Ain't been living here but three days. Who know I'm here? Open the door . . . devil standing there bigger than life. White fellow . . . got on good clothes and everything. Standing there with a clipboard in his hand. I ain't had to say nothing. First words come out of his mouth was . . . "I understand you need some furniture and can't get no credit." I liked to fell over. He say, "I'll give you all the credit you want, but you got to pay the interest on it." I told him, "Give me three rooms worth and charge whatever you want." Next day a truck pulled up here and two men unloaded them three rooms. Man what drove
320 the truck give me a book. Say send ten dollars, first of every month to the address in the book and everything will be alright. Say if I miss a payment the devil was coming back and it'll be hell to pay. That was fifteen years ago. To this day . . . the first of the month I send my ten dollars, Rose'll tell you.

ROSE: Troy lying.

TROY: I ain't never seen that man since. Now you tell me who else that could have been but the devil? I ain't sold my soul or nothing like that, you understand. Naw, I wouldn't have truck with the devil about nothing like that. I got my furniture and pays my ten dollars
330 the first of the month just like clockwork.

BONO: How long you say you been paying this ten dollars a month?

TROY: Fifteen years!

BONO: Hell, ain't you finished paying for it yet? How much the man done charged you.

TROY: Aw hell, I done paid for it. I done paid for it ten times over! The fact is I'm scared to stop paying it.

ROSE: Troy lying. He got that furniture from Mr. Glickman. He ain't paying no ten dollars a month to nobody.

TROY: Aw hell, woman. Bono know I ain't that big a fool.

340 LYONS: I was just getting ready to say . . . I know where there's a bridge for sale.

TROY: Look here, I'll tell you this . . . it don't matter to me if he was the devil. It don't matter if the devil give credit. Somebody had got to give it.

ROSE: It ought to matter. You going around talking about having truck with the devil . . . God's the one you gonna have to answer to. He's the one gonna be at the Judgment.

LYONS: Yeah, well, look here, Pop . . . let me have that ten dollars. I'll give it back to you. Bonnie got a job working at the hospital.

350 TROY: What I tell you, Bono? The only time I see this nigger is when he wants something. That's the only time I see him.

LYONS: Come on, Pop, Mr. Bono don't want to hear all that. Let me have the ten dollars. I told you Bonnie working.

TROY: What that mean to me? "Bonnie working." I don't care if she working. Go ask her for the ten dollars if she working. Talking about "Bonnie working." Why ain't you working?

LYONS: Aw, Pop, you know I can't find no decent job. Where am I gonna get a job at? You know I can't get no job.

360 TROY: I told you I know some people down there. I can get you on the rubbish if you want to work. I told you that the last time you came by here asking me for something.

LYONS: Naw, Pop . . . thanks. That ain't for me. I don't wanna be carrying nobody's rubbish. I don't wanna be punching nobody's time clock.

TROY: What's the matter, you too good to carry people's rubbish? Where you think that ten dollars you talking about come from? I'm just supposed to haul people's rubbish and give my money to you cause you too lazy to work. You too lazy to work and wanna know why you ain't got what I got.

ROSE: What hospital Bonnie working at? Mercy?

370 LYONS: She's down at Passavant working in the laundry.

TROY: I ain't got nothing as it is. I give you that ten dollars and I got to eat beans the rest of the week. Naw . . . you ain't getting no ten dollars here.

LYONS: You ain't got to be eating no beans. I don't know why you wanna say that.

TROY: I ain't got no extra money. Gabe done moved over to Miss Pearl's paying her the rent and things done got tight around here. I can't afford to be giving you every payday.

LYONS: I ain't asked you to give me nothing. I asked you to loan me ten
380   dollars. I know you got ten dollars.

TROY: Yeah. I got it. You know why I got it? Cause I don't throw my
money away out there in the streets. You living the fast life . . . wanna
be a musician . . . running around in them clubs and things . . . then,
you learn to take care of yourself. You ain't gonna find me going and
asking nobody for nothing. I done spent too many years without.

LYONS: You and me is two different people, Pop.

TROY: I done learned my mistake and learned to do what's right by it.
You still trying to get something for nothing. Life don't owe you
nothing. You owe it to yourself. Ask Bono. He'll tell you I'm right.

390   LYONS: You got your way of dealing with the world . . . I got mine. The
only thing that matters to me is the music.

TROY: Yeah, I can see that! It don't matter how you gonna eat . . . where
your next dollar is coming from. You telling the truth there.

LYONS: I know I got to eat. But I got to live too. I need something that
gonna help me to get out of the bed in the morning. Make me feel
like I belong in the world. I don't bother nobody. Just stay with my
music cause that's the only way I can find to live in the world. Otherwise there ain't no telling what I might do. Now I don't come criticizing you and how you live. I just come by to ask you for ten dollars.
400   I don't wanna hear all that about how I live.

TROY: Boy, your mama did a hell of a job raising you.

LYONS: You can't change me, Pop. I'm thirty-four years old. If you wanted
to change me, you should have been there when I was growing up.
I come by to see you . . . ask for ten dollars and you want to talk about
how I was raised. You don't know nothing about how I was raised.

ROSE: Let the boy have ten dollars, Troy.

TROY (to Lyons): What the hell you looking at me for? I ain't got no
ten dollars. You know what I do with my money. (To Rose) Give
him ten dollars if you want him to have it.

410   ROSE: I will. Just as soon as you turn it loose.

TROY (handing Rose the money): There it is. Seventy-six dollars and forty-two
cents. You see this, Bono? Now, I ain't gonna get but six of that back.

ROSE: You ought to stop telling that lie. Here, Lyons. (She hands him the
money.)

LYONS: Thanks, Rose. Look . . . I got to run . . . I'll see you later.

TROY: Wait a minute. You gonna say, "thanks, Rose" and ain't gonna look
to see where she got that ten dollars from? See how they do me, Bono?

LYONS: I know she got it from you, Pop. Thanks. I'll give it back to you.

TROY: There he go telling another lie. Time I see that ten dollars . . .
420   he'll be owing me thirty more.

LYONS: See you, Mr. Bono.

BONO: Take care, Lyons!

LYONS: Thanks, Pop. I'll see you again.

(Lyons exits the yard.)

TROY: I don't know why he don't go and get him a decent job and take
    care of that woman he got.

BONO: He'll be alright, Troy. The boy is still young.

TROY: The *boy* is thirty-four years old.

ROSE: Let's not get off into all that.

BONO: Look here . . . I got to be going. I got to be getting on. Lucille
430   gonna be waiting.

TROY (*puts his arm round Rose*): See this woman, Bono? I love this woman.
    I love this woman so much it hurts. I love her so much . . . I done
    run out of ways of loving her. So I got to go back to basics. Don't you
    come by my house Monday morning talking about time to go to
    work . . . 'cause I'm still gonna be stroking!

ROSE: Troy! Stop it now!

BONO: I ain't paying him no mind. Rose. That ain't nothing but gin-talk.
    Go on, Troy. I'll see you Monday.

TROY: Don't you come by my house, nigger! I done told you what I'm
440   gonna be doing.

(The lights go down to black.)

SCENE 2

*The lights come up on Rose hanging up clothes. She hums and sings softly to
herself. It is the following morning.*

ROSE (*sings*):
    Jesus, be a fence all around me every day
    Jesus, I want you to protect me as I travel on my way
    Jesus, be a fence all around me every day.

(Troy enters from the house.)

ROSE (*continues*):
    Jesus, I want you to protect me
    As I travel on my way.
    (To Troy) 'Morning. You ready for breakfast? I can fix it soon as I fin-
    ish hanging up these clothes.

TROY: I got the coffee on. That'll be all right. I'll just drink some of that
    this morning.

450 ROSE: That *651* hit yesterday. That's the second time this month. Miss
    Pearl hit for a dollar . . . seem like those that need the least always
    get lucky. Poor folks can't get nothing.

TROY: Them numbers don't know nobody. I don't know why you fool
    with them. You and Lyons both.

ROSE: It's something to do.

TROY: You ain't doing nothing but throwing your money away.

ROSE: Troy, you know I don't play foolishly. I just play a nickel here and
    a nickel there.

TROY: That's two nickels you done thrown away.

460 ROSE: Now I hit sometimes . . . that makes up for it. It always comes in handy when I do hit. I don't hear you complaining then.

TROY: I ain't complaining now. I just say it's foolish. Trying to guess out of six hundred ways which way the number gonna come. If I had all the money niggers, these Negroes, throw away on numbers for one week—just one week—I'd be a rich man.

ROSE: Well, you wishing and calling it foolish ain't gonna stop folks from playing numbers. That's one thing for sure. Besides . . . some good things come from playing numbers. Look where Pope done bought him that restaurant off of numbers.

470 TROY: I can't stand niggers like that. Man ain't had two dimes to rub together. He walking around with his shoes all run over bumming money for cigarettes. All right. Got lucky there and hit the numbers . . .

ROSE: Troy, I know all about it.

TROY: Had good sense, I'll say that for him. He ain't throwed his money away. I seen niggers hit the numbers and go through two thousand dollars in four days. Man bought him that restaurant down there . . . fixed it up real nice . . . and then didn't want nobody to come in it! A Negro go in there and can't get no kind of service. I seen a white fellow come in there and order a bowl of stew. Pope picked all the

480 meat out the pot for him. Man ain't had nothing but a bowl of meat! Negro come behind him and ain't got nothing but the potatoes and carrots. Talking about what numbers do for people, you picked a wrong example. Ain't done nothing but make a worser fool out of him than he was before.

ROSE: Troy, you ought to stop worrying about what happened at work yesterday.

TROY: I ain't worried. Just told me to be down there at the Commissioner's office on Friday. Everybody think they gonna fire me. I ain't worried about them firing me. You ain't got to worry about that.

490 *(Pause.)* Where's Cory? Cory in the house? *(Calls)* Cory?

ROSE: He gone out.

TROY: Out, huh? He gone out cause he know I want him to help me with this fence. I know how he is. That boy scared of work.

(Gabriel enters. He comes halfway down the alley and, hearing Troy's voice, stops.)

TROY *(continues):* He ain't done a lick of work in his life.

ROSE: He had to go to football practice. Coach wanted them to get in a little extra practice before the season start.

TROY: I got his practice . . . running out of here before he get his chores done.

ROSE: Troy, what is wrong with you this morning? Don't nothing set

500 right with you. Go on back in there and go to bed . . . get up on the other side.

TROY: Why something got to be wrong with me? I ain't said nothing wrong with me.

ROSE: You got something to say about everything. First it's the numbers . . .
then it's the way the man runs his restaurant . . . then you done got on
Cory. What's it gonna be next? Take a look up there and see if the
weather suits you . . . or is it gonna be how you gonna put up the fence
with the clothes hanging in the yard.

TROY: You hit the nail on the head then.

510 ROSE: I know you like I know the back of my hand. Go on in there and
get you some coffee . . . see if that straighten you up. 'Cause you ain't
right this morning.

*(Troy starts into the house and sees Gabriel. Gabriel starts singing. Troy's
brother, he is seven years younger than Troy. Injured in World War II, he has a
metal plate in his head. He carries an old trumpet tied around his waist and
believes with every fiber of his being that he is the Archangel Gabriel. He carries
a chipped basket with an assortment of discarded fruits and vegetables he has
picked up in the strip district and which he attempts to sell.)*

GABRIEL *(singing):*
Yes, ma'am, I got plums.
You ask me how I sell them
Oh ten cents apiece
Three for a quarter
Come and buy now
'Cause I'm here today
And tomorrow I'll be gone

(Gabriel enters.)

520 Hey, Rose!

ROSE: How you doing, Gabe?

GABRIEL: There's Troy . . . Hey, Troy!

TROY: Hey, Gabe. *(Exits into kitchen.)*

ROSE *(to Gabriel):* What you got there?

GABRIEL: You know what I got, Rose. I got fruits and vegetables.

ROSE *(looking in basket):* Where's all these plums you talking about?

GABRIEL: I ain't got no plums today, Rose. I was just singing that. Have
some tomorrow. Put me in a big order for plums. Have enough
plums tomorrow for St. Peter and everybody.

(Troy re-enters from kitchen, crosses to steps.)

530 *(To Rose)* Troy's mad at me.

TROY: I ain't mad at you. What I got to be mad at you about? You ain't
done nothing to me.

GABRIEL: I just moved over to Miss Pearl's to keep out from in your way.
I ain't mean no harm by it.

TROY: Who said anything about that? I ain't said anything about that.

GABRIEL: You ain't mad at me, is you?

TROY: Naw . . . I ain't mad at you, Gabe. If I was mad at you I'd tell you
about it.

GABRIEL: Got me two rooms. In the basement. Got my own door, too.
540   Wanna see my key? *(He holds up a key.)* That's my own key! Ain't
nobody else got a key like that. That's my key! My two rooms!

TROY: Well, that's good, Gabe. You got your own key . . . that's good.

ROSE: You hungry, Gabe? I was just fixing to cook Troy his breakfast.

GABRIEL: I'll take some biscuits. You got some biscuits? Did you know
when I was in heaven . . . every morning me and St. Peter would sit
down by the gate and eat some big fat biscuits? Oh, yeah! We had
us a good time. We'd sit there and eat us them biscuits and then
St. Peter would go off to sleep and tell me to wake him up when it's
time to open the gates for the judgment.

550   ROSE: Well, come on . . . I'll make up a batch of biscuits.

(Rose exits into the house.)

GABRIEL: Troy . . . St. Peter got your name in the book. I seen it. It
say . . . Troy Maxson. I say . . . I know him! He got the same name
like what I got. That's my brother!

TROY: How many times you gonna tell me that, Gabe?

GABRIEL: Ain't got my name in the book. Don't have to have my name.
I done died and went to heaven. He got your name though. One
morning St. Peter was looking at his book . . . marking it up for the
judgment . . . and he let me see your name. Got it in there under
M. Got Rose's name . . . I ain't seen it like I seen yours . . . but I know
560   it's in there. He got a great big book. Got everybody's name what was
ever been born. That's what he told me. But I seen your name. Seen
it with my own eyes.

TROY: Go on in the house there. Rose going to fix you something to eat.

GABRIEL: Oh, I ain't hungry. I done had breakfast with Aunt Jemimah.
She come by and cooked me up a whole mess of flapjacks. Remember how we used to eat them flapjacks?

TROY: Go on in the house and get you something to eat now.

GABRIEL: I got to sell my plums. I done sold some tomatoes. Got me two
quarters. Wanna see? *(He shows Troy his quarters.)* I'm gonna save
570   them and buy me a new horn so St. Peter can hear me when it's time
to open the gates. *(Gabriel stops suddenly. Listens.)* Hear that? That's
the hellhounds. I got to chase them out of here . . . Go on get out of
here! Get out! *(Gabriel exits singing.)*
Better get ready for the judgment
Better get ready for the judgment
My Lord is coming down

(Rose enters from the house.)

TROY: He gone off somewhere.

GABRIEL *(offstage):*
Better get ready for the judgment
580   Better get ready for the judgment morning
Better get ready for the judgment
My God is coming down

ROSE: He ain't eating right. Miss Pearl say she can't get him to eat nothing.

TROY: What you want me to do about it, Rose? I done did everything I can for the man. I can't make him get well. Man got half his head blown away . . . what you expect?

ROSE: Seem like something ought to be done to help him.

TROY: Man don't bother nobody. He just mixed up from that metal plate he got in his head. Ain't no sense for him to go back into the
590   hospital.

ROSE: Least he be eating right. They can help him take care of himself.

TROY: Don't nobody wanna be locked up, Rose. What you wanna lock him up for? Man go over there and fight the war . . . messin' around with them Japs . . . get half his head blown off . . . and they give him a lousy three thousand dollars. And I had to swoop down on that.

ROSE: Is you fixing to go into that again?

TROY: That's the only way I got a roof over my head . . . cause of that metal plate.

ROSE: Ain't no sense you blaming yourself for nothing. Gabe wasn't in
600   no condition to manage that money. You done what was right by him. Can't nobody say you ain't done what was right by him. Look how long you took care of him . . . till he wanted to have his own place and moved over there with Miss Pearl.

TROY: That ain't what I'm saying, woman! I'm just stating the facts. If my brother didn't have that metal plate in his head . . . I wouldn't have a pot to piss in or a window to throw it out of. And I'm fifty-three years old. Now see if you can understand that!

(Troy gets up from the porch and starts to exit the yard.)

ROSE: Where you going off to? You been running out of here every Saturday for weeks. I thought you was gonna work on this fence?
610   TROY: I'm gonna walk down to Taylors'. Listen to the ball game. I'll be back in a bit. I'll work on it when I get back.

(He exits the yard. The lights go to black.)

SCENE 3

The lights come up on the yard. It is four hours later. Rose is taking down the clothes from the line. Cory enters carrying his football equipment.

ROSE: Your daddy like to had a fit with you running out of here without doing your chores.

CORY: I told you I had to go to practice.

ROSE: He say you were supposed to help him with this fence.

CORY: He been saying that the last four or five Saturdays, and then he don't never do nothing, but go down to Taylors'. Did you tell him about the recruiter?

ROSE: Yeah, I told him.

620   CORY: What he say?

ROSE: He ain't said nothing too much. You get in there and get started on your chores before he gets back. Go on and scrub down them steps before he gets back here hollering and carrying on.

CORY: I'm hungry. What you got to eat, Mama?

ROSE: Go on and get started on your chores. I got some meat loaf in there. Go on and make you a sandwich . . . and don't leave no mess in there. (*Cory exits into the house. Rose continues to take down the clothes. Troy enters the yard and sneaks up and grabs her from behind.*) Troy! Go on, now. You liked to scared me to death. What was the score of the

630   game? Lucille had me on the phone and I couldn't keep up with it.

TROY: What I care about the game? Come here, woman. (*He tries to kiss her.*)

ROSE: I thought you went down Taylors' to listen to the game. Go on, Troy! You supposed to be putting up this fence.

TROY (*attempting to kiss her again*): I'll put it up when I finish with what is at hand.

ROSE: Go on, Troy. I ain't studying you.

TROY (*chasing after her*): I'm studying you . . . fixing to do my homework!

ROSE: Troy, you better leave me alone.

640   TROY: Where's Cory? That boy brought his butt home yet?

ROSE: He's in the house doing his chores.

TROY (*calling*): Cory! Get your butt out here, boy!

(*Rose exits into the house with the laundry. Troy goes over to the pile of wood, picks up a board, and starts sawing. Cory enters from the house.*)

TROY: You just now coming in here from leaving this morning?

CORY: Yeah, I had to go to football practice.

TROY: Yeah, what?

CORY: Yessir.

TROY: I ain't but two seconds off you noway. The garbage sitting in there overflowing . . . you ain't done none of your chores . . . and you come in here talking about "Yeah."

650   CORY: I was just getting ready to do my chores now, Pop . . .

TROY: Your first chore is to help me with this fence on Saturday. Every-thing else come after that. Now get that saw and cut them boards.

(*Cory takes the saw and begins cutting the boards. Troy continues working. There is a long pause.*)

CORY: Hey, Pop . . . why don't you buy a TV?

TROY: What I want with a TV? What I want one of them for?

CORY: Everybody got one. Earl, Ba Bra . . . Jesse!

TROY: I ain't asked you who had one. I say what I want with one?

CORY: So you can watch it. They got lots of things on TV. Baseball games and everything. We could watch the World Series.

TROY: Yeah . . . and how much this TV cost?

660 CORY: I don't know. They got them on sale for around two hundred dollars.

TROY: Two hundred dollars, huh?

CORY: That ain't that much, Pop.

TROY: Naw, it's just two hundred dollars. See that roof you got over your head at night? Let me tell you something about that roof. It's been over ten years since that roof was last tarred. See now . . . the snow come this winter and sit up there on that roof like it is . . . and it's gonna seep inside. It's just gonna be a little bit . . . ain't gonna hardly notice it. Then the next thing you know, it's gonna be leaking all over the house. Then the wood rot from all that water and you

670 gonna need a whole new roof. Now, how much you think it cost to get that roof tarred?

CORY: I don't know.

TROY: Two hundred and sixty-four dollars . . . cash money. While you thinking about a TV, I got to be thinking about the roof . . . and whatever else go wrong around here. Now if you had two hundred dollars, what would you do . . . fix the roof or buy a TV?

CORY: I'd buy a TV. Then when the roof started to leak . . . when it needed fixing . . . I'd fix it.

TROY: Where you gonna get the money from? You done spent it for a TV.

680 You gonna sit up and watch the water run all over your brand new TV.

CORY: Aw, Pop. You got money. I know you do.

TROY: Where I got it at, huh?

CORY: You got it in the bank.

TROY: You wanna see my bankbook? You wanna see that seventy-three dollars and twenty-two cents I got sitting up in there?

CORY: You ain't got to pay for it all at one time. You can put a down payment on it and carry it on home with you.

TROY: Not me. I ain't gonna owe nobody nothing if I can help it. Miss a payment and they come and snatch it right out of your house.

690 Then what you got? Now, soon as I get two hundred dollars clear, then I'll buy a TV. Right now, as soon as I get two hundred and sixty-four dollars, I'm gonna have this roof tarred.

CORY: Aw . . . Pop!

TROY: You go on and get your two hundred dollars and buy one if ya want it. I got better things to do with my money.

CORY: I can't get no two hundred dollars. I ain't never seen two hundred dollars.

TROY: I'll tell you what . . . you get a hundred dollars and I'll put the other hundred with it.

700 CORY: All right, I'm gonna show you.

TROY: You gonna show me how you can cut them boards right now.

(Cory begins to cut the boards. There is a long pause.)

CORY: The Pirates won today. That make five in a row.

TROY: I ain't thinking about the Pirates. Got an all-white team. Got that
boy . . . that Puerto Rican boy . . . Clemente. Don't even half-play
him. That boy could be something if they give him a chance. Play
him one day and sit him on the bench the next.

CORY: He gets a lot of chances to play.

TROY: I'm talking about playing regular. Playing every day so you can
get your timing. That's what I'm talking about.

CORY: They got some white guys on the team that don't play everyday.
You can't play everybody at the same time.

TROY: If they got a white fellow sitting on the bench . . . you can bet
your last dollar he can't play! The colored guy got to be twice as
good before he get on the team. That's why I don't want you to get
all tied up in them sports. Man on the team and what it get him?
They got colored on the team and don't use them. Same as not having them. All them teams the same.

CORY: The Braves got Hank Aaron and Wes Covington. Hank Aaron hit
two home runs today. That makes forty-three.

TROY: Hank Aaron ain't nobody. That's what you supposed to do. That's
how you supposed to play the game. Ain't nothing to it. It's just a
matter of timing . . . getting the right follow-through. Hell, I can hit
forty-three home runs right now!

CORY: Not off no major-league pitching, you couldn't.

TROY: We had better pitching in the Negro leagues. I hit seven home
runs off of Satchel Paige. You can't get no better than that!

CORY: Sandy Koufax. He's leading the league in strike-outs.

TROY: I ain't thinking of no Sandy Koufax.

CORY: You got Warren Spahn and Lew Burdette. I bet you couldn't hit
no home runs off of Warren Spahn.

TROY: I'm through with it now. You go on and cut them boards. (*Pause.*)
Your mama tell me you done got recruited by a college football
team? Is that right?

CORY: Yeah. Coach Zellman say the recruiter gonna be coming by to
talk to you. Get you to sign the permission papers.

TROY: I thought you supposed to be working down there at the A&P.
Ain't you suppose to be working down there after school?

CORY: Mr. Stawicki say he gonna hold my job for me until after the football season. Say starting next week I can work weekends.

TROY: I thought we had an understanding about this football stuff? You
suppose to keep up with your chores and hold that job down at the
A&P. Ain't been around here all day on a Saturday. Ain't none of
your chores done . . . and now you telling me you done quit your job.

CORY: I'm gonna be working weekends.

TROY: You damn right you are! And ain't no need for nobody coming
around here to talk to me about signing nothing.

CORY: Hey, Pop . . . you can't do that. He's coming all the way from
North Carolina.

750   TROY: I don't care where he coming from. The white man ain't gonna let you get nowhere with that football noway. You go on and get your book-learning so you can work yourself up in that A&P or learn how to fix cars or build houses or something, get you a trade. That way you have something can't nobody take away from you. You go on and learn how to put your hands to some good use. Besides hauling people's garbage.

CORY: I get good grades, Pop. That's why the recruiter wants to talk with you. You got to keep up your grades to get recruited. This way I'll be going to college. I'll get a chance . . .

760   TROY: First you gonna get your butt down there to the A&P and get your job back.

CORY: Mr. Stawicki done already hired somebody else cause I told him I was playing football.

TROY: You a bigger fool than I thought . . . to let somebody take away your job so you can play some football. Where you gonna get your money to take out your girlfriend and whatnot? What kind of fool-ishness is that to let somebody take away your job?

CORY: I'm still gonna be working weekends.

TROY: Naw . . . naw. You getting your butt out of here and finding you another job.

770

CORY: Come on, Pop! I got to practice. I can't work after school and play football, too. The team needs me. That's what Coach Zellman say . . .

TROY: I don't care what nobody else say. I'm the boss . . . you under-stand? I'm the boss around here. I do the only saying what counts.

CORY: Come on, Pop!

TROY: I asked you . . . did you understand?

CORY: Yeah . . .

TROY: What?!

780   CORY: Yessir.

TROY: You go on down there to that A&P and see if you can get your job back. If you can't do both . . . then you quit the football team. You've got to take the crookeds with the straights.

CORY: Yessir. *(Pause.)* Can I ask you a question?

TROY: What the hell you wanna ask me? Mr. Stawicki the one you got the questions for.

CORY: How come you ain't never liked me?

TROY: Liked you? Who the hell say I got to like you? What law is there say I got to like you? Wanna stand up in my face and ask a damn
790   foolass question like that. Talking about liking somebody. Come here, boy, when I talk to you.

(Cory comes over to where Troy is working. He stands slouched over and Troy shoves him on his shoulder.)

Straighten up, goddammit! I asked you a question . . . what law is there say I got to like you?

CORY: None.

TROY: Well, all right then! Don't you eat every day? *(Pause.)* Answer me when I talk to you! Don't you eat every day?

CORY: Yeah.

TROY: Nigger, as long as you in my house, you put that sir on the end of it when you talk to me!

800 CORY: Yes . . . sir.

TROY: You eat every day.

CORY: Yessir!

TROY: Got a roof over your head.

CORY: Yessir!

TROY: Got clothes on your back.

CORY: Yessir.

TROY: Why you think that is?

CORY: Cause of you.

TROY: Aw, hell I know it's cause of me . . . but why do you think that is?

810 CORY *(hesitant):* Cause you like me.

TROY: Like you? I go out of here every morning . . . bust my butt . . . putting up with them crackers every day . . . cause I like you? You about the biggest fool I ever saw. *(Pause.)* It's my job. It's my responsibility! You understand that? A man got to take care of his family. You live in my house . . . sleep you behind on my bedclothes . . . fill you belly up with my food . . . cause you my son. You my flesh and blood. Not cause I like you! Cause it's my duty to take care of you. I owe a responsibility to you!

Let's get this straight right here . . . before it go along any
820 further . . . I ain't got to like you. Mr. Rand don't give me money come payday cause he likes me. He gives me cause he owe me. I done give you everything I had to give you. I gave you your life! Me and your mama worked that out between us. And liking your black ass wasn't part of the bargain. Don't you try and go through life worrying about if somebody like you or not. You best be making sure they doing right by you. You understand what I'm saying, boy?

CORY: Yessir.

TROY: Then get the hell out of my face, and get on down to that A&P.

(Rose has been standing behind the screen door for much of the scene. She enters as Cory exits.)

ROSE: Why don't you let the boy go ahead and play football, Troy? Ain't
830 no harm in that. He's just trying to be like you with the sports.

TROY: I don't want him to be like me! I want him to move as far away from my life as he can get. You the only decent thing that ever happened to me. I wish him that. But I don't wish him a thing else from my life. I decided seventeen years ago that boy wasn't getting involved in no sports. Not after what they did to me in the sports.

ROSE: Troy, why don't you admit you was too old to play in the major leagues? For once . . . why don't you admit that?

TROY: What do you mean too old? Don't come telling me I was too old. I just wasn't the right color. Hell, I'm fifty-three years old and can do better then Selkirk's .269 right now!

ROSE: How's was you gonna play ball when you were over forty? Sometimes I can't get no sense out of you.

TROY: I got good sense, woman. I got sense enough not to let my boy get hurt over playing no sports. You been mothering that boy too much. Worried about if people like him.

ROSE: Everything that boy do . . . he do for you. He wants you to say "Good job, son." That's all.

TROY: Rose, I ain't got time for that. He's alive. He's healthy. He's got to make his own way. I made mine. Ain't nobody gonna hold his hand when he get out there in that world.

ROSE: Times have changed from when you was young, Troy. People change. The world's changing around you and you can't even see it.

TROY (*slow, methodical*): Woman . . . I do the best I can do. I come in here every Friday. I carry a sack of potatoes and a bucket of lard. You all line up at the door with your hand out. I give you the lint from my pockets. I give you my sweat and my blood. I ain't got no tears. I done spent them. We go upstairs in that room at night . . . and I fall down on you and try to blast a hole into forever. I get up Monday morning . . . find my lunch on the table. I go out. Make my way. Find my strength to carry me through to the next Friday. (*Pause.*) That's all I got, Rose. That's all I got to give. I can't give nothing else.

(*Troy exits into the house. The lights go down to black.*)

SCENE 4

It is Friday. Two weeks later. Cory starts out of the house with his football equipment. The phone rings.

CORY (*calling*): I got it!

(*He answers the phone and stands in the screen door talking.*)

Hello? Hey, Jesse. Naw . . . I was just getting ready to leave now.

ROSE (*calling*): Cory!

CORY: I told you, man, them spikes is all tore up. You can use them if you want, but they ain't no good. Earl got some spikes.

ROSE (*calling*): Cory!

CORY (*calling to Rose*): Mam? I'm talking to Jesse. (*Into phone*) When she say that? (*Pause.*) Aw, you lying, man. I'm gonna tell her you said that.

ROSE (*calling*): Cory, don't you go nowhere!

CORY: I got to go to the game, Ma! (*Into the phone*) Yeah, hey, look, I'll talk to you later. Yeah, I'll meet you over Earl's house. Later. Bye, Ma.

(*Cory exits the house and starts out the yard.*)

ROSE: Cory, where you going off to? You got that stuff all pulled out and thrown all over your room.

CORY *(in the yard):* I was looking for my spikes. Jesse wanted to borrow my spikes.

ROSE: Get up there and get that cleaned up before your daddy get back in here.

CORY: I got to go to the game! I'll clean it up when I get back.

(Cory exits.)

880 ROSE: That's all he need to do is see that room all messed up.

(Rose exits into the house. Troy and Bono enter the yard. Troy is dressed in clothes other than his work clothes.)

BONO: He told him the same thing he told you. Take it to the union.

TROY: Brownie ain't got that much sense. Man wasn't thinking about nothing. He wait until I confront them on it . . . then he wanna come crying seniority. *(Calls)* Hey Rose!

BONO: I wish I could have seen Mr. Rand's face when he told you.

TROY: He couldn't get it out of his mouth! Liked to bit his tongue! When they called me down there to the Commissioner's office . . . he thought they was gonna fire me. Like everybody else.

BONO: I didn't think they was gonna fire you. I thought they was gonna
890 put you on the warning paper.

TROY: Hey, Rose! *(To Bono)* Yeah, Mr. Rand like to bit his tongue.

(Troy breaks the seal on the bottle, takes a drink, and hands it to Bono.)

BONO: I see you run right down to Taylors' and told that Alberta gal.

TROY *(calling):* Hey Rose! *(To Bono)* I told everybody. Hey, Rose! I went down there to cash my check.

ROSE *(entering from the house):* Hush all that hollering, man! I know you out here. What they say down there at the Commissioner's office?

TROY: You supposed to come when I call you, woman. Bono'll tell you that. *(To Bono)* Don't Lucille come when you call her?

900 ROSE: Man, hush your mouth. I ain't no dog . . . talk about "come when you call me."

TROY *(puts his arm around Rose):* You hear this Bono? I had me an old dog used to get uppity like that. You say, "C'mere, Blue!" . . . and he just lay there and look at you. End up getting a stick and chasing him away trying to make him come.

ROSE: I ain't studying you and your dog. I remember you used to sing that old song.

TROY *(he sings):*
    Hear it ring! Hear it ring!
    I had a dog and his name was Blue.

910 ROSE: Don't nobody wanna hear you sing that old song.

TROY *(sings):* You know Blue was mighty true.

ROSE: Used to have Cory running around here singing that song.

BONO: Hell, I remember that song myself.

TROY *(sings):*

> You know Blue was a good old dog
> Blue treed a possum in a hollow log.

That was my daddy's song. My daddy made up that song.

ROSE: I don't care who made it up. Don't nobody wanna hear you sing it.

TROY *(makes a sound like calling a dog):* Come here, woman.

ROSE: You come in here carrying on, I reckon they ain't fired you. What
920   they say down there at the Commissioner's office?

TROY: Look here, Rose . . . Mr. Rand called me into his office today when
I got back from talking to them people down there . . . it come from
up top . . . he called me in and told me they was making me a driver.

ROSE: Troy, you kidding!

TROY: No I ain't. Ask Bono.

ROSE: Well, that's great, Troy. Now you don't have to hassle them people no more.

(Lyons enters from the street.)

TROY: Aw hell, I wasn't looking to see you today. I thought you was in
jail. Got it all over the front page of the *Courier* about them raiding
Sefus' place . . . where you be hanging out with all them thugs.

930 LYONS: Hey, Pop . . . that ain't got nothing to do with me. I don't go
down there gambling. I go down there to sit in with the band. I ain't
got nothing to do with the gambling part. They got some good
music down there.

TROY: They got some rogues . . . is what they got.

LYONS: How you been, Mr. Bono? Hi, Rose.

BONO: I see where you playing down at the Crawford Grill tonight.

ROSE: How come you ain't brought Bonnie like I told you. You should
have brought Bonnie with you, she ain't been over in a month of
Sundays.

940 LYONS: I was just in the neighborhood . . . thought I'd stop by.

TROY: Here he come . . .

BONO: Your daddy got a promotion on the rubbish. He's gonna be the
first colored driver. Ain't got to do nothing but sit up there and read
the paper like them white fellows.

LYONS: Hey, Pop . . . if you knew how to read you'd be all right.

BONO: Naw . . . naw . . . you mean if the nigger knew how to drive he'd
be all right. Been fighting with them people about driving and ain't
even got a license. Mr. Rand know you ain't got no driver's license?

TROY: Driving ain't nothing. All you do is point the truck where you
950   want it to go. Driving ain't nothing.

BONO: Do Mr. Rand know you ain't got no driver's license? That's what
I'm talking about. I ain't asked if driving was easy. I asked if Mr. Rand
know you ain't got no driver's license.

TROY: He ain't got to know. The man ain't got to know my business. Time he find out, I have two or three driver's licenses.

LYONS *(going into his pocket):* Say look here, Pop . . .

TROY: I knew it was coming. Didn't I tell you, Bono? I know what kind of "Look here, Pop" that was. The nigger fixing to ask me for some
960   money. It's Friday night. It's my payday. All them rogues down there on the avenue . . . the ones that ain't in jail . . . and Lyons is hopping in his shoes to get down there with them.

LYONS: See, Pop . . . if you give somebody else a chance to talk sometime, you'd see that I was fixing to pay you back your ten dollars like I told you. Here . . . I told you I'd pay you when Bonnie got paid.

TROY: Naw . . . you go ahead and keep that ten dollars. Put it in the bank. The next time you feel like you wanna come by here and ask me for something . . . you go on down there and get that.

LYONS: Here's your ten dollars, Pop. I told you I don't want you to give
970   me nothing. I just wanted to borrow ten dollars.

TROY: Naw . . . you go on and keep that for the next time you want to ask me.

LYONS: Come on, Pop . . . here go your ten dollars.

ROSE: Why don't you go on and let the boy pay you back, Troy?

LYONS: Here you go, Rose. If you don't take it I'm gonna have to hear about it for the next six months. *(He hands her the money.)*

ROSE: You can hand yours over here too, Troy.

TROY: You see this, Bono. You see how they do me.

BONO: Yeah, Lucille do me the same way.

(Gabriel is heard singing offstage. He enters.)

980   GABRIEL: Better get ready for the Judgment! Better get ready for . . . Hey! . . . Hey! . . . There's Troy's boy!

LYONS: How you doing, Uncle Gabe?

GABRIEL: Lyons . . . The King of the Jungle! Rose . . . hey, Rose. Got a flower for you. *(He takes a rose from his pocket.)* Picked it myself. That's the same rose like you is!

ROSE: That's right nice of you, Gabe.

LYONS: What you been doing, Uncle Gabe?

GABRIEL: Oh, I been chasing hellhounds and waiting on the time to tell St. Peter to open the gates.

990   LYONS: You been chasing hellhounds, huh? Well . . . you doing the right thing, Uncle Gabe. Somebody got to chase them.

GABRIEL: Oh, yeah . . . I know it. The devil's strong. The devil ain't no pushover. Hellhounds snipping at everybody's heels. But I got my trumpet waiting on the judgment time.

LYONS: Waiting on the Battle of Armageddon, huh?

GABRIEL: Ain't gonna be too much of a battle when God get to waving that Judgment sword. But the people's gonna have a hell of a time trying to get into heaven if them gates ain't open.

LYONS *(putting his arm around Gabriel):* You hear this, Pop. Uncle Gabe,
1000   you all right!

GABRIEL *(laughing with Lyons):* Lyons! King of the Jungle.

ROSE: You gonna stay for supper, Gabe. Want me to fix you a plate?

GABRIEL: I'll take a sandwich, Rose. Don't want no plate. Just wanna eat
     with my hands. I'll take a sandwich.

ROSE: How about you, Lyons? You staying? Got some short ribs cooking.

LYONS: Naw, I won't eat nothing till after we finished playing. *(Pause.)*
     You ought to come down and listen to me play, Pop.

TROY: I don't like that Chinese music. All that noise.

ROSE: Go on in the house and wash up, Gabe . . . I'll fix you a sandwich.

1010 GABRIEL *(to Lyons, as he exits):* Troy's mad at me.

LYONS: What you mad at Uncle Gabe for, Pop?

ROSE: He thinks Troy's mad at him cause he moved over to Miss Pearl's.

TROY: I ain't mad at the man. He can live where he want to live at.

LYONS: What he move over there for? Miss Pearl don't like nobody.

ROSE: She don't mind him none. She treats him real nice. She just don't
     allow all that singing.

TROY: She don't mind that rent he be paying . . . that's what she don't
     mind.

ROSE: Troy, I ain't going through that with you no more. He's over
1020   there cause he want to have his own place. He can come and go as
     he please.

TROY: Hell, he could come and go as he please here. I wasn't stopping
     him. I ain't put no rules on him.

ROSE: It ain't the same thing, Troy. And you know it. *(Gabriel comes to the
     door.)* Now that's the last I wanna hear about that. I don't wanna hear
     nothing else about Gabe and Miss Pearl. And next week . . .

GABRIEL: I'm ready for my sandwich, Rose.

ROSE: And next week when that recruiter come from that school . . .
     I want you to sign that paper and go on and let Cory play football.
1030   Then that'll be the last I have to hear about that.

TROY *(to Rose as she exits into the house):* I ain't thinking about Cory
     nothing.

LYONS: What . . . Cory got recruited? What school he going to?

TROY: That boy walking around here smelling his piss . . . thinking he's
     grown. Thinking he's gonna do what he want, irrespective of what
     I say. Look here, Bono . . . I left the Commissioner's office and went
     down to the A&P . . . that boy ain't working down there. He lying to
     me. Telling me he got his job back . . . telling me he working week-
     ends . . . telling me he working after school . . . Mr. Stawicki tell me
1040   he ain't working down there at all!

LYONS: Cory just growing up. He's just busting at the seams trying to fill
     out your shoes.

TROY: I don't care what he's doing. When he get to the point where he
     wanna disobey me . . . then it's time for him to move on. Bono'll tell

you that. I bet he ain't never disobeyed his daddy without paying the consequences.

BONO: I ain't never had a chance. My daddy came on through . . . but I ain't never knew him to see him . . . or what he had on his mind or where he went. Just moving on through. Searching out the New Land. That's what the old folks used to call it. See a fellow moving around from place to place . . . woman to woman . . . called it searching out the New Land. I can't say if he ever found it. I come along, didn't want no kids. Didn't know if I was gonna be in one place long enough to fix on them right as their daddy. I figured I was going searching, too. As it turned out I been hooked up with Lucille near about as long as your daddy been with Rose. Going on sixteen years.

TROY: Sometimes I wish I hadn't known my daddy. He ain't cared nothing about no kids. A kid to him wasn't nothing. All he wanted was for you to learn how to walk so he could start you to working. When it come time for eating . . . he ate first. If there was anything left over, that's what you got. Man would sit down and eat two chickens and give you the wing.

LYONS: You ought to stop that, Pop. Everybody feed their kids. No matter how hard times is . . . everybody care about their kids. Make sure they have something to eat.

TROY: The only thing my daddy cared about was getting them bales of cotton in to Mr. Lubin. That's the only thing that mattered to him. Sometimes I used to wonder why he was living. Wonder why the devil hadn't come and got him "Get them bales of cotton in to Mr. Lubin" and find out he owe him money . . .

LYONS: He should have just went on and left when he saw he couldn't get nowhere. That's what I would have done.

TROY: How he gonna leave with eleven kids? And where he gonna go? He ain't knew how to do nothing but farm. No, he was trapped and I think he knew it. But I'll say this for him . . . he felt a responsibility toward us. Maybe he ain't treated us the way I felt he should have . . . but without that responsibility he could have walked off and left us . . . made his own way.

BONO: A lot of them did. Back in those days what you talking about . . . they walk out their front door and just take on down one road or another and keep on walking.

LYONS: There you go! That's what I'm talking about.

BONO: Just keep on walking till you come to something else. Ain't you never heard of nobody having the walking blues? Well, that's what you call it when you just take off like that.

TROY: My daddy ain't had them walking blues! What you talking about? He stayed right there with his family. But he was just as evil as he could be. My mama couldn't stand him. Couldn't stand that evilness. She run off when I was about eight. She sneaked off one night after he had gone to sleep. Told me she was coming back for me. I ain't never seen her no more. All his women run off and left him. He wasn't good for nobody.

When my turn come to head out, I was fourteen and got to sniffing around Joe Canewell's daughter. Had us an old mule we called Greyboy. My daddy sent me out to do some plowing and I tied Greyboy and went to fooling around with Joe Canewell's daughter. We done found us a nice little spot, got real cozy with each other. She about thirteen and we done figured we was grown anyway . . . so we down there enjoying ourselves . . . ain't thinking about nothing. We didn't know Greyboy had got loose and wandered back to the house and my daddy was looking for me. We down there by the creek enjoying ourselves when my daddy come up on us. Surprised us. He had them leather straps off the mule and commenced to whupping me like there was no tomorrow. I jumped up, mad and embarrassed. I was scared of my daddy. When he commenced to whupping on me . . . quite naturally I run to get out of the way. *(Pause.)*

Now I thought he was mad cause I ain't done my work. But I see where he was chasing me off so he could have the gal for himself. When I see what the matter of it was, I lost all fear of my daddy. Right there is where I become a man . . . at fourteen years of age. *(Pause.)*

Now it was my turn to run him off. I picked up them same reins that he had used on me. I picked up them reins and commenced to whupping on him. The gal jumped up and run off . . . and when my daddy turned to face me, I could see why the devil had never come to get him . . . cause he was the devil himself. I don't know what happened. When I woke up, I was laying right there by the creek, and Blue . . . this old dog we had . . . was licking my face. I thought I was blind. I couldn't see nothing. Both my eyes were swollen shut. I layed there and cried. I didn't know what I was gonna do. The only thing I knew was the time had come for me to leave my daddy's house. And right there the world suddenly got big. And it was a long time before I could cut it down to where I could handle it.

Part of that cutting down was when I got to the place where I could feel him kicking in my blood and knew that the only thing that separated us was the matter of a few years.

(Gabriel enters from the house with a sandwich.)

LYONS: What you got there, Uncle Gabe?

GABRIEL: Got me a ham sandwich. Rose gave me a ham sandwich.

TROY: I don't know what happened to him. I done lost touch with everybody except Gabriel. But I hope he's dead. I hope he found some peace.

LYONS: That's a heavy story, Pop. I didn't know you left home when you was fourteen.

TROY: And didn't know nothing. The only part of the world I knew was the forty-two acres of Mr. Lubin's land. That's all I knew about life.

LYONS: Fourteen's kinda young to be out on your own. *(Phone rings.)* I don't even think I was ready to be out on my own at fourteen. I don't know what I would have done.

TROY: I got up from the creek and walked on down to Mobile. I was through with farming. Figured I could do better in the city. So I walked the two hundred miles to Mobile.

LYONS: Wait a minute . . . you ain't walked no two hundred miles, Pop. Ain't nobody gonna walk no two hundred miles. You talking about some walking there.

BONO: That's the only way you got anywhere back in them days.

LYONS: Shhh. Damn if I wouldn't have hitched a ride with somebody!

TROY: Who you gonna hitch it with? They ain't had no cars and things like they got now. We talking about 1918.

ROSE *(entering):* What you all out here getting into?

TROY *(to Rose):* I'm telling Lyons how good he got it. He don't know nothing about this I'm talking.

ROSE: Lyons, that was Bonnie on the phone. She say you supposed to pick her up.

LYONS: Yeah, okay, Rose.

TROY: I walked on down to Mobile and hitched up with some of them fellows that was heading this way. Got up here and found out . . . not only couldn't you get a job . . . you couldn't find no place to live. I thought I was in freedom. Shhh. Colored folks living down there on the riverbanks in whatever kind of shelter they could find for themselves. Right down there under the Brady Street Bridge. Living in shacks made of sticks and tarpaper. Messed around there and went from bad to worse. Started stealing. First it was food. Then I figure, hell, if I steal money I can buy me some food. Buy me some shoes, too! One thing led to another. Met your mama and had you. What I do that for? Now I got to worry about feeding you and her. Got to steal three times as much. Went out one day looking for somebody to rob . . . that's what I was, a robber. I'll tell you the truth. I'm ashamed of it today. But it's the truth. Went to rob this fellow . . . pulled out my knife . . . and he pulled out a gun. Shot me in the chest. It felt just like somebody had taken a hot branding iron and laid it on me. When he shot me I jumped at him with my knife. They told me I killed him and they put me in the penitentiary and locked me up for fifteen years. That's where I met Bono. That's where I learned how to play baseball. Got out that place and your mama had taken you and went on to make life without me. Fifteen years was a long time for her to wait. But that fifteen years cured me of that robbing stuff. Rose'll tell you. She asked me when I met her if I had gotten all that foolishness out of my system. And I told her "Baby, it's you and baseball all what count with me." You hear me, Bono? I meant it, too. She say, "Which one comes first?" I told her, "Baby, ain't no doubt it's baseball . . . but

you stick and get old with me and we'll both outlive this baseball."
Am I right, Rose? And it's true.

ROSE: Man, hush your mouth. You ain't said no such thing. Talking
about "Baby, you know you'll always be number one with me." That's
what you was talking.

TROY: You hear that, Bono. That's why I love her.

BONO: Rose'll keep you straight. You get off the track, she'll straighten
you up.

ROSE: Lyons, you better get on up and get Bonnie. She waiting on you.

1190 LYONS *(gets up to go):* Hey, Pop, why don't you come on down to the Grill
and hear me play?

TROY: I ain't going down there. I'm too old to be sitting around in
them clubs.

BONO: You got to be good to play down at the Grill.

LYONS: Come on, Pop . . .

TROY: I got to get up in the morning.

LYONS: You ain't got to stay long.

TROY: Naw, I'm gonna get my supper and go on to bed.

LYONS: Well, I got to go. I'll see you again.

1200 TROY: Don't you come around my house on my payday.

ROSE: Pick up the phone and let somebody know you coming. And
bring Bonnie with you. You know I'm always glad to see her.

LYONS: Yeah, I'll do that, Rose. You take care now. See you, Pop. See
you, Mr. Bono. See you, Uncle Gabe.

GABRIEL: Lyons! King of the Jungle!

(Lyons exits.)

TROY: Is supper ready, woman? Me and you got some business to take
care of. I'm gonna tear it up, too.

ROSE: Troy, I done told you now!

TROY *(puts his arm around Bono):* Aw hell, woman . . . this is Bono. Bono
1210 like family. I done known this nigger since . . . how long I done
know you?

BONO: It's been a long time.

TROY: I done known this nigger since Skippy was a pup. Me and him
done been through some times.

BONO: You sure right about that.

TROY: Hell, I done know him longer than I known you. And we still
standing shoulder to shoulder. Hey, look here, Bono . . . a man can't
ask for no more than that. *(Drinks to him.)* I love you, nigger.

BONO: Hell, I love you too . . . but I got to get home see my woman. You
1220 got yours in hand. I got to go get mine.

*(Bono starts to exit as Cory enters the yard, dressed in his football uniform. He
gives Troy a hard, uncompromising look.)*

CORY: What you do that for, Pop? *(He throws his helmet down in the direction of Troy.)*

ROSE: What's the matter? Cory . . . what's the matter?

CORY: Pa done went up to the school and told Coach Zellman I can't play football no more. Wouldn't even let me play the game. Told him to tell the recruiter not to come.

ROSE: Troy . . .

TROY: What you Troying me for. Yeah, I did it. And the boy know why I did it.

CORY: Why you wanna do that to me? That was the one chance I had.

1230   ROSE: Ain't nothing wrong with Cory playing football, Troy.

TROY: The boy lied to me. I told the nigger if he wanna play football . . . to keep up his chores and hold down that job at the A&P. That was the conditions. Stopped down there to see Mr. Stawicki . . .

CORY: I can't work after school during the football season, Pop! I tried to tell you that Mr. Stawicki's holding my job for me. You don't never want to listen to nobody. And then you wanna go and do this to me!

TROY: I ain't done nothing to you. You done it to yourself.

CORY: Just cause you didn't have a chance! You just scared I'm gonna be better than you, that's all.

1240   TROY: Come here.

ROSE: Troy . . .

(Cory reluctantly crosses over to Troy.)

TROY: All right! See. You done made a mistake.

CORY: I didn't even do nothing!

TROY: I'm gonna tell you what your mistake was. See . . . you swung at the ball and didn't hit it. That's strike one. See, you in the batter's box now. You swung and you missed. That's strike one. Don't you strike out!

(Lights fade to black.)

ACT 2

SCENE 1

The following morning. Cory is at the tree hitting the ball with the bat. He tries to mimic Troy, but his swing is awkward, less sure. Rose enters from the house.

ROSE: Cory, I want you to help me with this cupboard.

CORY: I ain't quitting the team. I don't care what Poppa say.

1250   ROSE: I'll talk to him when he gets back. He had to go see about your Uncle Gabe. The police done arrested him. Say he was disturbing the peace. He'll be back directly. Come on in here and help me clean out the top of this cupboard.

(Cory exits into the house. Rose sees Troy and Bono coming down the alley.)

Troy . . . what they say down there?

TROY: Ain't said nothing. I give them fifty dollars and they let him go. I'll talk to you about it. Where's Cory?

ROSE: He's in there helping me clean out these cupboards.

TROY: Tell him to get his butt out here.

(Troy and Bono go over to the pile of wood. Bono picks up the saw and begins sawing.)

TROY *(to Bono):* All they want is the money. That makes six or seven
1260   times I done went down there and got him. See me coming they stick out their *hands.*

BONO: Yeah. I know what you mean. That's all they care about . . . that money. They don't care about what's right. *(Pause.)* Nigger, why you got to go and get some hard wood? You ain't doing nothing but building a little old fence. Get you some soft pine wood. That's all you need.

TROY: I know what I'm doing. This is outside wood. You put pine wood inside the house. Pine wood is inside wood. This here is outside wood. Now you tell me where the fence is gonna be?

1270 BONO: You don't need this wood. You can put it up with pine wood and it'll stand as long as you gonna be here looking at it.

TROY: How you know how long I'm gonna be here, nigger? Hell, I might just live forever. Live longer than old man Horsely.

BONO: That's what Magee used to say.

TROY: Magee's a damn fool. Now you tell me who you ever heard of gonna pull their own teeth with a pair of rusty pliers.

BONO: The old folks . . . my granddaddy used to pull his teeth with pliers. They ain't had no dentists for the colored folks back then.

TROY: Get clean pliers! You understand? Clean, pliers! Sterilize them!
1280   Besides we ain't living back then. All Magee had to do was walk over to Doc Goldblum's.

BONO: I see where you and that Tallahassee gal . . . that Alberta . . . I see where you all done got tight.

TROY: What do you mean "got tight?"

BONO: I see where you be laughing and joking with her all the time.

TROY: I laughs and jokes with all of them, Bono. You know me.

BONO: That ain't the kind of laughing and joking I'm talking about.

(Cory enters from the house.)

CORY: How you doing, Mr. Bono?

TROY: Cory? Get that saw from Bono and cut some wood. He talking
1290   about the wood's too hard to cut. Stand back there, Jim, and let that young boy show you how it's done.

BONO: He's sure welcome to it.

(Cory takes the saw and begins to cut the wood.)

Whew-e-e! Look at that. Big old strong boy. Look like Joe Louis. Hell, must be getting old the way I'm watching that boy whip through that wood.

CORY: I don't see why Mama want a fence around the yard noways.

TROY: Damn if I know either. What the hell she keeping out with it? She ain't got nothing nobody want.

BONO: Some people build fences to keep people out . . . and other people build fences to keep people in. Rose wants to hold on to you all. She loves you.

TROY: Hell, nigger, I don't need nobody to tell me my wife loves me. Cory . . . go on in the house and see if you can find that other saw.

CORY: Where's it at?

TROY: I said find it! Look for it till you find it!

(Cory exits into the house.)

What's that supposed to mean? Wanna keep us in?

BONO: Troy . . . I done known you seem like damn near my whole life. You and Rose both. I done know both of you all for a long time. I remember when you met Rose. When you was hitting them baseball out the park. A lot of them old gals was after you then. You had the pick of the litter. When you picked Rose, I was happy for you. That was the first time I knew you had any sense. I said . . . My man Troy knows what he's doing . . . I'm gonna follow this nigger . . . he might take me somewhere. I been following you, too. I done learned a whole heap of things about life watching you. I done learned how to tell where the shit lies. How to tell it from the alfalfa. You done learned me a lot of things. You showed me how to not make the same mistakes . . . to take life as it comes along and keep putting one foot in front of the other. *(Pause.)* Rose a good woman, Troy.

TROY: Hell, nigger, I know she a good woman. I been married to her for eighteen years. What you got on your mind, Bono?

BONO: I just say she a good woman. Just like I say anything. I ain't got to have nothing on my mind.

TROY: You just gonna say she a good woman and leave it hanging out there like that? Why you telling me she a good woman?

BONO: She loves you, Troy. Rose loves you.

TROY: You saying I don't measure up. That's what you trying to say. I don't measure up cause I'm seeing this other gal. I know what you trying to say.

BONO: I know what Rose means to you, Troy. I'm just trying to say I don't want to see you mess up.

TROY: Yeah, I appreciate that, Bono. If you was messing around on Lucille I'd be telling you the same thing.

BONO: Well that's all I got to say. I just say that because I love you both.

TROY: Hell, you know me . . . I wasn't out there looking for nothing. You can't find a better woman than Rose. I know that. But seems like this woman just stuck onto me where I can't shake her loose. I done wrestled with it, tried to throw her off me . . . but she just stuck on tighter. Now she's stuck on for good.

1340 BONO: You's in control . . . that's what you tell me all the time. You responsible for what you do.

TROY: I ain't ducking the responsibility of it. As long as it sets right in my heart . . . then I'm okay. Cause that's all I listen to. It'll tell me right from wrong every time. And I ain't talking about doing Rose no bad turn. I love Rose. She done carried me a long ways and I love and respect her for that.

BONO: I know you do. That's why I don't want to see you hurt her. But what you gonna do when she find out? What you got then? If you try to juggle both of them . . . sooner or later you gonna drop one of
1350 them. That's common sense.

TROY: Yeah, I hear what you saying, Bono. I been trying to figure a way to work it out.

BONO: Work it out right, Troy. I don't want to be getting all up between you and Rose's business . . . but work it so it come out right.

TROY: Aw hell, I get all up between you and Lucille's business. When you gonna get that woman that refrigerator she been wanting? Don't tell me you ain't got no money now. I know who your banker is. Mellon don't need that money bad as Lucille want that refrigerator. I'll tell you that.

1360 BONO: Tell you what I'll do . . . when you finish building this fence for Rose . . . I'll buy Lucille that refrigerator.

TROY: You done stuck your foot in your mouth now! *(Troy grabs up a board and begins to saw. Bono starts to walk out the yard.)* Hey, nigger . . . where you going?

BONO: I'm going home. I know you don't expect me to help you now. I'm protecting my money. I wanna see you put that fence up by your-self. That's what I want to see. You'll be here another six months without me.

TROY: Nigger, you ain't right.

1370 BONO: When it comes to my money . . . I'm right as fireworks on the Fourth of July.

TROY: All right, we gonna see now. You better get out your bankbook.

(Bono exits, and Troy continues to work. Rose enters from the house.)

ROSE: What they say down there? What's happening with Gabe?

TROY: I went down there and got him out. Cost me fifty dollars. Say he was disturbing the peace. Judge set up a hearing for him in three weeks. Say to show cause why he shouldn't be recommitted.

ROSE: What was he doing that cause them to arrest him?

TROY: Some kids was teasing him and he run them off home. Say he was howling and carrying on. Some folks seen him and called the police. That's all it was.

ROSE: Well, what's you say? What'd you tell the Judge?

TROY: Told him I'd look after him. It didn't make no sense to recommit the man. He stuck out his big greasy palm and told me to give him fifty dollars and take him on home.

ROSE: Where's he at now? Where'd he go off to?

TROY: He's gone on about his business. He don't need nobody to hold his hand.

ROSE: Well, I don't know. Seem like that would be the best place for him if they did put him into the hospital. I know what you're gonna say. But that's what I think would be best.

TROY: The man done had his life ruined fighting for what? And they wanna take and lock him up. Let him be free. He don't bother nobody.

ROSE: Well, everybody got their own way of looking at it I guess. Come on and get your lunch. I got a bowl of lima beans and some corn-bread in the oven. Come on get something to eat. Ain't no sense you fretting over Gabe.

(Rose turns to go into the house.)

TROY: Rose . . . got something to tell you.

ROSE: Well, come on . . . wait till I get this food on the table.

TROY: Rose! *(She stops and turns around.)* I don't know how to say this. *(Pause.)* I can't explain it none. It just sort of grows on you till it gets out of hand. It starts out like a little bush . . . and the next thing you know it's a whole forest.

ROSE: Troy . . . what is you talking about?

TROY: I'm talking, woman, let me talk. I'm trying to find a way to tell you . . . I'm gonna be a daddy. I'm gonna be somebody's daddy.

ROSE: Troy . . . you're not telling me this? You're gonna be . . . what?

TROY: Rose . . . now . . . see . . .

ROSE: You telling me you gonna be somebody's daddy? You telling your *wife* this?

(Gabriel enters from the street. He carries a rose in his hand.)

GABRIEL: Hey, Troy! Hey, Rose!

ROSE: I have to wait eighteen years to hear something like this.

GABRIEL: Hey, Rose . . . I got a flower for you. *(He hands it to her.)* That's a rose. Same rose like you is.

ROSE: Thanks, Gabe.

GABRIEL: Troy, you ain't mad at me is you? Them bad mens come and put me away. You ain't mad at me is you?

TROY: Naw, Gabe, I ain't mad at you.

ROSE: Eighteen years and you wanna come with this.

1420   GABRIEL *(takes a quarter out of his pocket):* See what I got? Got a brand new quarter.

TROY: Rose . . . it's just . . .

ROSE: Ain't nothing you can say, Troy. Ain't no way of explaining that.

GABRIEL: Fellow that give me this quarter had a whole mess of them. I'm gonna keep this quarter till it stop shining.

ROSE: Gabe, go on in the house there. I got some watermelon in the frigidaire. Go on and get you a piece.

GABRIEL: Say, Rose . . . you know I was chasing hellhounds and them bad mens come and get me and take me away. Troy helped me. He

1430   come down there and told them they better let me go before he beat them up. Yeah, he did!

ROSE: You go on and get you a piece of watermelon, Gabe. Them bad mens is gone now.

GABRIEL: Okay, Rose . . . gonna get me some watermelon. The kind with the stripes on it.

(Gabriel exits into the house.)

ROSE: Why, Troy? Why? After all these years to come dragging this in to me now. It don't make no sense at your age. I could have expected this ten or fifteen years ago, but not now.

TROY: Age ain't got nothing to do with it, Rose.

1440   ROSE: I done tried to be everything a wife should be. Everything a wife could be. Been married eighteen years and I got to live to see the day you tell me you been seeing another woman and done fathered a child by her. And you know I ain't never wanted no half nothing in my family. My whole family is half. Everybody got different fathers and mothers . . . my two sisters and my brother. Can't hardly tell who's who. Can't never sit down and talk about Papa and Mama. It's your papa and your mama and my papa and my mama . . .

TROY: Rose . . . stop it now.

ROSE: I ain't never wanted that for none of my children. And now you

1450   wanna drag your behind in here and tell me something like this.

TROY: You ought to know. It's time for you to know.

ROSE: Well, I don't want to know, goddamn it!

TROY: I can't just make it go away. It's done now. I can't wish the cir-cumstance of the thing away.

ROSE: And you don't want to either. Maybe you want to wish me and my boy away. Maybe that's what you want? Well, you can't wish us away. I've got eighteen years of my life invested in you. You ought to have stayed upstairs in my bed where you belong.

TROY: Rose . . . now listen to me . . . we can get a handle on this thing.

1460   We can talk this out . . . come to an understanding.

ROSE: All of a sudden it's "we." Where was "we" at when you was down there rolling around with some god-forsaken woman? "We" should have come to an understanding before you started making a damn fool of yourself. You're a day late and a dollar short when it comes to an understanding with me.

TROY: It's just . . . She gives me a different idea . . . a different understanding about myself. I can step out of this house and get away from the pressures and problems . . . be a different man. I ain't got to wonder how I'm gonna pay the bills or get the roof fixed. I can just

1470   be a part of myself that ain't never been.

ROSE: What I want to know . . . is do you plan to continue seeing her. That's all you can say to me.

TROY: I can sit up in her house and laugh. Do you understand what I'm saying. I can laugh out loud . . . and it feels good. It reaches all the way down to the bottom of my shoes. *(Pause.)* Rose, I can't give that up.

ROSE: Maybe you ought to go on and stay down there with her . . . if she a better woman than me.

TROY: It ain't about nobody being a better woman or nothing. Rose,

1480   you ain't the blame. A man couldn't ask for no woman to be a better wife than you've been. I'm responsible for it. I done locked myself into a pattern trying to take care of you all that I forget about myself.

ROSE: What the hell was I there for? That was my job, not somebody else's.

TROY: Rose, I done tried all my life to live decent . . . to live a clean . . . hard . . . useful life. I tried to be a good husband to you. In every way I knew how. Maybe I come into the world backwards, I don't know. But . . . you born with two strikes on you before you come to the plate. You got to guard it closely . . . always looking for the curve-ball on the inside corner. You can't afford to let none get past you. You

1490   can't afford a call strike. If you going down . . . you going down swinging. Everything lined up against you. What you gonna do. I fooled them, Rose. I bunted. When I found you and Cory and a halfway decent job . . . I was safe. Couldn't nothing touch me. I wasn't gonna strike out no more. I wasn't going back to the penitentiary. I wasn't gonna lay in the streets with a bottle of wine. I was safe. I had me a family. A job. I wasn't gonna get that last strike. I was on first looking for one of them boys to knock me in. To get me home.

ROSE: You should have stayed in my bed, Troy.

TROY: Then when I saw that gal . . . she firmed up my backbone. And

1500   I got to thinking that if I tried . . . I just might be able to steal second. Do you understand after eighteen years I wanted to steal second.

ROSE: You should have held me tight. You should have grabbed me and held on.

TROY: I stood on first base for eighteen years and I thought . . . well, goddamn it . . . go on for it!

ROSE: We're not talking about baseball! We're talking about you going off to lay in bed with another woman . . . and then bring it home to me. That's what we're talking about. We ain't talking about no baseball.

TROY: Rose, you're not listening to me. I'm trying the best I can to
1510   explain it to you. It's not easy for me to admit that I been standing in
the same place for eighteen years.

ROSE: I been standing with you! I been right here with you, Troy. I got
a life too. I gave eighteen years of my life to stand in the same spot
with you. Don't you think I ever wanted other things? Don't you
think I had dreams and hopes? What about my life? What about me?
Don't you think it ever crossed my mind to want to know other men?
That I wanted to lay up somewhere and forget about my responsibilities? That I wanted someone to make me laugh so I could feel good?
You not the only one who's got wants and needs. But I held on to
1520   you, Troy. I took all my feelings, my wants and needs, my dreams . . .
and I buried them inside you. I planted a seed and watched and
prayed over it. I planted myself inside you and waited to bloom. And
it didn't take me no eighteen years to find out the soil was hard and
rocky and it wasn't never gonna bloom.

But I held on to you, Troy. I held on tighter. You was my husband.
I owed you everything I had. Every part of me I could find to give
you. And upstairs in that room . . . with the darkness falling in on
me . . . I gave everything I had to try and erase the doubt that you
wasn't the finest man in the world. And wherever you was going . . .
1530   I wanted to be there with you. Cause you was my husband. Cause
that's the only way I was gonna survive as your wife. You always talking about what you give . . . and what you don't have to give. But
you take, too. You take . . . and don't even know nobody's giving!

(Rose turns to exit into the house; Troy grabs her arm.)

TROY: You say I take and don't give!
ROSE: Troy! You're hurting me!
TROY: You say I take and don't give.
ROSE: Troy . . . you're hurting my arm! Let go!
TROY: I done give you everything I got. Don't you tell that lie on me.
ROSE: Troy!
1540   TROY: Don't you tell that lie on me!

(Cory enters from the house.)

CORY: Mama!
ROSE: Troy. You're hurting me.
TROY: Don't you tell me about no taking and giving.

*(Cory comes up behind Troy and grabs him. Troy, surprised, is thrown off bal-
ance just as Cory throws a glancing blow that catches him on the chest and
knocks him down. Troy is stunned, as is Cory.)*

ROSE: Troy. Troy. No!

(Troy gets to his feet and starts at Cory.)

Troy . . . no. Please! Troy!

(Rose pulls on Troy to hold him back. Troy stops himself.)

TROY: *(to Cory):* All right. That's strike two. You stay away from around me, boy. Don't you strike out. You living with a full count. Don't you strike out.

(Troy exits out the yard as the lights go down.)

SCENE 2

It is six months later, early afternoon. Troy enters from the house and starts to exit the yard. Rose enters from the house.

ROSE: Troy, I want to talk to you.

1550 TROY: All of a sudden, after all this time, you want to talk to me, huh? You ain't wanted to talk to me for months. You ain't wanted to talk to me last night. You ain't wanted no part of me then. What you wanna talk to me about now?

ROSE: Tomorrow's Friday.

TROY: I know what day tomorrow is. You think I don't know tomorrow's Friday? My whole life I ain't done nothing but look to see Friday coming and you got to tell me it's Friday.

ROSE: I want to know if you're coming home.

TROY: I always come home, Rose. You know that. There ain't never been

1560 a night I ain't come home.

ROSE: That ain't what I mean . . . and you know it. I want to know if you're coming straight home after work.

TROY: I figure I'd cash my check . . . hang out at Taylors' with the boys . . . maybe play a game of checkers . . .

ROSE: Troy, I can't live like this. I won't live like this. You livin' on borrowed time with me. It's been going on six months now you ain't been coming home.

TROY: I be here every night. Every night of the year. That's 365 days.

ROSE: I want you to come home tomorrow after work.

1570 TROY: Rose . . . I don't mess up my pay. You know that now. I take my pay and I give it to you. I don't have no money but what you give me back. I just want to have a little time to myself . . . a little time to enjoy life.

ROSE: What about me? When's my time to enjoy life?

TROY: I don't know what to tell you, Rose. I'm doing the best I can.

ROSE: You ain't been home from work but time enough to change your clothes and run out . . . and you wanna call that the best you can do?

TROY: I'm going over to the hospital to see Alberta. She went into the hospital this afternoon. Look like she might have the baby early. I won't be gone long.

1580 ROSE: Well, you ought to know. They went over to Miss Pearl's and got Gabe today. She said you told them to go ahead and lock him up.

TROY: I ain't said no such thing. Whoever told you that is telling a lie. Pearl ain't doing nothing but telling a big fat lie.

ROSE: She ain't had to tell me. I read it on the papers.

TROY: I ain't told them nothing of the kind.

ROSE: I saw it right there on the papers.

TROY: What it say, huh?

ROSE: It said you told them to take him.

TROY: Then they screwed that up, just the way they screw up everything. I ain't worried about what they got on the paper.

ROSE: Say the government send part of his check to the hospital and the other part to you.

TROY: I ain't got nothing to do with that if that's the way it works. I ain't made up the rules about how it work.

ROSE: You did Gabe just like you did Cory. You wouldn't sign the paper for Cory . . . but you signed for Gabe. You signed that paper.

(The telephone is heard ringing inside the house.)

TROY: I told you I ain't signed nothing, woman! The only thing I signed was the release form. Hell, I can't read, I don't know what they had on that paper! I ain't signed nothing about sending Gabe away.

ROSE: I said send him to the hospital . . . you said let him be free . . . now you done went down there and signed him to the hospital for half his money. You went back on yourself, Troy. You gonna have to answer for that.

TROY: See now . . . you been over there talking to Miss Pearl. She done got mad cause she ain't getting Gabe's rent money. That's all it is. She's liable to say anything.

ROSE: Troy, I seen where you signed the paper.

TROY: You ain't seen nothing I signed. What she doing got papers on my brother anyway? Miss Pearl telling a big fat lie. And I'm gonna tell her about it too! You ain't seen nothing I signed. Say . . . you ain't seen nothing I signed.

(Rose exits into the house to answer the telephone. Presently she returns.)

ROSE: Troy . . . that was the hospital. Alberta had the baby.

TROY: What she have? What is it?

ROSE: It's a girl.

TROY: I better get on down to the hospital to see her.

ROSE: Troy.

TROY: Rose . . . I got to see her now. That's only right . . . what's the matter . . . the baby's all right, ain't it?

ROSE: Alberta died having the baby.

TROY: Died . . . you say she's dead? Alberta's dead?

ROSE: They said they done all they could. They couldn't do nothing for her.

TROY: The baby? How's the baby?

ROSE: They say it's healthy. I wonder who's gonna bury her.

TROY: She had family, Rose. She wasn't living in the world by herself.

ROSE: I know she wasn't living in the world by herself.

TROY: Next thing you gonna want to know if she had any insurance.

ROSE: Troy, you ain't got to talk like that.

TROY: That's the first thing that jumped out your mouth. "Who's gonna
1630 bury her?" Like I'm fixing to take on that task for myself.

ROSE: I am your wife. Don't push me away.

TROY: I ain't pushing nobody away. Just give me some space. That's all.
Just give me some room to breathe.

(Rose exits into the house. Troy walks about the yard.)

TROY: *(with a quiet rage that threatens to consume him):* All right . . . Mr.
Death. See now . . . I'm gonna tell you what I'm gonna do. I'm
gonna take and build me a fence around this yard. See? I'm gonna
build me a fence around what belongs to me. And then I want you to
stay on the other side. See? You stay over there until you're ready for
me. Then you come on. Bring your army. Bring your sickle. Bring
1640 your wrestling clothes. I ain't gonna fall down on my vigilance this
time. You ain't gonna sneak up on me no more. When you ready for
me . . . when the top of your list say Troy Maxson . . . that's when you
come around here. You come up and knock on the front door. Ain't
nobody else got nothing to do with this. This is between you and me.
Man to man. You stay on the other side of that fence until you ready
for me. Then you come up and knock on the front door. Anytime
you want. I'll be ready for you.

(The lights go down to black.)

SCENE 3

*The lights come up on the porch. It is late evening three days later. Rose sits lis-
tening to the ball game waiting for Troy. The final out of the game is made and
Rose switches off the radio. Troy enters the yard carrying an infant wrapped in
blankets. He stands back from the house and calls.*
  *Rose enters and stands on the porch. There is a long, awkward silence, the
weight of which grows heavier with each passing second.*

TROY: Rose . . . I'm standing here with my daughter in my arms. She
ain't but a wee bittie little old thing. She don't know nothing about
1650 grownups' business. She innocent . . . and she ain't got no mama.

ROSE: What you telling me for, Troy?

(She turns and exits into the house.)

TROY: Well . . . I guess we'll just sit out here on the porch.

*(He sits down on the porch. There is an awkward indelicateness about the way
he handles the baby. His largeness engulfs and seems to swallow it. He speaks
loud enough for Rose to hear.)*

A man's got to do what's right for him. I ain't sorry for nothing I done. It felt right in my heart. *(To the baby):* What you smiling at? Your daddy's a big man. Got these great big old hands. But sometimes he's scared. And right now your daddy's scared cause we sitting out here and ain't got no home. Oh, I been homeless before. I ain't had no little baby with me. But I been homeless. You just be out on the road by your lonesome and you see one of them trains coming and you just kinda go like this . . . *(He sings as a lullaby):*
Please, Mr. Engineer let a man ride the line
Please, Mr. Engineer let a man ride the line
I ain't got no ticket please let me ride the blinds

(Rose enters from the house. Troy, hearing her steps behind him, stands and faces her.)

She's my daughter, Rose. My own flesh and blood. I can't deny her no more than I can deny them boys. *(Pause.)* You and them boys is my family. You and them and this child is all I got in the world. So I guess what I'm saying is . . . I'd appreciate it if you'd help me take care of her.

ROSE: Okay, Troy . . . you're right. I'll take care of your baby for you . . . cause . . . like you say . . . she's innocent . . . and you can't visit the sins of the father upon the child. A motherless child has got a hard time. *(She takes the baby from him.)* From right now . . . this child got a mother. But you a womanless man.

(Rose turns and exits into the house with the baby. Lights go down to black.)

Scene 4

It is two months later. Lyons enters from the street. He knocks on the door and calls.

LYONS: Hey, Rose! *(Pause.)* Rose!
ROSE *(from inside the house):* Stop that yelling. You gonna wake up Raynell. I just got her to sleep.
LYONS: I just stopped by to pay Papa this twenty dollars I owe him. Where's Papa at?
ROSE: He should be here in a minute. I'm getting ready to go down to the church. Sit down and wait on him.
LYONS: I got to go pick up Bonnie over her mother's house.
ROSE: Well, sit it down there on the table. He'll get it.
LYONS *(enters the house and sets the money on the table):* Tell Papa I said thanks. I'll see you again.
ROSE: All right, Lyons. We'll see you.

(Lyons starts to exit as Cory enters.)

CORY: Hey, Lyons.

LYONS: What's happening, Cory. Say man, I'm sorry I missed your graduation. You know I had a gig and couldn't get away. Otherwise, I would have been there, man. So what you doing?

1690 CORY: I'm trying to find a job.

LYONS: Yeah I know how that go, man. It's rough out here. Jobs are scarce.

CORY: Yeah, I know.

LYONS: Look here, I got to run. Talk to Papa . . . he know some people. He'll be able to help get you a job. Talk to him . . . see what he say.

CORY: Yeah . . . all right, Lyons.

LYONS: You take care. I'll talk to you soon. We'll find some time to talk.

(Lyons exits the yard. Cory wanders over to the tree, picks up the bat and assumes a batting stance. He studies an imaginary pitcher and swings. Dissatisfied with the result, he tries again. Troy enters. They eye each other for a beat. Cory puts the bat down and exits the yard. Troy starts into the house as Rose exits with Raynell. She is carrying a cake.)

TROY: I'm coming in and everybody's going out.

ROSE: I'm taking this cake down to the church for the bake sale. Lyons was by to see you. He stopped by to pay you your twenty dollars. It's

1700 laying in there on the table.

TROY *(going into his pocket)*: Well . . . here go this money.

ROSE: Put it in there on the table, Troy. I'll get it.

TROY: What time you coming back?

ROSE: Ain't no use you studying me. It don't matter what time I come back.

TROY: I just asked you a question, woman. What's the matter . . . can't I ask you a question?

ROSE: Troy, I don't want to go into it. Your dinner's in there on the stove. All you got to do is heat it up. And don't you be eating the rest

1710 of them cakes in there. I'm coming back for them. We having a bake sale at the church tomorrow.

(Rose exits the yard. Troy sits down on the steps, takes a pint bottle from his pocket, opens it and drinks. He begins to sing.)

TROY:
   Hear it ring! Hear it ring!
   Had an old dog his name was Blue
   You know Blue was mighty true
   You know Blue was a good old dog
   Blue treed a possum in a hollow log
   You know from that he was a good old dog
      (Bono enters the yard.)

BONO: Hey, Troy.

1720 TROY: Hey, what's happening, Bono?

BONO: I just thought I'd stop by to see you.

TROY: What you stop by and see me for? You ain't stopped by in a month of Sundays. Hell, I must owe you money or something.

BONO: Since you got your promotion I can't keep up with you. Used to see you every day. Now I don't even know what route you working.

TROY: They keep switching me around. Got me out in Greentree now . . . hauling white folks' garbage.

BONO: Greentree, huh? You lucky, at least you ain't got to be lifting them barrels. Damn if they ain't getting heavier. I'm gonna put in
1730   my two years and call it quits.

TROY: I'm thinking about retiring myself.

BONO: You got it easy. You can *drive* for another five years.

TROY: It ain't the same, Bono. It ain't like working the back of the truck. Ain't got nobody to talk to . . . feel like you working by yourself. Naw, I'm thinking about retiring. How's Lucille?

BONO: She all right. Her arthritis get to acting up on her sometime. Saw Rose on my way in. She going down to the church, huh?

TROY: Yeah, she took up going down there. All them preachers looking for somebody to fatten their pockets. *(Pause.)* Got some gin here.

1740 BONO: Naw, thanks. I just stopped by to say hello.

TROY: Hell, nigger . . . you can take a drink. I ain't never known you to say no to a drink. You ain't got to work tomorrow.

BONO: I just stopped by. I'm fixing to go over to Skinner's. We got us a domino game going over his house every Friday.

TROY: Nigger, you can't play no dominoes. I used to whup you four games out of five.

BONO: Well, that learned me. I'm getting better.

TROY: Yeah? Well, that's all right.

BONO: Look here . . . I got to be getting on. Stop by sometime, huh?

1750 TROY: Yeah, I'll do that, Bono. Lucille told Rose you bought her a new refrigerator.

BONO: Yeah, Rose told Lucille you had finally built your fence . . . so I figured we'd call it even.

TROY: I knew you would.

BONO: Yeah . . . okay. I'll be talking to you.

TROY: Yeah, take care, Bono. Good to see you. I'm gonna stop over.

BONO: Yeah. Okay, Troy.

(Bono exits. Troy drinks from the bottle.)

TROY:

> Old Blue died and I dig his grave
> Let him down with a golden chain
1760 > Every night when I hear old Blue bark
> I know Blue treed a possum in Noah's Ark.
> Hear it ring! Hear it ring!

(Cory enters the yard. They eye each other for a beat. Troy is sitting in the middle of the steps. Cory walks over.)

CORY: I got to get by.

TROY: Say what? What's you say?

CORY: You in my way. I got to get by.

TROY: You got to get by where? This is my house. Bought and paid for. Took me fifteen years. And if you wanna go in my house and I'm sitting on the steps . . . you say excuse me. Like your mama taught you.

CORY: Come on, Pop . . . I got to get by.

(Cory starts to maneuver his way past Troy. Troy grabs his leg and shoves him back.)

1770 TROY: You just gonna walk over top of me?

CORY: I live here, too!

TROY *(advancing toward him):* You just gonna walk over top of me in my own house?

CORY: I ain't scared of you.

TROY: I ain't asked if you was scared of me. I asked you if you was fixing to walk over top of me in my own house? That's the question. You ain't gonna say excuse me? You just gonna walk over top of me?

CORY: If you wanna put it like that.

TROY: How else am I gonna put it?

1780 CORY: I was walking by you to go into the house cause you sitting on the steps drunk, singing to yourself. You can put it like that.

TROY: Without saying excuse me???

(Cory doesn't respond.)

I asked you a question. Without saying excuse me???

CORY: I ain't got to say excuse me to you. You don't count around here no more.

TROY: Oh, I see . . . I don't count around here no more. You ain't got to say excuse me to your daddy. All of a sudden you done got so grown that your daddy don't count around here no more . . . Around here in his own house and yard that he done paid for with the sweat of his 1790 brow. You done got so grown to where you gonna take over. You gonna take over my house. Is that right? You gonna wear my pants. You gonna go in there and stretch out on my bed. You ain't got to say excuse me cause I don't count around here no more. Is that right?

CORY: That's right. You always talking this dumb stuff. Now, why don't you just get out my way.

TROY: I guess you got someplace to sleep and something to put in your belly. You got that, huh? You got that? That's what you need. You got that, huh?

CORY: You don't know what I got. You ain't got to worry about what I got.

1800 TROY: You right! You one hundred percent right! I done spent the last seventeen years worrying about what you got. Now it's your turn, see? I'll tell you what to do. You grown . . . we done established that. You a man. Now, let's see you act like one. Turn your behind around and walk out this yard. And when you get out there in the alley . . . you can forget about this house. See? Cause this is my house. You go on and be a man and get your own house. You can forget about this. Cause this is mine. You go on and get yours cause I'm through with doing for you.

CORY: You talking about what you did for me . . . what'd you ever give me?

1810 TROY:Them feet and bones! That pumping heart, nigger! I give you more than anybody else is ever gonna give you.

CORY: You ain't never gave me nothing! You ain't never done nothing but hold me back. Afraid I was gonna be better than you. All you ever did was try and make me scared of you. I used to tremble every time you called my name. Every time I heard your footsteps in the house. Wondering all the time . . . what's Papa gonna say if I do this? . . . What's he gonna say if I do that? . . . What's Papa gonna say if I turn on the radio? And Mama, too . . . she tries . . . but she's scared of you.

1820 TROY: You leave your mama out of this. She ain't got nothing to do with this.

CORY: I don't know how she stands you . . . after what you did to her.

TROY: I told you to leave your mama out of this!

(He advances toward Cory.)

CORY: What you gonna do . . . give me a whupping? You can't whup me no more. You're too old. You just an old man.

TROY *(shoves him on his shoulder):* Nigger! That's what you are. You just another nigger on the street to me!

CORY: You crazy! You know that?

TROY: Go on now! You got the devil in you. Get on away from me!

1830 CORY: You just a crazy old man . . . talking about I got the devil in me.

TROY: Yeah, I'm crazy! If you don't get on the other side of that yard . . . I'm gonna show you how crazy I am! Go on . . . get the hell out of my yard.

CORY: It ain't your yard. You took Uncle Gabe's money he got from the army to buy this house and then you put him out.

TROY *(advances on Cory):* Get your black ass out of my yard!

(Troy's advance backs Cory up against the tree. Cory grabs up the bat.)

CORY: I ain't going nowhere! Come on . . . put me out! I ain't scared of you.

TROY: That's my bat!

1840 CORY: Come on!

TROY: Put my bat down!

CORY: Come on, put me out.

(Cory swings at Troy, who backs across the yard.)

What's the matter? You so bad . . . put me out!

(Troy advances toward Cory.)

CORY *(backing up):* Come on! Come on!

TROY: You're gonna have to use it! You wanna draw that bat back on me . . . you're gonna have to use it.

CORY: Come on! . . . Come on!

(Cory swings the bat at Troy a second time. He misses. Troy continues to advance toward him.)

TROY: You're gonna have to kill me! You wanna draw that bat back on me. You're gonna have to kill me.

(Cory, backed up against the tree, can go no farther. Troy taunts him. He sticks out his head and offers him a target.)

1850   Come on! Come on!

(Cory is unable to swing the bat. Troy grabs it.)

TROY: Then I'll show you.

(Cory and Troy struggle over the bat. The struggle is fierce and fully engaged. Troy ultimately is the stronger, and takes the bat from Cory and stands over him ready to swing. He stops himself.)

Go on and get away from around my house.

(Cory, stung by his defeat, picks himself up, walks slowly out of the yard and up the alley.)

CORY: Tell Mama I'll be back for my things.

TROY: They'll be on the other side of that fence.

(Cory exits.)

TROY: I can't taste nothing. Helluljah! I can't taste nothing no more.

(Troy assumes a batting posture and begins to taunt Death, the fastball in the outside corner.) Come on! It's between you and me now! Come on! Anytime you want! Come on! I be ready for you . . . but I ain't gonna be easy.

(The lights go down on the scene.)

SCENE 5

The time is 1965. The lights come up in the yard. It is the morning of Troy's funeral. A funeral plaque with a light hangs beside the door. There is a small garden plot off to the side. There is noise and activity in the house as Rose, Lyons, and Bono have gathered. The door opens and Raynell, seven years old, enters dressed in a flannel nightgown. She crosses to the garden and pokes around with a stick. Rose calls from the house.

ROSE: Raynell!
RAYNELL: Mam?
ROSE: What you doing out there?
RAYNELL: Nothing.

(Rose comes to the door.)

1860 ROSE: Girl, get in here and get dressed. What you doing?
RAYNELL: Seeing if my garden growed.
ROSE: I told you it ain't gonna grow overnight. You got to wait.
RAYNELL: It don't look like it never gonna grow. Dag!
ROSE: I told you a watched pot never boils. Get in here and get dressed.
RAYNELL: This ain't even no pot, Mama.
ROSE: You just have to give it a chance. It'll grow. Now you come on and
do what I told you. We got to be getting ready. This ain't no morning
to be playing around. You hear me?
RAYNELL: Yes, Mam.

*(Rose exits into the house. Raynell continues to poke at her garden with a
stick. Cory enters. He is dressed in a Marine corporal's uniform, and carries
a duffel bag. His posture is that of a military man, and his speech has a
clipped sternness.)*

1870 CORY *(to Raynell):* Hi. *(Pause.)* I bet your name is Raynell.
RAYNELL: Uh huh.
CORY: Is your mama home?

(Raynell runs up on the porch and calls through the screen door.)

RAYNELL: Mama . . . there's some man out here. Mama?

(Rose comes to the door.)

ROSE: Cory? Lord have mercy! Look here, you all!

*(Rose and Cory embrace in a tearful reunion as Bono and Lyons enter from the
house dressed in funeral clothes.)*

BONO: Aw, looka here . . .
ROSE: Done got all grown up!
CORY: Don't cry, Mama. What you crying about?
ROSE: I'm just so glad you made it.
CORY: Hey, Lyons. How you doing, Mr. Bono.

(Lyons goes to embrace Cory.)

1880 LYONS: Look at you, man. Look at you. Don't he look good, Rose? Got
them Corporal stripes.
ROSE: What took you so long?
CORY: You know how the Marines are, Mama. They got to get all their
paperwork straight before they let you do anything.

ROSE: Well, I'm sure glad you made it. They let Lyons come. Your Uncle Gabe's still in the hospital. They don't know if they gonna let him out or not. I just talked to them a little while ago.

LYONS: A Corporal in the United States Marines.

BONO: Your daddy knew you had it in you. He used to tell me all the time.

1890   LYONS: Don't he look good, Mr. Bono?

BONO: Yeah, he remind me of Troy when I first met him. *(Pause.)* Say, Rose, Lucille's down at the church with the choir. I'm gonna go down and get the pallbearers lined up. I'll be back to get you all.

ROSE: Thanks, Jim.

CORY: See you, Mr. Bono.

LYONS *(with his arm around Raynell):* Cory . . . look at Raynell. Ain't she precious? She gonna break a whole lot of hearts.

ROSE: Raynell, come and say hello to your brother. This is your brother, Cory. You remember Cory.

1900   RAYNELL: No, Mam.

CORY: She don't remember me, Mama.

ROSE: Well, we talk about you. She heard us talk about you. *(To Raynell):* This is your brother, Cory. Come on and say hello.

RAYNELL: Hi.

CORY: Hi. So you're Raynell. Mama told me a lot about you.

ROSE: You all come on into the house and let me fix you some breakfast. Keep up your strength.

CORY: I ain't hungry, Mama.

LYONS: You can fix me something, Rose. I'll be in there in a minute.

1910   ROSE: Cory, you sure you don't want nothing? I know they ain't feeding you right.

CORY: No, Mama . . . thanks. I don't feel like eating. I'll get something later.

ROSE: Raynell . . . get on upstairs and get that dress on like I told you.

(Rose and Raynell exit into the house.)

LYONS: So . . . I hear you thinking about getting married.

CORY: Yeah, I done found the right one, Lyons. It's about time.

LYONS: Me and Bonnie been split up about four years now. About the time Papa retired. I guess she just got tired of all them changes I was putting her through. *(Pause.)* I always knew you was gonna make something out yourself. Your head was always in the right direction. So . . .

1920   you gonna stay in . . . make it a career . . . put in your twenty years?

CORY: I don't know. I got six already. I think that's enough.

LYONS: Stick with Uncle Sam and retire early. Ain't nothing out here. I guess Rose told you what happened with me. They got me down the workhouse. I thought I was being slick cashing other people's checks.

CORY: How much time you doing?

LYONS: They give me three years. I got that beat now. I ain't got but nine more months. It ain't so bad. You learn to deal with it like anything else. You got to take the crookeds with the straights. That's what Papa used to say. He used to say that when he struck out. I seen him

1930   strike out three times in a row . . . and the next time up he hit the
         ball over the grandstand. Right out there in Homestead Field. He
         wasn't satisfied hitting in the seats . . . he want to hit it over everything!
         After the game he had two hundred people standing around waiting
         to shake his hand. You got to take the crookeds with the straights.
         Yeah, Papa was something else.

CORY: You still playing?

LYONS: Cory . . . you know I'm gonna do that. There's some fellows
         down there we got us a band . . . we gonna try and stay together
         when we get out . . . but yeah, I'm still playing. It still helps me to get
1940   out of bed in the morning. As long as it do that I'm gonna be right
         there playing and trying to make some sense out of it.

ROSE *(calling):* Lyons, I got these eggs in the pan.

LYONS: Let me go on and get these eggs, man. Get ready to go bury
         Papa. *(Pause.)* How you doing? You doing all right?

         *(Cory nods. Lyons touches him on the shoulder and they share a moment of silent
         grief. Lyons exits into the house. Cory wanders about the yard. Raynell enters.)*

RAYNELL: Hi.

CORY: Hi.

RAYNELL: Did you used to sleep in my room?

CORY: Yeah . . . that used to be my room.

RAYNELL: That's what Papa call it. "Cory's room." It got your football in
1950   the closet.

         (Rose comes to the door.)

ROSE: Raynell, get in there and get them good shoes on.

RAYNELL: Mama, can't I wear these? Them other one hurt my feet.

ROSE: Well, they just gonna have to hurt your feet for a while. You ain't
         said they hurt your feet when you went down to the store and got
         them.

RAYNELL: They didn't hurt then. My feet done got bigger.

ROSE: Don't you give me no backtalk now. You get in there and get
         them shoes on. *(Raynell exits into the house.)* Ain't too much changed.
         He still got that piece of rag tied to that tree. He was out here swing-
1960   ing that bat. I was just ready to go back in the house. He swung that
         bat and then he just fell over. Seem like he swung it and stood there
         with this grin on his face . . . and then he just fell over. They carried
         him on down to the hospital, but I knew there wasn't no need . . .
         why don't you come on in the house?

CORY: Mama . . . I got something to tell you. I don't know how to tell you
         this . . . but I've got to tell you . . . I'm not going to Papa's funeral.

ROSE: Boy, hush your mouth. That's your daddy you talking about. I
         don't want hear that kind of talk this morning. I done raised you to
         come to this? You standing there all healthy and grown talking about
         you ain't going to your daddy's funeral?

1970 CORY: Mama . . . listen . . .

ROSE: I don't want to hear it, Cory. You just get that thought out of
   your head.

CORY: I can't drag Papa with me everywhere I go. I've got to say no to
   him. One time in my life I've got to say no.

ROSE: Don't nobody have to listen to nothing like that. I know you and
   your daddy ain't seen eye to eye, but I ain't got to listen to that kind
   of talk this morning. Whatever was between you and your daddy . . .
   the time has come to put it aside. Just take it and set it over there on
   the shelf and forget about it. Disrespecting your daddy ain't gonna
   make you a man, Cory. You got to find a way to come to that on your
   own. Not going to your daddy's funeral ain't gonna make you a man.

CORY: The whole time I was growing up . . . living in his house . . . Papa
   was like a shadow that followed you everywhere. It weighed on you
   and sunk into your flesh. It would wrap around you and lay there
   until you couldn't tell which one was you anymore. That shadow digging in your flesh. Trying to crawl in. Trying to live through you.
   Everywhere I looked, Troy Maxson was staring back at me . . . hiding
   under the bed . . . in the closet. I'm just saying I've got to find a way
   to get rid of that shadow, Mama.

ROSE: You just like him. You got him in you good.

CORY: Don't tell me that, Mama.

ROSE: You Troy Maxson all over again.

CORY: I don't want to be Troy Maxson. I want to be me.

ROSE: You can't be nobody but who you are, Cory. That shadow wasn't
   nothing but you growing into yourself. You either got to grow into it
   or cut it down to fit you. But that's all you got to make life with. That's
   all you got to measure yourself against that world out there. Your daddy
   wanted you to be everything he wasn't . . . and at the same time he
   tried to make you into everything he was. I don't know if he was right
   or wrong . . . but I do know he meant to do more good than he meant
   to do harm. He wasn't always right. Sometimes when he touched he
   bruised. And sometimes when he took me in his arms he cut.

   When I first met your daddy I thought . . . Here is a man I can lay
   down with and make a baby. That's the first thing I thought when
   I seen him. I was thirty years old and had done seen my share of men.
   But when he walked up to me and said, "I can dance a waltz that'll
   make you dizzy," I thought, Rose Lee, here is a man that you can
   open yourself up to and be filled to bursting. Here is a man that can
   fill all them empty spaces you been tipping around the edges of.
   One of them empty spaces was being somebody's mother.

   I married your daddy and settled down to cooking his supper and
   keeping clean sheets on the bed. When your daddy walked through
   the house he was so big he filled it up. That was my first mistake. Not
   to make him leave some room for me. For my part in the matter.
   But at that time I wanted that. I wanted a house that I could sing in.
   And that's what your daddy gave me. I didn't know to keep up his
   strength I had to give up little pieces of mine. I did that. I took on his

life as mine and mixed up the pieces so that you couldn't hardly tell which was which anymore. It was my choice. It was my life and I didn't have to live it like that. But that's what life offered me in the way of being a woman and I took it. I grabbed hold of it with both hands.

By the time Raynell came into the house, me and your daddy had done lost touch with one another. I didn't want to make my blessing off of nobody's misfortune . . . but I took on to Raynell like she was all them babies I had wanted and never had. *(The phone rings.)* Like I'd been blessed to relive a part of my life. And if the Lord see fit to keep up my strength . . . I'm gonna do her just like your daddy did you . . . I'm gonna give her the best of what's in me.

RAYNELL *(entering, still with her old shoes):* Mama . . . Reverend Tollivier on the phone.

(Rose exits into the house.)

RAYNELL: Hi.

CORY: Hi.

RAYNELL: You in the Army or the Marines?

CORY: Marines.

RAYNELL: Papa said it was the Army. Did you know Blue?

CORY: Blue? Who's Blue?

RAYNELL: Papa's dog what he sing about all the time.

CORY *(singing):*
　　Hear it ring! Hear it ring!
　　I had a dog his name was Blue
　　You know Blue was mighty true
　　You know Blue was a good old dog
　　Blue treed a possum in a hollow log
　　You know from that he was a good old dog.
　　Hear it ring! Hear it ring!

(Raynell joins in singing.)

CORY AND RAYNELL:
　　Blue treed a possum out on a limb
　　Blue looked at me and I looked at him
　　Grabbed that possum and put him in a sack
　　Blue stayed there till I came back
　　Old Blue's feets was big and round
　　Never allowed a possum to touch the ground.
　　Old Blue died and I dug his grave
　　I dug his grave with a silver spade
　　Let him down with a golden chain
　　And every night I call his name
　　Go on Blue, you good dog you
　　Go on Blue, you good dog you.

RAYNELL:
　　Blue laid down and died like a man
　　Blue laid down and died . . .

2060 BOTH:
>   Blue laid down and died like a man
>   Now he's treeing possums in the Promised Land
>   I'm gonna tell you this to let you know
>   Blue's gone where the good dogs go
>   When I hear old Blue bark
>   When I hear old Blue bark
>   Blue treed a possum in Noah's Ark
>   Blue treed a possum in Noah's Ark.

(Rose comes to the screen door.)

ROSE: Cory, we gonna be ready to go in a minute.
CORY *(to Raynell):* You go on in the house and change them shoes like
2070   Mama told you so we can go to Papa's funeral.
RAYNELL: Okay, I'll be back.

(Raynell exits into the house. Cory gets up and crosses over to the tree. Rose stands in the screen door watching him. Gabriel enters from the alley.)

GABRIEL *(calling):* Hey, Rose!
ROSE: Gabe?
GABRIEL: I'm here, Rose. Hey Rose, I'm here!

(Rose enters from the house.)

ROSE: Lord . . . Look here, Lyons!
LYONS: See, I told you, Rose . . . I told you they'd let him come.
CORY: How you doing, Uncle Gabe?
LYONS: How you doing, Uncle Gabe?
GABRIEL: Hey, Rose. It's time. It's time to tell St. Peter to open the gates.
2080   Troy, you ready? You ready, Troy. I'm gonna tell St. Peter to open the
gates. You get ready now.

(Gabriel, with great fanfare, braces himself to blow. The trumpet is without a mouthpiece. He puts the end of it into his mouth and blows with great force, like a man who has been waiting some twenty-odd years for this single moment. No sound comes out of the trumpet. He braces himself and blows again with the same result. A third time he blows. There is a weight of impossible description that falls away and leaves him bare and exposed to a frightful realization. It is a trauma that a sane and normal mind would be unable to withstand. He begins to dance. A slow, strange dance, eerie and life-giving. A dance of atavistic signature and ritual. Lyons attempts to embrace him. Gabriel pushes Lyons away. He begins to howl in what is an attempt at song, or perhaps a song turning back into itself in an attempt at speech. He finishes his dance and the gates of heaven stand open as wide as God's closet.)

That's the way that go!

Blackout

Questions for Discussion

Act I

Scene 1

1. In the introduction, Wilson describes Troy as "a large man with thick, heavy hands" and says it is "this largeness that he strives to fill out and make an accommodation with. Together with his blackness, his largeness informs his sensibilities and the choices he has made in his life." After you have read the play, interpret this description.

2. Why does Rose shop at the A&P and Troy at Bella's? Why are the prices at Bella's higher?

3. Rose tells Troy that "Times have changed since you was playing baseball." Why is he not comforted by this fact?

4. Troy says, "Death ain't nothing but a fastball on the outside corner." Explain what he means by this baseball imagery.

5. What does Troy's story about wrestling with death reveal about his attitude toward life?

6. Why does Troy call the man who gave him credit to buy furniture the devil? Explain similar financial practices that exist today.

7. Lyons says that he cannot find a job. What would be a more accurate statement about his situation? Why does Troy hassle him before giving him money?

8. Explain Lyons's statement to Troy: "You and me is two different people."

Scene 2

1. Compare Rose's and Troy's attitudes toward gambling.

2. Explain Troy's treatment of Gabriel.

Scene 3

1. What does Cory view as his two primary jobs? What does Troy believe Cory's responsibilities should be?

2. Troy asks Cory, "What law is there I got to like you?" What does this question reveal about Troy's concept of fatherhood?

3. Explain Troy's statement to Rose at the end of scene 3.

Scene 4

1. Why does Troy, who cannot read and has no driver's license, want to drive the garbage truck?

2. Gabriel's severance money, which he received as a result of his injury while fighting for his country, pays for the house Troy lives in. Why, then, does Gabriel want to live at Miss Pearl's, where he has to pay rent?

3. Both Rose and Lyons tell Troy that Cory is trying to live up to Troy's example. Why does this assertion not please Troy?

4. Describe Troy's father's behavior. In what ways has his experience with his father influenced Troy's behavior toward Lyons and Cory?

5. What does Lyons's comment that Troy's father "should have just went on and left when he saw he couldn't get nowhere" reveal about Lyons's attitude toward responsibility?

6. Why does Troy sabotage Cory's chances to play football?

7. Explain Troy's comment to Cory at the end of Act 1.

Act 2

Scene 1

1. How and why do Troy's and Rose's opinions about Gabriel's being institutionalized differ?

2. In what way does Troy's statement that the situation with Alberta "starts out like a little bush . . . and the next thing you know it's a whole forest" contradict his other statements about personal responsibility?

3. Explain Troy's statement that at Alberta's "I can . . . get away from the pressures and problems . . . and be a different man. . . . I can just be a part of myself that ain't never been."

4. Interpret the baseball analogy with which Troy tries to explain why he has been unfaithful to Rose.

5. Explain Rose's analogy about the seed.

Scene 2

1. Explain Rose's statement to Troy that "You did Gabe just like you did Cory. You wouldn't sign the paper for Cory . . . but you signed for Gabe." Why did Troy sign Gabriel's commitment papers?

2. Why, after Alberta's death, does Troy tell death that he is going to finish the fence?

Scene 3

1. Explain Rose's statement at the end of this scene: "From right now . . . this child got a mother. But you a womanless man."

Scene 4

1. Why does Cory threaten Troy with a baseball bat? Why does Troy drive his own son away from home?

Scene 5

1. Discuss the contrasting attitudes of Lyons and Cory about responsibility and their consequent adult roles.

2. Support or argue against Cory's statement that his father was "trying to live through" him when Cory was growing up and Rose's answer that "Your daddy wanted you to be everything he wasn't . . . and at the same time he tried to make you into everything he was."

3. Analyze Rose's explanation of her marriage to Troy.

4. Troy sings a favorite song, "Old Blue," when he is drinking, and Raynell and Cory sing "Old Blue" at the end of the play. What is the significance of this song?

THE DRAMATIC VISION OF AUGUST WILSON[1]

SANDRA SHANNON

According to Wilson, he began *Fences* "with the image of a man standing in his yard with a baby in his arms" (DeVries 25). From the play's inception, he was aware of the amount of dramatic leverage provided by this visually powerful image, born of his desire to prove that, contrary to myth, black men are responsible: "We have been told so many times how irresponsible we are as black males that I try and present positive images of responsibility" (25). But Troy appears not to pose much of a challenge to this myth. Although he heroically acknowledges the infant as his own— "She's my daughter, Rose. My own flesh and blood" (*F* 79)—his idea of responsibility is seen in his decision to hand over the child to someone who apparently is more responsible than he. Indeed, Wilson's perspective on responsibility might appear dubious to those unfamiliar with his decidedly male ethos, which he links to the history of black male-female relations in America. In an interview with Mark Rocha, Wilson states:

> You've got to understand the sociology of it. The transition from slavery to freedom was a cultural shock for blacks. All of a sudden black men had to ask themselves things like, "What is money?" "What is marriage?" Black women, for all their own struggles, were relatively stable. Economicially, they had control of the house. But what were black men supposed to do to make a living? (Rocha 38).

Still, for Wilson or any member of an audience to view Troy's actions as "responsible" depends on focusing not on the responsibility of the distraught middle-aged garbageman for the entire situation but on his responsibility in honoring his daughter and ultimately facing the evils of his own making. That he does not simply flee apparently saves him from the total damnation heaped upon so many black men caught in similar dilemmas.

Troy's entertaining anecdotes and searing monologues only seem incongruous with his station in life: in fact, language has become his most effective defense against victimization. That his own father was essentially a failure and a victim of the ruthless tenant farming system rests heavily upon Troy, for, as a young boy, he witnessed firsthand his father's destruction: "Sometimes I use to wonder why he was living. . . . He ain't knew how to do nothing but farm. No, he was trapped and I think he knew it" (*F* 51). Unfortunately, Troy's predicament is not very far removed from the bleak conditions that doomed his father—a dead-end job and no chance for a better life. Still, Troy's words portray him as the ultimate warrior, even though circumstances suggest otherwise. Expansive rhetoric justifies his wrongdoing, appeases his family, and apparently soothes his conscience.

[1]Sandra G. Shannon, *The Dramatic Vision of August Wilson* (Washington, DC: Howard UP, 1995), 103–17. Parenthetical references to play are pages from the New American Library edition.

Troy's fondness for talk is grounded in the African American oral tradition not yet affected by the cultural shock that followed the invention of the television and the spread of modern audiovisual devices. In fact, the Maxsons do not own a television set, and, as Troy explains to Cory, patching their leaky roof will most certainly take precedence over purchasing an electronic gadget. In the absence of such diversions, verbal communication becomes an art form for Troy. Rarely does he spare words when he has an opportunity to dominate center stage. When Rose cautions him against consuming too much liquor, he launches into a speech on death based upon a series of metaphors that provide a window to his character. By invoking the rules of baseball, he familiarizes death's power: "Death ain't nothing but a fastball on an outside corner" (10). By borrowing images from the military, he acknowledges and, to some extent, admires death's persistence: "I looked up one day and Death was marching straight at me. The middle of July, 1941" (11). And by alluding to wrestling, he suggests that he, as if heeding the speaker of Dylan Thomas's poem, will not "go gentle into that good night": "We wrestled for three days and three nights. I can't say where I found the strength from. Every time it seemed like he was gonna get the best of me, I'd reach way down deep inside myself and find the strength to do him one better" (12).

In addition to being a master at metaphors, Troy is skilled at using language to deflect attention from his faults. One of the most dramatically poignant moments in *Fences* occurs when Troy scrambles to find suitable words to explain to his wife of eighteen years that he has fathered a child with another woman: "I'm trying to find a way to tell you . . . I'm gonna be a daddy. I'm gonna be somebody's daddy" (66). He is moving as he justifies his relationship with Alberta, the "other woman": "I can sit up in her house and laugh. Do you understand what I'm saying. I can laugh . . . and it feels good. It reaches all the way down to the bottom of my shoes" (69). He even succeeds at presenting a convincing plea to Rose to take in and raise his orphaned daughter as her own. Apparently language creates a larger-than-life reality for Troy. In each of these situations, Troy's words redirect any feelings of guilt away from himself. He seems free from remorse and actually appears heroic against all charges while a less eloquent man might appear villainous.

Like all of Wilson's plays to date, *Fences* is very much a black man's story. Black women do have appreciable roles in his dramas; however, they seldom are as developed as the men, who freely commune with other black men, whether in a dingy bandroom, on a back porch stoop, at a kitchen table, or in a one-room cafe. Wilson's sharply drawn male characters are, no doubt, also the result of his early devotion to listening to their conversations in the barrooms and tobacco houses of Pittsburgh. As a young, inexperienced poet who admitted that his verse suffered because he knew nothing of the world, he unconsciously absorbed the larger-than-life narratives of these storytellers. Also, deep within the psyche of young Wilson was (and still is) an urge to search for and create the image of a father he never had, one who would fill his son's head with his wisdom and guide him toward a responsible adulthood. As evidenced by Troy, Wilson assembles from the variety of black men that he has encountered a paternal image—by no means angelic, but an image of a father nonetheless.

Regardless of the process behind Wilson's depictions of his characters, the women's realities are decidedly different from those of the men around them and are limited to those possibilities sustained and promoted by Western culture. Critic and novelist Marilyn French sees a general dualism in the portrayal of women: "This split in principle of nature, the feminine principle, still exists in our perception of actual women; there is the mother madonna, and the whore; the nourisher and the castrator. This split in the feminine principle I call inlaw and outlaw aspects of it" (23). According to French, the outlaw is described in terms of "darkness, chaos, flesh, the sinister, magic and above all, sexuality," while the inlaw suggests completely different values: "nutritiveness, compassion, mercy, and the ability to create felicity" (24).

These two categories can be usefully applied to the women in *Fences*. Consider Troy's mistress Alberta as an "outlaw": she disrupts the Maxson family circle, sundering relationships between husband and wife and father and son as well as the deeply fraternal bond between Troy and Bono. She represents everything that sticks its tongue out at the responsibility that Troy faces as a family man and as head of the household. She demands nothing of him—not his loyalty, not his money, not even his time. She provides a haven from the chronic concerns of survival weighing down upon the frustrated garbage collector and would-be Major Leaguer, a place where he can simply laugh out loud. Nevertheless, Alberta is not blamed as the "whore," though she is the key to the disintegration of the Maxson family and ultimately to Troy's tragic demise. When Rose finally does learn about Troy's affair, her fury is directed solely at her husband as a willing party, not at Alberta as his temptress. Never physically appearing in the play, known only through conversations about her, Alberta becomes merely a manifestation of Troy's own flawed character.

While the outlaw Alberta appeals to Troy's hedonistic nature, the "inlaw" Rose reminds him of responsibility. She manages the home, wrestles with daily worries over money, and single-handedly tries to keep the Maxson family together. She does all of this while willfully neglecting to establish time and space for her own growth. As her name suggests, Rose thrives amid adversity and stands out from the moral squalor around her. While few might be expected to withstand the amount of humiliation she endures, Rose seems to thrive upon it; she is able to transform a motherless infant into a stable young girl and pull the loose threads of her family together at the play's end.

Rose Maxson lingers half in the shadows during the entire first act of *Fences*, speaking largely in reaction to her husband's exaggerated stories about himself. However, when she finally discovers her voice, she is convincing even as her character transforms. Though before she was the predictable image of temperance, she suddenly becomes a woman who stands eye-to-eye with her egoistic husband: "I been standing with you! I been right here with you, Troy. I got a life too. I gave eighteen years of my life to stand in the same spot with you. Don't you think I ever wanted other things? Don't you think I had dreams and hopes?" (70–71). In one impassioned scene, Rose's entire history rushes forward out of nearly two decades of dormancy. Yet this moment of revelation does not lessen Rose Maxson's extreme altruism. She is so thoroughly and persistently moral that her character becomes more obviously symbolic than realistic. She is her husband's conscience, quite literally his better half. Like Alberta, she is basically an extension of Troy's ego, not one whose own story requires a full hearing. Her eighteen-year suppression of self and allegiance to family perfectly match the mold of the inlaw, for as French describes it, the inlaw prototype "requires volitional subordination[;] . . . it values above all the good of the whole . . . and finds pleasure in that good rather than in assertion of self" (24).

Wilson's symbolic depictions of black women such as Rose have their basis in his capabilities as a poet. Also a by-product of his grounding in poetry is a conscious tendency to incorporate powerful metaphors to communicate his plays' larger thematic concerns. He believes this to be an important part of his strength as a dramatist: "The idea of metaphor . . . is a very large idea in my plays and something that I find lacking in most other contemporary plays. . . . I think I write the kinds of plays that I do because I have twenty-six years of writing poetry underneath all that" (interview).

The title image of *Fences*, the third play in Wilson's black history chronicle, very appropriately conveys a number of realities for the black family of late '50s America. It raises issues ranging from economic and professional deprivation to emotional and moral isolation. The fence, which may either inhibit or protect, is both a positive and negative image to various members of the Maxson family. To Rose, who nags Troy about completing this wooden border, the fence promises to keep in those whom she loves, preventing them from leaving the fortress she so lovingly sustains for them. To Cory, however, the fence becomes a tangible symbol of all that stands in the way of his independence. His work on it is merely an exercise in obedience and a reminder that he is not yet a man—at least not to Troy. To Troy, the fence represents added restrictions placed upon him. Thus he half-heartedly erects one section of the fence at a time and completes the job only after accepting a challenge from Bono, who agrees to buy his wife, Lucille, a refrigerator as soon as Troy completes the fence. It takes Bono to explain to him the importance of the fence:

CORY: I don't know why Mama want a fence around the yard noways.
TROY: Damn if I know either. What the hell she keeping out with it? She
ain't got nothing nobody want.

BONO: Some people build fences to keep people out . . . and other people build fences to keep people in. Rose wants to hold on to you all. She loves you. (*F* 61)

On a deeper level, Troy sees the fence's completion as a reminder of his own mortality; he senses that he is erecting his own monument. His anxiety about death's inevitability emerges when his longtime friend questions Troy's choice of wood:

BONO: You don't need this wood [hard wood]. You can put it up with pine wood and it'll stand as long as you gonna be here looking at it.

TROY: How you know how long I'm gonna be here, nigger? Hell, I might just live forever. Live longer than old man Horsely. (60)

Troy's reluctance to complete the fence seems ominous, for shortly after finishing it for Rose, he dies. The fence, then, becomes a gauge for his life, during which he experiences both literal and figurative incarceration. He is fenced off from society during a lengthy prison term; he is fenced out of the Major Leagues because of racial segregation; and after he initiates the breakup of his family, he is fenced out of his home as well as out of the hearts of Rose and Cory.

Other metaphors that the poet-turned-playwright effectively weaves throughout *Fences* adopt their imagery from the game of baseball. Images of the game loom large in the consciousness of the onetime Negro Leaguer, Troy, who often borrows the behavioral codes of this game to suit various situations in his life. Part of the tragedy of *Fences* is Troy's belief that he would have surpassed current black players and the white Major League players of his youth had he been allowed to play among them. His ego and professional potential have been devastated because he has been cheated out of at least a chance to play Major League ball. As an outward manifestation of the blues he surely feels because of this loss, Troy adopts the language of the game in order to explain the "deprivation of possibility" (Reed 93) that has hurt him so deeply.

For Troy, life is a baseball game riddled with fast balls, curve balls, sacrifice flies, and an occasional strikeout, but too few homeruns. Although the conflict of the ball game lasts for only nine innings, Troy sees himself as being constantly at bat. From keeping death at bay to announcing a "full count" against his defiant son Cory, Troy flavors his conversation with baseball metaphors at every chance he gets. The various rules of the game become his basis for interpreting his actions and another avenue for expressing his blues. His preoccupation with images associated with the traditionally masculine, extremely competitive sport robs him of the candor necessary to handle the delicate relationships in his life. In one of the most intense moments of the play, Troy struggles to explain to his wife that he has not only been unfaithful to her but has also fathered a child outside of their marriage bed: "I fooled them, Rose. I bunted. When I found you and Cory and a halfway decent job . . . I was safe. Couldn't nothing touch me. I wasn't gonna strike out no more. . . . I stood on first base for eighteen years and I thought . . . well, goddamn it . . . go on for it!" (*F* 70). In using this second language, Troy comes to live it. He completely alienates both his son and his wife by forcing upon them his very selfish view of life. Consequently, he cannot see past immediate self-gratification; he cannot compromise, nor can he ask for forgiveness.

Wilson's use of metaphor in *Fences* extends to include Gabriel, Troy's disabled brother. Gabriel's war injury, a severe head wound, required that a metal plate be surgically implanted in his head. The brain-damaged Gabriel fantasizes that he is Archangel Gabriel, whose tasks are to open Heaven's pearly gates and to chase away hellhounds. When Troy is certain of Gabriel's irreversible condition, he claims the $3,000 compensation awarded his brother and uses it to purchase the home where he, Rose, Cory, and Gabriel live.

Gabriel is what Wilson refers to as a "spectacle character" (interview) whose role, as its label suggests, is to command attention and to force both acknowledgment and understanding of issues that are sooner ignored. Here, he serves as a glaring reminder of the crippling injustices black men endure at the hands of their own country. Wilson notes, "This black man had suffered this wound fighting for a country in which his brother could not play baseball." America cannot hide the shame of thousands of black veterans like Gabriel, who sacrificed dearly in the service of their country yet possibly faced homelessness, prison, or the insane asylum upon their return. Gabriel's payment of $3,000 is ludicrously low for an injury that has maimed him for life.

Although Gabriel is not crucial to the central conflict of *Fences,* his presence gives Troy another dimension. In addition to being an embarrassing emblem of America's darker side, Gabriel is also a manifestation of the worst in Troy. He exposes a man who has become immune to the emotions of self-pity and remorse; a man who, after capitalizing on his brother's misfortune, has him committed to a mental institution. Troy has become so devastated by his own deferred dreams that nothing, save pleasing himself, matters to him. He can sign papers to prevent his son from receiving free tuition as a football recruit; he can sign papers to put his brother away indefinitely. To Wilson, Gabriel has a significant function in *Fences,* and he is bothered by critics who dismiss this wounded man as a halfwit:

> They [critics] make me mad when I read the reviews and they would refer to Gabriel as an idiot. . . . Gabriel is one of those self-sufficient characters. He gets up and goes to work every day. He goes out and collects those discarded fruit and vegetables, but he's taking care of himself. He doesn't want Troy to take care of him. He moves out of Troy's house and lives down there and pays his rent to the extent that he is able. (interview)

Wilson plays upon the dramatic tension inherent in the spectacle of Gabriel's character, but he also relies upon this highly sensitive man to introduce an identifiable element of African American culture: belief in a spiritual world. Although Gabriel's perceptions of Christianity and images associated with the afterlife are apparently the results of his dementia, he articulates several myths that have their origins in traditional religious beliefs among African Americans. For example, he revives the myth of Saint Peter, so-called keeper of the pearly gates, and keeps alive the fear of Judgment Day: "Ain't gonna be too much of a battle when God get to waving that Judgment sword. But the people's gonna have a hell of a time trying to get into heaven if them gates ain't open" (*F* 47–48).

Gabriel also confirms the existence of a great Judgment Book in which Saint Peter records "everybody's name what was ever been born" (26). Gabriel, who believes he has already died and gone to Heaven, is a privileged soul, for, according to him, Saint Peter has allowed him to see both Troy and Rose's names recorded in the ledger. And, again, according to Gabriel, he sometimes relieves Saint Peter from the eternal task of guarding the pearly gates: "Did you know when I was in heaven . . . every morning me and St. Peter would sit down by the gate and eat some big fat biscuits? Oh, yeah! We had us a good time. We'd sit there and eat us them biscuits and then St. Peter would go off to sleep and tell me to wake him up when it's time to open the gates for the judgment" (26).

Each encounter with Gabriel convinces one to look beyond his surface disability and concentrate instead upon the spiritual and mythical worlds he creates and the realms of possibility that these worlds offer. Gabriel's ability to look beyond the literal is his own means of negotiating an indifferent world, yet it also exemplifies a long-standing Christian belief among African Americans to look toward things-not-seen for salvation. He has adopted both a frame of mind and a vision that get him through the daily drudgery of his condition. This special vision is most evident in the final scene of *Fences,* when the Maxson family prepares to bury Troy. At this time Gabriel experiences "a trauma that a sane and normal mind would be unable to withstand. He begins to dance. A slow, strange dance, eerie and life-giving. A dance of atavistic signature and ritual. . . . He finishes his dance and the gates of heaven stand open as wide as God's closet" (101). As a spectacle character, Gabriel's significance is in providing a flawed icon of African Americans' cultural past. He is a cultural paradox—not taken seriously by those around him yet conveying in his distorted sensibilities the cultural bedrock of generations past and to come.

Works Cited

De Vries, Hillary. "A Song in Search of Itself." *American Theater* January 1987, 22–25.

Reed, Ishmael. "In Search of August Wilson." *Connoisseur* 217 (March 1987): 92–97.

Rocha, Mark. "A Conversation with August Wilson." *Diversity: A Journal of Multicultural Issues* 1 (Spring 1993): 24–42.

Wilson, August. *Fences.* New York: New American Library, 1987.

✕

BOUNDARIES, LOGISTICS, AND IDENTITY: THE PROPERTY OF METAPHOR IN *FENCES* AND *JOE TURNER'S COME AND GONE*[1]

ALAN NADEL

In *Fences,* August Wilson [. . .] describes Troy Maxson's struggle to build a fence around his property. [. . .] A fifty-three-year-old garbageman who owns a small house in a run-down section of Pittsburgh, in 1957, Troy during the course of the play works at building a small fence around his meager back yard. At the same time, he works constantly to delineate his rights and responsibilities, as husband, brother, worker, friend, and father. His name, Maxson, suggests a shortened "Mason-Dixon,"[2] a personalized version of the national division over the properties of blackness. His character similarly embodies the personal divisions that come from living in a world where the Mason-Dixon line exists as the ubiquitous circumscription of black American claims to human rights.

Troy lives in a house with Rose, his wife of eighteen years, and their seventeen-year-old son, Cory. The down payment for the house came from the $3,000 his brother Gabriel received in compensation for a World War II head wound that left him a virtual half-wit, harboring the belief "with every fiber of his being that he is the Archangel Gabriel" (23). Troy takes pride at having housed and cared for Gabriel since the injury, and at the same time expresses shame at having had to rely on Gabriel's misfortune to provide the down payment he could never have acquired through years of honest labor. Having run away from a cruel and abusive father when he was a teenager, he found his way to the city, where he married and supported his family through theft until he was convicted of assault and armed robbery and sent to jail for fifteen years. There he learned to play baseball and give up robbery. By the time he was released, his wife having left him, he met Rose, remarried, and after playing baseball in the Negro Leagues, became a garbageman.

The central conflicts in the play arise from his refusal to let his son play football or accept a football scholarship to college, and from his having fathered a daughter through an extramarital affair. But these are framed

---

[1]Alan Nadel, "Boundaries, Logistics, and Identity: The Property of Metaphor in *Fences* and *Joe Turner's Come and Gone,*" *May All Your Fences Have Gates: Essays on the Drama of August Wilson,* ed. Alan Nadel (Iowa City: U of Iowa P, 1994), 86–95. Parenthetical page references are to the New American Library edition of *Fences.*

[2]In *Ma Rainey's Black Bottom,* in fact, Levee refers to it as the "Maxon-Dixon line" (82).

by conflicts with the father he fled, the major leagues that wouldn't let him play baseball, and Death himself, with whom Troy had once wrestled. Whatever else he loses, he vigilantly maintains his property and his property rights, demanding his authority within its confines, eventually building a fence around his yard and guarding the entrance with all of his human power against the force of Death, whose representation in human form is generally perceived to be metaphoric.

It is on these grounds—and on his home ground—that Troy chooses to be sized up. For in all other locales he is a large man who has been underestimated. As a baseball player and even as a garbageman, the world has not taken his measure. To "take the measure of a man" is to make a metaphor derived from a set of primary physical traits. "To measure up" means to fulfill a role in the same way one fills out a suit of clothes; "to take measure of oneself" means to assess one's ability to fill a specific role in the same way that one selects that suit of clothes. Implicit in all these metaphors is a set of objective physical standards— what Locke called primary characteristics—against which such intangibles as character, courage, loyalty, skill, or talent can be determined.

In the logistics of *Fences,* however, these standards form the variables measured against the standard of Troy Maxson's largeness. From the outset of the play, his size is a given: "Troy is fifty-three years old, a large man with thick heavy hands; it is this largeness that he strives to fill out and make an accommodation with. Together with his blackness, his largeness informs his sensibilities and the choices he has made in life" (1). And after his death, as Rose explains to Cory, "When I first met your daddy, . . . I thought here is a man you can open yourself up to and be filled to bursting. Here is a man that can fill all them empty spaces you been tipping around the edges of. . . .When your daddy walked through the house, he filled it up" (93). Cory perceived Troy as "a shadow that followed you everywhere. It weighed on you and sunk in your flesh. It would wrap around you and lay there until you couldn't tell which one was you any more" (93), but Rose argues that Cory is just like his father:

> That shadow wasn't nothing but you growing into yourself. You either got to grow into it or cut it down to fit you. But that's all you got to make life with. That's all you got to measure yourself against that world out there. Your daddy wanted you to be everything he wasn't . . . and at the same time he tried to make you into everything he was. (93)

In addition to establishing Troy's size as the standard, both negative and positive, Rose is setting that standard against the standards asserted by the dominant white culture. Cory, in other words, is being urged not to measure himself against Troy but to use Troy's size as a defense against the other, implicitly figurative, norms of "that world out there."

In so doing, Rose is asking him, in fact, to continue his father's quest. For the problem of the play can be seen as Troy's attempt to take measure of himself in a world that has denied him the external referents. His struggle is to act in the literal world in such a way as to become not just the literal but the figurative father, brother, husband, man he desires to be. The role of father is the most complex because he is the father of three children from three different women. The children, precisely seventeen years apart, represent Troy's paternal responsibilities to three successive generations of black children. As each of these children makes demands on him, he must measure up to his responsibilities, and for each generation he measures up differently.

When his older son, Lyons, a would-be musician, for example, regularly borrows money from him, Troy puts Lyons through a ritual of humiliation constructed out of the process of differentiating Lyons from himself: "I done learned my mistake and learned to do what's right by it. You still trying to get something for nothing. Life don't owe you nothing. You owe it to yourself." At issue here is not only Troy's sense of himself as role model but also his sense of himself as negative example. He is both the father to emulate and the father not to emulate: Lyons should be like Troy by not making Troy's mistake. This lesson has a double edge, though, because the earlier, error-ridden life that Troy has learned to reject included not only his criminal acts but also his marriage to Lyons's mother and his fathering of Lyons. At that point in his life, we later learn, he felt he was not ready to be a father or to accept the responsibilities of fatherhood. For Lyons to recognize Troy's mistakes, then, is for him to acknowledge the inappropriateness of his own existence.

Troy deals with his younger son, Cory, in the same way. Like Troy, Cory is a talented athlete. A superstar in the Negro baseball leagues, Troy was never given an opportunity to play in the white leagues. Believing that white America would never allow a black to be successful in professional sports, he refuses to allow his son to go to college on a football scholarship. Once again, he becomes what he sees as a positive example for his son by virtue of his ability to reject himself. In a completely self-contained economy, he becomes both the model of error and the model of correction.

In regard to sports, particularly, he does this by constructing a division between personal history and American history. An extraordinary baseball player whose talents are compared with those of Babe Ruth and Josh Gibson, Troy was unfortunately over forty years old when professional baseball was first integrated. Within the time frame of American history, as his friend Bono says, "Troy just come along too early" (9). Troy rejects Bono's opinion with a triple negative: "There ought not never have been no time called too early" (9). "I'm talking about," he explains, "if you could play ball then they ought to have let you play. Don't care what color you were. Come telling me I come along too early. If you could play, then they ought to have let you play" (9).

🍓

After the death in childbirth of his girlfriend [. . .] Troy issues his challenge to Death in terms of the wall he is constructing between himself and it:

> I'm gonna build me a fence around what belongs to me. And I want you to stay on the other side. See? You stay over there until you're ready for me. Then you come on. Bring your army. Bring your sickle. Bring your wrestling clothes. I ain't gonna fall down on my vigilance this time. You ain't gonna sneak up on me no more. When you ready for me . . . that's when you come around here. . . . Then we gonna find out what manner of man you are. . . . You stay on the other side of that fence until you ready for me.

This is the metaphoric fence constructed to complement the literal fence Rose had been requesting from the outset. When Death accepts Troy's challenge, he confirms Troy's mastery over the literal, his power to turn his property into the visible recognition of his human properties, such that his responsibilities to his family, his athletic prowess, and his physical presence confirm his ability to confront Death—and hence to construct his life—on his own terms. In his terms, as he stated earlier in the play, "Death ain't nothing but a fastball on the outside corner" (10). Rose's description of Troy's death confirms that terminology: "He was out there swinging that bat and then he just fell over. Seem like he swung it and stood there with this grin on his face . . . and then he just fell over" (91). The inference is not only that he had protected his family by striking a final blow at Death but, more significantly, that he was able to do so because Troy made Death come to him on Troy's terms. Although Troy's challenge may be seen as figurative, Death's accepting it makes it literal, and thus the man-to-man battle between Troy and Death becomes a literal fight and simultaneously affirms Troy's power to create a site—however small—in which the figurative becomes literal. The conversion not only reduces Death to a man but also affirms Troy's status as one.

Within the context of the play, moreover, Wilson affirms the literal status of that conversion by having Gabriel perform a similar feat. Released from the mental hospital in order to attend Troy's funeral, Gabriel arrives carrying his trumpet. Although it has no mouthpiece, he uses it to "tell St. Peter to open the gates" (99). After three attempts, with no sound coming from the trumpet, "he begins to dance. A slow, strange dance, eerie and life-giving. A dance of atavistic signature and ritual. He begins to howl in what is an attempt at song, or perhaps a song turning back into itself in an attempt at speech. He finishes his song and the gates of heaven stand open as wide as God's closet" (100).

Gabriel's ability to invert the literal and the figurative thus confirms our understanding of Troy's death, at the same time that it revises our understanding of Gabriel's marginality or "madness." For we can read his wound as a function of attributing literal power to such figurative institutions as nation and warfare. As a soldier in World War II, he invested his primary literal claim to human rights—his human life—in support of a figurative structure—the United States—that on the very site of his investment, the segregated armed forces, denied the status of that life as human. One can only assume that the part of his brain blown away in the war contained the beliefs and conceptions that allowed him to accept the figurative status of his own humanity. Lacking that part of his brain, he is not functional within the dominant white culture, as is evidenced by his numerous arrests as well as his institutionalizations.

The Mason-Dixon line, marking off the site where he may consider himself literally human, has become for Gabriel the walls of the mental institution. By the end of the play—providing a virtual survey of the institutionalized power critiqued by Michel Foucault—all the Maxsons are disciplined within figurative Mason-Dixon lines. With Gabriel in the mental hospital, Cory in the armed services, Lyons in prison (we could conceivably even add Rose's recent involvement with the church), they find only this moment of relief within the boundary of the fence that Troy built. In the play's final pronouncement, with Gabriel speaking now as prophet and miracle worker rather than as marginalized madman, he asserts and demonstrates that the order of things—the relationship of figurative to literal—should be reversed: "And that's the way that go!" (100).

This is a tactical victory, a method of subverting and resisting the strategic power of the dominant culture. For that culture has urged the black American man to flight with the implication that his humanity was the function of logistics; confined by sites that denied literal confirmation of that humanity, the culture has offered the promise of an elsewhere, a site where the literal and figurative reconfigure. To pursue that promise, to seek that site, often meant sacrificing familial responsibilities. Instead of pursuing that site at the expense of his family, Troy created it in order to protect them. As Rose, referring to the fence, noted to Cory: "Oh, that's been up there ever since Raynell wasn't but a wee little bitty old thing. Your daddy finally got around to putting that up to keep her in the yard" (91).

In this way, Troy fought not only Death, but also history. For the normative discourse of white American history, in 1957, was one of progress and assimilation. Textbooks promoted the idea of the melting pot and of upward mobility; historical films and dramas reinscribed the myth of the nuclear family; and despite the continued presence of Jim Crow laws, segregated schools and facilities, rampant denial of voter rights, and extensive discrimination in housing and employment, American history and, more important, its popularizations represented the United States as a land of equal opportunity, with liberty and justice for all. Those whose personal narratives failed to confirm this hegemonic discourse became invisible; as Ralph Ellison so dramatically illustrated in *Invisible Man,* they fell outside of history. Despairing of the possibility of altering dominant historical discourse, Troy devotes himself to reconfiguring the paternal patterns that compose his personal history.

In thus making himself both the positive and the negative model for his sons, he also makes his father a positive and a negative model. For unlike many men of his generation—Bono's father, for example—Troy's father refused to leave the family, however much he detested it. As Troy points out, "He felt a responsibility toward us. May be he ain't treated us the way I felt he should have, but without that responsibility he could have walked off and left us, made his own way" (49). In contrast, as Bono points out, "Back in those days what you talking about, niggers used to travel all over. They get up one day and see where the day ain't sitting right with them and they walk out their front door and just take on down one road or another and keep on walking. . . . Just walk on till you come to something else. Ain't you never heard of nobody having the walking blues?" (50–51).

Works Cited

Wilson, August. *Fences.* New York: New American Library, Plume, 1986.
——. *Ma Rainey's Black Bottom.* New York: New American Library, Plume, 1985.

FILLING THE TIME:
READING HISTORY IN THE DRAMA
OF AUGUST WILSON[1]

JOHN TIMPANE

In the prefatorial piece "The Play," Wilson locates *Fences* in a "big-city neighborhood" of an eastern industrial town—probably Pittsburgh—in 1957. In 1957, "the Milwaukee Braves won the World Series, and the hot winds of change that would make the sixties a turbulent, racing, dangerous, and provocative decade had not yet begun to blow full."[2] The year 1957, as Wilson does not mean us to forget, was the year of Little Rock,

---

[1] John Timpane, "Filling the Time: Reading History in the Drama of August Wilson," *May All Your Fences Have Gates: Essays on the Drama of August Wilson,* ed. Alan Nadel (Iowa City: U of Iowa P, 1994), 69–74. Parenthetical page numbers are from the Plume edition of *Fences.*

[2] Richards, Introduction, pp. vii, xviii.

when Eisenhower reluctantly ordered regular army paratroops to prevent interference with court-ordered racial integration at Little Rock Central High School. That was the year of H.R. 6127, the Civil Rights Act of 1957, passed after virulent debate and filibuster in the Senate. Texas, Tennessee, Delaware, Maryland, and other states were in the throes of court-ordered desegregation; Little Rock stood out because of the prospect that state and federal troops might face each other. The winds of change blew both hot and cold. The possibility of new positivities coexisted with the fact of ancient recalcitrance. Only three weeks before Little Rock, Ku Klux Klan members had castrated a black man outside of Zion, Alabama. And Louis "Satchmo" Armstrong, in a public gesture that attracted both widespread praise and widespread blame, canceled a much-publicized tour of the USSR, saying that "the way they are treating my people in the South, the government can go to hell. . . . It's getting almost so bad, a colored man hasn't got any country."

In *Fences*, baseball operates metonymically, as a metaphoric stand-in for the troubled changes of 1957. Much of the action takes place just before the Milwaukee Braves' victory over the New York Yankees in the 1957 World Series. That victory signified a year of many changes in baseball, changes that reflected the social upheavals of 1957. One change, very much in progress, was the emergence of the black ballplayer. Black players had played prominent roles in previous World Series—Willie Mays in the 1954 series and Jackie Robinson in the Brooklyn Dodgers' victory over the Yankees in 1955. Milwaukee was the first non–New York team led by a black star to win a World Series. Hank Aaron, the most powerful hitter in baseball history, played alongside Eddie Mathews, white and a great slugger, and alongside three excellent white pitchers: Warren Spahn, Bob Buhl, and Lew Burdette. Because of the quick rise to prominence of Mays, Aaron, Roberto Clemente, and Frank Robinson, the question was no longer whether blacks would play but whether they could become leaders. As the success of the Braves portended, the answer was yes: Aaron led the league in power statistics, hit a home run on the last day of the season to give the Braves the pennant, rampaged through Yankee pitching to give his team the World Series, and won the National League Most Valuable Player Award for 1957.

Yet the Braves were far from being a truly integrated team, and integration was far from complete in baseball. Though blacks had been playing in the major leagues since 1947, it would take until 1959 for each major league team to have at least one black player. Behind the grudging, piecemeal process of integration in sports lies a Foucaultian "disjunction"—World War II—and a resultant "redistribution": the postwar move west. Hard times in postwar Boston meant dwindling patronage for the Boston Braves, so the team moved west to Milwaukee in 1953. In 1957, the Dodgers left Brooklyn for Los Angeles, and the New York

Giants left for San Francisco. In so doing, these teams mirrored an accelerating westward shift in the center of population. Further, the war probably created new social potential (to this day not completely realized) for women and blacks. For baseball, all this meant new teams, new audiences, and new pressures to tap at last the large pool of talented black players. The National League led in this regard. Indeed, it was not until Frank Robinson was traded from the Cincinnati Reds to the Baltimore Orioles and won the Triple Crown in 1966 that a black player dominated American League pitching the way Mays, Clemente, and Aaron had done in the National League.

Changes in baseball and changes in American life complicate the ability of anyone who, like Troy, bases his assumptions about reality on the facts of a prewar world. In the first scene of *Fences*, Troy pits his reading of things against those of Bono, Rose, and Lyons. Troy intersperses lies with truths, claiming he has seen and contended with Death and the devil. Rose challenges the way Troy presents these tales: "Anything you can't understand, you want to call it the devil" (14). Rose and Bono are a chorus parenthesizing Troy's insistence on his reading:

> ROSE: Times have changed since you was playing baseball, Troy. That was before the war. Times have changed a lot since then.
> TROY: How in hell they done changed?
> ROSE: They got lots of colored boys playing ball now. Baseball and football.
> BONO: You right about that, Rose. Times have changed, Troy. You done come along too early.
> TROY: There ought not never have been no time called too early! (9)

James calls the present "a saddle-back . . . from which we look in two directions into time."[3] Throughout *Fences*, Troy Maxson straddles this saddle-back, constantly constructing a present selectively out of memory (the past) and desire (the future).

Desire figures most clearly in his conflict with his son, Cory. Troy is affronted by Cory's desire to try out before a college football recruiter from North Carolina. Troy's own sport, and the source of his personal language of metaphors, is baseball; Cory's choice of football galls him. American popular culture has forgotten that integration had come to major league football long before Jackie Robinson signed a baseball contract. Fritz Pollard had played with the Akron Indians beginning in 1919, and black players played professional football until 1933, when the disruption of the Depression made football a whites-only sport for thirteen years.

As with baseball, this redistribution was tied to the postwar westward push. The National Football League (NFL) had originally centered in the Midwest, gradually adding franchises in eastern industrial centers. Long-standing interest in starting a franchise on the West Coast was realized when the Cleveland Rams moved to Los Angeles after the war. A rival

[3]James, *Principles of Psychology*, p. 574.

league, the All-American Football Conference (AAFC), started up in 1946. Though the two leagues would soon merge, the AAFC forced some innovative moves, including the initiation of western franchises (the Los Angeles Dons and the San Francisco 49ers) and the signing of black players. That same year, the Los Angeles Rams signed Kenny Washington and Woody Strode, and the Cleveland Browns signed Bill Willis and Marion Motley. Motley became a record-breaking rusher, beginning a strong tradition of black running backs that included Joe Perry, who, while playing for the San Francisco 49ers and Baltimore Colts, broke all rushing records through the 1950s. (His heir-apparent was Jim Brown.) By 1953, a black collegiate running back, J. C. Caroline of the University of Illinois, had broken the hallowed records of "Red" Grange, a white runner of the 1920s and 1930s. By the late 1950s, black athletes had established a prominence in football that at least equaled the standing of Mays, Aaron, and the Robinsons in baseball.[4]

With the stronger tradition of integration, football was on the verge of becoming a truly national sport in 1957. Cory believes, as Troy does not, that a talented black athlete can get a chance. This disagreement emerges when they discuss Roberto Clemente, now in his third year with the local baseball club, the Pittsburgh Pirates.

> TROY: I ain't thinking about the Pirates. Got an all-white team. Got that boy . . . that Puerto Rican boy . . . Clemente. Don't even half-play him. That boy could be something if they give him a chance. Play him one day and sit him on the bench the next.
> CORY: He gets a lot of chances to play.
> TROY: I'm talking about playing regular. Playing every day so you can get your timing. That's what I'm talking about.
> CORY: They got some white guys on the team that don't play every day. You can't play everybody at the same time.
> TROY: If they got a white fellow sitting on the bench . . . you can bet your last dollar he can't play! The colored guy got to be twice as good before he get on the team. That's why I don't want you to get all tied up in them sports. Man on the team and what it get him? They got colored on the team and don't use them. Same as not having them. All them teams the same.
> CORY: The Braves got Hank Aaron and Wes Covington. Hank Aaron hit two home runs today. That makes forty-three.
> TROY: Hank Aaron ain't nobody. (33–34)

Far beyond baseball, the ulterior difference here is over whether a change has occurred in American society. Generational differences indicate a difference in reading. All Cory knows are the achievements of Aaron (who would hit forty-four home runs in 1957), Covington, and Clemente; these seem incontrovertible evidence that his dreams have a foundation.

[4]For a more detailed discussion about the vexed issue of integration in professional football, see Ocania Chalk, *Pioneers of Black Sport* (New York: Dodd, Mead, 1975).

What Troy knows is his own frustration as a great player in the Negro Leagues. His success was also his self-sacrifice: The Negro Leagues began to die as soon as black players began to be accepted in numbers into professional baseball. What killed Troy's career was, ironically, the *advent* of integrated baseball. Although he is clearly aware of these facts, and clearly damaged by them, Troy insists that history is continuous, that what was once true is still true. Cory assumes that what is true is new—that there is now a new form of positivity, a sudden redistribution—and this assumption on Cory's part outrages his father. For one the gap signifies the death he constantly pits himself against, and for the other it signifies a life in the future, liberated from his father's limitations. Granted, Troy's knowing dictum that "the colored guy got to be twice as good before he get on the team" was quite true in 1957 and is still a widely shared perception today. But Cory is not arguing that his chance is likely; he is arguing that it is possible.

Troy gives many names to his resistance. Compassion is one. As he says to Rose, "I got sense enough not to let my boy get hurt over playing no sports" (39). Jealousy is another. Cory is getting a chance while he is still young, whereas even in 1947 Troy was "too old to play in the major leagues" (39). Both these "reasons" are versions of his resistance to reading the change that is making Clemente and Aaron into national heroes. Both Troy's compassion for his son and his jealousy of him are ways to deny his own death.

Here, we may remember one of Foucault's more disturbing claims: that the traditional view of history as a seamless continuity really disguised the quest to construct the self as authoritative, continuous, integrated, and eternal. In *Archaeology of Knowledge* he pictures the outraged author crying, "Must I suppose that in my discourse I can have no survival? And that in speaking I am not banishing my death, but actually establishing it?"[5] For Troy, to acknowledge the possibility of Cory's success is to acknowledge that his own time has passed. Thus his repression of a fact that would have been available to any avid baseball fan in Pittsburgh—that Roberto Clemente really is getting a chance to play. Clemente had 543 at-bats in 1956 and 451 in 1957.[6] Thus his claim that Aaron is "nobody." Note the extreme care with which Wilson has placed the action of the third act: quite late in September 1957, seemingly to show that reality takes no heed of Troy's judgments. Aaron would win the home-run and runs-batted-in titles, earning him the Most Valuable Player Award. Clemente would go on to 3,000 hits and the Hall of Fame.

Works Cited

Foucault, Michel. *Archaeology of Knowledge.* Trans. by A. M. Sheridan Smith. New York: Pantheon, 1972.

[5]Foucault, *Archaeology of Knowledge*, p. 210.
[6]Neft and Cohen, *Sports Encyclopedia*, pp. 309, 312.

James, William. *Principles of Psychology.* Ed. by Frederick H. Burkhardt. Vol. 1. Cambridge: Harvard University Press, 1981.

Neft, David S., and Richard M. Cohen. *The Sports Encyclopedia: Baseball.* New York: St. Martin's Press, 1989.

Richards, Lloyd. Introduction to *Fences,* by August Wilson, vii–viii. New York: New American Library, Plume, 1986.

Wilson, August. *Fences.* New York: New American Library, Plume, 1986.

AUGUST WILSON'S WOMEN[1]

HARRY ELAM JR.

The idea of a woman "needing a man" is . . . implicit in the action of *Fences.* It underlines Rose Maxson's reasons for marrying her husband, Troy, and remaining married to him despite his infidelity. Rose Maxson in *Fences* reflects strong traditional values associated with black women and yet asserts a strong feminist voice. Unlike the other women discussed, she is both wife and mother. In these roles she sacrifices self, supports her family, and holds it together. Barbara Christian notes that in African American communities, "the idea that mothers should lead lives of sacrifice has become the norm."[2] Rose embodies this norm. Christian observes that the literature of black males has often perpetuated this image.[3] Yet with Rose, Wilson expands on the stereotype while exploring this question of need as well as consistent truths of black female experience as wife and mother.

Rose exudes both love and strength. Each Friday her husband, Troy, hands over his paycheck to Rose. He relinquishes this element of economic authority, and she controls the household budget. From a position of "outsider-within" she observes the weekly payday rituals of the men. When necessary and from a distance, she participates, playfully teasing Troy, always bolstering his authority and publicly demonstrating her support for her man. As mother she nurtures her son, Cory. Aggressively, she defends Cory against the stubborn will of his father.

Rose understands that she has consigned herself to the limits imposed upon her by marriage and social expectations. Unlike Risa or Berniece, Rose articulates her perspective and the motivation for her actions. When Troy rationalizes his infidelity to her, she reaffirms her commitment to the relationship and castigates him for not doing the same.

> But I held onto you, Troy. I took all my feelings, my wants and needs, my dreams and I buried them inside you. I planted a seed and watched and prayed over it. I planted myself inside you and waited to bloom. And it

---

[1]Harry Elam Jr. "August Wilson's Women," *May All Your Fences Have Gates: Essays on the Drama of August Wilson,* ed. Alan Nadel (Iowa City: U of Iowa P, 1994), 178–80. Parenthetical documentation is to Wilson's *Three Plays.*

[2]Christian, *Black Feminist Criticism,* p. 234.

[3]Ibid., p. 236.

didn't take me no eighteen years to find out the soil was hard and rocky and it wasn't never gonna bloom. But I held onto you, Troy. I held tighter. You was my husband. I owed you everything I had. Every part of me I could find to give you. And upstairs in that room, with the darkness falling in on me, I gave everything I had to try and erase the doubt that you wasn't the finest man in the world. And wherever you was going I wanted to be there with you. 'Cause you was my husband,' cause that's the only way I was gonna survive as your wife. (165)

Rose's verbal assault on Troy earns the audience's sympathy. Faced with the realities and imperfections of marriage, she is determined to make their marriage work. Still, Rose clearly accepts her own material oppression. "I *owed* you everything I had," she says. Troy's adultery provides that catalyst that propels her to reassess her position, to gain a greater self-awareness and to change.

Quite powerfully, Rose, hurt and betrayed, asserts her independence. When Troy presents her with his illegitimate, motherless daughter, Rose informs him, "Okay Troy. You're right. I'll take care of your baby for you 'cause, like you say, she's innocent and you can't visit the sins of the father upon the child. A motherless child has got a hard time. From right now . . . this child has a mother. But you a womanless man" (173). In the Broadway production, when Mary Alice as Rose accented this line by taking the baby and then slamming the back door in Troy's face, the audience, particularly black female spectators, erupted with cheers and applause. For at that moment Rose stands as a champion of black women, of any woman who has suffered under the constraints of a restrictive and inequitable marriage.

The avenues into which Rose channels her new freedom, nevertheless, affirm rather than assault traditional gender limitations and hegemonic legitimacy. She finds solace in the church and the mothering of her adopted daughter, Raynell. While Rose spiritually distances herself from Troy, she does not leave the marriage. The church becomes a surrogate. Collins argues that institutions such as the church can be "contradictory locations," where black women not only learn independence but also "learn to subordinate our interests as women to the allegedly greater good of the larger African American community."[4] Thus Rose, despite her spiritual independence, continues to conform to the traditional expectations and limitations placed on women. Black feminist scholar bell hooks criticizes the play and Rose for their conformity:

Fences poignantly portrays complex and negative contradictions within black masculinity in a white supremacist context. However, patriarchy is not critiqued, and even though tragic expressions of conventional masculinity are evoked, sexist values are re-inscribed via the black woman's redemption message as the play ends.[5]

[4]Collins, *Black Feminist Thought,* p. 86.
[5]hooks, *Yearning,* p. 18.

Rose's words at the end of the play, however, both critique and confirm the patriarchy. She tells Cory, who has returned for his father's funeral:

> That was my first mistake. Not to make him leave some room for me, for my part in the matter. But at that time I wanted that. I wanted a house that I could sing in. And that's what your daddy gave me. I didn't know to keep his strength I had to give up little pieces of mine. I did that. I took his life as mine and mixed up the pieces so that I couldn't hardly tell which was which anymore. It was my choice. It was my life and I didn't have to live it like that. But that's what life offered me in the way of being a woman, and I took it. (189–90)

As a black woman in 1957, Rose had extremely restricted options. Marriage required compromise and, quite often for women, a loss of self. The traditional nature of their marriage allowed Troy to dominate, while Rose suppressed her will and desires. Rose reflects on this reality, on a historic truth experienced by many black women. Thus her words call attention to the limitations of gender roles and critique the patriarchal system that created these limitations. Yet Rose also professes her own complicity. Rose's acceptance of the blame, her internalization of external conditions of oppression, prevent her from challenging the status quo. She chooses to accept her subservient position in her marriage; this she believes is what "life offers her as a woman."

Works Cited

Christian, Barbara. *Black Feminist Criticism.* New York: Pergamon Press, 1985.

Collins, Patricia Hill. *Black Feminist Thought.* Boston: Unwin Hyman, 1990.

hooks, bell. *Yearning: Race, Gender, and Cultural Politics.* Boston: South End Press, 1990.

Wilson, August. *Three Plays: "Ma Rainey's Black Bottom," "Fences," "Joe Turner's Come and Gone."* Pittsburgh: University of Pittsburgh Press, 1991.

AN INTERVIEW WITH AUGUST WILSON[1]

BONNIE LYONS

This interview took place in February 1997 in Merchants Cafe in Pioneer Square in downtown Seattle, near August Wilson's office. Dressed in a white dress shirt and tie coupled with a casual jacket and a cap, Wilson was soft-spoken and somewhat restrained at first. He became more and more animated as he spoke about his passion for black life in America and for his plays. Wilson is well aware that he created his characters, but

[1]Bonnie Lyons, "An Interview with August Wilson," *Contemporary Literature* 40.1 (Spring 1999): 1–21.

he spoke of them with such knowledge and affection that I was reminded of the famous story of Balzac calling for his characters on his deathbed.

Q. Elsewhere you've talked about writing as a way of effecting social change and said that all your plays are political, but that you try not to make them didactic or polemical. Can you talk a little about how plays can effect social change without being polemical or didactic?

A. I don't write primarily to effect social change. I believe writing can do that, but that's not why I write. I work as an artist. However, all art is political in the sense that it serves the politics of someone. Here in America whites have a particular view of blacks, and I think my plays offer them a different and new way to look at black Americans. For instance, in *Fences* they see a garbageman, a person they really don't look at, although they may see a garbageman every day. By looking at Troy's life, white people find out that the content of this black garbageman's life is very similar to their own, that he is affected by the same things—love, honor, beauty, betrayal, duty. Recognizing that these things are as much a part of his life as of theirs can be revolutionary and can affect how they think about and deal with black people in their lives.

Q. How would that same play, *Fences,* affect a black audience?

A. Blacks see the content of their lives being elevated into art. They don't always know that is possible, and it's important to know that.

Q. You've talked about how important black music was for your development. Was there any black literature that showed you that black lives can be the subject of great art?

A. *Invisible Man.* When I was fourteen I discovered the Negro section of the library. I read *Invisible Man,* Langston Hughes, and all the thirty or forty books in the section, including the sociology. I remember reading a book that talked about the "Negro's power of hard work" and how much that phrase affected me. . . . Forty years ago we had few black writers compared to today. There have been forty years of education and many more college graduates. And it's important to remember that blacks don't have a long history of writing. We come from an oral tradition. At one point in America it was a crime to teach blacks to read and write. So it's only in the past 150 years that we've been writing in this country.

Q. You're self-educated. How do you feel about schools and self-education?

A. The schools are horrible and don't teach anybody anything. From about the fifth grade on, I was always butting heads with my teachers. I would ask them questions and they would say, "Shut up. Sit down," because they didn't know the answers. So I'd go to the library to find out. When I quit school at fourteen, I didn't want my mother to know, so I'd get up and go to the library and stay there until three o'clock. My mother taught me to read when I was four years old, and in the library for the first time in my life I felt free. I could read whole books on subjects that interested me. I'd read about the Civil War or theology. By the time I left the library, I thought, "Okay, I'm ready. I know a lot of stuff." It always amazed me that libraries were free.

Q. When you look at your work as a whole, what patterns do you see?

A. *Fences* is the odd man out because it's about one individual and everything focuses around him. The others are ensemble plays. I think I need to write another one like *Fences* to balance it out.

Q. How were things better in the forties?

A. We used to have our own black baseball league, for example. Everything was black-owned. On a Sunday black families would go over to the field, and some would sell peanuts or chicken sandwiches and so on. We were more self-sufficient. When blacks were finally allowed to play in the white leagues, the loss for the black community was great. Similarly in the forties black women were not allowed to go downtown and try on dresses in the department stores. So we had our own dress stores in the neighborhood and the doctors and dentists and teachers and business owners all lived in the same neighborhood and we had a thriving community. Then the doctors and dentists started moving out, and the whole community began to fall down. So now we're in a situation in which the basketball league is 99 percent black, but it's owned by whites. If all the money made from black sports and black music were in black hands, if it were spent in our neighborhoods, things would be very different.

Q. Elsewhere you've said you want your audience to see your characters as Africans, not just black folks in America. Can you talk about that?

A. I'm talking about black Americans having uniquely African ways of participating in the world, of doing things, different ways of socializing. I have no fascination with Africa itself. I've never been to Africa and have no desire to go.

Q. You've said that you try not to create characters who are victims. Yet aren't all these scars a sign that they have been victimized? Is the issue how they deal with their victimization, how they respond to it?

A. We're all victims of white America's paranoia. My characters don't respond as victims. No matter what society does to them, they are engaged with life, wrestling with it, trying to make sense out of it. Nobody is sitting around saying, "Woe is me."

Baseball Metaphors in <u>Fences</u>

Jim Fowler

1   Many factors related to life experience work together to influence an individual's thought and character. In August Wilson's play <u>Fences</u>, the character Troy Maxson is an excellent portrayal of how numerous factors influence the complex personality of a black man in the 1950's. One very influential factor which is highlighted throughout the play involves Troy's experience as a former Negro league baseball player. Troy's baseball experience has a significant effect upon his language, his lifestyle, and even his character.

2   Troy Maxson uses the language of baseball to express many of his thoughts and emotions. As Sandra Shannon states, "Troy flavors his conversation with baseball metaphors at every chance he gets" (228). Troy deals with many issues in his personal life by using baseball terms and experiences to reflect how he feels. One illustration of how baseball affects his emotional expression occurs when he and his son Cory are fighting. Troy angrily informs Cory that he already has two strikes, and he cautions his son, "Don't you strike out" (207). On another occasion, Troy uses baseball lingo to reveal the thrill and excitement he experiences when he engages in an extramarital affair. Troy attempts to explain his infidelity by stating to his wife, "Do you understand after eighteen years I wanted to steal second" (205). When he refers to his more serious emotions involving the duties and responsibility of wife and family, he uses the analogy of bunting his way on base and states, "I was safe. I had me a family. A job. I wasn't gonna get that last strike" (205).

3   Troy's lifestyle is certainly affected in significant ways by his prior baseball experience. Playing the sport of baseball has

probably contributed to Troy's self-centered and egotistical behavior. His friend tells Troy, "When you was hitting them baseballs out the park. A lot of them old gals was after you then" (201). Troy seems to miss the excitement and fun of baseball, and at times he resents the demanding responsibilities of work and his family. Baseball also influenced Troy's lifestyle by affecting his parenting. Because of the injustice Troy experienced when he played in the Negro league before the integration of baseball, he robs his son Cory of a chance to enjoy and possibly make something of himself in sports. In response to his own personal experience, Troy states, "I got sense enough not to let my boy get hurt over playing no sports" (190). Troy's decision not to allow his son to make his own choices and decisions causes anger and resentment in their relationship.

4   His experiences with baseball also affect Troy's character in significant ways. Troy describes his perception of the black person's experience when he states, "you born with two strikes on you before you come to the plate" (205). Facing the obstacles of life as a black man in a hostile society makes Troy very strong-willed and independent. Because of his experiences in baseball, Troy believes that black athletes will always be treated unfairly. Unlike his son, Troy cannot believe that "a change has occurred in American society" (Timpane 239). He somewhat pessimistically accepts the unfairness of his life and tries to deal with his difficulties in his own manner. The way in which Troy views his life also strongly impacts his attitude toward death. Troy refers to death as a "fastball on the outside corner" (175). This analogy indicates that Troy believes that although he cannot hold power over death, he can try his best to fight it off. When he receives a fastball on the outside corner, he may not hit a home run, but he has a very good chance of defending the

plate. Troy is able "to confront Death—and hence to construct his life—on his own terms" (Nadel 234).

5   In the play <u>Fences</u>, August Wilson reveals how environmental factors contribute to the character formation of Troy Maxson. Troy Maxson's life is strongly affected by his experience of playing baseball in the Negro league prior to World War II. At this time in the history of the sport, Troy realized that having the athletic ability to play baseball did not guarantee African American players equal opportunities with white players. Troy's bitter disappointment over this experience of injustice has a great impact on shaping his perception of the world and his lifestyle choices. The baseball metaphors and images in the play provide excellent insight into the character of Troy Maxson.

~ Works Cited

Henderson, Gloria Mason, Bill Day, and Sandra Stevenson Waller, eds. <u>Literature and Ourselves.</u> 4th ed. New York: Longman, 2003.

Nadel, Alan. "Boundaries, Logistics, and Identity: The Property of Metaphor in <u>Fences</u> and <u>Joe Turner's Come and Gone.</u>" <u>May All Your Fences Have Gates: Essays on the Drama of August Wilson.</u> Ed. Alan Nadel. Iowa City: U of Iowa P, 1994. Henderson, Day, and Waller. 231-36.

Shannon, Sandra G. <u>The Dramatic Vision of August Wilson.</u> Washington, DC: Howard UP, 1995. 103-17. Henderson, Day, and Waller. 224-31.

Timpane, John. "Filling the Time: Reading History in the Drama of August Wilson." <u>May All Your Fences Have Gates: Essays on the Drama of August Wilson.</u> Ed. Alan Nadel. Iowa City: U of Iowa P, 1994. Henderson, Day, and Waller. 236-41.

Wilson, August. <u>Fences.</u> N.p.: New American Library, 1986.

Henderson, Day, and Waller. 169-221.

3

Suggestions for Exploration and Writing

1. Troy says to Rose, "Woman. . . I do the best I can do. I come in here every Friday. I carry a sack of potatoes and a bucket of lard. You all line up at the door with your hands out. I give you the lint from my pockets. I give you my sweat and my blood." What is Troy's conception of a husband's responsibilities? What does he lack as a husband? Why?

2. Explain the symbolism of fences in the play. Why is Troy building a fence? Why does it take him so long to finish it?

3. Discuss in detail how baseball has affected Troy's lifestyle, his language, and his character.

4. Analyze the means by which Troy uses language to justify himself and his behavior and thereby to protect his self-esteem.

5. Write an essay comparing Troy's sons.

6. Troy tells Rose that in Alberta's house he can "laugh out loud." Beginning with this idea, contrast Troy's relationship with Rose to his relationship with Alberta.

7. Analyze the relationship between Rose and Troy, comparing their marriage before and after Troy tells Rose about Alberta.

8. Using research on the treatment and condition of African Americans in northeastern industrial cities on the eve of the civil rights movement, analyze the effect of white oppression on Troy and / or other characters in the play.

9. After researching the "Negro Leagues" and the integration of baseball, discuss the impact that playing in the "Negro Leagues" and failing to make the major leagues has had on Troy.

10. Analyze the role of Gabriel in the play. How does he retain dignity and independence in spite of brain damage and mistreatment by the government and by Troy? What are the implications of his part in the final scene?

11. List examples of the **foreshadowing** of Troy's death, and write an essay on Wilson's use of foreshadowing in *Fences*.

12. Why, living and working in the midst of so many people, is Troy almost always lonely?   *Pick One.*

Family: Suggestions for Writing

1. We often tend to think of families as consisting of a mother, a father, and one or more children who relate to each other in various

conventional ways. Many of the families in this section are unconventional. Discuss any two unconventional families in this unit.

2. Write an essay comparing the mothers, fathers, or situations in any of the works in this unit.

3. Use at least two of the poems in this unit as a basis for an essay about a parent's feelings for a child or about a child's perception of a parent.

4. Discuss problems faced by members of dysfunctional families, using two of the short stories in this unit.

5. Write an essay exploring the ways in which family problems vary in different cultures, or discuss similarities of family situations between two cultures.

6. Write an essay on two families depicted in this unit, explaining how they deal successfully with crises.

7. Death is a difficult part of the life cycle for the survivors. The death of a child is especially traumatic. Examine the ways in which parents and/or children deal with the death of a child in "The Benchmark" and "Home Burial."

8. Compare any two mothers in this unit.

9. Write an essay describing the ways in which your own identity has been shaped by your family.

10. In several essays in this unit, the authors return to the past: a particular time or place, such as their childhood or their home. Using one of the essays as a guide, write an essay that describes a particular time in your past.

Family: Writing about Film

1. View a contemporary film in which the theme of family is central (*American Beauty, Boyz 'N the Hood, In the Bedroom, Double Happiness, Mi Familia, The Deep End, The Ice Storm, Eve's Bayou, Lone Star, What's Eating Gilbert Grape?* to name just a few). Do any of the poems and stories in this unit deal with similar events or characters? Select an event or character from a poem or story and compare it to an event or character in the film. What makes them similar? Don't worry too much about superficial characteristics; think in terms of relationships and problems. What is your response to each, and how has the author, director, or actor created that effect?

2. From *The Simpsons* to *Titus* to *Gilmore Girls*, families that put the "fun" in dysfunctional are a favorite setting for American situation comedies. Select one television show or film that is especially appealing to you. What is it about your own family experience that makes you like this show? Consider your family as characters and

how they might compare to two or three of the main characters on the show.

3. Imagine you've been hired to write a screenplay of one of the short stories or dramas in this unit. Your producer wants you to shoot an opening montage sequence—a three-minute series of shots to be shown with a musical soundtrack as background for the opening credits. You know that screen time is very valuable, so you want to design this montage to set the tone, introduce main characters and relationships, give a sense of setting, and foreshadow events or themes. Describe two or three shots in detail and decide on the music (pop, jazz, classical) that will accompany them; then explain why these shots and this music will work well to prepare for the rest of the story. Try to make every shot work with three specific purposes (tone, setting, character, relationship, event, or theme).

Men and Women

Pablo Picasso, "La Danse Villageoise," 1922. Musée Picasso, Paris. © 2003 Estate of Pablo Picasso/Artists Rights Society (ARS), New York.

Through the ages, men and women have treated each other respectfully and disrespectfully, honestly and dishonestly. They have loved and hated each other, fought and made up, understood and misunderstood each other. In literature, we can examine these complex relationships with an objectivity often impossible in real-life relationships. The attitudes of men and women toward each other portrayed in this anthology range from humorous to serious and from lightly sarcastic to bitter.

We can also examine the parameters of being a woman or of being a man. For example, Jamaica Kincaid's "Girl" focuses on the restrictions placed on girls. Rita Dove's "Courtship" and "Courtship, Diligence" reflect how two people see the same courtship: Thomas thinks he has made a lasting, positive impression; Beulah is unimpressed. Both David Osborne and Rose Del Castillo Guilbault in their essays discuss male stereotypes, he from personal experience and she from a language and cultural perspective. In *A Doll's House* and in "The Yellow Wallpaper," the authors explore the problems faced by women in the past—problems similar to those some women confront today.

Another part of learning to be a man or woman is learning to live in the generation to which we belong and to deal effectively with members of other generations. Janice Mirikitani in "Breaking Tradition" explores three generations of women and applauds their differences.

The tone of each selection also suggests attitudes toward gender. While Maya Angelou celebrates her phenomenal womanhood, Marge Piercy takes issue with the destructive outcome of a female's attempts to be attractive to others in society. Edna St. Vincent Millay shows the sometimes transitory nature of love in "What lips my lips have kissed, and where, and why." In contrast, Shakespeare's Sonnet 116 lauds the permanence of love. Similarly, the joy made possible when two people love unselfishly is celebrated by Elizabeth Barrett Browning in Sonnet 43, as she answers the question "How do I love thee?"

Literary treatment of relationships is not always humorous or light. The disasters that result from the failure of a man and a woman to understand one another are vividly portrayed by Ernest Hemingway in "Hills Like White Elephants," by Charlotte Perkins Gilman in "The Yellow Wallpaper," and by Robert Browning in "Porphyria's Lover" and "My Last Duchess." Similarly, Bobbie Ann Mason in "Shiloh" explores the battlefield that marriage can become when both partners feel unfulfilled.

In literature as in life, the roles of men and women are not always precisely defined. Perhaps the lesson most clearly revealed is that men and women are individuals who face insecurities, share romance, and struggle to understand themselves as well as members of the opposite sex.

Writing about Men and Women

The works in this unit offer many gender issues that would be good subjects for essays. For help in selecting a suitable topic, reread the questions at the end of this unit. For example, several of the selections could lead to an analysis of women. If you select a short story such as Zora Neale Hurston's "The Gilded Six-Bits" and an essay such as Shalmali Pal's "Looking for My Prince Charming," you might begin with two lists: one could be about the concerns of the central character or the author; the other would list the resolutions for these concerns. Then you could review the works to look for similarities or differences and write a rough outline for a comparison/contrast essay. You might choose to rewrite Jamaica Kincaid's "Girl" as an essay entitled "Boy," incorporating what most people would say a boy should be told by a parent, or write an expository essay explaining the differences between what boys and girls are told. Perhaps you would prefer to write about the stereotypes that men or women have to live by. Using "Barbie Doll" by Marge Piercy, "Beyond the Cult of Fatherhood" by David Osborne, or "Americanization Is Tough on 'Macho'" by Rose Del Castillo Guilbault, you might plan an argumentative essay in which you defend your position on these stereotypes.

Many of the poems in this section deal with love: imperfect love, perfect love, and love gone wrong. After reading Shakespeare's Sonnet 138 and Elizabeth Barrett Browning's Sonnet 43, you could write an essay about true love. If you prefer to write about disastrous love, you might use Robert Browning's "My Last Duchess" or "Porphyria's Lover." If your instructor asks for a personal essay, you might write an epistolary essay, one that explains your love ideal in the form of a letter.

This unit is also rich in showing relations between men and women. For an expository essay, you might list in separate columns the negative and positive characteristics of the relationships in "The Yellow Wallpaper" by Charlotte Perkins Gilman, "Hills Like White Elephants" by Ernest Hemingway, or "Shiloh" by Bobbie Ann Mason. Using one or more of the works from this list, you could write an essay that examines these relationships.

Brittney Victor chose to write a research paper on Langston Hughes. First, she looked at the portrayal of the women in three of his poems. At first, there did not seem to be enough information about the women, so she decided to look at the African American men as portrayed by Hughes.

Then she considered the relationship between the poet (a male), the mother and son in "Mother to Son," the female jazz dancer in "Jazzonia," the washerwoman in "A Song to a Negro Wash-Woman," and the blues player in "Weary Blues." She asked herself if common ground existed or if the era of the poems was a factor. Next, she reread the primary sources, the poems, and considered Hughes's audience. As she reread the secondary sources in *Literature and Ourselves,* she wrote down some quotations and paraphrases that could help her in explaining her ideas. The next step was to arrive at a thesis sentence and to construct an outline. Brittney knew that she could not begin to write without a plan. After discussing minor changes with her instructor, she polished the outline and essay, edited it, and printed the final copy.

ESSAYS

Virginia Woolf (1882–1941)

Though plagued throughout her lifetime by nervous breakdowns, Virginia Stephen Woolf became a major influence on English literature. Today she is considered one of the most significant writers in the field of women's literature. Woolf was a member of the famous Bloomsbury circle, a group that stressed culture and opposed many restrictive Victorian standards. She excelled as a novelist with such works as Mrs. Dalloway *(1925) and* To the Lighthouse *(1927); as a critic; and as an essayist with* A Room of One's Own *(1929) and* Three Guineas *(1938). This speech was presented to the Women's Service League, a group of career women, in 1936.*

PROFESSIONS FOR WOMEN   (1936)

1   When your secretary invited me to come here, she told me that your Society is concerned with the employment of women and she suggested that I might tell you something about my own professional experiences. It is true I am a woman; it is true I am employed; but what professional experiences have I had? It is difficult to say. My profession is literature; and in that profession there are fewer experiences for women than in any other, with the exception of the stage—fewer, I mean, that are peculiar to women. For the road was cut many years ago—by Fanny Burney, by Aphra Behn, by Harriet Martineau, by Jane Austen, by George Eliot—many famous women, and many more unknown and forgotten, have been before me, making the path smooth, and regulating my steps. Thus, when I came to write, there were very few material obstacles in my way. Writing was a reputable and harmless occupation. The family peace was not broken by the scratching of a pen. No demand was made upon the family purse. For ten and sixpence one can buy paper enough to write all the plays of Shakespeare—if one has a mind that way. Pianos and models, Paris, Vienna and Berlin, masters and mistresses, are not needed by a writer. The cheapness of writing paper is, of course, the reason why women have succeeded as writers before they have succeeded in the other professions.

2   But to tell you my story—it is a simple one. You have only got to figure to yourselves a girl in a bedroom with a pen in her hand. She had only to move that pen from left to right—from ten o'clock to one. Then it occurred to her to do what is simple and cheap enough after all—to slip a few of those pages into an envelope, fix a penny stamp in the corner, and drop the envelope in the red box at the corner. It was thus that I became a journalist; and my effort was rewarded on the first day of the following month—a very glorious day it was for me—by a letter from an editor containing a cheque for one pound ten shillings and sixpence. But to show you how little I deserve to be called a professional woman, how

little I know of the struggles and difficulties of such lives, I have to admit that instead of spending that sum upon bread and butter, rent, shoes and stockings, or butcher's bills, I went out and bought a cat—a beautiful cat, a Persian cat, which very soon involved me in bitter disputes with my neighbours.

3   What could be easier than to write articles and to buy Persian cats with the profits? But wait a moment. Articles have to be about something. Mine, I seem to remember, was about a novel by a famous man. And while I was writing this review, I discovered that if I were going to review books I should need to do battle with a certain phantom. And the phantom was a woman, and when I came to know her better I called her after the heroine of a famous poem, The Angel in the House. It was she who used to come between me and my paper when I was writing reviews. It was she who bothered me and wasted my time and so tormented me that at last I killed her. You who come of a younger and happier generation may not have heard of her—you may not know what I mean by the Angel in the House. I will describe her as shortly as I can. She was intensely sympathetic. She was immensely charming. She was utterly unselfish. She excelled in the difficult arts of family life. She sacrificed herself daily. If there was chicken, she took the leg; if there was a draught she sat in it— in short she was so constituted that she never had a mind or a wish of her own, but preferred to sympathize always with the minds and wishes of others. Above all—I need not say it—she was pure. Her purity was supposed to be her chief beauty—her blushes, her great grace. In those days—the last of Queen Victoria—every house had its Angel. And when I came to write I encountered her with the very first words. The shadow of her wings fell on my page; I heard the rustling of her skirts in the room. Directly, that is to say, I took my pen in hand to review that novel by a famous man, she slipped behind me and whispered: "My dear, you are a young woman. You are writing about a book that has been written by a man. Be sympathetic; be tender; flatter; deceive; use all the arts and wiles of our sex. Never let anybody guess that you have a mind of your own. Above all, be pure." And she made as if to guide my pen. I now record the one act for which I take some credit to myself, though the credit rightly belongs to some excellent ancestors of mine who left me a certain sum of money— shall we say five hundred pounds a year?—so that it was not necessary for me to depend solely on charm for my living. I turned upon her and caught her by the throat. I did my best to kill her. My excuse, if I were to be had up in a court of law, would be that I acted in self-defence. Had I not killed her she would have killed me. She would have plucked the heart out of my writing. For, as I found, directly I put pen to paper, you cannot review even a novel without having a mind of your own, without expressing what you think to be the truth about human relations, morality, sex. And all these questions, according to the Angel in the House, cannot be dealt with freely and openly by women; they must charm, they must conciliate, they must—to put it bluntly—tell lies if they are to succeed.

Thus, whenever I felt the shadow of her wing or the radiance of her halo upon my page, I took up the inkpot and flung it at her. She died hard. Her fictitious nature was of great assistance to her. It is far harder to kill a phantom than a reality. She was always creeping back when I thought I had despatched her. Though I flatter myself that I killed her in the end, the struggle was severe; it took much time that had better have been spent upon learning Greek grammar; or in roaming the world in search of adventures. But it was a real experience; it was an experience that was bound to befall all women writers at that time. Killing the Angel in the House was part of the occupation of a woman writer.

4   But to continue my story. The Angel was dead; what then remained? You may say that what remained was a simple and common object—a young woman in a bedroom with an inkpot. In other words, now that she had rid herself of falsehood, that young woman had only to be herself. Ah, but what is "herself"? I mean, what is a woman? I assure you, I do not know. I do not believe that you know. I do not believe that anybody can know until she has expressed herself in all the arts and professions open to human skill. That indeed is one of the reasons why I have come here—out of respect for you, who are in process of showing us by your experiments what a woman is, who are in process of providing us, by your failures and successes, with that extremely important piece of information.

5   But to continue the story of my professional experiences. I made one pound ten and six by my first review; and I bought a Persian cat with the proceeds. Then I grew ambitious. A Persian cat is all very well, I said; but a Persian cat is not enough. I must have a motor car. And it was thus that I became a novelist—for it is a very strange thing that people will give you a motor car if you will tell them a story. It is a still stranger thing that there is nothing so delightful in the world as telling stories. It is far pleasanter than writing reviews of famous novels. And yet, if I am to obey your secretary and tell you my professional experiences as a novelist, I must tell you about a very strange experience that befell me as a novelist. And to understand it you must try first to imagine a novelist's state of mind. I hope I am not giving away professional secrets if I say that a novelist's chief desire is to be as unconscious as possible. He has to induce in himself a state of perpetual lethargy. He wants life to proceed with the utmost quiet and regularity. He wants to see the same faces, to read the same books, to do the same things day after day, month after month, while he is writing, so that nothing may break the illusion in which he is living— so that nothing may disturb or disquiet the mysterious nosings about, feelings round, darts, dashes and sudden discoveries of that very shy and illusive spirit, the imagination. I suspect that this state is the same both for men and women. Be that as it may, I want you to imagine me writing a novel in a state of trance. I want you to figure to yourselves a girl sitting with a pen in her hand, which for minutes, and indeed for hours, she never dips into the inkpot. The image that comes to my mind when I think of this girl is the image of a fisherman lying sunk in dreams on the

verge of a deep lake with a rod held out over the water. She was letting her imagination sweep unchecked round every rock and cranny of the world that lies submerged in the depths of our unconscious being. Now came the experience, the experience that I believe to be far commoner with women writers than with men. The line raced through the girl's fingers. Her imagination had rushed away. It had sought the pools, the depths, the dark places where the largest fish slumber. And then there was a smash. There was an explosion. There was foam and confusion. The imagination had dashed itself against something hard. The girl was roused from her dream. She was indeed in a state of the most acute and difficult distress. To speak without figure she had thought of something, something about the body, about the passions which it was unfitting for her as a woman to say. Men, her reason told her, would be shocked. The consciousness of what men will say of a woman who speaks the truth about her passions had roused her from her artist's state of unconsciousness. She could write no more. The trance was over. Her imagination could work no longer. This I believe to be a very common experience with women writers—they are impeded by the extreme conventionality of the other sex. For though men sensibly allow themselves great freedom in these respects, I doubt that they realize or can control the extreme severity with which they condemn such freedom in women.

6   These then were two very genuine experiences of my own. These were two of the adventures of my professional life. The first—killing the Angel in the House—I think I solved. She died. But the second, telling the truth about my own experiences as a body, I do not think I solved. I doubt that any woman has solved it yet. The obstacles against her are still immensely powerful—and yet they are very difficult to define. Outwardly, what is simpler than to write books? Outwardly, what obstacles are there for a woman rather than for a man? Inwardly, I think, the case is very different; she has still many ghosts to fight, many prejudices to overcome. Indeed it will be a long time still, I think, before a woman can sit down to write a book without finding a phantom to be slain, a rock to be dashed against. And if this is so in literature, the freest of all professions for women, how is it in the new professions which you are now for the first time entering?

7   Those are the questions that I should like, had I time, to ask you. And indeed, if I have laid stress upon these professional experiences of mine, it is because I believe that they are, though in different forms, yours also. Even when the path is nominally open—when there is nothing to prevent a woman from being a doctor, a lawyer, a civil servant—there are many phantoms and obstacles, as I believe, looming in her way. To discuss and define them is I think of great value and importance; for thus only can the labour be shared, the difficulties be solved. But besides this, it is necessary also to discuss the ends and the aims for which we are fighting, for which we are doing battle with these formidable obstacles. Those aims cannot be taken for granted; they must be perpetually questioned and examined. The whole position, as I see it—

here in this hall surrounded by women practicing for the first time in history I know not how many different professions—is one of extraordinary interest and importance. You have won rooms of your own in the house hitherto exclusively owned by men. You are able, though not without great labour and effort, to pay the rent. You are earning your five hundred pounds a year. But this freedom is only a beginning; the room is your own, but it is still bare. It has to be furnished; it has to be decorated; it has to be shared. How are you going to furnish it, how are you going to decorate it? With whom are you going to share it, and upon what terms? These, I think are questions of the utmost importance and interest. For the first time in history you are able to ask them; for the first time you are able to decide for yourselves what the answers should be. Willingly would I stay and discuss those questions and answers—but not tonight. My time is up; and I must cease.

Questions for Discussion

1. According to Woolf, why have women "succeeded as writers before they have succeeded in the other professions"?

2. Who is the "Angel in the House," and what did she have to do with Woolf's writing? Why did the author have to kill the "Angel"?

3. What obstacle other than the "Angel in the House" did Woolf face? Why has she not overcome the obstacle?

4. What does Woolf mean when, after killing the "Angel," she asks herself "What is a woman?" and reports that she does not know?

5. What, according to Woolf, can a man talk about or write about that a woman cannot? What limits on free expression do women today face?

6. Explain Woolf's analogy between women pioneering in professions and an unfurnished room.

Suggestions for Exploration and Writing

1. In an essay, discuss the degree to which the "Angel in the House" haunts women you know.

2. Argue for or against the following statement from Woolf's essay: "Even when the path is nominally open—when there is nothing to prevent a woman from being a doctor, a lawyer, a civil servant—there are many phantoms and obstacles, as I believe, looming in her way."

3. Beginning with number 2 above, discuss other angels that a person might have to kill off, such as the Angel at Work, the Angel in School, the Angel in the Family, or the Angel of Friendship.

David Osborne (b. 1951)

David Osborne, a political journalist and a consultant to the Clinton presidential campaign in 1992, has published articles in many prestigious magazines. His book Reinventing Government (*1992*), *coauthored with Ted Gaebler, presents guidelines and suggestions for changes in government;* Banishing Bureaucracy (*1997*) *suggests strategies for implementing these changes. Osborne and his wife, Rose, an obstetrician and gynecologist, and their four children live in Dedham, Massachusetts.*

BEYOND THE CULT OF FATHERHOOD   (1985)

1   If I ever finish this article, it will be a miracle. Nicholas woke up this morning with an earache and a temperature, and I spent half the day at the doctor's office and pharmacy. Another ear infection.

2   Nicholas is my son. Twenty months old, a stout little bundle of energy and affection.

3   I will never forget the moment when I realized how completely Nick would change my life. My wife is a resident in obstetrics and gynecology, which means, among other things, that she works 100 hours a week, leaves the house every day by six and works all night several times a week, and often all weekend too. I'm not a househusband; I take Nick to day care five days a week. But I come about as close to househusbandry as I care to. I am what you might call a "nontraditional" father.

4   Nick was three weeks old when I learned what that actually meant. Rose had just gone back to work, and Nick and I were learning about bottles. I don't remember if it was Rose's first night back or her second, but she wasn't home.

5   I stayed up too late; I had not yet learned that, with a baby in the house, you grab sleep whenever you can—even if it means going to bed at nine. Just as I drifted off, about 11:30, Nick woke up. I fed him and rocked him and put him back to sleep. About 2 A.M. he woke again, crying, and I rocked him for 45 minutes before he quieted down.

6   When he started screaming at four, I was in the kitchen by the time I woke up. As every parent knows, the sound of an infant—your infant— screaming sends lightning bolts up the spine. Bells ring in the head; nerves jangle. Racing against my son's hunger, I boiled water, poured it into the little plastic sack, slipped the sack into the plastic bottle, put on the top, and plunged the bottle into a bowl of cold water to cool it. I had not yet learned that in Connecticut, where I live, the water need not be sterilized. (Fathers are the last to know.)

7   It takes a long time to boil water and cool it back to body temperature, and I was dead on my feet even before the screams rearranged my vertebrae. By the time the water had cooled, I was half-crazed, my motions rapid and jerky. I mixed in the powdered formula and slipped the nipple back on. I ran toward Nick's room, shaking the bottle as hard as I could

to make sure it was thoroughly mixed. As I reached his crib, the top flew off—and the contents sprayed all over the room.

8   At that point, I lost it. I swore at the top of my lungs, I stomped around the room, I slammed the changing table, and I swore some more. That was when I realized what I had gotten myself into—and how much I had to learn.

9   With baby boomers well ensconced in the nation's newsrooms, fatherhood is sweeping American journalism. You can pick up the *New York Times Magazine,* or *Esquire,* or Bob Greene's best-seller, *Good Morning, Merry Sunshine: A Father's Journal of His Child's First Year* (Penguin), and read all about the wonders of being a father.

10 By all accounts, today's fathers are more involved and more sensitive than their own fathers were. But as warm and tender as their writing may be, it rings false. Rosalie Ziomek, a mother in Evanston, Illinois, said it perfectly in a letter to the *New Republic,* after it printed a scathing review of Bob Greene's book. "I was enraged by Greene's book," Ziomek wrote. "Anyone taking care of a newborn infant doesn't have time to write about it. Greene was cashing in on the experiences that most women have quietly and painfully lived without the glorification of fame and money. Meanwhile, because of the structure of his work/social life, which he is unwilling to alter, he avoids the thing that is the hardest part of new motherhood: the moment-to-moment dependency of a tiny, helpless, and demanding human being. I have more to say on the subject, but I have three children to take care of and writing is a luxury I can't afford right now."

11 Ziomek is right. I've been trying to keep a journal as Greene did, and it's impossible. There's no time. And how do you capture the essence of an exhausting, never-ending 24-hour day in a few paragraphs? Snapshots work if you spend an hour or two with a child, but if you spend days, everything dissolves in a blur.

12 My experience is different from that of the fathers I read about. Certainly I am not fulfilling the role of a traditional mother, and certainly no child could ask for a more loving mother than Nick has. But I do fix most of the meals and do most of the laundry and change a lot of the diapers and get Nick up and dressed in the morning and shuttle him back and forth to day care and cart him to the grocery store and sing him to sleep and clean up his toys and wipe his nose and deal with his tantrums and cuddle with him and tickle him and all the other wonderful and exhausting things mothers do. If you ask me what it all means, I can't say. After 20 months, I'm still dizzy, still desperate for a free hour or two, and still hopelessly in love with my little boy. All I have to offer are fragments; profound thoughts are for people who have more time. But if you want to go beyond the cult of fatherhood, I think I've been there.

13 My day starts about 6:30 or 7 A.M., when Nick stands up in his crib and calls out for me. I stumble into his room, pick him up, give him a kiss and a "Good morning, Pumpkin," and carry him back to bed. I lay him down

on his mother's empty pillow, lie down beside him, and sometimes I drowse again before it's really time to get up. But most mornings Nick is ready to start his day, and he gradually drags me up toward consciousness. He smiles at me, climbs up on me, and rests his head against my cheek— even kisses me if I'm really lucky, or sits on my bladder and bounces, if I'm not. I tickle him, and he laughs and squirms and shrieks for more.

14   Sometimes he lies there for a few minutes, thinking his little boy thoughts, before sliding himself backward off the bed and going in search of something to do. Often he arrives back with a toy or two and asks to be picked "Up! Up!" Then he plays for a few minutes, making sure to keep an eye on my progress toward wakefulness. When he has waited long enough, he hands me my glasses, takes my hand, and pulls me out of bed.

15   While I shower, Nick plays in the bathroom, sitting on the floor with his toys. By the time I'm dressed, the kettle is whistling, and he's ready for breakfast. We always eat together, he has hot cereal, I have cold cereal, and often we share a bagel. I wish you could hear him say "cream cheese."

16   The rough times come on weekends. After 24 hours, I'm ready to be hung out on the line to dry. After 48 hours, I'm ready to pin medals on women who stay home every day with their kids. For single mothers, I'm ready to build monuments.

17   Don't let anyone tell you otherwise: traditional mothers work harder than anyone else can even imagine. They are on duty 24 hours a day, 365 days a year. I remember wondering, as a youth, why my own mother always rushed around with such urgency when she was cooking or cleaning. To me, she was like a woman possessed. Now I do the same thing. When you have a young child (or two, or three), you have very little time to get the dishes done, or cook dinner, or vacuum, or do the laundry so when you get a moment, you proceed with all possible haste. If your children are asleep, they might wake up. If they're playing, they might get bored and demand your attention.

18   Friends who visit me nowadays probably think I'm crazy, the way I rush compulsively to get dinner ready or mow the lawn or finish the laundry. I do feel somewhat self-conscious about it. But the fact is, if I'm cooking, Nick is going to start demanding his meal soon, and if it's not ready, he's going to get very cranky. And with all the chores that pile up on a weekend—the lawn, the laundry, the groceries, and so on—I have to seize every possible instant. If he naps, that may give me an hour and a half. If he wakes up before I'm done, whatever I'm doing will never get finished.

19   In any case, it is on weekends alone with Nick that I feel the full brunt of child-rearing. Consider a typical weekend: Nick wakes at 7:00, and we lie in bed and play for half an hour before getting up. But this morning he feels feverish, so I take his temperature. It is 101.6—not high for a young child, but a fever nonetheless.

20   The first thing I do is call Maureen, who takes care of him during the week. Both of her kids have a bug, and I want to find out what the symptoms are, to see if Nick has the same thing. From what we can tell, he does. On that basis, I decide to give him Tylenol for the fever, rather than taking him in to the pediatrician to see if he's got an ear infection. Besides, he wants to lie down for a nap at 10:00, before I have decided, and doesn't wake until 1:00. By then the office is closed.

21   After lunch he feels much better—cool, happy, and bubbling. We play with his lock-blocks for a while, then watch a basketball game. He's very cuddly, because he's not feeling well. After the game it's off to the bank and grocery store. He falls asleep on the way home, at 5:45. It's an awkward time for a nap, but he only sleeps until 6:30. He wakes up crying, with a high fever, feeling miserable.

22   To get him to swallow more Tylenol, which he hates, I promise him ice cream. I give him half an ice-cream sandwich while I rush around the kitchen cooking dinner, and when he finishes it, he cries for the other half. I tell him he can have it after he eats his dinner. But when dinner is ready, he won't eat; he just sits there pointing at the freezer, where the ice cream is, and wailing. This is a major tantrum—hot tears, red face. I can't help but sympathize, though, because it's born of feeling absolutely wretched. How should I respond? I don't want to give in and teach him he can get his way by screaming. I try to comfort him by holding him in my lap, but he just sobs. Finally I take him into his room and rock him, holding him close. Gradually the sobs subside, and after 10 minutes I take him back into the kitchen, hold him on my lap, and feed him myself. He doesn't eat much, but enough to deserve his ice cream.

23   Though Nick gets over the incident in no time, I am traumatized. The fever is frightening—it has hit 102 by dinnertime, and it only drops to 101.4 by 8 P.M. Should I have taken him to the doctor? Will he spike a really high fever tonight? Am I being too relaxed? And what will Rose say? I cannot stop worrying; I feel heartsick as I read him his bedtime stories, though he cools down as he drifts to sleep in my arms. Would a mother feel so uncertain, I wonder? Do mothers feel adequate at moments like this? Or am I in a father's territory here?

24   Sunday morning Nick wakes at 6:30 and devours his breakfast, but pretty soon his temperature begins to rise. I call our pediatrician, who reassures me that it doesn't sound like an ear infection, and that I'm doing the right thing. Still, Nick isn't feeling well, and it makes him more demanding. He wants to be held; he wants me with him constantly; he insists that I do what he wants me to do and cries if I balk. It is a wearing day. He naps late, and when I wake him at seven, he is again miserable—temperature at 102.4, crying, refusing to let me change his diaper. But after more Tylenol and a good dinner he feels better.

25   I haven't heard from Rose all weekend, so I decide to call her at the hospital. She is furious that I haven't taken Nick to the doctor. A child

who gets ear infections as often as he does has to be checked, she yells at me. He could blow out an eardrum! And why haven't I called her—she's his mother, for God's sake! I'm exhausted, I've been busting my hump all weekend, alone, doing the best I can, and now I'm being abused. I don't like it. My first impulse is to hang up on her, but instead I hand the phone to Nicholas, who has a long talk with her. He says "Mommy!" she says "Nicholas!" and he laughs and laughs.

26   Rose may be right, I know, but that doesn't help my anger. We part tersely, and I promise to take him to the pediatrician the next morning before I leave for California on an article assignment. After that's out of the way, Nick and I have a good evening. We read books, and several times he leads me into his room to get another handful. A short bath, more books, then off to bed. He wants to take two of his trucks to bed with him—a new wrinkle—but I finally convince him to say "night-night" to his trucks and turn out the lights.

27   I have several hours of work to do before I leave, so I don't get to bed until after midnight. I'm absolutely shot. When the alarm rings at 6:00, I haul myself out of bed, shower, get dressed, and get Nick up and fed and dressed. We speed down to the library to return several books, then to the doctor's office. No ear infection; it's just a bug, says the doc, and he should be over it by nightfall. I drop Nick off at Maureen's by 9:30, race home, and spend the next hour packing, vacuuming, cleaning up the dishes and defrosting something for Rose and Nick's dinner. When I get to the airport, I realize I've misread my ticket and I'm half an hour early. I'm exhausted, and the trip has yet to begin.

28   Two nights later I call Rose. When I ask how she is, she bursts into tears. Nicholas has fallen at Maureen's and cut his forehead on a metal toy. Rose was caught in an ice storm between the hospital and home, so Maureen had to take her own kids to a neighbor's and rush Nick to the pediatrician's office for stitches. They gave him a local anesthetic, but he screamed the whole time.

29   "I feel so awful," Rose sobs, over and over. "I should have been there. I just feel awful." Guilt floods in, but it is nothing to match Rose's guilt. This is one of the differences I have discovered between mothers and fathers.

30   Rose has felt guilty since the day she went back to work—the hardest single thing I've ever watched her do. Deep inside her psyche lies a powerful message that she belongs at home, that if she is not with her child she is terribly irresponsible.

31   I feel guilty only occasionally. When I dropped Nick off at day care the first day after returning from California, and he sobbed because he thought I was leaving him again, the guilt just about killed me. I turned into a classic mother: as soon as I got home, I called to see if he was still crying. (He was.) Two guilt-ridden hours later I called again, desperate to hear that everything was fine. (It was.)

32   Deep within my psyche, however, the most powerful message is that I belong at work, that if I am not out making my mark on the world I am worth nothing.

33   The contradiction between family and career is nothing new; it is perhaps the central unresolved conflict in the lives of American women today. What I did not expect was the force with which that conflict would erupt in my life.

34   Like an addict, I now find myself squeezing in every last minute of work that I can. I wait until the last possible instant before rushing out the door to pick Nick up in the afternoon. I dart out to my study while he naps on weekends, using a portable intercom to listen for his cries. At night I compulsively page through old newspapers that pile up because I can no longer read them over breakfast, afraid I've missed something important. As I hit deadline time, I pray that Nicholas doesn't get sick. I have even tried writing on a Saturday afternoon, with Nick playing in my studio. That experiment lasted half an hour, at which point he hit the reset button on the back of my computer and my prose was lost to the ages.

35   This frantic effort to keep up is clearly not good for me, but I cannot seem to abandon it. I constantly feel as if I live in a pressure cooker. I long for a free day, even a free hour. But my career has taken off just as my responsibilities as a father have hit their peak, and I cannot seem to scale down my commitment to either.

36   When Nick was four months old, I took him to a Christmas party, one Saturday when Rose was working. After an hour or so he got cranky, so I took him upstairs with a bottle. A little girl followed, and soon her brother and sister—equally bored by the goings-on downstairs—had joined us. It wasn't long before Dad came looking for them.

37   We introduced ourselves and talked for a bit. His wife, it turned out, was also a doctor. The curious part came when I asked what he did. First he told me all the things he had done in the past: carpentry, business, you name it. Then he said he'd done enough—he was about 40—and felt no need to prove himself any more. Finally he told me he stayed at home with the kids. And frankly, he pulled it off with far more dignity and less stammering than I would have, had our places been reversed.

38   I don't think I could do what he does. If I were to stay home full-time with Nick, I would quickly lose my self-esteem, and within months I would be deep into an identity crisis. Part of the reason I love my role as a father is that I am secure in my role as a writer. Without that, I would not feel good enough about myself to be the kind of father I am.

39   This is not simply a problem inside male heads. How many women would be content with men who stayed home with the kids? Not many, I'll wager. And not my wife, I know. From my experience, modern women want a man who will share the responsibilities at home but still be John Wayne in the outside world. They don't want any wimps wearing aprons. And men know it.

40   We are in a Burger King, in Fall River, Massachusetts. We are not having a good day. We drove two hours to shop in the factory outlets here, and all but a handful are closed because it's Sunday.

41   Nick likes Burger King, but he's not having a great day either. He has recently learned about tantrums, and as we get ready to leave, he decides to throw one. He doesn't want to leave; he doesn't want to put on his coat; he just doesn't want to be hauled around any more. So he stands up and wails.

42   Rose is mortified; she takes any misbehavior in public as an advertisement of her failings as a mother. It triggers all her guilt about working. This time, the timing couldn't be worse, because she is already on edge.

43   Our tantrum strategy is generally to let him yell, to ignore him, and thus to teach him that it does no good. But in a public restaurant, I don't have the stamina to ignore him, so I cross the room to pick him up.

44   Rose orders me away from him, in no uncertain terms. There are no negotiations, no consultations. We are going to do this her way or no way.

45   That lights my fuse, of course, and after simmering for 10 minutes, I bring it up. "Let it go," she tells me, almost in tears over Nicholas. "It's not important."

46   It's not important.

47   Ah, the double bind. You're in charge one day, playing mother and father all wrapped into one, depended upon to feed him and clothe him and change him and bathe him and rock him and meet his every need. And the next day you're a third wheel, because Mom is around. You are expected to put in the long hours, but to pretend in public that you don't, for fear of undercutting your wife's sense of self-worth as a mother. How could she be doing her job, her psyche seems to whisper, if she's letting someone else make half the decisions and give half the care? There are many double binds in modern relationships, and this is the one I like the least.

48   I didn't let it drop that day, of course. At home, when Rose asserts the traditional mother's prerogative to make decisions and handle problems alone, on her terms, I often let it go. But when it happens in public, or in front of family, it is too much. It is as if my entire contribution to raising Nicholas is being denied, as if the world is being told that I am nothing more than a spectator. Luckily, as Nick grows older, and it becomes clear to Rose that she will always be number one in his heart, she has begun to relax her public vigilance, and this problem seems to have abated.

49   This is the first time I've ever been part of a woman's world. I'm not really a part of it, of course; the chasm between the sexes is too wide to step across so lightly. But when it comes to children, I have instant rapport with most mothers. We talk about the same things, think about the same things, joke about the same things. With men, it is almost never that way, even when the men are fathers and the subject is kids. We can share enthusiasms, but the sense of being there, on the inside—the unspoken understanding that comes out of shared experience—that is missing.

50   In fact, most men don't have the slightest idea what my life with Nick is like. When I tell colleagues—even those with children—that I have no time to read, or to watch television, I get blank stares. (I never tell mothers that; they already know. Who has time to read?) One friend, also a writer, stopped in the middle of a recent conversation and said, "You have Nick at home while you're working, don't you? What do you do with him?" No such thought could pass a mother's lips.

51   None of this would have been possible had I not been forced into taking care of Nick on my own much of the time. In fact, my entire relationship with Nick would have been different had I not been forced off the sidelines. I am convinced that in our society, when Mom is home with the kids, it is almost impossible for Dad to be an equal partner in their upbringing, even if he wants to be.

52   I believe this because for three weeks, while Rose was home after Nick's birth, it felt impossible to me. Rose had carried Nick for nine months; Rose had been through labor; and Rose was nursing him. For nine months he had listened to her heartbeat, felt her pulse, been a part of her being. Now he hunted her scent and drank from her body, and the bond between them was awesome. I was like some voyeur, peeking through the window at an ancient and sacred rite.

53   Then Rose went back to work, and I had no choice but to get off the sidelines. I *had* to get Nick dressed in the morning. I *had* to feed him. I *had* to burp him and rock him and change him and get up with him in the night. He may have wanted his mother, but she wasn't there.

54   Gradually, it all began to come naturally. I learned to carry him on my (nonexistent) hip and do anything—or any combination of things—with one hand. I learned to whip up a bottle in no time, to change a diaper and treat diaper rash and calm his tears.

55   Even on vacation, it is remarkably easy to slip back into a traditional role—for both Rose and me. But the day Rose goes back to work, I am always yanked back to reality. I complain a lot, but in truth, this is my great good fortune.

56   Last night Nick asked to go to the beach—"Go? Beach? Go? Beach?" I walked him the two blocks down, one of his hands firmly in mine, the other proudly holding the leash for Sam, our dog. We played on the swings for a long time, then strolled along the beach while Sam went swimming. It was that very still hour before dark, when the world slows to a hush, and little boys and girls slowly wind down. It was almost dark when we returned. Nick asked his daddy to give him his bath, then his mommy to put him to bed.

57   This morning when I woke he was lying beside me, on his mother's empty pillow. I looked over and he gave me a big smile, his eyes shining with that special, undiluted joy one sees only in children. Then he propped himself up on his elbows, leaned over and kissed me. If there are any better moments in life, I've never found them.

Questions for Discussion

1. To what does the title of Osborne's essay refer?

2. Osborne's staying home with his son defies traditional family roles. What difficulties does this defiance create?

3. Osborne quotes a letter by Rosalie Ziomek to the *New Republic* as describing "'the hardest part of new motherhood: the moment-to-moment dependency of a tiny, helpless, and demanding human being.'" Precisely what does that dependency entail for the mother? How does Osborne's essay convincingly develop the consequences of that dependency?

4. Certainly, Osborne's role as father differs from that of other, traditional fathers. As he says, however, it also differs from that of traditional mothers. How?

5. Osborne spends much more time with Nicholas than does his wife, yet Rose feels greater guilt than Osborne when Nicholas is hurt or sick, or when he throws a tantrum. What do these different reactions reveal about their perceptions of their roles?

Suggestions for Exploration and Writing

1. Osborne calls the "contradiction between family and career [. . .] the central unresolved conflict in the lives of American women today." In an essay drawn from your experience or observation, develop this assertion.

2. Osborne declares that he could not stay at home full time: "Part of the reason I love my role as a father is that I am secure in my role as a writer. Without that, I would not feel good enough about myself to be the kind of father I am." Why must he prove himself in ways other than fatherhood? Do men share the "unresolved conflict" Osborne attributes to women?

Rose Del Castillo Guilbault (b. 1952)

Born in Sonora, Mexico, Rose Del Castillo Guilbault has directed in television and published in magazines. This essay is taken from her column in the San Francisco Chronicle.

AMERICANIZATION IS TOUGH ON "MACHO"   (1989)

1   What is *macho*? That depends which side of the border you come from.

2   Although it's not unusual for words and expressions to lose their subtlety in translation, the negative connotations of *macho* in this country are troublesome to Hispanics.

3   Take the newspaper descriptions of alleged mass murderer Ramon Salcido. That an insensitive, insanely jealous, hard-drinking, violent Latin male is referred to as *macho* makes Hispanics cringe.

4   *"Es muy macho,"* the women in my family nod approvingly, describing a man they respect. But in the United States, when women say, "He's so macho," it's with disdain.

5   The Hispanic *macho* is manly, responsible, hardworking, a man in charge, a patriarch. A man who expresses strength through silence. What the Yiddish language would call a *mensch.*

6   The American *macho* is a chauvinist, a brute, uncouth, selfish, loud, abrasive, capable of inflicting pain, and sexually promiscuous.

7   Quintessential *macho* models in this country are Sylvester Stallone, Arnold Schwarzenegger and Charles Bronson. In their movies, they exude toughness, independence, masculinity. But a closer look reveals their machismo is really violence masquerading as courage, sullenness disguised as silence and irresponsibility camouflaged as independence.

8   If the Hispanic ideal of *macho* were translated to American screen roles, they might be Jimmy Stewart, Sean Connery and Laurence Olivier.

9   In Spanish, *macho* ennobles Latin males. In English it devalues them. This pattern seems consistent with the conflicts ethnic minority males experience in this country. Typically the cultural traits other societies value don't translate as desirable characteristics in America.

10   I watched my own father struggle with these cultural ambiguities. He worked on a farm for twenty years. He laid down miles of irrigation pipe, carefully plowed long, neat rows in fields, hacked away at recalcitrant weeds and drove tractors through whirlpools of dust. He stoically worked twenty-hour days during harvest season, accepting the long hours as part of agricultural work. When the boss complained or upbraided him for minor mistakes, he kept quiet, even when it was obvious the boss had erred.

11   He handled the most menial tasks with pride. At home he was a good provider, helped out my mother's family in Mexico without complaint, and was indulgent with me. Arguments between my mother and him generally had to do with money, or with his stubborn reluctance to share his troubles. He tried to work them out in his own silence. He didn't want to trouble my mother—a course that backfired, because the imagined is always worse than the reality.

12   Americans regarded my father as decidedly un-*macho.* His character was interpreted as nonassertive, his loyalty non-ambition, and his quietness, ignorance. I once overheard the boss's son blame him for plowing crooked rows in a field. My father merely smiled at the lie, knowing the boy had done it, but didn't refute it, confident his good work was well known. But the boss instead ridiculed him for being "stupid" and letting a kid get away with a lie. Seeing my embarrassment, my father dismissed the incident, saying "They're the dumb ones. Imagine, me fighting with a kid."

13   I tried not to look at him with American eyes because sometimes the reflection hurt.

14   Listening to my aunts' clucks of approval, my vision focused on the qualities America overlooked. "He's such a hard worker. So serious, so responsible." My aunts would secretly compliment my mother. The unspoken comparison was that he was not like some of their husbands, who drank and womanized. My uncles represented the darker side of *macho*.

15   In a patriarchal society, few challenge their roles. If men drink, it's because it's the manly thing to do. If they gamble, it's because it's how men relax. And if they fool around, well, it's because a man simply can't hold back so much man! My aunts didn't exactly meekly sit back, but they put up with these transgressions because Mexican society dictated this was their lot in life.

16   In the United States, I believe it was the feminist movement of the early '70s that changed *macho*'s meaning. Perhaps my generation of Latin women was in part responsible. I recall Chicanas complaining about the chauvinistic nature of Latin men and the notion they wanted their women barefoot, pregnant and in the kitchen. The generalization that Latin men embodied chauvinistic traits led to this interesting twist of semantics. Suddenly a word that represented something positive in one culture became a negative prototype in another.

17   The problem with the use of *macho* today is that it's become an accepted stereotype of the Latin male. And like all stereotypes, it distorts truth.

18   The impact of language in our society is undeniable. And the misuse of *macho* hints at a deeper cultural misunderstanding that extends beyond mere word definitions.

Questions for Discussion

1. The author gives two contrasting meanings of the word *macho*. What does she believe are the origins of these meanings?

2. List other words that we use in stereotyping males or females. In what ways can these words be misleading or dangerous?

3. If you speak a language other than American English, explain a word that has different meanings in these two languages.

Suggestions for Exploration and Writing

1. Write an essay discussing the qualities you believe a "real man" or a "real woman" should have.

2. Write an essay discussing the qualities that men and women have in common.

Shalmali Pal

Writer Shalmali Pal lives in San Francisco. She wrote this article for the "My Turn" column in Newsweek *magazine.*

LOOKING FOR MY PRINCE CHARMING   (1999)

1   For some reason, an Indian mother finds it necessary to stretch the truth when it comes to her son's height. "You're very tall. That's good, because my son is six feet," said a potential mother-in-law while perched on my uncle's sofa in Calcutta. When I found myself face to face with the aforementioned son on a street corner in New York City about two months later, I couldn't help noticing that he had perhaps an inch or two on my 5 feet 7 inches. Taking into consideration this man's many appealing characteristics—he's a successful investment banker, well mannered, well traveled—it seems odd that his mother chose to describe him in terms of inches. Welcome to the world of arranged marriages, where height is only a few notches below moral rectitude on the desirability scale.

2   Born and raised in America by parents who moved from Calcutta more than 30 years ago, I grew up on the prevailing notion that first comes love, then comes marriage. I watched Prince Charming fall for Cinderella and her slipper, and followed Laurie Partridge, the oldest sister of television's *The Partridge Family,* on countless dates with her *beau d'épisode.*

3   Fast forward twenty years and I'm singing a slightly different tune. While I haven't gone so far as to allow my parents to pick a mate virtually sight unseen and cast my lot with a stranger (as is still the tradition in many Indian families), I have agreed to the occasional discreet introduction.

4   Fortunately, my parents have respected my preferences in a mate. I would prefer someone who also was raised outside of India. I'd like it if he weighed more than I do. I want no mustaches. But most important, I don't want to be featured in any matrimonial advertisements, such as this one I found on the Web: "Renowned Physicians Family seek Bengali surgeons, physicians, others, 32 to 42, for US Citizen, Bengali, Brahmin, bright, pretty, adorable, petite, US raised, educated daughter. Two degrees, Business Administration, Computer Science, 37—looks 20ish, 3 day unconsummated convenient marriage annulled."

5   When people ask why I've agreed to my family's setups, I could say it's about preserving my cultural heritage or maintaining a link to a homeland that my parents have fought to preserve. But in the end, I'm just lazy. Marrying an Indian means a lot less explaining: Why don't my parents call one another by their first names? Why do they eat with their hands? What is that red dot on my mother's forehead?

6   Marriage strikes me as stressful enough, what with having to learn the ins and outs of any "normal" (i.e., slightly dysfunctional) family. Fitting in to a family with ties that are several time zones away could be too much to ask.

7   In the last two years I've phoned, e-mailed and dined with three potential "ideal husbands." (This is according to the aunts or cousins who talk
up the suitors to my parents. Marriage brokering is a favorite pastime for
my extended family.) The investment banker was my first blind date. The
timing couldn't have been worse. He'd made his mark and was searching
for a full-fledged adult companion, not a recent journalism-school graduate who spent most of lunch whining about being unemployed.

8   After that came drinks with the San Francisco-based attorney. He rattled on about himself for an hour and then we said polite goodbyes. It
was a superficial meeting, as initial conversations usually are. Two days
later he sent me a long-winded e-mail explaining that he wasn't ready for
a serious commitment—which was a shame because I'd already mailed
the invitations, set up the bridal registry and commissioned the cake.

9   Finally, there was the multimedia artist raised in London. We had been
e-mailing each other for a few months and, for the most part, it was a
pleasant exchange. When we met in person, he complimented my apartment, but said he would like it better if I weren't in it (I think he was joking). He made me see *Deep Impact*. Enough said.

10   Obviously, none of these gentlemen wound up being "the one." And
compared with the agony that can follow a breakup after just a few
months of dating, I came out relatively unscathed. However, just
because there wasn't an emotional investment, the rejection didn't
smart any less.

11   In my most dire moments I consider surrendering my marital future
to the scientists at the University of Hawaii who successfully cloned a couple of mice. If I could take elements of my three suitors and fuse them
together, maybe I would have the perfect man. I could just relax while
genetic engineering caught up with my needs. Of course, I don't see the
anxious aunts and cousins waiting it out with me. In fact, my father seems
keen on sending me on an extended holiday to India. I can just picture
myself rolling out of Calcutta customs, bleary-eyed and jet-lagged, to be
greeted by a line of eligible young men, holding up little cards with their
respective heights printed on them, well-intentioned mothers hovering
close at hand.

Questions for Discussion

1. How does Pal's reference to being "born and raised in America" also
define her Indian roots?

2. In what ways does the content of the Web message contrast with what
Pal wants in a man?

3. Why would Pal prefer to be lazy than to pursue an American husband?
Would you be willing to accept an arranged marriage? Why or why not?

4. What are some advantages of an arranged marriage? What are some of its disadvantages?

5. What is the overall tone of this essay?

Suggestions for Exploration and Writing

1. In an essay, argue for or against arranged marriages. As you argue, be sure to consider the other side.

2. Compare the courtship and marriage customs in this essay with those in Bessie Head's "Snapshots of a Wedding."

FICTION

Geoffrey Chaucer (1343–1400)

The son of a London merchant, Geoffrey Chaucer became the greatest of medieval English poets. He served the court of King Edward III on numerous diplomatic missions, particularly to France and to such Italian city-states as Genoa and Florence. An urbane and learned court poet, Chaucer is best known for such long poems as The Book of the Duchess, The House of Fame, Troilus and Criseyde, *and, pre-eminently,* Canterbury Tales. *The latter, of which "The Wife of Bath's Tale" is a part, consists of a series of stories told by a strikingly diverse group of pilgrims traveling from London to Thomas à Becket's shrine at Canterbury. The Wife of Bath, who has outlived five husbands, appears to have joined the pilgrimage to find husband number six.*

THE WIFE OF BATH'S TALE   (1386–1400)

TRANSLATED BY THEODORE MORRISON

1   In the old days when King Arthur ruled the nation,
Whom Welshmen speak of with such veneration,
This realm we live in was a fairy land.
The fairy queen danced with her jolly band
On the green meadows where they held dominion.
This was, as I have read, the old opinion;
I speak of many hundred years ago.
But no one sees an elf now, as you know,
For in our time the charity and prayers
And all the begging of these holy friars
Who swarm through every nook and every stream
Thicker than motes of dust in a sunbeam,
Blessing our chambers, kitchens, halls, and bowers,
Our cities, towns, and castles, our high towers,

Our villages, our stables, barns, and dairies,
They keep us all from seeing any fairies,
For where you might have come upon an elf
There now you find the holy friar himself
Working his district on industrious legs
And saying his devotions while he begs.
Women are safe now under every tree.
No incubus is there unless it's he,
And all they have to fear from him is shame.

2   It chanced that Arthur had a knight who came
Lustily riding home one day from hawking,
And in his path he saw a maiden walking
Before him, stark alone, right in his course.
This young knight took her maidenhead by force,
A crime at which the outcry was so keen
It would have cost his neck, but that the queen,
With other ladies, begged the king so long
That Arthur spared his life, for right or wrong,
And gave him to the queen, at her own will,
According to her choice, to save or kill.

3   She thanked the king, and later told this knight,
Choosing her time, "You are still in such a plight
Your very life has no security.
I grant your life, if you can answer me
This question: what is the thing that most of all
Women desire? Think, or your neck will fall
Under the ax! If you cannot let me know
Immediately, I give you leave to go
A twelvemonth and a day, no more, in quest
Of such an answer as will meet the test.
But you must pledge your honor to return
And yield your body, whatever you may learn."

4   The knight sighed; he was rueful beyond measure.
But what! He could not follow his own pleasure.
He chose at last upon his way to ride
And with such answer as God might provide
To come back when the year was at the close.
And so he takes his leave, and off he goes.

5   He seeks out every house and every place
Where he has any hope, by luck or grace,
Of learning what thing women covet most.
But it seemed he could not light on any coast
Where on this point two people would agree,
For some said wealth and some said jollity,
Some said position, some said sport in bed
And often to be widowed, often wed.
Some said that to a woman's heart what mattered

Above all else was to be pleased and flattered.
That shaft, to tell the truth, was a close hit.
Men win us best by flattery, I admit,
And by attention. Some say our greatest ease
Is to be free and do just as we please,
And not to have our faults thrown in our eyes,
But always to be praised for being wise.
And true enough, there's not one of us all
Who will not kick if you rub us on a gall.
Whatever vices we may have within,
We won't be taxed with any fault or sin.

6   Some say that women are delighted well
If it is thought that they will never tell
A secret they are trusted with, or scandal.
But that tale isn't worth an old rake handle!
We women, for a fact, can never hold
A secret. Will you hear a story told?
Then witness Midas! For it can be read
In Ovid that he had upon his head
Two ass's ears that he kept out of sight
Beneath his long hair with such skill and sleight
That no one else besides his wife could guess.
He loved her well, and trusted her no less.
He begged her not to make his blemish known,
But keep her knowledge to herself alone.
She swore that never, though to save her skin,
Would she be guilty of so mean a sin,
And yet it seemed to her she nearly died
Keeping a secret locked so long inside.
It swelled about her heart so hard and deep
She was afraid some word was bound to leap
Out of her mouth, and since there was no man
She dared to tell, down to a swamp she ran—
Her heart, until she got there, all agog—
And like a bittern booming in the bog
She put her mouth close to the watery ground:
"Water, do not betray me with your sound!
I speak to you, and you alone," she said.
"Two ass's ears grow on my husband's head!
And now my heart is whole, now it is out.
I'd burst if I held it longer, past all doubt."
Safely, you see, awhile you may confide
In us, but it will out; we cannot hide
A secret. Look in Ovid if you care
To learn what followed; the whole tale is there.

7   This knight, when he perceived he could not find
What women covet most, was low in mind;
But the day had come when homeward he must ride,
And as he crossed a wooded countryside
Some four and twenty ladies there by chance
He saw, all circling in a woodland dance,
And toward this dance he eagerly drew near
In hope of any counsel he might hear.
But the truth was, he had not reached the place
When dance and all, they vanished into space.
No living soul remained there to be seen
Save an old woman sitting on the green,
As ugly a witch as fancy could devise.
As he approached her she began to rise
And said, "Sir knight, here runs no thoroughfare.
What are you seeking with such anxious air?
Tell me! The better may your fortune be.
We old folk know a lot of things," said she.

8   "Good mother," said the knight, "my life's to pay,
That's all too certain, if I cannot say
What women covet most. If you could tell
That secret to me, I'd requite you well."

9   "Give me your hand," she answered. "Swear me true
That whatsoever I next ask of you,
You'll do it if it lies within your might
And I'll enlighten you before the night."

10   "Granted, upon my honor," he replied.

11   "Then I dare boast, and with no empty pride,
Your life is safe," she told him. "Let me die
If the queen herself won't say the same as I.
Let's learn if the haughtiest of all who wear
A net or coverchief upon their hair
Will be so forward as to answer 'no'
To what I'll teach you. No more; let us go."
With that she whispered something in his ear,
And told him to be glad and have no fear.

12   When they had reached the court, the knight declared
That he had kept his day, and was prepared
To give his answer, standing for his life.
Many the wise widow, many the wife,
Many the maid who rallied to the scene,
And at the head as justice sat the queen.
Then silence was enjoined; the knight was told
In open court to say what women hold
Precious above all else. He did not stand

Dumb like a beast, but spoke up at command
And plainly offered them his answering word
In manly voice, so that the whole court heard.

13   "My liege and lady, most of all," said he,
"Women desire to have the sovereignty
And sit in rule and government above
Their husbands, and to have their way in love.
That is what most you want. Spare me or kill
As you may like; I stand here by your will."

14   No widow, wife, or maid gave any token
Of contradicting what the knight had spoken.
He should not die; he should be spared instead;
He was worthy of his life, the whole court said.

15   The old woman whom the knight met on the green
Sprang up at this. "My sovereign lady queen,
Before your court has risen, do me right!
It was I who taught this answer to the knight,
For which he pledged his honor in my hand,
Solemnly, that the first thing I demand,
He would do it, if it lay within his might.
Before the court I ask you, then, sir knight,
To take me," said the woman, "as your wife,
For well you know that I have saved your life.
Deny me, on your honor, if you can."

16   "Alas," replied this miserable man,
"That was my promise, it must be confessed.
For the love of God, though, choose a new request!
Take all my wealth, and let my body be."

17   "If that's your tune, then curse both you and me,"
She said. "Though I am ugly, old, and poor,
I'll have, for all the metal and the ore
That under earth is hidden or lies above,
Nothing, except to be your wife and love."

18   "My love? No, my damnation, if you can!
Alas," he said, "that any of my clan
Should be so miserably misallied!"

19   All to no good; force overruled his pride,
And in the end he is constrained to wed,
And marries his old wife and goes to bed.

20   Now some will charge me with an oversight
In failing to describe the day's delight,
The merriment, the food, the dress at least.
But I reply, there was no joy nor feast;
There was only sorrow and sharp misery.
He married her in private, secretly,

And all day after, such was his distress,
Hid like an owl from his wife's ugliness.
21   Great was the woe this knight had in his head
When in due time they both were brought to bed.
He shuddered, tossed, and turned, and all the while
His old wife lay and waited with a smile.
"Is every knight so backward with a spouse?
Is it," she said, "a law in Arthur's house?
I am your love, your own, your wedded wife,
I am the woman who has saved your life.
I have never done you anything but right.
Why do you treat me this way the first night?
You must be mad, the way that you behave!
Tell me my fault, and as God's love can save,
I will amend it, truly, if I can."

22   "Amend it?" answered this unhappy man.
"It can never be amended, truth to tell.
You are so loathsome and so old as well,
And your low birth besides is such a cross
It is no wonder that I turn and toss.
God take my woeful spirit from my breast!"

23   "Is this," she said, "the cause of your unrest?"

24   "No wonder!" said the knight. "It truly is."

25   "Now sir," she said, "I could amend all this
Within three days, if it should please me to,
And if you deal with me as you should do.

26   "But since you speak of that nobility
That comes from ancient wealth and pedigree,
As if *that* constituted gentlemen,
I hold such arrogance not worth a hen!
The man whose virtue is pre-eminent,
In public and alone, always intent
On doing every generous act he can,
Take him—he is the greatest gentleman!
Christ wills that we should claim nobility
From him, not from old wealth or family.
Our elders left us all that they were worth
And through their wealth and blood we claim high birth,
But never, since it was beyond their giving,
Could they bequeath to us their virtuous living;
Although it first conferred on them the name
Of gentlemen, they could not leave that claim!

27   "Dante the Florentine on this was wise:
'Frail is the branch on which man's virtues rise'—
Thus runs his rhyme—'God's goodness wills that we

Should claim from him alone nobility.'
Thus from our elders we can only claim
Such temporal things as men may hurt and maim.
28   "It is clear enough that true nobility
Is not bequeathed along with property,
For many a lord's son does a deed of shame
And yet, God knows, enjoys his noble name.
But though descended from a noble house
And elders who were wise and virtuous,
If he will not follow his elders, who are dead,
But leads, himself, a shameful life instead,
He is not noble, be he duke or earl.
It is the churlish deed that makes the churl.
And therefore, my dear husband, I conclude
That though my ancestors were rough and rude,
Yet may Almighty God confer on me
The grace to live, as I hope, virtuously.
Call me of noble blood when I begin
To live in virtue and to cast out sin.
29   "As for my poverty, at which you grieve,
Almighty God in whom we all believe
In willful poverty chose to lead his life,
And surely every man and maid and wife
Can understand that Jesus, heaven's king,
Would never choose a low or vicious thing.
A poor and cheerful life is nobly led;
So Seneca and others have well said.
The man so poor he doesn't have a stitch,
If he thinks himself repaid, I count him rich.
He that is covetous, he is the poor man,
Pining to have the things he never can.
It is of cheerful mind, true poverty.
Juvenal says about it happily:
'The poor man as he goes along his way
And passes thieves is free to sing and play.'
Poverty is a good we loathe, a great
Reliever of our busy worldly state,
A great amender also of our minds
As he that patiently will bear it finds.
And poverty, for all it seems distressed,
Is a possession no one will contest.
Poverty, too, by bringing a man low,
Helps him the better both God and self to know.
Poverty is a glass where we can see
Which are our true friends, as it seems to me.
So, sir, I do not wrong you on this score;

Reproach me with my poverty no more.

30 "Now, sir, you tax me with my age; but, sir,
You gentlemen of breeding all aver
That men should not despise old age, but rather
Grant an old man respect, and call him 'father.'

31 "If I am old and ugly, as you have said,
You have less fear of being cuckolded,
For ugliness and age, as all agree,
Are notable guardians of chastity.
But since I know in what you take delight,
I'll gratify your worldly appetite.

32 "Choose now, which of two courses you will try:
To have me old and ugly till I die
But evermore your true and humble wife,
Never displeasing you in all my life,
Or will you have me rather young and fair
And take your chances on who may repair
Either to your house on account of me
Or to some other place, it well may be.
Now make your choice, whichever you prefer."

33 The knight took thought, and sighed, and said to her
At last, "My love and lady, my dear wife,
In your wise government I put my life.
Choose for yourself which course will best agree
With pleasure and honor, both for you and me.
I do not care, choose either of the two;
I am content, whatever pleases you."

34 "Then have I won from you the sovereignty,
Since I may choose and rule at will?" said she.

35 He answered, "That is best, I think, dear wife."

36 "Kiss me," she said. "Now we are done with strife,
For on my word, I will be both to you,
That is to say, fair, yes, and faithful too.
May I die mad unless I am as true
As ever wife was since the world was new.
Unless I am as lovely to be seen
By morning as an empress or a queen
Or any lady between east and west,
Do with my life or death as you think best.
Lift up the curtain, see what you may see."

37 And when the knight saw what had come to be
And knew her as she was, so young, so fair,
His joy was such that it was past compare.
He took her in his arms and gave her kisses
A thousand times on end; he bathed in blisses.
And she obeyed him also in full measure

In everything that tended to his pleasure.
38   And so they lived in full joy to the end.
And now to all us women may Christ send
Submissive husbands, full of youth in bed,
And grace to outlive all the men we wed.
And I pray Jesus to cut short the lives
Of those who won't be governed by their wives;
And old, ill-tempered niggards who hate expense,
God promptly bring them down with pestilence!

[handwritten: is moment if we can't give it ... all she wants]

Questions for Discussion

1. Why does King Arthur leave the knight's fate to be decided by the queen? In what ways is his doing so appropriate?

2. What, according to the old woman, do women most desire? Do you agree with her assessment? Why or why not?

3. Should the knight's correct answer save him from the penalty of death for committing rape? Why or why not?

4. What attitude does the knight display in answering the old woman's demand that he marry her? What is the old woman's answer to his complaint that she is old, ugly, poor, and common?

5. In the end, the knight allows his wife to decide whether she will be beautiful or faithful. In what ways is this decision appropriate? What does it suggest that the knight has learned?

Suggestions for Exploration and Writing

1. In what ways is the knight's search for what women most want a quest? In what ways does this quest gently mock the traditional knightly quest?

2. What does this tale reveal about its teller, the Wife of Bath?

3. Write an essay arguing that the old woman's statement about what women want most is or is not accurate and suggesting other possible answers.

Nathaniel Hawthorne (1804–1864)

One of America's greatest fiction writers, Nathaniel Hawthorne was born in Salem, Massachusetts, and was strongly influenced by his Puritan heritage. The Scarlet Letter (1850) is considered an American classic. The House of Seven Gables (1851) and The Blithedale Romance (1852) continued his stories about New England, but in his last novel, The Marble Faun (1860), Hawthorne chose Italy as his setting. In his short story collections—Twice-Told Tales (1837), Mosses from an Old Manse (1846), and The Snow-Image, and Other Twice-Told Tales (1851)—Hawthorne gave American literature some of its most memorable short fiction.

Many of these stories, like "The Birth-Mark," portray men who over-estimate their own intelligence and power over science and consequently lose touch with the heart of humanity. Though Hawthorne seldom portrayed successful marriages in his fiction, his own marriage was a loving and lasting one.

THE BIRTH-MARK (1843)

1   In the latter part of the last century, there lived a man of science—an eminent proficient in every branch of natural philosophy—who, not long before our story opens, had made experience of a spiritual affinity, more attractive than any chemical one. He had left his laboratory to the care of an assistant, cleared his fine countenance from the furnace-smoke, washed the stain of acids from his fingers, and persuaded a beautiful woman to become his wife. In those days, when the comparatively recent discovery of electricity, and other kindred mysteries of nature, seemed to open paths into the region of miracle, it was not unusual for the love of science to rival the love of woman, in its depth and absorbing energy. The higher intellect, the imagination, the spirit, and even the heart, might all find their congenial aliment in pursuits which, as some of their ardent votaries believed, would ascend from one step of powerful intelligence to another, until the philosopher should lay his hand on the secret of creative force, and perhaps make new worlds for himself. We know not whether Aylmer possessed this degree of faith in man's ultimate control over nature. He had devoted himself, however, too unreservedly to scientific studies, ever to be weaned from them by any second passion. His love for his young wife might prove the stronger of the two; but it could only be by intertwining itself with his love of science, and uniting the strength of the latter to its own.

2   Such a union accordingly took place, and was attended with truly remarkable consequences, and a deeply impressive moral. One day, very soon after their marriage, Aylmer sat gazing at his wife, with a trouble in his countenance that grew stronger, until he spoke.

3   "Georgiana," said he, "has it never occurred to you that the mark upon your cheek might be removed?"

4   "No, indeed," said she, smiling; but perceiving the seriousness of his manner, she blushed deeply. "To tell you the truth, it has been so often called a charm, that I was simple enough to imagine it might be so."

5   "Ah, upon another face, perhaps it might," replied her husband. "But never on yours! No, dearest Georgiana, you came so nearly perfect from the hand of Nature, that this slightest possible defect—which we hesitate whether to term a defect or a beauty—shocks me, as being the visible mark of earthly imperfection."

6   "Shocks you, my husband!" cried Georgiana, deeply hurt; at first reddening with momentary anger, but then bursting into tears. "Then why did you take me from my mother's side? You cannot love what shocks you!"

7   To explain this conversation, it must be mentioned, that, in the centre of Georgiana's left cheek, there was a singular mark, deeply

interwoven, as it were, with the texture and substance of her face. In the usual state of her complexion,—a healthy, though delicate bloom,—the mark wore a tint of deeper crimson, which imperfectly defined its shape amid the surrounding rosiness. When she blushed, it gradually became more indistinct, and finally vanished amid the triumphant rush of blood, that bathed the whole check with its brilliant glow. But, if any shifting emotion caused her to turn pale, there was the mark again, a crimson stain upon the snow, in what Aylmer sometimes deemed an almost fearful distinctness. Its shape bore not a little similarity to the human hand, though of the smallest pigmy size. Georgiana's lovers were wont to say, that some fairy, at her birth-hour, had laid her tiny hand upon the infant's cheek, and left this impress there, in token of the magic endowments that were to give her such sway over all hearts. Many a desperate swain would have risked life for the privilege of pressing his lips to the mysterious hand. It must not be concealed, however, that the impression wrought by this fairy sign-manual varied exceedingly, according to the difference of temperament in the beholders. Some fastidious persons—but they were exclusively of her own sex—affirmed that the Bloody Hand, as they chose to call it, quite destroyed the effect of Georgiana's beauty, and rendered her countenance even hideous. But it would be as reasonable to say that one of those small blue stains, which sometimes occur in the purest statuary marble, would convert the Eve of Powers to a monster. Masculine observers, if the birth-mark did not heighten their admiration, contented themselves with wishing it away, that the world might possess one living specimen of ideal loveliness, without the semblance of a flaw. After his marriage—for he thought little or nothing of the matter before—Aylmer discovered that this was the case with himself.

8   Had she been less beautiful—if Envy's self could have found aught else to sneer at—he might have felt his affection heightened by the prettiness of this mimic hand, now vaguely portrayed, now lost, now stealing forth again and glimmering to-and-fro with every pulse of emotion that throbbed within her heart. But, seeing her otherwise so perfect, he found this one defect grow more and more intolerable, with every moment of their united lives. It was the fatal flaw of humanity, which Nature, in one shape or another, stamps ineffaceably on all her productions, either to imply that they are temporary and finite, or that their perfection must be wrought by toil and pain. The Crimson Hand expressed the ineludible gripe, in which mortality clutches the highest and purest of earthly mould, degrading them into kindred with the lowest, and even with the very brutes, like whom their visible frames return to dust. In this manner, selecting it as the symbol of his wife's liability to sin, sorrow, decay, and death, Alymer's sombre imagination was not long in rendering the birth-mark a frightful object, causing him more trouble and horror than ever Georgiana's beauty, whether of soul or sense, had given him delight.

9   At all the seasons which should have been their happiest, he invariable and without intending it—nay, in spite of a purpose to the contrary—

reverted to this one disastrous topic. Trifling as it at first appeared, it so connected itself with innumerable trains of thought, and modes of feeling, that it became the central point of all. With the morning twilight, Aylmer opened his eyes upon his wife's face, and recognized the symbol of imperfection; and when they sat together at the evening hearth, his eyes wandered stealthily to her cheek, and beheld, flickering with the blaze of the wood fire, the spectral Hand that wrote mortality, where he would fain have worshipped. Georgiana soon learned to shudder at his gaze. It needed but a glance, with the peculiar expression that his face often wore, to change the roses of her cheek into a deathlike paleness, amid which the Crimson Hand was brought strongly out, like a bas-relief of ruby on the whitest marble.

10   Late, one night, when the lights were growing dim, so as hardly to betray the stain on the poor wife's cheek, she herself, for the first time, voluntarily took up the subject.

11   "Do you remember, my dear Aylmer," said she, with a feeble attempt at a smile—"have you any recollection of a dream, last night, about this odious Hand?"

12   "None!—none whatever!" replied Aylmer, starting; but then he added in a dry, cold tone, affected for the sake of concealing the real depth of his emotion:—"I might well dream of it; for before I fell asleep, it had taken a pretty firm hold of my fancy."

13   "And you did dream of it," continued Georgiana, hastily; for she dreaded lest a gush of tears should interrupt what she had to say—"A terrible dream! I wonder that you can forget it. Is it possible to forget this one expression?—'It is in her heart now—we must have it out'—Reflect, my husband; for by all means I would have you recall that dream."

14   The mind is in a sad note, when Sleep, the all-involving, cannot confine her spectres within the dim region of her sway, but suffers them to break forth, affrighting this actual life with secrets that perchance belong to a deeper one. Aylmer now remembered his dream. He had fancied himself, with his servant Aminadab, attempting an operation for the removal of the birth-mark. But the deeper went the knife, the deeper sank the Hand, until at length its tiny grasp appeared to have caught hold of Georgiana's heart; whence, however, her husband was inexorably resolved to cut or wrench it away.

15   When the dream had shaped itself perfectly in his memory, Aylmer sat in his wife's presence with a guilty feeling. Truth often finds its way to the mind close-muffled in robes of sleep, and then speaks with uncompromising directness of matters in regard to which we practise an unconscious self-deception, during our waking moments. Until now, he had not been aware of the tyrannizing influence acquired by one idea over his mind, and of the lengths which he might find in his heart to go, for the sake of giving himself peace.

16   "Aylmer," resumed Georgiana, solemnly, "I know not what may be the cost to both of us, to rid me of this fatal birth-mark. Perhaps its removal

may cause cureless deformity. Or, it may be, the stain goes as deep as life itself. Again, do we know that there is a possibility, on any terms, of unclasping the firm gripe of this little Hand, which was laid upon me before I came into the world?"

17   "Dearest Georgiana, I have spent much thought upon the subject," hastily interrupted Aylmer—"I am convinced of the perfect practicability of its removal."

18   "If there be the remotest possibility of it," continued Georgiana, "let the attempt be made, at whatever risk. Danger is nothing to me; for life— while this hateful mark makes me the object of your horror and disgust— life is a burthen which I would fling down with joy. Either remove this dreadful Hand, or take my wretched life! You have deep science! All the world bears witness of it. You have achieved great wonders! Cannot you remove this little little mark, which I cover with the tips of two small fingers? Is this beyond your power, for the sake of your own peace, and to save your poor wife from madness?"

19   "Noblest—dearest—tenderest wife!" cried Aylmer, rapturously. "Doubt not my power. I have already given this matter the deepest thought— thought which might almost have enlightened me to create a being less perfect than yourself. Georgiana, you have led me deeper than ever into the heart of science. I feel myself fully competent to render this dear cheek as faultless as its fellow; and then, most beloved, what will be my triumph, when I shall have corrected what Nature left imperfect, in her fairest work! Even Pygmalion, when his sculptured woman assumed life, felt not greater ecstasy than mine will be."

20   "It is resolved, then," said Georgiana, faintly smiling,—"And, Aylmer, spare me not, though you should find the birth-mark take refuge in my heart at last."

21   Her husband tenderly kissed her cheek—her right cheek—not that which bore the impress of the Crimson Hand.

22   The next day, Aylmer apprized his wife of a plan that he had formed, whereby he might have opportunity for the intense thought and constant watchfulness, which the proposed operation would require; while Georgiana, likewise, would enjoy the perfect repose essential to its success. They were to seclude themselves in the extensive apartments occupied by Aylmer as a laboratory, and where, during his toilsome youth, he had made discoveries in the elemental powers of nature, that had roused the admiration of all the learned societies in Europe. Seated calmly in this laboratory, the pale philosopher had investigated the secrets of the highest cloud-region, and of the profoundest mines; he had satisfied himself of the causes that kindled and kept alive the fires of the volcano; and had explained the mystery of fountains, and how it is that they gush forth, some so bright and pure, and others with such rich medicinal virtues, from the dark bosom of the earth. Here, too, at an earlier period, he had studied the wonders of the human frame, and attempted to fathom the very process by which Nature assimilates all her precious influences from

earth and air, and from the spiritual world to create and foster Man, her masterpiece. The latter pursuit, however Aylmer had long laid aside, in unwilling recognition of the truth, against which all seekers sooner or later stumble, that our great creative Mother while she amuses us with apparently working in the broadest sunshine, is yet severely careful to keep her own secrets, and, in spite of her pretended openness, shows us nothing but results. She permits us indeed, to mar, but seldom to mend, and, like a jealous patentee, on no account to make. Now, however, Aylmer resumed these half-forgotten investigations; not, of course, with such hopes or wishes as first suggested them; but because they involved much physiological truth, and lay in the path of his proposed scheme for the treatment of Georgiana.

23   As he led her over the threshold of the laboratory, Georgiana was cold and tremulous. Aylmer looked cheerfully into her face, with intent to reassure her, but was so startled with the intense glow of the birth-mark upon the whiteness of her cheek, that he could not restrain a strong convulsive shudder. His wife fainted.

24   "Aminadab! Aminadab!" shouted Aylmer, stamping violently on the floor.

25   Forthwith, there issued from an inner apartment a man of low stature, but bulky frame, with shaggy hair hanging about his visage, which was grimed with the vapors of the furnace. This personage had been Aylmer's underworker during his whole scientific career, and was admirably fitted for that office by his great mechanical readiness, and the skill with which, while incapable of comprehending a single principle, he executed all the practical details of his master's experiments. With his vast strength, his shaggy hair, his smoky aspect, and the indescribable earthiness that incrusted him, he seemed to represent man's physical nature; while Aylmer's slender figure, and pale, intellectual face, were no less apt a type of the spiritual element.

26   "Throw open the door of the boudoir, Aminadab," said Aylmer, "and burn a pastille."

27   "Yes, master," answered Aminadab, looking intently at the lifeless form of Georgiana; and then he muttered to himself:—"If she were my wife, I'd never part with that birth-mark."

28   When Georgiana recovered consciousness, she found herself breathing an atmosphere of penetrating fragrance, the gentle potency of which had recalled her from her deathlike faintness. The scene around her looked like enchantment. Aylmer had converted those smoky, dingy, sombre rooms, where he had spent his brightest years in recondite pursuits, into a series of beautiful apartments, not unfit to be the secluded abode of a lovely woman. The walls were hung with gorgeous curtains, which imparted the combination of grandeur and grace, that no other species of adornment can achieve; and as they fell from the ceiling to the floor, their rich and ponderous folds, concealing all angles and straight lines, appeared to shut in the scene from infinite space. For aught Georgiana

knew, it might be a pavilion among the clouds. And Aylmer, excluding the sunshine, which would have interfered with his chemical processes, had supplied its place with perfumed lamps, emitting flames of various hue, but all uniting in a soft, empurpled radiance. He now knelt by his wife's side, watching her earnestly, but without alarm; for he was confident in his science, and felt that he could draw a magic circle round her, within which no evil might intrude.

29   "Where am I?—Ah, I remember!" said Georgiana, faintly; and she placed her hand over her cheek, to hide the terrible mark from her husband's eyes.

30   "Fear not, dearest!" exclaimed he. "Do not shrink from me! Believe me, Georgiana, I even rejoice in this single imperfection, since it will be such rapture to remove it."

31   "Oh, spare me!" sadly replied his wife—"Pray do not look at it again. I never can forget that convulsive shudder."

32   In order to soothe Georgiana, and, as it were, to release her mind from the burthen of actual things, Aylmer now put in practice some of the light and playful secrets, which science had taught him among its profounder lore. Airy figures, absolutely bodiless ideas, and forms of unsubstantial beauty came and danced before her, imprinting their momentary footsteps on beams of light. Though she had some indistinct idea of the method of these optical phenomena, still the illusion was almost perfect enough to warrant the belief that her husband possessed sway over the spiritual world. Then again, when she felt a wish to look forth from her seclusion, immediately, as if her thoughts were answered, the procession of external existence flitted across a screen. The scenery and the figures of actual life were perfectly represented, but with that bewitching, yet indescribable difference, which always makes a picture, an image, or a shadow, so much more attractive than the original. When wearied of this, Aylmer bade her cast her eyes upon a vessel, containing a quantity of earth. She did so, with little interest at first, but was soon startled, to perceive the germ of a plant, shooting upward from the soil. Then came the slender stalk—the leaves gradually unfolded themselves—and amid them was a perfect and lovely flower.

33   "It is magical!" cried Georgiana, "I dare not touch it."

34   "Nay, pluck it," answered Aylmer, "pluck it, and inhale its brief perfume while you may. The flower will wither in a few moments, and leave nothing save its brown seed-vessels—but thence may be perpetuated a race as ephemeral as itself."

35   But Georgiana had no sooner touched the flower than the whole plant suffered a blight, its leaves turning coal-black, as if by the agency of fire.

36   "There was too powerful a stimulus," said Aylmer thoughtfully.

37   To make up for this abortive experiment, he proposed to take her portrait by a scientific process of his own invention. It was to be effected by rays of light striking upon a polished plate of metal. Georgiana assented—but, on looking at the result, was affrighted to find the features of the

portrait blurred and indefinable; while the minute figure of a hand appeared where the cheek should have been. Aylmer snatched the metallic plate and threw it into a jar of corrosive acid.

38   Soon, however, he forgot these mortifying failures. In the intervals of study and chemical experiment, he came to her, flushed and exhausted, but seemed invigorated by her presence, and spoke in glowing language of the resources of his art. He gave a history of the long dynasty of the Alchemists, who spent so many ages in quest of the universal solvent, by which the Golden Principle might be elicited from all things vile and base. Aylmer appeared to believe that, by the plainest scientific logic, it was altogether within the limits of possibility to discover this long-sought medium; but, he added, a philosopher who should go deep enough to acquire the power would attain too lofty a wisdom to stoop to the exercise of it. Not less singular were his opinions in regard to the Elixir Vitae. He more than intimated that it was his option to concoct a liquid that should prolong life for years—perhaps interminably—but that it would produce a discord in nature, which all the world, and chiefly the quaffer of the immortal nostrum, would find cause to curse.

39   "Aylmer, are you in earnest?" asked Georgiana, looking at him with amazement and fear; "it is terrible to possess such power, or even to dream of possessing it!"

40   "Oh, do not tremble, my love!" said her husband, "I would not wrong either you or myself by working such inharmonious effects upon our lives. But I would have you consider how trifling, in comparison, is the skill requisite to remove this little Hand."

41   At the mention of the birth-mark, Georgiana, as usual, shrank, as if a red-hot iron had touched her cheek.

42   Again, Aylmer applied himself to his labors. She could hear his voice in the distant furnace-room, giving directions to Aminadab, whose harsh, uncouth, misshapen tones were audible in response, more like the grunt or growl of a brute than human speech. After hours of absence, Aylmer reappeared, and proposed that she should now examine his cabinet of chemical products and natural treasures of the earth. Among the former he showed her a small vial, in which, he remarked, was contained a gentle yet most powerful fragrance, capable of impregnating all the breezes that blow across a kingdom. They were of inestimable value, the contents of that little vial; and, as he said so, he threw some of the perfume into the air, and filled the room with piercing and invigorating delight.

43   "And what is this?" asked Georgiana, pointing to a small crystal globe, containing a gold-colored liquid. "It is so beautiful to the eye, that I could imagine it the Elixir of Life."

44   "In one sense it is," replied Aylmer, "or rather the Elixir of Immortality. It is the most precious poison that ever was concocted in this world. By its aid, I could apportion the lifetime of any mortal at whom you might point your finger. The strength of the dose would determine whether he were to linger out years, or drop dead in the midst of a breath. No king, on his

guarded throne, could keep his life, if I, in my private station, should deem that the welfare of millions justified me in depriving him of it."

45   "Why do you keep such a terrific drug?" inquired Georgiana in horror.

46   "Do not mistrust me, dearest!" said her husband, smiling; "its virtuous potency is yet greater than its harmful one. But, see! here is a powerful cosmetic. With a few drops of this, in a vase of water, freckles may be washed away as easily as the hands are cleansed. A stronger infusion would take the blood out of the cheek, and leave the rosiest beauty a pale ghost."

47   "Is it with this lotion that you intend to bathe my cheek?" asked Georgiana anxiously.

48   "Oh, no!" hastily replied her husband—"this is merely superficial. Your case demands a remedy that shall go deeper."

49   In his interviews with Georgiana, Aylmer generally made minute inquiries as to her sensations, and whether the confinement of the rooms, and the temperature of the atmosphere, agreed with her. These questions had such a particular drift that Georgiana began to conjecture that she was already subjected to certain physical influences, either breathed in with the fragrant air, or taken with her food. She fancied likewise—but it might be altogether fancy—that there was a stirring up of her system,— a strange indefinite sensation creeping through her veins, and tingling, half painfully, half pleasurably, at her heart. Still, whenever she dared to look into the mirror, there she beheld herself, pale as a white rose, and with the crimson birth-mark stamped upon her cheek. Not even Aylmer now hated it so much as she.

50   To dispel the tedium of the hours which her husband found it necessary to devote to the processes of combination and analysis, Georgiana turned over the volumes of his scientific library. In many dark old tomes, she met with chapters full of romance and poetry. They were the works of the philosophers of the middle ages, such as Albertus Magnus, Cornelius Agrippa, Paracelsus, and the famous friar who created the prophetic Brazen Head. All these antique naturalists stood in advance of their centuries, yet were imbued with some of their credulity, and therefore were believed, and perhaps imagined themselves, to have acquired from the investigation of nature a power above nature, and from physics a sway over the spiritual world. Hardly less curious and imaginative were the early volumes of the Transactions of the Royal Society, in which the members, knowing little of the limits of natural possibility, were continually recording wonders, or proposing methods whereby wonders might be wrought.

51   But, to Georgiana, the most engrossing volume was a large folio from her husband's own hand, in which he had recorded every experiment of his scientific career, with its original aim, the methods adopted for its development, and its final success or failure, with the circumstances to which either event was attributable. The book, in truth, was both the history and emblem of his ardent, ambitious, imaginative, yet practical and laborious life. He handled physical details, as if there were nothing

beyond them; yet spiritualized them all, and redeemed himself from materialism, by his strong and eager aspiration towards the infinite. In his grasp, the veriest clod of earth assumed a soul. Georgiana, as she read, reverenced Aylmer, and loved him more profoundly than ever, but with a less entire dependence on his judgment than heretofore. Much as he had accomplished, she could not but observe that his most splendid successes were almost invariably failures, if compared with the ideal at which he aimed. His brightest diamonds were the merest pebbles, and felt to be so by himself, in comparison with the inestimable gems which lay hidden beyond his reach. The volume, rich with achievements that had won renown for its author, was yet as melancholy a record as ever mortal hand had penned. It was the sad confession, and continual exemplification, of the short-comings of the composite man—the spirit burthened with clay and working in matter—and of the despair that assails the higher nature at finding itself so miserably thwarted by the earthly part. Perhaps every man of genius, in whatever sphere, might recognize the image of his own experience in Aylmer's journal.

52   So deeply did these reflections affect Georgiana that she laid her face upon the open volume and burst into tears. In this situation she was found by her husband.

53   "It is dangerous to read in a sorcerer's books," said he, with a smile, though his countenance was uneasy and displeased. "Georgiana, there are pages in that volume, which I can scarcely glance over and keep my senses. Take heed lest it prove as detrimental to you!"

54   "It has made me worship you more than ever," said she.

55   "Ah! wait for this one success," rejoined he, "then worship me if you will. I shall deem myself hardly unworthy of it. But, come! I have sought you for the luxury of your voice. Sing to me, dearest!"

56   So she poured out the liquid music of her voice to quench the thirst of his spirit. He then took his leave, with a boyish exuberance of gaiety, assuring her that her seclusion would endure but a little longer, and that the result was already certain. Scarcely had he departed, when Georgiana felt irresistibly impelled to follow him. She had forgotten to inform Aylmer of a symptom, which, for two or three hours past, had begun to excite her attention. It was a sensation in the fatal birth-mark, not painful, but which induced a restlessness throughout her system. Hastening after her husband, she intruded, for the first time, into the laboratory.

57   The first thing that struck her eye was the furnace, that hot and feverish worker, with the intense glow of its fire, which, by the quantities of soot clustered above it, seemed to have been burning for ages. There was a distilling apparatus in full operation. Around the room were retorts, tubes, cylinders, crucibles, and other apparatus of chemical research. An electrical machine stood ready for immediate use. The atmosphere felt oppressively close, and was tainted with gaseous odors, which had been tormented forth by the processes of science. The severe and homely simplicity of the apartment, with its naked walls and brick pavement, looked

strange, accustomed as Georgiana had become to the fantastic elegance of her boudoir. But what chiefly, indeed almost solely, drew her attention, was the aspect of Aylmer himself.

58 He was pale as death, anxious, and absorbed, and hung over the furnace as if it depended upon his utmost watchfulness whether the liquid, which it was distilling, should be the draught of immortal happiness or misery. How different from the sanguine and joyous mien that he had assumed for Georgiana's encouragement!

59 "Carefully now, Aminadab! Carefully, thou human machine! Carefully, thou man of clay!" muttered Aylmer, more to himself than his assistant. "Now, if there be a thought too much or too little, it is all over!"

60 "Ho! ho!" mumbled Aminadab—"look, master, look!"

61 Aylmer raised his eyes hastily, and at first reddened, then grew paler than ever, on beholding Georgiana. He rushed towards her, and seized her arm with a gripe that left the print of his fingers upon it.

62 "Why do you come hither? Have you no trust in your husband?" cried he impetuously. "Would you throw the blight of that fatal birth-mark over my labors? It is not well done. Go, prying woman, go!"

63 "Nay, Aylmer," said Georgiana, with the firmness of which she possessed no stinted endowment, "it is not you that have a right to complain. You mistrust your wife! You have concealed the anxiety with which you watch the development of this experiment. Think not so unworthily of me, my husband! Tell me all the risk we run; and fear not that I shall shrink, for my share in it is far less than your own!"

64 "No, no, Georgiana!" said Aylmer impatiently, "it must not be."

65 "I submit," replied she calmly. "And, Aylmer, I shall quaff whatever draught you bring me; but it will be on the same principle that would induce me to take a dose of poison, if offered by your hand."

"My noble wife," said Aylmer, deeply moved, "I knew not the height and depth of your nature, until now. Nothing shall be concealed. Know, then, that this Crimson Hand, superficial as it seems, has clutched its grasp into your being, with a strength of which I had no previous conception. I have already administered agents powerful enough to do aught except to change your entire physical system. Only one thing remains to be tried. If that fail us, we are ruined!"

66 "Why did you hesitate to tell me this?" asked she.

67 "Because, Georgiana," said Aylmer, in a low voice, "there is danger!"

68 "Danger? There is but one danger—that this horrible stigma shall be left upon my cheek!" cried Georgiana. "Remove it! remove it!—whatever be the cost—or we shall both go mad!"

69 "Heaven knows, your words are too true," said Aylmer, sadly. "And now, dearest, return to your boudoir. In a little while, all will be tested."

70 He conducted her back, and took leave of her with a solemn tenderness, which spoke far more than his words how much was now at stake. After his departure, Georgiana became wrapt in musings. She considered the character of Aylmer, and did it completer justice than at any previous

moment. Her heart exulted, while it trembled, at his honorable love, so pure and lofty that it would accept nothing less than perfection, nor miserably make itself contented with an earthlier nature than he had dreamed of. She felt how much more precious was such a sentiment, than that meaner kind which would have borne with the imperfection for her sake, and have been guilty of treason to holy love, by degrading its perfect idea to the level of the actual. And, with her whole spirit, she prayed, that, for a single moment, she might satisfy his highest and deepest conception. Longer than one moment, she well knew, it could not be; for his spirit was ever on the march—ever ascending—and each instant required something that was beyond the scope of the instant before.

71   The sound of her husband's footsteps aroused her. He bore a crystal goblet, containing a liquor colorless as water, but bright enough to be the draught of immortality. Aylmer was pale; but it seemed rather the consequence of a highly wrought state of mind, and tension of spirit, than of fear or doubt.

72   "The concoction of the draught has been perfect," said he, in answer to Georgiana's look. "Unless all my science have deceived me, it cannot fail."

73   "Save on your account, my dearest Aylmer," observed his wife, "I might wish to put off this birth-mark of mortality by relinquishing mortality itself, in preference to any other mode. Life is but a sad possession to those who have attained precisely the degree of moral advancement at which I stand. Were I weaker and blinder, it might be happiness. Were I stronger, it might be endured hopefully. But, being what I find myself, methinks I am of all mortals the most fit to die."

74   "You are fit for heaven without tasting death!" replied her husband. "But why do we speak of dying? The draught cannot fail. Behold its effect upon this plant!"

75   On the window-seat there stood a geranium, diseased with yellow blotches which had overspread all its leaves. Aylmer poured a small quantity of the liquid upon the soil in which it grew. In a little time, when the roots of the plant had taken up the moisture, the unsightly blotches began to be extinguished in a living verdure.

76   "There needed no proof," said Georgiana, quietly. "Give me the goblet. I joyfully stake all upon your word."

77   "Drink, then, thou lofty creature!" exclaimed Aylmer, with fervid admiration. "There is no taint of imperfection on thy spirit. Thy sensible frame, too, shall be all perfect!"

78   She quaffed the liquid, and returned the goblet to his hand.

79   "It is grateful," said she, with a placid smile. "Methinks it is like water from a heavenly fountain; for it contains I know not what of unobtrusive fragrance and deliciousness. It allays a feverish thirst that had parched me for many days. Now, dearest, let me sleep. My earthly senses are closing over my spirit like the leaves round the heart of a rose at sunset."

80   She spoke the last words with a gentle reluctance, as if it required almost more energy than she could command to pronounce the faint and

lingering syllables. Scarcely had they loitered through her lips, ere she was lost in slumber. Aylmer sat by her side, watching her aspect with the emotions proper to a man, the whole value of whose existence was involved in the process now to be tested. Mingled with this mood, however, was the philosophic investigation, characteristic of the man of science. Not the minutest symptom escaped him. A heightened flush of the cheek—a slight irregularity of breath—a quiver of the eyelid—a hardly perceptible tremor through the frame—such were the details which, as the moments passed, he wrote down in his folio volume. Intense thought had set its stamp upon every previous page of that volume; but the thoughts of years were all concentrated upon the last.

81   While thus employed, he failed not to gaze often at the fatal Hand, and not without a shudder. Yet once, by a strange and unaccountable impulse, he pressed it with his lips. His spirit recoiled, however, in the very act, and Georgiana, out of the midst of her deep sleep, moved uneasily and murmured as if in remonstrance. Again, Aylmer resumed his watch. Nor was it without avail. The Crimson Hand, which at first had been strongly visible upon the marble paleness of Georgiana's cheek now grew more faintly outlined. She remained not less pale than ever; but the birth-mark, with every breath that came and went, lost somewhat of its former distinctness. Its presence had been awful; its departure was more awful still. Watch the stain of the rainbow fading out of the sky; and you will know how that mysterious symbol passed away.

82   "By Heaven, it is well nigh gone!" said Aylmer to himself, in almost irrepressible ecstasy. "I can scarcely trace it now. Success! Success! And now it is like the faintest rose-color. The slightest flush of blood across her cheek would overcome it. But she is so pale!"

83   He drew aside the window-curtain and suffered the light of natural day to fall into the room and rest upon her cheek. At the same time, he heard a gross, hoarse chuckle, which he had long known as his servant Aminadab's expression of delight.

84   "Ah, clod! Ah, earthly mass!" cried Aylmer, laughing in a sort of frenzy. "You have served me well! Matter and Spirit—Earth and Heaven—have both done their part in this! Laugh, thing of senses! You have earned the right to laugh."

85   These exclamations broke Georgiana's sleep. She slowly unclosed her eyes and gazed into the mirror, which her husband had arranged for that purpose. A faint smile flitted over her lips, when she recognized how barely perceptible was now that Crimson Hand, which had once blazed forth with such disastrous brilliancy as to scare away all their happiness. But then her eyes sought Aylmer's face, with a trouble and anxiety that he could by no means account for.

86   "My poor Aylmer!" murmured she.

87   "Poor? Nay, richest! Happiest! Most favored!" exclaimed he. "My peerless bride, it is successful! You are perfect!"

88   "My poor Aylmer!" she repeated, with a more than human tenderness. "You have aimed loftily!—you have done nobly! Do not repent, that, with

so high and pure a feeling, you have rejected the best that earth could offer. Aylmer—dearest Aylmer—I am dying!"

89   Alas, it was too true! The fatal Hand had grappled with the mystery of life, and was the bond by which an angelic spirit kept itself in union with a mortal frame. As the last crimson tint of the birth-mark—that sole token of human imperfection—faded from her cheek, the parting breath of the now perfect woman passed into the atmosphere, and her soul, lingering a moment near her husband, took its heavenward flight. Then a hoarse, chuckling laugh was heard again! Thus ever does the gross Fatality of Earth exult in its invariable triumph over the immortal essence, which, in this dim sphere of half-development, demands the completeness of a higher state. Yet, had Aylmer reached a profounder wisdom, he need not thus have flung away the happiness, which would have woven his mortal life of the self-same texture with the celestial. The momentary circumstance was strong for him; he failed to look beyond the shadowy scope of Time, and living once for all in Eternity, to find the perfect Future in the present.

Questions for Discussion

1. Describe the elevated view of science that, according to Hawthorne, existed for some people at the end of the eighteenth century.

2. Explain why or how "the love of science" might "rival the love of woman." Why would the two be opposing forces? How does Aylmer try to blend the two?

3. Why did the birthmark not bother Aylmer when he courted Georgiana yet bother him after marriage? What does it represent to him? Why?

4. How do Aylmer's dream and the pattern of the results in Aylmer's experiments foreshadow the end of the story?

5. How and why do the views of women and men about the birthmark differ?

6. Why does Georgiana agree to submit to Aylmer's treatments? What does the wilting of the flower when Georgiana touches it suggest about these treatments?

7. Why is Aylmer upset when his wife enters his laboratory?

8. If Aylmer represents science, what does Aminadab represent?

9. Explain Georgiana's statement to Aylmer: "[Y]ou have aimed loftily; you have done nobly. Do not repent that with so high and pure a feeling, you have rejected the best the earth could offer."

10. How does the last sentence sum up one of Hawthorne's major points?

Suggestions for Exploration and Writing

1. Apply Hawthorne's statement, "She [Mother Nature] permits us indeed, to mar, but seldom to mend, and, like a jealous patentee, on no account to make," to one aspect of modern science, such as cloning.

2. The story is full of symbolic meaning from the birthmark itself to nature. In an essay, explain one or more of the symbols.

3. In an essay, explain what you think the theme of Hawthorne's story is.

4. Analyze the character of Aylmer, explaining whether or not he is guilty of hubris and examining his motivation.

5. Contrast Georgiana's situation with that of the girl child in "Barbie Doll."

Kate Chopin (1850–1904)

Katherine O'Flaherty was born in St. Louis, Missouri, but moved to Louisiana when she married Oscar Chopin in 1870. New Orleans and the Grande Isle are the setting for most of her stories and for her novel The Awakening *(1899), which shocked readers because of her treatment of adultery and suicide. Chopin's stories deal with marriages that are failing, women in the process of achieving independence, or subjects such as miscegenation and integration. "Désirée's Baby" deals honestly with women's emotions.*

Désirée's Baby   (1894)

1   As the day was pleasant, Madame Valmondé drove over to L'Abri to see Désirée and the baby.

2   It made her laugh to think of Désirée with a baby. Why, it seemed but yesterday that Désirée was little more than a baby herself; when Monsieur in riding through the gateway of Valmondé had found her lying asleep in the shadow of the big stone pillar.

3   The little one awoke in his arms and began to cry for "Dada." That was as much as she could do or say. Some people thought she might have strayed there of her own accord, for she was of the toddling age. The prevailing belief was that she had been purposely left by a party of Texans, whose canvas-covered wagon, late in the day, had crossed the ferry that Coton Maïs kept, just below the plantation. In time Madame Valmondé abandoned every speculation but the one that Désirée had been sent to her by a beneficent Providence to be the child of her affection, seeing that she was without child of the flesh. For the girl grew to be beautiful and gentle, affectionate and sincere—the idol of Valmondé.

4   It was no wonder, when she stood one day against the stone pillar in whose shadow she had lain asleep, eighteen years before, that Armand Aubigny riding by and seeing her there, had fallen in love with her. That was the way all the Aubignys fell in love, as if struck by a pistol shot. The wonder was that he had not loved her before; for he had known her since his father brought him home from Paris, a boy of eight, after his mother

died there. The passion that awoke in him that day, when he saw her at the gate, swept along like an avalanche, or like a prairie fire, or like anything that drives headlong over all obstacles.

5   Monsieur Valmondé grew practical and wanted things well considered: that is, the girl's obscure origin. Armand looked into her eyes and did not care. He was reminded that she was nameless. What did it matter about a name when he could give her one of the oldest and proudest in Louisiana? He ordered the *corbeille* from Paris, and contained himself with what patience he could until it arrived; then they were married.

6   Madame Valmondé had not seen Désirée and the baby for four weeks. When she reached L'Abri she shuddered at the first sight of it, as she always did. It was a sad looking place, which for many years had not known the gentle presence of a mistress, old Monsieur Aubigny having married and buried his wife in France, and she having loved her own land too well ever to leave it. The roof came down steep and black like a cowl, reaching out beyond the wide galleries that encircled the yellow stuccoed house. Big, solemn oaks grew close to it, and their thick-leaved, far-reaching branches shadowed it like a pall. Young Aubigny's rule was a strict one, too, and under it his negroes had forgotten how to be gay, as they had been during the old master's easygoing and indulgent lifetime.

7   The young mother was recovering slowly, and lay full length, in her soft white muslins and laces, upon a couch. The baby was beside her, upon her arm, where he had fallen asleep, at her breast. The yellow nurse woman sat beside a window fanning herself.

8   Madame Valmondé bent her portly figure over Désirée and kissed her, holding her an instant tenderly in her arms. Then she turned to the child.

9   "This is not the baby!" she exclaimed, in startled tones. French was the language spoken at Valmondé in those days.

10   "I knew you would be astonished," laughed Désirée, "at the way he has grown. The little *cochon de lait!* Look at his legs, mamma, and his hands and fingernails,—real finger-nails. Zandrine had to cut them this morning. Isn't it true, Zandrine?"

11   The woman bowed her turbaned head majestically, "Mais si, Madame."

12   "And the way he cries," went on Désirée, "is deafening. Armand heard him the other day as far away as La Blanche's cabin."

13   Madame Valmondé had never removed her eyes from the child. She lifted it and walked with it over to the window that was lightest. She scanned the baby narrowly, then looked as searchingly at Zandrine, whose face was turned to gaze across the fields.

14   "Yes, the child has grown, has changed," said Madame Valmondé, slowly, as she replaced it beside its mother. "What does Armand say?"

15   Désirée's face became suffused with a glow that was happiness itself.

16   "Oh, Armand is the proudest father in the parish, I believe, chiefly because it is a boy, to bear his name; though he says not,—that he would

have loved a girl as well. But I know it isn't true. I know he says that to please me. And mamma," she added, drawing Madame Valmondé's head down to her, and speaking in a whisper, "he hasn't punished one of them—not one of them—since baby is born. Even Négrillon, who pretended to have burnt his leg that he might rest from work—he only laughed, and said Négrillon was a great scamp. Oh, mamma, I'm so happy; it frightens me."

17 What Désirée said was true. Marriage, and later the birth of his son, had softened Armand Aubigny's imperious and exacting nature greatly. This was what made the gentle Désirée so happy, for she loved him desperately. When he frowned she trembled, but loved him. When he smiled, she asked no greater blessing of God. But Armand's dark, handsome face had not often been disfigured by frowns since the day he fell in love with her.

18 When the baby was about three months old, Désirée awoke one day to the conviction that there was something in the air menacing her peace. It was at first too subtle to grasp. It had only been a disquieting suggestion; an air of mystery among the blacks; unexpected visits from far-off neighbors who could hardly account for their coming. Then a strange, an awful change in her husband's manner, which she dared not ask him to explain. When he spoke to her, it was with averted eyes, from which the old love-light seemed to have gone out. He absented himself from home; and when there, avoided her presence and that of her child, without excuse. And the very spirit of Satan seemed suddenly to take hold of him in his dealings with the slaves. Désirée was miserable enough to die.

19 She sat in her room, one hot afternoon, in her *peignoir,* listlessly drawing through her fingers the strands of her long, silky brown hair that hung about her shoulders. The baby, half naked, lay asleep upon her own great mahogany bed, that was like a sumptuous throne, with its satin lined halfcanopy. One of La Blanche's little quadroon boys—half naked too—stood fanning the child slowly with a fan of peacock feathers. Désirée's eyes had been fixed absently and sadly upon the baby, while she was striving to penetrate the threatening mist that she felt closing about her. She looked from her child to the boy who stood beside him, and back again; over and over. "Ah!" It was a cry that she could not help, which she was not conscious of having uttered. The blood turned like ice in her veins, and a clammy moisture gathered upon her face.

20 She tried to speak to the little quadroon boy; but no sound would come, at first. When he heard his name uttered, he looked up, and his mistress was pointing to the door. He laid aside the great, soft fan, and obediently stole away, over the polished floor, on his bare tiptoes.

21 She stayed motionless, with gaze riveted upon her child, and her face the picture of fright.

22 Presently her husband entered the room, and without noticing her, went to a table and began to search among some papers which covered it.

23 "Armand," she called to him, in a voice which must have stabbed him, if he was human. But he did not notice. "Armand," she said again. Then

she rose and tottered toward him. "Armand," she panted once more, clutching his arm, "look at our child. What does it mean? tell me."

24 He coldly but gently loosened her fingers from about his arm and thrust the hand away from him. "Tell me what it means!" she cried despairingly.

25 "It means," he answered lightly, "that the child is not white; it means that you are not white."

26 A quick conception of all that this accusation meant for her nerved her with unwonted courage to deny it. "It is a lie; it is not true, I am white! Look at my hair, it is brown; and my eyes are gray, Armand, you know they are gray. And my skin is fair," seizing his wrist. "Look at my hand; whiter than yours, Armand," she laughed hysterically.

27 "As white as La Blanche's," he returned cruelly; and went away leaving her alone with their child.

28 When she could hold a pen in her hand, she sent a despairing letter to Madame Valmondé.

29 "My mother, they tell me I am not white. Armand has told me I am not white. For God's sake tell them it is not true. You must know it is not true. I shall die. I must die. I cannot be so unhappy, and live."

30 The answer that came was as brief:

31 "My own Désirée: Come home to Valmondé; back to your mother who loves you. Come with your child."

32 When the letter reached Désirée she went with it to her husband's study, and laid it open upon the desk before which he sat. She was like a stone image: silent, white, motionless after she placed it there.

33 In silence he ran his cold eyes over the written words. He said nothing. "Shall I go, Armand?" she asked in tones sharp with agonized suspense.

34 "Yes, go."

35 "Do you want me to go?"

36 "Yes, I want you to go."

37 He thought Almighty God had dealt cruelly and unjustly with him; and felt, somehow, that he was paying Him back in kind when he stabbed thus into his wife's soul. Moreover he no longer loved her, because of the unconscious injury she had brought upon his home and his name.

38 She turned away like one stunned by a blow, and walked slowly towards the door, hoping he would call her back.

39 "Good-by, Armand," she moaned.

40 He did not answer her. That was his last blow at fate.

41 Désirée went in search of her child. Zandrine was pacing the sombre gallery with it. She took the little one from the nurse's arms with no word of explanation, and descending the steps, walked away, under the live-oak branches.

42 It was an October afternoon; the sun was just sinking. Out in the still fields the negroes were picking cotton.

43 Désirée had not changed the thin white garment nor the slippers which she wore. Her hair was uncovered and the sun's rays brought a

golden gleam from its brown meshes. She did not take the broad, beaten road which led to the far-off plantation of Valmondé. She walked across a deserted field, where the stubble bruised her tender feet, so delicately shod, and tore her thin gown to shreds.

44   She disappeared among the reeds and willows that grew thick along the banks of the deep, sluggish bayou; and she did not come back again.

45   Some weeks later there was a curious scene enacted at L'Abri. In the centre of the smoothly swept back yard was a great bonfire. Armand Aubigny sat in the wide hallway that commanded a view of the spectacle; and it was he who dealt out to a half dozen negroes the material which kept this fire ablaze.

46   A graceful cradle of willow, with all its dainty furbishings, was laid upon the pyre, which had already been fed with the richness of a priceless *layette*. Then there were silk gowns, and velvet and satin ones added to these; laces, too, and embroideries; bonnets and gloves; for the *corbeille* had been of rare quality.

47   The last thing to go was a tiny bundle of letters; innocent little scribblings that Désirée had sent to him during the days of their espousal. There was the remnant of one back in the drawer from which he took them. But it was not Désirée's; it was part of an old letter from his mother to his father. He read it. She was thanking God for the blessing of her husband's love:—

48   "But, above all," she wrote, "night and day, I thank the good God for having so arranged our lives that our dear Armand will never know that his mother, who adores him, belongs to the race that is cursed with the brand of slavery."

Questions for Discussion

1. This story takes place in Louisiana in the latter part of the nineteenth century. Would the results of such a discovery about the baby be the same today? Why or why not?

2. Explain the phrase "cursed with the brand of slavery."

3. Define *white* and *quadroon*.

4. This story has a surprise ending. For such an ending to be artistically effective, the author should give readers clues that such an eventuality is possible. Were you sufficiently prepared for the end of the story? Explain your answer.

Suggestions for Exploration and Writing

1. Write an essay either on the social acceptability of interracial marriages or on your personal feelings toward them.

2. Go beyond the story to speculate on what happens to Désirée and her baby.

Charlotte Perkins Gilman (1860–1935)

Charlotte Perkins Gilman was best known during her lifetime as a lecturer and author of books on the rights of women and on socialism. Yet today she is most famous for what is generally acknowledged as her best short story, "The Yellow Wallpaper." According to Gilman, the story was written after she had suffered a nervous breakdown. A specialist in nervous diseases, consulted as a result of Gilman's depression, advised her first husband to allow her to participate only in domestic life and to terminate her painting and writing. After three months of this treatment, she was near a mental breakdown. Unlike the narrator of "The Yellow Wallpaper," Gilman went on to a successful second marriage and a career. She continued to suffer from depression at times and committed suicide in 1935 as a result of severe pain caused by cancer.

THE YELLOW WALLPAPER (1899)

1   It is very seldom that mere ordinary people like John and myself secure ancestral halls for the summer.

2   A colonial mansion, a hereditary estate, I would say a haunted house and reach the height of romantic felicity—but that would be asking too much of fate!

3   Still I will proudly declare that there is something queer about it.

4   Else, why should it be let so cheaply? And why have stood so long untenanted?

5   John laughs at me, of course, but one expects that.

6   John is practical in the extreme. He has no patience with faith, an intense horror of superstition, and he scoffs openly at any talk of things not to be felt and seen and put down in figures.

7   John is a physician, and *perhaps*—(I would not say it to a living soul, of course, but this is dead paper and a great relief to my mind)—*perhaps* that is one reason I do not get well faster.

8   You see, he does not believe I am sick! And what can one do?

9   If a physician of high standing, and one's own husband, assures friends and relatives that there is really nothing the matter with one but temporary nervous depression—a slight hysterical tendency—what is one to do?

10   My brother is also a physician, and also of high standing, and he says the same thing.

11   So I take phosphates or phosphites—whichever it is—and tonics, and air and exercise, and journeys, and am absolutely forbidden to "work" until I am well again.

12   Personally, I disagree with their ideas.

13   Personally, I believe that congenial work, with excitement and change, would do me good.

14   But what is one to do?

15   I did write for a while in spite of them; but it *does* exhaust me a good deal—having to be so sly about it, or else meet with heavy opposition.

16   I sometimes fancy that in my condition, if I had less opposition and more society and stimulus—but John says the very worst thing I can do is to think about my condition, and I confess it always makes me feel bad.

17   So I will let it alone and talk about the house.

18   The most beautiful place! It is quite alone, standing well back from the road, quite three miles from the village. It makes me think of English places that you read about, for there are hedges and walls and gates that lock, and lots of separate little houses for the gardeners and people.

19   There is a *delicious* garden! I never saw such a garden—large and shady, full of box-bordered paths, and lined with long grape-covered arbors with seats under them.

20   There were greenhouses, but they are all broken now.

21   There was some legal trouble, I believe, something about the heirs and co-heirs; anyhow, the place has been empty for years.

22   That spoils my ghostliness, I am afraid, but I don't care—there is something strange about the house—I can feel it.

23   I even said so to John one moonlight evening, but he said what I felt was a draught, and shut the window.

24   I get unreasonably angry with John sometimes. I'm sure I never used to be so sensitive. I think it is due to this nervous condition.

25   But John says if I feel so I shall neglect proper self-control; so I take pains to control myself—before him, at least, and that makes me very tired.

26   I don't like our room a bit. I wanted one downstairs that opened onto the piazza and had roses all over the window, and such pretty old-fashioned chintz hangings! But John would not hear of it.

27   He said there was only one window and not room for two beds, and no near room for him if he took another.

28   He is very careful and loving, and hardly lets me stir without special direction.

29   I have a schedule prescription for each hour in the day; he takes all care from me, and so I feel basely ungrateful not to value it more.

30   He said he came here solely on my account, that I was to have perfect rest and all the air I could get. "Your exercise depends on your strength, my dear," said he, "and your food somewhat on your appetite; but air you can absorb all the time." So we took the nursery at the top of the house.

31   It is a big, airy room, the whole floor nearly, with windows that look all ways, and air and sunshine galore. It was nursery first, and then playroom and gymnasium, I should judge, for the windows are barred for little children, and there are rings and things in the walls.

32   The paint and paper look as if a boys' school had used it. It is stripped off—the paper—in great patches all around the head of my bed, about as far as I can reach, and in a great place on the other side of the room low down. I never saw a worse paper in my life. One of those sprawling, flamboyant patterns committing every artistic sin.

33   It is dull enough to confuse the eye in following, pronounced enough constantly to irritate and provoke study, and when you follow

the lame uncertain curves for a little distance they suddenly commit suicide—plunge off at outrageous angles, destroy themselves in unheard-of contradictions.

34   The color is repellent, almost revolting: a smouldering unclean yellow, strangely faded by the slow-turning sunlight. It is a dull yet lurid orange in some places, a sickly sulphur tint in others.

35   No wonder the children hated it! I should hate it myself if I had to live in this room long.

36   There comes John, and I must put this away—he hates to have me write a word.

37   We have been here two weeks, and I haven't felt like writing before, since that first day.

38   I am sitting by the window now, up in this atrocious nursery, and there is nothing to hinder my writing as much as I please, save lack of strength.

39   John is away all day, and even some nights when his cases are serious.

40   I am glad my case is not serious!

41   But these nervous troubles are dreadfully depressing.

42   John does not know how much I really suffer. He knows there is no reason to suffer, and that satisfies him.

43   Of course it is only nervousness. It does weigh on me so not to do my duty in any way!

44   I meant to be such a help to John, such a real rest and comfort, and here I am a comparative burden already!

45   Nobody would believe what an effort it is to do what little I am able—to dress and entertain, and order things.

46   It is fortunate Mary is so good with the baby. Such a dear baby!

47   And yet I *cannot* be with him, it makes me so nervous.

48   I suppose John never was nervous in his life. He laughs at me so about this wallpaper!

49   At first he meant to repaper the room, but afterward he said that I was letting it get the better of me, and that nothing was worse for a nervous patient than to give way to such fancies.

50   He said that after the wallpaper was changed it would be the heavy bedstead, and then the barred windows, and then the gate at the head of the stairs, and so on.

51   "You know the place is doing you good," he said, "and really, dear, I don't care to renovate the house just for a three months' rental."

52   "Then do let us go downstairs," I said. "There are such pretty rooms there."

53   Then he took me in his arms and called me a blessed little goose, and said he would go down cellar, if I wished, and have it whitewashed into the bargain.

54   But he is right enough about the beds and windows and things.

55   It is as airy and comfortable a room as anyone need wish, and, of course, I would not be so silly as to make him uncomfortable just for a whim.

56   I'm really getting quite fond of the big room, all but that horrid paper.

57   Out of one window I can see the garden—those mysterious deep-shaded arbors, the riotous old-fashioned flowers, and bushes and gnarly trees.

58   Out of another I get a lovely view of the bay and a little private wharf belonging to the estate. There is a beautiful shaded lane that runs down there from the house. I always fancy I see people walking in these numerous paths and arbors, but John has cautioned me not to give way to fancy in the least. He says that with my imaginative power and habit of story-making, a nervous weakness like mine is sure to lead to all manner of excited fancies, and that I ought to use my will and good sense to check the tendency. So I try.

59   I think sometimes that if I were only well enough to write a little it would relieve the press of ideas and rest me.

60   But I find I get pretty tired when I try.

61   It is so discouraging not to have any advice and companionship about my work. When I get really well, John says we will ask Cousin Henry and Julia down for a long visit; but he says he would as soon put fireworks in my pillow-case as to let me have those stimulating people about now.

62   I wish I could get well faster.

63   But I must not think about that. This paper looks to me as if it *knew* what a vicious influence it had!

64   There is a recurrent spot where the pattern lolls like a broken neck and two bulbous eyes stare at you upside down.

65   I get positively angry with the impertinence of it and the everlasting-ness. Up and down and sideways they crawl, and those absurd unblinking eyes are everywhere. There is one place where two breadths didn't match, and the eyes go all up and down the line, one a little higher than the other.

66   I never saw so much expression in an inanimate thing before, and we all know how much expression they have! I used to lie awake as a child and get more entertainment and terror out of blank walls and plain furniture than most children could find in a toy-store.

67   I remember what a kindly wink the knobs of our big old bureau used to have, and there was one chair that always seemed like a strong friend.

68   I used to feel that if any of the other things looked too fierce I could always hop into that chair and be safe.

69   The furniture in this room is no worse than inharmonious, however, for we had to bring it all from downstairs. I suppose when this was used as a playroom they had to take the nursery things out, and no wonder! I never saw such ravages as the children have made here.

70   The wallpaper, as I said before, is torn off in spots, and it sticketh closer than a brother—they must have had perseverance as well as hatred.

71   Then the floor is scratched and gouged and splintered, the plaster itself is dug out here and there, and this great heavy bed, which is all we found in the room, looks as if it had been through the wars.

72   But I don't mind it a bit—only the paper.

73　There comes John's sister. Such a dear girl as she is, and so careful of me! I must not let her find me writing.

74　She is a perfect and enthusiastic housekeeper, and hopes for no better profession. I verily believe she thinks it is the writing which made me sick!

75　But I can write when she is out, and see her a long way off from these windows.

76　There is one that commands the road, a lovely shaded winding road, and one that just looks off over the country. A lovely country, too, full of great elms and velvet meadows.

77　This wallpaper has a kind of sub-pattern in a different shade, a particularly irritating one, for you can only see it in certain lights, and not clearly then.

78　But in the places where it isn't faded and where the sun is just so— I can see a strange, provoking, formless sort of figure that seems to skulk about behind that silly and conspicuous front design.

79　There's sister on the stairs!

80　Well, the Fourth of July is over! The people are all gone, and I am tired out. John thought it might do me good to see a little company, so we just had Mother and Nellie and the children down for a week.

81　Of course I didn't do a thing. Jennie sees to everything now.

82　But it tired me all the same.

83　John says if I don't pick up faster he shall send me to Weir Mitchell in the fall.

84　But I don't want to go there at all. I had a friend who was in his hands once, and she says he is just like John and my brother, only more so!

85　Besides, it is such an undertaking to go so far.

86　I don't feel as if it was worthwhile to turn my hand over for anything, and I'm getting dreadfully fretful and querulous.

87　I cry at nothing, and cry most of the time.

88　Of course I don't when John is here, or anybody else, but when I am alone.

89　And I am alone a good deal just now. John is kept in town very often by serious cases, and Jennie is good and lets me alone when I want her to.

90　So I walk a little in the garden or down that lovely lane, sit on the porch under the roses, and lie down up here a good deal.

91　I'm getting really fond of the room in spite of the wallpaper. Perhaps *because* of the wallpaper.

92　It dwells in my mind so!

93　I lie here on this great immovable bed—it is nailed down, I believe— and follow that pattern about by the hour. It is as good as gymnastics, I assure you. I start, we'll say, at the bottom, down in the corner over there where it has not been touched, and I determine for the thousandth time that I *will* follow that pointless pattern to some sort of a conclusion.

94　I know a little of the principle of design, and I know this thing was not arranged on any laws of radiation, or alternation, or repetition, or symmetry, or anything else that I ever heard of.

95   It is repeated, of course, by the breadths, but not otherwise.

96   Looked at in one way, each breadth stands alone; the bloated curves and flourishes—a kind of "debased Romanesque" with delirium tremens—go waddling up and down in isolated columns of fatuity.

97   But, on the other hand, they connect diagonally, and the sprawling outlines run off in great slanting waves of optic horror, like a lot of wallowing sea-weeds in full chase.

98   The whole thing goes horizontally, too, at least it seems so, and I exhaust myself trying to distinguish the order of its going in that direction.

99   They have used a horizontal breadth for a frieze, and that adds wonderfully to the confusion.

100   There is one end of the room where it is almost intact, and there, when the crosslights fade and the low sun shines directly upon it, I can almost fancy radiation after all—the interminable grotesque seems to form around a common center and rush off in headlong plunges of equal distraction.

101   It makes me tired to follow it. I will take a nap, I guess.

102   I don't know why I should write this.

103   I don't want to.

104   I don't feel able.

105   And I know John would think it absurd. But I *must* say what I feel and think in some way—it is such a relief!

106   But the effort is getting to be greater than the relief.

107   Half the time now I am awfully lazy, and lie down ever so much. John says I mustn't lose my strength, and has me take cod liver oil and lots of tonics and things, to say nothing of ale and wine and rare meat.

108   Dear John! He loves me very dearly, and hates to have me sick. I tried to have a real earnest reasonable talk with him the other day, and tell him how I wish he would let me go and make a visit to Cousin Henry and Julia.

109   But he said I wasn't able to go, nor able to stand it after I got there; and I did not make out a very good case for myself, for I was crying before I had finished.

110   It is getting to be a great effort for me to think straight. Just this nervous weakness, I suppose.

111   And dear John gathered me up in his arms, and just carried me upstairs and laid me on the bed, and sat by me and read to me till it tired my head.

112   He said I was his darling and his comfort and all he had, and that I must take care of myself for his sake, and keep well.

113   He says no one but myself can help me out of it, that I must use my will and self-control and not let any silly fancies run away with me.

114   There's one comfort—the baby is well and happy, and does not have to occupy this nursery with the horrid wallpaper.

115   If we had not used it, that blessed child would have! What a fortunate escape! Why, I wouldn't have a child of mine, an impressionable little thing, live in such a room for worlds.

116   I never thought of it before, but it is lucky that John kept me here after all; I can stand it so much easier than a baby, you see.

117   Of course I never mention it to them any more—I am too wise—but I keep watch for it all the same.

118   There are things in that wallpaper that nobody knows about but me, or ever will.

119   Behind that outside pattern the dim shapes get clearer every day.

120   It is always the same shape, only very numerous.

121   And it is like a woman stooping down and creeping about behind that pattern. I don't like it a bit. I wonder—I begin to think—I wish John would take me away from here!

122   It is so hard to talk with John about my case, because he is so wise, and because he loves me so.

123   But I tried it last night.

124   It was moonlight. The moon shines in all around just as the sun does.

125   I hate to see it sometimes, it creeps so slowly, and always comes in by one window or another.

126   John was asleep and I hated to waken him, so I kept still and watched the moonlight on that undulating wallpaper till I felt creepy.

127   The faint figure behind seemed to shake the pattern, just as if she wanted to get out.

128   I got up softly and went to feel and see if the paper *did* move, and when I came back John was awake.

129   "What is it, little girl?" he said. "Don't go walking about like that— you'll get cold."

130   I thought it was a good time to talk, so I told him that I really was not gaining here, and that I wished he would take me away.

131   "Why, darling!" said he. "Our lease will be up in three weeks, and I can't see how to leave before."

132   "The repairs aren't done at home, and I cannot possibly leave town just now. Of course, if you were in any danger, I could and would, but you really are better, dear, whether you can see it or not. I am a doctor, dear, and I know. You are gaining flesh and color, your appetite is better, I feel really much easier about you."

133   "I don't weigh a bit more," said I, "not as much; and my appetite may be better in the evening when you are here but it is worse in the morning when you are away!"

134   "Bless her little heart!" said he with a big hug. "She shall be as sick as she pleases! But now let's improve the shining hours by going to sleep, and talk about it in the morning!"

135   "And you won't go away?" I asked gloomily.

136   "Why, how can I, dear? It is only three weeks more and then we will take a nice little trip of a few days while Jennie is getting the house ready. Really, dear, you are better!"

137   "Better in body perhaps—" I began, and stopped short, for he sat up straight and looked at me with such a stern, reproachful look that I could not say another word.

138   "My darling," said he, "I beg of you, for my sake and for our child's sake, as well as for your own, that you will never for one instant let that idea enter your mind! There is nothing so dangerous, so fascinating, to a temperament like yours. It is a false and foolish fancy. Can you not trust me as a physician when I tell you so?"

139   So of course I said no more on that score, and we went to sleep before long. He thought I was asleep first, but I wasn't, and lay there for hours trying to decide whether that front pattern and the back pattern really did move together or separately.

140   On a pattern like this, by daylight, there is a lack of sequence, a defiance of law, that is a constant irritant to a normal mind.

141   The color is hideous enough, and unreliable enough, and infuriating enough, but the pattern is torturing.

142   You think you have mastered it, but just as you get well under way in following, it turns a back-somersault and there you are. It slaps you in the face, knocks you down, and tramples upon you. It is like a bad dream.

143   The outside pattern is a florid arabesque, reminding one of a fungus. If you can imagine a toadstool in joints, an interminable string of toadstools, budding and sprouting in endless convolutions—why, that is something like it.

144   That is, sometimes!

145   There is one marked peculiarity about this paper, a thing nobody seems to notice but myself, and that is that it changes as the light changes.

146   When the sun shoots in through the east window—I always watch for that first long, straight ray—it changes so quickly that I never can quite believe it.

147   That is why I watch it always.

148   By moonlight—the moon shines in all night when there is a moon— I wouldn't know it was the same paper.

149   At night in any kind of light, in twilight, candlelight, lamplight, and worst of all by moonlight, it becomes bars! The outside pattern, I mean, and the woman behind it is as plain as can be.

150   I didn't realize for a long time what the thing was that showed behind, that dim sub-pattern, but now I am quite sure it is a woman.

151   By daylight she is subdued, quiet. I fancy it is the pattern that keeps her so still. It is so puzzling. It keeps me quiet by the hour.

152   I lie down ever so much now. John says it is good for me, and to sleep all I can.

153   Indeed he started the habit by making me lie down for an hour after each meal.

154   It is a very bad habit, I am convinced, for you see, I don't sleep.

155   And that cultivates deceit, for I don't tell them I'm awake—oh, no!

156   The fact is I am getting a little afraid of John.

157   He seems very queer sometimes, and even Jennie has an inexplicable look.

158   It strikes me occasionally, just as a scientific hypothesis, that perhaps it is the paper!

159   I have watched John when he did not know I was looking, and come into the room suddenly on the most innocent excuses, and I've caught him several times *looking at the paper!* And Jennie too. I caught Jennie with her hand on it once.

160   She didn't know I was in the room, and when I asked her in a quiet, a very quiet voice, with the most restrained manner possible, what she was doing with the paper, she turned around as if she had been caught stealing, and looked quite angry—asked me why I should frighten her so!

161   Then she said that the paper stained everything it touched, that she had found yellow smooches on all my clothes and John's and she wished we would be more careful!

162   Did not that sound innocent? But I know she was studying that pattern, and I am determined that nobody shall find it out but myself!

163   Life is very much more exciting now than it used to be. You see, I have something more to expect, to look forward to, to watch. I really do eat better, and am more quiet than I was.

164   John is so pleased to see me improve! He laughed a little the other day, and said I seemed to be flourishing in spite of my wallpaper.

165   I turned it off with a laugh. I had no intention of telling him it was *because* of the wallpaper—he would make fun of me. He might even want to take me away.

166   I don't want to leave now until I have found it out. There is a week more, and I think that will be enough.

167   I'm feeling so much better!

168   I don't sleep much at night, for it is so interesting to watch developments; but I sleep a good deal during the daytime.

169   In the daytime it is tiresome and perplexing.

170   There are always new shoots on the fungus, and new shades of yellow all over it. I cannot keep count of them, though I have tried conscientiously.

171   It is the strangest yellow, the wallpaper! It makes me think of all the yellow things I ever saw—not beautiful ones like buttercups, but old, foul, bad yellow things.

172   But there is something else about that paper—the smell! I noticed it the moment we came into the room, but with so much air and sun it was not bad. Now we have had a week of fog and rain, and whether the windows are open or not, the smell is here.

173   It creeps all over the house.

174   I find it hovering in the dining-room, skulking in the parlor, hiding in the hall, lying in wait for me on the stairs.

175   It gets into my hair.

176   Even when I go to ride, if I turn my head suddenly and surprise it— there is that smell!

177   Such a peculiar odor, too! I have spent hours in trying to analyze it, to find what it smelled like.

178   It is not bad—at first—and very gentle, but quite the subtlest, most enduring odor I ever met.

179   In this damp weather it is awful. I wake up in the night and find it hanging over me.

180   It used to disturb me at first. I thought seriously of burning the house—to reach the smell.

181   But now I am used to it. The only thing I can think of that it is like is the *color* of the paper! A yellow smell.

182   There is a very funny mark on this wall, low down, near the mopboard. A streak that runs round the room. It goes behind every piece of furniture, except the bed, a long, straight, even *smooch*, as if it had been rubbed over and over.

183   I wonder how it was done and who did it, and what they did it for. Round and round and round—round and round and round—it makes me dizzy!

184   I really have discovered something at last.

185   Through watching so much at night, when it changes so, I have finally found out.

186   The front pattern *does* move—and no wonder! The woman behind shakes it!

187   Sometimes I think there are a great many women behind, and sometimes only one, and she crawls around fast, and her crawling shakes it all over.

188   Then in the very bright spots she keeps still, and in the very shady spots she just takes hold of the bars and shakes them hard.

189   And she is all the time trying to climb through. But nobody could climb through that pattern—it strangles so; I think that is why it has so many heads.

190   They get through and then the pattern strangles them off and turns them upside down, and makes their eyes white!

191   If those heads were covered or taken off it would not be half so bad.

192   I think that woman gets out in the daytime!

193   And I'll tell you why—privately—I've seen her!

194   I can see her out of every one of my windows!

195   It is the same woman, I know, for she is always creeping, and most women do not creep by daylight.

196   I see her in that long shaded lane, creeping up and down. I see her in those dark grape arbors, creeping all around the garden.

197   I see her on that long road under the trees, creeping along, and when a carriage comes she hides under the blackberry vines.

198   I don't blame her a bit. It must be very humiliating to be caught creeping by daylight!

199   I always lock the door when I creep by daylight. I can't do it at night, for I know John would suspect something at once.

200   And John is so queer now that I don't want to irritate him. I wish he would take another room! Besides, I don't want anybody to get that woman out at night but myself.

201   I often wonder if I could see her out of all the windows at once.

202   But, turn as fast as I can, I can only see out of one at one time.

203   And though I always see her, she *may* be able to creep faster than I can turn! I have watched her sometimes away off in the open country, creeping as fast as a cloud shadow in a wind.

204   If only that top pattern could be gotten off from the under one! I mean to try it, little by little.

205   I have found out another funny thing, but I shan't tell it this time! It does not do to trust people too much.

206   There are only two more days to get this paper off, and I believe John is beginning to notice. I don't like the look in his eyes.

207   And I heard him ask Jennie a lot of professional questions about me. She had a very good report to give.

208   She said I slept a good deal in the daytime.

209   John knows I don't sleep very well at night, for all I'm so quiet!

210   He asked me all sorts of questions, too, and pretended to be very loving and kind.

211   As if I couldn't see through him!

212   Still, I don't wonder he acts so, sleeping under this paper for three months.

213   It only interests me, but I feel sure John and Jennie are affected by it.

214   Hurrah! This is the last day, but it is enough. John is to stay in town over night, and won't be out until this evening.

215   Jennie wanted to sleep with me—the sly thing; but I told her I should undoubtedly rest better for a night all alone.

216   That was clever, for really I wasn't alone a bit! As soon as it was moonlight and that poor thing began to crawl and shake the pattern, I got up and ran to help her.

217   I pulled and she shook. I shook and she pulled, and before morning we had peeled off yards of that paper.

218   A strip about as high as my head and half around the room.

219   And then when the sun came and that awful pattern began to laugh at me, I declared I would finish it today!

220   We go away tomorrow, and they are moving all my furniture down again to leave things as they were before.

221   Jennie looked at the wall in amazement, but I told her merrily that I did it out of pure spite at the vicious thing.

222   She laughed and said she wouldn't mind doing it herself, but I must not get tired.

223   How she betrayed herself that time!

224   But I am here, and no person touches this paper but Me—not *alive!*

225   She tried to get me out of the room—it was too patent! But I said it was so quiet and empty and clean now that I believed I would lie down again

and sleep all I could, and not to wake me even for dinner—I would call when I woke.

226   So now she is gone, and the servants are gone, and the things are gone, and there is nothing left but that great bedstead nailed down, with the canvas mattress we found on it.

227   We shall sleep downstairs tonight, and take the boat home tomorrow.

228   I quite enjoy the room, now it is bare again.

229   How those children did tear about here!

230   This bedstead is fairly gnawed!

231   But I must get to work.

232   I have locked the door and thrown the key down into the front path.

233   I don't want to go out, and I don't want to have anybody come in, till John comes.

234   I want to astonish him.

235   I've got a rope up here that even Jennie did not find. If that woman does get out, and tries to get away, I can tie her!

236   But I forgot I could not reach far without anything to stand on!

237   This bed will *not* move!

238   I tried to lift and push it until I was lame, and then I got so angry I bit off a little piece at one corner—but it hurt my teeth.

239   Then I peeled off all the paper I could reach standing on the floor. It sticks horribly and the pattern just enjoys it! All those strangled heads and bulbous eyes and waddling fungus growths just shriek with derision!

240   I am getting angry enough to do something desperate. To jump out of the window would be admirable exercise, but the bars are too strong even to try.

241   Besides I wouldn't do it. Of course not. I know well enough that a step like that is improper and might be misconstrued.

242   I don't like to *look* out of the windows even—there are so many of those creeping women and they creep so fast.

243   I wonder if they all come out of that wallpaper as I did?

244   But I am securely fastened now by my well-hidden rope—you don't get *me* out in the road there!

245   I suppose I shall have to get back behind the pattern when it comes night, and that is hard!

246   It is so pleasant to be out in this great room and creep around as I please!

247   I don't want to go outside. I won't, even if Jennie asks me to.

248   For outside you have to creep on the ground, and everything is green instead of yellow.

249   But here I can creep smoothly on the floor, and my shoulder just fits in that long smooch around the wall, so I cannot lose my way.

250   Why, there's John at the door!

251   It is no use, young man, you can't open it!

252   How he does call and pound!

253   Now he's crying to Jennie for an axe.

254   It would be a shame to break down that beautiful door!

255   "John, dear!" said I in the gentlest voice. "The key is down by the front steps, under a plantain leaf!"

256   That silenced him for a few moments.

257   Then he said, very quietly indeed, "Open the door, my darling!"

258   "I can't," said I. "The key is down by the front door under a plantain leaf!" And then I said it again, several times, very gently and slowly, and said it so often that he had to go and see, and he got it of course, and came in. He stopped short by the door.

259   "What is the matter?" he cried. "For God's sake, what are you doing!"

260   I kept on creeping just the same, but I looked at him over my shoulder.

261   "I've got out at last," said I, "in spite of you and Jane. And I've pulled off most of the paper, so you can't put me back!"

262   Now why should that man have fainted? But he did, and right across my path by the wall, so that I had to creep over him every time!

Questions for Discussion

1. What kind of relationship does the **narrator** have with her husband John? How does he treat her? List the times that the narrator, after having given her opinion, adds "but John says" or a similar phrase.

2. What is the **point of view** of this story? Why is it crucial to the effectiveness of the story? How does the point of view create an **ironic** tone?

3. What is the role of John's sister in the story?

4. What is the significance of the narrator's not being allowed to see her baby?

5. What is the significance of the wallpaper's appeal to four of the five senses (touch, smell, sound, and sight)?

6. Why is the narrator unnamed for much of the story while John and Jennie have names? What is the significance of the name Jane?

Suggestions for Exploration and Writing

1. In what ways is John's attitude toward his wife typical of the attitudes of men toward women in the late nineteenth and early twentieth centuries in the United States? Does John love his wife? Support your answer.

2. Gilman's narrator says she feels "basely ungrateful" for not appreciating John's regulation of her days by the hour or his choice of their bedroom. Compare her feelings with those expressed by Missie May in "The Gilded Six-Bits."

3. Discuss the wallpaper. Why does it have an "everlastingness" about it? Why does the narrator's husband choose the nursery with the bars on the window and the ugly wallpaper rather than the first-floor room with the view?

4. In an essay, trace the changes in the narrator's attitudes toward John.

Zora Neale Hurston (1891–1960)

Born in Alabama, Hurston moved with her family to Eatonville, Florida, the first "Negro" community to be incorporated; from there she moved to Jacksonville, Baltimore, and then New York. In New York she received good reviews for "Spunk" in 1925 and became part of the Harlem Renaissance. Hurston published four novels, two volumes of poetry, and an autobiography. One of her novels, Their Eyes Were Watching God *(1937), has been praised by modern critics. Hurston spent five years traveling the rural South, collecting some of the folklore and music of her people, information she assimilated into her stories. Much of her writing uses as a setting the general store porch because she felt that that part of the community was the most interesting place in town, even though women were excluded from it.*

THE GILDED SIX-BITS (1933)

1   It was a Negro yard around a Negro house in a Negro settlement that looked to the payroll of the G. and G. Fertilizer works for its support.

2   But there was something happy about the place. The front yard was parted in the middle by a sidewalk from gate to doorstep, a sidewalk edged on either side by quart bottles driven neck down into the ground on a slant. A mess of homey flowers planted without a plan but blooming cheerily from their helter-skelter places. The fence and house were white-washed. The porch and steps scrubbed white.

3   The front door stood open to the sunshine so that the floor of the front room could finish drying after its weekly scouring. It was Saturday. Everything clean from the front gate to the privy house. Yard raked so that the strokes of the rake would make a pattern. Fresh newspaper cut in fancy edge on the kitchen shelves.

4   Missie May was bathing herself in the galvanized washtub in the bedroom. Her dark-brown skin glistened under the soapsuds that skittered down from her washrag. Her stiff young breasts thrust forward aggressively, like broad-based cones with the tips lacquered in black.

5   She heard men's voices in the distance and glanced at the dollar clock on the dresser.

6   "Humph! Ah'm way behind time t'day! Joe gointer be heah 'fore Ah git mah clothes on if Ah don't make haste."

7   She grabbed the clean mealsack at hand and dried herself hurriedly and began to dress. But before she could tie her slippers, there came the ring of singing metal on wood. Nine times.

8   Missie May grinned with delight. She had not seen the big tall man come stealing in the gate and creep up the walk grinning happily at the joyful mischief he was about to commit. But she knew that it was her husband throwing silver dollars in the door for her to pick up and pile beside her plate at dinner. It was this way every Saturday afternoon. The nine dollars hurled into the open door, he scurried to a hiding place behind the Cape jasmine bush and waited.

9   Missie May promptly appeared at the door in mock alarm.

10   "Who dat chunkin' money in mah do'way?" she demanded. No answer from the yard. She leaped off the porch and began to search the shrubbery. She peeped under the porch and hung over the gate to look up and down the road. While she did this, the man behind the jasmine darted to the chinaberry tree. She spied him and gave chase.

11   "Nobody ain't gointer be chunkin' money at me and Ah not do 'em nothin'," she shouted in mock anger. He ran around the house with Missie May at his heels. She overtook him at the kitchen door. He ran inside but could not close it after him before she crowded in and locked with him in a rough-and-tumble. For several minutes the two were a furious mass of male and female energy. Shouting, laughing, twisting, turning, tussling, tickling each other in the ribs; Missie May clutching onto Joe and Joe trying, but not too hard, to get away.

12   "Missie May, take yo' hand out mah pocket!" Joe shouted out between laughs.

13   "Ah ain't, Joe, not lessen you gwine gimme whateve' it is good you got in yo' pocket. Turn it go, Joe, do. Ah'll tear yo' clothes."

14   "Go on tear 'em. You de one dat pushes de needles round heah. Move yo' hand, Missie May."

15   "Lemme git dat paper sak out yo' pocket. Ah bet it's candy kisses."

16   "Tain't. Move yo' hand. Woman ain't got no business in a man's clothes nohow. Go way."

17   Missie May gouged way down and gave an upward jerk and triumphed.

18   "Unhhunh! Ah got it! It 'tis so candy kisses. Ah knowed you had somethin' for me in yo' clothes. Now Ah got to see whut's in every pocket you got."

19   Joe smiled indulgently and let his wife go through all of his pockets and take out the things that he had hidden there for her to find. She bore off the chewing gum, the cake of sweet soap, the pocket handkerchief as if she had wrested them from him, as if they had not been bought for the sake of this friendly battle.

20   "Whew! dat play-fight done got me all warmed up!" Joe exclaimed. "Got me some water in de kittle?"

21   "Yo' water is on de fire and yo' clean things is cross de bed. Hurry up and wash yo'self and get changed so we kin eat. Ah'm hongry." As Missie said this, she bore the steaming kettle into the bedroom.

22   "You ain't hongry, sugar," Joe contradicted her. "Youse jus' a little empty. Ah'm de one what's hongry. Ah could eat up camp meetin', back off 'ssociation, and drink Jurdan dry. Have it on de table when Ah get out de tub."

23   "Don't you mess wid mah business, man. You get in yo' clothes. Ah'm a real wife, not no dress and breath. Ah might not look lak one, but if you burn me, you won't git a thing but wife ashes."

24   Joe splashed in the bedroom and Missie May fanned around in the kitchen. A fresh red-and-white checked cloth on the table. Big pitcher

of buttermilk beaded with pale drops of butter from the churn. Hot fried mullet, crackling bread, ham hock atop a mound of string beans and new potatoes, and perched on the windowsill a pone of spicy potato pudding.

25   Very little talk during the meal but that little consisted of banter that pretended to deny affection but in reality flaunted it. Like when Missie May reached for a second helping of the tater pone. Joe snatched it out of her reach.

26   After Missie May had made two or three unsuccessful grabs at the pan, she begged, "Aw, Joe, gimme some mo' dat tater pone."

27   "Nope, sweetenin' is for us menfolks. Y'all pritty li'l frail eels don't need nothin' lak dis. You too sweet already."

28   "Please, Joe."

29   "Naw, naw. Ah don't want you to git no sweeter than whut you is already. We goin' down de road a lil piece t'night so you go put on yo' Sunday-go-to-meetin' things."

30   Missie May looked at her husband to see if he was playing some prank. "Sho nuff, Joe?"

31   "Yeah. We goin' to de ice cream parlor."

32   "Where de ice cream parlor at, Joe?"

33   "A new man done come heah from Chicago and he done got a place and took and opened it up for a ice cream parlor, and bein' as it's real swell, Ah wants you to be one de first ladies to walk in dere and have some set down."

34   "Do Jesus, Ah ain't knowed nothin' bout it. Who de man done it?"

35   "Mister Otis D. Slemmons, of spots and places—Memphis, Chicago, Jacksonville, Philadelphia and so on."

36   "Dat heavyset man wid his mouth full of gold teeths?"

37   "Yeah. Where did you see 'im at?"

38   "Ah went down to de sto' tuh git a box of lye and Ah seen 'im standin' on de corner talkin' to some of de mens, and Ah come on back and went to scrubbin' de floor, and he passed and tipped his hat whilst Ah was scourin' de steps. Ah thought 'Ah never seen *him* befo'.'"

39   Joe smiled pleasantly. "Yeah, he's up-to-date. He got de finest clothes Ah ever seen on a colored man's back."

40   "Aw, he don't look no better in his clothes than you do in yourn. He got a puzzlegut on 'im and he so chuckleheaded he got a pone behind his neck."

41   Joe looked down at his own abdomen and said wistfully: "Wisht Ah had a build on me lak he got. He ain't puzzlegutted, honey. He jes' got a cor-peration. Dat make 'm look lak a rich white man. All rich mens is got some belly on 'em."

42   "Ah seen de pitchers of Henry Ford and he's a spare-built man and Rockefeller look lak he ain't got but one gut. But Ford and Rockefeller and dis Slemmons and all de rest kin be as many-gutted as dey please, Ah'm satisfied wid you jes' lak you is, baby. God took pattern after a pine tree and built you noble. Youse a pritty still man, and if Ah knowed any way to make you mo' pritty Ah'd take and do it."

43   Joe reached over gently and toyed with Missie May's ear. "You jes' say dat cause you love me, but Ah know Ah can't hold no light to Otis D. Slemmons. Ah ain't never been nowhere and Ah ain't got nothin' but you."

44   Missie May got on his lap and kissed him and he kissed back in kind. Then he went on. "All de womens is crazy 'bout 'im everywhere he go."

45   "How you know dat, Joe?"

46   "He tole us so hisself."

47   "Dat don't make it so. His mouf is cut crossways, ain't it? Well, he kin lie jes' lak anybody else."

48   "Good Lawd, Missie! You womens sho is hard to sense into things. He's got a five-dollar gold piece for a stickpin and he got a ten-dollar gold piece on his watch chain and his mouf is jes' crammed full of gold teeths. Sho wisht it wuz mine. And what make it so cool, he got money 'cumulated. And womens give it all to 'im."

49   "Ah don't see whut de womens see on 'im. Ah wouldn't give 'im a wink if de sheriff wuz after 'im."

50   "Well, he tole us how de white womens in Chicago give 'im all dat gold money. So he don't 'low nobody to touch it at all. Not even put dey finger on it. Dey told 'im not to. You kin make 'miration at it, but don't tetch it."

51   "Whyn't he stay up dere where dey so crazy 'bout 'im?"

52   "Ah reckon dey done made 'im vast-rich and he wants to travel some. He says dey wouldn't leave 'im hit a lick of work. He got mo' lady people crazy 'bout him than he kin shake a stick at."

53   "Joe, Ah hates to see you so dumb. Dat stray nigger jes' tell y'all anything and y'all b'lieve it."

54   "Go 'head on now, honey, and put on yo' clothes. He talkin' 'bout his pritty womens—Ah wan 'im to see *mine*."

55   Missie May went off to dress and Joe spent the time trying to make his stomach punch out like Slemmons's middle. He tried the rolling swagger of the stranger, but found that his tall bone-and-muscle stride fitted ill with it. He just had time to drop back into his seat before Missie May came in dressed to go.

56   On the way home that night Joe was exultant. "Didn't Ah say ole Otis was swell? Can't he talk Chicago talk? Wuzn't dat funny whut he said when great big fat ole Ida Armstrong come in? He asted me, 'Who is dat broad wid de forty shake?' Dat's a new word. Us always thought forty was a set of figgers but he showed us where it means a whole heap of things. Sometimes he don't say forty, he jes' say thirty-eight and two and dat mean de same thing. Know whut he told me when Ah wuz payin' for our ice cream? He say, "Ah have to hand it to you, Joe. Dat wife of yours is jes' thirty-eight and two. Yessuh, she's forty!' Ain't he killin'?"

57   "He'll do in case of a rush. But he sho is got uh heap uh gold on 'im. Dat's de first time Ah ever seed gold money. It lookted good on him sho nuff, but it'd look a whole heap better on you."

58   "Who, me? Missie May, youse crazy! Where would a po' man lak me git gold money from?"

59   Missie May was silent for a minute, then she said, "Us might find some goin' long de road some time. Us could."

60   "Who would be losin' gold money round heah? We ain't even seen none dese white folks wearin' no gold money on dey watch chain. You must be figgerin' Mister Packard or Mister Cadillac goin' pass through heah."

61   "You don't know whut been lost 'round heah. Maybe somebody way back in memorial times lost they gold money and went on off and it ain't never been found. And then if we wuz to find it, you could wear some 'thout havin' no gang of womens lak dat Slemmons say he got."

62   Joe laughed and hugged her. "Don't be so wishful 'bout me. Ah'm satisfied de way Ah is. So long as Ah be yo' husband. Ah don't keer 'bout nothin' else. Ah'd ruther all de other womens in de world to be dead than for you to have de toothache. Less we go to bed and get our night rest."

63   It was Saturday night once more before Joe could parade his wife in Slemmons's ice cream parlor again. He worked the night shift and Saturday was his only night off. Every other evening around six o'clock he left home, and dying dawn saw him hustling home around the lake, where the challenging sun flung a flaming sword from east to west across the trembling water.

64   That was the best part of life—going home to Missie May. Their whitewashed house, the mock battle on Saturday, the dinner and ice cream parlor afterwards, church on Sunday nights when Missie outdressed any woman in town—all, everything, was right.

65   One night around eleven the acid ran out at the G. and G. The foreman knocked off the crew and let the steam die down. As Joe rounded the lake on his way home, a lean moon rode the lake in a silver boat. If anybody had asked Joe about the moon on the lake, he would have said he hadn't paid it any attention. But he saw it with his feelings. It made him yearn painfully for Missie. Creation obsessed him. He thought about children. They had been married more than a year now. They had money put away. They ought to be making little feet for shoes. A little boy child would be about right.

66   He saw a dim light in the bedroom and decided to come in through the kitchen door. He could wash the fertilizer dust off himself before presenting himself to Missie May. It would be nice for her not to know that he was there until he slipped into his place in bed and hugged her back. She always liked that.

67   He eased the kitchen door open slowly and silently, but when he went to set his dinner bucket on the table he bumped it into a pile of dishes, and something crashed to the floor. He heard his wife gasp in fright and hurried to reassure her.

68   "Iss me, honey. Don't git skeered."

69   There was a quick, large movement in the bedroom. A rustle, a thud, and a stealthy silence. The light went out.

70   What? Robbers? Murderers? Some varmint attacking his helpless wife, perhaps. He struck a match, threw himself on guard and stepped over the doorsill into the bedroom.

71   The great belt on the wheel of Time slipped and eternity stood still. By the match light he could see the man's legs fighting with his breeches in his frantic desire to get them on. He had both chance and time to kill the intruder in his helpless condition—half in and half out of his pants—but he was too weak to take action. The shapeless enemies of humanity that live in the hours of Time had waylaid Joe. He was assaulted in his weakness. Like Samson awakening after his haircut. So he just opened his mouth and laughed.

72   The match went out and he struck another and lit the lamp. A howling wind raced across his heart, but underneath its fury he heard his wife sobbing and Slemmons pleading for his life. Offering to buy it with all that he had. "Please, suh, don't kill me. Sixty-two dollars at de sto'. Gold money."

73   Joe just stood. Slemmons looked at the window, but it was screened. Joe stood out like a rough-backed mountain between him and the door. Barring him from escape, from sunrise, from life.

74   He considered a surprise attack upon the big clown that stood there laughing like a chessy cat. But before his fist could travel an inch, Joe's own rushed out to crush him like a battering ram. Then Joe stood over him.

75   "Git into yo' damn rags, Slemmons, and dat quick."

76   Slemmons scrambled to his feet and into his vest and coat. As he grabbed his hat, Joe's fury overrode his intentions and he grabbed at Slemmons with his left hand and struck at him with his right. The right landed. The left grazed the front of his vest. Slemmons was knocked a somersault into the kitchen and fled through the open door. Joe found himself alone with Missie May, with the golden watch charm clutched in his left fist. A short bit of broken chain dangled between his fingers.

77   Missie May was sobbing. Wails of weeping without words. Joe stood, and after a while he found out that he had something in his hand. And then he stood and felt without thinking and without seeing with his natural eyes. Missie May kept on crying and Joe kept on feeling so much, and not knowing what to do with all his feelings, he put Slemmons's watch charm in his pants pocket and took a good laugh and went to bed.

78   "Missie May, whut you cryin' for?"

79   "Cause Ah love you so hard and Ah know you don't love *me* no mo'."

80   Joe sank his face into the pillow for a spell, then he said huskily, "You don't know de feelings of dat yet, Missie May."

81   "Oh Joe, honey, he said he wuz gointer give me dat gold money and he jes' kept on after me—"

82   Joe was very still and silent for a long time. Then he said, "Well, don't cry no mo', Missie May. Ah got yo' gold piece for you."

83   The hours went past on their rusty ankles. Joe still and quiet on one bed rail and Missie May wrung dry of sobs on the other. Finally the sun's tide crept upon the shore of night and drowned all its hours. Missie May with her face stiff and streaked towards the window saw the dawn come into her yard. It was day. Nothing more. Joe wouldn't be coming home as usual. No need to fling open the front door and sweep off the porch,

making it nice for Joe. Never no more breakfast to cook; no more washing and starching of Joe's jumper-jackets and pants. No more nothing. So why get up?

84   With this strange man in her bed, she felt embarrassed to get up and dress. She decided to wait till he had dressed and gone. Then she would get up, dress quickly and be gone forever beyond reach of Joe's looks and laughs. But he never moved. Red light turned to yellow, then white.

85   From beyond the no-man's land between them came a voice. A strange voice that yesterday had been Joe's.

86   "Missie May, ain't you gonna fix me no breakfus'?"

87   She sprang out of bed. "Yeah, Joe. Ah didn't reckon you wuz hongry."

88   No need to die today. Joe needed her for a few more minutes anyhow.

89   Soon there was a roaring fire in the cookstove. Water bucket full and two chickens killed. Joe loved fried chicken and rice. She didn't deserve a thing and good Joe was letting her cook him some breakfast. She rushed hot biscuits to the table as Joe took his seat.

90   He ate with his eyes in his plate. No laughter, no banter.

91   "Missie May, you ain't eatin' yo' breakfus'."

92   "Ah don't choose none, Ah thank yuh."

93   His coffee cup was empty. She sprang to refill it. When she turned from the stove and bent to set the cup beside Joe's plate, she saw the yellow coin on the table between them.

94   She slumped into her seat and wept into her arms.

95   Presently Joe said calmly, "Missie May, you cry too much. Don't look back lak Lot's wife and turn to salt."

96   The sun, the hero of every day, the impersonal old man that beams as brightly on death as on birth, came up every morning and raced across the blue dome and dipped into the sea of fire every morning. Water ran downhill and birds nested.

97   Missie knew why she didn't leave Joe. She couldn't. She loved him too much, but she could not understand why Joe didn't leave her. He was polite, even kind at times, but aloof.

98   There were no more Saturday romps. No ringing silver dollars to stack beside her plate. No pockets to rifle. In fact, the yellow coin in his trousers was like a monster hiding in the cave of his pockets to destroy her.

99   She often wondered if he still had it, but nothing could have induced her to ask nor yet to explore his pockets to see for herself. Its shadow was in the house whether or no.

100   One night Joe came home around midnight and complained of pains in the back. He asked Missie to rub him down with liniment. It had been three months since Missie had touched his body and it all seemed strange. But she rubbed him. Grateful for the chance. Before morning youth triumphed and Missie exulted. But the next day, as she joyfully made up their bed, beneath her pillow she found the piece of money with the bit of chain attached.

101   Alone to herself, she looked at the thing with loathing, but look she must. She took it into her hands with trembling and saw first thing that it was no gold piece. It was a gilded half dollar. Then she knew why

Slemmons had forbidden anyone to touch his gold. He trusted village eyes at a distance not to recognize his stickpin as a gilded quarter, and his watch charm as a four-bit piece.

102   They were man and wife again. Then another thought came clawing at her. He had come home to buy from her as if she were any woman in the longhouse. Fifty cents for her love. As if to say that he could pay as well as Slemmons. She slid the coin into his Sunday pants pocket and dressed herself and left his house.

103   Halfway between her house and the quarters she met her husband's mother, and after a short talk she turned and went back home. Never would she admit defeat to that woman who prayed for it nightly. If she had not the substance of marriage she had the outside show. Joe must leave *her*. She let him see she didn't want his old gold four-bits, too.

104   She saw no more of the coin for some time though she knew that Joe could not help finding it in his pocket. But his health kept poor, and he came home at least every ten days to be rubbed.

105   The sun swept around the horizon, trailing its robes of weeks and days. One morning as Joe came in from work, he found Missie May chopping wood. Without a word he took the ax and chopped a huge pile before he stopped.

106   "You ain't got no business choppin' wood, and you know it."

107   "How come? Ah been choppin' it for the last longest."

108   "Ah ain't blind. You makin' feet for shoes."

109   "Won't you be glad to have a lil baby chile, Joe?"

110   "You know dat 'thout astin' me."

111   "Iss gointer be a boy chile and de very spit of you."

112   "You reckon, Missie May?"

113   "Who else could it look lak?"

114   Joe said nothing, but he thrust his hand deep into his pocket and fingered something there.

115   It was almost six months later Missie May took to bed and Joe went and got his mother to come wait on the house.

116   Missie May was delivered of a fine boy. Her travail was over when Joe came in from work one morning. His mother and the old woman were drinking great bowls of coffee around the fire in the kitchen.

117   The minute Joe came into the room his mother called him aside.

118   "How did Missie May make out?" he asked quickly.

119   "Who, dat gal? She strong as a ox. She gointer have plenty mo'. We done fixed her wid de sugar and lard to sweeten her for de nex' one."

120   Joe stood silent awhile.

121   "You ain't ask 'bout de baby, Joe. You oughter be mighty proud cause he sho is de spittin' image of yuh, son. Dat's yourn all right, if you never git another one, dat un is yourn. And you know Ah'm mighty proud too, son, cause Ah never thought well of you marryin' Missie May cause her ma used tuh fan her foot round right smart and Ah been mighty skeered dat Missie May wuz gointer git misput on her road."

122   Joe said nothing. He fooled around the house till late in the day, then, just before he went to work, he went and stood at the foot of the bed and asked his wife how she felt. He did this every day during the week.

123   On Saturday he went to Orlando to make his market. It had been a long time since he had done that.

124   Meat and lard, meal and flour, soap and starch. Cans of corn and tomatoes. All the staples. He fooled around town for a while and bought bananas and apples. Way after while he went around to the candy store.

125   "Hellow, Joe," the clerk greeted him. "Ain't seen you in a long time."

126   "Nope, Ah ain't been heah. Been round in spots and places."

127   "Want some of them molasses kisses you always buy?"

128   "Yessuh." He threw the gilded half dollar on the counter. "Will dat spend?"

129   "What is it, Joe? Well, I'll be doggone! A gold-plated four-bit piece. Where'd you git it, Joe?"

130   "Offen a stray nigger dat come through Eatonville. He had it on his watch chain for a charm—goin' round making out iss gold money. Ha ha! He had a quarter on his tiepin and it wuz all golded up too. Tryin' to fool people. Makin' out he so rich and everything. Ha! Ha! Tryin' to tole off folkses wives from home."

131   "How did you git it, Joe? Did he fool you, too?"

132   "Who, me? Naw suh! He ain't fooled me none. Know what Ah done? He come round me wid his smart talk. Ah hauled off and knocked 'im down and took his old four-bits away from 'im. Gointer buy my wife some good ole lasses kisses wid it. Gimme fifty cents worth of dem candy kisses."

133   "Fifty cents buys a mighty lot of candy kisses, Joe. Why don't you split it up and take some chocolate bars, too? They eat good, too."

134   "Yessuh, dey do, but Ah wants all dat is kisses. Ah got a lil boy chile home now. Tain't a week old yet, but he kin suck a sugar tit and maybe eat one them kisses hisself."

135   Joe got his candy and left the store. The clerk turned to the next customer. "Wisht I could be like these darkies. Laughin' all the time. Nothin' worries 'em."

136   Back in Eatonville, Joe reached his own front door. There was the ring of singing metal on wood. Fifteen times. Missie May couldn't run to the door, but she crept there as quickly as she could.

137   "Joe Banks, Ah hear you chunkin' money in mah do'way. You wait till Ah got mah strength back and Ah'm gointer fix you for dat."

Questions for Discussion

1. How does the first sentence set the stage for the story?

2. Missie May says to Joe, "'Ah'm a real wife, not no dress and breath.'" What does she mean? What evidence in her behavior suggests that she is a "real wife"?

3. Why does Joe feel inferior to Otis D. Slemmons and try to imitate him?

4. When Joe arrives home unexpectedly, he laughs at the scene before him. Why? Later, he acts with exaggerated politeness. Why?

5. What is the significance of the "gold piece" under the pillow? Why is the title of the story appropriate?

6. At the end, the white clerk in the store remarks that the "darkies" are always laughing without a care in the world. Explain the **irony** of this statement.

7. Why does Joe forgive Missie May? Does he act responsibly?

Suggestions for Exploration and Writing

1. In an essay, discuss the strengths and weaknesses in this marriage.

2. How does the happy Saturday ritual reveal the relationship between Missie May and Joe?

3. In a researched essay, show how Hurston reveals the complexity of characters who appear to the outside world to be simple and happy.

4. Should infidelity or adultery be grounds for divorce? Discuss.

5. This story involves a conflict in which one character's pursuit of unlimited freedom infringes on the dignity of a more responsible character. Discuss how the story explores and defines the limits of freedom.

Ernest Hemingway (1899–1961)

Hemingway began his literary career as a cub reporter for the Kansas City Star. *There he learned a style of writing that many critics believe had a lasting influence on his fiction: his frequent use of short, simple or compound sentences. Hemingway continued his newspaper writing as a foreign correspondent throughout much of his life. As his works became famous, Hemingway also became a celebrity, often living the kind of adventures he wrote about: he fought in World War I, supported the Spanish Civil War, hunted in Africa, and married four times. His most famous novels include* The Sun Also Rises *(1926),* A Farewell to Arms *(1929),* For Whom the Bell Tolls *(1940), and* The Old Man and the Sea *(1952). In 1954, Hemingway was awarded the Nobel Prize for Literature.*

HILLS LIKE WHITE ELEPHANTS   (1927)

1   The hills across the valley of the Ebro were long and white. On this side there was no shade and no trees and the station was between two lines of rails in the sun. Close against the side of the station there was the warm shadow of the building and a curtain, made of strings of bamboo beads, hung across the open door into the bar, to keep out flies. The American

and the girl with him sat at a table in the shade, outside the building. It was very hot and the express from Barcelona would come in forty minutes. It stopped at this junction for two minutes and went on to Madrid.

2   "What should we drink?" the girl asked. She had taken off her hat and put it on the table.

3   "It's pretty hot," the man said.

4   "Let's drink beer."

5   "Dos cervezas," the man said into the curtain.

6   "Big ones?" a woman asked from the doorway.

7   "Yes. Two big ones."

8   The woman brought two glasses of beer and two felt pads. She put the felt pads and the beer glasses on the table and looked at the man and the girl. The girl was looking off at the line of hills. They were white in the sun and the country was brown and dry.

9   "They look like white elephants," she said.

10   "I've never seen one," the man drank his beer.

11   "No, you wouldn't have."

12   "I might have," the man said. "Just because you say I wouldn't have doesn't prove anything."

13   The girl looked at the bead curtain. "They've painted something on it," she said. "What does it say?"

14   "Anis del Toro. It's a drink."

15   "Could we try it?"

16   The man called "Listen" through the curtain. The woman came out from the bar.

17   "Four reales."

18   "We want two Anis del Toro."

19   "With water?"

20   "Do you want it with water?"

21   "I don't know," the girl said. "Is it good with water?"

22   "It's all right."

23   "You want them with water?" asked the woman.

24   "Yes, with water."

25   "It tastes like licorice," the girl said and put the glass down.

26   "That's the way with everything."

27   "Yes," said the girl. "Everything tastes of licorice. Especially all the things you've waited so long for, like absinthe."

28   "Oh, cut it out."

29   "You started it," the girl said. "I was being amused. I was having a fine time."

30   "Well, let's try and have a fine time."

31   "All right. I was trying. I said the mountains looked like white elephants. Wasn't that bright?"

32   "That was bright."

33   "I wanted to try this new drink. That's all we do, isn't it—look at things and try new drinks?"

34   "I guess so."

35   The girl looked across at the hills.

36   "They're lovely hills," she said. "They don't really look like white elephants. I just meant the coloring of their skin through the trees."

37   "Should we have another drink?"

38   "All right."

39   The warm wind blew the bead curtain against the table.

40   "The beer's nice and cool," the man said.

41   "It's lovely," the girl said.

42   "It's really an awfully simple operation, Jig," the man said. "It's not really an operation at all."

43   The girl looked at the ground the table legs rested on.

44   "I know you wouldn't mind it, Jig. It's really not anything. It's just to let the air in."

45   The girl did not say anything.

46   "I'll go with you and I'll stay with you all the time. They just let the air in and then it's all perfectly natural."

47   "Then what will we do afterward?"

48   "We'll be fine afterward. Just like we were before."

49   "What makes you think so?"

50   "That's the only thing that bothers us. It's the only thing that's made us unhappy."

51   The girl looked at the bead curtain, put her hand out and took hold of two of the strings of beads.

52   "And you think then we'll be all right and be happy."

53   "I know we will. You don't have to be afraid. I've known lots of people that have done it."

54   "So have I," said the girl. "And afterward they were all so happy."

55   "Well," the man said, "if you don't want to you don't have to. I wouldn't have you do it if you didn't want to. But I know it's perfectly simple."

56   "And you really want to?"

57   "I think it's the best thing to do. But I don't want you to do it if you don't really want to."

58   "And if I do it you'll be happy and things will be like they were and you'll love me?"

59   "I love you now. You know I love you."

60   "I know. But if I do it, then it will be nice again if I say things are like white elephants, and you'll like it?"

61   "I'll love it. I love it now but I just can't think about it. You know how I get when I worry."

62   "If I do it you won't ever worry?"

63   "I won't worry about that because it's perfectly simple."

64   "Then I'll do it. Because I don't care about me."

65   "What do you mean?"

66   "I don't care about me."

67   "Well, I care about you."

68   "Oh, yes. But I don't care about me. And I'll do it and then everything will be fine."

69   "I don't want you to do it if you feel that way."

70   The girl stood up and walked to the end of the station. Across, on the other side, were fields of grain and trees along the banks of the Ebro. Far away, beyond the river, were mountains. The shadow of a cloud moved across the field of grain and she saw the river through the trees.

71   "And we could have all this," she said. "And we could have everything and every day we make it more impossible."

72   "What did you say?"

73   "I said we could have everything."

74   "We can have everything."

75   "No, we can't."

76   "We can have the whole world."

77   "No, we can't."

78   "We can go everywhere."

79   "No, we can't. It isn't ours any more."

80   "It's ours."

81   "No, it isn't. And once they take it away, you never get it back."

82   "But they haven't taken it away."

83   "We'll wait and see."

84   "Come on back in the shade," he said. "You mustn't feel that way."

85   "I don't feel any way," the girl said. "I just know things."

86   "I don't want you to do anything that you don't want to do—"

87   "Nor that isn't good for me," she said. "I know. Could we have another beer?"

88   "All right. But you've got to realize—"

89   "I realize," the girl said. "Can't we maybe stop talking?"

90   They sat down at the table and the girl looked across at the hills on the dry side of the valley and the man looked at her and at the table.

91   "You've got to realize," he said, "that I don't want you to do it if you don't want to. I'm perfectly willing to go through with it if it means anything to you."

92   "Doesn't it mean anything to you? We could get along."

93   "Of course it does. But I don't want anybody but you. I don't want any one else. And I know it's perfectly simple."

94   "Yes, you know it's perfectly simple."

95   "It's all right for you to say that, but I do know it."

96   "Would you do something for me now?"

97   "I'd do anything for you."

98   "Would you please please please please please please please stop talking?"

99   He did not say anything but looked at the bags against the wall of the station. There were labels on them from all the hotels where they had spent nights.

100   "But I don't want you to," he said, "I don't care anything about it."

101   "I'll scream," the girl said.

102   The woman came out through the curtains with two glasses of beer and put them down on the damp felt pads. "The train comes in five minutes," she said.

103   "What did she say?" asked the girl.

104   "That the train is coming in five minutes."

105   The girl smiled brightly at the woman, to thank her.

106   "I'd better take the bags over to the other side of the station," the man said. She smiled at him.

107   "All right. Then come back and we'll finish the beer."

108   He picked up the two heavy bags and carried them around the station to the other tracks. He looked up the tracks but could not see the train. Coming back, he walked through the barroom, where people waiting for the train were drinking. He drank an Anis at the bar and looked at the people. They were all waiting reasonably for the train. He went out through the bead curtain. She was sitting at the table and smiled at him.

109   "Do you feel better?" he asked.

110   "I feel fine," she said. "There's nothing wrong with me. I feel fine."

Questions for Discussion

1. What is the couple's relationship like at the beginning of the story? How has that relationship recently changed? Who dominates the relationship?

2. How does the man attempt to manipulate the woman into having a "simple operation"? How responsible does he seem? What does he mean by "'We'll be fine afterward. Just like we were before'"?

3. How would you describe the woman's tone in talking about a "simple operation"?

4. How do the landscapes on either side of the river differ? What might these contrasting landscapes suggest about the woman's state of mind?

5. Considering the symbolism of the landscapes, the man's references to the "simple operation," the recent changes in the couple's relationship, and the expected effect of the "operation" on the couple's relationship, what kind of operation do you think the couple are talking about? Why do they never openly name the operation?

6. In the course of the conversation, when does the relationship between the two seem to change?

7. How do you interpret the woman's final words?

Suggestions for Exploration and Writing

1. Clearly, in this story the man tries to manipulate the woman into doing what he wants done without himself taking any responsibility for her action. In an essay, discuss how a family member, friend, or acquaintance has similarly attempted to manipulate you.

2. In an essay, discuss how the relationship between the man and woman changes through the course of this very short story.

Jamaica Kincaid (b. 1949)

Born Elaine Potter Richardson on St. John's Island, Antigua, Jamaica Kincaid emigrated at age seventeen to New York, where she worked various menial jobs and attended college. From 1976 to 1995 she was a regular writer for the New Yorker. *While her stories often reveal the narrowness and provinciality of the island people among whom she grew up, they also reveal a love of country and family. Her books include* At the Bottom of the River *(1983), from which "Girl" is taken,* Annie John *(1985),* Lucy *(1990), and* My Brother *(1997). Kincaid now lives in Vermont with her husband and three children.*

GIRL   (1978)

1   Wash the white clothes on Monday and put them on the stone heap; wash the color clothes on Tuesday and put them on the clothes-line to dry; don't walk barehead in the hot sun; cook pumpkin fritters in very hot sweet oil; soak your little cloths right after you take them off; when buying cotton to make yourself a nice blouse, be sure that it doesn't have gum on it, because that way it won't hold up well after a wash; soak salt fish overnight before you cook it; is it true that you sing benna in Sunday school? always eat your food in such a way that it won't turn someone else's stomach; on Sundays try to walk like a lady and not like the slut you are so bent on becoming; don't sing benna in Sunday school; you mustn't speak to wharf-rat boys, not even to give directions; don't eat fruits on the street—flies will follow you; *but I don't sing benna on Sundays at all and never in Sunday school;* this is how to sew on a button; this is how to make a buttonhole for the button you have just sewed on; this is how to hem a dress when you see the hem coming down and so to prevent yourself from looking like the slut I know you are so bent on becoming; this is how you iron your father's khaki shirt so that it doesn't have a crease; this is how you iron your father's khaki pants so that they don't have a crease; this is how you grow okra—far from the house, because okra tree harbors red ants; when you are growing dasheen, make sure it gets plenty of water or else it makes your throat itch when you are eating it; this is how you sweep a corner; this is how you sweep a whole house; this is how you sweep a yard; this is how you smile to someone you don't like too much; this is how you smile to someone you don't like at all; this is how you smile to someone you like completely; this is how you set a table for tea; this is how you set a table for dinner; this is how you set a table for dinner with an important guest; this is how you set a table for lunch; this is how you set a table for breakfast; this is how to behave in the presence of men who don't know you very well, and this way they won't recognize immediately the slut I have

warned you against becoming; be sure to wash every day, even if it is with your own spit; don't squat down to play marbles—you are not a boy, you know; don't pick people's flowers—you might catch something; don't throw stones at blackbirds, because it might not be a blackbird at all; this is how to make a bread pudding; this is how to make doukona; this is how to make pepper pot; this is how to make a good medicine for a cold; this is how to make a good medicine to throw away a child before it even becomes a child; this is how to catch a fish; this is how to throw back a fish you don't like, and that way something bad won't fall on you; this is how to bully a man; this is how a man bullies you; this is how to love a man, and if this doesn't work there are other ways, and if they don't work don't feel too bad about giving up; this is how to spit up in the air if you feel like it, and this is how to move quick so that it doesn't fall on you; this is how to make ends meet; always squeeze bread to make sure it's fresh; *but what if the baker won't let me feel the bread?;* you mean to say that after all you are really going to be the kind of woman who the baker won't let near the bread?

Questions for Discussion

1. What words or phrases other than "this is how" are repeated? How do these repeated phrases define the girl's role?
2. What do you know about the relationship between the two people?
3. Why are two clauses italicized?

Suggestions for Exploration and Writing

1. Using a favorite, oft-repeated parental phrase, write an essay explaining why you resented, welcomed, or now understand this phrase.
2. Are men less frequently told what to do than women? As a male, write about what has been told to you. As a female, write about what should have been told to a boy and why.
3. Using the form of Kincaid's "Girl," write "Boy."

Bobbie Ann Mason (b. 1940)

Born in Kentucky, Bobbie Ann Mason has written fiction and literary criticism. Many of her stories were first published in magazines such as the New Yorker *and* Redbook. *Her first book of fiction,* Shiloh and Other Stories *(1982), received the Ernest Hemingway Award in 1983. Her subjects are usually the working-class people of western Kentucky. Mason's stories have been instrumental in the growth of regional fiction in a literary style labeled* shopping-mall realism. *Her two novels are* In Country *(1985) and* Spence and Lila *(1988). Her most recent collections of stories are* Midnight Magic

(1998) and Down a Wild Trail *(2001). In 1999, Mason published* Clear Springs: A Memoir.

SHILOH

(1982)

1   Leroy Moffitt's wife, Norma Jean, is working on her pectorals. She lifts three-pound dumbbells to warm up, then progresses to a twenty-pound barbell. Standing with her legs apart, she reminds Leroy of Wonder Woman.

2   "I'd give anything if I could just get these muscles to where they're real hard," says Norma Jean. "Feel this arm. It's not as hard as the other one."

3   "That's 'cause you're right-handed," says Leroy, dodging as she swings the barbell in an arc.

4   "Do you think so?"

5   "Sure."

6   Leroy is a truckdriver. He injured his leg in a highway accident four months ago, and his physical therapy, which involves weights and a pulley, prompted Norma Jean to try building herself up. Now she is attending a body-building class. Leroy has been collecting temporary disability since his tractor-trailer jackknifed in Missouri, badly twisting his left leg in its socket. He has a steel pin in his hip. He will probably not be able to drive his rig again. It sits in the backyard, like a gigantic bird that has flown home to roost. Leroy has been home in Kentucky for three months, and his leg is almost healed, but the accident frightened him and he does not want to drive any more long hauls. He is not sure what to do next. In the meantime, he makes things from craft kits. He started by building a miniature log cabin from notched Popsicle sticks. He varnished it and placed it on the TV set, where it remains. It reminds him of a rustic Nativity scene. Then he tried string art (sailing ships on black velvet), a macramé owl kit, a snap-together B-17 Flying Fortress, and a lamp made out of a model truck, with a light fixture screwed in the top of the cab. At first the kits were diversions, something to kill time, but now he is thinking about building a full-scale log house from a kit. It would be considerably cheaper than building a regular house, and besides, Leroy has grown to appreciate how things are put together. He has begun to realize that in all the years he was on the road he never took time to examine anything. He was always flying past scenery.

7   "They won't let you build a log cabin in any of the new subdivisions," Norma Jean tells him.

8   "They will if I tell them it's for you," he says, teasing her. Ever since they were married, he has promised Norma Jean he would build her a new home one day. They have always rented, and the house they live in is small and nondescript. It does not even feel like a home, Leroy realizes now.

9   Norma Jean works at the Rexall drugstore, and she has acquired an amazing amount of information about cosmetics. When she explains to Leroy the three stages of complexion care, involving creams, toners, and

moisturizers, he thinks happily of other petroleum products—axle grease, diesel fuel. This is a connection between him and Norma Jean. Since he has been home, he has felt unusually tender about his wife and guilty over his long absences. But he can't tell what she feels about him. Norma Jean has never complained about his traveling; she has never made hurt remarks, like calling his truck a "widow-maker." He is reasonably certain she has been faithful to him, but he wishes she would celebrate his permanent homecoming more happily. Norma Jean is often startled to find Leroy at home, and he thinks she seems a little disappointed about it. Perhaps he reminds her too much of the early days of their marriage, before he went on the road. They had a child who died as an infant, years ago. They never speak about their memories of Randy, which have almost faded, but now that Leroy is home all the time, they sometimes feel awkward around each other, and Leroy wonders if one of them should mention the child. He has the feeling that they are waking up out of a dream together—that they must create a new marriage, start afresh. They are lucky they are still married. Leroy has read that for most people losing a child destroys the marriage—or else he heard this on *Donahue*. He can't always remember where he learns things anymore.

10   At Christmas, Leroy bought an electric organ for Norma Jean. She used to play the piano when she was in high school. "It don't leave you," she told him once. "It's like riding a bicycle."

11   The new instrument had so many keys and buttons that she was bewildered by it at first. She touched the keys tentatively, pushed some buttons, then pecked out "Chopsticks." It came out in an amplified fox-trot rhythm, with marimba sounds.

12   "It's an orchestra!" she cried.

13   The organ had a pecan-look finish and eighteen preset chords, with optional flute, violin, trumpet, clarinet, and banjo accompaniments. Norma Jean mastered the organ almost immediately. At first she played Christmas songs. Then she bought *The Sixties Songbook* and learned every tune in it, adding variations to each with the rows of brightly colored buttons.

14   "I didn't like these old songs back then," she said. "But I have this crazy feeling I missed something."

15   "You didn't miss a thing," said Leroy.

16   Leroy likes to lie on the couch and smoke a joint and listen to Norma Jean play "Can't Take My Eyes Off You" and "I'll Be Back." He is back again. After fifteen years on the road, he is finally settling down with the woman he loves. She is still pretty. Her skin is flawless. Her frosted curls resemble pencil trimmings.

17   Now that Leroy has come home to stay, he notices how much the town has changed. Subdivisions are spreading across western Kentucky like an oil slick. The sign at the edge of town says "Pop: 11,500"—only seven hundred more than it said twenty years before. Leroy can't figure out who is

living in all the new houses. The farmers who used to gather around the courthouse square on Saturday afternoons to play checkers and spit tobacco juice have gone. It has been years since Leroy has thought about the farmers, and they have disappeared without his noticing.

18   Leroy meets a kid named Stevie Hamilton in the parking lot at the new shopping center. While they pretend to be strangers meeting over a stalled car, Stevie tosses an ounce of marijuana under the front seat of Leroy's car. Stevie is wearing orange jogging shoes and a T-shirt that says CHATTAHOOCHEE SUPER-RAT. His father is a prominent doctor who lives in one of the expensive subdivisions in a new white-columned brick house that looks like a funeral parlor. In the phone book under his name there is a separate number, with the listing "Teenagers."

19   "Where do you get this stuff?" asks Leroy. "From your pappy?"

20   "That's for me to know and you to find out," Stevie says. He is slit-eyed and skinny.

21   "What else you got?"

22   "What you interested in?"

23   "Nothing special. Just wondered."

24   Leroy used to take speed on the road. Now he has to go slowly. He needs to be mellow. He leans back against the car and says, "I'm aiming to build me a log house, soon as I get time. My wife, though, I don't think she likes the idea."

25   "Well, let me know when you want me again," Stevie says. He has a cigarette in his cupped palm, as though sheltering it from the wind. He takes a long drag, then stomps it on the asphalt and slouches away.

26   Stevie's father was two years ahead of Leroy in high school. Leroy is thirty-four. He married Norma Jean when they were both eighteen, and their child Randy was born a few months later, but he died at the age of four months and three days. He would be about Stevie's age now. Norma Jean and Leroy were at the drive-in, watching a double feature (*Dr. Strangelove* and *Lover Come Back*), and the baby was sleeping in the back seat. When the first movie ended, the baby was dead. It was the sudden infant death syndrome. Leroy remembers handing Randy to a nurse at the emergency room, as though he were offering her a large doll as a present. A dead baby feels like a sack of flour. "It just happens sometimes," said the doctor, in what Leroy always recalls as a nonchalant tone. Leroy can hardly remember the child anymore, but he still sees vividly a scene from *Dr. Strangelove* in which the President of the United States was talking in a folksy voice on the hot line to the Soviet premier about the bomber accidentally headed toward Russia. He was in the War Room, and the world map was lit up. Leroy remembers Norma Jean standing catatonically beside him in the hospital and himself thinking: Who is this strange girl? He had forgotten who she was. Now scientists are saying that crib death is caused by a virus. Nobody knows anything, Leroy thinks. The answers are always changing.

27   When Leroy gets home from the shopping center, Norma Jean's mother, Mabel Beasley, is there. Until this year, Leroy has not realized how much time she spends with Norma Jean. When she visits, she inspects the

closets and then the plants, informing Norma Jean when a plant is droopy or yellow. Mabel calls the plants "flowers," although there are never any blooms. She always notices if Norma Jean's laundry is piling up. Mabel is a short, overweight woman whose tight, brown-dyed curls look more like a wig than the actual wig she sometimes wears. Today she has brought Norma Jean an off-white dust ruffle she made for the bed; Mabel works in a custom-upholstery shop.

28   "This is the tenth one I made this year," Mabel says. "I got started and couldn't stop."

29   "It's real pretty," says Norma Jean.

30   "Now we can hide things under the bed," says Leroy, who gets along with his mother-in-law primarily by joking with her. Mabel has never really forgiven him for disgracing her by getting Norma Jean pregnant. When the baby died, she said that fate was mocking her.

31   "What's that thing?" Mabel says to Leroy in a loud voice, pointing to a tangle of yarn on a piece of canvas.

32   Leroy holds it up for Mabel to see. "It's my needlepoint," he explains. "This is a *Star Trek* pillow cover."

33   "That's what a woman would do," says Mabel. "Great day in the morning!"

34   "All the big football players on TV do it," he says.

35   "Why, Leroy, you're always trying to fool me. I don't believe you for one minute. You don't know what to do with yourself—that's the whole trouble. Sewing!"

36   "I'm aiming to build us a log house," says Leroy. "Soon as my plans come."

37   "Like *heck* you are," says Norma Jean. She takes Leroy's needlepoint and shoves it into a drawer. "You have to find a job first. Nobody can afford to build now anyway."

38   Mabel straightens her girdle and says, "I still think before you get tied down y'all ought to take a little run to Shiloh."

39   "One of these days, Mama," Norma Jean says impatiently.

40   Mabel is talking about Shiloh, Tennessee. For the past few years, she has been urging Leroy and Norma Jean to visit the Civil War battleground there. Mabel went there on her honeymoon—the only real trip she ever took. Her husband died of a perforated ulcer when Norma Jean was ten, but Mabel, who was accepted into the United Daughters of the Confederacy in 1975, is still preoccupied with going back to Shiloh.

41   "I've been to kingdom come and back in that truck out yonder," Leroy says to Mabel, "but we never yet set foot in that battleground. Ain't that something? How did I miss it?"

42   "It's not even that far," Mabel says.

43   After Mabel leaves, Norma Jean reads to Leroy from a list she has made. "Things you could do," she announces. "You could get a job as a guard at Union Carbide, where they'd let you set on a stool. You could get on at the lumberyard. You could do a little carpenter work, if you want to build so bad. You could—"

44   "I can't do something where I'd have to stand up all day."

45   "You ought to try standing up all day behind a cosmetics counter. It's amazing that I have strong feet, coming from two parents that never had strong feet at all." At the moment Norma Jean is holding on to the kitchen counter, raising her knees one at a time as she talks. She is wearing two-pound ankle weights.

46   "Don't worry," says Leroy. "I'll do something."

47   "You could truck calves to slaughter for somebody. You wouldn't have to drive any big old truck for that."

48   "I'm going to build you this house," says Leroy. "I want to make you a real home."

49   "I don't want to live in any log cabin."

50   "It's not a cabin. It's a house."

51   "I don't care. It looks like a cabin."

52   "You and me together could lift those logs. It's just like lifting weights."

53   Norma Jean doesn't answer. Under her breath, she is counting. Now she is marching through the kitchen. She is doing goose steps.

54   Before his accident, when Leroy came home he used to stay in the house with Norma Jean, watching TV in bed and playing cards. She would cook fried chicken, picnic ham, chocolate pie—all his favorites. Now he is home alone much of the time. In the mornings, Norma Jean disappears, leaving a cooling place in the bed. She eats a cereal called Body Buddies, and she leaves the bowl on the table, with the soggy tan balls floating in a milk puddle. He sees things about Norma Jean that he never realized before. When she chops onions, she stares off into a corner, as if she can't bear to look. She puts on her house slippers almost precisely at nine o'clock every evening and nudges her jogging shoes under the couch. She saves bread heels for the birds. Leroy watches the birds at the feeder. He notices the peculiar way goldfinches fly past the window. They close their wings, then fall, then spread their wings to catch and lift themselves. He wonders if they close their eyes when they fall. Norma Jean closes her eyes when they are in bed. She wants the lights turned out. Even then, he is sure she closes her eyes.

55   He goes for long drives around town. He tends to drive a car rather carelessly. Power steering and an automatic shift make a car feel so small and inconsequential that his body is hardly involved in the driving process. His injured leg stretches out comfortably. Once or twice he has almost hit something, but even the prospect of an accident seems minor in a car. He cruises the new subdivisions, feeling like a criminal rehearsing for a robbery. Norma Jean is probably right about a log house being inappropriate here in the new subdivisions. All the houses look grand and complicated. They depress him.

56   One day when Leroy comes home from a drive he finds Norma Jean in tears. She is in the kitchen making a potato and mushroom-soup casserole, with grated-cheese topping. She is crying because her mother caught her smoking.

57   "I didn't hear her coming. I was standing here puffing away pretty as you please," Norma Jean says, wiping her eyes.

58   "I knew it would happen sooner or later," says Leroy, putting his arm around her.

59   "She don't know the meaning of the word 'knock,'" says Norma Jean. "It's a wonder she hadn't caught me years ago."

60   "Think of it this way," Leroy says. "What if she caught me with a joint?"

61   "You better not let her!" Norma Jean shrieks. "I'm warning you, Leroy Moffitt!"

62   "I'm just kidding. Here, play me a tune. That'll help you relax."

63   Norma Jean puts the casserole in the oven and sets the timer. Then she plays a ragtime tune, with horns and banjo, as Leroy lights up a joint and lies on the couch, laughing to himself about Mabel's catching him at it. He thinks of Stevie Hamilton—a doctor's son pushing grass. Everything is funny. The whole town seems crazy and small. He is reminded of Virgil Mathis, a boastful policeman Leroy used to shoot pool with. Virgil recently led a drug bust in a back room at a bowling alley, where he seized ten thousand dollars' worth of marijuana. The newspaper had a picture of him holding up the bags of grass and grinning widely. Right now, Leroy can imagine Virgil breaking down the door and arresting him with a lungful of smoke. Virgil would probably have been alerted to the scene because of all the racket Norma Jean is making. Now she sounds like a hard-rock band. Norma Jean is terrific. When she switches to a Latin-rhythm version of "Sunshine Superman," Leroy hums along. Norma Jean's foot goes up and down, up and down.

64   "Well, what do you think?" Leroy says, when Norma Jean pauses to search through her music.

65   "What do I think about what?"

66   His mind has gone blank. Then he says, "I'll sell my rig and build us a house." That wasn't what he wanted to say. He wanted to know what she thought—what she *really* thought—about them.

67   "Don't start in on that again," says Norma Jean. She begins playing "Who'll Be the Next in Line?"

68   Leroy used to tell hitchhikers his whole life story—about his travels, his hometown, the baby. He would end with a question: "Well, what do you think?" It was just a rhetorical question. In time, he had the feeling that he'd been telling the same story over and over to the same hitchhikers. He quit talking to hitchhikers when he realized how his voice sounded— whining and self-pitying, like some teenage-tragedy song. Now Leroy has the sudden impulse to tell Norma Jean about himself, as if he had just met her. They have known each other so long they have forgotten a lot about each other. They could become reacquainted. But when the oven timer goes off and she runs to the kitchen, he forgets why he wants to do this.

69   The next day, Mabel drops by. It is Saturday and Norma Jean is cleaning. Leroy is studying the plans of his log house, which have finally come in the

mail. He has them spread out on the table—big sheets of stiff blue paper, with diagrams and numbers printed in white. While Norma Jean runs the vacuum, Mabel drinks coffee. She sets her coffee cup on a blueprint.

70   "I'm just waiting for time to pass," she says to Leroy, drumming her fingers on the table.

71   As soon as Norma Jean switches off the vacuum, Mabel says in a loud voice, "Did you hear about the datsun dog that killed the baby?"

72   Norma Jean says, "The word is 'dachshund.'"

73   "They put the dog on trial. It chewed the baby's legs off. The mother was in the next room all the time." She raises her voice. "They thought it was neglect."

74   Norma Jean is holding her ears. Leroy manages to open the refrigerator and get some Diet Pepsi to offer Mabel. Mabel still has some coffee and she waves away the Pepsi.

75   "Datsuns are like that," Mabel says. "They're jealous dogs. They'll tear a place to pieces if you don't keep an eye on them."

76   "You better watch out what you're saying, Mabel," says Leroy.

77   "Well, facts is facts."

78   Leroy looks out the window at his rig. It is like a huge piece of furniture gathering dust in the backyard. Pretty soon it will be an antique. He hears the vacuum cleaner. Norma Jean seems to be cleaning the living room rug again.

79   Later, she says to Leroy, "She just said that about the baby because she caught me smoking. She's trying to pay me back."

80   "What are you talking about?" Leroy says, nervously shuffling blueprints.

81   "You know good and well," Norma Jean says. She is sitting in a kitchen chair with her feet up and her arms wrapped around her knees. She looks small and helpless. She says, "The very idea, her bringing up a subject like that! Saying it was neglect."

82   "She didn't mean that," Leroy says.

83   "She might not have *thought* she meant it. She always says things like that. You don't know how she goes on."

84   "But she didn't really mean it. She was just talking."

85   Leroy opens a king-sized bottle of beer and pours it into two glasses, dividing it carefully. He hands a glass to Norma Jean and she takes it from him mechanically. For a long time, they sit by the kitchen window watching the birds at the feeder.

86   Something is happening. Norma Jean is going to night school. She has graduated from her six-week body-building course and now she is taking an adult-education course in composition at Paducah Community College. She spends her evenings outlining paragraphs.

87   "First you have a topic sentence," she explains to Leroy. "Then you divide it up. Your secondary topic has to be connected to your primary topic."

88   To Leroy, this sounds intimidating. "I never was any good in English," he says.

89   "It makes a lot of sense."

90   "What are you doing this for, anyhow?"

91   She shrugs. "It's something to do." She stands up and lifts her dumb-bells a few times.

92   "Driving a rig, nobody cared about my English."

93   "I'm not criticizing your English."

94   Norma Jean used to say, "If I lose ten minutes' sleep, I just drag all day." Now she stays up late, writing compositions. She got a B on her first paper—a how-to theme on soup-based casseroles. Recently Norma Jean has been cooking unusual foods—tacos, lasagna, Bombay chicken. She doesn't play the organ anymore, though her second paper was called "Why Music Is Important to Me." She sits at the kitchen table, concentrating on her outlines, while Leroy plays with his log house plans, practicing with a set of Lincoln Logs. The thought of getting a truckload of notched, numbered logs scares him, and he wants to be prepared. As he and Norma Jean work together at the kitchen table, Leroy has the hopeful thought that they are sharing something, but he knows he is a fool to think this. Norma Jean is miles away. He knows he is going to lose her. Like Mabel, he is just waiting for time to pass.

95   One day, Mabel is there before Norma Jean gets home from work, and Leroy finds himself confiding in her. Mabel, he realizes, must know Norma Jean better than he does.

96   "I don't know what's got into that girl," Mabel says. "She used to go to bed with the chickens. Now you say she's up all hours. Plus her a-smoking. I like to died."

97   "I want to make her this beautiful home," Leroy says, indicating the Lincoln Logs. "I don't think she even wants it. Maybe she was happier with me gone."

98   "She don't know what to make of you, coming home like this."

99   "Is that it?"

100   Mabel takes the roof off his Lincoln Log cabin. "You couldn't get *me* in a log cabin," she says. "I was raised in one. It's no picnic, let me tell you."

101   "They're different now," says Leroy.

102   "I tell you what," Mabel says, smiling oddly at Leroy.

103   "What?"

104   "Take her on down to Shiloh. Y'all need to get out together, stir a little. Her brain's all balled up over them books."

105   Leroy can see traces of Norma Jean's features in her mother's face. Mabel's worn face has the texture of crinkled cotton, but suddenly she looks pretty. It occurs to Leroy that Mabel has been hinting all along that she wants them to take her with them to Shiloh.

106   "Let's all go to Shiloh," he says. "You and me and her. Come Sunday."

107   Mabel throws up her hands in protest. "Oh, no, not me. Young folks want to be by theirselves."

108   When Norma Jean comes in with groceries, Leroy says excitedly, "Your mama here's been dying to go to Shiloh for thirty-five years. It's about time we went, don't you think?"

109   "I'm not going to butt in on anybody's second honeymoon," Mabel says.

110   "Who's going on a honeymoon, for Christ's sake?" Norma Jean says loudly.

111   "I never raised no daughter of mine to talk that-a-way," Mabel says.

112   "You ain't seen nothing yet," says Norma Jean. She starts putting away boxes and cans, slamming cabinet doors.

113   "There's a log cabin at Shiloh," Mabel says. "It was there during the battle. There's bullet holes in it."

114   "When are you going to *shut up* about Shiloh, Mama?" asks Norma Jean.

115   "I always thought Shiloh was the prettiest place, so full of history," Mabel goes on. "I just hoped y'all could see it once before I die, so you could tell me about it." Later, she whispers to Leroy, "You do what I said. A little change is what she needs."

116   "Your name means 'the king,'" Norma Jean says to Leroy that evening. He is trying to get her to go to Shiloh, and she is reading a book about another century.

117   "Well, I reckon I ought to be right proud."

118   "I guess so."

119   "Am I still king around here?"

120   Norma Jean flexes her biceps and feels them for hardness. "I'm not fooling around with anybody, if that's what you mean," she says.

121   "Would you tell me if you were?"

122   "I don't know."

123   "What does *your* name mean?"

124   "It was Marilyn Monroe's real name."

125   "No kidding!"

126   "Norma comes from the Normans. They were invaders," she says. She closes her book and looks hard at Leroy. "I'll go to Shiloh with you if you'll stop staring at me."

127   On Sunday, Norma Jean packs a picnic and they go to Shiloh. To Leroy's relief, Mabel says she does not want to come with them. Norma Jean drives, and Leroy, sitting beside her, feels like some boring hitchhiker she has picked up. He tries some conversation, but she answers him in monosyllables. At Shiloh, she drives aimlessly through the park, past bluffs and trails and steep ravines. Shiloh is an immense place, and Leroy cannot see it as a battleground. It is not what he expected. He thought it would look like a golf course. Monuments are everywhere, showing through the thick clusters of trees. Norma Jean passes the log cabin Mabel mentioned. It is surrounded by tourists looking for bullet holes.

128   "That's not the kind of log house I've got in mind," says Leroy apologetically.

129   "I know *that*."

130   "This is a pretty place. Your mama was right."

131   "It's O.K.," says Norma Jean. "Well, we've seen it. I hope she's satisfied."

132   They burst out laughing together.

133   At the park museum, a movie on Shiloh is shown every half hour, but they decide that they don't want to see it. They buy a souvenir Confederate flag for Mabel, and then they find a picnic spot near the cemetery. Norma Jean has brought a picnic cooler, with pimiento sandwiches, soft drinks, and Yodels. Leroy eats a sandwich and then smokes a joint, hiding it behind the picnic cooler. Norma Jean has quit smoking altogether. She is picking cake crumbs from the cellophane wrapper, like a fussy bird.

134   Leroy says, "So the boys in gray ended up in Corinth. The Union soldiers zapped 'em finally. April 7, 1862."

135   They both know that he doesn't know any history. He is just talking about some of the historical plaques they have read. He feels awkward, like a boy on a date with an older girl. They are still just making conversation.

136   "Corinth is where Mama eloped to," says Norma Jean.

137   They sit in silence and stare at the cemetery for the Union dead and, beyond, at a tall cluster of trees. Campers are parked nearby, bumper to bumper, and small children in bright clothing are cavorting and squealing. Norma Jean wads up the cake wrapper and squeezes it tightly in her hand. Without looking at Leroy, she says, "I want to leave you."

138   Leroy takes a bottle of Coke out of the cooler and flips off the cap. He holds the bottle poised near his mouth but cannot remember to take a drink. Finally he says, "No, you don't."

139   "Yes, I do."

140   "I won't let you."

141   "You can't stop me."

142   "Don't do me that way."

143   Leroy knows Norma Jean will have her own way. "Didn't I promise to be home from now on?" he says.

144   "In some ways, a woman prefers a man who wanders," says Norma Jean. "That sounds crazy, I know."

145   "You're not crazy."

146   Leroy remembers to drink from his Coke. Then he says, "Yes, you *are* crazy. You and me could start all over again. Right back at the beginning."

147   "We *have* started all over again," says Norma Jean. "And this is how it turned out."

148   "What did I do wrong?"

149   "Nothing."

150   "Is this one of those women's lib things?" Leroy asks.

151   "Don't be funny."

152   The cemetery, a green slope dotted with white markers, looks like a subdivision site. Leroy is trying to comprehend that his marriage is breaking up, but for some reason he is wondering about white slabs in a graveyard.

153   "Everything was fine till Mama caught me smoking," says Norma Jean, standing up. "That set something off."

154   "What are you talking about?"

155   "She won't leave me alone—*you* won't leave me alone." Norma Jean seems to be crying, but she is looking away from him. "I feel eighteen again. I can't face that all over again." She starts walking away. "No, it *wasn't* fine. I don't know what I'm saying. Forget it."

156   Leroy takes a lungful of smoke and closes his eyes as Norma Jean's words sink in. He tries to focus on the fact that thirty-five hundred soldiers died on the grounds around him. He can only think of that war as a board game with plastic soldiers. Leroy almost smiles, as he compares the Confederates' daring attack on the Union camps and Virgil Mathis's raid on the bowling alley. General Grant, drunk and furious, shoved the Southerners back to Corinth, where Mabel and Jet Beasley were married years later, when Mabel was still thin and good-looking. The next day, Mabel and Jet visited the battleground, and then Norma Jean was born, and then she married Leroy and they had a baby, which they lost, and now Leroy and Norma Jean are here at the same battleground. Leroy knows he is leaving out a lot. He is leaving out the insides of history. History was always just names and dates to him. It occurs to him that building a house out of logs is similarly empty—too simple. And the real inner workings of a marriage, like most of history, have escaped him. Now he sees that building a log house is the dumbest idea he could have had. It was clumsy of him to think Norma Jean would want a log house. It was a crazy idea. He'll have to think of something else, quickly. He will wad the blueprints into tight balls and fling them into the lake. Then he'll get moving again. He opens his eyes. Norma Jean has moved away and is walking through the cemetery, following a serpentine brick path.

157   Leroy gets up to follow his wife, but his good leg is asleep and his bad leg still hurts him. Norma Jean is far away, walking rapidly toward the bluff by the river, and he tries to hobble toward her. Some children run past him, screaming noisily. Norma Jean has reached the bluff, and she is looking out over the Tennessee River. Now she turns toward Leroy and waves her arms. Is she beckoning to him? She seems to be doing an exercise for her chest muscles. The sky is unusually pale—the color of the dust ruffle Mabel made for Leroy and Norma Jean's bed.

Questions for Discussion

1. The loss of his career as a truck driver has changed Leroy's life significantly. In what ways is his life better? In what ways is it worse?

2. How have the changes in Leroy's life also changed Norma Jean? Why?

3. Why does Leroy smoke marijuana? How does it affect his thinking and his actions?

4. After Norma Jean learns the songs and masters the organ, she says that she has "this craven feeling [she] missed something." What is the double meaning of this statement?

5. What is the significance of the baby's death? Could the presence of a child have changed their relationship?

6. Why does Mabel want Norma Jean and Leroy to go to Shiloh?

7. Leroy realizes that he and Norma Jean "have known each other so long they have forgotten a lot about each other. They could become reacquainted." Why does he not speak of or act on this realization?

8. Why is it ironic that at this point in their relationship, Norma Jean learns the meaning of Leroy's name? What is the significance of her name?

9. Explain the symbolism of Norma Jean's choosing to tell Leroy that she is leaving him at Shiloh.

Suggestions for Exploration and Writing

1. Write a cause-and-effect essay detailing the disintegration of this marriage.

2. Describe the appearance and analyze the personalities of the three main characters.

3. Write an essay explaining how the characters reverse the traditional male/female roles.

4. In an essay, explain the battles men and women sometimes fight.

POETRY

William Shakespeare (1564–1616)

The biography of William Shakespeare precedes Othello *in the Grief and Loss Unit.*

SONNET 116 (1609)

Let me not to the marriage of true minds
Admit impediments. Love is not love
Which alters when it alteration finds,
Or bends with the remover to remove:
5 O, no! it is an ever-fixed mark,
That looks on tempests and is never shaken;
It is the star to every wandering bark,
Whose worth's unknown, although his height be taken.
Love's not Time's fool, though rosy lips and cheeks
10 Within his bending sickle's compass come;
Love alters not with his brief hours and weeks,
But bears it out even to the edge of doom.
    If this be error, and upon me prov'd,
    I never writ, nor no man ever lov'd.

SONNET 130

(1609)

My mistress' eyes are nothing like the sun;
Coral is far more red than her lips' red:
If snow be white, why then her breasts are dun;
If hairs be wires, black wires grow on her head.
5   I have seen roses damask'd, red and white,
But no such roses see I in her cheeks;
And in some perfumes is there more delight
Than in the breath that from my mistress reeks.
I love to hear her speak, yet well I know
10 That music hath a far more pleasing sound:
I grant I never saw a goddess go;
My mistress, when she walks, treads on the ground:
    And yet, by heaven, I think my love as rare
    As any she belied with false compare.

SONNET 138

(1609)

When my love swears that she is made of truth,
I do believe her, though I know she lies,
That she might think me some untutor'd youth,
Unlearned in the world's false subtleties.
5   Thus vainly thinking that she thinks me young,
Although she knows my days are past the best,
Simply I credit her false-speaking tongue:
On both sides thus is simple truth supprest.
But wherefore says she not she is unjust?
10 And wherefore say not I that I am old?
O, love's best habit is in seeming trust,
And age in love loves not to have years told:
    Therefore I lie with her, and she with me,
    And in our faults by lies we flatter'd be.

Questions for Discussion

1. In Sonnet 116, what claims does the speaker make for love? What cannot change love? What can?

2. Sonnet 130 differs from most love poetry of Shakespeare's day in its
unflattering description of the loved woman's appearance. What does
the speaker claim for his love?

3. Why do the speaker and his beloved lie to each other in Sonnet 138?
What do you think of their behavior?

Suggestions for Exploration and Writing

1. Write a descriptive essay—either serious or humorous—about your love.

2. Explain the qualities, other than physical appearance, that attract members of the opposite sex to each other.

3. Examine one or more pairs of lovers in this section in light of Shakespeare's definition of love in Sonnet 116.

4. Discuss some of the pressures that are put on a man and/or a woman in a seemingly "good" marriage or in "true love."

5. Do you agree that the "marriage of true minds" is unaffected by change or time? Explain why marriage is or is not an "ever-fixed mark."

John Donne (1572–1631)

John Donne, an Anglican priest highly regarded for his sermons, wrote conversational, sometimes tortuous, but carefully controlled poetry. His works include cynical court poetry such as the Satires, *strikingly sensual love poems in* Songs and Sonnets, *and powerful, often anguished religious poems such as the* Holy Sonnets. *Foremost among those poets later called* **metaphysical** *by Samuel Johnson, Donne often joins quite disparate concepts in elaborate images or conceits. The speaker's comparison of himself and his beloved to a compass in "A Valediction: Forbidding Mourning" is among the most famous of Donne's conceits.*

A VALEDICTION: FORBIDDING MOURNING   (1611)

As virtuous men passe mildly away,
    And whisper to their soules, to goe,
Whilst some of their sad friends doe say,
    The breath goes now, and some say, no:

5 So let us melt, and make no noise,
    No teare-floods, nor sigh-tempests move,
'Twere prophanation of our joyes
    To tell the layetie our love.

Moving of th'earth brings harmes and feares,
10   Men reckon what it did and meant,
But trepidation of the spheares,
    Though greater farre, is innocent.

Dull sublunary lovers love
    (Whose soule is sense) cannot admit
15 Absence, because it doth remove
    Those things which elemented it.

But we by a love, so much refin'd,
    That our selves know not what it is,
Inter-assured of the mind,
20   Care lesse, eyes, lips, and hands to misse.

Our two soules therefore, which are one,
   Though I must goe, endure not yet
A breach, but an expansion,
   Like gold to airy thinnesse beate.
25 If they be two, they are two so
   As stiffe twin compasses are two,
Thy soule the fixt foot, makes no show
   To move, but doth, if th' other doe.

And though it in the center sit,
30   Yet when the other far doth rome,
It leanes, and hearkens after it,
   And growes erect, as it comes home.

Such wilt thou be to mee, who must
   Like th'other foot, obliquely runne;
35 Thy firmnes makes my circle just,
   And makes me end, where I begunne.

Questions for Discussion

1. What is the occasion for the poem?

2. How does the woman whom the speaker is addressing seem to feel about his impending departure? What, then, is the purpose of the poem?

3. How do the various images that define the couple's love help to fulfill the poem's purpose?

4. According to the speaker, how does this couple's love differ from that of other couples?

Suggestion for Exploration and Writing

1. Carefully analyze Donne's poem, showing how **diction, imagery,** sound, and **syntax** all contribute to the soothing, reassuring **tone** of the poem.

 Iambic tetra/meter

Andrew Marvell (1621–1678)

*Andrew Marvell was a Puritan, a vocal advocate of personal freedom, and a member of the British Parliament. He, like John Donne, was one of the poets whom Samuel Johnson later called **metaphysical.** Marvell is known today for the exquisite craftsmanship of such poems as "The Garden," "To His Coy Mistress," and "An Horatian Ode upon Cromwell's Return from Ireland."*

TO HIS COY MISTRESS   (1681)

Had we but world enough, and time,
This coyness, Lady, were no crime.
We would sit down, and think which way
To walk, and pass our long love's day.

5   Thou by the Indian Ganges' side
      Shouldst rubies find: I by the tide
      Of Humber would complain. I would
      Love you ten years before the flood:
      And you should, if you please, refuse
10   Till the conversion of the Jews.
      My vegetable love should grow
      Vaster than empires, and more slow.
      An hundred years should go to praise
      Thine eyes, and on thy forehead gaze.
15   Two hundred to adore each breast:
      But thirty thousand to the rest.
      An age at least to every part,
      And the last age should show your heart:
      For, Lady, you deserve this state;
20   Nor would I love at lower rate.
          But at my back I always hear
      Time's wingèd chariot hurrying near:
      And yonder all before us lie
      Deserts of vast eternity.
25   Thy beauty shall no more be found;
      Nor, in thy marble vault, shall sound
      My echoing song: then worms shall try
      That long-preserved virginity:
      And your quaint honour turn to dust;
30   And into ashes all my lust.
      The grave's a fine and private place,
      But none, I think, do there embrace.
          Now, therefore, while the youthful hew
      Sits on thy skin like morning dew,
35   And while thy willing soul transpires
      At every pore with instant fires,
      Now let us sport us while we may;
      And now, like amorous birds of prey,
      Rather at once our time devour,
40   Than languish in his slow-chapped power.
      Let us roll all our strength, and all
      Our sweetness, up into one ball:
      And tear our pleasures with rough strife,
      Thorough the iron gates of life.
45   Thus, though we cannot make our sun
      Stand still, yet we will make him run.

Questions for Discussion

1. How does the **tone** of the poem change from the first stanza to the second to the last?

2. Do you think the speaker genuinely loves his listener, or is he just feeding her a line? Defend your answer.

Suggestions for Exploration and Writing

1. Define *carpe diem,* and explain how Marvell's narrator uses this concept to further his seduction.

2. Analyze some techniques that men or women use to be coy or to play hard to get.

Elizabeth Barrett Browning (1806–1861)

Elizabeth Barrett was famous as a well-educated and precocious poet. By the time Robert Browning fell in love with her, she had become a semi-invalid forbidden by her tyrannical father to marry. After Elizabeth and Robert eloped to Italy, her health improved. The depth of her love for her husband is beautifully illustrated by the Sonnets from the Portuguese *(1850), forty-four verses tracing the progress of her love for Robert, who called her his little Portuguese. "How Do I Love Thee?" is the most famous of these sonnets.*

SONNET 43 (1850)

How do I love thee? Let me count the ways.
I love thee to the depth and breadth and height
My soul can reach, when feeling out of sight
For the ends of Being and ideal Grace.
5   I love thee to the level of everyday's
Most quiet need, by sun and candlelight.
I love thee freely, as men strive for Right;
I love thee purely, as they turn from Praise.
I love thee with the passion put to use
10   In my old griefs, and with my childhood's faith.
I love thee with a love I seemed to lose
With my lost saints—I love thee with the breath,
Smiles, tears, of all my life!—and, if God choose,
I shall but love thee better after death.

Questions for Discussion

1. Is this an English or an Italian **sonnet**?

2. According to this sonnet, what are the different types of love necessary for a marriage to last?

Suggestions for Exploration and Writing

1. Browning uses a series of **metaphorical** devices—**personification, metonymy,** and **synecdoche**—to describe her love. These are combined

with poetic sound devices such as **anaphora, alliteration, assonance,** and **caesura.** Write an essay explaining how these devices, as well as the **sonnet** form, enable Browning to express great depths of feeling in the confined space of a sonnet.

2. Compare and contrast the depth of love described in this sonnet with the depth of love in one of Shakespeare's sonnets.

Edgar Allan Poe (1809–1849)

Best known for his brilliantly macabre stories, Poe was one of the earliest masters of the modern short story and has been credited with inventing the detective story. Raised in the home of his godfather, John Allan, after both his parents died, Poe struggled in his personal life with alcoholism, serious gambling debts, and the loss of one promising job after another. Poe's stories create a world that is surreal, mysterious, and highly symbolic. In addition to his stories, Poe was also highly regarded as a literary critic and a poet. In its richness of music and imagery, "To Helen" is typical of his poems.

To Helen   (1831)

Helen, thy beauty is to me
   Like those Nicéan barks of yore,
That gently, o'er a perfumed sea,
   The weary, way-worn wanderer bore
5   To his own native shore.

On desperate seas long wont to roam,
   Thy hyacinth hair, thy classic face,
Thy Naiad airs have brought me home
   To the glory that was Greece,
10   And the grandeur that was Rome.

Lo! in yon brilliant window-niche
   How statue-like I see thee stand,
The agate lamp within thy hand!
   Ah, Psyche, from the regions which
15   Are Holy-Land!

Questions for Discussion:

1. What does the speaker appear most to appreciate about Helen's beauty?

2. To what does the speaker compare Helen? What qualities in her do these comparisons suggest?

3. What extravagant claim does the speaker make for Helen's beauty in the last stanza? Is she to him simply a lovely woman or is she something more?

Suggestions for Exploration and Writing

1. Discuss in an essay Poe's highly musical and suggestive use of sound in this poem. How does sound help convey the poem's **tone** of adoration and develop its meaning? Consider the effects of alliteration, assonance, and rhyme as well as the smooth vowels and liquids.

2. Research the poem's classical allusions and show how they contribute to the poem's meaning.

Robert Browning (1812–1889)

The English poet Robert Browning is famous for his perfection of the **dramatic monologue,** *for the depth and breadth of knowledge displayed in his poetry, for his ideas, and for his role in one of the most famous love stories of the nineteenth century. His wife, Elizabeth Barrett Browning, immortalized their love in her* Sonnets from the Portuguese. *Robert Browning's most admired books,* Men and Women *(1855) and* Dramatis Personae *(1864), contain many of his frequently read poems. His book-length poem* The Ring and the Book *(1868), an account of a murder trial in seventeenth-century Rome, experiments with multiple* **points of view** *and is a precursor of the* **nonfiction novel.**

PORPHYRIA'S LOVER   (1836)

The rain set early in tonight,
   The sullen wind was soon awake,
It tore the elm-tops down for spite,
   And did its worst to vex the lake:
5   I listened with heart fit to break.
When glided in Porphyria; straight
   She shut the cold out and the storm,
And kneeled and made the cheerless grate
   Blaze up, and all the cottage warm;
10   Which done, she rose, and from her form
Withdrew the dripping cloak and shawl,
   And laid her soiled gloves by, untied
Her hat and let the damp hair fall,
   And, last, she sat down by my side
15   And called me. When no voice replied,
She put my arm about her waist,
   And made her smooth white shoulder bare,
And all her yellow hair displaced,
   And, stooping, made my cheek lie there,
20   And spread, o'er all, her yellow hair,
Murmuring how she loved me—she
   Too weak, for all her heart's endeavor,
To set its struggling passion free
   From pride, and vainer ties dissever,

25   And give herself to me forever.
But passion sometimes would prevail,
    Nor could tonight's gay feast restrain
A sudden thought of one so pale
    For love of her, and all in vain:
30   So, she was come through wind and rain.
Be sure I looked up at her eyes
    Happy and proud; at last I knew
Porphyria worshiped me: surprise
    Made my heart swell, and still it grew
35   While I debated what to do.
That moment she was mine, mine, fair,
    Perfectly pure and good: I found
A thing to do, and all her hair
    In one long yellow string I wound
40   Three times her little throat around,
And strangled her. No pain felt she;
    I am quite sure she felt no pain.
As a shut bud that holds a bee,
    I warily oped her lids: again
45   Laughed the blue eyes without a stain.
And I untightened next the tress
    About her neck; her cheek once more
Blushed bright beneath my burning kiss:
    I propped her head up as before,
50   Only, this time my shoulder bore
Her head, which droops upon it still:
    The smiling rosy little head,
So glad it has its utmost will,
    That all it scorned at once is fled,
55   And I, its love, am gained instead!
Porphyria's love: she guessed not how
    Her darling one wish would be heard.
And thus we sit together now,
    And all night long we have not stirred,
60   And yet God has not said a word!

Questions for Discussion

1. To whom is the narrator speaking? In what tone of voice? What does the **tone** reveal about the speaker?

2. What, according to the **narrator,** is Porphyria's "darling one wish"? How has the **narrator** granted it?

Suggestion for Exploration and Writing

1. Contrast Porphyria with the Duchess.

MY LAST DUCHESS   (1842)

FERRARA

That's my last Duchess painted on the wall,
Looking as if she were alive. I call
That piece a wonder, now: Frà Pandolf's hands
Worked busily a day, and there she stands.
5 Will't please you sit and look at her? I said
"Frà Pandolf" by design, for never read
Strangers like you that pictured countenance,
The depth and passion of its earnest glance,
But to myself they turned (since none puts by
10 The curtain I have drawn for you, but I)
And seemed as they would ask me, if they durst,
How such a glance came there; so, not the first
Are you to turn and ask thus. Sir, 'twas not
Her husband's presence only, called that spot
15 Of joy into the Duchess' cheek: perhaps
Frà Pandolf chanced to say "Her mantle laps
Over my lady's wrist too much," or "Paint
Must never hope to reproduce the faint
Half-flush that dies along her throat": such stuff
20 Was courtesy, she thought, and cause enough
For calling up that spot of joy. She had
A heart—how shall I say?—too soon made glad,
Too easily impressed; she liked whate'er
She looked on, and her looks went everywhere.
25 Sir, 'twas all one! My favor at her breast,
The dropping of the daylight in the West,
The bough of cherries some officious fool
Broke in the orchard for her, the white mule
She rode with round the terrace—all and each
30 Would draw from her alike the approving speech,
Or blush, at least. She thanked men—good! but thanked
Somehow—I know not how—as if she ranked
My gift of a nine-hundred-years-old name
With anybody's gift. Who'd stoop to blame
35 This sort of trifling? Even had you skill
In speech—(which I have not)—to make your will
Quite clear to such an one, and say, "Just this
Or that in you disgusts me; here you miss,
Or there exceed the mark"—and if she let
40 Herself be lessoned so, nor plainly set
Her wits to yours, forsooth, and made excuse
—E'en then would be some stooping; and I choose
Never to stoop. Oh sir, she smiled, no doubt,
Whene'er I passed her; but who passed without

Much the same smile? This grew; I gave commands;
Then all smiles stopped together. There she stands
As if alive. Will't please you rise? We'll meet
The company below, then. I repeat,
The Count your master's known munificence
Is ample warrant that no just pretense
Of mine for dowry will be disallowed;
Though his fair daughter's self, as I avowed
At starting, is my object. Nay, we'll go
Together down, sir. Notice Neptune, though,
Taming a sea horse, thought a rarity,
Which Claus of Innsbruck cast in bronze for me!

Questions for Discussion

1. What qualities of the deceased Duchess annoyed the Duke? Why?

2. Why does the Duke want to make plain to this particular listener what he disliked about his deceased wife?

3. How do Ferrara's **diction** and sentence structure suggest his callous egotism?

Suggestion for Exploration and Writing

1. This **dramatic monologue** in which the Duke describes his deceased wife reveals more about him than about her. Write a **character sketch** of the Duke.

2. In a researched essay, explain how a relationship can be hurt or enhanced by the different kinds of love: obsessive, clinical or analytical, romantic, or platonic.

H[ilda] D[oolittle] (1886–1961)

H. D. is considered one of the finest of the Imagist poets. Born in Bethlehem, Pennsylvania, H.D. moved to England in 1911 and in 1913 married British novelist Richard Aldington. Her friendship with other Imagist poets, such as Marianne Moore, Ezra Pound, and Amy Lowell, influenced her poetry and furthered the publication of her work. Her poetry appeared in many of the influential magazines of the day, including the English Review, *the* Transatlantic Review, *and the* Egoist. *H.D. had a lifelong fascination with anything Greek, and many of her poems, like the one included here, reflect this interest.*

HELEN (1924)

All Greece hates
the still eyes in the white face,
the lustre as of olives

where she stands,
5   and the white hands.

All Greece reviles
the wan face when she smiles,
hating it deeper still
when it grows wan and white,
10   remembering past enchantments
and past ills.

Greece sees unmoved,
God's daughter, born of love,
the beauty of cool feet
15   and slenderest knees,
could love indeed the maid,
only if she were laid,
white ash amid funereal cypresses.

Questions for Discussion

1. Why would the Greeks hate Helen?
2. Why does the author describe Helen's physical attributes while revealing the Greeks' hatred for her?
3. Explain the references to Helen's conception in the third verse.
4. Under what conditions would the Greeks be willing to love Helen?

Suggestions for Exploration and Writing

1. Choose a modern Helen (male or female) and explain why this person, who is admired by many, would be hated by others. Use H.D.'s technique of giving one side's opinions about admirable qualities and contrasting these with the other side's reasons for hatred.

2. After researching the myths about Helen, write an essay comparing Poe's poem praising Helen's beauty with H.D.'s poem describing the hatred of the Greeks for her.

Edna St. Vincent Millay (1892–1950)

Edna St. Vincent Millay, winner of the 1923 Pulitzer Prize for Poetry, was talented as an actress, a musician, and a poet. After graduation from Vassar College, she moved to Greenwich Village, where she lived a bohemian life. Her poetry reflects this life and her later devotion to her husband, her zest for life, her sense of humor, her capability for great depths of feeling, and her love of beauty.

SONNET 42

(1923)

What lips my lips have kissed, and where, and why,
I have forgotten, and what arms have lain
Under my head till morning; but the rain
Is full of ghosts tonight, that tap and sigh
5   Upon the glass and listen for reply,
And in my heart there stirs a quiet pain
For unremembered lads that not again
Will turn to me at midnight with a cry.
Thus in the winter stands the lonely tree,
10   Nor knows what birds have vanished one by one,
Yet knows its boughs more silent than before:
I cannot say what loves have come and gone,
I only know that summer sang in me
A little while, that in me sings no more.

Questions for Discussion

1. In the **octave,** the poet describes her feelings. What is her mood?

2. In the **sestet,** rather than give an answer to her problem, as is traditional in the Italian **sonnet,** Millay uses a **metaphor** to repeat the same
   mood. What is the **metaphor,** and how does it apply to her?

3. What does the speaker regret the most about those lost "summers"?

Suggestions for Exploration and Writing

1. Write about a relationship that failed and explain the reasons for its
   failure.

2. Explain why remembered friendships or relationships seem so much
   sweeter than real, present ones.

3. Write an essay on the way the **sonnet** form, **onomatapoeia, alliteration,**
   and metaphors add to the meaning and create the mood of the poem.

Muriel Rukeyser (1913–1980)

*Poet, biographer, playwright, and activist Muriel Rukeyser was born in
New York City. She attended both Vassar College and Columbia University. Theory of Flight (1935), her first book of poems, was selected for
publication in the Yale Younger Poets Series. Poetry and political commitment were the primary moving forces in Rukeyser's life. She covered
the Scottsboro case in Alabama, was in Spain when the Spanish Civil
War broke out, and went to Gauley Bridge, West Virginia, to investigate
the cases of silicosis among miners. Her research on this situation resulted
in her powerful poem sequence The Book of the Dead, published in
U.S. 1 (1938). Among her other books of poetry are A Turning Wind
(1939), Beast in View (1944), The Green Wave (1948), Elegies*

(1949), Body of Waking *(1958)*, The Speed of Darkness *(1968)*, Breaking Open *(1973)*, and The Gates *(1976)*. *As a political activist as well as an artist, Rukeyser encouraged other writers, including Alice Walker and Anne Sexton.*

MYTH   (1973)

Long afterward, Oedipus, old and blinded, walked the
roads.   He smelled a familiar smell.   It was
the Sphinx.   Oedipus said, "I want to ask one question.
Why didn't I recognize my mother?"   "You gave the
5 wrong answer," said the Sphinx.   "But that was what
made everything possible," said Oedipus.   "No," she said
"When I asked, What walks on four legs in the morning,
two at noon, and three in the evening, you answered,
Man.   You didn't say anything about woman."
10 "When you say Man," said Oedipus, "you include women too.
Everyone knows that."   She said, "That's what you think."

Questions for Discussion

1. Why is Oedipus blind?

2. What did Oedipus get as a result of answering the Sphinx's question? What is the irony in this result?

3. Why does the word *man* not always include woman? What new twist does Rukeyser add to the myth?

Suggestions for Exploration and Writing

1. Define irony. Then write an interpretation of this poem, explaining the double use of irony.

2. Select another myth or popular story and rewrite it to make it conform to modern standards of sensitivity to individuals or groups.

Maya Angelou (b. 1928)

Marguerita Johnson, who later changed her name to Maya Angelou, was born in St. Louis but spent her childhood in Stamps, Arkansas, and in California. Before she became famous as a writer, she tried a wide variety of occupations, from streetcar conductor to cook to dancer and singer. Angelou has written five autobiographical books, the first, I Know Why the Caged Bird Sings *(1969), being the most popular. In addition, she excels in many areas: writing essays, novels, and short fiction; acting and directing; and participating in civil-rights activities. Maya Angelou is a colorful and popular speaker. At Bill Clinton's presidential inauguration, in January 1993, Angelou read her poem "On the Pulse of Morning," written for the occasion. Two of*

her recent books of essays are Wouldn't Take Nothing for My Journey Now *(1993) and* Even the Stars Look Lonesome *(1997).*

PHENOMENAL WOMAN   (1978)

Pretty women wonder where my secret lies.
I'm not cute or built to suit a fashion model's size
But when I start to tell them,
They think I'm telling lies.
5   I say,
It's in the reach of my arms,
The span of my hips,
The stride of my step,
The curl of my lips.
10   I'm a woman
Phenomenally.
Phenomenal woman,
That's me.

I walk into a room
15   Just as cool as you please,
And to a man,
The fellows stand or
Fall down on their knees.
Then they swarm around me,
20   A hive of honey bees.
I say,
It's the fire in my eyes,
And the flash of my teeth,
The swing in my waist,
25   And the joy in my feet.
I'm a woman
Phenomenally.
Phenomenal woman,
That's me.

30   Men themselves have wondered
What they see in me.
They try so much
But they can't touch
My inner mystery.
35   When I try to show them,
They say they still can't see.
I say,
It's in the arch of my back,
The sun of my smile,
40   The ride of my breasts,
The grace of my style.

I'm a woman
Phenomenally,
Phenomenal woman,
45   That's me.

Now you understand
Just why my head's not bowed.
I don't shout or jump about
Or have to talk real loud.
50   When you see me passing,
It ought to make you proud.
I say,
It's in the click of my heels,
The bend of my hair,
55   the palm of my hand,
The need for my care.
'Cause I'm a woman
Phenomenally.
Phenomenal woman,
60   That's me.

Questions for Discussion

1. What is the significance of the contrast between pretty women and the speaker? Why don't the women or the men understand her attractiveness?

2. What do others say is her attraction?

3. What does she believe is her secret?

4. In one or two words, give your opinion of what the attraction is. Can these words explain the truth about her attraction?

Suggestions for Exploration and Writing

1. Write an essay in which you explain your own womanliness or manliness.

2. Get the words to Helen Reddy's song "I Am Woman" and compare or contrast these words with Angelou's words.

3. In an essay, discuss the qualities that make women phenomenal, that enable them simultaneously to be wife, mother, homemaker, family social secretary, chauffeur, and sometimes breadwinner.

4. Write an essay entitled "Phenomenal Man."

Ted Hughes (1930–1999)

Edward James Hughes, Poet Laureate of England from 1984 to 1999, was born in Yorkshire, and his experiences on the moors of England greatly influenced the mythic framework for his literary world. He graduated from Pembroke College, having switched from English as a major field to archeology and anthropology. Hughes was a prolific writer, and his works cover a wide variety of forms. His first collection of poems, The Hawk in the Rain, *from which the following poem is taken, appeared in 1957. Probably his most famous poetry collections are* Crow: From the Life and the Songs of the Crow *(1971) and* Birthday Letters *(1998), a controversial book about his relationship with Sylvia Plath, his wife. In addition to poems, Hughes wrote plays, stories, and poems for children; translated and edited classical litera-ture; and edited his wife's poems and prose.*

INCOMPATIBILITIES   (1957)

Desire's a vicious separator in spite
    Of its twisting women round men:
Cold-chisels two selfs single as it welds hot
    Iron of their separates to one.

5   Old Eden commonplace: something magnets
    And furnaces and with fierce
Hammer-blows the one body on the other knits
    Till the division disappears.

But desire outstrips those hands that a nothing fills,
10   It dives into the opposite eyes,
Plummets through blackouts of impassables
    For the star that lights the face,

Each body still straining to follow down
    The maelstrom dark of the other, their limbs flail
15 Flesh and beat upon
    The inane everywhere of its obstacle,

Each, each second, lonelier and further
    Falling alone through the endless
Without-world of the other, through both here
20   Twist so close they choke their cries.

Questions for Discussion

1. According to Hughes, how does physical attraction (desire) separate two people? Explain.

2. Desire means several things in this poem. Explain at least two of them.

3. Analyze the images that suggest incompatibilities.

Suggestions for Exploration and Writing

1. In an essay, explain the last line as it relates to incompatibility of two people.

2. Analyze the tone in this poem, examining in particular the ways in which Hughes blends the ideas of love with a feeling of violence.

Octavio Paz (1914–1998)

Paz, a Mexican writer who won the 1990 Nobel Prize for Literature, was throughout his life committed to social reform in his native Mexico. Between 1945 and 1968, he served as a diplomat in France, Switzerland, and Tokyo and as ambassador to India. In 1968, when the Mexican government killed dissident students in Mexico City, Paz resigned his ambassadorship in protest. His most important works include The Labyrinth of Silence *(1950), a collection of essays;* The Bow and the Lyre *(1956), essays on poetry and critical theory; and* The Sun Stone *(1957), a long poem.*

TWO BODIES   (1984)

Two bodies face to face
are at times two waves
and night is an ocean.

Two bodies face to face
5   are at times two stones
and night a desert.

Two bodies face to face
are at times two roots
laced into night.

10   Two bodies face to face
are at times two knives
and night strikes sparks.

Two bodies face to face
are two stars falling
15   in an empty sky.

Questions for Discussion

1. Interpret the five metaphors in the five verses, explaining whether they are positive or negative.

2. Are the two bodies necessarily male and female?

Suggestion for Exploration and Writing

1. Write an essay using three or four metaphors to describe a variety of male-female relationships.

Adrienne Rich (b. 1929)

Adrienne Rich has won a Guggenheim fellowship and a National Book Award for her highly regarded poems, which often advocate the liberation of oppressed groups, especially women. From the clear and traditional A Change of Worlds *(1951) to the highly polemical* An Atlas of What's Difficult *(1992), her poems have become more difficult and more aggressively feminist. Among her many other volumes of poetry are* The Dream of a Common Language *(1978);* The Fact of a Doorframe: Poems Selected and New, 1950–1984 *(1984);* Time's Power: Poems 1985–1988 *(1989);* An Atlas of the Difficult World: Poems 1988–1991 *(1991);* Dark Fields of the Republic: Poems 1991–1995 *(1995);* Midnight Salvage: Poems 1995–1998 *(1999); and* Fox: Poems 1998–2000 *(2001). In 1997, Adrienne Rich was awarded the* Wallace Stevens Award *for outstanding and proven mastery in the art of poetry.*

LIVING IN SIN   (1975)

She had thought the studio would keep itself;
no dust upon the furniture of love.
Half heresy, to wish the taps less vocal,
the panes relieved of grime. A plate of pears,
5   a piano with a Persian shawl, a cat
stalking the picturesque amusing mouse
had risen at his urging.
Not that at five each separate stair would writhe
under the milkman's tramp; that morning light
10   so coldly would delineate the scraps
of last night's cheese and three sepulchral bottles;
that on the kitchen shelf among the saucers
a pair of beetle-eyes would fix her own—
envoy from some village in the moldings . . .
15   Meanwhile, he, with a yawn,
sounded a dozen notes upon the keyboard,
declared it out of tune, shrugged at the mirror,
rubbed at his beard, went out for cigarettes;
while she, jeered by the minor demons,
20   pulled back the sheets and made the bed and found
a towel to dust the table-top,
and let the coffee-pot boil over on the stove.
By evening she was back in love again,
though not so wholly but throughout the night
25   she woke sometimes to feel the daylight coming
like a relentless milkman up the stairs.

Marge Piercy (b. 1936)

Piercy was born in Detroit of a Jewish mother and a Presbyterian father. Leaving home at seventeen, she struggled through such jobs as secretary, switchboard operator, artist's model, and salesclerk while trying unsuccessfully to get her novels published. She and her second husband were very active in the civil rights movement and the movement against the Vietnam War. She has recently become involved in the Jewish renewal movement. Seriously involved in political causes all her life, Piercy considers herself a political writer. She has published over thirty books, including novels, poetry, essays, and a play. Her most recent works are The Art of Blessing the Day: Poems with a Jewish Theme *(1999) and the novel* Three Women *(1999).*

BARBIE DOLL   (1970)

This girlchild was born as usual
and presented dolls that did pee-pee
and miniature GE stoves and irons
and wee lipsticks the color of cherry candy.
5 Then in the magic of puberty, a classmate said:
You have a great big nose and fat legs.

She was healthy, tested intelligent,
possessed strong arms and back,
abundant sexual drive and manual dexterity.
10 She went to and fro apologizing.
Everyone saw a fat nose on thick legs.

She was advised to play coy,
exhorted to come on hearty,
exercise, diet, smile and wheedle.
15 Her good nature wore out
like a fan belt.
So she cut off her nose and her legs
and offered them up.

In the casket displayed on satin she lay
20 with the undertaker's cosmetics painted on,
a turned-up putty nose,
dressed in a pink and white nightie.
Doesn't she look pretty? everyone said.
Consummation at last.
25 To every woman a happy ending.

Questions for Discussion

1. What is significant about the gifts "this girlchild" received?

2. Why is she not named but rather referred to generically as "this girl-child"?

3. The "girlchild" seems to be crushed by what her classmate says to her "in the magic of puberty." In what ways is puberty magic? In what ways is it a time of vulnerability?

4. Why does she allow others' perceptions of her few "unattractive" qualities to outweigh her strengths?

5. Explain her statement "her good nature wore out / like a fan belt."

6. Explain the contradictory advice she is given in the third verse.

7. Explain the irony of the last verse. At what stereotypes is Piercy's satire directed?

Suggestions for Exploration and Writing

1. What does this poem say about society? Explain in an essay.

2. In an essay, contrast the girlchild in "Barbie Doll" with the speaker in "Phenomenal Woman."

3. Write an essay in which you show how physical attributes can have positive as well as negative influences on a person.

4. Write an essay examining the effects of gender stereotyping on teenage boys.

Janice Mirikitani (b. 1942)

Janice Mirikitani, a third-generation Japanese American who was interned during World War II, is president of the Glide Foundation, where she directs thirty-five programs that serve the poor and homeless of San Francisco. As a founding member of Third World Communications, Mirikitani has edited many works of struggling Japanese American writers. Her works, which express her outrage against racism, sexism, and oppression of any kind, include volumes of poetry: Awake in the River *(1978),* Shedding Silence *(1987), and* We the Dangerous *(1995). Much of her work shows a dichotomy between traditional Japanese customs and beliefs and a newer Japanese American or American identity.*

BREAKING TRADITION (1987)

for my Daughter

My daughter denies she is like me,
Her secretive eyes avoid mine.
    She reveals the hatreds of womanhood
    already veiled behind music and smoke and telephones.
5 I want to tell her about the empty room
    of myself.
    This room we lock ourselves in
    where whispers live like fungus,
    giggles about small breasts and cellulite,

10   where we confine ourselves to jealousies,
        bedridden by menstruation.
        This waiting room where we feel our hands
        are useless, dead speechless clamps
        that need hospitals and forceps and kitchens
15   and plugs and ironing boards to make them useful.
    I deny I am like my mother. I remember why:
        She kept her room neat with silence,
        defiance smothered in requirements to be otonashii,
        passion and loudness wrapped in an obi,
20   her steps confined to ceremony,
        the weight of her sacrifice she carried like
        a foetus. Guilt passed on in our bones.
    I want to break tradition—unlock this room
        where women dress in the dark.
25   Discover the lies my mother told me.
        The lies that we are small and powerless.
        that our possibilities must be compressed
        to the size of pearls, displayed only as
        passive chokers, charms around our neck.
30   Break Tradition.
        I want to tell my daughter of this room
        of myself
        filled with tears of violins,
        the light in my hands,
35   poems about madness,
        the music of yellow guitars—
        sounds shaken from barbed wire and
        goodbyes and miracles of survival.
        This room of open window where daring ones escape.
40 My daughter denies she is like me
        her secretive eyes are walls of smoke
        and music and telephones,
        her pouting ruby lips, her skirts
        swaying to salsa, teena marie and the stones,
45   her thighs displayed in carnivals of color.
        I do not know the contents of her room.
    She mirrors my aging.
    She is breaking tradition.

Questions for Discussion

1. To what is the speaker referring by "this room we lock ourselves in,"
   and "she kept her room neat with silence"? Why does she want to
   "unlock this room/where women dress in the dark"?

2. What are "the hatreds of womanhood" that the daughter expresses? What is the poem about other than the generation gap?

3. What does the speaker mean by "she mirrors my aging"?

4. What is the speaker's **tone?** Explain your answer.

5. Mirikitani addresses the poem "for my daughter." How does she also use addresses to her daughter to structure the poem?

Suggestions for Exploration and Writing

1. Discuss ways in which sons and daughters break tradition—for example, in music, career choices, lifestyles, or education.

2. Three generations are pictured in the poem. Discuss why each daughter denies being like her mother.

3. Write an essay discussing what details used to describe each generation reveal about changing standards and styles.

4. In some families, the parents are such high achievers that the children find it difficult to live up to their parents' standards. In other families, the children are encouraged not to emulate their parents. Discuss the importance of family role models for sons or daughters, or discuss the need for sons or daughters to be distinct individuals.

Judith Ortiz Cofer (b. 1952)

Born in Puerto Rico, Judith Cofer spent part of her childhood in Patterson, New Jersey, where the library became an oasis to her literary yearnings. In 1987, she published two books of poetry, Terms of Survival *and* Reaching for the Mainland, *and in 1990 she published personal essays and poems in* Silent Dancing: A Partial Remembrance of a Puerto Rican Childhood *and a novel,* The Line of the Sun. *Her 1993 book,* The Latin Deli, *vividly reveals the dichotomy of a woman who is pulled between two cultures. Her 1995 book,* An Island Like You: Stories of the Barrio, *was a Best Book of the Year selection of the American Library Association. Cofer is presently a professor of English and Creative Writing at the University of Georgia.*

ANNIVERSARY (1993)

Lying in bed late, you will sometimes read to me
about a past war that obsesses you;
about young men, like our brothers once,
who each year become more like our sons
5   because they died the year we met,
or the year we got married
or the year our child was born.
                    You read to me
about how they dragged their feet through a green maze
10 where they fell, again and again, victims

to an enemy wily enough to be the critter hero
of some nightmare folktale, with his booby traps
in the shape of human children, and his cities
under the earth; and how, even when they survived,
these boys left something behind
in the thick brush or muddy swamp where no one
can get it back—caught like a baseball cap
on a low-hanging tree branch.
                                    And I think about you and me,
nineteen, angry, and in love, in that same year
when America broke out in violence
like a late-blooming adolescent, deep in a turmoil
it could neither understand nor control;
how we marched in the rough parade
decorated with the insignias of our rebellion:
peace symbols and scenes of Eden
embroidered on our torn and faded jeans,
necks heavy with beads we did not count on
for patience, singing *Revolution*—
a song we misconstrued for years.
                                    Death was a slogan
to shout about with raised fists or hang on banners.
But here we are,
listening more closely than ever to the old songs,
sung for new reasons by new voices. We are survivors
of an undeclared war someone might decide to remake
like a popular tune. Sometimes, in the dark, alarmed
by too deep a silence, I will lay my hand on your chest,
for the familiar, steady beat to which I have attuned
my breathing for so many years.

Questions for Discussion

1. Why do the young men mentioned in the first verse not age with the narrator and her husband?

2. What war does the narrator describe? What clues identify the time and the war?

3. Explain why "young men, like our brothers once/[. . .] each year become more like our sons."

4. Explain the irony of "Death was a slogan / to shout about with raised fists or hang on banners."

5. What did the survivors of this war leave behind?

6. Explain the statement "We are survivors / of an undeclared war someone might decide to remake / like a popular tune."

7. What kind of marriage does this anniversary celebrate? How do you know?

8. This poem celebrates several anniversaries. List them in the order of importance. Defend the order of your list.

Suggestions for Exploration and Writing

1. Write an essay about one of your anniversaries that brings back significant memories.

2. Shakespeare in Sonnet 116 describes love as "an ever-fixed mark." Explain in an essay how this marriage fits his description.

Rita Dove (b. 1952)

The biography of Rita Dove appears in the Family Unit.

COURTSHIP   (1986)

FROM *BEULAH AND THOMAS*

1.

Fine evening may I have
the pleasure . . .
up and down the block
waiting—for what? A
5   magnolia breeze, someone
to trot out the stars?

But she won't set a foot
in his turtledove Nash,
it wasn't proper.
10   Her pleated skirt fans
softly, a circlet of arrows.

King of the Crawfish
in his yellow scarf,
mandolin belly pressed tight
15   to his hounds-tooth vest—
his wrist flicks for the pleats
all in a row, sighing . . .

2.

. . . so he wraps the yellow silk
still warm from his throat
20   around her shoulders. (He made
good money; he could buy another.)
A gnat flies
in his eye and she thinks
he's crying.

25   Then the parlor festooned

like a ship and Thomas
twirling his hat in his hands
wondering how did I get here.
China pugs guarding a fringed settee
30   where a father, half-Cherokee,
smokes and frowns.
I'll give her a good life—
what was he doing,
selling all for a song?
35   His heart fluttering shut
then slowly opening.

Questions for Discussion

1. Describe the events on this night or several nights of courtship from Thomas's viewpoint. What are some of the courting conventions employed by both Thomas and Beulah?

2. How is this courtship the same as or different from a courtship today?

3. To Thomas, what is the importance of wrapping his yellow silk scarf around Beulah's shoulders? What is the significance of the gnat in his eye and her misconception about what he was doing?

4. The fifth verse changes the tone and location. What has taken place between the fourth and the fifth verse? Why does Thomas wonder how he got there?

5. Thomas says to Beulah's father, "*I'll give her a good life—*." This sentence has become almost a cliche now. What are the connotations of this line, and why does he say these words?

6. Explain the meaning of the last two lines.

Suggestions for Exploration and Writing

1. Write a personal essay describing your first date. Then write another essay from the point of view of your date.

2. Write an essay on courtship past and present.

COURTSHIP, DILIGENCE   (1986)

A yellow scarf runs through his fingers
as if it were melting.
Thomas dabbing his brow.

And now his mandolin in a hurry
5   though the night, as they say,
is young,
though she is *getting on*.

Hush, the strings tinkle. *Pretty gal.*

Cigar-box music!
10   She'd much prefer a pianola
and scent in a sky-colored flask

Not that scarf, bright as butter.
Not his hands, cool as dimes.

Questions for Discussion

1. Contrast the first and last verses in this poem with the fourth verse in "Courtship."
2. Identify lines in the poem that reveal that both Thomas and Beulah had misgivings about one another or about their marriage.

DRAMA

Henrik Ibsen (1828–1906)

Norwegian playwright Henrik Ibsen is often called the father of modern drama. His early Romantic plays were written in verse. In his plays, Ibsen established the tradition of realism in drama, of plays that attempt to imitate life faithfully. His most famous realistic plays, A Doll's House *(1879),* Ghosts *(1881), and* Hedda Gabler *(1890), are also described as theater of ideas or* **problem plays,** *those that deal with social issues or depict social problems.*

A Doll's House *caused immediate controversy when it was first produced, for it was performed before audiences accustomed to viewing a wife as virtually the property of her husband. When* A Doll's House *was followed by* Ghosts, *a play about inherited venereal disease, Ibsen was forced to leave Norway. Later, when praised by leaders of the Women's Rights League for defending women's rights, Ibsen pointed out that he was describing all humanity in his plays. One reason for the continued popularity of* A Doll's House *is that it raises questions about the rights of women and about the multiple roles played by women—roles that sometimes pull women in different directions.*

A DOLL'S HOUSE   (1879)

TRANS. MICHAEL MEYER

List of Characters

TORVALD HELMER: a lawyer
NORA: his wife
DR. RANK
MRS. LINDE

NILS KROGSTAD: also a lawyer
THE HELMERS' THREE
SMALL CHILDREN
ANNE-MARIE: their nurse
HELEN: the maid
A PORTER

Scene

The action takes place in the Helmers' apartment.

ACT I

A comfortably and tastefully but not expensively furnished room. Backstage right, a door leads out to the hall; backstage left, another door to Helmer's study. Between these two doors stands a piano. In the middle of the left-hand wall is a door, with a window downstage of it. Near the window, a round table with armchairs and a small sofa. In the right-hand wall, slightly upstage, is a door; downstage of this, against the same wall, a stove lined with porcelain tiles, with a couple of armchairs and a rocking-chair in front of it. Between the stove and the side door is a small table. Engravings on the wall. A what-not with china and other bric-a-brac; a small bookcase with leather-bound books. A carpet on the floor; a fire in the stove. A winter day.

A bell rings in the hall outside. After a moment, we hear the front door being opened. Nora enters the room, humming contentedly to herself. She is wearing outdoor clothes and carrying a lot of parcels, which she puts down on the table right. She leaves the door to the hall open; through it, we can see a Porter carrying a Christmas tree and a basket. He gives these to the Maid, who had opened the door for them.

NORA: Hide that Christmas tree away, Helen. The children mustn't see it before I've decorated it this evening. (*To the Porter, taking out her purse.*) How much—?
PORTER: A shilling.
NORA: Here's half a crown. No, keep it.

(The Porter touches his cap and goes. Nora closes the door. She continues to laugh happily to herself as she removes her coat, etc. She takes from her pocket a bag containing macaroons and eats a couple. Then she tiptoes across and listens at her husband's door.)

NORA: Yes, he's here. (*Starts humming again as she goes over to the table, right.*)
HELMER (*from his room*): Is that my skylark twittering out there?
NORA (*opening some of the parcels*): It is!
HELMER: Is that my squirrel rustling?
10 NORA: Yes!
HELMER: When did my squirrel come home?
NORA: Just now. (*Pops the bag of macaroons in her pocket and wipes her mouth.*) Come out here, Torvald, and see what I've bought.

HELMER: You mustn't disturb me! *(Short pause; then he opens the door and looks in, his pen in his hand.)* Bought, did you say? All that? Has my little squanderbird been overspending again?

NORA: Oh, Torvald, surely we can let ourselves go a little this year! It's the first Christmas we don't have to scrape.

HELMER: Well, you know, we can't afford to be extravagant.

20 NORA: Oh yes, Torvald, we can be a little extravagant now. Can't we? Just a tiny bit? You've got a big salary now, and you're going to make lots and lots of money.

HELMER: Next year, yes. But my new salary doesn't start till April.

NORA: Pooh; we can borrow till then.

HELMER: Nora! *(Goes over to her and takes her playfully by the ear.)* What a little spendthrift you are! Suppose I were to borrow fifty pounds today, and you spent it all over Christmas, and then on New Year's Eve a tile fell off a roof on to my head—

NORA *(puts her hand over his mouth):* Oh, Torvald! Don't say such

30 dreadful things!

HELMER: Yes, but suppose something like that did happen? What then?

NORA: If anything as frightful as that happened, it wouldn't make much difference whether I was in debt or not.

HELMER: But what about the people I'd borrowed from?

NORA: Them? Who cares about them? They're strangers.

HELMER: Oh, Nora, Nora, how like a woman! No, but seriously, Nora, you know how I feel about this. No debts! Never borrow! A home that is founded on debts can never be a place of freedom and beauty. We two have stuck it out bravely up to now; and we shall con-

40 tinue to do so for the short time we still have to.

NORA *(goes over towards the stove):* Very well, Torvald. As you say.

HELMER *(follows her):* Now, now! My little songbird mustn't droop her wings. What's this? Is little squirrel sulking? *(Takes out his purse.)* Nora; guess what I've got here!

NORA *(turns quickly):* Money!

HELMER: Look. *(Hands her some banknotes.)* I know how these small expenses crop up at Christmas.

NORA *(counts them):* One—two—three—four. Oh, thank you, Torvald, thank you! I should be able to manage with this.

50 HELMER: You'll have to.

NORA: Yes, yes of course I will. But come over here, I want to show you everything I've bought. And so cheaply! Look, here are new clothes for Ivar—and a sword. And a horse and a trumpet for Bob. And a doll and a cradle for Emmy—they're nothing much, but she'll pull them apart in a few days. And some bits of material and handkerchiefs for the maids. Old Anne-Marie ought to have had something better, really.

HELMER: And what's in that parcel?

NORA *(cries):* No, Torvald, you mustn't see that before this evening!

60   HELMER: Very well. But now, tell me, you little spendthrift, what do you want for Christmas?

NORA: Me? Oh, pooh, I don't want anything.

HELMER: Oh, yes, you do. Now tell me, what, within reason, would you most like?

NORA: No, I really don't know. Oh, yes—Torvald—!

HELMER: Well?

NORA *(plays with his coat-buttons; not looking at him):* If you really want to give me something, you could—you could—

HELMER: Come on, out with it.

70   NORA *(quickly):* You could give me money, Torvald. Only as much as you feel you can afford; then later I'll buy something with it.

HELMER: But, Nora—

NORA: Oh yes, Torvald dear, please! Please! Then I'll wrap up the notes in pretty gold paper and hang them on the Christmas tree. Wouldn't that be fun!

HELMER: What's the name of that little bird that can never keep any money?

NORA: Yes, yes, squanderbird; I know. But let's do as I say, Torvald; then I'll have time to think about what I need most. Isn't that the best
80   way? Mm?

HELMER *(smiles):* To be sure it would be, if you could keep what I give you and really buy yourself something with it. But you'll spend it on all sorts of useless things for the house, and then I'll have to put my hand in my pocket again.

NORA: Oh, but Torvald—

HELMER: You can't deny it, Nora dear. *(Puts his arm round her waist.)* The squanderbird's a pretty little creature, but she gets through an awful lot of money. It's incredible what an expensive pet she is for a man to keep.

90   NORA: For shame! How can you say such a thing? I save every penny I can.

HELMER *(laughs):* That's quite true. Every penny you can. But you can't.

NORA *(hums and smiles, quietly gleeful):* Hm. If you only knew how many expenses we larks and squirrels have, Torvald.

HELMER: You're a funny little creature. Just like your father used to be. Always on the look-out for some way to get money, but as soon as you have any it just runs through your fingers, and you never know where it's gone. Well, I suppose I must take you as you are. It's in your blood. Yes, yes, yes, these things are hereditary, Nora.

NORA: Oh, I wish I'd inherited more of Papa's qualities.

100   HELMER: And I wouldn't wish my darling little songbird to be any different from what she is. By the way, that reminds me. You look awfully— how shall I put it?—awfully guilty today.

NORA: Do I?

HELMER: Yes, you do. Look me in the eyes.

NORA *(looks at him):* Well?

HELMER (*wags his finger*): Has my little sweet-tooth been indulging herself in town today, by any chance?

NORA: No, how can you think such a thing?

HELMER: Not a tiny little digression into a pastry shop?

110 NORA: No, Torvald, I promise—

HELMER: Not just a wee jam tart?

NORA: Certainly not.

HELMER: Not a little nibble at a macaroon?

NORA: No, Torvald—I promise you, honestly—

HELMER: There, there. I was only joking.

NORA (*goes over to the table, right*): You know I could never act against your wishes.

HELMER: Of course not. And you've given me your word— (*Goes over to her.*) Well, my beloved Nora, you keep your little Christmas secrets to

120 yourself. They'll be revealed this evening, I've no doubt, once the Christmas tree has been lit.

NORA: Have you remembered to invite Dr. Rank?

HELMER: No. But there's no need; he knows he'll be dining with us. Anyway, I'll ask him when he comes this morning. I've ordered some good wine. Oh, Nora, you can't imagine how I'm looking forward to this evening.

NORA: So am I. And, Torvald, how the children will love it!

HELMER: Yes, it's a wonderful thing to know that one's position is assured and that one has an ample income. Don't you agree? It's

130 good to know that, isn't it?

NORA: Yes, it's almost like a miracle.

HELMER: Do you remember last Christmas? For three whole weeks you shut yourself away every evening to make flowers for the Christmas tree, and all those other things you were going to surprise us with. Ugh, it was the most boring time I've ever had in my life.

NORA: I didn't find it boring.

HELMER (*smiles*): But it all came to nothing in the end, didn't it?

NORA: Oh, are you going to bring that up again? How could I help the cat getting in and tearing everything to bits?

140 HELMER: No, my poor little Nora, of course you couldn't. You simply wanted to make us happy, and that's all that matters. But it's good that those hard times are past.

NORA: Yes, it's wonderful.

HELMER: I don't have to sit by myself and be bored. And you don't have to tire your pretty eyes and your delicate little hands—

NORA (*claps her hands*): No, Torvald, that's true, isn't it—I don't have to any longer? Oh, it's really all just like a miracle. (*Takes his arm.*) Now, I'm going to tell you what I thought we might do, Torvald. As soon as Christmas is over—(*A bell rings in the hall.*) Oh, there's the doorbell.

150 (*Tidies up one or two things in the room.*) Someone's coming. What a bore.

HELMER: I'm not at home to any visitors. Remember!

MAID (*in the doorway*): A lady's called, madam. A stranger.

NORA: Well, ask her to come in.

MAID: And the doctor's here too, sir.

HELMER: Has he gone to my room?

MAID: Yes, sir.

(Helmer goes into his room. The Maid shows in Mrs. Linde, who is dressed in traveling clothes, and closes the door.)

MRS. LINDE (*shyly and a little hesitantly*): Good evening, Nora.

NORA (*uncertainly*): Good evening—

MRS. LINDE: I don't suppose you recognize me.

160   NORA: No, I'm afraid I—Yes, wait a minute—surely—*(Exclaims.)* Why, Christine! Is it really you?

MRS. LINDE: Yes, it's me.

NORA: Christine! And I didn't recognize you! But how could I—? *(More quietly.)* How you've changed, Christine!

MRS. LINDE: Yes, I know. It's been nine years—nearly ten—

NORA: Is it so long? Yes, it must be. Oh, these last eight years have been such a happy time for me! So you've come to town? All that way in winter! How brave of you!

MRS. LINDE: I arrived by the steamer this morning.

170   NORA: Yes, of course—to enjoy yourself over Christmas. Oh, how splendid! We'll have to celebrate! But take off your coat. You're not cold, are you? *(Helps her off with it.)* There! Now let's sit down here by the stove and be comfortable. No, you take the armchair. I'll sit here in the rocking chair. *(Clasps Mrs. Linde's hands.)* Yes, now you look like your old self. It was just at first that—you've got a little paler, though, Christine. And perhaps a bit thinner.

MRS. LINDE: And older, Nora. Much, much older.

NORA: Yes, perhaps a little older. Just a tiny bit. Not much. *(Checks herself suddenly and says earnestly.)* Oh, but how thoughtless of me to sit here

180   and chatter away like this! Dear, sweet Christine, can you forgive me?

MRS. LINDE: What do you mean, Nora?

NORA (*quietly*): Poor Christine, you've become a widow.

MRS. LINDE: Yes. Three years ago.

NORA: I know, I know—I read it in the papers. Oh, Christine, I meant to write to you so often, honestly. But I always put it off, and something else always cropped up.

MRS. LINDE: I understand, Nora dear.

NORA: No, Christine, it was beastly of me. Oh, my poor darling, what you've gone through! And he didn't leave you anything?

190   MRS. LINDE: No.

NORA: No children, either?

MRS. LINDE: No.

NORA: Nothing at all, then?

MRS. LINDE: Not even a feeling of loss or sorrow.

NORA (*looks incredulously at her*): But, Christine, how is that possible?

MRS. LINDE (*smiles sadly and strokes Nora's hair*): Oh, these things happen, Nora.

NORA: All alone. How dreadful that must be for you. I've three lovely children. I'm afraid you can't see them now, because they're out with nanny. But you must tell me everything—

MRS. LINDE: No, no, no. I want to hear about you.

NORA: No, you start. I'm not going to be selfish today, I'm just going to think about you. Oh, but there's one thing I *must* tell you. Have you heard of the wonderful luck we've just had?

MRS. LINDE: No. What?

NORA: Would you believe it—my husband's just been made manager of the bank!

MRS. LINDE: Your husband? Oh, how lucky—!

NORA: Yes, isn't it? Being a lawyer is so uncertain, you know, especially if one isn't prepared to touch any case that isn't—well—quite nice. And of course Torvald's been very firm about that—and I'm absolutely with him. Oh, you can imagine how happy we are! He's joining the bank in the New Year, and he'll be getting a big salary, and lots of percentages too. From now on we'll be able to live quite differently—we'll be able to do whatever we want. Oh, Christine, it's such a relief! I feel so happy! Well, I mean, it's lovely to have heaps of money and not to have to worry about anything. Don't you think?

MRS. LINDE: It must be lovely to have enough to cover one's needs, anyway.

NORA: Not just our needs! We're going to have heaps and heaps of money!

MRS. LINDE (*smiles*): Nora, Nora, haven't you grown up yet? When we were at school you were a terrible little spendthrift.

NORA (*laughs quietly*): Yes, Torvald still says that. (*Wags her finger.*) But "Nora, Nora" isn't as silly as you think. Oh, we've been in no position for me to waste money. We've both had to work.

MRS. LINDE: You too?

NORA: Yes, little things—fancy work, crocheting, embroidery and so forth. (*Casually.*) And other things too. I suppose you know Torvald left the Ministry when we got married? There were no prospects of promotion in his department, and of course he needed more money. But the first year he overworked himself quite dreadfully. He had to take on all sorts of extra jobs, and worked day and night. But it was too much for him, and he became frightfully ill. The doctors said he'd have to go to a warmer climate.

MRS. LINDE: Yes, you spent a whole year in Italy, didn't you?

NORA: Yes. It wasn't easy for me to get away, you know. I'd just had Ivar. But of course we had to do it. Oh, it was a marvelous trip! And it saved Torvald's life. But it cost an awful lot of money, Christine.

MRS. LINDE: I can imagine.

NORA: Two hundred and fifty pounds. That's a lot of money, you know.

MRS. LINDE: How lucky you had it.

NORA: Well, actually, we got it from my father.

MRS. LINDE: Oh, I see. Didn't he die just about that time?

NORA: Yes, Christine, just about then. Wasn't it dreadful, I couldn't go and look after him. I was expecting little Ivar any day. And then I had my poor Torvald to care for—we really didn't think he'd live. Dear, kind Papa! I never saw him again, Christine. Oh, it's the saddest thing that's happened to me since I got married.

MRS. LINDE: I know you were very fond of him. But you went to Italy—?

NORA: Yes. Well, we had the money, you see, and the doctors said we
250   mustn't delay. So we went the month after Papa died.

MRS. LINDE: And your husband came back completely cured?

NORA: Fit as a fiddle!

MRS. LINDE: But—the doctor?

NORA: How do you mean?

MRS. LINDE: I thought the maid said that the gentleman who arrived with me was the doctor.

NORA: Oh yes, that's Doctor Rank, but he doesn't come because anyone's ill. He's our best friend, and he looks us up at least once every day. No, Torvald hasn't had a moment's illness since we went away.
260   And the children are fit and healthy and so am I. (*Jumps up and claps her hands.*) Oh God, oh God, Christine, isn't it a wonderful thing to be alive and happy! Oh, but how beastly of me! I'm only talking about myself. (*Sits on a footstool and rests her arms on Mrs. Linde's knee.*) Oh, please don't be angry with me! Tell me, is it really true you didn't love your husband? Why did you marry him, then?

MRS. LINDE: Well, my mother was still alive; and she was helpless and bedridden. And I had my two little brothers to take care of. I didn't feel I could say no.

NORA: Yes, well, perhaps you're right. He was rich then, was he?

270   MRS. LINDE: Quite comfortably off, I believe. But his business was unsound, you see, Nora. When he died it went bankrupt, and there was nothing left.

NORA: What did you do?

MRS. LINDE: Well, I had to try to make ends meet somehow, so I started a little shop, and a little school, and anything else I could turn my hand to. These last three years have been just one endless slog for me, without a moment's rest. But now it's over, Nora. My poor dear mother doesn't need me any more; she's passed away. And the boys don't need me either; they've got jobs now and can look after themselves.

280   NORA: How relieved you must feel—

MRS. LINDE: No, Nora. Just unspeakably empty. No one to live for anymore. (*Gets up restlessly.*) That's why I couldn't bear to stay out there any longer, cut off from the world. I thought it'd be easier to find some work here that will exercise and occupy my mind. If only I could get a regular job—office work of some kind—

NORA: Oh, but, Christine, that's dreadfully exhausting; and you look practically finished already. It'd be much better for you if you could go away somewhere.

MRS. LINDE (*goes over to the window*): I have no Papa to pay for my holi-
290   days, Nora.

NORA (*gets up*): Oh, please don't be angry with me.

MRS. LINDE: My dear Nora, it's I who should ask you not to be angry.
That's the worst thing about this kind of situation—it makes one so
bitter. One has no one to work for; and yet one has to be continually
sponging for jobs. One has to live; and so one becomes completely
egocentric. When you told me about this luck you've just had with
Torvald's new job—can you imagine?—I was happy not so much on
your account, as on my own.

NORA: How do you mean? Oh, I understand. You mean Torvald might
300   be able to do something for you?

MRS. LINDE: Yes, I was thinking that.

NORA: He will too, Christine. Just you leave it to me. I'll lead up to it so
delicately, so delicately; I'll get him in the right mood. Oh, Christine,
I do so want to help you.

MRS. LINDE: It's sweet of you to bother so much about me, Nora. Especially since you know so little of the worries and hardships of life.

NORA: I? You say *I* know little of—?

MRS. LINDE (*smiles*): Well, good heavens—those bits of fancy work of
yours—well, really—! You're a child, Nora.

310   NORA (*tosses her head and walks across the room*): You shouldn't say that
so patronizingly.

MRS. LINDE: Oh?

NORA: You're like the rest. You all think I'm incapable of getting down
to anything serious—

MRS. LINDE: My dear—

NORA: You think I've never had any worries like the rest of you.

MRS. LINDE: Nora dear, you've just told me about all your difficulties—

NORA: Pooh—that! (*Quietly.*) I haven't told you about the big thing.

MRS. LINDE: What big thing? What do you mean?

320   NORA: You patronize me, Christine; but you shouldn't. You're proud
that you've worked so long and so hard for your mother.

MRS. LINDE: I don't patronize anyone, Nora. But you're right—I am
both proud and happy that I was able to make my mother's last
months on earth comparatively easy.

NORA: And you're also proud of what you've done for your brothers.

MRS. LINDE: I think I have a right to be.

NORA: I think so too. But let me tell you something, Christine. I too
have done something to be proud and happy about.

MRS. LINDE: I don't doubt it. But—how do you mean?

330   NORA: Speak quietly! Suppose Torvald should hear! He mustn't, at any
price—no one must know, Christine—no one but you.

MRS. LINDE: But what is this?

NORA: Come over here. (*Pulls her down on to the sofa beside her.*) Yes,
Christine—I too have done something to be happy and proud about.
It was I who saved Torvald's life.

MRS. LINDE: Saved his—? How did you save it?

NORA: I told you about our trip to Italy. Torvald couldn't have lived if he hadn't managed to get down there—

MRS. LINDE: Yes, well—your father provided the money—

340 NORA (*smiles*): So Torvald and everyone else thinks. But—

MRS. LINDE: Yes?

NORA: Papa didn't give us a penny. It was I who found the money.

MRS. LINDE: You? All of it?

NORA: Two hundred and fifty pounds. What do you say to that?

MRS. LINDE: But Nora, how could you? Did you win a lottery or something?

NORA (*scornfully*): Lottery? (*Sniffs.*) What would there be to be proud of in that?

MRS. LINDE: But where did you get it from, then?

NORA (*hums and smiles secretively*): Hm; tra-la-la-la!

350 MRS. LINDE: You couldn't have borrowed it.

NORA: Oh? Why not?

MRS. LINDE: Well, a wife can't borrow money without her husband's consent.

NORA (*tosses her head*): Ah, but when a wife has a little business sense, and knows how to be clever—

MRS. LINDE: But Nora, I simply don't understand—

NORA: You don't have to. No one has said I borrowed the money. I could have got it in some other way. (*Throws herself back on the sofa.*) I could have got it from an admirer. When a girl's as pretty as I am—

360 MRS. LINDE: Nora, you're crazy!

NORA: You're dying of curiosity now, aren't you, Christine?

MRS. LINDE: Nora dear, you haven't done anything foolish?

NORA (*sits up again*): Is it foolish to save one's husband's life?

MRS. LINDE: I think it's foolish if without his knowledge you—

NORA: But the whole point was that he mustn't know! Great heavens, don't you see? He hadn't to know how dangerously ill he was. I was the one they told that his life was in danger and that only going to a warm climate could save him. Do you suppose I didn't try to think of other ways of getting him down there? I told him how wonderful it

370 would be for me to go abroad like other young wives; I cried and prayed; I asked him to remember my condition, and said he ought to be nice and tender to me; and then I suggested he might quite easily borrow the money. But then he got almost angry with me, Christine. He said I was frivolous, and that it was his duty as a husband not to pander to my moods and caprices—I think that's what he called them. Well, well, I thought, you've got to be saved somehow. And then I thought of a way—

MRS. LINDE: But didn't your husband find out from your father that the money hadn't come from him?

380 NORA: No, never. Papa died just then. I'd thought of letting him into the plot and asking him not to tell. But since he was so ill—! And as things turned out, it didn't become necessary.

MRS. LINDE: And you've never told your husband about this?

NORA: For heaven's sake, no! What an idea! He's frightfully strict about such matters. And besides—he's so proud of being a *man*—it'd be so painful and humiliating for him to know that he owed anything to me. It'd completely wreck our relationship. This life we have built together would no longer exist.

MRS. LINDE: Will you never tell him?

390 NORA (*thoughtfully, half-smiling*): Yes—some time, perhaps. Years from now, when I'm no longer pretty. You mustn't laugh! I mean of course,when Torvald no longer loves me as he does now; when it no longer amuses him to see me dance and dress up and play the fool for him. Then it might be useful to have something up my sleeve. (*Breaks off.*) Stupid, stupid, stupid! That time will never come. Well, what do you think of my big secret, Christine? I'm not completely useless, am I? Mind you, all this has caused me a frightful lot of worry. It hasn't been easy for me to meet my obligations punctually. In case you don't know, in the world of business there are things
400 called quarterly installments and interest, and they're a terrible problem to cope with. So I've had to scrape a little here and save a little there as best I can. I haven't been able to save much on the housekeeping money, because Torvald likes to live well; and I couldn't let the children go short of clothes—I couldn't take anything out of what he gives me for them. The poor little angels!

MRS. LINDE: So you've had to stint yourself, my poor Nora?

NORA: Of course. Well, after all, it was my problem. Whenever Torvald gave me money to buy myself new clothes, I never used more than half of it; and I always bought what was cheapest and plainest. Thank
410 heaven anything suits me, so that Torvald's never noticed. But it made me a bit sad sometimes, because it's lovely to wear pretty clothes. Don't you think?

MRS. LINDE: Indeed it is.

NORA: And then I've found one or two other sources of income. Last winter I managed to get a lot of copying to do. So I shut myself away and wrote every evening, late into the night. Oh, I often got so tired, so tired. But it was great fun, though, sitting there working and earning money. It was almost like being a man.

MRS. LINDE: But how much have you managed to pay off like this?

420 NORA: Well, I can't say exactly. It's awfully difficult to keep an exact check on these kinds of transactions. I only know I've paid everything I've managed to scrape together. Sometimes I really didn't know where to turn. (*Smiles.*) Then I'd sit here and imagine some rich old gentleman had fallen in love with me—

MRS. LINDE: What! What gentleman?

NORA: Silly! And that now he'd died and when they opened his will it said in big letters: "Everything I possess is to be paid forthwith to my beloved Mrs. Nora Helmer in cash."

MRS. LINDE: But, Nora dear, who was this gentleman?

430   NORA: Great heavens, don't you understand? There wasn't any old gentleman; he was just something I used to dream up as I sat here
evening after evening wondering how on earth I could raise some
money. But what does it matter? The old bore can stay imaginary as
far as I'm concerned, because now I don't have to worry any longer!
(*Jumps up.*) Oh, Christine, isn't it wonderful? I don't have to worry
any more! No more troubles! I can play all day with the children, I
can fill the house with pretty things, just the way Torvald likes. And,
Christine, it'll soon be spring, and the air'll be fresh and the skies
blue,—and then perhaps we'll be able to take a little trip somewhere.
440   I shall be able to see the sea again. Oh, yes, yes, it's a wonderful
thing to be alive and happy!

(*The bell rings in the hall.*)

MRS. LINDE (*gets up*): You've a visitor. Perhaps I'd better go.
NORA: No, stay. It won't be for me. It's someone for Torvald—
MAID (*in the door*): Excuse me, madam, a gentleman's called who says
he wants to speak to the master. But I didn't know—seeing as the
doctor's with him—
NORA: Who is this gentleman?
KROGSTAD (*in the doorway*): It's me, Mrs. Helmer.

(*Mrs. Linde starts, composes herself, and turns away to the window.*)

NORA (*takes a step toward him and whispers tensely*): You? What is it? What
450   do you want to talk to my husband about?
KROGSTAD: Business—you might call it. I hold a minor post in the bank,
and I hear your husband is to become our new chief—
NORA: Oh—then it isn't—?
KROGSTAD: Pure business, Mrs. Helmer. Nothing more.
NORA: Well, you'll find him in his study.

(*Nods indifferently as she closes the hall door behind him. Then she walks across
the room and sees to the stove.*)

MRS. LINDE: Nora, who was that man?
NORA: A lawyer called Krogstad.
MRS. LINDE: It was him, then.
NORA: Do you know that man?
460   MRS. LINDE: I used to know him—some years ago. He was a solicitor's
clerk in our town, for a while.
NORA: Yes, of course, so he was.
MRS. LINDE: How he's changed!
NORA: He was very unhappily married, I believe.
MRS. LINDE: Is he a widower now?
NORA: Yes, with a lot of children. Ah, now it's alight.

(*She closes the door of the stove and moves the rocking-chair a little to one side.*)

MRS. LINDE: He does—various things now, I hear?

NORA: Does he? It's quite possible—I really don't know. But don't let's talk about business. It's so boring.

(Dr. Rank enters from Helmer's study.)

RANK: *(still in the doorway):* No, no, my dear chap, don't see me out. I'll go and have a word with your wife. *(Closes the door and notices Mrs. Linde.)* Oh, I beg your pardon. I seem to be *de trop* here too.

NORA: Not in the least. *(Introduces them.)* Dr. Rank. Mrs. Linde.

RANK: Ah! A name I have often heard in this house. I believe I passed you on the stairs as I came up.

MRS. LINDE: Yes. Stairs tire me; I have to take them slowly.

RANK: Oh, have you hurt yourself?

MRS. LINDE: No, I'm just a little run down.

RANK: Ah, is that all? Then I take it you've come to town to cure yourself by a round of parties?

MRS. LINDE: I have come here to find work.

RANK: Is that an approved remedy for being run down?

MRS. LINDE: One has to live, Doctor.

RANK: Yes, people do seem to regard it as a necessity.

NORA: Oh, really, Dr. Rank. I bet you want to stay alive.

RANK: You bet I do. However miserable I sometimes feel, I still want to go on being tortured for as long as possible. It's the same with all my patients; and with people who are morally sick, too. There's a moral cripple in with Helmer at this very moment—

MRS. LINDE *(softly):* Oh!

NORA: Whom do you mean?

RANK: Oh, a lawyer fellow called Krogstad—you wouldn't know him. He's crippled all right; morally twisted. But even he started off by announcing, as though it were a matter of enormous importance, that he had to live.

NORA: Oh? What did he want to talk to Torvald about?

RANK: I haven't the faintest idea. All I heard was something about the bank.

NORA: I didn't know that Krog—that this man Krogstad had any connection with the bank.

RANK: Yes, he's got some kind of job down there. *(To Mrs. Linde.)* I wonder if in your part of the world you too have a species of human being that spends its time fussing around trying to smell out moral corruption? And when they find a case they give him some nice, comfortable position so that they can keep a good watch on him. The healthy ones just have to lump it.

MRS. LINDE: But surely it's the sick who need care most?

RANK *(shrugs his shoulders):* Well, there we have it. It's that attitude that's turning human society into a hospital.

(Nora, lost in her own thoughts, laughs half to herself and claps her hands.)

RANK: Why are you laughing? Do you really know what society is?

NORA: What do I care about society? I think it's a bore. I was laughing at
510 something else—something frightfully funny. Tell me, Dr. Rank—
will everyone who works at the bank come under Torvald now?

RANK: Do you find that particularly funny?

NORA (*smiles and hums*): Never you mind! Never you mind! (*Walks around
the room.*) Yes, I find it very amusing to think that we—I mean, Torvald—
has obtained so much influence over so many people. (*Takes the paper
bag from her pocket.*) Dr. Rank, would you like a small macaroon?

RANK: Macaroons! I say! I thought they were forbidden here.

NORA: Yes, well, these are some Christine gave me.

MRS. LINDE: What? I—?

520 NORA: All right, all right, don't get frightened. You weren't to know
Torvald had forbidden them. He's afraid they'll ruin my teeth. But,
dash it—for once—! Don't you agree, Dr. Rank? Here! (*Pops a macaroon into his mouth.*) You too, Christine. And I'll have one too. Just
a little one. Two at the most. (*Begins to walk around again.*) Yes, now
I feel really, really happy. Now there's just one thing in the world
I'd really love to do.

RANK: Oh? And what is that?

NORA: Just something I'd love to say to Torvald.

RANK: Well, why don't you say it?

530 NORA: No, I daren't. It's too dreadful.

MRS. LINDE: Dreadful?

RANK: Well, then, you'd better not. But you can say it to us. What is it
you'd so love to say to Torvald?

NORA: I've the most extraordinary longing to say: "Bloody hell!"

RANK: Are you mad?

MRS. LINDE: My dear Nora—!

RANK: Say it. Here he is.

NORA (*hiding the bag of macaroons*): Ssh! Ssh!

(*Helmer, with his overcoat on his arm and his hat in his hand, enters from his
study.*)

NORA (*goes to meet him*): Well, Torvald dear, did you get rid of him?

540 HELMER: Yes, he's just gone.

NORA: May I introduce you—? This is Christine. She's just arrived in town.

HELMER: Christine—? Forgive me, but I don't think—

NORA: Mrs. Linde, Torvald dear. Christine Linde.

HELMER: Ah. A childhood friend of my wife's, I presume.

MRS. LINDE: Yes, we knew each other in earlier days.

NORA: And imagine, now she's traveled all this way to talk to you.

HELMER: Oh?

MRS. LINDE: Well, I didn't really—

NORA: You see, Christine's frightfully good at office work, and she's mad
550 to come under some really clever man who can teach her even more
than she knows already—

HELMER: Very sensible, madam.

NORA: So when she heard you'd become head of the bank—it was in her
local paper—she came here as quickly as she could and—Torvald, you
will, won't you? Do a little something to help Christine? For my sake?

HELMER: Well, that shouldn't be impossible. You are a widow, I take it,
Mrs. Linde?

MRS. LINDE: Yes.

HELMER: And you have experience of office work?

560 MRS. LINDE: Yes, quite a bit.

HELMER: Well then, it's quite likely I may be able to find some job for
you—

NORA *(claps her hands):* You see, you see!

HELMER: You've come at a lucky moment, Mrs. Linde.

MRS. LINDE: Oh, how can I ever thank you—?

HELMER: There's absolutely no need. *(Puts on his overcoat.)* But now I'm
afraid I must ask you to excuse me—

RANK: Wait. I'll come with you.

(He gets his fur coat from the hall and warms it at the stove.)

NORA: Don't be long, Torvald dear.

570 HELMER: I'll only be an hour.

NORA: Are you going too, Christine?

MRS. LINDE *(puts on her outdoor clothes):* Yes, I must start to look round for
a room.

HELMER: Then perhaps we can walk part of the way together.

NORA *(helps her):* It's such a nuisance we're so cramped here—I'm afraid
we can't offer to—

MRS. LINDE: Oh, I wouldn't dream of it. Goodbye, Nora dear, and
thanks for everything.

NORA: *Au revoir.* You'll be coming back this evening, of course. And you
580 too, Dr. Rank. What? If you're well enough? Of course you'll be well
enough. Wrap up warmly, though.

(They go out, talking, into the hall. Children's voices are heard from the stairs.)

NORA: Here they are! Here they are!

(She runs out and opens the door. Anne-Marie, the nurse, enters with the children.)

NORA: Come in, come in! *(Stoops down and kisses them.)* Oh, my sweet
darlings—! Look at them, Christine! Aren't they beautiful?

RANK: Don't stand here chattering in this draught!

HELMER: Come, Mrs. Linde. This is for mothers only.

*(Dr. Rank, Helmer, and Mrs. Linde go down the stairs. The nurse brings the
children into the room. Nora follows, and closes the door to the hall.)*

NORA: How well you look! What red cheeks you've got! Like apples and
roses! *(The children answer her inaudibly as she talks to them.)* Have you
had fun? That's splendid. You gave Emmy and Bob a ride on the

590 sledge? What, both together? I say! What a clever boy you are, Ivar! Oh, let me hold her for a moment, Anne-Marie! My sweet little baby doll! *(Takes the smallest child from the nurse and dances with her.)* Yes, yes, Mummy will dance with Bob too. What? Have you been throwing snowballs? Oh, I wish I'd been there! No, don't—I'll undress them myself, Anne-Marie. No, please let me; it's such fun. Go inside and warm yourself; you look frozen. There's some hot coffee on the stove. *(The nurse goes into the room on the left. Nora takes off the children's outdoor clothes and throws them anywhere while they all chatter simultaneously.)* What? A big dog ran after you? But he didn't bite you? No,
600 dogs don't bite lovely little baby dolls. Leave those parcels alone, Ivar. What's in them? Ah, wouldn't you like to know! No, no; it's nothing nice. Come on, let's play a game. What shall we play? Hide and seek. Yes, let's play hide and seek. Bob shall hide first. You want me to? All right, let me hide first.

(Nora and the children play around the room, and in the adjacent room to the left, laughing and shouting. At length Nora hides under the table. The children rush in, look, but cannot find her. Then they hear her half-stifled laughter, run to the table, lift up the cloth, and see her. Great excitement. She crawls out as though to frighten them. Further excitement. Meanwhile, there has been a knock on the door leading from the hall, but no one has noticed it. Now the door is half-opened and Krogstad enters. He waits for a moment; the game continues.)

KROGSTAD: Excuse me, Mrs. Helmer—
NORA *(turns with a stifled cry and half jumps up):* Oh! What do you want?
KROGSTAD: I beg your pardon; the front door was ajar. Someone must have forgotten to close it.
NORA *(gets up):* My husband is not at home, Mr. Krogstad.
610 KROGSTAD: I know.
NORA: Well, what do you want here, then?
KROGSTAD: A word with you.
NORA: With—? *(To the children, quietly.)* Go inside to Anne-Marie. What? No, the strange gentleman won't do anything to hurt Mummy. When he's gone we'll start playing again.

(She takes the children into the room on the left and closes the door behind them.)

NORA *(uneasy, tense):* You want to speak to me?
KROGSTAD: Yes.
NORA: Today? But it's not the first of the month yet.
KROGSTAD: No, it is Christmas Eve. Whether or not you have a merry
620 Christmas depends on you.
NORA: What do you want? I can't give you anything today—
KROGSTAD: We won't talk about that for the present. There's something else. You have a moment to spare?
NORA: Oh, yes. Yes, I suppose so; though—
KROGSTAD: Good. I was sitting in the café down below and I saw your husband cross the street—

NORA: Yes.

KROGSTAD: With a lady.

NORA: Well?

630 KROGSTAD: Might I be so bold as to ask: was not that lady a Mrs. Linde?

NORA: Yes.

KROGSTAD: Recently arrived in town?

NORA: Yes, today.

KROGSTAD: She is a good friend of yours, is she not?

NORA: Yes, she is. But I don't see—

KROGSTAD: I used to know her too once.

NORA: I know.

KROGSTAD: Oh? You've discovered that. Yes, I thought you would. Well then, may I ask you a straight question: is Mrs. Linde to be

640 employed at the bank?

NORA: How dare you presume to cross-examine me, Mr. Krogstad? You, one of my husband's employees? But since you ask, you shall have an answer. Yes, Mrs. Linde is to be employed by the bank. And I arranged it, Mr. Krogstad. Now you know.

KROGSTAD: I guessed right, then.

NORA (*walks up and down the room*): Oh, one has a little influence, you know. Just because one's a woman it doesn't necessarily mean that— When one is in a humble position, Mr. Krogstad, one should think twice before offending someone who—hm—

650 KROGSTAD: —who has influence?

NORA: Precisely.

KROGSTAD (*changes his tone*): Mrs. Helmer, will you have the kindness to use your influence on my behalf?

NORA: What? What do you mean?

KROGSTAD: Will you be so good as to see that I keep my humble position at the bank?

NORA: What do you mean? Who is thinking of removing you from your position?

KROGSTAD: Oh, you don't need to play innocent with me. I realize it can't

660 be very pleasant for your friend to risk bumping into me; and now I also realize whom I have to thank for being hounded out like this.

NORA: But I assure you—

KROGSTAD: Look, let's not beat about the bush. There's still time, and I'd advise you to use your influence to stop it.

NORA: But, Mr. Krogstad, I have no influence!

KROGSTAD: Oh? I thought you just said—

NORA: But I didn't mean it like that! I? How on earth could you imagine that I would have any influence over my husband?

KROGSTAD: Oh, I've known your husband since we were students

670 together. I imagine he has his weaknesses like other married men.

NORA: If you speak impertinently of my husband, I shall show you the door.

KROGSTAD: You're a bold woman, Mrs. Helmer.

NORA: I'm not afraid of you any longer. Once the New Year is in, I'll soon be rid of you.

KROGSTAD (*more controlled*): Now listen to me, Mrs. Helmer. If I'm forced to, I shall fight for my little job at the bank as I would fight for my life.

NORA: So it sounds.

KROGSTAD: It isn't just the money; that's the last thing I care about. There's something else—well, you might as well know. It's like this, you see. You know of course, as everyone else does, that some years ago I committed an indiscretion.

NORA: I think I did hear something—

KROGSTAD: It never came into court; but from that day, every opening was barred to me. So I turned my hand to the kind of business you know about. I had to do something; and I don't think I was one of the worst. But now I want to give up all that. My sons are growing up; for their sake, I must try to regain what respectability I can. This job in the bank was the first step on the ladder. And now your husband wants to kick me off that ladder back into the dirt.

NORA: But my dear Mr. Krogstad, it simply isn't in my power to help you.

KROGSTAD: You say that because you don't want to help me. But I have the means to make you.

NORA: You don't mean you'd tell my husband that I owe you money?

KROGSTAD: And if I did?

NORA: That'd be a filthy trick! (*Almost in tears.*) This secret that is my pride and my joy—that he should hear about it in such a filthy, beastly way—hear about it from you! It'd involve me in the most dreadful unpleasantness—

KROGSTAD: Only—unpleasantness?

NORA (*vehemently*): All right, do it! You'll be the one who'll suffer. It'll show my husband the kind of man you are, and then you'll never keep your job.

KROGSTAD: I asked you whether it was merely domestic unpleasantness you were afraid of.

NORA: If my husband hears about it, he will of course immediately pay you whatever is owing. And then we shall have nothing more to do with you.

KROGSTAD (*takes a step closer*): Listen, Mrs. Helmer. Either you've a bad memory or else you know very little about financial transactions. I had better enlighten you.

NORA: What do you mean?

KROGSTAD: When your husband was ill, you came to me to borrow two hundred and fifty pounds.

NORA: I didn't know anyone else.

KROGSTAD: I promised to find that sum for you—

NORA: And you did find it.

KROGSTAD: I promised to find that sum for you on certain conditions. You were so worried about your husband's illness and so keen to get

the money to take him abroad that I don't think you bothered much
about the details. So it won't be out of place if I refresh your memory. Well—I promised to get you the money in exchange for an
I.O.U., which I drew up.

NORA: Yes, and which I signed.

KROGSTAD: Exactly. But then I added a few lines naming your father as
security for the debt. This paragraph was to be signed by your father.

NORA: Was to be? He did sign it.

KROGSTAD: I left the date blank for your father to fill in when he signed
this paper. You remember, Mrs. Helmer?

NORA: Yes, I think so—

KROGSTAD: Then I gave you back this I.O.U. for you to post to your
father. Is that not correct?

NORA: Yes.

KROGSTAD: And of course you posted it at once; for within five or six
days you brought it along to me with your father's signature on it.
Whereupon I handed you the money.

NORA: Yes, well. Haven't I repaid the installments as agreed?

KROGSTAD: Mm—yes, more or less. But to return to what we were
speaking about—that was a difficult time for you just then, wasn't
it, Mrs. Helmer?

NORA: Yes, it was.

KROGSTAD: And your father was very ill, if I am not mistaken.

NORA: He was dying.

KROGSTAD: He did in fact die shortly afterwards?

NORA: Yes.

KROGSTAD: Tell me, Mrs. Helmer, do you by any chance remember the
date of your father's death? The day of the month, I mean.

NORA: Papa died on the twenty-ninth of September.

KROGSTAD: Quite correct; I took the trouble to confirm it. And that
leaves me with a curious little problem—*(Takes out a paper.)*—which I
simply cannot solve.

NORA: Problem? I don't see—

KROGSTAD: The problem, Mrs. Helmer, is that your father signed this
paper three days after his death.

NORA: What? I don't understand—

KROGSTAD: Your father died on the twenty-ninth of September. But
look at this. Here your father has dated his signature the second of
October. Isn't that a curious little problem, Mrs. Helmer? *(Nora is
silent.)* Can you suggest any explanation? *(She remains silent.)* And
there's another curious thing. The words "second of October" and
the year are written in a hand which is not your father's, but which
I seem to know. Well, there's a simple explanation to that. Your
father could have forgotten to write in the date when he signed, and
someone else could have added it before the news came of his death.
There's nothing criminal about that. It's the signature itself I'm

wondering about. It *is* genuine, I suppose, Mrs. Helmer? It was your father who wrote this name here?

NORA (*after a short silence, throws back her head and looks defiantly at him*): No, it was not. It was I who wrote Papa's name there.

KROGSTAD: Look, Mrs. Helmer, do you realize this is a dangerous
770   admission?

NORA: Why? You'll get your money.

KROGSTAD: May I ask you a question? Why didn't you send this paper to your father?

NORA: I couldn't. Papa was very ill. If I'd asked him to sign this, I'd have had to tell him what the money was for. But I couldn't have told him in his condition that my husband's life was in danger. I couldn't have done that!

KROGSTAD: Then you would have been wiser to have given up your idea of a holiday.

780   NORA: But I couldn't! It was to save my husband's life. I couldn't put it off.

KROGSTAD: But didn't it occur to you that you were being dishonest towards me?

NORA: I couldn't bother about that. I didn't care about you. I hated you because of all the beastly difficulties you'd put in my way when you knew how dangerously ill my husband was.

KROGSTAD: Mrs. Helmer, you evidently don't appreciate exactly what you have done. But I can assure you that it is no bigger nor worse a crime than the one I once committed, and thereby ruined my whole social position.

790   NORA: You? Do you expect me to believe that you would have taken a risk like that to save your wife's life?

KROGSTAD: The law does not concern itself with motives.

NORA: Then the law must be very stupid.

KROGSTAD: Stupid or not, if I show this paper to the police, you will be judged according to it.

NORA: I don't believe that. Hasn't a daughter the right to shield her father from worry and anxiety when he's old and dying? Hasn't a wife the right to save her husband's life? I don't know much about the law, but there must be something somewhere that says that
800   such things are allowed. You ought to know about that, you're meant to be a lawyer, aren't you? You can't be a very good lawyer, Mr. Krogstad.

KROGSTAD: Possibly not. But business, the kind of business we two have been transacting—I think you'll admit I understand something about that? Good. Do as you please. But I tell you this. If I get thrown into the gutter for a second time, I shall take you with me.

(*He bows and goes out through the hall.*)

NORA (*stands for a moment in thought, then tosses her head*): What nonsense! He's trying to frighten me! I'm not that stupid. (*Busies herself gathering*

together the children's clothes; then she suddenly stops.) But—? No, it's
impossible. I did it for love, didn't I?

CHILDREN *(in the doorway, left):* Mummy, the strange gentleman's gone
out into the street.

NORA: Yes, yes, I know. But don't talk to anyone about the strange gentleman. You hear? Not even to Daddy.

CHILDREN: No, Mummy. Will you play with us again now?

NORA: No, no. Not now.

CHILDREN: Oh but, Mummy, you promised!

NORA: I know, but I can't just now. Go back to the nursery. I've a lot
to do. Go away, my darlings, go away. *(She pushes them gently into
the other room, and closes the door behind them. She sits on the sofa, takes
up her embroidery, stitches for a few moments, but soon stops.)* No!
*(Throws the embroidery aside, gets up, goes to the door leading to the hall,
and calls.)* Helen! Bring in the Christmas tree! *(She goes to the table
on the left and opens the drawer in it; then pauses again.)* No, but it's
utterly impossible!

MAID *(enters with tree):* Where shall I put it, madam?

NORA: There, in the middle of the room.

MAID: Will you be wanting anything else?

NORA: No, thank you, I have everything I need.

(The maid puts down the tree and goes out.)

NORA *(busy decorating the tree):* Now—candles here—and flowers here.
That loathsome man! Nonsense, nonsense, there's nothing to be
frightened about. The Christmas tree must be beautiful. I'll do
everything that you like, Torvald. I'll sing for you, dance for you—

(Helmer, with a bundle of papers under his arm, enters.)

NORA: Oh—are you back already?

HELMER: Yes. Has anyone been here?

NORA: Here? No.

HELMER: That's strange. I saw Krogstad come out of the front door.

NORA: Did you? Oh yes, that's quite right—Krogstad was here for a few
minutes.

HELMER: Nora, I can tell from your face, he's been here and asked you
to put in a good word for him.

NORA: Yes.

HELMER: And you were to pretend you were doing it of your own
accord? You weren't going to tell me he'd been here? He asked you
to do that too, didn't he?

NORA: Yes, Torvald. But—

HELMER: Nora, Nora! And you were ready to enter into such a conspiracy?
Talking to a man like that, and making him promises—and then, on
top of it all, to tell me an untruth!

NORA: An untruth?

HELMER: Didn't you say no one had been here? *(Wags his finger.)* My
little songbird must never do that again. A songbird must have a
clean beak to sing with; otherwise she'll start twittering out of tune.
(Puts his arm round her waist.) Isn't that the way we want things? Yes,
of course it is. *(Lets go of her.)* So let's hear no more about that.
(Sits down in front of the stove.) Ah, how cozy and peaceful it is here.
(Glances for a few moments at his papers.)

NORA *(busy with the tree; after a short silence):* Torvald.

HELMER: Yes.

860   NORA: I'm terribly looking forward to that fancy dress ball at the
Stenborgs on Boxing Day.

HELMER: And I'm terribly curious to see what you're going to surprise
me with.

NORA: Oh, it's so maddening.

HELMER: What is?

NORA: I can't think of anything to wear. It all seems so stupid and
meaningless.

HELMER: So my little Nora's come to that conclusion, has she?

NORA *(behind his chair, resting her arms on its back):* Are you very busy,
870   Torvald?

HELMER: Oh—

NORA: What are those papers?

HELMER: Just something to do with the bank.

NORA: Already?

HELMER: I persuaded the trustees to give me authority to make certain
immediate changes in the staff and organization. I want to have
everything straight by the New Year.

NORA: Then that's why this poor man Krogstad—

HELMER: Hm.

880   NORA *(still leaning over his chair, slowly strokes the back of his head):* If you
hadn't been so busy, I was going to ask you an enormous favour,
Torvald.

HELMER: Well, tell me. What was it to be?

NORA: You know I trust your taste more than anyone's. I'm so anxious
to look really beautiful at the fancy dress ball. Torvald, couldn't
you help me to decide what I shall go as, and what kind of costume
I ought to wear?

HELMER: Aha! So little Miss Independent's in trouble and needs a man
to rescue her, does she?

890   NORA: Yes, Torvald. I can't get anywhere without your help.

HELMER: Well, well, I'll give the matter thought. We'll find something.

NORA: Oh, how kind of you! *(Goes back to the tree. Pause.)* How pretty
these red flowers look! But, tell me, is it so dreadful, this thing that
Krogstad's done?

HELMER: He forged someone else's name. Have you any idea what that
means?

NORA: Mightn't he have been forced to do it by some emergency?

HELMER: He probably just didn't think—that's what usually happens. I'm not so heartless as to condemn a man for an isolated action.

900   NORA: No, Torvald, of course not!

HELMER: Men often succeed in reestablishing themselves if they admit their crime and take their punishment.

NORA: Punishment?

HELMER: But Krogstad didn't do that. He chose to try and trick his way out of it; and that's what has morally destroyed him.

NORA: You think that would—?

HELMER: Just think how a man with that load on his conscience must always be lying and cheating and dissembling; how he must wear a mask even in the presence of those who are dearest to him, even

910   his own wife and children! Yes, the children. That's the worst danger, Nora.

NORA: Why?

HELMER: Because an atmosphere of lies contaminates and poisons every corner of the home. Every breath that the children draw in such a house contains the germs of evil.

NORA (*comes closer behind him*): Do you really believe that?

HELMER: Oh, my dear, I've come across it so often in my work at the bar. Nearly all young criminals are the children of mothers who are constitutional liars.

920   NORA: Why do you say mothers?

HELMER: It's usually the mother; though of course the father can have the same influence. Every lawyer knows that only too well. And yet this fellow Krogstad has been sitting at home all these years poisoning his children with his lies and pretenses. That's why I say that, morally speaking, he is dead. (*Stretches out his hands toward her.*) So my pretty little Nora must promise me not to plead his case. Your hand on it. Come, come, what's this? Give me your hand. There. That's settled, now. I assure you it'd be quite impossible for me to work in the same building as him. I literally feel physically ill in the presence of a man like that.

930   NORA (*draws her hand from his and goes over to the other side of the Christmas tree*): How hot it is in here! And I've so much to do.

HELMER (*gets up and gathers his papers*): Yes, and I must try to get some of this read before dinner. I'll think about your costume too. And I may even have something up my sleeve to hang in gold paper on the Christmas tree. (*Lays his hand on her head.*) My precious little songbird!

(*He goes into his study and closes the door.*)

NORA (*softly, after a pause*): It's nonsense. It must be. It's impossible. It must be impossible!

NURSE (*in the doorway, left*): The children are asking if they can come in to Mummy.

940   NORA: No, no, no; don't let them in! You stay with them, Anne-Marie.

NURSE: Very good, madam. *(Closes the door.)*

NORA *(pale with fear):* Corrupt my little children—! Poison my home! *(Short pause. She throws back her head.)* It isn't true! It *couldn't* be true!

ACT 2

The same room. In the corner by the piano the Christmas tree stands, stripped and disheveled, its candles burned to their sockets. Nora's outdoor clothes lie on the sofa. She is alone in the room, walking restlessly to and fro. At length she stops by the sofa and picks up her coat.

NORA *(drops the coat again):* There's someone coming! *(Goes to the door and listens.)* No, it's no one. Of course—no one'll come today, it's Christmas Day. Nor tomorrow. But perhaps—! *(Opens the door and looks out.)* No. Nothing in the letter-box. Quite empty. *(Walks across the room.)* Silly, silly. Of course he won't do anything. It couldn't happen. It isn't possible. Why, I've three small children.

(The Nurse, carrying a large cardboard box, enters from the room on the left.)

950 NURSE: I found those fancy dress clothes at last, madam.

NORA: Thank you. Put them on the table.

NURSE *(does so):* They're all rumpled up.

NORA: Oh, I wish I could tear them into a million pieces!

NURSE: Why, madam! They'll be all right. Just a little patience.

NORA: Yes, of course. I'll go and get Mrs. Linde to help me.

NURSE: What, out again? In this dreadful weather? You'll catch a chill, madam.

NORA: Well, that wouldn't be the worst. How are the children?

NURSE: Playing with their Christmas presents, poor little dears. But—

960 NORA: Are they still asking to see me?

NURSE: They're so used to having their Mummy with them.

NORA: Yes, but, Anne-Marie, from now on I shan't be able to spend so much time with them.

NURSE: Well, children get used to anything in time.

NORA: Do you think so? Do you think they'd forget their mother if she went away from them—for ever?

NURSE: Mercy's sake, madam! For ever!

NORA: Tell me, Anne-Marie—I've so often wondered. How could you bear to give your child away—to strangers?

970 NURSE: But I had to when I came to nurse my little Miss Nora.

NORA: Do you mean you wanted to?

NURSE: When I had the chance of such a good job? A poor girl what's got into trouble can't afford to pick and choose. That good-for-nothing didn't lift a finger.

NORA: But your daughter must have completely forgotten you.

NURSE: Oh no, indeed she hasn't. She's written to me twice, once when she got confirmed and then again when she got married.

NORA *(hugs her):* Dear old Anne-Marie, you were a good mother to me.

NURSE: Poor little Miss Nora, you never had any mother but me.

980 NORA: And if my little ones had no one else, I know you would—no, silly, silly, silly! *(Opens the cardboard box.)* Go back to them, Anne-Marie. Now I must—Tomorrow you'll see how pretty I shall look.

NURSE: Why, there'll be no one at the ball as beautiful as my Miss Nora.

(She goes into the room, left.)

NORA *(begins to unpack the clothes from the box, but soon throws them down again):* Oh, if only I dared to go out! If I could be sure no one would come, and nothing would happen while I was away! Stupid, stupid! No one will come. I just mustn't think about it. Brush this muff. Pretty gloves, pretty gloves! Don't think about it, don't think about it! One, two, three, four, five, six—*(Cries.)* Ah—they're coming—!

(She begins to run toward the door, but stops uncertainly. Mrs. Linde enters from the hall where she has been taking off her outdoor clothes.)

990 NORA: Oh, it's you, Christine. There's no one else out there, is there? Oh, I'm so glad you've come.

MRS. LINDE: I hear you were at my room asking for me.

NORA: Yes, I just happened to be passing. I want to ask you to help me with something. Let's sit down here on the sofa. Look at this. There's going to be a fancy dress ball tomorrow night upstairs at Consul Stenborg's, and Torvald wants me to go as a Neapolitan fisher-girl and dance the tarantella. I learned it on Capri.

MRS. LINDE: I say, are you going to give a performance?

NORA: Yes, Torvald says I should. Look, here's the dress. Torvald had it made for me in Italy; but now it's all so torn, I don't know—

1000 MRS. LINDE: Oh, we'll soon put that right; the stitching's just come away. Needle and thread? Ah, here we are.

NORA: You're being awfully sweet.

MRS. LINDE *(sews):* So you're going to dress up tomorrow, Nora? I must pop over for a moment to see how you look. Oh, but I've completely forgotten to thank you for that nice evening yesterday.

NORA *(gets up and walks across the room):* Oh, I didn't think it was as nice as usual. You ought to have come to town a little earlier, Christine. . . . Yes, Torvald understands how to make a home look attractive.

1010 MRS. LINDE: I'm sure you do, too. You're not your father's daughter for nothing. But, tell me. Is Dr. Rank always in such low spirits as he was yesterday?

NORA: No, last night it was very noticeable. But he's got a terrible disease; he's got spinal tuberculosis, poor man. His father was a frightful creature who kept mistresses and so on. As a result Dr. Rank has been sickly ever since he was a child—you understand—

MRS. LINDE *(puts down her sewing):* But, my dear Nora, how on earth did you get to know about such things?

NORA (*walks about the room*): Oh, don't be silly, Christine—when one has
1020   three children, one comes into contact with women who—well, who
        know about medical matters, and they tell one a thing or two.

MRS. LINDE (*sews again; a short silence*): Does Dr. Rank visit you every
        day?

NORA: Yes, every day. He's Torvald's oldest friend, and a good friend to
        me too. Dr. Rank's almost one of the family.

MRS. LINDE: But, tell me—is he quite sincere? I mean doesn't he rather
        say the sort of thing he thinks people want to hear?

NORA: No, quite the contrary. What gave you that idea?

MRS. LINDE: When you introduced me to him yesterday, he said he'd
1030   often heard my name mentioned here. But later I noticed your hus-
        band had no idea who I was. So how could Dr. Rank—?

NORA: Yes, that's quite right, Christine. You see, Torvald's so hopelessly
        in love with me that he wants to have me all to himself—those were
        his very words. When we were first married, he got quite jealous if I
        as much as mentioned any of my old friends back home. So natu-
        rally, I stopped talking about them. But I often chat with Dr. Rank
        about that kind of thing. He enjoys it, you see.

MRS. LINDE: Now listen, Nora. In many ways you're still a child; I'm a bit
        older than you and have a little more experience of the world.
1040   There's something I want to say to you. You ought to give up this
        business with Dr. Rank.

NORA: What business?

MRS. LINDE: Well, everything. Last night you were speaking about this
        rich admirer of yours who was going to give you money—

NORA: Yes, and who doesn't exist—unfortunately. But what's that got to
        do with—?

MRS. LINDE: Is Dr. Rank rich?

NORA: Yes.

MRS. LINDE: And he has no dependents?

1050   NORA: No, no one. But—

MRS. LINDE: And he comes here to see you every day?

NORA: Yes, I've told you.

MRS. LINDE: But how dare a man of his education be so forward?

NORA: What on earth are you talking about?

MRS. LINDE: Oh, stop pretending, Nora. Do you think I haven't guessed
        who it was who lent you that two hundred pounds?

NORA: Are you out of your mind? How could you imagine such a thing?
        A friend, someone who comes here every day! Why, that'd be an
        impossible situation!

1060   MRS. LINDE: Then it really wasn't him?

NORA: No, of course not. I've never for a moment dreamed of—anyway,
        he hadn't any money to lend then. He didn't come into that till later.

MRS. LINDE: Well, I think that was a lucky thing for you, Nora dear.

NORA: No, I could never have dreamed of asking Dr. Rank—Though
        I'm sure that if I ever did ask him—

MRS. LINDE: But of course you won't.

NORA: Of course not. I can't imagine that it should ever become necessary. But I'm perfectly sure that if I did speak to Dr. Rank—

MRS. LINDE: Behind your husband's back?

1070 NORA: I've got to get out of this other business; and *that's* been going on behind his back. I've *got* to get out of it.

MRS. LINDE: Yes, well, that's what I told you yesterday. But—

NORA (*walking up and down*): It's much easier for a man to arrange these things than a woman—

MRS. LINDE: One's own husband, yes.

NORA: Oh, bosh. (*Stops walking.*) When you've completely repaid a debt, you get your I.O.U. back, don't you?

MRS. LINDE: Yes, of course.

NORA: And you can tear it into a thousand pieces and burn the filthy,
1080 beastly thing!

MRS. LINDE (*looks hard at her, puts down her sewing, and gets up slowly*): Nora, you're hiding something from me.

NORA: Can you see that?

MRS. LINDE: Something has happened since yesterday morning. Nora, what is it?

NORA (*goes toward her*): Christine! (*Listens.*) Ssh! There's Torvald. Would you mind going into the nursery for a few minutes? Torvald can't bear to see sewing around. Anne-Marie'll help you.

MRS. LINDE (*gathers some of her things together*): Very well. But I shan't leave
1090 this house until we've talked this matter out.

(*She goes into the nursery, left. As she does so, Helmer enters from the hall.*)

NORA (*runs to meet him*): Oh, Torvald dear, I've been so longing for you to come back!

HELMER: Was that the dressmaker?

NORA: No, it was Christine. She's helping me mend my costume. I'm going to look rather splendid in that.

HELMER: Yes, that was quite a bright idea of mine, wasn't it?

NORA: Wonderful! But wasn't it nice of me to give in to you?

HELMER (*takes her chin in his hand*): Nice—to give in to your husband? All right, little silly, I know you didn't mean it like that. But I won't
1100 disturb you. I expect you'll be wanting to try it on.

NORA: Are you going to work now?

HELMER: Yes. (*Shows her a bundle of papers.*) Look at these. I've been down to the bank—(*Turns to go into his study.*)

NORA: Torvald.

HELMER (*stops*): Yes.

NORA: If little squirrel asked you really prettily to grant her a wish—

HELMER: Well?

NORA: Would you grant it to her?

HELMER: First I should naturally have to know what it was.

1110   NORA: Squirrel would do lots of pretty tricks for you if you granted her wish.

HELMER: Out with it, then.

NORA: Your little skylark would sing in every room—

HELMER: My little skylark does that already.

NORA: I'd turn myself into a little fairy and dance for you in the moonlight, Torvald.

HELMER: Nora, it isn't that business you were talking about this morning?

NORA (*comes closer*): Yes, Torvald—oh, please! I beg of you!

1120   HELMER: Have you really the nerve to bring that up again?

NORA: Yes, Torvald, yes, you must do as I ask! You must let Krogstad keep his place at the bank!

HELMER: My dear Nora, his is the job I'm giving to Mrs. Linde.

NORA: Yes, that's terribly sweet of you. But you can get rid of one of the other clerks instead of Krogstad.

HELMER: Really, you're being incredibly obstinate. Just because you thoughtlessly promised to put in a word for him, you expect me to—

NORA: No, it isn't that, Helmer. It's for your own sake. The man writes for the most beastly newspapers—you said so yourself. He could do

1130   you tremendous harm. I'm so dreadfully frightened of him—

HELMER: Oh, I understand. Memories of the past. That's what's frightening you.

NORA: What do you mean?

HELMER: You're thinking of your father, aren't you?

NORA: Yes, yes. Of course. Just think what those dreadful men wrote in the papers about Papa! The most frightful slanders. I really believe it would have lost him his job if the Ministry hadn't sent you down to investigate, and you hadn't been so kind and helpful to him.

HELMER: But my dear little Nora, there's a considerable difference

1140   between your father and me. Your father was not a man of unassailable reputation. But I am; and I hope to remain so all my life.

NORA: But no one knows what spiteful people may not dig up. We could be so peaceful and happy now, Torvald—we could be free from every worry—you and I and the children. Oh, please, Torvald, please—!

HELMER: The very fact of your pleading his cause makes it impossible for me to keep him. Everyone at the bank already knows that I intend to dismiss Krogstad. If the rumor got about that the new manager had allowed his wife to persuade him to change his mind—

NORA: Well, what then?

1150   HELMER: Oh, nothing, nothing. As long as my little Miss Obstinate gets her way—Do you expect me to make a laughing-stock of myself before my entire staff—give people the idea that I am open to outside influence? Believe me, I'd soon feel the consequences! Besides—there's something else that makes it impossible for Krogstad to remain in the bank while I am its manager.

NORA: What is that?

HELMER: I might conceivably have allowed myself to ignore his moral obloquies—

NORA: Yes, Torvald, surely?

1160   HELMER: And I hear he's quite efficient at his job. But we—well, we were schoolfriends. It was one of those friendships that one enters into over-hastily and so often comes to regret late in life. I might as well confess the truth. We—well, we're on Christian name terms. And the tactless idiot makes no attempt to conceal it when other people are present. On the contrary, he thinks it gives him the right to be famil- iar with me. He shows off the whole time, with "Torvald this," and "Torvald that." I can tell you, I find it damned annoying. If he stayed, he'd make my position intolerable.

NORA: Torvald, you can't mean this seriously.

1170   HELMER: Oh? And why not?

NORA: But it's so petty.

HELMER: What did you say? Petty? You think I am petty?

NORA: No, Torvald dear, of course you're not. That's just why—

HELMER: Don't quibble! You call my motives petty. Then I must be petty too. Petty! I see. Well, I've had enough of this. (*Goes to the door and calls into the hall.*) Helen!

NORA: What are you going to do?

HELMER (*searching among his papers*): I'm going to settle this matter once and for all. (*The Maid enters.*) Take this letter downstairs at once. Find

1180   a messenger and see that he delivers it. Immediately! The address is on the envelope. Here's the money.

MAID: Very good, sir. (*Goes out with the letter.*)

HELMER (*putting his papers in order*): There now, little Miss Obstinate.

NORA (*tensely*): Torvald—what was in that letter?

HELMER: Krogstad's dismissal.

NORA: Call her back, Torvald! There's still time. Oh, Torvald, call her back! Do it for my sake—for your own sake—for the children! Do you hear me, Torvald? Please do it! You don't realize what this may do to us all!

1190   HELMER: Too late.

NORA: Yes. Too late.

HELMER: My dear Nora, I forgive you this anxiety. Though it is a bit of an insult to me. Oh, but it is! Isn't it an insult to imply that I should be frightened by the vindictiveness of a depraved hack journalist? But I forgive you, because it so charmingly testifies to the love you bear me. (*Takes her in his arms.*) Which is as it should be, my own dearest Nora. Let what will happen, happen. When the real crisis comes, you will not find me lacking in strength or courage. I am man enough to bear the burden for us both.

1200   NORA (*fearfully*): What do you mean?

HELMER: The whole burden, I say—

NORA (*calmly*): I shall never let you do that.

HELMER: Very well. We shall share it, Nora—as man and wife. And that is as it should be. (*Caresses her.*) Are you happy now? There, there, there; don't look at me with those frightened little eyes. You're simply imagining things. You go ahead now and do your tarantella, and get some practice on that tambourine. I'll sit in my study and close the door. Then I won't hear anything, and you can make all the noise you want. (*Turns in the doorway.*) When Dr. Rank comes, tell him where to find me. (*He nods to her, goes into his room with his papers, and closes the door.*)

NORA (*desperate with anxiety, stands as though transfixed, and whispers*): He said he'd do it. He will do it. He will do it, and nothing'll stop him. No, never that. I'd rather anything. There must be some escape—Some way out—! (*The bell rings in the hall.*) Dr. Rank—! Anything but that! Anything, I don't care—!

(*She passes her hand across her face, composes herself, walks across, and opens the door to the hall. Dr. Rank is standing there, hanging up his fur coat. During the following scene, it begins to grow dark.*)

NORA: Good evening, Dr. Rank. I recognized your ring. But you mustn't go to Torvald yet. I think he's busy.

RANK: And—you?

NORA (*as he enters the room and she closes the door behind him*): Oh, you know very well I've always time to talk to you.

RANK: Thank you. I shall avail myself of that privilege as long as I can.

NORA: What do you mean by that? As long as you *can?*

RANK: Yes. Does that frighten you?

NORA: Well, it's rather a curious expression. Is something going to happen?

RANK: Something I've been expecting to happen for a long time. But I didn't think it would happen quite so soon.

NORA (*seizes his arm*): What is it? Dr. Rank, you must tell me!

RANK (*sits down by the stove*): I'm on the way out. And there's nothing to be done about it.

NORA (*sighs with relief*): Oh, it's you—?

RANK: Who else? No, it's no good lying to oneself. I am the most wretched of all my patients, Mrs. Helmer. These last few days I've been going through the books of this poor body of mine, and I find I am bankrupt. Within a month I may be rotting up there in the churchyard.

NORA: Ugh, what a nasty way to talk!

RANK: The facts aren't exactly nice. But the worst is that there's so much else that's nasty to come first. I've only one more test to make. When that's done I'll have a pretty accurate idea of when the final disintegration is likely to begin. I want to ask you a favour. Helmer's a sensitive chap, and I know how he hates anything ugly. I don't want him to visit me when I'm in hospital—

NORA: Oh but, Dr. Rank—

RANK: I don't want him there. On any pretext. I shan't have him
allowed in. As soon as I know the worst, I'll send you my visiting card
with a black cross on it, and then you'll know that the final filthy
process has begun.

NORA: Really, you're being quite impossible this evening. And I did
hope you'd be in a good mood.

RANK: With death on my hands? And all this to atone for someone else's
sin? Is there justice in that? And in every single family, in one way or
another, the same merciless law of retribution is at work—

NORA (*holds her hands to her ears*): Nonsense! Cheer up! Laugh!

RANK: Yes, you're right. Laughter's all the damned thing's fit for. My
poor innocent spine must pay for the fun my father had as a gay
young lieutenant.

NORA (*at the table, left*): You mean he was too fond of asparagus and
foie gras?

RANK: Yes, and truffles too.

NORA: Yes, of course, truffles, yes. And oysters too, I suppose?

RANK: Yes, oysters, oysters. Of course.

NORA: And all that port and champagne to wash them down. It's too sad
that all those lovely things should affect one's spine.

RANK: Especially a poor spine that never got any pleasure out of them.

NORA: Oh yes, that's the saddest thing of all.

RANK (*looks searchingly at her*): Hm—

NORA (*after a moment*): Why did you smile?

RANK: No, it was you who laughed.

NORA: No, it was you who smiled, Dr. Rank!

RANK (*gets up*): You're a worse little rogue than I thought.

NORA: Oh, I'm full of stupid tricks today.

RANK: So it seems.

NORA (*puts both her hands on his shoulders*): Dear, dear. Dr. Rank, you
mustn't die and leave Torvald and me.

RANK: Oh, you'll soon get over it. Once one is gone, one is soon forgotten.

NORA (*looks at him anxiously*): Do you believe that?

RANK: One finds replacements, and then—

NORA: Who will find a replacement?

RANK: You and Helmer both will, when I am gone. You seem to have
made a start already, haven't you? What was this Mrs. Linde doing
here yesterday evening?

NORA: Aha! But surely you can't be jealous of poor Christine?

RANK: Indeed I am. She will be my successor in this house. When I have
moved on, this lady will—

NORA: Ssh—don't speak so loud! She's in there!

RANK: Today again? You see!

NORA: She's only come to mend my dress. Good heavens, how unreasonable you are! (*Sits on the sofa.*) Be nice now, Dr. Rank. Tomorrow

1290   you'll see how beautifully I shall dance; and you must imagine that
        I'm doing it just for you. And for Torvald of course; obviously.
        (Takes some things out of the box.) Dr. Rank, sit down here and I'll
        show you something.

RANK *(sits):* What's this?

NORA: Look here! Look!

RANK: Silk stockings!

NORA: Flesh-colored. Aren't they beautiful? It's very dark in here now,
        of course, but tomorrow—No, no, no; only the soles. Oh well, I
        suppose you can look a bit higher if you want to.

1300   RANK: Hm—

NORA: Why are you looking so critical? Don't you think they'll fit me?

RANK: I can't really give you a qualified opinion on that.

NORA *(looks at him for a moment):* Shame on you! *(Flicks him on the ear with
        the stockings.)* Take that. *(Puts them back in the box.)*

RANK: What other wonders are to be revealed to me?

NORA: I shan't show you anything else. You're being naughty.

        (She hums a little and looks among the things in the box.)

RANK *(after a short silence):* When I sit here like this being so intimate
        with you, I can't think—I cannot imagine what would have become
        of me if I had never entered this house.

1310   NORA *(smiles):* Yes, I think you enjoy being with us, don't you?

RANK *(more quietly, looking into the middle distance):* And now to have to
        leave it all—

NORA: Nonsense. You're not leaving us.

RANK *(as before):* And not to be able to leave even the most wretched
        token of gratitude behind; hardly even a passing sense of loss; only
        an empty place, to be filled by the next comer.

NORA: Suppose I were to ask you to—? No—

RANK: To do what?

NORA: To give me proof of your friendship—

1320   RANK:: Yes, yes?

NORA: No, I mean—to do me a very great service—

RANK: Would you really for once grant me that happiness?

NORA: But you've no idea what it is.

RANK: Very well, tell me, then.

NORA: No, but, Dr. Rank, I can't. It's far too much—I want your help
        and advice, and I want you to do something for me.

RANK: The more the better. I've no idea what it can be. But tell me. You
        do trust me, don't you?

NORA: Oh, yes, more than anyone. You're my best and truest friend.

1330   Otherwise I couldn't tell you. Well then, Dr. Rank—there's something
        you must help me to prevent. You know how much Torvald loves
        me—he'd never hesitate for an instant to lay down his life for me—

RANK *(leans over toward her):* Nora—do you think he is the only one—?

NORA *(with a slight start):* What do you mean?

RANK: Who would gladly lay down his life for you?

NORA (*sadly*): Oh, I see.

RANK: I swore to myself I would let you know that before I go, I shall never have a better opportunity. . . . Well, Nora, now you know that. And now you also know that you can trust me as you can trust nobody else.

1340 NORA (*rises; calmly and quietly*): Let me pass, please.

RANK (*makes room for her but remains seated*): Nora—

NORA (*in the doorway to the hall*): Helen, bring the lamp. (*Goes over to the stove.*) Oh, dear Dr. Rank, this was really horrid of you.

RANK (*gets up*): That I have loved you as deeply as anyone else has? Was that horrid of me?

NORA: No—but that you should go and tell me. That was quite unnecessary—

RANK: What do you mean? Did you know, then—?

(*The Maid enters with the lamp, puts it on the table, and goes out.*)

RANK: Nora—Mrs. Helmer—I am asking you, did you know this?

1350 NORA: Oh, what do I know, what did I know, what didn't I know—I really can't say. How could you be so stupid, Dr. Rank? Everything was so nice.

RANK: Well, at any rate now you know that I am ready to serve you, body and soul. So—please continue.

NORA (*looks at him*): After this?

RANK: Please tell me what it is.

NORA: I can't possibly tell you now.

RANK: Yes, yes! You mustn't punish me like this. Let me be allowed to do what I can for you.

1360 NORA: You can't do anything for me now. Anyway, I don't need any help. It was only my imagination—you'll see. Yes, really. Honestly. (*Sits in the rocking chair, looks at him, and smiles.*) Well, upon my word you *are* a fine gentleman, Dr. Rank. Aren't you ashamed of yourself, now that the lamp's been lit?

RANK: Frankly, no. But perhaps I ought to say—*adieu*?

NORA: Of course not. You will naturally continue to visit us as before. You know quite well how Torvald depends on your company.

RANK: Yes, but you?

NORA: Oh, I always think it's enormous fun having you here.

1370 RANK: That was what misled me. You're a riddle to me, you know. I'd often felt you'd just as soon be with me as with Helmer.

NORA: Well, you see, there are some people whom one loves, and others whom it's almost more fun to be with.

RANK: Oh yes, there's some truth in that.

NORA: When I was at home, of course I loved Papa best. But I always used to think it was terribly amusing to go down and talk to the servants; because they never told me what I ought to do; and they were such fun to listen to.

RANK: I see. So I've taken their place?

1380 NORA (*jumps up and runs over to him*): Oh, dear, sweet Dr. Rank, I didn't mean that at all. But I'm sure you understand—I feel the same about Torvald as I did about Papa.

MAID (*enters from the hall*): Excuse me, madam. (*Whispers to her and hands her a visiting card.*)

NORA (*glances at the card*): Oh! (*Puts it quickly in her pocket.*)

RANK: Anything wrong?

NORA: No, no, nothing at all. It's just something that—it's my new dress.

RANK: What? But your costume is lying over there.

NORA: Oh—that, yes—but there's another—I ordered it specially—
1390 Torvald mustn't know—

RANK: Ah, so that's your big secret?

NORA: Yes, yes. Go in and talk to him—he's in his study—keep him talking for a bit—

RANK: Don't worry. He won't get away from me. (*Goes into Helmer's study.*)

NORA (*to the Maid*): Is he waiting in the kitchen?

MAID: Yes, madam, he came up the back way—

NORA: But didn't you tell him I had a visitor?

MAID: Yes, but he wouldn't go.

NORA: Wouldn't go?
1400 MAID: No, madam, not until he'd spoken with you.

NORA: Very well, show him in; but quietly. Helen, you mustn't tell anyone about this. It's a surprise for my husband.

MAID: Very good, madam. I understand. (*Goes.*)

NORA: It's happening. It's happening after all. No, no, no, it can't happen, it mustn't happen.

(*She walks across and bolts the door of Helmer's study. The Maid opens the door in the hall to admit Krogstad, and closes it behind him. He is wearing an overcoat, heavy boots, and a fur cap.*)

NORA (*goes towards him*): Speak quietly. My husband's at home.

KROGSTAD: Let him hear.

NORA: What do you want from me?

KROGSTAD: Information.
1410 NORA: Hurry up, then. What is it?

KROGSTAD: I suppose you know I've been given the sack.

NORA: I couldn't stop it, Mr. Krogstad. I did my best for you, but it didn't help.

KROGSTAD: Does your husband love you so little? He knows what I can do to you, and yet he dares to—

NORA: Surely you don't imagine I told him?

KROGSTAD: No. I didn't really think you had. It wouldn't have been like my old friend Torvald Helmer to show that much courage—

NORA: Mr. Krogstad, I'll trouble you to speak respectfully of my husband.
1420 KROGSTAD: Don't worry, I'll show him all the respect he deserves. But since you're so anxious to keep this matter hushed up, I presume

you're better informed than you were yesterday of the gravity of what you've done?

NORA: I've learned more than you could ever teach me.

KROGSTAD: Yes, a bad lawyer like me—

NORA: What do you want from me?

KROGSTAD: I just wanted to see how things were with you, Mrs. Helmer. I've been thinking about you all day. Even duns and hack journalists have hearts, you know.

1430 NORA: Show some heart, then. Think of my little children.

KROGSTAD: Have you and your husband thought of mine? Well, let's forget that. I just wanted to tell you, you don't need to take this business too seriously. I'm not going to take any action, for the present.

NORA: Oh, no—you won't, will you? I knew it.

KROGSTAD: It can all be settled quite amicably. There's no need for it to become public, We'll keep it among the three of us.

NORA: My husband must never know about this.

KROGSTAD: How can you stop him? Can you pay the balance of what you owe me?

1440 NORA: Not immediately.

KROGSTAD: Have you any means of raising the money during the next few days?

NORA: None that I would care to use.

KROGSTAD: Well, it wouldn't have helped anyway. However much money you offered me now I wouldn't give you back that paper.

NORA: What are you going to do with it?

KROGSTAD: Just keep it. No one else need ever hear about it. So in case you were thinking of doing anything desperate—

NORA: I am.

1450 KROGSTAD: Such as running away—

NORA: I am.

KROGSTAD: Or anything more desperate—

NORA: How did you know?

KROGSTAD: —just give up the idea.

NORA: How did you know?

KROGSTAD: Most of us think of that at first. I did. But I hadn't the courage—

NORA (*dully*): Neither have I.

KROGSTAD (*relieved*): It's true, isn't it? You haven't the courage either?

1460 NORA: No. I haven't. I haven't.

KROGSTAD: It'd be a stupid thing to do anyway. Once the first little domestic explosion is over. . . . I've got a letter in my pocket here addressed to your husband—

NORA: Telling him everything?

KROGSTAD: As delicately as possible.

NORA (*quickly*): He must never see that letter. Tear it up. I'll find the money somehow—

KROGSTAD: I'm sorry, Mrs. Helmer, I thought I'd explained—

NORA: Oh, I don't mean the money I owe you. Let me know how much

1470   you want from my husband, and I'll find it for you.

KROGSTAD: I'm not asking your husband for money.

NORA: What do you want, then?

KROGSTAD: I'll tell you. I want to get on my feet again, Mrs. Helmer. I want to get to the top. And your husband's going to help me. For eighteen months now my record's been clean. I've been in hard straits all that time; I was content to fight my way back inch by inch. Now I've been chucked back into the mud, and I'm not going to be satisfied with just getting back my job. I'm going to get to the top, I tell you. I'm going to get back into the bank, and it's going to be

1480   higher up. Your husband's going to create a new job for me—

NORA: He'll never do that!

KROGSTAD: Oh, yes he will. I know him. He won't dare to risk a scandal. And once I'm in there with him, you'll see! Within a year I'll be his right-hand man. It'll be Nils Krogstad who'll be running that bank, not Torvald Helmer!

NORA: That will never happen.

KROGSTAD: Are you thinking of—?

NORA: Now I *have* the courage.

KROGSTAD: Oh, you can't frighten me. A pampered little pretty like you—

1490   NORA: You'll see! You'll see!

KROGSTAD: Under the ice? Down in the cold, black water? And then, in the spring, to float up again, ugly, unrecognizable, hairless—?

NORA: You can't frighten me.

KROGSTAD: And you can't frighten me. People don't do such things, Mrs. Helmer. And anyway, what'd be the use? I've got him in my pocket.

NORA: But afterwards? When I'm no longer—?

KROGSTAD: Have you forgotten that then your reputation will be in my hands? (*She looks at him speechlessly.*) Well, I've warned you. Don't do anything silly. When Helmer's read my letter, he'll get in touch with

1500   me. And remember, it's your husband who's forced me to act like this. And for that I'll never forgive him. Goodbye, Mrs. Helmer. (*He goes out through the hall.*)

NORA (*runs to the hall door, opens it a few inches, and listens*): He's going. He's not going to give him the letter. Oh, no, no, it couldn't possibly happen. (*Opens the door a little wider.*) What's he doing? Standing outside the front door. He's not going downstairs. Is he changing his mind? Yes, he—!

(*A letter falls into the letter-box. Krogstad's footsteps die away down the stairs.*)

NORA (*with a stifled cry, runs across the room towards the table by the sofa. A pause*): In the letter-box. (*Steals timidly over towards the hall door.*)

1510   There it is! Oh, Torvald, Torvald! Now we're lost!

MRS. LINDE (*enters from the nursery with Nora's costume*): Well, I've done the best I can. Shall we see how it looks—?

NORA (*whispers hoarsely*): Christine, come here.

MRS. LINDE (*throws the dress on the sofa*): What's wrong with you? You look as though you'd seen a ghost!

NORA: Come here. Do you see that letter? There—look—through the glass of the letter-box.

MRS. LINDE: Yes, yes, I see it.

NORA: That letter's from Krogstad—

1520 MRS. LINDE: Nora! It was Krogstad who lent you the money!

NORA: Yes. And now Torvald's going to discover everything.

MRS. LINDE: Oh, believe me, Nora, it'll be best for you both.

NORA: You don't know what's happened. I've committed a forgery—

MRS. LINDE: But, for heaven's sake—!

NORA: Christine, all I want is for you to be my witness.

MRS. LINDE: What do you mean? Witness what?

NORA: If I should go out of my mind—and it might easily happen—

MRS. LINDE: Nora!

NORA: Or if anything else should happen to me—so that I wasn't here

1530 any longer—

MRS. LINDE: Nora, Nora, you don't know what you're saying!

NORA: If anyone should try to take the blame, and say it was all his fault—you understand—?

MRS. LINDE: Yes, yes—but how can you think—?

NORA: Then you must testify that it isn't true, Christine. I'm not mad— I know exactly what I'm saying—and I'm telling you, no one else knows anything about this. I did it entirely on my own. Remember that.

MRS. LINDE: All right. But I simply don't understand—

NORA: Oh, how could you understand? A—miracle—is about to happen.

1540 MRS. LINDE: Miracle?

NORA: Yes. A miracle. But it's so frightening, Christine. It *mustn't* happen, not for anything in the world.

MRS. LINDE: I'll go over and talk to Krogstad.

NORA: Don't go near him. He'll only do something to hurt you.

MRS. LINDE: Once upon a time he'd have done anything for my sake.

NORA: He?

MRS. LINDE: Where does he live?

NORA: Oh, how should I know—? Oh, yes, wait a moment—(*Feels in her pocket.*) Here's his card. But the letter, the letter—!

1550 HELMER (*in his study, knocks on the door*): Nora!

NORA (*cries in alarm*): What is it?

HELMER: Now, now, don't get alarmed. We're not coming in; you've closed the door. Are you trying on your costume?

NORA: Yes, yes—I'm trying on my costume. I'm going to look so pretty for you, Torvald.

MRS. LINDE (*who has been reading the card*): Why, he lives just around the corner.

NORA: Yes; but it's no use. There's nothing to be done now. The letter's lying there in the box.

1560   MRS. LINDE: And your husband has the key?

NORA: Yes, he always keeps it.

MRS. LINDE: Krogstad must ask him to send the letter back unread. He
must find some excuse—

NORA: But Torvald always opens the box at just about this time—

MRS. LINDE: You must stop him. Go in and keep him talking. I'll be back
as quickly as I can.

(She hurries out through the hall.)

NORA *(goes over to Helmer's door, opens it and peeps in):* Torvald!

1570   HELMER *(offstage):* Well, may a man enter his own drawing room again?
Come on, Rank, now we'll see what—*(In the doorway.)* But what's this?

NORA: What, Torvald dear?

HELMER: Rank's been preparing me for some great transformation scene.

RANK *(in the doorway):* So I understood. But I seem to have been mistaken.

NORA: Yes, no one's to be allowed to see me before tomorrow night.

HELMER: But, my dear Nora, you look quite worn out. Have you been
practicing too hard?

NORA: No, I haven't practiced at all yet.

HELMER: Well, you must.

NORA: Yes, Torvald, I must, I know. But I can't get anywhere without
your help. I've completely forgotten everything.

1580   HELMER: Oh, we'll soon put that to rights.

NORA: Yes, help me, Torvald. Promise me you will? Oh, I'm so nervous.
All those people—! You must forget everything except me this
evening. You mustn't think of business—I won't even let you touch a
pen. Promise me, Torvald?

HELMER: I promise. This evening I shall think of nothing but you—
my poor, helpless little darling. Oh, there's just one thing I must see
to—*(Goes toward the hall door.)*

NORA: What do you want out there?

HELMER: I'm only going to see if any letters have come.

NORA: No, Torvald, no!

HELMER: Why, what's the matter?

1590   NORA: Torvald, I beg you. There's nothing there.

HELMER: Well, I'll just make sure.

*(He moves towards the door. Nora runs to the piano and plays the first bar of
the tarantella.)*

HELMER *(at the door, turns):* Aha!

NORA: I can't dance tomorrow if I don't practice with you now.

HELMER *(goes over to her):* Are you really so frightened, Nora dear?

NORA: Yes, terribly frightened. Let me start practicing now, at once—
we've still time before dinner. Oh, do sit down and play for me,
Torvald dear. Correct me, lead me, the way you always do.

1600   HELMER: Very well, my dear, if you wish it.

(He sits down at the piano. Nora seizes the tambourine and a long multicolored shawl from the cardboard box, wraps the latter hastily around her, then takes a quick leap into the center of the room.)

NORA: Play for me! I want to dance!

(Helmer plays and Nora dances. Dr. Rank stands behind Helmer at the piano and watches her.)

HELMER: Slower, slower!

NORA: I can't!

HELMER: Not so violently, Nora.

NORA: I must!

HELMER *(stops playing):* No, no, this won't do at all.

NORA *(laughs and swings her tambourine):* Isn't that what I told you?

RANK: Let me play for her.

HELMER *(gets up):* Yes, would you? Then it'll be easier for me to show her.

(Rank sits down at the piano and plays. Nora dances more and more wildly. Helmer has stationed himself by the stove and tries repeatedly to correct her but she seems not to hear him. Her hair works loose and falls over her shoulders; she ignores it and continues to dance. Mrs. Linde enters.)

1610 MRS. LINDE *(stands in the doorway as though tongue-tied):* Ah—!

NORA *(as she dances):* Oh, Christine, we're having such fun!

HELMER: But, Nora darling, you're dancing as if your life depended on it.

NORA: It does.

HELMER: Rank, stop it! This is sheer lunacy. Stop it, I say!

(Rank ceases playing. Nora suddenly stops dancing.)

HELMER *(goes over to her):* I'd never have believed it. You've forgotten
    everything I taught you.

NORA *(throws away the tambourine):* You see!

HELMER: I'll have to show you every step.

NORA: You see how much I need you! You must show me every step of
1620   the way. Right to the end of the dance. Promise me you will, Torvald?

HELMER: Never fear. I will.

NORA: You mustn't think about anything but me—today or tomorrow.
    Don't open any letters—don't even open the letter-box—

HELMER: Aha, you're still worried about that fellow—

NORA: Oh, yes, yes, him too.

HELMER: Nora, I can tell from the way you're behaving, there's a letter
    from him already lying there.

NORA: I don't know. I think so. But you mustn't read it now. I don't
    want anything ugly to come between us till it's all over.

1630 RANK *(quietly, to Helmer):* Better give her her way.

HELMER *(puts his arm round her):* My child shall have her way. But tomor-
    row night, when your dance is over—

NORA: Then you will be free.

MAID (*appears in the doorway, right*): Dinner is served, madam.

NORA: Put out some champagne, Helen.

MAID: Very good, madam. *(Goes.)*

HELMER: I say! What's this, a banquet?

NORA: We'll drink champagne until dawn! *(Calls.)* And, Helen! Put out some macaroons! Lots of macaroons—for once!

1640 HELMER (*takes her hands in his*): Now, now, now. Don't get so excited. Where's my little songbird, the one I know?

NORA: All right. Go and sit down—and you too, Dr. Rank. I'll be with you in a minute. Christine, you must help me put my hair up.

RANK (*quietly, as they go*): There's nothing wrong, is there? I mean, she isn't—er—expecting—?

HELMER: Good heavens no, my dear chap. She just gets scared like a child sometimes—I told you before—

(They go out right.)

NORA: Well?

MRS. LINDE: He's left town.

1650 NORA: I saw it from your face.

MRS. LINDE: He'll be back tomorrow evening. I left a note for him.

NORA: You needn't have bothered. You can't stop anything now. Anyway, it's wonderful really, in a way—sitting here and waiting for the miracle to happen.

MRS. LINDE: Waiting for what?

NORA: Oh, you wouldn't understand. Go in and join them. I'll be with you in a moment.

(Mrs. Linde goes into the dining-room.)

NORA (*stands for a moment as though collecting herself. Then she looks at her watch*): Five o'clock. Seven hours till midnight. Then another twenty-

1660 four hours till midnight tomorrow. And then the tarantella will be finished. Twenty-four and seven? Thirty-one hours to live.

HELMER (*appears in the doorway, right*): What's happened to my little songbird?

NORA (*runs to him with her arms wide*): Your songbird is here!

ACT 3

The same room. The table which was formerly by the sofa has been moved into the center of the room; the chairs surround it as before. The door to the hall stands open. Dance music can be heard from the floor above. Mrs. Linde is seated at the table, absent-mindedly glancing through a book. She is trying to read, but seems unable to keep her mind on it. More than once she turns and listens anxiously towards the front door.

MRS. LINDE (*looks at her watch*): Not here yet. There's not much time left. Please God he hasn't—! *(Listens again.)* Ah, here he is. (*Goes out into the hall and cautiously opens the front door. Footsteps can be heard softly ascending the stairs. She whispers.)* Come in. There's no one here.

KROGSTAD (*in the doorway*): I found a note from you at my lodgings. What does this mean?

MRS. LINDE: I must speak with you.

KROGSTAD: Oh? And must our conversation take place in this house?

MRS. LINDE: We couldn't meet at my place; my room has no separate entrance. Come in. We're quite alone. The maid's asleep, and the Helmers are at the dance upstairs.

KROGSTAD (*comes into the room*): Well, well! So the Helmers are dancing this evening? Are they indeed?

MRS. LINDE: Yes. Why not?

KROGSTAD: True enough. Why not?

MRS. LINDE: Well, Krogstad. You and I must have a talk together.

KROGSTAD: Have we two anything further to discuss?

MRS. LINDE: We have a great deal to discuss.

KROGSTAD: I wasn't aware of it.

MRS. LINDE: That's because you've never really understood me.

KROGSTAD: Was there anything to understand? It's the old story, isn't it—a woman chucking a man because something better turns up?

MRS. LINDE: Do you really think I'm so utterly heartless? You think it was easy for me to give you up?

KROGSTAD: Wasn't it?

MRS. LINDE: Oh, Nils, did you really believe that?

KROGSTAD: Then why did you write to me the way you did?

MRS. LINDE: I had to. Since I had to break with you, I thought it my duty to destroy all the feelings you had for me.

KROGSTAD (*clenches his fists*): So that was it. And you did this for money!

MRS. LINDE: You mustn't forget I had a helpless mother to take care of, and two little brothers. We couldn't wait for you, Nils. It would have been so long before you'd had enough to support us.

KROGSTAD: Maybe. But you had no right to cast me off for someone else.

MRS. LINDE: Perhaps not. I've often asked myself that.

KROGSTAD (*more quietly*): When I lost you, it was just as though all solid ground had been swept from under my feet. Look at me. Now I am a shipwrecked man clinging to a spar.

MRS. LINDE: Help may be near at hand.

KROGSTAD: It was near. But then you came, and stood between it and me.

MRS. LINDE: I didn't know, Nils. No one told me till today that this job I'd found was yours.

KROGSTAD: I believe you, since you say so. But now you know, won't you give it up?

MRS. LINDE: No—because it wouldn't help you even if I did.

KROGSTAD: Wouldn't it? I'd do it all the same.

MRS. LINDE: I've learned to look at things practically. Life and poverty have taught me that.

KROGSTAD: And life has taught me to distrust fine words.

MRS. LINDE: Then it's taught you a useful lesson. But surely you still believe in actions?

KROGSTAD: What do you mean?

MRS. LINDE: You said you were like a shipwrecked man clinging to a spar.

KROGSTAD: I have good reason to say it.

MRS. LINDE: I'm in the same position as you. No one to care about, no
1720   one to care for.

KROGSTAD: You made your own choice.

MRS. LINDE: I had no choice—then.

KROGSTAD: Well?

MRS. LINDE: Nils, suppose we two shipwrecked souls could join hands?

KROGSTAD: What are you saying?

MRS. LINDE: Castaways have a better chance of survival together than on their own.

KROGSTAD: Christine!

MRS. LINDE: Why do you suppose I came to this town?

1730   KROGSTAD: You mean—you came because of me?

MRS. LINDE: I must work if I'm to find life worth living. I've always worked, for as long as I can remember; it's been the greatest joy of my life—my only joy. But now I'm alone in the world, and I feel so dreadfully lost and empty. There's no joy in working just for oneself. Oh, Nils, give me something—someone—to work for.

KROGSTAD: I don't believe all that. You're just being hysterical and romantic. You want to find an excuse for self-sacrifice.

MRS. LINDE: Have you ever known me to be hysterical?

KROGSTAD: You mean you really—? Is it possible? Tell me—you know
1740   all about my past?

MRS. LINDE: Yes.

KROGSTAD: And you know what people think of me here?

MRS. LINDE: You said just now that with me you might have become a different person.

KROGSTAD: I know I could have.

MRS. LINDE: Couldn't it still happen?

KROGSTAD: Christine—do you really mean this? Yes—you do—I see it in your face. Have you really the courage—?

MRS. LINDE: I need someone to be a mother to; and your children need
1750   a mother. And you and I need each other. I believe in you, Nils. I am afraid of nothing—with you.

KROGSTAD (*clasps her hands*): Thank you, Christine—thank you! Now I shall make the world believe in me as you do! Oh—but I'd forgotten—

MRS. LINDE (*listens*): Ssh! The tarantella! Go quickly, go!

KROGSTAD: Why? What is it?

MRS. LINDE: You hear that dance? As soon as it's finished, they'll be coming down.

KROGSTAD: All right, I'll go. It's no good, Christine. I'd forgotten—you don't know what I've just done to the Helmers.

1760 MRS. LINDE: Yes, Nils. I know.

KROGSTAD: And yet you'd still have the courage to—?

MRS. LINDE: I know what despair can drive a man like you to.

KROGSTAD: Oh, if only I could undo this!

MRS. LINDE: You can. Your letter is still lying in the box.

KROGSTAD: Are you sure?

MRS. LINDE: Quite sure. But—

KROGSTAD (*looks searchingly at her*): Is that why you're doing this? You want to save your friend at any price? Tell me the truth. Is that the reason?

MRS. LINDE: Nils, a woman who has sold herself once for the sake of oth-
1770 ers doesn't make the same mistake again.

KROGSTAD: I shall demand my letter back.

MRS. LINDE: No, no.

KROGSTAD: Of course I shall. I shall stay here till Helmer comes down. I'll tell him he must give me back my letter—I'll say it was only to do with my dismissal, and that I don't want him to read it—

MRS. LINDE: No, Nils, you mustn't ask for that letter back.

KROGSTAD: But—tell me—wasn't that the real reason you asked me to come here?

MRS. LINDE: Yes—at first, when I was frightened. But a day has passed
1780 since then, and in that time I've seen incredible things happen in this house. Helmer must know the truth. This unhappy secret of Nora's must be revealed. They must come to a full understanding; there must be an end of all these shiftings and evasions.

KROGSTAD: Very well. If you're prepared to risk it. But one thing I can do—and at once—

MRS. LINDE (*listens*): Hurry! Go, go! The dance is over. We aren't safe here another moment.

KROGSTAD: I'll wait for you downstairs.

MRS. LINDE: Yes, do. You can see me home.

1790 KROGSTAD: I've never been so happy in my life before!

(*He goes out through the front door. The door leading from the room into the hall remains open.*)

MRS. LINDE (*tidies the room a little and gets her hat and coat*): What a change! Oh, what a change! Someone to work for—to live for! A home to bring joy into! I won't let this chance of happiness slip through my fingers. Oh, why don't they come? (*Listens.*) Ah, here they are. I must get my coat on.

(*She takes her hat and coat. Helmer's and Nora's voices become audible outside. A key is turned in the lock and Helmer leads Nora almost forcibly into the hall. She is dressed in an Italian costume with a large black shawl. He is in evening dress, with a black cloak.*)

NORA (*still in the doorway, resisting him*): No, no, no—not in here! I want to go back upstairs. I don't want to leave so early.

HELMER: But my dearest Nora—

NORA: Oh, please, Torvald, please! Just another hour!

1800   HELMER: Not another minute, Nora, my sweet. You know what we
agreed. Come along, now. Into the drawing-room. You'll catch cold
if you stay out here.

(He leads her, despite her efforts to resist him, gently into the room.)

MRS. LINDE: Good evening.

NORA: Christine!

HELMER: Oh, hullo, Mrs. Linde. You still here?

MRS. LINDE: Please forgive me. I did so want to see Nora in her costume.

NORA: Have you been sitting here waiting for me?

MRS. LINDE: Yes. I got here too late, I'm afraid. You'd already gone up.
And I felt I really couldn't go back home without seeing you.

1810   HELMER (*takes off Nora's shawl*): Well, take a good look at her. She's
worth looking at, don't you think? Isn't she beautiful, Mrs. Linde?

MRS. LINDE: Oh, yes, indeed—

HELMER: Isn't she unbelievably beautiful? Everyone at the party said so.
But dreadfully stubborn she is, bless her pretty little heart. What's to
be done about that? Would you believe it, I practically had to use
force to get her away!

NORA: Oh, Torvald, you're going to regret not letting me stay—just
half an hour longer.

HELMER: Hear that, Mrs. Linde? She dances her tarantella—makes a
1820   roaring success—and very well deserved—though possibly a trifle
too realistic—more so than was aesthetically necessary, strictly speaking. But never mind that. Main thing is—she had a success—roaring
success. Was I going to let her stay on after that and spoil the impression? No, thank you. I took my beautiful little Capri signorina—my
capricious little Capricienne, what?—under my arm—a swift round
of the ballroom, a curtsey to the company, and, as they say in novels,
the beautiful apparition disappeared! An exit should always be dramatic, Mrs. Linde. But unfortunately that's just what I can't get Nora
to realize. I say, it's hot in here. (*Throws his cloak on a chair and opens*
1830   *the door to his study.*) What's this? It's dark in here. Ah, yes, of
course—excuse me. (*Goes in and lights a couple of candles.*)

NORA (*whispers swiftly, breathlessly*): Well?

MRS. LINDE (*quietly*): I've spoken to him.

NORA: Yes?

MRS. LINDE: Nora—you must tell your husband everything.

NORA (*dully*): I knew it.

MRS. LINDE: You've nothing to fear from Krogstad. But you must tell him.

NORA: I shan't tell him anything.

MRS. LINDE: Then the letter will.

1840   NORA: Thank you, Christine. Now I know what I must do. Ssh!

HELMER (*returns*): Well, Mrs. Linde, finished admiring her?

MRS. LINDE: Yes. Now I must say goodnight.

HELMER: Oh, already? Does this knitting belong to you?

MRS. LINDE *(takes it):* Thank you, yes. I nearly forgot it.

HELMER: You knit, then?

MRS. LINDE: Why, yes.

HELMER: Know what? You ought to take up embroidery.

MRS. LINDE: Oh? Why?

HELMER: It's much prettier. Watch me, now. You hold the embroidery in
1850   your left hand, like this, and then you take the needle in your right
hand and go in and out in a slow, steady movement—like this. I am
right, aren't I?

MRS. LINDE: Yes, I'm sure—

HELMER: But knitting, now—that's an ugly business—can't help it.
Look—arms all huddled up—great clumsy needles going up and
down—make you look like a damned Chinaman. I say, that really was
a magnificent champagne they served us.

MRS. LINDE: Well, good night, Nora. And stop being stubborn. Remember!

HELMER: Quite right, Mrs. Linde!

1860   MRS. LINDE: Good night, Mr. Helmer.

HELMER *(accompanies her to the door):* Good night, good night! I hope
you'll manage to get home all right? I'd gladly—but you haven't far
to go, have you? Good night, good night. *(She goes. He closes the door
behind her and returns.)* Well, we've got rid of her at last. Dreadful
bore that woman is!

NORA: Aren't you very tired, Torvald?

HELMER: No, not in the least.

NORA: Aren't you sleepy?

HELMER: Not a bit. On the contrary, I feel extraordinarily exhilarated.
1870   But what about you? Yes, you look very sleepy and tired.

NORA: Yes, I am very tired. Soon I shall sleep.

HELMER: You see, you see! How right I was not to let you stay longer!

NORA: Oh, you're always right, whatever you do.

HELMER *(kisses her on the forehead):* Now my little songbird's talking just
like a real big human being. I say, did you notice how cheerful Rank
was this evening?

NORA: Oh? Was he? I didn't have a chance to speak with him.

HELMER: I hardly did. But I haven't seen him in such a jolly mood for
ages. *(Looks at her for a moment, then comes closer.)* I say, it's nice to get
1880   back to one's home again, and be all alone with you. Upon my word,
you're a distractingly beautiful young woman.

NORA: Don't look at me like that, Torvald!

HELMER: What, not look at my most treasured possession? At all this
wonderful beauty that's mine, mine alone, all mine.

NORA *(goes round to the other side of the table):* You mustn't talk to me
like that tonight.

HELMER *(follows her):* You've still the tarantella in your blood, I see. And
that makes you even more desirable. Listen! Now the other guests

are beginning to go. *(More quietly.)* Nora—soon the whole house will
1890   be absolutely quiet.

NORA: Yes, I hope so.

HELMER: Yes, my beloved Nora, of course you do! Do you know—when
I'm out with you among other people like we were tonight, do you
know why I say so little to you, why I keep so aloof from you, and
just throw you an occasional glance? Do you know why I do that?
It's because I pretend to myself that you're my secret mistress, my
clandestine little sweetheart, and that nobody knows there's anything at all between us.

NORA: Oh, yes, yes, yes—I know you never think of anything but me.

1900   HELMER: And then when we're about to go, and I wrap the shawl round
your lovely young shoulders, over this wonderful curve of your
neck—then I pretend to myself that you are my young bride, that
we've just come from the wedding, that I'm taking you to my house
for the first time—that, for the first time, I am alone with you—quite
alone with you, as you stand there young and trembling and beautiful. All evening I've had no eyes for anyone but you. When I saw you
dance the tarantella, like a huntress, a temptress, my blood grew hot,
I couldn't stand it any longer! That was why I seized you and
dragged you down here with me—

1910   NORA: Leave me, Torvald! Get away from me! I don't want all this.

HELMER: What? Now, Nora, you're joking with me. Don't want, don't
want—? Aren't I your husband—?

(There is a knock on the front door.)

NORA *(starts):* What was that?

HELMER *(goes toward the hall):* Who is it?

RANK *(outside):* It's me. May I come in for a moment?

HELMER *(quietly, annoyed):* Oh, what does he want now? *(Calls.)* Wait a
moment. *(Walks over and opens the door.)* Well! Nice of you not to go by
without looking in.

RANK: I thought I heard your voice, so I felt I had to say goodbye. *(His*
1920   *eyes travel swiftly around the room.)* Ah, yes—these dear rooms, how well
I know them. What a happy, peaceful home you two have.

HELMER: You seemed to be having a pretty happy time yourself
upstairs.

RANK: Indeed I did. Why not? Why shouldn't one make the most of
this world? As much as one can, and for as long as one can. The
wine was excellent—

HELMER: Especially the champagne.

RANK: You noticed that too? It's almost incredible how much I managed to get down.

1930   NORA: Torvald drank a lot of champagne too, this evening.

RANK: Oh?

NORA: Yes. It always makes him merry afterwards.

RANK: Well, why shouldn't a man have a merry evening after a well-spent day?

HELMER: Well-spent? Oh, I don't know that I can claim that.

RANK (*slaps him across the back*): I can, though, my dear fellow!

NORA: Yes, of course, Dr. Rank—you've been carrying out a scientific experiment today, haven't you?

RANK: Exactly.

1940 HELMER: Scientific experiment! Those are big words for my little Nora to use!

NORA: And may I congratulate you on the finding?

RANK: You may indeed.

NORA: It was good, then?

RANK: The best possible finding—both for the doctor and the patient. Certainty.

NORA (*quickly*): Certainty?

RANK: Absolute certainty. So aren't I entitled to have a merry evening after that?

1950 NORA: Yes, Dr. Rank. You were quite right to.

HELMER: I agree. Provided you don't have to regret it tomorrow.

RANK: Well, you never get anything in this life without paying for it.

NORA: Dr. Rank—you like masquerades, don't you?

RANK: Yes, if the disguises are sufficiently amusing.

NORA: Tell me. What shall we two wear at the next masquerade?

HELMER: You little gadabout! Are you thinking about the next one already?

RANK: We two? Yes, I'll tell you. You must go as the Spirit of Happiness—

1960 HELMER: You try to think of a costume that'll convey that.

RANK: Your wife need only appear as her normal, everyday self—

HELMER: Quite right! Well said! But what are you going to be? Have you decided that?

RANK: Yes, my dear friend. I have decided that.

HELMER: Well?

RANK: At the next masquerade, I shall be invisible.

HELMER: Well, that's a funny idea.

RANK: There's a big, black hat—haven't you heard of the invisible hat? Once it's over your head, no one can see you any more.

1970 HELMER (*represses a smile*): Ah yes, of course.

RANK: But I'm forgetting what I came for. Helmer, give me a cigar. One of your black Havanas.

HELMER: With the greatest pleasure. (*Offers him the box.*)

RANK (*takes one and cuts off the tip*): Thank you.

NORA (*strikes a match*): Let me give you a light.

RANK: Thank you. (*She holds out the match for him. He lights his cigar.*) And now—goodbye.

HELMER: Goodbye, my dear chap, goodbye.

NORA: Sleep well, Dr. Rank.

1980   RANK: Thank you for that kind wish.

NORA: Wish me the same.

RANK: You? Very well—since you ask. Sleep well. And thank you for the light. *(He nods to them both and goes.)*

HELMER *(quietly):* He's been drinking too much.

NORA *(abstractedly):* Perhaps.

(Helmer takes his bunch of keys from his pocket and goes out into the hall.)

NORA: Torvald, what do you want out there?

HELMER: I must empty the letter-box. It's absolutely full. There'll be no room for the newspapers in the morning.

NORA: Are you going to work tonight?

1990   HELMER: You know very well I'm not. Hullo, what's this? Someone's been at the lock.

NORA: At the lock—?

HELMER: Yes, I'm sure of it. Who on earth—? Surely not one of the maids? Here's a broken hairpin. Nora, it's yours—

NORA *(quickly):* Then it must have been the children.

HELMER: Well, you'll have to break them of that habit. Hm, hm. Ah, that's done it. *(Takes out the contents of the box and calls into the kitchen.)* Helen! Put out the light on the staircase. *(Comes back into the drawing-room with the letters in his hand and closes the door to the hall.)* Look at

2000   this! You see how they've piled up? *(Glances through them.)* What on earth's this?

NORA *(at the window):* The letter! Oh, no, Torvald no!

HELMER: Two visiting cards—from Rank.

NORA: From Dr. Rank?

HELMER *(looks at them):* Peter Rank, M.D. They were on top. He must have dropped them in as he left.

NORA: Has he written anything on them?

HELMER: There's a black cross above his name. Look. Rather gruesome, isn't it? It looks just as though he was announcing his death.

2010   NORA: He is.

HELMER: What? Do you know something? Has he told you anything?

NORA: Yes. When these cards come, it means he's said goodbye to us. He wants to shut himself up in his house and die.

HELMER: Ah, poor fellow. I knew I wouldn't be seeing him for much longer. But so soon—! And now he's going to slink away and hide like a wounded beast.

NORA: When the time comes, it's best to go silently. Don't you think so, Torvald?

HELMER *(walks up and down):* He was so much a part of our life. I can't

2020   realize that he's gone. His suffering and loneliness seemed to pro- vide a dark background to the happy sunlight of our marriage. Well, perhaps it's best this way. For him, anyway. *(Stops walking.)* And per-

haps for us too, Nora. Now we have only each other. (*Embraces her.*)
Oh, my beloved wife—I feel as though I could never hold you close
enough. Do you know, Nora, often I wish some terrible danger
might threaten you, so that I could offer my life and my blood,
everything, for your sake.

NORA (*tears herself loose and says in a clear, firm voice*): Read your letters
now, Torvald.

2030   HELMER: No, no. Not tonight. Tonight I want to be with you, my darling
wife—

NORA: When your friend is about to die—?

HELMER: You're right. This news has upset us both. An ugliness has
come between us; thoughts of death and dissolution. We must try to
forget them. Until then—you go to your room; I shall go to mine.

NORA (*throws her arms round his neck*): Good night, Torvald! Good night!

HELMER (*kisses her on the forehead*): Good night, my darling little songbird. Sleep well, Nora. I'll go and read my letters.

(*He goes into the study with the letters in his hand, and closes the door.*)

NORA (*wild-eyed, fumbles around, seizes Helmer's cloak, throws it round
2040   herself and whispers quickly, hoarsely*): Never see him again. Never.
Never. Never. (*Throws the shawl over her head.*) Never see the children
again. Them too. Never. Never. Oh—the icy black water! Oh—that
bottomless—that—! Oh, if only it were all over! Now he's got it—
he's reading it. Oh, no, no! Not yet! Goodbye, Torvald! Goodbye,
my darlings!

(*She turns to run into the hall. As she does so, Helmer throws open his door
and stands there with an open letter in his hand.*)

HELMER: Nora!

NORA (*shrieks*): Ah—!

HELMER: What is this? Do you know what is in this letter?

NORA: Yes, I know. Let me go! Let me go!

2050   HELMER (*holds her back*): Go? Where?

NORA (*tries to tear herself loose*): You mustn't try to save me, Torvald!

HELMER (*staggers back*): Is it true? Is it true, what he writes? Oh, my God!
No, no—it's impossible, it can't be true!

NORA: It *is* true. I've loved you more than anything else in the world.

HELMER: Oh, don't try to make silly excuses.

NORA (*takes a step toward him*): Torvald—

HELMER: Wretched woman! What have you done?

NORA: Let me go! You're not going to suffer for my sake. I won't let you!

HELMER: Stop being theatrical. (*Locks the front door.*) You're going to stay
2060   here and explain yourself. Do you understand what you've done?
Answer me! Do you understand?

NORA (*looks unflinchingly at him and, her expression growing colder, says*):
Yes. Now I am beginning to understand.

HELMER (*walking around the room*): Oh, what a dreadful awakening! For eight whole years—she who was my joy and my pride—a hypocrite, a liar—worse, worse—a criminal! Oh, the hideousness of it! Shame on you, shame!

(*Nora is silent and stares unblinkingly at him.*)

HELMER (*stops in front of her*): I ought to have guessed that something of this sort would happen. I should have foreseen it. All your father's recklessness and instability—be quiet!—I repeat, all your father's recklessness and instability he had handed on to you. No religion, no morals, no sense of duty! Oh, how I have been punished for closing my eyes to his faults! I did it for your sake. And now you reward me like this.

NORA: Yes. Like this.

HELMER: Now you have destroyed all my happiness. You have ruined my whole future. Oh, it's too dreadful to contemplate! I am in the power of a man who is completely without scruples. He can do what he likes with me, demand what he pleases, order me to do anything—I dare not disobey him. I am condemned to humiliation and ruin simply for the weakness of a woman.

NORA: When I am gone from this world, you will be free.

HELMER: Oh, don't be melodramatic. Your father was always ready with that kind of remark. How would it help me if you were "gone from this world," as you put it? It wouldn't assist me in the slightest. He can still make all the facts public; and if he does, I may quite easily be suspected of having been an accomplice in your crime. People may think that I was behind it—that it was I who encouraged you! And for all this I have to thank you, you whom I have carried on my hands through all the years of our marriage! Now do you realize what you've done to me?

NORA (*coldly calm*): Yes.

HELMER: It's so unbelievable I can hardly credit it. But we must try to find some way out. Take off that shawl. Take it off, I say! I must try to buy him off somehow. This thing must be hushed up at any price. As regards our relationship—we must appear to be living together just as before. Only *appear*, of course. You will therefore continue to reside here. That is understood. But the children shall be taken out of your hands. I dare no longer entrust them to you. Oh, to have to say this to the woman I once loved so dearly—and whom I still—! Well, all that must be finished. Henceforth there can be no question of happiness; we must merely strive to save what shreds and tatters— (*The front bell rings. Helmer starts.*) What can that be? At this hour? Surely not—? He wouldn't—? Hide yourself, Nora. Say you're ill.

(*Nora does not move. Helmer goes to the door of the room and opens it. The maid is standing half-dressed in the hall.*)

MAID: A letter for madam.

HELMER: Give it to me. *(Seizes the letter and shuts the door.)* Yes, it's from
    him. You're not having it. I'll read this myself.

NORA: Read it.

HELMER *(by the lamp):* I hardly dare to. This may mean the end for us
2110   both. No, I must know. *(Tears open the letter hastily; reads a few lines;*
    looks at a piece of paper which is enclosed with it; utters a cry of joy.) Nora!
    (She looks at him questioningly.) Nora! No—I must read it once more.
    Yes, yes, it's true! I am saved! Nora, I am saved!

NORA: What about me?

HELMER: You too, of course. We're both saved, you and I. Look! He's
    returning your I.O.U. He writes that he is sorry for what has hap-
    pened—a happy accident has changed his life—oh, what does it
    matter what he writes? We are saved, Nora! No one can harm you
    now. Oh, Nora, Nora—no, first let me destroy this filthy thing. Let
2120   me see—! *(Glances at the I.O.U.)* No, I don't want to look at it. I shall
    merely regard the whole business as a dream. *(He tears the I.O.U.*
    and both letters into pieces, throws them into the stove, and watches them
    burn.) There. Now they're destroyed. He wrote that ever since
    Christmas Eve you've been—oh, these must have been three dread-
    ful days for you, Nora.

NORA: Yes. It's been a hard fight.

HELMER: It must have been terrible—seeing no way out except—no,
    we'll forget the whole sordid business. We'll just be happy and go on
    telling ourselves over and over again: "It's over! It's over!" Listen to
2130   me, Nora. You don't seem to realize. It's over! Why are you looking so
    pale? Ah, my poor little Nora, I understand. You can't believe that I
    have forgiven you. But I have, Nora. I swear it to you. I have forgiven
    you everything. I know that what you did you did for your love of me.

NORA: That is true.

HELMER: You have loved me as a wife should love her husband. It was
    simply that in your inexperience you chose the wrong means. But
    do you think I love you any the less because you don't know how
    to act on your own initiative? No, no. Just lean on me. I shall coun-
    sel you. I shall guide you. I would not be a true man if your femi-
2140   nine helplessness did not make you doubly attractive in my eyes.
    You mustn't mind the hard words I said to you in those first dread-
    ful moments when my whole world seemed to be tumbling about
    my ears. I have forgiven you, Nora. I swear it to you; I have for-
    given you.

NORA: Thank you for your forgiveness.

(She goes out through the door, right.)

HELMER: No, don't go—*(Looks in.)* What are you doing there?

NORA *(offstage):* Taking off my fancy dress.

HELMER *(by the open door):* Yes, do that. Try to calm yourself and get your
    balance again, my frightened little songbird. Don't be afraid. I have
2150   broad wings to shield you. *(Begins to walk around near the door.)* How

lovely and peaceful this little home of ours is, Nora. You are safe here;
I shall watch over you like a hunted dove which I have snatched
unharmed from the claws of the falcon. Your wildly beating little heart
shall find peace with me. It will happen, Nora; it will take time, but it
will happen, believe me. Tomorrow all this will seem quite different.
Soon everything will be as it was before. I shall no longer need to
remind you that I have forgiven you; your own heart will tell you that
it is true. Do you really think I could ever bring myself to disown you,
or even to reproach you? Ah, Nora, you don't understand what goes

2160   on in a husband's heart. There is something indescribably wonderful
and satisfying for a husband in knowing that he has forgiven his wife—
forgiven her unreservedly, from the bottom of his heart. It means that
she has become his property in a double sense; he has, as it were,
brought her into the world anew; she is now not only his wife but also
his child. From now on that is what you shall be to me, my poor, helpless, bewildered little creature. Never be frightened of anything again,
Nora. Just open your heart to me. I shall be both your will and your
conscience. What's this? Not in bed? Have you changed?

NORA (*in her everyday dress*): Yes, Torvald. I've changed.

2170 HELMER: But why now—so late—?

NORA: I shall not sleep tonight.

HELMER: But, my dear Nora—

NORA (*looks at her watch*): It isn't that late. Sit down here, Torvald. You
and I have a lot to talk about.

(*She sits down on one side of the table.*)

HELMER: Nora, what does this mean? You look quite drawn—

NORA: Sit down. It's going to take a long time. I've a lot to say to you.

HELMER (*sits down on the other side of the table*): You alarm me, Nora. I
don't understand you.

NORA: No, that's just it. You don't understand me. And I've never

2180   understood you—until this evening. No, don't interrupt me. Just listen to what I have to say. You and I have got to face facts, Torvald.

HELMER: What do you mean by that?

NORA (*after a short silence*): Doesn't anything strike you about the way
we're sitting here?

HELMER: What?

NORA: We've been married for eight years. Does it occur to you that this
is the first time that we two, you and I, man and wife, have ever had a
serious talk together?

HELMER: Serious? What do you mean, serious?

2190 NORA: In eight whole years—no, longer—ever since we first met—we
have never exchanged a serious word on a serious subject.

HELMER: Did you expect me to drag you into all my worries—worries
you couldn't possibly have helped me with?

NORA: I'm not talking about worries. I'm simply saying that we have
never sat down seriously to try to get to the bottom of anything.

HELMER: But, my dear Nora, what on earth has that got to do with you?

NORA: That's just the point. You have never understood me. A great wrong has been done to me, Torvald. First by Papa, and then by you.

HELMER: What? But we two have loved you more than anyone in the world!

NORA (*shakes her head*): You have never loved me. You just thought it was fun to be in love with me.

HELMER: Nora, what kind of a way is this to talk?

NORA: It's the truth, Torvald. When I lived with Papa, he used to tell me what he thought about everything, so that I never had any opinions but his. And if I did have any of my own, I kept them quiet, because he wouldn't have liked them. He called me his little doll, and he played with me just the way I played with my dolls. Then I came here to live in your house.

HELMER: What kind of a way is that to describe our marriage?

NORA (*undisturbed*): I mean, then I passed from Papa's hands into yours. You arranged everything the way you wanted it, so that I simply took over your taste in everything—or pretended I did—I don't really know—I think it was a little of both—first one and then the other. Now I look back on it, it's as if I've been living here like a pauper, from hand to mouth. I performed tricks for you, and you gave me food and drink. But that was how you wanted it. You and Papa have done me a great wrong. It's your fault that I have done nothing with my life.

HELMER: Nora, how can you be so unreasonable and ungrateful? Haven't you been happy here?

NORA: No; never. I used to think I was; but I haven't ever been happy.

HELMER: Not—not happy?

NORA: No. I've just had fun. You've always been very kind to me. But our home has never been anything but a playroom. I've been your doll-wife, just as I used to be Papa's doll-child. And the children have been my dolls. I used to think it was fun when you came in and played with me, just as they think it's fun when I go in and play games with them. That's all our marriage has been, Torvald.

HELMER: There may be a little truth in what you say, though you exaggerate and romanticize. But from now on it'll be different. Playtime is over. Now the time has come for education.

NORA: Whose education? Mine or the children's?

HELMER: Both yours and the children's, my dearest Nora.

NORA: Oh, Torvald, you're not the man to educate me into being the right wife for you.

HELMER: How can you say that?

NORA: And what about me? Am I fit to educate the children?

HELMER: Nora!

NORA: Didn't you say yourself a few minutes ago that you dare not leave them in my charge?

HELMER: In a moment of excitement. Surely you don't think I meant it seriously?

NORA: Yes. You were perfectly right. I'm not fitted to educate them. There's something else I must do first. I must educate myself. And you can't help me with that. It's something I must do by myself. That's why I'm leaving you.

HELMER (*jumps up*): What did you say?

NORA: I must stand on my own feet if I am to find out the truth about myself and about life. So I can't go on living here with you any longer.

2250   HELMER: Nora, Nora!

NORA: I'm leaving you now, at once. Christine will put me up for tonight—

HELMER: You're out of your mind! You can't do this! I forbid you!

NORA: It's no use your trying to forbid me any more. I shall take with me nothing but what is mine. I don't want anything from you, now or ever.

HELMER: What kind of madness is this?

NORA: Tomorrow I shall go home—I mean, to where I was born. It'll be easiest for me to find some kind of job there.

HELMER: But you're blind! You've no experience of the world—

NORA: I must try to get some, Torvald.

2260   HELMER: But to leave your home, your husband, your children! Have you thought what people will say?

NORA: I can't help that. I only know that I must do this.

HELMER: But this is monstrous! Can you neglect your most sacred duties?

NORA: What do you call my most sacred duties?

HELMER: Do I have to tell you? Your duties towards your husband, and your children.

NORA: I have another duty which is equally sacred.

HELMER: You have not. What on earth could that be?

NORA: My duty towards myself.

2270   HELMER: First and foremost you are a wife and a mother.

NORA: I don't believe that any longer. I believe that I am first and foremost a human being, like you—or anyway, that I must try to become one. I know most people think as you do, Torvald, and I know there's something of the sort to be found in books. But I'm no longer prepared to accept what people say and what's written in books. I must think things out for myself, and try to find my own answer.

HELMER: Do you need to ask where your duty lies in your own home? Haven't you an infallible guide in such matters—your religion?

NORA: Oh, Torvald, I don't really know what religion means.

2280   HELMER: What are you saying?

NORA: I only know what Pastor Hansen told me when I went to confirmation. He explained that religion meant this and that. When I get away from all this and can think things out on my own, that's one of the questions I want to look into. I want to find out whether what Pastor Hansen said was right—or anyway, whether it is right for me.

HELMER: But it's unheard of for so young a woman to behave like this! If religion cannot guide you, let me at least appeal to your conscience. I presume you have some moral feelings left? Or—perhaps you haven't? Well, answer me.

2290 NORA: Oh, Torvald, that isn't an easy question to answer. I simply don't know. I don't know where I am in these matters. I only know that these things mean something quite different to me from what they do to you. I've learned now that certain laws are different from what I'd imagined them to be; but I can't accept that such laws can be right. Has a woman really not the right to spare her dying father pain, or save her husband's life? I can't believe that.

HELMER: You're talking like a child. You don't understand how society works.

NORA: No, I don't. But now I intend to learn. I must try to satisfy myself
2300 which is right, society or I.

HELMER: Nora, you're ill; you're feverish. I almost believe you're out of your mind.

NORA: I've never felt so sane and sure in my life.

HELMER: You feel sure that it is right to leave your husband and your children?

NORA: Yes. I do.

HELMER: Then there is only one possible explanation.

NORA: What?

HELMER: That you don't love me any longer.

2310 NORA: No, that's exactly it.

HELMER: Nora! How can you say this to me?

NORA: Oh, Torvald, it hurts me terribly to have to say it, because you've always been so kind to me. But I can't help it. I don't love you any longer.

HELMER (*controlling his emotions with difficulty*): And you feel quite sure about this too?

NORA: Yes, absolutely sure. That's why I can't go on living here any longer.

HELMER: Can you also explain why I have lost your love?

NORA: Yes, I can. It happened this evening, when the miracle failed to
2320 happen. It was then that I realized you weren't the man I'd thought you to be.

HELMER: Explain more clearly. I don't understand you.

NORA: I've waited so patiently, for eight whole years—well, good heavens, I'm not such a fool as to suppose that miracles occur everyday. Then this dreadful thing happened to me, and then I *knew:* "Now the miracle will take place!" When Krogstad's letter was lying out there, it never occurred to me for a moment that you would let that man trample over you. I *knew* that you would say to him: "Publish the facts to the world." And when he had done this—

2330 HELMER: Yes, what then? When I'd exposed my wife's name to shame and scandal—

NORA: Then I was certain that you would step forward and take all the blame on yourself, and say: "I am the one who is guilty!"

HELMER: Nora!

NORA: You're thinking I wouldn't have accepted such a sacrifice from you? No, of course I wouldn't! But what would my word have counted for against yours? That was the miracle I was hoping for, and dreading. And it was to prevent it happening that I wanted to end my life.

HELMER: Nora, I would gladly work for you night and day, and endure

2340 sorrow and hardship for your sake. But no man can be expected to sacrifice his honor, even for the person he loves.

NORA: Millions of women have done it.

HELMER: Oh, you think and talk like a stupid child.

NORA: That may be. But you neither think nor talk like the man I could share my life with. Once you'd got over your fright—and you weren't frightened of what might threaten me, but only of what threatened you—once the danger was past, then as far as you were concerned it was exactly as though nothing had happened. I was your little songbird just as before—your doll whom henceforth you would take particular

2350 care to protect from the world because she was so weak and fragile. *(Gets up.)* Torvald, in that moment I realized that for eight years I had been living here with a complete stranger, and had borne him three children—! Oh, I can't bear to think of it! I could tear myself to pieces!

HELMER *(sadly)*: I see it, I see it. A gulf has indeed opened between us. Oh, but Nora—couldn't it be bridged?

NORA: As I am now, I am no wife for you.

HELMER: I have the strength to change.

NORA: Perhaps—if your doll is taken from you.

HELMER: But to be parted—to be parted from you! No, no, Nora, I can't

2360 conceive of it happening!

NORA *(goes into the room, right)*: All the more necessary that it should happen.

(She comes back with her outdoor things and a small traveling bag, which she puts down on a chair by the table.)

HELMER: Nora, Nora, not now! Wait till tomorrow!

NORA *(puts on her coat)*: I can't spend the night in a strange man's house.

HELMER: But can't we live here as brother and sister, then—?

NORA *(fastens her hat)*: You know quite well it wouldn't last. *(Puts on her shawl.)* Goodbye, Torvald. I don't want to see the children. I know they're in better hands than mine. As I am now, I can be nothing to them.

HELMER: But some time, Nora—some time—?

2370 NORA: How can I tell? I've no idea what will happen to me.

HELMER: But you are my wife, both as you are and as you will be.

NORA: Listen, Torvald. When a wife leaves her husband's house, as I'm doing now, I'm told that according to the law he is freed of any obligations towards her. In any case, I release you from any such obligations. You mustn't feel bound to me in any way, however small, just as I shall not feel bound to you. We must both be quite free. Here is your ring back. Give me mine.

HELMER: That too?

NORA: That too.

2380 HELMER: Here it is.

NORA: Good. Well, now it's over. I'll leave the keys here. The servants know about everything to do with the house—much better than I do. Tomorrow, when I have left town, Christine will come to pack the things I brought here from home. I'll have them sent on after me.

HELMER: This is the end then! Nora, will you never think of me any more?

NORA: Yes, of course. I shall often think of you and the children and this house.

HELMER: May I write to you, Nora?

NORA: No. Never. You mustn't do that.

2390 HELMER: But at least you must let me send you—

NORA: Nothing. Nothing.

HELMER: But if you should need help?—

NORA: I tell you, no. I don't accept things from strangers.

HELMER: Nora—can I never be anything but a stranger to you?

NORA (*picks up her bag*): Oh, Torvald! Then the miracle of miracles would have to happen.

HELMER: The miracle of miracles?

NORA: You and I would both have to change so much that—oh, Torvald, I don't believe in miracles any longer.

2400 HELMER: But I want to believe in them. Tell me. We should have to change so much that—?

NORA: That life together between us two could become a marriage. Goodbye.

(*She goes out through the hall.*)

HELMER (*sinks down on a chair by the door and buries his face in his hands*): Nora! Nora! (*Looks round and gets up.*) Empty! She's gone! (*A hope strikes him.*) The miracle of miracles—?

(*The street door is slammed shut downstairs.*)

Questions for Discussion

Act 1

1. Why does Nora want money for her Christmas gift?

2. When Torvald says, "I wouldn't wish my darling little songbird to be any different from what she is," what are the qualities he admires in Nora?

3. From the opening scene of the play until the last scene, Nora lies to Torvald. Why?

4. In what ways is Christine Linde a **dramatic foil** for Nora?

5. Why has Torvald not made a lot of money as a lawyer? In what ways does the knowledge of his attitude toward clients **foreshadow** his reaction to Nora's revelation?

6. Nora says of Torvald, "he's so proud of being a *man*—it'd be so painful and humiliating for him to know that he owed anything to me." What attitudes does Nora here reveal about male-female relationships?

7. Examine Torvald's statements about Krogstad near the end of Act 1. How do these opinions foreshadow Torvald's reaction to Nora's revelation in Act 3?

Act 2

1. Explain the **irony** of Torvald's statement, "When the real crisis comes, you will not find me lacking in strength or courage. I am man enough to bear the burden for us both."

2. Why does Dr. Rank refuse to let Torvald visit him in the hospital?

3. Explain Nora's statement to Dr. Rank that "there are some people whom one loves, and others whom it's almost more fun to be with."

Act 3

1. Why does Christine tell Krogstad *not* to take his letter back?

2. Explain Nora's statement to Torvald, "You don't understand me. And I've never understood you—until this evening."

3. Why would Nora's statement that she has a duty toward herself be so astonishing to a nineteenth-century audience? What would be the probable reaction of an audience today?

4. In what ways is Nora's situation at the end of the play more difficult than it would be for a woman today?

5. List the pet names that Torvald calls Nora and explain the implications of each.

6. Explain the significance of the play's title.

Suggestions for Exploration and Writing

1. Write an essay explaining how you, as a modern wife or husband, would deal with a situation such as that faced by Nora or Torvald, or explain how you would conduct your life in such a way as to avoid facing such a situation.

2. What does Nora think Torvald will do when he learns the truth? How does her expectation make the reality even worse?

3. In an essay, explain the ironic contrast between Torvald's statements to Nora about protecting her and his actual behavior toward her.

4. In a cause-and-effect essay, explain why Nora has been, as Torvald says, for eight years "a hypocrite, [and] a liar."

5. Write an essay explaining why Nora leaves her children, even though she loves them.

6. In what ways does Nora misjudge the males in her life? Explain.

7. In a documented paper, discuss the roles of Krogstad and Christine in Ibsen's play.

Casebook
on Three Poets

Emily Dickinson · Robert Frost · Langston Hughes

WRITING ABOUT LOVE AND GENDER

Emily Dickinson (1830–1886)

Although very sociable as a girl and young woman, Emily Dickinson slowly became reclusive. In fact, she and her younger sister Lavinia lived their whole lives in their father's house, with their only other sibling, Austin, living only a stone's throw away. Despite her later tendency to "dwell" only in her house and the grounds surrounding it, Dickinson maintained close friendships with her sister-in-law, Susan Gilbert Dickinson, and with people with whom she corresponded but whom she seldom or never saw. The reasons for the poet's seclusion are nowhere stated clearly, though literary critics and lovers of her poetry are fascinated by the possibilities: was she agoraphobic; was she suffering from a broken heart; or was she choosing to avoid a patriarchal world that little valued women's writing? Few people in Amherst, Massachusetts, where Emily Dickinson spent most of her life, would have dreamed that within the confines of her yard a revolution in American poetry was taking place. Her poetry was far ahead of her time in form and content. The great bulk of her work—close to two thousand poems—was discovered only after her death. In little packets sewn together with thread and on scraps of paper, Dickinson had enclosed an extraordinary outpouring of creativity. Her brief poems, rich in metaphor and punctuated primarily by dashes, present a wealth of startling images and an intensity of thought that make her one of America's most loved and studied poets.

106 (1890)

The Daisy follows soft the Sun—
And when his golden walk is done—
Sits shyly at his feet—
He—waking—finds the flower there—
5   Wherefore—Marauder—art thou here?
Because, Sir, love is sweet!

We are the Flower—Thou the Sun!
Forgive us, if as days decline—
We nearer steal to Thee!
10   Enamored of the parting West—
The peace—the flight—the Amethyst—
Night's possibility!

Questions for Discussion

1. What metaphor is used to represent the speaker? What metaphor represents the one for whom the poem seems to have been written?

2. How does the controlling metaphor characterize the relationship depicted in the poem?

3. What does "Marauder" mean? How does the use of this word affect the meaning of the poem?

4. To what does the phrase "night's possibility" refer?

199 (1890)

I'm "wife"—I've finished that—
That other state—
I'm Czar—I'm "Woman" now—
It's safer so—

5   How odd the Girl's life looks
Behind this soft Eclipse—
I think that Earth feels so
To folks in Heaven—now—

This being comfort—then
10   That other kind—was pain—
But why compare?
I'm "Wife"! Stop there!

Questions for Discussion

1. What two states does the poem speak about? How is each depicted? Does one seem to be drawn in a more positive way than the other?

2. What is "this soft Eclipse"? In what ways do the different meanings of "Eclipse" add richness to the poem's meaning?

3. The words "wife" and "Woman" are in quotation marks. How does this punctuation affect your interpretation of the poem?

284   (1945)

The Drop, that wrestles in the Sea—
Forgets her own locality—
As I—toward Thee—

She knows herself an incense small—
5   Yet *small*—she sighs—if *All*—is *All*—
How *larger*—be?

The Ocean—smiles—at her Conceit—
But *she,* forgetting Amphitrite—
Pleads—"Me"?

Questions for Discussion

1. Like poem 106, this poem uses a metaphor that speaks to qualities about the speaker and another. Explain the metaphor.

2. How does the drop feel about being a drop?

3. What are the implications of the word "wrestles"?

4. Dickinson frequently plays with language, using words whose secondary definitions add levels of meaning to her poems. Look up the word "Conceit" and then study its use in the poem and its relation to the whole poem. What do the different definitions add to your interpretation?

339   (1929)

I tend my flowers for thee—
Bright Absentee!
My Fuchsia's Coral Seams
Rip—while the Sower—dreams—

5   Geraniums—tint—and spot—
Low Daisies—dot—
My Cactus—splits her Beard
To show her throat—

Carnations—tip their spice—
10 And Bees—pick up—
A Hyacinth—I hid—
Puts out a Ruffled Head—
And odors fall

From flasks—so small—
15   You marvel how they held—

Globe Roses—break their satin flake—
Upon my Garden floor—
Yet—thou—not there—
I had as lief they bore
20   No Crimson—more—

Thy flower—be gay—
Her Lord—away!
It ill becometh me—
I'll dwell in Calyx—Gray—
25   How modestly—alway—
Thy Daisy—
Draped for thee!

Questions for Discussion

1. In this poem, the speaker, calling herself "Daisy," addresses a "Bright Absentee." Explain the metaphors she uses to speak to the absent one.

2. Stanzas 1 through 4 primarily describe; stanza 5 articulates the point the speaker wants to make about the earlier descriptions. What is the message?

732   (1890)

She rose to His Requirement—dropt
The Playthings of Her Life
To take the honorable Work
Of Woman, and of Wife—

5   If ought She missed in Her new Day,
Of Amplitude, or Awe—
Or first Prospective—Or the Gold
In using, wear away,

It lay unmentioned—as the Sea
10   Develop Pearl, and Weed,
But only to Himself—be known
The Fathoms they abide—

Questions for Discussion

1. Like poem 199, this poem seems to compare two states. What are they? How is each described?

2. In stanza 2, the speaker speaks of "Gold" that "In using, wear[s] away." What does Dickinson seem to suggest here? Why is this a particularly rich image for this poem?

3. Look closely at the last three lines. What do they mean? What do they add to your interpretation of the poem?

SUBVERTING THE CULT OF DOMESTICITY: EMILY DICKINSON'S CRITIQUE OF WOMEN'S WORK[1]

GERTRUDE REIF HUGHES

Womanhood and women's work were especially prominent topics in Emily Dickinson's time. Historians of the period have shown how the doctrine of separate spheres for women and men thrived between 1820 and 1860, when a whole canon of conventions governing women's domestic duties became codified.[2] This orthodoxy about women and women's work came to be called the cult of domesticity or of true womanhood. It was as accepted in Dickinson's culture as was New England Puritanism, and Dickinson's critique of it permeates her poetry as thoroughly, if perhaps less visibly.

Precisely when she is being most demure, conforming most fully to what is expected of a true woman, she is most rebelliously questioning what motivates those expectations. She uses her poems and her poetic imagination to ponder "her" gender and the assumptions that created it. This pondering and questioning occur memorably in another poem where Dickinson merges sewing and sowing. "I tend my flowers for thee— / Bright Absentee!" (339). The pun comes in the first stanza when one of her flowers rips its seams while she, "the Sower," dreams:

> I tend my flowers for thee—
> Bright Absentee!
> My Fuschia's Coral Seams
> Rip—while the Sower—dreams—

Then the poem burgeons into a riot of color, odor, and kinetic energy as the flowers she is tending enact various excesses of longing and allure:

> Geraniums—tint—and spot—
> Low Daisies—dot—
> My Cactus—splits her Beard
> To show her throat—

[1]Gertrude Reif Hughes, "Subverting the Cult of Domesticity: Emily Dickinson's Critique of Women's Work," *Legacy: A Journal of American Women Writers* 3.1 (Spring 1986): 17–28.

[2]Barbara Welter described the cult of domesticity in 1966. Since then, a number of historians have focused on the ideology that established separate arenas of activity for men and women, including: Nancy Cott, *The Bonds of Womanhood;* Carl Degler, *At Odds;* Kathryn Kish Sklar, *Catharine Beecher: A Study in American Domesticity;* and, more recently, Mary Kelley, *Private Woman, Public Stage.* Cott, 197–98, outlines three ways historians of domesticity tend to evaluate its effects on women.

Carnations—tip their spice—
And Bees—pick up—
A Hyacinth—I hid—
Puts out a Ruffled Head—
And odors fall
From flasks—so small—
You marvel how they held—

Globe Roses—break their satin flake—
Upon my Garden floor—
Yet—thou—not there—
I had as lief they bore
No Crimson—more—

Thy flower—be gay—
Her Lord—away!
It ill becometh me—
I'll dwell in Calyx—Gray—
How modestly—alway—
Thy Daisy—
Draped for thee!

Deputized by the absentee landlord to cultivate this brutal and erotic plot, Dickinson purports to disapprove of the misrule over which she presides. Coverings rip and split, tiny hidden vessels spill out their surprisingly heady contents, petals fall like satin remnants ruining the perfection they had composed, while Dickinson's Daisy-persona demurely disassociates herself from all this indecent exposure. But the Daisy's demure disclaimer actually carries the poem's devastating satire. While seeming to reproach her sister flowers for their excesses, she actually holds her Bright Absentee lord responsible, for he is the desired audience and he is absent. In his absence, what ought to be a glorious spectacle becomes a scandalous waste. "Her Lord—away" has failed to take emotional responsibility for the blossoming in the garden he purports to own, and his rioting flowers, including his demure Daisy, protest their Bright Absentee landlord's irresponsible, oppressive rule. Moreover, from the poem's dutiful opening stanza, through its erotic progression, to its final disclaimer, Dickinson is specifically satirizing a humiliation that she knew well but did not necessarily applaud—the humiliation of control-by-deprivation.

Works Cited

Cott, Nancy. *The Bonds of Womanhood: "Women's Sphere" in New England 1790–1835*. New Haven: Yale UP, 1977.

Degler, Carl N. *At Odds: Women and the Family in America from the Revolution to the Present.* New York: Oxford UP, 1980.

Kelley, Mary. *Private Woman, Public Stage: Literary Domesticity in Nineteenth-Century America.* New York: Oxford UP, 1984.

Sklar, Kathryn Kish. *Catherine Beecher: A Study in American Domesticity.* New Haven: Yale UP, 1973. Rpt., Norton, 1976.

Welter, Barbara. "The Cult of True Womanhood: 1820–1860." *American Quarterly* 18.2, pt. 1 (Summer 1966).

"The Invisible Lady": Emily Dickinson and Conventions of the Female Self[1]

Joanne Dobson

By choosing to be a writer in nineteenth-century America, Emily Dickinson, as a woman, placed herself squarely within a community of expression characterized by specific and often rigid constraints upon articulation of personal individuality. Although men as well as women were bound by a cultural decorum of personal reticence, restrictions on the presentation of women's lives, particularly in fiction and poetry, were especially strict, and cultural monitoring was intense. Nina Baym, in her recent study of book reviewing in nineteenth-century America, traces a clear differentiation between the critical treatment of male and female fictional characters. In the creation of character in general, reviewers over the course of the middle years of the century moved toward a preference for individualism (*Novels, Readers, and Reviewers* 88). But the preferred women characters, Baym notes, "are not individuals. [. . .] They are 'Woman.' In the discourse on characterization of women the substitution of norms for observation or discovery is so pervasive that one feels oneself close to a major cultural deception" (98).[2]

The significance of this ideology of expressive norms for women's writing was profound; it resulted in a dynamic of literary discourse that pitted the "feminine"—or the societal definition of womanhood—against the "female"—or the personal experience of womanhood—in a manner serving all but to eliminate the latter from women's texts. Female character was expected to conform to the cultural outlines of the feminine— had, in other words, to become 'Woman,' to become stereotyped. Although peripheral women characters were sometimes allowed their individuality, the woman at the center of a text, the one most likely to be identified with by her creator, and by the reader as well, became almost universally conventionalized.

[1]Joanne Dobson, "'The Invisible Lady': Emily Dickinson and Conventions of the Female Self," *Legacy: A Journal of American Women Writers* 3.1 (Spring 1986): 41–55.

[2]I wish to thank Nina Baym and Cheryl Walker, who read an earlier version of "The Invisible Lady." Their very helpful comments are reflected throughout the paper.

Higginson called the contemporary attitude toward female self-expression "a gospel of silence" (73). The expressive bind women writers found themselves in was this: they were writing prolifically and with great popular success, so they did have voices; yet as individuals they were expected to maintain a decorous silence within their texts, in essence, to become "invisible ladies," manifesting nothing that would reveal to the world the presence of any passion or aspiration beyond the ordained. In order to manage such expressive sleight of hand, to be both present as a feminine voice and absent as a uniquely female presence, women turned to specific images—that of the little girl was particularly popular—that would allow them at one and the same time to be somebody in the text, and yet remain, as Dickinson asserts in an often quoted poem, "Nobody."

I do not claim, of course, that Dickinson was a conventional nineteenth-century poet; in all the well-known ways she is indeed a modernist. And certainly her focus on personal female experience is intense. But Dickinson's connections to her own time and place and the ways in which she was acculturated to her era are important when we attempt to understand as fully as possible the cultural dynamics informing her work. As she set pen to paper Dickinson must have been aware to a significant degree of the decorum of "invisibility." Certainly this would have been a factor in her non-publication.[3] Yet, in spite of Dickinson's decision not to publish, she did not choose silence; she continued to write. In so doing she faced the same choices as her contemporaries; her options, if she were to speak about herself at all, were three: to speak in conventional cultural terms; to exploit conventions for personal use; to spurn conventions.

In the cultural mythos a new and transcendent identity awaited the married woman—one that was not available to the single woman. It is the seductive lure of this promised mystical transformation co-existing alongside the nagging awareness of identity loss in conventional marriage that informs the complex and self-contradictory figure of the wife/bride in Dickinson's highly charged marriage poems.[4]

> I'm "wife"—I've finished that—
> That other state—
> I'm Czar—I'm "Woman" now—
> It's safer so—

[3]Karen Dandurand's discovery of additional Dickinson publications in the poet's lifetime reveals that editors and the public were indeed responsive to Dickinson's work. According to Dandurand it now appears that Dickinson's non-publication was not forced upon her, but was a conscious choice.

[4]Poems using the wife/bride figure are: "I'm 'wife'—I've finished that—" 199: "A Wife—at Daybreak I shall be—" 461: "I am ashamed—I hide—" 473: "The World—stands—solemner—to me—" 493: "She rose to His Requirements—dropt" 732: "Given in Marriage unto Thee" 817: "Title divine—is mine!" 1072: "All that I do" 1496: "Rearrange a 'Wife's' affection!" 1737: "'Twas here my summer paused" 1756: and possibly "I'm ceded—I've stopped being Their's—" 508.

How odd the Girl's life looks
Behind this soft Eclipse—
I think that Earth feels so
To Folks in Heaven—now—

This being comfort—then
That other kind—was pain—
But why compare?
I'm "Wife"! Stop there!   (199)

Of the several "wife" poems in Dickinson's canon, this poem pays the most attention to defining the terms. The use of quotation marks around the two key terms, "wife" and "woman," focuses attention squarely upon them. The words do not announce themselves boldly as known entities, but rather float like protean bubbles in a sea of potential meaning. The known experience, on the other hand, "the Girl's life," while introduced hesitantly as "that— / That other state," immediately becomes the base term of reference, compared with Earth in contrast to Heaven, and thus, by analogy, with life in contrast to death.

Marriage, in Dickinson's metaphor. is the "soft Eclipse," which at one and the same time transforms the self *and* makes it invisible. In her investigation of the significance of this word "wife," which beyond all others defined the ideal female self in her era, Dickinson aligns the "safety" and "comfort" of marriage with a state of afterlife. While this afterlife is ostensibly heaven, it is a fairly ambiguous paradise: are safety and comfort worth the "eclipse" of a life? This question is implicit in the equation as Dickinson places marriage in contradistinction to "that— / That other state" for which society seems to offer no identifying term. Certainly "woman" does not seem to be available, having immediately equated itself with "wife."

This speaker, however, although initially stammering for want of a precise term, goes on to identify "that other state" as life, "the Girl's life." Further she is reluctant to recognize the "pain" that according to received definitions must have been attached to this solitary state: "This being comfort—then / That other kind/was pain—." The tone is one of hesitant acknowledgment of some "truth" not intuitively recognized as valid; she may well have found "the Girl's life" quite satisfactory. "But why compare?" she continues quickly, "I'm 'Wife'! Stop there!" The persona of "wife,"—or, more precisely, the persona trying on the role of "wife"—will not permit further investigation, suggesting by the abruptness of her termination of the discussion that she is afraid the results will be unfavorable. Having linguistically "tried on" this married identity, the speaker thinks it prudent, like the novels of her era, to "stop there." The poem, begun in a tone of triumph, closes in ambiguity.

In the poem above, the word "marriage" is never mentioned. The operative term is "this soft Eclipse." In other words, marriage as Dickinson sees it here means not only transformation, but also an obscuration—whether of life or of the self is not specified. This eclipse may be painless, even comfortable, perhaps even ecstatic, with suggestions of sexual transport, but it is nonetheless real. One cannot be seen when one is eclipsed. Other wife poems also contain elements of invisibility. Dickinson's most overt exploration of the effect of marriage on the individual woman is in poem 732:

> She rose to His Requirement—dropt
> The Playthings of Her Life
> To take the honorable Work
> Of Woman, and of Wife—
>
> If ought She missed in Her new Day.
> Of Amplitude, or Awe—
> Or first Prospective—Or the Gold
> In using, wear away.
>
> It lay unmentioned—as the Sea
> Develop Pearl, and Weed,
> But only to Himself—be known
> The Fathoms they abide—

Here being "Woman" and "Wife" is once again equated, and defined, sincerely I think, as "honorable Work." In order to attain this identity, however, the woman described in this poem must sink her own potential: "Fathoms" deep, in invisibility and silence, her capacity for "Amplitude, or Awe" lies unrecognized and "unmentioned." And in poem 461, "A Wife—at Daybreak I shall be—," the consummation of the marriage, the making of a wife, is implicitly equated with death. "Eternity, I'm coming—Sir," the bride says to her approaching husband, "Savior—I've seen the face—before!" Christ, Death and the husband are indistinguishable one from the other here, and the marriage experience is thoroughly overlaid with implications of death—the final invisibility.

Loss of consciousness, invisibility, silence; these are the qualities of death. They are also qualities that contemporary women's literature attached, if only in a secondary manner, to marriage. For Dickinson, too, these qualities are inextricably linked to the idea of marriage. *Her* dilemma in the face of marriage is heightened by her awareness of her own "Amplitude," of just how much it is she has to lose.

Works Cited

Baym, Nina. *Novels, Readers, and Reviewers: Responses to Fiction in Antebellum America.* Ithaca: Cornell UP, 1984.

Writing Doubly: Emily Dickinson
and Female Experience[1]
Suzanne Juhasz

1

In the following poem, Emily Dickinson portrays herself as she is situated in the world.

> Perhaps I asked too large—
> I take—no less than skies—
> For Earths, grow thick as
> Berries, in my native town—
>
> My Basket holds—just—Firmaments—
> Those—dangle easy—on my arm,
> But smaller bundles—Cram.   (352)

This is a manifesto about her own ambition, and yet it is expressed with that curious combination of authority and girlishness which so often defines the Dickinson persona. Or, to put it another way, we hear both bravado and coyness, confidence and timidity. Likewise, we see poetic images of the cosmic, and, at the same time, of the everyday. We notice, too, how syntax sustains seemingly contradictory attitudes or events: "perhaps" with "too large"; "Basket" with "Firmaments"; or even, "just" with "Firmaments." What are we to make of these contrasts, in a poem which depicts a young lady gathering earths and skies in her basket as she takes a walk outside of town?

We can interpret the poem as contrasting societal expectations for women with the speaker's different and altogether grander ambitions. She finds herself confined by the former, more suited to the latter. We know that the speaker is a woman, and that the poem concerns itself with gender norms and expectations, because the vocabulary is so pointedly "feminine." Only girls, after all, go around with baskets on their arms, berry-picking. Yet at the same time we are told how feminine "bundles cram": how she takes more readily to large things—earths, firmaments—not normally within the woman's sphere.

And yet, although she both aspires to and achieves "larger" matters, she does so in terms of her femaleness. The poem's opening line balances flamboyance with tentativeness: "*Perhaps* I asked *too large*" (my emphasis). We can't tell if the "perhaps" is guilty, or ironic. Having properly asked, in the past tense, she has, we discover next, not waited for permission: she *takes*. The most there is: no less than skies. In the situation in which she finds herself, or has created for herself, planets are accessible to her in the same way that berries would normally be to girls in their native towns. Here analogy conflates two sorts of round objects, earths and berries. The figure both contrasts them (girls' lives/this other life) and identifies them (berries and

[1]Suzanne Juhasz, "Writing Doubly: Emily Dickinson and Female Experience," *Legacy: A Journal of American Women Writers* 3.1 (Spring 1986): 5–15.

earths are equally spheres, just of different dimensions). But smallness is as much a matter of fit as of size, the concluding trope points out, for the relationship created between "just" and "cram" reverses societal notions of comfort. It is firmaments that dangle easy; smaller bundles that cram. But although the speaker is happier with these larger berries, she nonetheless construes her occupation as berry-picking and carries a basket to accomplish it. That is, she retains female forms as much as she eschews them.

Which brings us to the crucial ambiguity of the "native town." Is this Amherst, Massachusetts—or somewhere else? For of course earths do not grow, not literally, on New England bushes. These earths and skies are symbolic—of something like larger aspirations—and they exist vis-à-vis Amherst as bodies in the space of the mind or imagination: another sort of native town.

In other words, this poem takes place in two worlds; and however much it causes us to be aware of contradictions and conflicts between them, it also points to their congruence and simultaneity in the speaker's experience. Two native towns; two sorts of berries; two purposes for gathering them. The contradictions making for tension ("Perhaps I asked too large"), the congruence for facility ("My Basket holds—just Firmaments").

2

The doubleness present throughout this poem is an expression, I believe, of the ontological situation of women in patriarchal culture. "*Could you imagine a world of women only,* / the interviewer asked," writes Adrienne Rich in her poem "Natural Resources":

> . . . *Can you imagine*
> *a world where women are absent.* (He believed
> he was joking.) Yet I have to imagine
> at one and the same moment, both. Because I
> live in both.   (Rich 61)

Describing this same doubleness, the anthropologists Shirley and Edwin Ardener, in "Belief and the Problem of Women" (1972) and "The 'Problem' Revisited" (1975), have suggested that women constitute a muted group, the boundaries of whose culture and reality overlap, but are not wholly contained by, the dominant (male) group. This situation may be diagramed as follows:

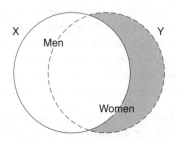

Elaine Showalter, who presents this diagram in her influential article, "Feminist Criticism in the Wilderness," comments,

> A model of the cultural situation of women is crucial to understanding both how they are perceived by the dominant group and how they perceive themselves and others. [. . .] Both muted and dominant groups generate beliefs or ordering ideas of social reality at the unconscious level, but dominant groups control the forms or structures in which consciousness can be articulated. Thus muted groups must mediate their beliefs through the allowable forms of dominant structures. Another way of putting this would be to say that all language is the language of the dominant order, and women, if they speak at all, must speak through it.   (262)

Describing women's writing, contemporary feminist criticism has consistently been aware of some kind of doubleness. Sandra Gilbert and Susan Gubar, for example, have identified the overt and covert texts of writing in disguise: "In short, she uses her art both to express and to camouflage herself" (81). [. . .] Seeing double, however, many feminist critics have wanted to see hierarchy as well. The covert text becomes the real story: truer, better, preferable. Yet it seems to me that female doubleness means not hierarchy or dichotomy but simultaneity, *both/and* rather than *either/or*, because that is closer to how female experience is constituted. [. . .]

Emily Dickinson's poetry is a good place to find this double vision, [. . .] In fact, an understanding of the presence of doubling in poems depicting her sense of self and world provides a perspective on her famous ambiguities. It is a commonplace that Dickinson will try to say at least two things at once: to our excitement and confusion. All of her critics have had to deal with this tantalizing feature of her art. One way to think about its cause—why it informs many poems at the most crucial moments—is that it reflects the central gestalt of her experience as a woman.

3

Love is the special province of women, we are told. Emily Dickinson, like most women throughout history, was raised not only according to the belief that her destined role in life was as wife and mother, but to be skillful at the role—to be empathetic, caring, deeply interested in personal relationships and for that matter, in love itself. Yet we know that Dickinson, a young woman who wanted to be a poet, emphatically resisted the kind of dominance and commensurate loss of self that love and marriage traditionally brought. In a famous letter to Susan Gilbert, she writes of wives, how "they know that the man of noon, is *mightier* than the morning and their life is henceforth to him. Oh, Susie, it is dangerous. [. . .] It does so rend me, Susie, the thought of it when it comes, that I tremble lest at sometime I, too, am yielded up" (L.93, p. 210). But we also know how often she intensely and romantically sought love—if not marriage. If love according to the patriarchy is characterized, as Dickinson well knew, by a dominance-submission paradigm, she often participated in the submissive role allotted to her as the woman. But again, at the same time, she resented and sought to alter the role that, in effect, silenced her voice, her authority, her precious selfhood. Her life itself is testimony to that denial. Her poetry, too, consistently seeks to sabotage, invert, destroy the very premises that it at the same time quite readily established. Poem 1736, for example, begins with a posture of supplication akin to masochism: "Proud of my broken heart, since thou didst break it." But by the conclusion of the poem the speaker has reinterpreted the power structure implicit in this arrangement so that she, not he, has the upper hand: "See! I usurped *thy* crucifix to honor mine!"

The following poem, "The Drop, that wrestles in the Sea—" (284), is one of the most extreme examples of this double consciousness, in that its meaning seems impossible to determine, since the interpretations available contradict one another. Read one way, the poem shows its speaker succumbing to the power of the male. Read another way, the same words show her challenging him, proposing an alternative model of love between equals.

> The Drop, that wrestles in the Sea—
> Forgets her own locality—
> As I—toward Thee—
>
> She knows herself an incense small—
> Yet *small*—she sighs—if *All*—is *All*—
> How *larger*—be?
>
> The Ocean—smiles—at her Conceit—
> But *she,* forgetting Amphitrite—
> Pleads—"Me"?

Doubleness in this poem is manifested in semantic tension and in profound ambiguity. In the first stanza, the complimentary and even supplicating tone of "As I—toward Thee—" jars with the word "wrestles," calling into question the very idea itself of "locality." In the second stanza, that matter of locality and its connection with power as well as identity comes into question by the syllogistic pairing of *"small"* and *"All."* In the final stanza, our interpretation of the message carried by the final word, "Me," depends upon how we hear its tone, and that in turn depends upon how we have read the poem that leads up to it.

The first stanza offers a conventional-sounding compliment, essential ingredient in love lyrics, of which Dickinson's are no exception. An anology between drop and sea, lover and beloved can be read as praise for the beloved's power and significance. The relation between drop and sea is like the one between you and me, says the speaker: even as the drop is soon swallowed up by the sea, so am I by you. What could be more natural, according to patriarchal definitions of romantic love? And yet, the fact that this drop is *wrestling* in the sea, wrestling against a powerful force that would cause her to *forget* her own locality, makes the compliment somewhat suspect. Is it in fact no compliment at all, but an accusation?

We assume the information offered in the second stanza is about the situation described in stanza one. Perhaps it will resolve the difficulty in interpretation of tone, of attitude. Here the organizing trope changes. The drop has become an incense—a pleasing scent, or perhaps a flame. What connects the two metaphors is their smallness, even as the "All" which follows is analogous to the "sea" of stanza one. Again, at issue is their relationship; here the speaker proposes an argument ("Yet") on behalf of her position. "Yet small": "if *All*—is *All*— / How *larger*—be?" The relationship between small and all may be interpreted as one of contrast or synchronicity, depending upon how we interpret the syllogism itself. Does it mean (1) that if the drop is consumed by the sea, so that the small becomes all, the drop assumes the sea's identity and hence a borrowed or second-hand power, in the way that the candidate's wife is his spokesperson and alter-ego, even "the power behind the throne"? Or, (2) that since one drop of water, by its nature, is equivalent to many drops of water, so is not she, as a drop, as "large" as the entire sea? Is she, in other words, already equal in essence if not size to him—as important as he is? In the first argument, she acquires identity, or "locality," through him; in the second, she asserts her own. Or, to put it yet another way, does the superimposition of the dominant mode (patriarchy) upon the muted (female) mode mean that the latter is absorbed into the former; or does the female world maintain its own locality, and value?

This is surely a matter of, among other things, language and silence. This drop speaks; speaks up on her own behalf. The Ocean, now further personified as Poseidon, God of the Sea (and husband of Amphitrite), acknowledges either her pride or her word-play (depending upon how one interprets the pun, "Conceit"), by smiling. Is this a pleased response to her compliment, an affectionate appreciation of a postulant who has conceitedly put herself forward in this way? Or his mocking laughter at her challenge, wherein he smiles because it is after all only words, only a clever conceit, and he knows the true state of affairs in the world. The "But" that begins line eight suggests that the smile is condescending; *but* she is coming back for another round. In any case, she forgets Amphitrite (his wife, token of his unavailability to *her*) and pleads, "'Me'?" This final gesture calling attention to herself may be read either as the ultimate indication of her posture of deference and adoration, as in "Oh, please love me, humble drop that I am!" Or it may be read as her final attempt to make him recognize her as a separate individual, and thus worthy of love: *me!*

Both readings really are possible, no matter how much I personally have always leaned towards the latter, the gesture of self-assertion. That would seem to be, after all, the "feminist" reading. But even as I know that Dickinson was such a challenger of patriarchal norms, I also know (even if I don't like it) that she was often sycophantic in her relations with powerful god-like men, the Poseidons of her life. If the poem itself presents two alternatives every step of the way, then the critical task seems to me not to try to choose one reading, but to accept the doubleness of the poem as its meaning. Nor is it, I would argue further, a question of seeing one meaning hidden or coded into the other with the poet *pretending* to be submissive while *actually* challenging that position. Rather, the poem incarnates contradictory albeit simultaneous interpretations of the same situation, as the speaker finds herself seeking to win the love of a powerful man both on his terms and on her own. This is, in fact, a feminist reading, because it recognizes the actual situation of a woman in patriarchy.

Works Cited

Dickinson, Emily. *The Letters of Emily Dickinson.* Ed. Thomas H. Johnson and Theodora Ward. Cambridge: Harvard UP, 1958.

_____. *The Poems of Emily Dickinson.* Ed. Thomas H. Johnson. Cambridge: Harvard UP, 1955.

Gilbert, Sandra, and Susan Gubar. *The Madwoman in the Attic.* New Haven: Yale UP, 1979.

Rich, Adrienne. *The Dream of a Common Language.* New York: Norton, 1978.

Showalter, Elaine. "Feminist Criticism in the Wilderness." *The New Feminist Criticism.* Ed. Elaine Showalter. New York: Pantheon, 1985. 243–70.

"Oh, Vision of Language!" Dickinson's Poems of Love and Death[1]

Margaret Homans

That her community held something of an established place for poetry in the form of valentines, even when written by young women, may be one reason why the first poems she was willing to show to others and to keep were love poems, but these poems are significant as a starting point for her poetry also because of their interdependency of metaphor and love. Poetry for her begins with romantic love and

[1]Margaret Homans, "'Oh, Vision of Language!' Dickinson's Poems of Love and Death," *Feminist Critics Read Emily Dickinson,* ed. Suzanne Juhasz (Bloomington: Indiana UP, 1983), 114–33.

specifically with the model of love that metaphor generates, where difference and subject-object relations structure what it is possible to say and to feel.

When Dickinson began to write more seriously several years after the date of the early love poems, she produced, more or less simultaneously, poems that confirm and poems that critique the hierarchical relationship between lovers that the earliest poems introduce. Most readers' predominant impression is of the first group, in which the self is figured as small, frail, and feminine in relation to a series of powerful, clearly male figures; as, typically, in "Mute thy Coronation—" (151), in which the speaker as a "meek" and reverent "tiny courtier" imagines herself, on the occasion of his coronation, enfolded in the Master's "Ermine."[2] In poems of this kind, Dickinson imagines a possibility for placing herself as a woman that is at once seductive (because traditional and comfortable) and dangerous (because it defines her as silent). Like the lowly and the small sought out by the high and the great in the first valentine, the tiny courtier takes her place with the object and the absent tenor in a hierarchical structure of romantic relations that is like the structure of metaphor. But in other poems written at the same time, Dickinson initiates a radical critique of conventional romantic relations between the sexes, through a simultaneous critique of the dualistic structure of language and of metaphor. The relation between subject and object necessary to the structures both of metaphor and of romantic love obtains as well and most fundamentally for Dickinson (as well as for contemporary criticism) in language's relation between signifier and signified, but as I have argued elsewhere,[3] in her endeavors to transcend or correct this oppositional structure of language, Dickinson pushes language to the border of meaninglessness. Her efforts to undo the subject-object structure of romantic love encounter similar obstacles. One group of poems appears to follow the pattern of the conventional love poems, the pattern begun in the earliest poems and continued in poems such as "Mute thy Coronation—." In this group of poems the powerful male figure (who incorporates attributes both of God and of the father) is figured as the sun, while the fragile female self is figured as a daisy. This conventional polarity, recalling the genuinely conventional male-female relations in the earlier love poems, is set up in these particular poems in order to be collapsed. At the same time, metaphor is shown to be integral to the structure of that relation, and is undercut as well.

In the love poem that begins, "The Daisy follows soft the Sun" (106), at the level of the theme of romantic love the daisy reverses the two figures'

---

[2]For the most salient discussion of Master and the other male figures of power, see Joanne Feit Diehl, *Dickinson and the Romantic Imagination* (Princeton: Princeton UP, 1981), ch. 1: " 'Come Slowly—Eden': The Woman Poet and Her Muse," 13–33.

[3]Margaret Homans, *Women Writers and Poetic Identity* (Princeton: UP, 1980), 176–88.

apparent relation of authority and humility, while at the level of rhetorical structure the metaphor that underlies both the poem's and the relationship's structure is exposed as illusion.

> The Daisy follows soft the Sun—
> And when his golden walk is done—
> Sits shily at his feet—
> He—waking—finds the flower there—
> Wherefore—Marauder—art thou here?
> Because, Sir, love is sweet!
>
> We are the Flower—Thou the Sun!
> Forgive us, if as days decline—
> We nearer steal to Thee!

As in the poem about Master and the tiny courtier, it is the distance and disparity between the sun and the daisy that structures their relationship, which is then acted out as the effort to bridge that distance. At the same time, as in the earliest valentine, their relation is structured by and as metaphor. As sun and moon are like lover in the valentine, here daisy and sun are like each other because of a minimal visual resemblance that is privileged by and formulated in her name: day's eye. The daisy's name makes her like the sun: a flower called a day's eye is being defined not as itself but in comparison to the sun. The bridging of the tremendous discrepancy between them in status and size structures both their romantic attraction and the metaphor that governs the poem. The perspectival illusion that, as the sun approaches the horizon, the daisy steals close to him visually enacts the way metaphor and romance are working here: she only seems to look like him, and their relation only seems intimate because of an optical illusion.

Through a strategy of mock humility the daisy gently dismantles the sun's pretensions to absolute power, but she can increase her power only by decreasing his. The transcendent third term beyond them both that would benefit both by permitting an escape from a closed system of opposed and relative power is found in the poem's final lines, where the daisy descries what she really wants:

> Enamored of the parting West—
> The peace—the flight—the Amethyst—
> Night's possibility!

"Night's possibility," gorgeous and compelling as it is, both removes the basis of their relationship (visual resemblance and optical illusion) and indeed requires the absence of the beloved sun himself. In moving away from the binary system in which two terms are related by opposition, by distance, and by illusory resemblance, toward the single term of night, the poem collapses its thematics of romance. It also collapses its own rhetorical structure: "Night's possibility" is beyond ordinary communication, which depends on the rhetorical dualism and on the tension between disparity and resemblance that this image rejects. "Night's possibility" is a theoretically ideal but effectively unhappy solution to the problem of hierarchical relations between genders.

The alternative to this self-defeating end to rhetoric, however, where a conventionally heterosexual paradigm is retained, is for Dickinson a silence that represents no improvement. When Dickinson turns to the more conventional conclusion of a male-female love relationship, she figures marriage as a "soft Eclipse" (199). Having imagined herself leaving "the Girl's life" behind, the speaker concludes,

> This being comfort—then
> That other kind—was pain—
> But why compare?
> I'm "Wife"! Stop there!

Being wife means stopping, both in the sense that the woman's life stops growing and in the sense that the poem comes to an end. Like the night that closes the poem about the daisy, heterosexuality is imaged as leading to an end to communication. The poem calls a halt to comparisons, especially the obviously disadvantageous one between being a wife and being a girl; but the alternative to comparisons is not to speak at all: "I'm 'Wife'! Stop there!" Without the possibility for the measurement of difference—which is the basis of metaphor as well as of this poem's thematics—language dwindles into silence.

Suggestions for Research, Exploration, and Writing

1. In an essay, discuss Emily Dickinson's use of primary and secondary definitions and the effect of this poetic strategy on her poetry.

2. Write an essay that explicates Dickinson's use of metaphor in one or more of the poems in this section.

3. Using the critical essays and Poems 284 and 106, write a documented paper that examines the effect on the female who finds herself in a male/female relationship.

4. Two of Dickinson's poems compare the woman's premarital state with her married state. In a documented essay, explain the comparison.

5. Write a documented paper that examines Dickinson's presentation of her speaker as a daisy, a drop, a girl concerned with "playthings," and an "incense small." Since she also uses the terms "Czar," "Marauder," "Amphitrite," and "the Sower," interpret her seeming contradictions.

6. Men in these poems are referred to as the sun, a sea, and an absent lord. In a documented essay, discuss Dickinson's portrayal of men.

7. Discuss in an essay the degree to which a woman gives up her sense of identity in a marriage. Or analyze the degree to which a man does so.

Robert Frost (1874–1963)

Robert Frost's life, like many of his poems, was filled with ironies. Known as a New England poet, Frost was born in San Francisco and named after Robert E. Lee. When his poetry was not recognized in the United States, he moved to England and there published his first books of poetry, A Boy's Will *(1913) and* North of Boston *(1914). When he returned to the United States, his fame as a poet was already established. Early criticism identified Frost with the kindly New England speaker of many of his poems, and even now his most famous poems are those about nature, which often emphasize rising above life's problems.*

Frost had more than his share of family tragedies, however, and was always aware of the darker side of life. Even his famous definition of poetry as a "momentary stay against confusion" in "The Figure a Poem Makes" emphasizes the complexities of life and the necessity of finding ways to manage life's ambiguities. For Frost, precise form in poetry is one of those ways; as a master craftsman, he uses traditional poetic form so skillfully that he seems to recreate the natural speech patterns of the New England characters in his **dialogues** *and* **monologues,** *and he adds to the meaning of his poems by using such tight forms as the* **sonnet** *and* **terza rima.**

HOME BURIAL   (1914)

He saw her from the bottom of the stairs
Before she saw him. She was starting down,
Looking back over her shoulder at some fear.
She took a doubtful step and then undid it
5   To raise herself and look again. He spoke
Advancing toward her: "What is it you see
From up there always?—for I want to know."
She turned and sank upon her skirts at that,
And her face changed from terrified to dull.
10   He said to gain time: "What is it you see?"
Mounting until she cowered under him.

"I will find out now—you must tell me, dear."
She, in her place, refused him any help,
With the least stiffening of her neck and silence.
15   She let him look, sure that he wouldn't see,
Blind creature; and awhile he didn't see.
But at last he murmured, "Oh," and again, "Oh."

"What is it—what?" she said.

      "Just that I see."

20   "You don't," she challenged. "Tell me what it is."

"The wonder is I didn't see at once.
I never noticed it from here before.
I must be wonted to it—that's the reason.
The little graveyard where my people are!
25   So small the window frames the whole of it.
Not so much larger than a bedroom, is it?
There are three stones of slate and one of marble,
Broad-shouldered little slabs there in the sunlight
On the sidehill. We haven't to mind *those*.
30   But I understand: it is not the stones,
But the child's mound—"

      "Don't, don't, don't,
  don't," she cried.

She withdrew, shrinking from beneath his arm
35   That rested on the banister, and slid downstairs;
And turned on him with such a daunting look,
He said twice over before he knew himself:
"Can't a man speak of his own child he's lost?"

"Not you!—Oh, where's my hat? Oh, I don't need it!
40   I must get out of here. I must get air.—
I don't know rightly whether any man can."

"Amy! Don't go to someone else this time.
Listen to me. I won't come down the stairs."
He sat and fixed his chin between his fists.
45   "There's something I should like to ask you, dear."

"You don't know how to ask it."

      "Help me, then."

Her fingers moved the latch for all reply.

"My words are nearly always an offense.
50   I don't know how to speak of anything
So as to please you. But I might be taught,

I should suppose. I can't say I see how.
A man must partly give up being a man
With womenfolk. We could have some arrangement
55 By which I'd bind myself to keep hands off
Anything special you're a-mind to name.
Though I don't like such things 'twixt those that love.
Two that don't love can't live together without them.
But two that do can't live together with them."
60 She moved the latch a little. "Don't—don't go.
Don't carry it to someone else this time.
Tell me about it if it's something human.
Let me into your grief. I'm not so much
Unlike other folks as your standing there
65 Apart would make me out. Give me my chance.
I do think, though, you overdo it a little.
What was it brought you up to think it the thing
To take your mother-loss of a first child
So inconsolably—in the face of love.
70 You'd think his memory might be satisfied—"

"There you go sneering now!"

                    "I'm not, I'm not!
You make me angry. I'll come down to you.
God, what a woman! And it's come to this,
75 A man can't speak of his own child that's dead."

"You can't because you don't know how to speak.
If you had any feelings, you that dug
With your own hand—how could you?—his little grave;
I saw you from that very window there,
80 Making the gravel leap and leap in air,
Leap up, like that, like that, and land so lightly
And roll back down the mound beside the hole.
I thought, Who is that man? I didn't know you.
And I crept down the stairs and up the stairs
85 To look again, and still your spade kept lifting.
Then you came in. I heard your rumbling voice
Out in the kitchen and I don't know why,
But I went near to see with my own eyes,
You could sit there with the stains on your shoes
90 Of the fresh earth from your own baby's grave
And talk about your everyday concerns.
You had stood the spade up against the wall
Outside there in the entry, for I saw it."

"I shall laugh the worst laugh I ever laughed.
95 I'm cursed. God, if I don't believe I'm cursed."

"I can repeat the very words you were saying:
'Three foggy mornings and one rainy day
Will rot the best birch fence a man can build.'
Think of it, talk like that at such a time!
100   What had how long it takes a birch to rot
To do with what was in the darkened parlor?
You *couldn't* care! The nearest friends can go
With anyone to death, comes so far short
They might as well not try to go at all.
105   No, from the time when one is sick to death,
One is alone, and he dies more alone.
Friends make pretense of following to the grave,
But before one is in it, their minds are turned
And making the best of their way back to life
110   And living people, and things they understand.
But the world's evil. I won't have grief so
If I can change it. Oh, I won't, I won't!"

"There, you have said it all and you feel better.
You won't go now. You're crying. Close the door.
115   The heart's gone out of it: why keep it up?
Amy! There's someone coming down the road!"

"*You*—oh, you think the talk is all. I must go—
Somewhere out of this house. How can I make you—"

"If—you—do!" She was opening the door wider.
120   "Where do you mean to go? First tell me that.
I'll follow and bring you back by force. I *will!*—"

Questions for Discussion

1. The husband says, "A man must partly give up being a man / With womenfolk." Explain these lines and agree or disagree with the husband's claim.

2. Explain the significance of Amy's statement about the rotting birch. Why does the husband's statement about the birch offend Amy? With whom do you agree?

3. In lines 105–06, Amy says, "No, from the time when one is sick to death, / One is alone, and he dies more alone." Agree or disagree with this statement.

4. Do you think Amy has grieved too long and blamed her husband unfairly? Explain.

5. Explain the double meaning of the title.

Suggestions for Exploration and Writing

1. Agree or disagree with this statement: It is a stereotype that men and women show distinctive differences in reaction to a tragedy.

2. Contrast Amy's view about death with the husband's view of death.

THE DEATH OF THE HIRED MAN   (1914)

Mary sat musing on the lamp-flame at the table,
Waiting for Warren. When she heard his step,
She ran on tiptoe down the darkened passage
To meet him in the doorway with the news
5   And put him on his guard. "Silas is back."
She pushed him outward with her through the door
And shut it after her. "Be kind," she said.
She took the market things from Warren's arms
And set them on the porch, then drew him down
10   To sit beside her on the wooden steps.

"When was I ever anything but kind to him?
But I'll not have the fellow back," he said.
"I told him so last haying, didn't I?
If he left then, I said, that ended it.
15   What good is he? Who else will harbor him
At his age for the little he can do?
What help he is there's no depending on.
Off he goes always when I need him most.
He thinks he ought to earn a little pay,
20   Enough at least to buy tobacco with,
So he won't have to beg and be beholden.
'All right,' I say, 'I can't afford to pay
Any fixed wages, though I wish I could.'
'Someone else can.' 'Then someone else will have to.'
25   I shouldn't mind his bettering himself
If that was what it was. You can be certain,
When he begins like that, there's someone at him
Trying to coax him off with pocket money—
In haying time, when any help is scarce.
30   In winter he comes back to us. I'm done."

"Sh! not so loud: he'll hear you," Mary said.

"I want him to: he'll have to soon or late."

"He's worn out. He's asleep beside the stove.
When I came up from Rowe's I found him here,
35   Huddled against the barn door fast asleep,
A miserable sight, and frightening, too—

You needn't smile—I didn't recognize him—
I wasn't looking for him—and he's changed.
Wait till you see."

40   "Where did you say he'd been?"

"He didn't say. I dragged him to the house,
And gave him tea and tried to make him smoke.
I tried to make him talk about his travels.
Nothing would do: he just kept nodding off."

45   "What did he say? Did he say anything?"

"But little."
"Anything? Mary confess
He said he'd come to ditch the meadow for me."

"Warren!"

50   "But did he? I just want to know."

"Of course he did. What would you have him say?
Surely you wouldn't grudge the poor old man
Some humble way to save his self-respect.
55   He added, if you really care to know,
He meant to clear the upper pasture, too.
That sounds like something you have heard before?
Warren, I wish you could have heard the way
He jumbled everything. I stopped to look
Two or three times—he made me feel so queer—
60   To see if he was talking in his sleep.
He ran on Harold Wilson—you remember—
The boy you had in haying four years since.
He's finished school, and teaching in his college.
Silas declares you'll have to get him back.
65   He says they two will make a team for work:
Between them they will lay this farm as smooth!
The way he mixed that in with other things.
He thinks young Wilson a likely lad, though daft
On education—you know how they fought
70   All through July under the blazing sun,
Silas up on the cart to build the load,
Harold along beside to pitch it on."

"Yes, I took care to keep well out of earshot."

"Well, those days trouble Silas like a dream.
75   You wouldn't think they would. How some things linger!
Harold's young college-boy's assurance piqued him.
After so many years he still keeps finding
Good arguments he sees he might have used.

I sympathize. I know just how it feels
80   To think of the right thing to say too late.
Harold's associated in his mind with Latin.
He asked me what I thought of Harold's saying
He studied Latin, like the violin,
Because he liked it—that an argument!
85   He said he couldn't make the boy believe
He could find water with a hazel prong—
Which showed how much good school had ever done him.
He wanted to go over that. But most of all
He thinks if he could have another chance
90   To teach him how to build a load of hay—"

"I know, that's Silas' one accomplishment.
He bundles every forkful in its place,
And tags and numbers it for future reference,
So he can find and easily dislodge it
95   In the unloading. Silas does that well.
He takes it out in bunches like big birds' nests.
You never see him standing on the hay
He's trying to lift, straining to lift himself."

"He thinks if he could teach him that, he'd be
100   Some good perhaps to someone in the world.
He hates to see a boy the fool of books.
Poor Silas, so concerned for other folk,
And nothing to look backward to with pride,
And nothing to look forward to with hope,
105   So now and never any different."

Part of a moon was falling down the west,
Dragging the whole sky with it to the hills.
Its light poured softly in her lap. She saw it
And spread her apron to it. She put out her hand
110   Among the harplike morning-glory strings,
Taut with the dew from garden bed to eaves,
As if she played unheard some tenderness
That wrought on him beside her in the night.
"Warren," she said, "he has come home to die:
115   You needn't be afraid he'll leave you this time."

"Home," he mocked gently.

                              "Yes, what else but home?
It all depends on what you mean by home.
Of course he's nothing to us, any more
120   Than was the hound that came a stranger to us
Out of the woods, worn out upon the trail."

"Home is the place where, when you have to go there,
They have to take you in."

                                 "I should have called it
125   Something you somehow haven't to deserve."

Warren leaned out and took a step or two,
Picked up a little stick, and brought it back
And broke it in his hand and tossed it by.
"Silas has better claim on us you think
130   Than on his brother? Thirteen little miles
As the road winds would bring him to his door.
Silas has walked that far no doubt today.
Why doesn't he go there? His brother's rich,
A somebody—director in the bank."

135   "He never told us that."

                             "We know it, though."

"I think his brother ought to help, of course.
I'll see to that if there is need. He ought of right
To take him in, and might be willing to—
140   He may be better than appearances.
But have some pity on Silas. Do you think
If he had any pride in claiming kin
Or anything he looked for from his brother,
He'd keep so still about him all this time?"

145   "I wonder what's between them."

                                "I can tell you.
Silas is what he is—we wouldn't mind him—
But just the kind that kinsfolk can't abide.
He never did a thing so very bad.
150   He don't know why he isn't quite as good
As anybody. Worthless though he is,
He won't be made ashamed to please his brother."

"*I* can't think Si ever hurt anyone."

"No, but he hurt my heart the way he lay
155   And rolled his old head on that sharp-edged chair-back.
He wouldn't let me put him on the lounge.
You must go in and see what you can do.
I made the bed up for him there tonight.
You'll be surprised at him—how much he's broken.
160   His working days are done; I'm sure of it."

"I'd not be in a hurry to say that."

"I haven't been. Go, look, see for yourself.
But, Warren, please remember how it is:

He's come to help you ditch the meadow.
165   He has a plan. You mustn't laugh at him.
He may not speak of it, and then he may.
I'll sit and see if that small sailing cloud
Will hit or miss the moon."

                    It hit the moon.
170   Then there were three there, making a dim row,
The moon, the little silver cloud, and she.

Warren returned—too soon, it seemed to her—
Slipped to her side, caught up her hand and waited.

"Warren?" she questioned.

175   "Dead," was all he answered.

Questions for Discussion

1. Examine the passages describing the cloud, the moon, and the stick, and explain their significance or **symbolism.**

2. Support or attack Mary's statement that Silas had "nothing to look backward to with pride, / And nothing to look forward to with hope."

Suggestions for Exploration and Writing

1. Silas thinks that Harold's studying "Latin, like the violin, / Because he liked it" is ridiculous. Write an essay supporting or opposing Harold's point of view.

2. Mary says, "I know just how it feels / To think of the right thing to say too late." Write an essay about an incident in which you thought of "the right thing to say too late."

3. Write an essay comparing the marriage in "The Death of the Hired Man" with that in "Home Burial."

4. Warren and Mary handle the same situation differently. Discuss in an essay how these differences define their personalities.

5. The two dialogue poems by Frost, "Home Burial" and "The Death of the Hired Man," depicting the conversation between a husband and wife, are written in blank verse. Write an essay on one or both of these poems illustrating Frost's skill in writing poetry that successfully imitates conversation.

THE SILKEN TENT   (1942)

She is as in a field a silken tent
At midday when a sunny summer breeze
Has dried the dew and all its ropes relent,

So that in guys it gently sways at ease,
5   And its supporting central cedar pole,
That is its pinnacle to heavenward
And signifies the sureness of the soul,
Seems to owe naught to any single cord,
But strictly held by none, is loosely bound
10   By countless silken ties of love and thought
To everything on earth the compass round,
And only by one's going slightly taut
In the capriciousness of summer air
Is of the slightest bondage made aware.

Questions for Discussion

1. Look at the structure of this sonnet. If the words were put into paragraph form, what would be the most striking point?

2. The silken tent is "loosely bound / By countless silken ties of love and thought" to earth. What is the contrast in the last three lines? What specific words show this contrast, and what is the significance of these words?

Suggestions for Exploration and Writing

1. The woman is portrayed as a silken tent. Analyze all the images conveyed by this simile. What type of person is this woman? What are her attitudes toward life? Write an essay analyzing her character.

2. Discuss in an essay how the boundaries of a marriage also provide freedom.

3. Agree or disagree with this statement: Women rule and men drool!

PUTTING IN THE SEED   (1916)

You come to fetch me from my work tonight
When supper's on the table, and we'll see
If I can leave off burying the white
Soft petals fallen from the apple tree
5   (Soft petals, yes, but not so barren quite,
Mingled with these, smooth bean and wrinkled pea),
And go along with you ere you lose sight
Of what you came for and become like me,
Slave to a springtime passion for the earth.
10   How Love burns through the Putting in the Seed
On through the watching for that early birth
When, just as the soil tarnishes with weed,
The sturdy seedling with arched body comes
Shouldering its way and shedding the earth crumbs.

Questions for Discussion

1. What is the situation in this poem?
2. What is the husband's attitude toward working in his orchard or garden? How does this attitude parallel his feelings toward his wife?
3. Explain the double meaning of the title.

Suggestion for Exploration and Writing

1. The two sonnets by Frost, "The Silken Tent" and "Putting in the Seed," describe the love between a man and a woman. Review the introductory section on poetry form. Then either select one of the two sonnets and show how Frost uses the sonnet form to create the love poem, or compare the relationships portrayed in the two sonnets.

MENDING WALL   (1914)

Something there is that doesn't love a wall,
That sends the frozen-ground-swell under it
And spills the upper boulders in the sun,
And makes gaps even two can pass abreast.
5   The work of hunters is another thing:
I have come after them and made repair
Where they have left not one stone on a stone,
But they would have the rabbit out of hiding,
To please the yelping dogs. The gaps I mean,
10 No one has seen them made or heard them made,
But at spring mending-time we find them there.
I let my neighbor know beyond the hill;
And on a day we meet to walk the line
And set the wall between us once again.
15 We keep the wall between us as we go.
To each the boulders that have fallen to each.
And some are loaves and some so nearly balls
We have to use a spell to make them balance:
"Stay where you are until our backs are turned!"
20 We wear our fingers rough with handling them.
Oh, just another kind of outdoor game,
One on a side. It comes to little more:
There where it is we do not need the wall:
He is all pine and I am apple orchard.
25 My apple trees will never get across
And eat the cones under his pines, I tell him.
He only says, "Good fences make good neighbors."
Spring is the mischief in me, and I wonder
If I could put a notion in his head:
30 "*Why* do they make good neighbors? Isn't it

Where there are cows? But here there are no cows.
Before I built a wall I'd ask to know
What I was walling in or walling out,
And to whom I was like to give offense.
35   Something there is that doesn't love a wall,
That wants it down." I could say "Elves" to him,
But it's not elves exactly, and I'd rather
He said it for himself. I see him there,
Bringing a stone grasped firmly by the top
40   In each hand, like an old-stone savage armed.
He moves in darkness as it seems to me,
Not of woods only and the shade of trees.
He will not go behind his father's saying,
And he likes having thought of it so well
45   He says again, "Good fences make good neighbors."

Questions for Discussion

1. What causes the wall to disintegrate?

2. Why does Frost call repairing the wall "just another kind of outdoor game"?

3. Explain Frost's description of his neighbor as "an old stone-savage armed" who "moves in darkness." Why does the neighbor choose not to answer the narrator's question?

4. Does the narrator want the wall rebuilt? Is his questioning the wall genuine or joking? Why, if he thinks the wall unnecessary, does he cooperate in rebuilding it?

Suggestion for Exploration and Writing

1. Write an essay in which you support one of the following quotations from the poem:

> Something there is that doesn't love a wall.
> "Good fences make good neighbors."

A New American Poet[1]

Edward Garnett

[. . . A] literary friend chanced to place in my hands a slim green volume, *North of Boston,* by Robert Frost. I read it, and reread it. It seemed to me that this poet was destined to take a permanent place in American literature. I asked myself why this book was issued by an English and not by an American publisher. And to this question I have found no answer. I

---

[1]Edward Garnett, "A New American Poet," *Atlantic Monthly* August 1915. Online. Internet. 14 July 1999. Available http://www.theatlantic.com/unbound/poetry/frost/garnett.htm.

may add here, in parenthesis, that I know nothing of Mr. Robert Frost save the three or four particulars I gleaned from the English friend who sent me *North of Boston*.

On opening *North of Boston* we see the first lines to be stamped with the magic of *style,* of a style that obeys its own laws of grace and beauty and inner harmony.

> Something there is that doesn't love a wall,
> That sends the frozen-ground-swell under it,
> And spills the upper boulders in the sun;
> And makes gaps even two can pass abreast.
> The work of hunters is another thing:
> I have come after them and made repair
> Where they have left not one stone on stone,
> But they would have the rabbit out of hiding,
> To please the yelping dogs.

Note the clarity of the images, the firm outline. How delicately the unobtrusive opening suggests the countryman's contemplative pleasure in his fields and woods. [. . .] And when we turn the page, the second poem, "The Death of the Hired Man," proves that this American poet has arrived, not indeed to challenge the English poet's possession of his territory, but to show how untrodden, how limitless are the stretching adjacent lands. "The Death of the Hired Man" is a dramatic dialogue between husband and wife, a dialogue characterized by an exquisite precision of psychological insight. [. . .]

Mr. Frost possesses a keen feeling for situation. And his fine, sure touch in clarifying our obscure instincts and clashing impulses, and in crystallizing them in sharp, precise images—for that we cannot be too grateful.

Yes, this is poetry, but of what order? the people may question, to whom for some reason poetry connotes the fervor of lyrical passion, the glow of romantic color, or the play of picturesque fancy. But it is precisely its quiet passion and spiritual tenderness that betray this to be poetry of a rare order, "the poetry of a true real natural vision of life," which, as Goethe declared, "demands descriptive power of the highest degree, rendering a poet's pictures so lifelike that they become actualities to every reader."

But it is best to give an example of Mr. Frost's emotional force, and in quoting a passage from "Home Burial" I say unhesitatingly that for tragic poignancy this piece stands by itself in American poetry. How dramatic is the action, in this moment of revelation of the tragic rift sundering man and wife! [. . .]

He entreats his wife to let him into her grief, and not to carry it, this time, to someone else. He entreats her to tell him why the loss of her first child has bred in her such rankling bitterness toward him, and why every word of his about the dead child gives her such offense. [. . .] Here is vision, bearing the flame of piercing feeling in the living word. How exquisitely the strain of the mother's anguish is felt in that naked image—

> "Making the gravel leap and leap in air,
> Leap up like that, like that, and land so lightly."

Perhaps some readers, deceived by the supreme simplicity of this passage, may not see what art has inspired its perfect naturalness. It is indeed the perfection of poetic realism, both in observation and in deep insight into the heart.

In nearly all Mr. Frost's quiet dramatic dialogues, his record of the present passing scene suggests how much has gone before, how much these people have lived through, what a lengthy chain of feelings and motives and circumstances has shaped their actions and mental attitudes.

TALKING ABOUT POEMS WITH ROBERT FROST[1]

WILLIAM G. O'DONNELL

When I met Frost unexpectedly outside the Lord Jeffery one Saturday afternoon in October—the Amherst football game had ended a few minutes earlier and people were drifting back to the center of town—he suggested a drink and led the way through the crowded lobby of the Inn to the cocktail lounge downstairs. [. . .] Unconcerned at the parties in progress all around us, he seemed determined to set a few things straight.

The idiomatic language of *North of Boston,* his breakthrough volume, what Edward Thomas in 1914 called "one of the most revolutionary books of modern times," marked the end of the old-fashioned diction and, beyond that, the end of a conventionality of mood occasionally found in the writing prior to 1912. In the future there would be no more "fens," no leaves blowing "alway," no suggestions of melancholy regret. In the second volume a different kind of language commenced and with it a rhythm marked by more heavily accentuated syllables: "Something there is that doesn't love a wall [. . .] " "The gaps I mean, / No one has seen them made or heard them made [. . .] " "Oh, just another kind of outdoor game, / One on a side." With these now familiar lines the forty-year-old Frost finally came into his own.

---

[1]William G. O'Donnell, "Talking About Poems with Robert Frost," *Massachusetts Review* 39.2 (Summer 1998): 225–49.

"Mending Wall" raises a question he preferred to leave unanswered: at what point before 1914 did he give up all trace of his earlier style?

When he spoke of poems he had composed before 1913, he would give the impression that in his first New Hampshire period he had written in two styles, one somewhat traditional, the other his personal, distinctive, ultimate style. Brief footnotes he added to individual volumes identified a few poems that existed for a long time as fragments and were completed years later, but he never attempted to fix the precise dates of composition of the more famous pieces in *North of Boston*, flatly refusing to give this information to Charles Green, his first bibliographer. Nor did he ever tell how it happened that in "The Hired Man," "Mending Wall," "The Wood-Pile," "A Servant to Servants," and the others, thirteen in all, he decided to write blank verse, a medium in which he had accomplished nothing of consequence earlier. The only example of blank verse in *A Boy's Will*, "Waiting," an echo of Milton's "Il Penseroso," provides no hint of a future genius in the form, no suggestion of a "Mending Wall."

At the readings he used to say that he liked all his poems without exception: if he lived long enough, he would eventually do each one in public several times. Talking with him privately, however, I learned of a special feeling he had for a few of the poems, above all those that won immediate popular approval and, in addition, were composed rapidly, in a day or two, or even at a single sitting. He liked "The Hired Man," "Stopping by Woods," "Directive," and several others that he had written, at least so he said, in a kind of "intoxication," an effortless glide of inspiration.

He would deny the existence of double meanings in the universally popular "Mending Wall": people had been finding far too much in that poem, discovering things he never intended when he composed it. Actually, multiple significances abound in the lines from beginning to end and give the poem a special quality; when the old-style farmer ("'Good fences make good neighbors'") is likened to "an old-stone savage" moving about in darkness, armed and dangerous, the way has been opened for a variety of readings regardless of what Frost himself may have intended.

I remember an unusual commentary he made on "The Silken Tent," one of the best of his twenty-seven sonnets, one that should have satisfied John Crowe Ransom's exacting demands for unity in the form. The free-ranging commentary came about as a result of his agreeing to make a half-hour taped recording of approximately fifteen of his poems as part of a series of eight radio programs entitled "New England Anthology" that several of us were preparing during the spring of 1954 under a grant from a national foundation. [. . .] I broke the news to Frost that I myself had selected the list of poems he would read, including "Directive" and "The Silken Tent." "Oh, I always select the poems I say," he said, and for upwards of half an hour I gave him a list of reasons why it had to be different this time, and he finally agreed, reluctantly, to do my list instead of his own. I then went on to explain that part way through the recording he would stop reciting poems and talk for eight minutes on the theme of our program, freedom. "I'll hold up a card saying, 'Now talk for eight minutes on freedom.'" "Oh, you know I can't do that," said Frost, and I thereupon spent a second half hour getting him to change his mind again—no small accomplishment in view of his stubbornness in such matters.

Later, he had me meet him at the Lord Jeff one afternoon a couple of days before the scheduled recording session so as to try out what he'd been considering as a commentary on what he called "your chosen subject." Perhaps he would talk a little about "The Silken Tent," he said, three lines in particular: "But strictly held by none, is loosely bound / By countless silken ties of love and thought / To everything on earth the compass round." You could take the poem as a tribute to a lady, and maybe that was the correct way of taking it, but this time he preferred to read it otherwise. Someone has said that we are the sum of our relationships. (He didn't identify the "someone" although it may have been William James.) You can imagine that an invisible silken thread goes out from each one of us to every person and thing we know, and the place where all those threads come together somewhere inside us, that little knot where they all converge, that's the soul; that's what we are, the sum of our relationships.

One purpose of the carefully prepared twenty-minute lecture he presented as an introduction to many of his readings at Amherst College was to persuade the younger generation in the audience to resist the English professors and the critics and enjoy poetry. He had a unique way of urging students not to be afraid of a particular poem, not to be afraid of poetry, not to be afraid of literature. He would read one of his familiar poems, perhaps "Stopping by Woods," pause for a moment or two and then, ignoring the faculty members in the audience, say, "I'd hate to tell you what the professors have been saying about that one." It was one of his charming stances: the old poet, sneaky as well as venerable, in alliance with the kids. Teaching poems, he seemed to believe, is a rather doubtful proceeding at best since someone else's comments, no matter how brilliant and profound, won't solve anyone's problem of learning how to read a poem. Although one person's interpretation may be superior to another's, sooner or later you have no choice but to venture out on your own and decide what, if anything, a particular poem is all about. It's an individual matter, like your sense of identity. Through the many years of successful performances on the platform at Amherst, that was a topic he kept returning to. His attitude wasn't without its dangers, of course, since suggestions of anti-intellectualism could sometimes be heard in the talks, as if Frost, privileged character in the academic world though he was, had grown weary, not only of literary criticism, but of the whole complicated enterprise of higher education in America. Still, there could be no denying a certain Socratic element in the poet as he began at Amherst and made his slow progress through the colleges each year, gently antagonizing the establishment, upsetting his good friends the professors, and reminding people that they would either discover poetry on their own or risk not discovering it at all.

Toward Robert Frost: The Reader and the Poet[1]

Judith Oster

If there is to be "salvation in surrender," there must be mutuality of surrender, not the selfless submission of the servant; there must be a balance between surrender and "keeping."—[L]oving, slight "bondage" is idealized in that magnificent tribute to woman-in-relation, "The Silken Tent". [. . .] This poem is not about a personified love, [. . .] but love as it is seen and felt in a loving woman, and thus the poem is a tribute to the kind of woman who, because of her loving and thoughtful ties to others, becomes proud, erect, and beautiful even as she exists as a shelter, creating a home, or providing a haven of privacy and emotional protection.

The silken tent swaying gently at ease presents an image not only of beauty but of dignity and free movement—the tent swaying "in guys" sways also in the "guise" of freedom of movement. But one guy going taut, a summer breeze, or increased moisture remind her occasionally of "the slightest bondage." Because these ties are ties of love and thought, however, because they are "silken ties," the slight bondage is not undesirable. What is necessary and positive about such bondage only becomes fully apparent when we realize that in giving she receives; that those "ties" to others are what keep her erect, that were those ties to snap, the tent would collapse; that heavenward pinnacle signifying the sureness of the soul would fall, for nothing emanates simply from the pole. The pole stands only in relation to the guys. It is important, too, that the ties are many, for that very diversity is what keeps the pole balanced at the center. In the relationship between heavenward pole and guys, it is almost as if the ties of love and thought are in fact her claim to heaven.

This poem of loving bondage and of an existence based upon it is a perfect example of form and words, form and idea, "embracing." It has been observed that the entire sonnet is a single sentence, but what seems

---

[1]From Judith Oster, *Toward Robert Frost: The Reader and the Poet* (Athens: U of Georgia P, 1991) 181–223. Throughout the essay, Oster uses CP for Frost's *Complete Poems* and SP for his *Selected Prose*.

so remarkable is the way in which the structure of this sentence is analogous to the metaphor itself and to the relationship that the metaphor expresses. The single sentence construction provides, even more firmly than the sonnet form, a unified tightness which corresponds to the tightness of the single image and the tightness of the ropes controlling the very existence of the silken structure. At the same time, the sentence comes perilously close to going out of control with its multiplication of subordinate clauses (a guise of freedom).

When one identifies the subordinate clauses, their subjects, verbs, and antecedents, one discovers that the sentence raises some real syntactical questions: for one, what is the main clause? For another, if "as" is used as a conjunction of comparison, it must introduce a clause—a subject and a predicate. Assuming the tent to be the subject, what verb completes the clause—what verb that is not inside another clause and governed by its own subject? We find that "tent" actually governs no verb in the poem. For example, the subject of "sways" in line 4 is "it"; the subject of "seems" and "is loosely bound" is really "pole." The "and" clause of the final three lines refers to "tent" as an implied subject of "is [. . .] made aware," but since the clause is a coordinate, not a subordinate clause, since "and" creates a compound sentence, we are still left with the question of what the verb should be of which "tent" is the subject in the "as" clause, that is, in the first half of the compound sentence that is contained in the larger complex one. It is interesting that the subtlety of control that is a subject of the poem is also carried out in the syntactic structure of the poem. Just as "tent" is the implied subject of "is [. . .] made aware," so is it the antecedent of "it" as the subject of "sways." Thus what the word "tent" does not do directly, "tent" as implied subject, as antecedent, does do indirectly—another "guise" of freedom, here freedom from the grammatical control of "tent" as subject.

One might so easily be tempted to identify "seems" (line 8) and "is loosely bound" as the verbs completing the clause whose subject is "tent," rendering it: "as [. . .] a silken tent [. . .] seems to owe naught to any single cord, but [. . .] is loosely bound by countless silken ties of love and thought." But then we run into problems of another kind in such a structure. The whole sentence would then essentially read: "She is as a tent seems to owe naught to any single cord, but [. . .] is loosely bound," which makes no sense. Even were we to insert "which" before "seems" we would still be left with an uncompleted clause. Were we to reverse the sentence— "As a tent seems to owe naught to one [. . .] but is loosely bound to many, she is"—we still have not solved the difficulty. The parallelism is faulty.

Further examination, of course, proves that it is not "tent" but "pole" that is the subject of the verbs under discussion. We find, too, that the "and" of line 12 really coordinates *within* the clause whose subject is "pole." The sentence reduced to simpler terms would read: "and its pole seems to owe naught to any single cord, but is loosely held by countless ties to earth, and only by one's going taut is of the slightest bondage made aware." What then is "made aware"? The pole, it seems; yet because of the word "its" we are forced to make the connection between pole and tent. What keeps up the pole—or binds it—is keeping up and binding the tent that it supports. Somehow the existence and erectness of the tent has become identified with the uprightness of the supporting pole, as if one cannot syntactically separate the pole from the tent any more than one can separate "sureness of the soul" from "her." Indeed we are forced back to "her" because there must be more than grammar operating in a sentence: there must also be sense—semantic sense—and this sense tells us that a pole cannot "be made aware." Just as a distinction is sometimes made between the grammatical subject of a sentence and its logical subject; so we find that a distinction must be drawn between a grammatical subject— even a logical subject—and an "emotional" one, one that we *feel* to be the subject, the dictates of grammar notwithstanding. "Pole" is the grammatical subject of "seems to owe naught," and as such it is logical as well; "tent," while it is not the grammatical subject, is also a logical subject of the same verb. When we get to "is made aware," however, we must reject both "pole" and "tent" as logical subjects. Only "she" can be made aware. The logic of our feelings has supplied the human subject, grammar and logic have supplied "tent" and "pole," and the operation of all three has forced the metaphoric fusion.

What of the original questions of main clause, though, and of verb to complete "tent"? They seem resolvable only if one can insert an implied "is" so that line 1 would essentially say: "She is as is [. . .] a silken tent in a field at midday" and on to the end. The parallelism then is one based on existence—analogous existence. And we must see this in relation to Frost's choice of "as" over "like."

The first line lends itself to two possible readings:

$$\text{(1) she is} \left\{ \begin{array}{l} \text{as} \\ \text{like} \end{array} \right\} \text{(in a field)} \quad \text{[pause]} \xrightarrow{\text{lowered pitch}} \text{a silken tent}$$

$$\text{(2) she} \left\{ \begin{array}{l} \text{is} \\ \text{exists} \end{array} \right\} \xrightarrow{\text{[sustained pitch and pause]}} \text{as [is] in a field a silken tent}$$

At first glance, (1) seems to have been intended. This would presume that "as" is being used for the preposition "like," a function that it actually does not have. Version (2), on the other hand, uses "as" correctly as a conjunction, and the result is the emphasis on existence and the necessity for assuming an implied "is." The whole grammatical problem would not have existed at all had Frost allowed the sentence to read: "She is like a silken tent in a field at midday, when a summer breeze has dried the dew, and all its ropes relent." It would make perfect sense, better sense, even, all the way to the end. By using "as," and thereby forcing us to supply the missing "is" for "tent," Frost has created a subtle distinction between "like" and "as." He has rejected the easier comparison between woman and tent and forced the comparison, not of nouns, but of relationships. She is not like a tent; she exists in the same manner as a tent does, by means of the same conflicting, balancing pulls. So the main clause can only be "she is"; and highlighting this clause at the very outset creates a compelling relationship between the fact and the manner of her existence.

As we have noted, only when one guy goes taut does the tent pole seem tied down; only when affairs are not proceeding smoothly, only when one "tie" of "love" pulls in an unusual way, is the woman made aware of "bondage" that she never feels when her "ties" are smooth and in balance. These countless ties, of course, are only countless when we apply the term to the ties of love and thought binding the woman, for surely actual tent guys *can* be counted. Once more, we have been deftly moved from a concrete tent to qualities and feelings that the tent as metaphor makes clear. Once more we are reminded that it is in the balance, in the manner of existence, that we find the analogy.

There is another aspect to the relationship between tent, pole, and guys. The tent depends for its uprightness, in fact for its very existence, upon the relationship between pole and guys. We are told that this "supporting central cedar pole" is "its pinnacle to heavenward / And signifies the sureness of the soul." We are not only told that these things of the spirit are bound by ties of love and thought but that they are bound by these ties "to everything on earth the compass round." Such a connection only serves to reinforce the relation of spirit to matter—in other words, that the spirit is dependent upon matter, that the spirit must rest on earth, that love is bound to earth or else its spirit cannot rise heavenward, cannot remain erect, and finally that the tent, and what it signifies as a loving woman, remains beautiful and erect by virtue of both the heavenward pole and the ties to earth, ultimately "the right place for love."

The one remaining problem involves the word "seems" ("seems to owe not to any single cord"), which raises the question: seems to whom? The fact that tent and pole are incapable of perception rules out these possibilities. The remaining possibilities are: (1) the casual observer of the scene, (2) the woman who has been metaphorically connected with tent and pole, or (3) the reader. If the reference is to the tent, then this is the way it seems to the casual observer; if it is to the woman, it may refer to the way it "seems" to her—the nature of seeming thus related to the "guise" of freedom that is, in reality, a complicated bondage. Psychologically this can refer to her self-delusion, her unawareness of bondage when there is no tension or pulling of a guy. In looking at the implications for the poem itself, however, "seems" reminds us of the manner in which we as readers are finding it difficult to keep tent, pole, and woman apart, the way in which metaphor works on us, and the way in which we depend upon illusion and manipulate illusion as metaphor ourselves. We can imagine the way in which the metaphor, once conceived, continued to work on—and for—Frost as he was working it into a poem, the ways he may have needed that metaphor, the needs he brought to his reading of the metaphor, and his reading of the relationship that created it. One need may have been of that very relationship. To be one of the guys is to play a relatively safe role, as the tent will not collapse if only one goes slack, for it is not dependent on any *one;* at the same time, if the guy does not slacken, it remains "tied" to the tent and benefits from the spiritual sureness of the pole, even as it contributes to its erectness. Because the dominant image is that of woman in relation, we tend to lose sight of how important the relationship is to the guys.

This need for relationship, for balanced, mutual support, makes even more dramatic its failure in a poem such as "Home Burial"; the need to keep by spending is best illustrated by the *un*willingness of either partner in that poem to give up any part of the self. Fierce possessiveness of one's feelings, of one's sense of who and what one is or should be, of one's self-conceived role, plays a large part in that disaster, the marriage in "Home Burial." So does a frustrating unwillingness on both their parts to respect, along with an inability to understand, what the other partner is feeling. "Who is that man? I didn't know you" (CP71), the wife said of her reaction to his digging of the grave. Indeed she did not seem to "know" him, not in any sense of the word, but then he did not "know" her either; neither did he know himself, or she, herself. The husband's offer of "some arrangement / by which I'd [. . .] keep hands off / anything special you've a mind to name" and his recognition that "two that don't love can't live together without [such restraints] / but two that do can't live together with them" (70–71) is exactly to the point. What he may not understand, however, is that what she wants his "hands off" are not peripheral possessions but what is fundamental to a love relationship—her person and her feelings. His plea, "Let me into *your* grief," is at the same time acknowledgment of this very separateness that he claims two who love cannot live with. It is as if this grief, "*your* grief," is a prized possession that she needs to feel exclusively hers, but he has allowed her to feel this way, letting it be *her* grief, never shouting, "This grief is *ours,* not yours," in just those words. Now is the one time, by saying "twice over *before he knew himself:* 'can't a man speak of his own child he's lost?'" (70), that he names the loss as his as well. He has been moved to speak out of character, an indication that this verbalizing of the loss has only just now come for the first time. He too can see it only as "his own," as if to imply the loss is his, the grief is hers.

She will not allow him the right to speak of the loss because of this distinction; one who does not *feel* the loss has no right to *express* the loss, and it is not only he but "any man" who cannot be allowed to enter the grief of a woman. He asks for help but seems to agree with her stereotypic view that to be a man is to fail in this arena of human emotions:

> My words are nearly always an offense.
> I don't know how to speak of anything
> So as to please you. But I might be taught

I should suppose. *I can't say I see how.*
A man must partly give up being a man
With women-folk. (CP 70; emphasis mine)

Deeper than the misunderstanding of each other's words and motives lies this fundamental misunderstanding about what manhood should be. It would require a woman of greater sensitivity and larger feeling than she to be the teacher of that verbal expression he requires, for to teach a new language, the teacher must try to understand the broken and sometimes incomprehensible attempts of the inarticulate learner.

It is here that gesture and action could potentially have bridged the gap in verbal communication. One of the horrors of this poem is that, when action takes the place of words, it is as inadequate as the words, and just as misunderstood. Action is used to reject communication, as in her silent stiffening of her neck, or in her "fingers mov[ing] the latch for all reply." He uses action in a mistaken attempt to force communication, mounting until she cowers under him. "I will find out now—you must tell me, dear" (69–70), that "dear" so incongruous and out of place with the forceful five consecutive stresses of "I will find out now"—and just as futile. As futile, too, is the threat of force in the last line: "I'll follow and bring you back by force. I *will!*" (73). It is just as clumsily that he used action to vent his feelings when he dug the little grave. We have her account of it. [. . .]

He did the "manly" thing in digging that little grave himself, and "manly" too was his ability to "sit there with the stains on [his] shoes / Of the fresh earth from [his] own baby's grave / And talk about [his] everyday concerns." (We could contrast him at this point with the unmistakably manly Macduff, who, dazed at the news of the death of "all [his] pretty ones, all," must reject Malcolm's appeal to "revenge it like a man" until he has had his opportunity to "feel it like a man." "He has no children," Macduff says of the man who thinks first of action before he allows for grief.) It is a very limited self-respect and a carefully circumscribed view of "manhood" that requires that a man's self-respect as a man deny feeling, deny verbal or emotional giving in to grief. Now the husband is ready "to laugh the worst laugh I have ever laughed," seeing himself as "cursed. God, if I don't believe I'm cursed" (72). He must mean a laugh of bitterness which could be at the irony of the way she saw that gravedigging, or it could be at himself for his emotional limitation.

Her view of his action must have been as literal-minded as her understanding of what he had said as he had come in from the digging of the grave:

I can repeat the very words you were saying.
'Three foggy mornings and one rainy day
Will rot the best birch fence a man can build.'
Think of it, talk like that at such a time!
What had how long it takes a birch to rot
To do with what was in the darkened parlor. (CP 72)

It has, of course, a great deal to do with it. It is ironic that she, who faults his inability to phrase questions, to "see," is herself totally unable to "see" and "hear"; that she seems capable only of understanding literal exclamations but is totally unable to understand metaphor; that he, nonverbal man that he is, finds expression in metaphor that she cannot interpret.

With all the grievances out on the table now, one could hope for the understanding that may come out of it to save the marriage, but the opportunity is irrevocably lost, again because of his inability to come out with a genuine expression of feeling, or his inability to understand or tolerate her grief. His assertion that she overdoes it a little is not necessarily untrue, but at this moment it is so tactless, so wrong. Worse still is his failure to explain why he shall laugh the worst laugh he ever laughed, his failure to explain what that rotting birch fence had to do with the little body in the parlor, his acceptance of her accusation, "you *couldn't* care!" In this revealing dialogue, he has finally noticed what it is she always looks at out there. He has finally found words to ask her for some explanation, and then, ironically, having found his tongue, he "think[s] the talk is all" (73).

Of course, as a man of action, he could have let his actions speak, but even his actions serve more to hide his feelings than to reveal them, assuming he is feeling grief or love. In his being more preoccupied with someone's seeing his wife crying than he is with the crying itself ("Amy! There's someone coming down the road!"), he has lost his last opportunity. The opening and closing of the door at the end, like the crossing of the stairs at the beginning, are actions that lead nowhere in the relationship. They are the empty gestures which throw into relief the crossing that took place rather than the meeting that should have; she responds to the plea to "let me in" by opening the door—not to let him in but to let herself out, for the home entraps her not only in marriage to this man but within a reality she tries desperately to escape.

In his digging the grave he demonstrates his acceptance of the death, his instinctive acceptance of the fact that he buries much as he plants. He accepts his own hard and bitter role and responsibility, rather than having anyone else take the burden from him. She, who cannot accept death, who "won't have grief so," cannot accept his acceptance. Her saying "the world's evil" is more extreme than saying the world is sad or unbearable. She introduces evil where there is perhaps only a hard fact of nature and life. She won't have grief so *if she can change it,* but of course she cannot change it; to see this she would have had to see that her own grief could be changed only by her ability to transcend it, to allow it some healing.

We can only assume that he does not explain or discuss these things because they have not formed as ideas in his mind. Rather he acts instinctively; he fails to understand that she cannot do the same, because he is not thinking of these things; he only lives by them. It is the husband who compares the graveyard to a bedroom in a smooth and calm speech that contrasts strongly with the nervous, staccato irregularity of the wife's speech rhythms. [. . .]

Surely without understanding the implications of what he has just said, he nevertheless instinctively grasps the relationship between the bedroom and the grave—the place of love, the place of birth, and the place of death as they all relate to each other in the process of life, which includes death as well as birth.

He can easily incorporate that physical fact of life into his own life by virtue of his own physicalness. This translates itself into his ability to dig without being emotionally paralyzed by what has necessitated that digging. It also shows in the physicalness of his responses to his wife's perverse stiffness. He *checks* his actions, he promises not to come down the stairs, then threatens again: "You make me angry. I'll come down to you / God, what a woman!" At the end, there is his inability to see any recourse other than brute force: "If—you—do! [. . .] I'll follow and bring you back by force. I *will!*"

Her cowering beneath him at the beginning of the poem suggests her fear of his brute force. Yet a moment before this, her face had "changed from terrified to dull"—dull as she faced him, terrified as she still was from having looked "back over her shoulder at some fear." The view that frightened her was that of the mound in the graveyard. Terror was probably compounded of this fear, fear of her husband's seeing it, and also, perhaps, fear of her husband's anger or strength, as we have already seen in her cowering. Still the realities of life and death are the sources of terror, and fear of him is only a part of this. It would seem that we have here still another example of failed communication, missed opportunity, and misunderstanding of manliness. The marriage is, among other things, a combination of a woman who seems unable to accept the hard facts of life and death and a man who is too completely physical, who feels that to express himself in words to womenfolk is "partly [to] give up being a man." Perhaps to express tenderness or gentleness physically may have been equally compromising to his perception of manhood. We cannot know, but it would be consistent with his mode of action and with her response. Just as she cannot meet him half way to help him express himself, just as she refuses to understand his mode of expression, so he cannot understand her needs in her grief or her inability to accept the brutal realities of life and death. Their home has been buried as surely as that child has been.

We have seen that Frost's poems often show a speaker identifying uncomfortably with aspects of nature which he wishes were not so reminiscent of his own inner nature; he may find in scenes of dissolution, disintegration, and destruction that which is too close to his fears of his own physical and psychic destruction. But binding humans even more closely to nature "outside" is an element in nature that he can recognize, not as analogous to him, but *within* him. In love, birth, and death, for example, we are one with nature, participating in the natural process, which operates within us as surely as in nonhuman nature, and it is here that we are not separate from nature but *of* it.

While in some poems Frost demonstrates the need for human beings to see themselves separate from nature, he also demonstrates the folly of being unwilling to recognize not only the similarities we share with nature but the actual connections.

❧

In Frost's poetry we see man seeking but only seldom finding harmony between himself and nature, and then it is usually by means of love. We have seen the creativity of love as it manifests itself in harvest, or human birth, or artistic creation. In these ways we can take comfort from our connection with nature and with others in love or communion. But we also share mortality with nature and may never feel reconciled with a reality that has as its inevitable end our own nonbeing—a state we cannot conceive—a return to earth as dust to dust, being "turned under" for future growth.[2] As conscious beings we cannot help resisting the notion of our being simply more organic matter in a nitrogen cycle; yet as humans we cannot help but be aware of this prospect.[. . . T]he very awareness of our mortality, our vulnerability, and our isolation is what informs our human vision. At the same time, while forcing us to confront painful reality—future and past, not merely present—this very humanness also seeks perpetually to fashion wholes from fragments, even if only to smash them once more; to make order out of the chaos, even if the order is "momentary"; to see patterns and connections, even if these too turn out to be illusory.

The poet sees connections, sees by means of metaphor what cannot be seen any other way, for there are perceptions and fears and feelings for which there is no logical explanation, no expression or description. With metaphor we are able to take in whole what cannot be made sensible by logical division and reconstruction of its parts; take intuitive, imaginative leaps, and bridge the gap between the known and the unknown by referring to what is known and concrete and within the range of our experience. We can deny, as did Frost, any comfort in death; we can resist, as he did, any reconciliation with it. We can put all the platitudinous statements about life and the continuity of life, love, and creation in any order we choose, and they remain unconvincing and wooden schemata that our feelings balk at and our minds cannot fathom. Yet "the sturdy seedling with arched body comes / shouldering its way and shedding the earth crumbs" says it all and says it in a manner that we can understand and, momentarily at least, accept. This is "the figure a poem makes [. . .] it assumes direction with the first line laid down, it runs a course of lucky events, and ends in a clarification of life—not necessarily a great clarification [. . .] but in a momentary stay against confusion" (SP 18).

[2]See "Build Soil" (CP 428).

The poem, however, does not simply clarify; it exists as a work of art whose creator gave it life. [. . . D]eath at our back provides a powerful stimulus to create—to leave something, to make what will outlive us. Then, too, death is the subject of our art. When we perceive the paradoxical dualities of life, we have something *from* which to fashion art, about which to write poetry. We also need to create order and harmony to provide for ourselves and our fellows that "momentary stay against confusion," to *create* meaning where we cannot see it. Our being human, then, not only impels awareness of our mortality but drives us to create. Like the rest of nature we die, but unlike the rest of nature we know of death and anticipate it. Limited by our humanity, however, we can neither understand this nor imagine it. Like the rest of nature we mate and reproduce; unlike the rest of nature, we seek to invest such union with communion; we see in procreation some kind of answer, unsatisfactory though it may be, to our individual dissolutions, and of course we see other ways to create, thereby hoping to achieve a measure of immortality. [. . .] Frost [. . .] goes further in making us feel that there is an identity between the creative urge and the sexual urge, artistic fulfillment and sexual fulfillment, the work of art and the product of tilling—sexually or agriculturally, [. . .] for example, in "Putting in the Seed."

Works Cited

Frost, Robert. *Complete Poems of Robert Frost.* New York: Holt, Rinehart, and Winston, 1949,

———. *Selected Prose of Robert Frost.* Ed. Hyde Cox and Edward Connery Latham. New York: Collier, 1966.

Suggestions for Exploration and Writing

1. Write an essay explaining the causes for the failed marriage in "Home Burial."

2. Write an essay comparing the attitudes of the husbands and wives in "Home Burial" and "The Death of the Hired Man" and discussing the relationships that result from these attitudes.

3. The husband in "Home Burial" says:

   > We could have some arrangement
   > By which I'd bind myself to keep hands off
   > Anything special you're a-mind to name.
   > Though I don't like such things 'twixt those that love.
   > Two that don't love can't live together without them.
   > But two that do can't live together with them.

   In an essay, oppose or defend the husband's position.

4. In an essay, explain the symbolism in "The Silken Tent."

Langston Hughes (1902–1967)

Born in Joplin, Missouri, James Langston Hughes was a novelist, poet, and play-wright who often wrote in dialect to reflect what he considered to be the language of the ordinary "Negro." He graduated from Lincoln University in 1929 after attending Columbia University and after working with some of the most famous black writers of the Harlem Renaissance. Hughes founded theaters, produced plays, and traveled to such locales as Haiti, the Soviet Union, and Spain, where he cov-ered the Spanish Civil War. His many works include the Semple tales, the novels Not Without Laughter *(1930) and* Ask Your Mama *(1961), and the gospel musical* Tambourines to Glory *(1959). Hughes's poetry reflects several recur-ring themes: the racial tension that the black man experiences, the glorification of the common man or woman, and the importance of music, especially jazz and the blues. The following poems represent these themes.*

MOTHER TO SON   (1922)

Well, son, I'll tell you:
Life for me ain't been no crystal stair.
It's had tacks in it,
And splinters,
5   And boards torn up,
And places with no carpet on the floor—
Bare.
But all the time
I'se been a-climbin' on,
10 And reachin' landin's,
And turnin' corners,
And sometimes goin' in the dark
Where there ain't been no light.
So boy, don't you turn back.
15 Don't you set down on the steps
'Cause you finds it's kinder hard.

Don't you fall now—
For I'se still goin', honey,
I'se still climbin',
20   And life for me ain't been no crystal stair.

Questions for Discussion

1. What is the significance of the stair as a metaphor? Explain the meaning of each part of the metaphor.
2. Who is the best example for the son of what a strong black man should be?
3. Instead of telling her son what life *has* been, the mother tells him what life *has not* been. Why?

Suggestions for Exploration and Writing

1. Write an essay in which you discuss what life has not been for you.
2. Reread the poem and discuss in an essay what you think have been the "tacks," "splinters," "boards torn up," and bare floors in the woman's life. What are they likely to be in the son's life as a man?

A SONG TO A NEGRO WASH-WOMAN   (1925)

Oh, wash-woman,
    Arms elbow-deep in white suds,
    Soul washed clean,
    Clothes washed clean,—
5   I have many songs to sing you
    Could I but find the words.

Was it four o'clock or six o'clock on a winter afternoon,
    I saw you wringing out the last shirt in Miss White
    Lady's kitchen? Was it four o'clock or six o'clock?
10   I don't remember.

But I know, at seven one spring morning you were on
    Vermont Street with a bundle in your arms going to
    wash clothes.
And I know I've seen you in a New York subway train in
15   the late afternoon coming home from washing clothes.

Yes, I know you, wash-woman.
I know how you send your children to school, and high-
    school, and even college.
I know how you work and help your man when times are
20   hard.
I know how you build your house up from the wash-tub
    and call it home.

And how you raise your churches from white suds for the
   service of the Holy God.

25   And I've seen you singing, wash-woman. Out in the backyard garden under the apple trees, singing, hanging
   white clothes on long lines in the sun-shine.
And I've seen you in church a Sunday morning singing,
   praising your Jesus, because some day you're going to
30   sit on the right hand of the Son of God and forget
   you ever were a wash-woman. And the aching back
   and the bundles of clothes will be unremembered
   then.
Yes, I've seen you singing.

35   And for you,
   O singing wash-woman,
   For you, singing little brown woman,
   Singing strong black woman,
   Singing tall yellow woman,
40   Arms deep in white suds,
   Soul clean,
   Clothes clean,—
   For you I have many songs to make
   Could I but find the words.

Questions for Discussion

1. Why does Hughes say that he could sing many songs to the wash-woman if he could "find the words"? Why would the songs be a difficult task?

2. Washing is often used symbolically in the poem. What are some double meanings of the word or of "clean"?

3. Why is the woman singing? What are her rewards for a hard day's work?

Suggestion for Exploration and Writing

1. Write an essay in which you praise a particular type of worker.

JAZZONIA   (1923)

Oh, silver tree!
Oh, shining rivers of the soul!

In a Harlem cabaret
Six long-headed jazzers play.
5   A dancing girl whose eyes are bold
Lifts high a dress of silken gold.

Oh, singing tree!
Oh, shining rivers of the soul!

Were Eve's eyes
10   In the first garden
Just a bit too bold?
Was Cleopatra gorgeous
In a gown of gold?

Oh, shining tree!
15   Oh, silver rivers of the soul!

In a whirling cabaret
Six long-headed jazzers play.

Questions for Discussion

1. What devices does Langston Hughes use to create the jazz tone?
2. Explain the references to Eve and Cleopatra.

Suggestions for Exploration and Writing

1. Gathering all of the clues from this poem, write a character analysis of the cabaret girl.
2. In an essay, explain how the images of the poem suggest the bold improvisation of jazz.

THE WEARY BLUES   (1925)

Droning a drowsy syncopated tune,
Rocking back and forth to a mellow croon,
    I heard a Negro play.
Down on Lenox Avenue the other night
5   By the pale dull pallor of an old gas light
        He did a lazy sway. . . .
        He did a lazy sway. . . .
To the tune o' those Weary Blues.
With his ebony hands on each ivory key
10   He made that poor piano moan with melody.
        O Blues!
Swaying to and fro on his rickety stool
He played that sad raggy tune like a musical fool.
        Sweet Blues!
15   Coming from a black man's soul.
        O Blues!
In a deep song voice with a melancholy tone
I heard that Negro sing, that old piano moan—
        "Ain't got nobody in all this world,
20   Ain't got nobody but ma self.
        I's gwine to quit ma frownin'
        And put ma troubles on the shelf."

Thump, thump, thump, went his foot on the floor.
He played a few chords then he sang some more—
25   "I got the Weary Blues
          And I can't be satisfied.
          Got the Weary Blues
          And can't be satisfied—
          I ain't happy no mo'
30   And I wish that I had died."
And far into the night he crooned that tune.
The stars went out and so did the moon.
The singer stopped playing and went to bed
While the Weary Blues echoed through his head.
35   He slept like a rock or a man that's dead.

Questions for Discussion

1. Why does the musician say that he is going to "put [his] troubles on the shelf" if later he says that he "can't be satisfied" and wishes "that [he] had died"? Why does Hughes say "O Blues!" and "Sweet Blues!" if things are so bad?

2. In what ways does the form of the poem suggest the blues?

3. Explain the significance of the last line.

Suggestions for Exploration and Writing

1. Compare the musician in this poem with the dancing girl in "Jazzonia." Do they have anything in common?

2. Research the term "blues." Then discuss in an essay why this poem qualifies beyond the title as a blues poem.

I, Too   (1925)

I, too, sing America.

I am the darker brother.
They send me to eat in the kitchen
When company comes,
5   But I laugh,
And eat well,
And grow strong.

Tomorrow,
I'll be at the table
10   When company comes.
Nobody'll dare
Say to me,
"Eat in the kitchen,"
Then.

15   Besides,
        They'll see how beautiful I am
        And be ashamed—

        I, too, am America.

Questions for Discussion

1. Why does Hughes call himself a "brother"? Why not a cousin, uncle, or man?
2. What is the irony of eating well in the kitchen?
3. When is "tomorrow"?
4. To whom is Hughes referring by using the term "they"?
5. What American poet is Hughes answering in this poem?

THE "CRYSTAL STAIR" WITHIN: THE APOCALYPTIC IMAGINATION[1]

R. BAXTER MILLER

Langston Hughes empowered his various renditions of the Black woman with a double-edged vision. At once it heroically faced the Jim Crow discrimination in the early part of the twentieth century, taking in some comic detachment as well, and showed Blacks transcending the social limitations some whites would impose upon them. What Hughes sensed in the folk source of woman was the dynamic will to epic heroism in both the physical and spiritual dimensions, and while the compulsion revealed itself in varying forms—the disciplined application to labor, the folk trickery that allows comic wit to circumvent defeat, the direct act of social defiance—Black woman incarnated the complex imagination and the masks through which it appeared. When her presence declined in his poetry, as in "Madrid—1937" and "Down Where I Am" (*Voices,* 1950), power and hope diminished somewhat as well. Whether in *The Ways of White Folks* (1934), *The Best of Simple* (1961), or the most telling of the short fiction, the eventual secularization of her previously religious image would increase irony as well as comic distance in the work. Though it was appropriate to Hughes' largesse, as an ethical writer, to restore complex humanity to Black woman in particular and woman in general, he had to replace the great void she had once occupied as idol and type. Then he would have to look at her as the well-rounded human being she was.

Even in the great lyrics such as "The Negro Speaks of Rivers" (*Crisis,* June 1921) and "Daybreak in Alabama" (*Unquote,* June 1940), where woman disappears as a persona, her symbolic yet invisible presence

[1]R. Baxter Miller, "The 'Crystal Stair' Within: The Apocalyptic Imagination," *The Art and Imagination of Langston Hughes* (Lexington, KY: UP of Kentucky, 1989), 33–46.

pervades (to speak in Hughes' metaphors) the fertility of the earth, the waters, and the rebirth of the morning. To trace the complex and rich design of woman in his world means to understand the symbolic movements enacted through the passage of his entire career, with varying degrees of free play back and forth from the great lyrics and monologues ("Mother to Son," *Crisis*, 1922), through his melodramas ("Father and Son," 1934; *Mulatto*, 1934–35) and comic detachments (the Madam poems; *One-Way Ticket*, 1949). The poems on women help to establish an overview for all his succeeding genres. They lead from his lighter humor and cryptic "warning" to white America in 1951 finally to the brilliant and underestimated stream of consciousness (*Ask Your Mama*, 1961), subsuming yet transcending them all.

For Langston Hughes the metaphor of woman marks the rise from the historical source, the folk expression of his grandmother in 1910, to the Civil Rights movement and the white backlash in late 1967. For Hughes, Black woman in particular signifies the cycle through which the poetic imagination emerges from history and transcends it but, as in "Fancy Free" (a tale of Simple), falls back to earth or history.[2]

In a statement by Maud Bodkin, one of the ablest critics of Hughes' time, we find a way to read some of his most accomplished poems. Bodkin explains the function of the female image in literature:

> Following the associations of the figure of the muse as communicated in Milton's poetry, we have reached a representation of yet wider significance—the figure of the divine mother appearing in varied forms, as Thetis mourning for Achilles, or Ishtar mourning and seeking for Tammuz. In this mother and child pattern the figure of the child, or youth, is not distinctively of either sex, though the male youth appears the older form. In historical times, the pattern as it enters poetry may be present, either as beautiful boy or warrior—Adonis, Achilles—or as maiden—Prosperpine, Kore—an embodiment of youth's bloom and transient splendor. In either case, the figure appears as the type-object of a distinctive emotion—a complex emotion within which we may recognize something of fear, pity and tender admiration, such as a parent may feel, but "distanced," as by relation to an object universal, an event inevitable.[3]

Not only does the code make for the coherence in "Mother to Son" (1922) and "The Negro Mother" (1931), possibly the two most famous of the matriarchal verses, but the exploration extends to some of the less well-known poems, thereby helping reveal finally the code of faith and redemption in contemporary American literature and thought.

"Mother to Son" begins the strong matriarchal portraits found in Hughes' poetry and fiction. In twenty lines of dramatic monologue a Black persona addresses her son. Making clear the hardships of Black life,

---

[2]Langston Hughes, "Fancy Free," in *Simple Takes a Wife* (New York: Simon & Schuster, 1953), 80–84.

[3]Maud Bodkin, *Archetypal Patterns in Poetry* (New York: Oxford UP, 1934), 165.

she asserts the paradox of the American mythmakers, who propose that all Americans are equal. Subsequently, she acknowledges the personal and racial progress through her metaphor of ascent. In a powerful refrain she teaches the child her moral of endurance as well as triumph: "And life for me ain't been no crystal stair."

In "Mother to Son" the complex of Christian myth informs the portrait of the woman. As a figure of mythic ascent, she becomes only typologically at one with the Vergil of the *Divine Comedy* or the Christ of the New Testament. But she is neither a great and ancient poet nor a god incarnate; rather, she is Woman struggling to merge with godhead. In more than making her way from failure to success, she moves from a worldly vision to a religious one, for hers is less a progression of the body than an evolution of the soul. Her last line—"And life for me ain't been no crystal stair"—repeats and reinforces her second. Yet through the power of her will and imagination, she has endowed the world far more richly by her inner light than society ever bequeathed opportunities to her. While the social world hardly ennobles her, she nevertheless ennobles it, and the quality of her grandeur marks the depth of her humanity. She cautions her son, "Don't you fall now." Because she associates the quest with her divine vision, any separation from it implies the fallen world, demarcating in itself the descent from heavenly grace.

While Christian myth is central to its complexity of meanings, the poem implies the interwoven designs of quest and self-realization. With the past participle of the durative verb *be,* the mother tells her offspring, "I's been a-climbin' on." As the vertical ascent anticipates her continued ascent, it looks forward to temporary success or to a respite from future quest ("reachin' landin's and turnin' corners").

Shrouded in religious myth, the Black woman must still confront secular reality, and the tension reveals the idea of Black oppression. The building, that synecdochical and metaphysical sign, becomes life itself as well as the questionable belief in any cosmic order. Dilapidated boards and bare feet imply the presence of deprivation or poverty in the house. Because the mother lived literally in a building that had loose tacks and splinters, she risked physical penetration and infection throughout her life. Yet she has withstood any fatal injury to the Black American soul. Her internal light illuminates the outer world.

"The Negro Mother" (*SP*, 288–89) resembles "Mother to Son" in code but differs from it in form. Once more the mixture of iambic and anapestic feet appears, while the rhythm results in a simulation of Black rhetoric.

> Chĭldrĕn, Ĭ come báck tŏdáy
> Tŏ téll yŏu ă stórў ŏf thĕ lóng dárk wáy
> Thăt Ĭ hád tŏ climb, thăt Ĭ hád tŏ knów
> Iň ordĕr thăt thĕ ráce mĭght líve aňd grów
> Lóok át mў fáce—dárk ăs thĕ níght—
> Yĕt shíniňg líke thĕ sún wĭth lóve's trúe líght.

Here the tetrameter and pentameter lines give a formal consistency.

"The Negro Mother" facilitates the division of itself into three parts. The first introduces the reader to the spirit or ghost of the mother, who represents the racial as well as historical consciousness of Blacks. In addressing her children or symbolic posterity, the mother identifies herself. The second shows that the mother's religious faith enabled her to endure adversity. Here she stands apart from her own monologue, and the moment becomes her awed reminiscence of personal accomplishment more than a speech to any particular listener.

> I couldn't read then. I couldn't write.
> I had nothing, back there in the night.
> Sometimes, the valley was filled with tears,
> But I kept trudging on through the lonely years.

In spirit the mother merges with her children to guarantee continued racial success. Part two prepares skillfully for part three, through which she returns from introspection to express herself in direct address once again. In the last section she cautions Blacks about the barriers still ahead: "Remember how the strong in struggle and strife / Still bar you the way [. . .]"

Myth means, in this instance, the religious overtones that cloak the parent-to-child monologue, implying pilgrimage. In opposing secular history—namely, the woman's being stolen from Africa—the tone heightens the tension between the real and the ideal. When the mother remembers the selling of her children after she "crossed the wide sea," the biblical cadence may remind the auditor of the human wanderings in Exodus.

The second part shows a shift in emphasis from the mother to the children who must continue the sacred quest. To express her belief in right, she prepares them by using metaphor, simile, and echo: "But God put a song and a prayer in my mouth. / God put a dream like steel in my soul." In identifying with a Christian woman, Hughes demonstrates his talent to create an autonomous persona. While more personal poems such as "Who But the Lord" indicate his own Christian humanism, as opposed to the mother's even deeper religiosity, her faith in the second part prepares for the lines near the end of the third: "Oh, my dark children, may my dream and my prayers / Impel you forever up the great stairs."

Christian images help to reveal her code of heroic sacrifice. When Hughes concentrates Christian images in the second and final sections, the "valley" complements the journey's "road." Subsequently, the narration lays out the goals and blessings that the mother urges the children to take. When she tells them to "look ever upward," the closure suggests once more the spatial duality that suggests both an embarkment and a place of departure. As in "Mother to Son," linear and vertical distances merge in the Christian metaphor of travel. Where she encourages the children to climb the "great stairs," she enhances the implication of ascent. Like the dilapidated stair in "Mother to Son," these stairs imply racial quest as well.

The female figure in "Negro Mother" functions much like that in "Mother to Son," for in being mythic it becomes a foil to secular reality. From an opposition of divine quest and earthly limitation emerges the theme of social restriction. The reader imagines the longevity of Black suffering in the United States for three hundred years. During that time, experience forged the "dream like steel" in the mother's soul; consequently, the dream inspired her to survive a valley "filled with tears" and a road "hot with sun." Though she has been beaten and mistreated, and though she warns her offspring that racial restrictions still exist, her spirit has triumphed. While we do not know the strength of the bars that represent the limitations in the third part, the tone suggests that these surpass neither the will of the mother nor the potential strength of the children whom she inspires. That in the second part the mother overcame her inability to read and write supports this reading. So do the sweat, pain, and despair she remembers in the third part, after having transcended them. She has withstood the whip of the slaver's lash. In combining social limits with Christian myth, Hughes uses his alliterative skill in fusing liquids with plosives: "Remember how the strong in struggle and strife / still bar you the way [. . .]"

In helping to illuminate the design of social confinement, the Black woman serves a third and equally important function; indeed, the imagery and idea of Nature rely on her presence. Pictures of light and dark, plants that grow or seeds that imply growth, all signify that presence—as does any place of growth. To unify the different parts as sections within an organic whole, Hughes distributes five images of the kind in the first part and three in the second as well as in the third. For example, the mother speaks of the "long dark way" that anticipates her self-reminiscence as the "dark girl." In the latter instance she becomes the image of the Black race transported across the sea. The darkness of the traveled way and the female figure who must travel it through time fuse with diurnal cycle. Consequently, the Black woman expresses the past in cyclic metaphor: "I had nothing, back there in the night," yet her advice to others will make for a different future, one of heroic progress as her "banner" is lifted from the "dust"— another echo of Christian myth, alluding to Ecclesiastes and suggesting mortality. In the third part the mother instructs her children to make of her past a "torch for tomorrow," thus teaching them the secret of Black art: the conversion of suffering into personal and social good. In lighting her way, the torch signals moral progression.

A natural complex unifies the first and second parts in "The Negro Mother." Like corn and cotton the Black race grows, though the analogy is ambiguous. While the products described grow for the purpose of human consumption, Hughes implies that the Black race develops in order to end exploitation. As corn and cotton grew in the field in which the mother worked, suffering enhanced her wisdom as well as her spirit. In tending the field outside herself, she nourished within herself the dream and seed of the free.

Other natural icons show that the unity of the poem depends upon the maternal portrait. The mother's general delineation as woman early on prepares for the particular depiction of her as the "Negro mother" in the second and third parts. Because, in the second part, the woman is the seed of an emerging free race, she becomes one with her children, who are young and free. Similarly, the Black woman's advice in the third part displays both her courage and the bond between a woman and her descendants: "Stand like free men." The banner that she urges her offspring to lift shares the firmness of her imperative verb, "stand." The first part makes clear the mother's place in the lineage of Black people, as through internal rhyme the color of her face blends with the history of the race.

Other poems about women preceded or followed "The Negro Mother"; "Mother to Son" is probably the most famous of the earlier verses and the "Madam Poems" the most memorable of the subsequent ones. The image of woman operates throughout these works in at least eleven diverse ways, which are not always separable. 1) In signaling stories about her yesterdays, 2) woman survives adversity and triumphs spiritually as well as artistically. 3) She presents an opportunity to admire the splendor of youth now departed or 4) to characterize a folk life-style of vibrant flare and color. 5) In providing a portrait of trouble, she cannot transcend adversity sometimes, but 6) she converts suffering into transcendence. 7) Sometimes she signifies the heavy yet affirmative tone through which humanity sublimates suffering into art; 8) at other times she clarifies a secular persona's comic and serious confrontation with death. 9) Even in emphasizing the dramatic situation of a deserted wife and 10) a matriarchal society, she 11) incarnates heroic determination.

What Langston Hughes dramatized so brilliantly in the auditor he must have discerned finally about himself and humanity. In the pursuit of some external decision, the seeker overlooks her own responsibility on earth. She needs always the sign of something beyond, the absent ideal of which the present realism reminds us only indirectly. Whereas the early poems mark, sometimes dramatically, an ascent from earth to heaven, the later ones embody often not only the redescent to earth but the closure of the great stairway. The vertical route that had never existed for woman or anybody else in physical space in the first place withdraws itself back from the external world now to the mind of the poet. In the process he recasts his fictional self as Madam. Though the auditor can read in her cards the obvious fortune only of what the teller narrates forthrightly, the teller reads the deeper irony of the human self ever in struggle with destiny and history. What separates the two women is Madam's human imagination.

In "Mother to Son" and "The Negro Mother," [. . .] which combine Christian myth and folk experience, Langston Hughes becomes one of several American poets to deal with a problem of religious belief. Our literary artists have believed (or disbelieved) in God, the American Dream, the Power of Transcendence, or the American Myth. Edward Taylor and William Cullen Bryant believed in God. Emerson believed in transcendence, and his contemporary, Whitman, believed in himself. Whitman had faith as well in a power that could rejuvenate or at least reinvigorate the world through enthusiastic perception. Wallace Stevens, who was humanistic like Whitman, believed more in man than in external divinity. To Stevens, indeed, man *was* divinity, since divinity must "live within herself."[4] Closer still to our own time, T.S. Eliot, through his Christian conservatism, restored to American poetry a sense of the divine.[5] Alan Ginsberg has laughed at American myth, now putting his "queer shoulder" to the country's wheel.[6]

But no American poet, I think, combines myth and pragmatism better than Langston Hughes does in the poems on women. Indeed, Hughes himself would never do so again. In the 1950s he would turn his attention more to prose than to poetry, and by the 1960s he would lose the sustained intensity of his once lyrical gift, for social injustice would almost never leave either him or his hopeful vision alone. But he never completely abandoned the folk source of his grandmother's stories. They had been the form through which his poetic spirit had taken shape most powerfully. Not always without stereotype, the poems about women were a very special genre for him. Even the most rabid feminist critics could admit that they radiate (whatever the almost inevitable limitations of Man) a profound sympathy and nearly unquestionable love.

Hughes indeed leaves to posterity his myth of the Black female who can tell tales about her yesterdays. Sometimes she becomes a means of discoursing on the youth that is gone forever. At other times, unable to transcend adversity, she personifies trouble sublimated often into art. We must laugh then at her confrontation with death, at her attempts to transcend hardship, if only to avoid crying at her weariness, at the bitterness surrounding the racial quest. But we must admire her heroic imagination. What empowers her creative energy as well as her moral force is the crystal stairway within. She isn't always well-rounded or even professional, but she is still Madam as much as Madonna. She is more human than almost any other female figure inscribed by a Black male writer in either Hughes' time or our own. And with her as a bulwark, we can go on to reconsider his lyrical power more profoundly.

[4]Wallace Stevens, "Sunday Morning," in *Poems* (New York: Viking Press, 1974), 5.
[5]See esp. "The Waste Land" and "Ash Wednesday" in T. S. Eliot, *Selected Poems* (New York: Haarcourt, Brace & World, 1930).
[6]See Alan Ginsberg, "America," in *The New Modern Poetry,* ed. M. L. Rosenthal (New York: Oxford UP, 1967), 67–70.

Langston Hughes: Poetry, Blues, and Gospel—Somewhere to Stand[1]

Steven C. Tracy

The fact that Hughes could throw one arm around spirituals and gospel music and the other around the blues simultaneously would seem remarkable, even blasphemous, in some circles, primarily Christian ones where the blues might be dubbed "the devil's music." But Hughes sat them rather comfortably side by side in his work and his ethos: "I liked the barrel houses of Seventh Street, the shouting churches, and the songs," he wrote in *The Big Sea* (209); the following year he called spirituals and blues the "two great Negro gifts to American music" ("Songs Called the Blues," 143). In the mid-fifties his devil figure Big Eye Buddy Lomax, in both the play and the novel *Tambourines to Glory*, asserted that "them gospel songs sound just like the blues," to which the holy sister managed only the feeble reply, "At least our words is different" (*Tambourines*, 126–27).

It is clear that Hughes did not exalt spirituals and gospel music based on any fervent belief in Christianity. The "Salvation" chapter in *The Big Sea* outlines his traumatic (non-) conversion experience that left him doubting the existence of a Jesus who had not come to help him (18–21); and his poem "Mystery" describes the feelings of an uninitiated thirteen-year-old, isolated by her confused uncertainty, yoking "The mystery / and the darkness / and the song / and me" (*Selected Poems*, 256). In "To Negro Writers" he called on his African American colleagues to "expose the sick-sweet smile of organized religion [. . .] and the half-voodoo, half-clown face of revivalism, dulling the mind with the clap of its empty hands" (139). His "first experience with censorship" he recounted in "My Adventures as a Social Poet," reporting how a preacher directed him not to read any more blues in his pulpit (206). Years later in a Simple story, "Gospel Singers," Simple compares churches to movie theaters, preachers to movie stars, and church services to shows during which gospel singers are "working in the vineyards of the Lord and digging in his gold mines," joking that when you hear gospel singers "crying 'I Cannot Bear My Burden Alone,' what they really mean is, 'Help me get my cross to my Cadillac.'" (*Simple's Uncle Sam*, 39). Significantly, though, Simple did not mind paying to hear the gospel singers—paying twice, even—because he felt that "the music that these people put down can't be beat" (39). For Simple, as for Hughes, it was not the meaning of the words so much as the wording of the means that carried him away. What Hughes said about the blues in "Songs Called the Blues" applies to gospel music as well: "You don't have to understand the words to know the meaning of the blues, or to feel their sadness or to hope their hopes"

[1]Steven C. Tracy, "Langston Hughes: Poetry, Blues, and Gospel—Somewhere to Stand," *Langston Hughes: The Man, His Art, and His Continuing Influence*, ed. C. James Trotman (New York: Garland Publishing, 1995), 51–61.

(145). Paul Oliver's description of gospel music captures the essence of the spark of gospel music that ignited Hughes:

> Gospel songs bring the message of "good news" and are so called, according to some preachers, because they state the "gospel truth." The promise of a better life hereafter still pervades them but their joyousness and extrovert behavior suggest happiness achieved in this life in preparation for the next. (199)

[. . .] Hughes heard the pulsing drama of the life of the spirit, the human spirit. It was a spirit he tried to capture in poems like "Fire" and "Sunday Morning Prophecy" and in gospel plays like *Tambourines to Glory*, the highly successful *Black Nativity* and *Jericho-Jim Crow*, and *The Gospel Glory*.

Hughes heard that pulse in the blues too, of course. Buddy Lomax was certainly right in hearing similarities between gospel and blues music. Robert Farris Thompson has pointed out the influence of the "Ancient African organizing principle of song and dance" on African American music as a whole, with its "dominance of a percussive performance attack, [. . .] propensity for multiple meter, [. . .] overlapping and response, [. . .] inner pulse control, [. . .] suspended accentuation pattern, [. . .] and songs and dances of social allusion" (xiii). It is not surprising that one of the founding fathers of gospel music, Thomas A. Dorsey, who came to religious prominence with the publication of *Gospel Pearls* in 1921 by the Sunday School Publishing Board of the National Baptist Convention, had been a blues and hokum singer. One of Dorsey's biggest hokum hits had been "It's Tight Like That" with singer-guitarist Tampa Red. Eventually, though, Dorsey went from being "tight like that" to being tight with God, penning such standards as "Precious Lord Take My Hand" and "Peace in the Valley." It was the *manner* of performing, the spirit of the performance, that transcended the sometimes artificial sacred, secular, and profane bounds and linked black musics together.

Certainly Hughes wrote more about blues than he did about gospel music in his lifetime. He recalled the first time he heard the blues in Kansas City on the appropriately named Independence Avenue, which provided him with material for his "The Weary Blues," one of the poems, with "Jazzonia" and "Negro Dancers," that Hughes placed beside Vachel Lindsay's plate at the Wardman Park Hotel; the blues of Ma Rainey and the boogie woogie and ragtime piano players on State Street in Chicago; the blues, ragtime, and jazz of Harlem from the twenties on; aboard the S.S. *Malone* bound for Africa, even at Le Grand Duc in France:

> Blues in the Rue Pigalle. Black and laughing, heartbreaking blues in the Paris dawn, pounding like a pulse beat, moving like the Mississippi. (*The Big Sea*, 162)

The yoking of the pulse beat, the river, and the singing links this description with another of Hughes's classic poems, "The Negro Speaks of Rivers," reminding us, as Hughes wrote with Milton Meltzer in *Black Magic*, that the "syncopated beat which the captive Africans brought with them" that found its first expression here in "the hand-clapping, feet-stomping, drum-beating rhythms (related, of course, to the rhythms of the human heart)" (4–5), is as "ancient as the world." After Le Grand Duc in Washington, D.C., and collecting with Zora Neale Hurston throughout the South—"All my life," Hughes wrote, "I've heard the blues" ("I Remember the Blues," 152). He continued to admire their expressive beauty, differentiating them clearly from the spirituals as being "sadder [. . .] because their sadness is not softened with tears, but hardened with laughter, the absurd, incongruous laughter of sadness without a god to appeal to" (Van Vechten, 86). To him they were "sad songs sung to the most despondent rhythm in the world" (review of *Blues: An Anthology,* 258), at times "as absurd as Krazy Kat" (Van Vechten, 86), but nearly always conveying "a kind of marching on syncopation, a gonna-make-it-somehow determination in spite of it all, that ever-present laughter-under-sorrow that indicates a love of life too precious to let it go" ("I Remember the Blues," 155), with "a steady rolling beat that seemed to be marching somewhere to something better, to something happy" (*First Book of Jazz,* 37). Despite the differences between spirituals and blues that Hughes enumerated in "Songs Called the Blues," he saw a greater inherent bond that transcended what he saw as the superficial discordances between the blues and spiritual and gospel music. The music, his art, black art, was not to be isolating but ultimately unifying, and if what Arnold Rampersad described as Hughes's "cloistered life" (16) with Mary Langston accentuated his solitude, the visceral drama of black music—tender, humorous, tragic, innocent, sexy, ecstatic, mundane, playful, lively and deadly serious—set the stage for his emergence as an artist.

Hughes delighted in reciting his poetry to musical accompaniment, seeing the performance as an occasion for meaningful group interaction that would enhance and strengthen communication. Ezra Pound wrote to Hughes about a poem Hughes sent to him: "Thank God; at last I come across a poem I can understand" (Hentoff, 27). The comment is ironic coming from Pound, but perfectly appropriate in regard to Hughes's intentions and achievement. Nat Hentoff reported Hughes's designs for his recitations with musical accompaniment:

> The music should not only be a background to the poetry, but should comment on it. I tell the musicians—and I've worked with several different modern and traditional groups—to improvise as much as they care around what I read. Whatever they bring of themselves to the poetry is welcome to me. I merely suggest the mood of each piece as a general orientation. Then I listen to what they say in their playing, and that affects my own rhythms when I read. We listen to each other. (27)

The performance of the poem, then, becomes a nexus, a dialogue, something as old as the inception of the poem but as new as the inflection of the impulse. Indeed, in the stage directions to *Tambourines to Glory* Hughes suggested that "audience participation might be encouraged— singing, foot-patting, handclapping—and in the program the lyrics of some of the songs might be printed with an invitation to sing the refrains along with the chorus of Tambourine Temple" (184). It would not likely take much to inspire participation for, as Hughes wrote in "Spirituals," "Song is a strong thing" (*Selected Poems*, 28).

Now Hughes had his limitations as a commentator on the blues. His discussions of the roots of the blues in African music and work songs and field hollers were often general and unsystematic early in his career, though his later work was somewhat more comprehensive. He overgeneralized a bit about the types of blues that males sang as opposed to females, and he did not adequately convey the breadth of themes or stanzaic patterns present in the blues. His lists of outstanding blues singers most often emphasized vaudeville blues singers, certainly urban blues singers at any rate, indicating more of a preference for sophisticated productions. Indeed, Hughes wrote that it was a desire of his to write the first libretto for a blues opera ("From the Blues to an Opera Libretto").[. . .] The blues poems that Hughes wrote were often thematic rather than associative, and they contained noticeably few references to drugs, sex, and violence in comparison to blues songs recorded both in the field and in the studio, opting for something of a via media in reflecting the themes and images of the folk tradition. His language and images, in fact, are not often as stark or startling as the best blues lyrics by performers within the oral tradition, but they make excellent use of both oral and written traditions in a way that adds materially to both, making his poetry something quite familiar, yet quite new.

Of course, not all of Hughes's blues poems did employ blues stanza forms. Hughes called his poem "Cross," for example, a poem whose "mood is that of the blues, although its lyric form lacks the folk repetition" ("From the Blues to an Opera Libretto"). If is not stanza form, repetition, or the number of measures in a stanza that makes the blues—but the feeling, spirit, attitude, and approach. And these, indeed, imbue much of the poetry of Langston Hughes to such an extent that the whine of a bottleneck, or the wail of a harmonica, or the trill of a piano may be regularly inferred as the subtext of his work.

Works Cited

Hentoff, Nat. "Langston Hughes: He Found Poetry in the Blues." *Mayfair* (August 1958): 26, 27, 43, 45–47, 49.

Hughes, Langston, *The Big Sea*. New York: Hill & Wang, 1963.

————. In *The First Book of Jazz*. Eds. Cliff Roberts and David Martin. New York: Franklin Watts, 1976.

————. "From the Blues to an Opera Libretto." *New York Times*. January 15, 1950.

————. *Selected Poems*. New York: Vintage Books, 1984.

————. *Simple's Uncle Sam*. New York: Hill & Wang, 1965.

————. "Songs Called the Blues." *Phylon* 2.2 (1941): 143–45.

————. *Tambourines to Glory*. In *Five Plays* by Langston Hughes. Bloomington: Indiana UP, 1968.

————. "To Negro Writers." *American Writer's Congress.* Ed. Henry Hart. New York: International Publisher, 1935. 139–41.

Oliver, Paul, Max Harrison, and William Bolcom. *The New Grove Gospel, Blues and Jazz, with Spirituals and Ragtime.* London: Macmillan, 1986.

Rampersad, Arnold. *The Life of Langston Hughes: Volume 1: 1902–1941: I, Too, Sing America.* New York: Oxford UP, 1986.

Thompson, Robert Farris. *Flash of the Spirit: African and AfroAmerican Art and Philosophy.* New York: Random House, 1983.

Van Vechten, Carl. "The Black Blues." *Vanity Fair* 24.6 (1925): 57, 86, 92.

THE HARLEM OF LANGSTON HUGHES' POETRY[1]

ARTHUR P. DAVIS

In a very real sense, Langston Hughes is the poet-laureate of Harlem. From his first publication down to his latest, Mr. Hughes has been concerned with the black metropolis. Returning to the theme again and again, he has written about Harlem oftener and more fully than any other poet. As Hughes has written about himself: "I live in the heart of Harlem. I have also lived in the heart of Paris, Madrid, Shanghai, and Mexico City. The people of Harlem seem not very different from others, except in language. I love the color of their language: and, being a Harlemite myself, their problems and interests are my problems and interests."

Knowing how deeply Langston Hughes loves Harlem and how intimately he understands the citizens of that community, I have long felt that a study of the Harlem theme in Hughes' poetry would serve a twofold purpose: it would give us insight into the growth and maturing of Mr. Hughes as a social poet; it would also serve as an index to the changing attitude of the Negro during the last quarter of a century.

When Mr. Hughes' first publication, *The Weary Blues* (1926), appeared, the New Negro Movement was in full swing; and Harlem, as the intellectual center of the movement, had become the Mecca of all aspiring young Negro writers and artists. This so-called Renaissance not only encouraged and inspired the black creative artist, but it served also to focus as never before the attention of America upon the Negro artist and scholar. As a result of this new interest, Harlem became a gathering place for downtown intellectuals and Bohemians—many of them honestly seeking a knowledge of Negro art and culture, others merely looking for exotic thrills in the black community. Naturally, the latter group was much the larger of the two; and Harlem, capitalizing on this new demand for "primitive" thrills, opened a series of spectacular

[1]Arthur P. Davis, "The Harlem of Langston Hughes' Poetry," *Phylon* 13 (1952): 276–83. Reprinted in *Critical Essays on Langston Hughes,* ed. Edward J. Mullen (Boston: G. K. Hall, 1986), 135–43.

cabarets. For a period of about ten years, the most obvious and the most sensational aspect of the New Negro Movement for downtown New York was the night life of Harlem. The 1925 Renaissance, of course, was not just a cabaret boom, and it would be decidedly unfair to give that impression. But the Harlem cabaret life of the period was definitely an important by-product of the new interest in the Negro created by the movement, and this life strongly influenced the early poetry of Langston Hughes.

Coming to Harlem, as he did, a twenty-two-year-old adventurer who had knocked around the world as sailor and beachcomber, it was only natural that Hughes should be attracted to the most exotic part of that city— its night life. The Harlem of *The Weary Blues* became therefore for him "Jazzonia," a new world of escape and release, an exciting never-never land in which "sleek black boys" blew their hearts out on silver trumpets in a "whirling cabaret." It was a place where the bold eyes of white girls called to black men, and "dark brown girls" were found "in blond men's arms." It was a city where "shameless gals" strutted and wiggled, and the "night dark girl of the swaying hips" danced beneath a papier-maché jungle moon. The most important inhabitants of this magic city are a "Nude Young Dancer," "Midnight Nan at Leroy's" a "Young Singer of *chansons vulgaires*," and a "Black Dancer in the Little Savoy."

This cabaret Harlem, this Jazzonia is a joyous city but this joyousness is not unmixed; it has a certain strident and hectic quality, and there are overtones of weariness and despair. "The long-headed jazzers" and whirling dancing girls are desperately trying to find some new delight, and some new escape. They seem obsessed with the idea of seizing the present moment as though afraid of the future: "Tomorrow [. . .] is darkness / Joy today!" "The rhythm of life / Is a jazz rhythm" for them, but it brings only "The broken heart of love / The weary, weary heart of pain." It is this weariness and this intensity that one hears above the laughter and even about the blare of the jazz bands.

There is no daytime in Jazzonia, no getting up and going to work. It is wholly a sundown city, illuminated by soft lights, spotlights, jewel-eyed sparklers, and synthetic stars in the scenery. Daylight is the one great enemy here, and when "the new dawn / Wan and pale / Descends like a white mist," it brings only an "aching emptiness," and out of this emptiness there often comes in the clear cool light of morning the disturbing thought that the jazz band may not be an escape, it may not be gay after all:

> Does a jazz-band ever sob?
> They say a jazz-band's gay . . .
> One said she heard the jazz-band sob
> When the little dawn was gray.

In this respect, the figure of the black piano player in the title poem is highly symbolic. Trying beneath "the pale dull pallor of an old gas light" to rid his soul of the blues that bedeviled it, he played all night, but when the dawn approached:

> The singer stopped playing and went to bed
> While the Weary Blues echoed through his head.
> He slept like a rock or a man that's dead.

It is hard to fool oneself in the honest light of dawn, but sleep, like dancing and singing and wild hilarity, is another means of escape. Unfortunately, it too is only a temporary evasion. One has to wake up sometime and face the harsh reality of daylight and everyday living. [. . .]

And in the final pages of *The Weary Blues*, the poet begins to sense this fact; he realizes that a "jazz-tuned" way of life is not the answer to the Negro's search for escape. The last poem on the Harlem theme in this work has the suggestive title "Disillusionment" and the even more suggestive lines:

> I would be simple again,
> Simple and clean . . .
> Nor ever know,
> Dark Harlem,
> The wild laughter
> Of your mirth . . .
> Be kind to me,
> Oh, great dark city.
> Let me forget.
> I will not come
> To you again.

Evidently Hughes did want to forget, at least temporarily, the dark city, for there is no mention of Harlem in his next work, *Fine Clothes to the Jew,* published the following year. Although several of the other themes treated in the first volume are continued in this the second, it is the only major production in which the name Harlem does not appear.

But returning to *The Weary Blues*—it is the eternal emptiness of the Harlem depicted in this work which depresses. In this volume, the poet has been influenced too strongly by certain superficial elements of the New Negro Movement. Like too many of his contemporaries, he followed the current vogue, and looking at Harlem through the "arty" spectacles of New Negro exoticism, he failed to see the everyday life about him. As charming and as fascinating as many of these poems undoubtedly are, they give a picture which is essentially false because it is one-dimensional and incomplete.

The picture of Harlem presented in *Shakespeare in Harlem* (1942) has very little in common with that found in *The Weary Blues*. By 1942 the black metropolis was a disillusioned city. The Depression of 1929, having struck the ghetto harder than any other section of New York, showed Harlem just how basically "marginal" and precarious its economic foundations were. Embittered by this knowledge, the black community had struck back blindly at things in general in the 1935 riot. The riot brought an end to the New Negro era; the Cotton Club, the most lavish of the uptown cabarets, closed its doors and moved to Broadway; and the black city settled down to the drab existence of WPA and relief living.

In the two groups of poems labeled "Death in Harlem" and "Lenox Avenue," Hughes has given us a few glimpses of this new Harlem. There are no bright colors in the scene, only the sombre and realistic shades appropriate to the depiction of a community that has somehow lost its grip on things. The inhabitants of this new Harlem impress one as a beaten people. A man loses his job because, "awake all night with loving," he cannot get to work on time. When he is discharged, his only comment is "So I went on back to bed [. . .] " and to the "sweetest dreams" ("Fired"). In another poem, a man and his wife wrangle over the family's last dime which he had thrown away gambling ("Early Evening Quarrel"). Harlem love has lost its former joyous abandon, and the playboy of the cabaret era has become a calculating pimp who wants to "share your bed / And your money too" ("50–50"). In fact all of the lovers in this section—men and women alike—are an aggrieved lot, whining perpetually about being "done wrong." Even the night spots have lost their jungle magic, and like Dixie's joint have become earthy and sordid places: "Dixie makes his money on two-bit gin"; he also "rents rooms at a buck a break." White folks still come to Dixie's seeking a thrill, but they find it unexpectedly in the cold-blooded shooting of Bessie by Arabella Johnson, in a fight over Texas Kid. As Arabella goes to jail and Bessie is taken to the morgue, Texas Kid, the cause of this tragedy, callously "picked up another woman and / Went to bed" ("Death in Harlem"). All of the fun, all of the illusion have gone from this new and brutal night life world; and as a fitting symbol of the change which has come about, we find a little cabaret girl dying forlornly as a ward of the city ("Cabaret Girl Dies on Welfare Island").

There is seemingly only one bright spot in this new Harlem—the spectrum-colored beauty of the girls on Sugar Hill ("Harlem Sweeties"); but this is only a momentary lightening of the mood. The prevailing tone is one of depression and futility:

> Down on the Harlem River
> > Two A.M.
> > Midnight
> > By yourself!
> Lawd, I wish I could die–
> But who would miss me if I left?

We see here the spectacle of a city feeling sorry for itself, the most dismal and depressing of all spectacles. Hughes has given us a whining Harlem. It is not yet the belligerent Harlem of the 1943 riot, but it is a city acquiring the mood from which this riot will inevitably spring.

The Harlem poems in *Fields of Wonder* (1947) are grouped under the title "Stars Over Harlem," but they do not speak out as clearly and as definitely as former pieces on the theme have done. The mood, however, continues in the sombre vein of *Shakespeare in Harlem,* and the idea of escape is stated or implied in each of the poems. In the first of the group, "Trumpet Player: 52nd Street," we find a curious shift in the African imagery used. Practically all former pieces having an African background tended to stress either the white-mooned loveliness of jungle nights or the pulse-stirring rhythm of the tom-tom. But from the weary eyes of the 52nd Street musician there blazes forth only "the smoldering memory of slave ships." In this new Harlem even the jazz players are infected with the sectional melancholy, and this performer finds only a vague release and escape in the golden tones he creates.

Transcendent Women, Earthbound Men
Brittney Victor

1   Langston Hughes, one of the most prolific writers of the early twentieth century, often blended the blues, gospel, and religious overtones in his poetry. Because all three areas fascinated him, his poetry reflects a mystical as well as a mythical portrayal of men and women who populated his Black neighborhoods. Drawing from his own background, Hughes wrote of man's soul and man's reality, a reality that each Black person had to face in order to survive. How each chose to survive was the subject of his poems. Four of Hughes's poems represent two types of personalities: those who chose to transcend the environment with their religion and those who lived on the earth in the glare of reality. In "Mother to Son" and "A Song to a Negro Wash-Woman," Hughes embodies the Black woman with the transcendent qualities that he saw in some of the women in his life. In "The Weary Blues" and "I, Too," he shows the reality of society's restrictions and oppression.

2   Hughes's poems "Mother to Son" and "A Song to a Negro Wash-Woman" exalt the archetypal, nurturing mother. Using the metaphor of the stairs as a lifelong journey to reach the top, the mother in the first poem cautions her son not to give up, to

obtain a goal, or to overcome adversity. As she says about her life: "Life for me ain't been no crystal stair" (2). Life has landings that she has "reached" and corners she has turned (9-10). On the surface she tries to inspire her son to endure in order to succeed; he must suffer the "tacks," "splinters," and "boards torn up," all suggesting a rather harsh reality of life (3, 4, 5). The mother's goal and her son's, if he chooses to imitate his mother, is to reach the top of the stairs. However, on another level, the mother is suggesting that the goal is far superior to the earthly one; it is the goal of reaching heaven, where the Black man or woman can obtain true happiness no matter how hard the journey. R. Baxter Miller states in "The 'Crystal Stair' Within: The Apocalyptic Imagination" that "In more than making her way from failure to success, she moves from a worldly vision to a religious one, for hers is less a progression of the body than an evolution of the soul.[. . .] While the social world hardly ennobles her, she nevertheless ennobles it, and the quality of her grandeur marks the depth of her humanity" (477). Her happiness depends on this aspect of her journey; life becomes a pilgrimage to transcend the earthly.

3   In "A Song to a Negro Wash-Woman," Langston Hughes writes of another mother who has the same transcendent personality. The woman with her "Arms elbow-deep in white suds, / Soul washed clean" (2-3) again is the archetypal Black woman who symbolizes every woman who sings her heart out as she rises early and goes to bed late so that her children can have a better life and receive an education. What is her goal? She will someday be "sit[ting] on the right hand of the Son of God and forget[ting] / [she] ever [was] a wash-woman" (22-23). R. Baxter Miller maintains that "the image of woman operates throughout these works in at least eleven diverse ways, which are not always separable.[. . . One of these ways is] woman survives adversity and triumphs spiritually as well as artistically" ("'Crystal Stair'

Within" 480). Hughes has portrayed the same kind of woman that he did in "Mother to Son," the admirable mother, the excellent worker. In doing so, Hughes, according to Miller, "sensed in the folk source of woman [. . .] the dynamic will to epic heroism in both the physical and spiritual dimensions, and while the compulsion revealed itself in varying forms [. . .] Black woman incarnated the complex imagination and the masks through which it appeared" ("'Crystal Stair' Within" 475). Even if the Black woman did not believe everything she said and sang, she still believed attainment of the top stair was possible and wore the mask to prove it.

4   What Hughes did not do in these poems was to deal with the reality of life in the real world. What was that son to do when he tried turning those stairs or the son to do when he was denied an education or opportunity because of the color of his skin?

5   Hughes's "The Weary Blues" captures the blues and the blues singer, but reverses the spectrum. To Hughes, the piano player whose songs are "Coming from a black man's soul" (15) sings night after night about his sorry state. For example, the player states that he has no one, "can't be satisfied," and wishes to die (25-30). Steven C. Tracy quotes Hughes as saying, "'You don't have to understand the words to know the meaning of the blues, or to feel their sadness or to hope their hopes'" (482). While the singer plays the piano and sings, his music fills the room with unspoken words and thoughts. For the Weary Blues singer, the "stars went out and so did the moon" (32), suggesting more than just the advent of night. A crystal stair does not exist for the blues player nor any hope for a splintered one that would eventually lead to the top. As long as he plays he can escape his earthly troubles. But unlike the wash-woman, his joy does not exist in seeing the next generation succeed or seeing a son survive. The body is exhausted. Arthur P. Davis says that "it is

this weariness and this intensity that one hears above the laughter and even about [sic] the blare of the jazz bands" (487). The immediate release is the music and then sleep, only to rise the next day and repeat the cycle: "He slept like a rock or a man that's dead" (35). In Hughes's Harlem or in any other large metropolitan Black community, Davis suggests, as Hughes does, that "it is hard to fool oneself in the honest light of dawn, but sleep, like dancing and singing and wild hilarity, is another means of escape. Unfortunately, it too is only a temporary evasion. One has to wake up sometime and face the harsh reality of daylight and everyday living" (488). So it is with the blues player.

6   "I, Too" emphasizes more the earthly existence of the ordinary black man, rather than the blues singer whose life may or may not represent everyman. Hughes's narrator states that he is "the darker brother" who must "eat in the kitchen / When company comes" (3-4). His use of the word "brother" implies a kinship with his "lighter" brothers; nevertheless, a distinction exists between the two. Bound to earth by these distinctions, the narrator hopes for a prosperous future, one that could have been provided for by his wash-woman or stair-climbing mother. One major difference between the son in "Mother to Son" and "I, Too" is that religious overtones do not apply. Life for the narrator is too real, too pervasive to escape.

7   Hughes's men and women share an awareness of reality, but while the women attempt to transcend their environment, the men are sometimes bound even more to earth. Hughes's women in these poems are indeed transcendent—they had to be to inspire their men to be more than they were. However, the men were more earth-bound—they had to be concerned with everyday life in order to provide for their families and to later participate in the Movements of the sixties.

Works Cited

Davis, Arthur P. "The Harlem of Langston Hughes' Poetry." <u>Pylon:</u>
<u>The Atlanta University Review of Race and Culture</u> 13 (1952):
276-83. Henderson, Day, and Waller. 486-90.

Henderson, Gloria Mason, Bill Day, and Sandra Stevenson Waller,
eds. <u>Literature and Ourselves.</u> 4th ed. New York: Longman,
2003.

Hughes, Langston. "I, Too." <u>The Collected Poems of Langston</u>
<u>Hughes.</u> New York: Knopf, 1995. Henderson, Day, and
Waller. 474-75.

- - -. "Mother to Son." <u>The Collected Poems.</u> Henderson,
Day, and Waller. 470-71.

- - -. "A Song to a Negro Wash-Woman." <u>The Collected Poems.</u>
Henderson, Day, and Waller. 471-72.

- - -. "The Weary Blues." <u>The Collected Poems.</u> Henderson, Day, and
Waller. 473-74.

Miller, R. Baxter. "The 'Crystal Stair' Within: The Apocalyptic
Imagination." <u>The Art and Imagination of Langston Hughes.</u>
Lexington, KY: UP of Kentucky, 1989. 33-46. Henderson, Day,
and Waller. 475-81.

Tracy, Steven C. "Langston Hughes: Poetry, Blues, and Gospel–
Somewhere to Stand." <u>Langston Hughes: The Man, His Art, and</u>
<u>His Continuing Influence.</u> Ed. C. James Trotman. New York:
Garland, 1995. 51-61. Henderson, Day, and Waller. 482-86.

Men and Women: Suggestions for Writing

1. Choose a character in one of the works in this unit and explain how
   this character dominates his or her spouse.

2. Several of the poems in this section deal with courtship. Use two or
   more of these poems to write an essay about the rituals of courtship.

3. Compare and/or contrast the problems faced by women and their
   methods of dealing with the problems in *A Doll's House,* "The Gilded
   Six-Bits," or "Shiloh."

4. Several of the poets use humor in their depiction of the male-female relationship. After rereading the poems and reviewing your own knowledge and experience about such relationships, write a humorous poem, story, or essay describing the complexities of such relationships.

5. Define **irony.** Using at least two selections from this unit, show how the authors use irony to enrich the meaning of their works.

6. Select two or three of the love poems in this unit and write an essay explaining what attributes of the loved one have caused the love to last and deepen.

Men and Women: Writing about Film

1. The essayists in this unit all have distinct ideas about the nature of male-female relationships. Select two essayists and consider what they might say about the man/woman relationships in your favorite film.

2. A romance relationship is often at the center of popular Hollywood films. Compare and contrast the roles of men and women in the romantic relationship in two films from very different genres (for instance: action/adventure compared to romantic comedy; thriller compared to family drama; detective movie compared to animated feature). What do these movies teach us about romantic love? Consider issues of who is choosing whom and why, what kinds of communications the characters have, how well they seem to know each other, or whether there is any indication of how the future relationship will work.

3. Romantic comedies (*Sleepless in Seattle, High Fidelity, The Wedding Planner, Serendipity, Never Been Kissed, Bridget Jones' Diary*) are staples of the popular film market, but why do we like them so much? What do they offer us that real life doesn't? If you have ever been in a serious relationship, what do the films add to or leave out of the actual dynamics of relationship? Compare and contrast your experiences or observations with the fictional world of a specific film.

Grief and Loss

Edward Hopper, "Automat," 1927. Des Moines Art Center, Iowa.

A news program on television recently reported that a construction worker was killed in an accident, crushed to nothing by the sheer weight of earth falling on him. That account brings home how vulnerable we all are. Mere quivering, soft, easily crushed masses that we are, how are we to live with the knowledge of our vulnerability and our mortality? Such questions have haunted writers since time immemorial, puzzling the ever-patient Job, the great tragedians of ancient Athens, and religious thinkers of quite diverse cultures and times. Something, Annie Dillard says, exulting in the sheer power of spirit, "pummels us."

No matter how we try to protect ourselves with security systems, storm warnings, airbags, and quake-resistant structures, violence constantly threatens us. It may threaten from outside ourselves, like the brutal violence Mark Mathabane describes in "The Road to Alexandra" and the ghastly devastation of war described in Wilfred Owen's *"Dulce et Decorum Est."* Perhaps more frighteningly, it may threaten us from within ourselves as well as from without, as it does the narrator in Madison Smartt Bell's "Customs of the Country," who reveals and must ultimately face the violence within that has led her to abuse her son and to assault the wife-abuser next door. Othello, in Shakespeare's tragedy, twisted and manipulated by the evil Iago, struggles with jealousy so violent that it leads him to kill his innocent wife, Desdemona. Like Othello, we may live in an illusion of security until the seductive face of evil draws us into its violent maw.

How we face our common and fearful vulnerability defines us as human beings. Confronted by the terrible brutality of Auschwitz, Pinhas, a rabbi in Elie Wiesel's essay "Yom Kippur: The Day without Forgiveness," doubts whether God knows what He is doing. Others, like Dylan Thomas's speaker in "Do Not Go Gentle into That Good Night," may fight death with every ounce of will and energy they can muster. Still others, like Shakespeare's Othello, may choose self-inflicted death over a life consumed with humiliation and guilt. However it may confront them, great literature does not ignore the horrors of evil in the world but reflects the extraordinary variety of our responses to them.

Writing about Grief and Loss

As you prepare your essay on one or more of the works in this section, you should consider that just as each genre allows you to take different approaches to the work, so too does each kind of essay. You might, for example, write an expository essay examining the language of fear—the angry commands and the denigrating comments—in the essay by Mathabane. You might examine one or more of the different kinds of discrimination portrayed in the works in this unit: for example, religious discrimination in Wiesel's "Yom Kippur," racial discrimination in Mathabane's "The Road to Alexandra" and Olds's "On the Subway," or class discrimination in Heker's "The Stolen Party." Another possibility would be a persuasive essay arguing that the narrator in Bell's "Customs of the Country" does or does not deserve custody of her son. You might prefer a comparison-contrast essay on the attitudes toward death expressed in Thomas's "Do Not Go Gentle into That Good Night." Because so much excellent scholarship on *Othello* is available, you might write a researched expository essay on the evil of Iago or a cause-and-effect essay on the changes in Othello's language and personality.

When Gael Fowler was asked to write a documented essay using the casebook on Amy Tan, she began by reading both stories and all of the critical essays. At first she considered writing on both of the stories, but as she tried several thesis statements, she could not decide on one that included both. She finally chose to write on the types of death in "Immortal Heart."

Gael wrote her first rough draft on paper but soon discarded that copy. She actually started several essays but in the end went back to her original idea. She wrote a partially completed draft of the essay on the computer and sent it to her professor by e-mail to see if she was following the directions of the assignment. The professor suggested adding a few different aspects to the paper. She also said that Gael needed to make it clear that the stories told by Precious Auntie were a retelling of things that happened in the past. At this point, Gael added to the introduction a part about what had happened to the main character of the story. The new version, because it focused more on the main character, made a better essay. Gael felt that this change caused the paper as a whole to flow more smoothly. This revision also solved a problem she had faced about the verb tenses because the whole paper now was written in present tense, except for the quotations. Next she polished the essay to make it read more smoothly. Her original conclusion had to be rearranged and reworded, but the content remained essentially the same. Gael chose her title after she wrote the first draft, and it is the title of the essay found at the end of the casebook.

ESSAYS

Elie Wiesel (b. 1928)

Elie Wiesel was born in the village of Sighet in a part of Romania often claimed by Hungary. In 1944, the Nazis sent Wiesel and his family, along with all the other Jews of their village and region, to Auschwitz, where Wiesel's mother and younger sister were killed. Moved to Buchenwald, Wiesel and his father worked as slaves under horrendous conditions, which ultimately killed his father. Wiesel survived to become the foremost chronicler of the horrors of the Holocaust. Naturalized as a U.S. citizen in 1963, Wiesel has served as a faculty member in humanities at Boston University since 1976 and in 1978 was named chair of the U.S. Holocaust Museum. In 1985, he was awarded the National Medal of Freedom and, in 1986, the Nobel Peace Prize. Among his books, all of which focus on the Holocaust, are And the World Has Remained Silent *(1956), a powerful novel of life in Auschwitz from the point of view of a young boy, later translated and abridged as* Night: The Town Beyond the Wall *(1962), a novel;* A Beggar in Jerusalem *(1968);* Souls on Fire *(1972);* The Forgotten *(1989); and* All Rivers Run to the Sea: A Memoir *(1995).*

YOM KIPPUR: THE DAY WITHOUT FORGIVENESS (1968)

1   With a lifeless look, a painful smile on his face, while digging a hole in the ground, Pinhas moved his lips in silence. He appeared to be arguing with someone within himself and, judging from his expression, seemed close to admitting defeat.

2   I had never seen him so downhearted. I knew that his body would not hold out much longer. His strength was already abandoning him, his movements were becoming more heavy, more chaotic. No doubt he knew it too. But death figured only rarely in our conversations. We preferred to deny its presence, to reduce it, as in the past, to a simple allusion, something abstract, inoffensive, a word like any other.

3   "What are you thinking about? What's wrong?"

4   Pinhas lowered his head, as if to conceal his embarrassment, or his sadness, or both, and let a long time go by before he answered, in a voice scarcely audible: "Tomorrow is Yom Kippur."

5   Then I too felt depressed. My first Yom Kippur in the camp. Perhaps my last. The day of judgment, of atonement. Tomorrow the heavenly tribunal would sit and pass sentence: "And like unto a flock, the creatures of this world shall pass before thee." Once upon a time—last year—the approach of this day of tears, of penitence and fear, had made me tremble. Tomorrow, we would present ourselves before God, who sees everything and who knows everything, and we would say: "Father, have pity on your children." Would I be capable of praying with fervor again? Pinhas shook himself abruptly. His glance plunged into mine.

6   "Tomorrow is the Day of Atonement and I have just made a decision: I am not going to fast. Do you hear? I am not going to fast."

7   I asked for no explanation. I knew he was going to die and suddenly I was afraid that by way of justification he might declare: "It is simple, I have decided not to comply with the law anymore and not to fast because in the eyes of man and of God I am already dead, and the dead can disobey the commandments of the Torah." I lowered my head and made believe I was not thinking about anything but the earth I was digging up under a sky more dark than the earth itself.

8   We belonged to the same Kommando. We always managed to work side by side. Our age difference did not stop him from treating me like a friend. He must have been past forty. I was fifteen. Before the war, he had been *Rosh-Yeshiva,* director of a rabbinical school somewhere in Galicia. Often, to outwit our hunger or to forget our reasons for despair, we would study a page of the Talmud from memory. I relived my childhood by forcing myself not to think about those who were gone. If one of my arguments pleased Pinhas, if I quoted a commentary without distorting its meaning, he would smile at me and say: "I should have liked to have you among my disciples."

9   And I would answer: "But I am your disciple, where we are matters little."

10   That was false, the place was of capital importance. According to the law of the camp I was his equal; I used the familiar form when I addressed him. Any other form of address was inconceivable.

11   "Do you hear?" Pinhas shouted defiantly. "I will not fast."

12   "I understand. You are right. One must not fast. Not at Auschwitz. Here we live outside time, outside sin. Yom Kippur does not apply to Auschwitz."

13   Ever since Rosh Hashana, the New Year, the question had been bitterly debated all over camp. Fasting meant a quicker death. Here everybody fasted all year round. Every day was Yom Kippur. And the book of life and death was no longer in God's hands, but in the hands of the executioner. The words *mi yichye umi yamut,* "who shall live and who shall die," had a terrible real meaning here, an immediate bearing. And all the prayers in the world could not alter the *Gzar-din,* the inexorable movement of fate. Here, in order to live, one had to eat, not pray.

14   "You are right, Pinhas," I said, forcing myself to withstand his gaze. "You *must* eat tomorrow. You've been here longer than I have, longer than many of us. You need your strength. You have to save your strength, watch over it, protect it. You should not go beyond your limits. Or tempt misfortune. That would be a sin."

15   Me, his disciple? I gave him lessons, I gave him advice, as if I were his elder, his guide.

16   "That is not it," said Pinhas, getting irritated. "I could hold out for one day without food. It would not be the first time."

17   "Then what is it?"

18   "A decision. Until now, I've accepted everything. Without bitterness, without reservation. I have told myself: 'God knows what he is

doing.' I have submitted to his will. Now I have had enough, I have reached my limit. If he knows what he is doing, then it is serious; and it is not any less serious if he does not. Therefore, I have decided to tell him: 'It is enough.'"

19   I said nothing. How could I argue with him? I was going through the same crisis. Every day I was moving a little further away from the God of my childhood. He had become a stranger to me; sometimes, I even thought he was my enemy.

20   The appearance of Edek put an end to our conversation. He was our master, our king. The Kapo. This young Pole with rosy cheeks, with the movements of a wild animal, enjoyed catching his slaves by surprise and making them shout with fear. Still an adolescent, he enjoyed possessing such power over so many adults. We dreaded his changeable moods, his sudden fits of anger: without unclenching his teeth, his eyes half-closed, he would beat his victims long after they had lost consciousness and had ceased to moan.

21   "Well?" he said, planting himself in front of us, his arms folded. "Taking a little nap? Talking over old times? You think you are at a resort? Or in the synagogue?"

22   A cruel flame lit his blue eyes, but it went out just as quickly. An aborted rage. We began to shovel furiously, not thinking about anything but the ground which opened up menacingly before us. Edek insulted us a few more times and then walked off.

23   Pinhas did not feel like talking anymore, neither did I. For him the die had been cast. The break with God appeared complete.

24   Meanwhile, the pit under our legs was becoming wider and deeper. Soon our heads would hardly be visible above the ground. I had the weird sensation that I was digging a grave. For whom? For Pinhas? For myself? Perhaps for our memories.

25   On my return to camp, I found it plunged in feverish anticipation: they were preparing to welcome the holiest and longest day of the year. My barracks neighbors, a father and son, were talking in low voices. One was saying: "Let us hope the roll-call does not last too long." The other added: "Let us hope that the soup is distributed before the sun sets, otherwise we will not have the right to touch it."

26   Their prayers were answered. The roll-call unfolded without incident, without delay, without public hanging. The section-chief hurriedly distributed the soup; I hurriedly gulped it down. I ran to wash, to purify myself. By the time the day was drawing to a close, I was ready.

27   Some days before, on the eve of Rosh Hashana, all the Jews in camp—Kapos included—had congregated at the square where roll was taken, and we had implored the God of Abraham, Isaac, and Jacob to end our humiliation, to change sides, to break his pact with the enemy. In unison we had said *Kaddish* for the dead and for the living as well. Officers and soldiers, machine guns in hand, had stood by, amused spectators, on the other side of the barbed wire.

28   Now, we did not go back there for *Kol Nidre*. We were afraid of a selection: in preceding years, the Day of Atonement had been turned into a day of mourning. Yom Kippur had become *Tisha b'Av*, the day the Temple was destroyed.

29   Thus, each barracks housed its own synagogue. It was more prudent. I was sorry, because Pinhas was in another block.

30   A Hungarian rabbi officiated as our cantor. His voice stirred my memories and evoked that legend according to which, on the night of Yom Kippur, the dead rise from their graves and come to pray with the living. I thought: "Then it is true; that is what really happens. The legend is confirmed at Auschwitz."

31   For weeks, several learned Jews had gathered every night in our block to transcribe from memory—by hand, on toilet paper—the prayers for the High Holy Days. Each cantor received a copy. Ours read in a loud voice and we repeated each verse after him. The *Kol Nidre*, which releases us from all vows made under constraint, now seemed to me anachronistic, absurd, even though it had been composed in similar circumstances, in Spain, right near the Inquisition stakes. Once a year the converts would assemble and cry out to God: "Know this, all that we have said is unsaid, all that we have done is undone." *Kol Nidre?* A sad joke. Here and now we no longer had any secret vows to make or to deny: everything was clear, irrevocable.

32   Then came the *Vidui*, the great confession. There again, everything rang false, none of it concerned us anymore. *Ashamnu*, we have sinned. *Bagadnu*, we have betrayed. *Gazalnu*, we have stolen. What? Us? *We* have sinned? Against whom? by doing what? *We* have betrayed? Whom? Undoubtedly this was the first time since God judged his creation that victims beat their breasts accusing themselves of the crimes of their executioners.

33   Why did we take responsibility for sins and offenses which not one of us could ever have had the desire or the possibility of committing? Perhaps we felt guilty despite everything. Things were simpler that way. It was better to believe our punishments had meaning, that we had deserved them; to believe in a cruel but just God was better than not to believe at all. It was in order not to provoke an open war between God and his people that we had chosen to spare him, and we cried out: "You are our God, blessed be your name. You smite us without pity, you shed our blood, we give thanks to you for it, O Eternal One, for you are determined to show us that you are just and that your name is justice!"

34   I admit having joined my voice to the others and implored the heavens to grant me mercy and forgiveness. At variance with everything my lips were saying, I indicted myself only to turn everything into derision, into farce. At any moment I expected the Master of the universe to strike me dumb and to say: "That is enough—you have gone too far." And I like to think I would have replied: "You, also, blessed be your name, you also."

35   Our services were dispersed by the camp bell. The section-chiefs began to yell: "Okay, go to sleep! If God hasn't heard you, it's because he is incapable of hearing."

36   The next day, at work, Pinhas joined another group. I thought: "He wants to eat without being embarrassed by my presence." A day later, he returned. His face even more pale, even more gaunt than before. Death was gnawing at him. I caught myself thinking: "He will die because he did not observe Yom Kippur."

37   We dug for several hours without looking at each other. From far off, the shouting of the Kapo reached us. He walked around hitting people relentlessly.

38   Toward the end of the afternoon, Pinhas spoke to me: "I have a confession to make."

39   I shuddered, but went on digging. A strange, almost child-like smile appeared on his lips when he spoke again: "You know, I fasted."

40   I remained motionless. My stupor amused him.

41   "Yes, I fasted. Like the others. But not for the same reasons. Not out of obedience, but out of defiance. Before the war, you see, some Jews rebelled against the divine will by going to restaurants on the Day of Atonement; here, it is by observing the fast that we can make our indignation heard. Yes, my disciple and teacher, know that I fasted. Not for love of God, but against God."

42   He left me a few weeks later, victim of the first selection.

43   He shook my hand: "I would have liked to die some other way and elsewhere. I had always hoped to make of my death, as of my life, an act of faith. It is a pity. God prevents me from realizing my dream. He no longer likes dreams."

44   Nonetheless, he asked me to say *Kaddish* for him after his death, which, according to his calculations, would take place three days after his departure from camp.

45   "But why?" I asked, "since you are no longer a believer?"

46   He took the tone he always used when he explained a passage in the Talmud to me: "You do not see the heart of the matter. Here and now, the only way to accuse him is by praising him."

47   And he went, laughing, to his death.

Questions for Discussion

1. What is Wiesel's relationship to Pinhas in the essay? What is Wiesel's age?

2. Yom Kippur is the one opportunity for divine forgiveness Pinhas will have during the year. He is unlikely to live until the next Day of Atonement. Why, then, does he tell the narrator that he will not fast and will thereby willfully disobey God?

3. The narrator says, "Once upon a time—last year—the approach of this day of tears, of penitence and fear, had made me tremble." Why

does he refer to a time as recently as "last year" as "once upon a time"? Why did he tremble? How and why has his attitude toward Yom Kippur changed?

4. Why would the inhabitants of Auschwitz want to reduce death to "a simple allusion, something abstract, inoffensive, a word like any other"?

5. Discuss Pinhas's statement "The only way to accuse him is by praising him."

6. Why does Pinhas die laughing?

Suggestions for Exploration and Writing

1. Write a character analysis of Edek, the "master of the camp."

2. Explain why both Pinhas and the narrator have such a hard time accepting God. Why might Pinhas doubt that God knows what He is doing? What are the implications of God's not knowing "what He is doing"? What are the implications of His knowing but nevertheless allowing a horror like the Holocaust to continue?

3. If you were asked to explain God's role (or lack of a role) in the treatment of Jews in Nazi concentration camps, what would your answer be? Defend your answer in an essay.

4. Research the treatment of prisoners at Auschwitz and write an essay explaining the accuracy of Wiesel's account.

5. Research the Jewish traditions referred to in Wiesel's essay. To what degree do the two characters in the tale remain faithful to those traditions?

6. Compare Pinhas's story to Job's. See especially Job 1, 2 (note particularly 1:22 and 2:10), 6, and 10.

7. What terrible contemporary events might lead one to doubt as Pinhas does? Why?

Annie Dillard (b. 1945)

Annie Dillard, born in Pittsburgh, Pennsylvania, is a poet and essayist. Her essays in Pilgrim at Tinker Creek *(1974), from which the following essay is taken, and* Teaching a Stone to Talk *(1982) reveal a profound interest in, even fascination with, the natural world, dwelling lovingly on its details. Aware not only of nature's violence but also of the transcendental mystery that infuses it, Dillard reveals a sense of awe at the power of the divine driving the physical world.*

HEAVEN AND EARTH IN JEST (1974)

1   I used to have a cat, an old fighting tom, who would jump through the open window by my bed in the middle of the night and land on my chest.

I'd half-awaken. He'd stick his skull under my nose and purr, stinking of urine and blood. Some nights he kneaded my bare chest with his front paws, powerfully, arching his back, as if sharpening his claws, or pummeling a mother for milk. And some mornings I'd wake in daylight to find my body covered with paw prints in blood; I looked as though I'd been painted with roses.

2   It was hot, so hot the mirror felt warm. I washed before the mirror in a daze, my twisted summer sleep still hung about me like sea kelp. What blood was this, and what roses? It could have been the rose of union, the blood of murder, or the rose of beauty bare and the blood of some unspeakable sacrifice or birth. The sign on my body could have been an emblem or a stain, the keys to the kingdom or the mark of Cain. I never knew. I never knew as I washed, and the blood streaked, faded and finally disappeared, whether I'd purified myself or ruined the blood sign of the passover. We wake, if we ever wake at all, to mystery, rumors of death, beauty, violence. . . . "Seem like we're just set down here," a woman said to me recently, "and don't nobody know why."

3   These are morning matters, pictures you dream as the final wave heaves you up on the sand to the bright light and drying air. You remember pressure, and a curved sleep you rested against, soft, like a scallop in its shell. But the air hardens your skin; you stand; you leave the lighted shore to explore some dim headland, and soon you're lost in the leafy interior, intent, remembering nothing.

4   I still think of that old tomcat, mornings, when I wake. Things are tamer now; I sleep with the window shut. The cat and our rites are gone and my life is changed, but the memory remains of something powerful playing over me. I wake expectant, hoping to see a new thing. If I'm lucky I might be jogged awake by a strange birdcall. I dress in a hurry, imagining the yard flapping with auks, or flamingos. This morning it was a wood duck, down at the creek. It flew away.

5   I live by a creek, Tinker Creek, in a valley in Virginia's Blue Ridge. An anchorite's hermitage is called an anchor-hold; some anchor-holds were simple sheds clamped to the side of a church like a barnacle to a rock. I think of this house clamped to the side of Tinker Creek as an anchor-hold. It holds me at anchor to the rock bottom of the creek itself and it keeps me steadied in the current, as a sea anchor does, facing the stream of light pouring down. It's a good place to live; there's a lot to think about. The creeks—Tinker and Carvin's—are an active mystery, fresh every minute. Theirs is the mystery of the continuous creation and all that providence implies: the uncertainty of vision, the horror of the fixed, the dissolution of the present, the intricacy of beauty, the pressure of fecundity, the elusiveness of the free, and the flawed nature of perfection. The mountains—Tinker and Brushy, McAfee's Knob and Dead Man— are a passive mystery, the oldest of all. Theirs is the one simple mystery

of creation from nothing, of matter itself, anything at all, the given. Mountains are giant, restful, absorbent. You can heave your spirit into a mountain and the mountain will keep it, folded, and not throw it back as some creeks will. The creeks are the world with all its stimulus and beauty; I live there. But the mountains are home.

6   The wood duck flew away. I caught only a glimpse of something like a bright torpedo that blasted the leaves where it flew. Back at the house I ate a bowl of oatmeal; much later in the day came the long slant of light that means good walking.

7   If the day is fine, any walk will do; it all looks good. Water in particular looks its best, reflecting blue sky in the flat, and chopping it into graveled shallows and white chute and foam in the riffles. On a dark day, or a hazy one, everything's washed-out and lack-luster but the water. It carries its own lights. I set out for the railroad tracks, for the hill the flocks fly over, for the woods where the white mare lives. But I go to the water.

8   Today is one of those excellent January partly cloudies in which light chooses an unexpected part of the landscape to trick out in gilt, and then shadow sweeps it away. You know you're alive. You take huge steps, trying to feel the planet's roundness arc between your feet. Kazantzakis says that when he was young he had a canary and a globe. When he freed the canary, it would perch on the globe and sing. All his life, wandering the earth, he felt as though he had a canary on top of his mind, singing.

9   West of the house, Tinker Creek makes a sharp loop, so that the creek is both in back of the house, south of me, and also on the other side of the road, north of me. I like to go north. There the afternoon sun hits the creek just right, deepening the reflected blue and lighting the sides of trees on the banks. Steers from the pasture across the creek come down to drink; I always flush a rabbit or two there; I sit on a fallen trunk in the shade and watch the squirrels in the sun. There are two separated wooden fences suspended from cables that cross the creek just upstream from my tree-trunk bench. They keep the steers from escaping up or down the creek when they come to drink. Squirrels, the neighborhood children, and I use the downstream fence as a swaying bridge across the creek. But the steers are there today.

10   I sit on the downed tree and watch the black steers slip on the creek bottom. They are all bred beef: beef heart, beef hide, beef hocks. They're a human product like rayon. They're like a field of shoes. They have cast-iron shanks and tongues like foam insoles. You can't see through to their brains as you can with other animals; they have beef fat behind their eyes, beef stew.

11   I cross the fence six feet above the water, walking my hands down the rusty cable and tightroping my feet along the narrow edge of the planks. When I hit the other bank and terra firma, some steers are bunched in a knot between me and the barbed-wire fence I want to cross: So I suddenly rush at them in an enthusiastic spring, flailing my arms and hollering,

"Lightning! Copperhead! Swedish meatballs!" They flee, still in a knot, stumbling across the flat pasture. I stand with the wind on my face.

12   When I slide under a barbed-wire fence, cross a field, and run over a sycamore trunk felled across the water, I'm on a little island shaped like a tear in the middle of Tinker Creek. On one side of the creek is a steep forested bank; the water is swift and deep on that side of the island. On the other side is the level field I walked through next to the steers' pasture; the water between the field and the island is shallow and sluggish. In summer's low water, flags and bulrushes grow along a series of shallow pools cooled by the lazy current. Water striders patrol the surface film, crayfish hump along the silt bottom eating filth, frogs shout and glare, and shiners and small bream hide among roots from the sulky green heron's eye. I come to this island every month of the year. I walk around it, stopping and staring, or I straddle the sycamore log over the creek, curling my legs out of the water in winter, trying to read. Today I sit on dry grass at the end of the island by the slower side of the creek. I'm drawn to this spot. I come to it as to an oracle; I return to it as a man years later will seek out the battlefield where he lost a leg or an arm.

13   A couple of summers ago I was walking along the edge of the island to see what I could see in the water, and mainly to scare frogs. Frogs have an inelegant way of taking off from invisible positions on the bank just ahead of your feet, in dire panic, emitting a froggy "Yike!" and splashing into the water. Incredibly, this amused me, and incredibly, it amuses me still. As I walked along the grassy edge of the island, I got better and better at seeing frogs both in and out of the water. I learned to recognize, slowing down, the difference in texture of the light reflected from mudbank, water, grass, or frog. Frogs were flying all around me. At the end of the island I noticed a small green frog. He was exactly half in and half out of the water, looking like a schematic diagram of an amphibian, and he didn't jump.

14   He didn't jump; I crept closer. At last I knelt on the island's winter-killed grass, lost, dumbstruck, staring at the frog in the creek just four feet away. He was a very small frog with wide, dull eyes. And just as I looked at him, he slowly crumpled and began to sag. The spirit vanished from his eyes as if snuffed. His skin emptied and drooped; his very skull seemed to collapse and settle like a kicked tent. He was shrinking before my eyes like a deflating football. I watched the taut, glistening skin on his shoulder ruck, and rumple, and fall. Soon, part of his skin, formless as a pricked balloon, lay in floating folds like bright scum on top of the water: it was a monstrous and terrifying thing. I gaped bewildered, appalled. An oval shadow hung in the water behind the drained frog; then the shadow glided away. The frog skin bag started to sink.

15   I had read about the giant water bug, but never seen one. "Giant water bug" is really the name of the creature, which is an enormous, heavy-bodied brown beetle. It eats insects, tadpoles, fish, and frogs. Its grasping forelegs are mighty and hooked inward. It seizes a victim with these legs,

hugs it tight, and paralyzes it with enzymes injected during a vicious bite. That one bite is the only bite it ever takes. Through the puncture shoot the poisons that dissolve the victim's muscle and bone and organs—all but the skin—and through it the giant water bug sucks out the victim's body, reduced to a juice. This event is quite common in warm fresh water. The frog I saw was being sucked by a giant water bug. I had been kneeling on the island grass; when the unrecognizable flap of frog skin settled on the creek bottom, swaying, I stood up and brushed the knees of my pants. I couldn't catch my breath.

16   Of course, many carnivorous animals devour their prey alive. The usual method seems to be to subdue the victim by downing or grasping it so it can't flee, then eating it whole or in a series of bloody bites. Frogs eat everything whole, stuffing prey into the mouths with their thumbs. People have seen frogs with their wide jaws so full of live dragonflies they couldn't close them. Ants don't even have to catch their prey: in the spring they swarm over newly hatched, featherless birds in the nest and eat them tiny bite by bite.

17   That it's rough out there and chancy is no surprise. Every live thing is a survivor on a kind of extended emergency bivouac. But at the same time we are also created. In the Koran, Allah asks, "The heaven and the earth and all in between, thinkest thou I made them *in jest?*" It's a good question. What do we think of the created universe, spanning an unthinkable void with an unthinkable profusion of forms? Or what do we think of nothingness, those sickening reaches of time in either direction? If the giant water bug was not made in jest, was it then made in earnest? Pascal uses a nice term to describe the notion of the creator's, once having called forth the universe, turning his back to it: "Deus Absconditus." Is that what we think happened? Was the sense of it there, and God absconded with it, ate it, like a wolf who disappears round the edge of the house with the Thanksgiving turkey? "God is subtle," Einstein said, "but not malicious." Again, Einstein said that "nature conceals her mystery by means of her essential grandeur, not by her cunning." It could be that God has not absconded but spread, as our vision and understanding of the universe have spread, to a fabric of spirit and sense so grand and subtle, so powerful in a new way, that we can only feel blindly of its hem. In making the thick darkness a swaddling band for the sea, God "set bars and doors" and said, "hitherto shalt thou come, but no further." But have we come even that far? Have we rowed out to the thick darkness, or are we all playing pinochle in the bottom of the boat?

18   Cruelty is a mystery, and the waste of pain. But if we describe a world to compass these things, a world that is a long, brute game, then we bump against another mystery: the inrush of power and light, the canary that sings on the skull. Unless all ages and races of men have been deluded by the same mass hypnotist (who?), there seems to be such a thing as beauty, a grace wholly gratuitous. About five years ago I saw a mockingbird make a straight vertical descent from the roof gutter of a four-story

building. It was an act as careless and spontaneous as the curl of a stem or the kindling of a star.

19   The mockingbird took a single step into the air and dropped. His wings were still folded against his sides as though he were singing from a limb and not falling, accelerating thirty-two feet per second per second, through empty air. Just a breath before he would have been dashed to the ground, he unfurled his wings with exact, deliberate care, revealing the broad bars of white, spread his elegant, white-banded tail, and so floated onto the grass. I had just rounded a corner when his insouciant step caught my eye; there was no one else in sight. The fact of his free fall was like the old philosophical conundrum about the tree that falls in the forest. The answer must be, I think, that beauty and grace are performed whether or not we will or sense them. The least we can do is try to be there.

20   Another time I saw another wonder: sharks off the Atlantic coast of Florida. There is a way a wave rises above the ocean horizon, a triangular wedge against the sky. If you stand where the ocean breaks on a shallow beach, you see the raised water in a wave is translucent, shot with lights. One late afternoon at low tide a hundred big sharks passed the beach near the mouth of a tidal river in a feeding frenzy. As each green wave rose from the churning water, it illuminated within itself the six- or eight-foot-long bodies of twisting sharks. The sharks disappeared as each wave rolled toward me; then a new wave would swell above the horizon, containing in it, like scorpions in amber, sharks that roiled and heaved. The sight held awesome wonders: power and beauty, grace tangled in a rapture with violence.

21   We don't know what's going on here. If these tremendous events are random combinations of matter run amok, the yield of millions of monkeys at millions of typewriters, then what is it in us, hammered out of those same typewriters, that they ignite? We don't know. Our life is a faint tracing on the surface of mystery, like the idle, curved tunnels of leaf miners on the face of a leaf. We must somehow take a wider view, look at the whole landscape, really see it, and describe what's going on here. Then we can at least wail the right question into the swaddling band of darkness, or, if it comes to that, choir the proper praise.

22   At the time of Lewis and Clark, setting the prairies on fire was a well-known signal that meant, "Come down to the water." It was an extravagant gesture, but we can't do less. If the landscape reveals one certainty, it is that the extravagant gesture is the very stuff of creation. After the one extravagant gesture of creation in the first place, the universe has continued to deal exclusively in extravagances, flinging intricacies and colossi down aeons of emptiness, heaping profusions on profligacies with everfresh vigor. The whole show has been on fire from the word go. I come down to the water to cool my eyes. But everywhere I look I see fire; that which isn't flint is tinder, and the whole world sparks and flames.

23   I have come to the grassy island late in the day. The creek is up; icy water sweeps under the sycamore log bridge. The frog skin, of course, is

utterly gone. I have stared at that one spot on the creek bottom for so long, focusing past the rush of water, that when I stand, the opposite bank seems to stretch before my eyes and flow grassily upstream. When the bank settles down I cross the sycamore log and enter again the big plowed field next to the steers' pasture.

24   The wind is terrific out of the west; the sun comes and goes. I can see the shadow on the field before me deepen uniformly and spread like a plague. Everything seems so dull I am amazed I can even distinguish objects. And suddenly the light runs across the land like a comber, and up the trees, and goes again in a wink: I think I've gone blind or died. When it comes again, the light, you hold your breath, and if it stays you forget about it until it goes again.

25   It's the most beautiful day of the year. At four o'clock the eastern sky is a dead stratus black flecked with low white clouds. The sun in the west illuminates the ground, the mountains, and especially the bare branches of trees, so that everywhere silver trees cut into the black sky like a photographer's negative of a landscape. The air and the ground are dry; the mountains are going on and off like neon signs. Clouds slide east as if pulled from the horizon, like a tablecloth whipped off a table. The hemlocks by the barbed wire fence are flinging themselves east as though their backs would break. Purple shadows are racing east; the wind makes me face east, and again I feel the dizzying, drawn sensation I felt when the creek bank reeled.

26   At four-thirty the sky in the east is clear; how could that big blackness be blown? Fifteen minutes later another darkness is coming overhead from the northwest; and it's here. Everything is drained of its light as if sucked. Only at the horizon do inky black mountains give way to distant, lighted mountains—lighted not by direct illumination but rather paled by glowing sheets of mist hung before them. Now the blackness is in the east; everything is half in shadow, half in sun, every clod, tree, mountain, and hedge. I can't see Tinker Mountain through the line of hemlock, till it comes on like a streetlight, ping, *ex nihilo*. Its sandstone cliffs pink and swell. Suddenly the light goes; the cliffs recede as if pushed. The sun hits a clump of sycamores between me and the mountains; the sycamore arms light up, and *I can't see the cliffs*. They're gone. The pale network of sycamore arms, which a second ago was transparent as a screen, is suddenly opaque, glowing with light. Now the sycamore arms snuff out, the mountains come on, and there are the cliffs again.

27   I walk home. By five-thirty the show has pulled out. Nothing is left but an unreal blue and a few banked clouds low in the north. Some sort of carnival magician has been here, some fast-talking worker of wonder who has the act backwards. "Something in this hand," he says, "something in this hand, something up my sleeve, something behind my back . . ." and abracadabra, he snaps his fingers, and it's all gone. Only the bland, blank-faced magician remains, in his unruffled coat, barehanded, acknowledging a smattering of baffled applause. When you look again the whole

show has pulled up stakes and moved on down the road. It never stops. New shows roll in from over the mountains and the magician reappears unannounced from a fold in the curtain you never dreamed was an opening. Scarves of clouds, rabbits in plain view, disappear into the black hat forever. Presto chango. The audience, if there is an audience at all, is dizzy from head-turning, dazed.

28   Like the bear who went over the mountain, I went out to see what I could see. And, I might as well warn you, like the bear, all that I could see was the other side of the mountain: more of the same. On a good day I might catch a glimpse of another wooded ridge rolling under the sun like water, another bivouac. I propose to keep here what Thoreau called "a meteorological journal of the mind," telling some tales and describing some of the sights of this rather tamed valley, and exploring, in fear and trembling, some of the unmapped dim reaches and unholy fastnesses to which those tales and sights so dizzyingly lead.

29   I am no scientist. I explore the neighborhood. An infant who has just learned to hold his head up has a frank and forthright way of gazing about him in bewilderment. He hasn't the faintest clue where he is, and he aims to learn. In a couple of years, what he will have learned instead is how to fake it: he'll have the cocksure air of a squatter who has come to feel he owns the place. Some unwonted, taught pride diverts us from our original intent, which is to explore the neighborhood, view the landscape, to discover at least *where* it is that we have been so startlingly set down, if we can't learn why.

30   So I think about the valley. It is my leisure as well as my work, a game. It is a fierce game I have joined because it is being played anyway, a game of both skill and chance, played against an unseen adversary— the conditions of time—in which the payoffs, which may suddenly arrive in a blast of light at any moment, might as well come to me as anyone else. I stake the time I'm grateful to have, the energies I'm glad to direct. I risk getting stuck on the board, so to speak, unable to move in any direction, which happens enough, God knows; and I risk the searing, exhausting nightmares that plunder rest and force me face down all night long in some muddy ditch seething with hatching insects and crustaceans.

31   But if I can bear the nights, the days are a pleasure. I walk out; I see something, some event that would otherwise have been utterly missed and lost; or something sees me, some enormous power brushes me with its clean wing, and I resound like a beaten bell.

32   I am an explorer, then, and I am also a stalker, or the instrument of the hunt itself. Certain Indians used to carve long grooves along the wooden shafts of their arrows. They called the grooves "lightning marks," because they resembled the curved fissure lightning slices down the trunks of trees. The function of lightning marks is this: if the arrow fails to kill the game, blood from a deep wound will channel along the lightning mark,

streak down the arrow shaft, and spatter to the ground, laying a trail dripped on broadleaves, on stone, that the barefoot and trembling archer can follow into whatever deep or rare wilderness it leads. I am the arrow shaft, carved along my length by unexpected lights and gashes from the very sky, and this book is the straying trail of blood.

33   Something pummels us, something barely sheathed. Power broods and lights. We're played on like a pipe; our breath is not our own. James Houston describes two young Eskimo girls sitting cross-legged on the ground, mouth on mouth, blowing by turns each other's throat cords, making a low, unearthly music. When I cross again the bridge that is really the steers' fence, the wind has thinned to the delicate air of twilight; it crumples the water's skin. I watch the running sheets of light raised on the creek's surface. The sight has the appeal of the purely passive, like the racing of light under clouds on a field, the beautiful dream at the moment of being dreamed. The breeze is the merest puff, but you yourself sail head-long and breathless under the gale force of the spirit.

Questions for Discussion

1. What does the blood, repeatedly left on her body by the cat, suggest about Dillard?

2. Dillard says that Nikos Kazantzakis "felt as though he had a canary on top of his mind, singing." What does he mean? How is this quotation appropriate to Dillard's essay?

3. Dillard asks whether the giant water bug was "made in jest" or "in earnest." What is your answer? Why?

4. "Cruelty is a mystery," Dillard says. What does she mean? What else does she see as a mystery?

5. What does Dillard mean when she defines beauty as "a grace wholly gratuitous"? What meanings of the word *grace* might she have in mind?

6. Explain Dillard's comparison of herself to an arrow shaft. What is she saying about herself and her environment?

7. What does Dillard mean when she says, "Something pummels us, something barely sheathed"?

Suggestions for Exploration and Writing

1. Dillard's essay is rich in **imagery**. Examine the relationships between images of violence, power, light, dark, and grace. What dominant impression of people's place in the universe do these images suggest?

2. Compare the questions Dillard asks in this essay with the question Frost's speaker asks in the poem "Design" or the questions Pinhas asks in "Yom Kippur."

Mark Mathabane (b. 1960)

Mark Mathabane, a black South African, grew up in Alexandra, a crowded, poverty-stricken ghetto outside Johannesburg. His autobiography, Kaffir Boy *(1986), from which the following selection comes, recounts his upbringing under the crushing weight of apartheid and his escape to the United States by means of a tennis scholarship. Since then he has lived in the United States. In 1997, he received a White House fellowship to visit South Africa and observe firsthand the changes in his homeland since the end of apartheid in 1993. The word* kaffir *in the title is a racial epithet, a term used by South African whites to degrade and disparage blacks.*

THE ROAD TO ALEXANDRA (1986)

1 It was early morning of a bitterly cold winter day in 1965. I was lying on a bed of cardboard, under a kitchen table, peering through a large hole in the blanket at the spooky darkness around me. I was wide awake and terrified. All night long I had been having nightmares in which throngs of black people sprawled dead in pools of red blood, surrounded by all sorts of slimy, creeping creatures. These nightmares had plagued me since I turned five two weeks ago. I thought of waking my mother in the next room, but my father's words of warning not to wake her on account of bad dreams stopped me. All was quiet, save for the snores of my sister Florah—three years old—huddled alongside me, under the same blanket, and the squeaks of rats in the cupboard. From time to time the moon shone eerily through the window. Afraid to go back to sleep lest I have another nightmare, I stayed awake, peering at the quivering blackness through the hole. The darkness seemed alive.

2 My father woke up and began arguing sharply with my mother in the bedroom. It was five o'clock by the *kikilihoo* (cock's crow), time for him to go to work. He always went to work at this time—and he was angry at my mother for forgetting to prepare his *scuffin* (food for work). Soon he emerged, holding a flickering tallow candle in one hand, and a worn-out Stetson hat in the other. He silently went about preparing his *scuffin* from what was left of yesterday's *pap'n vleis* (porridge and meat). He wrapped the *scuffin* in sheets of old newspapers, took the family's *waslap* (face-cloth) from the window, dampened it with water from a mug and wiped his face. He drank what was left of the water in the mug. Minutes later he was out through the door, on his way to work, but not before I had said to him: "Don't forget our fish and chips, Papa."

3 "Fish and chips is tomorrow, son. Today is Thursday. Payday is tomorrow."

4 "'Bye, 'bye, Papa."

5 "Go back to sleep."

6 As soon as he was out through the door my mother, clad only in her skimpy underwear, came into the kitchen, chamber pot in hand. The chamber pot dripped and had a bad smell, like the one which always

pervaded the yard whenever our neighbours hung urine-soaked blankets and cardboard on fences to dry under the blazing African sun.

7   "Where are you going, Mama?"

8   "To the outhouse."

9   "Those bad dreams came back, Mama."

10   "I'll be back soon."

11   Before she left, she blew out the candle to save it from burning out and took with her a book of matches. I lingered between sleep and wakefulness, anticipating my mother's speedy return. Twenty minutes passed without any sign of her. I grew more afraid of the darkness; I shut my eyes, pulled the blanket over my head and minutes later I was in dreamland. I had been asleep but a short while when my mother came bursting through the door, yelling, in a winded voice, "Get up, Johannes! Get up quickly!" And as she yelled she reached under the table and shook me vigorously.

12   "Hunh?" I mumbled sleepily, stirring but not waking up, thinking it a dream.

13   "Get up! Get up!" she yelled again, yanking the torn blanket covering Florah and me, and almost instantly I awoke and heard a door shut with a resounding slam. From then on things became rather entangled for me. Unaware that I was still under the table I jerked upward, and my head banged against the top of the table. I winced but didn't cry; my father had warned me that men and boys never cry, ever. Still only half awake, I began crawling upon my hands and knees from under the table, but the darkness was all around me, and I couldn't see where I was going.

14   As I was crawling blindly my face rammed into one of the concrete slabs propping one of the table's legs. I let out a scream and drew back momentarily, dazed and smarting. At this point half my mind still told me that I was in a dream, but the hot pain all over my face convinced me otherwise. I resumed groping for a way from under the table, to find out where my mother had suddenly gone, and why she had awakened me. Finally I was out. I leaned myself for a while against the side of the table and waited for the throbbing pain in my head to cease.

15   Suddenly, as I stood leaning against the table, from outside came a series of dreadful noises. Sirens blared, voices screamed and shouted, wood cracked and windows shattered, children bawled, dogs barked and foot-steps pounded. I was bewildered; I had never heard such a racket before. I was instantly seized by a feeling of terror.

16   "Mama! Where are you?" I screamed, groping about with one hand, the other clutching the table. I did not know whether my mother had gone back out, or was still in the house.

17   "Over here," a voice suddenly whispered from somewhere behind me. It was my mother's voice, but it sounded so faint I could barely hear it. I turned my head and strained to see where it was coming from and saw nothing but darkness. Where was my mother? Why was it so dark? Why the dreadful noises outside? My imagination ran wild. The pitch-black room seemed alive with the voodoo spirits of my mother's tales, ready to pounce upon me if I as much as took a step from where I was standing.

18   "Mama! Where are you?" I screamed again, fear mounting inside me.

19   "I'm over here," the disembodied voice of my mother said from somewhere in the dark.

20   I swung around and saw a candle coming out of the bedroom. It
stopped briefly by the door. It was my mother. In the dim candlelight, her
body, crouched like that of an animal cowering in fear, cast an oblong,
eerie shadow on the flaking whitewashed wall. She stole over to where I
stood transfixed, handed me the flickering candle and told me to keep it
down and away from the window.

21   "What's the matter, Mama?"

22   "Not so loud," she cautioned, a finger on her lips. Still clad only in her
underwear, she hurriedly draped a tattered black shawl, which had been
lying on a tin chair nearby, over her shoulders, but the shawl didn't cover
much. She reached under the kitchen table and grabbed the torn blanket and draped it in place of the shawl and took the shawl and spread it
over the newspapers and cardboard covering Florah.

23   "What's the matter, Mama?"

24   "Peri-Urban is here."

25   "Peri-Urban!" I gasped and stiffened at the name of the dreaded
Alexandra Police Squad. To me nothing, short of a white man, was
more terrifying; not even a bogeyman. Memories of previous encounters
with the police began haunting me. Will the two fat black policemen with
sjamboks[1] and truncheons burst open the door again? And will the one
with the twirled mustache and big hands grit his teeth at me while threatening, "Speak up, boy! or I'll let you taste my *sjambok!*" and thereafter
spit in my face and hit me on the head with a truncheon for refusing to
tell where my mother and father were hiding? And will the tall, carroty-
haired white man in fatigues stand by the doorjamb again, whistling a
strange tune and staring fear into Florah and me?

26   "W-where a-are t-they?" I stammered.

27   "Outside. Don't be afraid now. They're still in the next neighbourhood.
I was in the outhouse when the alarm came." "When the alarm came"
meant people leaping over fences in a mad dash to escape the police.

28   I nodded sheepishly, the sleep now completely gone from my eyes. I
was now standing—naked, cold and trembling—in the middle of the
room. My mother took the candle from my hand and told me to dress. I
reached under the kitchen table for my patched khaki shorts and dressed
hurriedly. Meanwhile the pandemonium outside was intensifying with
each minute; the raid, it seemed, was gathering momentum. Suddenly a
gust of wind puffed through the sackcloth covering the hole in the window; the candle flickered but did not go out. I felt something warm soak
my groin and trickle down my legs. I tried to stem the flow of urine by
pressing my thighs together, but I was too late; a puddle had formed
about my feet, and I scattered it with my toes. My mother handed me the
candle and headed toward the table in the corner. As she went along she

---

[1]An animal-hide whip used to enforce apartheid.

said, without turning to face me, "Take good care of your brother and sister while I'm gone, you hear?"

29   "Yes, Mama." I knew she had to leave, she had to flee from the police and leave us children alone as she had done so many times before. By now my mother had reached the table, and her big brown eyes darted about its top, searching for something.

30   "Where's my passbook?" she asked in a frantic voice, her tense body bent low over the table. "Bring the candle over here. Keep it down! Away from the window!" As I hurried the candle, which had now burnt to a stub, over to her, a loud scream leaped out from the dark outside. Alarmed, I stumbled and fell headlong into my mother's arms. As she steadied me she continued asking, "Where's my passbook? Where is it?" I did not know; I could not answer; I could not think; my mind had suddenly gone blank. She grabbed me by the shoulder and shook me, yelling frantically, "Where is it! Where is it! Oh, God. Where is it, child? Where is the book? Hurry, or they'll find me!"

31   "What book?" I said blankly.

32   "The little book I showed you and your sister last night, remember," she stared at me anxiously, but my eyes merely widened in confusion. No matter how hard I tried it seemed I could not rid my mind of the sinister force that had suddenly blotted out all memory.

33   "Remember the little black book with my picture in it. Where is it?" my mother said, again grabbing me and shaking me, begging me to remember. I could not snap out of my amnesia.

34   The noise outside had risen to a dreadful crescendo. Suddenly several gunshots rang out in quick succession. Shouts of "Follow that Kaffir! He can't get far! He's wounded!" followed the shots. Somehow it all jolted me back to consciousness, and I remembered where my mother's little black book was; under the pallet of cardboard where I had tucked it the night before, hoping to sneak it out the next day and show it to my friends at play—who had already shown me their mothers'—to see whose mother's picture was the most beautiful.

35   "It's under the table, Mama!" I cried out.

36   My mother thanked her ancestors. Hurriedly, she circled the table, reached under it, rolled Florah away from the damp cardboard, lifted them up, and underneath, on the earthen floor, she found her little black book. I heaved a great sigh of relief as I watched her tuck it into her bosom.

37   My sister's naked, frail body, now on the bare floor, shook from the icy cold seeping through a hole under the door. She coughed, then moaned—a prolonged rasping sound; but she did not wake up. My mother quickly straightened out the cardboard and rolled Florah back to sleep and covered her with more newspapers and cardboard. More screams came from outside as more doors and windows were being busted by the police; the vicious barking of dogs escalated, as did the thudding of running feet. Shouts of "*Mbambe! Mbambe!* (Grab him! Catch him!)" followed the screams of police whistles.

38   My mother was headed for the bedroom door when a shaft of very bright light flashed through the uncurtained window and fell upon her. Instantly she leaped behind the door and remained hidden behind it. Alarmed, I dropped the candle, spilling the molten wax on my feet; the room was plunged into utter darkness, for the bright light disappeared barely seconds after it had flashed. As I groped about for the candle, the bright light again flashed through the window and flooded the kitchen. This time it stayed. It seemed daylight.

39   My mother crept from behind the bedroom door and started toward the kitchen door, on tiptoe. As she neared it, my year-old brother, George, who slept with my mother and father on the only bed in the house, started screaming, piercing the tenuous stillness of the house. His screams stopped my mother dead in her tracks; she spun around and said to me; in a whisper, "Go quiet your brother."

40   "Yes, Mama," I said, but I did not go. I could not go. I seemed rooted to the spot by a terrifying fear of the unknown.

41   "I'll be gone a short while," my mother, now by the door, whispered. She stealthily opened it a crack, her blanketed body still in a crouch, her head almost touching the floor. She hesitated a moment or two before peering through the opening. The storm of screams that came through the door made me think that the world was somehow coming to an end. Through the opening I saw policemen, with flashlights and what looked like raised cavemen's clubs, move searchingly about several shacks across the street.

42   "Don't forget to lock the door securely behind me," my mother said as she ran her eyes up and down the street. More gunshots rang out; more screams and more shouts came from somewhere deep in the neighbourhood.

43   "Don't go, Mama!" I cried. "Please don't go! Don't leave us, please!"

44   She did not answer, but continued opening the door a little wider and inching her blanketed body, still bent low, slowly forward until she was halfway in and halfway out. Meantime in the bedroom George continued bawling. I hated it when he cried like that, for it heightened, and made more real, my feelings of confusion, terror and helplessness.

45   "Let him suck thumb," my mother said, now almost out of the house. She was still bent low. She spat on the doorknob twice, a ritual that, she once told me, protected the innocent and kept all evil spirits away, including the police. I felt vaguely reassured seeing her perform the ritual.

46   "And don't forget now," she said, "don't ever be afraid. I'll be back soon." Those were her last words; and as I watched her disappear behind the shacks, swallowed up by the ominous darkness and ominous sounds, her figure like that of a black-cloaked ghost, she seemed less of the mother I knew and loved, and more of a desperate fugitive fleeing off to her secret lair somewhere in the inky blackness.

47   I immediately slammed the door shut, bolted it in three places, blew out the candle and then scampered to the bedroom, where my brother was still crying. But as I flung open the bedroom door a new and more dreadful fear gripped me and made me turn and run back to the front door. I

suddenly remembered how the police had smashed open the door during a raid one morning even though it had been bolted. I must barricade the door this time, I told myself; that will stop them. I started dragging things from all over the kitchen and piling them up against the door—a barrel half-filled with drinking water, a scuttle half-filled with coal and several tin chairs. Satisfied that the door was now impregnable I then scuttled back to the bedroom and there leaped onto the bed by the latticed window.

48   "Shut up, you fool!" I yelled at my brother, but he did not quiet. I then uttered the phrase, "There's a white man outside," which to small black children had the same effect as "There's a bogeyman outside," but still he would not stop. I then stuck my thumb into his wide-open mouth, as my mother had told me. But George had other plans for my thumb; he sunk his teeth into it. Howling with pain, I grabbed him by the feet and tossed him over and spanked him on the buttocks.

49   "Don't ever do that!"

50   He became hysterical and went into a seizure of screams. His body writhed and his mouth frothed. Again I grabbed his tiny feet and shook him violently, begged him to stop screaming, but still he would not quiet. I screamed at him some more; that made him worse. In desperation I wrenched his ears, pinched him black and blue, but still he continued hollering. In despair I gave up, for the time being, attempts to quiet him. My head spun and did not know what to do.

51   I glanced at the window; it was getting light outside. I saw two black policemen breaking down a door at the far end of the yard. A half-naked, near-hysterical, jet-black woman was being led out of an outhouse by a fat laughing black policeman who, from time to time, prodded her private parts with a truncheon. The storm of noises had now subsided somewhat, but I could still hear doors and windows being smashed, and dogs barking and children screaming. I jerked George and pinned him against the window, hoping that he would somehow understand why I needed him to shut up; but that did not help, for his eyes were shut, and he continued to scream and writhe. My eyes roved frantically about the semidark room and came to rest on a heavy black blanket hanging limply from the side of the bed. Aha! I quickly grabbed it and pulled it over George's head to muffle his screams. I pinned it tightly with both hands over his small head as he lay writhing. It worked! For though he continued screaming, I could hardly hear him. He struggled and struggled and I pinned the blanket tighter and tighter. It never crossed my mind that my brother might suffocate. As he no longer screamed, I waited, from time to time glancing nervously at the window.

52   Suddenly I heard the bedroom door open and shut. Startled, I let go of my hold on the blanket and turned my head toward the door only to see Florah, her eyes wild with fear, come rushing in, screaming, her hands over her head. She came over to the bedside and began tugging frantically at the blanket.

53   "Where's Mama! I want Mama! Where's Mama!"

54   "Shut up!" I raged. "Go back to sleep before I hit you!"

55   She did not leave.

56   "I'm scared," she whimpered. "I want Mama."

57   "Shut up, you fool!" I screamed at her again. "The white man is out-side, and he's going to get you and eat you!" I should not have said that; my sister became hysterical. She flung herself at the bed and tried to claw her way up. Enraged, I slapped her hard across the mouth; she staggered but did not fall. She promptly returned to the bedside and resumed her tugging of the blanket more determinedly. My brother too was now screaming. My head felt hot with confusion and desperation; I did not know what to do; I wished my mother were present; I wished the police were blotted off the surface of the earth.

58   I could still hear footsteps pounding, children screaming and dogs barking, so I quickly hauled my sister onto the bed, seeing that she was resolved not to return to the kitchen. We coiled together on the narrow bed, the three of us, but because of all the awkward movements everyone was making, the bricks propping the legs of the bed shifted, and it wobbled as if about to collapse. I held my breath, and the bed did not fall. I carefully pulled the blanket tautly over the three of us. Under the blanket I saw nothing but darkness.

59   But the din outside after a temporary lull surged and made its way through the bolted door, through the barricade, through the kitchen, through the blanket, through the blackness and into my finger-plugged ear, as if the bed were perched in the midst of all the pandemonium. My mind blazed with questions. What was really going on outside? Were the barking dogs police dogs? Who was shooting whom? Were the *Msomi*[2] gangs involved? I had often been told that police dogs ate black people when given the order by white people—were they eating people this time? Suppose my mother had been apprehended, would the police dogs eat her up too? What was happening to my friends?

60   I ached with curiosity and fear. Should I go to the kitchen window and see what was going on in the streets? My sister had wet the bed, and it felt damp and cold. Childish curiosity finally overcame the fear, and I hopped out of bed and tiptoed to the kitchen window. I had barely reached the bedroom door when I heard my sister whimper.

61   "Where are you going? I'm scared." I looked over my shoulder and saw Florah on the edge of the bed, her legs dangling over the side, poised to follow.

62   "Shut up and go back to sleep!"

63   "I'm coming with you." She dropped her tiny feet to the floor.

64   "Dare and I'll whip you!"

65   She whined and retracted her body frame under the blanket. I slowly opened the bedroom door, taking care to keep low and away from the

[2]Legendary black gangsters of the fifties and early sixties in the mode of the Mafia.

shaft of light still streaming through the uncurtained window. I reached the window. What next? A piece of sackcloth covered the bottom half of the window where several panes were missing, the result of a rock hurled from the street one night long ago. My father hadn't replaced the window but used the flap as a watchpost whenever police raided the neighbourhood.

66   With mounting excitement I raised myself toward the window and reached for the flap. I carefully pushed it to one side as I had seen my father do and then poked my head through; all the time my eyes were on the prowl for danger. My head was halfway in and halfway out when my eyes fell upon two tall black policemen emerging from a shack across the street. They joined two others standing alongside a white man by the entrance gate to one of the yards. The white man had a holstered gun slung low about his waist, as in the movies, and was pacing briskly about, shouting orders and pointing in all different directions. Further on in the yard, another white man, also with a gun, was supervising a group of about ten black policemen as they rounded up half-naked black men and women from the shacks. Children's screams issued from some of the shacks.

67   The sight had me spellbound. Suddenly the white man by the entrance gate pointed in the direction of our house. Two black policemen jumped and started across the street toward me. They were quickly joined by a third. I gasped with fear. A new terror gripped me and froze me by the window, my head still sticking halfway out. My mind went blank; I shut my eyes; my heart thumped somewhere in my throat. I overheard the three black policemen, as they came across the street, say to each other:

68   "That's number thirty-seven."

69   "Yes. But I don't think we'll find any of the *Msomi* gang in there."

70   "*Umlungu* [the white man] thinks there may be a few hiding in there. If we don't find them, we can still make easy money. The yard is a haven for people without passbooks."

71   "But I think everybody has fled. Look at those busted doors."

72   "There's a few over there still shut."

73   "All right, then, let's go in."

74   Suddenly there was a tremendous thud, as of something heavy crashing against the floor, and I heard George's screams of pain pierce the air. I opened my eyes momentarily and saw the three black policemen, only a few steps from the door, stop and look at one another. I quickly retracted my head but remained crouched under the window, afraid of going anywhere lest I be seen. I heard the three policemen say to one another:

75   "You hear that?"

76   "Yes. It's an infant crying."

77   "I bet you they left that one alone too."

78   Suddenly my sister came screaming out of the bedroom, her hands over her head.

79   "Yowee! Yowee!" she bawled. "Johannes! Come an' see! Come an' see!"

80   I stared at her, unable to move, not wanting to move.

81   "It's G-george," she stammered with horror; "B-blood, d-dead, b-blood, d-dead!" her voice trailed into sobs. She rushed over to where I stood and began pulling my hand, imploring me to go see my brother who, she said dramatically, was bleeding to death. My mouth contorted into frantic, inaudible "Go aways" and "shut ups" but she did not leave. I heard someone pounding at the door. In the confusion that followed angry voices said:

82   "There's no point in going in. I've had enough of hollering infants."

83   "Me too."

84   "I bet you there's no one in there but the bloody children."

85   "You just took the words right out of my mouth."

86   "Then let's go back to the vans. We still have more streets to comb. This neighbourhood is about dry anyway."

87   They left. It turned out that George had accidentally fallen off the bed and smashed his head against a pile of bricks at the foot of the bed, sustaining a deep cut across the forehead. The gash swelled and bled badly, stopping only after I had swathed his forehead with pieces of rags. The three of us cowered together in silence another three hours until my mother returned from the ditch where she had been hiding.

Questions for Discussion

1. What details reveal the poverty of this family?

2. Why must the mother leave the house? Why is she so frantic to find her passbook? What was the significance of the passbook in apartheid South Africa?

3. Why are the police raiding the yard? If the family has done nothing wrong, why should the family fear the police?

4. The essay is told from the **point of view** of a five-year-old boy who seems wise for his age. What are the advantages of this point of view?

Suggestions for Exploration and Writing

1. People whose jobs or lifestyles require the frequent use of violence sometimes develop a tolerance for violence. In an essay, discuss the development of a tolerance for violence in a group of people, or propose methods for preventing the development of this tolerance.

2. Classify the fears of South African blacks as shown in this essay.

3. Could anything like this incident happen in the United States? In an essay, discuss the possibility.

4. Since apartheid ended in 1993, South Africa has worked to bring peace and reconciliation to its people. Research these efforts at reconciliation and write an essay based on your research.

Lee Stringer (b. 1957)

Lee Stringer was born in New York. Becoming addicted to drugs after the death of his brother, Stringer lived on the streets from the mid-1980s until the mid-1990s. Later he became editor and columnist for Street News. *He has published essays and articles in* The Nation, The New York Times, *and* Newsday. *Stringer now lives in Mamaroneck, New York. The piece included is from the first and second chapters in Stringer's* Grand Central Winter: Stories from the Street *(1998).*

GRAND CENTRAL WINTER   (1998)

1   What happened was I was digging around in my hole—there's this long, narrow, crawl space in Grand Central's lower regions, of which few people are aware and into which I moved some time ago. It is strung with lights and there is a water spigot just outside the cubbyhole through which I enter. It's on the chilly side in winter, and I baste down there in summer, but it is, as they say, home.

2   I have filled this place with blankets and books and have fortified it with enough cardboard baffles to hold any rats at bay (the secret being, of course, to never bring food down here. It's the food that attracts them). So, at the end of the day I come down here to polish off that last, lonely blast. Or just to sleep it off.

3   But as I said, I was digging around in this hole—lying flat on my back, reaching back and under the old blankets, newspapers, and clothes that I've amassed over time and that keep me insulated from the concrete floor, trying to find some small, dowellike instrument with which to push the screens from one end of my stem to the other, so that I could smoke the remaining resin caked up in the thing.

4   For those of you who have not had the pleasure, I point out that when you are piping up, the first thing to go is your patience. And I'm digging around under this mess, cursing and muttering under my breath like an old wino on a three-day drunk, when my fingers finally wrap around some sort of smooth, straight stick.

5   I pull it out and it's a pencil and it does the trick. I push my screens and take a hit and have a pleasurable half hour of sweaty trembling panic that at any second someone or something is going to jump out of the darkness—I get much too paranoid to smoke with the lights on—and stomp the living shit out of me or something.

6   That's the great thing about being a veteran crackhead.

7   Always a lot of fun.

8   Anyway, the point is, I start carrying this pencil around with me because I really hate like hell to be caught without something to push with and then have to go searching or digging around like I was doing when I found the thing.

9   The good thing about carrying a pencil is that it's a pencil. And if I get stopped and searched for any reason, it's just a pencil. Of course I carry

my stem around too. And there's no doubt about what that's for. But, hey, I'm not looking to strain my cerebral cortex on the subject. It's all I can do just to hustle up enough scratch every day and go cop something decent—without getting beat, arrested, or shot—so I can have a lovely time cowering in the dark for a couple of hours.

10   So I have this pencil with me all the time and then one day I'm sitting there in my hole with nothing to smoke and nothing to do and I pull the pencil out just to look at the film of residue stuck to the sides—you do that sort of thing when you don't have any shit—and it dawns on me that it's a pencil. I mean it's got a lead in it and all, and you can write with the thing.

11   So now I'm at it again. Digging around in my hole. Because I know there's an old composition book down there somewhere and I figure maybe I can distract myself for a little while by writing something.

12   The things a person will do when he's not smoking.

13   The funny thing is, I get into it.

14   I mean really get into it.

15   I start off just writing about a friend of mine. Just describing his cluttered apartment. How I kind of like the clutter. How it gives the place a lived-in look. How you can just about read his life by looking around.

16   So I'm writing away, and the more I write, the easier it gets. And the easier it gets, the better the writing gets, until it's like I'm just taking dictation.

17   Pretty soon I forget all about hustling and getting a hit. I'm scribbling like a maniac; heart pumping, adrenaline rushing, hands trembling. I'm so excited I almost crap on myself.

18   It's just like taking a hit.

19   Before I know it, I have a whole story.

20   I go to read the thing and it's a mess. The pages are all out of order. Parts are scratched out. Other parts are written sideways in the margins. But what I can read looks pretty good.

21   Even great in parts.

22   By the time I go back and carefully rewrite the thing, it's too late at night for me to bother going out, which is a remarkable thing for me because I don't think there's been a day since I started that I have gone without at least one hit.

23   So I read the story over and over.

24   Fix a few things.

25   And what I end up with reads like Tennessee Williams (I have a paperback with all his short stories in it) in the way it kind of comes in through the side door. I mean, Williams will start off talking about, say, what it smells like to work in a shoe factory and before you know it, he's going on about wanting to kill his father or something like that.

26   That's how my story went.

27   It started with my friend's house and then I have a guy sitting there with him who wants to get some pills from him so he can take himself out before the AIDS virus gets him—you see, he is HIV positive—and when

he gets the pills, he goes over to the park to just lie down and fade away on the grass.

28 Only he feels the need to apologize to the world because he has to die in public. And someone will have to come along and pick up his sorry, dead ass and all. But he's homeless, there's no place for him to go.

29 I guess they'll never make a musical out of it.

30 But the thing is—and this is what gets me—when I read the story, I can feel this guy's pain! I mean, I haven't been able to feel much of anything in years. And there I am, sitting down there under Grand Central, reading this thing scribbled in an old composition book, and I'm practically in tears.

31 The next day I take the story over to my friend's house and he reads it. All I'm expecting from him is a sarcastic remark because this guy is one of those snob alcoholics. He doesn't approve of anything.

32 Ever.

33 Least of all me.

34 But he just puts it down quietly when he finishes and gives me the slightest nod. Then he says,

35 "*Do* you love me?"

36 I know why he asks this.

37 Because in the story the two guys are friends but they would never admit it. They just hang around together putting each other down all the time—a lot like my friend and me—and in the end the one guy is sorry because he'll never have the chance to tell his buddy that he loves him—in a normal sort of way, I mean—and that he'll miss him.

38 He never realizes this until he's dying.

39 The only real difference between the story and me and my friend, come to think of it, is that I'm not HIV positive and I'm not dying.

40 But my friend is.

41 And when he asks me whether or not I love him, it gets to me because I would never have thought he gave a shit one way or the other. So I go over to him and hug him, and that weepy shit starts kicking up again.

42 What can I tell you?

43 It was one of those moments.

44 All because I sat in my hole and wrote this little story.

45 Next thing you know, I'm up at the *Street News* office with it, asking if anybody'd be interested in putting it in the paper, and—sure enough—damned if I don't open up the next issue and there's my story!

46 That's how I got my first thing published in *Street News*.

47 I think I called it "No Place to Call Home."

48 A couple of months later I had a regular column in there. And—one thing after the other—I had the writing bug.

49 After that there were *four* things I did every day. Hustle up money, cop some stuff, beam up, and write. And in the end I wound up dropping the other three.

50 When I was out there, it occurred to a great many people to ask what a guy like me was doing on the street. After all, I had the full use of all my

limbs, and I didn't appear to have any particular mental deficiencies. So, what, these people wanted to know, had happened?

51   I see it somewhat like a play, in three succinct acts.

52   **Act I. East Side, Fall, 1984.** *It is going on one o'clock on a Sunday afternoon when I exit the Lexington Avenue subway station at Thirty-third Street. The streets are awash with a bleak, gray light, which does nothing for my sour disposition. But at least the bracing September air keeps me from puking. My hangover has been at me ever since I reluctantly dragged myself out of bed.*

53   *The phone tried to summon me three times.*

54   *Seven, eight rings each time.*

55   *But I knew what would happen if I let in the light of day. The room would begin to float, my head would begin to pound, my teeth would begin to itch. . . .*

56   *I held on to sleep for as long as I could.*

57   *The phone be damned.*

58   *I am now on my way to Bellevue Hospital. I have a vague recollection of where it is. In one of its wings lies the city morgue. I know this because I have been there once before, in the dead of spring, to identify the corpse of my business partner, Barry. He stepped out the door one evening and his heart attacked him. The day after Easter two detectives came to the door.*

59   *"Do you know this man?" they wanted to know, and showed me the grim Polaroid. A death face. Eyes and mouth wide with surprise. Spooked by the reaper.*

60   *A wind has kicked up.*

61   *Swirls of litter dance at my feet as Bellevue's grimy brick facade looms up ahead of me. I am struck by how closely it resembles a prison. A short, gray-haired man walks solemnly toward me as I descend the entrance ramp. His head is swathed in bandages and his arm hangs in a sling. I imagine that I know what his Saturday night was about. I see rum, rancor, and rude contention. The scene plays vividly in my head.*

62   *I walk through the glass doors with this sudden prescience—almost an out-of-body experience. I can see not only the faces and bodies of the people milling through the veneered lobby but their lives as well. Each conveys to me some sense of where they live, what pictures are on their walls, who is beside them when they turn over in bed.*

63   *I find the starched, white efficiency of the nurse behind the reception desk intolerable for some reason. I survey her for a chink in her armor. A smudge, a wrinkle, a stray hair, something to connect her to humanity. But she seems seamless.*

64   *For a second I try imagining her in the throes of passion. Her hair splashed wildly against a pillow, her white, stockinged legs above her head. Moaning and growling in animal abandon with each blunt thrust. But the smile she puts on for me is all professional, conveying nothing more than—*

65   *"—Yes?"*

66   *"Visitor's pass for Wayne Stringer," I say, as curt and clipped as she.*

67   *Her thumb wanders through the index cards in front of her.*

68   *"One minute," she chirps, still looking.*

69   *But I discover that I know what she is about to tell me; that in fact I knew it even before I woke up. The minute the phone had started ringing for the third time.*

70   *"Are you related to the patient?" she wants to know.*

71 *"I'm his brother," I tell her.*

72 *"I'm sorry," she says. "Haven't you been notified? I'm afraid Mr. Stringer died late last night."*

73 *There is no shock or surprise. Just a strange, rehearsed raggedness to the moment. I am a director, and she has delivered her lines exactly right.*

74 *Cut!*

75 How characteristic of Wayne to make himself larger in absence than he was when present. To express displeasure, he often put on his disappearing act. Cross a certain line with him and ZAP! You'd be left confronting an impenetrable void, with little to do but wonder what you'd done wrong. In a family like ours, which shared loneliness like hand-me-down clothing, my brother's slow-burning pout was a particularly potent weapon.

76 And I was particularly vulnerable to it. I may have thought I had little use for Wayne most of the time, but when he'd cut me off like that, nothing in this world mattered as much as getting back on his good side. Usually I would resort to some verbal antics. For I was one of the very few people who could, when I put my mind to it, catch the abstract and slightly macabre rhythm of Wayne's sense of humor and make him laugh.

77 But Wayne could be one stubborn son of a bitch. When he didn't want to laugh, nothing on this earth could make him so much as crack a grin. Lord knows I never had anything near his resolve. And Lord knows how desperately I mined for the nuggets of his laughter.

78 Mostly Wayne disappeared into his piano. He would sit for hours, oblivious to the world, languidly picking at the keys. It got so you could travel the landscape of his shifting temperament by listening to the impromptu dance his fingers performed on the keyboard. They would twitch discordantly on the sharps and flats when he was annoyed, making the whole room ring with his impatience. When he was bored, they would meander the scales, aimless and atonal, off to nowhere in particular. And when they stalked the minor chords, somber and funereal, you could measure the depth of his glumness.

79 "Wayne lacked confidence," my mother would say, trying to make sense of the fact that he never made a profession of his music. My take on it was that what went on between Wayne and his piano was too personal for him to offer up for public consumption.

80 Although I was a year younger than Wayne, I was the first to leave home. A year or two after graduating high school I was gone, off in a rush. But Wayne was in no rush. He had taken a job at a hardware store down the street, and seemed perfectly content to remain where he was, buttoned down, bottled up, a shade too sober and conservative for his years.

81 When I returned home about two years later, having conquered considerably less of the world than I had imagined I would, I found that in the intervening time Wayne had started acting a lot more like me. At least as it concerned my less-than-wholesome facets.

82 He had gleefully interred his former icons—Messrs. Bach, Mozart, Beethoven, Schubert, Tchaikovsky, and company—beneath a deluge of

freshly minted rock and pop recordings—some six hundred of them. Sitting with Wayne in his room the day of my return, amid the whirlybird din of a Pink Floyd opus, as he juggled a joint, a cigarette, and a beer all at the same time, I should have seen the love in his overt bid for my approval. But what I felt was a terrible sadness. For even though I may have written him off as a fuddy-duddy and a square, the truth was I had always loved, admired and greatly respected Wayne as he was. And it unnerved me to bear witness to the rude influence I had had upon him.

83   Such was the persistent irony between us. Both of us routinely missing the obvious, always hovering just shy of real kinship, even while we each campaigned to win the other over. It was Wayne who finally openly took the initiative. And he did it just scant months before I would be faced once again, but this time irreversibly, with his absence.

84   I was still reeling from my partner's sudden demise, and the legal melee that resulted from it, when Wayne appeared at my door, thirty-four years old, penniless, pale, dangerously thin, a bewildered look on his face, black-and-blue blotches all over his legs. I told myself he had bruised himself somehow and I set him up on the living room couch, thinking, *This will soon blow over and then I will be free of this bother.*

85   But he could barely eat. And he tossed and turned the nights away. I dragged him to a high-rent doctor. He checked him over, but had nothing to offer but a grim, confounded shrug. When I could no longer bear seeing Wayne writhe in pain on the couch, I appealed to an acquaintance of mine, who forged prescriptions. But neither painkillers nor sleeping pills had much effect. Wayne just lay there, day after day, taking his agony as he did most everything else, in frightened silence.

86   I seem to remember starting to feel like something was chasing me. I hid from it during the day in my work. And there was no shortage of that, or of problems to go with it. My business partner and I had been sharing our two-bedroom, rent-stabilized apartment, which doubled as our office. But his name was on the eighteen-year-old lease. And the landlord couldn't wait to dump me so that he could enjoy full Upper West Side market value for the space. Barry's son—and executor of what there was of his estate—came sniffing around to see if there was any money to be wrung out of our graphic design company. I was about ready to pull in my shingle altogether and had been offered a job with a small consumer products company. That took care of the days. Nights I went out and drank myself numb.

87   One night I came fumbling through the door, head swimming with booze, to find Wayne, standing in the middle of the darkened living room, a near skeleton in dirty, drooping drawers. And it broke the spell of my denial. There was no more avoiding how very sick he was. And I realized that the thing that had been chasing me was a sense of guilt.

88   "I was waiting here to tell you," he said softly and sadly. "That I know you were always for me, I know you were always on my side."

89   I couldn't say anything. Just stood there blinking into the darkness as Wayne teetered over to me and kissed me, cracked, chalky lips and all.

90   I took him to Bellevue Hospital first thing the next day and stayed with him until someone would see him. Eight hours in the waiting room, Wayne squirming beside me all the while. But once they discovered he was unemployed and uninsured, they didn't want his bother any more than I had. And so long as it was apparent that Wayne could make it back out the door on his own two feet, they refused to admit him.

91   But I shamed them into it.

92   "I SUPPOSE YOU'LL BE HAPPY TO TAKE HIM WHEN HE'S DOA!" I roared at the top of my lungs. The whole floor came to a stop. They were left with no choice but to take him in.

93   It turned out Bellevue didn't have any solutions to offer either. They weren't even sure what the hell it was Wayne had. First they said vasculitis, then they said AIDS. One day I arrived to visit him and it's all about gloves and masks and quarantine, and the next time I come, all the precautions are off. He got a little better, then he got worse, and then he was dead.

94   Everybody has their share of bad news to swallow. But the thing with my brother caught me off guard. So long as he had been around, I was content to pretend I didn't give a rat's ass about him. But once he was gone, the jig was up on that game.

95   I was able to keep up my happy-camper act for almost two years after that. I immersed myself in my new job, and found myself an apartment.

96   Whatever money didn't go to rent I poured into diversion.

97   Then one night in my apartment, alone with a bottle of Georgi's, I found myself going ten rounds with a rolled-up carpet I had leaning against the wall. I laid into the thing, roundhouse swings, all my weight behind each one. But all it got me was bleeding knuckles. For there I was again after all, doing the thing I wanted to be done with, sitting on the floor, bawling into my sleeve.

98   [Two days later, Stringer became addicted to crack. Nine months later, he had lost his job and his apartment. He was homeless.]

Questions for Discussion

1. Describe the process through which Stringer becomes a writer. Why does writing give him such a rush? How could writing enable him to give up drugs as he said he did "in the end"?

2. Why is the friend's reaction to his story important?

3. Stringer says that he and his brother Wayne were "always hovering just shy of real kinship." What does he mean?

4. Why, after Wayne becomes sick, does Stringer feel guilty?

5. Why is Stringer's descent so swift?

6. What common stereotypes of the homeless does Stringer dispel?

Suggestions for Exploration and Writing

1. If you know someone who succumbed to an addiction, write a cause-and-effect essay describing the process. Or write an essay detailing the recovery and the qualities that made it possible.
2. Write a comparison-contrast essay on the two brothers.
3. Stringer implies in the beginning that homelessness liberated him. To what extent do possessions encumber us? To what extent do they increase our enjoyment of life? What makes the difference?
4. In an essay, discuss the fairness or unfairness of stereotypes of homeless people. Why do so many people appear to be afraid of the homeless?
5. In a researched essay, analyze the causes of homelessness.

FICTION

F. Scott Fitzgerald (1896–1940)

A native of St. Paul, Minnesota, educated at Princeton, Francis Scott Key Fitzgerald published his highly successful first novel, This Side of Paradise, *in 1920. Soon thereafter, he and his fashionable wife, Zelda, embraced an extravagant and hedonistic lifestyle of partying with the newly rich Americans of what Fitzgerald dubbed "the jazz age." Most of his fiction, including the short story collections* Flappers and Philosophers *(1920) and* Tales of the Jazz Age *(1922), chronicles the enthusiastic pursuit of pleasure among the wealthy partygoers he and Zelda encountered. He is perhaps best known for his novels, including* The Great Gatsby *(1925), surely one of the gems of modern American fiction, and* Tender Is the Night *(1934).*

WINTER DREAMS   (1922)

I

1   Some of the caddies were poor as sin and lived in one-room houses with a neurasthenic cow in the front yard, but Dexter Green's father owned the second best grocery-store in Black Bear—the best one was "The Hub," patronized by the wealthy people from Sherry Island—and Dexter caddied only for pocket-money.

2   In the fall when the days became crisp and gray, and the long Minnesota winter shut down like the white lid of a box, Dexter's skis moved over the snow that hid the fairways of the golf course. At these times the

country gave him a feeling of profound melancholy—it offended him that the links should lie in enforced fallowness, haunted by ragged sparrows for the long season. It was dreary, too, that on the tees where the gay colors fluttered in summer there were now only the desolate sand-boxes knee-deep in crusted ice. When he crossed the hills the wind blew cold as misery, and if the sun was out he tramped with his eyes squinted up against the hard dimensionless glare.

3   In April the winter ceased abruptly. The snow ran down into Black Bear Lake scarcely tarrying for the early golfers to brave the season with red and black balls. Without elation, without an interval of moist glory, the cold was gone.

4   Dexter knew that there was something dismal about this Northern spring, just as he knew there was something gorgeous about the fall. Fall made him clinch his hands and tremble and repeat idiotic sentences to himself, and make brisk abrupt gestures of command to imaginary audiences and armies. October filled him with hope which November raised to a sort of ecstatic triumph, and in this mood the fleeting brilliant impressions of the summer at Sherry Island were ready grist to his mill. He became a golf champion and defeated Mr. T. A. Hedrick in a marvellous match played a hundred times over the fairways of his imagination, a match each detail of which he changed about untiringly—sometimes he won with almost laughable ease, sometimes he came up magnificently from behind. Again, stepping from a Pierce-Arrow automobile, like Mr. Mortimer Jones, he strolled frigidly into the lounge of the Sherry Island Golf Club—or perhaps, surrounded by an admiring crowd, he gave an exhibition of fancy diving from the spring-board of the club raft. . . . Among those who watched him in open-mouthed wonder was Mr. Mortimer Jones.

5   And one day it came to pass that Mr. Jones—himself and not his ghost—came up to Dexter with tears in his eyes and said that Dexter was the —— best caddy in the club, and wouldn't he decide not to quit if Mr. Jones made it worth his while, because every other —— caddy in the club lost one ball a hole for him—regularly ——

6   "No, sir," said Dexter decisively, "I don't want to caddy any more." Then, after a pause: "I'm too old."

7   "You're not more than fourteen. Why the devil did you decide just this morning that you wanted to quit? You promised that next week you'd go over to the State tournament with me."

8   "I decided I was too old."

9   Dexter handed in his "A Class" badge, collected what money was due him from the caddy master, and walked home to Black Bear Village.

10   "The best —— caddy I ever saw," shouted Mr. Mortimer Jones over a drink that afternoon. "Never lost a ball! Willing! Intelligent! Quiet! Honest! Grateful!"

11   The little girl who had done this was eleven—beautifully ugly as little girls are apt to be who are destined after a few years to be inexpressibly lovely and bring no end of misery to a great number of men. The spark,

however, was perceptible. There was a general ungodliness in the way her lips twisted down at the corners when she smiled, and in the—Heaven help us!—in the almost passionate quality of her eyes. Vitality is born early in such women. It was utterly in evidence now, shining through her thin frame in a sort of glow.

12 She had come eagerly out on to the course at nine o'clock with a white linen nurse and five small new golf-clubs in a white canvas bag which the nurse was carrying. When Dexter first saw her she was standing by the caddy house, rather ill at ease and trying to conceal the fact by engaging her nurse in an obviously unnatural conversation graced by startling and irrelevant grimaces from herself.

13 "Well, it's certainly a nice day, Hilda," Dexter heard her say. She drew down the corners of her mouth, smiled, and glanced furtively around, her eyes in transit falling for an instant on Dexter.

14 Then to the nurse:

15 "Well, I guess there aren't very many people out here this morning, are there?"

16 The smile again—radiant, blatantly artificial—convincing.

17 "I don't know what we're supposed to do now," said the nurse, looking nowhere in particular.

18 "Oh, that's all right. I'll fix it up."

19 Dexter stood perfectly still, his mouth slightly ajar. He knew that if he moved forward a step his stare would be in her line of vision—if he moved backward he would lose his full view of her face. For a moment he had not realized how young she was. Now he remembered having seen her several times the year before—in bloomers.

20 Suddenly, involuntarily, he laughed, a short abrupt laugh—then, startled by himself, he turned and began to walk quickly away.

21 "Boy!"

22 Dexter stopped.

23 "Boy———"

24 Beyond question he was addressed. Not only that, but he was treated to that absurd smile, that preposterous smile—the memory of which at least a dozen men were to carry into middle age.

25 "Boy, do you know where the golf teacher is?"

26 "He's giving a lesson."

27 "Well, do you know where the caddy-master is?"

28 "He isn't here yet this morning."

29 "Oh." For a moment this baffled her. She stood alternately on her right and left foot.

30 "We'd like to get a caddy," said the nurse. "Mrs. Mortimer Jones sent us out to play golf, and we don't know how without we get a caddy."

31 Here she was stopped by an ominous glance from Miss Jones, followed immediately by the smile.

32 "There aren't any caddies here except me," said Dexter to the nurse, "and I got to stay here in charge until the caddy-master gets here."

33 "Oh."

34 Miss Jones and her retinue now withdrew, and at a proper distance from Dexter became involved in a heated conversation, which was concluded by Miss Jones taking one of the clubs and hitting it on the ground with violence. For further emphasis she raised it again and was about to bring it down smartly upon the nurse's bosom, when the nurse seized the club and twisted it from her hands.

35 "You damn little mean old *thing!*" cried Miss Jones wildly.

36 Another argument ensued. Realizing that the elements of the comedy were implied in the scene, Dexter several times began to laugh, but each time restrained the laugh before it reached audibility. He could not resist the monstrous conviction that the little girl was justified in beating the nurse.

37 The situation was resolved by the fortuitous appearance of the caddy-master, who was appealed to immediately by the nurse.

38 "Miss Jones is to have a little caddy, and this one says he can't go."

39 "Mr. McKenna said I was to wait here till you came," said Dexter quickly.

40 "Well, he's here now." Miss Jones smiled cheerfully at the caddy-master. Then she dropped her bag and set off at a haughty mince toward the first tee.

41 "Well?" The caddy-master turned to Dexter. "What you standing there like a dummy for? Go pick up the young lady's clubs."

42 "I don't think I'll go out to-day," said Dexter.

43 "You don't———"

44 "I think I'll quit."

45 The enormity of his decision frightened him. He was a favorite caddy, and the thirty dollars a month he earned through the summer were not to be made elsewhere around the lake. But he had received a strong emotional shock, and his perturbation required a violent and immediate outlet.

46 It is not so simple as that, either. As so frequently would be the case in the future, Dexter was unconsciously dictated to by his winter dreams.

II

47 Now, of course, the quality and the seasonability of these winter dreams varied, but the stuff of them remained. They persuaded Dexter several years later to pass up a business course at the State university—his father, prospering now, would have paid his way—for the precarious advantage of attending an older and more famous university in the East, where he was bothered by his scanty funds. But do not get the impression, because his winter dreams happened to be concerned at first with musings on the rich, that there was anything merely snobbish in the boy. He wanted not association with glittering things and glittering people—he wanted the glittering things themselves. Often he reached out for the best without knowing why he wanted it—and sometimes he ran up against the myste-

rious denials and prohibitions in which life indulges. It is with one of those denials and not with his career as a whole that this story deals.

48 He made money. It was rather amazing. After college he went to the city from which Black Bear Lake draws its wealthy patrons. When he was only twenty-three and had been there not quite two years, there were already people who liked to say: "Now *there's* a boy—". All about him rich men's sons were peddling bonds precariously, or investing patrimonies precariously, or plodding through the two dozen volumes of the "George Washington Commercial Course," but Dexter borrowed a thousand dollars on his college degree and his confident mouth, and bought a partnership in a laundry.

49 It was a small laundry when he went into it but Dexter made a specialty of learning how the English washed fine woollen golf-stockings without shrinking them, and within a year he was catering to the trade that wore knickerbockers. Men were insisting that their Shetland hose and sweaters go to his laundry just as they had insisted on a caddy who could find golf-balls. A little later he was doing their wives' lingerie as well—and running five branches in different parts of the city. Before he was twenty-seven he owned the largest string of laundries in his section of the country. It was then that he sold out and went to New York. But the part of his story that concerns us goes back to the days when he was making his first big success.

50 When he was twenty-three Mr. Hart—one of the gray-haired men who like to say "Now there's a boy"—gave him a guest card to the Sherry Island Golf Club for a week-end. So he signed his name one day on the register, and that afternoon played golf in a foursome with Mr. Hart and Mr. Sandwood and Mr. T. A. Hedrick. He did not consider it necessary to remark that he had once carried Mr. Hart's bag over this same links, and that he knew every trap and gully with his eyes shut—but he found himself glancing at the four caddies who trailed them, trying to catch a gleam or gesture that would remind him of himself, that would lessen the gap which lay between his present and his past.

51 It was a curious day, slashed abruptly with fleeting, familiar impressions. One minute he had the sense of being a trespasser—in the next he was impressed by the tremendous superiority he felt toward Mr. T. A. Hedrick, who was a bore and not even a good golfer any more.

52 Then, because of a ball Mr. Hart lost near the fifteenth green, an enormous thing happened. While they were searching the stiff grasses of the rough there was a clear call of "Fore!" from behind a hill in their rear. And as they all turned abruptly from their search a bright new ball sliced abruptly over the hill and caught Mr. T. A. Hedrick in the abdomen.

53 "By Gad!" cried Mr. T. A. Hedrick, "they ought to put some of these crazy women off the course. It's getting to be outrageous."

54 A head and a voice came up together over the hill:

55 "Do you mind if we go through?"

56 "You hit me in the stomach!" declared Mr. Hedrick wildly.

57 "Did I?" The girl approached the group of men. "I'm sorry. I yelled 'Fore!'"

58 Her glance fell casually on each of the men—then scanned the fairway for her ball.

59 "Did I bounce into the rough?"

60 It was impossible to determine whether this question was ingenuous or malicious. In a moment, however, she left no doubt, for as her partner came up over the hill she called cheerfully:

61 "Here I am! I'd have gone on the green except that I hit something."

62 As she took her stance for a short mashie shot, Dexter looked at her closely. She wore a blue gingham dress, rimmed at throat and shoulders with a white edging that accentuated her tan. The quality of exaggeration, of thinness, which had made her passionate eyes and down-turning mouth absurd at eleven, was gone now. She was arrestingly beautiful. The color in her cheeks was centered like the color in a picture—it was not a "high" color, but a sort of fluctuating and feverish warmth, so shaded that it seemed at any moment it would recede and disappear. This color and the mobility of her mouth gave a continual impression of flux, of intense life, of passionate vitality—balanced only partially by the sad luxury of her eyes.

63 She swung her mashie impatiently and without interest, pitching the ball into a sand-pit on the other side of the green. With a quick, insincere smile and a careless "Thank you!" she went on after it.

64 "That Judy Jones!" remarked Mr. Hedrick on the next tee, as they waited—some moments—for her to play on ahead. "All she needs is to be turned up and spanked for six months and then to be married off to an old-fashioned cavalry captain."

65 "My God, she's good-looking!" said Mr. Sandwood, who was just over thirty.

66 "Good-looking!" cried Mr. Hedrick contemptuously, "she always looks as if she wanted to be kissed! Turning those big cow-eyes on every calf in town!"

67 It was doubtful if Mr. Hedrick intended a reference to the maternal instinct.

68 "She'd play pretty good golf if she'd try," said Mr. Sandwood.

69 "She has no form," said Mr. Hedrick solemnly.

70 "She has a nice figure," said Mr. Sandwood.

71 "Better thank the Lord she doesn't drive a swifter ball," said Mr. Hart, winking at Dexter.

72 Later in the afternoon the sun went down with a riotous swirl of gold and varying blues and scarlets, and left the dry, rustling night of Western summer. Dexter watched from the veranda of the Golf Club, watched the even overlap of the waters in the little wind, silver molasses under the harvest-moon. Then the moon held a finger to her lips and the lake became a clear pool, pale and quiet. Dexter put on his bathing-suit and swam out to the farthest raft, where he stretched dripping on the wet canvas of the springboard.

73 There was a fish jumping and a star shining and the lights around the lake were gleaming. Over on a dark peninsula a piano was playing the songs

of last summer and of summers before that—songs from "Chin-Chin" and "The Count of Luxemburg" and "The Chocolate Soldier"—and because the sound of a piano over a stretch of water had always seemed beautiful to Dexter he lay perfectly quiet and listened.

74   The tune the piano was playing at that moment had been gay and new five years before when Dexter was a sophomore at college. They had played it at a prom once when he could not afford the luxury of proms, and he had stood outside the gymnasium and listened. The sound of the tune precipitated in him a sort of ecstasy and it was with that ecstasy he viewed what happened to him now. It was a mood of intense appreciation, a sense that, for once, he was magnificently attune to life and that everything about him was radiating a brightness and a glamour he might never know again.

75   A low, pale oblong detached itself suddenly from the darkness of the Island, spitting forth the reverberate sound of a racing motor-boat. Two white streamers of cleft water rolled themselves out behind it and almost immediately the boat was beside him, drowning out the hot tinkle of the piano in the drone of its spray. Dexter raising himself on his arms was aware of a figure standing at the wheel, of two dark eyes regarding him over the lengthening space of water—then the boat had gone by and was sweeping in an immense and purposeless circle of spray round and round in the middle of the lake. With equal eccentricity one of the circles flattened out and headed back toward the raft.

76   "Who's that?" she called, shutting off her motor. She was so near now that Dexter could see her bathing-suit, which consisted apparently of pink rompers.

77   The nose of the boat bumped the raft, and as the latter tilted rakishly he was precipitated toward her. With different degrees of interest they recognized each other.

78   "Aren't you one of those men we played through this afternoon?" she demanded.

79   He was.

80   "Well, do you know how to drive a motor-boat? Because if you do I wish you'd drive this one so I can ride on the surf-board behind. My name is Judy Jones"—she favored him with an absurd smirk—rather, what tried to be a smirk, for, twist her mouth as she might, it was not grotesque, it was merely beautiful—"and I live in a house over there on the Island, and in that house there is a man waiting for me. When he drove up at the door I drove out of the dock because he says I'm his ideal."

81   There was a fish jumping and a star shining and the lights around the lake were gleaming. Dexter sat beside Judy Jones and she explained how her boat was driven. Then she was in the water, swimming to the floating surfboard with a sinuous crawl. Watching her was without effort to the eye, watching a branch waving or a sea-gull flying. Her arms, burned to butternut, moved sinuously among the dull platinum ripples, elbow appearing first, casting the forearm back with a cadence of falling water, then reaching out and down, stabbing a path ahead.

82   They moved out into the lake; turning, Dexter saw that she was kneeling on the low rear of the now uptilted surf-board.

83   "Go faster," she called, "fast as it'll go."

84   Obediently he jammed the lever forward and the white spray mounted at the bow. When he looked around again the girl was standing up on the rushing board, her arms spread wide, her eyes lifted toward the moon.

85   "It's awful cold," she shouted. "What's your name?"

86   He told her.

87   "Well, why don't you come to dinner to-morrow night?"

88   His heart turned over like the fly-wheel of the boat, and, for the second time, her casual whim gave a new direction to his life.

III

89   Next evening while he waited for her to come down-stairs, Dexter peopled the soft deep summer room and the sun-porch that opened from it with the men who had already loved Judy Jones. He knew the sort of men they were—the men who when he first went to college had entered from the great prep schools with graceful clothes and the deep tan of healthy summers. He had seen that, in one sense, he was better than these men. He was newer and stronger. Yet in acknowledging to himself that he wished his children to be like them he was admitting that he was but the rough, strong stuff from which they eternally sprang.

90   When the time had come for him to wear good clothes, he had known who were the best tailors in America, and the best tailors in America had made him the suit he wore this evening. He had acquired that particular reserve peculiar to his university, that set it off from other universities. He recognized the value to him of such a mannerism and he had adopted it; he knew that to be careless in dress and manner required more confidence than to be careful. But carelessness was for his children. His mother's name had been Krimslich. She was a Bohemian of the peasant class and she had talked broken English to the end of her days. Her son must keep to the set patterns.

91   At a little after seven Judy Jones came down-stairs. She wore a blue silk afternoon dress, and he was disappointed at first that she had not put on something more elaborate. This feeling was accentuated when, after a brief greeting, she went to the door of a butler's pantry and pushing it open called: "You can serve dinner, Martha." He had rather expected that a butler would announce dinner, that there would be a cocktail. Then he put these thoughts behind him as they sat down side by side on a lounge and looked at each other.

92   "Father and mother won't be here," she said thoughtfully.

93   He remembered the last time he had seen her father, and he was glad the parents were not to be here to-night—they might wonder who he was. He had been born in Keeble, a Minnesota village fifty miles farther north, and he always gave Keeble as his home instead of Black Bear Village.

Country towns were well enough to come from if they weren't inconveniently in sight and used as footstools by fashionable lakes.

94 They talked of his university, which she had visited frequently during the past two years, and of the near-by city which supplied Sherry Island with its patrons, and whither Dexter would return next day to his prospering laundries.

95 During dinner she slipped into a moody depression which gave Dexter a feeling of uneasiness. Whatever petulance she uttered in her throaty voice worried him. Whatever she smiled at—at him, at a chicken liver, at nothing—it disturbed him that her smile could have no root in mirth, or even in amusement. When the scarlet corners of her lips curved down, it was less a smile than an invitation to a kiss.

96 Then, after dinner, she led him out on the dark sun-porch and deliberately changed the atmosphere.

97 "Do you mind if I weep a little?" she said.

98 "I'm afraid I'm boring you," he responded quickly.

99 "You're not. I like you. But I've just had a terrible afternoon. There was a man I cared about, and this afternoon he told me out of a clear sky that he was poor as a church-mouse. He'd never even hinted it before. Does this sound horribly mundane?"

100 "Perhaps he was afraid to tell you."

101 "Suppose he was," she answered. "He didn't start right. You see, if I'd thought of him as poor—well, I've been mad about loads of poor men, and fully intended to marry them all. But in this case, I hadn't thought of him that way, and my interest in him wasn't strong enough to survive the shock. As if a girl calmly informed her fiancé that she was a widow. He might not object to widows, but——

102 "Let's start right," she interrupted herself suddenly. "Who are you, anyhow?"

103 For a moment Dexter hesitated. Then:

104 "I'm nobody," he announced. "My career is largely a matter of futures."

105 "Are you poor?"

106 "No," he said frankly, "I'm probably making more money than any man my age in the Northwest. I know that's an obnoxious remark, but you advised me to start right."

107 There was a pause. Then she smiled and the corners of her mouth drooped and an almost imperceptible sway brought her closer to him, looking up into his eyes. A lump rose in Dexter's throat, and he waited breathless for the experiment, facing the unpredictable compound that would form mysteriously from the elements of their lips. Then he saw— she communicated her excitement to him, lavishly, deeply, with kisses that were not a promise but a fulfillment. They aroused in him not hunger demanding renewal but surfeit that would demand more surfeit . . . kisses that were like charity, creating want by holding back nothing at all.

108 It did not take him many hours to decide that he had wanted Judy Jones ever since he was a proud, desirous little boy.

IV

109   It began like that—and continued, with varying shades of intensity, on such a note right up to the dénouement. Dexter surrendered a part of himself to the most direct and unprincipled personality with which he had ever come in contact. Whatever Judy wanted, she went after with the full pressure of her charm. There was no divergence of method, no jockeying for position or premeditation of effects—there was a very little mental side to any of her affairs. She simply made men conscious to the highest degree of her physical loveliness. Dexter had no desire to change her. Her deficiencies were knit up with a passionate energy that transcended and justified them.

110   When, as Judy's head lay against his shoulder that first night, she whispered, "I don't know what's the matter with me. Last night I thought I was in love with a man and to-night I think I'm in love with you————" —it seemed to him a beautiful and romantic thing to say. It was the exquisite excitability that for the moment he controlled and owned. But a week later he was compelled to view this same quality in a different light. She took him in her roadster to a picnic supper, and after supper she disappeared, likewise in her roadster, with another man. Dexter became enormously upset and was scarcely able to be decently civil to the other people present. When she assured him that she had not kissed the other man, he knew she was lying—yet he was glad that she had taken the trouble to lie to him.

111   He was, as he found before the summer ended, one of a varying dozen who circulated about her. Each of them had at one time been favored above all others—about half of them still basked in the solace of occasional sentimental revivals. Whenever one showed signs of dropping out through long neglect, she granted him a brief honeyed hour, which encouraged him to tag along for a year or so longer. Judy made these forays upon the helpless and defeated without malice, indeed half unconscious that there was anything mischievous in what she did.

112   When a new man came to town every one dropped out—dates were automatically cancelled.

113   The helpless part of trying to do anything about it was that she did it all herself. She was not a girl who could be "won" in the kinetic sense—she was proof against cleverness, she was proof against charm; if any of these assailed her too strongly she would immediately resolve the affair to a physical basis, and under the magic of her physical splendor the strong as well as the brilliant played her game and not their own. She was entertained only by the gratification of her desires and by the direct exercise of her own charm. Perhaps from so much youthful love, so many youthful lovers, she had come, in self-defense, to nourish herself wholly from within.

114   Succeeding Dexter's first exhilaration came restlessness and dissatisfaction. The helpless ecstasy of losing himself in her was opiate rather than tonic. It was fortunate for his work during the winter that those moments of ecstasy came infrequently. Early in their acquaintance it had

seemed for a while that there was a deep and spontaneous mutual attraction—that first August, for example—three days of long evenings on her dusky veranda, of strange wan kisses through the late afternoon, in shadowy alcoves or behind the protecting trellises of the garden arbors, of mornings when she was fresh as a dream and almost shy at meeting him in the clarity of the rising day. There was all the ecstasy of an engagement about it, sharpened by his realization that there was no engagement. It was during those three days that, for the first time, he had asked her to marry him. She said "maybe some day," she said "kiss me," she said "I'd like to marry you," she said "I love you"—she said—nothing.

115   The three days were interrupted by the arrival of a New York man who visited at her house for half September. To Dexter's agony, rumor engaged them. The man was the son of the president of a great trust company. But at the end of a month it was reported that Judy was yawning. At a dance one night she sat all evening in a motor-boat with a local beau, while the New Yorker searched the club for her frantically. She told the local beau that she was bored with her visitor, and two days later he left. She was seen with him at the station, and it was reported that he looked very mournful indeed.

116   On this note the summer ended. Dexter was twenty-four, and he found himself increasingly in a position to do as he wished. He joined two clubs in the city and lived at one of them. Though he was by no means an integral part of the stag-lines at these clubs, he managed to be on hand at dances where Judy Jones was likely to appear. He could have gone out socially as much as he liked—he was an eligible young man, now, and popular with down-town fathers. His confessed devotion to Judy Jones had rather solidified his position. But he had no social aspirations and rather despised the dancing men who were always on tap for the Thursday or Saturday parties and who filled in at dinners with the younger married set. Already he was playing with the idea of going East to New York. He wanted to take Judy Jones with him. No disillusion as to the world in which she had grown up could cure his illusion as to her desirability.

117   Remember that—for only in the light of it can what he did for her be understood.

118   Eighteen months after he first met Judy Jones he became engaged to another girl. Her name was Irene Scheerer, and her father was one of the men who had always believed in Dexter. Irene was light-haired and sweet and honorable, and a little stout, and she had two suitors whom she pleasantly relinquished when Dexter formally asked her to marry him.

119   Summer, fall, winter, spring, another summer, another fall—so much he had given of his active life to the incorrigible lips of Judy Jones. She had treated him with interest, with encouragement, with malice, with indifference, with contempt. She had inflicted on him the innumerable little slights and indignities possible in such a case—as if in revenge for having ever cared for him at all. She had beckoned him and yawned at him and beckoned him again and he had responded often with bitterness

and narrowed eyes. She had brought him ecstatic happiness and intolerable agony of spirit. She had caused him untold inconvenience and not a little trouble. She had insulted him, and she had ridden over him, and she had played his interest in her against his interest in his work—for fun. She had done everything to him except to criticise him—this she had not done—it seemed to him only because it might have sullied the utter indifference she manifested and sincerely felt toward him.

120   When autumn had come and gone again it occurred to him that he could not have Judy Jones. He had to beat this into his mind but he convinced himself at last. He lay awake at night for a while and argued it over. He told himself the trouble and the pain she had caused him, he enumerated her glaring deficiencies as a wife. Then he said to himself that he loved her, and after a while he fell asleep. For a week, lest he imagined her husky voice over the telephone or her eyes opposite him at lunch, he worked hard and late, and at night he went to his office and plotted out his years.

121   At the end of a week he went to a dance and cut in on her once. For almost the first time since they had met he did not ask her to sit out with him or tell her that she was lovely. It hurt him that she did not miss these things—that was all. He was not jealous when he saw that there was a new man to-night. He had been hardened against jealousy long before.

122   He stayed late at the dance. He sat for an hour with Irene Scheerer and talked about books and about music. He knew very little about either. But he was beginning to be master of his own time now, and he had a rather priggish notion that he—the young and already fabulously successful Dexter Green—should know more about such things.

123   That was in October, when he was twenty-five. In January, Dexter and Irene became engaged. It was to be announced in June, and they were to be married three months later.

124   The Minnesota winter prolonged itself interminably, and it was almost May when the winds came soft and the snow ran down into Black Bear Lake at last. For the first time in over a year Dexter was enjoying a certain tranquility of spirit. Judy Jones had been in Florida, and afterward in Hot Springs, and somewhere she had been engaged, and somewhere she had broken it off. At first, when Dexter had definitely given her up, it had made him sad that people still linked them together and asked for news of her, but when he began to be placed at dinner next to Irene Scheerer people didn't ask him about her any more—they told him about her. He ceased to be an authority on her.

125   May at last. Dexter walked the streets at night when the darkness was damp as rain, wondering that so soon, with so little done, so much of ecstasy had gone from him. May one year back had been marked by Judy's poignant, unforgivable, yet forgiven turbulence—it had been one of those rare times when he fancied she had grown to care for him. That old penny's worth of happiness he had spent for this bushel of content. He knew that Irene would be no more than a curtain spread behind him, a hand moving among gleaming tea-cups, a voice calling to children . . .

fire and loveliness were gone, the magic of nights and the wonder of the varying hours and seasons . . . slender lips, down-turning, dropping to his lips and bearing him up into a heaven of eyes. . . . . The thing was deep in him. He was too strong and alive for it to die lightly.

126   In the middle of May when the weather balanced for a few days on the thin bridge that led to deep summer he turned in one night at Irene's house. Their engagement was to be announced in a week now—no one would be surprised at it. And to-night they would sit together on the lounge at the University Club and look on for an hour at the dancers. It gave him a sense of solidity to go with her—she was so sturdily popular, so intensely "great."

127   He mounted the steps of the brownstone house and stepped inside.

128   "Irene," he called.

129   Mrs. Scheerer came out of the living-room to meet him.

130   "Dexter," she said, "Irene's gone up-stairs with a splitting headache. She wanted to go with you but I made her go to bed."

131   "Nothing serious, I———"

132   "Oh, no. She's going to play golf with you in the morning. You can spare her for just one night, can't you, Dexter?"

133   Her smile was kind. She and Dexter liked each other. In the living-room he talked for a moment before he said good-night.

134   Returning to the University Club, where he had rooms, he stood in the doorway for a moment and watched the dancers. He leaned against the door-post, nodded at a man or two—yawned.

135   "Hello, darling."

136   The familiar voice at his elbow startled him. Judy Jones had left a man and crossed the room to him—Judy Jones, a slender enamelled doll in cloth of gold: gold in a band at her head, gold in two slipper points at her dress's hem. The fragile glow of her face seemed to blossom as she smiled at him. A breeze of warmth and light blew through the room. His hands in the pockets of his dinner-jacket tightened spasmodically. He was filled with a sudden excitement.

137   "When did you get back?" he asked casually.

138   "Come here and I'll tell you about it."

139   She turned and he followed her. She had been away—he could have wept at the wonder of her return. She had passed through enchanted streets, doing things that were like provocative music. All mysterious happenings, all fresh and quickening hopes, had gone away with her, come back with her now.

140   She turned in the doorway.

141   "Have you a car here? If you haven't, I have."

142   "I have a coupé."

143   In then, with a rustle of golden cloth. He slammed the door. Into so many cars she had stepped—like this—like that—her back against the leather, so—her elbow resting on the door—waiting. She would have been soiled long since had there been anything to soil her—except herself—but this was her own self outpouring.

144   With an effort he forced himself to start the car and back into the street. This was nothing, he must remember. She had done this before, and he had put her behind him, as he would have crossed a bad account from his books.

145   He drove slowly down-town and, affecting abstraction, traversed the deserted streets of the business section, peopled here and there where a movie was giving out its crowd or where consumptive or pugilistic youth lounged in front of pool halls. The clink of glasses and the slap of hands on the bars issued from saloons, cloisters of glazed glass and dirty yellow light.

146   She was watching him closely and the silence was embarrassing, yet in this crisis he could find no casual word with which to profane the hour. At a convenient turning he began to zigzag back toward the University Club.

147   "Have you missed me?" she asked suddenly.

148   "Everybody missed you."

149   He wondered if she knew of Irene Scheerer. She had been back only a day—her absence had been almost contemporaneous with his engagement.

150   "What a remark!" Judy laughed sadly—without sadness. She looked at him searchingly. He became absorbed in the dashboard.

151   "You're handsomer than you used to be," she said thoughtfully. "Dexter, you have the most rememberable eyes."

152   He could have laughed at this, but he did not laugh. It was the sort of thing that was said to sophomores. Yet it stabbed at him.

153   "I'm awfully tired of everything, darling." She called every one darling, endowing the endearment with careless, individual comraderie. "I wish you'd marry me."

154   The directness of this confused him. He should have told her now that he was going to marry another girl, but he could not tell her. He could as easily have sworn that he had never loved her.

155   "I think we'd get along," she continued, on the same note, "unless probably you've forgotten me and fallen in love with another girl."

156   Her confidence was obviously enormous. She had said, in effect, that she found such a thing impossible to believe, that if it were true he had merely committed a childish indiscretion—and probably to show off. She would forgive him, because it was not a matter of any moment but rather something to be brushed aside lightly.

157   "Of course you could never love anybody but me," she continued. "I like the way you love me. Oh, Dexter, have you forgotten last year?"

158   "No, I haven't forgotten."

159   "Neither have I!"

160   Was she sincerely moved—or was she carried along by the wave of her own acting?

161   "I wish we could be like that again," she said, and he forced himself to answer:

162   "I don't think we can."

163   "I suppose not. . . . I hear you're giving Irene Scheerer a violent rush."

164   There was not the faintest emphasis on the name, yet Dexter was suddenly ashamed.

165   "Oh, take me home," cried Judy suddenly; "I don't want to go back to that idiotic dance—with those children."

166   Then, as he turned up the street that led to the residence district, Judy began to cry quietly to herself. He had never seen her cry before.

167   The dark street lightened, the dwellings of the rich loomed up around them, he stopped his coupé in front of the great white bulk of the Mortimer Joneses house, somnolent, gorgeous, drenched with the splendor of the damp moonlight. Its solidity startled him. The strong walls, the steel of the girders, the breadth and beam and pomp of it were there only to bring out the contrast with the young beauty beside him. It was sturdy to accentuate her slightness—as if to show what a breeze could be generated by a butterfly's wing.

168   He sat perfectly quiet, his nerves in wild clamor, afraid that if he moved he would find her irresistibly in his arms. Two tears had rolled down her wet face and trembled on her upper lip.

169   "I'm more beautiful than anybody else," she said brokenly, "why can't I be happy?" Her moist eyes tore at his stability—her mouth turned slowly downward with an exquisite sadness: "I'd like to marry you if you'll have me, Dexter. I suppose you think I'm not worth having, but I'll be so beautiful for you, Dexter."

170   A million phrases of anger, pride, passion, hatred, tenderness fought on his lips. Then a perfect wave of emotion washed over him, carrying off with it a sediment of wisdom, of convention, of doubt, of honor. This was his girl who was speaking, his own, his beautiful, his pride.

171   "Won't you come in?" He heard her draw in her breath sharply.

172   Waiting.

173   "All right," his voice was trembling, "I'll come in."

V

174   It was strange that neither when it was over nor a long time afterward did he regret that night. Looking at it from the perspective of ten years, the fact that Judy's flare for him endured just one month seemed of little importance. Nor did it matter that by his yielding he subjected himself to a deeper agony in the end and gave serious hurt to Irene Scheerer and to Irene's parents, who had befriended him. There was nothing sufficiently pictorial about Irene's grief to stamp itself on his mind.

175   Dexter was at bottom hard-minded. The attitude of the city on his action was of no importance to him, not because he was going to leave the city, but because any outside attitude on the situation seemed superficial. He was completely indifferent to popular opinion. Nor, when he had seen that it was no use, that he did not possess in himself the power to move fundamentally or to hold Judy Jones, did he bear any malice toward her. He loved her, and he would love her until the day he was too old for loving—but he could not have her. So he tasted the deep pain that

is reserved only for the strong, just as he had tasted for a little while the deep happiness.

176   Even the ultimate falsity of the grounds upon which Judy terminated the engagement that she did not want to "take him away" from Irene—Judy, who had wanted nothing else—did not revolt him. He was beyond any revulsion or any amusement.

177   He went East in February with the intention of selling out his laundries and settling in New York—but the war came to America in March and changed his plans. He returned to the West, handed over the management of the business to his partner, and went into the first officers' training-camp in late April. He was one of those young thousands who greeted the war with a certain amount of relief, welcoming the liberation from webs of tangled emotion.

VI

178   This story is not his biography, remember, although things creep into it which have nothing to do with those dreams he had when he was young. We are almost done with them and with him now. There is only one more incident to be related here, and it happens seven years farther on.

179   It took place in New York, where he had done well—so well that there were no barriers too high for him. He was thirty-two years old, and, except for one flying trip immediately after the war, he had not been West in seven years. A man named Devlin from Detroit came into his office to see him in a business way, and then and there this incident occurred, and closed out, so to speak, this particular side of his life.

180   "So you're from the Middle West," said the man Devlin with careless curiosity. "That's funny—I thought men like you were probably born and raised on Wall Street. You know—wife of one of my best friends in Detroit came from your city. I was an usher at the wedding."

181   Dexter waited with no apprehension of what was coming.

182   "Judy Simms," said Devlin with no particular interest; "Judy Jones she was once."

183   "Yes, I knew her." A dull impatience spread over him. He had heard, of course, that she was married—perhaps deliberately he had heard no more.

184   "Awfully nice girl," brooded Devlin meaninglessly, "I'm sort of sorry for her."

185   "Why?" Something in Dexter was alert, receptive, at once.

186   "Oh, Lud Simms has gone to pieces in a way. I don't mean he ill-uses her, but he drinks and runs around———"

187   'Doesn't she run around?"

188   'No, Stays at home with her kids."

189   "Oh."

190   "She's a little too old for him," said Devlin.

191   "Too old!" cried Dexter. "Why, man, she's only twenty-seven."

192   He was possessed with a wild notion of rushing out into the streets and taking a train to Detroit. He rose to his feet spasmodically.

193   "I guess you're busy," Devlin apologized quickly. "I didn't realize————"

194   "No, I'm not busy," said Dexter, steadying his voice. "I'm not busy at all. Not busy at all. Did you say she was—twenty-seven? No, I said she was twenty-seven."

195   "Yes, you did," agreed Devlin dryly.

196   "Go on, then. Go on."

197   "What do you mean?"

198   "About Judy Jones."

199   Devlin looked at him helplessly.

200   "Well, that's—I told you all there is to it. He treats her like the devil. Oh, they're not going to get divorced or anything. When he's particularly outrageous she forgives him. In fact, I'm inclined to think she loves him. She was a pretty girl when she first came to Detroit."

201   A pretty girl! The phrase struck Dexter as ludicrous.

202   "Isn't she—a pretty girl, any more?"

203   "Oh, she's all right."

204   "Look here," said Dexter, sitting down suddenly, "I don't understand. You say she was a 'pretty girl' and now you say she's 'all right.' I don't understand what you mean—Judy Jones wasn't a pretty girl, at all. She was a great beauty. Why, I knew her, I knew her. She was————"

205   Devlin laughed pleasantly.

206   "I'm not trying to start a row," he said. "I think Judy's a nice girl and I like her. I can't understand how a man like Lud Simms could fall madly in love with her, but he did." Then he added: "Most of the women like her."

207   Dexter looked closely at Devlin, thinking wildly that there must be a reason for this, some insensitivity in the man or some private malice.

208   "Lots of women fade just like *that*," Devlin snapped his fingers. "You must have seen it happen. Perhaps I've forgotten how pretty she was at her wedding. I've seen her so much since then, you see. She has nice eyes."

209   A sort of dullness settled down upon Dexter. For the first time in his life he felt like getting very drunk. He knew that he was laughing loudly at something Devlin had said, but he did not know what it was or why it was funny. When, in a few minutes, Devlin went he lay down on his lounge and looked out the window at the New York sky-line into which the sun was sinking in dull lovely shades of pink and gold.

210   He had thought that having nothing else to lose he was invulnerable at last—but he knew that he had just lost something more, as surely as if he had married Judy Jones and seen her fade away before his eyes.

211   The dream was gone. Something had been taken from him. In a sort of panic he pushed the palms of his hands into his eyes and tried to bring up a picture of the waters lapping on Sherry Island and the moonlit veranda, and gingham on the golf-links and the dry sun and the gold color of her neck's soft down. And her mouth damp to his kisses and her

eyes plaintive with melancholy and her freshness like new fine linen in the morning. Why, these things were no longer in the world! They had existed and they existed no longer.

212   For the first time in years the tears were streaming down his face. But they were for himself now. He did not care about mouth and eyes and moving hands. He wanted to care, and he could not care. For he had gone away and he could never go back any more. The gates were closed, the sun was gone down, and there was no beauty but the gray beauty of steel that withstands all time. Even the grief he could have borne was left behind in the country of illusion, of youth, of the richness of life, where his winter dreams had flourished.

213   "Long ago," he said, "long ago, there was something in me, but now that thing is gone. Now that thing is gone, that thing is gone. I cannot cry. I cannot care. That thing will come back no more."

Questions for Discussion

1. Explain the meaning and the implications of the title.
2. Why does Dexter quit his caddying job? What characteristic of his personality is first revealed by this action?
3. List the things that attract Dexter to Judy. Then compare these to the qualities that attract Dexter to Irene.
4. What were Judy Jones's "casual whims," and how do they affect Dexter's life? Explain how "the helpless ecstasy of himself in her" is an "opiate rather than a tonic."
5. What knowledge does Dexter acquire at the end of the story? Why is this knowledge so important to him? How does it change him?

Suggestions for Exploration and Writing

1. If you have ever acted on impulse in a way that changed your life, either for a short while or forever, describe this action and analyze why you made that particular choice.
2. Dexter Green's dreams were "winter dreams." In an essay, describe your own dreams and explain why you would label them winter, spring, summer, or fall.
3. Explain why Dexter's behavior toward Judy is or is not typical of individuals who are infatuated.
4. Analyze Judy Jones's personality and motivation, from her attitudes as a child of eleven on the golf course to her later role as wife.
5. In an essay, compare the two women in Dexter's life.
6. Write a character analysis of Dexter, exploring his impulsiveness, his goals, and his talents.

Katherine Anne Porter (1890–1980)

Katherine Anne Porter was born in Texas and attended convent schools there and in Louisiana. She worked as a journalist in Chicago and in Mexico. Porter considered herself an artist, and in her short stories, short novels, and one full-length novel, Ship of Fools, *she proves her claim. Her mastery of style, even in her early stories, is at least partly a result of her almost endless polishing. Literary critics repeatedly praise her craftsmanship with language and her command of multiple-layered point of view. Through her skillful use of point of view, Porter probes deeply into the minds and hearts of her characters, revealing their dreams and aspirations and their disappointments and disillusionment. While most of Porter's works reflect events and locations from her own life, the character with whom she is most often identified is Miranda Gay. The seven short stories grouped together under the heading "The Old Order" in chronological order are "The Source," "The Journey," "The Witness," "The Circus," "The Last Leaf," "The Fig Tree," and "The Grave." These stories trace many of the people, events, and perceptions that shape Miranda into the young woman portrayed at the end of "The Grave" and in two longer stories—"Old Mortality" and "Pale Horse, Pale Rider."*

THE GRAVE (1935)

1   The grandfather, dead for more than thirty years, had been twice disturbed in his long repose by the constancy and possessiveness of his widow. She removed his bones first to Louisiana and then to Texas as if she had set out to find her own burial place, knowing well she would never return to the places she had left. In Texas she set up a small cemetery in a corner of her first farm, and as the family connection grew, and oddments of relations came over from Kentucky to settle, it contained at last about twenty graves. After the grandmother's death, part of her land was to be sold for the benefit of certain of her children, and the cemetery happened to lie in the part set aside for sale. It was necessary to take up the bodies and bury them again in the family plot in the big new public cemetery, where the grandmother had been buried. At last her husband was to lie beside her for eternity, as she had planned.

2   The family cemetery had been a pleasant small neglected garden of tangled rose bushes and ragged cedar trees and cypress, the simple flat stones rising out of uncropped sweet-smelling wild grass. The graves were lying open and empty one burning day when Miranda and her brother Paul, who often went together to hunt rabbits and doves, propped their twenty-two Winchester rifles carefully against the rail fence, climbed over and explored among the graves. She was nine years old and he was twelve.

3   They peered into the pits all shaped alike with such purposeful accuracy, and looking at each other with pleased adventurous eyes, they said in solemn tones: "These were graves!" trying by words to shape a special, suitable emotion in their minds, but they felt nothing except an agreeable

thrill of wonder: they were seeing a new sight, doing something they had not done before. In them both there was also a small disappointment at the entire commonplaceness of the actual spectacle. Even if it had once contained a coffin for years upon years, when the coffin was gone a grave was just a hole in the ground. Miranda leaped into the pit that had held her grandfather's bones. Scratching around aimlessly and pleasurably as any young animal, she scooped up a lump of earth and weighed it in her palm. It had a pleasantly sweet, corrupt smell, being mixed with the cedar needles and small leaves, and as the crumbs fell apart, she saw a silver dove no larger than a hazel nut, with spread wings and a neat fan-shaped tail. The breast had a deep round hollow in it. Turning it up to the fierce sunlight, she saw that the inside of the hollow was cut in little whorls. She scrambled out, over the pile of loose earth that had fallen back into one end of the grave, calling to Paul that she had found something, he must guess what . . . His head appeared smiling over the rim of another grave. He waved a closed hand at her. "I've got something too!" They ran to compare treasures, making a game of it, so many guesses each, all wrong, and a final show-down with opened palms. Paul had found a thin wide gold ring carved with intricate flowers and leaves. Miranda was smitten at sight of the ring and wished to have it. Paul seemed more impressed by the dove. They made a trade, with some little bickering. After he had got the dove in his hand, Paul said, "Don't you know what this is? This is a screw head for a *coffin!* . . . I'll bet nobody else in the world has one like this!"

4   Miranda glanced at it without covetousness. She had the gold ring on her thumb; it fitted perfectly. "Maybe we ought to go now," she said, "maybe one of the niggers 'll see us and tell somebody." They knew the land had been sold, the cemetery was no longer theirs, and they felt like trespassers. They climbed back over the fence, slung their rifles loosely under their arms—they had been shooting at targets with various kinds of firearms since they were seven years old—and set out to look for the rabbits and doves or whatever small game might happen along. On these expeditions Miranda always followed at Paul's heels along the path, obeying instructions about handling her gun when going through fences; learning how to stand it up properly so it would not slip and fire unexpectedly; how to wait her time for a shot and not just bang away in the air without looking, spoiling shots for Paul, who really could hit things if given a chance. Now and then, in her excitement at seeing birds whizz up suddenly before her face, or a rabbit leap across her very toes, she lost her head, and almost without sighting she flung her rifle up and pulled the trigger. She hardly ever hit any sort of mark. She had no proper sense of hunting at all. Her brother would be often completely disgusted with her. "You don't care whether you get your bird or not," he said. "That's no way to hunt." Miranda could not understand his indignation. She had seen him smash his hat and yell with fury when he had missed his aim. "What I like about shooting," said Miranda, with exasperating inconsequence, "is pulling the trigger and hearing the noise."

5   "Then, by golly," said Paul, "whyn't you go back to the range and shoot at bulls-eyes?"

6   "I'd just as soon," said Miranda, "only like this, we walk round more."

7   "Well, you just stay behind and stop spoiling my shots," said Paul, who, when he made a kill, wanted to be certain he had made it. Miranda, who alone brought down a bird once in twenty rounds, always claimed as her own any game they got when they fired at the same moment. It was tiresome and unfair and her brother was sick of it.

8   "Now, the first dove we see, or the first rabbit, is mine," he told her. "and the next will be yours. Remember that and don't get smarty."

9   "What about snakes?" asked Miranda idly. "Can I have the first snake?"

10   Waving her thumb gently and watching her gold ring glitter, Miranda lost interest in shooting. She was wearing her summer roughing outfit: dark blue overalls, a light blue shirt, a hired-man's straw hat, and thick brown sandals. Her brother had the same outfit except his was a sober hickory-nut color. Ordinarily Miranda preferred her overalls to any other dress, though it was making rather a scandal in the countryside, for the year was 1903, and in the back country the law of female decorum had teeth in it. Her father had been criticized for letting his girls dress like boys and go careering around astride barebacked horses. Big sister Maria, the really independent and fearless one, in spite of her rather affected ways, rode at a dead run with only a rope knotted around her horse's nose. It was said that the motherless family was running down, with the Grandmother no longer there to hold it together. It was known that she had discriminated against her son Harry in her will, and that he was in straits about money. Some of his old neighbors reflected with vicious satisfaction that now he would probably not be so stiffnecked, nor have any more high-stepping horses either. Miranda knew this, though she could not say how. She had met along the road old women of the kind who smoked corn-cob pipes, who had treated her grandmother with most sincere respect. They slanted their gummy old eyes side-ways at the granddaughter and said, "Ain't you ashamed of yoself, Missy? It's against the Scriptures to dress like that. Whut yo Pappy thinkin about?" Miranda, with her powerful social sense, which was like a fine set of antennae radiating from every pore of her skin, would feel ashamed because she knew well it was rude and ill-bred to shock anybody, even bad-tempered old crones, though she had faith in her father's judgment and was perfectly comfortable in the clothes. Her father had said, "They're just what you need, and they'll save your dresses for school . . ." This sounded quite simple and natural to her. She had been brought up in rigorous economy. Wastefulness was vulgar. It was also a sin. These were truths; she had heard them repeated many times and never once disputed.

11   Now the ring, shining with the serene purity of fine gold on her rather grubby thumb, turned her feelings against her overalls and sockless feet, toes sticking through the thick brown leather straps. She wanted to go back to the farmhouse, take a good cold bath, dust herself with plenty of

Maria's violet talcum powder—provided Maria was not present to object, of course—put on the thinnest, most becoming dress she owned, with a big sash, and sit in a wicker chair under the trees . . . These things were not all she wanted, of course; she had vague stirrings of desire for luxury and a grand way of living which could not take precise form in her imagination but were founded on family legend of past wealth and leisure. These immediate comforts were what she could have, and she wanted them at once. She lagged rather far behind Paul, and once she thought of just turning back without a word and going home. She stopped, thinking that Paul would never do that to her, and so she would have to tell him. When a rabbit leaped, she let Paul have it without dispute. He killed it with one shot.

12   When she came up with him, he was already kneeling, examining the wound, the rabbit trailing from his hands. "Right through the head," he said complacently, as if he had aimed for it. He took out his sharp, competent bowie knife and started to skin the body. He did it very cleanly and quickly. Uncle Jimbilly knew how to prepare the skins so that Miranda always had fur coats for her dolls, for though she never cared much for her dolls she liked seeing them in fur coats. The children knelt facing each other over the dead animal. Miranda watched admiringly while her brother stripped the skin away as if he were taking off a glove. The flayed flesh emerged dark scarlet, sleek, firm; Miranda with thumb and finger felt the long fine muscles with the silvery flat strips binding them to the joints. Brother lifted the oddly bloated belly. "Look," he said, in a low amazed voice. "It was going to have young ones."

13   Very carefully he slit the thin flesh from the center ribs to the flanks, and a scarlet bag appeared. He slit again and pulled the bag open, and there lay a bundle of tiny rabbits, each wrapped in a thin scarlet veil. The brother pulled these off and there they were, dark gray, their sleek wet down lying in minute even ripples, like a baby's head just washed, their unbelievably small delicate ears folded close, their little blind faces almost featureless.

14   Miranda said, "Oh, I want to *see*," under her breath. She looked and looked—excited but not frightened, for she was accustomed to the sight of animals killed in hunting—filled with pity and astonishment and a kind of shocked delight in the wonderful little creatures for their own sakes, they were so pretty. She touched one of them ever so carefully, "Ah, there's blood running over them," she said and began to tremble without knowing why. Yet she wanted most deeply to see and to know. Having seen, she felt at once as if she had known all along. The very memory of her former ignorance faded, she had always known just this. No one had ever told her anything outright, she had been rather unobservant of the animal life around her because she was so accustomed to animals. They seemed simply disorderly and unaccountably rude in their habits, but altogether natural and not very interesting. Her brother had spoken as if he had known about everything all along. He may have seen all this before. He had never

said a word to her, but she knew now a part at least of what he knew. She understood a little of the secret, formless intuitions in her own mind and body, which had been clearing up, taking form, so gradually and so steadily she had not realized that she was learning what she had to know. Paul said cautiously, as if he were talking about something forbidden. "They were just about ready to be born." His voice dropped on the last word. "I know," said Miranda, "like kittens. I know, like babies." She was quietly and terribly agitated, standing again with her rifle under her arm, looking down at the bloody heap. "I don't want the skin," she said, "I won't have it." Paul buried the young rabbits again in their mother's body, wrapped the skin around her, carried her to a clump of sage bushes, and hid her away. He came out again at once and said to Miranda, with an eager friendliness, a confidential tone quite unusual in him, as if he were taking her into an important secret on equal terms: "Listen now. Now you listen to me, and don't ever forget. Don't you ever tell a living soul that you saw this. Don't tell a soul. Don't tell Dad because I'll get into trouble. He'll say I'm leading you into things you ought not to do. He's always saying that. So now don't you go and forget and blab out sometime the way you're always doing . . . Now, that's a secret. Don't you tell."

15   Miranda never told, she did not even wish to tell anybody. She thought about the whole worrisome affair with confused unhappiness for a few days. Then it sank quietly in her mind and was heaped over by accumulated thousands of impressions, for nearly twenty years. One day she was picking her path among the puddles and crushed refuse of a market street in a strange city of a strange country, when without warning, plain and clear in its true colors as if she looked through a frame upon a scene that had not stirred nor changed since the moment it happened, the episode of that far-off day leaped from its burial place before her mind's eye. She was so reasonlessly horrified she halted suddenly staring, the scene before her eyes dimmed by the vision back of them. An Indian vendor had held up before her a tray of dyed sugar sweets, in the shapes of all kinds of small creatures: birds, baby chicks, baby rabbits, lambs, baby pigs. They were in gay colors and smelled of vanilla, maybe. . . . It was a very hot day and the smell in the market, with its piles of raw flesh and wilting flowers, was like the mingled sweetness and corruption she had smelled that other day in the empty cemetery at home: the day she had remembered always until now vaguely as the time she and her brother had found treasure in the opened graves. Instantly upon this thought the dreadful vision faded, and she saw clearly her brother, whose childhood face she had forgotten, standing again in the blazing sunshine, again twelve years old, a pleased sober smile in his eyes, turning the silver dove over and over in his hands.

Questions for Discussion

1. Why are the graves empty? What is the double significance of their being empty?

2. In what ways could Miranda's experiences in this story be described as an **epiphany?**

3. List the objects and phrases in the story that suggest death and/or rebirth.

4. We see this event through the double perception of Miranda's consciousness. Here she is first described at age nine, but at the end of the story she recalls the incident twenty years later. What triggers this memory? Why is she "reasonlessly horrified" by the memory? Why does the "dreadful vision" fade into a memory of her brother Paul's "childhood face [. . .], a pleased sober smile in his eyes"?

5. The story of the discoveries in the grave is framed by the description of moving the remains of Miranda's grandfather and the final scene in the Indian market. What significance do these framing scenes have?

Suggestions for Exploration and Writing

1. This story describes events in Miranda's life that shape her as an adult. Describe and tell the significance of a transforming event in your life.

2. After carefully rereading the descriptions in "The Grave" of the empty graves, the ring, the dove, and the rabbit, write an essay explaining and illustrating what each symbolizes.

3. Write an essay explaining how and why this story could be described as ending in an epiphany.

William Faulkner (1897–1962)

Born near Oxford, Mississippi, Faulkner used his home state as the setting for many of his short stories and novels. He invented an imaginary county—Yoknapatawpha—and peopled it with a variety of characters worthy of Shakespeare, from the noble members of the Sartoris family and the intellectual Quenton Compson to the Snopes family, most of whom are sneaky and self-serving. His most famous novels include The Sound and the Fury *(1929);* Light in August *(1932);* Absalom, Absalom! *(1936); and the Snopes trilogy:* The Hamlet *(1940),* The Town *(1957), and* The Mansion *(1958). In 1950, Faulkner was awarded the Nobel Prize for Literature.*

A ROSE FOR EMILY   (1930)

I

1   When Miss Emily Grierson died, our whole town went to her funeral: the men through a sort of respectful affection for a fallen monument, the women mostly out of curiosity to see the inside of her house, which no

one save an old manservant—a combined gardener and cook—had seen in at least ten years.

2   It was a big, squarish frame house that had once been white, decorated with cupolas and spires and scrolled balconies in the heavily lightsome style of the seventies, set on what had once been our most select street. But garages and cotton gins had encroached and obliterated even the august names of that neighborhood; only Miss Emily's house was left, lifting its stubborn and coquettish decay above the cotton wagons and the gasoline pumps—an eyesore among eyesores. And now Miss Emily had gone to join the representatives of those august names where they lay in the cedar-bemused cemetery among the ranked and anonymous graves of Union and Confederate soldiers who fell at the battle of Jefferson.

3   Alive, Miss Emily had been a tradition, a duty, and a care; a sort of hereditary obligation upon the town, dating from that day in 1894 when Colonel Sartoris, the mayor—he who fathered the edict that no Negro woman should appear on the streets without an apron—remitted her taxes, the dispensation dating from the death of her father on into perpetuity. Not that Miss Emily would have accepted charity. Colonel Sartoris invented an involved tale to the effect that Miss Emily's father had loaned money to the town, which the town, as a matter of business, preferred this way of repaying. Only a man of Colonel Sartoris' generation and thought could have invented it and only a woman could have believed it.

4   When the next generation, with its more modern ideas, became mayors and aldermen, this arrangement created some little dissatisfaction. On the first of the year they mailed her a tax notice. February came, and there was no reply. They wrote her a formal letter, asking her to call at the sheriff's office at her convenience. A week later the mayor wrote her himself, offering to call or to send his car for her, and received in reply a note on paper of an archaic shape, in a thin, flowing calligraphy in faded ink, to the effect that she no longer went out at all. The tax notice was also enclosed, without comment.

5   They called a special meeting of the Board of Aldermen. A deputation waited upon her, knocked at the door through which no visitor had passed since she ceased giving china painting lessons eight or ten years earlier. They were admitted by the old Negro into a dim hall from which a stairway mounted into still more shadow. It smelled of dust and disuse—a close, dank smell. The Negro led them into the parlor. It was furnished in heavy, leather-covered furniture. When the Negro opened the blinds of one window, they could see that the leather was cracked; and when they sat down, a faint dust rose sluggishly about their thighs, spinning with slow motes in the single sun-ray. On a tarnished gilt easel before the fireplace stood a crayon portrait of Miss Emily's father.

6   They rose when she entered—a small, fat woman in black, with a thin gold chain descending to her waist and vanishing into her belt, leaning on an ebony cane with a tarnished gold head. Her skeleton was small and spare; perhaps that was why what would have been merely plumpness in another

<u>was obesity in her.</u> She looked bloated, like a body long submerged in motionless water, and of that pallid hue. Her eyes, lost in the fatty ridges of her face, looked like two small pieces of coal pressed into a lump of dough as they moved from one face to another while the visitors stated their errand.

7   She did not ask them to sit. She just stood in the door and listened quietly until the spokesman came to a stumbling halt. Then they could hear the invisible watch ticking at the end of the gold chain.

8   Her voice was dry and cold. "I have no taxes in Jefferson. Colonel Sartoris explained it to me. Perhaps one of you can gain access to the city records and satisfy yourselves."

9   "But we have. We are the city authorities, Miss Emily. Didn't you get a notice from the sheriff, signed by him?"

10   "I received a paper, yes," Miss Emily said. "Perhaps he considers himself the sheriff . . . I have no taxes in Jefferson."

11   "But there is nothing on the books to show that, you see. We must go by the—"

12   "See Colonel Sartoris. I have no taxes in Jefferson."

13   "But, Miss Emily—"

14   "See Colonel Sartoris." (Colonel Sartoris had been dead almost ten years.) "I have no taxes in Jefferson. Tobe!" The Negro appeared. "Show these gentlemen out."

II

15   So she vanquished them, horse and foot, just as she had vanquished their fathers thirty years before about the smell. That was two years after her father's death and a short time after her sweetheart—the one we believed would marry her—had deserted her. After her father's death she went out very little; after her sweetheart went away, people hardly saw her at all. A few of the ladies had the temerity to call, but were not received, and the only sign of life about the place was the Negro man—a young man then—going in and out with a market basket.

16   "Just as if a man—any man—could keep a kitchen properly," the ladies said; so they were not surprised when the smell developed. It was another link between the gross, teeming world and the high and mighty Griersons.

17   A neighbor, a woman, complained to the mayor, Judge Stevens, eighty years old.

18   "But what will you have me do about it, madam?" he said.

19   "Why, send her word to stop it," the woman said. "Isn't there a law?"

20   "I'm sure that won't be necessary," Judge Stevens said. "It's probably just a snake or a rat that nigger of hers killed in the yard. I'll speak to him about it."

21   The next day he received two more complaints, one from a man who came in diffident deprecation. "We really must do something about it, Judge. I'd be the last one in the world to bother Miss Emily, but we've got to do something." That night the Board of Aldermen met—three graybeards and one younger man, a member of the rising generation.

22   "It's simple enough," he said. "Send her word to have her place cleaned up. Give her a certain time to do it in, and if she don't . . ."

23   "Dammit, sir," Judge Stevens said, "will you accuse a lady to her face of smelling bad?"

24   So the next night, after midnight, four men crossed Miss Emily's lawn and slunk about the house like burglars, sniffing along the base of the brick-work and at the cellar openings while one of them performed a regular sowing motion with his hand out of a sack slung from his shoulder. They broke open the cellar door and sprinkled lime there, and in all the outbuildings. As they recrossed the lawn, a window that had been dark was lighted and Miss Emily sat in it, the light behind her, and her upright torso motionless as that of an idol. They crept quietly across the lawn and into the shadow of the locusts that lined the street. After a week or two the smell went away.

25   That was when people had begun to feel really sorry for her. People in our town, remembering how old lady Wyatt, her great-aunt, had gone completely crazy at last, believed that the Griersons held themselves a little too high for what they really were. None of the young men were quite good enough for Miss Emily and such. We had long thought of them as a tableau, Miss Emily a slender figure in white in the background, her father a spraddled silhouette in the foreground, his back to her and clutching a horsewhip, the two of them framed by the back-flung front door. So when she got to be thirty and was still single, we were not pleased exactly, but vindicated; even with insanity in the family she wouldn't have turned down all of her chances if they had really materialized.

26   When her father died, it got about that the house was all that was left to her; and in a way, people were glad. At last they could pity Miss Emily. Being left alone, and a pauper, she had become humanized. Now she too would know the old thrill and the old despair of a penny more or less.

27   The day after his death all the ladies prepared to call at the house and offer condolence and aid, as is our custom. Miss Emily met them at the door, dressed as usual and with no trace of grief on her face. She told them that her father was not dead. She did that for three days, with the ministers calling on her, and the doctors, trying to persuade her to let them dispose of the body. Just as they were about to resort to law and force, she broke down, and they buried her father quickly.

28   We did not say she was crazy then. We believed she had to do that. We remembered all the young men her father had driven away, and we knew that with nothing left, she would have to cling to that which had robbed her, as people will.

III

29   She was sick for a long time. When we saw her again, her hair was cut short, making her look like a girl, with a vague resemblance to those angels in colored church windows—sort of tragic and serene.

30   The town had just let the contracts for paving the sidewalks, and in the summer after her father's death they began the work. The construction

company came with niggers and mules and machinery, and a foreman named Homer Barron, a Yankee—a big, dark, ready man, with a big voice and eyes lighter than his face. The little boys would follow in groups to hear him cuss the niggers, and the niggers singing in time to the rise and fall of picks. Pretty soon he knew everybody in town. Whenever you heard a lot of laughing anywhere about the square, Homer Barron would be in the center of the group. Presently we began to see him and Miss Emily on Sunday afternoons driving in the yellow-wheeled buggy and the matched team bays from the livery stable.

31   At first we were glad that Miss Emily would have an interest, because the ladies all said, "Of course a Grierson would not think seriously of a Northerner, a day laborer." But there were still others, older people, who said that even grief could not cause a real lady to forget *noblesse oblige*—without calling it *noblesse oblige*. They just said, "Poor Emily. Her kinsfolk should come to her." She had some kin in Alabama; but years ago her father her had fallen out with them over the estate of old lady Wyatt, the crazy woman, and there was no communication between the two families. They had not even been represented at the funeral.

32   And as soon as the old people said, "Poor Emily," the whispering began. "Do you suppose it's really so?" they said to one another. "Of course it is. What else could . . ." This behind their hands; rustling of craned silk and satin behind jalousies closed upon the sun of Sunday afternoon as the thin, swift clop-clop-clop of the matched team passed: "Poor Emily."

33   She carried her head high enough—even when we believed that she was fallen. It was as if she demanded more than ever the recognition of her dignity as the last Grierson; as if it had wanted that touch of earthiness to reaffirm her imperviousness. Like when she bought the rat poison, the arsenic. That was over a year after they had begun to say "Poor Emily," and while the two female cousins were visiting her.

34   "I want some poison," she said to the druggist. She was over thirty then, still a slight woman, though thinner than usual, with cold, haughty black eyes in a face the flesh of which was strained across the temples and about the eyesockets as you imagine a lighthouse-keeper's face ought to look. "I want some poison," she said.

35   "Yes, Miss Emily. What kind? For rats and such? I'd recom—"

36   "I want the best you have. I don't care what kind."

37   The druggist named several. "They'll kill anything up to an elephant. But what you want is—"

38   "Arsenic," Miss Emily said, "Is that a good one?"

39   "Is . . . arsenic? Yes, ma'am. But what you want—"

40   "I want arsenic."

41   The druggist looked down at her. She looked back at him, erect, her face like a strained flag. "Why, of course," the druggist said. "If that's what you want. But the law requires you to tell what you are going to use it for."

42   Miss Emily just stared at him, her head tilted back in order to look him eye for eye, until he looked away and went and got the arsenic and

wrapped it up. The Negro delivery boy brought her the package; the druggist didn't come back. When she opened the package at home there was written on the box, under the skull and bones: "For rats."

IV

43   So the next day we all said, "She will kill herself"; and we said it would be the best thing. When she had first begun to be seen with Homer Barron, we had said, "She will marry him." Then we said, "She will persuade him yet," because Homer himself had remarked—he liked men, and it was known that he drank with the younger men in the Elks' Club—that he was not a marrying man. Later we said, "Poor Emily" behind the jalousies as they passed on Sunday afternoon in the glittering buggy, Miss Emily with her head high and Homer Barron with his hat cocked and a cigar in his teeth, reins and whip in a yellow glove.

44   Then some of the ladies began to say that it was a disgrace to the town and a bad example to the young people. The men did not want to interfere, but at last the ladies forced the Baptist minister—Miss Emily's people were Episcopal—to call upon her. He would never divulge what happened during that interview, but he refused to go back again. The next Sunday they again drove about the streets, and the following day the minister's wife wrote to Miss Emily's relations in Alabama.

45   So she had blood-kin under her roof again and we sat back to watch the developments. At first nothing happened. Then we were sure that they were to be married. We learned that Miss Emily had been to the jeweler's and ordered a man's toilet set in silver, with the letters H. B. on each piece. Two days later we learned that she had bought a complete outfit of men's clothing, including a nightshirt, and we said, "They are married." We were really glad. We were glad because the two female cousins were even more Grierson than Miss Emily had ever been.

46   So we were not surprised when Homer Barron—the streets had been finished some time since—was gone. We were a little disappointed that there was not a public blowing-off, but we believed that he had gone on to prepare for Miss Emily's coming, or to give her a chance to get rid of the cousins. (By that time it was a cabal, and we were all Miss Emily's allies to help circumvent the cousins.) Sure enough, after another week they departed. And, as we had expected all along, within three days Homer Barron was back in town. A neighbor saw the Negro man admit him at the kitchen door at dusk one evening.

47   And that was the last we saw of Homer Barron. And of Miss Emily for some time. The Negro man went in and out with the market basket, but the front door remained closed. Now and then we would see her at a window for a moment, as the men did that night when they sprinkled the lime, but for almost six months she did not appear on the streets. Then we knew that this was to be expected too; as if that quality of her father which had thwarted her woman's life so many times had been too virulent and too furious to die.

48   When we next saw Miss Emily, she had grown fat and her hair was turning gray. During the next few years it grew grayer and grayer until it attained an even pepper-and-salt iron-gray, when it ceased turning. Up to the day of her death at seventy-four it was still that vigorous iron-gray, like the hair of an active man.

49   From that time on her front door remained closed, save for a period of six or seven years, when she was about forty, during which she gave lessons in china-painting. She fitted up a studio in one of the downstairs rooms, where the daughters and granddaughters of Colonel Sartoris' contemporaries were sent to her with the same regularity and in the same spirit that they were sent to church on Sundays with a twenty-five-cent piece for the collection plate. Meanwhile her taxes had been remitted.

50   Then the newer generation became the backbone and the spirit of the town, and the painting pupils grew up and fell away and did not send their children to her with boxes of color and tedious brushes and pictures cut from the ladies' magazines. The front door closed upon the last one and remained closed for good. When the town got free postal delivery, Miss Emily alone refused to let them fasten the metal numbers above her door and attach a mailbox to it. She would not listen to them.

51   Daily, monthly, yearly we watched the Negro grow grayer and more stooped, going in and out with the market basket. Each December we sent her a tax notice, which would be returned by the post office a week later, unclaimed. Now and then we would see her in one of the downstairs windows—she had evidently shut up the top floor of the house—like the carven torso of an idol in a niche, looking or not looking at us, we could never tell which. Thus she passed from generation to generation—dear, inescapable, impervious, tranquil, and perverse.

52   And so she died. Fell ill in the house filled with dust and shadows, with only a doddering Negro man to wait on her. We did not even know she was sick; we had long since given up trying to get any information from the Negro. He talked to no one, probably not even to her, for his voice had grown harsh and rusty, as if from disuse.

53   She died in one of the downstairs rooms, in a heavy walnut bed with a curtain, her gray head propped on a pillow yellow and moldy with age and lack of sunlight.

V

54   The Negro met the first of the ladies at the front door and let them in, with their hushed, sibilant voices and their quick curious glances, and then he disappeared. He walked right through the house and out the back and was not seen again.

55   The two female cousins came at once. They held the funeral on the second day, with the town coming to look at Miss Emily beneath a mass of bought flowers, with the crayon face of her father musing profoundly above the bier and the ladies sibilant and macabre; and the very old men—some in their brushed confederate uniforms—on the porch and

the lawn, talking of Miss Emily as if she had been a contemporary of theirs, believing that they had danced with her and courted her perhaps, confusing time with its mathematical progression, as the old do, to whom all the past is not a diminishing road but, instead, a huge meadow which no winter ever quite touches, divided from them now by the narrow bottleneck of the most recent decade of years.

56   Already we knew that there was one room in that region above stairs which no one had seen in forty years, and which would have to be forced. They waited until Miss Emily was decently in the ground before they opened it.

57   The violence of breaking down the door seemed to fill this room with pervading dust. A thin, acrid pall as of the tomb seemed to lie everywhere upon this room decked and furnished as for a bridal: upon the valance curtains of faded rose color, upon the rose-shaded lights, upon the dressing table, upon the delicate array of crystal and the man's toilet things backed with tarnished silver, silver so tarnished that the monogram was obscured. Among them lay a collar and tie, as if they had just been removed, which, lifted, left upon the surface a pale crescent in the dust. Upon a chair hung the suit, carefully folded; beneath it the two mute shoes and the discarded socks.

58   The man himself lay in the bed.

59   For a long while we just stood there, looking down at the profound and fleshless grin. The body had apparently once lain in the attitude of an embrace, but now the long sleep that outlasts love, that conquers even the grimace of love, had cuckolded him. What was left of him, rotted beneath what was left of the nightshirt, had become inextricable from the bed in which he lay; and upon him and upon the pillow beside him lay that even coating of the patient and biding dust.

60   Then we noticed that in the second pillow was the indentation of a head. One of us lifted something from it, and leaning forward, that faint and invisible dust dry and acrid in the nostrils, we saw a long strand of iron-gray hair.

Questions for Discussion

1. From whose **point of view** is the story told? How would you describe the narrator's attitude toward Miss Emily?

2. What is the relationship between the town and Miss Emily? In what sense(s) is she a "tradition, a duty, and a care"? Why does Colonel Sartoris feel obliged to remit her taxes and to make up an excuse for doing so?

3. Why is Miss Emily able to vanquish the authorities of Jefferson, to make them back down on taxes and on the smell? Why don't they just bring the force of the law to bear on her?

4. What does the description of the parlor reveal about the house and about Miss Emily?

5. What does the last sentence of the story reveal? What hints of the ending make it believable, if shocking?

Suggestions for Exploration and Writing

1. Write an essay about a person you know who has refused to adapt to changing times.
2. In terms of the time and the environment in which she lives, explain Miss Emily's treatment by, and response to, the two men in her life.

Arna Bontemps (1902–1973)

Bontemps was born in Alexandria, Louisiana, but moved to Los Angeles, California, as a child. Because his parents resented their African American heritage, they sent him to white schools, and he lived in white neighborhoods. Bontemps learned about his culture from his great-uncle Buddy. As a result of his upbringing, Bontemps spent the rest of his life trying to rectify omissions in the history books and trying to increase interest in African American literature and culture.

A SUMMER TRAGEDY   (1933)

1   Old Jeff Patton, the black share farmer, fumbled with his bow tie. His fingers trembled, and the high, stiff collar pinched his throat. A fellow loses his hand for such vanities after thirty or forty years of simple life. Once a year, or maybe twice if there's a wedding among his kin-folks, he may spruce up; but generally fancy clothes do nothing but adorn the wall of the big room and feed the moths. That had been Jeff Patton's experience. He had not worn his stiff-bosomed shirt more than a dozen times in all his married life. His swallowtailed coat lay on the bed beside him, freshly brushed and pressed, but it was as full of holes as the overalls in which he worked on week days. The moths had used it badly. Jeff twisted his mouth into a hideous toothless grimace as he contended with the obstinate bow. He stamped his good foot and decided to give up the struggle.

2   "Jennie," he called.

3   "What's that, Jeff?" His wife's shrunken voice came out of the adjoining room like an echo. It was hardly bigger than a whisper.

4   "I reckon you'll have to he'p me wid this heah bow tie, baby," he said meekly. "Dog if I can hitch it up."

5   Her answer was not strong enough to reach him, but presently the old woman came to the door, feeling her way with a stick. She had a wasted, dead-leaf appearance. Her body, as scrawny and gnarled as a stringbean, seemed less than nothing in the ocean of frayed and faded petticoats that surrounded her. These hung an inch or two above the tops of her heavy, unlaced shoes and showed little grotesque piles where the stockings had fallen down from her negligible legs.

6   "You oughta could do a heap mo' wid a thing like that 'n me–beingst as you got yo' good sight."

7   "Looks like I *oughta* could," he admitted. "But ma fingers is gone democrat on me. I get all mixed up in the looking glass an' can't tell whicha way to twist the devilish thing."

8   Jennie sat on the side of the bed and old Jeff Patton got down on one knee while she tied the bow knot. It was a slow and painful ordeal for each of them in this position. Jeff's bones cracked, his knee ached, and it was only after a half dozen attempts that Jennie worked a semblance of a bow into the tie.

9   "I got to dress maself now," the old woman whispered. "These is ma old shoes an' stockings, and I ain't so much as unwrapped ma dress."

10   "Well, don't worry 'bout me no mo', baby," Jeff said. "That 'bout finishes me. All I gotta do now is slip on that old coat 'n ves' an' I'll be fixed to leave."

11   Jennie disappeared again through the dim passage into the shed room. Being blind was no handicap to her in that black hole. Jeff heard the cane placed against the wall beside the door and knew that his wife was on easy ground. He put on his coat, took a battered top hat from the bed post, and hobbled to the front door. He was ready to travel. As soon as Jennie could get on her Sunday shoes and her old black silk dress, they would start.

12   Outside the tiny log house the day was warm and mellow with sunshine. A host of wasps was humming with busy excitement in the trunk of a dead sycamore. Grey squirrels were searching through the grass for hickory nuts and blue jays were in the trees, hopping from branch to branch. Pine woods stretched away to the left like a black sea. Among them were scattered scores of log houses like Jeff's, houses of black share farmers. Cows and pigs wandered freely among the trees. There was no danger of loss. Each farmer knew his own stock and knew his neighbor's as well as he knew his neighbor's children.

13   Down the slope to the right were the cultivated acres on which the colored folks worked. They extended to the river, more than two miles away, and they were today green with the unmade cotton crop. A tiny thread of a road, which passed directly in front of Jeff's place, ran through these green fields like a pencil mark.

14   Jeff, standing outside the door with his absurd hat in his left hand, surveyed the wide scene tenderly. He had been forty-five years on these acres. He loved them with the unexplained affection that others have for the countries to which they belong.

15   The sun was hot on his head, his collar still pinched his throat, and the Sunday clothes were intolerably hot. Jeff transferred the hat to his right hand and began fanning with it. Suddenly the whisper that was Jennie's voice came out of the shed room.

16   "You can bring the car round front whilst you's waitin'," it said feebly. There was a tired pause; then it added, "I'll soon be fixed to go."

17   "A'right, baby," Jeff answered. "I'll get it in a minute."

18   But he didn't move. A thought struck him that made his mouth fall open. The mention of the car brought to his mind, with new intensity,

the trip he and Jennie were about to take. Fear came into his eyes; excitement took his breath. Lord, Jesus!

19   "Jeff . . . Oh Jeff," the old woman's whisper called.

20   He awakened with a jolt. "Hunh, baby?"

21   "What you doin'?"

22   "Nuthin. Jes studyin'. I jes been turnin' things round 'n round in ma mind."

23   "You could be gettin' the car," she said.

24   "Oh yes, right away, baby."

25   He started round to the shed, limping heavily on his bad leg. There were three frizzly chickens in the yard. All his other chickens had been killed or stolen recently. But the frizzly chickens had been saved somehow. That was fortunate indeed, for these curious creatures had a way of devouring "poison" from the yard and in that way protecting against conjure and bad luck and spells. But even the frizzly chickens seemed now to be in a stupor. Jeff thought they had some ailment; he expected all three of them to die shortly.

26   The shed in which the old model-T Ford stood was only a grass roof held up by four corner poles. It had been built by tremulous hands at a time when the little rattle-trap car had been regarded as a peculiar treasure. And, miraculously, despite wind and downpour, it still stood.

27   Jeff adjusted the crank and put his weight on it. The engine came to life with a sputter and bang that rattled the old car from radiator to tail light. Jeff hopped into the seat and put his foot on the accelerator. The sputtering and banging increased. The rattling became more violent. That was good. It was good banging, good sputtering and rattling, and it meant that the aged car was still in running condition. She could be depended on for this trip.

28   Again Jeff's thought halted as if paralyzed. The suggestion of the trip fell into the machinery of his mind like a wrench. He felt dazed and weak. He swung the car out into the yard, made a half turn, and drove around to the front door. When he took his hands off the wheel, he noticed that he was trembling violently. He cut off the motor and climbed to the ground to wait for Jennie.

29   A few moments later she was at the window, her voice rattling against the pane like a broken shutter.

30   "I'm ready, Jeff."

31   He did not answer, but limped into the house and took her by the arm. He led her slowly though the big room, down the step, and across the yard.

32   "You reckon I'd oughta lock the do'?" he asked softly.

33   They stopped and Jennie weighed the question. Finally she shook her head.

34   "Ne' mind the do'," she said. "I don't see no cause to lock up things."

35   "You right," Jeff agreed. "No cause to lock up."

36   Jeff opened the door and helped his wife into the car. A quick shudder passed over him. Jesus! Again he trembled.

37   "How come you shaking so?" Jennie whispered.

38   "I don't know," he said.

39   "You mus' be scairt, Jeff."

40   "No, baby, I ain't scairt."

41   He slammed the door after her and went around to crank up again. The motor started easily. Jeff wished that it had not been so responsive. He would have liked a few more minutes in which to turn things around in his head. As it was, with Jennie chiding him about being afraid, he had to keep going. He swung the car into the little pencil-mark road and started off toward the river, driving very slowly, very cautiously.

42   Chugging across the green countryside, the small, battered Ford seemed tiny indeed. Jeff felt a familiar excitement, a thrill, as they came down the first slope to the immense levels on which the cotton was growing. He could not help reflecting that the crops were good. He knew what that meant, too; he had made forty-five of them with his own hands. It was true that he had worn out nearly a dozen mules, but that was the fault of old man Stevenson, the owner of the land. Major Stevenson had the odd notion that one mule was all a share farmer needed to work a thirty-acre plot. It was an expensive notion, the way it killed mules from overwork, but the old man held to it. Jeff thought it killed a good many share farmers as well as mules, but he had no sympathy for them. He had always been strong, and he had been taught to have no patience with weakness in men. Women or children might be tolerated if they were puny, but a weak man was a curse. Of course, his own children—

43   Jeff's thought halted there. He and Jennie never mentioned their dead children any more. And naturally he did not wish to dwell upon them in his mind. Before he knew it, some remark would slip out of his mouth and that would make Jennie feel blue. Perhaps she would cry. A woman like Jennie could not easily throw off the grief that comes from losing five grown children within two years. Even Jeff was still staggered by the blow. His memory had not been much good recently. He frequently talked to himself. And, although he had kept it a secret he knew that his courage had left him. He was terrified by the least unfamiliar sound at night. He was reluctant to venture far from home in the daytime. And that habit of trembling when he felt fearful was now far beyond his control. Sometimes he became afraid and trembled without knowing what had frightened him. The feeling would just come over him like a chill.

44   The car rattled slowly over the dusty road. Jennie sat erect and silent, with a little absurd hat pinned to her hair. Her useless eyes seemed very large and very white in their deep sockets. Suddenly Jeff heard her voice, and he inclined his head to catch the words.

45   "Is we passed Delia Moore's house yet?" she asked.

46   "Not yet," he said.

47   "You must be drivin' mighty slow, Jeff."

48   "We jes as well take our time, baby."

49   There was a pause. A little puff of steam was coming out of the radiator of the car. Heat wavered above the hood. Delia Moore's house was nearly half a mile away. After a moment Jennie spoke again.

50   "You ain't really scairt, is you, Jeff?"

51   "Nah, baby, I ain't scairt."

52   "You know how we agreed—we gotta keep on goin'."

53   Jewels of perspiration appeared on Jeff's forehead. His eyes rounded, blinked, became fixed on the road.

54   "I don't know," he said with a shiver. "I reckon it's the only thing to do."

55   "Hm."

56   A flock of guinea fowls, pecking in the road, were scattered by the passing car. Some of them took to their wings; others hid under bushes. A blue jay, swaying on a leafy twig, was annoying a roadside squirrel. Jeff held an even speed till he came near Delia's place. Then he slowed down noticeably.

57   Delia's house was really no house at all, but an abandoned store building converted into a dwelling. It sat near a crossroads, beneath a single black cedar tree. There Delia, a catlike old creature of Jennie's age, lived alone. She had been there more years than anybody could remember, and long ago had won the disfavor of such women as Jennie. For in her young days Delia had been gayer, yellower, and saucier than seemed proper in those parts. Her ways with menfolks had been dark and suspicious. And the fact that she had had as many husbands as children did not help her reputation.

58   "Yonder's old Delia," Jeff said as they passed.

59   "What she doin'?"

60   "Jes sittin' in the do'," he said.

61   "She see us?"

62   "Hm," Jeff said. "Musta did."

63   That relieved Jennie. It strengthened her to know that her old enemy had seen her pass in her best clothes. That would give the old she-devil something to chew her gums and fret about, Jennie thought. Wouldn't she have a fit if she didn't find out? Old evil Delia! This would be just the thing for her. It would pay her back for being so evil. It would also pay her, Jennie thought, for the way she used to grin at Jeff—long ago when her teeth were good.

64   The road became smooth and red, and Jeff could tell by the smell of the air that they were nearing the river. He could see the rise where the road turned and ran along parallel to the stream. The car chugged on monotonously. After a long silent spell, Jennie leaned against Jeff and spoke.

65   "How many bale o' cotton you think we got standin'?" she said.

66   Jeff wrinkled his forehead as he calculated.

67   "'Bout twenty-five, I reckon."

68   "How many you make las' year?"

69   "Twenty-eight," he said. "How come you ask that?"

70   "I's jes thinkin'," Jennie said quietly.

71   "It don't make a speck o' diff'ence though," Jeff reflected. "If we get much or if we get little, we still gonna be in debt to old man Stevenson when he gets through counting up agin us. It's took us a long time to learn that."

72   Jennie was not listening to these words. She had fallen into a trance-like meditation. Her lips twitched. She chewed her gums and rubbed her old gnarled hands nervously. Suddenly, she leaned forward, buried her face in the nervous hands, and burst into tears. She cried aloud in a dry, cracked voice that suggested the rattle of fodder on dead stalks. She cried aloud like a child, for she had never learned to suppress a genuine sob. Her slight old frame shook heavily and seemed hardly able to sustain such violent grief.

73   "What's the matter, baby?" Jeff asked awkwardly. "Why you cryin' like all that?"

74   "I's jes thinkin'," she said.

75   "So you the one what's scairt now, hunh?"

76   "I ain't scairt, Jeff. I's jes thinkin' 'bout leavin' eve'thing like this—eve'thing we been used to. It's right sad-like."

77   Jeff did not answer, and presently Jennie buried her face and continued crying.

78   The sun was almost overhead. It beat down furiously on the dusty wagon path road, on the parched roadside grass, and the tiny battered car. Jeff's hands, gripping the wheel, became wet with perspiration; his forehead sparkled. Jeff's lips parted and his mouth shaped a hideous grimace. His face suggested the face of a man being burned. But the torture passed and his expression softened again.

79   "You mustn't cry, baby," he said to his wife. "We gotta be strong. We can't break down."

80   Jennie waited a few seconds, then said, "You reckon we oughta do it, Jeff? You reckon we oughta go 'head an' do it really?"

81   Jeff's voice choked; his eyes blurred. He was terrified to hear Jennie say the thing that had been in his mind all morning. She had egged him on when he had wanted more than anything in the world to wait, to reconsider, to think things over a little longer. Now *she* was getting cold feet. Actually, there was no need of thinking the question through again. It would only end in making the same painful decision once more. Jeff knew that. There was no need of fooling around longer.

82   "We jes as well to do like we planned," he said. "They ain't nuthin else for us now—it's the bes' thing."

83   Jeff thought of the handicaps, the near impossibility, of making another crop with his leg bothering him more and more each week. Then there was always the chance that he would have another stroke, like the one that had made him lame. Another one might kill him. The least it could do would be to leave him helpless. Jeff gasped . . . Lord, Jesus! He could not bear to think of being helpless, like a baby, on Jennie's hands. Frail, blind Jennie.

84   The little pounding motor of the car worked harder and harder. The puff of steam from the cracked radiator became large. Jeff realized that they were climbing a little rise. A moment later the road turned abruptly and he looked down upon the face of the river.

85   "Jeff."

86   "Hunh?"

87   "Is that the water I hear?"

88   "Hm. That's it."

89   "Well, which way you goin' now?"

90   "Down this-a way," he answered. "The road runs 'long-side o' the water a lil piece."

91   She waited a while calmly. Then she said, "Drive faster."

92   "A'right, baby," Jeff said.

93   The water roared in the bed of the river. It was fifty or sixty feet below the level of the road. Between the road and the water there was a long smooth slope, sharply inclined. The slope was dry; the clay had been hardened by prolonged summer heat. The water below, roaring in a narrow channel, was noisy and wild.

94   "Jeff."

95   "Hunh?"

96   "How far you goin'?"

97   "Jes a lil piece down the road."

98   "You ain't scairt is you, Jeff?"

99   "Nah, baby," he was trembling. "I ain't scairt."

100   "Remember how we planned it, Jeff. We gotta do it like we said. Brave-like."

101   "Hm."

102   Jeff's brain darkened. Things suddenly seemed unreal, like figures in a dream. Thoughts swam in his mind foolishly, hysterically, like little blind fish in a pool within a dense cave. They rushed, crossed one another, jostled, collided, retreated, and rushed again. Jeff soon became dizzy. He shuddered violently and turned to his wife.

103   "Jennie, I can't do it. I can't." His voice broke pitifully.

104   She did not appear to be listening. All the grief had gone from her face. She sat erect, her unseeing eyes wide open, strained and frightful. Her glossy black skin had become dull. She seemed as thin and as sharp and bony as a starved bird. Now, having suffered and endured the sadness of tearing herself away from beloved things, she showed no anguish. She was absorbed with her own thoughts, and she didn't even hear Jeff's voice shouting in her ear.

105   Jeff said nothing more. For an instant there was light in his cavernous brain. That chamber was, for less than a second, peopled by characters he knew and loved. They were simple, healthy creatures, and they behaved in a manner that he could understand. They had quality. But since he had already taken leave of them long ago, the remembrance did not break his heart again. Young Jeff Patton was among them, the Jeff Patton of fifty years ago who went down to New Orleans with a crowd of country boys to the Mardi Gras doings. The gay young crowd—boys with candy-striped shirts and rouged brown girls in noisy silks—was like a picture in his head. Yet it did not make him sad. On that very trip Slim Burns had killed Joe Beasley—the crowd had been broken up. Since then Jeff Patton's work had been the Greenbrier Plantation. If there had been other

Mardi Gras carnivals, he had not heard of them. Since then there had been no time; the years had fallen on him like waves. Now he was old, worn out. Another paralytic stroke like the one he had already suffered would put him on his back for keeps. In that condition, with a frail blind woman to look after him, he would be worse off than if he were dead.

106   Suddenly Jeff's hands became steady. He actually felt brave. He slowed down the motor of the car and carefully pulled off the road. Below, the water of the stream boomed, a soft thunder in the deep channel. Jeff ran the car onto the clay slope, pointed it directly toward the stream, and put his foot heavily on the accelerator. The little car leaped furiously down the steep incline toward the water. The movement was nearly as swift and direct as a fall. The two old black folks, sitting quietly side by side, showed no excitement. In another instant the car hit the water and dropped immediately out of sight.

107   A little later it lodged in the mud of a shallow place. One wheel of the crushed and upturned little Ford became visible above the rushing water.

Questions for Discussion

1. What does "gone democrat" mean?

2. Why does Bontemps take so much time to describe the old couple, the **setting,** and the model-T Ford?

3. What **foreshadows** the ending?

4. Analyze the feelings of Jeff Patton. Why does Jeff shiver or feel dazed? Why does he say to himself, "Women or children might be tolerated if they were puny, but a weak man was a curse"?

5. Analyze the feelings of Jennie Patton. Why does she want to get even with Delia Moore? Why does she cry?

6. What causes Jeff and Jennie to despair? What is Mr. Stevenson's role in their decision?

Suggestions for Exploration and Writing

1. Bontemps says that "fear came into [Jeff Patton's] eyes; excitement took his breath." Sometimes fear is accompanied by excitement. Examine some activity that you are thrilled by and discuss both the thrill and the fear involved.

2. Jeff Patton thinks to himself: "Now he was old, worn out." Discuss why and how elderly people in some cultures are treated as if they are "worn out." Or write an essay contrasting such treatment of the elderly with the belief of some cultures that the elderly must be treated with respect.

3. Compare the attitude toward the elderly in this story with that shown in Capote's "A Christmas Memory."

Liliana Heker (b. 1943)

Liliana Heker, an Argentine writer, began writing as a teen. Her first volume of short stories, Those Who Beheld the Burning Bush, *was published when she was in her teens. As a political writer during the turbulent times in Argentina, Heker edited the literary magazine* The Platypus, *which published works that portrayed Argentinean social and political problems. In her collection of short stories,* The Stolen Party *(1982), Heker writes from a child's point of view. The short story by the same name examines a child's fears caused by inequality and injustice.*

THE STOLEN PARTY   (1982)

1   As soon as she arrived she went straight to the kitchen to see if the monkey was there. It was: what a relief! She wouldn't have liked to admit that her mother had been right. *Monkeys at a birthday?* her mother had sneered. *Get away with you, believing any nonsense you're told!* She was cross, but not because of the monkey, the girl thought; it's just because of the party.

2   "I don't like you going," she told her. "It's a rich people's party."

3   "Rich people go to Heaven too," said the girl, who studied religion at school.

4   "Get away with Heaven," said the mother. "The problem with you, young lady, is that you like to fart higher than your ass."

5   The girl didn't approve of the way her mother spoke. She was barely nine, and one of the best in her class.

6   "I'm going because I've been invited," she said. "And I've been invited because Luciana is my friend. So there."

7   "Ah yes, your friend," her mother grumbled. She paused. "Listen, Rosaura," she said at last. "That one's not your friend. You know what you are to them? The maid's daughter, that's what."

8   Rosaura blinked hard: she wasn't going to cry. Then she yelled: "Shut up! You know nothing about being friends!"

9   Every afternoon she used to go to Luciana's house and they would both finish their homework while Rosaura's mother did the cleaning. They had their tea in the kitchen and they told each other secrets. Rosaura loved everything in the big house, and she also loved the people who lived there.

9   "I'm going because it will be the most lovely party in the whole world, Luciana told me it would. There will be a magician, and he will bring a monkey and everything."

10   The mother swung around to take a good look at her child, and pompously put her hands on her hips.

12   "Monkeys at a birthday?" she said. "Get away with you, believing any nonsense you're told!"

13   Rosaura was deeply offended. She thought it unfair of her mother to accuse other people of being liars simply because they were rich. Rosaura too wanted to be rich, of course. If one day she managed to live in a

beautiful palace, would her mother stop loving her? She felt very sad. She wanted to go to that party more than anything else in the world.

14   "I'll die if I don't go," she whispered, almost without moving her lips.

15   And she wasn't sure whether she had been heard, but on the morning of the party she discovered that her mother had starched her Christmas dress. And in the afternoon, after washing her hair, her mother rinsed it in apple vinegar so that it would be all nice and shiny. Before going out, Rosaura admired herself in the mirror, with her white dress and glossy hair, and thought she looked terribly pretty.

16   Señora Ines also seemed to notice. As soon as she saw her, she said:

17   "How lovely you look today, Rosaura."

18   Rosaura gave her starched skirt a slight toss with her hands and walked into the party with a firm step. She said hello to Luciana and asked about the monkey. Luciana put on a secretive look and whispered into Rosaura's ear: "He's in the kitchen. But don't tell anyone, because it's a surprise."

19   Rosaura wanted to make sure. Carefully she entered the kitchen and there she saw it: deep in thought, inside its cage. It looked so funny that the girl stood there for a while, watching it, and later, every so often, she would slip out of the party unseen and go and admire it. Rosaura was the only one allowed into the kitchen. Señora Ines had said: "You yes, but not the others, they're much too boisterous, they might break something." Rosaura had never broken anything. She even managed the jug of orange juice, carrying it from the kitchen into the dining room. She held it carefully and didn't spill a single drop. And Señora Ines had said: "Are you sure you can manage a jug as big as that?" Of course she could manage. She wasn't a butterfingers, like the others. Like that blonde girl with the bow in her hair. As soon as she saw Rosaura, the girl with the bow had said:

20   "And you? Who are you?"

21   "I'm a friend of Luciana," said Rosaura.

22   "No," said the girl with the bow, "you are not a friend of Luciana because I'm her cousin and I know all her friends. And I don't know you."

23   "So what," said Rosaura. "I come here every afternoon with my mother and we do our homework together."

24   "You and your mother do your homework together?" asked the girl, laughing.

25   "I and Luciana do our homework together," said Rosaura, very seriously.

26   The girl with the bow shrugged her shoulders.

27   "That's not being friends," she said. "Do you go to school together?"

28   "No."

29   "So where do you know her from?" said the girl, getting impatient.

30   Rosaura remembered her mother's words perfectly. She took a deep breath.

31   "I'm the daughter of the employee," she said.

32   Her mother had said very clearly: "If someone asks, you say you're the daughter of the employee; that's all." She also told her to add: "And

proud of it." But Rosaura thought that never in her life would she dare say something of the sort.

33 "What employee?" said the girl with the bow. "Employee in a shop?"

34 "No," said Rosaura angrily. "My mother doesn't sell anything in any shop, so there."

35 "So how come she's an employee?" said the girl with the bow.

36 Just then Señora Ines arrived saying *shh shh*, and asked Rosaura if she wouldn't mind helping serve out the hotdogs, as she knew the house so much better than the others.

37 "See?" said Rosaura to the girl with the bow, and when no one was looking she kicked her in the shin.

38 Apart from the girl with the bow, all the others were delightful. The one she liked best was Luciana, with her golden birthday crown; and then the boys. Rosaura won the sack race, and nobody managed to catch her when they played tag. When they split into two teams to play charades, all the boys wanted her for their side. Rosaura felt she had never been so happy in all her life.

39 But the best was still to come. The best came after Luciana blew out the candles. First the cake. Señora Ines had asked her to help pass the cake around, and Rosaura had enjoyed the task immensely, because everyone called out to her, shouting "Me, me!" Rosaura remembered a story in which there was a queen who had the power of life or death over her subjects. She had always loved that, having the power of life or death. To Luciana and the boys she gave the largest pieces, and to the girl with the bow she gave a slice so thin one could see through it.

40 After the cake came the magician, tall and bony, with a fine red cape. A true magician: he could untie handkerchiefs by blowing on them and make a chain with links that had no openings. He could guess what cards were pulled out from a pack, and the monkey was his assistant. He called the monkey "partner." "Let's see here, partner," he would say, "turn over a card." And, "Don't run away, partner: time to work now."

41 The final trick was wonderful. One of the children had to hold the monkey in his arms and the magician said he would make him disappear.

42 "What, the boy?" they all shouted.

43 "No, the monkey!" shouted back the magician.

44 Rosaura thought that this was truly the most amusing party in the whole world.

45 The magician asked a small fat boy to come and help, but the small fat boy got frightened almost at once and dropped the monkey on the floor. The magician picked him up carefully, whispered something in his ear, and the monkey nodded almost as if he understood.

46 "You mustn't be so unmanly, my friend," the magician said to the fat boy.

47 "What's unmanly?" said the fat boy.

48 The magician turned around as if to look for spies.

49 "A sissy," said the magician. "Go sit down."

50   Then he stared at all the faces, one by one. Rosaura felt her heart tremble:

51   "You, with the Spanish eyes," said the magician. And everyone saw that he was pointing at her.

52   She wasn't afraid. Neither holding the monkey, nor when the magician made him vanish; not even when, at the end, the magician flung his red cape over Rosaura's head and uttered a few magic words . . . and the monkey reappeared, chattering happily, in her arms. The children clapped furiously. And before Rosaura returned to her seat, the magician said:

53   "Thank you very much, my little countess."

54   She was so pleased with the compliment that a while later, when her mother came to fetch her, that was the first thing she told her.

55   "I helped the magician and he said to me, 'Thank you very much, my little countess.'"

56   It was strange because up to then Rosaura had thought that she was angry with her mother. All along Rosaura had imagined that she would say to her: "See that the monkey wasn't a lie?" But instead she was so thrilled that she told her mother all about the wonderful magician.

57   Her mother tapped her on the head and said: "So now we're a countess!"

58   But one could see that she was beaming.

59   And now they both stood in the entrance, because a moment ago Señora Ines, smiling, had said: "Please wait here a second."

60   Her mother suddenly seemed worried.

61   "What is it?" she asked Rosaura.

62   "What is what?" said Rosaura. "It's nothing; she just wants to get the presents for those who are leaving, see?"

63   She pointed at the fat boy and at a girl with pigtails who were also waiting there, next to their mothers. And she explained about the presents. She knew, because she had been watching those who left before her. When one of the girls was about to leave, Señora Ines would give her a bracelet. When a boy left, Señora Ines gave him a yo-yo. Rosaura preferred the yo-yo because it sparkled, but she didn't mention that to her mother. Her mother might have said: "So why don't you ask for one, you blockhead?" That's what her mother was like. Rosaura didn't feel like explaining that she'd be horribly ashamed to be the odd one out. Instead she said:

64   "I was the best-behaved at the party."

65   And she said no more because Señora Ines came out into the hall with two bags, one pink and one blue.

66   First she went up to the fat boy, gave him a yo-yo out of the blue bag, and the fat boy left with his mother. Then she went up to the girl and gave her a bracelet out of the pink bag, and the girl with the pigtails left as well.

67   Finally she came up to Rosaura and her mother. She had a big smile on her face and Rosaura liked that. Señora Ines looked down at her, then looked up at her mother, and then said something that made Rosaura proud:

68   "What a marvelous daughter you have, Herminia."

69   For an instant, Rosaura thought that she'd give her two presents: the bracelet and the yo-yo. Señora Ines bent down as if about to look for something. Rosaura also leaned forward, stretching out her arm. But she never completed the movement.

70   Señora Ines didn't look in the pink bag. Nor did she look in the blue bag. Instead she rummaged in her purse. In her hand appeared two bills.

71   "You really and truly earned this," she said handing them over. "Thank you for all your help, my pet."

72   Rosaura felt her arms stiffen, stick close to her body, and then she noticed her mother's hand on her shoulder. Instinctively she pressed herself against her mother's body. That was all. Except her eyes. Rosaura's eyes had a cold, clear look that fixed itself on Señora Ines's face.

73   Señora Ines, motionless, stood there with her hand outstretched. As if she didn't dare draw it back. As if the slightest change might shatter an infinitely delicate balance.

Questions for Discussion

1. Explain the contrasting expectations of Rosaura and her mother. Does her mother want to be right?

2. What events or comments foreshadow the ending?

3. What is the significance of the magician's monkey? Why is the monkey mentioned at the beginning of the story?

4. Señora Ines is consistently kind and flattering to Rosaura. Why? How is her flattery offensive?

5. What is Señora Ines's intended message at the end of the party? Is Rosaura's reaction fair? What is meant by "an infinitely delicate balance" between Señora Ines and Rosaura?

6. In what ways will this experience probably change Rosaura?

7. Explain the significance of the title.

Suggestions for Exploration and Writing

1. Write an essay about an act of condescension you have seen or experienced that was similar to Señora Ines's offering Rosaura money.

2. Write a character analysis contrasting the two mothers.

3. This story describes a class system based upon money. Does such a system exist where you live? Explain.

4. Compare Weaver's concern about his son's entering a hostile world, in "Improvisation for Piano," to the mother's concern about her daughter in "The Stolen Party."

5. Compare the condescension in this story to the husband's condescension to his wife in Gilman's "The Yellow Wallpaper."

Madison Smartt Bell (b. 1957)

A prolific young writer, Madison Smartt Bell by the age of thirty-four had published six novels and two collections of short stories. His fiction creates a dark world of often violent characters who frequently, like the narrator-protagonist of "Customs of the Country," live or die in the face of apparent hopelessness. Among Bell's novels are Waiting for the World *(1985);* The Year of Silence *(1987);* Save Me, Joe Louis *(1993);* Soldier's Joy, *which received a Lillian Smith Award; and* All Souls' Rising, *which received a National Book Award nomination.*

Customs of the Country   (1988)

1   I don't remember much about that place anymore. It was nothing but somewhere I came to put in some pretty bad time, though that was not what I had planned on when I went there. I had it in mind to improve things, but I didn't think you could fairly claim that's what I did. So that's one reason I might just as soon forget about it. And I didn't stay there all that long, not more than about nine months or so, about the same time, come to think, that the child I was there to try to get back had lived inside my body.

2   It was a cluster-housing thing a little ways north out of town from Roanoke, on a two-lane road that crossed the railroad cut and went about a mile farther up through the woods. The buildings looked something like a motel, a little raw still, though they weren't new. My apartment was no more than a place that would barely look all right and yet cost me little enough so I had something left over to give the lawyer. There was fresh paint on the walls and the trim in the kitchen and bathroom was in fair shape. And it was real quiet mostly, except that the man next door used to beat up his wife a couple of times a week. The place was soundproof enough I couldn't usually hear talk but I could hear yelling plain as day and when he got going good he would slam her bang into our common wall. If she hit in just the right spot it would send my pots and pans flying off the pegboard where I'd hung them above the stove.

3   Not that it mattered to me that the pots fell down, except for the noise and the time it took to pick them up again. Living alone like I was, I didn't have the heart to do much cooking and if I did fix myself something I mostly used an old iron skillet that hung there on the same wall. All the others I only had out for show. The whole apartment was done about the same way, made into something I kept spotless and didn't much care to use. I wore my hands out scrubbing everything clean and then saw to it that it stayed that way. I sewed slipcovers for that threadbare batch of Goodwill furniture I'd put in the place, and I hung curtains and found some sunshiny posters to tack on the walls, and I never cared a damn about any of it. It was an act, and I wasn't putting it on for me or for Davey, but for all the other people I expected to come to see it and judge it. And however good I could get it looking, it never felt quite right.

4   I felt even less at home there than I did at my job, which was waitressing three snake-bends of the counter at the Truckstops of America out at

the I-81 interchange. The supervisor was a man named Tim that used to know my husband Patrick from before we had the trouble. He was nice about letting me take my phone calls there and giving me time off to see the lawyer, and in most other ways he was a decent man to work for, except that now and then he would have a tantrum over something or other and try to scream the walls down. Still, it never went beyond yelling, and he always acted sorry once he got through. The other waitress on my shift was an older lady named Prissy, and I liked her all right in spite of the name.

5   We were both on a swing shift that rolled over every ten days, which was the main thing I didn't like about that job. The six-to-two I hated the worst because it would have me getting back to my apartment building around three in the morning, not the time it looked its best. It was the kind of place where at that time of night I could expect to find the deputies out there looking for somebody, or else some other kind of trouble. I never got to know the neighbors any too well, but a lot of them were pretty sorry—small-time criminals, dope dealers and thieves, none of them much good at whatever it was they did. There was one check forger that I knew of, and a man who would break into the other apartments looking for whiskey. One thing and another, along that line.

6   The man next door, the one that beat up his wife, didn't do crimes or work either that I ever heard. He just seemed to lay around the place, maybe drawing some kind of welfare. There wasn't a whole lot of him, he was just a stringy little man, hair and mustache a dishwater-brown, cheap green tatoos running up his arms. Maybe he was stronger than he looked, but I did wonder how come his wife would take it from him, since she was about a head taller and must have outweighed him an easy ten pounds. I might have thought she was whipping on him—stranger things have been known to go on—but she was the one that seemed like she might break out crying if you looked at her crooked. She was a big fine-looking girl with a lovely shape, and long brown hair real smooth and straight and shiny. I guess she was too hammered down most of the time to pay much attention to how she dressed, but still she had pretty brown eyes, big and long-lashed and soft, sort of like a cow's eyes, except I never saw a cow that looked that miserable.

7   At first I thought maybe I might make a friend of her, she was about the only one around there I felt like I might want to. Our paths crossed pretty frequent, either around the apartment building or in the Kwik Sack back toward town, where I'd find her running the register some days. But she was shy of me, shy of anybody I suppose. She would flinch if you did so much as say hello. So after a while I quit trying. She'd get hers about twice a week, maybe other times I wasn't around to hear it happen. It's a wonder all the things you can learn to ignore, and after a month or so I was that accustomed I barely noticed when they would start in. I would just wait till I thought they were good and through, and then get up and hang those pans back on the wall where they were supposed to go. And all the while I would just be thinking about some other thing, like what might be going on with my Davey.

8   The place where he had been fostered out was not all that far away, just about ten or twelve miles up the road, out there in the farm country. The people were named Baker. I never got to first names with them, just called them Mr. and Mrs. They were older than me, both just into their forties, and they didn't have any children of their own. The place was only a small farm but Mr. Baker grew tobacco on the most of it and I'm told he made it a paying thing. Mrs. Baker kept a milk cow or two and she grew a garden and canned in the old-time way. Thrifty people. They were real sweet to Davey and he seemed to like being with them pretty well. He had been staying there almost the whole two years, which was lucky too, since most children usually got moved around a whole lot more than that.

9   And that was the trouble, like the lawyer explained to me, it was just too good. Davey was doing too well out there. He'd made out better in the first grade than anybody would have thought. So nobody really felt like he needed to be moved. The worst of it was the Bakers had got to like him well enough they were saying they wanted to adopt him if they could. Well, it would have been hard enough for me without that coming into it.

10   Even though he was so close, I didn't go out to see Davey near as much as I would have liked to. The lawyer kept telling me it wasn't a good idea to look like I was pressing too hard. Better take it easy till all the evaluations came in and we had our court date and all. Still, I would call and go on out there maybe a little more than once a month, most usually on the weekends, since that seemed to suit the Bakers better. They never acted like it was any trouble, and they were always pleasant to me, or polite might be a better word yet. The way it sometimes seemed they didn't trust me did bother me a little. I would have liked to take him out to the movies a time or two, but I could see plain enough the Bakers wouldn't have been easy about me having him off their place.

11   But I can't remember us having a bad time, any of those times I went. He was always happy to see me, though he'd be quiet when we were in the house, with Mrs. Baker hovering. So I would get us outside quick as ever I could and, once we were out, we would just play like both of us were children. There was an open pasture, a creek with a patch of woods, a hay barn where we would play hide-and-go-seek. I don't know what all else we did, silly things mostly. That was how I could get near him the easiest, he didn't get a whole lot of playing in, way out there. The Bakers weren't what you would call playful and there weren't any other children living near. So that was the thing I could give him that was all mine to give. When the weather was good we would stay outside together most all the day and he would just wear me out. But over the winter those visits seemed to get shorter and shorter, like the days.

12   Davey called me Momma still, but I suppose he had come to think your mother was something more like a big sister or just some kind of a friend. Mrs. Baker was the one doing for him all the time. I don't know just what he remembered from before, or if he remembered any of the bad part. He would always mind me but he never acted scared around me, and if anybody says he did they lie. But I never really did get to know what he had

going on in the back of his mind about the past. At first I worried the Bakers might have been talking against me, but after I had seen a little more of them I knew they wouldn't have done anything like that, wouldn't have thought it right. So I expect whatever Davey knew about the other time he remembered on his own. He never mentioned Patrick hardly and I think he really had forgotten about him. Thinking back I guess he never saw that much of Patrick even when we were all living together. But Davey had Patrick's mark all over him, the same eyes and the same red hair.

13   Patrick had thick wavy hair the shade of an Irish setter's, and a big rolling mustache the same color. Maybe that was his best feature, but he was a good-looking man altogether, still is I suppose, though the prison haircut don't suit him. If he ever had much of a thought in his head I suspect he had knocked it clean out with dope, yet he was always fun to be around. I wasn't but seventeen when I married him and I didn't have any better sense myself. Right to the end I never thought anything much was the matter, all his vices looked so small to me. He was good-tempered almost all the time, and good with Davey when he did notice him. Never once did he raise his hand to either one of us. In little ways he was unreliable, late, not showing up at all, gone out of the house for days sometimes. Hindsight shows me he ran with other women, but I managed not to know anything about that at the time. He had not quite finished high school and the best job he could hold was being an orderly down at the hospital, but he made a good deal of extra money stealing pills out of there and selling them on the street.

14   That was something else I didn't allow myself to think on much back then. Patrick never told me a lot about it anyhow, always acted real mysterious about whatever he was up to in that line. He would disappear on one of his trips and come back with a whole mess of money, and I would spend up my share and be glad I had it too. I never thought much about where it was coming from, the money or the pills either one. He used to keep all manner of pills around the house, Valium and ludes and a lot of different kinds of speed, and we both took what we felt like whenever we felt in the mood. But what Patrick made the most on was Dilaudid. I used to take it without ever knowing what it really was, but once everything fell in on us I found out it was a bad thing, bad as heroin they said, and not much different, and it was what they gave Patrick most of his time for.

15   I truly was surprised to find out that it was the strongest dope we had, because I never really even felt like it made you all that high. You would just take one and kick back on a long slow stroke and whatever trouble you might have, it would not be able to find you. It came on like nothing but it was the hardest habit to lose, and I was a long time shaking it. I might be thinking about it yet if I would let myself, and there were times, all through the winter I spent in that apartment, I'd catch myself remembering the feeling.

16   You couldn't call it a real bad winter, there wasn't much snow or anything, but I was cold just about all the time, except when I was at work.
All I had in the apartment was some electric baseboard heaters, and they
cost too much for me to leave them running very long at a stretch. I'd
keep it just warm enough so I couldn't see my breath, and spent my time
in a hot bathtub or under a big pile of blankets on the bed. Or else I
would just be cold.

17   There was some kind of strange quietness about that place all during
the cold weather. If the phone rang it would make me jump. Didn't seem
like there was any TV or radio ever playing next door. The only sound
coming out of there was Susan getting beat up once in a while. That was
her name, a sweet name, I think. I found it out from hearing him say it,
which he used to do almost every time before he started on her. "Su-*san*,"
he'd call out, loud enough I could hear him through the wall. He'd do it
a time or two, he might have been calling her to him, and I suppose she
went. After that would come a bad silence that reminded you of a snake
being somewhere around. Then a few minutes' worth of hitting sounds
and then the big slam as she hit the wall, and the clatter of my pots falling
on the floor. He'd throw her at the wall maybe once or twice, usually when
he was about to get rough. By the time the pots had quit spinning on the
floor it would be real quiet over there again, and the next time I saw Susan
she'd be walking in that ginger way people have when they're hiding a
hurt, and if I said hello to her she'd give a little jump and look away.

18   After a while I quit paying it much mind, it didn't feel any different to
me than hearing the news on the radio. All their carrying on was not any
more to me than a bump in the rut I had worked myself into, going back
and forth from the job, cleaning that apartment till it hurt, calling up the
lawyer about once a week to find out what was happening, which never
was much. He was forever trying to get our case before some particular
doctor or social worker or judge who'd be more apt to help us than
another, so he said. I would call him up from the TOA, all eager to hear
what news he had, and every time it was another delay. In the beginning
I used to talk it all over with Tim or Prissy after I hung up, but after a
while I got out of the mood to discuss it. I kept ahead making those calls
but every one of them just wore out my hope a little more, like a drip of
water wearing down a stone. And little by little I got in the habit of thinking that nothing really was going to change.

19   Somehow or other that winter passed by, with me going from one
phone call to the next, going out to wait on that TOA counter, coming
home to shiver and hold hands with myself and lie awake all through the
night, or the day, depending what shift I was on. It was springtime, well
into warm weather, before anything really happened at all. That was when
the lawyer called *me,* for a change, and told me he had some people lined
up to see me at last.

20   Well, I was all ready for them to come visit, come see how I'd fixed up
my house and all the rest of my business to get set for having Davey back

with me again. But as it turned out, nobody seemed to feel like they were called on to make that trip. "I don't think that will be necessary" was what one of them said, I don't recall which. They both talked about the same, in voices that sounded like filling out forms.

21   So all I had to do was drive downtown a couple of times and see them in their offices. That child psychologist was the first and I doubt he kept me more than half an hour. I couldn't tell the point of most of the questions he asked. My second trip I saw the social worker, who turned out to be a black lady once I got down there, though I never could have told it over the phone. Her voice sounded like it was coming out of the TV. She looked me in the eye while she was asking her questions, but I couldn't tell a thing about what she thought. It wasn't till I was back in the apartment that I understood that she must have already had her mind made up.

22   That came to me in a sort of a flash, while I was standing in the kitchen washing out a cup. Soon as I walked back in the door I saw my coffee mug left over from breakfast, and I kicked myself for letting it sit out. I was giving it a hard scrub with a scouring pad when I realized it didn't matter anymore. I might just as well have dropped it on the floor and got what kick I could out of watching it smash, because it wasn't going to make any difference to anybody now. But all the same I rinsed it and set it in the drainer, careful as if it was an eggshell. Then I stepped backward out of the kitchen and took a long look around that cold shabby place and thought it might be for the best that nobody was coming. How could I have expected it to fool anybody else when it wasn't even good enough to fool me? A lonesomeness came over me, I felt like I was floating all alone in the middle of cold air, and then I began to remember some things I would just as soon have had not.

23   No, I never did like to think about this part, but I have had to think about it time and again, with never a break for a long, long time, because I needed to get to understand it at least well enough to believe it never would ever happen anymore. And I had come to believe that, in the end. If I hadn't, I never would have come back at all. I had found a way to trust myself again, though it took me a full two years to do it, and though of course it still didn't mean that anybody else would trust me.

24   What had happened was that Patrick went off on one of his mystery trips and stayed gone a deal longer than usual. Two nights away, I was used to that, but on the third I did start to wonder. He normally would have called at least, if he was going to be gone that long of a stretch. But I didn't hear a peep until about halfway through the fourth day. And it wasn't Patrick himself that called, but one of those public-assistance lawyers from downtown.

25   Seemed like the night before Patrick had got himself stopped on the interstate loop down there. The troopers said he was driving like a blind man, and he was so messed up on whiskey and ludes I suppose he must have been pretty near blind at that. Well, maybe he would have just lost his license or something like that, only that the backseat of the car was loaded up with all he had lately stole out of the hospital.

26   So it was bad. It was so bad my mind just could not contain it, and every hour it seemed to be getting worse. I spent the next couple of days running back and forth between the jail and that lawyer, and I had to haul Davey along with me wherever I went. He was too little for school and I couldn't find anybody to take him right then, though all that running around made him awful cranky. Patrick was just grim, he would barely speak. He already knew pretty well for sure that he'd be going to prison. The lawyer had told him there wasn't no use in getting a bondsman, he might just as well stay on in there and start pulling his time. I don't know how much he really saved himself that way, though, since what they ended up giving him was twenty-five years.

27   That was when all my troubles found me, quick. Two days after Patrick got arrested, I came down real sick with something. I thought at first it was a bad cold or the flu. My nose kept running and I felt so wore out I couldn't hardly get up off the bed and yet at the same time I felt real restless, like all my nerves had been scraped bare. Well, I didn't really connect it up to the fact that I'd popped the last pill in the house a couple of days before. What was really the matter was me coming off that Dilaudid, but I didn't have any notion of that at the time.

28   I was laying there in bed not able to get up and about ready to jump right out of my skin at the same time when Davey got the drawer underneath the stove open. Of course he was getting restless himself with all that had been going on, and me not able to pay him much mind. All our pots and pans were down in that drawer then, and he began to take them out one at a time and throw them on the floor. It made a hell of a racket, and the shape I was in, I felt like he must be doing it on purpose to devil me. I called out to him and asked him to quit. Nice at first: "You stop that, now, Davey. Momma don't feel good." But he kept right ahead. All he wanted was to have my attention, I know, but my mind wasn't working right just then. I knew I should get up and just go lead him away from there, but I couldn't seem to get myself to move. I had a picture of myself doing the right thing, but I just wasn't doing it. I was still lying there calling to him to quit and he was still banging those pots around and before long I was screaming at him outright, and starting to cry at the same time. But he never stopped a minute. I guess I had scared him some already and he was just locked into doing it, or maybe he wanted to drown me out. Every time he flung a pot it felt like I was getting shot at. And the next thing I knew I got myself in the kitchen someway and I was snatching him up off the floor.

29   To this day I don't remember doing it, though I have tried and tried. I thought if I could call it back then maybe I could root it out of myself and be shed of it for good and all. But all I ever knew was one minute I was grabbing a hold of him and the next he was laying on the far side of the room with his right leg folded up funny where it was broke, not even crying, just looking surprised. And I knew that it had to be me that threw him over there because as sure as hell is real there was nobody else around that could have done it.

30   I drove him to the hospital myself. I laid him straight on the front seat beside me and drove with one hand all the way so I could hold on to him with the other. He was real quiet and real brave the whole time, never cried the least bit, just kept a tight hold on my hand with his. Well, after a while, we got there and they ran him off somewhere to get his leg set and pretty soon the doctor came back out and asked me how it had happened.

31   It was the same hospital where Patrick had worked and I even knew that doctor a little bit. Not that being connected to Patrick would have done me a whole lot of good around there at that time. Still, I have often thought since then that things might have come out better for me and Davey both if I just could have lied to that man, but I was not up to telling a lie that anybody would be apt to believe. All I could do was start to scream and jabber like a crazy person, and it ended up I stayed in that hospital quite a few days myself. They took me for a junkie and I guess I really was one too, though I hadn't known it till that very day. And I never saw Davey again for a whole two years, not till the first time they let me go out to the Bakers'.

32   Sometimes you don't get but one mistake, if the one you pick is bad enough. Do as much as step in the road one time without looking, and your life could be over with then and there. But during those two years I taught myself to believe that this mistake of mine could be wiped out, that if I struggled hard enough with myself and the world I could make it like it never had been.

33   Three weeks went by after I went to see that social worker, and I didn't have any idea what was happening, or if anything was. Didn't call anybody, I expect I was afraid to. Then one day the phone rang for me out there at the TOA. It was the lawyer and I could tell right off from the sound of his voice I wasn't going to care for his news. Well, he told me all the evaluations had come in now, sure enough and they weren't running in our favor. They weren't against *me*, he made sure to say that, it was more like they were *for* the Bakers. And his judgment was it wouldn't pay me anything if we went on to court. It looked like the Bakers would get Davey for good anyhow, and they were likely to be easier about visitation if there wasn't any big tussle. But if I drug them into court, then we would have to start going back over the whole case history—

34   That was the word he used, *case history,* and it was around about there that I hung up. I went walking stiff-legged back across to the counter and just let myself sort of drop on a stool. Prissy had been covering my station while I was on the phone and she came right over to me then.

35   "What is it?" she said. I guess she could tell it was something by the look on my face.

36   "I lost him," I said.

37   "Oh, hon, you know I'm so sorry," she said. She reached out for my hand but I snatched it back. I know she meant it well but I just was not in the mood to be touched.

38   "There's no forgiveness," I said. I felt bitter about it. It had been a hard road for me to come as near forgiving myself as I ever could. And Davey forgave me, I really knew that, I could tell it in the way he acted when we were together. And if us two could do it, I didn't feel like it ought to be anybody else's business but ours. Tim walked up then and Prissy whispered something to him, and then he took a step nearer to me.

39   "I'm sorry," he told me.

40   "Not like I am," I said. "You don't know the meaning of the word."

41   "Go ahead and take off the rest of your shift if you feel like it," he said. "I'll wait on these tables myself, need be."

42   "I don't know it would make any difference," I said.

43   "Better take it easy on yourself," he said. "No use in taking it so hard. You're just going to have to get used to it."

44   "Is that a fact?" I said. And I lit myself a cigarette and turned my face away. We had been pretty busy, it was lunchtime, and the people were getting restless seeing all of us standing around there not doing a whole lot about bringing them their food. Somebody called out something to Tim, I didn't hear just what it was, but it set off one of his temper fits.

45   "Go on and get out of here if that's how you feel," he said. He was getting red in the face and waving his arms around to include everybody there in what he was saying. "Go on and clear out of here, every last one of you, and we don't care if you never come back. There's not one of you couldn't stand to miss a meal anyhow. Take a look at yourselves, you're all fat as hogs . . ."

46   It seemed like he might be going to keep it up a good while, and he had already said I could leave, so I hung up my apron and got my purse and I left. It was the first time he ever blew up at the customers that way, it had always been me or Prissy or one of the cooks. I never did find out what came of it all because I never went back to that place again.

47   I drove home in such a poison mood I barely knew I was driving a car or that there were any others on the road. I was ripe to get killed or kill somebody, and I wouldn't have cared much either way. I kept thinking about what Tim had said about having to get used to it. It came to me that I was used to it already, I really hadn't been all that surprised. That's what I'd been doing all those months, just gradually getting used to losing my child forever.

48   When I got back to the apartment I just fell in a chair and sat there staring across at the kitchen wall. It was in my mind to pack my traps and leave that place, but I hadn't yet figured out where I could go. I sat there a good while, I guess. The door was ajar from me not paying attention, but it wasn't cold enough out to make any difference. If I turned my head that way I could see a slice of the parking lot. I saw Susan drive up and park and come limping toward the building with an armload of groceries. Because of the angle I couldn't see her go into their apartment but I heard the door open and shut and after that it was quiet as a tomb. I kept on sitting there thinking about how used to everything I had got. There must have been generous numbers of other people too, I thought, who

had got themselves accustomed to all kinds of things. Some were used to taking the pain and the rest were used to serving it up. About half of the world was screaming in misery, and it wasn't anything but a habit.

49   When I started to hear the hitting sounds come toward me through the wall, a smile came on my face like it was cut there with a knife. I'd been expecting it, you see, and the mood I was in I felt satisfied to see what I had expected was going to happen. So I listened a little more carefully than I'd been inclined to do before. It was *hit hit hit* going along together with a groan and a hiss of the wind being knocked out of her. I had to strain pretty hard to hear that breathing part, and I could hear him grunt too, when he got in a good one. There was about three minutes of that with some little breaks, and then a longer pause. When she hit the wall it was the hardest she had yet, I think. It brought down every last one of my pots at one time, including the big iron skillet that was the only one I ever used.

50   It was the first time they'd managed to knock that skillet down, and I was so impressed that I went over and stood looking down at it like I needed to make sure it was a real thing. I stared at the skillet so long it went out of focus and started looking more like a big black hole in the floor. That's when it dawned on me that this was one thing I didn't really have to keep on being used to.

51   It took three or four knocks before he came to the door, but that didn't worry me at all. I had faith, I knew he was going to come. I meant to stay right there till he did. When he came, he opened the door wide and stood there with his arms folded and his face all stiff with his secrets. It was fairly dark behind him, they had all the curtains drawn. I had that skillet held out in front of me in both my hands, like maybe I had come over to borrow a little hot grease or something. It was so heavy it kept wanting to dip down toward the floor like a water witch's rod. When I saw he wasn't expecting anything, I twisted the skillet back over my shoulder like baseball players do their bat, and I hit him bang across the face as hard as I knew how. He went down and out at the same time and fetched up on his back clear in the middle of the room.

52   Then I went in after him with the skillet cocked and ready in case he made to get up. But he didn't look like there was a whole lot of fight left in him right then. He was awake, at least partly awake, but his nose was just spouting blood and it seemed like I'd knocked out a few of his teeth. I wish I could tell you I was sorry or glad, but I didn't feel much of anything really, just that high lonesome whistle in the blood I used to get when I took all that Dilaudid. Susan was sitting on the floor against the wall, leaning down on her knees and sniveling. Her eyes were red but she didn't have any bruises where they showed. He never did hit her on the face, that was the kind he was. There was a big crack coming down the wall behind her and I remember thinking it probably wouldn't be too much longer before it worked through to my side.

53   "I'm going to pack and drive over to Norfolk," I told her. I hadn't thought of it before but once it came out my mouth I knew it was what I

would do. "You can ride along with me if you want to. With your looks you could make enough money serving drinks to the sailors to buy that Kwik Sack and blow it up."

54   She didn't say anything, just raised her head up and stared at me kind of bug-eyed. And after a minute I turned around and went out. It didn't take me any time at all to get ready. All I had was a suitcase and a couple of boxes of other stuff. The sheets and blankets I just pulled off the bed and stuffed in the trunk all in one big wad. I didn't care a damn about that furniture, I would have lit it on fire on a dare.

55   When I was done I stuck my head back into the other apartment. The door was still open like I had left it. What was she doing but kneeling down over that son of a bitch and trying to clean off his face with a washrag. I noticed he was making a funny sound when he breathed, and his nose was still bleeding pretty quick, so I thought maybe I had broke it. Well, I can't say that worried me much.

56   "Come on now if you're coming, girl," I said. She looked up at me, not telling me one word, just giving me a stare out of those big cow eyes of hers like I was the one had been beating on her that whole winter through. And I saw then that they were both of them stuck in their groove and that she would not be the one to step out of it. So I pulled back out of the doorway and went on down the steps to my car.

57   I was speeding on the road to Norfolk, doing seventy, seventy-five. I'd have liked to gone faster if the car had been up to it. I can't say I felt sorry for busting that guy, though I didn't enjoy the thought of it either. I just didn't know what difference it had made, and chances were it had made none at all. Kind of a funny thing, when you thought about it that way. It was the second time in my life I'd hurt somebody bad, and the other time I hadn't meant to do it at all. This time I'd known what I was doing for sure, but I still didn't know what I'd done.

Questions for Discussion

1. Why does the **narrator** clean up the apartment even though she says she does not care how it looks and does not feel at home there? How does she feel when the expected social worker and other experts do not come to her apartment?

2. What events led the narrator to abuse Davey?

3. What does the narrator mean when she says, "That's what I'd been doing all those months, just gradually getting used to losing my child forever"? How has she attempted to get used to losing her child? How successful has she been?

4. Should the narrator be given custody of her son?

5. What kind of future can the narrator anticipate?

6. How would this story be different if it were told from another **point of view**? Could it be as effective?

Suggestions for Exploration and Writing

1. Is the narrator, a child-abuser and drug addict, simply an evil person, or does she have some redeeming qualities? Do you feel sympathy for her? If you do, explain how the writer has caused you to do so. If you have no sympathy for the narrator, explain why, citing specific passages from the story.

2. In spite of his abuse, Susan is very tender toward her husband and refuses to leave him. Using research on spousal abuse, explain the reasons for Susan's behavior.

3. What factors are most often the causes of child abuse? In an essay, propose methods for stopping child abuse or treatments for abused children.

Eric Skipper (b. 1967)

Born in Burlington, North Carolina, Eric Skipper attended The Georgia Institute of Technology and Florida State University. A student of Hispanic literature and culture, he has worked with Mexican immigrants, traveled extensively in Puerto Rico and Spain, and lectured on Spanish literature at various national conferences. Skipper currently teaches Spanish at Augusta State University in Georgia. "The Runt," his second published work of fiction, first appeared in The Roanoke Review.

THE RUNT (2001)

1   The summer after my second year of college I found myself overseeing a crew of Mexican migrant workers in a small farming community called Garrett. I had envisioned a sexier form of employment, perhaps on the shrimp docks of New Orleans or a ranch in Arizona or Texas, but low traveling funds and a copy of *Farmer's Bulletin* which happened into my hands ultimately kept me in the state.

2   Garrett is in south Georgia, which is the dry, flat part of the state. Farmers consider its location ideal on two counts. It is close enough to Valdosta or Tallahassee for a same-day trip when parts or equipment are needed, but far enough away to deter workers from making same-night quests for debauchery. The population, on average, is one-fourth Mexican; the number rises during the harvest season and drops during the off-months. The Garrett community, made up mostly of farmers and their families, is very tolerant of the migrant workers and views them as a vital ingredient of the economic landscape. They work hard and for cheap, for the most part. Mexican-on-Mexican crime is generally ignored by local authorities. Conflicts that cross cultural lines are usually blown out of proportion for a day or two, but then are forgotten just as quickly and the community resumes its prosaic, work-a-day routine.

3   A fat, bleary-eyed man named Moss picked me up at the bus station in Valdosta and introduced himself as my new foreman. During the drive to Garrett he informed me that I would be staying in town, in a small apartment connected to the back of one Mr. Banks's house. I protested smally, telling him that I hoped to live near the Mexicans in order to improve my Spanish.

4   "Believe me," he said, regarding me with those large, bleary eyes, "you don't want to live in that hell-hole. Do yourself a favor and stay in town. You'll get plenty chance to practice your Spanish."

5   I followed Moss's advice and took up residence at 120 Fuller Street. The Banks house was one of several stately residences on the street. It sat directly across from the Methodist church and was three blocks from the town's main strip. Mr. Banks—a squat, pallid-faced man with glasses and wispy white hair—seemed friendly enough at first. He assured me I would have the utmost privacy. Then he proceeded to inform me that his previous boarder used to eat six meals a day, drank a cheap brand of vodka, and caught the clap from a local girl. He said all this with a voice that was a little hungry-sounding.

6   "I'm an active practitioner of witchcraft," I told him.

7   It seemed to hold him at bay. Mr. Banks forced a weak smile, dismissed himself, and went back around the hedgerow toward the front of the house. I don't know if he kept tabs on me during the next three months, but I never caught a trace of him except when I paid the rent.

8   After arranging my room I went out for dinner. Coming from the Banks house the tops of the town's old brick buildings, the courthouse belfry, and two church steeples are visible. From that angle and distance the establishment of Garrett makes for an appeasing view. But once downtown the magical quality disappears and drab reality, in the form of broken sidewalks and deserted buildings—a few of them completely gutted—sets in. I had supper in a trailer-diner called Rhonda's and went back to my flat and read until I fell asleep.

9   It was still dark when Moss came to pick me up the next morning.

10 "You've wrangled yourself a plumb easy job," he told me when we arrived at the fields. His breath had the rotten smell of stale tobacco and whisky. Suddenly I felt like the chicken-fried steak from Rhonda's was stuck in my esophagus. Moss flipped on the cab light and handed me a grid sheet.

11 "You put the names of the workers here. Out here you put a mark for each bucket they fill so we know how much to pay them at the end of the day. Make sure they fill them to the top. Keep an eye out for bruised fruit. Especially the tomatoes. Sometimes they get careless and just toss them in the bucket."

12 I nodded and said that it sounded easy enough.

13 "I know it sounds rather simplistic," Moss continued, "but somebody's got to do it. Somebody's got to be here to tell them when to take breaks and when to go back to work. Somebody's got to make sure they show up in the morning. You'll pay them at the end of the day. I'll give you a bank

this afternoon. The schedule goes like this . . ." Moss laid out the day for me. I expressed my amusement at the fact that there was a break from eleven-thirty to two for "siesta."

14   Moss explained, "It keeps them out of the sun during the hottest part of the day."

15   We got out of Moss's truck. Murky light had begun to crawl up the eastern sky. The morning air was warm and balmy. The tomato plants had a strong acrid smell that grew stronger when an occasional breeze stirred the leaves. A pair of headlights came bouncing down the rutted road that parted the fields. Moss looked at his watch. "Right on time."

16   A battered pick-up pulled up and nine sleepy Mexicans tumbled out of it.

17   "Who's missing?" asked Moss.

18   A young, athletic-looking Mexican with longish hair said, "Joaqúin." He looked at me. "Who is he?"

19   "This is Willis," said Moss. "He's come here to whip your sorry asses into shape."

20   The Mexican grinned and flashed a gold tooth. "She-it!" he said twangily.

21   The Mexicans filed automatically toward Moss's truck and each took two five-gallon buckets from the back. They straggled toward the edge of the field while pulling on canvas gloves. After a few moments of shoving and bickering, each took a row and bent silently to work. The leathery plants rustled in response. The ripe tomatoes made soft plopping noises in the buckets.

22   Moss said, "They're like little kids. They're funny in their ways sometimes." He hiccuped and pounded his chest with a beefy hand. He shrugged. "It's a different culture and they do things different. Leave them be and they usually work things out among themselves. Now, the one that asked about you—his name is Mauricio. He's a good kid and his English is pretty good. Actually, there's not a bad one in the lot. I'd set up shop under one of these trees if I were you. Help me unload these buckets, will you?"

23   We took several stacks of buckets from the truck bed and put them under an oak tree. Moss pulled out a folding chair and handed it to me along with a clipboard and a whistle on a string. He turned and pointed across the field at a dense line of trees.

24   "Sometimes they like to go to the river during break. Use the whistle when you need to. I'll be back by eleven to pick up what they've picked. We'll go get lunch in town. There's a great little place called Rhonda's."

25   Within a couple of days I learned all the Mexicans' names and there developed a healthy affection between us, expressed mostly through cursing or vulgarities. Needless to say, I was never able to use the Spanish I learned that summer in a practical setting. I grew bored watching the Mexicans' straw hats bobbing in the fields and got a membership at the local library and commenced a summer of wide and varied reading. This is not to say that I ceased to give proper attention to my Mexicans. They were an entertaining clan, to say the least. During breaks Mauricio took great

pleasure in relating the latest drunk-fest or amorous episode that had taken place in Village Heights, the trailer park in which most of Garrett's Mexicans lived. I was certain Mauricio embellished a good deal because of the outlandish nature of his stories. A fifth of tequila does not increase one's stamina and a deer stand is not a viable place for making love. The other workers, who knew minimal English, if any, had no way of keeping him in check. Nevertheless, they crowded around Mauricio and myself grinning and nodding as if they understood every word.

26   One worker in particular caught my attention from the first day. He was a skinny, black boy named Rafa. He could not have been more than sixteen, though he swore he was twenty. His complexion was rough and his eyes were large and black and mouse-like in their nervousness. There was always a lazy idiot's grin pasted across his thick, purple lips. His limbs were loose and gangly and he seemed to flop about whenever he went into motion. He was a very slow worker, the slowest in fact, and the lazy vacant smile gave the impression that somehow he was proud of the fact. He was last in line for everything: last to drop down from the old blue pick-up in the mornings, last to climb back in at eleven-thirty for the siesta break, last to collect his pay at the end of the day. The thing that perturbed me the most was the fact that he served as the butt of his coworkers' every joke. He was a proverbial goat for all occasions.

27   One morning after a week on the job I witnessed a terrible thing. One of the Mexicans—a sloppy, bearded man named Octavio—had lost a bet on some sporting event the night before. That morning he beat Rafa to near unconsciousness, out of principle it seemed. When he finished, he stepped back and laughed roughly. Then he commenced to cleaning his bloody knuckles on his shirttails. The other Mexicans picked up the laughter where Octavio had left it. They stepped over and around the lank form that lay in the dust and patted Octavio on the back and congratulated him. They ushered him toward the field like a boxer's entourage. I shivered despite the morning heat.

28   I helped Rafa over to my tree where he lay on the ground. He made croaking noises and rolled from side to side.

29   "Are you okay?" I asked.

30   "Jes, okay!" he grunted. He grinned up at me lazily.

31   In twenty minutes he was standing and ready to go back to work. I handed him his straw hat, which had been crushed during the fight.

32   "Take it easy," I said. I pointed at his eye, which was swollen shut. I spoke slowly, touched him on the shoulder. "That doesn't look so good. You'd better clean it up a little. Rest some more until you feel better."

33   He was a pathetic sight. His shirt had been ripped open and fresh welts stood up on his neck and chest. His lower lip was split open and shiny with fresh blood. He took his shapeless hat and pressed it down over his stiff black hair so the brim drooped limply over his eyes. He did not bother to tilt his head so he could see me when he spoke.

34   "Jew no tell Mister Moss nothing, okay?"

35   "You speak English," I said. "Why didn't you say so?"

36   Rafa did not respond. He stood there waiting. All I could see were his smiling cut mouth and his narrow, black chin smeared with drying blood.

37   "Sure, I won't tell Moss anything," I said finally.

38   Rafa retrieved his buckets and limped across the field. One of the workers raised his head and said something, and there resulted a chorus of laughter. Out in the open the laughter had a faint, metallic quality, like pebbles dropping into a pail. As I watched Rafa join the others, I tried to make sense of it. I came to the conclusion that I did not understand the mistreatment, but I resolved to do something nice for the kid.

39   That same afternoon Mauricio invited me to Village Heights for supper and drinking. After hearing the stories, curiosity had gotten the better of me and I accepted. That evening I stopped by Billy's Bait & Supply—one of those big country stores that carries almost every item imaginable—and purchased a straw cowboy hat for Rafa. I sized it by finding one that fit me and buying the next size down. It was a good hat, arrow shaped with a red feather protruding from the wide black band. I also bought a six-pack of beer and I set off walking.

40   I arrived at Village Heights in ten minutes. It was a squalid little community comprised of thirty or so run-down trailers facing in all directions and arranged in no particular order. It sat just outside the city limits and low off the road behind a narrow stretch of cedars and pines, as if whoever had put it there did not want it to be visible from the road. Ash heaps and rusty vehicles dotted the landscape. Clusters of spindly pines grew up here and there, and the grass grew tall and stiff against the trailers and brushed against the sides when the wind blew. The atmosphere was a festive one. Everyone was outside. Small, brown children ran about throwing and chasing balls and playing tag. Groups of men were clustered here and there, chatting or tinkering with cars. The spicy smells of meals cooking drifted smokily from the open doors of trailers. Brassy ranchero and cumbia music competed from several directions.

41   "Hey, gringo!"

42   Mauricio and several other Mexicans were standing near the open hood of a rusty Mustang. Mauricio approached and shook my hand.

43   "Maybe jew know some of these guys."

44   I nodded. Three of the Mexicans worked with our picking crew. The bearded Octavio was one of them. I shook hands with each of them, seven in all including Mauricio.

45   Mauricio noticed the new hat. "Ah. Jew buy one, I see."

46   I fingered the rigid brim of the hat, turning it in my hands. "This is for Rafa. His took a beating today. It wasn't in very good shape to begin with."

47   A shadow crossed Mauricio's face. "Rafa live there," he said, motioning toward the road. Then he pointed at the nearest trailer, a dingy yellow one with a square of cardboard in place of one of the windows. "This is my house," he said. "Come in and see. You meet now my wife."

48   I followed Mauricio toward the trailer and some of the other Mexicans fell in behind me. A faint, high-pitched whimpering came from beneath the trailer. I stopped.

49 "You got pups," I said.

50 "Jes," Mauricio said proudly. He moved from the steps and lifted one of the tin underpinnings. "Come see."

51 I squatted next to Mauricio and peered into the darkness under the trailer. A brown and white mongrel bitch was sprawled on her side in the cool dirt. Her puppies squirmed and writhed against her warm belly, suckling in one heavy mass. I reached my hand in and the mongrel began licking it slowly. She regarded me with wet, affectionate eyes.

52 "How many are there?" I asked.

53 "I don't know."

54 "Look at this little one," I said. I lifted by the scruff the only pup that was not participating in the feast. It drew its hind legs up and began whimpering hysterically. It was smaller and darker than the others. Its eyelids were still clamped shut. I cupped it against my chest and caressed it with my fingers.

55 "You know you can feed him with an eyedropper," I said. "He'll drink that way. He's still plenty lively."

56 Mauricio nodded. "Strong one live, weak one die," he said. "I no can do nothing." His face was pleasant but unyielding.

57 I made a little crease between the warm, wriggling bodies and placed the runt facing his mother's teats. He quickly disappeared beneath the squirming bodies of his livelier brothers and sisters. So he would not suffocate. I fished him out and put him on the edge where I had found him.

58 "Feed him warm milk with an eye dropper," I repeated. "He can live yet."

59 "Jes." Mauricio stood up and dropped the tin into place. "Come inside. Meet my wife."

60 I followed him up the steps into the trailer. Three of the Mexicans, including Octavio, were already sitting in the small living room. The others were gone. The walls of the living room were decorated with calendars and colorful drapery. The vinyl sofa that sat against one wall was torn in several places and the arms were peppered with cigarette burns. Several cheap, vinyl-colored kitchen chairs sat about the perimeter of the room. In the kitchen a broad-hipped, dark woman flitted adroitly about, transferring dishes from the stove to the table. Mauricio nodded in that direction.

61 "This is my wife, Yolanda."

62 Yolanda looked up from her steamy work and smiled at me. A few strands of hair were plastered to her moist forehead. Her large face was petal-shaped; her laughing, black eyes gave me the feeling that we shared in some secret.

63 I nodded. "Willis," I said.

64 "Give her the beer," said Mauricio. "She put in refrigerator." He spoke to Yolanda in Spanish. She laughed aloud and took my six-pack. She opened a bottle of Tecate and gave it to me.

65 "Please, sit," said Mauricio. "We eat now."

66 There was not room for all of us. Mauricio and I sat down. Octavio joined us and Yolanda took the seat closest to the stove. The other two Mexicans prepared their plates at the table and went to sit in the living

room. The table was laden with steaming dishes, a couple of which I did not recognize. We served ourselves.

67   "This *real* Mexican food," Mauricio told me. "Not like the food you get in a restaurant." He proceeded to identify nearly everything I put on my plate. "This—*real* enchilada; this—*real* chorizo; this here—*real* chiles rellenos." There was a plate of lettuce and freshly sliced tomatoes. "This," said Mauricio, picking up a cold slab of tomato and plopping it in his mouth, "this come from work."

68   It was the best food I had eaten since I arrived in Garrett. We ate quietly, ravenously, and drank long swigs of beer. Yolanda kept getting up to bring us more tortillas and beer. I noticed that Octavio's manners matched his appearance. He ate hunched over his plate so that all that was visible was the top of his dirty, matted head. He shoved food onto his tortilla with his round fingers and alternately made snorting and slurping noises. There was a warm, wet towel for us to clean our hands. I was happy to see that Octavio did not use it, as he occasionally cleaned his dripping beard on his shirtsleeve.

69   Mauricio said, "See this. I am one lucky man. *Buena suerte,* yeah? I have the good food, and I have *this.*" He whacked Yolanda's rump as she was sitting down. "You like this one, eh?"

70   Yolanda smiled coyly across the table at me.

71   Octavio gave one final snort and shoved his chair noisily away from the table. His eyes glazed over and his mouth curved into a satisfied smile. He slid down low in his chair and regarded us through half-closed eyelids. I swear he began to make a low growling noise, like the purring of a large cat. The noise did not let up once. I looked at his plate. He had mopped it clean with a tortilla so it looked like it had never been touched.

72   Yolanda giggled. Mauricio said, "Big man eat big, no?"

73   I nodded toward Octavio and the men in the living room. "Do they live here with you?"

74   "Jes," said Mauricio. "It make five of us."

75   "Do the others work?"

76   "Sometime. Sometime they here all day."

77   Yolanda got up with a stack of dirty dishes and began plunging them vigorously into the sudsy water in the sink.

78   As we spoke I noticed that Octavio's slotted eyes were focused on the new hat which I had left on the counter. Every so often his eyes glinted and shifted over to me as his fleshy lips flattened into an increased smile. The purring never stopped.

79   "Where does Rafa live?" I asked. "I want to take the hat to him before it gets late."

80   "You come back, jes?" Mauricio implored. He pointed at the row of cabinets over the sink. "I have here *real* tequila."

81   I went outside. Lilac-colored light was diminishing over the fields in the west. The buzz sawing of crickets rose and fell in perfect intervals. Most of the children had gone inside but the men were still standing about in their small groups. Their forms were dark and anonymous in the fading light.

Now and then the glower of a cigarette exposed one of their brooding faces. As I walked past them their voices were tinny and peaceful in the dark.

82   I found Rafa's trailer, number eighteen. I strode across the warped plywood of the porch and knocked on the door. There came a hollow booming of footsteps. An unfamiliar Mexican appeared at the door. The yellow light from inside flooded past his square frame.

83   "Is Rafa home?" I asked.

84   The man retreated inside and shortly Rafa's bruised, smiling face appeared at the door. He did not seem surprised to see me.

85   "Buenas noches," I said. "I brought you something."

86   Rafa's good eye flickered upon the hat I offered him. Then it resumed the flat, somber quality that matched his voice.

87   "Thank you. It is one good hat."

88   "It's nothing," I said. "I've been at Mauricio's eating dinner. We're going to drink tequila now. Come join us. Mauricio won't mind."

89   Rafa regarded me with a puzzled expression that I almost mistook for one of amusement. It was hard to tell with that grin. "No," he said. "No tequila for me." He stood there holding the hat against his chest, grinning stupidly and regarding me with his one good eye. His lip had swollen considerably, and the cut on it had opened a quarter inch and turned black.

90   "Suit yourself. You're not a pretty sight for going out anyway." I instinctively reached out and patted his thin shoulder. "If you change your mind, you know where we'll be."

91   "Jes," he said.

92   "Well, goodnight."

93   Rafa closed the door and I stood on the porch for a moment thinking that he had not even tried on the hat. I thought about knocking again, but decided against it.

94   I went back to Mauricio's and learned never to doubt the veracity of his stories again. We began doing shots of mescal. Mauricio and I made a grand ordeal of sharing the worm on the bottom. Mauricio played cumbia music and tried to teach me to dance. We must have made a pathetic sight because he was trying to dance the woman's part. All the while he was telling me, "Now jew do it. Now jew do it." He finally turned me over to Yolanda. The smell of her perfume and the feel of her broad, swinging hips made me feel dizzy. She kept leaning back and regarding me with those black, shining eyes. Her complexion was a bit rutty and over-done with make-up, but the smiling, eager expression superseded it. Octavio climbed on the flimsy kitchen table and began spinning in circles. When a heavy-set man named José tried to join him the table collapsed and Octavio hit his head on the broken refrigerator handle. It did not even faze him. He sat on the floor grinning and holding the back of his bleeding head and saying, "Lu, lu, lu, lu, lu, lu!"

95   If I had been in a bigger town I might have been picked up for public drunkenness during the walk home. Instead all I got were a few honks from passers-by and some unoriginal obscenities from a carful of cruising

teenagers. Once I got home I was cognizant enough to be thankful that the next day was Sunday. I lay down on my bed fully clothed. The first thing I saw upon closing my eyes was Yolanda's wide, tapered face and laughing eyes.

96   When I returned to work on Monday I was not surprised to see Octavio wearing the hat I had given Rafa, and Rafa wearing his old one. Octavio looked ridiculous in the new hat. It was too small for his big head but he had jammed it on anyway. It pinched and pulled his skin upward and gave his eyes a slanted Oriental's look. To make matters worse, Rafa's lip looked like it had been freshly burst open. And while the swelling in his injured eye had gone down, his opposite cheekbone was now blue and puffy. I was annoyed but tried to forget about it.

97   Due to the exceptional heat, the Mexicans took their morning break by the large river which twisted through the middle of the fields. The river was crowded by thick growth of cypress and oaks and its shade was damp and pleasant. The water stayed muddy from irrigating. Since it moved quickly it also stayed very cold. On hot afternoons some the Mexicans would go for a swim. After twenty minutes in the sun their clothes would be dry again.

98   When I blew the whistle for the nine o'clock break the Mexicans moved toward the line of lush green foliage that parted the thousands of acres that we harvested along with other crews. When I arrived a few of them were already wading barefoot on the slippery rocks where the water swirled and lapped against the craggy black rocks that jutted out of the water.

99   I sat on the high embankment overlooking the river beside Mauricio. As we watched down on the horseplay Mauricio poked me with an elbow.

100   "How jew feeling today, boss?"

101   "Fine, today," I said. "Yesterday was a different story though. I didn't get up till noon."

102   "Jew no like the mescal, eh?"

103   "It's fine when I'm drinking it."

104   Mauricio laughed. "When jew leave Octavio run naked outside. He scare the neighbors."

105   "Well, I'm glad I got out when I did."

106   While we were talking a splashing battle began. Within a few seconds it had escalated to a full-fledged war. The Mexicans that were standing on the bank got wet and began jumping in to exact revenge. The water boiled with flailing limbs as they climbed on each other's backs and tried to push one another into the deep part of the river. I saw Octavio drag Rafa to the deep water and hold his head under. The longer he held Rafa's head the less horseplay there was. The Mexicans stopped their roughhousing and began whooping and shouting encouragement. Octavio snatched the boy's head out of the water long enough for him to gasp briefly and submerged it again.

107   "Tell him to stop," I told Mauricio.

108   Mauricio held up a hand as if to silence me. The hooting and shouting continued.

109   I slid down the embankment and splashed into the water. "Let go of him," I said. I shoved Octavio hard and he sprawled backwards into the water. Rafa came up coughing and sputtering. He limped over to the bank

where he flopped down on the sand and continued to cough and wheeze. When he caught his breath and saw me standing in the water an expression of alarm came into his face. The Mexicans had grown silent and I could feel them watching me. A bird overhead sounded three shrill notes. I looked at my watch.

110   "Break's over," I said.

111   The Mexicans resumed their work. The sun climbed up the sky. I shifted my chair close to the trunk of the poplar I was sitting under. Periodically one of the Mexicans would lug his buckets full of tomatoes over to check them in. I tried to concentrate on Clark's *The Ox-Bow Incident* but my thoughts kept turning to Rafa.

112   When he finally came to check in, I demanded angrily, "What's wrong with you? Why do you take it?"

113   He gave me that lazy grin and didn't answer.

114   "For Christ's sake," I exclaimed. "Buck up. Don't let them run all over you."

115   I felt like giving him a good shaking. I grabbed both his shoulders, but then stopped. I reached into my pocket and withdrew a jack knife. It was curved, with a bone handle grooved for gripping. It had been a gift from my father. I seized Rafa's hand and placed the knife in it.

116   The insipid smile faded from Rafa's lips and his eyes flashed intently. He opened the knife and tilted it so the shiny blade glinted in the sun.

117   "Next time that troll messes with you, whip it out," I instructed. "Don't use it, for God's sake, but—at least it will make him think." I clapped him hard on the shoulder. "Grow a spine, for Christ's sake! Don't act like a señorita."

118   Rafa looked at the knife for a long time before folding it and sliding it into his pocket. He looked at me and his eyes shone with sharpness and purpose. They were a man's eyes, weighted with responsibility.

119   "It is one good knife," he said. He turned to the stacks of buckets, separated two of them, and strode across the field.

120   At eleven-thirty I whistled for the siesta break. I called Mauricio aside as he came from the field. "Why is everybody down on the kid?"

121   Mauricio regarded me questioningly for a moment and then broke into an easy laugh. "The river? It happen all the time. They like to play."

122   "I'm not just talking about the river," I said. I felt the anger beginning to well in me again.

123   "Rafa still one little kid," said Mauricio. "We make him grow up. We make him one man." He watched me closely and chuckled. "Jew no worry. He okay."

124   As the Mexicans piled into the old pick-up, I saw Octavio clamp a large hand around the back of Rafa's neck. He shoved the boy aside and climbed onto the tailgate ahead of him. I caught a glimpse of Rafa's face and saw that he was not smiling.

125   A week passed without a major incident. I felt I had played a part in bringing relative peace to our crew and rewarded myself by buying a bicycle at a garage sale. I rewarded Moss actually. I didn't want to burden him with

transporting me to and from work the rest of the summer, although I don't think he would have minded. Riding the bicycle felt good and the extra time in the sun turned me a walnut shade of brown. Every so often I felt obliged to step back and marvel at my exquisite freedom. I had my own place and was making money. I ate and read what I wanted, and the bicycle enabled me to come and go as I pleased. I had supper with Mauricio again and found Yolanda as captivating as ever. When I left she kissed me and left a burning sensation on my lips that lasted an hour. Garrett, Georgia, was certainly no New Orleans or Arizona, but it had a strange way of growing on you.

126   One afternoon Moss's truck came tearing in from the main road. It jerked to a stop beside my tree and the swirling dust from the road enveloped it momentarily.

127   Moss got out of the truck. He waved a clipboard at the dust. "I got a couple of discrepancies with the numbers."

128   "I'll take a look." I blew my whistle for the four o'clock break and watched the Mexicans move slowly toward the river and disappear into the foliage. I thought about asking Moss to walk across the field with me, but then I looked at his flushed, swollen face and his sweat-soaked shirt and thought better of it.

129   "How are they treating you?" Moss asked.

130   "Things are under control," I said.

131   Moss squinted after the Mexicans as they retreated into the trees. "They're funny in their ways," he mused. "They got their own codes and such."

132   I took the clipboard from Moss and winked at him. "Let's see what you've got. It's probably your math again."

133   After Moss drove away I was about to blow my whistle when the Mexicans came trailing out of the trees. They never started back to work without me telling them. I sensed something was wrong and started across the field in a half-run. I drew near and saw the confused look on Mauricio's face. He stepped in front of me and grabbed my arm.

134   "He no want to," he cried. "He no want to do it."

135   I made a quick head count, and tore away from Mauricio's grasp. I sprinted toward the river. I found Octavio curled in a ball on the bank. He was shivering and making a high-pitched whimpering noise like a wounded beast. His arm was sliced open. The blood that ran from it had formed a dark circle in the sand. He was oblivious to the cut. He stared at the water with bolted eyes.

136   "Where is he?" I demanded. I slid down the embankment and lifted Octavio by the shirt. "Where is he?" When he did not respond I struck him hard across the face. "Where is he?"

137   Octavio offered no resistance. He slouched against my grasp and continued to whimper as if I had never touched him. His glazed eyes remained fixed on the water.

138   I looked at the water and saw Rafa's straw hat bobbing against some rocks. I let go of Octavio and crawled numbly up the embankment. The other Mexicans stood in a huddle twenty yards from the trees.

139   "What happened?" I asked Mauricio.

140   His voice was frightened and distant. "They start to play like last time. Rafa take out one knife." He looked at me earnestly. "Octavio no want to do it."

141   I looked across the field, at the neat tree-tufts along the horizon. "Did Octavio use the knife?" I asked.

142   Mauricio shook his head. "One rock."

143   "Where is the knife?"

144   "In the water, I think."

145   I looked at the sky. It was overcast with silver, rugged-looking clouds. The air was too muggy for rain. The tomato plants rustled in a breeze and their smell came up sharp and peppery. The Mexicans stood behind Mauricio like a throng of damp puppies. They looked back and forth between Mauricio and myself with wide, frightened eyes.

146   "I'll call Moss in a few minutes," I said. "I'll think of what to tell him. Octavio can't go to a hospital. We'll have to patch him up ourselves."

147   Mauricio regarded me gratefully. "Jes, we fix it!"

148   "Go get him, then get these guys back to work."

149   After the Mexicans had hauled Octavio out of the gorge I picked up an empty bucket and returned to the river alone. The battered old hat was gone from the rocks. I walked downstream a hundred yards and could not find it. I went back up to the river, and as I washed the blood from the sand I felt as if I were covering up my own crime.

Questions for Discussion

1. Explain why, in this south Georgia town, "Mexican-on-Mexican crime" would be ignored. What attitude is suggested by the townspeople's ignoring of Mexican-on-Mexican crime and the idea that Mexicans are "like little kids"?

2. Why didn't Willis, the narrator, stop Octavio from beating Rafa instead of choosing just to be nice to him? Why doesn't he retrieve the cowboy hat from Octavio?

3. Why does Moss claim about the Mexicans, "It's a different culture and they do things different. Leave them be and they usually work things out among themselves"? What does this statement suggest about Moss? Why does Willis ignore it?

4. What is the significance of Willis's calling the laborers "my Mexicans"?

5. Why does Octavio beat Rafa? Why do the others then treat Octavio as a hero and laugh at Rafa? What tendency of some people is suggested by this situation?

6. How are the other laborers' attitudes toward Rafa mirrored by Mauricio's attitude toward the runt puppy?

7. Why does Willis give Rafa the new hat? the knife? Should he have anticipated the results of his gifts? Explain.

8. Why does Willis help to cover up the crime? Should he feel as though he is "covering up [his] own crime"? How much responsibility should Willis take for what has happened?

Suggestions for Exploration and Writing

1. If you have ever experienced a similar dilemma, write an essay describing it and telling how you resolved it.

2. In an essay, describe what you would have done if you had been in Willis's place, or write a character analysis of Willis.

3. After examining the structure and foreshadowing in the story, write an essay on the style.

4. Compare the lone puppy with Rafa. What characteristics do they have in common?

5. In an essay, define what you consider to be a *runt*.

POETRY

William Shakespeare (1564–1616)

The biography of William Shakespeare precedes Othello.

SONNET 73   (1609)

That time of year thou mayst in me behold
When yellow leaves, or none, or few, do hang
Upon those boughs which shake against the cold,
Bare ruined choirs, where late the sweet birds sang.
5   In me thou seest the twilight of such day
As after sunset fadeth in the west;
Which by and by black night doth take away,
Death's second self that seals up all in rest.
In me thou seest the glowing of such fire,
10   That on the ashes of his youth doth lie,
As the deathbed whereon it must expire,
Consumed with that which it was nourished by.
      This thou perceiv'st, which makes thy love more strong,
      To love that well, which thou must leave ere long.

Questions for Discussion

1. What three analogies does the speaker use in the poem?

2. What do these analogies suggest about the speaker's attitude toward growing old?

3. How does the concluding couplet change your perception of the speaker's attitude?

Suggestion for Exploration and Writing

1. Write an essay in which you explain what it would mean to you to grow old with someone or to love someone who is near death.

Percy Bysshe Shelley (1792–1822)

Shelley, born in Field Place, Sussex, England, was adored by his six brothers and sisters; consequently, he demanded adoration in later years. He was expelled from Oxford along with his friend Thomas Jefferson Hogg because of his revolutionary philosophy. From that point on, Shelley led a fascinating life, marrying twice and enjoying a friendship with Romantic hero George Gordon, Lord Byron. He is known for his propaganda writing, lovely lyrics, and intellectual convictions.

OZYMANDIAS   (1818)

I met a traveller from an antique land
Who said: Two vast and trunkless legs of stone
Stand in the desert . . . Near them, on the sand,
Half sunk, a shattered visage lies, whose frown,
5 And wrinkled lip, and sneer of cold command,
Tell that its sculptor well those passions read
Which yet survive, stamped on these lifeless things,
The hand that mocked them, and the heart that fed:
And on the pedestal these words appear:
10 "My name is Ozymandias, king of kings:
Look on my works, ye Mighty, and despair!"
Nothing beside remains. Round the decay
Of that colossal wreck, boundless and bare
The lone and level sands stretch far away.

Questions for Discussion

1. What kind of king must Ozymandias have been?

2. What is meant by "shattered visage" and "the heart that fed"?

3. How did the sculptor mock Ozymandias? What is ironic about the inscription on the pedestal?

4. Are *hand* and *heart* in line 8 **synecdoche** or **metonymy?**

5. What is the form of this poem?

6. What is the theme of "Ozymandias"?

Suggestions for Exploration and Writing

1. Write your epitaph. Then discuss the effect this epitaph might have on later generations of your family or on society in general.

2. Ozymandias is the Greek name for Ramses II, an Egyptian ruler who erected a huge statue in his likeness. In later generations, however, the statue does not reflect a favorable image of Ramses II. Discuss how art reflects an era.

Edwin Arlington Robinson (1869–1935)

Edwin Arlington Robinson's life provided him with a wealth of material for his poetic portraits of lonely and tragic misfits. After a series of financial and physical tragedies decimated his family, Robinson moved to Greenwich Village in New York City, where for a time he was practically destitute. Although he received Pulitzer prizes for his later work, primarily book-length **blank verse** *poems on the Arthurian legends, Robinson is best remembered for his Tilbury Town poems, portraits of imaginary misfits who inhabit a town based on his hometown of Gardiner, Maine.*

Richard Cory (1897)

Whenever Richard Cory went down town,
We people on the pavement looked at him:
He was a gentleman from sole to crown,
Clean favored, and imperially slim.

5 And he was always quietly arrayed,
And he was always human when he talked;
But still he fluttered pulses when he said,
"Good-morning," and he glittered when he walked.

And he was rich—yes, richer than a king—
10 And admirably schooled in every grace:
In fine, we thought that he was everything
To make us wish that we were in his place.

So on we worked, and waited for the light,
And went without the meat, and cursed the bread;
15 And Richard Cory, one calm summer night,
Went home and put a bullet through his head.

Questions for Discussion

1. From what **point of view** is the poem written?

2. What do the people see when they look at Richard Cory?

Suggestions for Exploration and Writing

1. Situations and appearances are sometimes deceiving. Using the poem as the basis for an essay, discuss why the public makes assumptions about the seemingly rich lives of public figures.

2. Write an essay on the **symbols, images,** and sound devices used in this poem—the overall symbolism of kingship; the **metonymy** and **metaphor;** the **alliteration, assonance, consonance, rhyme,** and **rhythm.** Explain how these devices help to emphasize the observers' misperception of Richard Cory.

Paul Laurence Dunbar (1872–1906)

Paul Dunbar was born in Dayton, Ohio, to former slaves; however, his father, Joshua, escaped to Canada and fought in the Union army. Dunbar later wrote for The Tattler, *printed by his classmate, Orville Wright. Wanting more than Dayton could offer, Dunbar toured Europe giving readings of his poetry. He wrote poems, among them the collection* Oak and Ivy *(1892); novels, such as* The Sport of Gods *(1902); and musicals, including* Dream Lovers: An Operatic Romance *(1898). Dunbar gained recognition for his diverse accomplishments and for the use of dialect in his poems. His themes include the overt oppression of African Americans in all aspects of life and the ramifications of brutality imposed on the human soul.*

WE WEAR THE MASK   (1913)

We wear the mask that grins and lies,
It hides our cheeks and shades our eyes,—
This debt we pay to human guile;
With torn and bleeding hearts we smile,
5   And mouth with myriad subtleties.

Why should the world be overwise,
In counting all our tears and sighs?
Nay, let them only see us, while
    We wear the mask.

10   We smile, but, O great Christ, our cries
To Thee from tortured souls arise.

> We sing, but oh, the clay is vile
> Beneath our feet, and long the mile;
> But let the world dream otherwise,
> 15   We wear the mask.

Questions for Discussion

1. To whom does the word *we* refer?

2. What does the speaker mean by "with torn and bleeding hearts we smile"? Why torn and bleeding? At another point the speaker refers to "tortured souls" and says, "the clay is vile." Is the **tone** bitter? If so, why?

3. Why does the speaker say African Americans wish to mask their true feelings? Do all races mask their feelings? Why is there a certain amount of fear involved in exposing the true feelings behind the mask?

4. What does Dunbar mean by "let the world dream otherwise, / We wear the mask"? Why does he use the word *dream*?

Suggestions for Exploration and Writing

1. Does the poem have to refer to just one racial or ethnic group? Discuss cultural, racial, or ethnic groups that wear masks. Then write an essay on why or how one group wears masks.

2. In an essay, discuss to what degree men and women wear masks that conceal parts of themselves from the opposite sex.

3. Explain why people have to hide behind masks. What is there in society that causes people to conceal their true identities?

John McCrae (1872–1918)

Canadian John McCrae had resigned from the military in 1904 and pursued a successful career as a physician, but in 1914, when Canada declared war on Germany, McCrae, then forty-one years old, immediately joined the war effort. After fighting on the Western Front, he was assigned to the medical corps in France. He was still on active duty when he died of pneumonia in 1918. His only book of poetry, In Flanders Fields and Other Poems, *was published in 1919, but "In Flanders Fields," a poem written immediately after the battlefield death of a close friend, had been published in* Punch, *the English magazine, in 1915 and was already the most popular poem about World War I.*

IN FLANDERS FIELDS   (1915)

In Flanders fields the poppies blow
Between the crosses, row on row,

That mark our place; and in the sky
The larks, still bravely singing, fly
5   Scarce heard amid the guns below.

We are the Dead. Short days ago
We lived, felt dawn, saw sunset glow,
Loved, and were loved, and now we lie
In Flanders fields.

10   Take up our quarrel with the foe:
To you from failing hands we throw
The torch; be yours to hold it high.
If ye break faith with us who die
We shall not sleep, though poppies grow
In Flanders fields.

Questions for Discussion

1. Who are the speakers in this poem?
2. What are Flanders fields?
3. How does nature provide a contrast to the activities of the men?
4. What is the challenge issued in the third verse?

Suggestions for Exploration and Writing

1. Using McCrae's poem as a pattern, write a poem using the first person plural to represent those who died in the September 11, 2001, attack.
2. One theme of the poem is that life goes on in spite of death and during war. Using this theme, write an essay describing what has happened to you since September 11, 2001.
3. Write an essay from the Dead at Ground Zero in New York. Who is the real foe, and how has America "[taken] up [their] quarrel with the foe"?
4. Write an essay interpreting the symbols in this poem.
5. Select at least two of the poems about war in this unit and write an essay comparing their tone.

Robert Frost (1874–1963)

A biograpghy of Robert Frost can be found in the casebook in the Men and Women Unit.

DESIGN   (1936)

I found a dimpled spider, fat and white,
On a white heal-all, holding up a moth
Like a white piece of rigid satin cloth—
Assorted characters of death and blight
5   Mixed ready to begin the morning right,

Like the ingredients of a witches' broth—
A snow-drop spider, a flower like a froth,
And dead wings carried like a paper kite.

What had that flower to do with being white,
10   The wayside blue and innocent heal-all?
What brought the kindred spider to that height,
Then steered the white moth thither in the night?
What but design of darkness to appall?—
If design govern in a thing so small.

Question for Discussion

1. The traditional Italian **sonnet** asks a question in the **octave** and answers it in the **sestet.** In "Design," Frost changes the traditional form by asking questions in the sestet. What do these questions imply? How does Frost's reversal of the traditional form emphasize the meaning of the poem?

ONCE BY THE PACIFIC   (1936)

The shattered water made a misty din.
Great waves looked over others coming in,
And thought of doing something to the shore
That water never did to land before.
5   The clouds were low and hairy in the skies,
Like locks blown forward in the gleam of eyes.
You could not tell, and yet it looked as if
The shore was lucky in being backed by cliff,
The cliff in being backed by continent;
10   It looked as if a night of dark intent
Was coming, and not only a night, an age.
Someone had better be prepared for rage.
There would be more than ocean-water broken
Before God's last *Put out the Light* was spoken.

Questions for Discussion

1. How does the **personification** of the ocean make the poem threatening?
2. What is the threat implied in the last five lines of the poem?

Suggestions for Exploration and Writing

1. Select an example from nature that reflects your opinion of what the world is like and write an essay explaining your choice.
2. Use these two poems to write an essay about Frost's frightening view of the world.

e. e. cummings (1894–1962)

[E]dward [E]stlin [C]ummings lived his early life in Cambridge, Mass-achusetts. During World War I, he spent several months in a French con-centration camp as a political prisoner, an experience he recalls in his first book, The Enormous Room *(1922). Best known for his poetry, which is highly experimental in typography and punctuation, cummings published twelve books of poems, including* Tulips and Chimneys *(1923),* 50 Poems *(1940), and* 95 Poems *(1958). His* Poems 1923–1954 *earned a special citation from the National Book Awards.*

BUFFALO BILL'S DEFUNCT (1923)

Buffalo Bill's
defunct
     who used to
     ride a watersmooth-silver
5   stallion
and break onetwothreefourfive pigeonsjustlikethat
                         Jesus

he was a handsome man
              and what i want to know is
10 how do you like your blueeyed boy
Mister Death

Questions for Discussion

1. What is the effect of cummings's using the word *defunct* instead of *dead*?
2. Why are the words run together in line 6?

Suggestion for Exploration and Writing

1. Research the cowboy of the 1800s and early 1900s. Then, write an epistolary essay to Mr. Death in which you explain what has been lost or gained by Buffalo Bill's death or the death of the cowboy spirit epitomized by Buffalo Bill.

ANYONE LIVED IN A PRETTY HOW TOWN (1940)

anyone lived in a pretty how town
(with up so floating many bells down)
spring summer autumn winter
he sang his didn't he danced his did.

5 Women and men(both little and small)
cared for anyone not at all
they sowed their isn't they reaped their same
sun moon stars rain

children guessed(but only a few
10 and down they forgot as up they grew
autumn winter spring summer)
that noone loved him more by more

when by now and tree by leaf
she laughed his joy she cried his grief
15 bird by snow and stir by still
anyone's any was all to her

someones married their everyones
laughed their cryings and did their dance
(sleep wake hope and then)they
20 said their nevers they slept their dream

stars rain sun moon
(and only the snow can begin to explain
how children are apt to forget to remember
with up so floating many bells down)

25 one day anyone died i guess
(and noone stooped to kiss his face)
busy folk buried them side by side
little by little and was by was

all by all and deep by deep
30 and more by more they dream their sleep
noone and anyone earth by april
wish by spirit and if by yes.

Women and men(both dong and ding)
summer autumn winter spring
35 reaped their sowing and went their came
sun moon stars rain

Questions for Discussion

1. List and interpret the repeated lines that emphasize the passage of
   time and the cycle of life.

2. What lines in the poem reveal the sadness and loneliness of the
   people?

3. Either alone or in groups, interpret each verse of the poem.

Suggestions for Exploration and Writing

1. Compare the people in this poem with J. Alfred Prufrock from T. S.
   Eliot's poem in the Quest unit.

2. Using the interpretations from question 3 above, write an essay on
   the joys and sorrows of "noone and anyone."

Claude McKay (1890–1948)

Claude McKay's poetry reflects his childhood in Jamaica and his adult life in America. His work is associated with the Harlem Renaissance, but he was often in conflict with the writers of that movement because of his political views. During the course of his life, McKay wrote lyrical poems, dialect poems, and sonnets.

IF WE MUST DIE (1922)

If we must die, let it not be like hogs
Hunted and penned in an inglorious spot,
While round us bark the mad and hungry dogs,
Making their mock at our accursed lot.
5   If we must die, O let us nobly die,
So that our precious blood may not be shed
In vain; then even the monsters we defy
Shall be constrained to honor us though dead!
O kinsmen! we must meet the common foe!
10 Though far outnumbered let us show us brave,
And for their thousand blows deal one deathblow!
What though before us lies the open grave?
Like men we'll face the murderous, cowardly pack,
Pressed to the wall, dying, but fighting back!

Questions for Discussion

1. Whom does McKay refer to as "we" in the poem? McKay uses the terms *kinsmen* and the *common foe.* Is his poem only about African Americans?
2. McKay has negative words for those he wants to oppose: "mad and hungry dogs," "the monsters," and "murderous, cowardly pack." Do you think McKay is being too biased or slanted?

Suggestions for Exploration and Writing

1. Is there any cause for which you would be willing to die? Discuss.
2. Martin Luther King Jr. preached nonviolence; however, Claude McKay, writing a generation earlier, preached violence. Using the poem as the basis for discussion, comment on McKay's justification for not backing down from retaliation or violence.

Wilfred Owen (1893–1918)

Wilfred Owen is recognized as one of the greatest English war poets. He joined the British Army in 1915, fought as an officer in World War I, and was killed in that war on November 4, 1918, just seven days before it ended. Most of Owen's poems, which powerfully evoke the terror and inhumanity of war, were not published until after his death.

Dulce et Decorum Est   (1920)

Bent double, like old beggars under sacks,
Knock-kneed, coughing like hags, we cursed through sludge,
Till on the haunting flares we turned our backs
And towards our distant rest began to trudge.
5   Men marched asleep. Many had lost their boots
But limped on, blood-shod. All went lame; all blind;
Drunk with fatigue; deaf even to the hoots
Of tired, outstripped Five-Nines that dropped behind.

Gas! GAS! Quick, boys!—An ecstasy of fumbling,
10   Fitting the clumsy helmets just in time;
But someone still was yelling out and stumbling
And flound'ring like a man in fire or lime . . .
Dim, through the misty panes and thick green light,
As under a green sea, I saw him drowning.

15   In all my dreams, before my helpless sight,
He plunges at me, guttering, choking, drowning.

If in some smothering dreams you too could pace
Behind the wagon that we flung him in,
And watch the white eyes writhing in his face,
20   His hanging face, like a devil's sick of sin;
If you could hear, at every jolt, the blood
Come gargling from the froth-corrupted lungs,
Obscene as cancer, bitter as the cud
Of vile, incurable sores on innocent tongues,—
25   My friend, you would not tell with such high zest
To children ardent for some desperate glory,
The old Lie: *Dulce et decorum est*
Pro patria mori.

Questions for Discussion

1. This poem's last sentence, from Horace, *Odes,* III, ii, 13, means "It is
   sweet and proper to die for one's country." How does the realistic
   portrayal of war in the first stanza contrast with the patriotic sentiments the speaker attacks in the last few lines of the poem?

2. Why does Owen use the Latin quotation at the end?

Suggestion for Exploration and Writing

1. Write a thorough analysis of this poem, examining how its **tone**
   changes from stanza to stanza and how **imagery,** sound, **diction,** and
   syntax develop tone.

2. Is war ever justified? Support your answer.

Langston Hughes (1902–1967)

Hughes's biography can be found in the casebook in the Men and Women Unit.

DRAMA FOR WINTER NIGHT (FIFTH AVENUE)   (1925)

You can't sleep here,
My good man,
You can't sleep here.
This is the house of God.

5   The usher opens the church door and he goes out.

You can't sleep in this car, old top,
Not here.
If Jones found you
He'd give you to the cops.
10   Get-the-hell out now,
This ain't home.
You can't stay here.

The chauffeur opens the door and he gets out.

Lord! You can't let a man lie
15   In the streets like this.
Find an officer quick.
Send for an ambulance.
Maybe he is sick but
He can't die on this corner,
20   Not here!
He can't die here.

Death opens a door.

Oh, God,
Lemme git by St. Peter.
25   Lemme sit down on the steps of your throne.
Lemme rest somewhere.
What did yuh say, God?
What did yuh say?
You can't sleep here. . . .
30   Bums can't stay. . . .

The man's raving.
Get him to the hospital quick.
He's attracting a crowd.
He can't die on this corner.
35   No, no, not here.

Questions for Discussion

1. Identify the speaker in each verse.
2. Explain the irony of the open doors.
3. What is the significance of the man's "ravings" about God and St. Peter?
4. Why do the speakers want the homeless person not to die in their vicinity? Why do they not offer to help him?

Suggestions for Exploration and Writing

1. What is your reaction to the people who would not allow a homeless man a place to sleep? Do you blame the homeless man? Who is at fault in this situation?
2. Is the poem realistic in its indictment of our society? To what degree is it true that a homeless man would not be allowed to sleep in a church, in a car, or on the street? What message is Hughes sending about the homeless? You might consider in your essay the NIMBY (not in my backyard) syndrome.
3. On what major problem of the homeless does this poem focus?

Countee Cullen (1903–1948)

A New Yorker by birth, Cullen was a Phi Beta Kappa graduate of New York University. He wrote his first collection of poems, Color *(1925), while he was in college. Cullen also wrote a novel,* One Way to Heaven *(1932), and a version of Euripides' play* Medea. *A member of the Harlem Renaissance, Cullen later turned to teaching to earn a living.*

INCIDENT   (1925)

(For Eric Walrond)
Once riding in old Baltimore,
   Heart-filled, head-filled with glee,
I saw a Baltimorean
   Keep looking straight at me.

5   Now I was eight and very small,
   And he was no whit bigger,
And so I smiled, but he poked out
   His tongue, and called me, "Nigger."

I saw the whole of Baltimore
10   From May until December;
Of all the things that happened there
   That's all that I remember.

Question for Discussion

1. Why does the speaker remember only this incident from a seven-month stay in the city?

Suggestion for Exploration and Writing

1. If you have had a similar experience, describe it in a narrative essay.

2. Discuss the impact that a word such as *nigger* or another derogatory term can have on the self-esteem of an individual or a group.

Henry Reed (1914–1986)

Born in Birmingham, England, and educated at Birmingham University, Reed spent a year in the Royal Army Ordnance Corps during World War II. Out of this military experience grew his most famous book of poems, Lessons of the War *(1945). After the war, he produced more poems, subsequently published in* A Map of Verona *(1946), and several successful comic plays for radio. The two poems included here are, in their mocking tone, typical of his war poems.*

NAMING OF PARTS (1945)

Today we have naming of parts. Yesterday,
We had daily cleaning. And tomorrow morning,
We shall have what to do after firing. But today,
Today we have naming of parts. Japonica
5   Glistens like coral in all of the neighboring gardens,
    And today we have naming of parts.

This is the lower sling swivel. And this
Is the upper sling swivel, whose use you will see,
When you are given your slings. And this is the piling swivel,
10   Which in your case you have not got. The branches
Hold in the gardens their silent, eloquent gestures,
    Which in our case we have not got.

This is the safety-catch, which is always released
With an easy flick of the thumb. And please do not let me
15   See anyone using his finger. You can do it quite easy
If you have any strength in your thumb. The blossoms
Are fragile and motionless, never letting anyone see
    Any of them using their finger.

And this you can see is the bolt. The purpose of this
20   Is to open the breech, as you see. We can slide it
Rapidly backwards and forwards: we call this
Easing the spring. And rapidly backwards and forwards
The early bees are assaulting and fumbling the flowers:
    They call it easing the Spring.

25   They call it easing the Spring: it is perfectly easy
If you have any strength in your thumb: like the bolt,

And the breech, and the cocking-piece, and the point of balance,
Which in our case we have not got; and the almond-blossom
Silent in all of the gardens and the bees going backwards and forwards,
30   For today we have naming of parts.

Questions for Discussion

1. How would you describe the language in the opening lines of each stanza? What tone or feeling does the language convey?

2. How do the closing lines of each stanza differ in language and tone from the other lines?

3. How do you account for this difference in tone?

4. What seems to be the situation? How does the speaker in the closing lines of each stanza react to the situation?

5. Why is the naming of the parts of a gun important to war even if the soldiers don't have the guns yet? Why are the soldiers being conditioned to the war?

Suggestion for Exploration and Writing

1. In Afghanistan, for the last decade, many children have gone to school only to learn the Muslim religion or to be told how to use a gun. In an essay, explain what the soldiers in this poem and the Afghan children have lost.

JUDGING DISTANCES   (1945)

Not only how far away, but the way that you say it
Is very important. Perhaps you may never get
The knack of judging a distance, but at least you know
How to report on a landscape: the central sector,
5   The right of arc and that, which we had last Tuesday,
    And at least you know

That maps are of time, not place, so far as the army
Happens to be concerned—the reason being,
Is one which need not delay us. Again, you know
10   There are three kinds of tree, three only, the fir and the poplar,
And those which have bushy tops to; and lastly
    That things only seem to be things.

A barn is not called a barn, to put it more plainly,
Or a field in the distance, where sheep may be safely grazing.
15   You must never be over-sure. You must say, when reporting:
At five o'clock in the central sector is a dozen

Of what appear to be animals; whatever you do,
    Don't call the bleeders *sheep*.

I am sure that's quite clear; and suppose, for the sake of example,
20   The one at the end, asleep, endeavors to tell us
What he sees over there to the west, and how far away,
After first having come to attention. There to the west,
On the fields of summer the sun and the shadows bestow
    Vestments of purple and gold.

25   The still white dwellings are like a mirage in the heat,
And under the swaying elms a man and a woman
Lie gently together. Which is, perhaps, only to say
That there is a row of houses to the left of the arc,
And that under some poplars a pair of what appear to be humans
30   Appear to be loving.

Well that, for an answer, is what we might rightly call
Moderately satisfactory only, the reason being,
Is that two things have been omitted, and those are important.
The human beings, now: in what direction are they,
35   And how far away, would you say? And do not forget
    There may be dead ground in between.

There may be dead ground in between; and I may not have got
The knack of judging a distance; I will only venture
A guess that perhaps between me and the apparent lovers,
40   (Who, incidentally, appear by now to have finished,)
At seven o'clock from the houses, is roughly a distance
    Of about one year and a half.

Questions for Discussion

1. What is the situation in this poem? How is it similar to the situation in "Naming of Parts"?

2. How clear and precise is the language of the "army" in the first four stanzas and stanza 6? What is lacking in this use of language? Why?

3. How does the language of stanzas 5 and 7 contrast to this "army" language? What is the state of mind of the speaker here?

4. What do you consider to be the point of the sharp contrasts in tone in Reed's two poems?

Suggestion for Exploration and Writing

1. Write an analysis of either "Naming of Parts" or "Judging Distances" in which you discuss in detail the contrasts in tone and their significance.

Dylan Thomas (1914–1953)

*Dylan Thomas was a Welsh poet known for his extraordinary reading voice. His most famous poems, exuberant and rich in sound and imagery, are nevertheless constructed with painstaking care, as the deceptively simple **villanelle** "Do Not Go Gentle into That Good Night" illustrates.*

Do Not Go Gentle into That Good Night   (1945)

Do not go gentle into that good night,
Old age should burn and rave at close of day;
Rage, rage against the dying of the light.

Though wise men at their end know dark is right,
5   Because their words had forked no lightning they
Do not go gentle into that good night.

Good men, the last wave by, crying how bright
Their frail deeds might have danced in a green bay,
Rage, rage against the dying of the light.

10   Wild men who caught and sang the sun in flight,
And learn, too late, they grieved it on its way,
Do not go gentle into that good night.

Grave men, near death, who see with blinding sight
Blind eyes could blaze like meteors and be gay,
15   Rage, rage against the dying of the light.

And you, my father, there on the sad height,
Curse, bless, me now with your fierce tears, I pray.
Do not go gentle into that good night.
Rage, rage against the dying of the light.

Questions for Discussion

1. What is the effect of Thomas's repeating the two lines "Do not go gentle into that good night" and "Rage, rage against the dying of the light"?

2. Each of the middle stanzas describes a different kind of man facing death. Besides resisting death, what do the men have in common?

3. How effective is the longer, more specific last stanza after the first five? Why are the first five stanzas necessary if the main subject is the father's death?

4. Why does the speaker ask his father to "curse, bless" him? What does the speaker mean?

5. This poem is a **villanelle**, a form that is extremely difficult and rare in English poetry because of its rigidly patterned rhyme scheme. How does the extremely rigid form contribute to the **tone** of Thomas's poem?

Suggestions for Exploration and Writing

1. Write an essay urging someone you love to fight for life.

2. Thomas repeats, "Rage, rage against the dying of the light." He obviously feels that everyone should live life to the fullest and challenge old age and eventual death. Using three of his reasons, discuss whether you would agree or disagree.

Wislawa Szymborska (b. 1923)

Szymborska, the 1996 Nobel Prize–winning poet from Cracow, the artistic and intellectual center of Poland, thinks of herself as a very ordinary person. She so dislikes pretension that she collects trashy postcards, commenting "trash does not pretend to be anything better than it is." Early in her career she embraced Stalinism, but later she came to find Stalin and Communism cold and inhuman. A very private person, she does not like literary gatherings, dresses very plainly, and prefers to spend most of her time out of the limelight with a few close friends. Her books of poetry include Questions Put to Myself *(1954),* Calling Out to the Yeti *(1957), and* The End and the Beginning *(1993).*

OUR ANCESTORS' SHORT LIVES (1986)

TRANS. BY STANISLAW BARAŃCZAK AND CLARE CAVANAUGH

Few of them made it to thirty.
Old age was the privilege of rocks and trees.
Childhood ended as fast as wolf cubs grow.
One had to hurry, to get on with life
5   before the sun went down,
before the first snow.

Thirteen-year-olds bearing children,
four-year-olds stalking birds' nests in the rushes,
leading the hunt at twenty—
10   they aren't yet, then they are gone.
Infinity's ends fused quickly.
Witches chewed charms
with all the teeth of youth intact.
A son grew to manhood beneath his father's eye.
15   Beneath the grandfather's blank sockets the grandson
      was born.

And anyway they didn't count the years.
They counted nets, pods, sheds, and axes.
Time, so generous toward any petty star in the sky,
offered them a nearly empty hand
20   and quickly took it back, as if the effort were too much.
One step more, two steps more
along the glittering river
that sprang from darkness and vanished into darkness.

There wasn't a moment to lose,
25 no deferred questions, no belated revelations,
just those experienced in time.
Wisdom couldn't wait for gray hair.
It had to see clearly before it saw the light
and to hear every voice before it sounded.

30 Good and evil—
they knew little of them, but knew all:
when evil triumphs, good goes into hiding;
when good is manifest, then evil lies low.
Neither can be conquered
35 or cast off beyond return.
Hence, if joy, then with a touch of fear;
if despair, then not without some quiet hope.
Life, however long, will always be short.
Too short for anything to be added.

Questions for Discussion

1. What contrasts does Szymborska imply between the concerns of the short-lived ancestors and the concerns of most people today?
2. Explain what Szymborska means by "Infinity's ends fused quickly."
3. Explain the imagery of time in the third stanza.
4. Explain the seeming contradiction in the last two lines of the poem.
5. The poem ends, "Life, however long, will always be short. / Too short for anything to be added." What might people seek to add to life that the speaker might consider superfluous?

Suggestions for Exploration and Writing

1. Write a contrast essay explaining how our ancestors' lives differed from our own.
2. In an essay, agree or disagree with Szymborska's statement that "life, however long, will always be short / Too short for anything to be added."

Derek Walcott (b. 1930)

Born in Saint Lucia of mixed heritage, Walcott received a B.A. from the University of the West Indies in Jamaica. He began writing at an early age and became a prolific writer. His books of poetry include Epitaph for the Young: A Poem in XII Cantos *(1949),* The Caribbean Poetry of Derek Walcott, and the Art of Romare Beardon *(1983),* The Arkansas Testament *(1987),* Omeros *(1989), and* The Bounty *(1997). In addition, he has written plays:* Ione: A Play with Music *(1957),* Dream on Monkey Mountain *(1967), and* Odyssey: A Stage Version *(1993). In 1992, he won the Nobel Prize in literature. Trying to find a creative means of synthe-sizing opposites in order to fashion a Caribbean identity of the recent past, Walcott wrote of the contrasts in life: black and white, British and West Indian, colonizer and colonized.*

THE YOUNG WIFE

(1987)

(FOR NIGEL)

Make all your sorrow neat.
Plump pillows, soothe the corners
of her favourite coverlet.
Write to her mourners.

5 At dusk, after the office, *week / office of marriage*
travel an armchair's ridge,
the valley of the shadow in the sofas,
the drapes' dead foliage.

Ah, but the mirror—the mirror
10 which you believe has seen
the traitor you feel you are—
clouds, though you wipe it clean! *crying*

The buds on the wallpaper *buds on wall*
do not shake at the muffled sobbing
15 the children must not hear,
or the drawers you dare not open.

She has gone with that visitor *death*
that sat beside her, like wind
clicking shut the bedroom door;
20 arm in arm they went,

leaving her wedding photograph in
its lace frame, a face smiling at
itself. And the telephone *Nobody calling*
without a voice. The weight

25 we bear on this heavier side
of the grave brings no comfort. *dead / alive side*
But the vow that was said
in white lace has brought

you now to the very edge
30 of that promise; now, for some,
the hooks in the hawthorn hedge
break happily into blossom *spring*

and the heart into grief.
The sun slants on a kitchen floor. *making dinner*
35 You keep setting a fork and knife
at her place for supper.

The children close in the space
made by a chair removed,
and nothing takes her place,
40   loved and now deeper loved.

The children accept your answer.
They startle you when they laugh.
She sits there smiling that cancer
kills everything but Love.

Questions for Discussion

1. How is the husband in the poem attempting to cope with death of his young wife?

2. Why does the husband want to make sorrow neat? Is this realistic? Explain.

3. What are the little reminders of his loss?

4. Explain why the wife is "loved and now deeper loved."

5. Explain the last two lines of the poem.

6. Explain the following allusions in the poem:

   "the valley of the shadow in the sofas"

   "the mirror[. . .] clouds, though you wipe it clean!"

   "the vow that was said / in white lace has brought / you now to the very edge / of that promise"

Suggestions for Exploration and Writing

1. Walcott writes that earth is the "heavier side / of the grave [and] brings no comfort." Explain.

2. The speaker refers to various objects he associates with the dead wife. Write an essay analyzing the mixture of emotions aroused by an object you associate with someone who died.

3. Compare the husband in this poem to the narrator of "The Benchmark."

Mary Oliver (b. 1935)

Mary Oliver, whose poetry has won the Pulitzer Prize and the National Book Award, has lived in Ohio and New England. Among her books are No Voyage and Other Poems *(1963);* New and Selected Poems *(1992);* A Poetry Handbook *(1995);* Blue Pastures *(1995), essays about nature; and* Winter Hours: Prose, Prose Poems, and Poems *(1999). Her book-length poem,* The Leaf and the Cloud, *appears in* The Best American Poetry *for 1999 and 2000. Oliver was awarded the Catharine Osgood Foster Chair for Distinguished Teaching at Bennington College. In her vivid and distinctive images, she shares both the inspiration and the wisdom found in nature.*

UNIVERSITY HOSPITAL, BOSTON   (1983)

The trees on the hospital lawn
are lush and thriving. They too
are getting the best of care,
like you, and the anonymous many,
5   in the clean rooms high above this city,
where day and night the doctors keep
arriving, where intricate machines
chart with cool devotion
the murmur of the blood,
10   the slow patching-up of bone,
the despair of the mind.

When I come to visit and we walk out
into the light of a summer day,
we sit under the trees—
15   buckeyes, a sycamore and one
black walnut brooding
high over a hedge of lilacs
as old as the red-brick building
behind them, the original
20   hospital built before the Civil War.
We sit on the lawn together, holding hands
while you tell me: you are better.

How many young men, I wonder,
came here, wheeled on cots off the slow trains
25   from the red and hideous battlefields
to lie all summer in the small and stuffy chambers
while doctors did what they could, longing
for tools still unimagined, medicines still unfound,
wisdoms still unguessed at, and how many died
30   staring at the leaves of the trees, blind
to the terrible effort around them to keep them alive?
I look into your eyes

which are sometimes green and sometimes gray,
and sometimes full of humor, but often not,
35   and tell myself, you are better,
because my life without you would be
a place of parched and broken trees.
Later, walking the corridors down to the street,
I turn and step inside an empty room.
40   Yesterday someone was here with a gasping face.
Now the bed is made all new,
the machines have been rolled away. The silence
continues, deep and neutral,
as I stand there, loving you.

Questions for Discussion

1. In what ways do the machines in hospitals "chart with cool devotion"? Why is their presence comforting?
2. What impression do the images of the first stanza convey about healing in a hospital? How do these images contrast to those in the second stanza describing the hospital grounds?
3. How do the trees contrast with the lives of the patients in the hospital? What would the narrator's life be like if the patient were to die?

Suggestion for Exploration and Writing

1. Using the poem as the basis for an essay, discuss the vulnerability of both the patient and the friend.

Angela de Hoyos (b. 1940)

Born in Coahuela, Mexico, Angela de Hoyos, who lives now in the San Antonio area, has written for newspapers, literary magazines, and anthologies. Her major works include Arise Chicano and Other Poems *(1975),* Chicano Poems for the Barrio *(1975),* Selecciones—Selected Poems *(1976), and* Woman, Woman *(1985). Although many of her earlier themes expressed anger and frustration at the plight of Chicanos in America, she has since tempered her themes to include Chicano traditions and cultural identity as well as experiments with language.*

How to Eat Crow on a Cold Sunday Morning (1985)

just start on the wings
nibbling
apologetic-like
because after all
5   it was you
who held the gun
and fired point-blank
the minute you saw the
whites of their eyes
10 just like the army sergeant
always instructed you.

—Damn it, this thing's
gonna make me sick!

—No it won't. Go on. Eat the
15 blasted thing
(for practice)

because you'll be sicker
later on
when your friends
20   start giving you
an iceberg for a shoulder.

. . . So the giblets are dry
and tough.
But you can
25   digest them.

It's the gall bladder
—that green bag of billiousness—
wants to gag your throat
in righteous retribution

30   refuses to budge
won't go up or down, just
sticks there

makes you wish that long ago
you'd learned how to eat
35   a pound of prudence
instead.

Questions for Discussion

1. What does it mean when someone says that he had to "eat crow"?
2. Explain the other metaphors in this poem.
3. Point out the examples of **alliteration.**
4. What is the tone of the poem?

Suggestions for Exploration and Writing

1. Angela de Hoyos uses a popular metaphor literally. Think of other metaphors and write a poem on one metaphor, using it literally.
2. Write an essay contrasting eating "a pound of prudence" and eating crow.

Billy Collins (b. 1941)

Award-winning poet Billy Collins was born in New York. Among his books of poetry are Pokerface *(1977),* The Art of Drowning *(1995),* The Apple That Astonished Paris *(1988),* Questions About Angels *(1991), which was selected for the Edward Hirsch National Poetry Series, and* Picnic, Lightning *(1998). In 1971, he received a Ph.D. from the University of California, Riverside; he presently teaches at Herbert H. Lehman College of the City University of New York. In 2001, Collins was appointed Poet Laureate of the United States.*

FORGETFULNESS   (1991)

The name of the author is the first to go
followed obediently by the title, the plot,
the heartbreaking conclusion, the entire novel
which suddenly becomes one you have never read, never
5   even heard of,

as if, one by one, the memories you used to harbor
decided to retire to the southern hemisphere of the brain,
to a little fishing village where there are no phones.

Long ago you kissed the names of the nine Muses goodbye
10   and watched the quadratic equation pack its bag,
and even now as you memorize the order of the planets,

something else is slipping away, a state flower perhaps,
the address of an uncle, the capital of Paraguay.

Whatever it is you are struggling to remember
15   it is not poised on the tip of your tongue,
not even lurking in some obscure corner of your spleen.

It has floated away down a dark mythological river
whose name begins with an *L* as far as you can recall,
well on your own way to oblivion where you will join those
20   who have even forgotten how to swim and how to ride a
      bicycle.

No wonder you rise in the middle of the night
to look up the date of a famous battle in a book on war.
No wonder the moon in the window seems to have drifted
25   out of a love poem that you used to know by heart.

Questions for Discussion

1. To whom does "you" refer in Collins's poem?

2. What kinds of things has the speaker forgotten?

3. Explain Collins's pun on "harbor" in the second verse.

4. What is the mythological river that begins with *L*?

5. Does this poem relate only to the elderly? When have you experienced the kind of forgetfulness the speaker describes? How does such forgetfulness make you feel?

6. Compare Collins's comments about forgetfulness with Mary's comment in Frost's poem "Death of the Hired Man": "I know just how it feels to think of the right thing to say too late."

Suggestion for Exploration and Writing

1. Write an essay, either humorous or serious, explaining your own forgetfulness or that of someone you know.

Sharon Olds (b. 1942)

Sharon Olds, a San Francisco–born poet, was educated at Stanford and Columbia universities. She has won a National Book Critics Circle Award for her poetry. Her books of poems include Satan Says *(1980);* Dead and the Living *(1983);* The Gold Cell *(1987), which includes the following poem;* The Father *(1992);* The Wellspring *(1995); and* Blood, Tin, Straw *(1999). Her poetry has appeared in* The New Yorker, The Paris Review, *and* Ploughshares. *She teaches poetry workshops at New York University.*

ON THE SUBWAY   (1987)

The boy and I face each other.
His feet are huge, in black sneakers
laced with white in a complex pattern like a
set of intentional scars. We are stuck on
5   opposite sides of the car, a couple of
molecules stuck in a rod of light
rapidly moving through darkness. He has the
casual cold look of a mugger,
alert under hooded lids. He is wearing
10   red, like the inside of the body
exposed. I am wearing dark fur, the
whole skin of an animal taken and
used. I look at his raw face,
he looks at my fur coat, and I don't
15   know if I am in his power—
he could take my coat so easily, my
briefcase, my life—
or if he is in my power, the way I am
living off his life, eating the steak
20   he does not eat, as if I am taking
the food from his mouth. And he is black
and I am white, and without meaning or
trying to I must profit from his darkness,
the way he absorbs the murderous beams of the
25   nation's heart, as black cotton
absorbs the heat of the sun and holds it. There is
no way to know how easy this
white skin makes my life, this
life he could take so easily and

30   break across his knee like a stick the way his
      own back is being broken, the
      rod of his soul that at birth was dark and
      fluid and rich as the heart of a seedling
      ready to thrust up into any available light.

Questions for Discussion

1. Examine the **images** of color and light in the poem. How are they important in creating the **tone** of the poem?

2. List the **images** of hurt and pain the speaker uses to describe the life of the man she meets. How do these and other images create a striking contrast between the speaker's life and that of the stranger?

3. Explain the contradiction of the speaker's saying:

   [. . .] I don't

   know if I am in his power—

   [. . . . .]

   or if he is in my power. [. . .]

   To be in another's control can be very frightening. Who is in control of the lives in this poem—the boy, the speaker, both, or neither?

Suggestions for Exploration and Writing

1. Write an essay explaining how the rich **similes** and **metaphors** add to the visual effect of the poem and the depth of meaning.

2. Using the poem as background, analyze the factors leading to the fear the black man may have of the white woman.

3. Discuss the meaning of the last three lines of the poem. According to Olds, what has happened to the rod of the black man's soul?

Shirley Geok-lin Lim (b. 1944)

Shirley Geok-lin Lim, award-winning poet, short story writer, and critic, was born in Malacca, Malaysia. Her childhood was marked by poverty, abuse, and abandonment. Educated at a convent school, Lim won a federal scholarship to the University of Malaya, where she earned a BA and an MA. In 1973, she completed her PhD at Brandeis University, specializing in English and American literature. Presently she is Chair Professor of English at the University of Hong Kong. Lim has been publishing poetry since she was ten years old, and she considers it her major form. Her five books of poetry include What the Fortune Teller Didn't Say *(1998);* Monsoon History: Selected Poems *(1994);* Modern Secrets *(1989);* No Man's Grove *(1985), the source of the following poem; and* Crossing the Peninsula and

Other Poems *(1980). In addition, she has published three collections of short stories and a memoir,* Among the White Moon Faces: An Asian-American Memoir of Homelands *(1996).*

PANTOUN FOR CHINESE WOMEN (1985)

At present, the phenomena of butchering, drowning and leaving to die female infants have been very serious.

THE PEOPLE'S DAILY, PEKING, MARCH 3RD, 1983

They say a child with two mouths is no good.
In the slippery wet, a hollow space,
Smooth, gumming, echoing wide for food.
No wonder my man is not here at his place.

5   In the slippery wet, a hollow space,
A slit narrowly sheathed within its hood.
No wonder my man is not here at his place:
He is digging for the dragon jar of soot.

That slit narrowly sheathed within its hood!
10 His mother, squatting, coughs by the fire's blaze
While he digs for the dragon jar of soot.
We had saved ashes for a hundred days.

His mother, squatting, coughs by the fire's blaze.
The child kicks against me mewing like a flute.
15 We had saved ashes for a hundred days,
Knowing, if the time came, that we would.

The child kicks against me crying like a flute
Through its two weak mouths. His mother prays
Knowing when the time comes that we would,
20 For broken clay is never set in glaze.

Through her two weak mouths his mother prays.
She will not pluck the rooster nor serve its blood,
For broken clay is never set in glaze:
Women are made of river sand and wood.

25 She will not pluck the rooster nor serve its blood.
My husband frowns, pretending in his haste
Women are made of river sand and wood.
Milk soaks the bedding. I cannot bear the waste.

My husband frowns, pretending in his haste.
30 Oh, clean the girl, dress her in ashy soot!
Milk soaks our bedding, I cannot bear the waste.
They say a child with two mouths is no good.

Questions for Discussion

1. Why would "They" describe a girl as "a child with two mouths"?
2. What is the purpose of the "dragon jar of soot"?
3. What are the implications of describing a girl child as "broken clay" and of saying "Women are made of river sand and wood"?
4. What is the significance of the woman's not being able to bear the dripping of breast milk?

Suggestions for Exploration and Writing

1. From the evidence found in the poem, analyze the roles of the mother-in-law and/or the husband/father.
2. Research the situation with respect to the treatment of girl children in China today. Then write an essay applying that research to the conditions portrayed in the poem.
3. Examine the pattern of repeated lines in this poem. In an essay, interpret these lines and explain the significance of Lim's selection of these lines to repeat.
4. In an essay, describe the vivid images in this poem and explain how they add to the poignancy of the poem.
5. Compare the Chinese custom of destroying female babies with the custom in many African countries of female mutilation/circumcision.

Victor Hernández Cruz (b. 1949)

Cruz was born in Aguas Buenas, Puerto Rico, but moved with his parents to New York in 1955. A high school dropout, Cruz has written many books of poetry, including Snaps *(1969),* Tropicalization *(1976),* Mainland *(1973), and* Rhythm, Content, and Flavor: New and Selected Poems *(1989). His 1991 book,* Red Beans, *was the winner of the* Publishers Weekly *"Ten Best Books of the Year" Award.* Panoramas *(1997) is a collection of poems, essays, and stories. Cruz belongs to a movement called "neo-rican" or "nuyorican," composed of writers who use English with accents of Spanish and African American idiomatic expressions. His poems are written in simple language, free of pretense. Cruz now lives and writes in his native Puerto Rico.*

PROBLEMS WITH HURRICANES   (1989)

A campesino looked at the air
And told me:
With hurricanes it's not the wind
or the noise or the water.
5   I'll tell you he said:
it's the mangoes, avocados

Green plantains and bananas
flying into town like projectiles.

How would your family
10 feel if they had to tell
The generations that you
got killed by a flying
Banana.

Death by drowning has honor
15 If the wind picked you up
and slammed you
Against a mountain boulder
This would not carry shame
But
20 to suffer a mango smashing
Your skull
or a plantain hitting your
Temple at 70 miles per hour
is the ultimate disgrace.
25 The campesino takes off his hat—
As a sign of respect
toward the fury of the wind
And says:
Don't worry about the noise
30 Don't worry about the water
Don't worry about the wind—
If you are going out
beware of mangoes
And all such beautiful
35 sweet things.

Questions for Discussion

1. Why would death by "beautiful / sweet things" be so ignominious?

2. Given your choice of ways to die, what would you pick?

Suggestion for Exploration and Writing

1. Both Cruz and de Hoyos use humor to deal with something unpleasant. Write an essay on the use of humor in these two poems.

Adam Zagajewski (b. 1945)

Zagajewski is a prolific and award-winning writer of poetry, fiction, and essays. Born in Poland and raised in Silesia and Cracow, he graduated from the Jagiellonian University. His early poetry, published in Communique *(1972) and* Meat Shops *(1975), features political and social issues; but later poetry, in* Traveling to Lowe *(1985) and* The Canvas *(1986), deals with the searching of young intellectuals. His novels, such as* Warm and Cold *(1975),* The Thin Line *(1983), and* Absolute Pitch, *published only in German translation, present the spiritual problems of the modern artist. His often autobiographical essays are included in* The Unpresented World *(1974),* Solidarity and Solitude *(1986),* Two Cities *(1991), and* In the Beauty of Others *(1998).*

TRY TO PRAISE THE MUTILATED WORLD (2002)

TRANSLATED FROM THE POLISH BY CLARE CAVANAGH

Try to praise the mutilated world.
Remember June's long days,
and wild strawberries, drops of wine, the dew.
The nettles that methodically overgrow
5   the abandoned homesteads of exiles.
You must praise the mutilated world.
You watched the stylish yachts and ships;
one of them had a long trip ahead of it,
while salty oblivion awaited others.
10 You've seen the refugees heading nowhere,
you've heard the executioners sing joyfully.
You should praise the mutilated world.
Remember the moments when we were together
in a white room and the curtain fluttered.
15 Return in thought to the concert where music flared.
You gathered acorns in the park in autumn
and leaves eddied over the earth's scars.
Praise the mutilated world
and the gray feather a thrush lost,
20 and the gentle light that strays and vanishes
and returns.

Questions for Discussion

1. Why does the speaker call the world "mutilated"? Who mutilated the world—when, and how? In what way can this world be "praised"?

2. What is the implication of the last two lines?

3. What is the tone of the poem? What words and images set this tone?

4. Why does Zagajewski advise praising the world even though it is mutilated? Explain why the poet wants the reader to remember pleasant things. Is this act of remembrance in fact a denial of reality?

5. What recent events could be appropriately included in this poem?

Suggestions for Exploration and Writing

1. Write an essay describing what you consider recurring mutilations or what you consider the major mutilations of the modern world.
2. List the kinds of mutilation described in the poem. Then divide these into slight mutilations and major mutilations. In an essay, contrast and illustrate these forms of mutilation. Then give your interpretation of what Zagajewski is implying by these contrasts.
3. In an expository essay, explain what Zagajewski is saying about grief and loss.

D R A M A

William Shakespeare (1564–1616)

William Shakespeare is generally regarded as the greatest writer ever to have written in English. Though Shakespeare also produced an often-admired sequence of 154 sonnets and several narrative poems, his extraordinary reputation rests primarily on his plays. Notable for their sheer number and diversity, the thirty-seven plays include thirteen **comedies,** *ten* **tragedies,** *ten* **history plays,** *and four* **romances.**

Using language that is rich and highly allusive yet conversational and informal, the plays reveal not only a sure sense of dramatic structure and tension but also a love of human diversity. As a member of an acting company that performed both in the outdoor Globe playhouse and in the indoor Blackfriars, Shakespeare was intimately familiar with the theater of his time and with its conventions. Among the most highly regarded of his plays are the comedies As You Like It, All's Well That Ends Well, *and* Twelfth Night; *the history plays* Henry IV, Part I *and* Henry IV, Part II; *the tragedies* Hamlet, Othello, King Lear, *and* Macbeth; *and* The Tempest, *a romance generally thought to have been Shakespeare's last play.* Othello *displays the richness of language, character, and dramatic tension for which Shakespeare is justly celebrated.*

About Tragedy

Shakespeare's Othello *is a* **tragedy.** *In its most general literary usage, the term* **tragedy** *refers to a particular kind of play in which a good person through some character flaw destroys himself or herself.*

The most famous definition of tragedy comes from the ancient Greek philosopher Aristotle (384–322 B.C.). In his Poetics, *Aristotle defines tragedy as*

> a representation *(mimesis)* of an action *(praxis)* that is serious, complete, and of a certain magnitude [. . .] presented, not narrated [i.e., a drama, not a story] [. . .] with incidents arousing pity and fear in such a way as to accomplish a purgation *(katharsis)* of such emotions. (296)

*The purpose of tragedy, according to Aristotle, then, is to make the audience feel "pity and fear" in order somehow to purge or cleanse these emotions. The most important elements of tragedy are **plot** and **character**. The plot must present an action that is complete, with a clear beginning and an ending that gives a sense of finality, and must be unified, so that every part contributes to the whole. The best plots feature reversal (**peripeteia**), a not improbable but unexpected 180-degree change in situation, and recognition (**anagnorisis**), the tragic hero's sudden understanding of his or her fate and its implications. A **tragic hero**, Aristotle maintains, must be good but flawed, must be aristocratic, must be believable, and must behave consistently.*

*Shakespeare, writing for a different audience in a different kind of theater at a different time, produced tragedies that are rich in language and character development but less dramatically unified than Aristotle prescribes. For example, Shakespeare did not hesitate to insert into his tragedies scenes containing the broadest farce, an impropriety of which Aristotle would almost certainly have disapproved. It is a testimony to Shakespeare's dramatic genius that he could include in his tragedies such richly comic scenes without disrupting their dramatic tension. Of all Shakespeare's tragedies, Othello is the most Aristotelian in its unity. Shakespearean in its **puns** and plays on words and in the diversity and fullness of such characters as Othello, Iago, Emilia, and Desdemona, Othello moves inexorably to its tragic conclusion.*

Work Cited

Aristotle. "The Art of Poetry." From *Aristotle*. Sel. & trans. Philip Wheelwright. New York: Odyssey, 1951.

OTHELLO, THE MOOR OF VENICE   (1604)

The Names of the Actors

OTHELLO:	the Moor
BRABANTIO:	[a senator,] father to Desdemona
CASSIO:	an honorable lieutenant [to Othello]
IAGO:	[Othello's ancient,] a villain
RODERIGO:	a gulled gentleman
DUKE OF VENICE	
SENATORS [OF VENICE]	
MONTANO:	Governor of Cyprus
GENTLEMEN OF CYPRUS	
LODOVICO AND GRATIANO:	[kinsmen to Brabantio,] two noble Venetians
SAILORS	
CLOWN	

DESDEMONA:	[daughter to Brabantio and wife to Othello]
EMILIA:	wife to Iago
BIANCA:	a courtesan [and mistress to Cassio]

A MESSENGER
A HERALD
A MUSICIAN
SERVANTS, ATTENDANTS, OFFICERS,
SENATORS, MUSICIANS, GENTLEMEN

Scene

Venice; a seaport in Cyprus

1.1

(Enter Roderigo and Iago.)

RODERIGO:

1   Tush, never tell me! I take it much unkindly
That thou, Iago, who has had my purse
3   As if the strings were thine, shouldst know of this.
4 IAGO: 'Sblood, but you'll not hear me.
If ever I did dream of such a matter,
Abhor me.

RODERIGO:

Thou toldst me thou didst hold him in thy hate.
IAGO: Despise me
If I do not. Three great ones of the city,
In personal suit to make me his lieutenant,
11   Off-capped to him; and by the faith of man,
I know my price, I am worth no worse a place.
But he, as loving his own pride and purposes,
14   Evades them with a bombast circumstance
15   Horribly stuffed with epithets of war,
And, in conclusion,
17   Nonsuits my mediators. For, "Certes," says he,
"I have already chose my officer."

1.1 Location: Venice. A street.
1 never tell me (An expression of incredulity, like "tell me another one.")
3 this i.e., Desdemona's elopement
4 'Sblood by His (Christ's) blood
11 him i.e., Othello
14 bombast circumstance wordy evasion. (*Bombast* is cotton padding.)
15 epithets of war military expressions
17 Nonsuits rejects the petition of. **Certes** certainly

And what was he?

20 Forsooth, a great arithmetician,
One Michael Cassio, a Florentine,

22 A fellow almost damned in a fair wife,
That never set a squadron in the field

24 Nor the division of a battle knows

25 More than a spinster unless the bookish theoric,

26 Wherein the togaed consuls can propose
As masterly as he. Mere prattle without practice
Is all his soldiership. But he, sir, had th' election;

29 And I, of whom his eyes had seen the proof
At Rhodes, at Cyprus, and on other grounds

31 Christened and heathen, must be beleed and calmed

32 By debitor and creditor. This countercaster,

33 He, in good time, must his lieutenant be,

34 And I—God bless the mark!—his Moorship's ancient.

RODERIGO:

35 By heaven, I rather would have been his hangman.

IAGO:

Why, there's no remedy. 'Tis the curse of service;

37 Preferment goes by letter and affection,

38 And not by old gradation, where each second
Stood heir to th' first. Now, sir, be judge yourself

40 Whether I in any just term am affined
To love the Moor.

RODERIGO: I would not follow him then.

43 IAGO: O sir, content you.

20 arithmetician i.e., a man whose military knowledge is merely theoretical, based on books of tactics
22 A [. . .] wife (Cassio does not seem to be married, but his counterpart in Shakespeare's source does have a woman in his house. See also 4.1.131.)
24 division of a battle disposition of a military unit
25 a spinster i.e., a housewife, one whose regular occupation is spinning. **theoric** theory
26 togaed wearing the toga. **consuls** counselors, senators. **propose** discuss
29 his i.e., Othello's
31 Christened Christian. **beleed and calmed** left to leeward without wind, becalmed. (A sailing metaphor.)
32 debitor and creditor (A name for a system of bookkeeping, here used as a contemptuous nickname for Cassio.) **countercaster** i.e., bookkeeper, one who tallies with *counters*, or "metal disks." (Said contemptuously.)
33 in good time opportunely, i.e., forsooth
34 God bless the mark (Perhaps originally a formula to ward off evil; here an expression of impatience,) **ancient** standard-bearer, ensign
35 his hangman the executioner of him
37 Preferment promotion. **letter and affection** personal influence and favoritism
38 old gradation step-by-step seniority, the traditional way
40 term respect. **affined** bound
43 content you don't you worry about that

I follow him to serve my turn upon him.
We cannot all be masters, nor all masters
46 Cannot be truly followed. You shall mark
Many a duteous and knee-crooking knave
That, doting on his own obsequious bondage,
Wears out his time, much like his master's ass,
50 For naught but provender, and when he's old, cashiered.
51 Whip me such honest knaves. Others there are
52 Who, trimmed in forms and visages of duty,
Keep yet their hearts attending on themselves,
And, throwing but shows of service on their lords,
55 Do well thrive by them, and when they have lined their coats,
56 Do themselves homage. These fellows have some soul,
And such a one do I profess myself. For, sir,
It is as sure as you are Roderigo,
59 Were I the Moor I would not be Iago.
In following him, I follow but myself—
Heaven is my judge, not I for love and duty,
62 But seeming so for my peculiar end.
For when my outward action doth demonstrate
64 The native act and figure of my heart
65 In compliment extern, 'tis not long after
But I will wear my heart upon my sleeve
67 For daws to peck at. I am not what I am.

RODERIGO:
68 What a full fortune does the thick-lips owe
69 If he can carry 't thus!

IAGO: Call up her father.
Rouse him, make after him, poison his delight,
Proclaim him in the streets; incense her kinsmen,

46 **truly** faithfully
50 **cashiered** dismissed from service
51 **Whip me** whip, as far as I'm concerned
52 **trimmed** [. . .] **duty** dressed up in the mere form and show of dutifulness
55 **lined their coats** i.e., stuffed their purses
56 **Do themselves homage** i.e., attend to self-interest solely
59 **Were** [. . .] **Iago** i.e., if *I* were able to assume command, *I* certainly would not choose to remain a subordinate, or, *I* would keep a suspicious eye on a flattering subordinate
62 **peculiar** particular, personal
64 **native** innate. **figure** shape, intent
65 **compliment extern** outward show (conforming in this case to the inner workings and intention of the heart)
67 **daws** small crowlike birds, proverbially stupid and avaricious. **I am not what I am** i.e., I am not one who wears his heart on his sleeve
68 **full** swelling. **thick-lips** (Elizabethans often applied the term "Moor" to Negroes.) **owe** own
69 **carry 't thus** carry this off

72 And, though he in a fertile climate dwell,
73 Plague him with flies. Though that his joy be joy,
74 Yet throw such chances of vexation on 't
75 As it may lose some color.
RODERIGO: Here is her father's house. I'll call aloud.
IAGO:
77 Do, with like timorous accent and dire yell
78 As when, by night and negligence, the fire
Is spied in populous cities.
RODERIGO: What ho, Brabantio! Signor Brabantio, ho!
IAGO:
Awake! What ho, Brabantio! Thieves, thieves, thieves!
Look to your house, your daughter, and your bags!
83 Thieves, thieves!

(Brabantio [enters] above [at a window].)

BRABANTIO:
What is the reason of this terrible summons?
85 What is the matter there?
RODERIGO: Signor, is all your family within?
IAGO: Are your doors locked?
BRABANTIO: Why, wherefore ask you this?
IAGO:
89 Zounds, sir, you're robbed. For shame, put on your gown!
Your heart is burst; you have lost half your soul.
Even now, now, very now, an old black ram
92 Is tupping your white ewe. Arise, arise!
93 Awake the snorting citizens with the bell,
94 Or else the devil will make a grandsire of you.
Arise, I say!
BRABANTIO: What, have you lost your wits?
RODERIGO: Most reverend signor, do you know my voice?
BRABANTIO: Not I. What are you?
RODERIGO: My name is Roderigo.
BRABANTIO: The worser welcome.

72–73 though [. . .] flies though he seems prosperous and happy now, vex him with misery
73 Though [. . .] be joy although he seems fortunate and happy. (Repeats the idea of line 72.)
74 chances of vexation vexing changes
75 As it may that may cause it to. **some color** some of its fresh gloss
77 timorous frightening
78 and negligence i.e., by negligence
83 s.d. at a window (This stage direction, from the Quarto, probably calls for an appearance on the gallery above and rearstage.)
85 the matter your business
89 Zounds by His (Christ's) wounds
92 tupping covering, copulating with. (Said of sheep.)
93 snorting snoring
94 the devil (The devil was conventionally pictured as black.)

I have charged thee not to haunt about my doors.
In honest plainness thou hast heard me say
My daughter is not for thee; and now, in madness,
104   Being full of supper and distempering drafts,
105   Upon malicious bravery dost thou come
106   To start my quiet.
RODERIGO: Sir, sir, sir—
BRABANTIO: But thou must needs be sure
109   My spirits and my place have in their power
To make this bitter to thee.
RODERIGO: Patience, good sir.
BRABANTIO:
What tell'st thou me of robbing? This is Venice;
113   My house is not a grange.
RODERIGO: Most grave Brabantio,
115   In simple and pure soul I come to you.
IAGO: Zounds, sir, you are one of those that will not serve God if the
    devil bid you. Because we come to do you service and you think we
118   are ruffians, you'll have your daughter covered with a Barbary horse;
119   you'll have your nephews neigh to you; you'll have coursers for
120   cousins and jennets for germans.
BRABANTIO: What profane wretch art thou?
IAGO: I am one, sir, that comes to tell you your daughter and the Moor
    are now making the beast with two backs.
BRABANTIO: Thou art a villain.
125   IAGO: You are a senator.
BRABANTIO:
126   This thou shalt answer. I know thee, Roderigo.
RODERIGO:
Sir, I will answer anything. But I beseech you,
128   If't be your pleasure and most wise consent—
As partly I find it is—that your fair daughter,
130   At this odd-even and dull watch o' the night,
131   Transported with no worse nor better guard

---

104 distempering intoxicating
105 Upon malicious bravery with hostile intent to defy me
106 start startle, disrupt
109 My spirits and my place my temperament and my authority of office. **have in** have it in
113 grange isolated country house
115 simple sincere
118 Barbary from northern Africa (and hence associated with Othello)
119 nephews i.e., grandsons. **coursers** powerful horses
120 cousins kinsmen. **jennets** small Spanish horses. **germans** near relatives
125 a senator (Said with mock politeness, as though the word itself were an insult.)
126 answer be held accountable for
128 wise well-informed
130 odd-even between one day and the next, i.e., about midnight
131 with by

132 But with a knave of common hire, a gondolier,
     To the gross clasps of a lascivious Moor—
134 If this be known to you and your allowance
135 We then have done you bold and saucy wrongs.
     But if you know not this, my manners tell me
     We have your wrong rebuke. Do not believe
138 That, from the sense of all civility,
139 I thus would play and trifle with your reverence.
     Your daughter, if you have not given her leave,
     I say again, hath made a gross revolt,
142 Tying her duty, beauty, wit, and fortunes
143 In an extravagant and wheeling stranger
144 Of here and everywhere. Straight satisfy yourself.
     If she be in her chamber or your house,
     Let loose on me the justice of the state
     For thus deluding you.
148 BRABANTIO: Strike on the tinder, ho!
     Give me a taper! Call up all my people!
150 This accident is not unlike my dream.
     Belief of it oppresses me already.
     Light, I say, light!   (*Exit* [*above*].)
     IAGO: Farewell, for I must leave you.
154 It seems not meet nor wholesome to my place
155 To be producted—as, if I stay, I shall—
     Against the Moor. For I do know the state,
157 However this may gall him with some check,
158 Cannot with safety cast him, for he's embarked
159 With such loud reason to the Cyprus wars,
160 Which even now stands in act, that, for their souls,
161 Another of his fathom they have none

132 But with a knave than by a low fellow, a servant
134 allowance permission
135 saucy insolent
138 from contrary to. **civility** good manners, decency
139 your reverence the respect due to you
142 wit intelligence
143 extravagant expatriate, wandering far from home. **wheeling** roving about, vagabond
stranger foreigner
144 Straight straightway
148 tinder charred linen ignited by a spark from flint and steel, used to light torches or
tapers (lines 145, 171)
150 accident occurrence, event
154 meet fitting. **place** position (as ensign)
155 producted produced (as a witness)
157 gall rub; oppress. **check** rebuke
158 cast dismiss. **embarked** engaged
159 loud reason unanimous shout of confirmation (in the Senate)
160 stands in act are going on. **for their souls** to save themselves
161 fathom i.e., ability, depth of experience

162 To lead their business; in which regard,
Though I do hate him as I do hell pains,
164 Yet for necessity of present life
I must show out a flag and sign of love,
Which is indeed but sign. That you shall surely find him,
167 Lead to the Sagittary the raisèd search,
168 And there will I be with him. So farewell.   (*Exit*)

(Enter [below] Brabantio [in his nightgown] with servants and torches.)

BRABANTIO:
It is too true an evil. Gone she is;
170 And what's to come of my despisèd time
Is naught but bitterness. Now, Roderigo,
Where didst thou see her?—O unhappy girl!—
With the Moor, sayst thou?—Who would be a father!—
How didst thou know 'twas she?—O, she deceives me
Past thought!—What said she to you?—Get more tapers.
Raise all my kindred.—Are they married, think you?
RODERIGO: Truly, I think they are.
BRABANTIO:
O heaven! How got she out? O treason of the blood!
Fathers, from hence trust not your daughters' minds
180 By what you see them act. Is there not charms
181 By which the property of youth and maidhood
182 May be abused? Have you not read, Roderigo,
Of some such thing?
RODERIGO: Yes, sir, I have indeed.
BRABANTIO: Call up my brother.—O, would you had had her!—
Some one way, some another.—Do you know
Where we may apprehend her and the Moor?
RODERIGO:
188 I think I can discover him, if you please
To get good guard and go along with me.
BRABANTIO:
Pray you, lead on. At every house I'll call;

---

162 **in which regard** out of regard for which
164 **life** livelihood
167 **Sagittary** (An inn or house where Othello and Desdemona are staying, named for its sign of Sagittarius, or Centaur.) **raisèd search** search party roused out of sleep
168 **s.d. nightgown** dressing gown. (This costuming is specified in the Quarto text.)
170 **time** i.e., remainder of life
180 **charms** spells
181 **property** special quality, nature
182 **abused** deceived
188 **discover** reveal, uncover

191   I may command at most.—Get weapons, ho!
      And raise some special officers of night.—
193   On, good Roderigo. I will deserve your pains.   (*Exeunt.*)

1.2

(Enter Othello, Iago, attendants with torches.)

IAGO: Though in the trade of war I have slain men,
2   Yet do I hold it very stuff o' the conscience
3   To do no contrived murder. I lack iniquity
      Sometimes to do me service. Nine or ten times
5   I had thought t' have yerked him here under the ribs.
OTHELLO: 'Tis better as it is.
IAGO: Nay, but he prated,
      And spoke such scurvy and provoking terms
      Against your honor
      That, with the little godliness I have,
11   I did full hard forbear him. But, I pray you, sir,
      Are you fast married? Be assured of this,
13   That the magnifico is much beloved,
14   And hath in his effect a voice potential
      As double as the Duke's. He will divorce you,
      Or put upon you what restraint or grievance
      The law, with all his might to enforce it on,
18   Will give him cable.
OTHELLO: Let him do his spite.
20   My services which I have done the seigniory
21   Shall out-tongue his complaints. 'Tis yet to know—
      Which, when I know that boasting is an honor,
      I shall promulgate—I fetch my life and being
24   From men of royal siege, and my demerits
25   May speak unbonneted to as proud a fortune

---

191 command demand assistance
193 deserve show gratitude for
1.2 Location: Venice. Another street, before Othello's lodgings.
2 very stuff essence, basic material (continuing the metaphor of *trade* from line 1)
3 contrived premeditated
5 yerked stabbed. **him** i.e., Roderigo
11 I [. . .] him *I* restrained myself with great difficulty from assaulting him
13 magnifico Venetian grandee, i.e., Brabantio
14 in his effect at his command. **potential** powerful
18 cable i.e., scope
20 seigniory Venetian government
21 yet to know not yet widely known
24 siege i.e., rank. (Literally, seat used by a person of distinction.) **demerits** deserts
25 unbonneted without removing the hat, i.e., on equal terms (? Or "with hat off," "in all due modesty.")

As this that I have reached. For know, Iago,
But that I love the gentle Desdemona,
28   I would not my unhousèd free condition
29   Put into circumscription and confine
30   For the sea's worth. But look, what lights come yond?

(Enter Cassio [and certain officers] with torches.)

IAGO: Those are the raisèd father and his friends.
    You were best go in.
OTHELLO: Not I. I must be found.
34   My parts, my title, and my perfect soul
    Shall manifest me rightly. Is it they?
36   IAGO: By Janus, I think no.
OTHELLO: The servants of the Duke? And my lieutenant?
    The goodness of the night upon you, friends!
    What is the news?
CASSIO: The Duke does greet you, General,
    And he requires your haste-post-haste appearance
    Even on the instant.
43   OTHELLO: What is the matter, think you?
CASSIO:
44   Something from Cyprus, as I may divine.
45   It is a business of some heat. The galleys
46   Have sent a dozen sequent messengers
    This very night at one another's heels,
48   And many of the consuls, raised and met,
    Are at the Duke's already. You have been hotly called for;
    When, being not at your lodging to be found,
51   The Senate hath sent about three several quests
    To search you out.
OTHELLO: 'Tis well I am found by you.
    I will but spend a word here in the house
    And go with you.   *(Exit.)*
56   CASSIO: Ancient, what makes he here?

---

28 unhousèd unconfined, undomesticated
29 circumscription and confine restriction and confinement
30 the sea's worth all the riches at the bottom of the sea. **s.d. officers** (The Quarto text calls for "Cassio with lights, officers with torches.")
34 My [. . .] soul my natural gifts, my position or reputation, and my unflawed conscience
36 Janus Roman two-faced god of beginnings
43 matter business
44 divine guess
45 heat urgency
46 sequent successive
48 consuls senators
51 about all over the city. **several** separate
56 makes does

IAGO:

57   Faith, he tonight hath boarded a land carrack.

58   If it prove lawful prize, he's made forever.

CASSIO:

I do not understand.

IAGO: He's married.

CASSIO: To who?

(Enter Othello.)

IAGO:

62   Marry, to—Come,—Captain, will you go?

63   OTHELLO: Have with you.

CASSIO:

64   Here comes another troop to seek for you.

(Enter Brabantio, Roderigo, with officers and torches.)

IAGO:

65   It is Brabantio. General, be advised.

He comes to bad intent.

OTHELLO: Holla! Stand there!

RODERIGO:

Signor, it is the Moor.

BRABANTIO: Down with him, thief!

(They draw on both sides.)

IAGO:

You, Roderigo! Come, sir, I am for you.

OTHELLO:

71   Keep up your bright swords, for the dew will rust them.

Good signor, you shall more command with years.

Than with your weapons.

BRABANTIO:

O thou foul thief, where hast thou stowed my daughter?

Damned as thou art, thou hast enchanted her!

76   For I'll refer me to all things of sense,

If she in chains of magic were not bound

Whether a maid so tender, fair, and happy,

---

57 boarded gone aboard and seized as an act of piracy (with sexual suggestion).
carrack large merchant ship
58 prize booty
62 Marry (An oath, originally "by the Virgin Mary"; here used with wordplay on *married.*)
63 Have with you i.e., let's go
64 s.d. officers and torches (The Quarto text calls for "others with lights and weapons.")
65 be advised be on your guard
71 Keep up keep in the sheath
76 refer me submit my case. **things of sense** common sense understandings, or, creatures
possessing common sense

So opposite to marriage that she shunned
The wealthy curlèd darlings of our nation,
Would ever have, t' incur a general mock,
82   Run from her guardage to the sooty bosom
Of such a thing as thou—to fear, not to delight.
84   Judge me the world if 'tis not gross in sense
That thou hast practiced on her with foul charms,
86   Abused her delicate youth with drugs or minerals
87   That weakens motion. I'll have 't disputed on;
'Tis probable and palpable to thinking.
89   I therefore apprehend and do attach thee
For an abuser of the world, a practicer
91   Of arts inhibited and out of warrant.—
Lay hold upon him! If he do resist,
Subdue him at his peril.

OTHELLO: Hold your hands,
95   Both you of my inclining and the rest.
Were it my cue to fight, I should have known it
Without a prompter.—Whither will you that I go
To answer this your charge?

BRABANTIO: To prison, till fit time
100   Of law and course of direct session
Call thee to answer.

OTHELLO: What if I do obey?
How may the Duke be therewith satisfied,
Whose messengers are here about my side
Upon some present business of the state
To bring me to him?

OFFICER: 'Tis true, most worthy signor.
The Duke's in council, and your noble self,
I am sure, is sent for.

BRABANTIO: How? The Duke in council?
111   In this time of the night? Bring him away.
112   Mine's not an idle cause. The Duke himself,
Or any of my brothers of the state,
Cannot but feel this wrong as 'twere their own;

---

82 her guardage my guardianship of her
84 gross in sense obvious
86 minerals i.e., poisons
87 weakens motion impair the vital faculties. **disputed on** argued in court by professional counsel, debated by experts
89 attach arrest
91 arts inhibited prohibited arts, black magic
95 inclining following, party
100 course of direct session regular or specially convened legal proceedings
111 away right along
112 idle trifling

115   For if such actions may have passage free,
        Bondslaves and pagans shall our statesmen be.   (*Exeunt.*)

1.3

(Enter Duke [and] Senators [and sit at a table, with lights], and Officers.)

[The Duke and Senators are reading dispatches.]

DUKE:

1   There is no composition in these news
      That gives them credit.

3   FIRST SENATOR: Indeed, they are disproportioned.
      My letters say a hundred and seven galleys.

DUKE:

      And mine, a hundred forty.

SECOND SENATOR: And mine, two hundred.

7   But though they jump not on a just account—

8   As in these cases, where the aim reports
      'Tis oft with difference—yet do they all confirm
      A Turkish fleet, and bearing up to Cyprus.

DUKE:

      Nay, it is possible enough to judgment.

12   I do not so secure me in the error
      But the main article I do approve
      In fearful sense.

SAILOR (*within*):   What ho, what ho, what ho!

      (Enter Sailor.)

OFFICER: A messenger from the galleys.

DUKE: Now, what's the business?

SAILOR:

18   The Turkish preparation makes for Rhodes.
      So was I bid report here to the state
      By Signor Angelo.

DUKE:

21   How say you by this change?

---

115 have passage free are allowed to go unchecked
1.3 Location: Venice. A council chamber. s.d. Enter [. . .] Officers (The Quarto text calls for the Duke and senators to "sit at a table with lights and attendants.")
1 composition consistency
3 disproportioned inconsistent
7 jump agree. **just** exact
8 the aim conjecture
12–13 I do not [. . .] approve *I* do not take such (false) comfort in the discrepancies that *I* fail to perceive the main point, i.e., that the Turkish fleet is threatening
18 preparation fleet prepared for battle
21 by about

FIRST SENATOR: This cannot be
23   By no assay of reason. 'Tis a pageant
24   To keep us in false gaze. When we consider
       Th' importancy of Cyprus to the Turk,
       And let ourselves again but understand
       That, as it more concerns the Turk than Rhodes,
28   So may he with more facile question bear it,
29   For that it stands not in such warlike brace,
30   But altogether lacks th' abilities
31   That Rhodes is dressed in—if we make thought of this,
32   We must not think the Turk is so unskillful
33   To leave the latest which concerns him first,
       Neglecting an attempt of ease and gain
35   To wake and wage a danger profitless,
DUKE:
       Nay, in all confidence, he's not for Rhodes.
OFFICER: Here is more news.

(Enter a Messenger.)

MESSENGER: The Ottomites, reverend and gracious,
       Steering with due course toward the isle of Rhodes,
40   Have there injointed them with an after fleet.
FIRST SENATOR:
       Ay, so I thought. How many, as you guess?
MESSENGER:
42   Of thirty sail; and now they do restem
43   Their backward course, bearing with frank appearance
       Their purposes toward Cyprus. Signor Montano,
45   Your trusty and most valiant servitor,
46   With his free duty recommends you thus,
       And prays you to believe him.
DUKE: 'Tis certain then for Cyprus.
       Marcus Luccicos, is not he in town?
FIRST SENATOR: He's now in Florence.

23 **assay** test. **pageant** mere show
24 **in false gaze** looking the wrong way
28 **So may [. . .] it** so also he (the Turk) can more easily capture it (Cyprus)
29 **For that** since. **brace** state of defense
30 **abilities** means of self-defense
31 **dressed in** equipped with
32 **unskillful** deficient in judgment
33 **latest** last
35 **wake** stir up. **wage** risk
40 **injointed them** joined themselves. **after** second, following
42–43 **restem [. . .] course** retrace their original course
43 **frank appearance** undisguised intent
45 **servitor** officer under your command
46 **free duty** freely given and loyal service. **recommends** commends himself and reports to

DUKE:
>Write from us to him, post-post-haste. Dispatch.

FIRST SENATOR: Here comes Brabantio and the valiant Moor.

(Enter Brabantio, Othello, Cassio, Iago, Roderigo, and officers.)

DUKE:
53
>Valiant Othello, we must straight employ you
54
>Against the general enemy Ottoman.
55
>(*To Brabantio.*) I did not see you; welcome, gentle signor.
>We lacked your counsel and your help tonight.

BRABANTIO:
>So did I yours. Good Your Grace, pardon me;
58
>Neither my place nor aught I heard of business
>Hath raised me from my bed, nor doth the general care
60
>Take hold on me, for my particular grief
61
>Is of so floodgate and o'erbearing nature
62
>That it engluts and swallows other sorrows
63
>And it is still itself.

DUKE: Why, what's the matter?

BRABANTIO: My daughter! O, my daughter!

DUKE AND SENATORS: Dead?

BRABANTIO: Ay, to me.
68
>She is abused, stol'n from me, and corrupted
>By spells and medicines bought of mountebanks;
>For nature so preposterously to err,
71
>Being not deficient, blind, or lame of sense,
72
>Sans witchcraft could not.

DUKE:
>Whoe'er he be that in this foul proceeding
>Hath thus beguiled your daughter of herself,
>And you of her, the bloody book of law
>You shall yourself read in the bitter letter
77
>After your own sense—yea, though our proper son
78
>Stood in your action.

---

53 straight straightway
54 general enemy universal enemy to all Christendom
55 gentle noble
58 place official position
60 particular personal
61 floodgate i.e., overwhelming (as when floodgates are opened)
62 engluts engulfs
63 is still itself remains undiminished
68 abused deceived
71 deficient defective. **lame of sense** deficient in sensory perception
72 Sans without
77 After [. . .] sense according to your own interpretation. **our proper** my own
78 Stood [. . .] action were under your accusation

BRABANTIO: Humbly I thank Your Grace.
     Here is the man, this Moor, whom now it seems
     Your special mandate for the state affairs
     Hath hither brought.
ALL: We are very sorry for 't.
DUKE (*to Othello*):What, in your own part, can you say to this?
BRABANTIO: Nothing, but this is so.
OTHELLO:
     Most potent, grave, and reverend signors,
87   My very noble and approved good masters:
     That I have ta'en away this old man's daughter,
     It is most true; true, I have married her.
90   The very head and front of my offending
91   Hath this extent, no more. Rude am I in my speech,
     And little blessed with the soft phrase of peace;
93   For since these arms of mine had seven years' pith,
94   Till now some nine moons wasted, they have used
95   Their dearest action in the tented field;
     And little of this great world can I speak
     More than pertains to feats of broils and battle,
     And therefore little shall I grace my cause
     In speaking for myself. Yet, by your gracious patience,
100 I will a round unvarnished tale deliver
     Of my whole course of love—what drugs, what charms,
     What conjuration, and what mighty magic,
103 For such proceeding I am charged withal,
     I won his daughter.
BRABANTIO: A maiden never bold;
106 Of spirit so still and quiet that her motion
     Blushed at herself; and she, in spite of nature,
108 Of years, of country, credit, everything,
     To fall in love with what she feared to look on!
     It is a judgment maimed and most imperfect
111 That will confess perfection so could err
     Against all rules of nature, and must be driven

87 approved proved, esteemed
90 head and front height and breadth, entire extent
91 Rude unpolished
93 since [. . .] pith i.e., since I was seven. **pith** strength, vigor
94 Till [. . .] wasted until some nine months ago (since when Othello has evidently not been on active duty, but in Venice)
95 dearest most valuable
100 round plain
103 withal with
106–107 her [. . .] herself i.e., she blushed easily at herself. (*Motion* can suggest the impulse of the soul or of the emotions, or physical movement.)
108 years i.e., difference in age. **credit** virtuous reputation
111 confess concede (that)

113	To find out practices of cunning hell

113   To find out practices of cunning hell
114   Why this should be. I therefore vouch again
115   That with some mixtures powerful o'er the blood,
116   Or with some dram conjured to this effect,
        He wrought upon her.
DUKE: To vouch this is no proof,
119   Without more wider and more overt test
120   Than these thin habits and poor likelihoods
121   Of modern seeming do prefer against him.
FIRST SENATOR: But Othello, speak.
123   Did you by indirect and forcèd courses
        Subdue and poison this young maid's affections?
125   Or came it by request and such fair question
        As soul to soul affordeth?
OTHELLO: I do beseech you,
        Send for the lady to the Sagittary
        And let her speak of me before her father.
        If you do find me foul in her report,
        The trust, the office I do hold of you
        Not only take away, but let your sentence
        Even fall upon my life.
DUKE: Fetch Desdemona hither.
OTHELLO:
        Ancient, conduct them. You best know the place.

(Exeunt Iago and attendants.)

        And, till she come, as truly as to heaven
137   I do confess the vices of my blood,
138   So justly to your grave ears I'll present
        How I did thrive in this fair lady's love,
        And she in mine.
DUKE: Say it, Othello.
OTHELLO:
        Her father loved me, oft invited me,
143   Still questioned me the story of my life
        From year to year—the battles, sieges, fortunes
        That I have passed.

---

113 practices plots
114 vouch assert
115 blood passions
116 dram [. . .] **effect** dose made by magical spells to have this effect
119 more wider fuller. **test** testimony
120 habits garments, i.e., appearances. **poor likelihoods** weak inferences
121 modern seeming commonplace assumption. **prefer** bring forth
123 forcèd courses means used against her will
125 question conversation
137 blood passions, human nature
138 justly truthfully, accurately
143 Still continually

I ran it through, even from my boyish days
To th' very moment that he bade me tell it,
Wherein I spoke of most disastrous chances,
149 Of moving accidents by flood and field,
150 Of hairbreadth scapes i' th' imminent deadly breach,
Of being taken by the insolent foe
And sold to slavery, of my redemption thence,
153 And portance in my travels' history,
154 Wherein of antres vast and deserts idle,
155 Rough quarries, rocks, and hills whose heads touch heaven,
156 It was my hint to speak—such was my process—
And of the Cannibals that each other eat,
158 The Anthropophagi, and men whose heads
Do grow beneath their shoulders. These things to hear
Would Desdemona seriously incline;
But still the house affairs would draw her thence,
Which ever as she could with haste dispatch
She'd come again, and with a greedy ear
Devour up my discourse. Which I, observing,
165 Took once a pliant hour, and found good means
To draw from her a prayer of earnest heart
167 That I would all my pilgrimage dilate,
168 Whereof by parcels she had something heard,
169 But not intentively. I did consent,
And often did beguile her of her tears,
When I did speak of some distressful stroke
That my youth suffered. My story being done,
She gave me for my pains a world of sighs.
174 She swore, in faith, 'twas strange, 'twas passing strange,
'Twas pitiful, 'twas wondrous pitiful.
She wished she had not heard it, yet she wished
177 That heaven had made her such a man. She thanked me,
And bade me, if I had a friend that loved her,
I should but teach him how to tell my story,
180 And that would woo her. Upon this hint I spake.

149 moving accidents stirring happenings
150 imminent [. . .] **breach** death-threatening gaps made in a fortification
153 portance conduct
154 antres caverns. **idle** barren, desolate
155 Rough quarries rugged rock formations
156 hint occasion, opportunity
158 Anthropophagi man-eaters. (A term from Pliny's *Natural History.*)
165 pliant well-suiting
167 dilate relate in detail
168 by parcels piecemeal
169 intentively with full attention, continuously
174 passing exceedingly
177 made her created her to be
180 hint opportunity. (Othello does not mean that she was dropping hints.)

> She loved me for the dangers I had passed,
> And I loved her that she did pity them.
> This only is the witchcraft I have used.
> Here comes the lady. Let her witness it.

(Enter Desdemona, Iago, [and] attendants.)

DUKE:
> I think this tale would win my daughter too.
> Good Brabantio,
187   Take up this mangled matter at the best.
> Men do their broken weapons rather use
> Than their bare hands.

BRABANTIO: I pray you, hear her speak.
> If she confess that she was half the wooer,
> Destruction on my head if my bad blame
> Light on the man!—Come hither, gentle mistress.
> Do you perceive in all this noble company
> Where most you owe obedience?

DESDEMONA: My noble Father,
> I do perceive here a divided duty.
198   To you I am bound for life and education;
199   My life and education both do learn me
200   How to respect you. You are the lord of duty;
> I am hitherto your daughter. But here's my husband,
> And so much duty as my mother showed
> To you, preferring you before her father,
204   So much I challenge that I may profess
> Due to the Moor my lord.

BRABANTIO: God be with you! I have done.
> Please it Your Grace, on to the state affairs.
208   I had rather to adopt a child than get it.
> Come hither, Moor.   *(He joins the hands of Othello and Desdemona.)*
210   I here do give thee that with all my heart
211   Which, but thou hast already, with all my heart
212   I would keep from thee.—For your sake, jewel,
> I am glad at soul I have no other child,
214   For thy escape would teach me tyranny,

---

187 **Take [. . .] best** make the best of a bad bargain
198 **education** upbringing
199 **learn** teach
200 **of duty** to whom duty is due
204 **challenge** claim
208 **get** beget
210 **with all my heart** wherein my whole affection has been engaged
211 **with all my heart** willingly, gladly
212 **For your sake** on your account
214 **escape** elopement

215   To hang clogs on them.—I have done, my lord.
DUKE:
216   Let me speak like yourself, and lay a sentence
217   Which, as a grece or step, may help these lovers
       Into your favor.
219   When remedies are past, the griefs are ended
220   By seeing the worst, which late on hopes depended.
221   To mourn a mischief that is past and gone
222   Is the next way to draw new mischief on.
223   What cannot be preserved when fortune takes,
224   Patience her injury a mockery makes.
       The robbed that smiles steals something from the thief;
226   He robs himself that spends a bootless grief.
BRABANTIO:
       So let the Turk of Cyprus us beguile,
       We lose it not, so long as we can smile.
229   He bears the sentence well that nothing bears
       But the free comfort which from thence he hears,
       But he bears both the sentence and the sorrow
       That, to pay grief, must of poor patience borrow.
233   These sentences, to sugar or to gall,
       Being strong on both sides, are equivocal.
       But words are words. I never yet did hear
236   That the bruised heart was piercèd through the ear.
       I humbly beseech you, proceed to th' affairs of state.
DUKE: The Turk with a most mighty preparation makes for Cyprus.
239   Othello, the fortitude of the place is best known to you; and though

---

215 clogs (Literally, blocks of wood fastened to the legs of criminals or convicts to inhibit escape.)
216 like yourself i.e., as you would, in your proper temper. **lay a sentence** apply a maxim
217 grece step
219 remedies hopes of remedy
220 which [. . .] **depended** which griefs were sustained until recently by hopeful anticipation
221 mischief misfortune, injury
222 next nearest
223 What whatever
224 Patience [. . .] **makes** patience laughs at the injury inflicted by fortune (and thus eases the pain)
226 spends a bootless grief indulges in unavailing grief
229–232 He bears [. . .] **borrow** a person well bears out your maxim who can enjoy its platitudinous comfort, free of all genuine sorrow, but anyone whose grief bankrupts his poor patience is left with your saying and his sorrow, too. (*Bears the sentence* also plays on the meaning, "receives judicial sentence.")
233–234 These [. . .] **equivocal** these fine maxims are equivocal, either sweet or bitter in their application
236 piercèd [. . .] **ear** i.e., surgically lanced and cured by mere words of advice
239 fortitude strength

240   we have there a substitute of most allowed sufficiency, yet opinion,
            a sovereign mistress of effects, throws a more safer voice on you.
242   You must therefore be content to slubber the gloss of your
243   new fortunes with this more stubborn and boisterous expedition.

OTHELLO:
        The tyrant custom, most grave senators,
        Hath made the flinty and steel couch of war
246   My thrice-driven bed of down. I do agnize
        A natural and prompt alacrity
248   I find in hardness, and do undertake
        These present wars against the Ottomites.
250   Most humbly therefore bending to your state,
        I crave fit disposition for my wife,
252   Due reference of place and exhibition,
253   With such accommodation and besort
254   As levels with her breeding.

DUKE:
        Why, at her father's.

BRABANTIO: I will not have it so.

OTHELLO:
           Nor I.

DESDEMONA: Nor I. I would not there reside,
        To put my father in impatient thoughts
        By being in his eye. Most gracious Duke,
261   To my unfolding lend your prosperous ear,
262   And let me find a charter in your voice,
        T' assist my simpleness.

DUKE: What would you, Desdemona?

DESDEMONA:
        That I did love the Moor to live with him,
266   My downright violence and storm of fortunes

---

240 substitute deputy. **allowed** acknowledged
240–241 opinion [. . .] **on you** general opinion, an important determiner of affairs, chooses you as the best man
242 slubber soil, sully
243 stubborn harsh, rough
246 thrice-driven thrice sifted, winnowed. **agnize** know in myself, acknowledge
248 hardness hardship
250 bending [. . .] **state** bowing or kneeling to your authority
252 reference [. . .] **exhibition** provision of appropriate place to live and allowance of money
253 accommodation suitable provision. **besort** attendance
254 levels equals, suits. **breeding** social position, upbringing
261 unfolding explanation, proposal. **prosperous** propitious
262 charter privilege, authorization
266 My [. . .] **fortunes** my plain and total breach of social custom, taking my future by storm and disrupting my whole life

267 May trumpet to the world. My heart's subdued
Even to the very quality of my lord.
I saw Othello's visage in his mind,
270 And to his honors and his valiant parts
Did I my soul and fortunes consecrate.
So that, dear lords, if I be left behind
273 A moth of peace, and he go to the war,
274 The rites for why I love him are bereft me,
And I a heavy interim shall support
276 By his dear absence. Let me go with him.
277 OTHELLO: Let her have your voice.
Vouch with me, heaven, I therefor beg it not
To please the palate of my appetite,
280 Nor to comply with heat—the young affects
281 In me defunct—and proper satisfaction,
282 But to be free and bounteous to her mind.
283 And heaven defend your good souls that you think
I will your serious and great business scant
When she is with me. No, when light-winged toys
286 Of feathered Cupid seel with wanton dullness
287 My speculative and officed instruments,
288 That my disports corrupt and taint my business,
Let huswives make a skillet of my helm,
290 And all indign and base adversities
291 Make head against my estimation!
DUKE:
Be it as you shall privately determine,
Either for her stay or going. Thè affair cries haste,
And speed must answer it.
A SENATOR: You must away tonight.

267–268 My heart's [. . .] lord my heart is brought wholly into accord with Othello's
virtues; I love him for his virtues
270 parts qualities
273 moth i.e., one who consumes merely
274 rites rites of love (with a suggestion, too, of "rights," sharing)
276 dear (1) heartfelt (2) costly
277 voice consent
280 heat sexual passion. **young affects** passions of youth, desires
281 proper personal
282 free generous
283 defend forbid. **think** should think
286 seel i.e., making blind (as in falconry, by sewing up the eyes of the hawk during
training)
287 speculative [. . .] instruments eyes and other faculties used in the performance of
duty
288 That so that. **disports** sexual pastimes. **taint** impair
290 indign unworthy, shameful
291 Make head raise an army. **estimation** reputation

DESDEMONA:

    Tonight, my lord?

DUKE: This night.

OTHELLO: With all my heart.

DUKE:

    At nine i' the morning here we'll meet again.

    Othello, leave some officer behind,

    And he shall our commission bring to you,

302   With such things else of quality and respect

303   As doth import you.

OTHELLO: So please Your Grace, my ancient;

    A man he is of honesty and trust.

    To his conveyance I assign my wife,

    With what else needful Your Good Grace shall think

    To be sent after me.

DUKE: Let it be so.

    Good night to everyone. (*To Brabantio.*) And, noble signor,

311   If virtue no delighted beauty lack,

    Your son-in-law is far more fair than black.

FIRST SENATOR:

    Adieu, brave Moor. Use Desdemona well.

BRABANTIO:

    Look to her, Moor, if thou hast eyes to see.

    She has deceived her father, and may thee.

(Exeunt [Duke, Brabantio, Cassio, Senators and officers].)

OTHELLO:

    My life upon her faith! Honest Iago,

    My Desdemona must I leave to thee.

    I prithee, let thy wife attend on her,

319   And bring them after in the best advantage.

    Come, Desdemona. I have but an hour

321   Of love, of worldly matters and direction,

322   To spend with thee. We must obey the time.

([Exit with Desdemona].)

RODERIGO: Iago—

IAGO: What sayst thou, noble heart?

RODERIGO: What will I do, think'st thou?

302 **of quality and respect** of importance and relevance
303 **import** concern
311 **delighted** capable of delighting
319 **in [. . .] advantage** at the most favorable opportunity
321 **direction** instructions
322 **the time** the urgency of the present crisis

IAGO: Why, go to bed and sleep.

327 RODERIGO: I will incontinently drown myself.

IAGO: If thou dost, I shall never love thee after. Why,
    thou silly gentleman?

RODERIGO: It is silliness to live when to live is torment;

331   and then have we a prescription to die when death is
    our physician.

333 IAGO: O villainous! I have looked upon the world for
    four times seven years, and, since I could distinguish
    betwixt a benefit and an injury, I never found man
    that knew how to love himself. Ere I would say I

337   would drown myself for the love of a guinea hen, I
    would change my humanity with a baboon.

RODERIGO: What should I do? I confess it is my shame

340   to be so fond, but it is not in my virtue to amend it.

341 IAGO: Virtue? A fig! 'Tis in ourselves that we are thus
    or thus. Our bodies are our gardens, to the which our
    wills are gardeners; so that if we will plant nettles or

344   sow lettuce, set hyssop and weed up thyme, supply it

345   with one gender of herbs or distract it with many,

346   either to have it sterile with idleness or manured with

347   industry—why, the power and corrigible authority of

348   this lies in our wills. If the beam of our lives had not

349   one scale of reason to poise another of sensuality, the

350   blood and baseness of our natures would conduct us
    to most preposterous conclusions. But we have reason

352   to cool our raging motions, our carnal stings, our

353   unbitted lusts, whereof I take this that you call love to

354   be a sect or scion.

RODERIGO: It cannot be.

---

327 incontinently immediately, without self-restraint
331 prescription (1) right based on long-established custom (2) doctor's prescription
333 villainous i.e., what perfect nonsense
337 guinea hen (A slang term for a prostitute.)
340 fond infatuated. **virtue** strength, nature
341 fig (To give a fig is to thrust the thumb between the first and second fingers in a vulgar and insulting gesture)
344 hyssop a herb of the mint family
345 gender kind. **distract it with** divide it among
346 idleness want of cultivation
347 corrigible authority power to correct
348 beam balance
349 poise counterbalance
350 blood natural passions
352 motions appetites
353 unbitted unbridled, uncontrolled
354 sect or scion cutting or offshoot

IAGO: It is merely a lust of the blood and a permission
    of the will. Come, be a man. Drown thyself? Drown
    cats and blind puppies. I have professed me thy friend,
    and I confess me knit to thy deserving with cables of
360   perdurable toughness. I could never better stead thee
    than now. Put money in thy purse. Follow thou the
362   wars; defeat thy favor with an usurped beard. I say,
    put money in thy purse. It cannot be long that Des-
    demona should continue her love to the Moor—put
    money in thy purse—nor he his to her. It was a vio-
366   lent commencement in her, and thou shalt see an
    answerable sequestration—put but money in thy purse.
368   These Moors are changeable in their wills—fill thy
    purse with money. The food that to him now is as
370   luscious as locusts shall be to him shortly as bitter as
371   coloquintida. She must change for youth; when she is
    sated with his body, she will find the error of her
    choice. She must have change, she must. Therefore
    put money in thy purse. If thou wilt needs damn thy-
375   self, do it a more delicate way than drowning. Make
376   all the money thou canst. If sanctimony and a frail vow
377   betwixt an erring barbarian and a supersubtle Vene-
    tian be not too hard for my wits and all the tribe of
    hell, thou shalt enjoy her. Therefore make money.
380   A pox of drowning thyself! It is clean out of the way.
381   Seek thou rather to be hanged in compassing thy joy
    than to be drowned and go without her.
383 RODERIGO: Wilt thou be fast to my hopes if I depend on
384   the issue?
IAGO: Thou art sure of me. Go, make money. I have
    told thee often, and I retell thee again and again, I hate
387   the Moor. My cause is hearted; thine hath no less reason.

---

360 perdurable very durable. **stead** assist
362 defeat thy favor disguise your face. **usurped** (The suggestion is that Roderigo is not man enough to have a beard of his own.)
366–367 an answerable sequestration a corresponding separation or estrangement
368 wills carnal appetites
370 locusts fruit of the carob tree (see Matthew 3:4), or perhaps honeysuckle
371 coloquintida colocynth or bitter apple, a purgative
375 Make raise, collect
376 sanctimony sacred ceremony
377 erring wandering, vagabond, unsteady
380 clean [. . .] way entirely unsuitable as a course of action
381 compassing encompassing, embracing
383 fast true
384 issue (successful) outcome
387 hearted fixed in the heart, heartfelt

388   Let us be conjunctive in our revenge against him.
       If thou canst cuckold him, thou dost thyself a pleasure,
       me a sport. There are many events in the womb of time
391   which will get delivered. Traverse, go, provide thy money.
       We will have more of this tomorrow. Adieu.

RODERIGO: Where shall we meet i' the morning?

IAGO: At my lodging.

395   RODERIGO: I'll be with thee betimes.   (*He starts to leave.*)

IAGO: Go to, farewell.—Do you hear, Roderigo?

RODERIGO: What say you?

IAGO: No more of drowning, do you hear?

RODERIGO: I am changed.

IAGO: Go to, farewell. Put money enough in your purse.

RODERIGO:
       I'll sell my land.   (*Exit.*)

IAGO:
       Thus do I ever make my fool my purse;
       For I mine own gained knowledge should profane
404   If I would time expend with such a snipe
       But for my sport and profit. I hate the Moor;
406   And it is thought abroad that twixt my sheets
407   He's done my office. I know not if 't be true;
       But I, for mere suspicion in that kind,
409   Will do as if for surety. He holds me well;
       The better shall my purpose work on him.
411   Cassio's a proper man. Let me see now:
412   To get his place and to plume up my will
       In double knavery—How, how?—Let's see:
414   After some time, to abuse Othello's ear
415   That he is too familiar with his wife.
416   He hath a person and a smooth dispose
       To be suspected, framed to make women false.
418   The Moor is of a free and open nature,
       That thinks men honest that but seem to be so,

---

388 conjunctive united
391 Traverse (A military marching term.)
395 betimes early
404 snipe woodcock, i.e., fool
406 it is thought abroad it is rumored
407 my office i.e., my sexual function as husband
409 do [. . .] surety act as if on certain knowledge. **holds me well** regards me favorably
411 proper handsome
412 plume up put a feather in the cap of, i.e., glorify, gratify
414 abuse deceive
415 he i.e., Cassio
416 dispose disposition
418 free frank, generous. **open** unsuspicious

420 And will as tenderly be led by the nose
As asses are.
I have 't. It is engendered. Hell and night
Must bring this monstrous birth to the world's light.

(Exit.)

2.1

(Enter Montano and two Gentlemen.)

MONTANO: What from the cape can you discern at sea?
FIRST GENTLEMAN:
2   Nothing at all. It is a high-wrought flood.
3   I cannot, twixt the heaven and the main,
Descry a sail.
MONTANO:
Methinks the wind hath spoke aloud at land;
A fuller blast ne'er shook our battlements.
7   If it hath ruffianed so upon the sea,
8   What ribs of oak, when mountains melt on them,
9   Can hold the mortise? What shall we hear of this?
SECOND GENTLEMAN:
10   A segregation of the Turkish fleet.
For do but stand upon the foaming shore,
12   The chidden billow seems to pelt the clouds;
13   The wind-shaked surge, with high and monstrous mane,
14   Seems to cast water on the burning Bear
And quench the guards of th' ever-fixèd pole.
16   I never did like molestation view
17   On the enchafèd flood.

420 tenderly readily
2.1 Location: A seaport in Cyprus. An open place near the quay.
2 high-wrought flood very agitated sea
3 main ocean (also at line 42)
7 ruffianed raged
8 mountains i.e., of water
9 hold the mortise hold their joints together. (A mortise is the socket hollowed out in fitting timbers.)
10 segregation dispersal
12 chidden i.e., rebuked, repelled (by the shore), and thus shot into the air
13 monstrous mane (The surf is like the mane of a wild beast.)
14 the burning Bear i.e., the constellation Ursa Minor or the Little Bear, which includes the polestar (and hence regarded as the *guards of th' ever-fixèd pole* in the next line; sometimes the term *guards* is applied to the two "pointers" of the Big Bear or Dipper, which may be intended here.)
16 like molestation comparable disturbance
17 enchafèd angry

18 MONTANO: If that the Turkish fleet
19   Be not ensheltered and embayed, they are drowned;
20   It is impossible to bear it out.

(Enter a [Third] Gentleman.)

THIRD GENTLEMAN: News, lads! Our wars are done.
    The desperate tempest hath so banged the Turks
23   That their designment halts. A noble ship of Venice
24   Hath seen a grievous wreck and sufferance
    On most part of their fleet.
MONTANO: How? Is this true?
THIRD GENTLEMAN: This ship is here put in,
28   A Veronesa; Michael Cassio,
    Lieutenant to the warlike Moor Othello,
    Is come on shore; the Moor himself at sea,
    And is in full commission here for Cyprus.
MONTANO:
    I am glad on 't. 'Tis a worthy governor.
THIRD GENTLEMAN:
    But this same Cassio, though he speak of comfort
34   Touching the Turkish loss, yet he looks sadly
    And prays the Moor be safe, for they were parted
    With foul and violent tempest.
MONTANO: Pray heaven he be,
    For I have served him, and the man commands
39   Like a full soldier. Let's to the seaside, ho!
    As well to see the vessel that's come in
    As to throw out our eyes for brave Othello,
42   Even till we make the main and the' aerial blue
43   An indistinct regard.
THIRD GENTLEMAN: Come, let's do so,
45   For every minute is expectancy
46   Of more arrivance.

(Enter Cassio.)

18 **If that** if
19 **embayed** sheltered by a bay
20 **bear it out** survive, weather the storm
23 **designment** design, enterprise. **halts** is lame
24 **wreck** shipwreck. **sufferance** damage, disaster
28 **Veronesa** i.e., fitted out in Verona for Venetian service, or possibly *Verennessa* (the Folio spelling), i.e., *verrinessa*, a cutter (from *verrinare*, "to cut through")
34 **sadly** gravely
39 **full** perfect
42 **the main** [. . .] **blue** the sea and the sky
43 **An indistinct regard** indistinguishable in our view
45 **is expectancy** gives expectation
46 **arrivance** arrival

CASSIO:

    Thanks, you the valiant of this warlike isle,

48   That so approve the Moor! O, let the heavens

    Give him defense against the elements,

    For I have lost him on a dangerous sea.

MONTANO: Is he well shipped?

CASSIO:

    His bark is stoutly timbered, and his pilot

53   Of very expert and approved allowance;

54   Therefore my hopes, not surfeited to death,

55   Stand in bold cure.

         (*A cry*) within: "A sail, a sail, a sail!"

CASSIO: What noise?

A GENTLEMAN:

58   The town is empty. On the brow o' the sea

    Stand ranks of people, and they cry "A sail!"

CASSIO:

60   My hopes do shape him for the governor.

                (*A shot within.*)

SECOND GENTLEMAN:

61   They do discharge their shot of courtesy;

    Our friends at least.

CASSIO: I pray you, sir, go forth,

    And give us truth who 'tis that is arrived.

SECOND GENTLEMAN: I shall. (*Exit.*)

MONTANO:

    But, good Lieutenant, is your general wived?

CASSIO:

    Most fortunately. He hath achieved a maid

68   That paragons description and wild fame,

69   One that excels the quirks of blazoning pens,

70   And in th' essential vesture of creation

    Does tire the enginer.

48 approve admire, honor

53 approved allowance tested reputation

54 surfeited to death i.e., overextended, worn thin through repeated application or delayed fulfillment

55 in bold cure in strong hopes of fulfillment

58 brow o' the sea cliff-edge

60 My [. . .] for I hope it is

61 discharge [. . .] courtesy fire a salute in token of respect and courtesy

68 paragons surpasses. **wild fame** extravagant report

69 quirks witty conceits. **blazoning** setting forth as though in heraldic language

70–71 in [. . .] enginer in her real, God-given, beauty, (she) defeats any attempt to praise her. **enginer** engineer, i.e, poet, one who devises. **s.d. Second Gentleman** (So identified in the Quarto text here and in lines 58, 61, 68, and 96; the Folio calls him a gentleman.)

(Enter [Second] Gentleman.)

72   How now? Who has put in?

SECOND GENTLEMAN:
    'Tis one Iago, ancient to the General.

CASSIO:
    He's had most favorable and happy speed.
    Tempests themselves, high seas, and howling winds,
76   The guttered rocks and congregated sands—
77   Traitors ensteeped to clog the guiltless keel—
78   As having sense of beauty, do omit
79   Their mortal natures, letting go safely by
    The divine Desdemona.

MONTANO: What is she?

CASSIO:
    She that I spake of, our great captain's captain,
    Left in the conduct of the bold Iago,
84   Whose footing here anticipates our thoughts
85   A sennight's speed. Great Jove, Othello guard,
    And swell his sail with thine own powerful breath,
87   That he may bless this bay with his tall ship,
    Make love's quick pants in Desdemona's arms,
    Give renewed fire to our extincted spirits,
    And bring all Cyprus comfort!

(Enter Desdemona, Iago, Roderigo, and Emilia.)

    O, behold,
    The riches of the ship is come on shore!
    You men of Cyprus, let her have your knees.

(The gentleman make curtsy to Desdemona.)

    Hail to thee, lady! And the grace of heaven
    Before, behind thee, and on every hand
    Enwheel thee round!

DESDEMONA: I thank you, valiant Cassio.
    What tidings can you tell me of my lord?

CASSIO:
    He is not yet arrived, nor know I aught.
    But that he's well and will be shortly here.

72 put in i.e., to harbor
76 guttered jagged, trenched
77 ensteeped lying under water
78 As as if. **omit** forbear to exercise
79 mortal deadly
84 footing landing
85 sennight's week's
87 tall splendid, gallant

DESDEMONA:

O, but I fear—How lost you company?

CASSIO:

The great contention of the sea and skies
Parted our fellowship.
                    (*Within*) "A sail, a sail!" (*A shot.*)
                    But hark. A sail!

SECOND GENTLEMAN:

They give their greeting to the citadel.
This likewise is a friend.

CASSIO: See for the news.

(Exit Second Gentleman.)

Good Ancient, you are welcome. (*Kissing Emilia.*)
        Welcome, mistress.
Let it not gall your patience, good Iago,
112   That I extend my manners; 'tis my breeding
        That gives me this bold show of courtesy.

IAGO:

Sir, would she give you so much of her lips
As of her tongue she often bestows on me,
You would have enough.

117   DESDEMONA: Alas, she has no speech!

IAGO: In faith, too much.

119   I find it still, when I have list to sleep.
        Marry, before your ladyship, I grant,
        She puts her tongue a little in her heart
122   And chides with thinking.

EMILIA: You have little cause to say so.

IAGO:

124   Come on, come on. You are pictures out of doors,
125   Bells in your parlors, wildcats in your kitchens,
126   Saints in your injuries, devils being offended,
127   Players in your huswifery, and huswives in your beds.

DESDEMONA: O, fie upon thee, slanderer!

---

112 extend give scope to. **breeding** training in the niceties of etiquette
117 she has no speech i.e., she's not a chatterbox, as you allege
119 still always. **list** desire
122 with thinking i.e., in her thoughts only
124 pictures out of doors i.e., silent and well-behaved in public
125 Bells i.e., jangling, noisy, and brazen. **in your kitchens** i.e., in domestic affairs. (Ladies would not do the cooking.)
126 Saints martyrs
127 Players idlers, triflers, or deceivers. **huswifery** housekeeping. **huswives** hussies (i.e., women are "busy" in bed, or unduly thrifty in dispensing sexual favors)

IAGO:

129   Nay, it is true, or else I am a Turk.

          You rise to play, and go to bed to work.

EMILIA:

          You shall not write my praise.

IAGO: No, let me not.

DESDEMONA:

          What wouldst write of me, if thou shouldst praise me?

IAGO:

          O gentle lady, do not put me to 't,

135   For I am nothing if not critical.

DESDEMONA:

136   Come on, essay.—There's one gone to the harbor?

IAGO: Ay, madam.

DESDEMONA:

          I am not merry, but I do beguile

139   The thing I am by seeming otherwise.

          Come, how wouldst thou praise me?

IAGO:

          I am about it, but indeed my invention

142   Comes from my pate as birdlime does from frieze—

143   It plucks out brains and all. But my Muse labors,

          And thus she is delivered:

          If she be fair and wise, fairness and wit,

146   The one's for use, the other useth it.

DESDEMONA:

147   Well praised! How if she be black and witty?

IAGO:

          If she be black, and thereto have a wit,

149   She'll find a white that shall her blackness fit.

DESDEMONA:

          Worse and worse.

EMILIA: How if fair and foolish?

          She never yet was foolish that was fair,

153   For even her folly helped her to an heir.

129 A Turk an infidel, not to be believed
135 critical censorious
136 essay try
139 The thing I am i.e., my anxious self
142 birdlime sticky substance used to catch small birds. **frieze** coarse woolen cloth
143 labors (1) exerts herself (2) prepares to deliver a child (with a following pun on *delivered* in line 144)
146 The one's [. . .] it i.e., her cleverness will make use of her beauty
147 black dark-complexioned, brunette
149 a white a fair person (with wordplay on "wight," a person). **fit** (with sexual suggestion of mating)
153 folly (with added meaning of "lechery, wantonness"). **to an heir** i.e., to bear a child

154   DESDEMONA: These are old fond paradoxes to make fools
            laugh i' th' alehouse. What miserable praise hast thou
156   for her that's foul and foolish?
        IAGO:

157   There's none so foul and foolish thereunto,
158   But does foul pranks which fair and wise ones do.
        DESDEMONA: O heavy ignorance! Thou praisest the worst
            best. But what praise couldst thou bestow on a deserving
            woman indeed, one that, in the authority of her merit,
162   did justly put on the vouch of very malice itself?
        IAGO:

            She that was ever fair, and never proud,
            Had tongue at will, and yet was never loud,
165   Never lacked gold and yet went never gay,
166   Fled from her wish, and yet said, "Now I may,"
            She that being angered, her revenge being nigh,
168   Bade her wrong stay and her displeasure fly,
            She that in wisdom never was so frail
170   To change the cod's head for the salmon's tail,
            She that could think and ne'er disclose her mind,
            See suitors following and not look behind,
            She was a wight, if ever such wight were—
        DESDEMONA: To do what?
        IAGO:

175   To suckle fools and chronicle small beer.
        DESDEMONA: O most lame and impotent conclusion! Do
            not learn of him, Emilia, though he be thy husband.
178   How say you, Cassio? Is he not a most profane and
179   liberal counselor?
180   CASSIO: He speaks home, madam. You may relish him
181   more in the soldier than in the scholar.

    (Cassio and Desdemona stand together, conversing intimately.)

154 fond foolish
156 foul ugly
157 thereunto in addition
158 foul sluttish
162 put [. . .] vouch compel the approval
165 gay extravagantly clothed
166 Fled [. . .] may avoided temptation where the choice was hers
168 Bade [. . .] stay i.e., resolved to put up with her injury patiently
170 To [. . .] tail i.e., to exchange a lackluster husband for a sexy lover (?) (*Cod's head* is slang for "penis," and *tail,* for "pudendum.")
175 suckle fools breastfeed babies. **chronicle small beer** i.e., keep petty household accounts, keep track of trivial matters
178 profane irreverent, ribald
179 liberal licentious, free-spoken
180 home right to the target. (A term from fencing.) **relish** appreciate
181 in in the character of

182 IAGO (*aside*): He takes her by the palm. Ay, well said,
whisper. With as little a web as this will I ensnare as
great a fly as Cassio. Ay, smile upon her, do; I will

185 gyve thee in thine own courtship. You say true; 'tis so,
indeed. If such tricks as these strip you out of your
lieutenantry, it had been better you had not kissed
your three fingers so oft, which now again you are

189 most apt to play the sir in. Very good; well kissed! An
excellent courtesy! 'Tis so, indeed. Yet again your fingers

191 to your lips? Would they were clyster pipes for your
sake! (*Trumpet within.*) The Moor! I know his trumpet.
CASSIO: 'Tis truly so.
DESDEMONA: Let's meet him and receive him.
CASSIO: Lo, where he comes!

(Enter Othello and attendants.)

OTHELLO:
    O my fair warrior!
DESDEMONA: My dear Othello!
OTHELLO:
    It gives me wonder great as my content
    To see you here before me. O my soul's joy,
    If after every tempest come such calms,
    May the winds blow till they have wakened death,
    And let the laboring bark climb hills of seas
    Olympus-high, and duck again as low
    As hell's from heaven! If it were now to die,
    'Twere now to be most happy, for I fear
    My soul hath her content so absolute
    That not another comfort like to this

208   Succeeds in unknown fate.
DESDEMONA: The heavens forbid
    But that our loves and comforts should increase
    Even as our days do grow!
OTHELLO: Amen to that, sweet powers!
    I cannot speak enough of this content.
    It stops me here; it is too much of joy.

215   And this, and this, the greatest discords be

(They kiss.)

---

182 well said well done
185 gyve fetter, shackle. **courtship** courtesy, show of courtly manners. **You say true** i.e.,
that's right, go ahead
189 the sir i.e., the fine gentleman
191 clyster pipes tubes used for enemas and douches
208 Succeeds [. . .] fate i.e., can follow in the unknown future
215 s.d. They kiss (The direction is from the Quarto.)

That e'er our hearts shall make!

IAGO (*aside*): O, you are well tuned now!

218   But I'll set down the pegs that make this music,

219   As honest as I am.

OTHELLO: Come, let us to the castle.

News, friends! Our wars are done, the Turks are drowned.

How does my old acquaintance of this isle?—

223   Honey, you shall be well desired in Cyprus;

I have found great love amongst them. O my sweet,

225   I prattle out of fashion, and I dote

In mine own comforts.—I prithee, good Iago,

227   Go to the bay and disembark my coffers.

228   Bring thou the master to the citadel;

He is a good one, and his worthiness

230   Does challenge much respect.—Come, Desdemona.—

Once more, well met at Cyprus!

(Exeunt Othello and Desdemona [and all but Iago and Roderigo].)

IAGO (*to an attendant*): Do thou meet me presently at

the harbor. (*To Roderigo.*) Come hither. If thou be'st

234   valiant—as, they say, base men being in love have

then a nobility in their natures more than is native to

236   them—list me. The Lieutenant tonight watches on

237   the court of guard. First, I must tell thee this:

Desdemona is directly in love with him.

RODERIGO: With him? Why, 'tis not possible.

240   IAGO: Lay thy finger thus, and let thy soul be instructed.

Mark me with what violence she first loved the Moor,

242   but for bragging and telling her fantastical lies. To love

him still for prating? Let not thy discreet heart think it.

Her eye must be fed; and what delight shall she have

to look on the devil? When the blood is made dull with

246   the act of sport, there should be, again to inflame it

247   and to give satiety a fresh appetite, loveliness in favor,

218 set down loosen (and hence untune the instrument)
219 As [. . .] I am for all my supposed honesty
223 desired welcomed
225 out of fashion irrelevantly, incoherently (?)
227 coffers chests, baggage
228 master ship's captain
230 challenge lay claim to, deserve
234 base men even lowly born men
236 list listen to
237 court of guard guardhouse. (Cassio is in charge of the watch.)
240 thus i.e., on your lips
242 but only
246 the act of sport sex
247 favor appearance

248 sympathy in years, manners, and beauties all which
the Moor is defective in. Now, for want of these
250 required conveniences, her delicate tenderness will
251 find itself abused, begin to heave the gorge, disrelish
252 and abhor the Moor. Very nature will instruct her in it
and compel her to some second choice. Now, sir, this
254 granted—as it is a most pregnant and unforced
255 position—who stands so eminent in the degree of this
256 fortune as Cassio does? A knave very voluble, no
257 further conscionable than in putting on the mere form
258 of civil and humane seeming for the better compass-
259 ing of his salt and most hidden loose affection. Why,
260 none, why, none. A slipper and subtle knave, a finder
261 out of occasions, that has an eye can stamp and
262 counterfeit advantages, though true advantage never
present itself; a devilish knave. Besides, the knave is
handsome, young, and hath all those requisites in him
265 that folly and green minds look after. A pestilent
266 complete knave, and the woman hath found him already.
RODERIGO: I cannot believe that in her. She's full of
268 most blessed condition.
269 IAGO: Blessed fig's end! The wine she drinks is made of
grapes. If she had been blessed, she would never have
271 loved the Moor. Blessed pudding! Didst thou not see
her paddle with the palm of his hand? Didst not mark that?
RODERIGO: Yes, that I did; but that was but courtesy.
274 IAGO: Lechery, by this hand. An index, an obscure prologue to the history of lust and foul thoughts. They
met so near with their lips that their breaths embraced

248 sympathy correspondence, similarity
250 required conveniences things conducive to sexual compatibility
251 abused cheated, revolted. **heave the gorge** experience nausea
252 Very nature her very instincts
254 pregnant evident, cogent
255 in [. . .] of as next in line for
256 voluble facile, glib
257 conscionable conscientious, conscience-bound
258 humane polite, courteous
259 salt licentious. **affection** passion
260 slipper slippery
261 an eye can stamp an eye that can coin, create
262 advantages favorable opportunities
265 folly wantonness. **green** immature
266 found him sized him up, perceived his intent
268 condition disposition
269 fig's end (See 1.3,341 for the vulgar gesture of the fig.)
271 pudding sausage
274 index table of contents. **obscure** (i.e., the *lust and foul thoughts,* line 275, are secret, hidden from view)

together. Villainous thoughts, Roderigo! When these
278   mutualities so marshal the way, hard at hand comes
279   the master and main exercise, th' incorporate conclusion. Pish! But, sir, be you ruled by me. I have brought
281   you from Venice. Watch you tonight; for the command,
I'll lay't upon you. Cassio knows you not. I'll not
be far from you. Do you find some occasion to
284   anger Cassio, either by speaking too loud, or tainting
his discipline, or from what other course you please,
286   which the time shall more favorably minister.

RODERIGO: Well.

288   IAGO: Sir, he's rash and very sudden in choler, and haply
may strike at you. Provoke him that he may, for even
290   out of that will I cause these of Cyprus to mutiny,
291   whose qualification shall come into no true taste again
but by the displanting of Cassio. So shall you have a
shorter journey to your desires by the means I shall
294   then have to prefer them, and the impediment most
profitably removed, without the which there were no
expectation of our prosperity.

RODERIGO: I will do this, if you can bring it to any opportunity.

298   IAGO: I warrant thee. Meet me by and by at the citadel.
I must fetch his necessaries ashore. Farewell.

RODERIGO: Adieu.   (*Exit.*)

IAGO: That Cassio loves her, I do well believe 't;
302   That she loves him, 'tis apt and of great credit.
The Moor, howbeit that I endure him not,
Is of a constant, loving, noble nature,
And I dare think he'll prove to Desdemona
A most dear husband. Now, I do love her too,
Not out of absolute lust—though peradventure
308   I stand accountant for as great a sin—
309   But partly led to diet my revenge

278 **mutualities** exchanges, intimacies. **hard at hand** closely following
279 **incorporate** carnal
281 **Watch you** stand watch
281–282 **for the command [. . .] you** I'll arrange for you to be appointed, given orders
284 **tainting** disparaging
286 **minister** provide
288 **choler** wrath **haply** perhaps
290 **mutiny** riot
291 **qualification** appeasement. **true taste** i.e., acceptable state
294 **prefer** advance
298 **warrant** assure. **by and by** immediately
302 **apt** probable. **credit** credibility
308 **accountant** accountable
309 **diet** feed

For that I do suspect the lusty Moor
Hath leaped into my seat, the thought whereof
Doth, like a poisonous mineral, gnaw my innards;
And nothing can or shall content my soul
Till I am evened with him, wife for wife,
Or failing so, yet that I put the Moor
At least into a jealousy so strong
That judgment cannot cure. Which thing to do,
318   If this poor trash of Venice, whom I trace
319   For his quick hunting, stand the putting on,
320   I'll have our Michael Cassio on the hip,
321   Abuse him to the Moor in the rank garb—
322   For I fear Cassio with my nightcap too—
Make the Moor thank me, love me, and reward me
For making him egregiously an ass
325   And practicing upon his peace and quiet
Even to madness. 'Tis here, but yet confused.
Knavery's plain face is never seen till used.   (*Exit.*)

2.2

(*Enter Othello's Herald with a proclamation.*)

HERALD: It is Othello's pleasure, our noble and valiant
general, that, upon certain tidings now arrived, im-
3   porting the mere perdition of the Turkish fleet, every
4   man put himself into triumph: some to dance, some to
make bonfires, each man to what sport and revels his
6   addiction leads him. For, besides these beneficial
news, it is the celebration of his nuptial. So much was
8   his pleasure should be proclaimed. All offices are open,
and there is full liberty of feasting from this present
hour of five till the bell have told eleven. Heaven bless
the isle of Cyprus and our noble general Othello!

(*Exit.*)

---

318 trace i.e., train, or follow (?), or perhaps *trash*, a hunting term, meaning to put
weights on a hunting dog in order to slow him down
319 For to make more eager. **stand [. . .] on** respond properly when I incite him to quarrel
320 on the hip at my mercy, where I can throw him. (A wrestling term.)
321 Abuse slander. **rank garb** coarse manner, gross fashion
322 with my nightcap i.e., as a rival in my bed, as one who gives me cuckold's horns
325 practicing upon plotting against
2.2 Location: Cyprus. A street.
3 mere perdition complete destruction
4 triumph public celebration
6 addiction inclination
8 offices rooms where food and drink are kept

2.3

(Enter Othello, Desdemona, Cassio, and attendants.)

OTHELLO:

Good Michael, look you to the guard tonight.

2   Let's teach ourselves that honorable stop

3   Not to outsport discretion.

CASSIO:

Iago hath direction what to do,

But notwithstanding, with my personal eye

Will I look to 't.

OTHELLO: Iago is most honest.

8   Michael, good night. Tomorrow with your earliest

Let me have speech with you. (*To Desdemona.*)

Come, my dear love,

11   The purchase made, the fruits are to ensue;

That profit's yet to come 'tween me and you.—

Good night.

(Exit [Othello, with Desdemona and attendants].)

(Enter Iago.)

CASSIO: Welcome, Iago. We must to the watch.

15   IAGO: Not this hour, Lieutenant; 'tis not yet ten o' the

16   clock. Our general cast us thus early for the love of his

17   Desdemona; who let us not therefore blame. He hath

not yet made wanton the night with her, and she is

sport for Jove.

CASSIO: She's a most exquisite lady.

IAGO: And, I'll warrant her, full of game.

CASSIO: Indeed, she's a most fresh and delicate creature.

23   IAGO: What an eye she has! Me thinks it sounds a parley

to provocation.

CASSIO: An inviting eye, and yet methinks right modest.

26   IAGO: And when she speaks, is it not an alarum to love?

CASSIO: She is indeed perfection.

2.3. Location: Cyprus. The citadel.
2 stop restraint
3 outsport celebrate beyond the bounds of
8 with your earliest at your earliest convenience
11–12 The purchase [. . .] you i.e., though married, we haven't yet consummated our love
15 Not this hour not for an hour yet
16 cast dismissed
17 who i.e., Othello
23 sounds a parley calls for a conference, issues an invitation
26 alarum signal calling men to arms (continuing the military metaphor of *parley*, line 23)

IAGO: Well, happiness to their sheets! Come, Lieutenant,
29   I have a stoup of wine, and here without are a brace of
30   Cyprus gallants that would fain have a measure to the
  health of black Othello.
CASSIO: Not tonight, good Iago. I have very poor and unhappy brains for drinking. I could well wish courtesy
  would invent some other custom of entertainment.
35 IAGO: O, they are our friends. But one cup! I'll drink for you.
CASSIO: I have drunk but one cup tonight and that was
37   craftily qualified too, and behold what innovation it
38   makes here. I am unfortunate in the infirmity and
  dare not task my weakness with any more.
IAGO: What, man? 'Tis a night of revels. The gallants
  desire it.
CASSIO: Where are they?
IAGO: Here at the door. I pray you, call them in.
44 CASSIO: I'll do 't, but it dislikes me.   (*Exit.*)
IAGO: If I can fasten but one cup upon him,
  With that which he hath drunk tonight already,
47   He'll be as full of quarrel and offense
  As my young mistress' dog. Now, my sick fool Roderigo,
  Whom love hath turned almost the wrong side out,
50   To Desdemona hath tonight caroused
51   Potations pottle-deep; and he's to watch.
52   Three lads of Cyprus—noble swelling spirits,
53   That hold their honors in a wary distance,
54   The very elements of this warlike isle—
  Have I tonight flustered with flowing cups,
56   And they watch too. Now, 'mongst this flock of drunkards
  Am I to put our Cassio in some action
  That may offend the isle. But here they come.

(*Enter Cassio, Montano, and gentlemen; [servants following with wine].*)

---

29 stoup measure of liquor, two quarts. **without** outside. **brace** pair
30 fain have a measure gladly drink a toast
35 for you in your place. (Iago will do the steady drinking to keep the gallants company while Cassio has only one cup.)
37 qualified diluted. **innovation** disturbance, insurrection
38 here i.e., in my head
44 it dislikes me i.e., I'm reluctant
47 offense readiness to take offense
50 caroused drunk off
51 pottle-deep to the bottom of the tankard. **watch** stand watch
52 swelling proud
53 hold [. . .] distance i.e., are extremely sensitive of their honor
54 very elements typical sort
56 watch are members of the guard

59   If consequence do but approve my dream,
60   My boat sails freely both with wind and stream.
61 CASSIO: 'Fore God, they have given me a rouse already,
   MONTANO: Good faith, a little one; not past a pint, as I
       am a soldier.
   IAGO: Some wine, ho!
65   (*He sings.*) "And let me the cannikin clink, clink,
               And let me the cannikin clink.
                   A soldier's a man,
68   O, man's life's but a span;
               Why, then, let a soldier drink."
           Some wine, boys!
   CASSIO: 'Fore God, an excellent song.
   IAGO: I learned it in England, where indeed they are
73   most potent in potting. Your Dane, your German,
           and your swag-bellied Hollander—drink, ho!—are
           nothing to your English.
   CASSIO: Is your Englishman so exquisite in his drinking?
77 IAGO: Why, he drinks you, with facility, your Dane
78   dead drunk; he sweats not to overthrow your Almain;
           he gives your Hollander a vomit ere the next pottle
           can be filled.
   CASSIO: To the health of our general!
82 MONTANO: I am for it, Lieutenant, and I'll do you justice.
   IAGO: O sweet England!   (*He sings.*)
               "King Stephen was and-a worthy peer,
                   His breeches cost him but a crown;
               He held them sixpence all too dear,
87   With that he called the tailor lown.
               He was a wight of high renown,
                   And thou art but of low degree.
               'Tis pride that pulls the country down;
91   Then take thy auld cloak about thee."
           Some wine, ho!
   CASSIO: 'Fore God, this is a more exquisite song than
       the other.

59 If [. . .] dream if subsequent events will only substantiate my scheme
60 stream current
61 rouse full draft of liquor
65 cannikin small drinking vessel
68 span brief span of time. (Compare Psalm 39:5 as rendered in the Book of Common
Prayer: "Thou hast made my days as it were a span long.")
73 potting drinking
77 drinks you drinks. **your Dane** your typical Dane
78 sweats not i.e., need not exert himself. **Almain** German
82 I'll [. . .] justice i.e., I'll drink as much as you
87 lown lout, rascal
91 auld old

IAGO: Will you hear't again?

CASSIO: No, for I hold him to be unworthy of his place
that does those things. Well, God's above all; and
there be souls must be saved, and there be souls must
not be saved.

IAGO: It's true, good Lieutenant.

CASSIO: For mine own part—no offense to the General,
nor any man of quality—I hope to be saved.

IAGO: And so do I too, Lieutenant.

CASSIO: Ay, but, by your leave, not before me; the lieutenant is to be saved before the ancient. Let's have no
more of this; let's to our affairs.—God forgive us our
sins!—Gentlemen, let's look to our business. Do not
think, gentlemen, I am drunk. This is my ancient; this
is my right hand, and this is my left. I am not drunk
now. I can stand well enough, and speak well enough.

GENTLEMEN: Excellent well.

CASSIO: Why, very well then; you must not think then
that I am drunk.   (*Exit.*)

MONTANO:

To th' platform, masters. Come, let's set the watch.

(*Exeunt Gentlemen.*)

IAGO:

You see this fellow that is gone before.
He's a soldier fit to stand by Caesar
And give direction; and do but see his vice.
'Tis to his virtue a just equinox,
The one as long as the other. 'Tis pity of him.
I fear the trust Othello puts him in,
On some odd time of his infirmity,
Will shake this island.

MONTANO: But is he often thus?

IAGO:

'Tis evermore the prologue to his sleep.
He'll watch the horologe a double set,
If drink rock not his cradle.

MONTANO: It were well
The General were put in mind of it.
Perhaps he sees it not, or his good nature
Prizes the virtue that appears in Cassio
And looks not on his evils. Is not this true?

(*Enter Roderigo.*)

---

102 quality rank
114 set the watch mount the guard
118 just equinox exact counterpart. (*Equinox* is an equal length of days and nights.)
125 watch [. . .] **set** stay awake twice around the clock or *horologe*

IAGO (*aside to him*): How now, Roderigo?
    I pray you, after the Lieutenant; go.   (*Exit Roderigo.*)
MONTANO:
    And 'tis great pity that the noble Moor
135   Should hazard such a place as his own second
136   With one of an engraffed infirmity.
    It were an honest action to say so
    To the Moor.
IAGO: Not I, for this fair island.
    I do love Cassio well and would do much
    To cure him of this evil.   (*Cry within:* "Help! Help!")
142   But, hark! What noise?

(Enter Cassio, pursuing Roderigo.)

CASSIO: Zounds, you rogue! You rascal!
MONTANO: What's the matter, Lieutenant?
CASSIO: A knave teach me my duty? I'll beat the knave
146   into a twiggen bottle.
RODERIGO: Beat me?
CASSIO: Dost thou prate, rogue?   (*He strikes Roderigo.*)
MONTANO: Nay, good Lieutenant.   (*Restraining him.*)
    I pray you, sir, hold your hand.
CASSIO: Let me go, sir, or I'll knock you o'er
152   the mazard.
MONTANO: Come, come, you're drunk.
CASSIO: Drunk?   (*They fight.*)
IAGO (*aside to Roderigo*):
155   Away, I say. Go out and cry a mutiny.

(*Exit Roderigo.*)

    Nay, good Lieutenant—God's will, gentlemen—
    Help, ho!—Lieutenant—sir—Montano—sir—
158   Help, masters!—Here's a goodly watch indeed!

(*A bell rings.*)
159   Who's that which rings the bell?—Diablo, ho!

135–136 hazard [. . .] With risk giving such an important position as his second in command to
136 engraffed engrafted, inveterate
142 s.d. pursuing (The Quarto text reads, "driving in.")
146 twiggen wicker-covered. (Cassio vows to assail Roderigo until his skin resembles wickerwork or until he has driven Roderigo through the holes in a wickerwork.)
152 mazard i.e., head. (Literally, a drinking vessel.)
155 mutiny riot
158 masters sirs. **s.d. A bell rings** (This direction is from the Quarto, as are *Exit Roderigo* pat line 133, *They fight* at line 154, and *with weapons* at line 161.)
159 Diablo the devil

160 The town will rise. God's will, Lieutenant, hold!
You'll be ashamed forever.

(Enter Othello and attendants [with weapons].)

OTHELLO:
What is the matter here?

MONTANO: Zounds, I bleed still.
I am hurt to th' death. He dies! (*He thrusts at Cassio.*)

OTHELLO: Hold, for your lives!

IAGO:
Hold, ho! Lieutenant—sir—Montano—gentlemen—
Have you forgot all sense of place and duty?
Hold! The General speaks to you. Hold, for shame!

OTHELLO:
Why, how now, ho! From whence ariseth this?

170 Are we turned Turks, and to ourselves do that
Which heaven hath forbid the Ottomites?
For Christian shame, put by this barbarous brawl!

173 He that stirs next to carve for his own rage

174 Holds his soul light; he dies upon his motion.
Silence that dreadful bell. It frights the isle

176 From her propriety. What is the matter, masters?
Honest Iago, that looks dead with grieving,
Speak. Who began this? On thy love, I charge thee.

IAGO:
I do not know. Friends all but now, even now,

180 In quarter and in terms like bride and groom

181 Devesting them for bed; and then, but now—
As if some planet had unwitted men—
Swords out, and tilting one at others' breasts

184 In opposition bloody. I cannot speak

185 Any beginning to this peevish odds;
And would in action glorious I had lost
Those legs that brought me to a part of it!

OTHELLO:

188 How comes it, Michael, you are thus forgot?

---

160 rise grow riotous
170–171 to ourselves [. . .] **Ottomites** inflict on ourselves the harm that heaven has prevented the Turks from doing (by destroying their fleet)
173 carve for i.e., indulge, satisfy with his sword
174 Holds [. . .] **light** i.e., places little value on his life. **upon his motion** if he moves
176 propriety proper state or condition
180 In quarter in friendly conduct, within bounds. **in terms** on good terms
181 Devesting them undressing themselves
184 speak explain
185 peevish odds childish quarrel
188 are thus forgot have forgotten yourself thus

CASSIO: I pray you, pardon me. I cannot speak.

OTHELLO:

190   Worthy Montano, you were wont be civil;
191   The gravity and stillness of your youth
      The world hath noted, and your name is great
193   In mouths of wisest censure. What's the matter
194   That you unlace your reputation thus
195   And spend your rich opinion for the name
      Of a night-brawler? Give me answer to it.

MONTANO:

      Worthy Othello, I am hurt to danger.
      Your officer, Iago, can inform you—
199   While I spare speech, which something now offends me—
      Of all that I do know; nor know I aught
      By me that's said or done amiss this night,
      Unless self-charity be sometimes a vice,
      And to defend ourselves it be a sin
      When violence assails us.

OTHELLO: Now, by heaven,
206   My blood begins my safer guides to rule,
207   And passion, having my best judgment collied,
208   Essays to lead the way. Zounds, if I stir,
      Or do but lift this arm, the best of you
      Shall sink in my rebuke. Give me to know
211   How this foul rout began, who set it on;
212   And he that is approved in this offense,
      Though he had twinned with me, both at a birth,
214   Shall lose me. What? In a town of war
      Yet wild, the people's hearts brim full of fear,
216   To manage private and domestic quarrel?
217   In night, and on the court and guard of safety?
      'Tis monstrous. Iago, who began 't?

190 **wont** be accustomed to be
191 **stillness** sobriety
193 **censure** judgment
194 **unlace** undo, lay open (as one might loose the strings of a purse containing reputation)
195 **opinion** reputation
199 **something** somewhat. **offends** pains
206 **blood** passion (of anger). **guides** i.e., reason
207 **collied** darkened
208 **Essays** undertakes
211 **rout** riot
212 **approved** in found guilty of
214 **town of** town garrisoned for
216 **manage** undertake
217 **on [. . .] safety** at the main guardhouse or headquarters and on watch

MONTANO (*to Iago*):

219   If partially affined, or leagued in office,
Thou dost deliver more or less than truth,
Thou art no soldier.

IAGO: Touch me not so near.
I had rather have this tongue cut from my mouth
Than it should do offense to Michael Cassio;
Yet, I persuade myself, to speak the truth
Shall nothing wrong him. Thus it is, General.
Montano and myself being in speech,
There comes a fellow crying out for help,
And Cassio following him with determined sword

230   To execute upon him. Sir, this gentleman

                          (*indicating Montano*)

231   Steps in to Cassio and entreats his pause.
Myself the crying fellow did pursue,
Lest by his clamor—as it so fell out—
The town might fall in fright. He, swift of foot,

235   Outran my purpose, and I returned, the rather
For that I heard the clink and fall of swords
And Cassio high in oath, which till tonight
I ne'er might say before. When I came back—
For this was brief—I found them close together
At blow and thrust, even as again they were
When you yourself did part them.
More of this matter cannot I report.

243   But men are men; the best sometimes forget.
Though Cassio did some little wrong to him,

245   As men in rage strike those that wish them best,
Yet surely Cassio, I believe, received
From him that fled some strange indignity,

248   Which patience could not pass.

OTHELLO: I know, Iago,
Thy honesty and love doth mince this matter,
Making it light to Cassio. Cassio, I love thee,
But nevermore be officer of mine.

(*Enter Desdemona, attended.*)

---

219 partially affined made partial by some personal relationship. **leagued in office** in
league as fellow officers
230 execute give effect to (his anger)
231 his pause him to stop
235 rather sooner
243 forget forget themselves
245 those [. . .] best i.e., even those who are well disposed
248 pass pass over, overlook

Look if my gentle love be not raised up.
I'll make thee an example.

DESDEMONA:

What is the matter, dear?

OTHELLO: All's well now, sweeting;
Come away to bed. (*To Montano.*) Sir, for your hurts,
258   Myself will be your surgeon.—Lead him off.

(Montano is led off.)

Iago, look with care about the town
And silence those whom this vile brawl distracted.
Come, Desdemona. 'Tis the soldiers' life
To have their balmy slumbers waked with strife.

(Exit [with all but Iago and Cassio].)

IAGO: What, are you hurt, Lieutenant?

CASSIO: Ay, past all surgery.

IAGO: Marry, God forbid!

CASSIO: Reputation, reputation, reputation! O, I have
lost my reputation! I have lost the immortal part of
myself, and what remains is bestial. My reputation,
Iago, my reputation!

IAGO: As I am an honest man, I thought you had
received some bodily wound; there is more sense in
that than in reputation. Reputation is an idle and most
273   false imposition, oft got without merit and lost without deserving. You have lost no reputation at all,
unless you repute yourself such a loser. What, man,
276   there are more ways to recover the General again. You
277   are but now cast in his mood—a punishment more in
278   policy than in malice, even so as one would beat his
279   offenseless dog to affright an imperious lion. Sue to
him again and he's yours.

CASSIO: I will rather sue to be despised than to deceive
282   so good a commander with so slight, so drunken, and
283   so indiscreet an officer. Drunk? And speak parrot?

258 be your surgeon i.e., make sure you receive medical attention
273 false imposition thing artificially imposed and of no real value
276 recover regain favor with
277 cast in his mood dismissed in a moment of anger
277–278 in policy done for expediency's sake and as a public gesture
278–279 would [. . .] lion i.e., would make an example of a minor offender in order to
deter more important and dangerous offenders
279 Sue petition
282 slight worthless
283 speak parrot talk nonsense, rant. (*Discourse fustian,* lines 284–285, has much the same
meaning.)

And squabble? Swagger? Swear? And discourse fustian with one's own shadow? O thou invisible spirit
of wine, if thou hast no name to be known by, let us
call thee devil!

IAGO: What was he that you followed with your sword?
What had he done to you?

CASSIO: I know not.

IAGO: Is 't possible?

CASSIO: I remember a mass of things, but nothing
293   distinctly; a quarrel, but nothing wherefore. O God,
that men should put an enemy in their mouths to steal
away their brains! That we should with joy, pleasance,
296   revel, and applause transform ourselves into beasts!

IAGO: Why, but you are now well enough. How came
you thus recovered?

CASSIO: It hath pleased the devil drunkenness to give
place to the devil wrath. One unperfectness shows me
another, to make me frankly despise myself.

302 IAGO: Come, you are too severe a moraler. As the time,
the place, and the condition of this country stand, I
could heartily wish this had not befallen; but since it is
as it is, mend it for your own good.

CASSIO: I will ask him for my place again; he shall tell
307   me I am a drunkard. Had I as many mouths as Hydra,
such an answer would stop them all. To be now a
sensible man, by and by a fool, and presently a beast!
O, strange! Every inordinate cup is unblessed, and the
ingredient is a devil.

IAGO: Come, come, good wine is a good familiar
creature, if it be well used. Exclaim no more against it.
And, good Lieutenant, I think you think I love you.

315 CASSIO: I have well approved it, sir. I drunk!

316 IAGO: You or any man living may be drunk at a time,
man. I'll tell you what you shall do. Our general's wife
318   is now the general—I may say so in this respect, for
that he hath devoted and given up himself to the
320   contemplation, mark, and denotement of her parts
and graces. Confess yourself freely to her; importune

---

293 wherefore why
296 applause desire for applause
302 moraler moralizer
307 Hydra the Lernaean Hydra, a monster with many heads and the ability to grow two
heads when one was cut off, slain by Hercules as the second of his twelve labors
315 approved proved
316 at a time at one time or another
318–319 in [. . .] that in view of this fact, that
320 mark, and denotement (Both words mean "observation.") **parts** qualities

323   her help to put you in your place again. She is of so
       free, so kind, so apt, so blessed a disposition, she
       holds it a vice in her goodness not to do more than she
       is requested. This broken joint between you and her
326   husband entreat her to splinter; and, my fortunes
327   against any lay worth naming, this crack of your love
       shall grow stronger than it was before.

CASSIO: You advise me well.

330 IAGO: I protest, in the sincerity of love and honest
       kindness.

332 CASSIO: I think it freely; and betimes in the morning I
       will beseech the virtuous Desdemona to undertake for
334   me. I am desperate of my fortunes if they check me here.

IAGO: You are in the right. Good night, Lieutenant. I
       must to the watch.

CASSIO: Good night, Honest Iago.   (*Exit Cassio.*)

IAGO:
       And what's he then that says I play the villain,
339   When this advice is free I give, and honest,
340   Probal to thinking, and indeed the course
       To win the Moor again? For 'tis most easy
342   Th' inclining Desdemona to subdue
343   In any honest suit; she's framed as fruitful
344   As the free elements. And then for her
       To win the Moor—were't to renounce his baptism,
       All seals and symbols of redeemèd sin—
       His soul is so enfettered to her love
       That she may make, unmake, do what she list,
349   Even as her appetite shall play the god
350   With his weak function. How am I then a villain,
351   To counsel Cassio to this parallel course
352   Directly to his good? Divinity of hell!

323 **free** generous
326 **splinter** bind with splints
327 **lay** stake, wager
330 **protest** insist, declare
332 **freely** unreservedly
334 **check** repulse
339 **free** (1) free from guile (2) freely given
340 **Probal** probable, reasonable
342 **inclining** favorably disposed. **subdue** persuade
343 **framed as fruitful** created as generous
344 **free elements** i.e., earth, air, fire, and water, unrestrained and spontaneous
349 **her appetite** her desire, or, perhaps, his desire for her
350 **function** exercise of faculties (weakened by his fondness for her)
351 **parallel** corresponding to these facts and to his best interests
352 **Divinity of hell** inverted theology of hell (which seduces the soul to its damnation)

353 When devils will the blackest sins put on,
354 They do suggest at first with heavenly shows,
As I do now. For whiles this honest fool
Plies Desdemona to repair his fortune,
And she for him pleads strongly to the Moor,
I'll pour this pestilence into his ear,
359 That she repeals him for her body's lust;
And by how much she strives to do him good,
She shall undo her credit with the Moor.
362 So will I turn her virtue into pitch,
And out of her own goodness make the net
That shall enmesh them all.

(Enter Roderigo.)

How now, Roderigo?
RODERIGO: I do follow here in the chase, not like a
367 hound that hunts, but one that fills up the cry. My
money is almost spent; I have been tonight exceedingly well cudgeled; and I think the issue will be I shall
370 have so much experience for my pains, and so,
with no money at all and a little more wit, return again
to Venice.

IAGO:
How poor are they that have not patience!
What wound did ever heal but by degrees?
Thou know'st we work by wit, and not by witchcraft,
And wit depends on dilatory time.
Does't not go well? Cassio hath beaten thee,
378 And thou, by that small hurt, hast cashiered Cassio.
379 Though other things grow fair against the sun,
Yet fruits that blossom first will first be ripe.
Content thyself awhile. By the Mass, 'tis morning!
Pleasure and action make the hours seem short.
Retire thee; go where thou art billeted.
Away, I say! Thou shalt know more hereafter.
Nay, get thee gone.   *(Exit Roderigo.)*
Two things are to be done.

---

353 put on further, instigate
354 suggest tempt
359 repeals him attempts to get him restored
362 pitch i.e., (1) foul blackness (2) a snaring substance
367 fills up the cry merely takes part as one of the pack
370 so much just so much and no more
378 cashiered dismissed from service
379–380 Though [. . .] ripe i.e., plans that are well prepared and set expeditiously in
motion will soonest ripen into success

387 My wife must move for Cassio to her mistress;
I'll set her on;
Myself the while to draw the Moor apart
390 And bring him jump when he may Cassio find
Soliciting his wife. Ay, that's the way.
392 Dull not device by coldness and delay. (*Exit.*)

3.1

(Enter Cassio [and] Musicians.)

1 CASSIO: Masters, play here—I will content your pains—
Something that's brief, and bid "Good morrow, General."
(*They play.*)

([Enter] Clown)

CLOWN: Why, masters, have your instruments been in
4 Naples, that they speak i' the nose thus?
A MUSICIAN: How, sir, how?
CLOWN: Are these, I pray you, wind instruments?
A MUSICIAN: Ay, marry, are they, sir.
CLOWN: O, thereby hangs a tail.
A MUSICIAN: Whereby hangs a tale, sir?
10 CLOWN: Marry, sir, by many a wind instrument that I know.
But, masters, here's money for you. (*He gives money.*)
And the General so likes your music that he desires
13 you, for love's sake, to make no more noise with it.
A MUSICIAN: Well, sir, we will not.
15 CLOWN: If you have any music that may not be heard,
to 't again; but, as they say, to hear music the General
does not greatly care.
A MUSICIAN: We have none such, sir.
19 CLOWN: Then put up your pipes in your bag, for I'll away.
Go, vanish into air, away!   (*Exeunt Musicians.*)
CASSIO: Dost thou hear, mine honest friend?

---

387 move plead
390 jump precisely
392 device plot. **coldness** lack of zeal
3.1 Location: Before the chamber of Othello and Desdemona.
1 content your pains reward your efforts
4 speak i' the nose (1) sound nasal (2) sound like one whose nose has been attacked by syphilis. (Naples was popularly supposed to have a high incidence of venereal disease.)
10 wind instrument (With a joke on flatulence. The *tail,* line 8, that hangs nearby the *wind instrument* suggests the penis.)
13 for love's sake (1) out of friendship and affection (2) for the sake of lovemaking in Othello's marriage
15 may not cannot
19 I'll away (Possibly a misprint, or a snatch of song?)

CLOWN: No, I hear not your honest friend; I hear you.

23 CASSIO: Prithee, keep up thy quillets. There's a poor
piece of gold for thee. (*He gives money.*) If the gentle-
woman that attends the General's wife be stirring, tell
26 her there's one Cassio entreats her a little favor of
speech. Wilt thou do this?

28 CLOWN: She is stirring, sir. If she will stir hither, I
29 shall seem to notify unto her.

CASSIO:
Do, good my friend.   (*Exit Clown.*)

(*Enter Iago.*)

31   In happy time, Iago.

IAGO: You have not been abed, then?

CASSIO: Why, no. The day had broke
Before we parted. I have made bold, Iago,
To send in to your wife. My suit to her
Is that she will to virtuous Desdemona
Procure me some access.

IAGO: I'll send her to you presently;
And I'll devise a means to draw the Moor
Out of the way, that your converse and business
May be more free.

CASSIO:
I humbly thank you for 't.   (*Exit Iago*).
                    I never knew
44   A Florentine more kind and honest.

(*Enter Emilia.*)

EMILIA: Good morrow, good Lieutenant. I am sorry
46   For your displeasure; but all will sure be well.
The General and his wife are talking of it,
48   And she speaks for you stoutly. The Moor replies
49   That he you hurt is of great fame in Cyprus
50   And great affinity, and that in wholesome wisdom
51   He might not but refuse you; but he protests he loves you

---

23 keep up do not bring out, do not use. **quillets** quibbles, puns
26–27 a little [. . .] speech the favor of a brief talk
28 stir bestir herself (with a play on *stirring*, "rousing herself from rest")
29 seem deem it good, think fit
31 In happy time i.e., well met
44 Florentine i.e., even a fellow Florentine. (Iago is a Venetian; Cassio is a Florentine.)
46 displeasure fall from favor
48 stoutly spiritedly
49 fame reputation, importance
50 affinity kindred, family connection
51 protests insists

And needs no other suitor but his likings

53 To take the safest occasion by the front

To bring you in again.

CASSIO: Yet I beseech you,

If you think fit, or that it may be done,

Give me advantage of some brief discourse

With Desdemona alone.

EMILIA: Pray you, come in.

I will bestow you where you shall have time

61 To speak your bosom freely.

CASSIO: I am much bound to you.   (*Exeunt.*)

3.2

(Enter Othello, Iago, and Gentlemen.)

OTHELLO (*giving letters*): These letters give, Iago, to the pilot,

2 And by him do my duties to the Senate.

3 That done, I will be walking on the works;

4 Repair there to me.

IAGO: Well, my good lord, I'll do't.

OTHELLO:

This fortification, gentlemen, shall we see't?

7 GENTLEMEN: We'll wait upon your lordship.   (*Exeunt.*)

3.3

(Enter Desdemona, Cassio, and Emilia.)

DESDEMONA:

Be thou assured, good Cassio, I will do

All my abilities in thy behalf.

EMILIA:

Good madam, do. I warrant it grieves my husband

As if the cause were his.

DESDEMONA:

O, that's an honest fellow. Do not doubt, Cassio,

But I will have my lord and you again

As friendly as you were.

---

53 occasion [. . .] front opportunity by the forelock

61 bosom inmost thoughts

3.2 Location: The citadel.

2 do my duties convey my respects

3 works breastworks, fortifications

4 Repair return, come

7 wait upon attend

3.3 Location: The garden of the citadel.

CASSIO: Bounteous madam,
     Whatever shall become of Michael Cassio,
     He's never anything but your true servant.

DESDEMONA:
     I know't. I thank you. You do love my lord;
     You have known him long, and be you well assured

13   He shall in strangeness stand no farther off
14   Than in a politic distance.

CASSIO: Ay, but lady,
     That policy may either last so long,

17   Or feed upon such nice and waterish diet,
18   Or breed itself so out of circumstance,
19   That, I being absent and my place supplied,
     My general will forget my love and service.

DESDEMONA:
21   Do not doubt that. Before Emilia here
22   I give thee warrant of thy place. Assure thee,
     If I do vow a friendship I'll perform it
     To the last article. My lord shall never rest.

25   I'll watch him tame and talk him out of patience;
26   His bed shall seem a school, his board a shrift;
     I'll intermingle everything he does
     With Cassio's suit. Therefore be merry, Cassio,

29   For thy solicitor shall rather die
30   Than give thy cause away.

(Enter Othello and Iago [at a distance].)

EMILIA: Madam, here comes my lord.
CASSIO: Madam, I'll take my leave.
DESDEMONA: Why, stay, and hear me speak.
CASSIO:
     Madam, not now. I am very ill at ease,
     Unfit for mine own purposes.

---

13 strangeness aloofness
14 politic required by wise policy
17 Or [. . .] diet or sustain itself at length upon such trivial and meager technicalities
18 breed [. . .] circumstance continually renew itself so out of chance events, or yield so few chances for my being pardoned
19 supplied filled by another person
21 doubt fear
22 warrant guarantee
25 watch him tame tame him by keeping him from sleeping (A term from falconry.)
out of patience past his endurance
26 board dining table. **shrift** confessional
29 solicitor advocate
30 away up

36 DESDEMONA: Well, do your discretion.   (*Exit Cassio.*)

IAGO: Ha? I like not that.

OTHELLO: What dost thou say?

IAGO:

    Nothing, my lord; or if—I know not what.

OTHELLO: Was not that Cassio parted from my wife?

IAGO:

    Cassio, my lord? No, sure, I cannot think it,

    That he would steal away so guiltylike,

    Seeing you coming.

OTHELLO: I do believe 'twas he.

DESDEMONA: How now, my lord?

    I have been talking with a suitor here.

    A man that languishes in your displeasure.

OTHELLO: Who is 't you mean?

DESDEMONA:

    Why, your lieutenant, Cassio. Good my lord,

    If I have any grace or power to move you,

51   His present reconciliation take;

    For if he be not one that truly loves you,

53   That errs in ignorance and not in cunning,

    I have no judgment in an honest face.

    I prithee, call him back.

OTHELLO: Went he hence now?

DESDEMONA: Yes, faith, so humbled

    That he hath left part of his grief with me

    To suffer with him. Good love, call him back.

OTHELLO:

    Not now, sweet Desdemon. Some other time.

DESDEMONA: But shall 't be shortly?

OTHELLO: The sooner, sweet, for you.

DESDEMONA: Shall 't be tonight at supper?

OTHELLO: No, not tonight.

65 DESDEMONA: Tomorrow dinner, then?

OTHELLO: I shall not dine at home.

    I meet the captains at the citadel.

DESDEMONA:

    Why, then, tomorrow night, or Tuesday morn,

    Or Tuesday noon, or night, or Wednesday morn.

    I prithee, name the time, but let it not

    Exceed three days. I' faith, he's penitent;

---

36 do your discretion act according to your own discretion

51 His [. . .] take let him be reconciled to you right away

53 in cunning wittingly

65 dinner (the noontime meal)

72 And yet his trespass, in our common reason—
73 Save that, they say, the wars must make example
74 Out of her best—is not almost a fault
75 T'incur a private check. When shall he come?
    Tell me, Othello. I wonder in my soul
    What you would ask me that I should deny,
78 Or stand so mammering on. What? Michael Cassio,
    That came a-wooing with you, and so many a time,
    When I have spoke of you dispraisingly,
    Hath ta'en your part—to have so much to do
82 To bring him in! By 'r Lady, I could do much—

OTHELLO:
    Prithee, no more. Let him come when he will;
    I will deny thee nothing.

DESDEMONA: Why, this is not a boon.
    'Tis as I should entreat you wear your gloves,
    Or feed on nourishing dishes, or keep you warm,
88 Or sue to you to do a peculiar profit
    To your own person. Nay, when I have a suit
90 Wherein I mean to touch your love indeed,
91 It shall be full of poise and difficult weight,
    And fearful to be granted.

OTHELLO: I will deny thee nothing.
94 Whereon, I do beseech thee, grant me this,
    To leave me but a little to myself.

DESDEMONA:
    Shall I deny you? No. Farewell, my lord.

OTHELLO:
97 Farewell, my Desdemona. I'll come to thee straight.

DESDEMONA:
98 Emilia, come.—Be as your fancies teach you;
    Whate'er you be, I am obedient.   (*Exit* [*with Emilia*].)

---

72 common reason everyday judgments
73–74 Save [. . .] best were it not that, as the saying goes, military discipline requires making an example of the very best men. (*Her* refers to *wars* as a singular concept.)
74 not almost scarcely
75 a private check even a private reprimand
78 mammering on wavering about
82 bring him in restore him to favor
88 peculiar particular, personal
90 touch test
91 poise weight, heaviness; or equipoise, delicate balance involving hard choice
94 Whereon in return for which
97 straight straightway
98 fancies inclinations

OTHELLO:

¹⁰⁰   Excellent wretch! Perdition catch my soul

¹⁰¹   But I do love thee! And when I love thee not,

      Chaos is come again.

IAGO: My noble lord—

OTHELLO: What doest thou say, Iago?

IAGO:

      Did Michael Cassio, when you wooed my lady,

      Know of your love?

OTHELLO:

      He did, from first to last. Why dost thou ask?

IAGO:

      But for a satisfaction of my thought;

      No further harm.

OTHELLO: Why of thy thought, Iago?

IAGO:

      I did not think he had been acquainted with her.

OTHELLO:

      O, yes, and went between us very oft.

IAGO: Indeed?

OTHELLO:

      Indeed? Ay, indeed. Discern'st thou aught in that? Is he not honest?

IAGO: Honest, my lord?

OTHELLO: Honest. Ay, honest?

IAGO: My lord, for aught I know.

OTHELLO: What dost thou think?

IAGO: Think, my lord?

OTHELLO:

      "Think, my lord?" By heaven, thou echo'st me,

      As if there were some monster in thy thought

      Too hideous to be shown. Thou dost mean something.

      I heard thee say even now, thou lik'st not that,

      When Cassio left my wife. What didst not like?

¹²⁵   And when I told thee he was of my counsel

      In my whole course of wooing, thou criedst "Indeed?"

¹²⁷   And didst contract and purse thy brow together

      As if thou then hadst shut up in thy brain

¹²⁹   Some horrible conceit. If thou dost love me,

      Show me thy thought.

---

100 wretch (A term of affectionate endearment.)

101–102 And [. . .] again, i.e., my love for you will last forever, until the end of time when chaos will return. (But with an unconscious, ironic suggestion that, if anything should induce Othello to cease loving Desdemona, the result would be chaos.)

125 of my counsel in my confidence

127 purse knit

129 conceit fancy

IAGO: My lord, you know I love you.

OTHELLO: I think thou dost;

133   And for I know thou'rt full of love and honesty,
    And weigh'st thy words before thou giv'st them breath,

135   Therefore these stops of thine fright me the more;
    For such things in a false disloyal knave

137   Are tricks of custom, but in a man that's just

138   They're close dilations, working from the heart

139   That passion cannot rule.

IAGO: For Michael Cassio,
    I dare be sworn I think that he is honest.

OTHELLO:
    I think so too.

IAGO: Men should be what they seem;

144   Or those that be not, would they might seem none!

OTHELLO:
    Certain, men should be what they seem.

IAGO:
    Why, then, I think Cassio's an honest man.

OTHELLO: Nay, yet there's more in this.
    I prithee, speak to me as to thy thinkings,
    As thou dost ruminate, and give thy worst of thoughts
    The worst of words.

IAGO: Good my lord, pardon me.
    Though I am bound to every act of duty,

153   I am not bound to that all slaves are free to.
    Utter my thoughts? Why, say they are vile and false,
    As where's that palace where into foul things
    Sometimes intrude not? Who has that breast so pure
    But some uncleanly apprehensions

158   Keep leets and law days, and in sessions sit

159   With meditations lawful?

OTHELLO:

160   Thou dost conspire against thy friend, Iago,
    If thou but think'st him wronged and mak'st his ear

133 for because
135 stops pauses
137 of custom customary
138 close dilations secret or involuntary expressions or delays
139 That passion cannot rule i.e., that are too passionately strong to be restrained (referring to the workings), or, that cannot rule its own passions (referring to the heart). **For** as for
144 none i.e., not to be men, or not seem to be honest
153 that that which. **free to** free with respect to
158 Keep leets and law days i.e., hold court, set up their authority in one's heart. (*Leets* are a kind of manor court; *law days* are the days courts sit in session, or those sessions.)
159 With along with. **lawful** innocent
160 thy friend i.e., Othello

A stranger to thy thoughts.

IAGO: I do beseech you,

164   Though I perchance am vicious in my guess—
          As I confess it is my nature's plague
166   To spy into abuses, and oft my jealousy
167   Shapes faults that are not—that your wisdom then,
168   From one that so imperfectly conceits,
          Would take no notice, nor build yourself a trouble
170   Out of his scattering and unsure observance.
          It were not for your quiet nor your good,
          Nor for my manhood, honesty, and wisdom,
          To let you know my thoughts.

OTHELLO: What dost thou mean?

IAGO:

          Good name in man and woman, dear my lord,
176   Is the immediate jewel of their souls.
          Who steals my purse steals trash; 'tis something, nothing;
          'Twas mine, 'tis his, and has been slave to thousands;
          But he that filches from me my good name
          Robs me of that which not enriches him
          And makes me poor indeed.

OTHELLO: By heaven, I'll know thy thoughts.

IAGO:

183   You cannot, if my heart were in your hand,
          Nor shall not, whilst 'tis in my custody.

OTHELLO: Ha?

IAGO: O, beware, my lord, of jealousy.

187   It is the green-eyed monster which doth mock
          The meat it feeds on. That cuckold lives in bliss
189   Who, certain of his fate, loves not his wronger;
190   But O, what damnèd minutes tells he o'er
          Who dotes, yet doubts, suspects, yet fondly loves!

OTHELLO: O misery!

193   IAGO: Poor and content is rich, and rich enough,

164 vicious wrong
166 jealousy suspicious nature
167 then on that account
168 one i.e., myself, Iago. **conceits** judges, conjectures
170 scattering random
176 immediate essential, most precious
183 if even if
187–188 doth mock [. . .] on mocks and torments the heart of its victim, the man who suffers jealousy
189 his wronger i.e., his faithless wife. (The unsuspecting cuckold is spared the misery of loving his wife only to discover she is cheating on him.)
190 tells counts
193 Poor [. . .] enough to be content with what little one has is the greatest wealth of all. (Proverbial.)

194 But riches fineless is as poor as winter
To him that ever fears he shall be poor.
Good God, the souls of all my tribe defend
From jealousy!

OTHELLO: Why, why is this?
Think'st thou I'd make a life of jealousy,
200 To follow still the changes of the moon
With fresh suspicions? No! To be once in doubt
202 Is once to be resolved. Exchange me for a goat
When I shall turn the business of my soul
204 To such exsufflicate and blown surmises
205 Matching thy inference. 'Tis not to make me jealous
To say my wife is fair, feeds well, loves company,
Is free of speech, sings, plays, and dances well;
Where virtue is, these are more virtuous.
Nor from mine own weak merits will I draw
210 The smallest fear or doubt of her revolt,
For she had eyes, and chose me. No, Iago,
I'll see before I doubt; when I doubt, prove;
And on the proof, there is no more but this—
Away at once with love or jealousy.

IAGO:
I am glad of this, for now I shall have reason
To show the love and duty that I bear you
With franker spirit. Therefore, as I am bound,
Receive it from me. I speak not yet of proof.
Look to your wife; observe her well with Cassio.
220 Wear your eyes thus, not jealous nor secure.
I would not have your free and noble nature,
222 Out of self-bounty, be abused. Look to 't.
I know our country disposition well;
In Venice they do let God see the pranks
They dare not show their husbands; their best conscience
Is not to leave 't undone, but keep 't unknown.

OTHELLO: Dost thou say so?

---

194 fineless boundless
200–201 To follow [. . .] suspicions to be constantly imagining new causes for suspicion, changing incessantly like the moon
202 once once and for all. **resolved** free of doubt, having settled the matter
204 exsufflicate and blown inflated and blown up, rumored about, or spat out and fly-blown, hence loathsome, disgusting
205 inference description or allegation
210 doubt [. . .] revolt fear of her unfaithfulness
220 not neither. **secure** free from uncertainty
222 self-bounty inherent or natural goodness and generosity. **abused** deceived

IAGO:

> She did deceive her father, marrying you;
> And when she seemed to shake and fear your looks,
> She loved them most.

OTHELLO: And so she did.

232   IAGO:

233   Why, go to, then!

234   She that, so young, could give out such a seeming,

> To seel her father's eyes up close as oak,
> He thought 'twas witchcraft! But I am much to blame.
> I humbly do beseech you of your pardon
> For too much loving you.

238   OTHELLO: I am bound to thee forever.

IAGO:

> I see this hath a little dashed your spirits.

OTHELLO: Not a jot, not a jot.

IAGO: I' faith, I fear it has.

> I hope you will consider what is spoke
> Comes from my love. But I do see you're moved.
> I am to pray you not to strain my speech

245   To grosser issues nor to larger reach

> Than to suspicion.

OTHELLO: I will not.

IAGO: Should you do so, my lord,

249   My speech should fall into such vile success

> Which my thoughts aimed not. Cassio's my worthy friend.
> My lord, I see you're moved.

OTHELLO: No, not much moved.

253   I do not think but Desdemona's honest.

IAGO:

> Long live she so! And long live you to think so!

OTHELLO:

> And yet, how nature erring from itself—

IAGO:

> Ay, there's the point! As—to be bold with you—

257   Not to affect many proposèd matches

258   Of her own clime, complexion, and degree,

> Whereto we see in all things nature tends—

---

232 go to (An expression of impatience.)
233 seeming false appearance
234 seel blind. (A term from falconry.) **oak** (A close-grained wood.)
238 bound indebted (but perhaps with ironic sense of "tied")
245 issues significance. **reach** meaning, scope
249 success effect, result
253 honest chaste
257 affect prefer, desire
258 clime [. . .] **degree** country, color, and social position

260	Foh! One may smell in such a will most rank,
261	Foul disproportion, thoughts unnatural.
262	But pardon me. I do not in position
	Distinctly speak of her, though I may fear
264	Her will, recoiling to her better judgment,
265	May fall to match you with her country forms
266	And happily repent.

OTHELLO: Farewell, farewell!
If more thou dost perceive, let me know more.
Set on thy wife to observe. Leave me, Iago.

IAGO (*going*): My lord, I take my leave.

OTHELLO:
Why did I marry? This honest creature doubtless
Sees and knows more, much more, than he unfolds.

IAGO (*returning*):
My Lord, I would I might entreat your honor

274   To scan this thing no farther. Leave it to time.
Although 'tis fit that Cassio have his place—
For, sure, he fills it up with great ability—
Yet, if you please to hold him off awhile,

278   You shall by that perceive him and his means.
279   Note if your lady strain his entertainment
With any strong or vehement importunity;
Much will be seen in that. In the meantime,

282   Let me be thought too busy in my fears—
As worthy cause I have to fear I am—

284   And hold her free, O do beseech your honor.

285   OTHELLO: Fear not my government.

IAGO: I once more take my leave.   (*Exit.*)

OTHELLO:
This fellow's of exceeding honesty,

288   And knows all qualities, with a learnèd spirit,
289   Of human dealings. If I do prove her haggard,

---

260 will sensuality, appetite
261 disproportion abnormality
262 position argument, proposition
264 recoiling reverting. **better** i.e., more natural and reconsidered
265 fall [. . .] forms undertake to compare you with Venetian norms of handsomeness
266 happily repent haply repent her marriage
274 scan scrutinize
278 his means the method he uses (to regain his post)
279 strain his entertainment urge his reinstatement
282 busy interfering
284 hold her free regard her as innocent
285 government self-control, conduct
288 qualities natures, types
289 haggard wild (like a wild female hawk)

290 Though that her jesses were my dear heartstrings,
291 I'd whistle her off and let her down the wind
292 To prey at fortune. Haply, for I am black
293 And have not those soft parts of conversation
294 That chamberers have, or for I am declined
Into the vale of years—yet that's not much—
296 She's gone. I am abused, and my relief
Must be to loathe her. O curse of marriage,
That we can call these delicate creatures ours
And not their appetites! I had rather be a toad
And live upon the vapor of a dungeon
Than keep a corner in the thing I love
For others' uses. Yet, 'tis the plague of great ones;
303 Prerogatived are they less than the base.
'Tis destiny unshunnable, like death.
305 Even then this forkèd plague is fated to us
306 When we do quicken. Look where she comes.

(Enter Desdemona and Emilia.)

If she be false, O, then heaven mocks itself!
I'll not believe 't.
DESDEMONA: How now, my dear Othello?
310 Your dinner, and the generous islanders
311 By you invited, do attend your presence.
OTHELLO:
I am to blame.
DESDEMONA: Why do you speak so faintly?
Are you not well?
OTHELLO:
I have a pain upon my forehead here.

---

290 jesses straps fastened around the legs of a trained hawk
291 I'd [. . .] wind i.e., I'd let her go forever. (To release a hawk downwind was to invite it not to return.)
292 prey at fortune fend for herself in the wild. **Haply, for** perhaps, because
293 soft [. . .] conversation pleasing graces of social behavior
294 chamberers gallants
296 abused deceived
303 Prerogatived privileged (to have honest wives). **the base** ordinary citizens. (Socially prominent men are especially prone to the unavoidable destiny of being cuckolded and to the public shame that goes with it.)
305 forkèd (An allusion to the horns of the cuckold.)
306 quicken receive life. (*Quicken* may also mean to swarm with maggots as the body festers, as in 4.2.76, in which case lines 305–306 suggest that *even then*, in death, we are cuckolded by *forkèd* worms.)
310 generous noble
311 attend await

DESDEMONA:

316   Faith, that's with watching. 'Twill away again.
(She offers her handkerchief.)
Let me but bind it hard, within this hour
It will be well.

319 OTHELLO: Your napkin is too little.

320   Let it alone. Come, I'll go in with you.

(He puts the handkerchief from him, and it drops.)

DESDEMONA:

I am very sorry that you are not well.

(Exit [with Othello].)

EMILIA *(picking up the handkerchief)*: I am glad I have found this napkin.
This was her first remembrance from the Moor.
324   My wayward husband hath a hundred times
Wooed me to steal it, but she so loves the token—
For he conjured her she should ever keep it—
That she reserves it evermore about her
328   To kiss and talk to. I'll have the work ta'en out,
And give 't Iago. What he will do with it
Heaven knows, not I;
331   I nothing but to please his fantasy.

(Enter Iago.)

IAGO:

How now? What do you here alone?

EMILIA:

Do not you chide. I have a thing for you.

IAGO:

334   You have a thing for me? It is a common thing—

EMILIA: Ha?

IAGO: To have a foolish wife.

EMILIA:

O, is that all? What will you give me now
For that same handkerchief?

---

316 watching too little sleep
319 napkin handkerchief
320 Let it alone i.e., never mind
324 wayward capricious
328 work ta'en out design of the embroidery copied
331 fantasy whim
334 common thing (With bawdy suggestion; *common* suggests coarseness and availability to all comers, and *thing* is a slang term for the pudendum.)

IAGO: What handkerchief?

EMILIA: What handkerchief?

> Why, that the Moor first gave to Desdemona;
> That which so often you did bid me steal.

IAGO: Hast stolen it from her?

EMILIA:

> No, faith. She let it drop by negligence,
345 > And to th' advantage, I, being here, took 't up.
> Look, here 'tis.

IAGO: A good wench! Give it me.

EMILIA: What will you do with 't, that you have been so earnest
> To have me filch it?

IAGO (*snatching it*): Why, what is that to you?

EMILIA:

> If it be not for some purpose of import,
> Give 't me again. Poor lady, she'll run mad
353 > When she shall lack it.
354 IAGO: Be not acknown on 't.

> I have use for it. Go, leave me. (*Exit Emilia.*)
356 > I will in Cassio's lodging lose this napkin
> And let him find it. Trifles light as air
> Are to the jealous confirmations strong
> As proofs of Holy Writ. This may do something.
> The Moor already changes with my poison.
361 > Dangerous conceits are in their natures poisons,
362 > Which at the first are scarce found to distaste,
363 > But with a little act upon the blood
> Burn like the mines of sulfur.

(*Enter Othello.*)

>   I did say so.
366 > Look where he comes! Not poppy nor mandragora
> Nor all the drowsy syrups of the world
> Shall ever medicine thee to that sweet sleep
369 > Which thou owedst yesterday.

OTHELLO: Ha, ha, false to me?

---

345 to th' advantage taking the opportunity
353 lack miss
354 Be [. . .] on 't do not confess knowledge of it
356 lose (The Folio spelling, *loose,* is a normal spelling for "lose," but may also contain the idea of "let go," "release.")
361 conceits fancies, ideas
362 distaste be distasteful
363 act action, working
366 mandragora an opiate made of the mandrake root
369 thou owedst you did own

IAGO:

>Why, how now, General? No more of that.

OTHELLO:

>Avaunt! Begone! Thou hast set me on the rack.
>I swear 'tis better to be much abused
>Than but to know 't a little.

IAGO: How now, my lord?

OTHELLO:

>What sense had I of her stolen hours of lust?
>I saw 't not, thought it not, it harmed not me.

378
>I slept the next night well, fed well, was free and merry;
>I found not Cassio's kisses on her lips.

380
>He that is robbed, not wanting what is stolen,
>Let him not know 't and he's not robbed at all.

IAGO: I am sorry to hear this.

OTHELLO:

>I had been happy if the general camp,

384
>Pioners and all, had tasted her sweet body,

385
>So I had nothing known. O, now, forever
>Farewell the tranquil mind! Farewell content!

387
>Farewell the plumèd troops and the big wars
>That makes ambition virtue! Oh, farewell!
>Farewell the neighing steed and the shrill trump,
>The spirit-stirring drum, th' ear-piercing fife,

391
>The royal banner, and all quality,

392
>Pride, pomp, and circumstance of glorious war!

393
>And O, you mortal engines, whose rude throats

394
>Th' immortal Jove's dread clamors counterfeit,
>Farewell! Othello's occupation's gone.

IAGO: Is 't possible, my lord?

OTHELLO:

>Villain, be sure thou prove my love a whore!
>Be sure of it. Give me the ocular proof,
>Or, by the worth of mine eternal soul,
>Thou hadst been better have been born a dog
>Than answer my waked wrath!

IAGO: Is 't come to this?

---

378 free carefree
380 wanting missing
384 Pioners diggers of mines, the lowest grade of soldiers
385 So provided
387 big stately
391 quality character, essential nature
392 Pride rich display. **circumstance** pageantry
393 mortal engines i.e., cannon. (*Mortal* means "deadly.")
394 Jove's dread clamors i.e., thunder

OTHELLO:

> Make me to see 't, or at least so prove it
> 404   That the probation bear no hinge nor loop
> To hang a doubt on, or woe upon thy life!

IAGO: My noble lord—

OTHELLO:

> If thou dost slander her and torture me,
> 408   Never pray more; abandon all remorse;
> 409   On horror's head horrors accumulate;
> 410   Do deeds to make heaven weep, all earth amazed;
> For nothing canst thou to damnation add
> Greater than that.

IAGO: O grace! O heaven forgive me!

> Are you a man? Have you a soul or sense?
> 415   God b' wi' you; take mine office. O wretched fool,
> 416   That lov'st to make thine honesty a vice!
> O monstrous world! Take note, take note, O world,
> To be direct and honest is not safe.
> 419   I thank you for this profit, and from hence
> 420   I'll love no friend, sith love breeds such offense.

421 OTHELLO: Nay, stay. Thou shouldst be honest.

IAGO:

> I should be wise, for honesty's a fool
> And loses that it works for.

OTHELLO: By the world,

> I think my wife be honest and think she is not;
> 426   I think that thou art just and think thou are not.
> I'll have some proof. My name, that was as fresh
> 428   As Dian's visage, is now begrimed and black
> As mine own face. If there be cords, or knives,
> Poison, or fire, or suffocating streams,
> I'll not endure it. Would I were satisfied!

IAGO:

> I see, sir, you are eaten up with passion.
> I do repent me that I put it to you.
> You would be satisfied?

404 probation proof
408 remorse pity, penitent hope for salvation
409 horrors accumulate add still more horrors
410 amazed confounded with horror
415 O wretched fool (Iago addresses himself as a fool for having carried honesty too far.)
416 vice failing, something overdone
419 profit profitable instruction. **hence** henceforth
420 sith since. **offense** i.e., harm to the one who offers help and friendship
421 Thou shouldst be It appears that you are. (But Iago replies in the sense of "ought to be.")
426 that what
428 Dian Diana, goddess of the moon and of chastity

OTHELLO:	Would? Nay, and I will.

IAGO:

And may; but how? How satisfied, my lord?

437 Would you, the supervisor, grossly gape on?

Behold her topped?

OTHELLO:	Death and damnation! O!

IAGO:

It were a tedious difficulty, I think,

441 To bring them to that prospect. Damn them then,

442 If ever mortal eyes do see them bolster

443 More than their own. What then? How then?

What shall I say? Where's satisfaction?

It is impossible you should see this,

446 Were they as prime as goats, as hot as monkeys,

447 As salt as wolves in pride, and fools as gross

As ignorance made drunk. But yet I say,

449 If imputation and strong circumstances

Which lead directly to the door of truth

Will give you satisfaction, you might have 't.

OTHELLO:

Give me a living reason she's disloyal.

IAGO: I do not like the office.

454 But sith I am entered in this cause so far,

455 Pricked to 't by foolish honesty and love,

I will go on. I lay with Cassio lately,

And being troubled with a raging tooth

I could not sleep. There are a kind of men

So loose of soul that in their sleeps will mutter

Their affairs. One of this kind is Cassio.

In sleep I heard him say, "Sweet Desdemona,

Let us be wary, let us hide our loves!"

And then, sir, would he grip and wring my hand,

Cry "O sweet creature!", then kiss me hard,

As if he plucked up kisses by the roots

That grew upon my lips; then laid his leg

Over my thigh, and sighed, and kissed, and then

Cried, "Cursèd fate that gave thee to the Moor!"

---

437 supervisor onlooker
441 Damn them then i.e., they would have to be really incorrigible
442 bolster go to bed together, share a bolster
443 More other. **own** own eyes
446 prime lustful
447 salt wanton, sensual. **pride** heat
449 imputation [. . .] **circumstances** strong circumstantial evidence
454 sith since
455 Pricked spurred

OTHELLO:

O monstrous! Monstrous!

IAGO: Nay, this was but his dream.

OTHELLO:

471   But this denoted a foregone conclusion.

472   'Tis a shrewd doubt, though it be but a dream.

IAGO:

And this may help to thicken other proofs
That do demonstrate thinly.

OTHELLO: I'll tear her all to pieces.

IAGO:

Nay, but be wise. Yet we see nothing done;
She may be honest yet. Tell me but this:
Have you not sometimes seen a handkerchief

479   Spotted with strawberries in your wife's hand?

OTHELLO:

I gave her such a one. 'Twas my first gift.

IAGO:

I know not that; but such a handkerchief—
I am sure it was your wife's—did I today
See Cassio wipe his beard with.

OTHELLO: If it be that—

IAGO:

If it be that, or any that was hers,
It speaks against her with the other proofs.

OTHELLO:

487   O, that the slave had forty thousand lives!
One is too poor, too weak for my revenge.
Now do I see 'tis true. Look here, Iago,

490   All my fond love thus do I blow to heaven.
'Tis gone.
Arise, black vengeance, from the hollow hell!

493   Yield up, O love, thy crown and hearted throne

494   To tyrannous hate! Swell, bosom, with thy freight,

495   For 'tis of aspics' tongues!

496   IAGO: Yet be content.

OTHELLO: O, blood, blood, blood!

471 **foregone conclusion** concluded experience or action
472 **shrewd doubt** suspicious circumstance
479 **Spotted with strawberries** embroidered with a strawberry pattern
487 **the slave** i.e., Cassio
490 **fond** foolish (but also suggesting "affectionate")
493 **hearted** fixed in the heart
494 **freight** burden
495 **aspics'** venomous serpents'
496 **content** calm

IAGO:

> Patience, I say. Your mind perhaps may change.

OTHELLO:

499
> Never, Iago. Like to the Pontic Sea,
> Whose icy current and compulsive course
> Ne'er feels retiring ebb, but keeps due on

502
> To the Propontic and the Hellespont,
> Even so my bloody thoughts with violent pace
> Shall ne'er look back, ne'er ebb to humble love,

505
> Till that a capable and wide revenge

506
> Swallow them up. Now, by yond marble heaven,
> (*Kneeling*) In the due reverence of a sacred vow
> I here engage my words.

IAGO: Do not rise yet.

510
> (*He kneels.*) Witness, you ever-burning lights above,

511
> You elements that clip us round about,
> Witness that here Iago doth give up

513
> The execution of his wit, hands, heart,
> To wronged Othello's service. Let him command,

515
> And to obey shall be in me remorse,

516
> What bloody business ever.   (*They rise.*)

OTHELLO: I greet thy love,
> Not with vain thanks, but with acceptance bounteous,

519
> And will upon the instant put thee to 't.
> Within these three days let me hear thee say
> That Cassio's not alive.

IAGO: My friend is dead;
> 'Tis done at your request. But let her live.

OTHELLO:

524
> Damn her, lewd minx! O, damn her, damn her!
> Come, go with me apart. I will withdraw
> To furnish me with some swift means of death
> For the fair devil. Now art thou my lieutenant.

IAGO: I am your own forever.   (*Exeunt.*)

---

499 Pontic Sea Black Sea
502 Propontic Sea of Marmora, between the Black Sea and the Aegean. **Hellespont**
Dardanelles, straits where the Sea of Marmora joins with the Aegean
505 capable ample, comprehensive
506 marble i.e., gleaming like marble and unrelenting
510 s.d. He kneels (In the Quarto text, Iago kneels here after Othello has knelt at line 506.)
511 clip encompass
513 execution exercise, action. **wit** mind
515 remorse pity (for Othello's wrongs)
516 ever soever
519 to 't to the proof
524 minx wanton

3.4

(Enter Desdemona, Emilia, and Clown.)

1   DESDEMONA: Do you know, sirrah, where Lieutenant
2   Cassio lies?
    CLOWN: I dare not say he lies anywhere.
    DESDEMONA: Why, man?
    CLOWN: He's a soldier, and for me to say a soldier lies,
        'tis stabbing.
    DESDEMONA: Go to. Where lodges he?
    CLOWN: To tell you where he lodges is to tell you where I lie.
    DESDEMONA: Can anything be made of this?
    CLOWN: I know not where he lodges, and for me to devise a lodging and
11   say he lies here, or he lies there, were to lie in mine own throat.
    DESDEMONA: Can you inquire him out, and be edified
        by report?
    CLOWN: I will catechize the world for him; that is, make questions,
        and by them answer.
16 DESDEMONA: Seek him, bid him come hither. Tell him I have moved my
        lord on his behalf and hope all will be well.
    CLOWN: To do this is within the compass of man's wit, and therefore I
        will attempt the doing it. *(Exit Clown.)*
    DESDEMONA:
        Where should I lose that handkerchief, Emilia?
    EMILIA: I know not, madam.
    DESDEMONA:
        Believe me, I had rather have lost my purse
23   Full of crusadoes; and but my noble Moor
        Is true of mind and made of no such baseness
        As jealous creatures are, it were enough
        To put him to ill thinking.
    EMILIA: Is he not jealous?
    DESDEMONA:
        Who, he? I think the sun where he was born
29   Drew all such humors from him.
    EMILIA: Look where he comes.

        (Enter Othello.)

3.4. Location: Before the citadel.
1 sirrah (A form of address to an inferior.)
2 lies lodges. (But the Clown makes the obvious pun.)
11 lie [. . .] throat (1) lie egregiously and deliberately (2) use the windpipe to speak a lie
16 moved petitioned
23 crusadoes Portuguese gold coins
29 humors (Refers to the four bodily fluids thought to determine temperament.)

DESDEMONA:
> I will not leave him now till Cassio
> Be called to him. How is 't with you, my lord?

OTHELLO:
> Well, my good lady. (*Aside.*) O, hardness to dissemble!—
> How do you, Desdemona?

DESDEMONA: Well, my good lord.

OTHELLO:
> Give me your hand. (*She gives her hand.*) This hand is moist, my
> lady.

DESDEMONA: It yet hath felt no age nor known no sorrow.

39   OTHELLO: This argues fruitfulness and liberal heart.
> Hot, hot, and moist. This hand of yours requires

41   A sequester from liberty, fasting and prayer,

42   Much castigation, exercise devout;
> For here's a young and sweating devil here
> That commonly rebels. 'Tis a good hand,

45   A frank one.

DESDEMONA: You may indeed say so,
> For 'twas that hand that gave away my heart.

OTHELLO:

48   A liberal hand. The hearts of old gave hands,

49   But our new heraldry is hands, not hearts.

DESDEMONA:
> I cannot speak of this. Come now, your promise.

51   OTHELLO: What promise, chuck?

DESDEMONA:
> I have sent to bid Cassio come speak with you.

OTHELLO:

53   I have a salt and sorry rheum offends me;
> Lend me thy handkerchief.

DESDEMONA: Here, my lord. (*She offers a handkerchief.*)

OTHELLO:
> That which I gave you.

DESDEMONA: I have it not about me.

---

39 argues gives evidence of. **fruitfulness** generosity, amorousness, and fecundity. **liberal**
generous and sexually free
41 sequester separation, sequestration
42 castigation corrective discipline. **exercise devout** i.e., prayer, religious meditation, etc.
45 frank generous, open (with sexual suggestion)
48 The hearts [. . .] hands i.e., in former times, people would give their hearts when they
gave their hands to something
49 But [. . .] hearts i.e., in our decadent times, the joining of hands is no longer a badge
to signify the giving of hearts
51 chuck (A term of endearment.)
53 salt [. . .] rheum distressful head cold or watering of the eyes

OTHELLO: Not?

DESDEMONA: No, faith, my lord.

OTHELLO:

> That's a fault. That handkerchief
> Did an Egyptian to my mother give.
>
> 62 She was a charmer, and could almost read
> The thoughts of people. She told her, while she kept it
> 'Twould make her amiable and subdue my father
> Entirely to her love, but if she lost it
> Or made a gift of it, my father's eye
> Should hold her loathèd and his spirits should hunt
>
> 68 After new fancies. She, dying, gave it me,
> And bid me, when my fate would have me wived,
>
> 70 To give it her. I did so; and take heed on 't;
> Make it a darling like your precious eye.
>
> 72 To lose 't or give 't away were such perdition
> As nothing else could match.

DESDEMONA: Is 't possible?

OTHELLO:

> 'Tis true. There's magic in the web of it.
> A sibyl, that had numbered in the world
>
> 77 The sun to course two hundred compasses,
>
> 78 In her prophetic fury sewed the work;
> The worms were hallowed that did breed the silk,
>
> 80 And it was dyed in mummy which the skillful
> 81 Conserved of maiden's hearts.

DESDEMONA: I' faith! Is 't true?

OTHELLO:

> Most veritable. Therefore look to 't well.

DESDEMONA: Then would to God that I had never seen 't!

OTHELLO: Ha? Wherefore?

DESDEMONA:

> 86 Why do you speak so startingly and rash?

OTHELLO:

> 87 Is 't lost? Is 't gone? Speak, is 't out o' the way?

DESDEMONA: Heaven bless us!

---

62 charmer sorceress
68 fancies loves
70 her i.e., to my wife
72 perdition loss
77 compasses annual circlings. (The *sibyl*, or prophetess, was two hundred years old.)
78 prophetic fury frenzy of prophetic inspiration. **work** embroidered pattern
80 mummy medicinal or magical preparation drained from mummified bodies
81 Conserved of prepared or preserved out of
86 startingly and rash disjointedly and impetuously, excitedly
87 out o' the way lost, misplaced

OTHELLO: Say you?

90   DESDEMONA: It is not lost; but what an if it were?

OTHELLO: How?

DESDEMONA:
     I say it is not lost.

OTHELLO: Fetch 't, let me see 't.

DESDEMONA:
     Why, so I can, sir, but I will not now.
     This is a trick to put me from my suit.
     Pray you, let Cassio be received again.

OTHELLO:
     Fetch me the handkerchief! My mind misgives.

DESDEMONA: Come, come,

99   You'll never meet a more sufficient man.

OTHELLO:
     The handkerchief!

101   DESDEMONA: I pray, talk me of Cassio.

OTHELLO:
     The handkerchief!

103   DESDEMONA: A man that all his time
     Hath founded his good fortunes on your love,
     Shared dangers with you—

OTHELLO: The handkerchief!

DESDEMONA: I' faith, you are to blame.

OTHELLO: Zounds! (*Exit Othello.*)

EMILIA: Is not this man jealous?

DESDEMONA: I ne'er saw this before.
     Sure, there's some wonder in this handkerchief.
     I am most unhappy in the loss of it.

EMILIA:

113   'Tis not a year or two shows us a man.

114   They are all but stomachs, and we all but food;

115   They eat us hungerly, and when they are full
     They belch us.

     (*Enter Iago and Cassio.*)

          Look you, Cassio and my husband.

---

90 an if if
99 sufficient able, complete
101 talk talk to
103 all his time throughout his career
113 'Tis [. . .] man i.e., you can't really know a man even in a year or two of experience
(?), or, real men come along seldom (?)
114 but nothing but
115 hungerly hungrily

IAGO (*to Cassio*):

    There is no other way; 'tis she must do 't.

₁₁₉   And, lo, the happiness! Go and importune her.

DESDEMONA:

    How now, good Cassio? What's the news with you?

CASSIO:

    Madam, my former suit. I do beseech you

₁₂₂   That by your virtuous means I may again

    Exist and be a member of his love

₁₂₄   Whom I, with all the office of my heart,

    Entirely honor. I would not be delayed.

₁₂₆   If my offense be of such mortal kind

₁₂₇   That nor my service past, nor present sorrows,

    Nor purposed merit in futurity

    Can ransom me into his love again,

₁₃₀   But to know so must be my benefit;

    So shall I clothe me in a forced content,

₁₃₂   And shut myself up in some other course,

₁₃₃   To fortune's alms.

DESDEMONA: Alas, thrice-gentle Cassio,

₁₃₅   My advocation is not now in tune.

    My lord is not my lord; nor should I know him,

₁₃₇   Were he in favor as in humor altered.

    So help me every spirit sanctified

    As I have spoken for you all my best

₁₄₀   And stood within the blank of his displeasure

    For my free speech! You must awhile be patient.

    What I can do I will, and more I will

    Than for myself I dare. Let that suffice you.

IAGO:

    Is my lord angry?

EMILIA: He went hence but now.

    And certainly in strange unquietness.

IAGO:

    Can he be angry? I have seen the cannon

    When it hath blown his ranks into the air,

---

119 the happiness in happy time, fortunately met
122 virtuous efficacious
124 office loyal service
126 mortal fatal
127 nor [. . .] **nor** neither [. . .] nor
130 But [. . .] **benefit** merely to know that my case is hopeless will have to content me (and will be better than uncertainty)
132 shut [. . .] **in** confine myself to
133 To fortune's alms throwing myself on the mercy of fortune
135 advocation advocacy
137 favor appearance. **humor** mood
140 within the blank within point-blank range. (The *blank* is the center of the target.)

And like the devil from his very arm
Puffed his own brother—and is he angry?
151   Something of moment then. I will go meet him.
There's matter in 't indeed, if he be angry.

DESDEMONA:
     I prithee, do so.   (*Exit* [*Iago*].)
154   Something, sure of state,
155 Either from Venice, or some unhatched practice
Made demonstrable here in Cyprus to him,
157 Hath puddled his clear spirit; and in such cases
Men's natures wrangle with inferior things,
Though great ones are their object. 'Tis even so;
160 For let our finger ache, and it indues
Our other, healthful members even to a sense
Of pain. Nay, we must think men are not gods,
163 Nor of them look for such observancy
164 As fits the bridal. Beshrew me much, Emilia,
165 I was, unhandsome warrior as I am,
166 Arraigning his unkindness with my soul;
167 But now I find I had suborned the witness,
And he's indicted falsely.

EMILIA: Pray heaven it be
State matters, as you think, and no conception
171 Nor no jealous toy concerning you.

DESDEMONA:
     Alas the day! I never gave him cause.

EMILIA:
     But jealous souls will not be answered so;
They are not ever jealous for the cause,
175 But jealous for they're jealous. It is a monster
176 Begot upon itself, born on itself.

DESDEMONA:
     Heaven keep that monster from Othello's mind!

EMILIA: Lady, amen.

---

151 of moment of immediate importance, momentous
154 of state concerning state affairs
155 unhatched practice as yet unexecuted or undiscovered plot
157 puddled muddied
160 indues brings to the same condition
163 observancy attentiveness
164 bridal wedding (when a bridegroom is newly attentive to his bride). **Beshrew me** (A mild oath.)
165 unhandsome insufficient, unskillful
166 with before the bar of
167 suborned the witness induced the witness to give false testimony
171 toy fancy
175 for because
176 Begot upon itself generated solely from itself

DESInterMONA:

DESDEMONA:

> I will go seek him. Cassio, walk hereabout.
> If I do find him fit, I'll move your suit
> And seek to effect it to my uttermost.

CASSIO:

> I humbly thank your ladyship.

(Exit [Desdemona with Emilia].)

(Enter Bianca.)

BIANCA:

183   Save you, friend Cassio!

184   CASSIO: What make you from home?

> How is 't with you, my most fair Bianca?
> I' faith, sweet love, I was coming to your house.

BIANCA:

> And I was going to your lodging, Cassio.
> What, keep a week away? Seven days and nights?

189   Eightscore-eight hours? And lovers' absent hours

190   More tedious than the dial eightscore times?

> O weary reckoning!

CASSIO: Pardon me, Bianca.

> I have this while with leaden thoughts been pressed;

194   But I shall, in a more continuate time,

195   Strike off this score of absence. Sweet Bianca,

> *(giving her Desdemona's handkerchief)*

196   Take me this work out.

BIANCA: O Cassio, whence came this?

198   This is some token from a newer friend.

> To the felt absence now I feel a cause.
> Is 't come to this? Well, well.

CASSIO: Go to, woman!

> Throw your vile guesses in the devil's teeth,
> From whence you have them. You are jealous now
> That this is from some mistress, some remembrance.
> No, by my faith, Bianca.

BIANCA: Why, whose is it?

CASSIO:

> I know not, neither. I found it in my chamber.

---

183 Save God save.
184 make do
189 Eightscore-eight one hundred sixty-eight, the number of hours in a week
190 the dial a complete revolution of the clock
194 continuate uninterrupted
195 Strike [. . .] score settle this account
196 Take [. . .] out copy this embroidery for me
198 friend mistress

208   I like the work well. Ere it be demanded—
209   As like enough it will—I would have it copied.
        Take it and do 't, and leave me for this time.

BIANCA: Leave you? Wherefore?

CASSIO:
      I do attend here on the General,
213   And think it no addition, nor my wish,
      To have him see me womaned.

BIANCA: Why, I pray you?

CASSIO: Not that I love you not.

BIANCA: But that you do not love me.
218   I pray you, bring me on the way a little,
      And say if I shall see you soon at night.

CASSIO:
      'Tis but a little way that I can bring you,
      For I attend here; but I'll see you soon.

BIANCA:
      'Tis very good. I must be circumstanced.

(Exeunt omnes.)

4.1

(Enter Othello and Iago.)

IAGO: Will you think so?

OTHELLO: Think so, Iago?

IAGO: What,
      To kiss in private?

OTHELLO: An unauthorized kiss!

IAGO:
      Or to be naked with her friend in bed
      An hour or more, not meaning any harm?

OTHELLO:
      Naked in bed, Iago, and not mean harm?
      It is hypocrisy against the devil.
      They that mean virtuously and yet do so,
      The devil their virtue tempts, and they tempt heaven.

IAGO:
12   If they do nothing, 'tis a venial slip.
      But if I give my wife a handkerchief—

---

208 demanded inquired for
209 like likely
213 addition i.e., addition to my reputation
218 bring accompany
4.1 Location: Before the citadel.
12 venial pardonable

OTHELLO: What then?

IAGO:

> Why then, 'tis hers, my lord, and being hers,
> She may, I think, bestow 't on any man.

OTHELLO:

> She is protectress of her honor too.
> May she give that?

IAGO:

> Her honor is an essence that's not seen;
20 > They have it very oft that have it not.
> But, for the handkerchief—

OTHELLO:

> By heaven, I would most gladly have forgot it.
> Thou saidst—O, it comes o'er my memory
24 > As doth the raven o'er the infectious house,
> Boding to all—he had my handkerchief.

IAGO: Ay, what of that?

OTHELLO: That's not so good now.

IAGO: What

> If I had said I had seen him do you wrong?
30 > Or heard him say—as knaves by such abroad,
> Who having, by their own importunate suit,
32 > Or voluntary dotage of some mistress,
33 > Convincèd or supplied them, cannot choose
> But they must blab—

OTHELLO: Hath he said anything?

IAGO:

> He hath, my lord; but, be you well assured,
> No more than he'll unswear.

OTHELLO: What hath he said?

IAGO:

> Faith, that he did—I know not what he did.

OTHELLO: What? What?

IAGO:

> Lie—

OTHELLO: With her?

IAGO: With her, on her; what you will.

OTHELLO: Lie with her? Lie on her? We say "lie on her"
45 > when they belie her. Lie with her? Zounds, that's fulsome.

---

20 They have it i.e., they enjoy a reputation for it
24 raven [. . .] house (Allusion to the belief that the raven hovered over a house of sickness or infection, such as one visited by the plague.)
30 abroad around about
32 voluntary dotage willing infatuation
33 Convincèd or supplied seduced or sexually gratified
45 belie slander. **fulsome** foul

47 —Handkerchief—confessions—handkerchief!
48 —To confess and be hanged for his labor—first to be
hanged and then to confess.—I tremble at it. Nature
would not invest herself in such shadowing passion
50 without some instruction. It is not words that shakes
me thus. Pish! Noses, ears, and lips.—Is 't possible?
—Confess—handkerchief!—O devil!

(Falls in a trance.)

IAGO: Work on,
My medicine, work! Thus credulous fools are caught,
And many worthy and chaste dames even thus,
All guiltless, meet reproach.—What, ho! My lord!
My lord, I say! Othello!

(Enter Cassio.)

How now, Cassio?
CASSIO: What's the matter?
IAGO:
My lord is fall'n into an epilepsy.
This is his second fit. He had one yesterday.
CASSIO:
Rub him about the temples.
IAGO: No, forbear.
64 The lethargy must have his quiet course.
If not, he foams at mouth, and by and by
Breaks out to savage madness. Look, he stirs.
Do you withdraw yourself a little while.
He will recover straight. When he is gone,
69 I would on great occasion speak with you.

(Exit Cassio.)

How is it, General? Have you not hurt your head?
OTHELLO:
71 Dost thou mock me?
IAGO: I mock you not, by heaven.

47–48 first [. . .] to confess (Othello reverses the proverbial *confess and be hanged;* Cassio is to be given no time to confess before he dies.)
48–50 Nature [. . .] instruction i.e., without some foundation in fact, nature would not have dressed herself in such an overwhelming passion that comes over me now and fills my mind with images, or in such a lifelike fantasy as Cassio had in his dream of lying with Desdemona
50 words mere words
64 lethargy coma. **his** its
69 on great occasion on a matter of great importance
71 mock me (Othello takes Iago's question about hurting his head to be a mocking reference to the cuckold's horns)

Would you would bear your fortune like a man!
OTHELLO:
    A hornèd man's a monster and a beast.
IAGO:
    There's many a beast then in a populous city,
76   And many a civil monster.
OTHELLO: Did he confess it?
IAGO: Good sir, be a man.
79   Think every bearded fellow that's but yoked
80   May draw with you. There's millions now alive
81   That nightly lie in those unproper beds
82   Which they dare swear peculiar. Your case is better.
    O, 'tis the spite of hell, the fiend's arch-mock,
84   To lip a wanton in a secure couch
    And to suppose her chaste! No, let me know,
86   And knowing what I am, I know what she shall be.
OTHELLO: O, thou art wise. 'Tis certain.
IAGO: Stand you awhile apart;
89   Confine yourself but in a patient list.
    Whilst you were here o'erwhelmèd with your grief—
    A passion most unsuiting such a man—
92   Cassio came hither. I shifted him away,
93   And laid good 'scuse upon your ecstasy,
    Bade him anon return and here speak with me,
95   The which he promised. Do but encave yourself
96   And mark the fleers, the gibes, and notable scorns
    That dwell in every region of his face;
    For I will make him tell the tale anew,
    Where, how, how oft, how long ago, and when
100   He hath and is again to cope your wife.
    I say, but mark his gesture. Marry, patience!
102   Or I shall say you're all-in-all in spleen,
    And nothing of a man.

---

76 civil i.e., dwelling in a city
79 yoked (1) married (2) put into the yoke of infamy and cuckoldry
80 draw with you pull as you do, like oxen who are yoked, i.e., share your fate as cuckold
81 unproper not exclusively their own
82 peculiar private, their own. **better** i.e., because you know the truth
84 lip kiss. **secure** free from suspicion
86 what I am i.e., a cuckold. **she shall be** will happen to her
89 in [. . .] list within the bounds of patience
92 shifted him away used a dodge to get rid of him
93 ecstasy trance
95 encave conceal
96 fleers sneers. **notable** obvious
100 cope encounter with, have sex with
102 all-in-all in spleen utterly governed by passionate impulses

OTHELLO: Dost thou hear, Iago?
    I will be found most cunning in my patience;
    But dost thou hear?—most bloody.
IAGO: That's not amiss;
108   But yet keep time in all. Will you withdraw?

(Othello stands apart.)

    Now will I question Cassio of Bianca,
110   A huswife that by selling her desires.
    Buys herself bread and clothes. It is a creature
    That dotes on Cassio—as 'tis the strumpet's plague
    To beguile many and be beguiled by one.
114   He, when he hears of her, cannot restrain
    From the excess of laughter. Here he comes.

(Enter Cassio.)

    As he shall smile, Othello shall go mad;
117   And his unbookish jealousy must conster
    Poor Cassio's smiles, gestures, and light behaviors
    Quite in the wrong.—How do you now, Lieutenant?
CASSIO:
120   The worser that you give me the addition
121   Whose want even kills me.
IAGO:
    Ply Desdemona well and you are sure on 't.
    (*Speaking lower.*) Now, if this suit lay in Bianca's power,
    How quickly should you speed!
125 CASSIO (*laughing*): Alas, poor caitiff!
OTHELLO (*aside*): Look how he laughs already!
IAGO:
    I never knew a woman love man so.
CASSIO:
    Alas, poor rogue! I think, i' faith, she loves me.
OTHELLO:
    Now he denies it faintly, and laughs it out.
IAGO:
    Do you hear, Cassio?
OTHELLO: Now he importunes him

---

108 keep time keep yourself steady (as in music)
110 huswife hussy
114 restrain refrain
117 unbookish uninstructed. **conster** construe
120 addition title
121 Whose want the lack of which
125 caitiff wretch

132   To tell it o'er. Go to! Well said, well said.

IAGO:

She gives it out that you shall marry her.
Do you intend it?

CASSIO: Ha, ha, ha!

OTHELLO:

136   Do you triumph, Roman? Do you triumph?

137 CASSIO: I marry her? What? A customer? Prithee, bear
some charity to my wit; do not think it so unwholesome. Ha, ha, ha!

140 OTHELLO: So, so, so, so! They laugh that win.

141 IAGO: Faith, the cry goes that you shall marry her.

CASSIO: Prithee, say true.

143 IAGO: I am a very villain else.

144 OTHELLO: Have you scored me? Well.

CASSIO: This is the monkey's own giving out. She is
persuaded I will marry her out of her own love and

147   flattery, not out of my promise.

148 OTHELLO: Iago beckons me. Now he begins the story.

CASSIO: She was here even now; she haunts me in every

150   place. I was the other day talking on the seabank with

151   certain Venetians, and thither comes the bauble, and,

152   by this hand, she falls thus about my neck—

[*He embraces Iago.*]

OTHELLO: Crying, "O dear Cassio!" as it were; his gesture imports it.

CASSIO: So hangs and lolls and weeps upon me, so shakes
and pulls me. Ha, ha, ha!

OTHELLO: Now he tells how she plucked him to my

158   chamber. O, I see that nose of yours, but not that dog
I shall throw it to.

CASSIO: Well, I must leave her company.

---

132 Go to (An expression of remonstrance.) **Well said** well done
136 Roman (The Romans were noted for their *triumphs* or triumphal processions.)
137 customer i.e., prostitute
137–138 bear [. . .] wit be more charitable to my judgment
140 They [. . .] win i.e., they that laugh last laugh best
141 cry rumor
143 I [. . .] else call me a complete rogue if I'm not telling the truth
144 scored me scored off me, beaten me, made up my reckoning, branded me
147 flattery self-flattery, self-deception
148 beckons signals
150 seabank seashore
151 bauble plaything
152 by this hand I make my vow
158–159 not [. . .] to (Othello imagines himself cutting off Cassio's nose and throwing
it to a dog.)

161   IAGO: Before me, look where she comes.

(Enter Bianca [with Othello's handkerchief].)

162   CASSIO: 'Tis such another fitchew! Marry, a perfumed
         one. What do you mean by this haunting of me?

164   BIANCA: Let the devil and his dam haunt you! What did
         you mean by that same handkerchief you gave me
         even now? I was a fine fool to take it. I must take out

167   the work? A likely piece of work, that you should find
         it in your chamber and know not who left it there!
         This is some minx's token, and I must take out the

170   work? There; give it your hobbyhorse. [*She gives him
         the handkerchief.*] Wheresoever you had it, I'll take out
         no work on't.

       CASSIO: How now, my sweet Bianca? How now? How now?

174   OTHELLO: By heaven, that should be my handkerchief!

       BIANCA: If you'll come to supper tonight, you may; if

176   you will not, come when you are next prepared for.

(Exit.)

       IAGO: After her, after her.

       CASSIO: Faith, I must. She'll rail in the streets else.

       IAGO: Will you sup there?

       CASSIO: Faith, I intend so.

       IAGO: Well, I may chance to see you, for I would very fain speak with you.

       CASSIO: Prithee, come. Will you?

183   IAGO: Go to. Say no more.   *(Exit Cassio.)*

       OTHELLO (*advancing*): How shall I murder him, Iago?

       IAGO: Did you perceive how he laughed at his vice?

       OTHELLO: O, Iago!

       IAGO: And did you see the handkerchief?

       OTHELLO: Was that mine?

       IAGO: Yours, by this hand. And to see how he prizes
         the foolish woman your wife! She gave it him, and he
         hath given it his whore.

       OTHELLO: I would have him nine years a-killing. A fine
         woman! A fair woman! A sweet woman!

---

161 Before me i.e., on my soul
162 'Tis [. . .] fitchew what a polecat she is! Just like all the others. **fitchew** (Polecats
were often compared with prostitutes because of their rank smell and presumed lechery.)
164 dam mother
167 A likely [. . .] work a fine story
170 hobbyhorse harlot
174 should be must be
176 when [. . .] for when I'm ready for you (i.e., never)
183 Go to (An expression of remonstrance.)

IAGO: Nay, you must forget that.

OTHELLO: Ay, let her rot and perish, and be damned
      tonight, for she shall not live. No, my heart is turned
      to stone; I strike it, and it hurts my hand. O, the world
      hath not a sweeter creature! She might lie by an em-
      peror's side and command him tasks.

200 IAGO: Nay, that's not your way.

OTHELLO: Hang her! I do but say what she is. So delicate
      with her needle! An admirable musician! O, she will
      sing the savageness out of a bear. Of so high and plen-
204   teous wit and invention!

IAGO: She's the worse for all this.

OTHELLO: O, a thousand, a thousand times! And then,
207   of so gentle a condition!

208 IAGO: Ay, too gentle.

OTHELLO: Nay, that's certain. But yet the pity of it, Iago!
      O, Iago, the pity of it, Iago!

211 IAGO: If you are so fond over her iniquity, give her patent
      to offend, for if it touch not you it comes near nobody.

213 OTHELLO: I will chop her into messes. Cuckold me?

IAGO: O, 'tis foul in her.

OTHELLO: With mine officer?

IAGO: That's fouler.

OTHELLO: Get me some poison, Iago, this night. I'll not
218   expostulate with her, lest her body and beauty unpro-
      vide my mind again. This night, Iago.

IAGO: Do it not with poison. Strangle her in her bed,
      even the bed she hath contaminated.

OTHELLO: Good, good! The justice of it pleases. Very good.

223 IAGO: And for Cassio, let me be his undertaker. You shall
      hear more by midnight.

OTHELLO:
      Excellent good. [*A trumpet within.*] What trumpet is that same?

IAGO: I warrant, something from Venice.

    (*Enter Lodovico, Desdemona, and attendants.*)

      'Tis Lodovico. This comes from the Duke.
      See, your wife's with him.

---

200 your way i.e. the way you should think of her
204 invention imagination
207 gentle a condition wellborn and well-bred
208 gentle generous, yielding (to other men)
211 fond foolish. **patent** license
213 messes portions of meat, i.e., bits
218–219 unprovide weaken, render unfit
223 be his undertaker undertake to dispatch him

LODOVICO:
    God save you, worthy General!

230 OTHELLO: With all my heart, sir.

LODOVICO *(giving him a letter)*:
    The duke and the senators of Venice greet you.

OTHELLO:
    I kiss the instrument of their pleasures.

(He opens the letter, and reads.)

DESDEMONA:
    And what's the news, good cousin Lodovico?

IAGO:
    I am very glad to see you, signor. Welcome to Cyprus.

LODOVICO:
    I thank you. How does Lieutenant Cassio?

IAGO: Lives, sir.

DESDEMONA:
    Cousin, there's fall'n between him and my lord

238   An unkind breach; but you shall make all well.

OTHELLO: Are you sure of that?

DESDEMONA: My lord?

OTHELLO *(reads)*: "This fail you not to do, as you will—"

LODOVICO:
    He did not call; he's busy in the paper.
    Is there division twixt my lord and Cassio?

DESDEMONA:
    A most unhappy one. I would do much

245   T' atone them, for the love I bear to Cassio.

OTHELLO: Fire and brimstone!

DESDEMONA: My lord?

OTHELLO: Are you wise?

DESDEMONA:
    What, is he angry?

LODOVICO: Maybe the letter moved him;
    For, as I think, they do command him home,

252   Deputing Cassio in his government.

253 DESDEMONA: By my troth, I am glad on 't.

OTHELLO: Indeed?

DESDEMONA: My lord?

256 OTHELLO: I am glad to see you mad.

230 With all my heart i.e., I thank you most heartily
238 unkind unnatural, contrary to their natures; hurtful
254 atone reconcile
252 government office
253 on 't of it
256 I am [. . .] mad i.e., I am glad to see that you are insane enough to rejoice in Cassio's promotion (? Othello bitterly plays on Desdemona's *I am glad.*)

DESDEMONA: Why, sweet Othello—

OTHELLO (*striking her*): Devil!

DESDEMONA: I have not deserved this.

LODOVICO:

261
My lord, this would not be believed in Venice,
Though I should swear I saw 't. 'Tis very much.
Make her amends; she weeps.

OTHELLO: O devil, devil!

264
If that the earth could teem with woman's tears,

265
Each drop she falls would prove a crocodile.
Out of my sight!

DESDEMONA: I will not stay to offend you.   (*Going.*)

LODOVICO: Truly, an obedient lady.
I do beseech your lordship, call her back.

OTHELLO: Mistress!

DESDEMONA (*returning*): My lord?

272
OTHELLO: What would you with her, sir?

LODOVICO: Who, I, my lord?

OTHELLO:

Ay, you did wish that I would make her turn.
Sir, she can turn, and turn, and yet go on
And turn again; and she can weep, sir, weep;

277
And she's obedient, as you say, obedient,
Very obedient.—Proceed you in your tears.—

279
Concerning this, sir—O well-painted passion!—
I am commanded home.—Get you away;
I'll send for you anon.—Sir, I obey the mandate
And will return to Venice.—Hence, avaunt!

(*Exit Desdemona.*)

Cassio shall have my place. And, sir, tonight
I do entreat that we may sup together.

285
You are welcome, sir, to Cyprus.—Goats and monkeys!

(*Exit.*)

---

261 very much too much, outrageous

264 teem breed, be impregnated

265 falls lets fall. **crocodile** (Crocodiles were supposed to weep hypocritical tears for their victims.)

272 What [. . .] sir (Othello implies that Desdemona is pliant and will do a *turn*, lines 274–76, for any man.)

277 obedient (With much the same sexual connotation as *turn* in lines 274–76.)

279 passion i.e., grief

285 Goats and monkeys (See 3.3.446.)

LODOVICO:

> Is this the noble Moor whom our full Senate
> Call all in all sufficient? Is this the nature
> Whom passion could not shake? Whose solid virtue
> The shot of accident nor dart of chance
> Could neither graze nor pierce?

IAGO: He is much changed.

LODOVICO:

> Are his wits safe? Is he not light of brain?

IAGO:

293
> He's that he is. I may not breathe my censure
> What he might be. If what he might he is not,
> I would to heaven he were!

LODOVICO: What, strike his wife?

IAGO:

> Faith, that was not so well; yet would I knew
> That stroke would prove the worst!

299 LODOVICO: Is it his use?

300
> Or did the letters work upon his blood
> And new-create his fault?

IAGO: Alas, alas!

> It is not honesty in me to speak
> What I have seen and known. You shall observe him,

305
> And his own courses will denote him so
> That I may save my speech. Do but go after,
> And mark how he continues.

LODOVICO:

> I am sorry that I am deceived in him. (*Exeunt.*)

4.2

(Enter Othello and Emilia.)

OTHELLO: You have seen nothing then?

EMILIA:

> Nor ever heard, nor ever did suspect.

OTHELLO:

> Yes, you have seen Cassio and she together.

293–295 I may [. . .] were i.e., I dare not venture an opinion as to whether he's of unsound mind, as you suggest, but, if he isn't, then it might be better to wish he were in fact insane, since only that could excuse his wild behavior
299 use custom
300 blood passions
305 courses will denote actions will reveal
4.2 Location: The citadel.

EMILIA:
> But then I saw no harm, and then I heard
> Each syllable that breath made up between them.

OTHELLO: What, did they never whisper?

EMILIA: Never, my lord.

OTHELLO: Nor send you out o' the way?

EMILIA: Never.

OTHELLO:
> To fetch her fan, her gloves, her mask, nor nothing?

EMILIA: Never, my lord.

OTHELLO: That's strange.

EMILIA:
> I durst, my lord, to wager she is honest,
14   Lay down my soul at stake. If you think other,
15   Remove your thought; it doth abuse your bosom.
> If any wretch have put this in your head,
17   Let heaven requite it with the serpent's curse!
> For if she be not honest, chaste, and true,
> There's no man happy; the purest of their wives
> Is foul as slander.

OTHELLO: Bid her come hither. Go.
>   (*Exit Emilia.*)

22   She says enough; yet she's a simple bawd
23   That cannot say as much. This is a subtle whore,
24   A closet lock and key of villainous secrets.
> And yet she'll kneel and pray; I have seen her do't.

(Enter Desdemona and Emilia.)

DESDEMONA: My lord, what is your will?

OTHELLO: Pray you, chuck, come hither.

DESDEMONA:
> What is your pleasure?

OTHELLO: Let me see your eyes.
> Look in my face.

DESDEMONA: What horrible fancy's this?

32   OTHELLO (*to Emilia*): Some of your function, mistress.

33   Leave procreants alone and shut the door;

14 at stake as the wager
15 abuse your bosom deceive you
17 the serpent's curse the curse pronounced by God on the serpent for deceiving Eve, just as some man has done to Othello and Desdemona. (See Genesis 3:14.)
22–23 she's [. . .] much i.e., any procuress or go-between who couldn't make up as plausible a story as Emilia's would have to be pretty stupid
23 This i.e., Desdemona
24 closet lock and key i.e, concealer
32 Some [. . .] function i.e., practice your chosen profession, that of bawd (by guarding the door)
33 procreants mating couples

Cough or cry "hem" if anybody come.
35   Your mystery, your mystery! Nay, dispatch.

(Exit Emilia.)

DESDEMONA (*kneeling*):
Upon my knees, what doth your speech import?
I understand a fury in your words,
But not the words.
OTHELLO:
Why, what art thou?
DESDEMONA: Your wife, my lord, your true
And loyal wife.
OTHELLO: Come, swear it, damn thyself,
43   Lest, being like one of heaven, the devils themselves
Should fear to seize thee. Therefore be double damned:
Swear thou art honest.
DESDEMONA: Heaven doth truly know it
OTHELLO:
Heaven truly knows that thou art false as hell.
DESDEMONA:
To whom, my lord? With whom? How am I false?
OTHELLO [*weeping*]:
Ah, Desdemon! Away, away, away!
DESDEMONA:
Alas the heavy day! Why do you weep?
51   Am I the motive of these tears, my lord?
If haply you my father do suspect
An instrument of this your calling back,
Lay not your blame on me. If you have lost him,
I have lost him too.
OTHELLO: Had it pleased heaven
57   To try me with affliction, had they rained
All kinds of sores and shames on my bare head,
Steeped me in poverty to the very lips,
Given to captivity me and my utmost hopes,
I should have found in some place of my soul
A drop of patience. But, alas, to make me
63   A fixèd figure for the time of scorn
64   To point his slow and moving finger at!

---

35 mystery trade, occupation
43 being [. . .] heaven looking like an angel
51 motive cause
57 they i.e., heavenly powers
63 time of scorn i.e., scornful world
64 his its. **slow and moving finger** i.e., hour hand of the clock, moving so slowly it seems hardly to move at all. (Othello envisages himself as being eternally pointed at by the scornful world as the numbers on a clock are pointed at by the hour hand.)

Yet could I bear that too, well, very well.
66 But there where I have garnered up my heart,
Where either I must live or bear no life,
68 The fountain from the which my current runs
Or else dries up to be discarded thence!
70 Or keep it as a cistern for foul toads
71 knot and gender in! Turn thy complexion there,
72 Patience, thou young and rose-lipped cherubin—
Ay, there look grim as hell!

DESDEMONA:
74 I hope my noble lord esteems me honest.

OTHELLO:
75 O, ay, as summer flies are in the shambles,
76 That quicken even with blowing. O thou weed,
Who art so lovely fair and smell'st so sweet
That the sense aches at thee, would thou hadst ne'er been born!

DESDEMONA:
79 Alas, what ignorant sin have I committed?

OTHELLO:
Was this fair paper, this most goodly book,
Made to write "whore" upon? What committed?
82 Committed? O thou public commoner!
I should make very forges of my cheeks,
That would to cinders burn up modesty,
Did I but speak thy deeds. What committed?
86 Heaven stops the nose at it and the moon winks;
87 The bawdy wind, that kisses all it meets,
88 Is hushed within the hollow mine of earth
And will not hear 't. What committed?
Impudent strumpet!

DESDEMONA: By heaven, you do me wrong.

OTHELLO:
Are not you a strumpet?

66 garnered stored
68 fountain spring
70 cistern cesspool
71 knot couple. **gender** engender. **Turn** [. . .] **there** change your color, grow pale, at such a sight
72–73 Patience [. . .] **hell** (Even Patience, that rose-lipped cherub, will look grim and pale at this spectacle.)
74 honest chaste
75 shambles slaughterhouse
76 quicken come to life. **with blowing** i.e., with the puffing up of something rotten in which maggots are breeding
79 ignorant sin sin in ignorance
82 commoner prostitute
86 winks closes her eyes. (The moon symbolizes chastity.)
87 bawdy kissing one and all
88 mine cave (where the winds were thought to dwell)

DESDEMONA: No, as I am a Christian.
94   If to preserve this vessel for my lord
From any other foul unlawful touch
Be not to be a strumpet, I am none.
OTHELLO: What, not a whore?
DESDEMONA: No, as I shall be saved.
OTHELLO: Is 't possible?
DESDEMONA:
    O, heaven forgive us!
101   OTHELLO: I cry you mercy, then.
I took you for that cunning whore of Venice
That married with Othello. (*Calling out.*) You, mistress,
That have the office opposite to Saint Peter
And keep the gate of hell!

(*Enter Emilia.*)

    You, you, ay, you!
107   We have done our course. There's money for your pains.
        (*He gives money.*)
I pray you, turn the key and keep our counsel. (*Exit.*)
EMILIA:
109   Alas, what does this gentleman conceive?
How do you, madam? How do you, my good lady?
111   DESDEMONA: Faith, half asleep.
EMILIA:
    Good madam, what's the matter with my lord?
DESDEMONA: With who?
EMILIA: Why, with my lord, madam.
DESDEMONA:
    Who is thy lord?
EMILIA: He that is yours, sweet lady.
DESDEMONA:
    I have none. Do not talk to me, Emilia.
I cannot weep, nor answers have I none
119   But what should go by water. Prithee, tonight
Lay on my bed my wedding sheets, remember;
And call thy husband hither.
EMILIA: Here's a change indeed!   (*Exit.*)
DESDEMONA:
    'Tis meet I should be used so, very meet.

94 **vessel** body
101 **cry you mercy** beg your pardon
107 **course** business (with an indecent suggestion of "trick," turn at sex)
109 **conceive** suppose, think
111 **half asleep** i.e., dazed
119 **go by water** be expressed by tears

124   How have I been behaved, that he might stick
125   The small'st opinion on my least misuse?

(Enter Iago and Emilia.)

IAGO:
    What is your pleasure, madam? How is 't with you?
DESDEMONA:
    I cannot tell. Those that do teach young babes
    Do it with gentle means and easy tasks.
    He might have chid me so, for, in good faith,
    I am a child to chiding.
IAGO: What is the matter, lady?
EMILIA:
    Alas, Iago, my lord hath so bewhored her,
    Thrown such despite and heavy terms upon her,
    That true hearts cannot bear it.
DESDEMONA: Am I that name, Iago?
IAGO: What name, fair lady?
DESDEMONA:
    Such as she said my lord did say I was.
EMILIA:
    He called her whore. A begger in his drink
139   Could not have laid such terms upon his callet.
IAGO: Why did he so?
DESDEMONA *(weeping)*:
    I do not know. I am sure I am none such.
IAGO: Do not weep, do not weep. Alas the day!
EMILIA:
    Hath she forsook so many noble matches,
    Her father and her country and her friends,
    To be called whore? Would it not make one weep?
DESDEMONA:
    It is my wretched fortune.
147 IAGO: Beshrew him for 't!
148   How comes this trick upon him?
DESDEMONA: Nay, heaven doth know.
EMILIA:
150   I will be hanged if some eternal villain,
151   Some busy and insinuating rogue,

---

124 stick attach
125 opinion censure. **least misuse** slightest misconduct
139 callet whore
147 Beshrew curse
148 trick strange behavior, delusion
150 eternal inveterate
151 insinuating ingratiating, fawning, wheedling

152 Some cogging, cozening slave, to get some office,
Have not devised this slander. I will be hanged else.

IAGO:
Fie, there is no such man. It is impossible.

DESDEMONA:
If any such there be, heaven pardon him!

EMILIA:
156 A halter pardon him! And hell gnaw his bones!
Why should he call her whore? Who keeps her company?
158 What place? What time? What form? What likelihood?
The Moor's abused by some most villainous knave,
Some base notorious knave, some scurvy fellow.
161 O heaven, that such companions thou'dst unfold,
And put in every honest hand a whip
To lash the rascals naked through the world
Even from the east to th' west!

165 IAGO: Speak within door.

EMILIA:
166 O, fie upon them! Some such squire he was
167 That turned your wit the seamy side without
And made you to suspect me with the Moor.

IAGO:
169 You are a fool. Go to.

DESDEMONA: Alas, Iago,
What shall I do to win my lord again?
Good friend, go to him; for, by this light of heaven,
I know not how I lost him. Here I kneel.   (*She kneels.*)
If e'er my will did trespass 'gainst his love,
175 Either in discourse of thought or actual deed,
176 Or that mine eyes, mine ears, or any sense
177 Delighted them in any other form;
178 Or that I do not yet, and ever did,
And ever will—though he do shake me off
To beggarly divorcement love him dearly,

---

152 cogging cheating. **cozening** defrauding
156 halter hangman's noose
158 form appearance, circumstance
161 that would that. **companions** fellows. **unfold** expose
165 within door i.e., not so loud
166 squire fellow
167 seamy side without wrong side out
169 Go to i.e., that's enough
175 discourse of thought process of thinking
176 that if. (Also in line 178.)
177 Delighted them took delight
178 yet still

181   Comfort forswear me! Unkindness may do much,
182   And his unkindness may defeat my life,
    But never taint my love. I cannot say "whore."
184   It does abhor me now I speak the word;
185   To do the act that might the addition earn
186   Not the world's mass of vanity could make me.
          (*She rises.*)

IAGO:

187   I pray you, be content. 'Tis but his humor.
    The business of the state does him offense,
    And he does chide with you.

DESDEMONA: If 'twere no other—

IAGO: It is but so, I warrant.   (*Trumpets within.*)
    Hark, how these instruments summon you to supper!
193   The messengers of Venice stays the meat.
    Go in, and weep not. All things shall be well.

                    (*Exeunt Desdemona and Emilia.*)

    (*Enter Roderigo.*)

    How now, Roderigo?

RODERIGO: I do not find that thou deal'st justly with me.

IAGO: What in the contrary?

198   RODERIGO: Every day thou dafft'st me with some device,
    Iago, and rather, as it seems to me now, keep'st
200   from me all conveniency than suppliest me with the
201   least advantage of hope. I will indeed no longer
202   endure it, nor am I yet persuaded to put up in peace
    what already I have foolishly suffered.

IAGO: Will you hear me, Roderigo?

RODERIGO: Faith, I have heard too much, for your words
    and performances are no kin together.

IAGO: You charge me most unjustly.

RODERIGO: With naught but truth. I have wasted myself
    out of my means. The jewels you have had from me to

---

181 Comfort forswear may heavenly comfort forsake
182 defeat destroy
184 abhor (1) fill me with abhorrence (2) make me whorelike
185 addition title
186 vanity showy splendor
187 humor mood
193 stays the meat are waiting to dine
198 thou dafft'st me you put me off **device** excuse, trick
200 conveniency advantage, opportunity
201 advantage increase
202 put up submit to, tolerate

210   deliver Desdemona would half have corrupted a votarist.
        You have told me she hath received them and returned
212   me expectations and comforts of sudden respect and
        acquaintance, but I find none.

IAGO: Well, go to, very well.

215 RODERIGO: "Very well"! "Go to"! I cannot go to, man,
        nor 'tis not very well. By this hand, I think it is scurvy,
217   and begin to find myself fopped in it.

IAGO: Very well.

219 RODERIGO: I tell you 'tis not very well. I will make myself
        known to Desdemona. If she will return me my jewels,
        I will give over my suit and repent my unlawful solicita-
222   tion; if not, assure yourself I will seek satisfaction of you.

223 IAGO: You have said now?

RODERIGO: Ay, and said nothing but what I protest
225   intendment of doing.

IAGO: Why, now I see there's mettle in thee, and even
        from this instant do build on thee a better opinion
        than ever before. Give me thy hand, Roderigo. Thou
        hast taken against me a most just exception; but yet I
        protest I have dealt most directly in thy affair.

RODERIGO: It hath not appeared.

IAGO: I grant indeed it hath not appeared, and your
        suspicion is not without wit and judgment. But,
        Roderigo, if thou hast that in thee indeed which I have
        greater reason to believe now than ever—I mean
        purpose, courage, and valor—this night show it. If
        thou the next night following enjoy not Desdemona,
        take me from this world with treachery and devise
239   engines for my life.

RODERIGO: Well, what is it? Is it within reason and compass?

IAGO: Sir, there is especial commission come from Venice
        to depute Cassio in Othello's place.

RODERIGO: Is that true? Why, then Othello and Desdemona
        return again to Venice.

---

210 deliver deliver to **votarist** nun
212 sudden respect immediate consideration
215 I cannot go to (Roderigo changes Iago's *go to,* an expression urging patience, to *I cannot go to,* "I have no opportunity for success in wooing.")
217 fopped fooled, duped
219 not very well (Roderigo changes Iago's *very well,* "all right then," to *not very well,* "not at all good.")
222 satisfaction repayment. (The term normally means settling of accounts in a duel.)
223 You [. . .] now have you finished?
225 intendment intention
239 engines for plots against

IAGO: O, no; he goes into Mauritania and takes away
       with him the fair Desdemona, unless his abode be
       lingered here by some accident; wherein none can be
248   so determinate as the removing of Cassio.
RODERIGO: How do you mean, removing of him?
IAGO: Why, by making him uncapable of Othello's
       place—knocking out his brains.
RODERIGO: And that you would have me to do?
IAGO: Ay, if you dare do yourself a profit and a right.
254   He sups tonight with a harlotry, and thither will I go to
       him. He knows not yet of his honorable fortune. If
       you will watch his going thence, which I will fashion
257   to fall out between twelve and one, you may take him
       at your pleasure. I will be near to second your attempt,
       and he shall fall between us. Come, stand not amazed
       at it, but go along with me. I will show you such a
       necessity in his death that you shall think yourself
262   bound to put it on him. It is now high suppertime,
263   and the night grows to waste. About it.
RODERIGO: I will hear further reason for this.
IAGO: And you shall be satisfied.   (*Exeunt.*)

4.3

(*Enter Othello, Lodovico, Desdemona, Emilia, and attendants.*)

LODOVICO:
       I do beseech you, sir, trouble yourself no further.
OTHELLO:
       O, pardon me; 'twill do me good to walk.
LODOVICO:
       Madam, good night. I humbly thank your ladyship.
DESDEMONA:
       Your honor is most welcome.
OTHELLO: Will you walk, sir?
       O, Desdemona!
DESDEMONA: My lord?
OTHELLO: Get you to bed on th' instant. I will be returned forthwith.
       Dismiss your attendant there. Look 't be done.

---

248 **determinate** conclusive
254 **harlotry** slut
257 **fall out** occur
262 **high** fully
263 **grows to waste** wastes away
4.3. **Location: The citadel.**

DESDEMONA: I will my lord.

(Exit [Othello, with Lodovico and attendants].)

EMILIA: How goes it now? He looks gentler than he did.
DESDEMONA:

12   He says he will return incontinent,
        And hath commanded me to go to bed,
        And bid me to dismiss you.
EMILIA: Dismiss me?
DESDEMONA:
        It was his bidding. Therefore, good Emilia,
        Give me my nightly wearing, and adieu.
        We must not now displease him.
EMILIA: I would you had never seen him!
DESDEMONA:
        So would not I. My love doth so approve him
21   That even his stubbornness, his checks, his frowns—
        Prithee, unpin me—have grace and favor in them.

(Emilia prepares Desdemona for bed.)

EMILIA: I have laid those sheets you bade me on the bed.
DESDEMONA:
24   All's one. Good faith, how foolish are our minds!
        If I do die before thee, prithee shroud me
        In one of these same sheets.
27 EMILIA: Come, come, you talk.
DESDEMONA:
        My mother had a maid called Barbary.
29   She was in love, and he she loved proved mad
        And did forsake her. She had a song of "Willow."
        An old thing 'twas, but it expressed her fortune,
        And she died singing it. That song tonight
33   Will not go from my mind; I have much to do
        But to go hang my head all at one side
        And sing it like poor Barbary. Prithee, dispatch.
36 EMILIA: Shall I go fetch your nightgown?
DESDEMONA: No, unpin me here.
38   This Lodovico is a proper man.

---

12 incontinent immediately
21 stubbornness roughness. **checks** rebukes
24 All's one all right. It doesn't really matter
27 talk i.e., prattle
29 mad wild, i.e., faithless
33–34 I [. . .] hang I can scarcely keep myself from hanging
36 nightgown dressing gown
38 proper handsome

EMILIA: A very handsome man.

DESDEMONA: He speaks well.

EMILIA: I know a lady in Venice would have walked barefoot to Palestine
for a touch of his nether lip.

DESDEMONA (*singing*):

"The poor soul sat sighing by a sycamore tree,
44   Sing all a green willow;
Her hand on her bosom, her head on her knee,
Sing willow, willow, willow.
The fresh streams ran by her and murmured her moans;
Sing willow, willow, willow;
Her salt tears fell from her, and softened the stones—"
Lay by these.
(*Singing.*) "Sing willow, willow, willow—"
52   Prithee, hie thee. He'll come anon.
(*Singing.*) "Sing all a green willow must be my garland.
Let nobody blame him; his scorn I approve—"
Nay, that's not next.—Hark! Who is 't that knocks?

EMILIA: It's the wind.

DESDEMONA (*singing*):

"I called my love false love; but what said he then?
Sing willow, willow, willow;
If I court more women, you'll couch with more men."
So, get thee gone. Good night. Mine eyes do itch;
Doth that bode weeping?

EMILIA: 'Tis neither here nor there.

DESDEMONA: I have heard it said so. O, these men, these men!
Dost thou in conscience think—tell me, Emilia—
65   That there be women do abuse their husbands
In such gross kind?

EMILIA: There be some such, no question.

DESDEMONA:

Wouldst thou do such a deed for all the world?

EMILIA:

Why, would not you?

DESDEMONA: No, by this heavenly light!

EMILIA:

Nor I neither by this heavenly light;
I might do 't as well i' the dark.

DESDEMONA: Wouldst thou do such a deed for all the world?

EMILIA:

The world's a huge thing. It is a great price
For a small vice.

---

44 willow (A conventional emblem of disappointed love.)
52 hie thee hurry. **anon** right away
65 abuse deceive

DESDEMONA:
>
> Good troth, I think thou wouldst not.

EMILIA: By my troth, I think I should, and undo 't when
>
> I had done. Marry, I would not do such a thing for a

79   joint ring, nor for measures of lawn, nor for gowns,

80   petticoats, nor caps, nor any petty exhibition. But for

81   all the whole world! Uds pity, who would not make
>
> her husband a cuckold to make him a monarch? I
>
> should venture purgatory for 't.

DESDEMONA:
>
> Beshrew me if I would do such a wrong
>
> For the whole world.

EMILIA: Why, the wrong is but a wrong i' the world, and
>
> having the world for your labor, 'tis a wrong in your
>
> own world, and you might quickly make it right.

DESDEMONA:
>
> I do not think there is any such woman.

EMILIA: Yes, a dozen, and as many

91   To th' vantage as would store the world they played for.
>
> But I do think it is their husbands' faults

93   If wives do fall. Say that they slack their duties

94   And pour our treasures into foreign laps,
>
> Or else break out in peevish jealousies,

96   Throwing restraint upon us? Or say they strike us,

97   Or scant our former having in despite?

98   Why, we have galls, had though we have some grace,
>
> Yet have we some revenge. Let husbands know

100   Their wives have sense like them. They see, and smell,
>
> And have their palates both for sweet and sour,
>
> As husbands have. What is it that they do

103   When they change us for others? Is it sport?

104   I think it is. And doth affection breed it?
>
> I think it doth. Is 't frailty that thus errs?
>
> It is so, too. And have not we affections,
>
> Desires for sport, and frailty, as men have?

---

79 joint ring a ring made in separate halves. **lawn** fine linen
80 exhibition gift
81 Uds God's
91 To th' vantage in addition, to boot. **store** populate. **played** (1) gambled (2) sported
sexually
93 duties marital duties
94 pour [. . .] laps i.e., are unfaithful, give what is rightfully ours (semen) to other women
96 Throwing [. . .] us i.e., jealously restricting our freedom to see other men
97 scant [. . .] despite reduce our allowance to spite us
98 have galls i.e., are capable of resenting injury and insult
100 sense physical sense
103 sport sexual pastime
104 affection passion

Then let them sue us well; else let them know,
The ills we do, their ills instruct us so.

DESDEMONA:

110   Good night, good night. God me such uses send
111   Not to pick bad from bad, but by bad mend!

                                                            (Exeunt.)

5.1

(Enter Iago and Roderigo.)

IAGO:

1   Here stand behind this bulk. Straight will he come.
2   Wear thy good rapier bare, and put it home.
        Quick, quick! Fear nothing. I'll be at thy elbow.
        It makes us or it mars us. Think on that,
        And fix most firm thy resolution.

RODERIGO:

        Be near at hand. I may miscarry in 't.

IAGO:

        Here, at thy hand. Be bold, and take thy stand.

(Iago stands aside. Roderigo conceals himself.)

RODERIGO:

        I have no great devotion to the deed;
        And yet he hath given me satisfying reasons.
        'Tis but a man gone. Forth, my sword! He dies.

                                                            (He draws.)

IAGO:

11   I have rubbed this young quat almost to the sense,
        And he grows angry. Now, whether he kill Cassio
        Or Cassio him, or each do kill the other,
14   Every way makes my gain. Live Roderigo,
        He calls me to a restitution large
16   Of gold and jewels that I bobbed from him

---

110 uses habit, practice
111 Not [. . .] mend i.e, not to learn bad conduct from others' badness (as Emilia has suggested women learn from men), but to mend my ways by perceiving what badness is, making spiritual benefit out of evil and adversity
5.1 Location: A street in Cyprus.
1 bulk framework projecting from the front of a shop
2 bare unsheathed
11 quat pimple, pustule. **to the sense** to the quick
14 Live Roderigo if Roderigo lives
16 bobbed swindled

As gifts to Desdemona.
It must not be. If Cassio do remain,
He hath a daily beauty in his life
That makes me ugly; and besides, the Moor
21   May unfold me to him; there stand I in much peril.
No, he must die. Be 't so. I hear him coming.

(Enter Cassio.)

RODERIGO (*coming forth*):
I know his gait, 'tis he.—Villain, thou diest!
                              (*He attacks Cassio.*)

CASSIO:
That thrust had been mine enemy indeed,
25   But that my coat is better than thou know'st.
26   I will make proof of thine.
                  (*He draws, and wounds Roderigo.*)

RODERIGO: O, I am slain! (*He falls.*)
        (Iago, from behind, wounds Cassio in the leg, and exit.)

CASSIO:
I am maimed forever. Help, ho! Murder! Murder!

(Enter Othello.)

OTHELLO:
The voice of Cassio! Iago keeps his word.
RODERIGO: O, villain that I am!
OTHELLO: It is even so.
CASSIO: O, help, ho! Light! A surgeon!
OTHELLO:
'Tis he. O brave Iago, honest and just,
That hast such noble sense of thy friend's wrong!
35   Thou teachest me. Minion, your dear lies dead,
36   And your unblest fate hies. Strumpet, I come.
37   Forth of my heart those charms, thine eyes, are blotted;
Thy bed, lust-stained, shall with lust's blood be spotted.
            (*Exit Othello.*)

(Enter Lodovico and Gratiano.)

---

21 unfold expose
25 coat (Possibly a garment of mail under the outer clothing, or simply a tougher coat
than Roderigo expected.)
26 proof a test
35 Minion hussy (i.e., Desdemona)
36 hies hastens on
37 Forth of from out

CASSIO:
39   What ho! No watch? No passage? Murder! Murder!
GRATIANO:
      'Tis some mischance. The voice is very direful.
CASSIO: O, help!
LODOVICO: Hark!
RODERIGO: O wretched villain!
LODOVICO:
44   Two or three groan. 'Tis heavy night;
      These may be counterfeits. Let's think 't unsafe
46   To come in to the cry without more help.

      (They remain near the entrance.)

RODERIGO:
      Nobody come? Then shall I bleed to death.

      (Enter Iago [in his shirtsleeves, with a light].)

LODOVICO: Hark!
GRATIANO:
      Here's one comes in his shirt, with light and weapons.
IAGO:
50   Who's there? Whose noise is this that cries on murder?
LODOVICO:
      We do not know.
IAGO: Did not you hear a cry?
CASSIO:
      Here, here! for heaven's sake, help me!
IAGO: What's the matter?
      (He moves toward Cassio.)
GRATIANO *(to Lodovico)*:
      This is Othello's ancient, as I take it.
LODOVICO *(to Gratiano)*:
      The same indeed, a very valiant fellow.
IAGO *(to Cassio)*:
57   What are you here that cry so grievously?
CASSIO:
58   Iago? O, I am spoiled, undone by villains!
      Give me some help.
IAGO:
      O me, Lieutenant! What villains have done this?

39 passage people passing by
44 heavy thick, dark
46 come in to approach
50 cries on cries out
57 What who (also at lines 64 and 72)
58 spoiled ruined, done for

CASSIO:
    I think that one of them is hereabout,
62   And cannot make away.
  IAGO: O treacherous villains!
    (To Lodovico and Gratiano.) What are you there? Come
    in, and give me some help.   (*They advance.*)
RODERIGO: O, help me there!
CASSIO:
    That's one of them.
  IAGO: O murderous slave! O villain!
    (He stabs Roderigo.)
RODERIGO:
    O damned Iago! O inhuman dog!
IAGO:
    Kill men i' the dark?—Where be these bloody thieves?—
    How silent is this town!—Ho! Murder, murder!—
    (To Lodovico and Gratiano.) What may you be? Are you of good
    or evil?
74 LODOVICO: As you shall prove us, praise us.
  IAGO: Signor Lodovico?
LODOVICO: He, sir.
  IAGO:
77   I cry you mercy. Here's Cassio hurt by villains.
GRATIANO: Cassio?
IAGO: How is 't, brother?
CASSIO: My leg is cut in two.
IAGO: Marry, heaven forbid!
    Light, gentlemen! I'll bind it with my shirt.

    (He hands them the light, and tends to Cassio's wound.)

    (Enter Bianca.)

BIANCA:
    What is the matter, ho? Who is 't that cried?
IAGO: Who is 't that cried?
  BIANCA: O my dear Cassio!
    My sweet Cassio! O Cassio, Cassio, Cassio!
IAGO:
    O notable strumpet! Cassio, may you suspect
    Who they should be that have thus mangled you?
CASSIO: No.
GRATIANO:
    I am sorry to find you thus. I have been to seek you.

---

62 make get
74 praise appraise
77 I cry you mercy I beg your pardon

IAGO:

91   Lend me a garter. (*He applies a tourniquet.*) So.—O, for a chair,
        To bear him easily hence!

BIANCA:

        Alas, he faints! O Cassio, Cassio, Cassio!

IAGO:

        Gentlemen all, I do suspect this trash
        To be a party in this injury.—
        Patience awhile, good Cassio.—Come, come;
        Lend me a light. (*He shines the light on Roderigo.*)
        Know we this face or no?
        Alas, my friend and my dear countryman
        Roderigo! No.—Yes, sure.—O heaven! Roderigo!

GRATIANO: What, of Venice?

IAGO: Even he, sir. Did you know him?

GRATIANO: Know him? Ay.

IAGO:

104   Signor Gratiano? I cry your gentle pardon.
105   These bloody accidents must excuse my manners
        That so neglected you.

GRATIANO: I am glad to see you.

IAGO:

        How do you, Cassio? O, a chair, a chair!

GRATIANO: Roderigo!

IAGO:

110   He, he, 'tis he. (*A litter is brought in.*) O, that's well said;
        the chair.
        Some good man bear him carefully from hence;
        I'll fetch the General's surgeon. (*To Bianca.*) For you, mistress,
114   Save you your labor.—He that lies slain here, Cassio,
115   Was my dear friend. What malice was between you?

CASSIO:

        None in the world, nor do I know the man.

IAGO (*to Bianca*):

117   What, look you pale?—O, bear him out o' th' air.

        (*Cassio and Roderigo are borne off.*)

118   Stay you, good gentlemen.—Look you pale, mistress?—

---

91 chair litter
104 gentle noble
105 accidents sudden events
110 well said well done
114 Save [. . .] labor i.e., never you mind tending Cassio
115 malice enmity
117 bear [. . .] air (Fresh air was thought to be dangerous for a wound.)
118 Stay you (Lodovico and Gratiano are evidently about to leave.)

119   Do you perceive the gastness of her eye?—
120   Nay, if you stare, we shall hear more anon.—
        Behold her well; I pray you, look upon her.
        Do you see, gentlemen? Nay, guiltiness
        Will speak, though tongues were out of use.

(Enter Emilia.)

EMILIA:
    'Las, what's the matter? What's the matter, husband?
IAGO:
    Cassio hath here been set on in the dark
    By Roderigo and fellows that are scaped.
    He's almost slain, and Roderigo dead.
EMILIA:
    Alas, good gentleman! Alas, good Cassio!
IAGO:
    This is the fruits of whoring. Prithee, Emilia,
130   Go know of Cassio where he supped tonight.
        (To Bianca.) What, do you shake at that?
BIANCA:
    He supped at my house, but I therefore shake not.
IAGO:
    O, did he so? I charge you go with me.
EMILIA: O, fie upon thee, strumpet!
BIANCA:
135   I am no strumpet, but of life as honest
        As you that thus abuse me.
EMILIA: As I? Faugh! Fie upon thee!
IAGO:
138   Kind gentlemen, let's go see poor Cassio dressed.—
        Come, mistress, you must tell's another tale.
        Emilia, run you to the citadel
        And tell my lord and lady what hath happed.—
        Will you go on afore? *(Aside.)* This is the night
143   That either makes me or fordoes me quite.   *(Exeunt.)*

---

119 gastness terror
120 stare (Iago pretends to interpret Bianca's wild looks as an involuntary confession of guilt.)
130 know learn
135 honest chaste
138 Cassio dressed Cassio's wounds dressed
143 fordoes undoes, ruins

5.2

(Enter Othello [with a light], and Desdemona in her bed.)

OTHELLO:

1   It is the cause, it is the cause, my soul.
       Let me not name it to you, you chaste stars!
       It is the cause. Yet I'll not shed her blood,
       Nor scar that whiter skin of hers than snow,
5   And smooth as monumental alabaster.
       Yet she must die, else she'll betray more men.
7   Put out the light, and then put out the light.
8   If I quench thee, thou flaming minister,
       I can again thy former light restore,
10   Should I repent me; but once put out thy light,
11   Thou cunning'st pattern of excelling nature,
12   I know not where is that Promethean heat
13   That can thy light relume. When I have plucked thy rose,
       I cannot give it vital growth again;
       It needs must wither. I'll smell thee on the tree.

                              (He kisses her.)

       O balmy breath, that dost almost persuade
       Justice to break her sword! One more, one more.
       Be thus when thou art dead, and I will kill thee,
       And love thee after. One more, and that's the last.

                              (He kisses her.)

       So sweet was ne'er so fatal. I must weep,
21   But they are cruel tears. This sorrow's heavenly;
22   It strikes where it doth love. She wakes.

DESDEMONA: Who's there? Othello?
OTHELLO: Ay, Desdemona.
DESDEMONA: Will you come to bed, my lord?
OTHELLO: Have you prayed tonight, Desdemon?
DESDEMONA: Ay, my lord.

5.2 Location: A bedchamber in the citadel. s.d. in her bed (Either the curtains are drawn back to reveal the bed in a recessed area backstage, or the bed is "thrust out" onstage as the scene begins.)
1 cause i.e., cause of justice, the offense itself, which Othello must correct as an agent of justice
5 monumental i.e., used in making tombs and funeral monuments
7 the light [. . .] light the torch or lamp [. . .] Desdemona's life
8 flaming minister torch or lamp that serves me
10 repent me change my mind
11 Thou [. . .] pattern you skillfully wrought perfect example
12 Promethean heat divine fire (Alluding to the theft of fire from heaven by Prometheus.)
13 relume rekindle
21 cruel unrelenting
22 It [. . .] love (Compare Hebrews 12:6: "For whom the Lord loveth he chasteneth.")

OTHELLO:

28   If you bethink yourself of any crime

Unreconciled as yet to heaven and grace,

30   Solicit for it straight.

DESDEMONA:

Alack, my lord, what may you mean by that?

OTHELLO:

Well, do it, and be brief. I will walk by.

I would not kill thy unpreparèd spirit.

34   No, heaven forfend! I would not kill thy soul.

DESDEMONA:

Talk you of killing?

OTHELLO: Ay, I do.

DESDEMONA: Then heaven

Have mercy on me!

OTHELLO: Amen, with all my heart!

DESDEMONA:

If you say so, I hope you will not kill me.

OTHELLO: Humh!

DESDEMONA:

And yet I fear you; for you're fatal then

When your eyes roll so. Why I should fear I know not,

Since guiltiness I know not; but yet I feel I fear.

OTHELLO:

Think on thy sins.

46   DESDEMONA: They are loves I bear to you.

OTHELLO: Ay, and for that thou diest.

DESDEMONA:

That death's unnatural that kills for loving.

Alas, why gnaw you so your nether lip?

Some bloody passion shakes your very frame.

These are portents; but yet I hope, I hope,

52   They do not point on me.

OTHELLO: Peace, and be still!

DESDEMONA: I will so. What's the matter?

OTHELLO:

That handkerchief which I so loved and gave thee

Thou gav'st to Cassio.

DESDEMONA: No, by my life and soul!

Send for the man and ask him.

---

28 crime sin

30 Solicit petition, pray. **straight** immediately

34 forfend forbid

46 They are [. . .] you i.e., if I sinned, it was in loving you more than my father or more than God

52 point on point at, predict what is to happen to

OTHELLO:

Sweet soul, take heed, take heed of perjury.

Thou art on thy deathbed.

DESDEMONA:

Ay, but not yet to die.

62   OTHELLO: Yes, presently.

Therefore confess thee freely of thy sin;

For to deny each article with oath

65   Cannot remove nor choke the strong conception

66   That I do groan withal. Thou art to die.

DESDEMONA:

Then Lord have mercy on me!

OTHELLO: I say, amen.

DESDEMONA:

And have you mercy too! I never did

70   Offend you in my life; never loved Cassio

71   But with such general warranty of heaven

As I might love. I never gave him token.

OTHELLO:

By heaven, I saw my handkerchief in 's hand.

74   O perjured woman! Thou dost stone my heart,

And makes me call what I intend to do

A murder, which I thought a sacrifice.

I saw the handkerchief.

DESDEMONA: He found it, then.

I never gave it him. Send for him hither;

Let him confess a truth.

OTHELLO: He hath confessed.

DESDEMONA: What, my lord?

OTHELLO:

That he hath used thee.

DESDEMONA: How? Unlawfully?

OTHELLO: Ay.

DESDEMONA:

He will not say so.

OTHELLO: No, his mouth is stopped;

88   Honest Iago hath ta'en order for't.

DESDEMONA:

O, my fear interprets. What, is he dead?

---

62 presently immediately
65 conception (1) belief in your guilt (2) plan in my mind
66 groan withal (1) groan at in sorrow (2) as in giving birth
70 Offend wrong
71 warranty sanction
74 stone turn to stone, harden
88 ta'en order taken measures

OTHELLO:
    Had all his hairs been lives, my great revenge
    Had stomach for them all.
DESDEMONA:
    Alas, he is betrayed and I undone!   (*She weeps.*)
OTHELLO:
    Out, strumpet! Weep'st thou for him to my face?
DESDEMONA:
    O, banish me, my lord, but kill me not!
OTHELLO: Down, strumpet!
DESDEMONA:
    Kill me tomorrow; let me live tonight!
OTHELLO: Nay, if you strive—
DESDEMONA:
    But half an hour!
99 OTHELLO: Being done, there is no pause.
DESDEMONA:
    But while I say one prayer!
OTHELLO: It is too late.

(*Smothers her.*)

EMILIA (*at the door*):
    My lord, my lord! What, ho! My lord, my lord!
OTHELLO:
    What noise is this? Not dead? Not yet quite dead?
    I that am cruel am yet merciful;
    I would not have thee linger in thy pain.
                (*He dispatches her.*)
    So, so.
EMILIA (*within*): What, ho! My lord, my lord!
OTHELLO: Who's there?
EMILIA (*within*):
    O, good my lord, I would speak a word with you!
OTHELLO:
    Yes, 'tis Emilia.—By and by—She's dead.
    'Tis like she comes to speak of Cassio's death.—
112 The noise was here. Ha! No more moving?
    Still as the grave. Shall she come in? Were 't good?—
    I think she stirs again. No. What's best to do?
    If she come in, she'll sure speak to my wife.
    My wife! My wife! What wife? I have no wife.
    O, insupportable! O heavy hour!
    Methinks it should be now a huge eclipse

99 Being done i.e., since justice has begun its relentless course
112 here (The Folio's *high* is possible, suggesting that the commotion of the attack on Cassio was loud.)

Of sun and moon, and that th' affrighted globe
120   Should yawn at alteration.
EMILIA (*within*):   I do beseech you
That I may speak with you, O, good my lord!
OTHELLO:
I had forgot thee. O, come in, Emilia.—
124   Soft, by and by. Let me the curtains draw.—
(He closes the bed-curtains and opens the door.)
Where art thou?

(Enter Emilia.)

What's the matter with thee now?
EMILIA:
O, my good lord, yonder's foul murders done!
OTHELLO: What, now?
EMILIA: But now, my lord.
OTHELLO:
130   It is the very error of the moon;
She comes more nearer earth than she was wont,
And makes men mad.
EMILIA:
Cassio, my lord, hath killed a young Venetian
Called Roderigo.
OTHELLO: Roderigo killed?
And Cassio killed?
EMILIA: No, Cassio is not killed.
OTHELLO:
Not Cassio killed? Then murder's out of tune,
And sweet revenge grows harsh.
DESDEMONA: O, falsely, falsely murdered!
EMILIA: O Lord, what cry is that?
OTHELLO: That? What?
EMILIA:
143   Out and alas, that was my lady's voice.

(She opens the bed-curtains.)

Help, help, ho, help! O lady, speak again!
Sweet Desdemona! O sweet mistress, speak!
DESDEMONA: A guiltless death I die.
EMILIA: O, who hath done this deed?

---

120 yawn gape in amazement, i.e., move in an earthquake. (According to Pliny, earth-
quakes often happen during eclipses.) **at alteration** at these cataclysmic events in nature,
well suited to express the horror of Desdemona's death
124 Soft wait a minute
130 error aberration, irregularity
143 Out (A cry of dismay, intensifying *alas*.)

DESDEMONA: Nobody; I myself. Farewell.
　　Commend me to my kind lord. O, farewell! (*She dies.*)

OTHELLO:
　　Why, how should she be murdered?

EMILIA: 　　　　　　　　　　　　Alas, who knows?

OTHELLO:
　　You heard her say herself it was not I.

EMILIA:
　　She said so. I must needs report the truth.

OTHELLO:
　　She's like a liar gone to burning hell!
　　'Twas I that killed her.

EMILIA: 　　　　　　　O, the more angel she,
　　And you the blacker devil!

OTHELLO:
158　　She turned to folly, and she was a whore.

EMILIA:
159　　Thou dost belie her, and thou art a devil.

OTHELLO: She was false as water.

EMILIA: Thou art rash as fire to say
　　That she was false. O, she was heavenly true!

OTHELLO:
163　　Cassio did top her. Ask thy husband else.
　　O, I were damned beneath all depth in hell
　　But that I did proceed upon just grounds
　　To this extremity. Thy husband knew it all.

EMILIA: My husband?

OTHELLO: Thy husband.

EMILIA: That she was false to wedlock?

OTHELLO:
　　Ay, with Cassio. Nay, had she been true,
　　If heaven would make me such another world
172　　Of one entire and perfect chrysolite,
　　I'd not have sold her for it.

EMILIA: My husband?

OTHELLO:
　　Ay, 'twas he that told me on her first.
　　An honest man he is, and hates the slime
　　That sticks on filthy deeds.

EMILIA: My husband?

OTHELLO:
179　　What needs this iterance, woman? I say thy husband.

---

158 folly i.e., wantonness, fleshly sin
159 belie slander
163 else i.e., if you don't believe me
172 chrysolite precious topaz
179 iterance iteration, repetition

EMILIA:

180

O mistress, villainy hath made mocks with love!
My husband say she was false?

OTHELLO: He, woman;

I say thy husband. Dost understand the word?
My friend, thy husband, honest, honest Iago.

EMILIA:

If he say so, may his pernicious soul
Rot half a grain a day! He lies to th' heart.
She was too fond of her most filthy bargain.

OTHELLO: Ha?   (*He draws.*)

EMILIA: Do thy worst!

This deed of thine is no more worthy heaven
Than thou wast worthy her.

192   OTHELLO: Peace, you were best.

EMILIA:

Thou hast not half that power to do me harm

194

As I have to be hurt. O gull! O dolt!
As ignorant as dirt! Thou hast done a deed—
I care not for thy sword; I'll make thee known,
Though I lost twenty lives.—Help! Help, ho, help!
The Moor hath killed my mistress! Murder, murder!

(*Enter Montano, Gratiano, and Iago.*)

MONTANO:

What is the matter? How now, General?

EMILIA:

O, are you come, Iago? You have done well,
That men must lay their murders on your neck.

GRATIANO: What is the matter?

EMILIA (*to Iago*):

Disprove this villain, if thou be'st a man.
He says thou toldst him that his wife was false.
I know thou didst not; thou'rt not such a villain.
Speak, for my heart is full.

IAGO:

I told him what I thought, and told no more

208

Than what he found himself was apt and true.

EMILIA:

But did you ever tell him she was false?

IAGO: I did.

---

180 made mocks with derided, made sport of
192 you were best it would be best for you
194 to be hurt i.e, to endure hurt. **gull** dupe
208 apt plausible

EMILIA:

> You told a lie, an odious, damnèd lie!
>
> Upon my soul, a lie, a wicked lie.
>
> She false with Cassio? Did you say with Cassio?

IAGO:

214   With Cassio, mistress. Go to, charm your tongue.

EMILIA:

> I will not charm my tongue; I am bound to speak.
>
> My mistress here lies murdered in her bed—

ALL: O heavens forfend!

EMILIA:

> And your reports have set the murder on.

OTHELLO:

> Nay, stare not, masters. It is true indeed.

GRATIANO: 'Tis a strange truth.

MONTANO:

> O monstrous act!

EMILIA: Villainy, villainy, villainy!

> I think upon 't—I think I smell 't! O villainy!

224   I thought so then—I'll kill myself for grief—

> O villainy, villainy!

IAGO:

> What, are you mad? I charge you, get you home.

EMILIA:

> Good gentlemen, let me have leave to speak.
>
> 'Tis proper I obey him, but not now.
>
> Perchance, Iago, I will ne'er go home.

OTHELLO:

230   O! O! O!   (*Othello falls on the bed.*)

EMILIA: Nay, lay thee down and roar,

> For thou hast killed the sweetest innocent

233   That e'er did lift up eye.

OTHELLO (*rising*):   O, she was foul!

> I scarce did know you, uncle. There lies your niece,
>
> Whose breath indeed these hands have newly stopped.

237   I know this act shows horrible and grim.

GRATIANO:

> Poor Desdemon! I am glad thy father's dead.
>
> Thy match was mortal to him, and pure grief

---

214 charm keep silent (as though by a magic spell)
224 then (Perhaps at 3.3.347–349 and 4.2.150–169.)
230 s.d. Othello [. . .] bed (This direction is from the Quarto, as also *He kisses her* at line 19 and *She dies* at line 149.)
233 lift up eye i.e., lift her eyes to heaven
237 shows looks

240 Shore his old thread in twain. Did he live now,
241 This sight would make him do a desperate turn,
     Yea, curse his better angel from his side,
243 And fall to reprobance.

OTHELLO:
     'Tis pitiful. But yet Iago knows.
     That she with Cassio hath the act of shame
     A thousand times committed. Cassio confessed it;
247 And she did gratify his amorous works
248 With that recognizance and pledge of love
     Which I first gave her. I saw it in his hand;
     It was a handkerchief, an antique token
     My father gave my mother.

EMILIA: O God! O heavenly God!

IAGO:
     Zounds, hold your peace.

EMILIA: 'Twill out, 'twill out! I peace?
255 No, I will speak as liberal as the north.
     Let heaven and men and devils, let them all,
     All, all, cry shame against me, yet I'll speak.

IAGO:
     Be wise, and get you home.

EMILIA: I will not.

                    (Iago threatens Emilia.)

GRATIANO: Fie,
     Your sword upon a woman?

EMILIA:
     O thou dull Moor! That handkerchief thou speak'st of
     I found by fortune and did give my husband;
     For often, with a solemn earnestness,
265 More than indeed belonged to such a trifle,
     He begged of me to steal 't.

IAGO: Villainous whore!

EMILIA:
     She give it Cassio? No, alas! I found it,
     And I did give 't my husband.

IAGO: Filth, thou liest!

---

240 Shore [. . .] thread sheared the thread of his old age (as Atropos, one of the three
Fates, was thought to do)
241 turn deed
243 reprobance damnation, i.e., suicide
247 gratify reward
248 recognizance token
255 liberal as the north freely as the north wind (blows)
265 belonged was appropriate

EMILIA:
>By heaven, I do not, I do not, gentlemen.

272
>O murderous coxcomb! What should such a fool
>Do with so good a wife?

274 OTHELLO: Are there no stones in heaven
275
>But what serves for the thunder?—Precious villain!

(He runs at Iago; Montano disarms Othello, Iago, from behind, stabs Emilia.)

GRATIANO:
>The woman falls! Sure he hath killed his wife.

EMILIA:
>Ay, ay. O, lay me by my mistress' side.
>>*(Exit Iago.)*

GRATIANO: He's gone, but his wife's killed.

MONTANO:
>'Tis a notorious villain. Take you this weapon,
>Which I have here recovered from the Moor.
>Come, guard the door without. Let him not pass,
>But kill him rather. I'll after that same villain,
>For 'tis a damnèd slave.

>>*(Exit [with all but Othello and Emilia, who has been laid by Desdemona's side].)*

OTHELLO: I am not valiant neither,
285
>But every puny whipster gets my sword.
286
>But why should honor outlive honesty?
>Let it go all.

EMILIA: What did thy song bode, lady?
>Hark, canst thou hear me? I will play the swan,
>And die in music. (*She sings.*) "Willow, willow, willow."
>Moor, she was chaste. She loved thee, cruel Moor.
>So come my soul to bliss as I speak true.
>So speaking as I think, alas, I die.   (*She dies.*)

OTHELLO:
>I have another weapon in this chamber;
295
>It was a sword of Spain, the ice-brook's temper—

272 coxcomb fool. (Addressed to Othello.)
274 stones bolts, such as those used for thunderbolts
275 Precious i.e., arrant, utter, **s.d. He [. . .] Emilia** (The Quarto text reads, "The Moor runs at Iago. Iago kills his wife." The Quarto also specifies the exit of Iago at line 277 and the death of Emilia at line 293.)
285 whipster contemptible fellow (one who is always ready to whip out his sword)
286 honor i.e., the bravery for which one enjoys a soldier's reputation. **honesty** true integrity
295 the ice-brook's temper tempered in ice-cold water

O, here it is. (*He finds a sword.*) Uncle, I must come forth.

GRATIANO (*within*):

 If thou attempt it, it will cost thee dear.

 Thou hast no weapon, and perforce must suffer.

OTHELLO:

 Look in upon me then and speak with me,

300 Or, naked as I am, I will assault thee.

   (Enter Gratiano.)

GRATIANO:

 What is the matter?

OTHELLO: Behold, I have a weapon;

 A better never did itself sustain

 Upon a soldier's thigh. I have seen the day

 That, with this little arm and this good sword,

 I have made my way through more impediments

307 Than twenty times your stop. But O, vain boast!

 Who can control his fate? 'Tis not so now.

 Be not afraid, though you do see me weaponed;

310 Here is my journey's end, here is my butt

311 And very seamark of my utmost sail.

    (Gratiano steps back.)

312 Do you go back dismayed? 'Tis a lost fear;

313 Man but a rush against Othello's breast

 And he retires. Where should Othello go?

    (He turns to Desdemona.)

 Now, how dost thou look now? O ill-starred wench!

316 Pale as thy smock! When we shall meet at compt,

 This look of thine will hurl my soul from heaven,

 And fiends will snatch at it. Cold, cold, my girl?

319 Even like thy chastity. O cursèd, cursèd slave!

 Whip me, ye devils,

 From the possession of this heavenly sight!

 Blow me about in winds! Roast me in sulfur!

 Wash me in steep-down gulfs of liquid fire!

 O Desdemon! Dead, Desdemon! Dead! O! O!

---

300 naked unarmed
307 stop power (to stop)
310 butt goal, limit (An archery term.)
311 seamark beacon (marking his destination or limit)
312 lost wasted, unneeded
313 Man [. . .] rush wield no more than a reed
316 compt account, judgment day
319 slave i.e., Othello himself

(Enter Lodovico, Cassio [carried in a litter], Montano, and Iago [prisoner], with officers.)

LODOVICO:

325   Where is this rash and most unfortunate man?

OTHELLO:

That's he that was Othello. Here I am.

LODOVICO:

Where is that viper? Bring the villain forth.

(Iago is led forward.)

OTHELLO:

328   I look down towards his feet; but that's a fable.

If that thou be'st a devil, I cannot kill thee.

(He wounds Iago.)

LODOVICO:

Wrench his sword from him.   (*Othello is disarmed.*)

IAGO: I bleed, sir, but not killed.

OTHELLO:

I am not sorry neither. I'd have thee live,

333   For in my sense 'tis happiness to die.

LODOVICO:

O thou Othello that was once so good,

335   Fall'n in the practice of a cursèd slave,

What shall be said to thee?

OTHELLO: Why, anything.

An honorable murderer, if you will,

For naught I did in hate, but all in honor.

LODOVICO:

This wretch hath part confessed his villainy.

341   Did you and he consent in Cassio's death?

OTHELLO: Ay.

CASSIO:

Dear General, I never gave you cause.

OTHELLO:

I do believe it, and I ask your pardon.

Will you, I pray, demand that demi-devil

Why he hath thus ensnared my soul and body?

---

324 s.d. in a litter (The Quarto specifies that Cassio is "in a chair.")
328 towards his feet i.e., to see if they are cloven, as the devil's are fabled to be
333 in my sense to one who feels as I do
335 in the practice through the plotting, into the snare. **slave** villain
341 consent agree

IAGO:

> Demand me nothing. What you know, you know.
> From this time forth I never will speak word.

LODOVICO: What, not to pray?

350 GRATIANO: Torments will ope your lips.

OTHELLO: Well, thou dost best.

LODOVICO:

> Sir, you shall understand what hath befall'n,
> Which, as I think, you know not. Here is a letter
> Found in the pocket of the slain Roderigo;
> And here another. (*He produces letters.*) The one of them imports
> The death of Cassio, to be undertook
> By Roderigo.

OTHELLO: O villain!

359 CASSIO: Most heathenish and most gross!

LODOVICO (*showing another paper*):

360
> Now here's another discontented paper
> Found in his pocket too. And this, it seems,
> Roderigo meant t' have sent this damnèd villain;

363
> But that belike Iago in the interim

364
> Came in and satisfied him.

OTHELLO: O thou pernicious caitiff!—

> How came you, Cassio, by that handkerchief
> That was my wife's?

CASSIO: I found it in my chamber;

> And he himself confessed but even now
> That there he dropped it for a special purpose

371
> Which wrought to his desire.

OTHELLO: O fool, fool, fool!

CASSIO:

> There is besides in Roderigo's letter
> How he upbraids Iago, that he made him

375
> Brave me upon the watch, whereon it came

376
> That I was cast; and even but now he spake,
> After long seeming dead, Iago hurt him,
> Iago set him on.

---

350 Torments torture

359 gross monstrous

360 discontented full of discontent

363 belike most likely

364 Came [. . .] him interposed and gave him satisfactory explanation

371 wrought [. . .] desire worked out as he wished, fitted in with his plan

375 Brave defy. **whereon it came** whereof it came about

376 cast dismissed

LODOVICO (*to Othello*):
You must forsake this room and go with us.
380 Your power and your command is taken off,
And Cassio rules in Cyprus. For this slave,
If there be any cunning cruelty
383 That can torment him much and hold him long,
384 It shall be his. You shall close prisoner rest
Till that the nature of your fault be known
To the Venetian state.—Come, bring away.

OTHELLO:
387 Soft you; a word or two before you go.
I have done the state some service, and they know 't.
No more of that. I pray you, in your letters,
390 When you shall these unlucky deeds relate,
Speak of me as I am; nothing extenuate,
Nor set down aught in malice. Then must you speak
Of one that loved not wisely but too well;
394 Of one not easily jealous but, being wrought,
395 Perplexed in the extreme; of one whose hand,
396 Like the base Indian, threw a pearl away
397 Richer than all his tribe; of one whose subdued eyes,
Albeit unusèd to the melting mood,
Drops tears as fast as the Arabian trees
400 Their medicinable gum. Set you down this;
And say besides that in Aleppo once,
Where a malignant and a turbaned Turk
Beat a Venetian and traduced the state,
I took by th' throat the circumcisèd dog
And smote him, thus. (*He stabs himself.*)
406 LODOVICO: O bloody period!
GRATIANO: All that is spoke is marred.

380 taken off taken away
383 hold him long keep him alive a long time (during his torture)
384 rest remain
387 Soft you one moment
390 unlucky unfortunate
394 wrought worked upon, worked into a frenzy
395 Perplexed distraught
396 Indian (This reading from the Quarto pictures an ignorant savage who cannot recognize the value of a precious jewel. The Folio reading, *Iudean* or *Judean,* i.e., infidel or disbeliever, may refer to Herod, who slew Miriamne in a fit of jealousy, or to Judas Iscariot, the betrayer of Christ.)
397 subdued i.e., overcome by grief
400 gum i.e., myrrh
405 s.d. He stabs himself (This direction is in the Quarto text).
406 period termination, conclusion

OTHELLO:

> I kissed thee ere I killed thee. No way but this,
> Killing myself, to die upon a kiss.

> *(He kisses Desdemona and dies.)*

CASSIO:

412
> This did I fear, but thought he had no weapon;
413
> For he was great of heart.

LODOVICO (*to Iago.*):   O Spartan dog,
> More fell than anguish, hunger, or the sea!
416
> Look on the tragic loading of this bed.
> This is thy work. The object poisons sight;
> Let it be hid. Gratiano, keep the house,

417
418
> *(The bed curtains are drawn.)*

419
> And seize upon the fortunes of the Moor,
> For they succeed on you. (*To Cassio.*) To you, Lord Governor,
> Remains the censure of this hellish villain,
> The time, the place, the torture. O, enforce it!

---

412 Spartan dog (Spartan dogs were noted for their savagery and silence.)
413 fell cruel
416 Let it be hid i.e., draw the bed curtains. (No stage direction specifies that the dead are to be carried offstage at the end of the play.) **keep** remain in
417 seize upon take legal possession of
418 succeed on pass as though by inheritance to
419 censure sentencing

Questions for Discussion

Act I

1. What are Iago's motives for disliking Othello? What does he mean by "'Tis in ourselves that we are thus or thus" (1.3.341)? Why does Iago tell Roderigo he hates Othello, then advise Othello of danger in the next scene?

2. How does Iago feel about Othello's ethnic background? Support your answer with quotations from the play.

3. When Brabantio and Roderigo draw swords to attack Othello, the latter says, "Keep up your bright swords, for the dew will rust them" (1.2.71). What does this line reveal about Othello's character?

4. What are the qualities in Othello that cause Desdemona to fall in love with him?

5. What in Iago's character makes him particularly dangerous?

6. Why does Othello trust Iago more than he trusts Desdemona?

Act II

1. Why must Othello punish Cassio so severely? Is Cassio to blame? Is Othello punishing Cassio unjustly?

2. Why is Iago adept when talking to Roderigo but inept in producing flattering verses to please Desdemona? How do Iago's apparent ineptness in flattery and bluntness of speech serve his purpose?

3. What seems to be Iago's attitude toward women and sexuality? How does the **imagery** he uses reveal this attitude?

4. Why does Shakespeare have the ordinarily deceptive Iago reveal his true character in his **soliloquies?**

Act III

1. How does Iago lead Othello to begin doubting and suspecting Cassio?

2. Iago says in 3.3.360, "The Moor already changes with my poison." When Othello begins to doubt Desdemona, how else does his character change? Does his language change? If so, how does that reveal a character change? See 3.3.287–306 and 3.3.383–95.

3. Explain the significance of the handkerchief.

4. Iago has what he initially sought—the position of lieutenant. Why then does he continue his efforts to destroy Othello?

5. Explain the **foreshadowing** of Othello's speech:

> Perdition catch my soul
>
> But I do love thee! And when I love thee not,
>
> Chaos is come again. (3.3.100–02)

6. Explain the truth and the **irony** of Iago's speech:

> Who steals my purse steals trash; 'tis something, nothing;
>
> 'Twas mine, 'tis his, and has been slave to thousands;
>
> But he that filches from me my good name

> Robs me of that which not enriches him
> And makes me poor indeed. (3.3.177–81)

Act IV

1. How does Iago manipulate Cassio into incriminating himself and Desdemona?

2. Do Othello's speech and actions in this act make sense? What has happened to him? How does Lodovico's speech in 4.1.286–90 reflect the extent of Othello's fall?

3. Does Desdemona show the slightest sign of disobedience or unfaithfulness to Othello? How innocent is she? How does she respond to bad treatment from him? Support your response with references to the text. See, in particular, 4.3.63–66 and 4.3.84–85.

4. In what ways is Emilia a **dramatic foil** for Desdemona?

Act V

1. Why does Othello say, "Put out the light, and then put out the light" (5.2.7)?

2. How does Othello feel about killing Desdemona as he prepares to do so? See his soliloquy at 5.2.1–22.

3. How does Othello's speech at 5.2.302–24 reflect the extent of his fall?

4. What is Othello's motivation to kill Desdemona? Would he have been justified in doing so even if he had incontrovertible evidence of her infidelity? What flaw in his character leads him to fall into Iago's trap?

5. Why, after having explained his motives in **soliloquies** and conversations earlier in the play, does Iago now (5.2.348) say, "From this time forth I never will speak word"?

6. In what sense is Othello's death a triumph? Has he managed to retain any of his former dignity?

Suggestions for Exploration and Writing

1. Examine Iago's **motivation.** Is there any adequate motive that can explain the intensity of his malevolence? Is his evil ultimately explainable? Is it diabolic?

2. Analyze the means by which Iago poisons Othello's mind.

3. Examine in detail the change Othello undergoes. How does jealousy change not only his attitude toward Desdemona and Cassio but also

his language, his sleep, and his attitudes toward his work as a soldier—
his entire personality?

4. Discuss in detail how **imagery** defines one or more of the major characters—Iago, Desdemona, Othello, or Cassio. For example, you
might choose to show how Iago's use of animal imagery reveals his
character.

5. In *Poetics,* Aristotle describes the **tragic hero** as a good man who holds
a high position and falls because of a flaw within himself. Write an essay
explaining how Othello does or does not fit this definition.

Casebook
on Amy Tan

WRITING ABOUT VULNERABILITY

The two excerpts from Amy Tan's novels *The Hundred Secret Senses* and *The Bonesetter's Daughter* are excellent examples of the theme of vulnerability. They are connected to each other through the characters' and Tan's physical, emotional, and cultural experiences that determine the revelations about the self. The three articles will allow you to write critically about this theme using both primary and secondary sources. They will also provide insight into Chinese and Chinese American feelings of alienation.

Amy Tan (b. 1952)

Born in Oakland, Tan moved frequently to other cities in California while her father was a Baptist minister. After the deaths of her father and her brother Peter within months of each other, her mother moved the family to Montreaux, Switzerland, where Tan graduated from high school. Returning to the United States in 1969, Tan attended Linfield College but graduated from San Jose State University with a degree in linguistics. Despite her mother's admonitions against a low-paying profession, Tan decided to become a full-time writer. After an insightful trip to China, she rewrote a collection of short stories into a novel called The Joy Luck Club *(1986), which won the National Book Award in 1989 and later became a hit movie. Her second and third novels,* The Kitchen God's Wife *(1991) and* The Hundred Secret Senses *(1996), won critical acclaim also. The former portrays displacement and tension between life in two cultures, Chinese and American. The latter shows the real and the imaginary as the present and the past war within the two female characters. Tan's latest novel,* The Bonesetter's Daughter *(2001), combines these two themes and*

expands on the subject of relationships between mothers and daughters and the strug-
gle for identity. Tan also is an acclaimed writer of children's books: The Moon Lady
(1992) and The Chinese Siamese Cat *(1994).*

YOUNG GIRL'S WISH (1996)

1   My first morning in China, I awake in a dark hotel room in Guilin and
see a figure leaning over my bed, staring at me with the concentrated look
of a killer. I'm about to scream, when I hear my sister Kwan saying, in Chinese, "Sleeping on your side—so *this* is the reason your posture is so bad.
From now on, you must sleep on your back. Also, do exercises."

2   She snaps on the light and proceeds to demonstrate, hands on hips,
twisting at the waist like a sixties P.E. teacher. I wonder how long she's
been standing by my bed, waiting for me to waken so she can present her
latest bit of unsolicited advice. Her bed is already made.

3   I look at my watch and say, in a grumpy voice, "Kwan, it's only five in
the morning."

4   "This is China. Everyone else is up. Only you're asleep."

5   "Not anymore."

6   We've been in China less than eight hours, and already she's taking
control of my life. We're on her terrain; we have to go by her rules, speak
her language. She's in Chinese heaven.

7   Snatching my blankets, she laughs. "Libby-ah, hurry and get up." Kwan
has never been able to correctly pronounce my name, Olivia. "I want to
go see my village and surprise everyone. I want to watch Big Ma's mouth
fall open and hear her words of surprise: 'Hey, I thought I chased you
away. Why are you back?'"

8   Kwan pushes open the window. We're staying at the Sheraton Guilin,
which faces the Li River. Outside it's still dark. I can hear the *trnnng!*
trnnng! of what sounds like a noisy pachinko parlor. I go to the window
and look down. Peddlers on tricycle carts are ringing their bells, greeting
one another as they haul their baskets of grain, melons, and turnips to
market. The boulevard is bristling with the shadows of bicycles and cars,
workers and schoolchildren—the whole world chirping and honking,
shouting and laughing, as though it were the middle of the day. On the
handlebar of a bicycle dangle the gigantic heads of four pigs, roped
through the nostrils, their white snouts curled in death grins.

9   "Look." Kwan points down the street to a set of stalls lit by low-watt
bulbs. "We can buy breakfast there, cheap and good. Better than paying
nine dollars each for hotel food—and for what? Doughnut, orange juice,
bacon, who wants it?"

10   I recall the admonition in our guidebooks to steer clear of food sold
by street venders. "Nine dollars, that's not much," I reason.

11   "Wah! You can't think this way anymore. Now you're in China. Nine
dollars is lots of money here, one week's salary."

12   "Yeah, but cheap food might come with food poisoning."

13   Kwan gestures to the street. "You look. All those people there, do they have food poisoning?"

14   Kwan is right. Who am I to begrudge carrying home a few parasites? I slip some warm clothes on and go into the hallway to knock on my husband's door. Simon answers immediately, fully dressed. "I couldn't sleep," he admits.

15   In five minutes, the three of us are on the sidewalk. We pass dozens of food stalls, some with portable propane burners, others with makeshift grills. In front of the stalls, customers squat in semicircles eating noodles and dumplings. Kwan chooses a vender who is slapping what look like floury pancakes onto the sides of a blazing-hot oil drum. "Give me three," she says, in Chinese. The vender pries the pancakes off with his blackened fingers, and Simon and I yelp as we toss the hot pancakes up and down like circus jugglers.

16   "How much?" Kwan opens her change purse.

17   "Six yuan," the pancake vender tells her.

18   I calculate the cost is a little more than a dollar, dirt cheap. By Kwan's estimation, this is tantamount to extortion. "Wah!" She points to another customer. "You charged him only fifty fen a pancake."

19   "Of course! He's a local worker. You three are tourists."

20   "What are you saying! I'm also local."

21   "You?" The vender snorts and gives her a cynical once-over. "From where, then?"

22   "Changmian."

23   His eyebrows rise in suspicion. "Really, now! Who do you know in Changmian?"

24   Kwan rattles off some names.

25   The vender slaps his thigh. "Wu Ze-min? You know Wu Ze-min?"

26   "Of course. As children, we lived across the lane from each other. I haven't seen him in over thirty years."

27   "His daughter married my son."

28   "Nonsense!"

29   The man laughs. "It's true. Two years ago. My wife and my mother opposed the match—just because the girl was from Changmian. But they have old countryside ideas, they still believe Changmian is cursed. Not me, I'm not superstitious, not anymore. And now a baby's been born, last spring, a girl, but I don't mind."

30   "Hard to believe Wu Ze-min's a grandfather. How is he?"

31   "Lost his wife twenty years ago, when they were sent to the cowsheds for counter-revolutionary thinking. They smashed his hands, but not his mind. Later he married another woman, Yang Ling-fang."

32   "That's not possible! She was the little sister of an old schoolmate of mine. I still see her as a tender young girl."

33   "Not so tender anymore. She's got *jiaoban* skin, tough as leather, been through plenty of hardships, let me tell you."

34   Kwan and the vender continue to gossip while Simon and I eat our pancakes. They taste like a cross between focaccia and a green-onion omelette. By now Kwan and the vender act like old friends, and he advises her how to get a good price on a driver to take us to Changmian.

35   "All right, older brother," Kwan says, "how much do I owe you?"

36   "Six yuan."

37   "Wah! Still six yuan? Too much, too much. I'll give you two, no more than that."

38   "Make it three, then."

39   Kwan grunts, settles up, and we leave. When we're half a block away, I whisper to Simon, "That man said Changmian is cursed."

40   Kwan overhears me. "*Tst!* That's just a story, a thousand years old. Only stupid people still think Changmian is a bad-luck place to live."

41   I translate for Simon, then ask, "What kind of bad luck?"

42   "You don't want to know."

43   I am about to insist she tell me, when Simon points to my first photo opportunity—an open-air market overflowing with wicker baskets of thick-skinned pomelos, dried beans, cassia tea, chilies. I pull out my Nikon and am soon busy shooting, while Simon jots down notes.

44   "Plumes of acrid breakfast smoke mingled with the morning mist," he says aloud. "Hey, Olivia, can you do a shot from this direction? Get the turtles, the turtles would be great."

45   I inhale deeply and imagine that I'm filling my lungs with the very air that inspired my ancestors, whoever they might have been. Because we arrived late the night before, we haven't yet seen the Guilin landscape, its fabled karst peaks, its magical limestone caves, and all the other sites listed in our guidebook as the reasons this is known in China as "the most beautiful place on earth."

46   Looking up toward cloud level, we see the amazing peaks, which resemble prehistoric shark's teeth, the clichéd subject of every Chinese calendar and scroll painting. But tucked in the gums of these ancient stone formations is the blight of high-rises, their stucco exteriors grimy with industrial pollution, their signboards splashed with garish red and gilt characters. Between these are lower buildings from an earlier era, all of them painted a proletarian toothpaste-green. And here and there is the rubble of prewar houses and impromptu garbage dumps. The whole scene gives Guilin the look and stench of a pretty face marred by tawdry lipstick, gapped teeth, and an advanced case of periodontal disease.

47   "Boy, oh boy," whispers Simon. "If Guilin is China's most beautiful city, I can't wait to see what the cursed village of Changmian looks like."

48   We catch up with Kwan. "Everything is entirely different, no longer the same." Kwan must be sad to see how horribly Guilin has changed over the past thirty years. But then she says, in a proud and marvelling voice, "So much progress, everything is so much better."

49   A couple of blocks farther on, we come upon a bird market. Hanging from tree limbs are hundreds of decorative cages containing singing finches, and exotic birds with gorgeous plumage, punk crests, and fan-like tails. On the ground are cages of huge birds, perhaps eagles or hawks, magnificent, with menacing talons and beaks. There are also the ordinary fowl—chickens and ducks, destined for the stewpot.

50   I see a man hissing at me. "*Sssss!*" He sternly motions me to come over. What is he, the secret police?

51   The man solemnly reaches underneath a table and brings out a cage. "You like," he says, in English. Facing me is a snowy-white owl with milk-chocolate highlights. It looks like a fat Siamese cat with wings. The owl blinks its golden eyes and I fall in love.

52   "Hey, Simon, Kwan, come here. Look at this."

53   "One hundred dollar, U.S.," the man says. "Very cheap."

54   Simon shakes his head and says in a weird combination of pantomime and broken English: "Take bird on plane, not possible, customs official will say stop, not allowed, must pay big fine—"

55   "How much?" the man asks brusquely. "You say. I give you morning price, best price."

56   "There's no use bargaining," Kwan tells the man in Chinese. "We're tourists. We can't bring birds back to the United States, no matter how cheap."

57   "Aaah, who's talking about bringing it back?" the man replies in rapid Chinese. "Buy it today, then take it to that restaurant, over there. For a small price, they can cook it tonight for your dinner."

58   "Oh, my God!" I turn to Simon. "He's selling this owl as food!"

59   "That's disgusting. Tell him he's a fucking goon."

60   "You tell him!"

61   "I can't speak Chinese."

62   The man must think I am urging my husband to buy me an owl for dinner. "You're very lucky I even have *one*. The cat-eagle is rare, very rare," he brags. "Took me three weeks to catch it."

63   "I don't believe this," I tell Simon. "I'm going to be sick."

64   Then I hear Kwan saying, "A cat-eagle is not that rare, just hard to catch. Besides, I hear the flavor is ordinary."

65   "To be honest," says the man, "it's not as pungent as, say, a pangolin. But you eat a cat-eagle to give you strength and ambition, not to be fussy over taste. Also, it's good for improving your eyesight. One of my customers was nearly blind. After he ate a cat-eagle, he could see his wife for the first time in twenty years. The customer came back and cursed me: 'Shit! She's ugly enough to scare a monkey. Fuck your mother for letting me eat that cat-eagle!'"

66   Kwan laughs heartily. "Yes, yes, I've heard this about cat-eagles. It's a good story." She pulls out her change purse and holds up a hundred-yuan note.

67   "Kwan, what are you doing?" I cry. "We are *not* going to eat this owl!"

68   The man waves away the hundred yuan. "Only American money," he says firmly. "One hundred *American* dollars."

69   Kwan pulls out an American ten-dollar bill.

70   "Kwan!" I shout.

71   The man shakes his head, refusing the ten. Kwan shrugs, then starts to walk away. The man shouts to her to give him fifty, then. She comes back and holds out a ten and a five, and says, "That's my last offer."

72   "This is insane!" Simon mutters.

73   The man sighs, then relinquishes the cage, complaining, "What a shame, so little money for so much work. Look at my hands, three weeks of climbing and cutting down bushes to catch this bird."

74   As we walk away, I grab Kwan's free arm: "There's no way I'm going to let you eat this owl. I don't care if we are in China."

75   "Shh! Shh! You'll scare him!" Kwan pulls the cage out of my reach. She gives me a maddening smile, then walks over to a concrete wall, over-looking the river and sets the cage on top. She meows to the owl. "Oh, lit-tle friend, you want to go to Changmian? You want to climb with me to the top of the mountain, let my little sister watch you fly away?" The owl twists his head and blinks.

76   I almost cry with joy and guilt. Why do I think such bad things about Kwan?

77   "See that?" I hear Kwan say. "Over there." She's pointing to a cone-shaped peak off in the distance. "Just outside my village stands a sharp-headed mountain, taller than that one, even. We call it Young Girl's Wish, after a slave girl who ran away to the top of it, then flew off with a phoenix who was her lover." Kwan looks at me. "It's a story, just superstition."

78   I'm amused that she thinks she has to explain.

79   Kwan continues, "Yet all the girls in our village believed in that tale, not because they were stupid but because they wanted to hope for a bet-ter life. We thought that if we climbed to the top and made a wish, it might come true. So we raised little hatchlings, and when the birds were ready to fly we climbed to the top of Young Girl's Wish and let them go. The birds would then fly to where the phoenixes lived and tell them our wishes." Kwan sniffs. "Big Ma told me the peak was named Young Girl's Wish because a crazy girl climbed to the top. But when she tried to fly, she fell all the way down and lodged herself so firmly into the earth she became a boulder. Big Ma said that's why you can see so many boulders at the bottom of that peak—they're all the stupid girls who followed her kind of crazy thinking, wishing for hopeless things."

80   I laugh. Kwan stares at me fiercely, as if I were Big Ma, the aunt who raised her. "You can't stop young girls from wishing. No! Everyone must dream. To stop dreaming—well, that's like saying you can never change your fate. Isn't that true?"

81   "I suppose."

82   "So now you guess what I wished for."

83   "I don't know. What?"

84   "Come on, you guess."

85   "A handsome husband."

86   "No."

87   "A car."

88   Kwan laughs and slaps my arm. "You guessed wrong! O.K., I'll tell you." She looks toward the mountain peaks. "Before I left for America, I raised three birds, not just one, so I could make three wishes at the top of the peak. I told myself, If these three wishes come true, my life is complete,

I can die happy. My first wish: to have a sister I could love with all my heart, only that, and I would ask for nothing more from her. My second wish: to return to China with my sister. My third wish"—Kwan's voice now quavers—"for Big Ma to see this and say she was sorry she sent me away."

89   This is the first time Kwan's ever shown me how deeply she can resent someone who's treated her wrong. "I opened the cage," she continues, "and let my three birds go free." She flings out her hand in demonstration. "But one of them beat its wings uselessly, drifting in half-circles, before it fell like a stone all the way to the bottom. Now you see, two of my wishes have already happened: I have you, and together we are in China. Last night, I realized my third wish would never come true. Big Ma will never tell me she is sorry."

90   She holds up the cage with the owl. "But now I have a beautiful cat-eagle that can carry with him my new wish. When he flies away, all my old sadnesses will go with him. Then both of us will be free."

91   Actually, Kwan is my half sister, but I never mention that publicly. That would be an insult, as if she deserved only fifty per cent of my love. She was born in China. I was born in San Francisco, after our father immigrated there and married my mother.

92   Mom calls herself "American mixed grill, a bit of everything white, fatty, and fried." She was born in Moscow, Idaho, where she was a champion baton twirler and once won a county-fair prize for growing a deformed potato that had the profile of Jimmy Durante. She told me she dreamed she'd one day grow up to be different—thin, exotic, and noble, like Luise Rainer, who won an Oscar playing O-lan in "The Good Earth." When Mom moved to San Francisco and became a Kelly girl instead, she did the next-best thing. She married our father. Mom thinks that her marrying out of the Anglo race makes her a liberal. "When Jack and I met," she still tells people, "there were laws against mixed marriages. We broke the law for love." She neglects to mention that those laws didn't apply in California.

93   None of us, including my mom, even knew that Kwan *existed* until shortly before my father died, of renal failure. I was not quite four when he passed away. But I still remember the last day I saw him in the hospital.

94   I was sitting on a sticky vinyl chair, eating a bowl of strawberry Jell-O cubes that my father had given me from his lunch tray. He was propped up in bed, breathing hard. Mom would cry one minute, then act cheerful. The next thing I remember, my father was whispering and Mom leaned in close to listen. Her mouth opened wider and wider. Then her head turned sharply toward me, all twisted with horror.

95   "Your daughter?" I heard my mom say. "Bring her back?"

96   What I remember after that is a jumble: the bowl of Jell-O crashing to the floor, Mom staring at a photo, then me seeing the black-and-white snapshot of a skinny baby with patchy hair.

97   It turned out that my father had been a university student in Guilin. He used to buy live frogs for his supper at the outdoor market from a

young woman named Li Chen. He later married her, and in 1944 she gave birth to a daughter. In 1948, my father's first wife died, of a lung disease, perhaps t.b. He went to Hong Kong to search for work and left Kwan in the care of his wife's younger sister, Li Bin-bin, who lived in a small mountain village called Changmian. He sent money for their support—but in 1949, after the Communists took over, it was impossible for my father to return. What else could he do? With a heavy heart, he left for America to start a new life and forget about the sadness he left behind.

98   Eleven years later, while he was dying in the hospital, the ghost of his first wife appeared at the foot of his bed. "Claim back your daughter," she warned, "or suffer the consequences after death!"

99   Looking back, I can imagine how my mom must have felt when she first heard this. Another wife? A daughter in China? We were a modern American family. We spoke English. Sure, we ate Chinese food, but take-out, like everyone else. And we lived in a ranch-style house in Daly City. My father worked for the Government Accounting Office. My mother went to P.T.A. meetings. She had never heard my father talk about Chinese superstitions before; they attended church and bought life insurance instead.

100   After my father died, my mother kept telling everyone how he had treated her "just like a Chinese empress." She made all sorts of grief-stricken promises to God and my father's grave. My mother vowed never to remarry. She vowed to teach us children to do honor to the family name. She vowed to find my father's firstborn child, Kwan, and bring her to the United States. The last promise was the only one she kept.

101   I was nearly six when Kwan arrived.

102   We head to the hotel, in search of a car that will take one local, two tourists, and a cat-eagle to Changmian village. By nine, we've procured the services of a driver, an amiable young man who knows how to do the capitalist hustle. "Clean, cheap, fast," he declares, in Chinese. And then he makes an aside for Simon's benefit.

103   "What'd he say?" Simon asks.

104   "He's letting you know he speaks English."

105   Our driver reminds me of the slick Hong Kong youths who hang out in the trendy pool halls of San Francisco, the same pomaded hair, his inch-long pinkie nail, perfectly manicured, symbolizing that his lucky life is one without backbreaking work. He flashes us a smile, revealing a set of nicotine-stained teeth. "You call me Rocky," he says, in heavily accented English. "Like famous movie star." He opens the door with a flourish, and we climb into a black Nissan, a late-model sedan that, curiously, lacks seat belts and safety headrests. Do the Japanese think Chinese lives aren't worth saving? "China has either better drivers or no liability lawyers," Simon concludes.

106   Rocky happily assumes we like loud music and slips in a Eurythmics tape, a gift from one of his other "excellent American customers." And

so, with Kwan in the front seat and Simon, the owl, and me in back, we start our journey to Changmian, blasted by the beat of "Sisters Are Doing It for Themselves."

107   Rocky's excellent American customers have also taught him select phrases, which he recites to us: "Where you go? I know it. Jump in, let's go." "Go faster? Too fast? No way, José." "How far? Not far. Too far." "Park car? Wait a sec. Back in flash." "Not lost. No problem. Chill out."

108   Rocky explains that he is teaching himself English so he can one day go to America.

109   "My idea," he says, in Chinese, "is to become a famous movie actor, specializing in martial arts. Of course, I don't expect a big success from the start. Maybe I'll have to take a job as a taxi-driver. But I'm hardworking. In America, people don't know how to be as hardworking as we Chinese. We also know how to suffer. What's unbearable to Americans would be ordinary for me. Don't you think that's true, older sister?"

110   Kwan gives an ambiguous "Hmm." I wonder whether she is thinking of her brother-in-law, a former chemist, who immigrated to the States and now works as a dishwasher because he's too scared to speak English, lest people think he is stupid. Just then Simon's eyes grow round, and I shout, "Holy shit!" as the car nearly sideswipes two schoolgirls holding hands. Rocky blithely goes on about his dream.

111   "When I live in America, I'll save most of my money, spend only a little on food, cigarettes, maybe the movies every now and then, and, of course, a car for my taxi business. My needs are simple. Even if I don't become a movie star, I can still come back to China and live like a rich man."

112   He looks at us through the rearview mirror and gives us a thumbs-up. A second later, Simon grips the front seat, and I shout, "Holy Jesus shit!" We are about to hit a young woman on a bicycle with her baby perched on the handlebar. At the last possible moment, the cyclist wobbles to the right and out of our way.

113   Rocky laughs. "Chill out," he says. And then he explains, in Chinese, why we shouldn't worry. Kwan turns around and translates for Simon: "He said in China if driver run over somebody, driver always at fault, no matter how careless other person."

114   Simon looks at me. "This is supposed to reassure us? Did something get lost in the translation?"

115   "It doesn't make any sense," I tell Kwan, as Rocky veers in and out of traffic. "A dead pedestrian is a dead pedestrian, no matter whose fault it is."

116   "*Tst!* This American thinking," Kwan replies. The owl swings his head and stares at me, as if to say, Wise up, gringa, this is China, your American ideas don't work here. "In China," Kwan goes on, "you always responsible for someone else, no matter what. You get run over, this my fault, you my little sister. Now you understand?"

117   We drive by a strip of shops selling rattan furniture and straw hats. And then we're in the outskirts of town, both sides of the road lined with mile after mile of identical one-room restaurants. Some are in the stages of

being built, their walls layers of brick, mud plaster, and whitewash. They advertise the same specialties: orange soda pop and steamy-hot noodle soup. Idle waitresses squat outside, watching our car whizz by.

118 A few miles farther on, the restaurants give way to simple wooden stalls with thatched roofs, and, even farther, peddlers, without any shelter, stand by the road, yelling at the top of their lungs, waving their string bags of pomelos, their bottles of homemade hot sauce.

119 As the stretches between villages grow longer, Kwan falls asleep, her head bobbing lower and lower. She half awakens with a snort every time we hit a pothole. After a while, she emits long, rhythmical snores, blissfully unaware that Rocky is driving faster and faster down the two-lane road. Each time he accelerates, the owl opens his wings slightly, then settles down again in the cramped cage. I'm gripping my knees, then sucking air between clenched teeth whenever Rocky swings into the left lane.

120 We are now tailgating a truck filled with soldiers in green uniforms. They wave to us. Rocky honks his horn, then swerves sharply to pass. As we go by the truck, I can see an oncoming bus bearing down on us, the urgent blare of its horn growing louder and louder. "Oh, my God, oh, my God," I whimper. I close my eyes, and Simon grabs my hand. The car jerks back into the right lane. I hear a *whoosh,* then the blare of the bus horn receding.

121 "That's it," I say in a tense whisper. "I'm going to tell him to slow down."

122 "I don't know, Olivia. He might be offended."

123 I glare at Simon. "What? You'd rather die than be rude?"

124 He affects an attitude of nonchalance. "They all drive like that."

125 "So mass suicide makes it O.K.?"

126 "Well, we haven't seen any accidents."

127 Simon stares at me. At that moment, Rocky brakes abruptly. Kwan and the owl awake with a flutter of arms and wings. Rocky rolls down the window and sticks out his head. He curses under his breath, then starts punching the car horn with the heel of his hand.

128 After a few minutes, we see the source of our delay: an accident, a bad one, to judge from the spray of glass, metal, and personal belongings that litters the road. The smells of spilled gasoline and scorched rubber hang in the air. Just as I am about to say to Simon, "See?" our car inches past a black minivan, belly up, its doors splayed like the broken wings of a squashed insect. A tire lies in a nearby vegetable field. Seconds later, we go by the other half of the impact: a red-and-white bus. The large front window is smashed, the hound-nosed hood twisted and smeared with a hideous swath of blood. About fifty gawkers, farm tools still in hand, mill around, staring and pointing at various parts of the crumpled bus as if it were a science exhibit. And then I see a dozen or so injured people, some clutching themselves and bellowing in pain, others lying quietly in shock. Or perhaps they are already dead.

129 "Shit, I can't believe this," says Simon. "There's no ambulance, no doctors."

130   "Stop the car," I order Rocky, in Chinese. "We should help them." Why did I say that? What can I possibly do? I can barely look at the victims, let alone touch them.

131   "*Ai-ya.*" Kwan stares at the field. "So many yin people." Yin people? Kwan believes she can see ghosts, those who have died and now dwell in the World of Yin. Is she now saying there are dead people out there? The owl coos mournfully, and my hands turn slippery-cold.

132   Rocky keeps his eyes on the road ahead, driving forward, leaving the tragedy behind us. "We'd be of no use," he says, in Chinese. "We have no medicine, no bandages. Besides, it's not good to interfere, especially since you're foreigners. Don't worry, the police will be along soon."

133   I'm secretly relieved he isn't heeding my instructions.

134   "You're Americans," he continues, his voice deep with Chinese authority. "You're not used to seeing tragedies. You pity us, yes, because you can later go home to a comfortable life and forget what you've seen. For us, this type of disaster is commonplace. We have so many people, no room left for pity."

135   "Would someone please tell me what's going on!" Simon exclaims. "Why aren't we stopping?"

136   "Don't ask questions," I snap. "Remember?"

137   When we get back on the open road, Kwan gives Rocky some advice. He solemnly nods, then slows down.

138   "What'd she say?" Simon asks.

139   "Chinese logic. If we're killed, no payment. And in the next life, he'll owe us big time."

140   Another three hours pass. I know we have to be getting close to Changmian. Kwan is pointing out landmarks. "There! There!" she cries huskily, bouncing up and down like a little child. "Those two peaks. The village they surround is called Wife Waiting for Husband's Return. But where is the tree? What happened to the tree? Next to that house, there was a very big tree, maybe a thousand years old."

141   She scans ahead. "That place there! We used to hold a big market. But now look, it's just an empty field. And there—that mountain up ahead! That's the one we called Young Girl's Wish."

142   Kwan laughs, but the next second she seems puzzled. "Funny, now that mountain looks so small. Why is that? Did it shrink, washed down by the rain? Or maybe the peak was worn down by too many girls running up there to make a wish. Or maybe it's because I've become too American and now. I see things with different eyes, everything looking smaller poorer, not as good."

143   All at once, Kwan shouts to Rocky to turn down a small dirt road we have just passed. He makes an abrupt U-turn, knocking Simon and me into each other, and causing the owl to shriek. We are rumbling along a rutted lane, past fields with pillows of moist red dirt. "Turn left, turn left!" Kwan orders. She has her hands clasped in her lap. "Too many years, too many years," she says, as if chanting.

144   We approach a stand of trees, and then, as soon as Kwan announces, "Changmian," I see it: a village nestled between two jagged peaks, their hillsides a velvety moss-green with folds deepening into emerald. More comes into view: crooked rows of buildings whitewashed with lime, their pitched tile roofs laid in the traditional pattern of dragon coils. Surrounding the village are well-tended fields and mirrorlike ponds neatly divided by stone walls and irrigation trenches. We jump out of the car. Miraculously, Changmian has avoided the detritus of modernization. I see no tin roofs or electrical power lines. In contrast to other villages we've passed, the outlying lands here haven't become dumping grounds for garbage, the alleys aren't lined with crumpled cigarette packs or pink plastic bags. Clean stone pathways crisscross the village, then thread up a cleft between the two peaks and disappear through a stone archway. In the distance is another pair of tall peaks, dark jade in color, and beyond those the purple shadows of two more. Simon and I stare at each other, wide-eyed.

145   I feel as though we've stumbled on a fabled misty land, half memory, half illusion. Are we in Chinese Nirvana? Changmian looks like the carefully cropped photos found in travel brochures advertising "a charmed world of the distant past, where visitors can step back in time." There must be something wrong, I keep warning myself. Around the corner we'll stumble on reality: the fast-food market, the tire junkyard, the signs indicating this village is really a Chinese fantasyland for tourists.

146   "I feel like I've seen this place before," I whisper to Simon.

147   "Me, too. Maybe it was in a documentary." He laughs. "Or a car commercial."

148   I gaze at the mountains and realize why Changmian seems so familiar. It's the setting for Kwan's stories, the ones that filter into my dreams. There they are: the archways, the cassia trees, the hills leading to Thistle Mountain. And being here, I feel as if the membrane separating the two halves of my life has finally been shed.

149   From out of nowhere we hear squeals and cheers. Fifty tiny schoolchildren race toward the perimeter of a fenced-in yard. As we draw closer, the children shriek, turn on their heels, and run back to the school building, laughing. After a few seconds, they come screaming toward us like a flock of birds, followed by their smiling teacher. They stand at attention, and then shout all together, in English, "A-B-C! One-two-three! How are you! Hello goodbye!"

150   We continue along the path. Two young men on bicycles slow down and stop to stare at us. We keep walking and round a corner. Kwan gasps. Farther up the path, in front of an arched gateway, stand a dozen smiling people. Kwan puts her hand to her mouth, then runs toward them. When she reaches the group, she grabs each person's hand between her two palms, then hails a stout woman and slaps her on the back.

151   "Fat!" Kwan says. "You've grown unbelievably fat!"

152   "Hey, look at you—what happened to your hair? Did you ruin it on purpose?"

153   "This is the style! What, have you been in the countryside so long you don't recognize good style?"

154   "Oh, listen to her, she's still bossy, I can tell."

155   "You were always the bossy one, not—"

156   Kwan stops in midsentence, transfixed by a stone wall. You would think it's the most fascinating sight she's ever seen.

157   "Big Ma," she murmurs. "What's happened? How can this be?"

158   A man in the crowd guffaws. "Ha! She was so anxious to see you she got up early this morning, then jumped on a bus to meet you in Guilin. And now look—you're here, she's there. Won't she be mad!"

159   Everyone laughs, except Kwan. She walks closer to the wall, calling hoarsely, "Big Ma, Big Ma." Several people whisper, and everyone draws back, frightened.

160   "Uh-oh," I say.

161   "Why is Kwan crying?" Simon whispers.

162   "Big Ma, oh, Big Ma." Tears are streaming down Kwan's cheeks. "You must believe me, this is not what I wished. How unlucky that you died on the day that I've come home." A few women gasp and cover their mouths.

163   I walk over to Kwan. "What are you saying? Why do you think she's dead?"

164   "Why is everyone so freaked?" Simon glances about.

165   I hold up my hand. "I'm not sure." I turn back to her. "Kwan?" I say gently. "Kwan?" But she does not seem to hear me. She is looking tenderly at the wall, laughing and crying.

166   "Yes, I knew this," she is saying. "Of course, I knew. In my heart, I knew all the time."

167   In the afternoon, the villagers hold an uneasy homecoming party for Kwan in the community hall. The news has spread through Changmian that Kwan has seen Big Ma's ghost. Yet she has not announced this to the village, and since there is no proof that Big Ma has died, there is no reason to call off a food-laden celebration that evidently took her friends days to prepare. During the festivities, Kwan does not brag about her car, her sofa, her English. She listens quietly as her former childhood playmates recount major events of their lives: the birth of twin sons, a railway trip to a big city, and the time a group of student intellectuals was sent to Changmian for reëducation during the Cultural Revolution.

168   "They thought they were smarter than us," recounts one woman, whose hands are gnarled by arthritis. "They wanted us to raise a fast-growing rice, three crops a year instead of two. They gave us special seeds. They brought us insect poison. Then the little frogs that swam in the rice fields and ate the insects, they all died. And the ducks that ate the frogs, they all died, too. Then the rice died."

169   A man with bushy hair shouts, "So we said, 'What good is it to plant three crops of rice that fail rather than two that are successful?'"

170   The woman with arthritic hands continues: "These same intellectuals tried to breed our mules! Ha! Can you believe it? For two years, every

week, one of us would ask them, 'Any luck?' And they'd say, 'Not yet, not yet.' And we'd try to keep our faces serious but encouraging. 'Try harder, comrade,' we'd say. 'Don't give up.' "

171   We are still laughing when a young boy runs into the hall, shouting that an official from Guilin has arrived in a fancy black car. Silence. The official comes into the hall, and everyone stands. He solemnly holds up the identity card of Li Bin-bin and asks if she belonged to the village. Several people glance nervously at Kwan. She walks slowly toward the official, looks at the identity card, and nods. The official makes an announcement, and a ripple of moans and then wails fills the room.

172   Simon leans toward me. "What's wrong?"

173   "Big Ma's dead. She was killed in that bus accident we saw this morning."

174   Simon and I walk over and each put a hand on one of Kwan's shoulders. She feels so small.

175   "I'm sorry," Simon stammers.

176   Kwan gives him a teary smile. As Li Bin-bin's closest relative, she has volunteered to perform the necessary bureaucratic ritual of bringing the body back to the village the next day. The three of us are returning to Guilin.

177   As soon as Rocky sees us, he stubs out his cigarette and turns off the car radio. Someone must have told him the news. "What a tragedy," he says. "I'm sorry, big sister, I should have stopped. I'm to blame—"

178   Kwan waves off his apologies. "No one's to blame. Anyway, regrets are useless, always too late."

179   When Rocky opens the car door, we see that the owl is still in his cage on the backseat. Kwan lifts the cage gently and stares at the bird. "No need to climb the mountain anymore," she says. She sets the cage on the ground, then opens its door. The owl sticks out his head, hops to the edge of the doorway and onto the ground. He twists his head and, with a great flap of wings, takes off toward the peaks. Kwan watches him until he disappears.

180   As Rocky warms the engine, I ask Kwan, "When we passed the bus accident this morning, did you see someone who looked like Big Ma? Is that how you knew she'd died?"

181   "What are you saying? I didn't know she was dead until I saw her yin self standing by the wall."

182   "Then why did you tell her that you knew?"

183   Kwan frowns, puzzled. "I knew what?"

184   "You were telling her you knew, in your heart you knew it was true. Weren't you talking about the accident?"

185   "Ah," she says, understanding at last. "No, not the accident." She sighs. "I told Big Ma that what *she* was saying was true."

186   "What did she say?"

187   Kwan turns to the window, and I can see the reflection of her stricken face. "She said she was wrong about the story of Young Girl's Wish. She said all my wishes had already come true. She was always sorry she sent me away. But she could never tell me this. Otherwise, I wouldn't have left her for a chance at a better life."

188   I search for some way to console Kwan. "At least you can still see her," I say.

189   "Ah?"

190   "I mean as a yin person. She can visit you."

191   Kwan stares out the car window. "But it's not the same. We can no longer make new memories together. We can't change the past. Not until the next lifetime." She exhales heavily, releasing all her unsaid words.

Questions for Discussion

1. Why is Kwan in "Chinese heaven" at the beginning of the story?

2. Describe the street scenes in Guilin. What does Olivia mean when she says that the city of Guilin was "a pretty face marred by tawdry lipstick, gapped teeth, and an advanced case of periodontal disease"?

3. Explain the importance of the "cat-eagle," the owl, and of what Kwan wants to do with it.

4. List some of the foreshadowing elements and explain what they foreshadow.

5. What is the tale of the "Young Girl's Wish"? What are Kwan's three wishes?

6. Explain Kwan's and Olivia's relationship. How did Olivia discover this relationship?

7. Who are "yin people"? What other Chinese legends does the story include?

8. In Eric Skipper's "The Runt," Willis is told not to interfere in the Mexicans' affairs. In this story, Olivia and Kwan are told by Rocky, the cab driver, not to interfere because they are foreigners. What is implied by these statements?

9. How does Kwan know that Big Ma is dead before anyone else does?

10. Why doesn't Kwan brag about her American possessions after Big Ma's death?

11. What is the significance of the owl at the end of the story?

IMMORTAL HEART   (2001)

1   These are the things I must not forget: I was raised among the Liu clan in the rocky Western Hills south of Peking, in Immortal Heart village. My nursemaid, Precious Auntie, who could speak only by making signs with her hands, taught me how to write the character for heart on my chalkboard. *Watch now, Lu Ling,* she ordered, and began to draw: *See this curving stroke? That's the bottom of the heart, where blood gathers.* And as I traced the character, she asked, *Whose dead heart gave shape to this word? How did it begin?*

2   Immortal Heart village lay in a valley that dropped into a deep limestone ravine. The ravine was shaped like the curved chamber of a heart, and the three streams that had once fed and drained the ravine were the heart's artery and veins. Now nothing was left of the waterways but cracked gullies and the stench of a fart.

3   The Liu clan had lived in Immortal Heart for six centuries. During that time, they had been ink stick makers who sold their goods to travellers. All in all, our family was successful—we now had a shop in Peking, where Father and his brothers and their sons worked—but not so successful that we caused great envy. The family home, on Pig's Head Lane, had grown from a simple house into a compound, with five-pillar wings, and outbuildings perched above the deepest end of the ravine. The Liu family had once owned twenty *mu* of land, but over the centuries, with each heavy rainfall, the walls of the ravine had collapsed and widened, rumbled and deepened, and the cliff crept closer to the back of our house. We called the ravine the End of the World. What lay below was too unlucky to name out loud: unwanted babies, suicide maidens, and beggar ghosts.

4   Precious Auntie was born in a town called Mouth of the Mountain, in the foothills on the other side of the ravine. In Mouth of the Mountain, poor men collected dragon bones from the nearby caves and then sold them to medicine shops for high prices, and the shops sold them to sick people for still higher prices. The bones were known to cure anything, from wasting diseases to stupidity. Plenty of doctors sold them. And so did Precious Auntie's father, the Famous Bonesetter in the Mouth of the Mountain. He used bones to heal bones.

5   Her father's customers were mostly men and boys who had been injured in the coal mines and limestone quarries. The bonesetter had learned his skill from watching his father, and his father had learned from his father before him. That was their inheritance. They also passed along a secret: the location of a cave called the Monkey's Jaw, where many dragon bones could be found.

6   I can still remember the directions to the Monkey's Jaw. It was between the Mouth of the Mountain and Immortal Heart, far from the other caves in the foothills, where everyone else went to dig up dragon bones. Precious Auntie took me there several times, always in the spring or the autumn. We went down into the End of the World and walked along the middle of the ravine, away from the walls, where the grown-ups said there were things that were bad to see. Sometimes we passed by a skein of weeds, shards of a bowl, a quagmire of twigs. In my childish mind, those sights became parched flesh, a baby's skull, a soup of maidens' bones.

7   When we stood in front of the cave itself, a split in the mountain that was no taller than a broom, Precious Auntie pulled aside the dead bushes that hid the entrance. The two of us took big breaths and went in. It was like trying to get inside an ear. By the time I was in the cave, I was crying and Precious Auntie was grunting to reassure me, because I could not see her inkstained fingers to know what she was saying. I had to follow her

handclaps, crawling like a dog so I would not hit my head. When we finally reached the larger part of the cave, Precious Auntie lit the candle lamp and hung it on a pole left by one of her clan long ago.

8   On the cave's floor, there were digging tools—iron wedges of different sizes, hammers and claws—as well as sacks for dragging out the dirt. The walls of the cave were many layers, like an eight-treasure rice pudding cut in half, with lighter, crumbly things on top, then a thicker, muddy part like bean paste below, growing heavier toward the bottom. After centuries of people's digging, there was an overhang waiting to crash down and bite you in two, which was why the cave was called the Monkey's Jaw.

9   While we rested, Precious Auntie talked with her inky hands. *Stay away from that side of the monkey's teeth. Once they chomped down on an ancestor, and he was ground up and gobbled down with stones. My father found his skull over there. We put it back right away. Bad luck to separate a man's head from his body.*

10   Hours later, we climbed back out of the Monkey's Jaw with a sack of dirt and, if we had been lucky, one or two dragon bones. Precious Auntie held them up to the sky and bowed, thanking the gods. The bones from this cave, she believed, were the reason her family had become famous as bonesetters.

11   Precious Auntie's father was so talented that patients from the five surrounding mountain villages travelled to see him. Skilled and famous though he was, he could not prevent all tragedies. When Precious Auntie was four, her mother and older brothers died of an intestine-draining disease. The bonesetter was so ashamed of being unable to save his own family members that he spent his entire fortune and went into a lifetime of debt to pay for their funerals.

12   *Because of grief,* Precious Auntie said with her hands, *he spoiled me, let me do whatever a son might do. I learned to read and write, to ask questions, to play riddle games, to write eight-legged essays, to walk alone and admire nature. The old biddies used to warn him that it was dangerous, and they asked why he didn't bind my feet. My father was used to seeing pain of the worst kinds. But with me he was helpless. He couldn't bear to see me cry.*

13   So Precious Auntie freely followed her father around in his study and shop. A customer could point to any jar on the shelves and she could read the name of its contents. By the time she passed into maidenhood, she had heard every kind of scream and curse. She had touched so many bodies, living, dying, and dead, that few families would consider her as a bride for their sons.

14   One night, as we ate dinner in the Liu compound, with Mother, my younger sister Gao Ling, and the rest of the family, Precious Auntie told me a story with her hands, which only I could understand. *A rich lady came to my father and told him to unbind her feet and mold them into modern ones. She said she wanted to wear high-heeled shoes. "But don't make the new feet too big,"* she said, *"not like a slave girl's or a foreigner's. Make them naturally small like hers."* *And she pointed to my feet.*

15   I'd forgotten that Mother and my other aunts were at the dinner table, and I said aloud, "Do bound feet look like white lilies, the way the romantic books say?" Mother, who had bound feet, frowned at me. How could I talk so openly about a woman's most private parts? So Precious Auntie pretended to scold me with her hands for asking such a question, but what she really said was this: *They're usually cramped like flower-twist bread. But if they're dirty and knotty with calluses, they look like rotten ginger roots and smell like the snouts of pigs three days dead.*

16   In this way, Precious Auntie taught me to be naughty, just like her. She taught me to be curious, just like her. She taught me to be spoiled. And because I was all these things, she could not teach me to be a better daughter, though she tried to.

17   I remember how she tried. The last week we were together, she did not speak to me. Instead, she wrote and wrote and wrote. Finally she handed me a bundle of pages laced together with cord. *This is my true story, Lu Ling,* she told me, *and yours as well.* Later, when I read them, this is what I learned.

18   One late-autumn day, when Precious Auntie was nineteen, her Chinese age, her father had two new patients. The first was a screaming baby from a family that lived in Immortal Heart. The second was my father's youngest brother. We called him Baby Uncle. They would both cause Precious Auntie everlasting sorrow, but in entirely different ways.

19   The bawling baby was the youngest son of a big-chested man named Chang, a coffin-maker who had grown rich in times of plague. The carved outsides of his coffins were camphor wood. But the insides were cheap pine, painted and lacquered to look and smell like the better wood.

20   Some of that camphor wood had fallen onto the baby and knocked his shoulder out of its socket. That's why the baby was now howling, Chang's wife reported with a frightened face. Two years before, she had visited the bonesetter's shop because her eye and jaw had been broken by a stone that, she said, must have dropped out of the open sky. Now she was here with her husband, who was slapping the baby's leg, telling him to stop his racket. Precious Auntie shouted at Chang, "First the shoulder, now you want to break his leg as well!" Chang scowled. Precious Auntie rubbed a little bit of medicine inside the baby's cheeks. Soon the baby quieted down, yawned once, and fell asleep. Then the bonesetter snapped the small shoulder into place.

21   "What's the medicine?" the coffin-maker asked Precious Auntie. She didn't answer.

22   "Traditional things," the bonesetter said. "A little opium, a few herbs, and a special kind of dragon bone we dig out from the Monkey's Jaw, a secret place only our family knows."

23   "Special dragon bone, eh?" Chang dipped his finger in the medicine bowl, then dabbed it inside his cheek. He offered some to Precious Auntie, who sniffed in disgust, and then he laughed and gave Precious Auntie

a bold look, as if he owned her and could do whatever he pleased. In those days, a well-to-do husband was always looking for a second wife.

24   Right after the Changs and their baby left, Baby Uncle limped in. His name was Liu, he said, Liu Hu Sen. He had been on his way from his family's ink shop in Peking to their home in Immortal Heart, when his horse spooked, throwing him, so he decided, "Better take myself right to the Famous Bonesetter in the Mouth of the Mountain." Precious Auntie was in the back room and could see the young ink-maker through a parted curtain. He was a thin man in his early twenties. His face was refined, but he did not act pompous or overly formal, and, while his gown was not that of a rich gentleman, he was well groomed. She heard him joke with her father about his accident: "My mare was so crazy with fright I thought she was going to gallop straight to the underworld with me stuck astride."

25   When Precious Auntie stepped into the room, she said, "But fate brought you here instead." Baby Uncle fell quiet. When she smiled, he forgot his pain. When she put a dragon-bone poultice on his naked foot, he decided to marry her. That was Precious Auntie's version of how fast their love grew.

26   The next morning, Baby Uncle came back with three stemfuls of lychees for Precious Auntie, to show his gratitude. He peeled off the shell of one, and she ate the white-fleshed fruit in front of him. The morning was warm for late autumn, they both remarked. He asked if he could recite a poem he had written that morning. "You speak," he said, "the language of shooting stars, more surprising than sunrise, more brilliant than the sun, as brief as sunset. I want to follow your trail to eternity."

27   Later that week, unbeknownst to each other, both men went to fortune-tellers to find out if there were any bad omens for marriage.

28   Chang went to a fortune-teller in Immortal Heart, a man who walked about the village with a divining stick. The marriage signs were excellent for a second wife, this fortune-teller said. See here, Precious Auntie was born in a Rooster year, and Chang was a Snake—nearly the best match possible. The old man said that Precious Auntie also had a lucky number of strokes in her name. And as a bonus, she had a mole in position eleven, near the fatty part of her cheek, indicating that only sweet words fell from her obedient mouth. Chang was so happy to hear this that he gave the fortune-teller a big tip.

29   Baby Uncle went to a fortune-teller in the Mouth of the Mountain, an old lady with a face more wrinkled than her palm. She saw nothing but calamity. The first sign was the mole on Precious Auntie's face. It was in position twelve, she told Baby Uncle, and it dragged the girl's mouth down, meaning that her life would always bring her sadness. What's more, she was a fire Rooster, and he a wood Horse, and the combination of birth years was inharmonious. The girl would ride his back and peck him apart piece by piece. The fortune-teller confided to Baby Uncle that she knew the girl quite well. She often saw her on market days, walking by

herself; the girl did fast calculations in her head and argued with merchants. She was arrogant and headstrong, too educated. Better find another match, the fortune-teller said. This one will lead to disaster.

30   Baby Uncle gave the fortune-teller more money, to make her think harder. The fortune-teller kept shaking her head. But after Baby Uncle had given her a total of a thousand coppers, the old lady finally had another thought. When the girl smiled, which was often, her mole was in a luckier position, number eleven. The fortune-teller consulted an almanac, matched it to the hour of the girl's birth. Good news. The Hour of the Rabbit was peace-loving. Her inflexibility was just a bluff. And any leftover righteousness could be beaten down with a strong stick. "But don't marry in the Dragon Year. Bad year for a Horse."

31   The first marriage proposal came from Chang's matchmaker, who went to the bonesetter and related the good omens. The matchmaker boasted of the coffin-maker's standing, as an artisan descended from noted artisans. She described his house, his rock gardens, his fish ponds, the furniture in his many rooms, how the wood was of the best color, purple like a fresh bruise. As to the matter of a dowry, the coffin-maker was willing to be more than generous. Since the girl was to be a second wife and not a first, couldn't her dowry be a jar of opium and a jar of dragon bones? This was not much, yet it was priceless, and therefore not insulting to the girl.

32   The bonesetter considered the offer. He was growing old. Where would his daughter go when he died? What man would want her? She was too spirited, too set in her ways. She had no mother to teach her the manners of a wife. True, the coffin-maker was not the bonesetter's first choice for a son-in-law, but he did not want to stand in the way of his daughter's future happiness. So he told Precious Auntie about Chang's generous offer.

33   Precious Auntie huffed. "The man's a brute," she said. "I'd rather eat worms than be his wife."

34   The bonesetter had to give Chang's matchmaker an awkward answer. "I'm sorry," he said, "but my daughter cried herself sick, unable to bear the thought of leaving her worthless father." The lie would have been swallowed without disgrace, if only Baby Uncle's offer had not been accepted the following week.

35   A few days after the betrothal was announced, the coffin-maker went back to the Mouth of the Mountain and surprised Precious Auntie as she was returning from the well. "You think you can insult me, then walk away laughing?"

36   "Who insulted whom? You asked me to be your concubine, a servant to your wife. I'm not interested in being a slave in a feudal marriage."

37   As she tried to leave, Chang grabbed her by the neck, pinched it, saying he should break it, then shook her as if he truly might snap off her head like a winter twig. But instead he threw her to the ground, cursing her and her dead mother's private parts. And he said these words, which she never forgot: "You'll soon be sorry every day of your miserable life."

38   Precious Auntie did not tell her father or her beloved Baby Uncle what had happened. No sense in worrying them. And why lead her future husband to wonder if Chang had reason to feel insulted? Too many people had said she was too strong, accustomed to having her own way. And perhaps this was true.

39   A month before the wedding, Baby Uncle came to her room late at night. "I want to hear your voice in the dark," he whispered. "I want to hear the language of shooting stars." She let him into her *kang* and he eagerly began the nuptials. But as Baby Uncle caressed her, a wind blew over her skin and she began to tremble and shake. For the first time, she realized, she was afraid, frightened by unknown joy.

40   The wedding was supposed to take place in the Liu family compound in Immortal Heart. It was soon after the start of the New Year, a bare spring day. For the journey there from Mouth of the Mountain, Precious Auntie changed her clothes to her bridal costume—a red jacket and skirt, the fancy headdress with a scarf that she had to drape over her face once she left her father's home. For the journey, the bonesetter had procured only the best for his daughter: an enclosed sedan chair for the bride herself, four sedan carriers, two men with carts, a flute player, and two of the strongest bodyguards, with real pistols and gunpowder, to watch out for bandits. In one of the carts was the dowry—the jar of opium and the jar of dragon bones, the last of his supply. He assured his daughter many times that she need not worry about the cost. After her wedding, he could go to the Monkey's Jaw and gather more bones.

41   Halfway to Immortal Heart, two bandits wearing hoods sprang out of the bushes. "I'm the famous Mongol Bandit!" one of them bellowed. Right away, Precious Auntie recognized the voice of Chang the coffin-maker. What kind of ridiculous joke was this? But before she could say anything, the guards threw down their pistols, the carriers dropped their poles, and Precious Auntie was thrown to the floor of the sedan and knocked out.

42   When she came to, Baby Uncle was lifting her out of the sedan. She looked around and saw that the wedding trunks had been ransacked and that the guards and carriers had fled. And then she noticed her father lying in a ditch, his head and neck at an odd angle, the life gone from his face. Was she in a dream? "My father," she moaned. As she bent over the body, unable to make sense of what had happened, Baby Uncle picked up a pistol that one of the guards had dropped.

43   "I swear I'll find the demons who caused my bride so much grief!" he—shouted, and then he fired the pistol toward Heaven, startling his horse.

44   Precious Auntie did not see the kick that killed Baby Uncle, but she heard it—a terrible crack, like the opening of the earth. For the rest of her life she was to hear it in the breaking of twigs, the crackling of fire, whenever a melon was split in two.

45   That was how Precious Auntie became a widow and an orphan on the same day. Baby Uncle's family took her into their home in Immortal

Heart—how could they not?—until plans for a double funeral could be made. For three sleepless days, Precious Auntie apologized to the corpses of her father and Baby Uncle. She talked to their still faces. She touched their mouths, though this was forbidden.

46   On the third day, Chang arrived at the Liu family home with two coffins. "He killed them!" Precious Auntie cried when she caught sight of him. She picked up a fire poker and tried to strike him. She beat at the coffins. Baby Uncle's brothers had to wrestle her away. They apologized to Chang for the girl's lunacy, and Chang replied that grief of this magnitude was admirable. Because Precious Auntie continued to be wild with admirable grief, the women of the house had to bind her from elbows to knees with strips of cloth. Then they laid her on Baby Uncle's *kang*, where she wiggled and twisted like a butterfly stuck in its cocoon until Great Granny forced her to drink a bowl of medicine that made her body grow limp. For two days and nights she dreamed she was with Baby Uncle, lying on the *kang* as his bride.

47   When she revived, she was alone in the dark. Her arms and legs had been unbound, but they were weak. The house was quiet. Weeping, she vowed to join her father and Baby Uncle in the yellow earth. In the ink-making studio, she went looking for a length of rope, a sharp knife, matches she could swallow, anything to cause pain greater than what she already felt. And then she saw a pot of black resin. She lowered a dipper into the liquid and put it in the maw of the stove. The oily ink became a soup of blue flames. She tipped the ladle and swallowed.

48   Great Granny was the first to hear the thump-bumping sounds, and she hurried to the studio with the other women of the household. They found Precious Auntie thrashing on the floor, hissing air out of a mouth blackened with blood and ink. "Like eels are swimming in the bowl of her mouth," Mother said. "Better if she dies."

49   But Great Granny did not let this happen. Baby Uncle's ghost had come to her in a dream and warned that if Precious Auntie died, he and his ghost bride would roam the house and seek revenge on those who had not pitied her. Day in and day out, Great Granny dipped cloths into ointments and laid these over Precious Auntie's burns. Over the next few months, the wounds changed from pus to scars. Precious Auntie had once been a fine-looking girl. Now all except blind beggars shuddered at the sight of her. But Great Granny continued to care for Precious Auntie: she bought dragon bones, crushed them, and sprinkled them into her swollen mouth. And eventually she noticed that another part of Precious Auntie had become swollen: her womb.

50   In the year 1929, my fourteenth year, I read Precious Auntie's story for the first time. Earlier that same year, the scientists, both Chinese and foreign, came to Dragon Bone Hill, at the Mouth of the Mountain. They wore sun hats and Wellington boots. They brought shovels and poking sticks, sorting pans and fizzing liquids. They dug in the quarries; they burrowed in the caves. They went from medicine shop to medicine shop,

buying up all the old bones. Then some of the Chinese workers who dug for the scientists passed along a rumor that two of the dragon bones might have been teeth from a human head. Some people stopped buying dragon bones. Big signs in the medicine shops declared, "None of our remedies contain human parts."

51   At the time, Precious Auntie still had four or five dragon bones left from our visits to the cave at the Monkey's Jaw. Soon after this, her father, the Famous Bonesetter, came to her in a dream. "The bones you have are not from dragons," he said. "They are from our own clan, an ancestor who was crushed in the Monkey's Jaw. That's why nearly everyone in our family has died—your mother, your brother, myself, your future husband—because of this curse. Return the bones, or he'll continue to plague us."

52   The next morning, Precious Auntie rose early to return the dragon bones to the Monkey's Jaw. When she returned, she seemed more at ease. But then the workmen passed along this news: "The teeth are not only human but belong to a piece of skull from our oldest ancestors, one million years old!" Peking Man was what the scientists decided to call the section of skull. They needed to find just a few more pieces to make a whole skull, and a few more after that to connect his skull to his jaw, his jaw to his neck, his neck to his shoulders, and so on, until he was a complete man. That was why the scientists were asking the villagers to bring all the dragon bones they had lying around their houses and medicine shops. If the dragon bones proved to be from ancient humans, the owner would receive a reward.

53   I knew where there were human bones, and yet I could say nothing. I had to watch as others gouged the ground where their sheep chewed grass. From the muck, they yanked out roots and worms. They guessed that these might be ancient men's finger and toes, or even the fossilized tongue that spoke the first words of our ancestors. In a short while, our village looked worse than a burial ground dug up by grave robbers.

54   Day and night, the family talked of Peking Man and almost nothing else. "Million years?" Mother wondered aloud. "How can anyone know the age of someone who has been dead that long? *Hnh,* when my grandfather died, no one knew if he was sixty-eight or sixty-nine."

55   I, too, had something to say: "Why are they calling him Peking Man? The teeth came from the Mouth of the Mountain. And now the scientists are saying that skull was a woman's. So it should be called Woman from the Mouth of the Mountain." My aunts and uncles looked at me, and one of them said, "Wisdom from a child's lips, simple yet true." I was embarrassed to hear my words spoken of so highly. Then my sister Gao Ling added, "I think he should be called Immortal Heart Man. Then our town would be famous and so would we." Mother praised her suggestion to the skies, and the others joined in. To my mind, her idea made no sense, but I could not say this.

56   I was often jealous when Gao Ling received more attention from our mother. I was the elder daughter. I was smarter. I had done better in

school. Yet Gao Ling had the honor of sitting next to Mother, of sleeping in her *kang*, while I shared Precious Auntie's room and her *kang*.

57   When I was younger, that had not bothered me. I felt I was lucky to have my nursemaid by my side. I thought the words "Precious Auntie" were what others meant by "Ma." I could not bear to be separated from Precious Auntie for even one moment. I admired her and was proud that she could write the names of every flower, seed, and bush, as well as explain their medicinal uses. But the bigger I grew, the more she shrank in importance: Precious Auntie was only a servant, a woman who held no great position in our household, a person no one liked.

58   Often I complained to Precious Auntie that Mother did not love me. *Stop your nonsense,* Precious Auntie would answer. *Didn't you hear her today? She said your sewing was sloppy. And she mentioned your skin was getting too dark. If she didn't love you, why did she bother to criticize you for your own good?* And then Precious Auntie went on to say how selfish I was, always thinking about myself. She criticized me so much that, although I did not realize it then, I now know that she was saying she loved me even more.

59   One day—this was sometime before Spring Festival—Old Cook came back from the market and said big news was flying through Immortal Heart. We were working in the ink studio as usual, all the women and girls of our family, everyone except Precious Auntie, who was in the root cellar, counting the ink sticks she had already carved. Old Cook went on: Chang the coffin-maker had become famous and was soon to be very rich. Those dragon bones he had given to the scientists? The results had come back: they were human. How old was not certain yet, but everyone guessed they were at least a million years, maybe even two.

60   "What a peculiar coincidence," one of my aunts now said. "The same Mr. Chang who sells us wood. His luck could have been ours just as easily."

61   "Our association goes back even further than that," Mother boasted. "He was the man who stopped his cart to help after Baby Uncle was killed by the Mongol bandits. A man of good deeds, that Mr. Chang."

62   Precious Auntie came back to the ink studio, and in a short while she realized who was being talked about. She stamped her feet and punched the air. *Chang is evil,* she said, her arms flailing. *He killed my father. He is the reason Baby Uncle is dead. And the bones, those are the ones he stole from my dowry, the bones of our ancestors who died in the Monkey's Jaw.*

63   That was not true, I thought. Her father had fallen off a cart when he was drunk, and Baby Uncle had been kicked by his own horse. Mother and my aunts had told me so. The Liu family had taken her in because they were too kindhearted for their own good.

64   I remember the day Mother received a surprise letter from Peking. It was the period of Great Heat, when mosquitoes were happiest. Great Granny had been dead for more than ninety days. We sat in the shade of the big tree in the courtyard, waiting to hear the news.

65   We all knew the letter writer, Old Widow Lau. She was a cousin, within eight degrees of kinship on Father's side and five degrees on Mother's side. She had come to Great Granny's funeral, and had wailed as loudly as the rest of us.

66   Since Mother could not read, she asked Gao Ling to, and I had to hide my disappointment. Gao Ling smoothed her hair, cleared her throat, and licked her lips. "Dear Cousin," she read, "I send greetings from all those who have asked after you with deep feeling." Gao Ling then stumbled through a long list of names, from those of brand new babies to people Mother was sure were already dead. On the next page, our old cousin wrote something like this: "I know you are still in mourning and barely able to eat because of grief. So it is not a good time to invite everyone to come visit in Peking. But I have been thinking about what you and I discussed when we last saw each other, and I wish humbly to suggest that your number-one daughter"—she was speaking of me, and my heart swelled—"come to Peking and accidentally meet a distant relation of mine." Gao Ling threw me a scowl, and I was pleased that she was jealous. "This relation," Gao Ling continued, in a less enthusiastic voice, "has four sons who are seventh cousins of mine. They live in your same village, but are barely related to you, if at all."

67   When I heard the words "barely related," I knew this accidental meeting meant she wanted to see whether I might be a marriage match for a certain family. Most girls my age were already married. As to which family she was speaking of, Old Widow Lau did not want to say, unless she knew for certain that our family believed such a meeting could be beneficial. "To be honest," she wrote, "I would not have thought of this family on my own. But the father came to me and asked about Lu Ling. Apparently, they have seen the girl and are impressed with her beauty and sweet nature."

68   My face flushed. At last, Mother knew what others were saying about me. Perhaps she might finally see these good qualities in me.

69   "I want to go to Peking, too," Gao Ling said like a complaining cat.

70   Mother scolded her: "Did anyone invite you? No? Shut your mouth, then." Mother yanked her braid before handing me the letter to finish reading.

71   I sat up straight, facing Mother, and read with much expression, "The family suggests a meeting at your ink shop in Peking." I stopped a moment and smiled at Gao Ling. I had never seen the shop, nor had she. "In this way," I continued, "if there is any disharmony of interest, there will be no public embarrassment for either family. If both families are in agreement about the match, then this will be a blessing from the gods, for which I can take no credit."

72   "No credit," Mother said with a snort, "just a lot of gifts."

73   The next part of the letter went like this: "My daughter-in-law suggested that your daughter's nursemaid should not accompany her to Peking. If a person were to see the two together, he would remember only the shocking ugliness of the nursemaid and not the emerging beauty of the maiden. I told her that was nonsense, and scolded her for being

coldhearted. But as I write this letter, I realize now that it would be inconvenient to accommodate another servant, since mine already complain that there is not enough room to sleep in the bed they share. . . ."

74   Only when I was done reading did I look up at Precious Auntie, embarrassed. *Never mind,* she signed to me. *I'll tell her, later, that I can sleep on the floor.* I turned to Mother, waiting to hear what she had to say.

75   "Write back. Tell Old Widow Lau that I will have you go in a week. I'd take you myself, but it's our busiest season and we have too much to do. I'll ask Mr. Wei to take you in his cart. He always makes a medical delivery to Peking on the first and won't mind an extra passenger in exchange for a little cash."

76   Precious Auntie flapped her hands for my attention. *Now is the time to tell her you can't go alone. Who will make sure it's a good marriage? What if that busybody idiot cousin tries to barter you off as a second wife to a poor family? Ask her to consider that.* I shook my head. I was afraid to anger Mother with a lot of unnecessary questions and ruin my chance to visit Peking.

77   Later, Precious Auntie handed me a letter, which I was supposed to give to Gao Ling so she could read it to Mother. I nodded, and as soon as I was out of the room, I read it: "The summer air in Peking is full of diseases, and there are strange ailments we have never even experienced here, maladies that could make the tips of Lu Ling's nose and fingers fall off. Luckily, I know the remedies for such problems, so Lu Ling will not return bringing an epidemic with her. . . ." When Precious Auntie asked me if I had given Gao Ling the letter for Mother, I made my face and heart a stone wall. "Yes," I lied. Precious Auntie sighed, relieved. This was the first time she believed a lie of mine.

78   The night before I was to leave, Precious Auntie stood before me with the letter, which she had found in a pocket of my jacket. *What is the meaning of this?* She grabbed my arm.

79   "Leave me alone," I protested. "You can't tell me what to do anymore."

80   *You think you're so smart? You're still a silly baby.*

81   "I'm not. I don't need you now."

82   *If you had a brain, then you wouldn't need me.*

83   "You want to keep me here only so you won't lose your position as nursemaid."

84   Her face turned dark, as if she were choking. *Position? You think I am here only for a lowly position as your nursemaid? Ai-ya! Why am I still alive to hear this child say such things?*

85   Our chests were heaving. And I shouted back what I had often heard Mother and my aunts say: "You're alive because our family was good and took pity on you and saved your life. We didn't have to. Baby Uncle never should have tried to marry you. It was bad luck. That's why he was killed by his own horse. Everyone knows it."

86   Her whole body slumped, and I thought she was acknowledging that I was right. At that moment, I pitied her in the same way I pitied beggars I could not look in the eye. I felt I had grown up at last, and she had lost

her power over me. It was as if the old me were looking at the new me, admiring how much I had changed.

87   The next morning, Precious Auntie did not help me with my bundle of clothes. She did not prepare a lunch I could take along. Instead, she sat on the edge of the *kang*, refusing to look at me. Two hours before day-break, Mr. Wei came by, his donkey loaded with cages of snakes for med-icine shops. I tied on a scarf, to keep the sun off my face. As I climbed into the cart next to him, everyone except Precious Auntie was standing at the gate to see me off. Even Gao Ling was there, with her face unwashed. "Bring me back a doll," she shouted. At thirteen, she was still such a baby.

88   The day was a long ride of never-ending dust. Whenever the donkey stopped to drink water, Mr. Wei dipped a large rag into the stream and wrapped it around his head to keep himself cool. Soon I was doing the same with my scarf.

89   In the late afternoon, we approached Peking, and I instantly revived from the effects of the heat and my hunger. When we entered the inspec-tion station, a policeman with a cap poked through my small bundle and looked inside the cages with Mr. Wei's snakes.

90   "What is your reason for being in Peking?" the policeman asked.

91   "Delivery of medicine." Mr. Wei nodded to the snake cages.

92   "Marriage," I answered truthfully, and the policeman turned to another and called out my answer and they both laughed. After that, they let us continue. Soon I saw a tall memorial archway in the distance, its gold letters glinting like the sun. We passed through and entered a road-way as wide as the greatest of rivers. Rickshaws raced by, more than I had seen in a lifetime. I saw men in loose-weave long jackets, others in West-ern suits. Those men looked more impatient, more important than the men in our village. And there were many girls in floating dresses, wear-ing hair styles like those of famous actresses, the fringe in front crimped like dried noodles. I heard a crisp crack, saw the freshly opened gut of a more delicious-looking melon than any we could buy in our town.

93   "If you gawk any more, your head will twist right off," Mr. Wei said. I kept tallying the sights in my head so I could tell everyone all that I had seen. I was imagining their awe, Mother's admiration, Gao Ling's envy. I could also see the disappointment in Precious Auntie's face. So I pushed her out of my mind.

94   Finally we stood in front of the gate on Lantern Market Street that led into the cramped courtyard of Old Widow Lau's house. Two dogs ran toward me, barking.

95   "*Ai!* Are you a girl or a yellow-mud statue?" Old Widow Lau said in greeting. Dirt ringed my neck, my hands, every place where my body had a crease or a bend. I stood in a four-walled courtyard compound that was so chaotic that my arrival attracted almost no notice. Right away, Old Widow Lau handed me a beat-up bucket and told me where the well pump

was. As I filled the bucket, I took a sip of the water, but it was brackish, terrible-tasting. No wonder Precious Auntie had told me that Peking was once the wasteland of the bitter sea. Just then, I realized this was the first time she had not been there to help me with my bath. Where was the tub? Where was the stove for warming the water? I was too scared to touch anything. I squatted behind a mat shed and poured cold water over my neck, angry with Precious Auntie for turning me into such a stupid girl.

96   When I next appeared before Old Widow Lau, she exclaimed, "Is your head just an empty eggshell? Why are you wearing a padded jacket and winter trousers? And what's the matter with your hair?"

97   How could I answer? That Precious Auntie had refused to help me prepare for the trip, and that I'd forgotten even a comb?

98   "What a disaster!" Old Widow Lau muttered. "Pity the family that takes in this stupid girl for a daughter-in-law." She hurried to her trunks to search among the slim dresses of her youth. At last she settled on a dress borrowed from one of her daughters-in-law, a lightweight *qipao* that was not too old-fashioned. It had a high collar, short sleeves, and was woven in the colors of summer foliage, lilac for the body, and leafy green for the trim and frog clasps. Old Widow Lau then undid my messy braids and dragged a wet comb through my hair.

99   Lantern Market Street was not far from our family's ink shop, where the meeting with the interested family was to take place. I soon found myself standing in front of its door, anxious to see Father. Old Widow Lau was paying the rickshaw driver—or rather, arguing with him that he should not charge us so much for an extra passenger, since I was still a small child. "Small child?" the driver said with a snort. "Where are your eyes, old woman?" I stared at the hem of the lilac dress I had borrowed, patted the neatly knotted bun at the back of my head. I was embarrassed but also proud that the driver thought I was a grownup woman.

100   The ink shop faced north and was quite dim inside. Father was busy with a customer, and did not see us at first. Big Uncle welcomed us and invited us to be seated. From his formal tone, I knew he did not recognize me. So I called his name in a shy voice. And he squinted at me, then laughed and announced our arrival to Little Uncle, who apologized many times for not rushing over sooner to greet us. They urged us to be seated at one of two tea tables for customers. Little Uncle brought hot tea and sweet oranges.

101   I tried to notice everything. Along the walls were display cases made of wood and glass, with silk-wrapped boxes inside. Father opened a box, took out an ink stick, set it on top of the glass case, and leaned over it with a customer. The stick had a top shaped like a fairy boat, and my father said, with graceful importance, "Your writing will flow as smoothly as a keel cutting through a glassy lake."

102   As he said this, Precious Auntie came back into my mind. I was remembering how she'd taught me that everything, even ink, had a purpose and a meaning. You cannot be an artist if your work comes without effort.

That is the problem with modern bottled ink. You do not have to think. You simply write what is swimming on the top of your brain, which is nothing but pond scum, dead leaves, and mosquito spawn. But when you push an ink stick along an inkstone, you take the first step to cleansing your mind and your heart. You push and you ask yourself, What are my intentions? What is in my heart that matches my mind?

103   Just as Old Widow Lau had planned, my prospective mother-in-law accidentally passed by the shop promptly at the scheduled time. The woman was younger than Mother. She had a stern countenance and she wore much gold and jade on her wrists, to show how valuable she was. When Old Widow Lau called to her, she acted puzzled at first, then delighted.

104   "What luck that we should run into you here," Old Widow Lau cried in a high voice. "When did you arrive in Peking ?. . . Oh, visiting a cousin? How are things back in Immortal Heart?" After we had recovered from our fake surprise, Old Widow Lau introduced the woman to Father and my uncles. I was concentrating so hard on not showing any expression whatsoever that I did not hear her name.

105   "This is my cousin's Elder Daughter, Liu Lu Ling," Old Widow Lau said. "She is visiting Peking this week. The family lives in Immortal Heart village, like yours, but they sell their ink in Peking. And as you can see," she said, sweeping her hand out to indicate the shop, "their business is not doing too bad."

106   "In part, we have your husband to thank," Father then said. "We buy much of our excellent wood from him."

107   "Really?" Old Widow Lau and the woman said at once.

108   "Burns down to the best resin. And he has also supplied us with coffins on less fortunate occasions, always of the best quality," Father continued.

109   So this was the wife of Chang the coffin-maker. As more exclamations of surprise rang out, I realized that Precious Auntie would never allow me to marry into this family. Then I reminded myself that this was not her decision to make.

110   "We, too, are thinking of starting a business in Peking," Mrs. Chang said.

111   "Is that so? Perhaps we can help you in some way," Father said politely.

112   As Mrs. Chang paused to consider the excellence of this idea, Father added, "In any case, I've been eager to talk to your husband about the dragon bones he contributed to the great scientific discovery of Peking Man."

113   Mrs. Chang nodded. "We were astonished that those ugly little bones were so valuable. Lucky we didn't eat them up as medicine."

114   Two evenings later, we went to the Changs' cousin's house for a Viewing the Moon party. I wore another borrowed dress. I sat quietly and did not eat much and talked even less. Mr. Chang had come up from Immortal Heart, and he and Father discussed Peking Man.

115   "All the pieces of the skull must stay in China," Father said. "That is not only proper, it's the agreement with the foreigners."

116   "Those foreigners," Chang said, "you can't trust them to keep their word. They'll find a way to sneak out some pieces. They'll find excuses, make new treaties, apply pressure."

117   "No treaty can change the fact that Peking Man is a Chinese man and should stay where he lived and died."

118   Suddenly Mr. Chang turned toward me. "Maybe one day you and I can collect more bones of Peking Man together. Then we can both be famous. How would you like that?"

119   I nodded eagerly.

120   The next day, I was a contented girl as I rode home. I had never felt so important. I had not shamed Old Widow Lau or my family. In fact, I had been a great success. My father had criticized me in small ways about unimportant matters. So I knew he was proud of me. Old Widow Lau had bragged to her daughters-in-law that I had the looks and manners to warrant ten proposals. She was certain I would receive an offer from the Changs within the week.

121   Though I had yet to meet the Changs' fourth son, who was back in Immortal Heart, I knew he was two years older than I was, and an apprentice in his father's coffin-making business. What's more, there had been talk of his expanding the business, just as our family had done, which meant I would live in Peking. During all these discussions, I did not ask if my future husband was smart, if he was educated, if he was kind. I did not think about romantic love. I knew nothing of that. But I did know that marriage had to do with whether I improved my station in life or made it worse. And, to judge by the Changs' manners and the jewelry the Chang wife wore, I was about to become a more important person. What could be wrong with that?

122   Mr. Wei came before dawn to take me back to Immortal Heart. On the way home, I began to dream about all the ways in which I had to change my life. I needed new clothes. And I should be more careful to keep my face out of the sun. I did not want to look like a dark little peasant girl. After all, we were artisans and merchants from an old clan, greatly respected.

123   Hours later, the cart climbed the last hill that hid Immortal Heart. I could hear the crowing of cocks, the yowling of dogs, all the familiar sounds of our village. As quickly as it takes to snap a twig—that's how fast the mind can turn against what is familiar and dear. There I was, about to arrive at my old home, and I was not filled with sentimental fondness for all I had grown up with. Instead, I noticed the ripe stench of a pig pasture, the pockmarked land dug up by dragon-bone dream-seekers. I saw how the women we passed had the same bland face, with sleepy eyes that were mirrors of their sleepy minds. They were country people, both naïve and practical, slow to change but quick to think that a disturbance of ants on the ground was a sign of bad luck from the gods. Even Precious Auntie seemed, to my mind, a sleepy-headed greasy hat from the country.

124   But as I pushed open the gate to our house my heart flew back into my chest, and I was filled with a longing to see Precious Auntie. I dashed into the front courtyard: "I'm home! I'm home already!" I went into the ink

studio, where I saw Mother and Gao Ling. "Ah, back so soon?" Mother said, not bothering to stop her work. "Cousin Lau sent me a note that the meeting went well, and the Changs will probably take you." Gao Ling wrinkled her nose and said, "*Cho!* You smell like the hind end of a donkey."

125   I went to the room I shared with Precious Auntie. Everything was in its usual place, the quilt folded just so at the bottom of the *kang*. But Precious Auntie was not there. I wandered from room to room, from little courtyard to little courtyard. With each passing moment, I felt more anxious to see her.

126   And then I heard a pot banging. She was in the root cellar, eager that I should know she was there. I peered down the steep ladder and into the tunnel. She waved, and as she climbed up from the shadows, I saw that she still had the figure of a girl. In the brief moment of seeing only half her face lit by the sun, she was again as beautiful as she had seemed to me when I was a small child. When she emerged from the hole, she put the pot down and stroked my face, then said with her hands, *Have you really come back to me?* She pulled my tangled braid and snorted. *Didn't take your comb? No one to remind you?* With spit on her finger, she rubbed dirt from my cheek.

127   I pulled away. "I can clean myself," I said.

128   She began to make hissing sounds. *Gone one week and now you're so grownup?*

129   I snapped back: "Of course. After all. I'm about to be a married woman."

130   *I heard. And not as a concubine but as a wife. That's good. I raised you well, and everyone can see that.*

131   I knew then that Mother had not told her the name of the family. She had to hear it sooner or later. "The family is the Changs," I said.

132   She made a choking sound, as if she were drowning. She rocked her head like a clanging bell. And then she told me with slashing hands, *You cannot. I forbid you.*

133   "It's not for you to decide!" I shouted back.

134   She slapped me, then pushed me against the wall. I pushed her back and stood tall, draining all expression out of my face, and this surprised her. We stared at each other, breathing hard and fast, until we no longer recognized each other. She dropped onto her knees, pounding her chest over and over, her sign for *useless.*

135   "I need to go help Mother and Gao Ling," I said, then turned from her and walked away.

136   Just as expected, the Changs asked our family if I could join theirs as a daughter-in-law. Mother decided that a few weeks would give her and my aunts enough time to sew quilts and clothes suitable for my new life. After Mother announced this news, she cried for joy. "I've done well by you," she said proudly. "No one can complain." Gao Ling cried as well. And though I shed some tears, not all of them were for joy. I would leave my

family, my home. I would change from a girl to a wife. And no matter how happy I was sure to be, I would still be sad to say goodbye to my old self.

137   Precious Auntie and I continued to share the same room, the same bed. But she no longer drew my bath or brought me sweet water from the well. She did not help me with my hair or worry over my daily health and the cleanliness of my fingernails. We slept at the farthest ends of the *kang*. And if I found myself huddled next to her familiar form, I quietly moved away before she awoke. Every morning she had red eyes, so I knew she had been crying. Sometimes my eyes were red, too.

138   A few days before I was supposed to leave to join the Changs, I awoke to find Precious Auntie sitting up, staring at me. She raised her hands and began to talk. *Now I will show you the truth.* She went to the small wooden cupboard and removed a package wrapped in blue cloth. She put this in my lap. Inside was a thick wad of pages, threaded together with string. She stared at me with an odd expression, then left the room.

139   I looked at the first page. "I was born the daughter of the Famous Bonesetter from the Mouth of the Mountain," it began. I glanced through the next few pages. And then I saw where it said, "Now I will tell you how bad this man Chang really is." I threw the pages down. I did not want Precious Auntie poisoning my mind anymore. So I did not read to the end; I did not get to the part where she said she was my mother.

140   During our evening meal, Precious Auntie acted as if I were once again helpless. She pinched pieces of food with her chopsticks and added these to my bowl. *Eat more,* she ordered. *Why aren't you eating? Are you ill? You seem warm. Your forehead is hot. Why are you so pale?*

141   After dinner, we all drifted to the courtyard as usual. Mother and my aunts were embroidering my bridal clothes. Precious Auntie was repairing a hole in my old trousers. She put down the needle and tugged my sleeve. *Did you already read what I wrote?*

142   I nodded, not wishing to argue in front of the others. My cousins, Gao Ling, and I played weaving games with strings looped around our fingers, and the evening wore on. All too soon it was time for bed. I waited for Precious Auntie to go first. After a long while, when I thought she might already be asleep, I went into the dark room.

143   Immediately Precious Auntie sat up and was talking to me with her hands.

144   "I can't see what you're saying," I said. And when she went to light the kerosene lamp, I protested, "Don't bother, I'm sleepy. I don't want to talk right now." She lit the lamp anyway. I went to the *kang* and lay down. She followed me and set the lamp on the ledge, crouched, and stared at me with a glowing face. *Now that you have read my story, what do you feel toward me? Be honest.*

145   I grunted. And that little grunt was enough for her to clasp her hands, then bow and praise the Goddess of Mercy for saving me from the Changs. Before she could give too many thanks, I added, "I'm still going."

146   For a long time, she did not move. Then she began to cry and beat her chest. Her hands moved fast: *Don't you have feelings for who I am?*

147   And I remember exactly what I said to her: "Even if the whole Chang family were murderers and thieves, I would join them just to get away from you."

148   She slapped her palms against the wall. And then she finally blew out the lamp and left the room.

149   In the morning, she was gone. But I was not worried. A few times in the past when she had become angry with me she had left like this, but she'd always come back. Let her be angry, then, I said to myself. She doesn't care about my future happiness. Only Mother does. That is the difference between a nursemaid and a mother.

150   These were my very thoughts as my aunts, Gao Ling, and I followed Mother to the ink-making studio to begin our work. As we entered the dim room, we saw a mess. There were stains on the walls. Stains on the bench. Long spills along the floor. Had a wild animal broken in? And what was that rotten, sweet smell? Then Mother began to wail. "She's dead! She's dead!" In the next moment, I saw Precious Auntie, the top half of her face limestone white, her eyes wild and staring at me. She was sitting propped up against the far wall.

151   "Who's dead?" I called to Precious Auntie. "What happened?" I walked toward her. Her hair was unbound and matted, and then I saw that her neck was clotted with flies. Her eyes followed me as I moved toward her, but her hands did not move. One held a knife that was used to carve ink sticks. Before I could reach her, a cousin pushed me aside so she could better gawk.

152   Of that day, this is all I remember. I didn't know how I came to be in my room, lying on the *kang*. When I woke up again, it was morning and Gao Ling was sitting on the edge of my *kang*. "No matter what," she said with a tearful face, "I promise to always treat you like a sister." Then she told me what had happened.

153   The day before, Mrs. Chang had come over. She was clutching a letter from Precious Auntie. It had arrived in the middle of the night. "What is the meaning of this?" the Chang woman wanted to know. The letter said that if I joined the Chang household, Precious Auntie would come to stay as a live-in ghost, haunting them forever. "Where is the woman who sent this?" Mrs. Chang demanded. And when Mother told her that the nurse-maid who'd written it had just killed herself, Mrs. Chang was terrified. She left scared out of her wits.

154   After that, Mother rushed over to the body, Gao Ling said. Precious Auntie was still propped up against the wall. "This is how you repay me?" Mother cried. "I treated you like a sister. I treated your daughter like my own." And she kicked the body, again and again, for not saying *thank you, sorry, I beg your pardon a thousand times.* "Mother was crazy with anger," Gao Ling said. "She told Precious Auntie's body, 'If you haunt us, I'll sell Lu Ling as a whore.'" After that, Mother ordered Old Cook to put the

body in a pushcart and throw it over the cliff. "She's down there," Gao Ling said. "Your Precious Auntie is lying in the End of the World."

155   When Gao Ling left, I still did not understand everything she had said, and yet I knew. I found the pages Precious Auntie had written for me. I finished reading them. At last, I read her words. *Your mother, your mother, I am your mother.*

156   That day, I went to the End of the World to look for her. As I slid down, branches and thorns tore at my skin. When I reached the bottom, I was feverish to find her. I heard the drumming of cicadas, the beating of vulture wings. I walked toward the thick brush, to where trees grew sideways just as they had fallen with the crumbling cliff. I saw moss, or was that her hair? I saw a nest high in the branches, or was that her body stuck on a limb? I came to a wasteland with rocky mounds, ten thousand pieces of her skull and bones. Everywhere I looked, it was as if I were seeing her, torn and smashed. I had done this. I was remembering the curse of her family, my family, the dragon bones that had not been returned to their burial place. Chang, that terrible man, wanted me to marry his son only so I would tell him where to find more of the dragon bones. How could I be so stupid as not to have realized this before?

157   I searched for her until dusk. By then, my eyes were swollen with dust and tears. I never found her. And as I climbed back up, I was a girl who had lost part of herself in the End of the World.

158   For five days I could not move. I could not eat. I could not cry. I lay in the lonely *kang* and felt the air leaving my chest. When I thought I had nothing left, my body still continued to be sucked empty. On the sixth day, I began to cry and did not stop, from morning until night. When I had no more feeling, I rose from my bed and went back to my life. I thought about what Precious Auntie had written, what she must have been thinking as she pushed the ink stick along the inkstone. She was taking the first step to clearing her mind and her heart. She pushed and pushed, asking herself, "What are my intentions? What is in my heart that will trickle into my daughter's foolish mind?"

159   *I am your mother,* she wrote. I read these words after she died. Yet I have a memory of her telling me with her hands. I can see her telling me with her eyes. When it is dark, she says this to me in a clear voice I have never heard. She speaks in the language of shooting stars.

Questions for Discussion

1. Explain the duties of a bonesetter.

2. Give examples of the geographically descriptive names of the Chinese cities and areas.

3. Why does Precious Auntie consider Chang's proposal of marriage an insult?

4. What do Chang and Baby Uncle have in common and what are their differences? What are the results of these commonalities? Why does Precious Auntie choose Baby Uncle instead of Chang, the coffin-maker?

5. How does Precious Auntie lose the ability to speak?

6. Why does Lu Ling reject Precious Auntie's advice about the trip to Peking?

7. In what ways is Lu Ling dependent on her nursemaid, Precious Auntie?

8. What is the source of Lu Ling's contentment after meeting the Changs? Why is she excited at the prospect of marrying into their family?

9. How and why does her trip to Peking change Lu Ling's attitude toward her home village of Immortal Heart and its people? Why is Lu Ling's trip to the End of the World both ironic and tragic?

10. What indicators early in the story suggest the true relationship between Precious Auntie and Lu Ling?

11. Explain the last line.

AMY TAN: A CRITICAL COMPANION [1]

E. D. HUNTLEY

Like a growing number of contemporary writers, Amy Tan crafts novels that resist facile and definitive classification into any of the conventional fictional genres. That the books are novels is widely acknowledged, although Tan has said that she intended *The Joy Luck Club* to be a collection of short stories. Readers and critics alike do, however, agree that Tan's work incorporates or echoes other genres including nonfiction and poetry. In fact, a significant source of the charm and artistry of the three Tan novels is their shape as fictional narratives that embrace elements of biography and autobiography, history and mythology, folk tale and Asian talk story, personal reminiscence and memoir. Tan's novels reify and reinterpret traditional genres by casting them in a variety of modes—realistic, comic, tragic, tragicomic, allegorical, fantastic, naturalistic, and heroic—that metamorphose seamlessly into each other in Tan's signature narrative style. Commentary is juxtaposed with memory, fable with history, pidgin English with California-speak, American culture with Chinese tradition, past with present in a collision of stories and voices and personalities, filtered through the point of view of an Asian American author who lives between worlds, who inhabits that border country known only to those in whose minds and sensibilities cultures clash and battle for dominance. Although Amy Tan's prose style is distinctively her own, she also owes a literary debt to other writers who, like her, inhabit the border country that shapes and inspires so many minority writers—writers who

---

[1]E. D. Huntley, *Amy Tan: A Critical Companion* (Westfort, Conn.: Greenwood Press, 1998. 219–31, 115–21.

derive their voices and narrative structures from their experiences in the neighborhoods of America's diaspora cultures.

Asian American Literature: A Definition

In 1982, Elaine Kim's ground-breaking study, *Asian American Literature: An Introduction to the Writings and Social Context,* essentially brought an entire body of little known literature into the American literary consciousness, and helped Asian American literature gain recognition as a significant body of writing with both a "new tradition" of literary creation and a discernible—and very fluid—canon. In her work, Kim defined Asian American literature as "published creative writings in English by Americans of Chinese, Japanese, Korean, and Filipino descent" (xi). Although that definition lost its currency as immigrants from Cambodia, Vietnam, India, Pakistan, and other Asian countries began to make their homes in the United States and to write about their experiences, one crucial element of Kim's definition still holds true. Asian American literature is the creative work of writers of Asian descent who identify themselves as Americans and who view their own experiences and the world through the dual lenses of their American identities and their ethnic roots. More specifically, Asian American literature "elucidates the social history of Asians in the United States" (xiii). Although, as Kim points out, Asian American literature "shares with most other literature thematic concerns such as love, desire for personal freedom and acceptance, and struggles against oppression and injustice" (xii–xiii), this body of literature also is the product of other distinctive cultural forces. Like African American writing, fiction, poetry, and drama by Asian Americans is shaped by racism—both overt and disguised—and its corollaries, prejudice and discrimination. Moreover, for most Asian American writers, the Old Country and its culture are neither ancient nor buried history but very much alive and integral to the present, either in their own lives or in those of their parents and grandparents. The immigrant experience looms large in the writing of Asian Americans, and with that experience comes questions about marginality and life on the border, as well as explorations of issues of biculturalism and language, and decisions about identity.

The Asian American Literary Tradition

The history of Asian Americans goes back to the nineteenth century when thousands of men left their families and homes in China, Japan, Korea, and the Philippines to seek their fortunes in the United States, a country that the Chinese referred to as *gum san* or "the Gold Mountain." Seeking opportunity and possibly wealth, these men found ready work on the railroad, in gold- and silver-mining towns, and in lumber camps in the Western United States, industriously setting about making lives for themselves and for the picture brides from China and Japan who eventually traveled to the United States to marry men they had never met. The earliest official immigrant arrivals seem to have been men from Guang-dong Province in China, although there exist records of Chinese sailors who stopped briefly in Baltimore in the late eighteenth century. Perhaps because they were first to arrive, the Chinese formed the largest Asian immigrant group, and they became the first Asians to experience insti-tutionalized discrimination when the Chinese Exclusion Act of 1882 was passed by Congress, barring the majority of Chinese from entering the United States. The only exceptions to the ban were businessmen, diplo-mats, teachers, and students. When the law expired, it was renewed for another decade. Similar laws passed in 1902 and 1904 made the Chinese exclusion permanent, and Chinese who were already in the United States not only were denied citizenship but also were abused, publicly denounced in the press and from the pulpit, vilified, and physically attacked and even killed. Not until 1943 was exclusion legally ended with the passage of the Magnuson Act, which allowed 105 Chinese immigrants to enter the United States legally each year and gave Chinese the privi-lege of earning citizenship through naturalization. The older generation that is portrayed in Amy Tan's novels represents that group of new Chinese immigrants—especially the women who had long been denied entry—who entered the United States after the war in the years immediately following the Magnuson Act.

Not surprisingly, Asian immigrants—whose straight black hair and yel-low-brown skin made them look different and who spoke languages that had no relation to Indo-European—seemed exotic and thus oddly fas-cinating to most Americans who were of European ancestry. Conse-quently, a number of stereotypical Asian characters became fixtures in certain forms of popular entertainment and literature. Racist images—the result of fear, ignorance, and xenophobia—were dominant, dissem-inated, and encouraged in a culture that feared that the increasing numbers of Chinese laborers, who were willing to work long hours at dif-ficult tasks for low wages, posed a threat to employment opportunities for white men. Many of these fictional Asians were "inscrutable," humor-lessly industrious, humble, patient, and inclined to say "Ah so" in response to nearly any comment or question that they presumably did not understand. The few who differed were aristocratic mandarins whose haughty demeanor and elegant carriage hinted at long acquaintance with a more ceremonious way of life in a mythical Old China. For decades, Charlie Chan, Fu Manchu, and Anna May Wong were the only Asians that many Americans had ever encountered, and their images remained indelibly etched into the American imagination and popular culture until well into the twentieth century.

Despite the popularity of Asian stock characters on stage and screen and in fiction, literary work by authors of Asian ancestry, while not unknown, was not particularly accessible or available, and much of what was published rapidly went out of print. Before their arrival in the United States, most Asian immigrants had belonged to economic or social classes that, in their home countries, would have provided them with little or no exposure to education, and certainly not to art and poetry, although a few might have learned some rudimentary reading and writing. On their arrival in America, they found employment that required them to labor up to twenty hours each day, often seven days a week, focusing all of their energies on the struggle to earn livelihoods for themselves as well as for their families who remained in China or Japan or Korea. Ignored on the job, and left to socialize among themselves, few Asian immigrants learned much English beyond the few phrases that were essential to basic communication in their jobs. Overworked, underpaid, housed in barely habitable structures in labor camps, deprived of educational opportunities, and widely discriminated against, most Asian immigrants endured bleak and joyless existences that stifled all creative or imaginative impulses. Hence, the dearth of imaginative writing from the earliest Asian Americans. Early immigrant writing—when it existed at all—generally took the form of letters and journals in languages other than English. Creative efforts, which were rare, resulted mainly in unfamiliar poetic genres such as *haiku* or *tanka*. In a poignantly significant series of attempts at artistic expression, anonymous Chinese immigrants who were detained at the Angel Island Detention Center after the passage of the Exclusion Act scrawled poetry on the walls, giving vent to their emotions and disappointments (Lim and Ling 5).

Although the Exclusion Act was directed at Chinese immigrants, negative Asian stereotypes were applied indiscriminately for decades not only to Chinese but also to Japanese, Korean, and Filipino immigrants. World War II changed those perceptions when international hostilities and American military losses in the Pacific unleashed waves of anti-Japanese propaganda, accompanied by sympathy for China and the Philippines. Because China was suffering the ravages of America's enemy, the Japanese army, the Chinese in America found themselves suddenly accepted as members of a "model minority" that was praised for loyalty to the United States.

In spite of the obstacles that barred the way to an Asian literary tradition in the United States, a few pieces of writing—chiefly memoirs—by Asians did appear as early as the end of the nineteenth century. The authors—mainly Chinese—had come to the United States as students, diplomats, or merchants, and were thus exempt from the Exclusion Act. Among the early books was a series of volumes by Western-educated young men of different countries, including two from China and Korea. These books, which were commissioned by the D. Lothrop Publishing Company, focused on elucidating for the benefit of the average American reader the cultural mores and traditional customs of the writers' native countries. Other autobiographies, written in the 1930s and 1940s, attempted to perform much the same anthropological function—to describe and explain to Western readers the more attractive elements of life in China: dress, food, festivals, sports, rituals and ceremonies, leisure activities, and daily life. Common to all of these personal accounts of life in China was their limited focus on the experiences of a privileged class, the members of which had nothing in common with the hordes of Asian laborers who spent their days patiently enduring their work in America's railroads, mines, and lumber camps. These early autobiographies and memoirs entranced American readers with descriptions of Chinese houses furnished with silk carpets and decorated with jade and porcelain artifacts, surrounded by gardens burgeoning with exotic blooms, meticulously maintained by happy, smiling servants who existed to make life easy and pleasant for the family who owned the house and land.

Among the most widely read of the Asian memoir-writers between the wars were three immigrant Chinese authors whose work is representative of the style of immigrant writing that American readers—and critics and reviewers—found not only acceptable but also immensely fascinating. The most prolific of these writers was Lin Yutang, who churned out scores of essays that are most notable for their gentle self-deprecating humor— at the expense not only of the author but also of his fellow Chinese—and for their genially superficial treatment of cultural issues and questions.

In a writing career that spanned about forty years, Lin Yutang claimed that his main purpose was to explain China and her people to Western readers. That he succeeded in reaching his target audience is evident in the popularity of his works, especially *My Country and My People* (1935), a book that went through four editions. The appeal of Lin's book for the majority of readers from the 1930s through the 1960s lies in its validation of a popular myth—the stereotype of the gently bred Chinese as naive, unworldly people who desired nothing more than to focus their energies and time on artistic and literary activities, and who submitted docilely to colonial rule because they lacked the motivation to govern themselves. Not surprisingly, more than a few Asian American readers took exception to Lin Yutang's portraits of China and the Chinese, claiming that Lin's books privileged a tiny percentage of the Chinese population—the affluent classes—and ignored the reality of the impoverished majority from whose ranks most Chinese immigrants came.

With a literary output that was far less voluminous than Lin Yutang's, Pardee Lowe and Jade Snow Wong nevertheless published highly regarded and extremely well-received memoirs of their experiences as Chinese immigrants growing up in America. Like Lin Yutang's books, Pardee Lowe's *Father and Glorious Descendant* (1943) and Jade Snow Wong's *Fifth Chinese Daughter* (1945 and 1950) describe an ethnic world in which existing stereotypes are confirmed and sanitized. Both books provided the predominantly white readership of the war years with a picture of Chinese American life that was both intriguing and easy to accept as genuine because it conformed to the mythical China that already existed in the popular American consciousness. Because he had enlisted in the U.S. Army, Lowe was praised for his patriotism and for the message of accommodation and assimilation that he disseminated through his memoirs.

As valuable as these works are in the history of Asian writing in the United States, they focus mainly on those immigrants whose antecedents had belonged to the privileged classes, and the prose and images appear dated to the late twentieth-century reader. The world of Lowe and Wong is populated with tea-sipping, poetry-writing aristocrats in beautiful, alien settings that exist only in a world that has receded into memory or survives only in the pages of forgotten volumes on neglected library shelves.

After the successes of Lowe and Wong, little by Asian American writers appeared for over two decades. In 1963, however, Virginia Lee's *The House That Tai Ming Built* revived the semi-autobiographical strain of immigrant writing popularized by Lowe and Wang. Like her predecessors, Lee portrayed a Chinese culture that did not represent the experience of the majority of Chinese Americans; nevertheless, like those earlier writers, Lee is important in the history of Asian American literary production. In their introduction to the first anthology of Asian American writing, Kai-yu Hsu and Helen Palubinskas comment on the work of Lowe, Wong, and Lee, which they describe as autobiographical and suggestive of

> the Chinese culture described in the connoisseurs' manuals of Chinese jade or oolong tea, and the stereotype of the Chinese immigrant, either withdrawn and totally Chinese, or quietly assimilated and unobtrusively American. (10)

Hsu and Palubinskas also caution against dismissing those early memoirs as irrelevant, pointing out that they have value for the student of Asian American literature. They assert that the three volumes of memoirs have a genuine claim to be considered landmarks in the development of a literary tradition by Asian Americans because "the authors wrote about the Chinese in America as they saw and understood them." Hsu and Palubinskas go on to issue a challenge: "Other Chinese-American writers, if they have different perceptions, should come forth with their stories" (10). Less than a decade after the publication of Lee's book, a vocal group of those "other [. . .] writers" emerged onto the American literary scene. But before they did so, their work was anticipated by Louis Chu whose 1961 novel, *Eat a Bowl of Tea*, first articulated some of the major concerns that would inform the work of later Asian writers.

Eat a Bowl of Tea is remarkable for its early treatment of the debilitating effects of racism and the patriarchal culture in Asian American communities. Set in 1947, two years after the War Bride Act of 1945 opened U.S. immigration to Chinese women, the novel examines the conflict between old-world patriarchal immigrant elders and their American-born children, a struggle that Ruth Hsiao describes as involving "emotionally damaged sons and daughters locked in battles of independence with their fathers or with the tradition that gives the fathers power" (54). Louis Chu foregrounds a nascent antipatriarchal movement through a complicated plot that portrays the traditional authoritarian father as a mere parody of the traditional patriarch. Hsiao points out that many consider Chu to be "a herald of the new Asian American sensibility" (153), although she criticizes his novel for suggesting in the end that patriarchy is an incurable condition in bicultural Asian communities and for positing "the birth of a new age patriarchy" (152). Nonetheless, it is clear that Chu does indeed prefigure not only the work of the writer-activists who would follow him in the next decade, but also the even more significant explosion of writing by Asian women that would mark the 1980s and 1990s.

The new Asian American writers of the 1970s were neither completely Asian nor definitively Western, but considered themselves to be members of a distinct new culture or set of cultures. Frank Chin, one of the new writers, articulated his position vis-à-vis the dominant landscape into which he was expected to assimilate by explaining the cultural force behind his writing:

> The sensibility, the kind of sensibility that is neither Chinese of China nor white-American. The sensibility derived from the peculiar experience of a Chinese born in this country some thirty years ago, with all the stigmas attached to his race, but felt by himself alone as an individual human being. (quoted in Hsu and Palubinskas 47)

The "sensibility" of which Chin speaks was shared by his peers, all of whom had grown up in a kind of ethnic limbo, belonging by heritage to a culture and homeland in which they were strangers, yet living and maturing in a culture that persisted in viewing them as Other, as alien and marginal. These writers incorporated their paradoxical condition—they were bicultural yet estranged from both cultures—into their poetry, fiction, and drama, producing a body of work that reflected a new Asian American voice that refused to mythologize ethnic origins or perpetuate stereotypes, yet avoided complete assimilation and in fact embraced difference on its own terms. For many of these writers, a crucial initiative of the decade was the attempt to redefine Asian American manhood and to counteract through their published writing what they perceived to have been the progressive cultural and psychological emasculation of the Asian male by the dominant culture.

Central to the activity of the 1970s was the work of a group called the Combined Asian Resources Project (CARP), whose members—Chin, Jeffery Paul Chan, Lawson Fusao Inada, Nathan Lee, Benjamin R. Tong, and Shawn Hsu Wong—actively sought publishing venues and performance spaces for the works of Asian American writers, created a collection of materials about those writers, found support for reissuing out-of-print works by the earliest Asian American writers, and sponsored literary conferences that focused on literary texts by Asian Americans. In addition, several valuable anthologies of writing by Asian Americans were published in the 1970s. The three best known of these anthologies are *Asian American Authors* (1972), edited by Kai-yu Hsu and Helen Palubinskas; *Aiiieeeee! An Anthology of Asian-American Writers* (1974), edited by CARP members

Frank Chin, Jeffery Paul Chan, Lawson Fusao Inada, and Shawn Hsu Wong; and *Asian American Heritage: An Anthology of Prose and Poetry* (1974), edited by David Hsin-fu Wand.

Although these anthologies made some Asian writing more accessible to larger numbers of readers, Asian American literature had its first significant impact on the popular American consciousness in 1976 when Maxine Hong Kingston published *The Woman Warrior,* her rivetingly powerful memoir about growing up Chinese in America. Kingston's book was well-received in literary circles, winning the National Book Critics Circle Award for the best nonfiction of 1976, and paved the way for the young writers of the next decade to prove conclusively that the Asian American voice had a powerful resonance far beyond Chinatown or Little Tokyo or the neighborhood enclaves of Korean or Filipino immigrants. Unfortunately, Kingston was condemned by some Asian American writers who accused her of trying to "cash in" on the "feminist fad," of writing only for financial gain by creating "white-pleasing autobiography passing for pop cultural anthropology" (Kim 198). However, Kingston's detractors, although articulate and vocal, are few—limited mainly to a few male writers of Asian descent who have continued to argue that the tremendous sales and widespread popularity enjoyed by Asian American women writers undermines the masculinity of their male colleagues.

Kingston ushered in the 1980s with *China Men* (1980), winning the American Book Award. During that decade, Asian American writers earned recognition for the excellence and importance of their work. Among poets, Cathy Song won the Yale Series of Younger Poets competition for *Picture Bride* in 1982, Garrett Hongo was awarded the Lamont Poetry prize of the Academy of American Poets in 1987, and Li-Young Lee was invited to read his poetry on National Public Radio. A new generation of playwrights graced the American stage: Genny Lim's *Island* (1985) was featured on National Public Television, and David Henry Hwang entranced Broadway audiences and won several Tony Awards for *M. Butterfly* in 1988. Into the growing market for and interest in Asian American writing came Amy Tan and *The Joy Luck Club* in 1989. The publication of that novel helped to catapult Asian American fiction into the literary mainstream when it appeared on national bestseller lists and became a featured book-club selection. By the end of the decade, many writers, including David Mura, Jessica Hagedorn, Philip Kan Gotanda, Ping Chong, Gish Jen, and Cynthia Kadohata discovered their work— along with that of Kingston and Tan—in textbook anthologies and on required reading lists for literature courses. Years later, the final pieces of evidence that Asian American writing has entrenched itself in the popular mind are the popular film versions of works by writers as diverse as Tan and Hwang, and memoir-writer Le-Ly Hayslip.

Partly because of the volume of their work and certainly because they write about subjects that resonate with so many mainstream readers, Chinese American women writers have been largely but inadvertently responsible for the new and sudden popularity of Asian American writing, a development that is made more startling because Chinese women were an almost invisible minority in American society until the early 1950s. Because most of them were kept out of the United States by laws specifically excluding Chinese women (including those who were married to American-born Chinese men) from immigration quotas, these women were outnumbered by Chinese men by approximately twenty to one. Given those numbers, we should not be surprised at the relatively small number of Chinese women writers in the first half of the twentieth century—in fact, we should be amazed that so many of the significant early Chinese American writers were women.

Chinese American Women Writers

The earliest successful Chinese American women authors were the Eurasian sisters Edith and Winnifred Eaton, daughters of an English artist and his Chinese wife. Although born in England, both Edith and Winnifred emigrated to the United States as adults, and it was as Americans that they began their writing careers. Despite their Caucasian features, the Eaton sisters used Asian pseudonyms: Edith became Sui Sin Far, Cantonese for "Narcissus," and Winnifred became the faux-Japanese Onoto Watanna. The sisters' choices are intriguing, particularly because Edith decided to emphasize their Chinese heritage despite the Chinese Exclusion Act and widespread prejudice against the Chinese, while Winnifred, by contrast, assumed the more acceptable Japanese identity. During the decades before World War II, the Japanese enjoyed widespread respect in the United States, and Winnifred enhanced the prestige of her assumed identity by claiming that her mother belonged to a noble Japanese family from Nagasaki.

The Eaton sisters' writing paralleled their pseudonymous identities. As Sui Sin Far, Edith wrote in defense of the much maligned Chinese, taking up the fight against racism and injustice, attempting in her short stories to portray Chinese characters sympathetically and without resorting to prevalent stereotypes. Her ironic examinations of American culture are not limited to the plight of the Chinese immigrant; she also focuses attention on prejudice based on gender and class, or on that cultural phenomenon that she exemplified—the individual of mixed heritage who belongs neither to one culture nor to the other. Winnifred's career was markedly different from that of her sister. Onoto Watanna's "Japanese novels" were romances set in exotic Orientalized landscapes, featuring delicate, winsome Japanese women and influential powerful men—often white men—to whom the heroine must appeal for help or protection. Unlike Edith, who used her pen as a weapon of protest, Winnifred's writing foregrounded and supported the status quo with its prejudices and cultural assumptions. So popular were Onoto Watanna's novels that they were translated into several European languages and went through several printings. They were adapted for the stage as well, and Winnifred eventually moved on to a highly successful career as a Hollywood scriptwriter.

Japan's attack on Pearl Harbor destroyed American readers' fascination with things Japanese and created a new acceptance of the Chinese, who were suddenly recognized as fellow victims of Japan's aggression. Several women—immigrants, American-born Chinese, American-raised Chinese—wrote novels and personal accounts about the devastating effects of the war on China, and about the strength and resilience of the Chinese people. Amy Ling points out that much of the war literature has a specifically defined purpose: "demonstration to the United States, a country superior in arms and supplies, that China was a worthy ally" ("Chinese American" 227). Among these writers were the three daughters of Lin Yutang—Adet and Anor, both of whom would have literary careers, and Mei-mei, the youngest and most Americanized. Also beginning their writing careers with personal accounts of the war were Han Suyin, Mai-mai Sze, and Helena Kuo. Although the war pieces received attention from readers who were chiefly concerned with discovering how the war was affecting some of America's Asian friends, it was Jade Snow Wong's *Fifth Chinese Daughter* that garnered the popularity and wide readership that the other works did not.

When the Exclusion Act was finally repealed in 1943, the increase in Chinese emigrating to the United States included significant numbers of women, and, as a result, the number of Chinese American women writers increased. Amy Ling and Elaine Kim, among others, have pointed out that despite the growing numbers of writers, Asian Americans' novels continued for a time to cater to the tastes of the predominantly white readership, looking with polite disfavor on Asian culture and enthusiastically embracing the American lifestyle.

There are two interesting exceptions to the tendency among early Asian writers in America to apologize for their ethnic backgrounds while commenting approvingly on Western culture. Han Suyin and Chuang Hua deserve mention for unapologetically examining the precarious balancing act performed by not only individuals who have both Asian and European or American blood but also Asians who are involved in interracial relationships. Herself of mixed blood, Han Suyin is a prolific writer with nearly two dozen titles—written over nearly half a century—in her oeuvre. Central to her most powerful novels are the problematic relationships between couples of different—and often antagonistic—ethnic and cultural backgrounds; and she underscores the tensions in such relationships by setting her novels in inherently contested territory that is unfamiliar to most of her readers. In Han Suyin's fiction, the cultural clashes involve Eurasian, American, Chinese, English, and Indian characters in settings as geographically diverse as Nepal, China under communism, and Hong Kong. Another writer, Chuang Hua, focuses her experimental novel, *Crossings* (1968), on life in that border country between cultures. Her protagonist, a Chinese woman who has grown up in England and the United States and spends time in France, falls in love with a European journalist, and their doomed affair is played out against the backdrop of the Korean War, which pits China and America against each other. Formally and structurally, Hua's novel is a forerunner of Maxine Hong Kingston's and Amy Tan's multiple genre approach to storytelling. In *Crossings,* the line of the narrative is ruptured time and again by autobiographical reminiscences, biographical elements, recounted dreams and nightmares, interior monologues, resulting in what Amy Ling calls "a highly original expression of the Chinese American hyphenated condition" (235).

As noted earlier, Maxine Hong Kingston's *Woman Warrior* took the American literary establishment as well as the reading public by surprise in 1975. In her text—which has been labeled variously talk-story memoir, autobiography, biography, novel—Kingston rejects the traditional linear fictional narrative structure, privileging instead a polyvocal mosaic of genres and styles that work together by both completing and contradicting each other, thus illustrating through content as well as form the collision between distinct and complex cultures. Writing about Kingston's work as the beginning of a new tradition in Asian American writing, Marlene Goldman points out that "Kingston's novel constitutes an alternative system for organizing experience, an activity directly related to the inscription of identity" (225). Kingston herself asserts that although *Woman Warrior* privileges women's circular narratives based on cultural memory and "old myths," the work itself is "much more American than Chinese" with characters who are "American people" (179). Indeed, the central theme in all of Kingston's writing is the attempt to sort out what being Chinese American means through the exploration of her experiences as an American-born child of immigrant parents.

By the time Amy Tan published her first novel, Maxine Hong Kingston had already introduced the general reading public to the talk-story narrative style. With her multiperspectival text, Tan was not only working in the traditions of her Chinese heritage and her Western training, but she also was following in the literary footsteps of a significant and powerful Asian American writer who had already begun to mine the rich vein of oral and written literary genres and traditions that exists within America's immigrant communities.

❧

Plot Development

The plot of *The Hundred Secret Senses* follows two narrative threads: Olivia's search for an integrated self, and Kwan's desire to undo the damage of a century-old mistake. Although the two are closely related, the connections between them do not immediately become obvious but emerge gradually as elements of each plot come to light and reveal echoes of the other.

Borrowing a technique from the classical epic, Amy Tan begins the novel *in medias res*, or—colloquially translated—in the middle of the action. Over a century earlier in China, Kwan—with the very best intentions—told a lie, fabricating a story that had the unforeseen effect of disrupting the lives of two people and abruptly terminating the romance that had begun between them. The plot that has Kwan at its center is the history of her previous existence as Nunumu; the events of her life gradually reveal the incidents that lead inexorably toward the mistake that separates Miss Banner and Yiban. Now in California, Kwan is devoting her energies to the cause of rectifying her mistake and reuniting the lovers. Meanwhile, in the narrative of Olivia's efforts to discover what she wants her life to become, Olivia and Simon already are separated and have initiated the legal transactions that will lead to divorce. Both women tell their stories, but whereas Olivia's narratives suggest interior monologues with a pervasive component of self-questioning and no identifiable audience, Kwan's stories—which are embedded in Olivia's—are clearly addressed to Olivia.

As Olivia sorts through the emotional chaos resulting from her separation from Simon, she repeatedly is reminded of the events of their courtship, the early years of their marriage, and their more recent attempts to revive the companionship they felt when they were younger. Because Simon was and is her first and only love, Olivia is not dealing well with the break-up of her marriage, and Kwan, who is still the protective older sister although they are both adults, worries constantly about Olivia, inviting her to dinner, dropping in for brief visits, offering the opinion that the separation is a mistake and that Olivia and Simon should reconcile. In the first half of the novel, each overture by Kwan prompts Olivia to remember a story that Kwan has told her, and each story told by Kwan in turn somehow returns the narrative to Olivia's emotional dilemma. With each new story, the outlines of connections become clearer. Initially, it appears that Kwan wants to bring the couple back together because she was responsible for the evening during which Elza—a *yin* person and Simon's first love who had been dead for a while—supposedly told Simon to forget her and to find happiness with Olivia. But Kwan's stories and everyday conversation are laced with oblique references to her belief that the rightness of Olivia's and Simon's union was determined by events in the distant past, and eventually Kwan manages to persuade Simon and Olivia to join her on a trip to China where, she points out mysteriously, they will discover the true pattern of their lives.

During the China trip, Olivia's and Kwan's narratives abruptly change. Removed from the familiar and confronted with a new culture, Olivia curtails her litany of past rejections and begins instead to detail events as they happen; and because she is in China, Olivia no longer has to rely on her memory of Kwan's stories—China is all around her to be experienced. Kwan, for her part, increases the number and frequency of her stories about Nunumu and Miss Banner, adding stories that Olivia has never heard—for instance, the story of Yiban and the last days in the Ghost

Merchant's house, or the tale of the flight to the mountains. Early in the novel, Kwan's stories emerge as Olivia's memories, but in the final chapters, Kwan tells her stories in the immediate present. Gone is the slow gentle rhythm of memory; each tale now is urgent, immediate, triggered by the sight of a mountain or the taste of a special dish or, ultimately, the very palpable presence of a music box that Kwan claims to have hidden in a cave over a century earlier. Kwan's final stories clarify connections: Olivia and Simon are Miss Banner and Yiban, and Kwan has brought them to Changmian to reunite them. The novel ends with an epilogue narrated by Olivia. She and Simon are working toward reconciliation. More important, they have a daughter who was conceived in China, and who is—Olivia firmly believes—Kwan's final gift to them.

Narrative Strategies

Tan employs the juxtaposition of past and present as a narrative device for her story of the indestructibility of love and loyalty. Past and present are so closely interrelated that Olivia ultimately admits to being occasionally confused about whether an event actually occurred or is merely an episode in one of Kwan's frequently recounted stories. Toward the end of the novel, as Olivia and Kwan turn over the contents of the ancient music box that the latter says she hid in a cave more than a hundred years earlier, Olivia's logical mind races from one explanation to another. Always the rational American woman of the 1990s, Olivia is inclined to doubt what her senses suggest; nevertheless, she cannot dismiss the fact of Kwan's unflinching candor. In their time together, Olivia has never known Kwan to lie; in fact, Kwan says only what she truly believes to be true. And although Olivia knows that she should believe Kwan even now, another question surfaces: "[I]f I believe what she says, does that mean I now believe she has *yin* eyes?" (320). At that moment, Olivia realizes what she has known, has in fact believed all along—since childhood—that Kwan does remember events, the memory of which defies rational explanation.

Events in the past clearly and significantly influence the lives of both Olivia and Kwan. They are sisters, thanks to Jack Yee's two marriages and the shameful act of thievery that provided him with the wherewithal to abandon a wife and child, to discard an identity, and to begin a new life and new family in America. Through her conversations with her *yin* friends about Olivia's marital problems, Kwan bridges the chronological gap between her two lives, and Olivia is forced to endure advice and comments on her marriage from a certain Lao Lu, a friend of Kwan's from the Taiping days in the Ghost Merchant's house. Not even Olivia's marriage is immune to the influence of the past: after nearly two decades of marriage, Simon still appears to be obsessed with his first love who was killed in an avalanche.

During the visit to China, Kwan becomes more and more insistent that she and Olivia have had a previous life together, and when the sisters are together on the mountain, Olivia begins to half believe that she does

indeed recognize in her present circumstances a series of strong reso-
nances from another time. Whether these frissons of memory are remnants of Kwan's stories or genuine recollections from Olivia's past is
immaterial. What is clear is that Olivia finds the more distinctive elements
of the Guilin landscape disturbingly familiar.

Present and past finally collide on a rain-drenched mountain just
beyond Changmian. Assailed from all directions by a cascade of sensory
and emotional stimuli (Kwan's final story about her last hours in the
nineteenth century, a hilly landscape that possesses a dreamlike familiarity combined with jarring strangeness, Simon's disappearance into the
cold mist, Kwan's rediscovery of the music box that she last saw when she
was Nunumu, and finally Kwan's revelation of the truth about Simon and
Elza), Olivia is drawn into an admission that her history with Kwan could
have begun near this mountain in an earlier century. It remains only for
Olivia to unearth the jars full of duck eggs that Kwan says Nunumu
buried during the Taiping troubles. As Olivia holds the ancient crumbling duck eggs in her cupped hands, the act liberates her from the
doubts that have undermined all of her relationships. And although
Kwan vanishes into the Changmian caves and is never found despite an
intensive and protracted search, Olivia believes that the daughter who is
born to her and Simon nine months later is a gift from Kwan. The child
is not Kwan, exactly, but she is connected with Kwan in some mysterious
way—and in that little girl, the past and the present are fused into wholeness and the future.

As she does in her other novels, Tan relies on formal storytelling as a
narrative strategy in *The Hundred Secret Senses*. Both Kwan's nineteenth-
century existence as Nunumu and her twentieth-century childhood in
Changmian before her emigration to America emerge through narrative
set pieces that Kwan performs as though they are legends or folktales,
artifacts of an oral tradition that she feels impelled to pass on to Olivia
who is her captive audience.

Tan uses the flashback technique to superb effect in the novel. New
words, chance remarks, familiar objects and mementos, the taste of traditional Chinese dishes, and celebrations trigger Kwan's recollections,
prompting her to narrate vignettes, brief tales, events, the particulars of
specific episodes in her former lives. In one instance, when she overhears the neighborhood children referring to her as "a retard" and
forces Olivia to define the word, Kwan suddenly is reminded of Miss Banner's early attempts to speak Chinese, and she tells Olivia that Nunumu
initially thought that Miss Banner's inability to speak or understand Chinese indicated a lack of intelligence. On occasion, Kwan says, Nunumu
actually laughed at Miss Banner's feeble attempts to converse in the ver-
nacular. The memory prompts Kwan immediately to launch into an
account of Miss Banner's first garbled description of her early life.
Because Miss Banner cannot speak adequate Chinese, she ends up thoroughly confusing Nunumu by telling an impossibly surrealistic story

about her origins, but Nunumu's patience with her mistress eventually results in her success at teaching Miss Banner how to view the world "exactly as a Chinese person" would (49).

By providing multiple versions of and varying perspectives on events that are central to the novel, Tan explores the ways through which storytellers create meaning on many levels and from different points of view. In some cases, the plurality of versions is the inadvertent result of misunderstandings, incomplete information, or even partial fabrication; in other cases, variant editions of a story signal the storyteller's intent to deceive. Tan seems to be suggesting that the truth exists both in each version of a story and somewhere in the unspoken narrative or in the spaces between stories.

A hallmark of *The Hundred Secret Senses* is the novel's precarious position somewhere between the real and the surreal, between the prosaic and the magical. When Kwan as Nunumu first hears Miss Banner's life story told in fractured stumbling Chinese, she forms the impression that Miss Banner has come from a peculiarly skewed and topsy-turvy universe. Miss Banner's little brothers chase a chicken into a deep hole and fall all the way to the other side of the world; her father picks scented money that grows like flowers and makes people happy; her mother puffs out her neck like a rooster, calls for her sons, and climbs down the hole that has swallowed them. After her mother's disappearance, Miss Banner's father takes her first to a palace governed by little Jesuses, and later to an island ruled by mad dogs. At length, the father vanishes and Miss Banner lives with a succession of uncles, including one who cuts off pieces of China and sails off on a floating island. The reality—which Kwan learns after Miss Banner becomes more fluent in Chinese—is that Miss Banner's brothers died of chicken pox and her mother of a goiter disease; her father was an opium trader who put her in a school for Jesus-worshipping children in India; father and daughter left India for Malacca; and the uncles were actually a series of lovers. Tan's clever juxtaposition of fact and whimsy complements the surrealism that pervades the entire novel and validates for the reader the simultaneous existence of twentieth century and nineteenth century, Chinese and American, Kwan and Nunumu, and the *yin* people in Tan's fictional universe.

Tan also employs multiple versions of a story to create uncertainty and to describe a world in which no definite answers are possible. Jack Yee, the shadowy father that Kwan and Olivia barely remember, is an enigma to both daughters, but for different reasons. In Olivia's version of Jack's story—passed on to her by the American-born adults in the family—Jack was a good-looking university student in Guilin who was forced to marry a young market vendor when she became pregnant with his child. Five years later, when his wife died of a lung disease, the grief-stricken Jack left his young daughter with an aunt and went to Hong Kong to begin a new life. Before he could send for his beloved daughter, the Communist takeover in China destroyed all hope for a reunion between father and child, and the despondent Jack emigrated to America. Kwan's arrival replaces the sad story with an even more disturbing one. According to Kwan, her mother did not die of a lung disease; she died of "heartsickness" when her husband abandoned her with a four-year-old daughter and another child on the way. Kwan tells Olivia that all the water in her mother's belly "poured out as tears from her eyes.[. . .] That poor starving baby in her belly ate a hole in my mother's heart, and they both died" (14). In this way, years later, Olivia learns what Kwan has always known. Their father had no legal or hereditary claim to the name Jack Yee. The name belonged to the owner of a stolen overcoat that the young university student who became their father purloined from a drunken man who had been trying to sell it for whatever cash he could get. In the coat's pockets were immigration permits, academic records, notification of admission to an American university, a ticket for passage on a ship, and cash—documents that would facilitate a new life in a wealthy country full of opportunity, far away from poverty, factory work, a pregnant wife, and a child. Donning the coat and the spectacles he found in one pocket, and appropriating the documents, the student became Jack Yee. But Amy Tan does not privilege Kwan's version. Kwan, in fact, prefaces her tale by saying that she heard it from Li Bin-bin, her mother's sister who raised her—and who, under the circumstances, would be unlikely to feel kindly toward the bogus Jack Yee. Thus the question remains: Who is the man behind the identity of Jack Yee? Kwan says that she has never known his true name, and she clearly knows almost nothing of his origins. And by extension, then, who are Olivia and Kwan? Who are their true ancestors? And who are Miss Banner and Nunumu? And, ultimately, how are all of these individuals connected?

Finally, Tan employs the many-layered triple narrative to interrogate the accounts of actual historical events, perhaps even to suggest that such accounts are unstable because they are the productions of gendered, class-defined, or racially constructed language. The Taiping Rebellion of the mid-nineteenth century is well known to Sinologists as well as to historians and geographers, but the standard texts tend toward factual, Westernized accounts of military battles, descriptions of territory gained or lost, and tallies of victories and defeats. Kwan's version of the Rebellion privileges the perspective of a half-blind orphan who notices far more than battles between Manchu and Hakka. For one-eyed Nunumu, the Rebellion means the loss of her entire family, and life in a half-deserted village populated only by the elderly and the very young, the physically and mentally disabled, and the cowardly; the Heavenly King and his armies succeed only in bringing her hunger and cold, and a life of servitude in a house full of missionaries. Nunumu's experiences factor the personal element into a historical equation, revealing the frequently overlooked truth that military and political battles are always won or lost at the expense of thousands of individuals whose lives are forever disrupted by the ambitions of a powerful minority and their followers.

Works Cited

Goldman, Marlene. "Naming the Unspeakable: The Mapping of Female Identity in Maxine Hong Kingston's *The Woman Warrior.*" *International Women's Writing: New Landscapes of Identity.* Eds. Anne E. Brown and Marjanne E. Goozé. Westport, CT: Greenwood Press, 1995. 223–32.

Hsaio, Ruth. "Facing the Incurable: Patriarchy in *Eat a Bowl of Tea.*" *Reading the Literature of Asian America.* Eds. Shirley Geok-lin Lim and Amy Ling. Philadelphia: Temple University Press, 1992. 151–62.

Kim, Elaine. *Asian American Literature: An Introduction to the Writings and their Social Context.* Philadelphia: Temple University Press, 1982.

Lim, Shirley G., and Amy Ling. *Reading the Literatures of Asian America.* Philadelphia: Temple University Press, 1992.

Ling, Amy. *Between Worlds: Women Writers of Chinese Ancestry.* New York: Pergamon, 1990.

CHINESE AMERICAN WOMEN, LANGUAGE, AND MOVING SUBJECTIVITY[1]

VICTORIA CHEN

To imagine a language means to imagine a form of life.

WITTGENSTEIN, *PHILOSOPHICAL INVESTIGATIONS*

Philosophical Investigations

It was not until the 1970s that Asian American literature became recognized as a separate canon and a "new tradition" of writing. While this "new" form of expression created a new political consciousness and identity, the images and stories that abound in pioneer literature such as Maxine Hong Kingston's *The Woman Warrior* and *China Men* are paradoxically located in "recovered" ethnic history. More recently, Amy Tan's *The Joy Luck Club* also takes the reader through a journey back to a specific set of ethnic memories as the mothers in the stories interweave their experiences struggling for survival and dignity in China and for coherence and hope in America. Part of the reason for the celebration of Asian American women's literature is that it provides an alternative way to think about issues such as language, subjectivity, cultural voice, and ethnic/gender identity.

For Chinese American women such as Kingston, Tan, and the female characters in *The Joy Luck Club,* speaking in a double voice and living in a bicultural world characterize their dual cultural enmeshment. While striving to maintain a relationship with their Chinese immigrant parents, the Chinese American daughters also live in a society where one is expected to speak in a "standard" form of English and to "succeed" in the middle class Euro-American way. For Kingston and Tan, writing about their immigrant mothers' neglected pasts and their own tumultuous presents

[1]From *Women & Language* 18.1 (Spring 1995). © 1995 by *Women & Language.*

becomes a powerful way to recreate their own identities as Chinese Americans and to confront the dilemma of living biculturally in a society that insists on a homogeneous identity. If a language indeed is intrinsically connected with a form of life, and speaking and writing in a given language necessitates one to participate in that cultural world, how then do these Chinese American women authors position themselves in linguistic/cultural borderlands through the use of language? What are some forms of language and life that make their storytelling possible and intelligible? How do different languages function in their own lives and in their storytelling? How do they use languages to interweave and mediate their multiple identities? This essay attempts to address some of these issues. I will draw upon essays written by and about Kingston and Tan as well as narratives from *The Joy Luck Club* and *The Woman Warrior* in my discussion.

Amy Tan (1991) in her essay "Mother Tongue" discusses that as someone who has always loved language, she celebrates using "all the Englishes I grew up with" in her living and her writing. The English that she hears from her mother, despite its "imperfection," has become their "language of intimacy, a different sort of English that relates to family talk, the language I grew up with." There is a discrepancy, both linguistically and culturally, between the "standard" English that she learns from school and uses in her professional world and the "simple" and "broken" English that is used in her interaction with her mother. However, as Tan points out, speaking her mother's version of English gives her bicultural insight and strength, and she sees the beauty and wisdom in her mother's language: "Her language, as I hear it, is vivid, direct, full of observation and imagery"; "I wanted to capture what language ability tests can never reveal: her intent, her passion, her imagery, the rhythms of her speech and the nature of her thoughts." Kingston also grew up in two languages, her family's Chinese dialect and the public American English in which she was educated. *The Woman Warrior* reveals the disjunction that Kingston experienced in moving between these two languages. While her mother marked her growing up with stories of nameless Chinese women, multiple cultural ghosts, Kingston wrote, "To make my waking life American-normal [. . .] I push the deformed into my dreams, which are in Chinese, the language of impossible stories." The entire book is devoted to Kingston's ongoing struggle to enter the Chinese cultural world composed of impossible stories and to figure out what it meant to be a Chinese American woman in this society.

Tan's *The Joy Luck Club* is a segmented novel, set in San Francisco in the 1980s, powerfully blending the voices of four Chinese immigrant mothers and their American-born daughters. The book opens with a story of a swan and a woman sailing across an ocean toward America saying, "In America I will have a daughter just like me. But over there [. . .] nobody will look down on her, because I will make her speak only perfect American English. And over there she will always be too full to swallow any sorrow! She will know my meaning.[. . .]" The tale symbolizes not only the geographic separation from the woman's motherland but also the alienation later felt by both the mother and daughter in America. The woman's desire for her daughter to speak perfect American English foregrounds the problems and difficulties of communicating and translating between the different languages that they speak. The American dream eventually eludes the immigrant woman beyond her best intentions. Mastering this imaginary perfect English for the American-born daughter turns out not to be a simple ticket to American success. This linguistic competency, ironically, signifies her departure from her mother (and her motherland), deepening the chasm between generations and cultures. Moreover, learning to speak perfect American English may also entail the complex journey of "successful" acculturation which often masks the racism and sexism that belie the American dream.

Although Tan's essay celebrates the two Englishes with which she grew up, and that dual languages and cultures can indeed enrich and enlighten one's life, coherence and double voice do not always come without personal struggle and emotional trauma. As we enter the hyphenated world of the "Chinese-American" women in *The Joy Luck Club,* much of the mothers' and daughters' conversations seem to be focused on debating, negotiating, and wandering between the two disparate cultural logics. Lindo shared her daughter's concern that she cannot say whether her Chinese or American face is better: "I think about our two faces. I think about my intentions. Which one is American? Which one is Chinese? Which one is better? If you show one, you must always sacrifice the other." Tan (1990), in her essay "The Language of Discretion," pointed out a special kind of double bind attached to knowing two languages and vehemently rebelled against seeing cultural descriptions as dichotomous categories: "It's dangerous business, this sorting out of language and behavior. Which one is English? Which is Chinese? [. . .] Reject them all!" "Having listened to both Chinese and English, I also tend to be suspicious of any comparisons between Chinese and English languages." Tan argued: "Typically, one language—that of the person doing the comparing—is often used as the standard, the benchmark for a logical form of explanation."

Speaking a language is inherently political. In the case of Chinese American women, while straddling and juggling along the fault lines of gender and culture, the truth is that the two Englishes that Tan cherished are not valued equally in this society. Despite the creative use of imaginative metaphors in her English, as Tan humorously presented, her mother would never score high in a standard English test that insists on one correct way of linguistic construction. It is no secret that in much of our social discourse and communication practice, the myth persists that what counts as the "normal" standards and criteria for comparing and discussing cultural difference is still the mainstream Eurocentric mode of thinking and doing. In her writing about Asian American women's experience of racism, Shah (1994) said, "For me, the experience of 'otherness,' the formative discrimination in my life, has resulted from culturally different people thinking they were culturally central; thinking that *my* house smelled funny, that *my* mother talked weird, that *my* habits were strange. They were normal; I wasn't." Similarly, in a discussion of the difficult dialogues between black and white women, Houston (1994) points out that when a white woman says "We're all alike," she usually means "I can see how you, a black woman, are like me, a white woman." She does not mean "I can see how I am like you." In other words, whether explicitly or implicitly, "just people" often means "just white people."

Language and identity are always positioned within a hierarchical power structure in which the Chinese American immigrants' form of life has never been granted a status equal to that of their European counterparts in the history of this country. It is one thing to embrace the philosophical wisdom of "having the best of both worlds" but another to confront the real ongoing struggle between languages and identities that most Chinese Americans experience. Bicultural identity cannot be reduced to two neutral, pristine, and equal linguistic domains that one simply picks and chooses to participate in without personal, relational, social, and political consequences. We need to understand the tension and conflict between generations of Chinese American women within the ideological cultural context of racial and sexual inequality and their ongoing contestation of their positions in it.

Through Tan's storytelling in *The Joy Luck Club,* the meaning of "perfect English" is transformed from the mother's naive American dream to the daughter's awakening bicultural disillusionment, as the daughter June laments: "These kinds of explanations made me feel my mother and I spoke two different languages, which we did. I talked to her in English, she answered back in Chinese," and later, "My mother and I never really understood one another. We translated each other's meanings and I seemed to hear less than what was said, while my mother heard more." The lack of shared languages and cultural logics remains a central theme throughout all the narratives in Tan's book. This absence transcends the simple linguistic dichotomies or cultural misunderstandings; both mothers and daughters are negotiating their relational and social positions and contesting their identities as Chinese American women in the languages that can enhance or undermine their power, legitimacy, and voice.

In a similar vein, in *The Woman Warrior* Kingston describes "abnormal" discourse as constructed and experienced by both parents and children in her family. The children in Kingston's family often spoke in English language which their parents "didn't seem to hear"; "the Chinese can't hear American at all; the language is too soft and Western music unhearable." Exasperated and bemused by their Chinese aunt's behavior, the children told each other that "Chinese people are very weird." Angry at the fact that the Chinese were unable, unwilling, or did not see the need to explain things to the children, Kingston writes, "I thought talking and not talking made the differences between sanity and insanity. Insane people were the ones who couldn't explain themselves." While the Chinese American children were frustrated by the impenetrable wisdom spoken or unspoken in the Chinese language, the parents teased the children about the way they spoke in the "ghost's" language and of the craziness and absurdity of doing things in American ways. Insane and absurd in what language(s) and from what cultural perspective(s)? Who has the authority to tell Kingston that Chinese girls are worthless growing up in a society that is supposed to be more egalitarian and liberating for women? What constitutes "normal" and "abnormal" discourse for Chinese American women? What price do they have to pay for being a full participant in either or both cultural worlds?

One intriguing feature in learning to speak and hear incommensurate languages is the process of adjudicating conflicting voices. In Chinese American families, communication can often be characterized by a lack of a shared universe of discourse or a set of mutually intelligible vocabularies. For Kingston, even attempting to engage in a meaningful dialogue with her parents about her confusions and their conflicts became a problem, as she told us, "I don't know any Chinese I can ask without getting myself scolded or teased." Silent and silenced, Kingston was angry at the sexist trivialization of her intellectual interests and academic accomplishment. She writes, "I've stopped checking 'bilingual' on job applications. I could not understand any of the dialects the interviewer at China Airlines tried on me, and he didn't understand me either." Family language almost became a "burden" as Kingston strived to make sense of what it meant to occupy two linguistic and cultural spaces as a Chinese American woman in a patriarchal system. Could her surrender allude to the disappointment and frustration that Chinese Americans as a group feel within the larger society?

In Tan's novel, when one of the daughters, June, did not comply with her mother's wishes, her mother shouted at her in Chinese: "Only two kinds of daughters. Those who are obedient and those who follow their own mind! Only one kind of daughter can live in this house. Obedient daughter!" The mother's injunction is an enactment of her personal power within the family structure, and in this language and cultural logic, June is powerless even if she could speak "perfect" American English, which would give her positional power in a different situation.

Toward the end of the book when Kingston finally confronted her mother with her long list of feelings of guilt being a Chinese American daughter, the linguistic gap and cultural intranslatability resonated throughout their shouting match. Angry, frustrated, hurt, sad, and disappointed, Kingston realized that the confrontation was futile: "And suddenly I got very confused and lonely because I was at the moment telling her my list, and in the telling, it grew. No higher listener. No listener but myself." Once again, their voices did not intermesh, and neither could enter the cultural logic that was specifically structured within the primary language that they spoke. There was no possibility for Kingston to articulate her silence, nor was there space for displaying her mother's good intentions. The celebration of the multiple languages and polyphonic voices seemed elusive. Two generations of women were ultimately torn apart and yet inextricably bonded by the unspeakable cultural tongue. Each in their own way sounded strange, incoherent, crazy, abnormal, and stubborn to the other.

The end of the story of the swan in *The Joy Luck Club* says, "Now the woman was old. And she had a daughter who grew up speaking only English and swallowing more Coca-Cola than sorrow. For a long time now the woman had wanted to give her daughter the single swan feather and tell her, 'This feather may look worthless, but it comes from afar and carries with it all my good intentions.' And she waited, year after year, for the day she could tell her daughter this in perfect American English." As one of the mothers Lindo lamented, "I wanted my children to have the best combination, American circumstances and Chinese character. How could I know these two things do not mix?"

If indeed Chinese Americans are steeped in two languages and two forms of life, one public and dominant, another private and submerged, what is the symbolic significance of using these languages as constructed from various social positions? For the immigrant parents, educating their American-born children to speak the family language is a way to continue the cultural tradition and to instill ethnic pride. Speaking a private language is also an attempt to mark one's difference from the mainstream culture and to resist racism, hegemony, and the overwhelming power of homogenization in this society. In Tan's and Kingston's storytelling, speaking Chinese also becomes simply functional for the older immigrants who do not want to participate or/and are not perceived as full participants in the public language. As a result, they remain outsiders within the system; their use of private language marks the central feature of their identity.

Although for many American-born Chinese, using family language can affirm their cultural ties to their ancestors, Kingston also grew up hearing all the derogatory comments about girls in Chinese, the language of foreign and impossible stories to her ear. While speaking her family dialect gives her a sense of connection and intimacy, the private language also symbolizes the oppression, confusion, frustration, madness, and silence that were associated with her coming of age. Using English to speak and write signifies Kingston's rebellion against the patriarchal tradition; it forced her to take a non-Chinese and non-female position in her family and community. For Chinese American women, speaking English affirms their public identity and gives them a legitimate cultural voice to claim for a space in this society. English gives them a means to assert their independence and a tool to fight against sexism and racism that they encounter. Trinh Minh-ha, in an interview, insisted that identity remains as a political/personal strategy of resistance and survival; "the reflexive question asked [. . .] is no longer: who am I? but when, where, how am I (so and so)?"

It is important to remember that a discussion of uses of language needs to be understood in a political context. Chinese Americans strive for polyphonic coherence within a society that celebrates conformity and homogeneity despite its rhetoric of diversity and pluralism. To mainstream ears, Chinese languages may sound a cacophony of unfamiliar tones and words; this unintelligibility can be associated with foreignness, exotic cultural others, lack of education, or powerlessness. This perceived absence of a shared language and culture (and therefore of disparate social and national interests) can lead to hostility or discrimination toward Chinese Americans.

Through the use of language we create and maintain our social relationships. We accomplish this goal only if an intersubjective discourse exists so that our words and actions are intelligible to others within the community. In Chinese American bicultural experience, this shared language often cannot be taken for granted. In *The Woman Warrior,* Kingston confronted her mother about telling her that she was ugly all the time, to which her mother replied, "That's what we're supposed to say. That's what Chinese say. We like to say the opposite." Here in the mother's language, "truth" is characterized by the logic of the opposite; this "indirect" approach works only if one knows how to hear the statement within the context of a certain kind of relationship. Saying the opposite is what the mother felt obligated to perform; in fact, it was the only language that she could use in order to demonstrate her affection and care for her daughter. Unfortunately, lacking the cultural insight to reverse the logic of her mother's statement, Kingston felt shamed, outraged, and was in turn accused by her mother of not being able to "tell a joke from real life"; her mother shouts at her, "You're not so smart. Can't even tell real from false." Real from false in what language? Where does the humor of this apparent joke for the mother—and humiliation for the daughter—lie in perfect American English?

In *The Joy Luck Club,* the young women's innocence, ignorance, and apathy toward their mother's language seemed to frighten the mothers. June tried to understand her three aunties at the mah jong table:

> And then it occurs to me. They are frightened. In me, they see their own daughters, just as ignorant, just as unmindful of all the truths and hopes they have brought to America. They see daughters who grow impatient when their mothers talk in Chinese, who think they are stupid when they explain things in fractured English. They see that joy and luck do not mean the same to their daughters, that to these closed American-born minds "joy luck" is not a word, it does not exist. They see daughters who will bear grandchildren born without any connecting hope passed from generation to generation

Failure to translate between languages can cost emotional turmoil; it can also silence someone who depends on the English translation to negotiate or accomplish his/her goals. In one of the stories in *The Joy*

Luck Club, the daughter Lena was unable to translate her mother's words to her Caucasian stepfather who did not speak Chinese. Since Lena understood the Chinese words spoken by her mother but not the implications, she made up something in her translation and as a result rewrote her mother's story in that episode. Tan intentionally constructed this scene to illustrate the nature of the mother-daughter relationship. Lena was ignorant of both the story that her mother was hinting at and of the Chinese language that her mother was speaking. Kingston's and Tan's writings are characterized by untold stories written in untranslatable language between the two generations of women. McAlister (1992) argued that by failing to translate between languages and stories, Chinese American daughters can participate in the silencing of their mothers. This position seems incongruous in view of Tan's overall agenda in her storytelling. By having all the women narrate their own stories, Tan treats language not just as a tool to reflect upon the past or to celebrate the present, but as a political means to allow Chinese American women to articulate their silenced lives, their otherwise voiceless positions in this society.

Tan writes *The Joy Luck Club* in a language that demands the reader recognize the distinctness of each character, each story and voice, and each mother-daughter relationship. The women in her creation are not just nameless, faceless, or interchangeable Chinese Americans. The interrelated narratives make sense only if readers can discern the specificities of each woman's story as located within the novel. Therefore, "Tan confronts an Orientalist discourse that depends on the sameness of Chinese difference." By granting subjectivity to each woman, Tan compels each to tell her own story in her own words, thus (re)creating the meanings of her life. The mother-daughter tensions as constructed in their own discourse are fraught with complexities of racial, gender, and class issues, not just the simple binary opposition of Americanness and Chineseness, mothers and daughters.

The ability to tell one's own story, to speak one's mind, is the best antidote to powerlessness. Tan's writing instills agency and visibility in Chinese American women. The silence is broken, and their new voices are constructed in collective storytelling, a language of community, without denying or erasing the different positions such collaboration encounters. In a similar vein, Kingston gave the no name woman in her mother's storytelling a voice and a life, a permanent place in American culture; she immortalized this silent woman through her writing: "My aunt haunts me—her ghost drawn to me because now, after fifty years of neglect, I alone devote pages of paper to her." Both Tan and Kingston allow their female characters to reclaim and recreate their identity. "Storytelling heals past experiences of loss and separation; it is also a medium for rewriting stories of oppression and victimization into parables of self-affirmation and individual empowerment." It is possible to celebrate the present without forgetting the past. In an interview when Kingston was contrasting her own American voice in *Tripmaster Monkey* and her translation of Chinese voices in her previous two books, she said, "When I wrote *The Woman Warrior* and *China Men*, as I look back on it, I was trying to find an American language that would translate the speech of the people who are living their lives with the Chinese language. They carry on their adventures and their emotional life and everything in Chinese. I had to find a way to translate all that into a graceful American language, which is my language." Perhaps the boundary between Kingston's two languages/voices is not so clear; of *Tripmaster Monkey*, [a Chinese poet] she said that "I was writing in the tradition of the past." "And I spent this lifetime working on roots. So what they were saying was that I was their continuity."

Both Kingston's and Tan's writings point to the multiplicity and instability of cultural identity for Chinese American women, oscillating and crisscrossing between different Englishes and Chinese dialects that they speak. Although cultural borderlands can be a useful metaphor for "home" for these individuals, we must realize that this home does not rest in a fixed location, nor is it constructed in any one unified language or perfect American English. Neither of the authors is searching for a definitive Chinese American voice. Through interweaving their own bicultural tongues and multiple imaginative voices, Kingston and Tan focus on women's experiences in their writings and position their uses of languages as central to our understanding of Chinese American women's bicultural world.

Ultimately we see the transformation of double voice in both *The Woman Warrior* and *The Joy Luck Club*. As Trinh put it nicely, "the fact one is always marginalized in one's own language and areas of strength is something that one has to learn to live with." Therefore, fragmentation in one's identity becomes "a way of living with differences without turning them into opposites, nor trying to assimilate them out of insecurity." Chinese American women need to cultivate not simply multiple subjectivities but also the ability to move between different languages and positions. As Trinh suggested, this fluidity is a form of challenge and reconstruction of power relations, and women need to learn to use language as a poetic arena of struggle of possibility for transformation. "Ethnic identity is twin skin to linguistic identity—I am my language." Unless Chinese American women acknowledge and celebrate all the Englishes that they grew up with, they cannot accept the legitimacy of their bicultural identity. When asked if she still felt the same contradictions that the protagonist did in *The Woman Warrior*, Kingston said "No, no. I feel much more integrated [. . .] It takes decades of struggle. When you are a person who comes from a multicultural background it just means that you have more information coming in from the universe. And it's your task to figure out how it all integrates, figure out its order and its beauty. It's a harder, longer struggle."

Man Must Die

Gael Fowler

1   The short story "Immortal Heart," written by the Chinese-American author Amy Tan, illustrates the theme of grief and loss resulting from the deaths of close family members. Three tragic deaths portrayed in this story are the loss of a child, a spouse, and a parent. The narrator, Lu Ling, reveals her nursemaid's experiences with these types of losses throughout the story. Lu Ling and Precious Auntie, her nursemaid, have a terrible argument toward the end of the story, and Lu Ling speaks harshly to her servant. Lu Ling realizes that she has been unkind to her friend and wants to apologize for her cruel behavior. Lu Ling discovers Precious Auntie dead in a ravine and mourns the loss of the woman she has known as her nursemaid. Later, she learns that Precious Auntie was actually her biological mother. Both mother and daughter experience tragic losses and have to deal with intense grief throughout their lives.

2   The most painful event that a parent can ever experience is the death of his child. In this story, Precious Auntie's father is an extremely gifted bonesetter who fails to save his four sons from a deadly disease. The loss of his children is devastating to him, and as a result "he spent his entire fortune and went into a lifetime of debt to pay for their funerals" (Tan 768). The death of Precious Auntie's brothers causes her father to be plagued with grief for the remainder of his life. The bone-setter survives the death of his sons by living through the happiness of his daughter. According to Precious Auntie, "*he spoiled me, let me do whatever a son might do*" (Tan 768). She also comments, "*My father was used to seeing pain of the worst kinds. But with me he was helpless. He couldn't bear to see me cry*" (Tan 768). Losing four sons is

extremely difficult for the bonesetter, but this tragedy results in the birth of a stronger relationship with his daughter as he struggles to endure the pain.

3   The loss of an intended spouse is also a catastrophic and traumatic experience. On the day of Precious Auntie's marriage to Baby Uncle, a horse kicks Baby Uncle in the head. This fatal blow changes Precious Auntie's life drastically. She continually hears the horrendous sound of the accident "in the breaking of twigs, the crackling of fire, [and] whenever a melon was split in two" (Tan 772). Precious Auntie is hysterical for days and weeks after her lover's death. She even tries to commit suicide in order "to cause pain greater than what she already felt" (Tan 773). Fortunately, Precious Auntie has a daughter who gives her a purpose for living during the remainder of her years.

4   Losing a mother or a father is extremely desolating for a child. When a parent dies, a child feels as if a vital part of her existence is missing. Precious Auntie never really knows her mother because she loses her mother at a young age. Therefore, her relationship with her father becomes that much closer. Seeing her father "lying [dead] in a ditch" (Tan 772) is the worst nightmare that Precious Auntie can imagine. For days, she "apologized to the [corpse] of her father" (Tan 773) because she feels responsible for her father's death. Even though Precious Auntie cannot prevent the accident that kills her father, she lives the rest of her life with agonizing feelings of guilt.

5   Death has always been a dominant theme in literature. Amy Tan's excellence at portraying such basic literary themes is seen throughout her writing. According to Elaine Kim, Asian authors like Tan write masterfully about the topics of "'love, desire for personal freedom and acceptance, and struggles against oppression and injustice'" (qtd. in Huntley 787). Several of Tan's

stories depict the lives of common people who experience severe tragedies, such as the loss of loved ones. Some people will lose a child like the bonesetter. Many people like Precious Auntie will watch in horror as their lovers or parents slip away from them. Even a few unfortunate people like Lu Ling will have to learn devastating secrets about their family relationships. Amy Tan addresses these classic themes of literature by delving into her own personal and cultural history. Amy Tan's style of writing is perfectly described with the following statement by E.D. Huntley:

> Tan's novels reify and reinterpret traditional genres by casting them in a variety of modes—realistic, comic, tragic, tragicomic, allegorical, fantastic, naturalistic, and heroic—that metamorphose seamlessly into each other in Tan's signature narrative style. (786)

Amy Tan's greatest strength as an author is the ability to make readers identify with her characters by writing from her heart.

Works Cited

Henderson, Gloria Mason, Bill Day, and Sandra Stevenson Waller, eds. <u>Literature and Ourselves</u>. 4th ed. New York: Longman, 2003.

Huntley, E. D. <u>Amy Tan: A Critical Companion</u>. Westport, Connecticut: Greenwood P, 1998. Henderson, Day, and Waller. 786–802.

Tan, Amy. "Immortal Heart." <u>The New Yorker</u>. 25 Dec. 2000–1 Jan. 2001: 134–52. Henderson, Day, and Waller. 766–85.

Suggestions for Research, Exploration, and Writing

1. Most people have an image of a childhood place that, when revisited as an adult, turned out different from memories and expectations.

Think back to your childhood and write an essay describing an event that left you happier, sadder, or wiser.

2. Write an essay explaining Simon's role in "Young Girl's Wish."

3. "Young Girl's Wish" and "Immortal Heart" portray grief and loss on many levels. Choose one or more levels of grief and write an essay explaining this theme.

4. When Lu Ling complains that her (apparent) mother does not love her, Precious Auntie says, "*If she didn't love you, why did she bother to criticize you for your own good?*" In an essay, discuss the degree to which criticism is an expression of love.

5. In a researched essay, discuss the differences in marriage customs between Lu Ling's culture and your own. Alternatively, research marriage customs in the Far and Near East. Then write an essay categorizing these customs.

Grief and Loss: Suggestions for Writing

1. One consistent **theme** in many of the works in this unit is that death is the ultimate equalize, as everyone has to die. Discuss the use of this theme in one or more of the works.

2. Write an essay on racial, cultural, or gender vulnerability, examining one of the selections that deals with a race, culture, or gender other than your own.

3. Use two of the short stories to show how people try to deal with their own vulnerability by clinging to others.

4. Select at least two poems that deal with the reaction of the living to the death of a loved one. Write an essay discussing the survivors' emotions.

5. Human beings often react violently when they realize their own vulnerability. Using one or more of the selections in this unit to illustrate and support your points, classify and describe these violent reactions.

6. Write an essay using three poems that illustrate three types of human vulnerability.

7. People are constantly susceptible to fears, prejudice, discrimination, and abuse of one sort or another. Describe an incident in which you were a victim of, or a witness to, one of these kinds of human vulnerability.

8. Four of the works in this unit—Faulkner's "A Rose for Emily," Robinson's "Richard Cory," Dunbar's "We Wear the Mask," and McCrae's "In Flander's Field"—are written in first person plural. After carefully rereading each work, analyze each author's reasons for choosing this particular point of view.

Grief and Loss: Writing about Film

1. Select a short lyric poem and design a silent screenplay to depict the images of the poem in such a way that they imply the meaning of the poem. Your screenplay should state in images the words of the poem you want to depict. Be sure to describe how each shot is framed (closeup, medium, or long shot), what exactly the camera sees, how the camera moves, how the images cut together, and what important design elements such as colors, details, props, or effects you want to include. Don't worry too much about telling the story of the poem, but try to create images that will work as visual poetry that honors the written poem.

2. Many contemporary films touch on the theme of loss (*Memento, In the Bedroom, Crouching Tiger, Hidden Dragon, Traffic, The Limey, Titanic*). View or re-view a loss-themed film, watching for specific cinematic methods: What design elements contribute to creating a mood of mourning or unhappiness? What scene is central to understanding how the main character is affected by loss or misfortune? How do the design elements assist the script in making this a particularly effective scene? What is the effect of music?

3. There are several film versions of *Othello*. Watch two, then compare the bedroom scenes in which Othello murders Desdemona. Is one more effective than the other? Which film-making element is most effective: pace, framing, camera movement, setting? No doubt the actors must make convincing choices as well. What are the actors doing that make you believe they are Othello and Desdemona? What information in the text justifies your judgment?

Freedom
and Responsibility

Marc Chagall, "The Promenade," 1917. Russian State Museum, St. Petersburg, Russia.
© 2003 Artist Rights Society (ARS), New York/ADAGP, Paris.

We are accustomed to celebrating our freedom as Americans without much thought. Seldom do we stop to realize what that freedom means or requires of us. The most seminal of American documents, the Declaration of Independence, espouses a doctrine that even today in this country seems astoundingly revolutionary— the idea that governments "derive their just powers from the consent of the governed" and that when they fail to serve their purpose in protecting citizens' rights, those citizens have the right, even the responsibility, to overthrow such governments. When Martin Luther King Jr. led peaceful protests against the segregation and brutal treatment of African Americans, he was simply acting on ideas contained in Jefferson's great founding document.

Often we fail to realize the extent to which those great American values, freedom and equality, both of which originate in the Declaration of Independence, may be mutually exclusive. As Kurt Vonnegut's "Harrison Bergeron" demonstrates, an exact and universal equality may not only reduce our freedom but produce a world that is culturally sterile. Asserting our freedom, as the fate of Harrison Bergeron illustrates, may be very costly. In John Updike's "A & P," Sammy's refusal to conform and his assertion of independence cost him his job. And in Vaclav Havel's "The Trial," a Czech rock band, guilty only of failure to conform to government-prescribed norms, faces trial as a menace to society. On the other hand, nowhere is the terrible cost of freedom more graphically exemplified than in Ursula Le Guin's "The Ones Who Walk Away from Omelas," where the freedom and comfortable lives of a whole society depend on the brutal suffering of a single poor wretch. One person's freedom may mean another's subjugation.

What, then, are the limits to freedom? To what degree should we be subject to our government, and to what degree should the government be subject to us? Sometimes the desire for freedom may compete with personal responsibilities to family and community. In "On the Rainy River," Tim O'Brien faces an agonizing choice. If he goes to Canada because of his opposition to the Vietnam War, he fears being perceived by his parents, friends, and neighbors as a coward, not a principled objector. On the other hand, to fight in a war he considers wrong will violate his conscience. Hence, O'Brien's story raises extremely important issues. When must we submerge our individuality in deference to the community? Where does our individual freedom end, and where do the perceived needs of the community begin? When should communal decisions, expressed as government policy, supersede individual conscience?

Writing about Freedom and Responsibility

In writing about the selections in Freedom and Responsibility, you will have a wide variety of choices. As you study the types of essays and subjects, you will probably notice that several of the stories and essays use satire or irony. You might start by reviewing the definitions of these two terms included in the glossary. Then you might use Jonathan Swift's "A Modest Proposal," which offers a perfect example of a caustic satire written about a real-life situation, to write a definition essay, an essay illustrating the literary devices that Swift uses to make his points, or a researched paper about the situation in Ireland that is the subject of Swift's satire. If you prefer to write about short stories, and especially if you enjoy fantasy, you might choose one of two stories that provide excellent examples of satire. Both Vonnegut's "Harrison Bergeron" and Asimov's "Frustration" combine satire with humor; therefore, you might examine the real-life tendencies that they satirize and explore the ways in which the authors use humor in their satire.

After reviewing the questions from the introduction on Writing about Poetry, you might write an essay comparing or classifying the choices and lack of choices recognized by the speakers in Randall Jarrell's "The Woman at the Washington Zoo," Anne Sexton's "Ringing the Bells," or Alicia Ostriker's "Watching the Feeder." Or you might discuss the theme of problems faced by immigrants portrayed in Pat Mora's "Immigrants" and Dwight Okita's "In Response to Executive Order 9066." As in any of the thematic units, you might write an essay examining the distinctive tone or the sound and metaphorical devices used by the poets to create the overall effects they desire.

If your professor asks you to use the casebook on Tim O'Brien to write a documented paper, you should, of course, begin by reading the stories. You might list ideas for topics as you read and then add to the list when you have completed your reading and have a more complete view of the possibilities. After writing down some of your own ideas for future reference, you should then read the critical essays. Using this technique will help you remember which ideas were yours and which were influenced by the essays. When Nick Hembree was asked to write a documented essay using some of the stories and critical essays in the casebook, he began by trying to detail the interesting and provocative techniques used by O'Brien. He also wanted to emphasize the meanings of the stories. Nick decided to use three of the stories to write an essay about the nature of truth and its general elusiveness and complexity. He e-mailed the first draft of the essay to his professor, who made a few suggestions. Then he polished the final draft, checked his documentation, and proofread it before e-mailing it to the professor. After you have read the O'Brien stories, you will probably enjoy reading Nick's essay to see if your perceptions are similar to his.

ESSAYS

Jonathan Swift (1667–1745)

*Though Jonathan Swift's parents were English, he was born in Dublin
and became one of the most ardent defenders of Ireland. As dean of
St. Patrick's Cathedral in Dublin from 1726 to 1739, Swift was a
major force in the religious and political affairs of Ireland. A man of
great intellect, Swift is recognized as a true master of style and as one
of the world's foremost satirists. His most famous work,* Gulliver's
Travels, *satirizes many of the social, political, and religious practices
of his time. "A Modest Proposal" reveals the extreme hardships the
peasants of Ireland suffered at the hands of greedy English landlords.*

A MODEST PROPOSAL   (1729)

FOR PREVENTING THE CHILDREN OF POOR PEOPLE IN IRELAND
FROM BEING A BURDEN TO THEIR PARENTS OR COUNTRY,
AND FOR MAKING THEM BENEFICIAL TO THE PUBLIC

1   It is a melancholy object to those who walk through this great town, or
travel in the country, when they see the streets, the roads and cabin-doors
crowded with beggars of the female sex, followed by three, four, or six
children, all in rags, and importuning every passenger for an alms. These
mothers, instead of being able to work for their honest livelihood, are
forced to employ all their time in strolling, to beg sustenance for their
helpless infants, who, as they grow up, either turn thieves for want of
work, or leave their dear native country to fight for the Pretender in
Spain, or sell themselves to the Barbadoes.

2   I think it is agreed by all parties that this prodigious number of children, in the arms, or on the backs, or at the heels of their mothers, and
frequently of their fathers, is in the present deplorable state of the kingdom a very great additional grievance; and therefore whoever could find
out a fair, cheap, and easy method of making these children sound and
useful members of the commonwealth would deserve so well of the public as to have his statue set up for a preserver of the nation.

3   But my intention is very far from being confined to provide only for
the children of professed beggars; it is of a much greater extent, and shall
take in the whole number of infants at a certain age who are born of parents in effect as little able to support them as those who demand our charity in the streets.

4   As to my own part, having turned my thoughts for many years upon
this important subject, and maturely weighed the several schemes of
other projectors, I have always found them grossly mistaken in their com-
putation. It is true a child just dropped from its dam may be supported
by her milk for a solar year with little other nourishment, at most not
above the value of two shillings, which the mother may certainly get, or

the value in scraps, by her lawful occupation of begging, and it is exactly at one year old that I propose to provide for them, in such a manner as, instead of being a charge upon their parents, or the parish, or wanting food and raiment for the rest of their lives, they shall, on the contrary, contribute to the feeding and partly to the clothing of many thousands.

5   There is likewise another great advantage in my scheme, that it will prevent those voluntary abortions, and that horrid practice of women murdering their bastard children, alas, too frequent among us, sacrificing the poor innocent babes, I doubt, more to avoid the expense than the shame, which would move tears and pity in the most savage and inhuman breast.

6   The number of souls in Ireland being usually reckoned one million and a half, of these I calculate there may be about two hundred thousand couples whose wives are breeders, from which number I subtract thirty thousand couples who are able to maintain their own children, although I apprehend there cannot be so many under the present distresses of the kingdom, but this being granted, there will remain an hundred and seventy thousand breeders. I again subtract fifty thousand for those women who miscarry, or whose children die by accident or disease within the year. There only remain an hundred and twenty thousand children of poor parents annually born: the question therefore is, how this number shall be reared, and provided for, which, as I have already said, under the present situation of affairs is utterly impossible by all the methods hitherto proposed, for we can neither employ them in handicraft or agriculture; we neither build houses (I mean in the country), nor cultivate land: they can very seldom pick up a livelihood by stealing until they arrive at six years old, except where they are of towardly parts, although I confess they learn the rudiments much earlier, during which time they can however be properly looked upon only as probationers, as I have been informed by a principal gentleman in the County of Cavan, who protested to me that he never knew above one or two instances under the age of six, even in a part of the kingdom so renowned for the quickest proficiency in that art.

7   I am assured by our merchants that a boy or a girl before twelve years old, is no saleable commodity, and even when they come to this age, they will not yield above three pounds, or three pounds and half-a-crown at most on the Exchange, which cannot turn to account either to the parents or the kingdom, the charge of nutriment and rags having been at least four times that value.

8   I shall now therefore humbly propose my own thoughts, which I hope will not be liable to the least objection.

9   I have been assured by a very knowing American of my acquaintance in London, that a young healthy child well nursed is at a year old a most delicious, nourishing and wholesome food, whether stewed, roasted, baked, or boiled, and I make no doubt that it will equally serve in a fricassee, or a ragout.

10   I do therefore humbly offer it to public consideration, that of the hundred and twenty thousand children already computed, twenty thousand may be reserved for breed, whereof only one fourth part to be males,

which is more than we allow to sheep, black-cattle, or swine, and my reason is that these children are seldom the fruits of marriage, a circumstance not much regarded by our savages, therefore one male will be sufficient to serve four females. That the remaining hundred thousand may at a year old be offered in sale to the persons of quality, and fortune, through the kingdom, always advising the mother to let them suck plentifully in the last month, so as to render them plump, and fat for a good table. A child will make two dishes at an entertainment for friends, and when the family dines alone, the fore or hind quarter will make a reasonable dish, and seasoned with a little pepper or salt will be very good boiled on the fourth day, especially in winter.

11   I have reckoned upon a medium, that a child just born will weigh twelve pounds, and in a solar year if tolerably nursed increaseth to twenty-eight pounds.

12   I grant this food will be somewhat dear, and therefore very proper for landlords, who, as they have already devoured most of the parents, seem to have the best title to the children.

13   Infant's flesh will be in season throughout the year, but more plentiful in March, and a little before and after, for we are told by a grave author,[1] an eminent French physician, that fish being a prolific diet, there are more children born in Roman Catholic countries about nine months after Lent than at any other season; therefore reckoning a year after Lent, the markets will be more glutted than usual, because the number of Popish infants is at least three to one in this kingdom, and therefore it will have one other collateral advantage by lessening the number of Papists among us.

14   I have already computed the charge of nursing a beggar's child (in which list I reckon all cottagers, labourers, and four-fifths of the farmers) to be about two shillings *per annum*, rags included, and I believe no gentleman would repine to give ten shillings for the carcass of a good fat child, which, as I have said, will make four dishes of excellent nutritive meat, when he hath only some particular friend or his own family to dine with him. Thus the Squire will learn to be a good landlord and grow popular among his tenants, the mother will have eight shillings net profit, and be fit for work until she produces another child.

15   Those who are more thrifty (as I must confess the times require) may flay the carcass; the skin of which artificially dressed, will make admirable gloves for ladies, and summer boots for fine gentlemen.

16   As to our city of Dublin, shambles may be appointed for this purpose, in the most convenient parts of it, and butchers we may be assured will not be wanting, although I rather recommend buying the children alive, and dressing them hot from the knife, as we do roasting pigs.

17   A very worthy person, a true lover of his country, and whose virtues I highly esteem, was lately pleased, in discoursing on this matter to offer a refinement upon my scheme. He said that many gentlemen of this

[1]Rabelais.

kingdom, having of late destroyed their deer, he conceived that the want of venison might be well supplied by the bodies of young lads and maidens, not exceeding fourteen years of age, nor under twelve, so great a number of both sexes in every county being now ready to starve, for want of work and service: and these to be disposed of by their parents if alive, or otherwise by their nearest relations. But with due deference to so excellent a friend, and so deserving a patriot, I cannot be altogether in his sentiments. For as to the males, my American acquaintance assured me from frequent experience that their flesh was generally tough and lean, like that of our schoolboys, by continual exercise, and their taste disagreeable, and to fatten them would not answer the charge. Then as to the females, it would, I think with humble submission, be a loss to the public, because they soon would become breeders themselves: and besides, it is not improbable that some scrupulous people might be apt to censure such a practice (although indeed very unjustly) as a little bordering upon cruelty, which I confess, hath always been with me the strongest objection against any project, howsoever well intended.

18   But in order to justify my friend, he confessed that this expedient was put into his head by the famous Psalmanazar, a native of the island Formosa, who came from thence to London, above twenty years ago, and in conversation told my friend that in his country when any young person happened to be put to death, the executioner sold the carcass to persons of quality, as a prime dainty, and that, in his time, the body of a plump girl of fifteen, who was crucified for an attempt to poison the emperor, was sold to his Imperial Majesty's Prime Minister of State, and other great Mandarins of the Court, in joints from the gibbet, at four hundred crowns. Neither indeed can I deny that if the same use were made of several plump young girls in this town who, without one single groat to their fortunes, cannot stir abroad without a chair, and appear at the playhouse and assemblies in foreign fineries, which they never will pay for, the kingdom would not be the worse.

19   Some persons of a desponding spirit are in great concern about that vast number of poor people, who are aged, diseased, or maimed, and I have been desired to employ my thoughts what course may be taken to ease the nation of so grievous an encumbrance. But I am not in the least pain upon that matter, because it is very well known that they are every day dying, and rotting, by cold, and famine, and filth, and vermin, as fast as can be reasonably expected. And as to the younger labourers they are now in almost as hopeful a condition. They cannot get work, and consequently pine away from want of nourishment, to a degree that if at any time they are accidentally hired to common labour, they have not strength to perform it; and thus the country and themselves are in a fair way of being soon delivered from the evils to come.

20   I have too long digressed, and therefore shall return to my subject. I think the advantages by the proposal which I have made are obvious and many, as well as of the highest importance.

21   For first, as I have already observed, it would greatly lessen the number of Papists, with whom we are yearly over-run, being the principal breeders of the nation, as well as our most dangerous enemies, and who stay at home on purpose with a design to deliver the kingdom to the Pretender, hoping to take their advantage by the absence of so many good Protestants, who have chosen rather to leave their country than stay at home and pay tithes against their conscience to an idolatrous Episcopal curate.

22   Secondly, the poorer tenants will have something valuable of their own, which by law may be made liable to distress, and help to pay their landlord's rent, their corn and cattle being already seized, and money a thing unknown.

23   Thirdly, whereas the maintenance of an hundred thousand children, from two years old, and upwards, cannot be computed at less than ten shillings a piece *per annum,* the nation's stock will be thereby increased fifty thousand pounds *per annum* besides the profit of a new dish, introduced to the tables of all gentlemen of fortune in the kingdom, who have any refinement in taste, and the money will circulate among ourselves, the goods being entirely of our own growth and manufacture.

24   Fourthly, the constant breeders, besides the gain of eight shillings sterling *per annum,* by the sale of their children, will be rid of the charge of maintaining them after the first year.

25   Fifthly, this food would likewise bring great custom to taverns, where the vintners will certainly be so prudent as to procure the best receipts for dressing it to perfection, and consequently have their houses frequented by all the fine gentlemen, who justly value themselves upon their knowledge in good eating; and a skilful cook, who understands how to oblige his guests, will contrive to make it as expensive as they please.

26   Sixthly, this would be a great inducement to marriage, which all wise nations have either encouraged by rewards, or enforced by laws and penalties. It would increase the care and tenderness of mothers towards their children, when they were sure of a settlement for life, to the poor babes, provided in some sort by the public to their annual profit instead of expense. We should soon see an honest emulation among the married women, which of them could bring the fattest child to the market. Men would become as fond of their wives, during the time of their pregnancy, as they are now of their mares in foal, their cows in calf, or sows when they are ready to farrow, nor offer to beat or kick them (as it is too frequent a practice) for fear of a miscarriage.

27   Many other advantages might be enumerated. For instance, the addition of some thousand carcasses in our exportation of barrelled beef; the propagation of swine's flesh, and improvement in the art of making good bacon, so much wanted among us by the great destruction of pigs, too frequent at our tables, which are no way comparable in taste or magnificence to a well-grown, fat, yearling child, which roasted whole will make a considerable figure at a Lord Mayor's feast, or any other public entertainment.

28   Supposing that one thousand families in this city would be constant customers for infants' flesh, besides others who might have it at merry meetings, particularly weddings and christenings; I compute that Dublin would take off annually about twenty thousand carcasses, and the rest of the kingdom (where probably they will be sold somewhat cheaper) the remaining eighty thousand.

29   I can think of no one objection that will possibly be raised against this proposal, unless it should be urged that the number of people will be thereby much lessened in the kingdom. This I freely own, and it was indeed one principal design in offering it to the world. I desire the reader will observe, that I calculate my remedy *for this one individual Kingdom of* Ireland, *and for no other that ever was, is, or, I think, ever can be upon earth.* Therefore let no man talk to me of other expedients: *Of taxing our absentees at five shillings a pound: Of using neither clothes, nor household furniture, except what is of our own growth and manufacture: Of utterly rejecting the materials and instruments that promote foreign luxury: Of curing the expensiveness of pride, vanity, idleness, and gaming in our women: Of introducing a vein of parsimony, prudence, and temperance: Of learning to love our country, wherein we differ even from* Laplanders, *and the inhabitants of* Topinamboo: *Of quitting our animosities and factions, nor act any longer like the* Jews, *who were murdering one another at the very moment their city was taken: Of being a little cautious not to sell our country and consciences for nothing: Of teaching landlords to have at least one degree of mercy towards their tenants.* Lastly, *of putting a spirit of honesty, industry, and skill into our shopkeepers, who, if a resolution could now be taken to buy only our native goods, would immediately unite to cheat and exact upon us in the price, the measure and the goodness, nor could ever yet be brought to make one fair proposal of just dealing, though often and earnestly invited to it.*

30   Therefore I repeat, let no man talk to me of these and the like expedients, till he hath at least a glimpse of hope that there will ever be some hearty and sincere attempt to put them in practice.

31   But as to myself, having been wearied out for many years with offering vain, idle, visionary thoughts, and at length utterly despairing of success, I fortunately fell upon this proposal, which as it is wholly new, so it hath something solid and real, of no expense and little trouble, full in our own power, and whereby we can incur no danger in disobliging England. For this kind of commodity will not bear exportation, the flesh being of too tender a consistence to admit a long continuance in salt, *although perhaps I could name a country which would be glad to eat up our whole nation without it.*

32   After all I am not so violently bent upon my own opinion as to reject any offer, proposed by wise men, which shall be found equally innocent, cheap, easy and effectual. But before some thing of that kind shall be advanced in contradiction to my scheme, and offering a better, I desire the author, or authors, will be pleased maturely to consider two points. First, as things now stand, how they will be able to find food and raiment for a hundred thousand useless mouths and backs? And secondly, there being a round million of creatures in human figure, throughout this kingdom, whose whole subsistence put into a common stock would leave

them in debt two millions of pounds sterling; adding those who are beggars by profession, to the bulk of farmers, cottagers, and labourers with their wives and children, who are beggars in effect; I desire those politicians who dislike my overture, and may perhaps be so bold to attempt an answer, that they will first ask the parents of these mortals whether they would not at this day think it a great happiness to have been sold for food at a year old, in the manner I prescribe, and thereby have avoided such a perpetual scene of misfortunes as they have since gone through, by the oppression of landlords, the impossibility of paying rent without money or trade, the want of common sustenance, with neither house nor clothes to cover them from the inclemencies of weather, and the most inevitable prospect of entailing the like, or greater miseries upon their breed for ever.

33   I profess in the sincerity of my heart that I have not the least personal interest in endeavouring to promote this necessary work, having no other motive than the *public good of my country, by advancing our trade, providing for infants, relieving the poor, and giving some pleasure to the rich.* I have no children by which I can propose to get a single penny; the youngest being nine years old, and my wife past child-bearing.

Questions for Discussion

1. What is the tone of this essay?
2. At what point in the essay does Swift's narrator present his shocking proposal?
3. Why would older children not be just as good as younger children for Swift's plan?
4. Outline the "advantages" of the "Modest Proposal," according to the narrator.
5. List the other suggestions for solving Ireland's problem included in paragraph 29. Swift, in other essays, had suggested all of these solutions. Why does the narrator reject them?
6. Would the money and benefits from the sale of children indeed "trickle down" to the less fortunate or the most needy?

Suggestions for Exploration and Writing

1. Write a character sketch of the narrator of this proposal.
2. Write your own modest proposal: an ironic solution to a current problem. Follow Swift's style: build a case, state your proposal, list and explain the advantages with one or more disadvantages, and end with the statement that the proposal is "solid and real, of no expense and little trouble." Possible topics might be the treatment of the homeless or the elderly, deadbeat fathers (or mothers), or drug dealers.
3. Analzye Swift's essay as an indictment of both the Irish and the English.

4. Someone has said that the more things change, the more they stay the same. Apply this saying to the situation Swift is discussing and to a similar situation today.

5. In what ways are we metaphorically cannibals today?

Thomas Jefferson (1743–1826)

Thomas Jefferson, the third president of the United States and author of the Declaration of Independence, was truly a Renaissance man— a statesman, a scientist, an architect, and an author. The son of a successful planter and a member of the famous Randolph family of Virginia, Jefferson spent most of his life in Virginia. As an architect, he designed both his home, Monticello, and the buildings of the University of Virginia. Jefferson is considered by many historians to be the foremost symbol of the American desire for individual freedom.

THE DECLARATION OF INDEPENDENCE   (1776)

1   When in the course of human events, it becomes necessary for one people to dissolve the political bands which have connected them with another, and to assume among the powers of the earth, the separate and equal station to which the Laws of Nature and of Nature's God entitle them, a decent respect to the opinions of mankind requires that they should declare the causes which impel them to the separation.

2   We hold these truths to be self-evident, that all men are created equal, that they are endowed by their Creator with certain inalienable rights, that among these are life, liberty, and the pursuit of happiness. That to secure these rights, governments are instituted among men, deriving their just powers from the consent of the governed. That whenever any form of government becomes destructive of these ends, it is the right of the people to alter or to abolish it, and to institute new government, laying its foundation on such principles and organizing its powers in such form, as to them shall seem most likely to effect their safety and happiness. Prudence, indeed, will dictate that governments long established should not be changed for light and transient causes; and accordingly all experience hath shown, that mankind are more disposed to suffer, while evils are sufferable, than to right themselves by abolishing the forms to which they are accustomed. But when a long train of abuses and usurpations, pursuing invariably the same object, evinces a design to reduce them under absolute despotism, it is their right, it is their duty, to throw off such government, and to provide new guards for their future security. Such has been the patient sufferance of these Colonies; and such is now the necessity which constrains them to alter their former systems of government. The history of the present King of Great Britain is a history of repeated injuries and usurpations, all having in direct object the establishment of an absolute tyranny over these States. To prove this, let facts be submitted to a candid world.

3   He has refused his assent to laws, the most wholesome and necessary for the public good.

4   He has forbidden his Governors to pass laws of immediate and pressing importance, unless suspended in their operation till his assent should be obtained; and when so suspended, he has utterly neglected to attend to them.

5   He has refused to pass other laws for the accommodation of large districts of people, unless those people would relinquish the right of representation in the legislature, a right inestimable to them and formidable to tyrants only.

6   He has called together legislative bodies at places unusual, uncomfortable, and distant from the depository of their public records, for the sole purpose of fatiguing them into compliance with his measures.

7   He has dissolved representative houses repeatedly, for opposing with manly firmness his invasions on the rights of the people.

8   He has refused for a long time, after such dissolutions, to cause others to be elected; whereby the legislative powers, incapable of annihilation, have returned to the people at large for their exercise; the State remaining in the meantime exposed to all the dangers of invasion from without and convulsions within.

9   He has endeavoured to prevent the population of these states; for that purpose obstructing the laws for naturalization of foreigners; refusing to pass others to encourage their migration hither, and raising the conditions of new appropriations of lands.

10   He has obstructed the administration of justice, by refusing his assent to laws for establishing judiciary powers.

11   He has made judges dependent on his will alone, for the tenure of their office, and the amount and payment of their salaries.

12   He has erected a multitude of new offices, and sent hither swarms of officers to harass our people, and eat out their substance.

13   He has kept among us, in times of peace, standing armies without the consent of our legislatures.

14   He has affected to render the military independent of and superior to the civil power.

15   He has combined with others to subject us to a jurisdiction foreign of our constitution, and unacknowledged by our laws; giving his assent to their acts of pretended legislation:

16   For quartering large bodies of armed troops among us:

17   For protecting them, by a mock trial, from punishment for any murders which they should commit on the inhabitants of these States:

18   For cutting off our trade with all parts of the world:

19   For imposing taxes on us without our consent:

20   For depriving us in many cases of the benefits of trial by jury:

21   For transporting us beyond seas to be tried for pretended offenses:

22   For abolishing the free system of English laws in a neighbouring Province, establishing therein an arbitrary government, and enlarging its boundaries so as to render it at once an example and fit instrument for introducing the same absolute rule into these Colonies:

23   For taking away our Charters, abolishing our most valuable laws, and altering fundamentally the forms of our governments:

24   For suspending our own legislatures, and declaring themselves invested with power to legislate for us in all cases whatsoever.

25   He has abdicated government here, by declaring us out of his protection and waging war against us.

26   He has plundered our seas, ravaged our coasts, burnt our towns, and destroyed the lives of our people.

27   He is at this time transporting large armies of foreign mercenaries to complete the works of death, desolation, and tyranny, already begun with circumstances of cruelty and perfidy scarcely paralleled in the most barbarous ages, and totally unworthy the head of a civilized nation.

28   He has constrained our fellow citizens taken captive on the high seas to bear arms against their country, to become the executioners of their friends and brethren, or to fall themselves by their hands.

29   He has excited domestic insurrections amongst us, and has endeavored to bring on the inhabitants of our frontiers, the merciless Indian savages, whose known rule of warfare, is an undistinguished destruction of all ages, sexes, and conditions.

30   In every stage of these oppressions we have petitioned for redress in the most humble terms: our repeated petitions have been answered only by repeated injury. A prince whose character is thus marked by every act which may define a tyrant is unfit to be the ruler of a free people.

31   Nor have we been wanting in attention to our British brethren. We have warned them from time to time of attempts by their legislature to extend an unwarrantable jurisdiction over us. We have reminded them of the circumstances of our emigration and settlement here. We have appealed to their native justice and magnanimity, and we have conjured them by the ties of our common kindred to disavow these usurpations, which would inevitably interrupt our connections and correspondence. They too have been deaf to the voice of justice and of consanguinity. We must, therefore, acquiesce in the necessity, which denounces our separation, and hold them, as we hold the rest of mankind, enemies in war, in peace friends.

32   We, therefore, the Representatives of the United States of America, in General Congress assembled, appealing to the Supreme Judge of the world for the rectitude of our intentions, do, in the name, and by authority of the good people of these Colonies, solemnly publish and declare, That these United Colonies are, and of right ought to be, Free and Independent States; that they are absolved from all allegiance to the British Crown, and that all political connection between them and the state of Great Britain, is and ought to be totally dissolved; and that as Free and Independent States, they have full power to levy war, conclude peace, contract alliances, establish commerce, and to do all other acts and things which Independent States may of right do. And for the support of this declaration, with a firm reliance on the protection of Divine Providence, we mutually pledge to each other our lives, our fortunes, and our sacred honor.

Questions for Discussion

1. Since the outcome of the rebellion will be determined by war in any case, why do Jefferson and his fellow patriots feel compelled to explain their reasons for rebellion?
2. What are the premises of Jefferson's argument?
3. What, according to Jefferson, is the purpose of government?
4. What are the abuses of power with which the Declaration charges King George III of England?

Suggestions for Exploration and Writing

1. Jefferson says that when government ceases to be responsive to the people, the people have the right to abolish the government. What offenses would cause you to advocate overthrowing the government? Discuss.
2. Jefferson says government derives its "just powers from the consent of the governed." In what ways have government agencies treated you as a subject rather than a person who is the source of their authority? Discuss.
3. To what degree have governments and government agencies in the United States today—local, state, and federal—failed in their purpose and ignored the source of their power?

Harriet Jacobs (1813–1897)

Harriet Jacobs was born into slavery in North Carolina and was orphaned as a child. Her owner's wife taught her to read, but her owner abused her. Consequently, she ran away and hid in a crawl-space in her grandmother's home. In 1842, she escaped to the North and became active in the antislavery movement. Her Incidents in the Life of a Slave Girl, *published in Boston in 1860, is a forceful and revealing account of the abuse endured by female slaves.*

THE SLAVE WHO DARED TO FEEL LIKE A MAN   (1860)

1   Two years had passed since I entered Dr. Flint's family, and those years had brought much of the knowledge that comes from experience, though they had afforded little opportunity for any other kinds of knowledge.

2   My grandmother had, as much as possible, been a mother to her orphan grandchildren. By perseverance and unwearied industry, she was now mistress of a snug little home, surrounded with the necessaries of life. She would have been happy could her children have shared them with her. There remained but three children and two grandchildren, all slaves. Most earnestly did she strive to make us feel that it was the will of

God: that He had seen fit to place us under such circumstances; and though it seemed hard, we ought to pray for contentment.

3   It was a beautiful faith, coming from a mother who could not call her children her own. But I, and Benjamin, her youngest boy, condemned it. We reasoned that it was much more the will of God that we should be situated as she was. We longed for a home like hers. There we always found sweet balsam for our troubles. She was so loving, so sympathizing! She always met us with a smile, and listened with patience to all our sorrows. She spoke so hopefully, that unconsciously the clouds gave place to sunshine. There was a grand big oven there, too, that baked bread and nice things for the town, and we knew there was always a choice bit in store for us.

4   But, alas! even the charms of the old oven failed to reconcile us to our hard lot. Benjamin was now a tall, handsome lad, strongly and gracefully made, and with a spirit too bold and daring for a slave. My brother William, now twelve years old, had the same aversion to the word master that he had when he was an urchin of seven years. I was his confidant. He came to me with all his troubles. I remember one instance in particular. It was on a lovely spring morning, and when I marked the sunlight dancing here and there, its beauty seemed to mock my sadness. For my master, whose restless, craving, vicious nature roved about day and night, seeking whom to devour, had just left me, with stinging, scorching words; words that scathed ear and brain like fire. O, how I despised him! I thought how glad I should be, if some day when he walked the earth, it would open and swallow him up, and disencumber the world of a plague.

5   When he told me that I was made for his use, made to obey his command in *every* thing; that I was nothing but a slave, whose will must and should surrender to his, never before had my puny arm felt half so strong.

6   So deeply was I absorbed in painful reflections afterwards, that I neither saw nor heard the entrance of any one, till the voice of William sounded close beside me. "Linda," he said, "what makes you look so sad? I love you. O, Linda, isn't this a bad world? Every body seems so cross and unhappy. I wish I had died when poor father did."

7   I told him that every body was *not* cross, or unhappy; that those who had pleasant homes, and kind friends, and who were not afraid to love them, were happy. But we, who were slave-children, without father or mother, could not expect to be happy. We must be good; perhaps that would bring us contentment.

8   "Yes," he said, "I try to be good; but what's the use? They are all the time troubling me." Then he proceeded to relate his afternoon's difficulty with young master Nicholas. It seemed that the brother of master Nicholas had pleased himself with making up stories about William. Master Nicholas said he should be flogged, and he would do it. Whereupon he went to work; but William fought bravely, and the young master, finding he was getting the better of him, undertook to tie his hands

behind him. He failed in that likewise. By dint of kicking and fisting, William came out of the skirmish none the worse for a few scratches.

9   He continued to discourse on his young master's *meanness;* how he whipped the *little* boys, but was a perfect coward when a tussle ensued between him and white boys of his own size. On such occasions he always took to his legs. William had other charges to make against him. One was his rubbing up pennies with quicksilver, and passing them off for quarters of a dollar on an old man who kept a fruit stall. William was often sent to buy fruit, and he earnestly inquired of me what he ought to do under such circumstances. I told him it was certainly wrong to deceive the old man, and that it was his duty to tell him of the impositions practised by his young master. I assured him the old man would not be slow to comprehend the whole, and there the matter would end. William thought it might with the old man, but not with *him.* He said he did not mind the smart of the whip, but he did not like the *idea* of being whipped.

10   While I advised him to be good and forgiving I was not unconscious of the beam in my own eye. It was the very knowledge of my own short-comings that urged me to retain, if possible, some sparks of my brother's God-given nature. I had not lived fourteen years in slavery for nothing. I had felt, seen, and heard enough, to read the characters, and question the motives, of those around me. The war of my life had begun; and though one of God's most powerless creatures, I resolved never to be con-quered. Alas, for me!

11   If there was one pure, sunny spot for me, I believed it to be in Ben-jamin's heart, and in another's, whom I loved with all the ardor of a girl's first love. My owner knew of it, and sought in every way to render me mis-erable. He did not resort to corporal punishment, but to all the petty, tyrannical ways that human ingenuity could devise.

12   I remember the first time I was punished. It was in the month of Feb-ruary. My grandmother had taken my old shoes, and replaced them with a new pair. I needed them; for several inches of snow had fallen, and it still continued to fall. When I walked through Mrs. Flint's room, their creaking grated harshly on her refined nerves. She called me to her, and asked what I had about me that made such a horrid noise. I told her it was my new shoes. "Take them off," said she; "and if you put them on again, I'll throw them into the fire."

13   I took them off, and my stockings also. She then sent me a long dis-tance, on an errand. As I went through the snow, my bare feet tingled. That night I was very hoarse; and I went to bed thinking the next day would find me sick, perhaps dead. What was my grief on waking to find myself quite well!

14   I had imagined if I died, or was laid up for some time, that my mistress would feel a twinge of remorse that she had so hated "the little imp," as she styled me. It was my ignorance of that mistress that gave rise to such extravagant imaginings.

15   Dr. Flint occasionally had high prices offered for me; but he always said, "She don't belong to me. She is my daughter's property, and I have no right to sell her." Good, honest man! My young mistress was still a child, and I could look for no protection from her. I loved her, and she returned my affection. I once heard her father allude to her attachment to me; and his wife promptly replied that it proceeded from fear. This put unpleasant doubts into my mind. Did the child feign what she did not feel? or was her mother jealous of the mite of love she bestowed on me? I concluded it must be the latter. I said to myself, "Surely, little children are true."

16   One afternoon I sat at my sewing, feeling unusual depression of spirits. My mistress had been accusing me of an offence, of which I assured her I was perfectly innocent; but I saw, by the contemptuous curl of her lip, that she believed I was telling a lie.

17   I wondered for what wise purpose God was leading me through such thorny paths, and whether still darker days were in store for me. As I sat musing thus, the door opened softly, and William came in. "Well, brother," said I, "what is the matter this time?"

18   "O Linda, Ben and his master have had a dreadful time!" said he.

19   My first thought was that Benjamin was killed. "Don't be frightened, Linda," said William; "I will tell you all about it."

20   It appeared that Benjamin's master had sent for him, and he did not immediately obey the summons. When he did, his master was angry, and began to whip him. He resisted. Master and slave fought, and finally the master was thrown. Benjamin had cause to tremble; for he had thrown to the ground his master—one of the richest men in town. I anxiously awaited the result.

21   That night I stole to my grandmother's house, and Benjamin also stole thither from his master's. My grandmother had gone to spend a day or two with an old friend living in the country.

22   "I have come," said Benjamin, "to tell you good by. I am going away."

23   I inquired where.

24   "To the north," he replied.

25   I looked at him to see whether he was in earnest. I saw it all in his firm, set mouth. I implored him not to go, but he paid no heed to my words. He said he was no longer a boy, and every day made his yoke more galling. He had raised his hand against his master, and was to be publicly whipped for the offence. I reminded him of the poverty and hardships he must encounter among strangers. I told him he might be caught and brought back; and that was terrible to think of.

26   He grew vexed, and asked if poverty and hardships with freedom, were not preferable to our treatment in slavery. "Linda," he continued, "we are dogs here; foot-balls, cattle, every thing that's mean. No, I will not stay. Let them bring me back. We don't die but once."

27   He was right; but it was hard to give him up. "Go," said I, "and break your mother's heart."

28   I repented of my words ere they were out.

29   "Linda," said he, speaking as I had not heard him speak that evening, "how *could* you say that? Poor mother! be kind to her, Linda; and you, too, cousin Fanny."

30   Cousin Fanny was a friend who had lived some years with us.

31   Farewells were exchanged, and the bright, kind boy, endeared to us by so many acts of love, vanished from our sight.

32   It is not necessary to state how he made his escape. Suffice it to say, he was on his way to New York when a violent storm overtook the vessel. The captain said he must put into the nearest port. This alarmed Benjamin, who was aware that he would be advertised in every port near his own town. His embarrassment was noticed by the captain. To port they went. There the advertisement met the captain's eye. Benjamin so exactly answered its description, that the captain laid hold on him, and bound him in chains. The storm passed, and they proceeded to New York. Before reaching that port Benjamin managed to get off his chains and throw them overboard. He escaped from the vessel, but was pursued, captured, and carried back to his master.

33   When my grandmother returned home and found her youngest child had fled, great was her sorrow; but, with characteristic piety, she said, "God's will be done." Each morning, she inquired if any news had been heard from her boy. Yes, news *was* heard. The master was rejoicing over a letter, announcing the capture of his human chattel.

34   That day seems but as yesterday, so well do I remember it. I saw him led through the streets in chains, to jail. His face was ghastly pale, yet full of determination. He had begged one of the sailors to go to his mother's house and ask her not to meet him. He said the sight of her distress would take from him all self-control. She yearned to see him, and she went; but she screened herself in the crowd, that it might be as her child had said.

35   We were not allowed to visit him; but we had known the jailer for years, and he was a kind-hearted man. At midnight he opened the jail door for my grandmother and myself to enter, in disguise. When we entered the cell not a sound broke the stillness. "Benjamin, Benjamin!" whispered my grandmother. No answer. "Benjamin!" she again faltered. There was a jingle of chains. The moon had just risen, and cast an uncertain light through the bars of the window. We knelt down and took Benjamin's cold hands in ours. We did not speak. Sobs were heard, and Benjamin's lips were unsealed; for his mother was weeping on his neck. How vividly does memory bring back that sad night! Mother and son talked together. He asked her pardon for the suffering he had caused her. She said she had nothing to forgive; she could not blame his desire for freedom. He told her that when he was captured, he broke away, and was about casting himself into the river, when thoughts of *her* came over him, and he desisted. She asked if he did not also think of God. I fancied I saw his face grow fierce in the moonlight. He answered, "No, I did not think of him. When a man is hunted like a wild beast he forgets there is a God, a heaven. He forgets every thing in his struggle to get beyond the reach of the bloodhounds."

36   "Don't talk so, Benjamin," said she. "Put your trust in God. Be humble, my child, and your master will forgive you."

37   "Forgive me for *what,* mother? For not letting him treat me like a dog? No! I will never humble myself to him. I have worked for him for nothing all my life, and I am repaid with stripes and imprisonment. Here I will stay till I die, or till he sells me."

38   The poor mother shuddered at his words. I think he felt it; for when he next spoke, his voice was calmer. "Don't fret about me, mother. I ain't worth it," said he. "I wish I had some of your goodness. You bear every thing patiently, just as though you thought it was all right. I wish I could."

39   She told him she had not always been so; once, she was like him; but when sore troubles came upon her, and she had no arm to lean upon, she learned to call on God, and he lightened her burdens. She besought him to do likewise.

40   We overstaid our time, and were obliged to hurry from the jail.

41   Benjamin had been imprisoned three weeks, when my grandmother went to intercede for him with his master. He was immovable. He said Benjamin should serve as an example to the rest of his slaves; he should be kept in jail till he was subdued, or be sold if he got but one dollar for him. However, he afterwards relented in some degree. The chains were taken off, and we were allowed to visit him.

42   As his food was of the coarsest kind, we carried him as often as possible a warm supper, accompanied with some little luxury for the jailer.

43   Three months elapsed, and there was no prospect of release or of a purchaser. One day he was heard to sing and laugh. This piece of indecorum was told to his master, and the overseer was ordered to re-chain him. He was now confined in an apartment with other prisoners, who were covered with filthy rags. Benjamin was chained near them, and was soon covered with vermin. He worked at his chains till he succeeded in getting out of them. He passed them through the bars of the window, with a request that they should be taken to his master, and he should be informed that he was covered with vermin.

44   This audacity was punished with heavier chains, and prohibition of our visits.

45   My grandmother continued to send him fresh changes of clothes. The old ones were burned up. The last night we saw him in jail his mother still begged him to send for his master, and beg his pardon. Neither persuasion nor argument could turn him from his purpose. He calmly answered, "I am waiting his time."

46   Those chains were mournful to hear.

47   Another three months passed, and Benjamin left his prison walls. We that loved him waited to bid him a long and last farewell. A slave trader had bought him. You remember, I told you what price he brought when ten years of age. Now he was more than twenty years old, and sold for three hundred dollars. The master had been blind to his own interest. Long confinement had made his face too pale, his form too thin; moreover, the

trader had heard something of his character, and it did not strike him as suitable for a slave. He said he would give any price if the handsome lad was a girl. We thanked God that he was not.

48   Could you have seen that mother clinging to her child, when they fastened the irons upon his wrists; could you have heard her heart-rending groans, and seen her bloodshot eyes wander wildly from face to face, vainly pleading for mercy; could you have witnessed that scene as I saw it, you would exclaim, *Slavery is damnable!*

49   Benjamin, her youngest, her pet, was forever gone! She could not realize it. She had had an interview with the trader for the purpose of ascertaining if Benjamin could be purchased. She was told it was impossible, as he had given bonds not to sell him till he was out of the state. He promised that he would not sell him till he reached New Orleans.

50   With a strong arm and unvaried trust, my grandmother began her work of love. Benjamin must be free. If she succeeded, she knew they would still be separated; but the sacrifice was not too great. Day and night she labored. The trader's price would treble that he gave; but she was not discouraged.

51   She employed a lawyer to write to a gentleman, whom she knew, in New Orleans. She begged him to interest himself for Benjamin, and he willingly favored her request. When he saw Benjamin, and stated his business, he thanked him; but said he preferred to wait a while before making the trader an offer. He knew he had tried to obtain a high price for him, and had invariably failed. This encouraged him to make another effort for freedom. So one morning, long before day, Benjamin was missing. He was riding over the blue billows, bound for Baltimore.

52   For once his white face did him a kindly service. They had no suspicion that it belonged to a slave; otherwise, the law would have been followed out to the letter, and the *thing* rendered back to slavery. The brightest skies are often overshadowed by the darkest clouds. Benjamin was taken sick, and compelled to remain in Baltimore three weeks. His strength was slow in returning; and his desire to continue his journey seemed to retard his recovery. How could he get strength without air and exercise? He resolved to venture on a short walk. A by-street was selected, where he thought himself secure of not being met by any one that knew him; but a voice called out, "Halloo, Ben, my boy! what are you doing *here?*"

53   His first impulse was to run; but his legs trembled so that he could not stir. He turned to confront his antagonist, and behold, there stood his old master's next door neighbor! He thought it was all over with him now; but it proved otherwise. That man was a miracle. He possessed a goodly number of slaves, and yet was not quite deaf to that mystic clock, whose ticking is rarely heard in the slaveholder's breast.

54   "Ben, you are sick," said he. "Why, you look like a ghost. I guess I gave you something of a start. Never mind, Ben, I am not going to touch you. You had a pretty tough time of it, and you may go on your way rejoicing for all me. But I would advise you to get out of this place plaguy quick,

for there are several gentlemen here from our town." He described the nearest and safest route to New York, and added, "I shall be glad to tell your mother I have seen you. Good by, Ben."

55   Benjamin turned away, filled with gratitude, and surprised that the town he hated contained such a gem—a gem worthy of a purer setting.

56   This gentleman was a Northerner by birth, and had married a southern lady. On his return, he told my grandmother that he had seen her son, and of the service he had rendered him.

57   Benjamin reached New York safely, and concluded to stop there until he had gained strength enough to proceed further. It happened that my grandmother's only remaining son had sailed for the same city on business for his mistress. Through God's providence, the brothers met. You may be sure it was a happy meeting. "O Phil," exclaimed Benjamin, "I am here at last." Then he told him how near he came to dying, almost in sight of free land, and how he prayed that he might live to get one breath of free air. He said life was worth something now, and it would be hard to die. In the old jail he had not valued it; once, he was tempted to destroy it; but something, he did not know what, had prevented him; perhaps it was fear. He had heard those who profess to be religious declare there was no heaven for self-murderers; and as his life had been pretty hot here, he did not desire a continuation of the same in another world. "If I die now," he exclaimed, "thank God, I shall die a freeman!"

58   He begged my uncle Phillip not to return south; but stay and work with him, till they earned enough to buy those at home. His brother told him it would kill their mother if he deserted her in her trouble. She had pledged her house, and with difficulty had raised money to buy him. Would he be bought?

59   "No, never!" he replied. "Do you suppose, Phil, when I have got so far out of their clutches, I will give them one red cent? No! And do you suppose I would turn mother out of her home in her old age? That I would let her pay all those hard-earned dollars for me, and never to see me? For you know she will stay south as long as her other children are slaves. What a good mother! Tell her to buy *you*, Phil. You have been a comfort to her, and I have been a trouble. And Linda, poor Linda; what'll become of her? Phil, you don't know what a life they lead her. She has told me something about it, and I wish old Flint was dead, or a better man. When I was in jail, he asked her if she didn't want *him* to ask my master to forgive me, and take me home again. She told him, No; that I didn't want to go back. He got mad, and said we were all alike. I never despised my own master half as much as I do that man. There is many a worse slaveholder than my master; but for all that I would not be his slave."

60   While Benjamin was sick, he had parted with nearly all his clothes to pay necessary expenses. But he did not part with a little pin I fastened in his bosom when we parted. It was the most valuable thing I owned, and I thought none more worthy to wear it. He had it still.

61   His brother furnished him with clothes, and gave him what money he had.

62   They parted with moistened eyes; and as Benjamin turned away, he said, "Phil, I part with all my kindred." And so it proved. We never heard from him again.

63   Uncle Phillip came home; and the first words he uttered when he entered the house were, "Mother, Ben is free! I have seen him in New York." She stood looking at him with a bewildered air. "Mother, don't you believe it?" he said, laying his hand softly upon her shoulder. She raised her hands, and exclaimed, "God be praised! Let us thank him." She dropped on her knees, and poured forth her heart in prayer. Then Phillip must sit down and repeat to her every word Benjamin had said. He told her all; only he forbore to mention how sick and pale her darling looked. Why should he distress her when she could do him no good?

64   The brave old woman still toiled on, hoping to rescue some of her other children. After a while she succeeded in buying Phillip. She paid eight hundred dollars, and came home with the precious document that secured his freedom. The happy mother and son sat together by the old hearthstone that night, telling how proud they were of each other, and how they would prove to the world that they could take care of themselves, as they had long taken care of others. We all concluded by saying, "He that is *willing* to be a slave, let him be a slave."

Questions for Discussion

1. Why did the grandmother try to convince her children and grandchildren that they should be content to be slaves?

2. What does Linda imply about her master in saying that his "restless, craving, vicious nature raved about day and night, seeking whom to devour"?

3. Explain the irony of the title. List the qualities that make Benjamin ill suited to be a slave.

4. What does the ordeal in the jail reveal about Benjamin's character?

5. What does Linda mean when she says of Benjamin's master that he had been "blind to his own interest"?

6. Why does Benjamin refuse to be bought by his mother?

7. Why did the slave owner's neighbor treat Benjamin kindly and report his whereabouts to his mother? Do you think this behavior typical of slave owners? Explain.

Suggestions for Exploration and Writing

1. Benjamin asks Linda "if poverty and hardships with freedom, were not preferable to our treatment in slavery." What would your answer be? Write an essay defending your position.

2. Discuss the last sentence in the essay. Who is willing to be a slave? Why?

3. Benjamin says, "When a man is hunted like a wild beast, he forgets there is a God." Compare Benjamin's attitude to Pinhas's attitude in Wiesel's "Yom Kippur."

4. The grandmother and Benjamin represent two distinctly different ways of dealing with injustice: passive contentment and resistance. Which would you be most likely to choose? Defend your answer in an essay.

5. Phil neglects to tell his mother "how sick and pale" Benjamin looked in order to spare his mother's feelings. Why? Would you hide the truth in order to spare someone pain? Why or why not?

Abraham Lincoln (1809–1865)

Abraham Lincoln, the sixteenth president of the United States, led his country through the difficult times of the Civil War. With the Emancipation Proclamation on January 1, 1863, Lincoln declared that all slaves were free. Even before he became president, Lincoln was noted for his powerful speeches; probably his most famous is The Gettysburg Address, delivered on November 19, 1863, at the site of the Battle of Gettysburg in honor of those who had died there for their country. This speech combines the best of Lincoln's rhetorical abilities in a powerful tribute and challenge. On April 14, 1865, while attending a performance of Our American Cousin *at Ford's Theatre in Washington, D.C., Lincoln was assassinated.*

THE GETTYSBURG ADDRESS (1863)

1   Four score and seven years ago our fathers brought forth on this continent a new nation, conceived in liberty and dedicated to the proposition that all men are created equal. Now we are engaged in a great civil war, testing whether that nation or any nation so conceived and so dedicated can long endure. We are met on a great battlefield of that war. We have come to dedicate a portion of that field as a final resting-place for those who here gave their lives that the nation might live. It is altogether fitting and proper that we should do this. But in a larger sense, we cannot dedicate, we cannot consecrate, we cannot hallow this ground. The brave men, living and dead, who struggled here have consecrated it far above our poor power to add or detract. The world will little note nor long remember what we say here, but it can never forget what they did here. It is for us the living rather to be dedicated here to the unfinished work which they who fought here have thus far so nobly advanced. It is rather for us to be here dedicated to the great task remaining before us— that from these honored dead we take increased devotion to that cause for which they gave the last full measure of devotion—that we here highly resolve that these dead shall not have died in vain, that this nation under God shall have a new birth of freedom, and that government of the people, by the people, for the people shall not perish from the earth.

Questions for Discussion

1. Why does Lincoln say that "we cannot consecrate, we cannot hallow this ground"? Explain.

2. What is the irony of his statement that "The world will little note nor long remember what we say here"? 50 yrs later we're still discussing it

3. Notice the many examples of parallel structure in this famous speech. How does this parallelism affect the meaning of Lincoln's speech?

Suggestions for Exploration and Writing

1. In an essay, defend Lincoln's description of the American government as "of the people, by the people, for the people."

2. Write an essay comparing Lincoln's challenge here with that in McCrae's "In Flanders Fields" or with the concluding paragraph of Henderson's "As Simple as That."

3. Write a speech in which you dedicate the sites of the September 11, 2001, attacks on the World Trade Center or the Pentagon.

Martin Luther King Jr. (1929–1968)

Martin Luther King Jr., an ordained minister at the age of eighteen, was born in Atlanta, Georgia. He received degrees from Morehouse College, Crozer Theological Seminary, and Boston University. A leader of the civil rights movement, King organized the Montgomery, Alabama, bus boycott after Rosa Parks refused to give up her seat. He was also the founder and president of the Southern Christian Leadership Conference (SCLC), which espoused his philosophy of nonviolence. This letter from jail was written in response to the local clergy who had questioned King's approach and methodology.

LETTER FROM BIRMINGHAM CITY JAIL   (1963)

1   My dear Fellow Clergymen,

2   While confined here in Birmingham city jail, I came across your recent statement calling our present activities "unwise and untimely." Seldom, if ever, do I pause to answer criticism of my work and ideas. If I sought to answer all of the criticisms that cross my desk, my secretaries would be engaged in little else in the course of the day, and I would have no time for constructive work. But since I feel that you are men of genuine good will and your criticisms are sincerely set forth, I would like to answer your statement in what I hope will be patient and reasonable terms.

3   I think I should give the reason for my being in Birmingham, since you have been influenced by the argument of "outsiders coming in." I have the honor of serving as president of the Southern Christian Leadership

Conference, an organization operating in every southern state, with headquarters in Atlanta, Georgia. We have some eighty-five affiliate organizations all across the South—one being the Alabama Christian Movement for Human Rights. Whenever necessary and possible we share staff, educational and financial resources with our affiliates. Several months ago our local affiliate here in Birmingham invited us to be on call to engage in a nonviolent direct-action program if such were deemed necessary. We readily consented and when the hour came we lived up to our promises. So I am here, along with several members of my staff, because we were invited here. I am here because I have basic organizational ties here.

4   Beyond this, I am in Birmingham because injustice is here. Just as the eighth century prophets left their little villages and carried their "thus saith the Lord" far beyond the boundaries of their hometowns; and just as the Apostle Paul left his little village of Tarsus and carried the gospel of Jesus Christ to practically every hamlet and city of the Graeco-Roman world, I too am compelled to carry the gospel of freedom beyond my particular hometown. Like Paul, I must constantly respond to the Macedonian call for aid.

5   Moreover, I am cognizant of the interrelatedness of all communities and states. I cannot sit idly by in Atlanta and not be concerned about what happens in Birmingham. Injustice anywhere is a threat to justice everywhere. We are caught in an inescapable network of mutuality, tied in a single garment of destiny. Whatever affects one directly affects all indirectly. Never again can we afford to live with the narrow, provincial "outside agitator" idea. Anyone who lives in the United States can never be considered an outsider anywhere in this country.

6   You deplore the demonstrations that are presently taking place in Birmingham. But I am sorry that your statement did not express a similar concern for the conditions that brought the demonstrations into being. I am sure that each of you would want to go beyond the superficial social analyst who looks merely at effects, and does not grapple with underlying causes. I would not hesitate to say that it is unfortunate that so-called demonstrations are taking place in Birmingham at this time, but I would say in more emphatic terms that it is even more unfortunate that the white power structure of this city left the Negro community with no other alternative.

7   In any nonviolent campaign there are four basic steps: (1) collection of the facts to determine whether injustices are alive, (2) negotiation, (3) self-purification, and (4) direct action. We have gone through all of these steps in Birmingham. There can be no gainsaying of the fact that racial injustice engulfs this community.

8   Birmingham is probably the most thoroughly segregated city in the United States. Its ugly record of police brutality is known in every section of this country. Its injust treatment of Negroes in the courts is a notorious reality. There have been more unsolved bombings of Negro homes and churches in Birmingham than any city in this nation. These are the

hard, brutal and unbelievable facts. On the basis of these conditions Negro leaders sought to negotiate with the city fathers. But the political leaders consistently refused to engage in good faith negotiation.

9   Then came the opportunity last September to talk with some of the leaders of the economic community. In these negotiating sessions certain promises were made by the merchants—such as the promise to remove the humiliating racial signs from the stores. On the basis of these promises Rev. Shuttlesworth and the leaders of the Alabama Christian Movement for Human Rights agreed to call a moratorium on any type of demonstrations. As the weeks and months unfolded we realized that we were the victims of a broken promise. The signs remained. Like so many experiences of the past we were confronted with blasted hopes, and the dark shadow of a deep disappointment settled upon us. So we had no alternative except that of preparing for direct action, whereby we would present our very bodies as a means of laying our case before the conscience of the local and national community. We were not unmindful of the difficulties involved. So we decided to go through a process of self-purification. We started having workshops on nonviolence and repeatedly asked ourselves the questions, "Are you able to accept blows without retaliating?" "Are you able to endure the ordeals of jail?" We decided to set our direct-action program around the Easter season, realizing that with the exception of Christmas, this was the largest shopping period of the year. Knowing that a strong economic withdrawal program would be the by-product of direct action, we felt that this was the best time to bring pressure on the merchants for the needed changes. Then it occurred to us that the March election was ahead and so we speedily decided to postpone action until after election day. When we discovered that Mr. Connor was in the run-off, we decided again to postpone action so that the demonstrations could not be used to cloud the issues. At this time we agreed to begin our nonviolent witness the day after the run-off.

10   This reveals that we did not move irresponsibly into direct action. We too wanted to see Mr. Connor defeated; so we went through postponement after postponement to aid in this community need. After this we felt that direct action could be delayed no longer.

11   You may well ask, "Why direct action? Why sit-ins, marches, etc.? Isn't negotiation a better path?" You are exactly right in your call for negotiation. Indeed, this is the purpose of direct action. Nonviolent direct action seeks to create such a crisis and establish such creative tension that a community that has constantly refused to negotiate is forced to confront the issue. It seeks so to dramatize the issue that it can no longer be ignored. I just referred to the creation of tension as a part of the work of the nonviolent resister. This may sound rather shocking. But I must confess that I am not afraid of the word tension. I have earnestly worked and preached against violent tension, but there is a type of constructive nonviolent tension that is necessary for growth. Just as Socrates felt that it was necessary

to create a tension in the mind so that individuals could rise from the bondage of myths and half-truths to the unfettered realm of creative analysis and objective appraisal, we must see the need of having nonviolent gadflies to create the kind of tension in society that will help men to rise from the dark depths of prejudice and racism to the majestic heights of understanding and brotherhood. So the purpose of the direct action is to create a situation so crisis-packed that it will inevitably open the door to negotiation. We, therefore, concur with you in your call for negotiation. Too long has our beloved Southland been bogged down in the tragic attempt to live in monologue rather than dialogue.

12   One of the basic points in your statement is that our acts are untimely. Some have asked, "Why didn't you give the new administration time to act?" The only answer that I can give to this inquiry is that the new administration must be prodded about as much as the outgoing one before it acts. We will be sadly mistaken if we feel that the election of Mr. Boutwell will bring the millennium to Birmingham. While Mr. Boutwell is much more articulate and gentle than Mr. Connor, they are both segregationists, dedicated to the task of maintaining the status quo. The hope I see in Mr. Boutwell is that he will be reasonable enough to see the futility of massive resistance to desegregation. But he will not see this without pressure from the devotees of civil rights. My friends, I must say to you that we have not made a single gain in civil rights without determined legal and nonviolent pressure. History is the long and tragic story of the fact that privileged groups seldom give up their privileges voluntarily. Individuals may see the moral light and voluntarily give up their unjust posture; but as Reinhold Niebuhr has reminded us, groups are more immoral than individuals.

13   We know through painful experience that freedom is never voluntarily given by the oppressor; it must be demanded by the oppressed. Frankly, I have never yet engaged in a direct action movement that was "well-timed," according to the timetable of those who have not suffered unduly from the disease of segregation. For years now I have heard the words "Wait!" It rings in the ear of every Negro with a piercing familiarity. This "Wait" has almost always meant "Never." It has been a tranquilizing thalidomide, relieving the emotional stress for a moment, only to give birth to an ill-formed infant of frustration. We must come to see with the distinguished jurist of yesterday that "justice too long delayed is justice denied." We have waited for more than 340 years for our constitutional and God-given rights. The nations of Asia and Africa are moving with jetlike speed toward the goal of political independence, and we still creep at horse and buggy pace toward the gaining of a cup of coffee at a lunch counter. I guess it is easy for those who have never felt the stinging darts of segregation to say, "Wait." But when you have seen vicious mobs lynch your mothers and fathers at will and drown your sisters and brothers at whim; when you have seen hate-filled policemen curse, kick, brutalize and even kill your black brothers and sisters with impunity; when

you see the vast majority of your twenty million Negro brothers smothering in an airtight cage of poverty in the midst of an affluent society; when you suddenly find your tongue twisted and your speech stammering as you seek to explain to your six-year-old daughter why she can't go to the public amusement park that has just been advertised on television, and see tears welling up in her little eyes when she is told that Funtown is closed to colored children, and see the depressing clouds of inferiority begin to form in her little mental sky, and see her begin to distort her little personality by unconsciously developing a bitterness toward white people; when you have to concoct an answer for a five-year-old son asking in agonizing pathos: "Daddy, why do white people treat colored people so mean?"; when you take a cross-country drive and find it necessary to sleep night after night in the uncomfortable corners of your automobile because no motel will accept you; when you are humiliated day in and day out by nagging signs reading "white" and "colored"; when your first name becomes "nigger" and your middle name becomes "boy" (however old you are) and your last name becomes "John," and when your wife and mother are never given the respected title "Mrs."; when you are harried by day and haunted by night by the fact that you are a Negro, living constantly at tiptoe stance never quite knowing what to expect next, and plagued with inner fears and outer resentments; when you are forever fighting a degenerating sense of "nobodiness"; then you will understand why we find it difficult to wait. There comes a time when the cup of endurance runs over, and men are no longer willing to be plunged into an abyss of injustice where they experience the blackness of corroding despair. I hope, sirs, you can understand our legitimate and unavoidable impatience.

14   You express a great deal of anxiety over our willingness to break laws. This is certainly a legitimate concern. Since we so diligently urge people to obey the Supreme Court's decision of 1954 outlawing segregation in the public schools, it is rather strange and paradoxical to find us consciously breaking laws. One may well ask, "How can you advocate breaking some laws and obeying others?" The answer is found in the fact that there are two types of laws: there are *just* and there are *unjust* laws. I would agree with Saint Augustine that "An unjust law is no law at all."

15   Now what is the difference between the two? How does one determine when a law is just or unjust? A just law is a man-made code that squares with the moral law or the law of God. An unjust law is a code that is out of harmony with the moral law. To put it in the terms of Saint Thomas Aquinas, an unjust law is a human law that is not rooted in eternal and natural law. Any law that uplifts human personality is just. Any law that degrades human personality is unjust. All segregation statutes are unjust because segregation distorts the soul and damages the personality. It gives the segregator a false sense of superiority, and the segregated a false sense of inferiority. To use the words of Martin Buber, the great Jewish philosopher, segregation substitutes an "I-it" relationship for the "I-thou" relationship, and ends up relegating persons to the status of things. So

segregation is not only politically, economically and sociologically unsound, but it is morally wrong and sinful. Paul Tillich has said that sin is separation. Isn't segregation an existential expression of man's tragic separation, an expression of his awful estrangement, his terrible sinfulness? So I can urge men to disobey segregation ordinances because they are morally wrong.

16   Let us turn to a more concrete example of just and unjust laws. An unjust law is a code that a majority inflicts on a minority that is not binding on itself. This is difference made legal. On the other hand a just law is a code that a majority compels a minority to follow that it is willing to follow itself. This is sameness made legal.

17   Let me give another explanation. An unjust law is a code inflicted upon a minority which that minority had no part in enacting or creating because they did not have the unhampered right to vote. Who can say that the legislature of Alabama which set up the segregation laws was democratically elected? Throughout the state of Alabama all types of conniving methods are used to prevent Negroes from becoming registered voters and there are some counties without a single Negro registered to vote despite the fact that the Negro constitutes a majority of the population. Can any law set up in such a state be considered democratically structured?

18   These are just a few examples of unjust and just laws. There are some instances when a law is just on its face and unjust in its application. For instance, I was arrested Friday on a charge of parading without a permit. Now there is nothing wrong with an ordinance which requires a permit for a parade, but when the ordinance is used to preserve segregation and to deny citizens the First Amendment privilege of peaceful assembly and peaceful protest, then it becomes unjust.

19   I hope you can see the distinction I am trying to point out. In no sense do I advocate evading or defying the law as the rabid segregationist would do. This would lead to anarchy. One who breaks an unjust law must do it *openly, lovingly* (not hatefully as the white mothers did in New Orleans when they were seen on television screaming, "nigger, nigger, nigger"), and with a willingness to accept the penalty. I submit that an individual who breaks a law that conscience tells him is unjust, and willingly accepts the penalty by staying in jail to arouse the conscience of the community over its injustice, is in reality expressing the very highest respect for law.

20   Of course, there is nothing new about this kind of civil disobedience. It was seen sublimely in the refusal of Shadrach, Meshach and Abednego to obey the laws of Nebuchadnezzar because a higher moral law was involved. It was practiced superbly by the early Christians who were willing to face hungry lions and the excruciating pain of chopping blocks, before submitting to certain unjust laws of the Roman Empire. To a degree academic freedom is a reality today because Socrates practiced civil disobedience.

21   We can never forget that everything Hitler did in Germany was "legal" and everything the Hungarian freedom fighters did in Hungary was

"illegal." It was "illegal" to aid and comfort a Jew in Hitler's Germany. But I am sure that if I had lived in Germany during that time I would have aided and comforted my Jewish brothers even though it was illegal. If I lived in a Communist country today where certain principles dear to the Christian faith are suppressed, I believe I would openly advocate disobeying these anti-religious laws. I must make two honest confessions to you, my Christian and Jewish brothers. First, I must confess that over the last few years I have been gravely disappointed with the white moderate. I have almost reached the regrettable conclusion that the Negro's great stumbling block in the stride toward freedom is not the White Citizen's Counciler or the Ku Klux Klanner, but the white moderate who is more devoted to "order" than to justice; who prefers a negative peace which is the absence of tension to a positive peace which is the presence of justice; who constantly says, "I agree with you in the goal you seek, but I can't agree with your methods of direct action"; who paternalistically feels that he can set the timetable for another man's freedom; who lives by the myth of time and who constantly advised the Negro to wait until a "more convenient season." Shallow understanding from people of good will is more frustrating than absolute misunderstanding from people of ill will. Lukewarm acceptance is much more bewildering than outright rejection.

22 I had hoped that the white moderate would understand that law and order exist for the purpose of establishing justice, and that when they fail to do this they become dangerously structured dams that block the flow of social progress. I had hoped that the white moderate would understand that the present tension of the South is merely a necessary phase of the transition from an obnoxious negative peace, where the Negro passively accepted his unjust plight, to a substance-filled positive peace, where all men will respect the dignity and worth of human personality. Actually, we who engage in nonviolent direct action are not the creators of tension. We merely bring to the surface the hidden tension that is already alive. We bring it in the open where it can be seen and dealt with. Like a boil that can never be cured as long as it is covered up but must be opened with all its pus-flowing ugliness to the natural medicines of air and light, injustice must likewise be exposed, with all of the tension its exposing creates, to the light of human conscience and the air of national opinion before it can be cured.

23 In your statement you asserted that our actions, even though peaceful, must be condemned because they precipitate violence. But can this assertion be logically made? Isn't this like condemning the robbed man because his possession of money precipitated the evil act of robbery? Isn't this like condemning Socrates because his unswerving commitment to truth and his philosophical delvings precipitated the misguided popular mind to make him drink the hemlock? Isn't this like condemning Jesus because His unique God-consciousness and never-ceasing devotion to his will precipitated the evil act of crucifixion? We must come to see, as federal courts have consistently affirmed, that it is immoral to urge an individual

to withdraw his efforts to gain his basic constitutional rights because the quest precipitates violence. Society must protect the robbed and punish the robber.

24   I had also hoped that the white moderate would reject the myth of time. I received a letter this morning from a white brother in Texas which said: "All Christians know that the colored people will receive equal rights eventually, but it is possible that you are in too great of a religious hurry. It has taken Christianity almost two thousand years to accomplish what it has. The teachings of Christ take time to come to earth." All that is said here grows out of a tragic misconception of time. It is the strangely irrational notion that there is something in the very flow of time that will inevitably cure all ills. Actually time is neutral. It can be used either destructively or constructively. I am coming to feel that the people of ill will have used time much more effectively than the people of good will. We will have to repent in this generation not merely for the vitriolic words and actions of the bad people, but for the appalling silence of the good people. We must come to see that human progress never rolls in on wheels of inevitability. It comes through the tireless efforts and persistent work of men willing to be co-workers with God, and without this hard work time itself becomes an ally of the forces of social stagnation. We must use time creatively, and forever realize that the time is always ripe to do right. Now is the time to make real the promise of democracy, and transform our pending national elegy into a creative psalm of brotherhood. Now is the time to lift our national policy from the quicksand of racial injustice to the solid rock of human dignity.

25   You spoke of our activity in Birmingham as extreme. At first I was rather disappointed that fellow clergymen would see my nonviolent efforts as those of the extremist. I started thinking about the fact that I stand in the middle of two opposing forces in the Negro community. One is a force of complacency made up of Negroes who, as a result of long years of oppression, have been so completely drained of self-respect and a sense of "somebodiness" that they have adjusted to segregation, and, of a few Negroes in the middle class who, because of a degree of academic and economic security, and because at points they profit by segregation, have unconsciously become insensitive to the problems of the masses. The other force is one of bitterness and hatred, and comes perilously close to advocating violence. It is expressed in the various black nationalist groups that are springing up over the nation, the largest and best known being Elijah Muhammad's Muslim movement. This movement is nourished by the contemporary frustration over the continued existence of racial discrimination. It is made up of people who have lost faith in America, who have absolutely repudiated Christianity, and who have concluded that the white man is an incurable "devil." I have tried to stand between these two forces, saying that we need not follow the "do-nothingism" of the complacent or the hatred and despair of the black nationalist. There is the more excellent way of love and nonviolent protest.

I'm grateful to God that, through the Negro church, the dimension of nonviolence entered our struggle. If this philosophy had not emerged, I am convinced that by now many streets of the South would be flowing with floods of blood. And I am further convinced that if our white brothers dismiss us as "rabble-rousers" and "outside agitators," those of us who are working through the channels of nonviolent direct action, and refuse to support our nonviolent efforts, millions of Negroes, out of frustration and despair, will seek solace and security in black nationalist ideologies, a development that will lead inevitably to a frightening racial nightmare.

26   Oppressed people cannot remain oppressed forever. The urge for freedom will eventually come. This is what happened to the American Negro. Something within has reminded him of his birthright of freedom; something without has reminded him that he can gain it. Consciously and unconsciously, he has been swept in by what the Germans call the *Zeitgeist,* and with his black brothers of Africa, and his brown and yellow brothers of Asia, South America and the Caribbean, he is moving with a sense of cosmic urgency toward the promised land of racial justice. Recognizing this vital urge that has engulfed the Negro community, one should readily understand public demonstrations. The Negro has many pent-up resentments and latent frustrations. He has to get them out. So let him march sometime; let him have his prayer pilgrimages to the city hall; understand why he must have sit-ins and freedom rides. If his repressed emotions do not come out in these nonviolent ways, they will come out in ominous expressions of violence. This is not a threat; it is a fact of history. So I have not said to my people "get rid of your discontent." But I have tried to say that this normal and healthy discontent can be channelized through the creative outlet of nonviolent direct action. Now this approach is being dismissed as extremist. I must admit that I was initially disappointed in being so categorized.

27   But as I continued to think about the matter I gradually gained a bit of satisfaction from being considered an extremist. Was not Jesus an extremist in love—"Love your enemies, bless them that curse you, pray for them that despitefully use you." Was not Amos an extremist for justice—"Let justice roll down like waters and righteousness like a mighty stream." Was not Paul an extremist for the gospel of Jesus Christ—"I bear in my body the marks of the Lord Jesus." Was not Martin Luther an extremist—"Here I stand; I can do none other so help me God." Was not John Bunyan an extremist—"I will stay in jail to the end of my days before I make a butchery of my conscience." Was not Abraham Lincoln an extremist—"This nation cannot survive half slave and half free." Was not Thomas Jefferson an extremist—"We hold these truths to be self-evident, that all men are created equal." So the question is not whether we will be extremists but what kind of extremist will we be. Will we be extremists for hate or will we be extremists for love? Will we be extremists for the preservation of injustice—or will we be extremists for the cause of justice? In that dramatic scene on Calvary's hill, three men were

crucified. We must not forget that all three were crucified for the same crime—the crime of extremism. Two were extremists for immorality, and thusly fell below their environment. The other, Jesus Christ, was an extremist for love, truth and goodness, and thereby rose above his environment. So, after all, maybe the South, the nation and the world are in dire need of creative extremists.

28   I had hoped that the white moderate would see this. Maybe I was too optimistic. Maybe I expected too much. I guess I should have realized that few members of a race that has oppressed another race can understand or appreciate the deep groans and passionate yearnings of those that have been oppressed and still fewer have the vision to see that injustice must be rooted out by strong, persistent and determined action. I am thankful, however, that some of our white brothers have grasped the meaning of this social revolution and committed themselves to it. They are still all too small in quantity, but they are big in quality. Some like Ralph McGill, Lillian Smith, Harry Golden and James Dabbs have written about our struggle in eloquent, prophetic and understanding terms. Others have marched with us down nameless streets of the South. They have languished in filthy roach-infested jails, suffering the abuse and brutality of angry policemen who see them as "dirty nigger-lovers." They, unlike so many of their moderate brothers and sisters, have recognized the urgency of the moment and sensed the need for powerful "action" antidotes to combat the disease of segregation.

29   Let me rush on to mention my other disappointment. I have been so greatly disappointed with the white church and its leadership. Of course, there are some notable exceptions. I am not unmindful of the fact that each of you has taken some significant stands on this issue. I commend you, Rev. Stallings, for your Christian stance on this past Sunday, in welcoming Negroes to your worship service on a non-segregated basis. I commend the Catholic leaders of this state for integrating Springhill College several years ago.

30   But despite these notable exceptions I must honestly reiterate that I have been disappointed with the church. I do not say that as one of the negative critics who can always find something wrong with the church. I say it as a minister of the gospel, who loves the church; who was nurtured in its bosom; who has been sustained by its spiritual blessing and who will remain true to it as long as the cord of life shall lengthen.

31   I had the strange feeling when I was suddenly catapulted into the leadership of the bus protest in Montgomery several years ago that we would have the support of the white church. I felt that the white ministers, priests and rabbis of the South would be some of our strongest allies. Instead, some have been outright opponents, refusing to understand the freedom movement and misrepresenting its leaders; all too many others have been more cautious than courageous and have remained silent behind the anesthetizing security of the stained-glass windows.

32   In spite of my shattered dreams of the past, I came to Birmingham with the hope that the white religious leadership of this community would see

the justice of our cause, and with deep moral concern, serve as the channel through which our just grievances would get to the power structure. I had hoped that each of you would understand. But again I have been disappointed. I have heard numerous religious leaders of the South call upon their worshippers to comply with a desegregation decision because it is the *law*, but I have longed to hear white ministers say, "Follow this decree because integration is morally *right* and the Negro is your brother." In the midst of blatant injustices inflicted upon the Negro, I have watched white churches stand on the sideline and merely mouth pious irrelevancies and sanctimonious trivialities. In the midst of a mighty struggle to rid our nation of racial and economic injustice, I have heard so many ministers say, "Those are social issues with which the gospel has no concern," and I have watched so many churches commit themselves to a completely otherworldly religion which made a strange distinction between body and soul, the sacred and the secular.

33   So here we are moving toward the exit of the twentieth century with a religious community largely adjusted to the status quo, standing as a taillight behind other community agencies rather than a headlight leading men to higher levels of justice.

34   I have traveled the length and breadth of Alabama, Mississippi and all the other southern states. On sweltering summer days and crisp autumn mornings I have looked at her beautiful churches with their lofty spires pointing heavenward. I have beheld the impressive outlay of her massive religious education buildings. Over and over again I have found myself asking: "What kind of people worship here? Who is their God? Where were their voices when the lips of Governor Barnett dripped with words of interposition and nullification? Where were they when Governor Wallace gave the clarion call for defiance and hatred? Where were their voices of support when tired, bruised and weary Negro men and women decided to rise from the dark dungeons of complacency to the bright hills of creative protest?"

35   Yes, these questions are still in my mind. In deep disappointment, I have wept over the laxity of the church. But be assured that my tears have been tears of love. There can be no deep disappointment where there is not deep love. Yes, I love the church; I love her sacred walls. How could I do otherwise? I am in the rather unique position of being the son, the grandson and the great-grandson of preachers. Yes, I see the church as the body of Christ. But, oh! How we have blemished and scarred that body through social neglect and fear of being nonconformists.

36   There was a time when the church was very powerful. It was during that period when the early Christians rejoiced when they were deemed worthy to suffer for what they believed. In those days the church was not merely a thermometer that recorded the ideas and principles of popular opinion; it was a thermostat that transformed the mores of society. Wherever the early Christians entered a town the power structure got disturbed and immediately sought to convict them for being "disturbers of the peace" and "outside agitators." But they went on with the conviction that

they were "a colony of heaven," and had to obey God rather than man. They were small in number but big in commitment. They were too God-intoxicated to be "astronomically intimidated." They brought an end to such ancient evils as infanticide and gladiatorial contests.

37   Things are different now. The contemporary church is often a weak, ineffectual voice with an uncertain sound. It is so often the arch-supporter of the status quo. Far from being disturbed by the presence of the church, the power structure of the average community is consoled by the church's silent and often vocal sanction of things as they are.

38   But the judgment of God is upon the church as never before. If the church of today does not recapture the sacrificial spirit of the early church, it will lose its authentic ring, forfeit the loyalty of millions, and be dismissed as an irrelevant social club with no meaning for the twentieth century. I am meeting young people every day whose disappointment with the church has risen to outright disgust.

39   Maybe again, I have been too optimistic. Is organized religion too inextricably bound to the status quo to save our nation and the world? Maybe I must turn my faith to the inner spiritual church, the church within the church, as the true *ecclesia* and the hope of the world. But again I am thankful to God that some noble souls from the ranks of organized religion have broken loose from the paralyzing chains of conformity and joined us as active partners in the struggle for freedom. They have left their secure congregations and walked the streets of Albany, Georgia, with us. They have gone through the highways of the South on tortuous rides for freedom. Yes, they have gone to jail with us. Some have been kicked out of their churches, and lost support of their bishops and fellow ministers. But they have gone with the faith that right defeated is stronger than evil triumphant. These men have been the leaven in the lump of the race. Their witness has been the spiritual salt that has preserved the true meaning of the gospel in these troubled times. They have carved a tunnel of hope through the dark mountain of disappointment.

40   I hope the church as a whole will meet the challenge of this decisive hour. But even if the church does not come to the aid of justice, I have no despair about the future. I have no fear about the outcome of our struggle in Birmingham, even if our motives are presently misunderstood. We will reach the goal of freedom in Birmingham and all over the nation, because the goal of America is freedom. Abused and scorned though we may be, our destiny is tied up with the destiny of America. Before the Pilgrims landed at Plymouth we were here. Before the pen of Jefferson etched across the pages of history the majestic words of the Declaration of Independence, we were here. For more than two centuries our foreparents labored in this country without wages; they made cotton king; and they built the homes of their masters in the midst of brutal injustice and shameful humiliation—and yet out of a bottomless vitality they continued to thrive and develop. If the inexpressible cruelties of slavery could

not stop us, the opposition we now face will surely fail. We will win our freedom because the sacred heritage of our nation and the eternal will of God are embodied in our echoing demands.

41   I must close now. But before closing I am impelled to mention one other point in your statement that troubled me profoundly. You warmly commended the Birmingham police force for keeping "order" and "preventing violence." I don't believe you would have so warmly commended the police force if you had seen its angry violent dogs literally biting six unarmed, nonviolent Negroes. I don't believe you would so quickly commend the policemen if you would observe their ugly and inhuman treatment of Negroes here in the city jail; if you would watch them push and curse old Negro women and young Negro girls; if you would see them slap and kick old Negro men and young boys; if you will observe them, as they did on two occasions, refuse to give us food because we wanted to sing our grace together. I'm sorry that I can't join you in your praise for the police department.

42   It is true that they have been rather disciplined in their public handling of the demonstrators. In this sense they have been rather publicly "nonviolent." But for what purpose? To preserve the evil system of segregation. Over the last few years I have consistently preached that nonviolence demands that the means we use must be as pure as the ends we seek. So I have tried to make it clear that it is wrong to use immoral means to attain moral ends. But now I must affirm that it is just as wrong, or even more so, to use moral means to preserve immoral ends. Maybe Mr. Connor and his policemen have been rather publicly nonviolent, as Chief Pritchett was in Albany, Georgia, but they have used the moral means of nonviolence to maintain the immoral end of flagrant racial injustice. T. S. Eliot has said that there is no greater treason than to do the right deed for the wrong reason.

43   I wish you had commended the Negro sit-inners and demonstrators of Birmingham for their sublime courage, their willingness to suffer and their amazing discipline in the midst of the most inhuman provocation. One day the South will recognize its real heroes. They will be the James Merediths, courageously and with a majestic sense of purpose facing jeering and hostile mobs and the agonizing loneliness that characterizes the life of the pioneer. They will be old, oppressed, battered Negro women, symbolized in the seventy-two-year-old woman of Montgomery, Alabama, who rose up with a sense of dignity and with her people decided not to ride the segregated buses, and responded to one who inquired about her tiredness with ungrammatical profundity: "My feet is tired, but my soul is rested." They will be the young high school and college students, young ministers of the gospel and a host of their elders courageously and nonviolently sitting-in at lunch counters and willingly going to jail for conscience's sake. One day the South will know that when these disinherited children of God sat down at lunch counters they were in reality standing up for the best in the

American dream and the most sacred values in our Judeo-Christian heritage, and thusly, carrying our whole nation back to those great wells of democracy which were dug deep by the Founding Fathers in the formulation of the Constitution and the Declaration of Independence.

44 Never before have I written a letter this long (or should I say a book?). I'm afraid that it is much too long to take your precious time. I can assure you that it would have been much shorter if I had been writing from a comfortable desk, but what else is there to do when you are alone for days in the dull monotony of a narrow jail cell other than write long letters, think strange thoughts, and pray long prayers?

45 If I have said anything in this letter that is an overstatement of the truth and is indicative of an unreasonable impatience, I beg you to forgive me. If I have said anything in this letter that is an understatement of the truth and is indicative of my having a patience that makes me patient with anything less than brotherhood, I beg God to forgive me.

46 I hope this letter finds you strong in the faith. I also hope that circumstances will soon make it possible for me to meet each of you, not as an integrationist or a civil rights leader, but as a fellow clergyman and a Christian brother. Let us all hope that the dark clouds of racial prejudice will soon pass away and the deep fog of misunderstanding will be lifted from our fear-drenched communities and in some not too distant tomorrow the radiant stars of love and brotherhood will shine over our great nation with all of their scintillating beauty.

47 Yours for the cause of Peace and Brotherhood,

48 Martin Luther King Jr.

Questions for Discussion

1. What are the conditions King and others in Birmingham are protesting? How does King respond to the charge that he is an "outside agitator"?

2. What are the four basic steps in a nonviolent action campaign? How were they carried out in Birmingham?

3. How does King use the word *untimely*? How does he prove invalid the charge that the demonstrations are untimely? Explain how "wait" becomes "never."

4. Under what circumstances does King consider breaking the law justified? What precedents does he cite for doing so? Discuss the dichotomy between *just* and *unjust* law and the difference between "*difference* made legal" and "*sameness* made legal."

5. Explain King's claim that "Injustice anywhere is a threat to justice everywhere."

6. Explain the "tension in the mind" that King discusses. How can it "help men to rise from the dark depths of prejudice and racism to the majestic heights of understanding and brotherhood"?

7. King was accused of extremism. Which do you consider more extreme, King's essay or the Declaration of Independence? Justify your answer.

Suggestions for Exploration and Writing

1. Agree or disagree with this statement: If the cause is right or just, I would participate in a boycott, march, or other nonviolent action.

2. Select one of the following quotations from King's letter and agree or disagree with it:

   History is the long and tragic story of the fact that privileged groups seldom give up their privileges voluntarily.

   Shallow understanding from people of good will is more frustrating than absolute misunderstanding from people of ill will. Lukewarm acceptance is much more bewildering than outright rejection.

3. King was influenced by both the Bible and the Declaration of Independence. In an essay, show how King's letter reflects the ideas and styles of these documents.

4. Analyze the style of this letter, showing how the rhythmic cadences of a sermon, the rhetorical questions, and the metaphors help to make the letter persuasive.

5. Write an essay explaining how poverty can be "an airtight cage."

6. King says that if people's frustrations and contained anger are not released, people will resort to violence. Discuss this concept.

7. Argue for or against this statement: Churches and their leaders have a moral responsibility to speak out against hatred and injustice and to speak for love and justice.

Vaclav Havel (b. 1936)

In such plays as The Garden Party *(1963) and* The Memorandum *(1966) and in a provocative collection of essays,* Protocols *(1966), Czech writer Havel, early in his career, angered the ruling Communist party of Czechoslovakia. In 1976, after attending the trial of a nonconformist Czech rock group,* The Plastic People of the Universe, *Havel became more overtly critical of his country's government and took a leading role in founding Charter 77, a loosely organized group of Czech dissidents. Havel's involvement in Charter 77, along with his portraying in his plays and poems the absurd, mechanical conformity of Czech society under communism, led the Czech government to imprison him from 1979 to 1983. After helping lead the overthrow of Czech communism in the "velvet revolution" of 1989, Havel was elected president of Czechoslovakia, and, in 1993, when Slovakia and the Czech Republic became separate nations, he was elected*

*to the presidency of the Czech Republic. Reelected in 1998, he contin-
ues to serve as his country's president and as an articulate international spokesman for human rights.*

THE TRIAL   (1976)

1   It doesn't often happen and when it does it usually happens when least
expected: somewhere, something slips out of joint and suddenly a particular event, because of an unforeseen interplay between its inner
premises and more or less fortuitous external circumstances, crosses the
threshold of its usual place in the everyday world, breaks through
the shell of what it is supposed to be and what it seems, and reveals its
innermost symbolic significance. And something originally quite ordinary
suddenly casts a surprising light on the time and the world we live in, and
dramatically highlights its fundamental questions.

2   On the surface of things, nothing special happened. The trial took
place on schedule, lasted as long as it was supposed to, and turned out as
intended: with the conviction of the defendants. Yet everything one saw
here was clearly and compellingly more than that, so much so that even
those who had the least reason to admit it could feel it. This sensation was
in the air from the start, and it intensified relentlessly from hour to hour.
The strangest thing of all was that nothing could be done about it. Once
begun, the game had to be played out, only to reveal, ultimately, how terribly entangled those who started it had become in the web of their own
prestige: rather than simply calling a halt and admitting their error, they
let this disgraceful spectacle carry on to the end.

3   The players in this spectacle found themselves in a paradoxical situation. The more candidly they played their role, the more clearly they
revealed its unpremeditated significance, and thus they gradually became
co-creators of a drama utterly different from the one they thought they
were playing in, or wanted to play in.

4   What was the public prosecutor originally supposed to have been in
this trial? Undoubtedly a plausible spokesman and guardian of society's
interests, convincingly demonstrating how offensive, vulgar, immoral, and
antisocial the defendants' creative work was.

5   But what did this man become? The symbol of an inflated, narrow-
minded power, persecuting everything that does not fit into its sterile
notions of life, everything unusual, risky, self-taught, and unbribable,
everything that is too artless and too complex, too accessible and too mysterious, everything in fact that is different from itself. He was a mouthpiece for the world of spiritual manipulation, opportunism, emotional
sterility, banality, and moral prudery. In short, he represented the world
of the "masters," those masters who for as long as we can remember—
whether they spoke in religious, liberal, patriotic, or socialist platitudes—
have always tried to turn artists into lackeys, and whom artists have always
rebelled against, or at least ridiculed. At the same time this cramped,

unimaginative, and humorless man stood cloaked in the garb that "masters" traditionally don when they try to deal with an unclassifiable creative phenomenon: the garb of histrionic disgust at moral degeneration and lack of respect for traditional values.

6   What did Ivan Jirous and his friends in the dock wish to be? Certainly not heroes who, like Dimitrov, would rise from the dock to become prosecutors and condemn the world that was trying to condemn them. I doubt they had any other aim in mind than persuading the court of their innocence and defending their right to compose and sing the songs they wanted. What did the author of the scenario want them to be? Repulsive, long-haired hooligans from the "underworld," as they were treated by the director of Czechoslovak Television, to be rejected in disgust by all serious people.

7   But what did they ultimately become? The unintentional personification of those forces in man that compel him to search for himself, to determine his own place in the world freely, and in his own way, not to make deals with his heart and not to cheat his conscience, to call things by their true names and to penetrate—as Pavel Zajíček said at the trial—to the "deeper level of being," and to do so at one's own risk, aware that at any time one may come up against the disfavor of the "masters," the incomprehension of the dull-witted, or their own limitations.

8   And what, finally, did the presiding judge try to be? My feeling is that at the outset, she simply wanted to be an objective arbiter, listening without prejudice to the arguments of the prosecution and the defense, the testimony of the witnesses and the defendants, and come to a just decision.

9   But what did the trial turn her into? The tragic symbol of a judiciary incapable of maintaining its independence and handing down the kind of verdicts that flow from the human, civil, and legal conscience of the judges; a judiciary fully aware of how it is manipulated by power, but incapable of defying that power and so, ultimately, accepting the pitiful role of a subordinated employee of the "masters."

10   And what was the whole trial meant to be? Obviously no more than an ordinary element in the practice of justice that traditionally converts human lives, actions, and crimes into a boring pile of documents, files, reports, and articles, a routine treatment of one of hundreds of similar crimes. This superficial similarity to ordinary criminal cases, by the way, was maintained for some time. A great deal of time was spent hearing dozens of written and oral eyewitness accounts that dealt at great length with questions such as whether, at a concert of "The Plastic People of the Universe" in Bojanovice or Postupice, the doors to the hall were open or closed.

11   Soon, however, this facade of judicial thoroughness and objectivity began to appear as a mere smokescreen to hide what the trial really was: an impassioned debate about the meaning of human existence, an urgent questioning of what one should expect from life, whether one should silently accept the world as it is presented to one and slip obediently into

one's prearranged place in it, or whether one has the strength to exercise free choice in the matter; whether one should be "reasonable" and take one's place in the world, or whether one has the right to resist in the name of one's own human convictions.

12   For a long time, I sought, without much success, for the best way to characterize this process of "slipping out of joint."

13   Was it depressing? Of course it was: what other feelings could have been aroused when the most humanly authentic impression was made by those who sat in the dock, surrounded by policemen and even taken to the toilet in handcuffs? Or by the fact that the defense lawyers presented an excellent and exhaustive defense, the accused pleaded their innocence convincingly, and the case for the prosecution gradually fell into disarray, all in a situation where—as every one must have known—the accused had already been found guilty long before? And anyway, the whole case was depressing simply because it had slipped out of joint. How could it have been otherwise, when this controversy over the meaning of human life took place here, in the district court for the Prague-West region, and when no one present could do the one thing that was appropriate in this situation: stand up and shout: "Enough of this comedy! Case dismissed!"?

14   Was it moving? Naturally. There were moments when a lump came to one's throat, such as when Svatopluk Karásek said quietly that if Jirous was found guilty, he wanted to be found guilty, too. From the legal point of view, this was obvious nonsense, but at that moment and in those circumstances, it was so humanly right that it told us more in a single second about the essence of the case than a whole pile of official documents.

15   At times it was tense, at times disturbing, at times agonizing (there were moments when one felt like shouting); very often, on the contrary, it flung one back into the world of sheer absurdity.

16   But none of this does justice to the experience. At a deeper level it was, oddly enough, not depressing at all. There was even something elevating about it. This was perhaps because of the very awareness that we were participants in a unique illumination of the world. But chiefly, I suppose, it was the exciting realization that there are still people among us who assume the existential responsibility for their own truth and are willing to pay a high price for it. (Whereas those who judge them can only depend on the collective backing of a colossal social power and would rather send someone to prison for no reason at all than risk even a minor blemish on their record.)

17   Somewhere deep down, however, I discerned yet another element in this experience, perhaps the most important of all. It was something that aroused me, a challenge that was all the more urgent for being unintentional. It was the challenge of example. Suddenly, much of the wariness and caution that marks my behavior seemed petty to me. I felt an increased revulsion toward all forms of guile, all attempts at painlessly worming one's way out of vital dilemmas. Suddenly, I discovered in myself more determination in one direction, and more independence in

another. Suddenly, I felt disgusted with a whole world, in which—as I realized then—I still have one foot: the world of emergency exits.

18   As we have seen, if a certain event slips out of joint—and if it does so in the deeper sense that I have in mind here—then inevitably something slips out of joint in ourselves, too: a new view of the world gives us a new view of our own human potential, of what we are and might be. Abruptly jerked out of our "routine humanness," we stand once more face to face with the most important question of all: How do we settle accounts with ourselves?

19   I would probably not be writing about this challenging aspect of things at all were I not convinced that it is not simply a product of my tendency to dramatize (for which I am often taken to task, by the way). But it was not. The universality of this feeling was underlined as well by the fact that it seeped out of the hermetically sealed courtroom into the corridors and stairwells of the courthouse. Only the exalting awareness of an important, shared experience, and only the urgency of the challenge that everyone felt in it, could have explained the rapid genesis of that very special, improvised community that came into being here for the duration of the trial, and which was definitely something more than an accidental assembly of friends of the accused and people who were interested in the trial. For instance, a new and quite unusual etiquette appeared: no one bothered with introductions, getting acquainted, or feeling one another out. The usual conventions were dropped and the usual reticence disappeared, and this happened right before the eyes of several squads of those "others" (though they wore no uniforms, they were identifiable at once). Dozens of things were discussed that many of us, in other circumstances, might have been afraid to talk about even with one other person. It was a community of people who were not only more considerate, communicative, and trusting toward each other, they were in a strange way democratic. A distinguished, elderly gentleman, a former member of the praesidium of the Communist Party of Czechoslovakia, spoke with long-haired youths he'd never seen in his life before, and they spoke uninhibitedly with him, though they had known him only from photographs. In this situation, all reserve and inner reticence seemed to lose its point; in this atmosphere, all the inevitable "buts" seemed ridiculous, insignificant, and evasive. Everyone seemed to feel that at a time when all the chips are down, there are only two things one can do: gamble everything, or throw in the cards.

20   On the second day of the trial, when I left the courthouse on Karmelitská Street and walked to the Malá Strana Café (where we all went, us and the "others"), and I was still so full of impressions that I could scarcely think of anything else, I met a certain Czech film director of the middle generation. When he asked me how I was, I replied, none too logically, that I had just been at a trial of the Czech underground. He asked whether it was about those drugs. I said that it had nothing to do with drugs at all, and I tried, succinctly, to explain the essence of things. When I had finished, he nodded and then said, "Apart from that, what else are you up to?"

21   Perhaps I'm doing him an injustice, but at that moment, I was overwhelmed by an intense feeling that this dear man belonged to a world that I no longer wish to have anything to do with—and Mr. Public Prosecutor Kovařík, pay attention, because here comes a vulgar word—I mean the world of cunning shits.

Questions for Discussion

1. Havel says the trial "turned out as intended: with the conviction of the defendants" and "the accused had already been found guilty long before." What does he mean?

2. Why does Havel call the parties in the trial "players"? Why and how are the prosecutors representative of the "masters"? To what degree are prosecutors the "guardian[s] of society's interests"?

3. Havel says artists have always rebelled against "the masters." Cite examples of such rebellion and of its cost to the artists themselves.

4. Judging from various clues in the essay, what are Ivan Jirous and his band on trial for?

5. In the course of the trial, what do Ivan and his friends come to symbolize?

6. Havel describes the trial at different times as "depressing," "moving," "intense," and "disgusting." Explain why he feels each of these emotions.

7. What does Havel mean by "people who assume the existential responsibility for their own truth and are willing to pay a high price for it"?

8. How did this trial build community among the spectators?

9. What does Havel mean by "the world of emergency exits"?

10. Why was Havel disgusted at the film director he met after the second day of the trial?

Suggestions for Exploration and Writing

1. Havel sums up the trial as being about a fundamental choice:

> [. . .] whether one should silently accept the world as it is presented to one and slip obediently into one's prearranged place in it, or whether one has the strength to exercise free choice in the matter, whether one should be "reasonable" and take one's place in the world, or whether one has the right to resist in the name of one's own human conscience.

In an essay, explain your position on this issue and give your reasons, supporting them with examples from your own experience.

2. Explain in an essay to what degree you would be willing to go along with unethical actions in order to preserve your job or position in your community or group.

3. Discuss in detail a situation where you had "one foot" in "the world of emergency exits." Explain how or whether you used an exit and how using it or rejecting it made you feel.

4. Imagine you are the prosecutor or a defendant in the trial Havel is discussing. Write a speech you would present to the judge.

5. From today's news, write an essay showing that "something originally quite ordinary casts a surprising light on the time and the world we live in, and dramatically highlights its fundamental questions."

FICTION

Richard Wright (1908–1960)

Richard Wright, born in Natchez, Mississippi, settled after high school in New York, where he became a journalist. He began to write seriously about the plight of African American men when he wrote Uncle Tom's Children *(1938), a collection of five stories;* Native Son *(1940), a story of racial conflict in urban America; and* Black Boy *(1945), an autobiography. In 1946, Wright moved to Paris, where he lived the rest of his life. He wrote realistically but often experimented with various literary techniques, including the mix of dialect and standard English.*

THE MAN WHO WAS ALMOST A MAN (1939)

1   Dave struck out across the fields, looking homeward through paling light. Whut's the use talkin wid em niggers in the field? Anyhow, his mother was putting supper on the table. Them niggers can't understan nothing. One of these days he was going to get a gun and practice shooting, then they couldn't talk to him as though he were a little boy. He slowed, looking at the ground. Shucks, Ah ain scareda them even of they are biggern me! Aw, Ah know whut Ahma do. Ahm going by ol Joe's sto n git that Sears Roebuck catlog n look at them guns. Mebbe Ma will lemme buy one when she gits mah pay from ol man Hawkins. Ahma beg her t gimme some money. Ahm ol ernough to hava gun. Ahm seventeen. Almost a man. He strode, feeling his long loose-jointed limbs. Shucks, a man oughta hava little gun aftah he done worked hard all day.

2   He came in sight of Joe's store. A yellow lantern glowed on the front porch. He mounted the steps and went through the screen door, hearing it bang behind him. There was a strong smell of coal oil and mackerel fish. He felt very confident until he saw fat Joe walk in through the rear door, then his courage began to ooze.

3   "Howdy Dave! Whutcha want?"

4   "How yuh, Mistah Joe? Aw, Ah don wanna buy nothing. Ah jus wanted t see ef yuhd lemme look at tha catlog erwhile."

5   "Sure! You wanna see it here?"

6   "Nawsuh. Ah wans t take it home wid me. Ah'll bring it back termorrow when Ah come in from the fiels."

7   "You plannin on buying something?"

8   "Yessuh."

9   "Your ma lettin you have your own money now?"

10   "Shucks. Mistah Joe, Ahm gittin t be a man like anybody else!"

11   Joe laughed and wiped his greasy white face with a red bandanna.

12   "Whut you plannin on buyin?"

13   Dave looked at the floor, scratched his head, scratched his thigh, and smiled. Then he looked up shyly.

14   "Ah'll tell yuh, Mistah Joe, ef yuh promise yuh won't tell."

15   "I promise."

16   "Waal, Ahma buy a gun."

17   "A gun? Whut you want with a gun?"

18   "Ah wanna keep it."

19   "You ain't nothing but a boy. You don't need a gun."

20   "Aw, lemme have the catlog, Mistah Joe. Ah'll bring it back."

21   Joe walked through the rear door. Dave was elated. He looked around at barrels of sugar and flour. He heard Joe coming back. He craned his neck to see if he were bringing the book. Yeah, he's got it. Gawddog, he's got it!

22   "Here, but be sure you bring it back. It's the only one I got."

23   "Sho, Mistah Joe."

24   "Say, if you wanna buy a gun, why don't you buy one from me? I gotta gun to sell."

25   "Will it shoot?"

26   "Sure it'll shoot."

27   "Whut kind is it?"

28   "Oh, it's kinda old . . . a left-hand Wheeler. A pistol. A big one."

29   "Is it got bullets in it?"

30   "It's loaded."

31   "Kin Ah see it?"

32   "Where's your money?"

33   "Whut yuh wan fer it?"

34   "I'll let you have it for two dollars."

35   "Just two dollahs? Shucks, Ah could buy tha when Ah git mah pay."

36   "I'll have it here when you want it."

37   "Awright, suh. Ah be in fer it."

38   He went through the door, hearing it slam again behind him. Ahma git some money from Ma n buy me a gun! Only two dollahs! He tucked the thick catalogue under his arm and hurried.

39   "Where yuh been, boy?" His mother held a steaming dish of black-eyed peas.

40   "Aw, Ma, Ah jus stopped down the road t talk wid the boys."

41   "Yuh know bettah t keep suppah waitin."

42   He sat down, resting the catalogue on the edge of the table.

43   "Yuh git up from there and git to the well n wash yosef! Ah ain feedin no hogs in mah house!"

44   She grabbed his shoulder and pushed him. He stumbled out of the room, then came back to get the catalogue.

45   "Whut this?"

46   "Aw, Ma, it's jusa catlog."

47   "Who yuh git it from?"

48   "From Joe, down at the sto."

49   "Waal, thas good. We kin use it in the outhouse."

50   "Naw, Ma." He grabbed for it. "Gimme ma catlog, Ma."

51   She held onto it and glared at him.

52   "Quit hollerin at me! Whut's wrong wid yuh? Yuh crazy?"

53   "But Ma, please. It ain mine! It's Joe's! He tol me t bring it back t im termorrow."

54   She gave up the book. He stumbled down the back steps, hugging the thick book under his arm. When he had splashed water on his face and hands, he groped back to the kitchen and fumbled in a corner for the towel. He bumped into a chair; it clattered to the floor. The catalogue sprawled at his feet. When he had dried his eyes he snatched up the book and held it again under his arm. His mother stood watching him.

55   "Now, ef yuh gonna act a fool over that ol book, Ah'll take it n burn it up."

56   "Naw, Ma, please."

57   "Waal, set down n be still!"

58   He sat down and drew the oil lamp close. He thumbed page after page, unaware of the food his mother set on the table. His father came in. Then his small brother.

59   "Whutcha got there, Dave?" his father asked.

60   "Jusa catlog," he answered, not looking up.

61   "Yeah, here they is!" His eyes glowed at blue-and-black revolvers. He glanced up, feeling sudden guilt. His father was watching him. He eased the book under the table and rested it on his knees. After the blessing was asked, he ate. He scooped up peas and swallowed fat meat without chewing. Buttermilk helped to wash it down. He did not want to mention money before his father. He would do much better by cornering his mother when she was alone. He looked at his father uneasily out of the edge of his eye.

62   "Boy, how com yuh don quit foolin wid tha book n eat yo suppah?"

63   "Yessuh."

64   "How you n ol man Hawkins gitten erlong?"

65   "Suh?"

66   "Can't yuh hear? Why don yuh lissen? Ah ast yu how wuz yuh n ol man Hawkins gittin erlong?"

67   "Oh, swell, Pa. Ah plows mo lan than anybody over there."

68   "Waal, yuh oughta keep yo mind on whut yuh doin."

69   "Yessuh."

70   He poured his plate full of molasses and sopped it up slowly with a chunk of cornbread. When his father and brother had left the kitchen, he still sat and looked again at the guns in the catalogue, longing to muster courage enough to present his case to his mother. Lawd, ef Ah only had tha pretty one! He could almost feel the slickness of the weapon with his fingers. If he had a gun like that he would polish it and keep it shining so it would never rust. N Ah'd keep it loaded, by Gawd!

71   "Ma?" His voice was hesitant.

72   "Hunh?"

73   "Ol man Hawkins give yuh mah money yit?"

74   "Yeah, but ain no usa yuh thinking bout throwin nona it erway. Ahm keepin tha money sos yuh kin have cloes t go to school this winter."

75   He rose and went to her side with the open catalogue in his palms. She was washing dishes, her head bent low over a pan. Shyly he raised the book. When he spoke, his voice was husky, faint.

76   "Ma, Gawd knows Ah wans one of these."

77   "One of whut?" she asked, not raising her eyes.

78   "One of these," he said again, not daring even to point. She glanced up at the page, then at him with wide eyes.

79   "Nigger, is yuh gone plumb crazy?"

80   "Aw, Ma—"

81   "Git outta here! Don yuh talk t me bout no gun! Yuh a fool!"

82   "Ma, Ah kin buy one fer two dollahs."

83   "Not ef Ah knows it, yuh ain!"

84   "But yuh promised me one—"

85   "Ah don care whut Ah promised! Yuh ain nothing but a boy yit!"

86   "Ma, ef yuh lemme buy one Ah'll *never* ast yuh fer nothing no mo."

87   "Ah tol yuh t git outta here! Yuh ain gonna toucha penny of tha money for no gun! Thas how come Ah has Mistah Hawkins t pay yo wages t me, cause Ah knows yuh ain got no sense."

88   "But, Ma, we needa gun. Pa ain got no gun. We needa gun in the house. Yuh kin never tell whut might happen."

89   "Now don yuh try to maka fool outta me, boy! Ef we did hava gun, yuh wouldn't have it!"

90   He laid the catalogue down and slipped his arm around her waist.

91   "Aw, Ma, Ah done worked hard alla summer n ain ast yuh fer nothin, is Ah, now?"

92   "Thas whut yuh spose to do!"

93   "But Ma, Ah wans a gun. Yuh kin lemme have two dollahs outta mah money. Please, Ma. I kin give it to Pa . . . Please, Ma! Ah loves yuh, Ma."

94   When she spoke her voice came soft and low.

95   "Whut yu wan wida gun, Dave? Yuh don need no gun. Yuh'll git in trouble. N ef yo pa jus thought Ah let yuh have money t buy a gun he'd hava fit."

96 "Ah'll hide it, Ma. It ain but two dollahs."

97 "Lawd, chil, whut's wrong wid yuh?"

98 "Ain nothin wrong, Ma. Ahm almos a man now. Ah wans a gun."

99 "Who gonna sell yuh a gun?"

100 "Ol Joe at the sto."

101 "N it don cos but two dollahs?"

102 "Thas all, Ma. Jus two dollahs. Please, Ma."

103 She was stacking the plates away; her hands moved slowly, reflectively. Dave kept an anxious silence. Finally, she turned to him.

104 "Ah'll let yuh git the gun ef yuh promise me one thing."

105 "Whut's tha, Ma?"

106 "Yuh bring it straight back t me, yuh hear? It be fer Pa."

107 "Yessum! Lemme go now, Ma."

108 She stooped, turned slightly to one side, raised the hem of her dress, rolled down the top of her stocking, and came up with a slender wad of bills.

109 "Here," she said. "Lawd knows yuh don need no gun. But yer pa does. Yuh bring it right back to me, yuh hear? Ahma put it up. Now ef yuh don, Ahma have yuh pa lick yuh so hard yuh won fergit it."

110 "Yessum."

111 He took the money, ran down the steps, and across the yard.

112 "Dave! Yuuuuuh Daaaaave!"

113 He heard, but he was not going to stop now. "Naw, Lawd!"

114 The first movement he made the following morning was to reach under his pillow for the gun. In the gray light of dawn he held it loosely, feeling a sense of power. Could kill a man with a gun like this. Kill anybody, black or white. And if he were holding his gun in his hand, nobody could run over him; they would have to respect him. It was a big gun, with a long barrel and a heavy handle. He raised and lowered it in his hand, marveling at its weight.

115 He had not come straight home with it as his mother had asked; instead he had stayed out in the fields, holding the weapon in his hand, aiming it now and then at some imaginary foe. But he had not fired it; he had been afraid that his father might hear. Also he was not sure he knew how to fire it.

116 To avoid surrendering the pistol he had not come into the house until he knew that they were all asleep. When his mother had tiptoed to his bedside later that night and demanded the gun, he had first played possum; then he had told her that the gun was hidden outdoors, that he would bring it to her in the morning. Now he lay turning it slowly in his hands. He broke it, took out the cartridges, felt them, and then put them back.

117 He slid out of bed, got a long strip of old flannel from a trunk, wrapped the gun in it, and tied it to his naked thigh while it was still loaded. He did not go in to breakfast. Even though it was not yet daylight, he started for Jim Hawkins' plantation. Just as the sun was rising he reached the barns where the mules and plows were kept.

118 "Hey! That you, Dave?"

119   He turned. Jim Hawkins stood eyeing him suspiciously.

120   "What're yuh doing here so early?"

121   "Ah didn't know Ah wuz gittin up so early, Mistah Hawkins. Ah wuz fixin t hitch up ol Jenny n take her t the fiels."

122   "Good. Since you're so early, how about plowing that stretch down by the woods?"

123   "Suits me, Mistah Hawkins."

124   "O.K. Go to it!"

125   He hitched Jenny to a plow and started across the fields. Hot dog! This was just what he wanted. If he could get down by the woods, he could shoot his gun and nobody would hear. He walked behind the plow, hearing the traces creaking, feeling the gun tied tight to his thigh.

126   When he reached the woods, he plowed two whole rows before he decided to take out the gun. Finally, he stopped, looked in all directions, then untied the gun and held it in his hand. He turned to the mule and smiled.

127   "Know whut this is, Jenny? Naw, yuh wouldn know! Yuhs jusa old mule! Anyhow, this is a gun, n it kin shoot, by Gawd!"

128   He held the gun at arm's length. Whut t hell, Ahma shoot this thing! He looked at Jenny again.

129   "Lissen here, Jenny! When Ah pull this ol trigger, Ah don wan yuh t run n acka fool now!"

130   Jenny stood with head down, her short ears pricked straight. Dave walked off about twenty feet, held the gun far out from him at arm's length, and turned his head. Hell, he told himself, Ah ain afraid. The gun felt loose in his fingers; he waved it wildly for a moment. Then he shut his eyes and tightened his forefinger. Bloom! A report half deafened him and he thought his right hand was torn from his arm. He heard Jenny whinnying and galloping over the field, and he found himself on his knees, squeezing his fingers hard between his legs. His hand was numb; he jammed it into his mouth, trying to warm it, trying to stop the pain. The gun lay at his feet. He did not quite know what had happened. He stood up and stared at the gun as though it were a living thing. He gritted his teeth and kicked the gun. Yuh almos broke mah arm! He turned to look for Jenny; she was far over the fields, tossing her head and kicking wildly.

131   "Hol on there, ol mule!"

132   When he caught up with her she stood trembling, walling her big white eyes at him. The plow was far away; the traces had broken. Then Dave stopped short, looking, not believing. Jenny was bleeding. Her left side was red and wet with blood. He went closer. Lawd, have mercy! Wondah did Ah shoot this mule? He grabbed for Jenny's mane. She flinched, snorted, whirled, tossing her head.

133   "Hol on now! Hol on."

134   Then he saw the hole in Jenny's side, right between the ribs. It was round, wet, red. A crimson stream streaked down the front leg, flowing fast. Good Gawd! Ah wuzn't shootin at tha mule. He felt panic. He knew

he had to stop that blood, or Jenny would bleed to death. He had never seen so much blood in all his life. He chased the mule for half a mile, trying to catch her. He caught her mane and led her back to where the plow and gun lay. Then he stooped and grabbed handfuls of damp black earth and tried to plug the bullet hole. Jenny shuddered, whinnied, and broke from him.

135   "Hol on! Hol on now!"

136   He tried to plug it again, but blood came anyhow. His fingers were hot and sticky. He rubbed dirt into his palms, trying to dry them. Then again he attempted to plug the bullet hole, but Jenny shied away, kicking her heels high. He stood helpless. He had to do something. He ran at Jenny; she dodged him. He watched a red stream of blood flow down Jenny's leg and form a bright pool at her feet.

137   "Jenny . . . Jenny," he called weakly.

138   His lips trembled. She's bleeding t death! He looked in the direction of home, wanting to go back, wanting to get help. But he saw the pistol laying in the damp black clay. He had a queer feeling that if he only did something, this would not be; Jenny would not be there bleeding to death.

139   When he went to her this time, she did not move. She stood with sleepy, dreamy eyes; and when he touched her she gave a low-pitched whinny and knelt to the ground, her front knees slopping in blood.

140   "Jenny . . . Jenny . . ." he whispered.

141   For a long time she held her neck erect; then her head sank, slowly. Her ribs swelled with a mighty heave and she went over.

142   Dave's stomach felt empty, very empty. He picked up the gun and held it gingerly between his thumb and forefinger. He buried it at the foot of a tree. He took a stick and tried to cover the pool of blood with dirt—but what was the use? There was Jenny lying with her mouth open and her eyes walled and glassy. He could not tell Jim Hawkins he had shot his mule. But he had to tell something. Yeah, Ah'll tell em Jenny started gittin wil n fell on the joint of the plow. . . . But that would hardly happen to a mule. He walked across the field slowly, head down.

143   It was sunset. Two of Jim Hawkins' men were over near the edge of the woods digging a hole in which to bury Jenny. Dave was surrounded by a knot of people, all of whom were looking down at the dead mule.

144   "I don't see how in the world it happened," said Jim Hawkins for the tenth time.

145   The crowd parted and Dave's mother, father, and small brother pushed into the center.

146   "Where Dave?" his mother called.

147   "There he is," said Jim Hawkins.

148   His mother grabbed him.

149   "Whut happened, Dave? Whut yuh done?"

150   "Nothin."

151   "C mon, boy, talk," his father said.

152   Dave took a deep breath and told the story he knew nobody believed.

153   "Waal," he drawled. "Ah brung ol Jenny down here sos Ah could do mah plowing. Ah plowed bout two rows, just like yuh see." He stopped and pointed at the long rows of upturned earth. "Then somethin musta been wrong wid ol Jenny. She wouldn ack right a-tall. She started snortin n kickin her heels. Ah tried t hol her, but she pulled erway, rearin n goin in. Then when the point of the plow was stickin up in the air, she swung erroun n twisted herself back on it . . . She stuck herself n started t bleed. N fo Ah could do anything, she wuz dead."

154   "Did you ever hear of anything like that in all your life?" asked Jim Hawkins.

155   There were white and black standing in the crowd. They murmured. Dave's mother came close to him and looked hard into his face. "Tell the truth, Dave," she said.

156   "Looks like a bullet hole to me," said one man.

157   "Dave, whut yuh do wid the gun?" his mother asked.

158   The crowd surged in, looking at him. He jammed his hands into his pockets, shook his head slowly from left to right, and backed away. His eyes were wide and painful.

159   "Did he hava gun?" asked Jim Hawkins.

160   "By Gawd, Ah tol yuh tha wuz a gun wound," said a man, slapping his thigh.

161   His father caught his shoulders and shook him till his teeth rattled.

162   "Tell whut happened, yuh rascal! Tell whut . . ."

163   Dave looked at Jenny's stiff legs and began to cry.

164   "Whut yuh do wid tha gun?" his mother asked.

165   "Whut wuz he doin wida gun?" his father asked.

166   "Come on and tell the truth," said Hawkins. "Ain't nobody going to hurt you . . ."

167   His mother crowded close to him.

168   "Did yuh shoot that mule, Dave?"

169   Dave cried, seeing blurred white and black faces.

170   "Ahh ddinn gggo tt sshooot hher . . . Ah ssswear ffo Gawd Ahh ddin. . . . Ah wuz a-tryin t sssee ef the old gggun would sshoot—"

171   "Where yuh git the gun from?" his father asked.

172   "Ah got it from Joe, at the sto."

173   "Where yuh git the money?"

174   "Ma give it t me."

175   "He kept worryin me, Bob. Ah had t. Ah tol im t bring the gun right back t me . . . It was fer yuh, the gun."

176   "But how yuh happen to shoot that mule?" asked Jim Hawkins.

177   "Ah wuzn shootin at the mule, Mistah Hawkins. The gun jumped when Ah pulled the trigger . . . N fo Ah knowed anythin Jenny was there a-bleedin."

178   Somebody in the crowd laughed. Jim Hawkins walked close to Dave and looked into his face.

179   "Well, looks like you have bought you a mule, Dave."

180   "Ah swear fo Gawd, Ah didn go t kill the mule, Mistah Hawkins!"

181   "But you killed her!"

182   All the crowd was laughing now. They stood on tiptoe and poked heads over one another's shoulders.

183   "Well, boy, looks like yuh done bought a dead mule! Hahaha!"

184   "Ain tha ershame."

185   "Hohohohoho."

186   Dave stood, head down, twisting his feet in the dirt.

187   "Well, you needn't worry about it, Bob," said Jim Hawkins to Dave's father. "Just let the boy keep on working and pay me two dollars a month."

188   "Whut yuh wan fer yo mule, Mistah Hawkins?"

189   Jim Hawkins screwed up his eyes.

190   "Fifty dollars."

191   "Whut yuh do wid tha gun?" Dave's father demanded.

192   Dave said nothing.

193   "Yuh wan me t take a tree n beat yuh till yuh talk!"

194   "Nawsuh!"

195   "Whut yuh do wid it?"

196   "Ah throwed it erway."

197   "Where?"

198   "Ah . . . Ah throwed it in the creek."

199   "Waal, c mon home. N firs thing in the mawnin git to tha creek n fin tha gun."

200   "Yessuh."

201   "Whut yuh pay fer it?"

202   "Two dollahs."

203   "Take tha gun n git yo money back n carry it to Mistah Hawkins, yuh hear? N don fergit Ahma lam you black bottom good fer this! Now march yosef on home, suh!"

204   Dave turned and walked slowly. He heard people laughing. Dave glared, his eyes welling with tears. Hot anger bubbled in him. Then he swallowed and stumbled on.

205   That night Dave did not sleep. He was glad that he had gotten out of killing the mule so easily, but he was hurt. Something hot seemed to turn over inside him each time he remembered how they had laughed. He tossed on his bed, feeling his hard pillow. N Pa says he's gonna beat me . . . He remembered other beatings, and his back quivered. Naw, naw, Ah sho don wan im t beat me tha way no mo. Dam em all! Nobody ever gave him anything. All he did was work. They treat me like a mule, n then they beat me. He gritted his teeth. N Ma had t tell on me.

206   Well, if he had to, he would take old man Hawkins that two dollars. But that meant selling the gun. And he wanted to keep that gun. Fifty dollars for a dead mule.

207   He turned over, thinking how he had fired the gun. He had an itch to fire it again. Ef other men kin shoota gun, by Gawd, Ah kin! He was still,

listening. Mebbe they all sleepin now. The house was still. He heard the soft breathing of his brother. Yes, now! He would go down and get that gun and see if he could fire it! He eased out of bed and slipped into overalls.

208   The moon was bright. He ran almost all the way to the edge of the woods. He stumbled over the ground, looking for the spot where he had buried the gun. Yeah, here it is. Like a hungry dog scratching for a bone, he pawed it up. He puffed his black cheeks and blew dirt from the trigger and barrel. He broke it and found four cartridges unshot. He looked around; the fields were filled with silence and moonlight. He clutched the gun stiff and hard in his fingers. But, as soon as he wanted to pull the trigger, he shut his eyes and turned his head. Naw, Ah can't shoot wid mah eyes closed n mah head turned. With effort he held his eyes open; then he squeezed. *Blooooom!* He was stiff, not breathing. The gun was still in his hands. Dammit, he'd done it! He fired again. *Blooooom!* He smiled. *Blooooom! Blooooom! Click, click.* There! It was empty. If anybody could shoot a gun, he could. He put the gun into his hip pocket and started across the fields.

209   When he reached the top of a ridge he stood straight and proud in the moonlight, looking at Jim Hawkins' big white house, feeling the gun sagging in his pocket. Lawd, ef Ah had just one mo bullet Ah'd taka shot at tha house. Ah'd like t scare ol man Hawkins jusa little . . . Jusa enough t let im know Dave Saunders is a man.

210   To his left the road curved, running to the tracks of the Illinois Central. He jerked his head, listening. From far off came a faint *hoooof-hoooof; hoooof-hoooof; hoooof-hoooof.* . . . He stood rigid. Two dollahs a mont. Les see now . . . Tha means it'll take bout two years. Shucks! Ah'll be dam!

211   He started down the road, toward the tracks. Yeah, here she comes! He stood beside the track and held himself stiffly. Here she comes, erroun the ben . . . C mon, yuh slow poke! C mon! He had his hand on his gun; something quivered in his stomach. Then the train thundered past, the gray and brown box cars rumbling and clinking. He gripped the gun tightly; then he jerked his hand out of his pocket. Ah betcha Bill wouldn't do it! Ah betcha . . . The cars slid past, steel grinding upon steel. Ahm ridin yuh ternight, so hep me Gawd! He was hot all over. He hesitated just a moment; then he grabbed, pulled atop of a car, and lay flat. He felt his pocket; the gun was still there. Ahead the long rails were glinting in the moonlight, stretching away, away to somewhere, somewhere where he could be a man . . .

Questions for Discussion

1. The African Americans in the story call each other "nigger" at various times. Why?

2. Why does Dave want a gun? What does the gun symbolize to him? Is his mother right to give in to Dave's desire to have a gun? Is Joe right to sell Dave the gun?

3. Why does Dave lie about the gun? Why does the laughter bother him?

4. Explain why Dave sneaks out of his house to fire the gun and uses up all the bullets?

5. What would having to work two years for Hawkins to pay for the dead mule do to Dave? Why does Dave hop the train to leave home?

Suggestions for Exploration and Writing

1. Discuss the various **ironies** of the story, including the irony of the title.

2. Do guns still play a role in the manhood of some people? Discuss.

3. What responsibilities should accompany the freedom to own guns? Use the story as a basis for an essay.

Zenna Henderson (1917–1983)

Zenna Chlarson Henderson was born in Tucson, Arizona, graduated from Arizona State University in 1940, and taught in the state for most of her life. She is noted not only for being one of the first women writers of science fiction but also for producing short stories that reveal a great depth of understanding of young people. The most famous of these are the stories about The People, kind and friendly aliens who have psychic and telekinetic powers. These collections include Pilgrimage: The Book of the People *(1961) and* The People: No Different Flesh *(1967). Many later science fiction writers credit her as a major influence on their writing. Two other short story collections are* The Anything Box *(1965) and* Holding Wonder *(1971), from which "As Simple As That" is taken.*

AS SIMPLE AS THAT   (1971)

1   "I won't read it." Ken sat staring down at his open first grade book.

2   I took a deep, wavery breath and, with an effort, brought myself back to the classroom and the interruption in the automatic smooth flow of the reading group.

3   "It's your turn, Ken," I said, "Don't you know the place?"

4   "Yes," said Ken, his thin, unhappy face angling sharply at the cheek bones as he looked at me. "But I won't read it."

5   "Why not?" I asked gently. Anger had not yet returned. "You know all the words. Why don't you want to read it?"

6   "It isn't true," said Ken. He dropped his eyes to his book as tears flooded in. "It isn't true."

7   "It never was true," I told him. "We play like it's true, just for fun." I flipped the four pages that made up the current reading lesson. "Maybe this city isn't true, but it's like a real one, with stores and—" My voice trailed off as the eyes of the whole class centered on me—seven pairs of eyes and the sightless, creamy oval of Maria's face—all seeing our city.

8   "The cities," I began again. "The cities—" By now the children were used to grown-ups stopping in mid-sentence. And to the stunned look on adult faces.

9   "It isn't true," said Ken. "I won't read it."

10   "Close your books," I said, "And go to your seats." The three slid quietly into their desks—Ken and Victor and Gloryanne. I sat at my desk, my elbows on the green blotter, my chin in the palms of my hands, and looked at nothing. I didn't want anything true. The fantasy that kept school as usual is painful enough. How much more comfortable to live unthinking from stunned silence to stunned silence. Finally I roused myself.

11   "If you don't want to read your book, let's write a story that *is* true, and we'll have that for reading."

12   I took the staff liner and drew three lines at a time across the chalk board, with just a small jog where I had to lift the chalk over the jagged crack that marred the board diagonally from top to bottom.

13   "What shall we name our story?" I asked. "Ken, what do you want it to be about?"

14   "About Biff's house," said Ken promptly.

15   "Biff's house," I repeated, my stomach tightening sickly as I wrote the words, forming the letters carefully in manuscript printing, automatically saying, "Remember now, all titles begin with—"

16   And the class automatically supplying, "—capital letters."

17   "Yes," I said. "Ken, what shall we say first?"

18   "Biff's house went up like an elevator," said Ken.

19   "Right up into the air?" I prompted.

20   "The ground went up with it," supplied Gloryanne.

21   I wrote the two sentences. "Victor? Do you want to tell what came next?" The chalk was darkening in my wet, clenched hand.

22   "The groun'—it comed down, more fast nor Biff's house," supplied Victor hoarsely. I saw his lifted face and the deep color of his heavily fringed eyes for the first time in a week.

23   "With noise!" shouted Maria, her face animated. "With lots of noise!"

24   "You're not in our group!" cried Ken. "This is our story!"

25   "It's everyone's story," I said and wrote carefully. "And every sentence ends with a—"

26   "Period," supplied the class.

27   "And then?" I paused, leaning my forehead against the coolness of the chalk board, blinking my eyes until the rich green alfalfa that was growing through the corner of the room came back into focus. I lifted my head.

28   Celia had waited. "Biff fell out of his house," she suggested.

29   I wrote. "And then?" I paused, chalk raised.

30   "Biff's house fell on him," said Ken with a rush. "And he got dead."

31   "I saw him!" Bobby surged up out of his seat, speaking his first words of the day. "There was blood, but his face was only asleep."

32   "He was dead!" said Ken fiercely. "And the house broke all to pieces!"

33   "And the pieces all went down in that deep, deep hole with Biff!" cried Bobby.

34   "And the hole went shut!" Celia triumphantly capped the recital.

35   "Dint either!" Victor whirled on her. "Ohney part! See! See!" He jabbed his finger toward the window. We all crowded around as though this was something new. And I suppose it was—new to our tongues, new to our ears, though long scabbed over unhealthily inside us.

36   There at the edge of the playground, just beyond the twisted tangle of the jungle gym and the sharp jut of the slide, snapped off above the fifth rung of the ladder, was the hole containing Biff's house. We solemnly contemplated all that was visible—the small jumble of shingles and the wadded TV antenna. We turned back silently to our classroom.

37   "How did you happen to see Biff when his house fell on him, Bobby?" I asked.

38   "I was trying to go to his house to play until my brother got out of fourth grade," said Bobby. "He was waiting for me on the porch. But all at once the ground started going up and down and it knocked me over. When I got up, Biff's house was just coming down and it fell on Biff. All but his head. And he looked asleep. He did! He did! And then everything went down and it shut. But not all!" he hastened to add before Victor gave tongue again.

39   "Now," I said—we had buried Biff—"Do we have it the way we want so it can be a story for reading? Get your pencils—"

40   "Teacher! Teacher!" Maria was standing, her sightless eyes wide, one hand up as high as she could reach. "Teacher! Malina!"

41   "Bobby! Quickly—help me!" I scrambled around my desk, knocking the section of four-by-four out from under the broken front leg. I was able to catch Malina because she had stopped to fumble for the door knob that used to be there. Bobby stumbled up with the beach towel and, blessedly, I had time to wind it securely around Malina before the first scream of her convulsions began. Bobby and I held her lightly, shoulder and knees, as her body rolled and writhed. We had learned bitterly how best to protect her against herself and the dangerous place she made for herself of the classroom. I leaned my cheek against my shoulder as I pressed my palms against Malina. I let my tears wash down my face untouched. Malina's shaking echoed through me as though I were sobbing.

42   The other children were righting my fallen desk and replacing the chunk of four-by-four, not paying any attention to Malina's gurgling screams that rasped my ears almost past enduring. So quickly do children adjust. So quickly. I blinked to clear my eyes. Malina was quieting. Oh, how blessedly different from the first terrified hour we had had to struggle with her! I quickly unwrapped her and cradled her against me as her face smoothed and her ragged breath quieted. She opened her eyes.

43   "Daddy said next time he had a vacation he'd take us to Disneyland again. Last time we didn't get to go in the rocket. We didn't get to go in anything in that land." She smiled her normal, front-tooth-missing smile at me and fell asleep. We went back to work, Bobby and I.

44   "Her daddy's dead," said Bobby matter-of-factly as he waited his turn at the pencil sharpener. "She knows her daddy's dead and her mother's dead and her baby brother's—"

45   "Yes, Bobby, we all know," I said. "Let's go back to our story. We just about have time to go over it again and write it before lunchtime."

46   So I stood looking out of the gap in the wall above the Find Out Table—currently, *What Did This Come From?* while the children wrote their first true story after the Torn Time.

BIFF'S HOUSE

Biff's house went up like an elevator.
The ground went up with it.
The ground came down before Biff's house did.
Biff fell out of his house.
The house fell on him and he was dead.
He looked asleep.
The house broke all to pieces with a lot of noise.
It went down into the deep, deep hole.
Biff went, too.
The hole went shut, but not all the way.
We can see the place by our playground.

47   It was only a few days later that the children asked to write another story. The rain was coming down again—a little less muddy, a little less torrential, so that the shards of glass in our windows weren't quite so smeary and there was an area unleaked upon in the room large enough to contain us all closely—minus Malina.

48   "I think she'll come tomorrow," said Celia. "This morning she forgot Disneyland 'cause she remembered all her family got mashed by the water tower when it fell down and she was crying when we left the sleeping place and she wasn't screaming and kicking and this time she was crying and—"

49   "Heavens above!" I cried, "You'll run out of breath completely!"

50   "Aw naw I won't!" Celia grinned up at me and squirmed in pleased embarrassment. "I breathe in between!"

51   "I didn't hear any in-betweens," I smiled back. "Don't use so many 'ands'!"

52   "Can we write another real story?" asked Willsey. ("Not Willie!" His mother's voice came back to me, tiny and piercing and never to be heard aloud again. "His name is Willsey. W-i-l-l-s-e-y. Please teach him to write it in full!")

53   "If you like," I said. "Only do we say, 'Can we?'"

54   "May we?" chorused the class.

55   "That's right," I said. "Did you have something special in mind, Willsey?"

56   "No," he said. "Only, this morning we had bread for breakfast. Mine was dry. Bobby's daddy said that was lucky 'relse it would have rotted away

a long time ago." Bread. My mouth watered. There must not have been enough to pass around to our table—only for the children.

57   "Mine was dry, too," said Ken. "And it had blue on the edge of it."

58   "Radioactive," nodded Victor wisely.

59   "Huh-uh!" contradicted Bobby quickly. "Nothing's radioactive around here! My daddy says—"

60   "You' daddy! You' daddy!" retorted Victor. "Once I gots daddy, too!"

61   "Everybody had a daddy," said Maria calmly. "'Relsn you couldn't get born. But some daddies die."

62   "All daddies die," said Bobby, "Only mine isn't dead yet. I'm *glad* he isn't dead!"

63   "We all are," I said, "Bobby's daddy helps us all—"

64   "Yeah," said Willsey, "he found the bread for us."

65   "Anyway, the blue was mold," Bobby broke in. "And it's good for you. It grows peni—pencil—"

66   "Penicillin?" I suggested. He nodded and subsided, satisfied. "Okay, Willsey, what shall we name our story?"

67   He looked at me blankly, "What's it about?" I asked.

68   "Eating," he said.

69   "Fine. That'll do for a title," I said. "Who can spell it for me? It's an ing ending."

70   I wrote it carefully with a black marking pencil on the chart paper as Gloryanne spelled it for me, swishing her long black hair back triumphantly as she did so. Our chalk board was a green cascade of water under the rain pouring down through the ragged, sagging ceiling. The bottom half of the board was sloughing slowly away from its diagonal fracture.

71   "Now, Willsey—" I waited, marker poised.

72   "We had bread for breakfast," he composed. "It was hard, but it was good."

73   "Mine wasn't," objected Ken. "It was awful."

74   "Bread isn't awful," said Maria. "Bread's good."

75   "Mine wasn't!" Ken was stubborn.

76   "Even if we don't ever get any more?" asked Maria.

77   "Aw! Who ever heard of not no more bread?" scoffed Ken.

78   "What is bread made of?" I asked.

79   "Flour," volunteered Bobby.

80   "Cornbread's with cornmeal," said Victor quickly.

81   "Yes, and flour's made from—" I prompted.

82   "From wheat," said Ken.

83   "And wheat—"

84   "Grows in fields," said Ken.

85   "Thee, Thmarty!" said Gloryanne. "And whereth any more fieldth?"

86   "Use your teeth, Gloryanne," I reminded. "Teeth and no tongue. Say, 'see.'"

87   Gloryanne clenched her teeth and curled her lips back. "S-s-s-thee!" she said, confidently. Bobby and I exchanged aware looks and our eyes smiled above our sober lips.

88   "Let's go on with the story," I suggested.

EATING

> We had bread for breakfast.
> It was hard but it was good.
> Bobby's daddy found it under some boards.
> We had some good milk to put it in.
> It was goat's milk.
> It made the bread soft.
> Once we had a cow.
> She was a nice cow but a man killed her
>   because he wanted to eat her.
> We all got mad at him.
> We chased him away.
> No one got to eat our cow
>   because it rained red mud
>   all over her and spoiled the meat.
> We had to push her into a big hole.

89   I looked over the tight huddle of studious heads before me as they all bent to the task of writing the story. The rain was sweeping past the windows like long curtains billowing in the wind. The raindrops were so fine but so numerous that it seemed I could reach out and stroke the swelling folds. I moved closer to the window, trying several places before I found one where no rain dripped on me from above and none sprayed me from outside. But it was an uncomfortable spot. I could see the nothing across the patio where the rest of the school used to be. Our room was the only classroom in the office wing. The office wing was the only one not gulped down in its entirety, lock, stock and student body. Half of the office wing was gone. We had the restrooms—non-operational—the supply room— half roofed—and our room. We were the school. We were the whole of the sub-teen generation—and the total faculty.

90   The total faculty wondered—was it possible that someone—some *one*— had caused all this to happen? Some one who said, "Now!" Or said, "Fire!" Or said, "If I can't have my way, then—" Or maybe some stress inside the world casually adjusted itself, all unknowing of the skim of life clinging to its outsides. Or maybe some One said, "I repent Me—"

91   "Teacher, Teacher!" Maria's voice called me back to the classroom. "The roof! The roof!" Her blind face was urgent. I glanced up, my arm lifting protectively.

92   "Down!" I shouted. "Get down flat!" and flung myself across the room, mowing my open-mouthed children down as I plunged. We made it to

the floor below the level of my desk before what was left of the ceiling peeled off and slammed soggily over us, humped up just enough by the desk and chairs to save our quivering selves.

93 Someone under me was sobbing, "My paper's all tore! My paper's all tore!" And I heard Bobby say with tight, controlled anguish, "Everything breaks! Any more, every thing breaks!"

94 We wrote another story—later. Quite a bit later. The sun, halo-ed broadly about by its perpetual haze, shone milkily down into our classroom. The remnants of the roof and ceiling had been removed and a canvas tarp draped diagonally over the highest corner of the remaining walls to give us shade in the afternoon. On the other side of the new, smaller playground our new school was shaping from adobe and reclaimed brick. Above the humming stillness of the classroom, I could hear the sound of blackbirds calling as they waded in the water that seeped from the foot of the knee-deep stand of wheat that covered the old playground. Maybe by Fall there would be bread again. Maybe. Everything was still maybe. But 'maybe' is a step—a big one—beyond 'never.'

95 Our chalk board was put back together and, except for a few spots that refused to accept any kind of impression, it functioned well with our smudgy charcoal sticks from the Art Supplies shelf.

96 "Has anyone the answer yet?" I asked.

97 "I gots it," said Victor, tentatively. "It's two more days."

98 "Huh-uh!" said Celia. "Four more days!"

99 "Well, we seem to have a difference of opinion," I said. "Let's work it out together.

100 "Now, first, how many people, Victor?"

101 "Firs' they's ten people," he said, checking the chalk board.

102 "That's right," I said, "And how many cans of beans? Malina?"

103 "Five," she said. "And each can is for two people for one day."

104 "Right," I said. "And so that'll be lunch for how many days for ten people?"

105 "For one day," said Malina.

106 "That's right. Then what happened?"

107 "All but two people fell in the West Crack," said Bobby. "Right—straight—down—farther than you can hear a rock fall." He spoke with authority. He had composed that part of our math problem.

108 "So?" I said.

109 "There were five cans of beans and that's ten meals and only two people," said Willsey.

110 "So?" I prompted.

111 "So two people can have five meals each."

112 "So?"

113 "So they gots dinners for five days and that's *four* days more than one day! So there!" cried Victor.

114   "Hey!" Celia was outraged. "That's what *I* said! You said *two* more days!"

115   "Aw!" said Victor. "Dumb problem! Nobody's gunna fa' down West Crack eenyway!"

116   "A lot of people fell in there," said Gloryanne soberly. "My gramma did and my Aunt Glory—"

117   In the remembering silence, the sweet creaking calls of the blackbirds could be heard again. A flash of brilliance from the sky aroused us. A pie-shaped wedge had suddenly cleared in the sun's halo, and there was bright blue and glitter, briefly, before the milky came back.

118   "A whole bright day," said Maria dreamily. "And the water in Briney Lake so shiny I can't look at it."

119   "You can't look anyway," said Ken. "How come you always talk about seeing when you can't even?"

120   "'Cause I can. Ever since the Torn Time," said Maria. "I got blind almost as soon as I got born. All blind. No anything to see. But now I can watch and I can see—inside me, somewhere. But I don't see now. I see some-time—after while. But what I see comes! It isn't, when I see it, but it bees pretty quick!" Her chin tilted a 'so there!'

121   The children all looked at her silently and I wondered. We had lost so much—so much! And Maria had lost, too—her blindness. Maybe more of our losses were gains—

122   Then Bobby cried out, "What happened, teacher? What happened? And why do we stay here? I can remember on the other side of West Crack. There was a town that wasn't busted. And bubble gum and ham-burgers and a—a escalator thing to go upstairs to buy color TV. Why don't we go there? Why do we stay here where everything's busted?"

123   "Broken," I murmured automatically.

124   The children were waiting for an answer. These child faces were turned to me, waiting for me to fill a gap they suddenly felt now, in spite of the endless discussions that were forever going on around them.

125   "What do *you* think?" I asked. "What do you think happened? Why *do* we stay here? Think about it for a while, then let's write another story."

126   I watched the wind flow across the wheat field and thought, too. Why do we stay? The West Crack is one reason. It's still unbridged, partly because to live has been more important than to go, partly because no one wants to leave anyone yet. The fear of separation is still too strong. We *know* people are here. The unknown is still too lonely to face.

127   South are the Rocks—jagged slivers of basalt or something older than that—that rocketed up out of the valley floor during the Torn Time and splintered into points and pinnacles. As far as we can see, they rise, rigidly vertical, above the solid base that runs out of sight east and west. And the base is higher than our tallest tree.

128   And north. My memory quivered away from north—

129   East. Town used to be east. The edge of it is Salvage now. Someday when the stench is gone, the whole of it will be salvage. Most of the stench is only a lingering of memory now, but we still stay away except when need drives us.

130   North. North. Now it is Briney Lake. During the Torn Time, it came from out of nowhere, all that wetness, filling a dusty, desert cup to brimming and more. It boiled and fumed and swallowed the land and spat out parts of it again.

131   Rafe and I had gone up to watch the magical influx of water. In this part of the country, any water, free of irrigation or conservation restrictions, was a wonder to be watched with fascinated delight. We stood, hand in hand, on the Point where we used to go at nights to watch the moonlight on the unusually heavy stand of cholla cactus on the hillsides—moonlight turning all those murderous, puncturing thorns to silvery fur and snowy velvet. The earth around us had firmed again from its shakenness and the half of the Point that was left was again a solid Gibraltar.

132   We watched the water rise and rise until our delight turned to apprehension. I had started to back away when Rafe pulled me to him to see a sudden silvery slick that was welling up from under the bubbling swells of water. As he leaned to point, the ground under our feet gave a huge hiccough, jerked him off balance and snatched his hand from my wrist. He hit the water just as the silvery slick arrived.

133   And the slick swallowed Rafe before my eyes. Only briefly did it let go of one of his arms—a hopelessly reaching arm that hadn't yet realized that its flesh was already melted off and only bones were reaching.

134   I crouched on the Point and watched half my boulder dissolve into the silver and follow Rafe down into the dark, convulsed depths. The slick was gone and Rafe was gone. I knelt, nursing my wrist with my other hand. My wrist still burned where Rafe's fingernails had scratched as he fell. My wrist carries the scars still, but Rafe is gone.

135   My breath shuddered as I turned back to the children.

136   "Well," I said, "what *did* happen? Shall we write our story now?"

What Happened?

Bobby's daddy thinks maybe the magnetic poles changed
   and north is west now or maybe east.
Gloryanne's mother says it must have been an atom bomb.
Malina's Uncle Don says the San Andreas fault did it.
That means a big earthquake all over everywhere.
Celia's grandfather says the Hand of God smote a wicked
   world.
Victor thinks maybe it was a flying saucer.
Ken thinks maybe the world just turned over and we are
   Australia now.
Willsey doesn't want to know what happened.
Maria doesn't know.
She couldn't see when it was happening.

137   "So you see," I summed up. "Nobody knows for sure what happened. Maybe we'll never know. Now, why do we stay here?"

138   "Because"—Bobby hesitated—"because maybe if here is like this, maybe everywhere is like this. Or maybe there isn't even anywhere else anymore."

139   "Maybe there isn't," I said, "But whether there is or not and whatever really happened, it doesn't matter to us now. We can't change it. We have to make do with what we have until we can make it better.

140   "Now, paper monitor," I was briskly routine. "Pass the paper. All of you write as carefully as you can so when you take your story home and let people read it, they'll say, 'Well! What an interesting story!' instead of 'Yekk! Does this say something?' Writing is no good unless it can be read. The eraser's here on my desk in case anyone goofs. You may begin."

141   I leaned against the window sill, waiting. If only we adults would admit that we'll probably never know what really happened—and that it really doesn't matter. Inexplicable things are always happening, but life won't wait for answers—it just keeps going. Do you suppose Adam's grandchildren knew what really happened to close Eden? Or that Noah's grandchildren sat around wondering why the earth was so empty? They contented themselves with very simple, home-grown explanations—or none at all—because what was, was. We don't want to accept what happened and we seem to feel that if we could find an explanation that it would undo what has been done. It won't. Maybe some day someone will come along who will be able to put a finger on one of the points in the children's story and say, "There! That's the explanation." Until then, though, explanation or not, we have our new world to work with.

142   No matter what caused the Torn Time, we go on from here—building or not-building, becoming or slipping back. It's as simple as that.

Questions for Discussion

1. What clues does the author give even before the children start to write their story that a catastrophe has occurred?

2. Describe the classroom. Why does this description suggest about the fragility of life?

3. Tell the story of Biff's house.

4. Why do Ken, Bobby, and some of the other children insist on the truth and facts? Why do the others live in the past and deny the truth?

5. Explain the teacher's comments that "maybe" is a big step beyond "never" and that "Maybe more of our losses were gains." What are some other *maybe's* in the story?

6. What are the teacher's theories about what happened? What theories do the children suggest?

7. Explain the pathos of the children's saying everything in their lives is either "busted" or "broken" and of Bobby's saying, "Anymore everything breaks!"

8. Why do they "stay here" rather than try to go to another area?

9. Why is the catastrophe through which they lived called the "Torn Time"?

10. Ultimately, what are the teacher's and the students' responsibilities?

11. In what ways is the story simple?

Suggestions for Exploration and Writing

1. Write an essay explaining why it is better sometimes not to speculate on *why* something happened and instead to focus on what Henderson's narrator says: "[. . .] what was, was." Use specific examples from your experience or from historical events.

2. Using specific examples from the story, prove that the narrator is a kind and caring teacher who makes learning relevant to her students.

3. Explain why and how the answers to Bobby's question—"Why do we stay here where everything's busted?"—reflect a universal human tendency.

4. Using the clues from the story, explain your theories about what happened in the Torn Time.

5. In an essay, defend the teacher's observation in the last paragraph.

6. Compare the hope for the future in this story with the hope or lack of hope in Bradbury's "There Will Come Soft Rain."

Isaac Asimov (1920–1992)

Isaac Asimov was one of the most prolific writers of the twentieth century, with works ranging from textbooks to children's books to scientific treatises to science fiction. Born in Petrovichi, Russia, Asimov earned a doctorate in chemistry at Columbia University and taught for much of his life at Boston University. He won seven Hugo Awards, among them awards for the Foundation Series (1966) and a posthumous award for I. Asimov: A Memoir (1995). Perhaps more than any other writer, Asimov helped familiarize readers with scientific concepts and science fiction.

FRUSTRATION (1995)

1   Herman Gelb turned his head to watch the departing figure. Then he said, "Wasn't that the Secretary?"

2   "Yes, that was the Secretary of Foreign Affairs. Old man Hargrove. Are you ready for lunch?"

3   "Of course. What was he doing here?"

4   Peter Jonsbeck didn't answer immediately. He merely stood up, and beckoned Gelb to follow. They walked down the corridor and into a room that had the steamy smell of spicy food.

5   "Here you are," said Jonsbeck. "The whole meal has been prepared by computer. Completely automated. Untouched by human hands. And my own programming. I promised you a treat, and here you are."

6   It *was* good. Gelb could not deny it and didn't want to. Over dessert, he said, "But what was Hargrove doing here?"

7   Jonsbeck smiled. "Consulting me on programming. What else am I good for?"

8   "But why? Or is it something you can't talk about?"

9   "It's something I suppose I *shouldn't* talk about, but it's a fairly open secret. There isn't a computer man in the capital who doesn't know what the poor frustrated simp is up to."

10   "What is he up to then?"

11   "He's fighting wars."

12   Gelb's eyes opened wide. "With whom?"

13   "With nobody, really. He fights them by computer analysis. He's been doing it for I don't know how long."

14   "But why?"

15   "He wants the world to be the way we are—noble, honest, decent, full of respect for human rights and so on."

16   "So do I. So do we all. We have to keep up the pressure on the bad guys, that's all."

17   "And they're keeping the pressure on us, too. They don't think we're perfect."

18   "I suppose we're not, but we're better than they are. You know that."

19   Jonsbeck shrugged. "A difference in point of view. It doesn't matter. We've got a world to run, space to develop, computerization to extend. Cooperation puts a premium on continued cooperation and there is slow improvement. We'll get along. It's just that Hargrove doesn't want to wait. He hankers for quick improvement—by force. You know, *make* the bums shape up. We're strong enough to do it."

20   "By force? By war, you mean. We don't fight wars any more."

21   "That's because it's gotten too complicated. Too much danger. We're all too powerful. You know what I mean? Except that Hargrove thinks he can find a way. You punch certain starting conditions into the computer and let it fight the war mathematically and yield the results."

22   "How do you make equations for war?"

23   "Well, you try, old man. Men. Weapons. Surprise. Counterattack. Ships. Space stations. Computers. We mustn't forget computers. There are a hundred factors and thousands of intensities and millions of combinations. Hargrove thinks it is possible to find *some* combination of starting conditions and courses of development that will result in clear victory for us and not too much damage to the world, and he labors under constant frustration."

24   "But what if he gets what he wants?"

25   "Well, if he can find the combination—if the computer says, 'This is it,' then I suppose he thinks he can argue our government into fighting exactly the war the computer has worked out so that, barring random events that upset the indicated course, we'd have what we want."

26   "There'd be casualties."

27   "Yes, of course. But the computer will presumably compare the casualties and other damage—to the economy and ecology, for instance—to the benefits that would derive from our control of the world, and if it decides the benefits will outweigh the casualties, then it will give the go-ahead for a 'just war.' After all, it may be that even the losing nations would benefit from being directed by us, with our stronger economy and stronger moral sense."

28   Gelb stared his disbelief and said, "I never knew we were sitting at the lip of a volcanic crater like that. What about the 'random events' you mentioned?"

29   "The computer program tries to allow for the unexpected, but you never can, of course. So I don't think the go-ahead will come. It hasn't so far, and unless old man Hargrove can present the government with a computer simulation of a war that is totally satisfactory, I don't think there's much chance he can force one."

30   "And he comes to you, then, for what reason?"

31   "To improve the program, of course."

32   "And you help him?"

33   "Yes, certainly. There are big fees involved, Herman."

34   Gelb shook his head, "Peter! Are you going to try to arrange a war, just for money?"

35   "There won't be a war. There's no realistic combination of events that would make the computer decide on war. Computers place a greater value on human lives than human beings do themselves, and what will seem bearable to Secretary Hargrove, or even to you and me, will never be passed by a computer."

36   "How can you be sure of that?"

37   "Because I'm a programmer and I don't know of any way of programming a computer to give it what is most needed to start any war, any persecution, any devilry, while ignoring any harm that may be done in the process. And because it lacks what is most needed, the computers will always give Hargrove, and all others who hanker for war, nothing but frustration."

38   "What is it that a computer doesn't have, then?"

39   "Why, Gelb. It totally lacks a sense of self-righteousness."

Questions for Discussion

1. What are the implications of Gelb and Jonsbeck's assumption that "we're better than they are"? What do they mean by "better"?

2. What does Gelb mean when he says that "we don't fight wars any more"? Why and how does the analogy to computer games sound so much like PlayStation 2 or the X Box?

3. What is the irony of fighting a computer war?

4. Why does Jonsbeck add the phrase "barring random events that upset the indicated course" after his statement that Hargrove wants the computer

to find "*some* combination of starting conditions and courses of development that will result in clear victory for us and not too much damage to the world"? Who gets to decide how much damage is too much?

5. When, according to Jonsbeck, is a war "just"? In reality, how does money alter the discussion of a "just war"?

6. How is it possible that "Computers place a greater value on human lives than human beings do"? Do you agree with this claim?

7. Explain the significance of the last sentence.

8. Why is the story entitled "Frustration"? Who is frustrated?

Suggestions for Exploration and Writing

1. Write an essay explaining how you would feel if you had lost someone you love—or if you have in reality lost a loved one—in a "just war."

2. Argue for or against "Star Wars"—a computer-generated war.

3. Research the causes or the results of two twentieth-century wars, such as World War I, World War II, the Korean War, the Vietnam War, or the Persian Gulf War. Then write a comparison or contrast of two of them.

Kurt Vonnegut Jr. (b. 1922)

Kurt Vonnegut Jr., a self-acknowledged pessimist, is one of America's foremost science fiction writers. In his short stories and novels, he satirizes the dilemmas people have created: unimaginably destructive wars, out-of-control technology, pollution, and racism. His most famous novels are Cat's Cradle *(1963), which ends with the freezing of the world, and* Slaughterhouse-Five *(1969), inspired by his experiences as a prisoner of war in Germany during the Dresden bombings. Vonnegut's novel* Timequake *(1999), and an autobiography,* Fates Worse Than Death *(1991), are his latest works. Vonnegut also writes essays, plays, and television adaptations of his works. He is a popular speaker on college campuses, where he challenges students to become critical thinkers.*

HARRISON BERGERON   (1961)

1   The year was 2081, and everybody was finally equal. They weren't only equal before God and the law. They were equal every which way. Nobody was smarter than anybody else. Nobody was better looking than anybody else. Nobody was stronger or quicker than anybody else. All this equality was due to the 211th, 212th, and 213th Amendments to the Constitution, and to the unceasing vigilance of agents of the United States Handicapper General.

2   Some things about living still weren't quite right, though. April, for instance, still drove people crazy by not being springtime. And it was in

that clammy month that the H-G men took George and Hazel Bergeron's fourteen-year-old son, Harrison, away.

3   It was tragic, all right, but George and Hazel couldn't think about it very hard. Hazel had a perfectly average intelligence, which meant she couldn't think about anything except in short bursts. And George, while his intelligence was way above normal, had a little mental handicap radio in his ear. He was required by law to wear it at all times. It was tuned to a government transmitter. Every twenty seconds or so, the transmitter would send out some sharp noise to keep people like George from taking unfair advantage of their brains.

4   George and Hazel were watching television. There were tears on Hazel's cheeks, but she'd forgotten for the moment what they were about.

5   On the television screen were ballerinas.

6   A buzzer sounded in George's head. His thoughts fled in panic, like bandits from a burglar alarm.

7   "That was a really pretty dance, that dance they just did," said Hazel.

8   "Huh?" said George.

9   "That dance—it was nice," said Hazel.

10   "Yup," said George. He tried to think a little about the ballerinas. They weren't really very good—no better than anybody else would have been, anyway. They were burdened with sashweights and bags of birdshot, and their faces were masked, so that no one, seeing a free and graceful gesture or a pretty face, would feel like something the cat drug in. George was toying with the vague notion that maybe dancers shouldn't be handicapped. But he didn't get very far with it before another noise in his ear radio scattered his thoughts.

11   George winced. So did two out of the eight ballerinas.

12   Hazel saw him wince. Having no mental handicap herself, she had to ask George what the latest sound had been.

13   "Sounded like somebody hitting a milk bottle with a ball peen hammer," said George.

14   "I'd think it would be real interesting, hearing all the different sounds," said Hazel, a little envious. "All the things they think up."

15   "Um," said George.

16   "Only, if I was Handicapper General, you know what I would do?" said Hazel. Hazel, as a matter of fact, bore a strong resemblance to the Handicapper General, a woman named Diana Moon Glampers. "If I was Diana Moon Glampers," said Hazel, "I'd have chimes on Sunday—just chimes. Kind of in honor of religion."

17   "I could think, if it was just chimes," said George.

18   "Well—maybe make 'em real loud," said Hazel. "I think I'd make a good Handicapper General."

19   "Good as anybody else," said George.

20   "Who knows better'n I do what normal is?" said Hazel.

21   "Right," said George. He began to think glimmeringly about his abnormal son who was now in jail, about Harrison, but a twenty-one-gun salute in his head stopped that.

22   "Boy!" said Hazel, "that was a doozy, wasn't it?"

23   It was such a doozy that George was white and trembling, and tears stood on the rims of his red eyes. Two of the eight ballerinas had collapsed to the studio floor, were holding their temples.

24   "All of a sudden you look so tired," said Hazel. "Why don't you stretch out on the sofa, so's you can rest your handicap bag on the pillows, honeybunch." She was referring to the forty-seven pounds of birdshot in a canvas bag, which was padlocked around George's neck. "Go on and rest the bag for a little while," she said. "I don't care if you're not equal to me for a while."

25   George weighed the bag with his hands. "I don't mind it," he said. "I don't notice it any more. It's just a part of me."

26   "You been so tired lately—kind of wore out," said Hazel. "If there was just some way we could make a little hole in the bottom of the bag, and just take out a few of them lead balls. Just a few."

27   "Two years in prison and two thousand dollars fine for every ball I took out," said George. "I don't call that a bargain."

28   "If you could just take a few out when you came home from work," said Hazel. "I mean—you don't compete with anybody around here. You just set around."

29   "If I tried to get away with it," said George, "then other people'd get away with it—and pretty soon we'd be right back to the dark ages again, with everybody competing against everybody else. You wouldn't like that, would you?"

30   "I'd hate it," said Hazel.

31   "There you are," said George. "The minute people start cheating on laws, what do you think happens to society?"

32   If Hazel hadn't been able to come up with an answer to this question, George couldn't have supplied one. A siren was going off in his head.

33   "Reckon it'd fall all apart," said Hazel.

34   "What would?" said George blankly.

35   "Society," said Hazel uncertainly. "Wasn't that what you just said?"

36   "Who knows?" said George.

37   The television program was suddenly interrupted for a news bulletin. It wasn't clear at first as to what the bulletin was about, since the announcer, like all announcers, had a serious speech impediment. For about half a minute, and in a state of high excitement, the announcer tried to say, "Ladies and gentlemen—"

38   He finally gave up, handed the bulletin to a ballerina to read.

39   "That's all right—" Hazel said of the announcer, "he tried. That's the big thing. He tried to do the best he could with what God gave him. He should get a nice raise for trying so hard."

40   "Ladies and gentlemen—" said the ballerina, reading the bulletin. She must have been extraordinarily beautiful, because the mask she wore was hideous. And it was easy to see that she was the strongest and most graceful of all the dancers, for her handicap bags were as big as those worn by two-hundred-pound men.

41   And she had to apologize at once for her voice, which was a very unfair voice for a woman to use. Her voice was a warm, luminous, timeless

melody. "Excuse me—" she said, and she began again, making her voice absolutely uncompetitive.

42   "Harrison Bergeron, age fourteen," she said in a grackle squawk, "has just escaped from jail, where he was held on suspicion of plotting to over- throw the government. He is a genius and an athlete, is underhandi- capped, and should be regarded as extremely dangerous."

43   A police photograph of Harrison Bergeron was flashed on the screen—upside down, then sideways, upside down again, then right side up. The picture showed the full length of Harrison against a background calibrated in feet and inches. He was exactly seven feet tall.

44   The rest of Harrison's appearance was Halloween and hardware. Nobody had ever borne heavier handicaps. He had outgrown hin- drances faster than the H-G men could think them up. Instead of a lit- tle ear radio for a mental handicap, he wore a tremendous pair of earphones, and spectacles with thick wavy lenses. The spectacles were intended to make him not only half blind, but to give him whanging headaches besides.

45   Scrap metal was hung all over him. Ordinarily, there was a certain sym- metry, a military neatness to the handicaps issued to strong people, but Harrison looked like a walking junkyard. In the race of life, Harrison car- ried three hundred pounds.

46   And to offset his good looks, the H-G men required that he wear at all times a red rubber ball for a nose, keep his eyebrows shaved off, and cover his even white teeth with black caps at snaggle-tooth random.

47   "If you see this boy," said the ballerina, "do not—I repeat, do not—try to reason with him."

48   There was the shriek of a door being torn from its hinges.

49   Screams and barking cries of consternation came from the television set. The photograph of Harrison Bergeron on the screen jumped again and again, as though dancing to the tune of an earthquake.

50   George Bergeron correctly identified the earthquake, and well he might have—for many was the time his own home had danced to the same crashing tune. "My God—" said George, "that must be Harrison."

51   The realization was blasted from his mind instantly by the sound of an automobile collision in his head.

52   When George could open his eyes again, the photograph of Harrison was gone. A living, breathing Harrison filled the screen.

53   Clanking, clownish, and huge, Harrison stood in the center of the stu- dio. The knob of the uprooted studio door was still in his hand. Balleri- nas, technicians, musicians, and announcers cowered on their knees before him, expecting to die.

54   "I am the Emperor!" cried Harrison. "Do you hear? I am the Emperor! Everybody must do what I say at once!" He stamped his foot and the stu- dio shook.

55   "Even as I stand here—" he bellowed, "crippled, hobbled, sickened— I am a greater ruler than any man who ever lived! Now watch me become what I *can* become!"

56   Harrison tore the straps of his handicap harness like wet tissue paper, tore straps guaranteed to support five thousand pounds.

57   Harrison's scrap-iron handicaps crashed to the floor.

58   Harrison thrust his thumbs under the bar of the padlock that secured his head harness. The bar snapped like celery. Harrison smashed his headphones and spectacles against the wall.

59   He flung away his rubber-ball nose, revealed a man that would have awed Thor, the god of thunder.

60   "I shall now select my Empress!" he said, looking down on the cowering people. "Let the first woman who dares rise to her feet claim her mate and her throne!"

61   A moment passed, and then a ballerina arose, swaying like a willow.

62   Harrison plucked the mental handicap from her ear, snapped off her physical handicaps with marvellous delicacy. Last of all, he removed her mask.

63   She was blindingly beautiful.

64   "Now—" said Harrison, taking her hand, "shall we show the people the meaning of the word dance? Music!" he commanded.

65   The musicians scrambled back into their chairs, and Harrison stripped them of their handicaps, too. "Play your best," he told them, "and I'll make you barons and dukes and earls."

66   The music began. It was normal at first—cheap, silly, false. But Harrison snatched two musicians from their chairs, waved them like batons as he sang the music as he wanted it played. He slammed them back into their chairs.

67   The music began again and was much improved.

68   Harrison and his Empress merely listened to the music for a while—listened gravely, as though synchronizing their heartbeats with it.

69   They shifted their weights to their toes.

70   Harrison placed his big hands on the girl's tiny waist, letting her sense the weightlessness that would soon be hers.

71   And then, in an explosion of joy and grace, into the air they sprang!

72   Not only were the laws of the land abandoned, but the law of gravity and the laws of motion as well.

73   They reeled, whirled, swiveled, flounced, capered, gamboled, and spun.

74   They leaped like deer on the moon.

75   The studio ceiling was thirty feet high, but each leap brought the dancers nearer to it.

76   It became their obvious intention to kiss the ceiling.

77   They kissed it.

78   And then, neutralizing gravity with love and pure will, they remained suspended in air inches below the ceiling, and they kissed each other for a long, long time.

79   It was then that Diana Moon Glampers, the Handicapper General, came into the studio with a double-barreled ten-gauge shotgun. She fired twice, and the Emperor and the Empress were dead before they hit the floor.

80   Diana Moon Glampers loaded the gun again. She aimed it at the musicians and told them they had ten seconds to get their handicaps back on.

81   It was then that the Bergerons' television tube burned out.

82   Hazel turned to comment about the blackout to George. But George had gone out into the kitchen for a can of beer.

83   George came back in with the beer, paused while a handicap signal shook him up. And then he sat down again. "You been crying?" he said to Hazel.

84   "Yup," she said.

85   "What about?" he said.

86   "I forget," she said. "Something real sad on television."

87   "What was it?" he said.

88   "It's all kind of mixed up in my mind," said Hazel.

89   "Forget sad things," said George.

90   "I always do," said Hazel.

91   "That's my girl," said George. He winced. There was the sound of a riveting gun in his head.

92   "Gee—I could tell that one was a doozy," said Hazel.

93   "You can say that again," said George.

94   "Gee—" said Hazel, "I could tell that one was a doozy."

Questions for Discussion

1. What are the effects of enforced equality in this story? What is lost in this society because of enforced equality?

2. What is the effect of seeing the story through George's and Hazel's eyes? How would the story be different if told from Harrison's point of view?

3. Explain what effect 213 amendments would have on the U.S. Constitution.

4. What is the significance of Hazel's repeating herself at the end of the story?

Suggestions for Exploration and Writing

1. The society of "Harrison Bergeron" extends to its logical conclusion Jefferson's premise that "all men are created equal." In what ways does the society described in this story violate other principles enunciated in the Declaration of Independence?

2. Write an essay comparing George and Harrison.

3. George Bergeron says, "'The minute people start cheating on laws, what do you think happens to society?'" Hazel responds, "'Reckon it'd fall all apart.'" Argue for or against Hazel's assessment.

4. "Harrison Bergeron" makes a statement about the clash between equality and competition. In an essay, discuss the conflict between equality and competition in a free society.

5. Discuss current trends in education or society that parallel the kind of equality established in this story.

Ursula K. Le Guin (b. 1929)

Ursula K. Le Guin is one of the most prolific writers of this century and one of the hardest to classify. She has written poetry, short stories, novels, and children's books. At times, the genres seem to overlap, for her fiction is beautifully lyric, often symbolic, and philosophically titillating. Though she is usually classified as a writer of science fiction or fantasy, Le Guin's works are also realistic. Her fiction is sometimes based on recorded mythology, but often the myths are Le Guin originals. Her most famous and most admired novels are those included in The Earthsea Series—A Wizard of Earthsea *(1968),* The Tombs of Atuan *(1971),* The Farthest Shore *(1972),* Tehanu *(1990), and* The Other Wind *(2001)—and the Hainish Series, which includes two of her most famous novels—*The Left Hand of Darkness *(1969), and* The Dispossessed *(1974). Her most recent work is* The Telling *(2000).*

THE ONES WHO WALK AWAY FROM OMELAS   (1973)

1   With a clamor of bells that set the swallows soaring, the Festival of Summer came to the city Omelas, bright-towered by the sea. The rigging of the boats in harbor sparkled with flags. In the streets between houses with red roofs and painted walls, between old moss-grown gardens and under avenues of trees, past great parks and public buildings, processions moved. Some were decorous: old people in long stiff robes of mauve and grey, grave master workmen, quiet, merry women carrying their babies and chatting as they walked. In other streets the music beat faster, a shimmering of gong and tambourine, and the people went dancing, the procession was a dance. Children dodged in and out, their high calls rising like the swallows' crossing flights over the music and the singing. All the processions wound towards the northside of the city, where on the great water-meadow called the Green Fields boys and girls, naked in the bright air, with mud-stained feet and ankles and long, lithe arms, exercised their restive horses before the race. The horses wore no gear at all but a halter without bit. Their manes were braided with streamers of silver, gold, and green. They flared their nostrils and pranced and boasted to one another; they were vastly excited, the horse being the only animal who has adopted our ceremonies as his own. Far off to the north and west the mountains stood up half encircling Omelas on her bay. The air of morning was so clear that the snow still crowning the Eighteen Peaks burned with white-gold fire across the miles of sunlit air, under the dark blue of the sky. There was just enough wind to make the banners that marked the race-course snap and flutter now and then. In the silence of the broad green meadows one could hear the music winding through the city streets, farther and nearer and ever approaching, a cheerful faint sweetness of the air that from time to time trembled and gathered together and broke into the great joyous clanging of the bells.

2   Joyous! How is one to tell about joy? How describe the citizens of Omelas?

3   They were not simple folk, you see, though they were happy. But we do not say the words of cheer much any more. All smiles have become archaic. Given a description such as this one tends to make certain assumptions. Given a description such as this one tends to look next for the King, mounted on a splendid stallion and surrounded by his noble knights, or perhaps in a golden litter borne by great-muscled slaves. But there was no king. They did not use swords, or keep slaves. They were not barbarians. I do not know the rules and laws of their society, but I suspect that they were singularly few. As they did without monarchy and slavery, so they also got on without the stock exchange, the advertisement, the secret police, and the bomb. Yet I repeat that these were not simple folk, not dulcet shepherds, noble savages, bland utopians. They were not less complex than us. The trouble is that we have a bad habit, encouraged by pedants and sophisticates, of considering happiness as something rather stupid. Only pain is intellectual, only evil interesting. This is the treason of the artist: a refusal to admit the banality of evil and the terrible boredom of pain. If you can't lick 'em, join 'em. If it hurts, repeat it. But to praise despair is to condemn delight, to embrace violence is to lose hold of everything else. We have almost lost hold; we can no longer describe a happy man, nor make any celebration of joy. How can I tell you about the people of Omelas? They were not naïve and happy children—though their children were, in fact, happy. They were mature, intelligent, passionate adults whose lives were not wretched. O miracle! but I wish I could describe it better. I wish I could convince you. Omelas sounds in my words like a city in a fairy tale, long ago and far away, once upon a time. Perhaps it would be best if you imagined it as your own fancy bids, assuming it will rise to the occasion, for certainly I cannot suit you all. For instance, how about technology? I think that there would be no cars or helicopters in and above the streets; this follows from the fact that the people of Omelas are happy people. Happiness is based on a just discrimination of what is necessary, what is neither necessary nor destructive, and what is destructive. In the middle category, however—that of the unnecessary but undestructive, that of comfort, luxury, exuberance, etc.—they could perfectly well have central heating, subway trains, washing machines, and all kinds of marvelous devices not yet invented here, floating light-sources, fuelless power, a cure for the common cold. Or they could have none of that: it doesn't matter. As you like it. I incline to think that people from towns up and down the coast have been coming in to Omelas during the last days before the Festival on very fast little trains and double-decked trams, and that the train station of Omelas is actually the handsomest building in town, though plainer than the magnificent Farmer's Market. But even granted trains, I fear that Omelas so far strikes some of you as goody-goody. Smiles, bells, parades, horses, bleh. If so, please add an orgy. If an orgy would help, don't hesitate. Let us not, however, have temples from

which issue beautiful nude priests and priestesses already half in ecstasy and ready to copulate with any man or woman, lover or stranger, who desires union with the deep godhead of the blood, although that was my first idea. But really it would be better not to have any temples in Omelas—at least, not manned temples. Religion yes, clergy no. Surely the beautiful nudes can just wander about, offering themselves like divine soufflés to the hunger of the needy and the rapture of the flesh. Let them join the processions. Let tambourines be struck above the copulations, and the glory of desire be proclaimed upon the gongs, and (a not unimportant point) let the offspring of these delightful rituals be beloved and looked after by all. One thing I know there is none of in Omelas is guilt. But what else should there be? I thought at first there were no drugs, but that is puritanical. For those who like it, the faint insistent sweetness of *drooz* may perfume the ways of the city, *drooz* which first brings a great lightness and brilliance to the mind and limbs, and then after some hours a dreamy languor, and wonderful visions at least of the very arcana and inmost secrets of the Universe, as well as exciting the pleasure of sex beyond all belief; and it is not habit-forming. For more modest tastes I think there ought to be beer. What else, what else belongs in the joyous city? The sense of victory, surely, the celebration of courage. But as we did without clergy, let us do without soldiers. The joy built upon successful slaughter is not the right kind of joy; it will not do; it is fearful and it is trivial. A boundless and generous contentment, a magnanimous triumph felt not against some outer enemy but in communion with the finest and fairest in the souls of all men everywhere and the splendor of the world's summer: this is what swells the hearts of the people of Omelas, and the victory they celebrate is that of life. I really don't think many of them need to take *drooz*.

4   Most of the processions have reached the Green Fields by now. A marvelous smell of cooking goes forth from the red and blue tents of the provisioners. The faces of small children are amiably sticky; in the benign grey beard of a man a couple of crumbs of rich pastry are entangled. The youths and girls have mounted their horses and are beginning to group around the starting line of the course. An old woman, small, fat, and laughing, is passing out flowers from a basket, and tall young men wear her flowers in their shining hair. A child of nine or ten sits at the edge of the crowd, alone, playing on a wooden flute. People pause to listen, and they smile, but they do not speak to him, for he never ceases playing and never sees them, his dark eyes wholly rapt in the sweet, thin magic of the tune.

5   He finishes, and slowly lowers his hands holding the wooden flute.

6   As if that little private silence were the signal, all at once a trumpet sounds from the pavilion near the starting line: imperious, melancholy, piercing. The horses rear on their slender legs, and some of them neigh in answer. Sober-faced, the young riders stroke the horses' necks and soothe them, whispering, "Quiet, quiet, there my beauty, my hope. . . ." They begin to form in rank along the starting line. The crowds along the race-course are like a field of grass and flowers in the wind. The Festival of Summer has begun.

7　　Do you believe? Do you accept the festival, the city, the joy? No? Then let me describe one more thing.

8　　In a basement under one of the beautiful public buildings of Omelas, or perhaps in the cellar of one of its spacious private homes, there is a room. It has one locked door, and no window. A little light seeps in dustily between cracks in the boards, secondhand from a cobwebbed window somewhere across the cellar. In one corner of the little room a couple of mops, with stiff, clotted, foul-smelling heads, stand near a rusty bucket. The floor is dirt, a little damp to the touch, as cellar dirt usually is. The room is about three paces long and two wide: a mere broom closer or disused tool room. In the room a child is sitting. It could be a boy or a girl. It looks about six, but actually is nearly ten. It is feeble-minded. Perhaps it was born defective, or perhaps it has become imbecile through fear, malnutrition, and neglect. It picks its nose and occasionally fumbles vaguely with its toes or genitals, as it sits hunched in the corner farthest from the bucket and the two mops. It is afraid of the mops. It finds them horrible. It shuts its eyes, but it knows the mops are still standing there; and the door is locked; and nobody will come. The door is always locked; and nobody ever comes, except that sometimes—the child has no understanding of time or interval—sometimes the door rattles terribly and opens, and a person, or several people, are there. One of them may come in and kick the child to make it stand up. The others never come close, but peer in at it with frightened, disgusted eyes. The food bowl and the water jug are hastily filled, the door is locked, the eyes disappear. The people at the door never say anything, but the child, who has not always lived in the tool room, and can remember sunlight and its mother's voice, sometimes speaks. "I will be good," it says. "Please let me out. I will be good!" They never answer. The child used to scream for help at night, and cry a good deal, but now it only makes a kind of whining, "eh-haa, eh-haa," and it speaks less and less often. It is so thin there are no calves to its legs; its belly protrudes; it lives on a half-bowl of corn meal and grease a day. It is naked. Its buttocks and thighs are a mass of festered sores, as it sits in its own excrement continually.

9　　They all know it is there, all the people of Omelas. Some of them have come to see it, others are content merely to know it is there. They all know that it has to be there. Some of them understand why, and some do not, but they all understand that their happiness, the beauty of their city, the tenderness of their friendships, the health of their children, the wisdom of their scholars, the skill of their makers, even the abundance of their harvest and the kindly weathers of their skies, depend wholly on this child's abominable misery.

10　　This is usually explained to children when they are between eight and twelve, whenever they seem capable of understanding; and most of those who come to see the child are young people, though often enough an adult comes, or comes back, to see the child. No matter how well the matter has been explained to them, these young spectators are always shocked and sickened at the sight. They feel disgust, which they had thought themselves superior to. They feel anger, outrage, impotence, despite all the explanations. They would like to do something for the child. But there is nothing they can do. If the child were brought up into the sunlight out of that vile place, if it were cleaned and fed and comforted, that would be a good thing, indeed; but if it were done, in that day and hour all the prosperity and beauty and delight of Omelas would wither and be destroyed. Those are the terms. To exchange all the goodness and grace of every life in Omelas for that single, small improvement: to throw away the happiness of thousands for the chance of the happiness of one: that would be to let guilt within the walls indeed.

11   The terms are strict and absolute; there may not even be a kind word spoken to the child.

12   Often the young people go home in tears, or in a tearless rage, when they have seen the child and faced this terrible paradox. They may brood over it for weeks or years. But as time goes on they begin to realize that even if the child could be released, it would not get much good of its freedom: a little vague pleasure of warmth and food, no doubt, but little more. It is too degraded and imbecile to know any real joy. It has been afraid too long ever to be free of fear. Its habits are too uncouth for it to respond to humane treatment. Indeed, after so long it would probably be wretched without walls about it to protect it, and darkness for its eyes, and its own excrement to sit in. Their tears at the bitter injustice dry when they begin to perceive the terrible justice of reality, and to accept it. Yet it is their tears and anger, the trying of their generosity and the acceptance of their helplessness, which are perhaps the true source of the splendor of their lives. Theirs is no vapid, irresponsible happiness. They know that they, like the child, are not free. They know compassion. It is the existence of the child, and their knowledge of its existence, that makes possible the nobility of their architecture, the poignancy of their music, the profundity of their science. It is because of the child that they are so gentle with children. They know that if the wretched one were not there snivelling in the dark, the other one, the flute-player, could make no joyful music as the young riders line up in their beauty for the race in the sunlight of the first morning of summer.

13   Now do you believe in them? Are they not more credible? But there is one more thing to tell, and this is quite incredible.

14   At times one of the adolescent girls or boys who go to see the child does not go home to weep or rage, does not, in fact, go home at all. Sometimes also a man or woman much older falls silent for a day or two, and then leaves home. These people go out into the street, and walk down the street alone. They keep walking, and walk straight out of the city of Omelas, through the beautiful gates. They keep walking across the farmlands of Omelas. Each one goes alone, youth or girl, man or woman. Night falls; the traveler must pass down village streets, between the houses with yellow-lit windows, and on out into the darkness of the fields. Each alone, they go west or north, towards the mountains. They go on. They leave Omelas, they walk ahead into the darkness, and they do not come

back. The place they go towards is a place even less imaginable to most of us than the city of happiness. I cannot describe it at all. It is possible that it does not exist. But they seem to know where they are going, the ones who walk away from Omelas.

Questions for Discussion

1. What descriptive details might lead you to infer that Omelas is a utopia? How does Le Guin involve you in making her description of Omelas believable? What is the significance of telling you what the people are *not?*

2. Le Guin's narrator accuses writers and artists of having a bias against happiness and joy, of seeing happiness as simple-minded. Which writers whom you have read in this anthology seem to have such a bias?

3. Why does the happiness of Omelas depend on the misery of a feeble-minded child locked in a closet? Why is the child referred to as "it"?

4. Why are the young offended, and why do some eventually walk away from Omelas? Why does the story emphasize the people who stay and the title emphasize those who walk away?

5. Omelas has religion but no clergy. What is the logic behind this proposal? Similarly, Omelas has no soldiers. Why?

Suggestions for Exploration and Writing

1. Would you walk away from Omelas? Give detailed reasons for your position. If you left Omelas, where would you go?

2. Should the prosperity of the majority be considered over the "rights" of the minority? Apply this story to the United States today.

John Updike (b. 1932)

Born in Reading, Pennsylvania, John Updike attended Harvard and wrote for and was later editor of the Harvard Lampoon. *As a Knox Fellow, he traveled and studied in England; as a Fulbright Lincoln Lecturer, he traveled to Ghana, Nigeria, Tanzania, Kenya, and Ethiopia. His short story collections include* The Same Door (1958) *and* Pigeon Feathers (1959); *his poetry includes* The Carpentered Hen and Other Tame Creatures (1958). *However, Updike is best known for his novels.* The Poorhouse Fair (1959) *won the Rosenthal Foundation Award, and* The Witches of Eastwick (1984) *was later made into a movie.* The Rabbit series won Updike critical acclaim: Rabbit, Run (1960); Rabbit Redux (1971); Rabbit Is Rich (1981), *which won the Pulitzer Prize in 1982; and* Rabbit at Rest (1990). *In 1998, Updike was awarded the National Book Foundation Medal for Distinguished Contribution to American Letters.*

A & P   (1959)

1   In walks these three girls in nothing but bathing suits. I'm in the third checkout slot, with my back to the door, so I don't see them until they're over by the bread. The one that caught my eye first was the one in the plaid green two-piece. She was a chunky kid, with a good tan and a sweet broad soft-looking can with those two crescents of white just under it, where the sun never seems to hit, at the top of the backs of her legs. I stood there with my hand on a box of HiHo crackers trying to remember if I rang it up or not. I ring it up again and the customer starts giving me hell. She's one of these cash-register-watchers, a witch about fifty with rouge on her cheekbones and no eyebrows, and I know it made her day to trip me up. She'd been watching cash registers for fifty years and probably never seen a mistake before.

2   By the time I got her feathers smoothed and her goodies into a bag— she gives me a little snort in passing, if she'd been born at the right time they would have burned her over in Salem—by the time I get her on her way the girls had circled around the bread and were coming back, without a pushcart, back my way along the counters, in the aisle between the checkouts and the Special bins. They didn't even have shoes on. There was this chunky one, with the two-piece—it was bright green and the seams on the bra were still sharp and her belly was still pretty pale so I guessed she just got it (the suit)—there was this one, with one of those chubby berry-faces, the lips all bunched together under her nose, this one, and a tall one, with black hair that hadn't quite frizzed right, and one of these sunburns right across under the eyes, and a chin that was too long—you know, the kind of girl other girls think is very "striking" and "attractive" but never quite makes it, as they very well know, which is why they like her so much—and then the third one, that wasn't quite so tall. She was the queen. She kind of led them, the other two peeking around and making their shoulders round. She didn't look around, not this queen, she just walked straight on slowly, on these long white prima-donna legs. She came down a little hard on her heels, as if she didn't walk in her bare feet that much, putting down her heels and then letting the weight move along to her toes as if she was testing the floor with every step, putting a little deliberate extra action into it. You never know for sure how girls' minds work (do you really think it's a mind in there or just a little buzz like a bee in a glass jar?) but you got the idea she had talked the other two into coming in here with her, and now she was showing them how to do it, walk slow and hold yourself straight.

3   She had on a kind of dirty-pink—beige maybe, I don't know—bathing suit with a little nubble all over it and, what got me, the straps were down. They were off her shoulders looped loose around the cool tops of her arms, and I guess as a result the suit had slipped a little on her, so all around the top of the cloth there was this shining rim. If it hadn't been there you wouldn't have known there could have been anything whiter than those shoulders. With the straps pushed off, there was nothing between the top

of the suit and the top of her head except just *her,* this clean bare plane of the top of her chest down from the shoulder bones like a dented sheet of metal tilted in the light. I mean, it was more than pretty.

4   She had sort of oaky hair that the sun and salt had bleached, done up in a bun that was unravelling, and a kind of prim face. Walking into the A & P with your straps down, I suppose it's the only kind of face you *can* have. She held her head so high her neck, coming up out of those white shoulders, looked kind of stretched, but I didn't mind. The longer her neck was, the more of her there was.

5   She must have felt in the corner of her eye me and over my shoulder Stokesie in the second slot watching, but she didn't tip. Not this queen. She kept her eyes moving across the racks, and stopped, and turned so slow it made my stomach rub the inside of my apron, and buzzed to the other two, who kind of huddled against her for relief, and then they all three of them went up the cat-and-dog-food-breakfast-cereal-macaroni-rice-raisins-season-ings-spreads-spaghetti-soft-drinks-crackers-and-cookies aisle. From the third slot I look straight up this aisle to the meat counter, and I watched them all the way. The fat one with the tan sort of fumbled with the cookies, but on second thought she put the package back. The sheep pushing their carts down the aisle—the girls were walking against the usual traffic (not that we have one-way signs or anything)—were pretty hilarious. You could see them, when Queenie's white shoulders dawned on them, kind of jerk, or hop, or hiccup, but their eyes snapped back to their own baskets and on they pushed. I bet you could set off dynamite in an A & P and the people would by and large keep reaching and checking oatmeal off their lists and mut-tering "Let me see, there was a third thing, began with A, asparagus, no, ah, yes, applesauce!" or whatever it is they do mutter. But there was no doubt, this jiggled them. A few houseslaves in pin curlers even looked around after pushing their carts past to make sure what they had seen was correct.

6   You know, it's one thing to have a girl in a bathing suit down on the beach, where what with the glare nobody can look at each other much anyway, and another thing in the cool of the A & P, under the fluorescent lights, against all those stacked packages, with her feet paddling along naked over our checkerboard green-and-cream rubber-tile floor.

7   "Oh Daddy," Stokesie said beside me. "I feel so faint."

8   "Darling," I said. "Hold me tight." Stokesie's married, with two babies chalked up on his fuselage already, but as far as I can tell that's the only difference. He's twenty-two, and I was nineteen this April.

9   "Is it done?" he asks, the responsible married man finding his voice. I forgot to say he thinks he's going to be manager some sunny day, maybe in 1990 when it's called the Great Alexandrov and Petrooshki Tea Com-pany or something.

10   What he meant was, our town is five miles from a beach, with a big sum-mer colony out on the Point, but we're right in the middle of town, and the women generally put on a shirt or shorts or something before they get out of the car into the street. And anyway these are usually women with six

children and varicose veins mapping their legs and nobody, including them, could care less. As I say, we're right in the middle of town, and if you stand at our front doors you can see two banks and the Congregational church and the newspaper store and three real-estate offices and about twenty-seven old freeloaders tearing up Central Street because the sewer broke again. It's not as if we're on the Cape; we're north of Boston and there's people in this town haven't seen the ocean for twenty years.

11   The girls had reached the meat counter and were asking McMahon something. He pointed, they pointed, and they shuffled out of sight behind a pyramid of Diet Delight peaches. All that was left for us to see was old McMahon patting his mouth and looking after them sizing up their joints. Poor kids, I began to feel sorry for them, they couldn't help it.

12   Now here comes the sad part of the story, at least my family says it's sad, but I don't think it's so sad myself. The store's pretty empty, it being Thursday afternoon, so there was nothing much to do except lean on the register and wait for the girls to show up again. The whole store was like a pinball machine and I didn't know which tunnel they'd come out of. After a while they come around out of the far aisle, around the light bulbs, records at discount of the Caribbean Six or Tony Martin Sings or some such gunk you wonder they waste the wax on, sixpacks of candy bars, and plastic toys done up in cellophane that fall apart when a kid looks at them anyway. Around they come, Queenie still leading the way, and holding a little gray jar in her hand. Slots Three through Seven are unmanned and I could see her wondering between Stokes and me, but Stokesie with his usual luck draws an old party in baggy gray pants who stumbles up with four giant cans of pineapple juice (what do these bums *do* with all that pineapple juice? I've often asked myself) so the girls come to me. Queenie puts down the jar and I take it into my fingers icy cold. Kingfish Fancy Herring Snacks in Pure Sour Cream: 49¢. Now her hands are empty, not a ring or a bracelet, bare as God made them, and I wonder where the money's coming from. Still with that prim look she lifts a folded dollar bill out of the hollow at the center of her nubbled pink top. The jar went heavy in my hand. Really, I thought that was so cute.

13   Then everybody's luck begins to run out. Lengel comes in from haggling with a truck full of cabbages on the lot and is about to scuttle into that door marked MANAGER behind which he hides all day when the girls touch his eye. Lengel's pretty dreary, teaches Sunday school and the rest, but he doesn't miss that much. He comes over and says, "Girls, this isn't the beach."

14   Queenie blushes, though maybe it's just a brush of sunburn I was noticing for the first time, now that she was so close. "My mother asked me to pick up a jar of herring snacks." Her voice kind of startled me, the way voices do when you see the people first, coming out so flat and dumb yet kind of tony, too, the way it ticked over "pick up" and "snacks." All of a sudden I slid right down her voice into her living room. Her father and the other men were standing around in ice-cream coats and

bow ties and the women were in sandals picking up herring snacks on toothpicks off a big glass plate and they were all holding drinks the color of water with olives and sprigs of mint in them. When my parents have somebody over they get lemonade and if it's a real racy affair Schlitz in tall glasses with "They'll Do It Every Time" cartoons stencilled on.

15   "That's all right," Lengel said. "But this isn't the beach." His repeating this struck me as funny, as if it had just occurred to him, and he had been thinking all these years the A & P was a great big dune and he was the head lifeguard. He didn't like my smiling—as I say he doesn't miss much—but he concentrates on giving the girls that sad Sunday-school-superintendent stare.

16   Queenie's blush is no sunburn now, and the plump one in plaid, that I liked better from the back—a really sweet can—pipes up. "We weren't doing any shopping. We just came in for the one thing."

17   "That makes no difference," Lengel tells her, and I could see from the way his eyes went that he hadn't noticed she was wearing a two-piece before. "We want you decently dressed when you come in here."

18   "We *are* decent," Queenie says suddenly, her lower lip pushing, getting sore now that she remembers her place, a place from which the crowd that runs the A & P must look pretty crummy. Fancy Herring Snacks flashed in her very blue eyes.

19   "Girls, I don't want to argue with you. After this come in here with your shoulders covered. It's our policy." He turns his back. That's policy for you. Policy is what the kingpins want. What the others want is juvenile delinquency.

20   All this while, the customers had been showing up with their carts but, you know, sheep, seeing a scene, they had all bunched up on Stokesie, who shook open a paper bag as gently as peeling a peach, not wanting to miss a word. I could feel in the silence everybody getting nervous, most of all Lengel, who asks me, "Sammy, have you rung up their purchase?"

21   I thought and said "No" but it wasn't about that I was thinking. I go through the punches, 4, 9, GROC, TOT—it's more complicated than you think, and after you do it often enough, it begins to make a little song, that you hear words to, in my case "Hello (*bing*) there, you (*gung*) hap-py pee-pul (*splat*)!"—the *splat* being the drawer flying out. I uncrease the bill, tenderly as you may imagine, it just having come from between the two smoothest scoops of vanilla I had ever known were there, and pass a half and a penny into her narrow pink palm, and nestle the herrings in a bag and twist its neck and hand it over, all the time thinking.

22   The girls, and who'd blame them, are in a hurry to get out, so I say "I quit" to Lengel quick enough for them to hear, hoping they'll stop and watch me, their unsuspected hero. They keep right on going, into the electric eye; the door flies open and they flicker across the lot to their car, Queenie and Plaid and Big Tall Goony-Goony (not that as raw material she was so bad), leaving me with Lengel and a kink in his eyebrow.

23   "Did you say something, Sammy?"

24   "I said I quit."

25   "I thought you did."

26   "You didn't have to embarrass them."

27   "It was they who were embarrassing us."

28   I started to say something that came out "Fiddle-de-doo." It's a saying of my grandmother's, and I know she would have been pleased.

29   "I don't think you know what you're saying," Lengel said.

30   "I know you don't," I said. "But I do." I pull the bow at the back of my apron and start shrugging it off my shoulders. A couple customers that had been heading for my slot begin to knock against each other, like scared pigs in a chute.

31   Lengel sighs and begins to look very patient and old and gray. He's been a friend of my parents for years. "Sammy, you don't want to do this to your Mom and Dad," he tells me. It's true, I don't. But it seems to me that once you begin a gesture it's fatal not to go through with it. I fold the apron, "Sammy" stitched in red on the pocket, and put it on the counter, and drop the bow tie on top of it. The bow tie is theirs, if you've ever wondered. "You'll feel this for the rest of your life," Lengel says, and I know that's true, too, but remembering how he made that pretty girl blush makes me so scrunchy inside I punch the No Sale tab and the machine whirs "pee-pul" and the drawer splats out. One advantage to this scene taking place in summer, I can follow this up with a clean exit, there's no fumbling around getting your coat and galoshes, I just saunter into the electric eye in my white shirt that my mother ironed the night before, and the door heaves itself open, and outside the sunshine is skating around on the asphalt.

32   I look around for my girls, but they're gone, of course. There wasn't anybody but some young married screaming with her children about some candy they didn't get by the door of a powder-blue Falcon station wagon. Looking back in the big windows, over the bags of peat moss and aluminum lawn furniture stacked on the pavement, I could see Lengel in my place in the slot, checking the sheep through. His face was dark gray and his back stiff, as if he'd just had an injection of iron, and my stomach kind of fell as I felt how hard the world was going to be to me hereafter.

Questions for Discussion

1. How does Sammy feel about his job?

2. Other than the obvious physical attraction, what is appealing to Sammy about the three girls "in nothing but bathing suits"? What does Sammy see as the significance of their wearing bathing suits in the A & P?

3. How do Sammy's customers behave? Why does Sammy call them sheep?

4. Describe Sammy's family.

5. Do you agree with Sammy's parents that his quitting his job is "sad"?

6. Why does Sammy quit?

Suggestions for Exploration and Writing

1. In an essay, analyze Sammy's reasons for quitting his job at the A & P.

2. Write a detailed contrast of the lifestyles of Sammy's family, the A & P customers, and the girls.

POETRY

William Blake (1757–1827)

William Blake was an English mystical poet and engraver. He sought to release Christianity from the constraints of early industrial materialism, Enlightenment rationalism, and puritanical sexual repression. He developed his own philosophical and mythological system expressed in such long, complex, and extremely difficult prophetic works as The Book of Thel *(1789) and* Jerusalem *(1804–1820). Much more accessible are the lyrics in* Songs of Innocence *(1789) and its companion volume,* Songs of Experience *(1794), poems that express Blake's sympathy with the oppressed and his rage at the human institutions that perpetuate oppression.*

LONDON   (1794)

I wander through each chartered street,
Near where the chartered Thames does flow,
And mark in every face I meet
Marks of weakness, marks of woe.

5 In every cry of every man,
In every infant's cry of fear,
In every voice, in very ban,
The mind-forged manacles I hear.

How the chimney-sweeper's cry
10 Every black'ning church appalls
And the hapless soldier's sigh
Runs in blood down palace walls.

But most through midnight streets I hear
How the youthful harlot's curse
15 Blasts the new born infant's tear
And blights with plagues the marriage hearse.

Questions for Discussion

1. What does Blake mean by calling the London streets and the Thames River "chartered"?

2. Look up the word *appalls*. What different meanings of the word seem appropriate here?

3. What is the "youthful harlot's curse"? What are the "plagues"?

4. How, according to Blake's poem, is the revolt of the oppressed expressed?

Suggestions for Exploration and Writing

1. Discuss what Blake means by "The mind-forged manacles I hear."

2. Observe the faces of the people in a city near you. What "marks of weakness, marks of woe" as well as marks of strength and marks of happiness do you find in these faces? Discuss.

William Wordsworth (1770–1850)

William Wordsworth was a leading poet of the Romantic movement in England. His collaboration with Samuel Taylor Coleridge on the book of poems Lyrical Ballads *in 1798 is often cited as the beginning of the Romantic movement in England. Wordsworth rebelled against the order and restraint of the Enlightenment, supported the French Revolution, and sought in nature and in the lives of ordinary people an answer to the complexity and materialism of industrial England. In his poetry, he tried to use the plain language of ordinary people. As the supreme English nature poet, Wordsworth changed forever the view of nature in his culture and in ours.*

THE WORLD IS TOO MUCH WITH US   (1807)

The world is too much with us; late and soon,
Getting and spending, we lay waste our powers;
Little we see in Nature that is ours;
We have given our hearts away, a sordid boon!
5 This Sea that bares her bosom to the moon;
The winds that will be howling at all hours,
And are up-gathered now like sleeping flowers;
For this, for everything, we are out of tune;
It moves us not. Great God! I'd rather be
10 A Pagan suckled in a creed outworn;
So might I, standing on this pleasant lea,
Have glimpses that would make me less forlorn;
Have sight of Proteus rising from the sea;
Or hear old Triton blow his wreathed horn.

Questions for Discussion

1. According to Wordsworth, what has the world made us "out of tune" for? In what sense have we "given our hearts away"?

2. What does Wordsworth mean by "a Pagan suckled in a creed outworn"? Why would he prefer being a pagan?

3. Proteus was an ancient Greek god of the sea who could change his shape whenever and however he wished. Triton, another ancient Greek sea god, had the upper body of a man and the lower body of a fish. In what ways might the sight of Proteus and the sound of Triton's horn be consoling to the poem's speaker?

4. Compare the **theme** and subject of this poem to those of Hopkins's "God's Grandeur" in the Quest unit.

Suggestion for Exploration and Writing

1. Wordsworth speaks of a former time when nature still awed humanity and life was simple. He says, however, "we have given our hearts away, a sordid boon!" Discuss some of the ways that people have given their hearts away.

Stephen Crane (1871–1900)

In his brief life, Stephen Crane produced a remarkable variety of literature. The son of a Methodist minister, Crane was born in Newark, New Jersey, and attended Lafayette College and Syracuse University. As a newspaper reporter, he traveled to Cuba and to Greece. His first novel, Maggie: A Girl of the Streets *(1893), shocked readers with its realistic depiction of slum life in the Bowery of New York, and his second,* The Red Badge of Courage *(1895), considered his masterpiece, told a remarkably true-to-life story about the American Civil War. Crane's poems, usually written in free verse, have been described as miniature parables.*

A MAN SAID TO THE UNIVERSE   (1899)

A man said to the universe:
"Sir, I exist!"
"However," replied the universe,
"The fact has not created in me
5   A sense of obligation."

Questions for Discussion

1. What does the man's statement imply about his opinion of himself?

2. What does this brief poem suggest about man's responsibility for his own fate?

Suggestions for Exploration and Writing

1. Write an epistolary essay from the man in response to the universe.
2. Write an essay in which the universe details the man's responsibilities for his own behavior and his obligations, or lack of obligations, to other human beings.

Rudyard Kipling (1865–1936)

Born in Bombay, India, Kipling was educated in England; in 1882, he returned to India to work as an editor of a newspaper. In 1889, he went back to England to continue his writing career. Some of his early poems were collected in Departmental Ditties *(1886) and* Barrack-Room Ballads *(1892); his short stories from this period were* Soldiers Three *(1888) and* Plain Tales from the Hills *(1888). His novel,* The Light That Failed *(1890), met with success. Kipling's stories of India made him a popular writer because of his romantic notions of the Englishman and the Indian people. These views are reflected in some of his poems such as "Mandalay," "The White Man's Burden," "Gunga Din," and in* Recessional *(1897). After marrying an American, Kipling moved to Vermont, where he lived for four years and wrote the children's stories:* The Jungle Book *(1894) and* Second Jungle Book *(1895);* Captains Courageous *(1897);* Kim *(1901); and* Just So Stories *(1902). In 1900, he returned to England and continued to write. His later works include* Puck of Pook's Hill *(1906) and his famous poem "If" (1910). Kipling was England's first Nobel Prize winner in literature (1907).*

If

(1910)

If you can keep your head when all about you
Are losing theirs and blaming it on you,
If you can trust yourself when all men doubt you
But make allowance for their doubting too,
5   If you can wait and not be tired by waiting,
Or being lied about, don't deal in lies,
Or being hated, don't give way to hating,
And yet don't look too good, nor talk too wise:

If you can dream—and not make dreams your
10   master,
If you can think—and not make thoughts your aim;
If you can meet with Triumph and Disaster
And treat those two impostors just the same;
If you can bear to hear the truth you've spoken
15   Twisted by knaves to make a trap for fools,
Or watch the things you gave your life to, broken,
And stoop and build 'em up with worn-out tools:

If you can make one heap of all your winnings
And risk it all on one turn of pitch-and-toss,
20   And lose, and start again at your beginnings
And never breathe a word about your loss;
If you can force your heart and nerve and sinew
To serve your turn long after they are gone,
And so hold on when there is nothing in you
25   Except the Will which says to them: "Hold on!"

If you can talk with crowds and keep your virtue,
Or walk with kings—nor lose the common touch,
If neither foes nor loving friends can hurt you;
If all men count with you, but none too much,
30   If you can fill the unforgiving minute
With sixty seconds' worth of distance run,
Yours is the Earth and everything that's in it,
And—which is more—you'll be a Man, my son!

Questions for Discussion

1. How many sentences make up this poem? Examine the sentence structure and explain the effect of this structure on the poem.

2. Look at each one of the "If" clauses and try to select one noun that
names the characteristic you would have if you could accomplish the
task described.

Suggestions for Exploration and Writing

1. Use the nouns listed in the question above to write an expository essay
about what qualities, according to Kipling, would make "a Man." Alternatively, use these nouns or others that you add to write an essay
describing what you consider the qualities that make any person—
whether male or female—a responsible and admirable adult.

2. Make a list of the qualities that you consider most important to manhood and to womanhood. Then write an essay explaining why those
lists are or are not the same.

3. Compare the qualities suggested here with those described by Maya
Angelou in "Phenomenal Woman."

W. H. Auden (1907–1973)

*W. H. Auden, a major twentieth-century poet who was born in Eng-
land, became a citizen of the United States in 1946. A precocious
writer, he published* Poems *in 1930 and* Orators *in 1932. Also in
the 1930s, Auden experimented with different forms of drama, including verse plays and plays that used music. A winner of many literary*

prizes, he was praised for his expertise in lyrical poetry and for his technical proficiency. Auden, who influenced many of the poets of his age, is noted as a poet, critic, essayist, and playwright.

THE UNKNOWN CITIZEN   (1940)

(TO JS/07/M/378

THIS MARBLE MONUMENT IS ERECTED BY THE STATE)

He was found by the Bureau of Statistics to be
One against whom there was no official complaint,
And all the reports on his conduct agree
That, in the modern sense of an old-fashioned word, he was a saint,
5   For in everything he did he served the Greater Community.
Except for the War till the day he retired
He worked in a factory and never got fired
But satisfied his employers, Fudge Motors Inc.
Yet he wasn't a scab or odd in his views,
10   For his Union reports that he paid his dues,
(Our report on his Union shows it was sound)
And our Social Psychology workers found
That he was popular with his mates and liked a drink.
The Press are convinced that he bought a paper every day
15   And that his reactions to advertisements were normal in every way.
Policies taken out in his name prove that he was fully insured,
And his Health-card shows he was once in hospital but left it cured.
Both Producers Research and High-Grade Living declare
He was fully sensible to the advantages of the Installment Plan
20   And had everything necessary to the Modern Man,
A phonograph, a radio, a car and a frigidaire.
Our researchers into Public Opinion are content
That he held the proper opinions for the time of year;
When there was peace, he was for peace; when there was war, he went.
25   He was married and added five children to the population,
Which our Eugenist says was the right number for a parent of his
    generation.
And our teachers report that he never interfered with their education.
Was he free? Was he happy? The question is absurd:
Had anything been wrong, we should certainly have heard.

Questions for Discussion

1. What, according to the poem, is the modern sense of the word "saint"? In what ways is this man saintly?

2. What adjectives seem best to describe the "unknown citizen"? In what way is he unknown?

3. What does the name of the unknown citizen's employer suggest?

4. Explain the implication of the statement that because he "was fully sensible to the advantages of the Installment Plan," he "had everything necessary to the Modern Man."

5. Why does the speaker call the questions "Was he free? Was he happy?" absurd? How would you answer these questions about the unknown citizen?

6. What is Auden mocking in this poem?

Suggestions for Exploration and Writing

1. Write an essay about efforts of your peers to conform and appear "normal in every way."

2. In an essay, describe the character traits that are admired by the speaker of the poem.

Karl Shapiro (1913–2000)

American poet and literary critic Karl Shapiro was born in Baltimore, Maryland. He is known for his independence and iconoclasm. He disliked and opposed the great modern poets Ezra Pound, William Butler Yeats, and T. S. Eliot, regarding Eliot's Christianity as a sellout to an outmoded worldview. Shapiro taught at many universities, including Johns Hopkins, the University of Nebraska, the University of Illinois at Chicago, and the University of California, Davis. His collections of poems include V-Letter and Other Poems *(1945), a collection of poems about World War II that won a Pulitzer Prize;* Poems of a Jew *(1958); and* The Bourgeois Poet *(1964).*

THE CONSCIENTIOUS OBJECTOR (1978)

The gates clanged and they walked you into jail
More tense than felons but relieved to find
The hostile world shut out, flags that dripped
From every mother's windowpane, obscene
5   The bloodlust sweating from the public heart,
The dog authority slavering at your throat.
A sense of quiet, of pulling down the blind
Possessed you. Punishment you felt was clean.

The decks, the catwalks, and the narrow light
10   Composed a ship. This was a mutinous crew
Troubling the captains for plain decencies,
A *Mayflower* brim with pilgrims headed out
To establish new theocracies to west,
A Noah's ark coasting the topmost seas
15   Ten miles above the sodomites and fish.
These inmates loved the only living doves.

Like all men hunted from the world you made
A good community, voyaging the storm
To no safe Plymouth or green Ararat;
20   Trouble or calm, the men with Bibles prayed,
The gaunt politicals construed our hate.
The opposite of all armies, you were best
Opposing uniformity and yourselves;
Prison and personality were your fate.

25   You suffered not so physically but knew
Maltreatment, hunger, ennui of the mind.
Well might the soldier kissing the hot beach
Erupting in his face damn all your kind.
Yet you who saved neither yourselves nor us
30   Are equally with those who shed the blood
The heroes of our cause. Your conscience is
What we come back to in the armistice.

Questions for Discussion

1. What is a conscientious objector?
2. Why and how is the prisoner "relieved" to be in prison?
3. What are the implications of Shapiro's comparing the prisoners to the pilgrims and to Noah on the ark?
4. The speaker says, "Well might the soldier [. . .] damn all your kind" but also calls the conscientious objector a kind of hero. Explain this apparent contradiction.

Suggestions for Exploration and Writing

1. In an essay, contrast the conscientious objector to the "unknown citizen" of Auden's poem.
2. O'Brien in "On the Rainy River" describes his agonizing decision to allow himself to be drafted. In an essay, discuss the relative merits of O'Brien's decision and the conscientious objector's decision.

Randall Jarrell (1914–1965)

Randall Jarrell was an American poet and critic. While some of his poems like the following one present a bleak, almost tragic vision, others present an innocent, almost childlike one. Early war poems such as "The Death of the Ball Turret Gunner" arose out of Jarrell's brief service as a pilot in World War II. Jarrell washed out as a pilot, partially because he was bored by having to stay in formation and to fly at one unvarying speed.

The Woman at the Washington Zoo (1960)

The saris go by me from the embassies.

Cloth from the moon. Cloth from another planet.
They look back at the leopard like the leopard.

And I. . . .

5   this print of mine, that has kept its color
Alive through so many cleanings; this dull null
Navy I wear to work, and wear from work, and so
To my bed, so to my grave, with no
Complaints, no comment: neither from my chief,
10 The Deputy Chief Assistant, nor his chief—
Only I complain. . . . this serviceable
Body that no sunlight dyes, no hand suffuses
But, dome-shadowed, withering among columns,
Wavy beneath fountains—small, far-off, shining
15 In the eyes of animals, these beings trapped
As I am trapped but not, themselves, the trap,
Aging, but without knowledge of their age,
Kept safe here, knowing not of death, for death—
Oh, bars of my own body, open, open!

20 The world goes by my cage and never sees me.
And there come not to me, as come to these,
The wild beasts, sparrows pecking the llamas' grain,
Pigeons settling on the bears' bread, buzzards
Tearing the meat the flies have clouded. . . .
25   Vulture,
When you come for the white rat that the foxes left,
Take off the red helmet of your head, the black
Wings that have shadowed me, and step to me as man:
The wild brother at whose feet the white wolves fawn,
30 To whose hand of power the great lioness
Stalks, purring. . . .
        You know what I was,
You see what I am: change me, change me!

Questions for Discussion

1. How does the speaker contrast with the other women she sees?
   What does she mean by "They look back at the leopard like the
   leopard"?

2. How does such repetition as "so / To my bed, so to my grave" reveal
   the speaker's feeling of entrapment?

3. How does the speaker compare herself to the animals she sees?

4. Briefly **paraphrase** the speaker's concluding **apostrophe** to the vulture. Why would she choose to address this short speech to such a bird?

Suggestions for Exploration and Writing

1. How does the speaker feel about her condition? How do sound, **diction, syntax,** and **imagery** develop her feeling?

2. What does Jarrell's narrator mean by "Oh, bars of my own body, open, open!"? Using this poem and Blake's "London," write an essay about the cages and/or bars that people build for themselves.

3. At one point the woman thinks, "change me, change me!" To what extent is she not free to change? Discuss.

4. Would you have noticed the woman at the zoo? Why are some people almost invisible while others are not? Write an essay classifying people according to their degree of visibility.

Gwendolyn Brooks (1917–2001)

Born in Topeka, Kansas, Gwendolyn Brooks began writing while still a teenager. In high school, she met Langston Hughes, who encouraged her to write and follow her literary ambitions. Brooks is the author of more than twenty books of poetry, including A Street in Bronzeville (1945); The Bean Eaters (1960); *and* Children Coming Home (1991). *She also wrote other works such as the novel* Maud Martha (1953) *and a book of essays,* Young Poet's Primer (1981). *In 1950, Brooks became the first African American to win the Pulitzer Prize in literature, for* Annie Allen. *In 1968, she became the poet laureate for the state of Illinois, and from 1985 to 1986 she was Consultant in Poetry for the Library of Congress.*

WE REAL COOL   (1966)

THE POOL PLAYERS.

SEVEN AT THE GOLDEN SHOVEL.

We real cool. We
Left school. We

Lurk late. We
Strike straight. We
5 Sing sin. We
Thin gin. We

Jazz June. We
Die soon.

Questions for Discussion

1. Why does Brooks omit the verb *are* in the statement "We real cool"?

2. Why do the speakers believe they are "cool"? What is their definition of cool?

3. Explain the meaning of the phrases "strike straight" and "Jazz June."

4. What is the basis for the statement that concludes the poem: "We / Die soon"?

Suggestion for Exploration and Writing

1. This poem was published in 1966, and reflects what Gwendolyn Brooks thought about the youth of that year and the preceding years. Write an essay comparing your generation or Generation X or Y with Brooks's assessment.

Anne Sexton (1928–1974)

Anne Sexton believed that as a child she had been unwanted and rejected. Before she was twenty years old, she married Alfred Muller Sexton III. In 1954, shortly after the birth of her first daughter, Sexton suffered her first mental breakdown. The birth of her second daughter in 1955 was followed by a second breakdown. The psychiatrist who treated her at this time convinced her that she was intelligent and talented, and he encouraged her to write poetry. Sexton found a form of salvation in writing poems about her tendency toward suicide, her mental breakdowns, and the problems she faced as a woman. In 1974, after a lifetime of feeling that death was calling her, Sexton committed suicide. The following poem was included in her first collection, To Bedlam and Part Way Back *(1960).*

RINGING THE BELLS   (1960)

And this is the way they ring
the bells in Bedlam
and this is the bell-lady
who comes each Tuesday morning
5   to give us a music lesson
and because the attendants make you go
and because we mind by instinct,
like bees caught in the wrong hive,
we are the circle of the crazy ladies
10 who sit in the lounge of the mental house
and smile at the smiling woman
who passes us each a bell,
who points at my hand

that holds my bell, E flat,
15   and this is the gray dress next to me
who grumbles as if it were special
to be old, to be old,
and this is the small hunched squirrel girl
on the other side of me
20   who picks at the hairs over her lip.
who picks at the hairs over her lip all day,
and this is how the bells really sound,
as untroubled and clean
as a workable kitchen,
25   and this is always my bell responding
to my hand that responds to the lady
who points at me, E flat;
and although we are no better for it,
they tell you to go. And you do.

Questions for Discussion

1. What is the music lesson supposed to do for the "crazy ladies"? What does it actually do for them?

2. How does the speaker feel about the music lesson? How do the structure and **diction** of the poem reveal feeling? What does Sexton's use of **anaphora** add to the poem?

3. What does the animal imagery reveal about the women in the poem?

Suggestion for Exploration and Writing

1. Research the symptoms of Alzheimer's disease. Then write an essay comparing some of these symptoms to the symptoms of the "crazy ladies" in the poem.

Adrienne Rich (b. 1929)

A brief biography of Adrienne Rich precedes "Living in Sin" in the Men and Women unit.

AUNT JENNIFER'S TIGERS   (1951)

Aunt Jennifer's tigers prance across a screen,
Bright topaz denizens of a world of green.
They do not fear the men beneath the tree;
They pace in sleek chivalric certainty.

5   Aunt Jennifer's fingers fluttering through her wool
Find even the ivory needle hard to pull.

The massive weight of Uncle's wedding band
Sits heavily upon Aunt Jennifer's hand.

When Aunt is dead, her terrified hands will lie
10   Still ringed with ordeals she was mastered by.
The tigers in the panel that she made
Will go on prancing, proud and unafraid.

Alicia Ostriker (b. 1937)

*A brief biography of Alicia Ostriker precedes "First Love" in the
Family unit.*

WATCHING THE FEEDER   (1989)

Snow has been falling, and the purple finches
Attack the feeder, diving like air aces.
A half a dozen squirrels
Do their Olympic leaps through the weak sunlight
5   Spilling sunflower seeds and seedhusks
Together over the drifts. The doves are pacing
And nodding, with the utmost
Placidity, like bourgeois wives and husbands.
Apparently they are going shopping—
10   I can almost see the stoutness of their billfolds,
Their station wagons, their wine cellars.
Snow falls through standing trees, my patch of the world's
      hair.

I have Vivaldi on the stereo,
15   Another cup of coffee. It is peaceful but hard
Growing older, no
Birds in my nest.

Now I can ask: What about my life?
What do I desire, now
20   That it has come to this? Snow coming down
Harder and harder this morning, the back yard
Becomes mysterious, the feeder
Is finally deserted.
I remember that I was hoping to be grateful
25   For existence itself.

Questions for Discussion

1. Identify and explain the two **similes** Ostriker uses to personify the
birds.

2. What do the birds, and later the deserted feeder, suggest to the speaker? Now that she has the freedom and the time to ask herself "What about my life? / What do I desire[. . .]:" why is she sad?

3. Explain the last two lines of the poem.

Suggestions for Exploration and Writing

1. How can women prepare themselves for the time when their nests are empty?

2. What responsibilities, if any, do children have to their parents after the children are grown?

Pat Mora (b. 1942)

Pat Mora, a Southwestern poet from El Paso, Texas, was educated at Texas Western College and University of Texas, El Paso. Of Mexican American parentage, she has written several books of poems, including Borders *(1986), which includes the following poem. Her poems and her memoirs about her family,* Voices from the Garden: Voces del Jardin *(1997), explore her heritage and the theme of identity, especially of female identity.*

IMMIGRANTS   (1986)

wrap their babies in the American flag,
feed them mashed hot dogs and apple pie,
name them Bill and Daisy,
buy them blonde dolls that blink blue
5   eyes or a football and tiny cleats
before the baby can even walk,
speak to them in thick English,
  hallo, babee, hallo,
whisper in Spanish or Polish
10   when the babies sleep, whisper
in a dark parent bed, that dark
parent fear, "Will they like
our boy, our girl, our fine american
boy, our fine american girl?"

Questions for Discussion

1. What American qualities do the immigrants seek for their children? Why?

2. Why do immigrants "whisper in Spanish or Polish / when the babies sleep"?

3. What is the source of the immigrants' anxiety?

4. The United States is often described as a "melting pot." What does this poem imply may be melted away?

Suggestions for Exploration and Writing

1. Explain the advantages and disadvantages of individuals' conforming to the society to which they have immigrated.

2. Mora speaks of the ultimate fear of the immigrant parents: that their children will not fit in despite all attempts to Americanize them. Discuss your attitude or the attitudes of your community toward people who are different.

3. In an essay, discuss the responsibilities of immigrants to their new country and the responsibilities of citizens to newcomers.

4. Discuss whether all immigrants in the United States should be expected to learn English.

Joy Harjo (b. 1951)

Joy Harjo, a Creek Indian born in Tulsa, Oklahoma, has won wide acclaim for her poetry. Her books of poetry include The Woman Who Fell from the Sky *(1994), which received the Oklahoma Book Arts Award;* In Mad Love and War *(1990), which received an American Book Award; and* What Moon Drove Me to This? *(1997). Harjo has received many honors such as the William Carlos Williams Award, the National Endowment for the Arts, and the American Indian Distinguished Achievement in the Arts Award. She lives in Albuquerque, New Mexico, where she recites her poetry and plays saxophone with her band, Poetic Justice, now called Joy Harjo and the Real Revolution. Most of her poems deal with her Creek heritage or the struggles of her people to avoid assimilation. Harjo's style usually mirrors the rhythm of the Creek language.*

The Woman Hanging from
the Thirteenth Floor Window   (1983)

She is the woman hanging from the 13th floor
window. Her hands are pressed white against the
concrete moulding of the tenement building. She
hangs from the 13th floor window in east Chicago,
5   with a swirl of birds over her head. They could
be a halo, or a storm of glass waiting to crush her.

She thinks she will be set free.

The woman hanging from the 13th floor window
on the east side of Chicago is not alone.

10 She is a woman of children, of the baby, Carlos,
and of Margaret, and of Jimmy who is the oldest.
She is her mother's daughter and her father's son.
She is several pieces between the two husbands
she has had. She is all the women of the apartment
15 building who stand watching her, watching themselves.

When she was young she ate wild rice on scraped down
plates in warm wood rooms. It was in the farther
north and she was the baby then. They rocked her.

She sees Lake Michigan lapping at the shores of
20 herself. It is a dizzy hole of water and the rich
live in tall glass houses at the edge of it. In some
places Lake Michigan speaks softly, here, it just sputters
and butts itself against the asphalt. She sees
other buildings just like hers. She sees other
25 women hanging from many-floored windows
counting their lives in the palms of their hands
and in the palms of their children's hands.

She is the woman hanging from the 13th floor window
on the Indian side of town. Her belly is soft from
30 her children's births, her worn levis swing down below
her waist, and then her feet, and then her heart.
She is dangling.

The woman hanging from the 13th floor hears voices.
They come to her in the night when the lights have gone
35 dim. Sometimes they are little cats mewing and scratching
at the door, sometimes they are her grandmother's voice,
and sometimes they are gigantic men of light whispering
to her to get up, to get up, to get up. That's when she wants
to have another child to hold onto in the night, to be able
40 to fall back into dreams.

And the woman hanging from the 13th floor window
hears other voices. Some of them scream out from below
for her to jump, they would push her over. Others cry softly
from the sidewalks, pull their children up like flowers and gather
45 them into their arms. They would help her, like themselves.

But she is the woman hanging from the 13th floor window,
and she knows she is hanging by her own fingers, her
own skin, her own thread of indecision.

She thinks of Carlos, of Margaret, of Jimmy.
50 She thinks of her father, and of her mother.

She thinks of all the women she has been, of all
the men. She thinks of the color of her skin, and
of Chicago streets, and of waterfalls and pines.
She thinks of moonlight nights, and of cool spring storms.
55   Her mind chatters like neon and northside bars.
She thinks of the 4 a.m. lonelinesses that have folded
her up like death, discordant, without logical and
beautiful conclusion. Her teeth break off at the edges.
She would speak.

60   The woman hangs from the 13th floor window crying for
the lost beauty of her own life. She sees the
sun falling west over the grey plane of Chicago.
She thinks she remembers listening to her own life
break loose, as she falls from the 13th floor
65   window on the east side of Chicago, or as she
climbs back up to claim herself again.

Questions for Discussion

1. Explain the significance of "13th floor window," "a tenement building [. . .] in east Chicago," and "on the Indian side of town"?

2. Why does the hanging woman represent all the watching women?
What do the references to the children mean in the overall context
of the poem?

3. Explain why the woman thinks she "will be set free."

4. Why does Harjo end the poem with two choices? What do you think
she is saying about freedom and responsibility?

Suggestions for Exploration and Writing

1. Using the poem to support your opinion, write an essay explaining
what the woman's decision is and why she makes that decision.

2. From the poem, select one passage that makes a political statement. Write an essay that discusses the significance of this passage,
or write an essay that discusses whether you agree or disagree with
the passage.

Dwight Okita (b. 1958)

*Dwight Okita, a native of Chicago, is a poet of Japanese American
descent. His mother spent World War II in a relocation center, one
of ten such centers in the Western states. In response to the Japanese attack on Pearl Harbor, the United States government, without
due process, forced over 100,000 Japanese Americans into these*

centers. Okita's Crossing with the Light *was published in paperback in 1992.*

IN RESPONSE TO EXECUTIVE ORDER 9066: ALL AMERICANS OF JAPANESE DESCENT MUST REPORT TO RELOCATION CENTERS   (1983)

Dear Sirs:
Of course I'll come. I've packed my galoshes
and three packets of tomato seeds. Janet calls them
"love apples." My father says where we're going
5   they won't grow.

I am a fourteen-year-old girl with bad spelling
and a messy room. If it helps any, I will tell you
I have always felt funny using chopsticks
and my favorite food is hot dogs.
10   My best friend is a white girl named Denise—
we look at boys together. She sat in front of me
all through grade school because of our names:
O'Connor, Ozawa. I know the back of Denise's head very well.
I tell her she's going bald. She tells me I copy on tests.
15   We're best friends.

I saw Denise today in Geography class.
She was sitting on the other side of the room.
"You're trying to start a war," she said, "giving secrets away
to the Enemy, Why can't you keep your big mouth shut?"
20   I didn't know what to say.
I gave her a packet of tomato seeds
and asked her to plant them for me, told her
when the first tomato ripened
she'd miss me.

Questions for Discussion

1. What seems to be the speaker's attitude toward the executive order to report to a relocation center? Why does she say that she likes hot dogs and feels uncomfortable using chopsticks?

2. Contrast the relationship between the speaker and Denise in stanza 2 with their relationship in stanza 3. What has happened to their friendship? Why does Denise sit on the other side of the room?

3. How does the speaker's attitude here compare to that of the speaker in "Immigrants"?

4. Why does the speaker give Denise tomato seeds?

Suggestions for Exploration and Writing

1. Discuss some of the consequences of relocation centers as shown by this letter from the fourteen-year-old Japanese girl and by the behavior of her friend Denise.

2. How appropriate is it to refer to people born in the United States as Japanese Americans, African Americans, Native Americans, and so forth? In what ways is the United States a melting pot of different cultures homogenized and blended? In what ways is it a stew of different cultures maintaining their distinctiveness? Discuss.

DRAMA

Sophocles (496?–406 B.C.)

Sophocles, the second of the three great Greek tragedians, wrote at least 120 plays and won first place at the festival of Dionysus twenty-four times. Sophocles' long life spanned the time in history when the culture of Athens was at its peak. Born to a wealthy Athenian family, Sophocles was honored as a producer of tragedies and as a citizen. He was selected for the highest elective office as one of the ten generals of Athens and was awarded priesthoods for his religious piety. Sophocles won first place in the festival of Dionysus for the first time in 468 B.C. and remained intellectually and artistically active until his death at the age of ninety. Three of the seven extant plays of Sophocles, Oedipus the King, Oedipus at Colonus, *and* Antigone, *tell the story of the royal family of Thebes. Aristotle gave* Oedipus the King *the highest praise of any extant Greek tragedy, and it is often described as the best example of* **dramatic irony** *in literature. Although written first,* Antigone *is the last play in the Thebes cycle. Because it portrays the conflict between individual rights and the rights of the state, a common dilemma that has spanned the years,* Antigone *is the most often performed of Sophocles's plays.*

Ancient Greek Drama

Ancient Greek drama was performed in huge outdoor amphitheaters that seated as many as 20,000 spectators on great semicircular stone benches that climbed the slope of a hill. At the bottom center was the skene building, which served both as a dressing room for the actors and as the scenery, most often as the front of a palace or temple. In front of the skene was a circular acting space, the orchestra.

Because of the massive size of such amphitheaters, where many spectators would have been hundreds of feet from the stage, ancient Greek drama empha-

sizes large, clearly visible, and stylized effects. Actors declaimed their lines through the amplifying mouthpieces of masks and apparently later, in tragedies, wore elevated shoes to enhance their stature. Probably, because of the size of the theaters and the masks, ancient Greek drama relied on bold and dramatic movements rather than on subtle gestures, facial expressions, and asides.

Deriving from the worship of the god Dionysus, Athenian drama was a community celebration. Audiences apparently were quite volatile and deeply involved in the drama. Because almost the only subjects accepted for performance were the Greek myths, the audience already knew the stories behind each play; therefore, Greek drama provided the perfect vehicle for **dramatic irony,** *a form of irony made possible by the audience's knowledge of events and relationships of which the characters were often ignorant. In* **dramatic irony,** *the character's words have a double meaning unknown to the character but known to the audience or to other characters. Apparently, too, the audience had extraordinary attention spans; on each of the last three days of the Dionysian festival, they would sit through five plays—three tragedies, one satyr play, and one comedy.*

ANTIGONE (5TH CENTURY B.C.)
TRANSLATED BY ROBERT FAGLES

Characters

ANTIGONE:	daughter of Oedipus and Jocasta
ISMENE:	sister of Antigone
A *CHORUS:*	of old Theban citizens and their *LEADER*
CREON:[1]	king of Thebes, uncle of Antigone and Ismene
A *SENTRY*	
HAEMON:	son of Creon and Eurydice
TIRESIAS:	a blind prophet
A *MESSENGER*	
EURYDICE:	wife of Creon
	Guards, attendants, and a boy

Time and Scene

The royal house of Thebes. It is still night, and the invading armies of Argos have just been driven from the city. Fighting on opposite sides, the sons of Oedipus, Eteocles and Polynices, have killed each other in combat. Their uncle, Creon, is now king of Thebes.

---

[1]The Kreon of *Oedipus the King*. The names in this translation sometimes are spelled differently.

Enter ANTIGONE, *slipping through the central doors of the palace.*
She motions to her sister, ISMENE, *who follows her cautiously toward an*
altar at the center of the stage.

ANTIGONE: My own flesh and blood—dear sister, dear Ismene,
how many griefs our father Oedipus handed down![2]
Do you know one, I ask you, one grief
that Zeus will not perfect for the two of us
while we still live and breathe? There's nothing,
no pain—our lives are pain—no private shame,
no public disgrace, nothing I haven't seen
in your griefs and mine. And now this:
an emergency decree, they say, the Commander
10   has just now declared for all of Thebes.
What, haven't you heard? Don't you see?
The doom reserved for enemies
marches on the ones we love the most.

ISMENE: Not I, I haven't heard a word, Antigone.
Nothing of loved ones,
no joy or pain has come my way, not since
the two of us were robbed of our two brothers,[3]
both gone in a day, a double blow—
not since the armies of Argos vanished,
20   just this very night. I know nothing more,
whether our luck's improved or ruin's still to come.

ANTIGONE: I thought so. That's why I brought you out here,
past the gates, so you could hear in private.

ISMENE: What's the matter? Trouble, clearly . . .
you sound so dark, so grim.

ANTIGONE: Why not? Our own brothers' burial![4]
Hasn't Creon graced one with all the rites,
disgraced the other? Eteocles, they say,
has been given full military honors,

[2]The two sisters had accompanied their self-blinded father Oedipus's in his wanderings and sufferings after his banishment from Thebes. (The banishment is described at
the end of *Oedipus the King.*) Possibly we are to regard Oedipus's lineage as afflicted by
an inherited curse. Oedipus's crimes, committed unwillingly, had been to kill his father
Laius, the king of Thebes, and to marry his mother.

[3]Oedipus' two sons, Eteocles and Polynices, had been rivals for the rulership of the
city. After being exiled by Eteocles, Polynices had recruited a military force in Argos to
attack Thebes. In the ensuing battle, the Thebans had defeated the Argives and the
brothers Eteocles and Polynices had killed each other, leaving Creon to rule Thebes.

[4]It was believed that the unburied were treated with contempt in the underground
realm of the dead. Moreover, to mourn and to prepare bodies for proper burial was the
special duty of the women.

30 rightly so—Creon has laid him in the earth
and he goes with glory down among the dead.
But the body of Polynices, who died miserably—
why, a city-wide proclamation, rumor has it,
forbids anyone to bury him, even mourn him.
He's to be left unwept, unburied, a lovely treasure
for birds that scan the field and feast to their heart's content.

Such, I hear, is the martial law our good Creon
lays down for you and me—yes, me, I tell you—
and he's coming here to alert the uninformed
40 in no uncertain terms,
and he won't treat the matter lightly. Whoever
disobeys in the least will die, his doom is sealed: stoning to death
inside the city walls!

There you have it. You'll soon show what you are,
worth your breeding, Ismene, or a coward—
for all your royal blood.

ISMENE: My poor sister, if things have come to this,
who am I to make or mend them, tell me,
what good am I to you?

ANTIGONE: Decide.
50 Will you share the labor, share the work?

ISMENE: What work, what's the risk? What do you mean?

ANTIGONE (*Raising her hands.*): Will you lift up his body with these bare
hands and lower it with me?

ISMENE: What? You'd bury him—
when a law forbids the city?

ANTIGONE: Yes!
He is my brother and—deny it as you will—
your brother too.
No one will ever convict me for a traitor.

ISMENE: So desperate, and Creon has expressly—

ANTIGONE: No,
he has no right to keep me from my own.

60 ISMENE: Oh my sister, think—
think how our own father died,[5] hated,
his reputation in ruins, driven on

---

[5]The version in *Oedipus at Colonus* is that Oedipus, after long suffering, died a holy
and mysterious death. The events Ismene describes here (her mother Jocasta's suicide
and Oedipus's self-blinding) take place in *Oedipus the King*.

by the crimes he brought to light himself
to gouge out his eyes with his own hands—
then mother . . . his mother and wife, both in one,
mutilating her life in the twisted noose—
and last, our two brothers dead in a single day,
both shedding their own blood, poor suffering boys,
battling out their common destiny hand-to-hand.
70   Now look at the two of us, left so alone . . .
think what a death we'll die, the worst of all
if we violate the laws and override
the fixed decree of the throne, its power—
we must be sensible. Remember we are women,
we're not born to contend with men. Then too,
we're underlings, ruled by much stronger hands,
so we must submit in this, and things still worse.

I, for one, I'll beg the dead to forgive me—
I'm forced, I have no choice—I must obey
80   the ones who stand in power. Why rush to extremes?
It's madness, madness.

ANTIGONE: I won't insist,
no, even if you should have a change of heart,
I'd never welcome you in the labor, not with me.
So, do as you like, whatever suits you best—
I will bury him myself.
And even if I die in the act, that death will be a glory.
I will lie with the one I love and loved by him—
an outrage sacred to the gods! I have longer
to please the dead than please the living here.
90   In the kingdom down below I'll lie forever.
Do as you like, dishonor the laws
the gods hold in honor.

ISMENE: I'd do them no dishonor . . .
but defy the city? I have no strength for that.

ANTIGONE: You have your excuses. I am on my way,
I will raise a mound for him, for my dear brother.

ISMENE: Oh Antigone, you're so rash—I'm so afraid for you!

ANTIGONE: Don't fear for me. Set your own life in order.

ISMENE: Then don't, at least, blurt this out to anyone.
Keep it a secret. I'll join you in that, I promise.

100   ANTIGONE: Dear god, shout it from the rooftops. I'll hate you
all the more for silence—tell the world!

ISMENE: So fiery—and it ought to chill your heart.

ANTIGONE: I know I please where I must please the most.

ISMENE: Yes, if you can, but you're in love with impossibility.

ANTIGONE: Very well, then, once my strength gives out
I will be done at last.

ISMENE: You're wrong from the start,
you're off on a hopeless quest.

ANTIGONE: If you say so, you will make me hate you,
and the hatred of the dead, by all rights,
110   will haunt you night and day.
But leave me to my own absurdity, leave me
to suffer this—dreadful thing. I will suffer
nothing as great as death without glory.

(Exit to the side.)

ISMENE: Then go if you must, but rest assured,
wild, irrational as you are, my sister,
you are truly dear to the ones who love you.

(Withdrawing to the palace. Enter a CHORUS, *the old citizens of Thebes,
chanting as the sun begins to rise.)*

CHORUS: Glory!—great beam of the sun, brightest of all
that ever rose on the seven gates of Thebes,
        you burn through night at last!
120   Great eye of the golden day,
mounting the Dirce's[6] banks you throw him back—
the enemy out of Argos, the white shield, the man of bronze—
he's flying headlong now
            the bridle of fate stampeding him with pain!

And he had driven against our borders,
launched by the warring claims of Polynices—
like an eagle screaming, winging havoc
over the land, wings of armor
shielded white as snow,
130   a huge army massing,
crested helmets bristling for assault.

He hovered above our roofs, his vast maw gaping
closing down around our seven gates,
        his spears thirsting for the kill
            but now he's gone, look,

---

[6]A river near Thebes.

before he could glut his jaws with Theban blood
or the god of fire put our crown of towers to the torch.
He grappled the Dragon[7] none can master—Thebes—
  the clang of our arms like thunder at his back!

140   Zeus hates with a vengeance all bravado,
the mighty boasts of men. He watched them
coming on in a rising flood, the pride
of their golden armor ringing shrill—
and brandishing his lightning
blasted the fighter just at the goal,
rushing to shout his triumph from our walls.[8]
Down from the heights he crashed, pounding down on the earth!
And a moment ago, blazing torch in hand—
  mad for attack, ecstatic
150   he breathed his rage, the storm
of his fury hurling at our heads!
But now his high hopes have laid him low
and down the enemy ranks the iron god of war
deals his rewards, his stunning blows—Ares[9]
rapture of battle, our right arm in the crisis.

Seven captains marshaled at seven gates
seven against their equals, gave
their brazen trophies up to Zeus,
god of the breaking rout of battle,
160   all but two: those blood brothers,
one father, one mother—matched in rage,
spears matched for the twin conquest—
clashed and won the common prize of death.

But now for Victory! Glorious in the morning,
joy in her eyes to meet our joy
  she is winging down to Thebes,
our fleets of chariots wheeling in her wake—
  Now let us win oblivion from the wars,
thronging the temples of the gods
170   in singing, dancing choirs through the night!
  Lord Dionysus,[10] god of the dance
  that shakes the land of Thebes, now lead the way!

(Enter CREON *from the palace, attended by his guard.)*

---

[7]According to myth, the Thebans were descendants of men metamorphosed from the teeth of a dragon killed by Cadmus, founder of the city.

[8]The fighter is Capaneus. Having scaled the walls of Thebes, he boasted that not even Zeus, king of the gods, could stop him, but Zeus killed him with a thunderbolt.

[9]God of war and of destruction.

[10]God of wine; his mother, Semele, who was ravished by Zeus in the form of lightning, was a Theban.

But look, the king of the realm is coming,
Creon, the new man for the new day,
whatever the gods are sending now . . .
what new plan will he launch?
Why this, this special session?
Why this sudden call to the old men
summoned at one command?

CREON: My countrymen,
180   the ship of state is safe. The gods who rocked her,
after a long, merciless pounding in the storm,
have righted her once more.
                                        Out of the whole city
I have called you here alone. Well I know,
first, your undeviating respect
for the throne and royal power of King Laius.
Next, while Oedipus steered the land of Thebes,
and even after he died, your loyalty was unshakable,
you still stood by their children. Now then,
since the two sons are dead—two blows of fate
190   in the same day, cut down by each other's hands,
both killers, both brothers stained with blood—
as I am next in kin to the dead,[11]
I now possess the throne and all its powers.

Of course you cannot know a man completely,
his character, his principles, sense of judgment,
not till he's shown his colors, ruling the people,
making laws. Experience, there's the test.
As I see it, whoever assumes the task,
the awesome task of setting the city's course,
200   and refuses to adopt the soundest policies
but fearing someone, keeps his lips locked tight,
he's utterly worthless. So I rate him now,
I always have. And whoever places a friend
above the good of his own country, he is nothing:
I have no use for him.[12] Zeus my witness,
Zeus who sees all things, always—
I could never stand by silent, watching destruction
march against our city, putting safety to rout,
nor could I ever make that man a friend of mine
210   who menaces our country. Remember this:

---

[11]Creon is the brother of the dead rivals' mother, Jocasta; he is also a cousin of the former king, Laius.
    [12]Creon here states his side of the play's central moral and political issue. The word "friend" has also the meaning of "kindred."

our country *is* our safety.
Only while she voyages true on course
can we establish friendships, truer than blood itself.
Such are my standards. They make our city great.

Closely akin to them I have proclaimed,
just now, the following decree to our people
concerning the two sons of Oedipus.
Eteocles, who died fighting for Thebes,
excelling all in arms: he shall be buried,
220   crowned with a hero's honors, the cups we pour
to soak the earth and reach the famous dead.

But as for his blood brother, Polynices,
who returned from exile, home to his father-city
and the gods of his race, consumed with one desire—
to burn them roof to roots—who thirsted to drink
his kinsmen's blood and sell the rest to slavery:
that man—a proclamation has forbidden the city
to dignify him with burial, mourn him at all.
No, he must be left unburied, his corpse
230   carrion for the birds and dogs to tear,
an obscenity for the citizens to behold!

These are my principles. Never at my hands
will the traitor be honored above the patriot.
But whoever proves his loyalty to the state—
I'll prize that man in death as well as life.

LEADER: If this is your pleasure, Creon, treating
our city's enemy and our friend this way . . .
The power is yours, I suppose, to enforce it
with the laws, both for the dead and all of us,
the living.

240 CREON: Follow my orders closely then,
be on your guard.

LEADER: We are too old.
Lay that burden on younger shoulders.

CREON: No, no,
I don't mean the body—I've posted guards already.

LEADER: What commands for us then? What other service?

CREON: See that you never side with those who break my orders.

LEADER: Never. Only a fool could be in love with death.

250 CREON: Death is the price—you're right. But all too often
the mere hope of money has ruined many men.

(A Sentry *enters from the side.)*

SENTRY: My lord,
 I can't say I'm winded from running, or set out
250 with any spring in my legs either—no sir,
 I was lost in thought, and it made me stop, often,
 dead in my tracks, wheeling, turning back,
 and all the time a voice inside me muttering,
 "Idiot, why? You're going straight to your death."
 Then muttering, "Stopped again, poor fool?
 If somebody gets the news to Creon first,
 what's to save your neck?"
       And so,
 mulling it over, on I trudged, dragging my feet,
 you can make a short road take forever . . .
260 but at last, look, common sense won out,
 I'm here, and I'm all yours,
 and even though I come empty-handed
 I'll tell my story just the same, because
 I've come with a good grip on one hope,
 what will come will come, whatever fate—

CREON: Come to the point!
 What's wrong—why so afraid?

SENTRY: First, myself, I've got to tell you,
 I didn't do it, didn't see who did—
270 Be fair, don't take it out on me.

CREON: You're playing it safe, soldier,
 barricading yourself from any trouble.
 It's obvious, you've something strange to tell.

SENTRY: Dangerous too, and danger makes you delay
 for all you're worth.

CREON: Out with it—then dismiss!

SENTRY: All right, here it comes. The body—
 someone's just buried it, then run off . . .
 sprinkled some dry dust on the flesh,
 given it proper rites.

280 CREON: What?
 What man alive would dare—

SENTRY: I've no idea, I swear it.
 There was no mark of a spade, no pickaxe there,
 no earth turned up, the ground packed hard and dry,
 unbroken, no tracks, no wheelruts, nothing,

the workman left no trace. Just at sunup
the first watch of the day points it out—
it was a wonder! We were stunned . . .
a terrific burden too, for all of us, listen;
you can't see the corpse, not that it's buried,
290   really, just a light cover of road-dust on it,
as if someone meant to lay the dead to rest
and keep from getting cursed.
Not a sign in sight that dogs or wild beasts
had worried the body, even torn the skin.
But what came next! Rough talk flew thick and fast,
guard grilling guard—we'd have come to blows
at last, nothing to stop it; each man for himself
and each the culprit, no one caught red-handed,
all of us pleading ignorance, dodging the charges,
300   ready to take up red-hot iron in our fists,
go through fire, swear oaths to the gods—
"I didn't do it, I had no hand in it either,
not in the plotting, not the work itself!"

Finally, after all this wrangling came to nothing,
one man spoke out and made us stare at the ground,
hanging our heads in fear. No way to counter him,
no way to take his advice and come through
safe and sound. Here's what he said:
"Look, we've got to report the facts to Creon,
310   we can't keep this hidden." Well, that won out,
and the lot fell to me, condemned me,
unlucky as ever, I got the prize. So here I am,
against my will and yours too, well I know—
no one wants the man who brings bad news.

LEADER: My king,
ever since he began I've been debating in my mind,
could this possibly be the work of the gods?

CREON: Stop—
before you make me choke with anger—the gods![13]
You, you're senile, must you be insane?
You say—why it's intolerable—say the gods
320   could have the slightest concern for that corpse?
Tell me, was it for meritorious service
they proceeded to bury him, prized him so? The hero

---

[13]The Chorus's surmise about divine intervention in this first burial is conceivably true; the play is somewhat ambiguous on the matter.

who came to burn their temples ringed with pillars,
their golden treasures—scorch their hallowed earth
and fling their laws to the winds.
Exactly when did you last see the gods
celebrating traitors? Inconceivable!

No, from the first there were certain citizens
who could hardly stand the spirit of my regime,
330   grumbling against me in the dark, heads together,
tossing wildly, never keeping their necks beneath
the yoke, loyally submitting to their king.
These are the instigators, I'm convinced—
they've perverted my own guard, bribed them
to do their work.
                    Money! Nothing worse
in our lives, so current, rampant, so corrupting.
Money—you demolish cities, root men from their homes,
you train and twist good minds and set them on
to the most atrocious schemes. No limit,
340   you make them adept at every kind of outrage,
every godless crime—money!
                              Everyone—
the whole crew bribed to commit this crime,
they've made one thing sure at least: sooner or
later they will pay the price.

(Wheeling on the SENTRY.*)*
                                  You—
I swear to Zeus as I still believe in Zeus,
if you don't find the man who buried that corpse,
the very man, and produce him before my eyes,
simple death won't be enough for you,
not till we string you up alive
350   and wring the immorality out of you.
Then you can steal the rest of your days,
better informed about where to make a killing.
You'll have learned, at last, it doesn't pay
to itch for rewards from every hand that beckons.
Filthy profits wreck most men, you'll see—
they'll never save your life.

SENTRY: Please,
may I say a word or two, or just turn and go?

CREON: Can't you tell? Everything you say offends me.

SENTRY: Where does it hurt you, in the ears or in the heart?

360   CREON: And who are you to pinpoint my displeasure?

SENTRY: The culprit grates on your feelings,
    I just annoy your ears.

CREON: Still talking?
    You talk too much! A born nuisance—

SENTRY: Maybe so,
    but I never did this thing, so help me!

CREON: Yes you did—
    what's more, you squandered your life for silver!

SENTRY: Oh it's terrible when the one who does the judging
    judges things all wrong.

CREON: Well now,
    you just be clever about your judgments—
    if you fail to produce the criminals for me,
370   you'll swear your dirty money brought you pain.

(Turning sharply, reentering the palace.)

SENTRY: I hope he's found. Best thing by far.
    But caught or not, that's in the lap of fortune:
    I'll never come back, you've seen the last of me.
    I'm saved, even now, and I never thought,
    I never hoped—
    dear gods, I owe you all my thanks!

(Rushing out.)

CHORUS: Numberless wonders
    terrible wonders walk the world but none the match for man—
    that great wonder crossing the heaving gray sea,
               driven on by the blasts of winter
380   on through breakers crashing left and right,
        holds his steady course
    and the oldest of the gods he wears away—
    the Earth, the immortal, the inexhaustible—
    as his plows go back and forth, year in, year out
        with the breed of stallions turning up the furrows.

And the blithe, lightheaded race of birds he snares,
    the tribes of savage beasts, the life that swarms the depths—
                 with one fling of his nets
    woven and coiled tight, he takes them all,
390   man the skilled, the brilliant!
    He conquers all, taming with his techniques
    the prey that roams the cliffs and wild lairs,
    training the stallion, clamping the yoke across
        his shaggy neck, and the tireless mountain bull.

And speech and thought, quick as the wind
and the mood and mind for law that rules the city—
   all these he has taught himself
and shelter from the arrows of the frost
when there's rough lodging under the cold clear sky
400   and the shafts of lashing rain—
     ready, resourceful man!
         Never without resources
never an impasse as he marches on the future—
only Death, from Death alone he will find no rescue
but from desperate plagues he has plotted his escapes.

Man the master, ingenious past all measure
past all dreams, the skills within his grasp—
   he forges on, now to destruction
now again to greatness. When he weaves in
410   the laws of the land, and the justice of the gods
that binds his oaths together
     he and his city rise high—
       but the city casts out
that man who weds himself to inhumanity
thanks to reckless daring. Never share my hearth
never think my thoughts, whoever does such things.

(Enter ANTIGONE *from the side, accompanied by the* SENTRY.*)*

Here is a dark sign from the gods—
what to make of this? I know her,
how can I deny it? That young girl's Antigone!
420   Wretched, child of a wretched father,
Oedipus. Look, is it possible?
They bring you in like a prisoner—
why? did you break the king's laws?
Did they take you in some act of mad defiance?

SENTRY: She's the one, she did it single-handed—
   we caught her burying the body. Where's Creon?

(Enter CREON *from the palace.)*

LEADER: Back again, just in time when you need him.

CREON: In time for what? What is it?

SENTRY: My king,
   there's nothing you can swear you'll never do—
430   second thoughts make liars of us all.
   I could have sworn I wouldn't hurry back
   (what with your threats, the buffeting I just took),
   but a stroke of luck beyond our wildest hopes,

what a joy, there's nothing like it. So,
back I've come, breaking my oath, who cares?
I'm bringing in our prisoner—this young girl—
we took her giving the dead the last rites.
But no casting lots this time; this is *my* luck,
my prize, no one else's.
                          Now, my lord,
440   here she is. Take her, question her,
cross-examine her to your heart's content.
But set me free, it's only right—
I'm rid of this dreadful business once for all.

CREON: Prisoner! Her? You took her—where, doing what?

SENTRY: Burying the man. That's the whole story.

CREON: What?
You mean what you say, you're telling me the truth?

SENTRY: She's the one. With my own eyes I saw her
bury the body, just what you've forbidden.
There. Is that plain and clear?

450   CREON: What did you see? Did you catch her in the act?

SENTRY: Here's what happened. We went back to our post,
those threats of yours breathing down our necks—
we brushed the corpse clean of the dust that covered it,
stripped it bare . . . it was slimy, going soft,
and we took to high ground, backs to the wind
so the stink of him couldn't hit us;
jostling, baiting each other to keep awake,
shouting back and forth—no napping on the job,
not this time. And so the hours dragged by
460   until the sun stood dead above our heads,
a huge white ball in the noon sky, beating,
blazing down, and then it happened—
suddenly, a whirlwind!
Twisting a great dust-storm up from the earth,
a black plague of the heavens, filling the plain,
ripping the leaves off every tree in sight,
choking the air and sky. We squinted hard
and took our whipping from the gods.

And after the storm passed—it seemed endless—
470   there, we saw the girl!
And she cried out a sharp, piercing cry,
like a bird come back to an empty nest,
peering into its bed, and all the babies gone . . .
Just so, when she sees the corpse bare

she bursts into a long, shattering wail
and calls down withering curses on the heads
of all who did the work. And she scoops up dry dust,
handfuls, quickly, and lifting a fine bronze urn,
lifting it high and pouring, she crowns the dead
with three full libations.[14]

480   Soon as we saw
we rushed her, closed on the kill like hunters,
and she, she didn't flinch. We interrogated her,
charging her with offenses past and present—
she stood up to it all, denied nothing. I tell you,
it made me ache and laugh in the same breath.
It's pure joy to escape the worst yourself,
it hurts a man to bring down his friends.
But all that, I'm afraid, means less to me
than my own skin. That's the way I'm made.

CREON (*Wheeling on* ANTIGONE.):   You,
490   with your eyes fixed on the ground—speak up.
Do you deny you did this, yes or no?

ANTIGONE. I did it. I don't deny a thing.

CREON (*To the* SENTRY.): You, get out, wherever you please—
you're clear of a very heavy charge.

(*He leaves;* CREON *turns back to* ANTIGONE.)

You, tell me briefly, no long speeches—
were you aware a decree had forbidden this?

ANTIGONE: Well aware. How could I avoid it? It was public.

CREON: And still you had the gall to break this law?

ANTIGONE: Of course I did.[15] It wasn't Zeus, not in the least,
500   who made this proclamation—not to me.
Nor did that Justice, dwelling with the gods
beneath the earth, ordain such laws for men.
Nor did I think your edict had such force
that you, a mere mortal, could override the gods,
the great unwritten, unshakable traditions.
They are alive, not just today or yesterday;

---

[14]Ritual pourings of liquids.

[15]In the following lines Antigone states her creed; compare Creon's maxim in lines 203–205. Both antagonists can cite religious or political principles. A major question in the play is whether Antigone and Creon are actually governed by these large principles or by more personal motives (good or bad).

they live forever, from the first of time,
and no one knows when they first saw the light.
These laws—I was not about to break them,
510   not out of fear of some man's wounded pride,
and face the retribution of the gods.
Die I must, I've known it all my life—
how could I keep from knowing?—even without
your death-sentence ringing in my ears.
And if I am to die before my time
I consider that a gain. Who on earth,
alive in the midst of so much grief as I,
could fail to find his death a rich reward?
So for me, at least, to meet this doom of yours
520   is precious little pain. But if I had allowed
my own mother's son to rot, an unburied corpse—
that would have been an agony! This is nothing.
And if my present actions strike you as foolish,
let's just say I've been accused of folly
by a fool.

LEADER: Like father like daughter,
passionate, wild . . .
she hasn't learned to bend before adversity.

CREON: No? Believe me, the stiffest stubborn wills
fall the hardest; the toughest iron,
530   tempered strong in the white-hot fire,
you'll see it crack and shatter first of all.
And I've known spirited horses you can break
with a light bit—proud, rebellious horses.
There's no room for pride, not in a slave,[16]
not with the lord and master standing by.

This girl was an old hand at insolence
when she overrode the edicts we made public.
But once she had done it—the insolence,
twice over—to glory in it, laughing,
540   mocking us to our face with what she'd done.
I am not the man, not now: she is the man
if this victory goes to her and she goes free.

Never! Sister's child or closer in blood
than all my family clustered at my altar
worshiping Guardian Zeus—she'll never escape,
she and her blood sister, the most barbaric death.

---

[16]This is arrogantly false; Antigone is not in fact a slave.

Yes, I accuse her sister of an equal part
in scheming this, this burial.

(To his attendants.)

                          Bring her here!
I just saw her inside, hysterical, gone to pieces.
550   It never fails; the mind convicts itself
in advance, when scoundrels are up to no good,
plotting in the dark. Oh but I hate it more
when a traitor, caught red-handed,
tries to glorify his crimes.

ANTIGONE: Creon, what more do you want
than my arrest and execution?

CREON: Nothing. Then I have it all.

ANTIGONE: Then why delay? Your moralizing repels me,
every word you say—pray god it always will.
So naturally all I say repels you too.
560   Enough.
Give me glory! What greater glory could I win
than to give my own brother decent burial?
These citizens here would all agree,

(To the CHORUS.)

they would praise me too
if their lips weren't locked in fear.

(Pointing to CREON.)

Lucky tyrants—the perquisites of power!
Ruthless power to do and say whatever pleases *them*.

CREON: You alone, of all the people in Thebes,
see things that way.

ANTIGONE: They see it just that way
570   but defer to you and keep their tongues in leash.

CREON: And you, aren't you ashamed to differ so from them?
So disloyal!

ANTIGONE: Not ashamed for a moment,
not to honor my brother, my own flesh and blood.

CREON: Wasn't Eteocles a brother too—cut down, facing him?

ANTIGONE: Brother, yes, by the same mother, the same father.

CREON: Then how can you render his enemy such honors,
such impieties in his eyes?

ANTIGONE: He will never testify to that,
Eteocles dead and buried.

CREON: He will—
580   if you honor the traitor just as much as him.

ANTIGONE: But it was his brother, not some slave that died—

CREON: Ravaging our country!—
but Eteocles died fighting in our behalf.

ANTIGONE: No matter—Death longs for the same rites for all.

CREON: Never the same for the patriot and the traitor.

ANTIGONE: Who, Creon, who on earth can say the ones below
don't find this pure and uncorrupt?

CREON: Never. Once an enemy, never a friend,
not even after death.

590   ANTIGONE: I was born to join in love, not hate—
that is my nature.

CREON: Go down below and love,
if love you must—love the dead! While I'm alive,
no woman is going to lord it over me.

(Enter ISMENE from the palace, under guard.)

CHORUS: Look,
Ismene's coming, weeping a sister's tears,
loving sister, under a cloud . . .
her face is flushed, her cheeks streaming.
Sorrow puts her lovely radiance in the dark.

CREON: You—
in my own house, you viper, slinking undetected,
sucking my life-blood! I never knew
600   I was breeding twin disasters, the two of you
rising up against my throne. Come, tell me,
will you confess your part in the crime or not?
Answer me. Swear to me.

ISMENE: I did it, yes—
if only she consents—I share the guilt,
the consequences too.

ANTIGONE: No,
Justice will never suffer that—not you,
you were unwilling. I never brought you in.

ISMENE: But now you face such dangers . . . I'm not ashamed

to sail through trouble with you,
make your troubles mine.

610 ANTIGONE: Who did the work?
Let the dead and the god of death bear witness!
I have no love for a friend who loves in words alone.

ISMENE: Oh no, my sister, don't reject me, please,
let me die beside you, consecrating
the dead together.

ANTIGONE: Never share my dying,
don't lay claim to what you never touched.
My death will be enough.

ISMENE: What do I care for life, cut off from you?

ANTIGONE: Ask Creon. Your concern is all for him.

ISMENE: Why abuse me so? It doesn't help you now.

620 ANTIGONE: You're right—
if I mock you, I get no pleasure from it,
only pain.

ISMENE: Tell me, dear one,
what can I do to help you, even now?

ANTIGONE: Save yourself. I don't grudge you your survival.

ISMENE: Oh no, no, denied my portion in your death?

ANTIGONE: You chose to live, I chose to die.

ISMENE: Not, at least,
without every kind of caution I could voice.

ANTIGONE: Your wisdom appealed to one world—mine, another.

ISMENE: But look, we're both guilty, both condemned to death.

630 ANTIGONE: Courage! Live your life. I gave myself to death,
long ago, so I might serve the dead.

CREON: They're both mad, I tell you, the two of them.
One's just shown it, the other's been that way
since she was born.

ISMENE: True, my king,
the sense we were born with cannot last forever . . .
commit cruelty on a person long enough
and the mind begins to go.

CREON: Yours did,
when you chose to commit your crimes with her.

ISMENE: How can I live alone, without her?

CREON: Her?

640   Don't even mention her—she no longer exists.

ISMENE: What? You'd kill your own son's bride?

CREON: Absolutely:
there are other fields for him to plow.

ISMENE: Perhaps,
but never as true, as close a bond as theirs.

CREON: A worthless woman for my son? It repels me.

ISMENE: Dearest Haemon, your father wrongs you so![17]

CREON: Enough, enough—you and your talk of marriage!

ISMENE: Creon—you're really going to rob your son of Antigone?

CREON: Death will do it for me—break their marriage off.

LEADER: So, it's settled then? Antigone must die?

650   CREON: Settled, yes—we both know that.

   (To the guards.)

Stop wasting time. Take them in.
From now on they'll act like women.
Tie them up, no more running loose;
even the bravest will cut and run,
once they see Death coming for their lives.

(The guards escort ANTIGONE *and* ISMENE *into the palace.* CREON *remains while the old citizens form their* CHORUS.*)*

CHORUS: Blest, they are the truly blest who all their lives
have never tasted devastation. For others, once
the gods have rocked a house to its foundations
      the ruin will never cease, cresting on and on
from one generation on throughout the race—
like a great mounting tide
driven on by savage northern gales,
660   surging over the dead black depths
roiling up from the bottom dark heaves of sand
and the headlands, taking the storm's onslaught full-force,
roar, and the low moaning
                  echoes on and on
                        and now

---

[17]In some versions, this line is given to Antigone.

as in ancient times I see the sorrows of the house,[18]
the living heirs of the old ancestral kings,
piling on the sorrows of the dead
670   and one generation cannot free the next—
some god will bring them crashing down,
the race finds no release.
And now the light, the hope
              springing up from the late last root
in the house of Oedipus, that hope's cut down in turn
by the long, bloody knife swung by the gods of death
by a senseless word
                    by fury at the heart.
                                        Zeus,
yours is the power, Zeus, what man on earth
can override it, who can hold it back?
680   Power that neither Sleep, the all-ensnaring
     no, nor the tireless months of heaven
can ever overmaster—young through all time,
mighty lord of power, you hold fast
     the dazzling crystal mansions of Olympus.
And throughout the future, late and soon
as through the past, your law prevails:
no towering form of greatness
     enters into the lives of mortals
                              free and clear of ruin.
                                        True,
690   our dreams, our high hopes voyaging far and wide
bring sheer delight to many, to many others
     delusion, blithe, mindless lusts
and the fraud steals on one slowly . . . unaware
till he trips and puts his foot into the fire.
     He was a wise old man who coined
the famous saying: "Sooner or later
foul is fair, fair is foul
to the man the gods will ruin"—
     He goes his way for a moment only
700   free of blinding ruin.

(Enter HAEMON *from the palace.)*

Here's Haemon now, the last of all your sons.[19]
Does he come in tears for his bride,

---

[18]The sorrows of the family extend farther into the past than to Oedipus's acts of patricide and incest; for example, his father, Laius, had been cursed by Pelops (the ancestor of the cursed family treated in Aeschylus's Orestes trilogy) after Laius had wronged Pelops, his protector during a period of exile, by stealing his son.

[19]According to one version of the Thebes saga, Haemon's brother Megareus had committed suicide in order to propitiate the war-god Ares and thus save Thebes.

his doomed bride, Antigone—
bitter at being cheated of their marriage?

CREON: We'll soon know, better than seers could tell us.
   (Turning to HAEMON.*)*
Son, you've heard the final verdict on your bride?
Are you coming now, raving against your father?
Or do you love me, no matter what I do?

HAEMON: Father, I'm your *son* . . . you in your wisdom
710   set my bearings for me—I obey you.
No marriage could ever mean more to me than you,
whatever good direction you may offer.

CREON: Fine, Haemon.
That's how you ought to feel within your heart,
subordinate to your father's will in every way.
That's what a man prays for: to produce good sons—
a household full of them, dutiful and attentive,
so they can pay his enemy back with interest
and match the respect their father shows his friend.
But the man who rears a brood of useless children,
720   what has he brought into the world, I ask you?
Nothing but trouble for himself, and mockery
from his enemies laughing in his face.
                                          Oh Haemon,
never lose your sense of judgment over a woman.
The warmth, the rush of pleasure, it all goes cold
in your arms, I warn you . . . a worthless woman
in your house, a misery in your bed.
What wound cuts deeper than a loved one
turned against you? Spit her out,
like a mortal enemy—let the girl go.
730   Let her find a husband down among the dead.
Imagine it: I caught her in naked rebellion,
the traitor, the only one in the whole city.
I'm not about to prove myself a liar,
not to my people, no, I'm going to kill her!
That's right—so let her cry for mercy, sing her hymns
to Zeus who defends all bonds of kindred blood.
Why, if I bring up my own kin to be rebels,
think what I'd suffer from the world at large.
Show me the man who rules his household well:
740   I'll show you someone fit to rule the state.
That good man, my son,
I have every confidence he and he alone
can give commands and take them too. Staunch
in the storm of spears he'll stand his ground,
a loyal, unflinching comrade at your side.

But whoever steps out of line, violates the laws
or presumes to hand out orders to his superiors,
he'll win no praise from me. But that man
the city places in authority, his orders
750   must be obeyed, large and small,
right and wrong.
                 Anarchy—
show me a greater crime in all the earth!
She, she destroys cities, rips up houses,
breaks the ranks of spearmen into headlong rout.
But the ones who last it out, the great mass of them
owe their lives to discipline. Therefore
we must defend the men who live by law,
never let some woman triumph over us.
Better to fall from power, if fall we must,
760   at the hands of a man—never be rated
inferior to a woman, never.

LEADER: To us,
unless old age has robbed us of our wits,
you seem to say what you have to say with sense.

HAEMON: Father, only the gods endow a man with reason,
the finest of all their gifts, a treasure.
Far be it from me—I haven't the skill,
and certainly no desire, to tell you when,
if ever, you make a slip in speech . . . though
someone else might have a good suggestion.

770   Of course it's not for you,
in the normal run of things, to watch
whatever men say or do, or find to criticize.
The man in the street, you know, dreads your glance
he'd never say anything displeasing to your face.
But it's for me to catch the murmurs in the dark,
the way the city mourns for this young girl.
"No woman," they say, "ever deserved death less,
and such a brutal death for such a glorious action.
She, with her own dear brother lying in his blood—
780   she couldn't bear to leave him dead, unburied,
food for the wild dogs or wheeling vultures.
Death? She deserves a glowing crown of gold!"
So they say, and the rumor spreads in secret,
darkly . . .
                I rejoice in your success, father—
nothing more precious to me in the world.
What medal of honor brighter to his children
than a father's growing glory? Or a child's

to his proud father? Now don't, please,
be quite so single-minded, self-involved,
790   or assume the world is wrong and you are right.
Whoever thinks that he alone possesses intelligence,
the gift of eloquence, he and no one else,
and character too . . . such men, I tell you,
spread them open—you will find them empty.

                                             No,

it's no disgrace for a man, even a wise man,
to learn many things and not to be too rigid.
You've seen trees by a raging winter torrent,
how many sway with the flood and salvage every twig,
but not the stubborn—they're ripped out, roots and all.
800   Bend or break. The same when a man is sailing:
haul your sheets too taut, never give an inch,
you'll capsize, and go the rest of the voyage
keel up and the rowing-benches under.

Oh give way. Relax your anger—change!
I'm young, I know, but let me offer this:
it would be best by far, I admit,
if a man were born infallible, right by nature.
If not—and things don't often go that way,
it's best to learn from those with good advice.

810 LEADER: You'd do well, my lord, if he's speaking to the point,
to learn from him,
        (Turning to HAEMON.*)*
                and you, my boy, from him.
You both are talking sense.

CREON: So,
men our age, we're to be lectured, are we?—
schooled by a boy his age?

HAEMON: Only in what is right. But if I seem young,
look less to my years and more to what I do.

CREON: Do? Is admiring rebels an achievement?

HAEMON: I'd never suggest that you admire treason.

CREON: Oh?—
isn't that just the sickness that's attacked her?

820 HAEMON: The whole city of Thebes denies it, to a man.

CREON: And is Thebes about to tell me how to rule?

HAEMON: Now, you see? Who's talking like a child?

CREON: Am I to rule this land for others—or myself?

HAEMON: It's no city at all, owned by one man alone.

CREON: What? The city *is* the king's—that's the law!

HAEMON: What a splendid king you'd make of a desert island—
you and you alone.

CREON (*To the* CHORUS.):   This boy, I do believe,
is fighting on her side, the woman's side.

HAEMON: If you are a woman, yes—
830   my concern is all for you.

CREON: Why, you degenerate—bandying accusations,
threatening me with justice, your own father!

HAEMON: I see my father offending justice—wrong.

CREON: Wrong?
To protect my royal rights?

HAEMON: Protect your rights?
When you trample down the honors of the gods?

CREON: You, you soul of corruption, rotten through—
woman's accomplice!

HAEMON: That may be,
but you will never find me accomplice to a criminal.

CREON: That's what *she* is,
840   and every word you say is a blatant appeal for her—

HAEMON: And you, and me, and the gods beneath the earth.

CREON: You will never marry her, not while she's alive.

HAEMON: Then she will die . . . but her death will kill another.

CREON: What, brazen threats? You go too far!

HAEMON: What threat?
Combating your empty, mindless judgments with a word?

CREON: You'll suffer for your sermons, you and your empty wisdom!

HAEMON: If you weren't my father, I'd say you were insane.

CREON: Don't flatter me with Father—you woman's slave!

HAEMON: You really expect to fling abuse at me
and not receive the same?

850 CREON: Is that so!
Now, by heaven, I promise you, you'll pay—
taunting, insulting me! Bring her out,

that hateful—she'll die now, here,
in front of his eyes, beside her groom!

HAEMON: No, no, she will never die beside me—
don't delude yourself. And you will never
see me, never set eyes on my face again.
Rage your heart out, rage with friends
who can stand the sight of you.
(Rushing out.)

LEADER: Gone, my king, in a burst of anger.
860   A temper young as his . . . hurt him once,
he may do something violent.

CREON: Let him do—
dream up something desperate, past all human limit!
Good riddance. Rest assured,
he'll never save those two young girls from death.

LEADER: Both of them, you really intend to kill them both?

CREON: No, not her, the one whose hands are clean—
you're quite right.

LEADER: But Antigone—
what sort of death do you have in mind for her?

870 CREON: I will take her down some wild, desolate path
never trod by men, and wall her up alive
in a rocky vault, and set out short rations,
just the measure piety demands
to keep the entire city free of defilement.[20]
There let her pray to the one god she worships:
Death[21]—who knows?—may just reprieve her from death.
Or she may learn at last, better late than never,
what a waste of breath it is to worship Death.
(Exit to the palace.)

CHORUS: Love, never conquered in battle
880   Love the plunderer laying waste the rich!
Love standing the night-watch
               guarding a girl's soft cheek,
you range the seas, the shepherds' steadings off in the wilds—

---

[20]This method of execution is inconsistent with the earlier passage that decrees death by stoning (lines 41–43). Creon apparently believes, legalistically, that he can avoid the crime of shedding kindred blood by merely shutting Antigone up alone and by providing her with food. Technically no act of execution will have been committed.

[21]Hades, king of the realm of the dead.

not even the deathless gods can flee your onset,
nothing human born for a day—
whoever feels your grip is driven mad.

                  Love!—
you wrench the minds of the righteous into outrage,
swerve them to their ruin—you have ignited this,
this kindred strife, father and son at war

890   and Love alone the victor—
warm glance of the bride triumphant, burning with desire!
Throned in power, side-by-side with the mighty laws!
Irresistible Aphrodite,[22] never conquered—
Love, you mock us for your sport

(ANTIGONE *is brought from the palace under guard.*)

    But now, even I would rebel against the king,
    I would break all bounds when I see this—
    I fill with tears, I cannot hold them back,
    not any more . . . I see Antigone make her way
    to the bridal vault where all are laid to rest.

900 ANTIGONE: Look at me, men of my fatherland,
      setting out on the last road
    looking into the last light of day
    the last I will ever see . . .
    the god of death who puts us all to bed
    takes me down to the banks of Acheron[23] alive—
      denied my part in the wedding-songs,
    no wedding-song in the dusk has crowned my marriage—
    I go to wed the lord of the dark waters.

CHORUS: Not crowned with glory or with a dirge,
910   you leave for the deep pit of the dead.
    No withering illness laid you low,
    no strokes of the sword—a law to yourself,
    alone, no mortal like you, ever, you go down
    to the halls of Death alive and breathing.

ANTIGONE: But think of Niobe[24]—well I know her story—
      think what a living death she died,

---

[22]Goddess of love.

[23]A river in the land of the dead.

[24]Niobe, originally from Phrygia in Asia Minor, was the wife of Amphion, a former ruler of Thebes. Mother of fourteen children, she boasted of her superiority to the goddess Leto, who had only two, Apollo and Artemis. In revenge for her impiety, all of Niobe's children were killed and she was turned into a stone from which flowed a perpetual stream of her tears. There is an irony: Niobe was punished for flouting the gods, while Antigone is being killed for her piety.

Tantalus's daughter, stranger queen from the east:
there on the mountain heights, growing stone
binding as ivy, slowly walled her round
920　　and the rains will never cease, the legends say
the snows will never leave her . . .
　　　　wasting away, under her brows the tears
showering down her breasting ridge and slopes—
a rocky death like hers puts me to sleep.

CHORUS: But she was a god, born of gods,[25]
and we are only mortals born to die.
And yet, of course, it's a great thing
for a dying girl to hear, even to hear
she shares a destiny equal to the gods,
during life and later, once she's dead.

930　ANTIGONE:　　　　　　　　　　　　　O you mock me!
Why, in the name of all my fathers' gods
why can't you wait till I am gone—
　　　must you abuse me to my face?[26]
O my city, all your fine rich sons!
And you, you springs of the Dirce,
holy grove of Thebes where the chariots gather,
　　　you at least, you'll bear me witness, look,
unmourned by friends and forced by such crude laws
I go to my rockbound prison, strange new tomb—
940　　　always a stranger, O dear god,
　　　I have no home on earth and none below,
　　　not with the living, not with the breathless dead.

CHORUS: You went too far, the last limits of daring—
smashing against the high throne of Justice!
　　　Your life's in ruins, child—I wonder . . .
do you pay for your father's terrible ordeal?

ANTIGONE: There—at last you've touched it, the worst pain
the worst anguish! Raking up the grief for father
　　　three times over, for all the doom
950　　that's struck us down, the brilliant house of Laius.
O mother, your marriage-bed
the coiling horrors, the coupling there—
　　　you with your own son, my father—doomstruck mother!
Such, such were my parents, and I their wretched child.

---

[25]Niobe was the daughter of Tantalus, whose father was Zeus.

[26]Antigone's protest probably reflects her bitter reaction to the elders' implication that she is lucky (in sharing the fate of the famed Niobe.)

I go to them now, cursed, unwed, to share their home—
   I am a stranger! O dear brother, doomed
   in your marriage—your marriage murders mine,[27]
     your dying drags me down to death alive!

(Enter CREON.*)*

CHORUS: Reverence asks some reverence in return—
960   but attacks on power never go unchecked,
       not by the man who holds the reins of power.
   Your own blind will, your passion has destroyed you.

ANTIGONE: No one to weep for me, my friends,
   no wedding-song—they take me away
   in all my pain . . . the road lies open, waiting.
   Never again, the law forbids me to see
   the sacred eye of day. I am agony!
   No tears for the destiny that's mine,
   no loved one mourns my death.

CREON: Can't you see?
970   If a man could wail his own dirge *before* he dies,
   he'd never finish.
     (To the guards.)
               Take her away, quickly!
   Wall her up in the tomb, you have your orders.
   Abandon her there, alone, and let her choose—
   death or a buried life with a good roof for shelter.
   As for myself, my hands are clean. This young girl—
   dead or alive, she will be stripped of her rights,
   her stranger's rights, here in the world above.

ANTIGONE: O tomb, my bridal-bed—my house, my prison
   cut in the hollow rock, my everlasting watch!
980   I'll soon be there, soon embrace my own,
   the great growing family of our dead
   Persephone[28] has received among her ghosts.

                                    I,

   the last of them all, the most reviled by far,
   go down before my destined time's run out.
   But still I go, cherishing one good hope:
   my arrival may be dear to father,
   dear to you, my mother,
   dear to you, my loving brother, Eteocles—

---

[27]Polynices, as part of his plan to enlist the aid of Argos in attacking Thebes, married a daughter of the Argive king. The war, and Polynices' death, have brought death to Antigone too.

[28]Consort of Hades, king of the dead.

When you died I washed you with my hands,
990   I dressed you all, I poured the sacred cups
across your tombs. But now, Polynices,
because I laid your body out as well,
this, this is my reward. Nevertheless
I honored you—the decent will admit it—
well and wisely too.
                Never, I tell you,
if I had been the mother of children
or if my husband died, exposed and rotting—
I'd never have taken this ordeal upon myself,
never defied our people's will. What law,
1000   you ask, do I satisfy with what I say?
A husband dead, there might have been another.
A child by another too, if I had lost the first.
But mother and father both lost in the halls of Death,
no brother could ever spring to light again.[29]
For this law alone I held you first in honor.
For this, Creon, the king, judges me a criminal
guilty of dreadful outrage, my dear brother!
And now he leads me off, a captive in his hands,
with no part in the bridal-song, the bridal-bed,
1010   denied all joy of marriage, raising children—
deserted so by loved ones, struck by fate,
I descend alive to the caverns of the dead.

What law of the mighty gods have I transgressed?
Why look to the heavens any more, tormented as I am?
Whom to call, what comrades now? Just think,
my reverence only brands me for irreverence!
Very well: if this is the pleasure of the gods,
once I suffer I will know that I was wrong.
But if these men are wrong, let them suffer
1020   nothing worse than they mete out to me—
these masters of injustice!

LEADER: Still the same rough winds, the wild passion
    raging through the girl.

CREON (*To the guards.*):   Take her away.
    You're wasting time—you'll pay for it too.

[29]For various reasons, including the opinion that Antigone's fine distinctions and perhaps insensitivity here are inconsistent with the rest of the play, some editors and translators reject lines 995–1004. The appropriateness of the passage has been defended on grounds of dramatic psychology (for example, the marital and maternal roles must be merely imagined by Antigone, while her role of sister is one she has experienced) and more technical grounds (for example, the notion that the sibling-bond is closer than either the marital one which involves no blood-kinship or the "half-interest" bond of blood-kinship that links a child with one of its two parents).

ANTIGONE: Oh god, the voice of death. It's come, it's here.

CREON: True. Not a word of hope—your doom is sealed.

ANTIGONE: Land of Thebes, city of all my fathers—
    O you gods, the first gods of the race![30]
    They drag me away, now, no more delay.
1030   Look on me, you noble sons of Thebes—
    the last of a great line of kings,
    I alone, see what I suffer now
    at the hands of what breed of men—
    all for reverence, my reverence for the gods!

(She leaves under guard: the CHORUS *gathers.)*

CHORUS: Danaë,[31] Danaë—
    even she endured a fate like yours,
      in all her lovely strength she traded
    the light of day for the bolted brazen vault—
    buried within her tomb, her bridal-chamber,
1040   wed to the yoke and broken.
    But she was of glorious birth
             my child, my child
  and treasured the seed of Zeus within her womb,
  and cloudburst streaming gold!
    The power of fate is a wonder,
    dark, terrible wonder—
    neither wealth nor armies
    towered walls nor ships
    black hulls lashed by the salt
1050   can save us from that force.

The yoke tamed him too
    young Lycurgus[32] flaming in anger
king of Edonia, all for his mad taunts
Dionysus clamped him down, encased
in the chain-mail of rock
    and there his rage
        his terrible flowering rage burst—

---

[30]According to the myths, several of Antigone's forebears in the Theban dynasty were related to the gods, by blood or marriage.

[31]Danaë's father, Acrisius, a king of Argos, had imprisoned her because of a prophecy that she would bear a son who would kill him. Zeus came to her in a shower of golden rain, begetting Perseus, who did later kill Acrisius.

[32]Lycurgus, a legendary Thracian king, had been imprisoned after being driven to madness by the gods for opposing the worship of Bacchus (Dionysus). Maenads (line 1063) were orgiastic female worshipers of the god.

sobbing, dying away . . . at last that madman
came to know his god—
1060   the power he mocked, the power
he taunted in all his frenzy
trying to stamp out
the women strong with the god—
the torch, the raving sacred cries—
enraging the Muses who adore the flute.
And far north where the Black Rocks[33]
   cut the sea in half
and murderous straits
split the coast of Thrace
1070   a forbidding city stands
where once, hard by the walls
the savage Ares thrilled to watch
a king's new queen, a Fury rearing in rage
   against his two royal sons—
     her bloody hands, her dagger-shuttle
stabbing out their eyes—cursed, blinding wounds—
their eyes blind sockets screaming for revenge!

They wailed in agony, cries echoing cries
    the princes doomed at birth . . .
1080   and their mother doomed to chains,
walled up in a tomb of stone—
   but she traced her own birth back
to a proud Athenian line and the high gods
and off in caverns half the world away,
born of the wild North Wind
   she sprang on her father's gales,
     racing stallions up the leaping cliffs—
child of the heavens. But even on her the Fates
the gray everlasting Fates rode hard
my child, my child.

(*Enter* TIRESIAS, *the blind prophet, led by a boy.*)

TIRESIAS: Lords of Thebes,
1090 I and the boy have come together,
hand in hand. Two see with the eyes of one . . .
so the blind must go, with a guide to lead the way.

CREON: What is it, old Tiresias? What news now?

---

[33]The following lines allude to a third story of imprisonment; most interpreters have found the story itself and its application to Antigone obscure. Phineus, a king of Thrace, divorced his wife Cleopatra (daughter of Boreas, the north wind), who had borne him two sons, and cast her into prison; his second wife blinded the two children and entombed them.

TIRESIAS: I will teach you. And you obey the seer.

CREON: I will,
   I've never wavered from your advice before.

TIRESIAS: And so you kept the city straight on course.

CREON: I owe you a great deal, I swear to that.

TIRESIAS: Then reflect, my son: you are poised,
1100   once more, on the razor-edge of fate.

CREON: What is it? I shudder to hear you.

TIRESIAS: You will learn
   when you listen to the warnings of my craft.
   As I sat on the ancient seat of augury,
   in the sanctuary where every bird I know
   will hover at my hands—suddenly I heard it,
   a strange voice in the wingbeats, unintelligible,
   barbaric, a mad scream! Talons flashing, ripping,
   they were killing each other—that much I knew—
   the murderous fury whirring in those wings
   made that much clear!
1110   I was afraid,
   I turned quickly, tested the burnt-sacrifice,
   ignited the altar at all points—but no fire,
   the god in the fire never blazed.
   Not from those offerings . . . over the embers
   slid a heavy ooze from the long thighbones,
   smoking, sputtering out, and the bladder
   puffed and burst—spraying gall into the air—
   and the fat wrapping the bones slithered off
   and left them glistening white. No fire!
1120   The rites failed that might have blazed the future
   with a sign. So I learned from the boy here:
   he is my guide, as I am guide to others.
                                    And it is you—
   your high resolve that sets this plague on Thebes.
   The public altars and sacred hearths are fouled,
   one and all, by the birds and dogs with carrion
   torn from the corpse, the doomstruck son of Oedipus!
   And so the gods are deaf to our prayers, they spurn
   the offerings in our hands, the flame of holy flesh.
   No birds cry out an omen clear and true—
1130   they're gorged with the murdered victim's blood and fat.
   Take these things to heart, my son, I warn you.
   All men make mistakes, it is only human.
   But once the wrong is done, a man

can turn his back on folly, misfortune too,
if he tries to make amends, however low he's fallen,
and stops his bullnecked ways. Stubbornness
brands you for stupidity—pride is a crime.
No, yield to the dead!
Never stab the fighter when he's down.
1140   Where's the glory, killing the dead twice over?

I mean you well. I give you sound advice.
It's best to learn from a good adviser
when he speaks for your own good:
it's pure gain.

CREON: Old man—all of you! So,
you shoot your arrows at my head like archers at the target—
I even have *him* loosed on me, this fortune-teller.
Oh his ilk has tried to sell me short
and ship me off for years.[34] Well,
drive your bargains, traffic—much as you like—
1150   in the gold of India, silver-gold of Sardis.
You'll never bury that body in the grave,
not even if Zeus's eagles rip the corpse
and wing their rotten pickings off to the throne of god!
Never, not even in fear of such defilement
will I tolerate his burial, that traitor.
Well I know, we can't defile the gods—
no mortal has the power.
                    No,
reverend old Tiresias, all men fall,
it's only human, but the wisest fall obscenely
1160   when they glorify obscene advice with rhetoric—
all for their own gain.

TIRESIAS: Oh god, is there a man alive
who knows, who actually believes . . .

CREON: What now?
What earth-shattering truth are you about to utter?

TIRESIAS: . . . just how much a sense of judgment, wisdom
is the greatest gift we have?

CREON: Just as much, I'd say,
as a twisted mind is the worst affliction known.

TIRESIAS: You are the one who's sick, Creon, sick to death.

CREON: I am in no mood to trade insults with a seer.

---

[34]Ironically, Oedipus (in *Oedipus the King*) had accused Tiresias and Creon himself of a similar, and equally imaginary, mercenary plot.

TIRESIAS: You have already, calling my prophecies a lie.

1170 CREON: Why not?
You and the whole breed of seers are mad for money!

TIRESIAS: And the whole race of tyrants lusts for filthy gain.

CREON: This slander of yours—
are you aware you're speaking to the king?

TIRESIAS: Well aware. Who helped you save the city?

CREON: You—
you have your skills, old seer, but you lust for injustice!

TIRESIAS: You will drive me to utter the dreadful secret in my heart.

CREON: Spit it out! Just don't speak it out for profit.

TIRESIAS: Profit? No, not a bit of profit, not for you.

1180 CREON: Know full well, you'll never buy off my resolve.

TIRESIAS: Then know this too, learn this by heart!
The chariot of the sun will not race through
so many circuits more, before you have surrendered
one born of your own loins, your own flesh and blood,
a corpse for corpses given in return, since you have thrust
to the world below a child sprung for the world above,
ruthlessly lodged a living soul within the grave—
then you've robbed the gods below the earth,
keeping a dead body here in the bright air,
1190 unburied, unsung, unhallowed by the rites.

You, you have no business with the dead,
nor do the gods above—this is violence
you have forced upon the heavens.
And so the avengers, the dark destroyers late
but true to the mark, now lie in wait for you,
the Furies[35] sent by the gods and the god of death
to strike you down with the pains that you perfected!

There. Reflect on that, tell me I've been bribed.
The day comes soon, no long test of time, not now,
1200 when the mourning cries for men and women break
throughout your halls. Great hatred rises against you—
cities in tumult,[36] all whose mutilated sons
the dogs have graced with burial, or the wild beasts

---

[35]Primitive personifications of vengeance, especially for crimes against kindred.
[36]The cities that organized the army to attack Thebes.

or a wheeling crow that wings the ungodly stench of carrion
back to each city, each warrior's hearth and home.

These arrows for your heart! Since you've raked me
I loose them like an archer in my anger,
arrows deadly true. You'll never escape
their burning, searing force.
(Motioning to his escort.)
1210   Come, boy, take me home.
So he can vent his rage on younger men,
and learn to keep a gentler tongue in his head
and better sense than what he carries now.
(Exit to the side.)

LEADER: The old man's gone, my king—
terrible prophecies. Well I know,
since the hair on this old head went gray,
he's never lied to Thebes.

CREON: I know it myself—I'm shaken, torn.
It's a dreadful thing to yield . . . but resist now?
1220   Lay my pride bare to the blows of ruin?
That's dreadful too.

LEADER: But good advice,
Creon, take it now, you must.

CREON: What should I do? Tell me . . . I'll obey.

LEADER: Go! Free the girl from the rocky vault
and raise a mound for the body you exposed.

CREON: That's your advice? You think I should give in?

LEADER: Yes, my king, quickly. Disasters sent by the gods
cut short our follies in a flash.

CREON: Oh it's hard,
giving up the heart's desire . . . but I will do it—
1230   no more fighting a losing battle with necessity.

LEADER: Do it now, go, don't leave it to others.

CREON: Now—I'm on my way! Come, each of you,
take up axes, make for the high ground,
over there, quickly! I and my better judgment
have come round to this—I shackled her,
I'll set her free myself. I am afraid . . .
it's best to keep the established laws
to the very day we die.
(Rushing out, followed by his entourage. The CHORUS *clusters around the altar.)*

CHORUS: God of a hundred names![37]
                    Great Dionysus—
1240   Son and glory of Semele! Pride of Thebes—
Child of Zeus whose thunder rocks the clouds—
Lord of the famous lands of evening—
King of the Mysteries!
                    King of Eleusis,[38] Demeter's plain
her breasting hills that welcome in the world—
Great Dionysus!
                    Bacchus, living in Thebes
the mother-city of all your frenzied women—
                    Bacchus
living along the Ismenus' rippling waters
standing over the field sown with the Dragon's teeth!

You—we have seen you through the flaring smoky fires,
1250   your torches blazing over the twin peaks[39]
where nymphs of the hallowed cave climb onward
                    fired with you, your sacred rage—
we have seen you at Castalia's running spring[40]
and down from the heights of Nysa[41] crowned with ivy
the greening shore rioting vines and grapes
        down you come in your storm of wild women
                    ecstatic, mystic cries—
                    Dionysus—
down to watch and ward the roads of Thebes!
First of all cities, Thebes you honor first
1260   you and your mother, bride of the lightning—
come, Dionysus! now your people lie
in the iron grip of plague,
come in your racing, healing stride
                    down Parnassus's slopes
or across the moaning straits.
                    Lord of the dancing—
dance, dance the constellations breathing fire!
Great master of the voices of the night!
Child of Zeus, God's offspring, come, come forth!
Lord, king, dance with your nymphs, swirling, raving

[37]The Chorus invokes Dionysus as the patron deity of Thebes.

[38]Eleusis, a town near Athens, was the center of the mysterious fertility rites of Demeter, goddess of the fields and harvest.

[39]Parnassus, a mountain near Apollo's shrine at Delphi; one of the peaks was sacred to Apollo, one to Bacchus (Dionysus).

[40]A spring and pool on Mount Parnassus.

[41]A mountain where Dionysus had been reared by nymphs.

1270   arm-in-arm in frenzy through the night
                    they dance you, Iacchus—
                                    Dance, Dionysus
       giver of all good things!

(Enter a MESSENGER *from the side.)*

MESSENGER: Neighbors,
       friends of the house of Cadmus and the kings,
       there's not a thing in this mortal life of ours
       I'd praise or blame as settled once for all.
       Fortune lifts and Fortune fells the lucky
       and unlucky every day. No prophet on earth
       can tell a man his fate. Take Creon:
       there was a man to rouse your envy once,
1280   as I see it. He saved the realm from enemies,
       taking power, he alone, the lord of the fatherland,
       he set us true on course—he flourished like a tree
       with the noble line of sons he bred and reared . . .
       and now it's lost, all gone.
                              Believe me,
       when a man has squandered his true joys,
       he's good as dead, I tell you, a living corpse.
       Pile up riches in your house, as much as you like—
       live like a king with a huge show of pomp,
       but if real delight is missing from the lot,
1290   I wouldn't give you a wisp of smoke for it,
       not compared with joy.

LEADER: What now?
       What new grief do you bring the house of kings?

MESSENGER: Dead, dead—and the living are guilty of their death!

LEADER: Who's the murderer? Who is dead? Tell us.

MESSENGER: Haemon's gone, his blood spilled by the very hand—

LEADER: His father's or his own?

MESSENGER: His own . . .
       raging mad with his father for the death—

LEADER: Oh great seer,
       you saw it all, you brought your word to birth!

MESSENGER: Those are the facts. Deal with them as you will.
       (As he turns to go, EURYDICE *enters from the palace.)*

1300   LEADER: Look, Eurydice. Poor woman, Creon's wife,
       so close at hand. By chance perhaps,
       unless she's heard the news about her son.

EURYDICE: My countrymen,
    all of you—I caught the sound of your words
    as I was leaving to do my part,
    to appeal to queen Athena with my prayers.
    I was just loosing the bolts, opening the doors,
    when a voice filled with sorrow, family sorrow,
    struck my ears, and I fell back, terrified,
    into the women's arms—everything went black.
1310   Tell me the news, again, whatever it is . . .
    sorrow and I are hardly strangers.
    I can bear the worst.

MESSENGER: I—dear lady,
    I'll speak as an eye-witness. I was there.
    And I won't pass over one word of the truth.
    Why should I try to soothe you with a story,
    only to prove a liar in a moment?
    Truth is always best.
                        So,
    I escorted your lord, I guided him
    to the edge of the plain where the body lay,
1320   Polynices, torn by the dogs and still unmourned.
    And saying a prayer to Hecate of the Crossroads,
    Pluto[42] too, to hold their anger and be kind,
    we washed the dead in a bath of holy water
    and plucking some fresh branches, gathering . . .
    what was left of him, we burned them all together
    and raised a high mound of native earth, and then
    we turned and made for that rocky vault of hers,
    the hollow, empty bed of the bride of Death.
    And far off, one of us heard a voice,
1330   a long wail rising, echoing
    out of that unhallowed wedding-chamber,
    he ran to alert the master and Creon pressed on,
    closer—the strange, inscrutable cry came sharper,
    throbbing around him now, and he let loose
    a cry of his own, enough to wrench the heart,
    "Oh god, am I the prophet now? going down
    the darkest road I've ever gone? My son—
    it's *his* dear voice, he greets me! Go, men,
    closer, quickly! Go through the gap,
1340   the rocks are dragged back—
    right to the tomb's very mouth—and look,
    see if it's Haemon's voice I think I hear,
    or the gods have robbed me of my senses."

---

[42]Hecate, associated with crossroads, was a goddess of night, magic, and the underworld; Pluto is another name for Hades, god of the dead.

The king was shattered. We took his orders,
went and searched, and there in the deepest,
dark recesses of the tomb we found her . . .
hanged by the neck in a fine linen noose,
strangled in her veils—and the boy,
his arms flung around her waist,
1350   clinging to her, wailing for his bride,
dead and down below, for his father's crimes
and the bed of his marriage blighted by misfortune.
When Creon saw him, he gave a deep sob,
he ran in, shouting, crying out to him,
"Oh my child—what have you done? what seized you,
what insanity? what disaster drove you mad?
Come out, my son! I beg you on my knees!"
But the boy gave him a wild burning glance,
spat in his face, not a word in reply,
1360   he drew his sword—his father rushed out,
running as Haemon lunged and missed!—
and then, doomed, desperate with himself,
suddenly leaning his full weight on the blade,
he buried it in his body, halfway to the hilt.
And still in his senses, pouring his arms around her,
he embraced the girl and breathing hard,
released a quick rush of blood,
bright red on her cheek glistening white.
And there he lies, body enfolding body . . .
1370   he has won his bride at last, poor boy,
not here but in the houses of the dead.

Creon shows the world that of all the ills
afflicting men the worst is lack of judgment.

(EURYDICE *turns and reenters the palace.*)

LEADER: What do you make of that? The lady's gone,
without a word, good or bad.

MESSENGER: I'm alarmed too
but here's my hope—faced with her son's death
she finds it unbecoming to mourn in public.
Inside, under her roof, she'll set her women
to the task and wail the sorrow of the house.
1380   She's too discreet. She won't do something rash.

LEADER: I'm not so sure. To me, at least,
a long heavy silence promises danger,
just as much as a lot of empty outcries.

MESSENGER: We'll see if she's holding something back,
hiding some passion in her heart.

I'm going in. You may be right—who knows?
Even too much silence has its dangers.

(Exit to the palace. Enter CREON *from the side, escorted by attendants carrying* HAEMON'S *body on a bier.)*

LEADER: The king himself! Coming toward us,
　　　look, holding the boy's head in his hands.
1390　　Clear, damning proof, if it's right to say so—
　　　proof of his own madness, no one else's,
　　　　　　no, his own blind wrongs.

CREON:　　　　　　　　　　　　Ohhh,
　　　so senseless, so insane . . . my crimes,
　　　my stubborn, deadly—
　　　Look at us, the killer, the killed,
　　　father and son, the same blood—the misery!
　　　My plans, my mad fanatic heart,
　　　my son, cut off so young!
　　　Ai, dead, lost to the world,
　　　not through your stupidity, no, my own.

1400　LEADER:　　　　　　　　　　　　Too late,
　　　too late, you see what justice means.

CREON:　　　　　　　　　　　　Oh I've learned
　　　through blood and tears! Then, it was then,
　　　when the god came down and struck me—a great weight
　　　shattering, driving me down that wild savage path,
　　　ruining, trampling down my joy. Oh the agony,
　　　　　the heartbreaking agonies of our lives.

(Enter the MESSENGER *from the palace.)*

MESSENGER:　　　　　　　　　　　　Master,
　　　what a hoard of grief you have, and you'll have more.
　　　The grief that lies to hand you've brought yourself—
　　　　(Pointing to HAEMON'S *body.)*
　　　the rest, in the house, you'll see it all too soon.

CREON: What now? What's worse than this?

1410　MESSENGER:　　　　　　　　　　The queen is dead.
　　　The mother of this dead boy . . . mother to the end—
　　　poor thing, her wounds are fresh.

CREON:　　　　　　　　　　　　No, no,
　　　harbor of Death, so choked, so hard to cleanse!—
　　　why me? why are you killing me?
　　　Herald of pain, more words, more grief?
　　　I died once, you kill me again and again!

What's the report, boy . . . some news for me?
My wife dead? O dear god!
Slaughter heaped on slaughter?

(The doors open; the body of EURYDICE *is brought out on her bier.)*

MESSENGER: See for yourself:
   now they bring her body from the palace.

1420   CREON: Oh no,
   another, a second loss to break the heart.
   What next, what fate still waits for me?
   I just held my son in my arms and now,
   look, a new corpse rising before my eyes—
      wretched, helpless mother—O my son!

MESSENGER: She stabbed herself at the altar,
   then her eyes went dark, after she'd raised
   a cry for the noble fate of Megareus,[43] the hero
   killed in the first assault, then for Haemon,
1430   then with her dying breath she called down
   torments on your head—you killed her sons.

CREON: Oh the dread,
   I shudder with dread! Why not kill me too?—
   run me through with a good sharp sword?
   Oh god, the misery, anguish—
   I, I'm churning with it, going under.

MESSENGER: Yes, and the dead, the woman lying there,
   piles the guilt of all their deaths on you.

CREON: How did she end her life, what bloody stroke?

MESSENGER: She drove home to the heart with her own hand,
1440   once she learned her son was dead . . . that agony.

CREON: And the guilt is all mine—
   can never be fixed on another man,
   no escape for me. I killed you,
   I, god help me, I admit it all!
   (To his attendants.)
   Take me away, quickly, out of sight.
   I don't even exist—I'm no one. Nothing.

LEADER: Good advice, if there's any good in suffering.
   Quickest is best when troubles block the way.

---

[43]The other son of Creon and Eurydice; he had bravely committed suicide to save Thebes.

CREON (*Kneeling in prayer.*): Come, let it come!—that best of fates
   for me
1450   that brings the final day, best fate of all.
   Oh quickly, now—
   so I never have to see another sunrise.

LEADER: That will come when it comes;
   we must deal with all that lies before us.
   The future rests with the ones who tend the future.

CREON: That prayer—I poured my heart into that prayer!

LEADER: No more prayers now. For mortal men
   there is no escape from the doom we must endure.

CREON: Take me away, I beg you, out of sight.
1460   A rash, indiscriminate fool!
   I murdered you, my son, against my will—
   you too, my wife . . .
                  Wailing wreck of a man,
   whom to look to? where to lean for support?
      (*Desperately turning from* HAEMON *to* EURYDICE *on their biers.*)
   Whatever I touch goes wrong—once more
   a crushing fate's come down upon my head!

   (*The* MESSENGER *and attendants lead* CREON *into the palace.*)

CHORUS: Wisdom is by far the greatest part of joy,
   and reverence toward the gods must be safeguarded.
   The mighty words of the proud are paid in full
   with mighty blows of fate, and at long last
1470   those blows will teach us wisdom.
      (*The old citizens exit to the side.*)

Questions for Discussion

1. What is the conflict between Antigone and Ismene? Ismene says,
   "Remember we are women" to her sister. What do Ismene's words tell
   you about Ismene and the time of the drama?

2. Why, knowing as he does that by refusing Polynices's body a proper
   burial he is denying him entrance into the world of the dead, does
   Creon decree that no one must bury the body? What does he hope to
   accomplish?

3. Why does the sentry fear telling his news to Creon? Are his fears justified? What characteristics of Creon's behavior are revealed by his reaction to the sentry? by his reaction to Antigone?

4. Why does Creon suspect money and bribery have corrupted the sentry and, later, Tiresias? What has he failed to see from the beginning?

5. What attitudes and opinions of Creon's are revealed in his speech telling Haemon that Antigone must die? How are these attitudes reemphasized in Haemon's answer to him?

6. What is Tiresias's advice to Creon? What reasons does he give for this advice? Why does Creon reject his suggestions?

7. Throughout the play, Creon emphasizes his role as king and his reactions to Antigone: "While I'm alive, / no woman is going to lord it over me" (ll. 592–93); "never let some woman triumph over us" (l. 758); and "you woman's slave! [to Haemon]" (l. 848). Why, then, does he rush to the cave to save Antigone's life?

8. Explain the reasons for the three deaths at the end of the drama.

9. Explain Creon's last speech.

Suggestions for Exploration and Writing

1. Write an essay explaining the ways in which Antigone and Creon are alike.

2. In the beginning, Ismene says to Antigone, "you're in love with impossibility." Explain how Ismene's statement describes Antigone.

3. Define dramatic foil and explain which characters in the play are dramatic foils to Antigone and to Creon.

4. The messenger says, "Creon shows the world that of all the ills / afflicting men the worst is lack of judgment." Write an essay in which you argue that this or some other quality is Creon's tragic flaw.

5. Antigone claims that her justification is from the gods; Creon claims that as head of state, his main duty is to the state. In an essay, examine the sometimes conflicting claims of individual rights, religion, and state.

6. The Chorus is composed of elderly Thebans. In an essay, explain their role in the drama.

Casebook
on Tim O'Brien

WRITING ABOUT WAR

Perhaps more vividly and convincingly than any other writer, Tim O'Brien, in his stories and novels on Vietnam, graphically illustrates William Tecumseh Sherman's statement, "War is hell." This casebook, containing four of O'Brien's stories as well as critical analyses of O'Brien's work, enables you to explore in class discussion and in writing the soul-searching, sometimes gut-wrenching dilemma of young men unwillingly drafted to fight in the Vietnam War, a war many did not believe in and very few understood.

Tim O'Brien (b. 1946)

Upon graduation from Macalester College in Minnesota in 1968, O'Brien was drafted into the infantry and, though he strongly opposed the war, went to Vietnam as a foot soldier. During part of his time in Vietnam, O'Brien and his platoon were stationed at My Lai, where, the previous year, panicking American soldiers had killed in cold blood every living thing in the village. Vietnam has been the primary focus of O'Brien's fiction. His books include If I Die in a Combat Zone, Box Me Up and Ship Me Home *(1973);* Northern Lights *(1975);* Going After Cacciato *(1978), which won the National Book Award;* The Things They Carried *(1990) a collection of interconnected stories, including the four printed here;* In the Lake of the Woods *(1990), which, in an effort to portray the tragic truth of the My Lai massacre, mixes fact and fiction; and* Tomcat in Love *(1998), a comic novel.*

ON THE RAINY RIVER   (1990)

1   This is one story I've never told before. Not to anyone. Not to my parents, not to my brother or sister, not even to my wife. To go into it, I've always thought, would only cause embarrassment for all of us, a sudden need to be elsewhere, which is the natural response to a confession. Even now, I'll admit, the story makes me squirm. For more than twenty years I've had to live with it, feeling the shame, trying to push it away, and so by this act of remembrance, by putting the facts down on paper, I'm hoping to relieve at least some of the pressure on my dreams. Still, it's a hard story to tell. All of us, I suppose, like to believe that in a moral emergency we will behave like the heroes of our youth, bravely and forthrightly, without thought of personal loss or discredit. Certainly that was my conviction back in the summer of 1968. Tim O'Brien: a secret hero. The Lone Ranger. If the stakes ever became high enough—if the evil were evil enough, if the good were good enough—I would simply tap a secret reservoir of courage that had been accumulating inside me over the years. Courage, I seemed to think, comes to us in finite quantities, like an inheritance, and by being frugal and stashing it away and letting it earn interest, we steadily increase our moral capital in preparation for that day when the account must be drawn down. It was a comforting theory. It dispensed with all those bothersome little acts of daily courage; it offered hope and grace to the repetitive coward; it justified the past while amortizing the future.

2   In June of 1968, a month after graduating from Macalester College, I was drafted to fight a war I hated. I was twenty-one years old. Young, yes, and politically naive, but even so the American war in Vietnam seemed to me wrong. Certain blood was being shed for uncertain reasons. I saw no unity of purpose, no consensus on matters of philosophy or history or law. The very facts were shrouded in uncertainty: Was it a civil war? A war of national liberation or simple aggression? Who started it, and when, and why? What really happened to the USS *Maddox* on that dark night in the Gulf of Tonkin? Was Ho Chi Minh a Communist stooge, or a nationalist savior, or both, or neither? What about the Geneva Accords? What about SEATO and the Cold War? What about dominoes? America was divided on these and a thousand other issues, and the debate had spilled out across the floor of the United States Senate and into the streets, and smart men in pinstripes could not agree on even the most fundamental matters of public policy. The only certainty that summer was moral confusion. It was my view then, and still is, that you don't make war without knowing why. Knowledge, of course, is always imperfect, but it seemed to me that when a nation goes to war it must have reasonable confidence in the justice and imperative of its cause. You can't fix your mistakes. Once people are dead, you can't make them undead.

3   In any case those were my convictions, and back in college I had taken a modest stand against the war. Nothing radical, no hothead stuff, just ringing a few doorbells for Gene McCarthy, composing a few tedious, uninspired editorials for the campus newspaper. Oddly, though, it was

almost entirely an intellectual activity. I brought some energy to it, of course, but it was the energy that accompanies almost any abstract endeavor; I felt no personal danger; I felt no sense of an impending crisis in my life. Stupidly, with a kind of smug removal that I can't begin to fathom, I assumed that the problems of killing and dying did not fall within my special province.

4   The draft notice arrived on June 17, 1968. It was a humid afternoon, I remember, cloudy and very quiet, and I'd just come in from a round of golf. My mother and father were having lunch out in the kitchen. I remember opening up the letter, scanning the first few lines, feeling the blood go thick behind my eyes. I remember a sound in my head. It wasn't thinking, just a silent howl. A million things all at once—I was too *good* for this war. Too smart, too compassionate, too everything. It couldn't happen. I was above it. I had the world dicked—Phi Beta Kappa and summa cum laude and president of the student body and a full-ride scholarship for grad studies at Harvard. A mistake, maybe—a foul-up in the paperwork. I was no soldier. I hated Boy Scouts. I hated camping out. I hated dirt and tents and mosquitoes. The sight of blood made me queasy, and I couldn't tolerate authority, and I didn't know a rifle from a slingshot. I was a *liberal*, for Christ sake: If they needed fresh bodies, why not draft some back-to-the-stone-age hawk? Or some dumb jingo in his hard hat and Bomb Hanoi button, or one of LBJ's pretty daughters, or Westmoreland's whole handsome family—nephews and nieces and baby grandson. There should be a law, I thought. If you support a war, if you think it's worth the price, that's fine, but you have to put your own precious fluids on the line. You have to head for the front and hook up with an infantry unit and help spill the blood. And you have to bring along your wife, or your kids, or your lover. A law, I thought.

5   I remember the rage in my stomach. Later it burned down to a smoldering self-pity, then to numbness. At dinner that night my father asked what my plans were.

6   "Nothing," I said. "Wait."

7   I spent the summer of 1968 working in an Armour meatpacking plant in my hometown of Worthington, Minnesota. The plant specialized in pork products, and for eight hours a day I stood on a quarter-mile assembly line—more properly, a disassembly line—removing blood clots from the necks of dead pigs. My job title, I believe, was Declotter. After slaughter, the hogs were decapitated, split down the length of the belly, pried open, eviscerated, and strung up by the hind hocks on a high conveyer belt. Then gravity took over. By the time a carcass reached my spot on the line, the fluids had mostly drained out, everything except for thick clots of blood in the neck and upper chest cavity. To remove the stuff, I used a kind of water gun. The machine was heavy, maybe eighty pounds, and was suspended from the ceiling by a heavy rubber cord. There was some bounce to it, and elastic up-and-down give, and the trick was to maneuver the gun with your whole body, not lifting with the arms, just letting the rubber cord do the work for you. At one end

was a trigger; at the muzzle end was a small nozzle and a steel roller brush. As a carcass passed by, you'd lean forward and swing the gun up against the clots and squeeze the trigger, all in one motion, and the brush would whirl and water would come shooting out and you'd hear a quick splattering sound as the clots dissolved into a fine red mist. It was not pleasant work. Goggles were a necessity, and a rubber apron, but even so it was like standing for eight hours a day under a lukewarm blood-shower. At night I'd go home smelling of pig. It wouldn't go away. Even after a hot bath, scrubbing hard, the stink was always there—like old bacon, or sausage, a dense greasy pig-stink that soaked deep into my skin and hair. Among other things, I remember, it was tough getting dates that summer. I felt isolated; I spent a lot of time alone. And there was also that draft notice tucked away in my wallet.

8   In the evenings I'd sometimes borrow my father's car and drive aimlessly around town, feeling sorry for myself, thinking about the war and the pig factory and how my life seemed to be collapsing toward slaughter. I felt paralyzed. All around me the options seemed to be narrowing, as if I were hurtling down a huge black funnel, the whole world squeezing in tight. There was no happy way out. The government had ended most graduate school deferments; the waiting lists for the National Guard and Reserves were impossibly long; my health was solid; I didn't qualify for CO status— no religious grounds, no history as a pacifist. Moreover, I could not claim to be opposed to war as a matter of general principle. There were occasions, I believed, when a nation was justified in using military force to achieve its ends, to stop a Hitler or some comparable evil, and I told myself that in such circumstances I would've willingly marched off to the battle. The problem, though, was that a draft board did not let you choose your war.

9   Beyond all this, or at the very center, was the raw fact of terror. I did not want to die. Not ever. But certainly not then, not there, not in a wrong war. Driving up Main Street, past the courthouse and the Ben Franklin store, I sometimes felt the fear spreading inside me like weeds. I imagined myself dead. I imagined myself doing things I could not do—charging an enemy position, taking aim at another human being.

10   At some point in mid-July I began thinking seriously about Canada. The border lay a few hundred miles north, an eight-hour drive. Both my conscience and my instincts were telling me to make a break for it, just take off and run like hell and never stop. In the beginning the idea seemed purely abstract, the word Canada printing itself out in my head; but after a time I could see particular shapes and images, the sorry details of my own future—a hotel room in Winnipeg, a battered old suitcase, my father's eyes as I tried to explain myself over the telephone. I could almost hear his voice, and my mother's. Run, I'd think. Then I'd think, Impossible. Then a second later I'd think, *Run*.

11   It was a kind of schizophrenia. A moral split. I couldn't make up my mind. I feared the war, yes, but I also feared exile. I was afraid of walking away from my own life, my friends and my family, my whole history, everything that mattered to me. I feared losing the respect of my parents. I

feared the law. I feared ridicule and censure. My hometown was a conservative little spot on the prairie, a place where tradition counted, and it was easy to imagine people sitting around a table down at the old Gobbler Café on Main Street, coffee cups poised, the conversation slowly zeroing in on the young O'Brien kid, how the damned sissy had taken off for Canada. At night, when I couldn't sleep, I'd sometimes carry on fierce arguments with those people. I'd be screaming at them, telling them how much I detested their blind, thoughtless, automatic acquiescence to it all, their simple-minded patriotism, their prideful ignorance, their love-it-or-leave-it platitudes, how they were sending me off to fight a war they didn't understand and didn't want to understand. I held them responsible. By God, yes, I *did.* All of them—I held them personally and individually responsible—the polyestered Kiwanis boys, the merchants and farmers, the pious churchgoers, the chatty housewives, the PTA and the Lions club and the Veterans of Foreign Wars and the fine upstanding gentry out at the country club. They didn't know Bao Dai from the man in the moon. They didn't know history. They didn't know the first thing about Diem's tyranny, or the nature of Vietnamese nationalism, or the long colonialism of the French—this was all too damned complicated, it required some reading—but no matter, it was a war to stop the Communists, plain and simple, which was how they liked things, and you were a treasonous pussy if you had second thoughts about killing or dying for plain and simple reasons.

12   I was bitter, sure. But it was so much more than that. The emotions went from outrage to terror to bewilderment to guilt to sorrow and then back again to outrage. I felt a sickness inside me. Real disease.

13   Most of this I've told before, or at least hinted at, but what I have never told is the full truth. How I cracked. How at work one morning, standing on the pig line, I felt something break open in my chest. I don't know what it was. I'll never know. But it was real, I know that much, it was a physical rupture—a cracking-leaking-popping feeling. I remember dropping my water gun. Quickly, almost without thought, I took off my apron and walked out of the plant and drove home. It was midmorning, I remember, and the house was empty. Down in my chest there was still that leaking sensation, something very warm and precious spilling out, and I was covered with blood and hog-stink, and for a long while I just concentrated on holding myself together. I remember taking a hot shower. I remember packing a suitcase and carrying it out to the kitchen, standing very still for a few minutes, looking carefully at the familiar objects all around me. The old chrome toaster, the telephone, the pink and white Formica on the kitchen counters. The room was full of bright sunshine. Everything sparkled. My house, I thought. My life. I'm not sure how long I stood there, but later I scribbled out a short note to my parents.

14   What it said, exactly, I don't recall now. Something vague. Taking off, will call, love Tim.

15   I drove north.

16   It's a blur now, as it was then, and all I remember is a sense of high velocity and the feel of the steering wheel in my hands. I was riding on adrenaline. A giddy feeling, in a way, except there was the dreamy edge of impossibility to it—like running a dead-end maze—no way out—it couldn't come to a happy conclusion and yet I was doing it anyway because it was all I could think of to do. It was pure flight, fast and mindless. I had no plan. Just hit the border at high speed and crash through and keep on running. Near dusk I passed through Bemidji, then turned northeast toward International Falls. I spent the night in the car behind a closed-down gas station a half mile from the border. In the morning, after gassing up, I headed straight west along the Rainy River, which separates Minnesota from Canada, and which for me separated one life from another. The land was mostly wilderness. Here and there I passed a motel or bait shop, but otherwise the country unfolded in great sweeps of pine and birch and sumac. Though it was still August, the air already had the smell of October, football season, piles of yellow-red leaves, everything crisp and clean. I remember a huge blue sky. Off to my right was the Rainy River, wide as a lake in places, and beyond the Rainy River was Canada.

17   For a while I just drove, not aiming at anything, then in the late morning I began looking for a place to lie low for a day or two. I was exhausted, and scared sick, and around noon I pulled into an old fishing resort called the Tip Top Lodge. Actually it was not a lodge at all, just eight or nine tiny yellow cabins clustered on a peninsula that jutted northward into the Rainy River. The place was in sorry shape. There was a dangerous wooden dock, an old minnow tank, a flimsy tar paper boathouse along the shore. The main building, which stood in a cluster of pines on high ground, seemed to lean heavily to one side, like a cripple, the roof sagging toward Canada. Briefly, I thought about turning around, just giving up, but then I got out of the car and walked up to the front porch.

18   The man who opened the door that day is the hero of my life. How do I say this without sounding sappy? Blurt it out—the man saved me. He offered exactly what I needed, without questions, without any words at all. He took me in. He was there at the critical time—a silent, watchful presence. Six days later, when it ended, I was unable to find a proper way to thank him, and I never have, and so, if nothing else, this story represents a small gesture of gratitude twenty years overdue.

19   Even after two decades I can close my eyes and return to that porch at the Tip Top Lodge. I can see the old guy staring at me. Elroy Berdahl: eighty-one years old, skinny and shrunken and mostly bald. He wore a flannel shirt and brown work pants. In one hand, I remember, he carried a green apple, a small paring knife in the other. His eyes had the bluish gray color of a razor blade, the same polished shine, and as he peered up at me I felt a strange sharpness, almost painful, a cutting sensation, as if his gaze were somehow slicing me open. In part, no doubt, it was my own

sense of guilt, but even so I'm absolutely certain that the old man took one look and went right to the heart of things—a kid in trouble. When I asked for a room, Elroy made a little clicking sound with his tongue. He nodded, led me out to one of the cabins, and dropped a key in my hand. I remember smiling at him. I also remember wishing I hadn't. The old man shook his head as if to tell me it wasn't worth the bother.

20   "Dinner at five-thirty," he said. "You eat fish?"

21   "Anything," I said.

22   Elroy grunted and said, "I'll bet."

23   We spent six days together at the Tip Top Lodge. Just the two of us. Tourist season was over, and there were no boats on the river, and the wilderness seemed to withdraw into a great permanent stillness. Over those six days Elroy Berdahl and I took most of our meals together. In the mornings we sometimes went out on long hikes into the woods, and at night we played Scrabble or listened to records or sat reading in front of his big stone fireplace. At times I felt the awkwardness of an intruder, but Elroy accepted me into his quiet routine without fuss or ceremony. He took my presence for granted, the same way he might've sheltered a stray cat—no wasted sighs or pity—and there was never any talk about it. Just the opposite. What I remember more than anything is the man's willful, almost ferocious silence. In all that time together, all those hours, he never asked the obvious questions: Why was I there? Why alone? Why so preoccupied? If Elroy was curious about any of this, he was careful never to put it into words.

24   My hunch, though, is that he already knew. At least the basics. After all, it was 1968, and guys were burning draft cards, and Canada was just a boat ride away. Elroy Berdahl was no hick. His bedroom, I remember, was cluttered with books and newspapers. He killed me at the Scrabble board, barely concentrating, and on those occasions when speech was necessary he had a way of compressing large thoughts into small, cryptic packets of language. One evening, just at sunset, he pointed up at an owl circling over the violet-lighted forest to the west.

25   "Hey, O'Brien," he said. "There's Jesus."

26   The man was sharp—he didn't miss much. Those razor eyes. Now and then he'd catch me staring out at the river, at the far shore, and I could almost hear the tumblers clicking in his head. Maybe I'm wrong, but I doubt it.

27   One thing for certain, he knew I was in desperate trouble. And he knew I couldn't talk about it. The wrong word—or even the right word—and I would've disappeared. I was wired and jittery. My skin felt too tight. After supper one evening I vomited and went back to my cabin and lay down for a few moments and then vomited again; another time, in the middle of the afternoon, I began sweating and couldn't shut it off. I went through whole days feeling dizzy with sorrow. I couldn't sleep; I couldn't lie still. At night I'd toss around in bed, half awake, half

dreaming, imagining how I'd sneak down to the beach and quietly push one of the old man's boats out into the river and start paddling my way toward Canada. There were times when I thought I'd gone off the psychic edge. I couldn't tell up from down, I was just falling, and late in the night I'd lie there watching weird pictures spin through my head. Getting chased by the Border Patrol—helicopters and searchlights and barking dogs—I'd be crashing through the woods, I'd be down on my hands and knees—people shouting out my name—the law closing in on all sides—my hometown draft board and the FBI and the Royal Canadian Mounted Police. It all seemed crazy and impossible. Twenty-one years old, an ordinary kid with all the ordinary dreams and ambitions, and all I wanted was to live the life I was born to—a mainstream life—I loved baseball and hamburgers and cherry Cokes—and now I was off on the margins of exile, leaving my country forever, and it seemed so impossible and terrible and sad.

28   I'm not sure how I made it through those six days. Most of it I can't remember. On two or three afternoons, to pass some time, I helped Elroy get the place ready for winter, sweeping down the cabins and hauling in the boats, little chores that kept my body moving. The days were cool and bright. The nights were very dark. One morning the old man showed me how to split and stack firewood, and for several hours we just worked in silence out behind his house. At one point, I remember, Elroy put down his maul and looked at me for a long time, his lips drawn as if framing a difficult question, but then he shook his head and went back to work. The man's self-control was amazing. He never pried. He never put me in a position that required lies or denials. To an extent, I suppose, his reticence was typical of that part of Minnesota, where privacy still held value, and even if I'd been walking around with some horrible deformity—four arms and three heads—I'm sure the old man would've talked about everything except those extra arms and heads. Simple politeness was part of it. But even more than that, I think, the man understood that words were insufficient. The problem had gone beyond discussion. During that long summer I'd been over and over the various arguments, all the pros and cons, and it was no longer a question that could be decided by an act of pure reason. Intellect had come up against emotion. My conscience told me to run, but some irrational and powerful force was resisting, like a weight pushing me toward the war. What it came down to, stupidly, was a sense of shame. Hot, stupid shame. I did not want people to think badly of me. Not my parents, not my brother and sister, not even the folks down at the Gobbler Café. I was ashamed to be there at the Tip Top Lodge. I was ashamed of my conscience, ashamed to be doing the right thing.

29   Some of this Elroy must've understood. Not the details, of course, but the plain fact of crisis.

30   Although the old man never confronted me about it, there was one occasion when he came close to forcing the whole thing out into the open. It was early evening, and we'd just finished supper, and over coffee

and dessert I asked him about my bill, how much I owed so far. For a long while the old man squinted down at the tablecloth.

31   "Well, the basic rate," he said, "is fifty bucks a night. Not counting meals. This makes four nights, right?"

32   I nodded. I had three hundred and twelve dollars in my wallet.

33   Elroy kept his eyes on the tablecloth. "Now that's an onseason price. To be fair, I suppose we should knock it down a peg or two." He leaned back in his chair. "What's a reasonable number, you figure?"

34   "I don't know," I said. "Forty?"

35   "Forty's good. Forty a night. Then we tack on food—say another hundred? Two hundred sixty total?"

36   "I guess."

37   He raised his eyebrows. "Too much?"

38   "No, that's fair. It's fine. Tomorrow, though . . . I think I'd better take off tomorrow."

39   Elroy shrugged and began clearing the table. For a time he fussed with the dishes, whistling to himself as if the subject had been settled. After a second he slapped his hands together.

40   "You know what we forgot?" he said. "We forgot wages. Those odd jobs you done. What we have to do, we have to figure out what your time's worth. Your last job—how much did you pull in an hour?"

41   "Not enough," I said.

42   "A bad one?"

43   "Yes. Pretty bad."

44   Slowly then, without intending any long sermon, I told him about my days at the pig plant. It began as a straight recitation of the facts, but before I could stop myself I was talking about the blood clots and the water gun and how the smell had soaked into my skin and how I couldn't wash it away. I went on for a long time. I told him about wild hogs squealing in my dreams, the sounds of butchery, slaughter-house sounds, and how I'd sometimes wake up with that greasy pig-stink in my throat.

45   When I was finished, Elroy nodded at me.

46   "Well, to be honest," he said, "when you first showed up here, I wondered about all that. The aroma, I mean. Smelled like you was awful damned fond of pork chops." The old man almost smiled. He made a snuffling sound, then sat down with a pencil and a piece of paper. "So what'd this crud job pay? Ten bucks an hour? Fifteen?"

47   "Less."

48   Elroy shook his head. "Let's make it fifteen. You put in twenty-five hours here, easy. That's three hundred seventy-five bucks total wages. We subtract the two hundred sixty for food and lodging, I still owe you a hundred and fifteen."

49   He took four fifties out of his shirt pocket and laid them on the table.

50   "Call it even," he said.

51   "No."

52   "Pick it up. Get yourself a haircut."

53   The money lay on the table for the rest of the evening. It was still there when I went back to my cabin. In the morning, though, I found an envelope tacked to my door. Inside were the four fifties and a two-word note that said EMERGENCY FUND.

54   The man knew.

55   Looking back after twenty years, I sometimes wonder if the events of that summer didn't happen in some other dimension, a place where your life exists before you've lived it, and where it goes afterward. None of it ever seemed real. During my time at the Tip Top Lodge I had the feeling that I'd slipped out of my own skin, hovering a few feet away while some poor yo-yo with my name and face tried to make his way toward a future he didn't understand and didn't want. Even now I can see myself as I was then. It's like watching an old home movie: I'm young and tan and fit. I've got hair—lots of it. I don't smoke or drink. I'm wearing faded blue jeans and a white polo shirt. I can see myself sitting on Elroy Berdahl's dock near dusk one evening, the sky a bright shimmering pink, and I'm finishing up a letter to my parents that tells what I'm about to do and why I'm doing it and how sorry I am that I'd never found the courage to talk to them about it. I ask them not to be angry. I try to explain some of my feelings, but there aren't enough words, and so I just say that it's a thing that has to be done. At the end of the letter I talk about the vacations we used to take up in this north country, at a place called White-fish Lake, and how the scenery here reminds me of those good times. I tell them I'm fine. I tell them I'll write again from Winnipeg or Montreal or wherever I end up.

56   On my last full day, the sixth day, the old man took me out fishing on the Rainy River. The afternoon was sunny and cold. A stiff breeze came in from the north, and I remember how the little fourteen-foot boat made sharp rocking motions as we pushed off from the dock. The current was fast. All around us, I remember, there was a vastness to the world, an unpeopled rawness, just the trees and the sky and the water reaching out toward nowhere. The air had the brittle scent of October.

57   For ten or fifteen minutes Elroy held a course upstream, the river choppy and silver-gray, then he turned straight north and put the engine on full throttle. I felt the bow lift beneath me. I remember the wind in my ears, the sound of the old outboard Evinrude. For a time I didn't pay attention to anything, just feeling the cold spray against my face, but then it occurred to me that at some point we must've passed into Canadian waters, across that dotted line between two different worlds, and I remember a sudden tightness in my chest as I looked up and watched the far shore come at me. This wasn't a daydream. It was tangible and real. As we came in toward land, Elroy cut the engine, letting the boat fishtail lightly about twenty yards off shore. The old man didn't look at me or speak. Bending down, he opened up his tackle box

and busied himself with a bobber and a piece of wire leader, humming to himself, his eyes down.

58   It struck me then that he must've planned it. I'll never be certain, of course, but I think he meant to bring me up against the realities, to guide me across the river and to take me to the edge and to stand a kind of vigil as I chose a life for myself.

59   I remember staring at the old man, then at my hands, then at Canada. The shoreline was dense with brush and timber. I could see tiny red berries on the bushes. I could see a squirrel up in one of the birch trees, a big crow looking at me from a boulder along the river. That close—twenty yards—and I could see the delicate latticework of the leaves, the texture of the soil, the browned needles beneath the pines, the configurations of geology and human history. Twenty yards. I could've done it. I could've jumped and started swimming for my life. Inside me, in my chest. I felt a terrible squeezing pressure. Even now, as I write this, I can still feel that tightness. And I want you to feel it—the wind coming off the river, the waves, the silence, the wooded frontier. You're at the bow of a boat on the Rainy River. You're twenty-one years old, you're scared, and there's a hard squeezing pressure in your chest.

60   What would you do?

61   Would you jump? Would you feel pity for yourself? Would you think about your family and your childhood and your dreams and all you're leaving behind? Would it hurt? Would it feel like dying? Would you cry, as I did?

62   I tried to swallow it back. I tried to smile, except I was crying.

63   Now, perhaps, you can understand why I've never told this story before. It's not just the embarrassment of tears. That's part of it, no doubt, but what embarrasses me much more, and always will, is the paralysis that took my heart. A moral freeze: I couldn't decide, I couldn't act, I couldn't comport myself with even a pretense of modest human dignity.

64   All I could do was cry. Quietly, not bawling, just the chest-chokes.

65   At the rear of the boat Elroy Berdahl pretended not to notice. He held a fishing rod in his hands, his head bowed to hide his eyes. He kept humming a soft, monotonous little tune. Everywhere, it seemed, in the trees and water and sky, a great worldwide sadness came pressing down on me, a crushing sorrow, sorrow like I had never known it before. And what was so sad, I realized, was that Canada had become a pitiful fantasy. Silly and hopeless. It was no longer a possibility. Right then, with the shore so close, I understood that I would not do what I should do. I would not swim away from my hometown and my country and my life. I would not be brave. That old image of myself as a hero, as a man of conscience and courage, all that was just a threadbare pipe dream. Bobbing there on the Rainy River, looking back at the Minnesota shore, I felt a sudden swell of helplessness come over me, a drowning sensation, as if I had toppled overboard and was being swept away by the silver waves. Chunks of my own history flashed by. I saw a seven-year-old boy in a white cowboy hat and a Lone Ranger mask and a pair of holstered six-shooters; I saw a twelve-year-old

Little League shortstop pivoting to turn a double play; I saw a sixteen-year-old kid decked out for his first prom, looking spiffy in a white tux and a black bow tie, his hair cut short and flat, his shoes freshly polished. My whole life seemed to spill out into the river, swirling away from me, everything I had ever been or ever wanted to be. I couldn't get my breath; I couldn't stay afloat; I couldn't tell which way to swim. A hallucination, I suppose, but it was as real as anything I would ever feel. I saw my parents calling to me from the far shoreline. I saw my brother and sister, all the townsfolk, the mayor and the entire Chamber of Commerce and all my old teachers and girlfriends and high school buddies. Like some weird sporting event: everybody screaming from the side-lines, rooting me on— a loud stadium roar. Hotdogs and popcorn—stadium smells, stadium heat. A squad of cheer-leaders did cartwheels along the banks of the Rainy River; they had megaphones and pompoms and smooth brown thighs. The crowd swayed left and right. A marching band played fight songs. All my aunts and uncles were there, and Abraham Lincoln, and Saint George, and a nine-year-old girl named Linda who had died of a brain tumor back in fifth grade, and several members of the United States Senate, and a blind poet scribbling notes, and LBJ, and Huck Finn, and Abbie Hoffman, and all the dead soldiers back from the grave, and the many thousands who were later to die—villagers with terrible burns, little kids without arms or legs—yes, and the Joint Chiefs of Staff were there, and a couple of popes, and a first lieutenant named Jimmy Cross, and the last surviving veteran of the American Civil War, and Jane Fonda dressed up as Barbarella, and an old man sprawled beside a pigpen, and my grandfather, and Gary Cooper, and a kind-faced woman carrying an umbrella and a copy of Plato's *Republic,* and a million ferocious citizens waving flags of all shapes and colors—people in hard hats, people in headbands—they were all whooping and chanting and urging me toward one shore or the other. I saw faces from my distant past and distant future. My wife was there. My unborn daughter waved at me, and my two sons hopped up and down, and a drill sergeant named Blyton sneered and shot up a finger and shook his head. There was a choir in bright purple robes. There was a cabbie from the Bronx. There was a slim young man I would one day kill with a hand grenade along a red clay trail outside the village of My Khe.

66   The little aluminum boat rocked softly beneath me. There was the wind and the sky.

67   I tried to will myself overboard.

68   I gripped the edge of the boat and leaned forward and thought, *Now.*

69   I did try. It just wasn't possible.

70   All those eyes on me—the town, the whole universe—and I couldn't risk the embarrassment. It was as if there were an audience to my life, that swirl of faces along the river, and in my head I could hear people screaming at me. Traitor! they yelled. Turncoat! Pussy! I felt myself blush. I couldn't tolerate it. I couldn't endure the mockery, or the disgrace, or the patriotic ridicule. Even in my imagination, the shore just twenty yards

away, I couldn't make myself be brave. It had nothing to do with morality. Embarrassment, that's all it was.

71   And right then I submitted.

72   I would go to the war—I would kill and maybe die—because I was embarrassed not to.

73   That was the sad thing. And so I sat in the bow of the boat and cried.

74   It was loud now. Loud, hard crying.

75   Elroy Berdahl remained quiet. He kept fishing. He worked his line with the tips of his fingers, patiently, squinting out at his red and white bobber on the Rainy River. His eyes were flat and impassive. He didn't speak. He was simply there, like the river and the late-summer sun. And yet by his presence, his mute watchfulness, he made it real. He was the true audience. He was a witness, like God, or like the gods, who look on in absolute silence as we live our lives, as we make our choices or fail to make them.

76   "Ain't biting," he said.

77   Then after a time the old man pulled in his line and turned the boat back toward Minnesota.

78   I don't remember saying goodbye. That last night we had dinner together, and I went to bed early, and in the morning Elroy fixed breakfast for me. When I told him I'd be leaving, the old man nodded as if he already knew. He looked down at the table and smiled.

79   At some point later in the morning it's possible that we shook hands—I just don't remember—but I do know that by the time I'd finished packing the old man had disappeared. Around noon, when I took my suitcase out to the car, I noticed that his old black pickup truck was no longer parked in front of the house. I went inside and waited for a while, but I felt a bone certainty that he wouldn't be back. In a way, I thought, it was appropriate. I washed up the breakfast dishes, left his two hundred dollars on the kitchen counter, got into the car, and drove south toward home.

80   The day was cloudy. I passed through towns with familiar names, through the pine forests and down to the prairie, and then to Vietnam, where I was a soldier, and then home again. I survived, but it's not a happy ending. I was a coward. I went to the war.

Questions for Discussion

1. Explain O'Brien's youthful theory about courage.

2. Describe O'Brien's summer job. How does it influence his decision? What causes him to leave the job and drive north?

3. Explain O'Brien's imagery of the pig stench and relate it to the stench of war.

4. In what way is the Tip Top Lodge misnamed? In what way is the name appropriate?

5. O'Brien chose to allow himself to be drafted and sent to Vietnam. Why does O'Brien consider his decision cowardly?

6. Why did O'Brien oppose the war in Vietnam? Referring to the summer of 1968 when he received his draft notice, O'Brien says, "The only certainty that summer was moral confusion." What does he mean? What were some of the uncertainties that contributed to his opposition to the war?

7. What is a conscientious objector? Why could O'Brien not apply for conscientious objector status?

8. How does the fishing trip on Rainy River precipitate O'Brien's decision not to flee to Canada?

9. What does Elroy Berdahl do for O'Brien that causes O'Brien to regard Berdahl as "the hero of [his] life"?

Suggestions for Exploration and Writing

1. O'Brien says that he thought, "There should be a law. [. . .] If you support a war, if you think it's worth the price, [. . .] you have to put your own precious fluids on the line. You have to head for the front and hook up with an infantry unit and help spill the blood." Write an essay explaining why you agree or disagree with this statement.

2. In an essay, analyze O'Brien's moral dilemma.

3. Write a character sketch of Elroy Berdahl, explaining his wisdom and understanding.

4. Analyze a moral dilemma you have faced and give the reason(s) for your final decision

5. Research the draft system in the 1960s. When did this system start? When did it end?

HOW TO TELL A TRUE WAR STORY   (1990)

1   This is true.

2   I had a buddy in Vietnam. His name was Bob Kiley, but everybody called him Rat.

3   A friend of his gets killed, so about a week later Rat sits down and writes a letter to the guy's sister. Rat tells her what a great brother she had, how together the guy was, a number one pal and comrade. A real soldier's soldier, Rat says. Then he tells a few stories to make the point, how her brother would always volunteer for stuff nobody else would volunteer for in a million years, dangerous stuff, like doing recon or going out on these really badass night patrols. Stainless steel balls, Rat tells her. The guy was a little crazy, for sure, but crazy in a good way, a real daredevil, because he liked the challenge of it, he liked testing himself, just man against gook. A great, great guy, Rat says.

4   Anyway, it's a terrific letter, very personal and touching. Rat almost bawls writing it. He gets all teary telling about the good times they had together, how her brother made the war seem almost fun, always raising hell and lighting up villes and bringing smoke to bear every which way. A great sense of humor, too. Like the time at this river when he went fishing with a whole damn crate of hand grenades. Probably the funniest thing in world history, Rat says, all that gore, about twenty zillion dead gook fish. Her brother, he had the right attitude. He knew how to have a good time. On Halloween, this real hot spooky night, the dude paints up his body all different colors and puts on this weird mask and hikes over to a ville and goes trick-or-treating almost stark naked, just boots and balls and an M–16. A tremendous human being, Rat says. Pretty nutso sometimes, but you could trust him with your life.

5   And then the letter gets very sad and serious. Rat pours his heart out. He says he loved the guy. He says the guy was his best friend in the world. They were like soul mates, he says, like twins or something, they had a whole lot in common. He tells the guy's sister he'll look her up when the war's over.

6   So what happens?

7   Rat mails the letter. He waits two months. The dumb cooze never writes back.

8   A true war story is never moral. It does not instruct, nor encourage virtue, nor suggest models of proper human behavior, nor restrain men from doing the things men have always done. If a story seems moral, do not believe it. If at the end of a war story you feel uplifted, or if you feel that some small bit of rectitude has been salvaged from the larger waste, then you have been made the victim of a very old and terrible lie. There is no rectitude whatsoever. There is no virtue. As a first rule of thumb, therefore, you can tell a true war story by its absolute and uncompromising allegiance to obscenity and evil. Listen to Rat Kiley. Cooze, he says. He does not say bitch. He certainly does not say woman, or girl. He says cooze. Then he spits and stares. He's nineteen years old—it's too much for him—so he looks at you with those big sad gentle killer eyes and says cooze, because his friend is dead, and because it's so incredibly sad and true: she never wrote back.

9   You can tell a true war story if it embarrasses you. If you don't care for obscenity, you don't care for the truth; if you don't care for the truth, watch how you vote. Send guys to war, they come home talking dirty.

10   Listen to Rat: "Jesus Christ, man, I write this beautiful fuckin' letter, I slave over it, and what happens? The dumb cooze never writes back."

11   The dead guy's name was Curt Lemon. What happened was, we crossed a muddy river and marched west into the mountains, and on the third day we took a break along a trail junction in deep jungle. Right away, Lemon and Rat Kiley started goofing. They didn't understand about the

spookiness. They were kids; they just didn't know. A nature hike, they thought, not even a war, so they went off into the shade of some giant trees—quadruple canopy, no sunlight at all—and they were giggling and calling each other yellow mother and playing a silly game they'd invented. The game involved smoke grenades, which were harmless unless you did stupid things, and what they did was pull out the pin and stand a few feet apart and play catch under the shade of those huge trees. Whoever chickened out was a yellow mother. And if nobody chickened out, the grenade would make a light popping sound and they'd be covered with smoke and they'd laugh and dance around and then do it again.

12   It's all exactly true.

13   It happened, to *me*, nearly twenty years ago, and I still remember that trail junction and those giant trees and a soft dripping sound somewhere beyond the trees. I remember the smell of moss. Up in the canopy there were tiny white blossoms, but no sunlight at all, and I remember the shadows spreading out under the trees where Curt Lemon and Rat Kiley were playing catch with smoke grenades. Mitchell Sanders sat flipping his yo-yo. Norman Bowker and Kiowa and Dave Jensen were dozing, or half dozing, and all around us were those ragged green mountains.

14   Except for the laughter things were quiet.

15   At one point, I remember, Mitchell Sanders turned and looked at me, not quite nodding, as if to warn me about something, as if he already *knew*, then after a while he rolled up his yo-yo and moved away.

16   It's hard to tell you what happened next.

17   They were just goofing. There was a noise, I suppose, which must've been the detonator, so I glanced behind me and watched Lemon step from the shade into bright sunlight. His face was suddenly brown and shining. A handsome kid, really. Sharp gray eyes, lean and narrow-waisted, and when he died it was almost beautiful, the way the sunlight came around him and lifted him up and sucked him high into a tree full of moss and vines and white blossoms.

18   In any war story, but especially a true one, it's difficult to separate what happened from what seemed to happen. What seems to happen becomes its own happening and has to be told that way. The angles of vision are skewed. When a booby trap explodes, you close your eyes and duck and float outside yourself. When a guy dies, like Curt Lemon, you look away and then look back for a moment and then look away again. The pictures get jumbled; you tend to miss a lot. And then afterward, when you go to tell about it, there is always that surreal seemingness, which makes the story seem untrue, but which in fact represents the hard and exact truth as it *seemed*.

19   In many cases a true war story cannot be believed. If you believe it, be skeptical. It's a question of credibility. Often the crazy stuff is true and the normal stuff isn't, because the normal stuff is necessary to make you believe the truly incredible craziness.

20   In other cases you can't even tell a true war story. Sometimes it's just beyond telling.

21   I heard this one, for example, from Mitchell Sanders. It was near dusk and we were sitting at my foxhole along a wide muddy river north of Quang Ngai. I remember how peaceful the twilight was. A deep pinkish red spilled out on the river, which moved without sound, and in the morning we would cross the river and march west into the mountains. The occasion was right for a good story.

22   "God's truth," Mitchell Sanders said. "A six-man patrol goes up into the mountains on a basic listening-post operation. The idea's to spend a week up there, just lie low and listen for enemy movement. They've got a radio along, so if they hear anything suspicious—anything—they're supposed to call in artillery or gunships, whatever it takes. Otherwise they keep strict field discipline. Absolute silence. They just listen."

23   Sanders glanced at me to make sure I had the scenario. He was playing with his yo-yo, dancing it with short, tight little strokes of the wrist.

24   His face was blank in the dusk.

25   "We're talking regulation, by-the-book LP. These six guys, they don't say boo for a solid week. They don't got tongues. *All* ears."

26   "Right," I said.

27   "Understand me?"

28   "Invisible."

29   Sanders nodded.

30   "Affirm," he said. "Invisible. So what happens is, these guys get themselves deep in the bush, all camouflaged up, and they lie down and wait and that's all they do, nothing else, they lie there for seven straight days and just listen. And man, I'll tell you—it's spooky. This is mountains. You don't *know* spooky till you been there. Jungle, sort of, except it's way up in the clouds and there's always this fog—like rain, except it's not raining—everything's all wet and swirly and tangled up and you can't see jack, you can't find your own pecker to piss with. Like you don't even have a body. Serious spooky. You just go with the vapors—the fog sort of takes you in . . . And the sounds, man. The sounds carry forever. You hear stuff nobody should *ever* hear."

31   Sanders was quiet for a second, just working the yo-yo, then he smiled at me.

32   "So after a couple days the guys start hearing this real soft, kind of wacked-out music. Weird echoes and stuff. Like a radio or something, but it's not a radio, it's this strange gook music that comes right out of the rocks. Faraway, sort of, but right up close, too. They try to ignore it. But it's a listening post, right? So they listen. And every night they keep hearing that crazyass gook concert. All kinds of chimes and xylophones. I mean, this is wilderness—no way, it can't be real—but there it *is,* like the mountains are tuned in to Radio fucking Hanoi. Naturally they get nervous. One guy sticks Juicy Fruit in his ears. Another guy almost flips. Thing is, though, they can't report music. They can't get on the horn and

call back to base and say, 'Hey, listen, we need some firepower, we got to blow away this weirdo gook rock band.' They can't do that. It wouldn't go down. So they lie there in the fog and keep their mouths shut. And what makes it extra bad, see, is the poor dudes can't horse around like normal. Can't joke it away. Can't even talk to each other except maybe in whispers, all hush-hush, and that just revs up the willies. All they do is listen."

33   Again there was some silence as Mitchell Sanders looked out on the river. The dark was coming on hard now, and off to the west I could see the mountains rising in silhouette, all the mysteries and unknowns.

34   "This next part," Sanders said quietly, "you won't believe."

35   "Probably not," I said.

36   "You won't. And you know why?" He gave me a long, tired smile. "Because it happened. Because every word is absolutely dead-on true."

37   Sanders made a sound in his throat, like a sigh, as if to say he didn't care if I believed him or not. But he did care. He wanted me to feel the truth, to believe by the raw force of feeling. He seemed sad, in a way.

38   "These six guys," he said, "they're pretty fried out by now, and one night they start hearing voices. Like at a cocktail party. That's what it sounds like, this big swank gook cocktail party somewhere out there in the fog. Music and chitchat and stuff. It's crazy, I know, but they hear the champagne corks. They hear the actual martini glasses. Real hoity-toity, all very civilized, except this isn't civilization. This is Nam.

39   "Anyway, the guys try to be cool. They just lie there and groove, but after a while they start hearing—you won't believe this—they hear chamber music. They hear violins and cellos. They hear this terrific mama-san soprano. Then after a while they hear gook opera and a glee club and the Haiphong Boys Choir and a barbershop quartet and all kinds of weird chanting and Buddha-Buddha stuff. And the whole time, in the background, there's still that cocktail party going on. All these different voices. Not human voices, though. Because it's the mountains. Follow me? The rock—it's *talking*. And the fog, too, and the grass and the goddamn mongooses. Everything talks. The trees talk politics, the monkeys talk religion. The whole country. Vietnam. The place talks. It talks. Understand? Nam—it truly *talks*.

40   "The guys can't cope. They lose it. They get on the radio and report enemy movement—a whole army, they say—and they order up the firepower. They get arty and gunships. They call in air strikes. And I'll tell you, they fuckin' crash that cocktail party. All night long, they just smoke those mountains. They make jungle juice. They blow away trees and glee clubs and whatever else there is to blow away. Scorch time. They walk napalm up and down the ridges. They bring in the Cobras and F-4s, they use Willie Peter and HE and incendiaries. It's all fire. They make those mountains burn.

41   "Around dawn things finally get quiet. Like you never even *heard* quiet before. One of those real thick, real misty days—just clouds and fog, they're off in this special zone—and the mountains are absolutely

dead-flat silent. Like *Brigadoon*—pure vapor, you know? Everything's all sucked up inside the fog. Not a single sound, except they still *hear* it.

42   "So they pack up and start humping. They head down the mountain, back to base camp, and when they get there they don't say diddly. They don't talk. Not a word, like they're deaf and dumb. Later on this fat bird colonel comes up and asks what the hell happened out there. What'd they hear? Why all the ordnance? The man's ragged out, he gets down tight on their case. I mean, they spent six trillion dollars on firepower, and this fatass colonel wants answers, he wants to know what the fuckin' story is.

43   "But the guys don't say zip. They just look at him for a while, sort of funny like, sort of amazed, and the whole war is right there in that stare. It says everything you can't ever say. It says, man, you got *wax* in your ears. It says, poor bastard, you'll never know—wrong frequency—you don't *even* want to hear this. Then they salute the fucker and walk away, because certain stories you don't ever tell."

44   You can tell a true war story by the way it never seems to end. Not then, not ever. Not when Mitchell Sanders stood up and moved off into the dark.

45   It all happened.

46   Even now, at this instant, I remember that yo-yo. In a way, I suppose, you had to be there, you had to hear it, but I could tell how desperately Sanders wanted me to believe him, his frustration at not quite getting the details right, not quite pinning down the final and definitive truth.

47   And I remember sitting at my foxhole that night, watching the shadows of Quang Ngai, thinking about the coming day and how we would cross the river and march west into the mountains, all the ways I might die, all the things I did not understand.

48   Late in the night Mitchell Sanders touched my shoulder. "Just came to me," he whispered. "The moral, I mean. Nobody listens. Nobody hears nothin'. Like that fatass colonel. The politicians, all the civilian types. Your girlfriend. My girlfriend. Everybody's sweet little virgin girlfriend. What they need is to go out on LP. The vapors, man. Trees and rocks—you got to *listen* to your enemy."

49   And then again, in the morning, Sanders came up to me. The platoon was preparing to move out, checking weapons, going through all the little rituals that preceded a day's march. Already the lead squad had crossed the river and was filing off toward the west.

50   "I got a confession to make," Sanders said. "Last night, man, I had to make up a few things."

51   "I know that."

52   "The glee club. There wasn't any glee club."

53   "Right."

54   "No opera."

55   "Forget it, I understand."

56   "Yeah, but listen, it's still true. Those six guys, they heard wicked sound out there. They heard sound you just plain won't believe."

57   Sanders pulled on his rucksack, closed his eyes for a moment, then almost smiled at me. I knew what was coming.

58   "All right," I said, "what's the moral?"

59   "Forget it."

60   "No, go ahead."

61   For a long while he was quiet, looking away, and the silence kept stretching out until it was almost embarrassing. Then he shrugged and gave me a stare that lasted all day.

62   "Hear that quiet, man?" he said. "That quiet—just listen. There's your moral."

63   In a true war story, if there's a moral at all, it's like the thread that makes the cloth. You can't tease it out. You can't extract the meaning without unraveling the deeper meaning. And in the end, really, there's nothing much to say about a true war story, except maybe "Oh."

64   True war stories do not generalize. They do not indulge in abstraction or analysis.

65   For example: War is hell. As a moral declaration the old truism seems perfectly true, and yet because it abstracts, because it generalizes, I can't believe it with my stomach. Nothing turns inside.

66   It comes down to gut instinct. A true war story, if truly told, makes the stomach believe.

67   This one does it for me. I've told it before—many times, many versions—but here's what actually happened.

68   We crossed that river and marched west into the mountains. On the third day, Curt Lemon stepped on a booby-trapped 105 round. He was playing catch with Rat Kiley, laughing, and then he was dead. The trees were thick; it took nearly an hour to cut an LZ for the dustoff.

69   Later, higher in the mountains, we came across a baby VC water buffalo. What it was doing there I don't know—no farms or paddies—but we chased it down and got a rope around it and led it along to a deserted village where we set up for the night. After supper Rat Kiley went over and stroked its nose.

70   He opened up a can of C rations, pork and beans, but the baby buffalo wasn't interested.

71   Rat shrugged.

72   He stepped back and shot it through the right front knee. The animal did not make a sound. It went down hard, then got up again, and Rat took careful aim and shot off an ear. He shot it in the hindquarters and in the little hump at its back. He shot it twice in the flanks. It wasn't to kill; it was to hurt. He put the rifle muzzle up against the mouth and shot the mouth away. Nobody said much. The whole platoon stood there watching, feeling all kinds of things, but there wasn't a great deal of pity for the baby water buffalo. Curt Lemon was dead. Rat Kiley had lost his best friend in

the world. Later in the week he would write a long personal letter to the guy's sister, who would not write back, but for now it was a question of pain. He shot off the tail. He shot away chunks of meat below the ribs. All around us there was the smell of smoke and filth and deep greenery, and the evening was humid and very hot. Rat went to automatic. He shot randomly, almost casually, quick little spurts in the belly and butt. Then he reloaded, squatted down, and shot it in the left front knee. Again the animal fell hard and tried to get up, but this time it couldn't quite make it. It wobbled and went down sideways. Rat shot it in the nose. He bent forward and whispered something, as if talking to a pet, then he shot it in the throat. All the while the baby buffalo was silent, or almost silent, just a light bubbling sound where the nose had been. It lay very still. Nothing moved except the eyes, which were enormous, the pupils shiny black and dumb.

73   Rat Kiley was crying. He tried to say something, but then cradled his rifle and went off by himself.

74   The rest of us stood in a ragged circle around the baby buffalo. For a time no one spoke. We had witnessed something essential, something brand-new and profound, a piece of the world so startling there was not yet a name for it.

75   Somebody kicked the baby buffalo.

76   It was still alive, though just barely, just in the eyes.

77   "Amazing," Dave Jensen said. "My whole life, I never seen anything like it."

78   "Never?"

79   "Not hardly. Not once."

80   Kiowa and Mitchell Sanders picked up the baby buffalo. They hauled it across the open square, hoisted it up, and dumped it in the village well.

81   Afterward, we sat waiting for Rat to get himself together.

82   "Amazing," Dave Jensen kept saying. "A new wrinkle. I never seen it before."

83   Mitchell Sanders took out his yo-yo. "Well, that's Nam," he said. "Garden of Evil. Over here, man, every sin's real fresh and original."

84   How do you generalize?

85   War is hell, but that's not the half of it, because war is also mystery and terror and adventure and courage and discovery and holiness and pity and despair and longing and love. War is nasty; war is fun. War is thrilling; war is drudgery. War makes you a man; war makes you dead.

86   The truths are contradictory. It can be argued, for instance, that war is grotesque. But in truth war is also beauty. For all its horror, you can't help but gape at the awful majesty of combat. You stare out at tracer rounds unwinding through the dark like brilliant red ribbons. You crouch in ambush as a cool, impassive moon rises over the nighttime paddies. You admire the fluid symmetries of troops on the move, the harmonies of sound and shape and proportion, the great sheets of metal-fire streaming down from a gunship, the illumination rounds, the white

phosphorus, the purply orange glow of napalm, the rocket's red glare. It's not pretty, exactly. It's astonishing. It fills the eye. It commands you. You hate it, yes, but your eyes do not. Like a killer forest fire, like cancer under a microscope, any battle or bombing raid or artillery barrage has the aesthetic purity of absolute moral indifference—a powerful, implacable beauty—and a true war story will tell the truth about this, though the truth is ugly.

87   To generalize about war is like generalizing about peace. Almost everything is true. Almost nothing is true. At its core, perhaps, war is just another name for death, and yet any soldier will tell you, if he tells the truth, that proximity to death brings with it a corresponding proximity to life. After a firefight, there is always the immense pleasure of aliveness. The trees are alive. The grass, the soil—everything. All around you things are purely living, and you among them, and the aliveness makes you tremble. You feel an intense, out-of-the-skin awareness of your living self—your truest self, the human being you want to be and then become by the force of wanting it. In the midst of evil you want to be a good man. You want decency. You want justice and courtesy and human concord, things you never knew you wanted. There is a kind of largeness to it, a kind of godliness. Though it's odd, you're never more alive than when you're almost dead. You recognize what's valuable. Freshly, as if for the first time, you love what's best in yourself and in the world, all that might be lost. At the hour of dusk you sit at your foxhole and look out on a wide river turning pinkish red, and at the mountains beyond, and although in the morning you must cross the river and go into the mountains and do terrible things and maybe die, even so, you find yourself studying the fine colors on the river, you feel wonder and awe at the setting of the sun, and you are filled with a hard, aching love for how the world could be and always should be, but now is not.

88   Mitchell Sanders was right. For the common soldier, at least, war has the feel—the spiritual texture—of a great ghostly fog, thick and permanent. There is no clarity. Everything swirls. The old rules are no longer binding, the old truths no longer true. Right spills over into wrong. Order blends into chaos, love into hate, ugliness into beauty, law into anarchy, civility into savagery. The vapors suck you in. You can't tell where you are, or why you're there, and the only certainty is overwhelming ambiguity.

89   In war you lose your sense of the definite, hence your sense of truth itself, and therefore it's safe to say that in a true war story nothing is ever absolutely true.

90   Often in a true war story there is not even a point, or else the point doesn't hit you until twenty years later, in your sleep, and you wake up and shake your wife and start telling the story to her, except when you get to the end you've forgotten the point again. And then for a long time you lie there watching the story happen in your head. You listen to your wife's breathing. The war's over. You close your eyes. You smile and think, Christ, what's the *point*?

91   This one wakes me up.

92   In the mountains that day, I watched Lemon turn sideways. He laughed and said something to Rat Kiley. Then he took a peculiar half step, moving from shade into bright sunlight, and the booby-trapped 105 round blew him into a tree. The parts were just hanging there, so Dave Jensen and I were ordered to shinny up and peel him off. I remember the white bone of an arm. I remember pieces of skin and something wet and yellow that must've been the intestines. The gore was horrible, and stays with me. But what wakes me up twenty years later is Dave Jensen singing "Lemon Tree" as we threw down the parts.

93   You can tell a true war story by the questions you ask. Somebody tells a story, let's say, and afterward you ask, "Is it true?" and if the answer matters, you've got your answer.

94   For example, we've all heard this one. Four guys go down a trail. A grenade sails out. One guy jumps on it and takes the blast and saves his three buddies.

95   Is it true?

96   The answer matters.

97   You'd feel cheated if it never happened. Without the grounding reality, it's just a trite bit of puffery, pure Hollywood, untrue in the way all such stories are untrue. Yet even if it did happen—and maybe it did, anything's possible—even then you know it can't be true, because a true war story does not depend upon that kind of truth. Absolute occurrence is irrelevant. A thing may happen and be a total lie; another thing may not happen and be truer than the truth. For example: Four guys go down a trail. A grenade sails out. One guy jumps on it and takes the blast, but it's a killer grenade and everybody dies anyway. Before they die, though, one of the dead guys says, "The fuck you do *that* for?" and the jumper says, "Story of my life, man," and the other guy starts to smile but he's dead.

98   That's a true story that never happened.

99   Twenty years later, I can still see the sunlight on Lemon's face. I can see him turning, looking back at Rat Kiley, then he laughed and took that curious half step from shade into sunlight, his face suddenly brown and shining, and when his foot touched down, in that instant, he must've thought it was the sunlight that was killing him. It was not the sunlight. It was a rigged 105 round. But if I could ever get the story right, how the sun seemed to gather around him and pick him up and lift him high into a tree, if I could somehow re-create the fatal whiteness of that light, the quick glare, the obvious cause and effect, then you would believe the last thing Curt Lemon believed, which for him must've been the final truth.

100   Now and then, when I tell this story, someone will come up to me afterward and say she liked it. It's always a woman. Usually it's an older woman of kindly temperament and humane politics. She'll explain that as a rule

she hates war stories; she can't understand why people want to wallow in all the blood and gore. But this one she liked. The poor baby buffalo, it made her sad. Sometimes, even, there are little tears. What I should do, she'll say, is put it all behind me. Find new stories to tell.

101   I won't say it but I'll think it.

102   I'll picture Rat Kiley's face, his grief, and I'll think, *You dumb cooze.*

103   Because she wasn't listening.

104   It *wasn't* a war story. It was a *love* story.

105   But you can't say that. All you can do is tell it one more time, patiently, adding and subtracting, making up a few things to get at the real truth. No Mitchell Sanders, you tell her. No Lemon, no Rat Kiley. No trail junction. No baby buffalo. No vines or moss or white blossoms. Beginning to end, you tell her, it's all made up. Every goddamn detail—the mountains and the river and especially that poor dumb baby buffalo. None of it happened. *None* of it. And even if it did happen, it didn't happen in the mountains, it happened in this little village on the Batangan Peninsula, and it was raining like crazy, and one night a guy named Stink Harris woke up screaming with a leech on his tongue. You can tell a true war story if you just keep on telling it.

106   And in the end, of course, a true war story is never about war. It's about sunlight. It's about the special way that dawn spreads out on a river when you know you must cross the river and march into the mountains and do things you are afraid to do. It's about love and memory. It's about sorrow. It's about sisters who never write back and people who never listen.

Questions for Discussion

1. How does war appear to affect the men's behavior? What do they do that they would not have done at home?

2. Why would a story that instructs on moral virtues, teaches the right way to do things, and causes a listener or reader to "feel uplifted" not be "a true war story"? What does O'Brien mean when he says the "stomach [must] believe" for a war story to be true? How do the stories the narrator tells exemplify what he says about the nature of a "true war story"?

3. Mitchell Sanders tells a story about a platoon on a listening post hearing strange music from a village. What about the music makes the men uncomfortable? What does the narrator mean when he comments that the trees, the monkeys, the fog, the grass—"everything talks"? Why did the men call down air strikes on the village from which the music emanates? Do you think they should have been held accountable for doing so? Why or why not?

4. Mitchell Sanders says of his story that he had made up the parts about the "glee club" and the "opera." Why does the narrator still regard Sanders' story as true? What does Sanders mean when he says the meaning of his story is in the "quiet"?

5. Why does Rat Kiley shoot and torture the baby water buffalo? Why does he cry as he does so? Why do the men watch in silence? Elie Wiesel, who wrote the story "Yom Kippur" printed in the Grief and Loss unit of this text, who spent part of his childhood in a Nazi concentration camp, and whose family died in the camp, has written and spoken at length against indifference and against refusal to get involved in stopping violence or injustice. Do you think the men in O'Brien's story should be held accountable for their failure to stop Kiley from shooting the buffalo? Why or why not?

6. The narrator describes war as having "a powerful, implacable beauty" that is simultaneously an "ugly" "truth." What does he mean?

7. What does the narrator mean by "in the end [. . .] a true war story is never about war"?

8. Do you believe O'Brien is telling the truth about war?

THE MAN I KILLED   (1990)

His jaw was in his throat, his upper lip and teeth were gone, his one eye was shut, his other eye was a star-shaped hole, his eyebrows were thin and arched like a woman's, his nose was undamaged, there was a slight tear at the lobe of one ear, his clean black hair was swept upward into a cowlick at the rear of the skull, his forehead was lightly freckled, his fingernails were clean, the skin at his left cheek was peeled back in three ragged strips, his right cheek was smooth and hairless, there was a butterfly on his chin, his neck was open to the spinal cord and the blood there was thick and shiny and it was this wound that had killed him. He lay face-up in the center of the trail, a slim, dead, almost dainty young man. He had bony legs, a narrow waist, long shapely fingers. His chest was sunken and poorly muscled—a scholar, maybe. His wrists were the wrists of a child. He wore a black shirt, black pajama pants, a gray ammunition belt, a gold ring on the third finger of his right hand. His rubber sandals had been blown off. One lay beside him, the other a few meters up the trail. He had been born, maybe, in 1946 in the village of My Khe near the central coastline of Quang Ngai Province, where his parents farmed, and where his family had lived for several centuries, and where, during the time of the French, his father and two uncles and many neighbors had joined in the struggle for independence. He was not a Communist. He was a citizen and a soldier. In the village of My Khe, as in all of Quang Ngai, patriotic resistance had the force of tradition, which was partly the force of legend, and from his earliest boyhood the man I killed would have listened to stories about the heroic Trung sisters and Tran Hung Dao's famous rout of the Mongols and Le Loi's final victory against the Chinese at Tot Dong. He would have been taught that to defend the land was a man's highest duty and highest privilege. He had accepted this. It was never open to question. Secretly, though, it also frightened him. He was not a fighter. His health was poor, his body small and frail. He liked books. He wanted some-day to be a teacher of mathematics. At night, lying on his mat, he could not picture himself doing the brave things his father had done, or his uncles, or the heroes of the stories. He hoped in his heart that he would never be tested. He hoped the Americans would go away. Soon, he hoped. He kept hoping and hoping, always, even when he was asleep.

2   "Oh, man, you fuckin' trashed the fucker," Azar said. "You scrambled his sorry self, look at that, you *did*, you laid him out like Shredded fuckin' Wheat."

3   "Go away," Kiowa said.

4   "I'm just saying the truth. Like oatmeal."

5   "Go," Kiowa said.

6   "Okay, then. I take it back," Azar said. He started to move away, then stopped and said, "Rice Krispies, you know? On the dead test, this par-ticular individual gets A-plus."

7   Smiling at this, he shrugged and walked up the trail toward the village behind the trees.

8   Kiowa kneeled down.

9   "Just forget that crud," he said. He opened up his canteen and held it out for a while and then sighed and pulled it away. "No sweat, man. What else could you do?"

10 Later, Kiowa said, "I'm serious. Nothing *anybody* could do. Come on, stop staring."

11 The trail junction was shaded by a row of trees and tall brush. The slim young man lay with his legs in the shade. His jaw was in his throat. His one eye was shut and the other was a star-shaped hole.

12 Kiowa glanced at the body.

13 "All right, let me ask a question," he said. "You want to trade places with him? Turn it all upside down—you *want* that? I mean, be honest."

14 The star-shaped hole was red and yellow. The yellow part seemed to be getting wider, spreading out at the center of the star. The upper lip and gum and teeth were gone. The man's head was cocked at a wrong angle, as if loose at the neck, and the neck was wet with blood.

15 "Think it over," Kiowa said.

16 Then later he said, "Tim, it's a *war*. The guy wasn't Heidi—he had a weapon, right? It's a tough thing, for sure, but you got to cut out that star-ing."

17 Then he said, "Maybe you better lie down a minute."

18 Then after a long empty time he said, "Take it slow. Just go wherever the spirit takes you."

19 The butterfly was making its way along the young man's forehead, which was spotted with small dark freckles. The nose was undamaged. The skin on the right cheek was smooth and fine-grained and hairless. Frail-looking, delicately boned, the young man would not have wanted to be a soldier and in his heart would have feared performing badly in bat-tle. Even as a boy growing up in the village of My Khe, he had often wor-ried about this. He imagined covering his head and lying in a deep hole

and closing his eyes and not moving until the war was over. He had no stomach for violence. He loved mathematics. His eyebrows were thin and arched like a woman's, and at school the boys sometimes teased him about how pretty he was, the arched eyebrows and long shapely fingers, and on the playground they mimicked a woman's walk and made fun of his smooth skin and his love for mathematics. The young man could not make himself fight them. He often wanted to, but he was afraid, and this increased his shame. If he could not fight little boys, he thought, how could he ever become a soldier and fight the Americans with their airplanes and helicopters and bombs? It did not seem possible. In the presence of his father and uncles, he pretended to look forward to doing his patriotic duty, which was also a privilege, but at night he prayed with his mother that the war might end soon. Beyond anything else, he was afraid of disgracing himself, and therefore his family and village. But all he could do, he thought, was wait and pray and try not to grow up too fast.

20   "Listen to me," Kiowa said. "You feel terrible, I know that."

21   Then he said, "Okay, maybe I *don't* know."

22   Along the trail there were small blue flowers shaped like bells. The young man's head was wrenched sideways, not quite facing the flowers, and even in the shade a single blade of sunlight sparkled against the buckle of his ammunition belt. The left cheek was peeled back in three ragged strips. The wounds at his neck had not yet clotted, which made him seem animate even in death, the blood still spreading out across his shirt.

23   Kiowa shook his head.

24   There was some silence before he said, "Stop *staring.*"

25   The young man's fingernails were clean. There was a slight tear at the lobe of one ear, a sprinkling of blood on the forearm. He wore a gold ring on the third finger of his right hand. His chest was sunken and poorly muscled—a scholar, maybe. His life was now a constellation of possibilities. So, yes, maybe a scholar. And for years, despite his family's poverty, the man I killed would have been determined to continue his education in mathematics. The means for this were arranged, perhaps, through the village liberation cadres, and in 1964 the young man began attending classes at the university in Saigon, where he avoided politics and paid attention to the problems of calculus. He devoted himself to his studies. He spent his nights alone, wrote romantic poems in his journal, took pleasure in the grace and beauty of differential equations. The war, he knew, would finally take him, but for the time being he would not let himself think about it. He had stopped praying; instead, now, he waited. And as he waited, in his final year at the university, he fell in love with a classmate, a girl of seventeen, who one day told him that his wrists were like the wrists of a child, so small and delicate, and who admired his narrow waist and the cowlick that rose up like a bird's tail at the back of his head. She liked his quiet manner; she laughed at his freckles and bony legs. One evening, perhaps, they exchanged gold rings.

26   Now one eye was a star.

27   "You okay?" Kiowa said.

28   The body lay almost entirely in shade. There were gnats at the mouth, little flecks of pollen drifting above the nose. The butterfly was gone. The bleeding had stopped except for the neck wounds.

29   Kiowa picked up the rubber sandals, clapping off the dirt, then bent down to search the body. He found a pouch of rice, a comb, a fingernail clipper, a few soiled piasters, a snapshot of a young woman standing in front of a parked motorcycle. Kiowa placed these items in his rucksack along with the gray ammunition belt and rubber sandals.

30   Then he squatted down.

31   "I'll tell you the straight truth," he said. "The guy was dead the second he stepped on the trail. Understand me? We all had him zeroed. A good kill—weapon, ammunition, everything." Tiny beads of sweat glistened at Kiowa's forehead. His eyes moved from the sky to the dead man's body to the knuckles of his own hands. "So listen, you best pull your shit together. Can't just sit here all day."

32   Later he said, "Understand?"

33   Then he said, "Five minutes, Tim. Five more minutes and we're moving out."

34   The one eye did a funny twinkling trick, red to yellow. His head was wrenched sideways, as if loose at the neck, and the dead young man seemed to be staring at some distant object beyond the bell-shaped flowers along the trail. The blood at the neck had gone to a deep purplish black. Clean fingernails, clean hair—he had been a soldier for only a single day. After his years at the university, the man I killed returned with his new wife to the village of My Khe, where he enlisted as a common rifleman with the 48th Vietcong Battalion. He knew he would die quickly. He knew he would see a flash of light. He knew he would fall dead and wake up in the stories of his village and people.

35   Kiowa covered the body with a poncho.

36   "Hey, you're looking better," he said. "No doubt about it. All you needed was time—some mental R&R."

37   Then he said, "Man, I'm sorry."

38   Then later he said, "Why not talk about it?"

39   Then he said, "Come on, man, talk."

40   He was a slim, dead, almost dainty young man of about twenty. He lay with one leg bent beneath him, his jaw in his throat, his face neither expressive nor inexpressive. One eye was shut. The other was a star-shaped hole.

41   "Talk," Kiowa said.

GOOD FORM   (1990)

1   It's time to be blunt.

2   I'm forty-three years old, true, and I'm a writer now, and a long time ago I walked through Quang Ngai Province as a foot soldier.

3   Almost everything else is invented.

4   But it's not a game. It's a form. Right here, now, as I invent myself, I'm thinking of all I want to tell you about why this book is written as it is. For instance, I want to tell you this: twenty years ago I watched a man die on a trail near the village of My Khe. I did not kill him. But I was present, you see, and my presence was guilt enough. I remember his face, which was not a pretty face, because his jaw was in his throat, and I remember feeling the burden of responsibility and grief. I blamed myself. And rightly so, because I was present.

5   But listen. Even *that* story is made up.

6   I want you to feel what I felt. I want you to know why story-truth is truer sometimes than happening-truth.

7   Here is the happening-truth. I was once a soldier. There were many bodies, real bodies with real faces, but I was young then and I was afraid to look. And now, twenty years later, I'm left with faceless responsibility and faceless grief.

8   Here is the story-truth. He was a slim, dead, almost dainty young man of about twenty. He lay in the center of a red clay trail near the village of My Khe. His jaw was in his throat. His one eye was shut, the other eye was a star-shaped hole. I killed him.

9   What stories can do, I guess, is make things present.

10   I can look at things I never looked at. I can attach faces to grief and love and pity and God. I can be brave. I can make myself feel again.

11   "Daddy, tell the truth," Kathleen can say, "did you ever kill anybody?" And I can say, honestly, "Of course not."

12   Or I can say, honestly, "Yes."

Questions for Discussion

1. What is the effect of O'Brien's opening "The Man I Killed" with sometimes gruesome details about the dead man? Why does O'Brien mix ordinary and brutal details?

2. Why does the narrator discuss in detail the past life of the dead Vietnamese, a past that is obviously fictional, as the narrator could have no way of knowing it? What effect does O'Brien create by using these details?

3. Kiowa insists that the narrator had no choice but to kill the Vietnamese soldier. Do you agree? Why or why not?

4. How does the narrator feel about the death of the Vietnamese soldier? If he had no choice, why does he dwell so extensively on the killing?

5. In "Good Form," the narrator says he did not personally kill the Vietnamese soldier. Why, then does he say he killed the man in "The Man I Killed"? Why does he feel responsibility for the man's death?

6. What distinction does the narrator make between "story-truth" and "happening-truth"?

7. Do you think the narrator killed the Vietnamese man? Why or why not?

The Undying Uncertainty of the Narrator in Tim O'Brien's
The Things They Carried[1]

Steven Kaplan, University of Southern Colorado

Before the United States became militarily involved in defending the sovereignty of South Vietnam, it had to, as one historian recently put it, "invent" (Baritz 142–43) the country and the political issues at stake there. The Vietnam War was in many ways a wild and terrible work of fiction written by some dangerous and frightening storytellers. First the United States decided what constituted good and evil, right and wrong, civilized and uncivilized, freedom and oppression for Vietnam, according to American standards; then it traveled the long physical distance to Vietnam and attempted to make its own notions about these things clear to the Vietnamese people—ultimately by brute, technological force. For the U.S. military and government, the Vietnam that they had in effect invented became fact. For the soldiers that the government then sent there, however, the facts that their government had created about who was the enemy, what were the issues, and how the war was to be won were quickly overshadowed by a world of uncertainty. Ultimately, trying to stay alive long enough to return home in one piece was the only thing that made any sense to them. As David Halberstam puts it in his novel, *One Very Hot Day*, the only fact of which an American soldier in Vietnam could be certain was that "yes was no longer yes, no was no longer no, maybe was more certainly maybe" (127). Almost all of the literature on the war, both fictional and nonfictional, makes clear that the only certain thing during the Vietnam War was that nothing was certain. Philip Beidler has pointed out in an impressive study of the literature of that war that "most of the time in Vietnam, there were some things that seemed just too terrible and strange to be true and others that were just too terrible and true to be strange" (4).

The main question that Beidler's study raises is how, in light of the overwhelming ambiguity that characterized the Vietnam experience, could any sense or meaning be derived from what happened and, above all, how could this meaning, if it were found, be conveyed to those who had not experienced the war? The answer Beidler's book offers, as Beidler himself recently said at a conference on writing about the war, is that "words are all we have. In the hands of true artists [. . .] they may yet preserve us against the darkness" (Lomperis 87). Similarly, for the novelist Tim O'Brien, the language of fiction is the most accurate means for conveying, as Beidler so incisively puts it, "what happened [in Vietnam] [. . .] what might have happened, what could have happened, what should have happened, and maybe also what can be kept from happening or what can be made to happen" (87). If the experience of Vietnam and its

[1]*Critique* 35.1 (Fall 1993) 43–52, online, Galileo, Academic Search Premier, 15 February 2002 <http://chostvgw21.epnet.com>.

accompanying sense of chaos and confusion can be shown at all, then for Tim O'Brien it will not be in the fictions created by politicians but in the stories told by writers of fiction.

One of Tim O'Brien's most important statements about the inherent problems of understanding and writing about the Vietnam experience appears in a chapter of his novel, *Going After Cacciato*, appropriately titled "The Things They Didn't Know." The novel's protagonist, Paul Berlin, briefly interrupts his fantasy about chasing the deserter Cacciato, who is en route from Vietnam to Paris, to come to terms with the fact that although he is physically in Vietnam and fighting a war, his understanding of where he is and what he is doing there is light-years away. At the center of the chapter is a long catalogue of the things that Berlin and his comrades did not know about Vietnam, and the chapter closes with the statement that what "they" knew above all else were the "uncertainties never articulated in war stories" (319). In that chapter Tim O'Brien shows that recognizing and exploring the uncertainties about the war is perhaps the closest one can come to finding anything certain at all. Paul Berlin, in his fantasy about escaping the war and chasing Cacciato to Paris, is in fact attempting to confront and, as far as possible, understand the uncertainties of the Vietnam War through the prism of his imagination. Once inside his make-believe world, Berlin has the opportunity to explore all of the things that he did not know about the war: The elusive enemy suddenly becomes his partner in a long debate about the meaning of the war; he explores the mysterious tunnels of the Vietcong; one of the victims of the war becomes Berlin's tour guide as he and his fellow soldiers go after Cacciato; and, most important of all, Berlin is given a chance to test and ultimately reject his own thoughts of desertion by imagining how he would react to the desertion of another soldier.

In his most recent work of fiction, *The Things They Carried*,[2] Tim O'Brien takes the act of trying to reveal and understand the uncertainties about the war one step further, by looking at it through the imagination. He completely destroys the fine line dividing fact from fiction and tries to show, even more so than in *Cacciato*, that fiction (or the imagined world) can often be truer, especially in the case of Vietnam, than fact. In the first chapter, an almost documentary account of the items referred to in the book's title, O'Brien introduces the reader to some of the things, both imaginary and concrete, emotional and physical, that the average foot soldier had to carry through the jungles of Vietnam. All of the "things" are depicted in a style that is almost scientific in its precision. We are told how much each subject weighs, either

---

[2]The reviewers of this book are split on whether to call it a novel or a collection of short stories. In a recent interview, I asked Tim O'Brien what he felt was the most adequate designation. He said that *The Things They Carried* is neither a collection of stories nor a novel; he preferred to call it a work of fiction.

psychologically or physically, and, in the case of artillery, we are even told how many ounces each round weighed:

> As PFCs or Spec 4s, most of them were common grunts and carried the standard M-16 gas operated assault rifle. The weapon weighed 7.5 pounds, 8.2 pounds with its full 20-round magazine. Depending on numerous factors, such as topography and psychology, the rifleman carried anywhere from 12 to 20 magazines, usually in cloth bandoliers, adding on another 8.4 pounds at minimum, 14 pounds at maximum. (Carried 7)

Even the most insignificant details seem worth mentioning. One main character is not just from Oklahoma City but from "Oklahoma City, Oklahoma" (5), as if mentioning the state somehow makes the location more factual, more certain. More striking than this obsession with even the minutest detail, however, is the academic tone that at times makes the narrative sound like a government report. We find such transitional phrases as "for instance" (5) and "in addition" (7), and whole paragraphs are dominated by sentences that begin with "because" (5). These strengthen our impression that the narrator is striving, above all else, to convince us of the reality, of the concrete certainty, of the things they carried.

In the midst of this factuality and certainty, however, are signals that all the information in this opening chapter will not amount to much: that the certainties are merely there to conceal uncertainties and that the words following the frequent "becauses" do not provide an explanation of anything. We are told in the opening page that the most important thing that First Lieutenant Jimmy Cross carried were some letters from a girl he loved. The narrator, one of Cross's friends in the war and now a forty-three-year-old writer named Tim O'Brien, tells us that the girl did not love Cross, but that he constantly indulged in "hoping" and "pretending" (3) in an effort to turn her love into fact. We are also told "she was a virgin," but this is immediately qualified by the statement that "he was almost sure" of this (3). On the next page, Cross becomes increasingly uncertain as he sits at "night and wonder(s) if Martha was a virgin" (4). Shortly after this, Cross wonders who had taken the pictures he now holds in his hands "because he knew she had boyfriends" (5), but we are never told how he "knew" this. At the end of the chapter, after one of Cross's men has died because Cross was too busy thinking of Martha, Cross sits at the bottom of his foxhole crying, not so much for the member of his platoon who has been killed "but mostly it was for Martha, and for himself, because she belonged to another world, and because she was [. . .] a poet and a virgin and uninvolved" (17).

This pattern of stating facts and then quickly calling them into question that is typical of Jimmy Cross's thoughts in these opening pages characterizes how the narrator portrays events throughout this book; the facts about an event are given; they then are quickly qualified or called into question; from this uncertainty emerges a new set of facts about the same subject that are again called into question—

on and on, without end. O'Brien catalogues the weapons that the soldiers carried, down to their weight, thus making them seem important
and their protective power real. However, several of these passages are
introduced by the statement that some of these same weapons were
also carried by the character Ted Lavender; each of the four sections
of the first chapter that tells us what he carried is introduced by a qual-
ifying phrase that reveals something about which Lavender himself
was not at all certain when he was carrying his weapons: "Until he was
shot [. . .]" (4, 7, 10).

Conveying the average soldier's sense of uncertainty about what
actually happened in Vietnam by presenting the what-ifs and maybes as
if they were facts, and then calling these facts back into question again,
can be seen as a variation of the haunting phrase used so often by American soldiers to convey their own uncertainty about what happened in
Vietnam: "there it is." They used it to make the unspeakable and indescribable and the uncertain real and present for a fleeting moment.
Similarly, O'Brien presents facts and stories that are only temporarily
certain and real; the strange "balance" in Vietnam between "crazy and
almost crazy" (20) always creeps back in and forces the mind that is
remembering and retelling a story to remember and retell it one more
time in a different form, adding different nuances, and then to tell it
again one more time.

Storytelling in this book is something in which "the whole world is
rearranged" (39) in an effort to get at the "full truth" (49) about events
that themselves deny the possibility of arriving at something called the
"full," meaning certain and fixed, "truth." By giving the reader facts and
then calling those facts into question, by telling stories and then saying
that those stories happened (147), and then that they did not happen
(203), and then that they might have happened (204), O'Brien puts
more emphasis in *The Things They Carried* on the question that he first
posed in *Going After Cacciato:* how can a work of fiction become paradoxically more real than the events upon which it is based, and how can the
confusing experiences of the average soldier in Vietnam be conveyed in
such a way that they will acquire at least a momentary sense of certainty?
In *The Things They Carried,* this question is raised even before the novel
begins. The book opens with a reminder: "This is a work of fiction. Except
for a few details regarding the author's own life, all the incidents, names,
and characters are imaginary." Two pages later we are told that "this book
is lovingly dedicated to the men of Alpha Company, and in particular to
Jimmy Cross, Norman Bowker, Rat Kiley, Mitchell Sanders, Henry Dobbins, and Kiowa." We discover only a few pages after this dedication that
those six men are the novel's main characters.

These prefatory comments force us simultaneously to consider the
unreal (the fictions that follow) as real because the book is dedicated to
the characters who appear in it, and the "incidents, names, and characters" are unreal or "imaginary." O'Brien informs us at one point that in

telling these war stories he intends to get at the "full truth" (49) about them; yet from the outset he has shown us that the full truth as he sees it is in itself something ambiguous. Are these stories and the characters in them real or imaginary, or does the "truth" hover somewhere between the two? A closer look at the book's narrative structure reveals that O'Brien is incapable of answering the questions that he initially raises, because the very act of writing fiction about the war, of telling war stories, as he practices it in *The Things They Carried,* is determined by the nature of the Vietnam War and ultimately by life in general where "the only certainty is overwhelming ambiguity" (88).

The emphasis on ambiguity behind O'Brien's narrative technique in *The Things They Carried* is thus similar to the pattern used by Joseph Conrad's narrator, Marlow, in *Heart of Darkness,* so incisively characterized by J. Hillis Miller as a lifting of veils to reveal a truth that is quickly obscured again by the dropping of a new veil (158). Over and over again, O'Brien tells us that we are reading "the full and exact truth" (181), and yet, as we make our way through this book and gradually find the same stories being retold with new facts and from a new perspective, we come to realize that there is no such thing as the full and exact truth. Instead, the only thing that can be determined at the end of the story is its own indeterminacy.

O'Brien calls telling stories in this manner "Good Form" in the title of one of the chapters of *The Things They Carried:* This is good form because "telling stories" like this "can make things present" (204). The stories in this book are not truer than the actual things that happened in Vietnam because they contain some higher, metaphysical truth: "True war stories do not generalize. They do not indulge in abstractions or analysis" (84). Rather, these stories are true because the characters and events within them are being given a new life each time they are told and retold. This approach to storytelling echoes Wolfgang Iser's theory of representation in his essay "Representation: A Performative Act":

> Whatever shape or form these various (philosophical or fictional) conceptualizations (of life) may have, their common denominator is the attempt to explain origins. In this respect they close off those very potentialities that literature holds open. Of course literature also springs from the same anthropological need, since it stages what is inaccessible, thus compensating for the impossibility of knowing what it is to be. But literature is not an explanation of origins; it is a staging of the constant deferment of explanation, which makes the origin explode into its multifariousness.

It is at this point that aesthetic semblance makes its full impact. Representation arises out of and thus entails the removal of difference, whose irremovability transforms representation into a performative act of staging something. This staging is almost infinitely variable, for in contrast to explanations, no single staging could ever remove difference and so explain origin. On the contrary, its very multiplicity facilitates an unending mirroring of what man is, because no mirrored manifestation can ever coincide with our actual being. (245)

When we conceptualize life, we attempt to step outside ourselves and look at who we are. We constantly make new attempts to conceptualize our lives and uncover our true identities because looking at who we might be is as close as we can come to discovering who we actually are. Similarly, representing events in fiction is an attempt to understand them by detaching them from the "real world" and placing them in a world that is being staged. In *The Things They Carried,* Tim O'Brien desperately struggles to make his readers believe that what they are reading is true because he wants them to step outside their everyday reality and partici-pate in the events that he is portraying; he wants us to believe in his sto-ries to the point where we are virtually in the stories so that we might gain a more thorough understanding of, or feeling for, what is being portrayed in them. Representation as O'Brien practices it in this book is not a mimetic act but a "game," as Iser also calls it in a more recent essay, "The Play of the Text," a process of acting things out:

> Now since the latter [the text] is fictional, it automatically invokes a con-vention-governed contract between author and reader indicating that the textual world is to be viewed not as reality but as if it were reality. And so whatever is repeated in the text is not meant to denote the world, but merely a world enacted. This may well repeat an identifiable reality, but it contains one all-important difference: what happens within it is relieved of the consequences inherent in the real world referred to. Hence in disclos-ing itself, fictionality signalizes that everything is only to be taken as if it were what it seems to be, to be taken—in other words—as play. (251)

In *The Things They Carried,* representation includes staging what might have happened in Vietnam while simultaneously questioning the accu-racy and credibility of the narrative act itself. The reader is thus made fully aware of being made a participant in a game, in a "performative act," and thereby also is asked to become immediately involved in the incred-ibly frustrating act of trying to make sense of events that resist under-standing. The reader is permitted to experience at first hand the uncertainty that characterized being in Vietnam. We are being forced to "believe" (79) that the only "certainty" was the "overwhelming ambiguity."

This process is nowhere clearer than in a chapter appropriately called "How to Tell A True War Story." O'Brien opens this chapter by telling us "This Is True." Then he takes us through a series of variations of the story about how Curt Lemon stepped on a mine and was blown up into a tree. The only thing true or certain about the story, however, is that it is being constructed and then deconstructed and then reconstructed right in front of us. The reader is given six different versions of the death of Curt Lemon, and each version is so discomforting that it is difficult to come up with a more accurate statement to describe his senseless death than "there it is," or as O'Brien puts it—"in the end, really there's nothing much to say about a true war story, except maybe 'oh'" (84).

Before we learn in this chapter how Curt Lemon was killed, we are told the "true" story that Rat Kiley apparently told to the character-narrator O'Brien about how Kiley wrote to Lemon's sister and "says he loved the guy. He says the guy was his best friend in the world" (76). Two months after writing the letter, Kiley has not heard from Lemon's sister, and so he writes her off as a "dumb cooze" (76). This is what happened according to Kiley, and O'Brien assures us that the story is "incredibly sad and true" (77). However, when Rat Kiley tells a story in another chapter we are warned that he

> swore up and down to its truth, although in the end, I'll admit, that doesn't amount to much of a warranty. Among the men in Alpha Company, Rat had a reputation for exaggeration and overstatement, a compulsion to rev up the facts, and for most of us it was normal procedure to discount sixty or seventy percent of anything he had to say. (101)

Rat Kiley is an unreliable narrator, and his facts are always distorted, but this does not affect storytelling truth as far as O'Brien is concerned. The passage above on Rat Kiley's credibility as a storyteller concludes: "It wasn't a question of deceit. Just the opposite: he wanted to heat up the truth, to make it burn so hot that you would feel exactly what he felt" (101). This summarizes O'Brien's often confusing narrative strategy in *The Things They Carried;* the facts about what actually happened, or whether anything happened at all, are not important. They cannot be important because they themselves are too uncertain, too lost in a world in which certainty had vanished somewhere between the "crazy and almost crazy." The important thing is that any story about the war, any "true war story," must "burn so hot" when it is told that it becomes alive for the listener-reader in the act of its telling.

In Rat Kiley's story about how he wrote to Curt Lemon's sister, the details we are initially given are exaggerated to the point where, in keeping with O'Brien's fire metaphor, they begin to heat up. Curt Lemon, we are told, "would always volunteer for stuff nobody else would volunteer for in a million years" (75). And once Lemon went fishing with a crate of hand grenades, "the funniest thing in world history . . . about twenty zillion dead gook fish" (76). But the story does not get so hot that it burns, it does not become so "incredibly sad and true," as O'Brien puts it, until we find out at the story's close that, in Rat's own words, "I write this beautiful fuckin' letter, I slave over it, and what happens? The dumb cooze never writes back" (77). It is these words and not the facts that come before them that make the story true for O'Brien.

At the beginning of this chapter, O'Brien asks us several times to "Listen to Rat," to listen how he says things more than to what he says. And of all of the words that stand out in his story, it is the word "cooze," (which is repeated four times in two pages), that makes his story come alive for O'Brien. "You can tell a true war story by its absolute and uncompromising allegiance to obscenity and evil" (76). This is just one way that O'Brien gives for determining what constitutes a true war story. The unending list of possibilities includes reacting to a story with the ambiguous words "Oh" and "There it is." Rat Kiley's use of "cooze" is another in the sequence of attempts to utter some truth about the Vietnam experience and, by extension, about war in general. There is no moral to be derived from this word, such as war is obscene or corrupt: "A true war story is never moral. It does not instruct" (76). There is simply the real and true fact that the closest thing to certainty and truth in a war story is a vague utterance, a punch at the darkness, an attempt to rip momentarily through the veil that repeatedly re-covers the reality and truth of what actually happened.

It is thus probably no coincidence that in the middle of this chapter on writing a true war story, O'Brien tells us that "Even now, at this instant," Mitchell Sanders's "yo-yo" is the main thing he can remember from the short time encompassing Lemon's death (83). This object, associated with games and play, becomes a metaphor for the playful act of narration that O'Brien practices in this book, a gamestory that he plays by necessity. The only way to tell a true war story, according to O'Brien, is to keep telling it "one more time, patiently, adding and subtracting, making up a few things to get at the real truth" (91), which ultimately is impossible because the real truth, the full truth, as the events themselves, are lost forever in "a great ghostly fog, thick and permanent" (88). You only "tell a true war story" "if you just keep on telling it" (91) because "absolute occurrence is irrelevant" (89). The truth, then, is clearly not something that can be distinguished or separated from the story itself, and the reality or non-reality of the story's events is not something that can be determined from a perspective outside of the story. As the critic Geoffrey Hartman says about poetry: "To keep a poem in mind is to keep it there, not to resolve it into available meanings" (274). Similarly, for O'Brien it is not the fact that a story happened that makes it true and worth remembering, any more than the story itself can be said to contain a final truth. The important thing is that a story becomes so much a part of the present that "there is nothing to remember (while we are reading it) except the story" (40). This is why O'Brien's narrator is condemned, perhaps in a positive sense, to telling and then retelling numerous variations of the same story over and over and over again. This is also why he introduces each new version of a story with such comments as: "This one does it for me. I have told it before many times, many versions—but here is what actually happened" (85). What actually happened, the story's truth, can only become apparent for the fleeting moment in which it is being told; that truth will vanish back into the fog just as quickly as the events that occurred in Vietnam were sucked into a realm of uncertainty the moment they occurred.

O'Brien demonstrates nothing new about trying to tell war stories—that the "truths" they contain "are contradictory" (87), elusive, and thus indeterminate. Two hundred years ago, Goethe, as he tried to depict the senseless bloodshed during the allied invasion of revolutionary France, also reflected in his autobiographical essay "Campaign in France" on the same inevitable contradictions that arise when one speaks of what happened or might have happened in battle. Homer's *Iliad* is, of course, the ultimate statement on the contradictions inherent in war. However, what is new in O'Brien's approach in *The Things They Carried* is that he makes the axiom that in war "almost everything is true. Almost nothing is true" (87) the basis for the act of telling a war story.

The narrative strategy that O'Brien uses in this book to portray the uncertainty of what happened in Vietnam is not restricted to depicting war, and O'Brien does not limit it to the war alone. He concludes his book with a chapter titled "The Lives of the Dead" in which he moves from his experiences in Vietnam back to when he was nine years old. On the surface, the book's last chapter is about O'Brien's first date, his first love, a girl named Linda who died of a brain tumor a few months after he had taken her to see the movie *The Man Who Never Was*. What this chapter is really about, however, as its title suggests, is how the dead (which also includes people who may never have actually existed) can be given life in a work of fiction. In a story, O'Brien tells us, "memory and imagination and language combine to make spirits in the head. There is the illusion of aliveness" (260). Like the man who never was in the film of that title, the people that never were except in memories and the imagination can become real or alive, if only for a moment, through the act of storytelling.

According to O'Brien, when you tell a story, really tell it, "you objectify your own experience. You separate it from yourself" (178). By doing this you are able to externalize "a swirl of memories that might otherwise have ended in paralysis or worse" (179). However, the storyteller does not just escape from the events and people in a story by placing them on paper; as we have seen, the act of telling a given story is an on-going and never-ending process. By constantly involving and then re-involving the reader in the task of determining what "actually" happened in a given situation, in a story, and by forcing the reader to experience the impossibility of ever knowing with any certainty what actually happened, O'Brien liberates himself from the lonesome responsibility of remembering and trying to understand events. He also creates a community of individuals immersed in the act of experiencing the uncertainty or indeterminacy of all events, regardless of whether they occurred in Vietnam, in a small town in Minnesota (253–273), or somewhere in the reader's own life.

O'Brien thus saves himself, as he puts it in the last sentence of his book, from the fate of his character Norman Bowker who, in a chapter called "Speaking of Courage," kills himself because he cannot find some lasting meaning in the horrible things he experienced in Vietnam. O'Brien saves himself by demonstrating in this book that the most important thing is to be able to recognize and accept that events have no fixed or final meaning and that the only meaning that events can have is one that emerges momentarily and then shifts and changes each time that the events come alive as they are remembered or portrayed.

The character Norman Bowker hangs himself in the locker room of the local YMCA after playing basketball with some friends (181), partially because he has a story locked up inside of himself that he feels he cannot tell because no one would want to hear it. It is the story of how he failed to save his friend Kiowa[3] from drowning in a field of human excrement: "A good war story, he thought, but it was not a war for war stories, not for talk of valor, and nobody in town wanted to know about the stink. They wanted good intentions and good deeds" (169). Bowker's dilemma is remarkably similar to that of Krebs in Hemingway's story "Soldier's Home": "At first Krebs [. . .] did not want to talk about the war at all. Later he felt the need to talk but no one wanted to hear about it. His town had heard too many atrocity stories to be thrilled by actualities" (Hemingway 145).

O'Brien, after his war, took on the task "of grabbing people by the shirt and explaining exactly what had happened to me" (179). He explains in *The Things They Carried* that it is impossible to know "exactly what had happened." He wants us to know all of the things he/they/we did not know about Vietnam and will probably never know. He wants us to feel the sense of uncertainty that his character/narrator Tim O'Brien experiences twenty years after the war when he returns to the place where his friend Kiowa sank into a "field of shit" and tries to find "something meaningful and right" (212) to say but ultimately can only say, "well . . . there it is" (212). Each time we, the readers of *The Things They Carried*, return to Vietnam through O'Brien's labyrinth of stories, we become more and more aware that this statement is the closest we probably ever will come to knowing the "real truth," the undying uncertainty of the Vietnam War.

Works Cited

Baritz, Loren. *Backfire: A History of How American Culture Led Us into Vietnam and Made Us Fight the Way We Did.* New York: Morrow, 1985.

Beidler, Philip. *American Literature and the Experience of Vietnam.* Athens: U of Georgia P, 1982.

Halberstam, David. *One Very Hot Day.* New York: Houghton, 1967.

Hartman, Geoffrey. *Criticism in the Wilderness: The Study of Literature Today.* New Haven: Yale UP, 1980.

Hemingway, Ernest. *Short Stories.* New York: Scribner, 1953.

Iser, Wolfgang. *Prospecting: From Reader Response to Literary Anthropology.* Baltimore: Johns Hopkins UP, 1989.

Lomperis, Timothy, *"Reading the Wind": The Literature of the Vietnam War: An Interpretative Critique.* Durham: Duke UP, 1989.

---

[3]In the "Notes" to this chapter, O'Brien typically turns the whole story upside down "in the interest of truth" and tells us that Norman Bowker was not responsible for Kiowa's horrible death: "That part of the story is my own" (182). This phrase could be taken to mean that this part of the story is his own creation or that he was the one responsible for Kiowa's death.

Miller, J. Hillis. "Heart of Darkness Revisited." *Heart of Darkness: A Case Study in Contemporary Criticism.* Ed. Ross C. Murfin. New York: St. Martin's, 1989.

O'Brien, Tim. *Going After Cacciato.* New York: Dell, 1978.

———. *The Things They Carried.* Boston: Houghton, 1990.

"How to Tell a True War Story": Metafiction
in *The Things They Carried*[1]

Catherine Calloway

Tim O'Brien's most recent book, *The Things They Carried*, begins with a litany of items that the soldiers "hump" in the Vietnam War—assorted weapons, dog tags, flak jackets, car plugs, cigarettes, insect repellent, letters, can openers, C-rations, jungle boots, maps, medical supplies, and explosives as well as memories, reputations, and personal histories. In addition, the reader soon learns, the soldiers also carry stories: stories that connect "the past to the future" (40), stories that can "make the dead talk" (261), stories that "never seem [. . .] to end" (83), stories that are "beyond telling" (79), and stories "that swirl back and forth across the border between trivia and bedlam, the mad and the mundane" (101). Although perhaps few of the stories in *The Things They Carried* are as brief as the well-known Vietnam War tale related by Michael Herr in *Dispatches*—"Patrol went up the mountain. One man came back. He died before he could tell us what happened," (6)—many are in their own way as enigmatic. The tales included in O'Brien's twenty-two chapters range from several lines to many pages and demonstrate well the impossibility of knowing the reality of the war in absolute terms. Sometimes stories are abandoned, only to be continued pages or chapters later. At other times, the narrator begins to tell a story, only to have another character finish the tale. Still other stories are told as if true accounts, only for their validity to be immediately questioned or denied. O'Brien draws the reader into the text, calling the reader's attention to the process of invention and challenging him to determine which, if any, of the stories are true. As a result, the stories become epistemological tools, multidimensional windows through which the war, the world, and the ways of telling a war story can be viewed from many different angles and visions.

The epistemological ambivalence of the stories in *The Things They Carried* is reinforced by the book's ambiguity of style and structure. What exactly is *The Things They Carried* in terms of technique? Many reviewers refer to the work as a series of short stories, but it is much more than that. *The Things They Carried* is a combat novel, yet it is not a combat novel. It is also a blend of traditional and untraditional forms—a collection, Gene Lyons says, of "short stories, essays, anecdotes, narrative fragments, jokes,

[1] *Critique* 36.4 (Summer 1995) 249–57, Galileo, Academic Search Premier, 15 January 2002 <http://chostvgw21.epnet.com>.

fables, biographical and autobiographical sketches, and philosophical asides" (52). It has been called both "a unified narrative with chapters that stand perfectly on their own" (Coffey 60) and a series of "22 discontinuous sections" (Bawer A 13).

Also ambiguous is the issue of how much of the book is autobiography. The relationship between fiction and reality arises early in the text when the reader learns the first of many parallels that emerge as the book progresses: that the protagonist and narrator, like the real author of *The Things They Carried,* is named Tim O'Brien. Both the real and the fictional Tim O'Brien are in their forties and are natives of Minnesota, writers who graduated Phi Beta Kappa from Macalester College, served as grunts in Vietnam after having been drafted at age twenty-one, attended graduate school at Harvard University, and wrote books entitled *If I Die in a Combat Zone* and *Going After Cacciato.* Other events of the protagonist's life are apparently invention. Unlike the real Tim O'Brien, the protagonist has a nine-year-old daughter named Kathleen and makes a return journey to Vietnam years after the war is over.[2] However, even the other supposedly fictional characters of the book sound real because of an epigraph preceding the stories that states, "This book is lovingly dedicated to the men of Alpha Company, and in particular to Jimmy Cross, Norman Bowker, Rat Kiley, Mitchell Sanders, Henry Dobbins, and Kiowa," leading the reader to wonder if the men of Alpha Company are real or imaginary.

Clearly O'Brien resists a simplistic classification of his latest work. In both the preface to the book and in an interview with Elizabeth Mehren, he terms *The Things They Carried* "fiction [. . .] a novel" (Mehren E1), but in an interview with Martin Naparsteck, he refers to the work as a "sort of half novel, half group of stories. It's part nonfiction, too," he insists (7). And, as Naparsteck points out, the work "resists easy categorization: it is part novel, part collection of stories, part essays, part journalism; it is, more significantly, all at the same time" (1).

As O'Brien's extensive focus on storytelling indicates, *The Things They Carried* is also a work of contemporary metafiction, what Robert Scholes first termed fabulation or "ethically controlled fantasy" (3). According to Patricia Waugh,

> Metafiction is a term given to fictional writing which self-consciously and systematically draws attention to its status as an artefact in order to pose questions about the relationship between fiction and reality. In providing a critique of their own methods of construction, such writings not only examine the fundamental structures of narrative fiction, they also explore the possible fictionality of the world outside the literary fictional text. (2)

---

[2]Biographical information on the real Tim O'Brien is taken from published facts of his life. See, for instance, Michael Coffey, "Tim O'Brien," *Publishers Weekly,* 237, 16 Feb. 1990, 60–61, and Everett C. Wilkie Jr., "Tim O'Brien." *Dictionary of Literary Biography Yearbook: 1980,* eds. Karen L. Rood, Jean W. Ross, and Richard Ziegfeld. Detroit: Gale, 1981, 286–290.

Like O'Brien's earlier novel, the critically acclaimed *Going After Cacciato*,[3] *The Things They Carried* considers the process of writing; it is, in fact, as much about the process of writing as it is the text of a literary work. By examining imagination and memory, two main components that O'Brien feels are important to a writer of fiction (Schroeder 143), and by providing so many layers of technique in one work, O'Brien delves into the origins of fictional creation. In focusing so extensively on what a war story is or is not, O'Brien writes a war story as he examines the process of writing one. To echo what Philip Beidler has stated about *Going After Cacciato*, "the form" of *The Things They Carried* thus becomes "its content" (172); the medium becomes the message.

"I'm forty-three years old, and a writer now," O'Brien's protagonist states periodically throughout the book, directly referring to his role as author and to the status of his work as artifice. "Much of it [the war] is hard to remember," he comments. "I sit at this typewriter and stare through my words and watch Kiowa sinking into the deep muck of a shit field, or Curt Lemon hanging in pieces from a tree, and as I write about these things, the remembering is turned into a kind of rehappening" (36). The "rehappening" takes the form of a number of types of stories: some happy, some sad, some peaceful, some bloody, some wacky. We learn of Ted Lavender, who is "zapped while zipping" (17) after urinating, of the paranoid friendship of Dave Jensen and Lee Strunk, of the revenge plot against Bobby Jorgenson, an unskilled medic who almost accidentally kills the narrator, of the moral confusion of the protagonist who fishes on the Rainy River and dreams of desertion to Canada, and Mary Ann Bell, Mark Fossie's blue-eyed, blonde, seventeen-year-old girlfriend, who is chillingly attracted to life in a combat zone.

Some stories only indirectly reflect the process of writing; other selections include obvious metafictional devices. In certain sections of the book, entire chapters are devoted to discussing form and technique. A good example is "Notes," which elaborates on "Speaking of Courage," the story that precedes it. The serious reader of the real Tim O'Brien's fiction recognizes "Speaking of Courage" as having first been published in the Summer 1976 issue of *Massachusetts Review*.[4] This earlier version of the story plays off chapter 14 of *Going After Cacciato*, "Upon Almost Winning the Silver Star," in which the protagonist, Paul Berlin, is thinking about how he might have won the Silver Star for bravery in Vietnam had he had the courage to rescue Frenchie Tucker, a character shot while searching a tunnel. However, in *The Things They Carried*'s version of "Speaking of Courage," the protagonist is not Paul Berlin, but Norman Bowker, who

---

[3]New York: Delta/Seymour Lawrence, 1978. *Going After Cacciato* received the National Book Award in 1979.

[4]Vol. 17, pp. 243–253. The earlier version of the story has also been published in *Prize Stories 1978: The O'Henry Awards*. Ed. and intro. William Abrahams. Garden City: Doubleday, 1978: 159–168. A later version of "Speaking of Courage" appeared in *Granta* 29 (Winter 1989): 135–154, along with "Notes."

wishes he had had the courage to save Kiowa, a soldier who dies in a field of excrement during a mortar attack.[5] Such shifts in character and events tempt the reader into textual participation, leading him to question the ambiguous nature of reality. Who really did not win the Silver Star for bravery? Paul Berlin, Norman Bowker, or Tim O'Brien? Who actually needed saving? Frenchie Tucker or Kiowa? Which version of the story, if either, is accurate? The inclusion of a metafictional chapter presenting the background behind the tale provides no definite answers or resolutions. We learn that Norman Bowker, who eventually commits suicide, asks the narrator to compose the story and that the author has revised the tale for inclusion in *The Things They Carried* because a postwar story is more appropriate for the later book than for *Going After Cacciato*. However, O'Brien's admission that much of the story is still invention compels the reader to wonder about the truth. The narrator assures us that the truth is that "Norman did not experience a failure of nerve that night [. . .] or lose the Silver Star for valor" (182). Can even this version be believed? Was there really a Norman Bowker, or is he, too, only fictional?

Even more significant, the reader is led to question the reality of many, if not all, of the stories in the book. The narrator insists that the story of Curt Lemon's death, for instance, is "all exactly true" (77), then states eight pages later that he has told Curt's story previously—"many times, many versions" (85)—before narrating yet another version. As a result, any and all accounts of the incident are questionable. Similarly, the reader is led to doubt the validity of many of the tales told by other characters in the book. The narrator remarks that Rat Kiley's stories, such as the one about Mary Ann Bell in "Sweetheart of the Song Tra Bong," are particularly ambiguous:

> For Rat Kiley [. . .] facts were formed by sensation, not the other way around, and when you listened to one of his stories, you'd find yourself performing rapid calculations in your head, subtracting superlatives, figuring the square root of an absolute and then multiplying by maybe. (101)

Still other characters admit the fictionality of their stories. Mitchell Sanders, in the ironically titled "How to Tell a True War Story," confesses to the protagonist that although his tale is the truth, parts of it are pure

---

[5]O'Brien frequently makes changes between versions of his stories that are published in literary magazines and chapters of his books. The version of "Spin" that was published in the Spring 1990 issue of *The Quarterly* (3–13), for example, combines several of the individual stories from *The Things They Carried* into one longer tale. In addition, O'Brien makes changes between the hardback and paperback versions of his books. In both the "Field Trip" chapter of the hardback edition of *The Things They Carried* and the short story version of "Field Trip" (*McCalls* 17, August 1990: 78–79), the narrator returns Kiowa's hatchet to the site of Kiowa's death, but in the paperback edition of *The Things They Carried* (New York: Penguin, 1990), the narrator carries a pair of Kiowa's moccasins. For references to changes in O'Brien's earlier works, see my "Pluralities of Vision: *Going After Cacciato* and Tim O'Brien's Short Fiction," *America Rediscovered: Critical Essays on Literature and Film of the Vietnam War.* Eds. Owen W. Gilman Jr. and Lorrie Smith. New York: Garland, 1990: 213–224.

invention. "Last night, man," Sanders states, "I had to make up a few things [. . .] The glee club. There wasn't any glee club . . . No opera," either (83–84). "But," he adds, "it's still true" (84).

O'Brien shares the criteria with which the writer or teller and the reader or listener must be concerned by giving an extended definition of what a war story is or is not. The chapter "How to Tell a True War Story" focuses most extensively on the features that might be found in a "true" war tale. "A true war story is never moral," the narrator states. "It does not instruct, nor encourage virtue, nor suggest models of proper human behavior, nor restrain men from doing the things men have always done" (76).

Furthermore, a true war story has an "absolute and uncompromising allegiance to obscenity and evil" (76), is embarrassing, may not be believable, seems to go on forever, does "not generalize" or "indulge in abstraction or analysis" (84), does not necessarily make "a point" (88), and sometimes cannot even be told. True war stories, the reader soon realizes, are like the nature of the Vietnam War itself; "the only certainty is overwhelming ambiguity" (88). "The final and definitive truth" (83) cannot be derived, and any "truths are contradictory" (87).

By defining a war story so broadly, O'Brien writes more stories, interspersing the definitions with examples from the war to illustrate them. What is particularly significant about the examples is that they are given in segments, a technique that actively engages the readers in the process of textual creation. Characters who are mentioned as having died early in the work are brought back to life through flashbacks in other parts of the text so that we can see who these characters are, what they are like, and how they die. For instance, in the story "Spin," the narrator first refers to the death of Curt Lemon, a soldier blown apart by a booby trap, but the reader does not learn the details of the tragedy until four stories later, in "How to Tell a True War Story." Even then, the reader must piece together the details of Curt's death throughout that particular tale. The first reference to Lemon appears on the third page of the story, when O'Brien matter-of-factly states, "The dead guy's name was Curt Lemon" (77). Lemon's death is briefly mentioned a few paragraphs later, but additional details surrounding the incident are not given at once but are revealed gradually throughout the story, in between digressive stories narrated by two other soldiers, Rat Kiley and Mitchell Sanders. Each fragment about Curt's accident illustrates the situation more graphically. Near the beginning of the tale, O'Brien describes the death somewhat poetically. Curt is "a handsome kid, really. Sharp grey eyes, lean and narrow-waisted, and when he died it was almost beautiful, the way the sunlight came around him and lifted him up and sucked him high into a tree full of moss and vines and white blossoms" (78). Lemon is not mentioned again for seven pages, at which time O'Brien illustrates the effect of Lemon's death upon the other soldiers by detailing how Rat Kiley, avenging Curt's death, mutilates and kills a baby water buffalo. When later in the story Lemon's accident is narrated for the third time, the reader is finally told what was briefly alluded to in the earlier tale "Spin": how the soldiers had to peel Curt Lemon's body parts from a tree.

The story of Curt Lemon does not end with "How to Tell a True War Story" but is narrated further in two other stories, "The Dentist" and "The Lives of the Dead." In "The Lives of the Dead," for example, Curt is resurrected through a story of his trick-or-treating in Vietnamese hootches on Halloween for whatever goodies he can get: "candles and joss sticks and a pair of black pajamas and statuettes of the smiling Buddha" (268). To hear Rat Kiley tell it, the narrator comments, "you'd never know that Curt Lemon was dead. He was still out there in the dark, naked and painted up, trick-or-treating, sliding from hootch to hootch in that crazy white ghost mask" (268). To further complicate matters, in "The Lives of the Dead," O'Brien alludes to a soldier other than Curt, Stink Harris, from a previous literary work, *Going After Cacciato,* written over a decade before *The Things They Carried.* Thus, the epistemological uncertainty in the stories is mirrored by the fact that O'Brien presents events that take place in a fragmented form rather than in a straightforward, linear fashion. The reader has to piece together information, such as the circumstances surrounding the characters' deaths, in the same manner that the characters must piece together the reality of the war, or, for that matter, Curt Lemon's body.

The issue of truth is particularly a main crux of the events surrounding "The Man I Killed," a story that O'Brien places near the center of the book. Gradually interspersed throughout the stories that make up *The Things They Carried* are references to a Vietnamese soldier, "A slim, dead, dainty young man of about twenty" (40) with "a star-shaped hole" (141) in his face, who is first mentioned in the story "Spin" and whose death still haunts the narrator long after the end of the war. Nine chapters after "Spin," in "The Man I Killed," the protagonist graphically describes the dead Vietnamese youth as well as creates a personal history for him; he envisions the young man to have been a reluctant soldier who hated violence and "loved mathematics" (142), a university-educated man who "had been a soldier for only a single day" (144) and who, like the narrator, perhaps went to war only to avoid "disgracing himself, and therefore his family and village" (142).[6] "Ambush," the story immediately following "The Man I Killed," provides yet another kaleidoscopic fictional frame of the incident, describing in detail the events that lead up to the narrator's killing of the young soldier and ending with a version of the event that suggests that the young man does not die at all. The reader is forced to connect the threads of the story in between several chapters that span over a hundred pages; not until a later chapter, "Good Form," where the protagonist narrates three more stories of the event, does the reader fully question the truth of the incident. In the first version in "Good Form,"

---

[6]O'Brien develops the figure of the young Vietnamese youth who opposes the war more fully in *Going After Cacciato,* where Li Van Hgoc, a Vietnamese major, has been imprisoned in a tunnel complex for ten years for fleeing from the war and refusing to fight. The major, in a sense, mirrors Paul Berlin and the Third Squad. Theoretically, the soldiers have one main factor in common with Li Van Hgoc; they are all deserters from the war.

the narrator reverses the details of the earlier stories and denies that he was the thrower of the grenade that killed the man. "Twenty years ago I watched a man die on a trail near the village of My Khe," he states. "I did not kill him. But I was present, you see, and my presence was guilt enough" (203). However, he immediately admits that "Even that story is made up" (203) and tells instead what he terms "the happening-truth":

> I was once a soldier. There were many bodies, real bodies with real faces, but I was young then and I was afraid to look. And now, twenty years later, I'm left with faceless responsibility and faceless grief. (203)

In still a third version, "the happening-truth" is replaced with "the story-truth." According to the protagonist, the Vietnamese soldier

> was a slim, dead, almost dainty young man of about twenty. He lay in the center of a red clay trail near the village of My Khe. His jaw was in his throat. His one eye was shut, the other eye was a star-shaped hole. I killed him. (204)

But the reader wonders, did the narrator kill the young man? When the narrator's nine-year-old daughter demands, "Daddy, tell the truth [. . .] did you ever kill anybody?" the narrator reveals that he "can say, honestly, 'Of course not,'" or he "can say, honestly, 'Yes'" (204).

According to Inger Christensen, one of the most important elements of metafiction is "the novelist's message" (10). At least one reviewer has reduced O'Brien's message in *The Things They Carried* to the moral "'Death sucks'" (Melmoth H6); the book, however, reveals an even greater thematic concern. "Stories can save us," asserts the protagonist in "The Lives of the Dead," the concluding story of the text (255), where fiction is used as a means of resurrecting the deceased. In this multiple narrative, O'Brien juxtaposes tales of death in Vietnam with an account of the death of Linda, a nine-year-old girl who had a brain tumor. As the protagonist tells Linda's story, he also comments on the nature and power of fiction. Stories, he writes, are "a kind of dreaming, [where] the dead sometimes smile and sit up and return to the world" (255). The narrator of "The Lives of the Dead" thus seeks to keep his own friends alive through the art of storytelling. "As a writer now," he asserts,

> I want to save Linda's life. Not her body—her life [. . .] in a story I can steal her soul. I can revive, at least briefly, that which is absolute and unchanging [. . .] in a story, miracles can happen. Linda can smile and sit up. She can reach out, touch my wrist, and say, "Timmy, stop crying." (265)

Past, present, and future merge into one story as through fiction O'Brien zips "across the surface of [. . .] [his] own history, moving fast, riding the melt beneath the blades, doing loops and spins [. . .] as Tim trying to save Timmy's life with a story" (273). His story mirrors his own creative image of history, "a blade tracing loops on ice" (265), as his metafictive narrative circles on three levels: the war of a little boy's soul as he tries to understand the death of a friend, the Vietnam War of a twenty-three-year-old infantry sergeant, and the war of "guilt and sorrow" (265) faced by "a middle-aged writer" (265) who must deal with the past.

In focusing so extensively on the power of fiction and on what a war story is or is not in *The Things They Carried,* O'Brien writes a multidimensional war story even as he examines the process of writing one. His tales become stories within stories or multilayered texts within texts within texts. The book's genius is a seeming inevitability of form that perfectly embodies its theme—the miracle of vision—the eternally protean and volatile capacity of the imagination, which may invent that which it has the will and vision to conceive.[7] "In the end," the narrator states,

> a true war story is never about war. It's about sunlight. It's about the special way that dawn spreads out on a river when you know you must cross the river and march into the mountains and do things you are afraid to do. It's about love and memory. It's about sorrow. It's about sisters who never write back and people who never listen. (91)

How, then, can a true war story be told? Perhaps the best way, O'Brien says, is to "just keep on telling it" (91).

Works Cited

Bawer, Bruce. "Confession or Fiction? Stories from Vietnam." *Wall Street Journal* 215, 23 Mar 1990: A13.

Beidler, Philip D. *American Literature and the Experience of Vietnam.* Athens: U of Georgia P, 1982.

Christensen, Inger. *The Meaning of Metafiction.* Bergen: Universitetsforlaget, 1981.

Herr, Michael. *Dispatches.* New York: Vintage, 1977.

Lyons, Gene. "No More Bugles, No More Drums." *Entertainment Weekly* 23 Feb. 1990: 50–52.

Mehren, Elizabeth. "Short War Stories." *Los Angeles Times* 11 Mar. 1990: E1, E12.

Melmoth, John. "Muck and Bullets." *The Sunday Times* (London) 20 May 1990: H6.

Naparsteck, Martin. "An Interview with Tim O'Brien." *Contemporary Literature* 32 (Spring 1991): 1–11.

O'Brien, Tim. *The Things They Carried.* New York: Houghton, 1990.

Scholes, Robert. *Fabulation and Metafiction.* Urbana: U of Illinois P, 1983.

Schroeder, Eric James. "Two Interviews: Talks with Tim O'Brien and Robert Stone." *Modern Fiction Studies* 30 (Spring 1984): 135–64.

Waugh, Patricia. *Metafiction: The Theory and Practice of Self-Conscious Fiction.* New York: Methuen, 1984.

---

[7]This theme is also a main theme of *Going After Cacciato,* which examines issues such as how war affects the imagination and how the imagination affects war, how reality cannot be escaped, even in the imagination, how the imagination is used to invent rather than to discover, how the imagination must be used as a responsible tool, and how the imagination can be a force for remaking reality.

Getting It Right: The Short Fiction of Tim O'Brien[1]

Daniel Robinson

But it's true even if it didn't happen—

—Ken Kesey

In his introduction to *Men at War*, Ernest Hemingway states that a "writer's job is tell the truth. His standard of fidelity to the truth should be so high that his inventions [. . .] should produce a truer account than anything factual can be" (xi). Tim O'Brien, for whose writing the Vietnam War is the informing principle, returns to this notion of truth in his short fiction.[2] His stories revolve around multiple centers of interest—at once stories in the truest sense, with a core of action and character, and also metafictional stories on the precise nature of writing war stories.

For O'Brien, like Hemingway in his introduction, the notion of absolute fidelity to facts almost becomes a non sequitur when considering truth. Facts might provide a chronology of events (and even then, we may disagree on the validity of the facts), but alone they cannot reveal the hidden truths found in a true war story. As Hemingway writes, facts "can be observed badly; but when a good writer is creating something, he has time and scope to make of it an absolute truth" (xi–xii). That is also true for O'Brien: He sometimes writes stories that contradict the facts of other stories; yet the essential, underlying truth of each story is intact and illuminating. Those truths lie as much in the fragmented, impressionistic stories he tells as in the narrative technique he chooses for the telling. O'Brien does not deliver Vietnam in neatly packaged truisms. The same words that rang obscene for Frederic Henry in Hemingway's *A Farewell to Arms*, "abstract words such as glory, honor, courage, or hallow," become empty in O'Brien's fiction. Those words imply a rational order to war that does not exist, and the absence of those words mirrors the horror of a world at its most irrational. As O'Brien writes in "How to Tell a True War Story," "[O]ften in a true war story there is not even a point" (88). What O'Brien prefers are the images that make "the stomach believe" (89), images of men at war who are too afraid not to kill.

The true reasons that bring O'Brien's characters to Vietnam are far from the abstract words that Frederic Henry dismisses and equally far from the Hollywood notion of heroism so prevalent in war movies prior to American involvement in Vietnam. The average age of the company of foot soldiers O'Brien writes about is nineteen or twenty, and most were probably

---

[1] *Critique* 40.3 (Spring 1999) 257–64, Galileo, Academic Search Premier, 15 January 2002 <http://ehostvgw2.epnet.com>.

[2] In this essay, I consider only those stories of Tim O'Brien's that were previously published as separate short stories and are substantially different from any counterparts in later novels. Thus, I exclude stories that appeared in *Going After Cacciato* in much the same form as when they were published earlier as well as those stories in *The Things They Carried* that were not separately published.

drafted, as is the case of the fictional Tim O'Brien through whom author O'Brien often tells his stories. Thus, we see boys becoming men before they have had the opportunity to understand what manhood involves. And among the many things each soldier carried—the weapons, charms, diseases, and emotions—they "carried the soldier's greatest fear, which was the fear of blushing. Men killed, and died, because they were embarrassed not to" ("Things" 20–21). Even the enemy soldiers, the Viet Cong, exhibit that moral dichotomy and fight out of fear as much as nationalism:

> In the presence of his father and uncles, he pretended to look forward to doing his patriotic duty, which was also a privilege, but at night he prayed with his mother that the war might end soon. Beyond anything else, he was afraid of disgracing himself, and therefore his family and village. ("Man" 142)

However, quite different from most of O'Brien's characters driven by fear is Azar, the nineteen-year-old draftee who straps a puppy to a Claymore antipersonnel mine and blows the dog to pieces. Azar, still a teenager, loves Vietnam because it makes him "feel like a kid again." "The Vietnam experience," he says, "I mean, wow, I love this shit" ("Ghost" 237). O'Brien's characters choose war for entirely negative reasons, not for unselfish love of country or of basic freedoms but from fear of embarrassment and cowardice or the love of war as if it were a child's game. Even the decision to go to Vietnam is determined not through an examination of positive motives but, again, for negative reasons: "I would go to the war [. . .] because I was embarrassed not to. [. . .] I was a coward. I went to war" ("River" 63).

That inability in O'Brien's characters to establish a positive purpose in their reasons for going to war mirrors the historical ambiguities surrounding American involvement in Vietnam. Like the chaotic and morally ambiguous war they fight, O'Brien's characters are unsure of their purpose or even their actions. Azar explains blowing up the puppy as simple childish exuberance: "What's everybody so upset about? I mean, Christ, I'm just a boy" ("Spin" 40). After one of his men dies, "Lieutenant Jimmy Cross led his men into the village of Than Ke. They burned everything. They shot chickens and dogs, they trashed the village well, they called in artillery and watched the wreckage, then they marched for several hours through the hot afternoon" to a place where they set up camp for the night ("Things" 16). Those men act not from forethought but from some measure of selective emotion: Azar, the sadist, experiences delight from torturing the puppy and, in "The Ghost Soldiers," torture-prankstering a medic on guard duty who had nearly allowed another soldier to die through inaction; and the troop, following Lavender's sniper-death, razes the nearest village not for some strategic reason but out of an apparent need for revenge. The chauvinistic clichés that so often accompany patriotic fervor are missing. These characters have no center around which they can construct a reason for their involvement, and the only absolute is that resupply helicopters will arrive soon with more things for them to carry: For "all the ambiguities of Vietnam, all the mysteries and unknowns, there was at least the single abiding certainty that they would never be at a loss for things to carry" ("Things" 16).

As Lorrie Smith writes in "Disarming the War Story," "The 'story' of World War II [. . .]has meaning for our culture as a heroic quest, and it forms a coherent narrative in which the soldier's sacrifices are redemptive" (90). All of that coherence of purpose is lost in O'Brien's stories of Vietnam, as his characters stumble through a landscape of disjointed experiences and realities. And though we may, as Smith asserts, "feel acutely the disjunction between ideals and realities" (90) when we attempt to consider Vietnam in terms of heroic quests, coherent actions, and redemptive sacrifices, O'Brien's characters seldom articulate any distinctions. For them, the realities are too overpowering to place against any abstract notions based upon cultural and societal ideals. Only Lt. Jimmy Cross, in "The Things They Carried," and Tim,[3] in "On the Rainy River," consider that disjunction, and then only in personal terms, excluding any real notion of established codes.

One often expects writers of war stories to present antithetical abstractions in a concrete form to establish some moral or ethical base. O'Brien, however, fuses abstracts such as reality and surreality and right and wrong in an effort to emphasize the lack of firm moral ground supporting his characters in a war lacking in definable purposes. To stop his own pain at seeing his best friend blown up, Rat Kiley systematically dismembers a baby water buffalo by shooting pieces from its body—its mouth, tail, ears, nose—until all that remains alive and moving are its eyes. The reaction by Rat's stunned comrades is restrained amazement: "A new wrinkle. I never seen it before. [. . .] Well, that's Nam" (86). A group of Green Berets keep a pile of enemy bones stacked in a corner of their barracks underneath a sign that reads, "ASSEMBLE YOUR OWN GOOK!! FREE SAMPLE KIT!" ("Sweetheart" 119). That distillation of moral or ethical standards, an "aesthetic purity of moral indifference" ("True" 87), illustrates a general loss of humanity in any war, but possibly more so in a war that lacks any underlying absolutes, any real reasons for having gone to war. Thus the moral confusion Tim feels (in "On the Rainy River") after finding out he has been drafted becomes a moral indifference once exposed to the brutalities and absurdities of war.

Those apparent indifferences extend even to how the soldiers deal with the death of their comrades. When a man dies, he is not killed, but

---

[3]Any use of "Tim" in this essay refers to the fictional character, and the use of "O'Brien" refers to Tim O'Brien the author. In an interview with Steven Kaplan, O'Brien discusses the similarities and differences between him and his fictional character: "Everything I have written has come partly out of my own concerns [. . .] but the story lines themselves, the events [. . .] the characters [. . .] the places [. . .] are almost all invented. [. . .] Ninety percent or more of the material [. . .] is invented, and I invented ninety percent of a new Tim O'Brien, maybe even more than that" (95).

"greased. [. . .] offed, lit up, zapped." ("Things" 19). Somehow, by verbally denying the reality of death through hyperbolic misnomers, they reject the death itself. At one point in "The Lives of the Dead," Tim's unit enters a village it has calmly watched being bombed and burned by air strikes for thirty minutes. When the unit enters, the only person in the village is a dead old man who is missing an arm and whose face is covered by swarming flies and gnats. Each man, as he walks past the dead Vietnamese, offers a greeting and shakes the remaining hand: "How-dee-doo. [. . .] Gimme five.[. . .] A real honor.[. . .] Pleased as punch" (256). After Tim refuses to introduce himself or even offer a toast to the old man's health, he is ridiculed for not showing respect for his elders: "Maybe it's too real for you?" he is asked. "That's right," he replies. "Way too real" (256). It is only his fourth day, and Tim soon realizes that he must develop the cynical sense of humor he will eventually need to cope with the realities of death. Paul Berlin, on his first day in Vietnam, in "Where Have You Gone, Charming Billy?" watches one of his comrades die of a heart attack brought on by the fear of dying. In his attempt to deal with witnessing his first death, he tries to transform the event into something that had not happened. Eventually, however, as the realities of the experience eat at him, he places the death in comic terms by imagining the official death notification:

SORRY TO INFORM YOU THAT YOUR SON BILLY BOY WAS YESTERDAY SCARED TO DEATH IN ACTION IN THE REPUBLIC OF VIETNAM, VALIANTLY SUCCUMBING TO A HEART ATTACK SUFFERED WHILE UNDER ENORMOUS STRESS. [. . .] (130)

Berlin finally concludes that the death will make "a good joke" and "a funny war story" for his father (132). Not superficial male posturing, but overwhelming fear forces O'Brien's characters purposefully to detach themselves from death. They use any method possible, from keeping the dead alive through absurd ceremonial greetings to parodying government form letters to, as Albert Wilhelm writes, "keep the horrors of war at bay" (221).

Ironically, one of the deaths that breaks through the fabricated veneer of insulation is the death of an enemy in "The Man I Killed." In explicit detail bordering on the religious, Tim vividly recalls the man he killed—maybe the first man or maybe just the first he had an opportunity to study afterwards. Azar dismisses the death in the common distancing dialogue discussed above, "Oh, man, you fuckin' trashed the fucker. [. . .] You laid him out like Shredded fuckin' Wheat. [. . .] Rice Krispies, you know? On the dead test, this particular individual gets A-plus" (140); And Kiowa tries moving Tim beyond his dumbstruck staring at the bloody corpse to talk about his emotions. Only here and in "Speaking of Courage," where Norman Bowker, back home in Iowa on the Fourth of July, recounts the death of Kiowa in a swampy field, is the examination of death not covered under false layers of fear. O'Brien the writer must now dredge up those deaths that Tim the young soldier tried so hard to bury, which may explain why O'Brien returns to Vietnam in his fiction with such force and passion: he is reliving the horrors he suppressed decades earlier.

As in "The Man I Killed" and "Speaking of Courage," O'Brien often uses a spiraling narrative technique to draw out the realism of death, even if this characters continue to refute that death. O'Brien revolves those stories around a specific death, as Joseph Heller revolves the first part of *Catch–22* around Snowden's death, covering the same ground yet illuminating the moment's particular horror with each movement back to the death. The effect is at once numbing and oddly positive. We sense the overwhelming totality of death on the one hand, but we also imagine the narrator attempting to place a new order to his story, one that will somehow exclude the death. In "The Man I Killed," the effect is an increasing horror at seeing the dead man; whereas in "Speaking Of Courage," Norman realizes that he failed to save his friend's life. "The Things They Carried" revolves around the sniper death of Lavender, and in so doing shows Lt. Jimmy Cross's movement from the innocence of his insular world in which, to keep the war at a distance, he pretends that a girl back home in the United States is in love with him. However, with Lavender's death, he must face the reality that his lack of focus in leading his men may in part have caused that death. As many initiations do, Cross's initiation into the realities surrounding him results also in his need to destroy something of his past, which he does when he burns Martha's letters and photographs.

Kiowa's death becomes the center point for Norman Bowker in "Speaking of Courage" and is also the death around which the action revolves in "In the Field." Ironically, here two other soldiers feel the responsibility for Kiowa's death, which adds an interesting layer of multiplicity of perception to O'Brien's stories. O'Brien further explores that notion of multiplicity of perception through Jimmy Cross's drafting a letter to Kiowa's parents. His first draft places blame on some ubiquitous "They" who sent him and his men to bivouac in a tactically indefensible position; in his second draft, he accepts the blame; and finally, he revises the letter to express "an officer's condolences. No apologies necessary" (197–98). All three drafts are accurate and true, underscoring the inability to write about war in absolute terms.

O'Brien's cyclical pattern that places death as the center point around which many of his stories revolve reinforces a permanence to war that a more linear narrative structure would necessarily exclude. O'Brien's characters cannot leave the deaths behind them and trudge on through a strictly chronological story. "The bad stuff," O'Brien writes in "Spin," "never stops happening: it lives in its own dimension, replaying itself over and over" (36). And even when the war is over, it is not over; even though "the war occurred half a lifetime ago, [. . .] the remembering makes it now" (40). So the cyclical pattern established in many of these stories continues to revolve long after the story stops, and the things they carried during the war become eclipsed by the things they carry following the war.

The deaths, of course, form the most visually unforgettable parts of O'Brien's stories. They are, first of all, not Hollywood war deaths: They are not scripted to show grace under pressure or to elevate the human reaction to the horrors of war. O'Brien's characters do not die filled with the notions of courage, honor, and camaraderie: they just die. Ted Lavender dies while zipping up his pants after urinating on a bus; Kiowa dies from drowning in the muddy human filth of a village's sewage field; Billy Boy Watkins dies of a heart attack brought on by the fear of dying after stepping on a land mine; Lemon dies from stepping on a land mine while playing an innocent game of catch and is literally blown into a nearby tree; and Jorgenson, who dies after eluding enemy patrols and taking a midnight swim, swallows bad water. None of the deaths are the deaths of heroes; and like the ritualized shooting of the water buffalo following Lemon's death, they serve to show a major theme connecting O'Brien's work—how isolated events of cruelty define war. Azar killing the puppy, Bowker shooting the water buffalo, a little girl dancing to an unheard rhythm outside her burned-out hut following a napalm raid, the first enemy killed, and the singular deaths of friends accrue as acts of cruelty to, as O'Brien says, "touch [the] reader's heart more than a grandiose description of the fire bombing of a village, or the napalming of a village, where you don't see corpses, you don't know the corpses, you don't witness the death in any detail. It is somehow made abstract, bloodless" (Kaplan 102). By focusing on the character—the individual coming in close contact with what death looks like—and allowing the surrounding scenes and events to take secondary importance, O'Brien increases the absurdity and horror. His plots are determined not by incident and event, but by the changing moral attitudes and development of his characters.

Likewise, "declarations about war, such as war is hell" (Kaplan 101) or war is immoral seem, in O'Brien's fiction, just as hollow as the declarations of war that place men in battle. These declarations, while possibly true, are little more than abstract generalities that fail to turn something deep within the reader. "A true war story," as O'Brien wrote, "if truly told, makes the stomach believe" (84). A true war story, then, may not have a point, and it certainly does not exist in the narrative vacuum of beginning-middle-end, but it functions at a level of truth beyond that found in the story's words. Often, you doubt whether an O'Brien story can be true. Can a man actually transport his girlfriend to an isolated medical post in the Central Highlands and then lose her to the war as she slowly matriculates into the jungle? Some things, Pederson says in "Keeping Watch by Night," "you just see and you got to believe in what you see" (66). A true war story has no moral, no instruction, no virtue, no suggestion of proper behavior; there is only a revelation of the possible evil in the nature of man: "You can tell a true war story," O'Brien tells us, "by its absolute and uncompromising allegiance to obscenity and evil" ("True" 76). True war stories, as O'Brien writes in his nonfiction narrative *If I Die in a Combat Zone,* offer "simple, unprofound scraps of truth" that lack any lessons to teach about war. The writer, then, according to O'Brien, must "simply tell stories" (32). However, within that apparent lack of pretense to message lies the phenomenological truths of O'Brien's fiction, which strike much deeper than, as Lorrie Smith writes, an exploitation of "war's larger political implications" (94). By suppressing the abstract in favor of the concrete, O'Brien allows his stories to exist as commentary through the "complex tangles and nuances of actual experience" (Calloway 222).

Beyond that, moreover, as O'Brien tells Steven Kaplan, "good stories somehow have to do with an awakening into a new world, something new and true, where someone is jolted out of [. . .] complacency and forced to confront a new set of circumstances or a new self " (99). The archetypal pattern that O'Brien here alludes to of initiation into the complexities of the real world forms an underlying basis of much of O'Brien's fiction. Paul Berlin's witnessing Billy Boy's death signals his loss of innocence, his transition into manhood, and an unwelcome realization of the world's potential for cruelty. And Tim, who may realize that his only options are kill or be killed, cannot be comforted by that knowledge as his world of relative innocence is shattered by the realities of this new world he inhabits. Correspondingly, that separation between men and boys is also shown by the physical appearance of the soldiers as they trudge along under the weight of all they carry: "The most recent arrivals had pasty skin burnt at the shoulder blades and clavicle and neck; their boots were not yet red with clay, and they walked more carefully than the rest, and they looked more vulnerable" ("Spin" 36). As their appearance evolves and their movements change, so, too, their character changes in the "effort to establish a new order" to their life (Kaplan 99)—one in which the vulnerability of youth is replaced by the cynicism and hardness of manhood.

That also may be why O'Brien still returns to Vietnam in his fiction— because he is still trying to make sense of the new order established in his life over twenty years ago. In his stories, in the futile attempt to regain what he had before the war, he can still dream alive the people who died; unfortunately, though, that also necessitates his reliving their deaths. That need may be what still hits O'Brien: "twenty years later, in your sleep, and you wake up and shake your wife and start telling the story to her, except when you get to the end you've forgotten the point again. And then for a long time you lie there watching the story happen in your head. You listen to your wife's breathing. The war's over. You close your eyes. You smile and think, Christ, what's the point?" ("True" 88–89). The point, however, is all in the telling, as is the healing. In his stories, O'Brien answers his characters' desire to make sense out of their experiences: Kiowa imploring Tim to just talk after killing an enemy soldier instead of dumbly staring at the corpse, or Rat Kiley—not wanting to have to listen to the silence of the night—asking Kiowa to tell once again how Lavender fell like a sack of cement, or the platoon waiting once more for Rat to tell his story about the sweetheart of Song Tra Bong. O'Brien's characters, like O'Brien himself, carry their stories with them, sometimes damning the unimaginable weight of relived experience and sometimes extolling the outlet allowed through storytelling, which becomes at times a life-support system and a salvation from the moral complexities of the war.

Those moral complexities required of O'Brien "an innovative form rather than the conventional chronological narrative" (Slabey 206). In presenting stories from a war that lacked a traditional progression or a logical structure, O'Brien demands more from his writing than strict realism can provide. He blurs the distinctions in his stories to present truths coalesced in memory and imagination to, "get things right"—not in the absolute terms of packaged truisms and simplistic judgments but through the inner landscape of experiential truth telling.

Works Cited

Beidler, Philip D. *Re-Writing America: Vietnam Authors in Their Generation.* Athens: U Georgia P, 1991.

Calloway, Catherine. "Pluralities of Vision: *Going After Cacciato* and *Tim O'Brien's* Short Fiction." Gilman and Smith 213–22.

Gilman, Owen W., and Lorrie Smith. *America Rediscovered: Critical Essays on Literature and Film of the Vietnam War.* New York: Garland, 1990.

Kaplan, Steven. "An Interview with *Tim O'Brien.*" *Missouri Review* 14.3 (1991): 95–108.

O'Brien, Tim. "The Ghost Soldiers." O'Brien, *Things* 215–44.

———. "How to Tell a True War Story." O'Brien, *Things* 73–92.

———. "In the Field." O'Brien, *Things* 183–200.

———. "Keeping Watch by Night." *Redbook* 148 (Dec. 1976) 65–67.

———. "The Lives of the Dead." O'Brien, *Things* 253–73.

———. "The Man I Killed." O'Brien, *Things* 137–44.

———. "On the Rainy River." O'Brien, *Things* 41–64.

———. "Speaking of Courage." O'Brien, *Things* 155–74.

———. "Spin." O'Brien, *Things* 33–40.

———. "Style." O'Brien, *Things* 151–54.

———. "Sweetheart of Song Tra Bong." O'Brien, *Things* 99–126.

———. "The Things They Carried." O'Brien, *Things* 1–26.

———. *The Things They Carried.* New York: Penguin, 1991.

———. "Where Have You Gone, Charming Billy?" *Redbook* 145 (May 1975) 81, 127–32.

Slabey, Robert M. "*Going After Cacciato:* Tim O'Brien's 'Separate Peace.'" Gilman and Smith 205–11.

Smith, Lorrie. "Disarming the War Story." Gilman and Smith 87–99.

Wilhelm, Albert. "Ballad Allusions in Tim O'Brien's 'Where Have You Gone, Charming Billy?'" *Studies in Short Fiction* 28.2 (Spring 1991): 218–22.

Dreams of Truth, Reality, and War

Nick Hembree

1   Tim O'Brien seamlessly blends fact and fiction in his stories set in the Vietnam conflict, weaving a horridly beautiful tapestry of war and of life. He creates truths that transcend what is and what is not, and in his own words, "[w]hat stories can do, I guess, is make things present" ("Good Form" 990). Many critics of his work agree that his masterful storytelling ability confers some special sense of what it was like to be there, deep in the foggy mountains and torrid jungles of Vietnam. Catherine Calloway says, "Clearly O'Brien resists a simplistic classification of his latest work [The Things They Carried]" (1002), and Daniel Robinson comments, "[Tim O'Brien] sometimes writes stories that contradict the facts of other stories; yet the essential underlying truth of each story is intact and illuminating" (1009).

2   As O'Brien himself often repeats throughout his works, there are no morals to his stories—only truths. A moral is a simple truism that can be applied to a limited situation; a truth, on the other hand, allows those who understand it properly to be more aware of the nature of humanity. With that idea in mind, O'Brien probes deeply into his own inner psyche in "On the Rainy River," delving deeply into powerful emotional currents that sweep past all of the thoughts and ideals that he has tried to construct around them. He begins the story with an explanation of why he has never told this particular tale to anyone before:

> To go into it, I always thought, would only cause
> embarrassment for all of us, a sudden need to be
> elsewhere, which is the natural response to a
> confession [. . .] For nearly twenty years I've had to
> live with it, feeling the shame, trying to push it away,

and so by this act of remembrance, by putting the
facts down on paper, I hope to relieve at least some of
the pressure of my dreams. (963)

This passage gives the reader some small idea of how
profoundly O'Brien's acts in the story have affected even his
present day life. The price of cowardice to one's self is one not
easily repaid, as O'Brien discovers from the events of his past.
Morally and intellectually against the fighting in Vietnam, Tim
O'Brien has found himself suddenly with a draft notice and
having finally to come to grips with who he is and what he is
personally going to do about the war, yet indecision is the only
solution he can come up with, and "[b]eyond all this, or at the
very center, was the raw fact of terror" (965), the terror of
facing death for a reason that cannot be understood or believed
in. Eventually, O'Brien heads north in a vain attempt to escape
his reality, only to find the Canadian border, and the ultimate
need to make a decision to run from the war or to take a part
in it. At the very end of the story, the choice is made: "[e]ven in
my imagination, the shore [of Canada] just twenty yards away,
I couldn't make myself be brave. It had nothing to do with
morality. Embarrassment, that's all it was" (973-74). It is nice
to believe in ideals of what is right and what is wrong, but in
the end, sometimes we simply do what our overwhelming
internal forces drive us to, for better or for worse. Tim O'Brien
would likely argue for the worst, yet the past has already been,
and we can only take care of the present.

3   Of all his stories, "On the Rainy River" rings with the clearest
sound of fact, yet this is not always the case with O'Brien's

writings. In fact, one of his greatest attributes as a writer is his excellent use of metafiction, drawing the reader's attention to a fundamental truth that might otherwise be missed. All throughout the story "How to Tell a True War Story," in <u>The Things They Carried</u>, O'Brien repeats the account of how Curt Lemon came to die: "he must've thought it was the sunlight killing him. It was not the sunlight. It was a rigged 105 round" (984). Every time he repeats the story, it comes a small step closer to a truth, becoming more full with the telling, yet also becoming less believable. Rat Kiley, a friend of Curt, writes to his sister after he dies, expressing his love and anguish for Curt, yet the "dumb cooze" never writes back, despite Rat's pouring his heart out into the letter. The reader later learns that Curt is the same man who trick-or-treated completely nude (save only his boots and gun) in a small Vietnamese village, and he is also the same man who traipses about the jungle, as if on a school field trip instead of a military mission. Later on, after Curt's death, Rat mercilessly tortures a water buffalo, shooting it in various places and watching it collapse, as all of his fellow soldiers sit back and watch, sickened at the display, yet simply letting it pass. Finally, O'Brien tells of how whenever he tells this particular story, someone will always come up and say to him how touching it was and that he should also move on with his life, but "[a]ll you can do is tell it one more time, patiently, adding and subtracting, making up a few things to get at the real truth [. . .] No Lemon, no Rat Kiley. No trail junction. No baby buffalo" (985). Simply telling the facts can be a poor way of getting people to understand what the speaker is trying to tell them; rather, it is when he changes the way that he tells a story, the exact details of it, that he can more easily allow people to understand truth, and not simple truisms or facts.

4   Yet another technique that O'Brien uses in his writings is that
of complete focus upon one thing all throughout a story, such as
in "The Man I Killed," as well as a complete rejection of the facts
to his readers, making them completely uncertain that the story
has any factual base yet at the same time, reinforcing the abstract
idea behind the story. In "The Man I Killed," O'Brien begins with
telling the physical details of a dead body lying on a trail, a man
stripped of his very life, moving on to personal details of the
Vietnamese youth that he could not possibly know, such as where
he was born, where he went to school, who his fiancée was.
Throughout the story, a mental image of what the youth was like
slowly collects in the reader's mind: "He was not a fighter. His
health was poor, his body small and frail. He liked books. He
wanted someday to be a teacher of mathematics" (986-87). There is
nothing especially evil about the youth, as he was not unlike
O'Brien himself, afraid of war, but more afraid to fight tradition
and ridicule; nevertheless, he has been killed, and O'Brien sits and
ponders the death of the youth, wondering who the young
Vietnamese boy was, what his future might have been. However,
in another short story in <u>The Things They Carried</u>, O'Brien
refutes the fact that the incident ever occurred, yet at the same
time making it clear that the story-truth is more real than the
happening-truth:

> Here is the happening-truth. I was once a soldier.
> There were many bodies, real bodies with real faces,
> but I was young then and I was afraid to look. And
> now, twenty years later, I'm left with faceless
> responsibility and faceless grief.
>
> Here is the story-truth. He was a slim, dead, almost
> dainty young man of about twenty. He lay in the center

of a red clay trail near the village of My Khe. His jaw was in his throat. His one eye was shut, the other eye was a star-shaped hole. I killed him. ("Good Form" 990)

O'Brien manages again to twist reality and fiction into something more real than either, and transcending both, reaching for some celestial absolute that tantalizes the mind.

5   Tim O'Brien's use of fiction and storytelling is a work of genius, extracting and manipulating its reader's thoughts and feelings in an incredibly powerful way. His stories do not have morals; as he says in "How to Tell a True War Story": "A true war story is never moral. It does not instruct, nor encourage virtue, nor suggest models of proper human behavior, nor restrain men from doing the things that men have always done" (976). A good story merely tells truth, and O'Brien has done the job elegantly in his savagely beautiful <u>The Things They Carried</u>, a book that should be read by anyone who wants to understand better the workings of the human mind under the stresses of war and conflict, be they physical, mental, or emotional.

Works Cited

Calloway, Catherine. "'How To Tell a True War Story': Metafiction in the Things They Carried." <u>Critique</u> 36.4 (Summer 1995): 249ff. Henderson, Day, and Waller. 1001-008.

Henderson, Gloria Mason, Bill Day, and Sandra Stevenson Waller. <u>Literature and Ourselves</u>. 4th ed. New York: Longman, 2003.

O'Brien, Tim. "Good Form." <u>The Things They Carried</u>. New York: Broadway Books, 1990. Henderson, Day, and Waller. 989-90.

- - -. "How to Tell a True War Story." <u>The Things They Carried</u>. New York: Broadway Books, 1990. Henderson, Day, and Waller. 975-85.

O'Brien, Tim. "The Man I Killed." <u>The Things They Carried</u>. New York: Broadway Books, 1990. Henderson, Day, and Waller. 986-89.

---. "On the Rainy River." <u>The Things They Carried</u>. New York: Broadway Books, 1990. Henderson, Day, and Waller. 963-74.

Robinson, Daniel. "Getting It Right: The Short Fiction of Tim O'Brien." <u>Critique</u> 40.3 (Spring 1999): 257-64. Henderson, Day, and Waller. 1009-016.

Suggestions for Exploration and Writing

1. If you have been in a war or in a confrontational situation comparable to war, write a war story that is "true," according to O'Brien's criteria.

2. Write an essay analyzing a situation in which "story-truth" is truer than "happening-truth."

3. Discuss in detail a situation where you felt responsible for a wrong you did not commit.

4. The men in O'Brien's stories have both extraordinary restrictions on their freedom and simultaneously the freedom to commit acts they would never consider at home. In a researched essay, using O'Brien's stories, analyze how war changes men's sense of freedom and responsibility.

5. Write an argumentative essay assessing responsibility for the brutal violence the men commit.

6. Using the stories and critical essays, write a researched essay arguing the truth of the narrator's assertion that "the truths [about war] are contradictory."

7. The narrator says of war, "The old rules are no longer binding, the old truths no longer hold true. Right spills over into wrong." Develop this idea in an essay.

Freedom and Responsibility: Suggestions for Writing

1. Using one selection from this unit, discuss how the author shows the delicate balance between freedom and responsibility.

2. Choose one short story from this section and relate what that work says about the responsibilities a person has to others in society.

3. When is a person obligated to disobey government regulations or laws? Using at least one work from this section, write an essay answering this question.

4. Select one of the stories in this unit and defend the protagonist's decision to defy or to obey the government.

5. Use one or more of the works in this unit to discuss how one's responsibilities change during a lifetime.

6. From your own experience or knowledge, explain how one's own freedom may be limited by the obligation to allow others to be free.

7. Write an essay describing the responsibilities to others that members of a civilized and organized society are expected to fulfill. Or write an essay describing the results, in the United States or in another country, of a failure to fulfill such responsibilities.

8. In an essay, discuss the ways in which individuals let their desire to be accepted limit their freedom.

Freedom and Responsibility: Writing about Film

1. The Western movie genre is often concerned with themes of freedom and responsibility. In fact, the western frontier was metaphor for a land where a man (rarely a woman) could be free and discover his true nature. View a classic Western made between 1938 and 1958 (*Stagecoach, Drums Along the Mohawk, The Man Who Shot Liberty Valence, My Darling Clementine, Red River, High Noon, The Searchers*). Then watch a contemporary Western (*Unforgiven, Black Robe, Dances with Wolves, Lone Star, The Last of the Mohicans*) and consider how the films from different periods reflect different cultural beliefs about freedom and responsibility in regard to the land, white "civilization," native and/or Hispanic people, cowboys, violence, and man/woman relationships.

2. An event that occurs in the plot of most American films is a choice made by the main character. This choice ultimately determines the outcome of the film and is central to determining the point of view of the film. Watch one or two films and see if you can locate the scene in which the character makes such a decision. Is it a reasoned choice or an emotional choice? How much control does the character have up to that point? after that point? In an essay, analyze the scene, explaining why it is or is not effectively presented. Have you ever experienced a similar choice-making/transformative event? If so, describe it in detail; if not, explain the difference between your real-life experience and the fictional story-world of the film.

Imagination
and Discovery

Charles Demuth, "Acrobats," 1919. The Museum of Modern Art,
New York.

One might broadly define art as an expression of the human imagination as it plays with various materials, called *media*, discovering new and intriguing collages of meaning. Such imaginative play is, paradoxically, serious business. Though we may think of work as serious and play as trivial, we often take play much more seriously than work and concentrate on play much more of our attention. We are often far more passionate about playing golf well or making the right cast with the right fly in the right spot to catch a trout or even about our favorite football team's latest victory than about anything we do at work. Art, then, the imagination in the process of discovery, is a particularly serious and concentrated form of play. It is also intensely pleasurable. In "Persimmons," for example, Li-Young Lee has great fun exploring the full implications of the word *persimmons* at the expense of his pedantic teacher.

So defined, art is for all of us, and we are all artists. As surely as in the painting by Renoir, the Beethoven played to dutifully hushed audience, the Shakespeare play delivered in resonant British tones, art is to be found in the street guitarist, the joke artfully told with perfect timing between (or even during) classes, the sinister makeup of Arnold Friend in Oates's "Where Are You Going, Where Have You Been?" and the graceful skating of Mr. Lacey in "Valentine." As Paul Theroux maintains, even so apparently passive an endeavor as travel, if accompanied by a delight in discovery, can be "a creative act" like "writing a novel." As Chinua Achebe shows in his essay "Africa and Her Writers," in most traditional cultures, art has been produced by and for people, not for an initiated elite. In the elaborate Yoruban art festival called *mbari*, Achebe finds art that embodies the heritage and values of, and that is produced for and even in a sense by, a whole people. The great twentieth-century Irish poet W. B. Yeats longed for a similar communal mythology that could integrate his art with the practical and religious life of his people.

Because it balances both inner experience and outer experience, both the human imagination and the world it discovers, art raises profound questions about the nature of truth, the essence of reality. Arnold Friend's makeup, for example, while intended as a kind of disguise, simultaneously reveals much about his character. Does he actually visit Connie? Or does she simply imagine their encounter? If he is simply a product of her imagination, is her experience any less real or true? Similar questions might be asked about Erin's encounter with Mr. Lacey in "Valentine." In Woody Allen's hilarious story "The Kugelmass Episode," the line between fiction and reality is obscured as Kugelmass enters the fictional world of

Gustave Flaubert's *Madame Bovary* to have an affair with the title character. So powerful is the human imagination that art may even threaten to consume the reader, as it does at the end of Allen's story and in Ishmael Reed's "beware : do not read this poem."

As Tim O'Brien's narrator in "How to Tell a True War Story" insists, the truth of art, empowered by the imagination, does not depend on factual accuracy. Art is free to render a higher kind of truth, a truth that transcends the mere phenomena of fact.

Writing about Imagination and Discovery

If you are asked to write about the theme of Imagination and Discovery, you might begin by asking yourself about the nature of reality. Several of the works in this section use science fiction or fantasy to explore the nature of truth. You might choose to explore what Ray Bradbury is implying about our present by showing us one version of the future in "There Will Come Soft Rains," or you might ask what Mark Bourne is saying about human nature as he describes people who fill their lives primarily with vicarious experiences. Obviously you are not limited to the modern works in exploring this theme; one of the greatest examples of the use of fantasy to portray reality is Shakespeare's *The Tempest*. You might use this play to write about fantastic characters such as Ariel or Caliban, or you might examine the character of Prospero, theorizing about the qualities that allow him to acquire magical powers and then to renounce them without taking revenge on those who have harmed him.

Another aspect of imagination and discovery involves the creation of literary works. You might use the works in this unit to form a definition of a literary genre. If you choose to describe poetry, you might use Archibald MacLeish's "Ars Poetica" as a starting point, or you might examine what Billy Collins is saying about poetry in his poems and analyze Lawrence Ferlinghetti's description of what it means to be a poet in "Constantly Risking Absurdity." Or you might ask what qualities of poetry allow John Keats to explore the meaning of beauty in his "Ode on a Grecian Urn."

When Kim Prevett was assigned a documented essay using the casebook on Joyce Carol Oates, she first read the two stories. She decided to write her essay before reading what other writers said about the stories because she did not want the other essays to influence her own interpretation. She was having difficulty deciding what to write about until she noticed the many parallels in the two stories. Once she had decided to compare these similarities, she wrote the body paragraphs of her essay. When the first draft was finished, she read the critical essays. In these she found several ideas that paralleled or illustrated some of her points, and she selected several quotations to add to her essay. Like many other writers, Kim found the introductory and concluding paragraphs much more difficult to write. For help with the introduction, she went to a biography of Oates, where she found a quotation that made an effective contribution. She asked her professor for help with ideas for the conclusion, finally deciding to stress the dreamlike qualities and the mystery and horror mentioned in her introduction. Before submitting her essay, Kim checked to make sure that her quotations were accurate and that her paraphrases reflected the authors' ideas without quoting them. Her final essay is included at the end of the Oates casebook.

E S S A Y S

Frederick Douglass (c. 1817–1895)

Frederick Douglass grew up as a slave in Maryland. In spite of his enslavement, he learned to read and write and became a powerful speaker and debator. Escaping slavery in 1838, he fled to Massachusetts, where he began to speak out for abolition. Fearing capture as a fugitive slave, he fled in 1845 to England, where he spoke not only for abolition of slavery but also for women's suffrage, Irish home rule, and prison reform. After English friends bought his freedom, he returned to the United States in 1847 and founded the North Star, *an abolitionist paper, which he edited until the end of the Civil War. After the Civil War, he served as U.S. Marshall in the District of Columbia and as minister to Haiti. He published his autobiography,* Narrative of the Life of Frederick Douglass, *in 1845.*

FROM *MY BONDAGE AND MY FREEDOM* (1855)

1   The frequent hearing of my mistress reading the bible—for she often read aloud when her husband was absent—soon awakened my curiosity in respect to this *mystery* of reading, and roused in me the desire to learn. Having no fear of my kind mistress before my eyes, (she had then given me no reason to fear,) I frankly asked her to teach me to read; and, without hesitation, the dear woman began the task, and very soon, by her assistance, I was master of the alphabet, and could spell words of three or four letters. My mistress seemed almost as proud of my progress, as if I had been her own child; and, supposing that her husband would be as well pleased, she made no secret of what she was doing for me. Indeed, she exultingly told him of the aptness of her pupil, of her intention to persevere in teaching me, and of the duty which she felt it to teach me, at least to read *the bible*. Here arose the first cloud over my Baltimore prospects, the precursor of drenching rains and chilling blasts.

2   Master Hugh was amazed at the simplicity of his spouse, and, probably for the first time, he unfolded to her the true philosophy of slavery, and the peculiar rules necessary to be observed by masters and mistresses, in the management of their human chattels. Mr. Auld promptly forbade continuance of her instruction; telling her, in the first place, that the thing itself was unlawful; that it was also unsafe, and could only lead to mischief. To use his own words, further, he said, "if you give a nigger an inch, he will take an ell;" "he should know nothing but the will of his master, and learn to obey it." "if you teach that nigger—speaking of myself—how to read the bible, there will be no keeping him;" "it would forever unfit him for the duties of a slave;" and "as to himself, learning would do him no good, but probably, a great deal of harm—making him

disconsolate and unhappy." "If you learn him now to read, he'll want to know how to write; and, this accomplished, he'll be running away with himself." Such was the tenor of Master Hugh's oracular exposition of the true philosophy of training a human chattel; and it must be confessed that he very clearly comprehended the nature and the requirements of the relation of master and slave. His discourse was the first decidedly antislavery lecture to which it had been my lot to listen. Mrs. Auld evidently felt the force of his remarks; and, like an obedient wife, began to shape her course in the direction indicated by her husband. The effect of his words, *on me*, was neither slight nor transitory. His iron sentences—cold and harsh—sunk deep into my heart, and stirred up not only my feelings into a sort of rebellion, but awakened within me a slumbering train of vital thought. It was a new and special revelation, dispelling a painful mystery, against which my youthful understanding had struggled, and struggled in vain, to wit: the *white* man's power to perpetuate the enslavement of the *black* man. "Very well," thought I; "knowledge unfits a child to be a slave." I instinctively assented to the proposition; and from that moment I understood the direct pathway from slavery to freedom. This was just what I needed; and I got it at a time, and from a source, whence I least expected it. I was saddened at the thought of losing the assistance of my kind mistress; but the information, so instantly derived, to some extent compensated me for the loss I had sustained in this direction. Wise as Mr. Auld was, he evidently underrated my comprehension, and had little idea of the use to which I was capable of putting the impressive lesson he was giving to his wife. *He* wanted me to be *a slave;* I had already voted against that on the home plantation of Col. Lloyd. That which he most loved I most hated; and the very determination which he expressed to keep me in ignorance, only rendered me the more resolute in seeking intelligence. In learning to read, therefore, I am not sure that I do not owe quite as much to the opposition of my master, as to the kindly assistance of my amiable mistress. I acknowledge the benefit rendered me by the one, and by the other; believing, that but for my mistress, I might have grown up in ignorance.

3   I lived in the family of Master Hugh, at Baltimore, seven years, during which time—as the almanac makers say of the weather—my condition was variable. The most interesting feature of my history here, was my learning to read and write, under somewhat marked disadvantages. In attaining this knowledge, I was compelled to resort to indirections by no means congenial to my nature, and which were really humiliating to me. My mistress—who, as the reader has already seen, had begun to teach me—was suddenly checked in her benevolent design, by the strong advice of her husband. In faithful compliance with this advice, the good lady had not only ceased to instruct me, herself, but had set her face as a flint against my learning to read by any means. It is due, however, to my mistress to say, that she did not adopt this course in all its stringency at the

first. She either thought it unnecessary, or she lacked the depravity indispensable to shutting me up in mental darkness. It was, at least, necessary for her to have some training, and some hardening, in the exercise of the slaveholder's prerogative, to make her equal to forgetting my human nature and character, and to treating me as a thing destitute of a moral or an intellectual nature. Mrs. Auld—my mistress—was, as I have said, a most kind and tender-hearted woman; and, in the humanity of her heart, and the simplicity of her mind, she set out, when I first went to live with her, to treat me as she supposed one human being ought to treat another.

4   It is easy to see, that, in entering upon the duties of a slaveholder, some little experience is needed. Nature has done almost nothing to prepare men and women to be either slaves or slaveholders. Nothing but rigid training, long persisted in, can perfect the character of the one or the other. One cannot easily forget to love freedom; and it is as hard to cease to respect that natural love in our fellow creatures. On entering upon the career of a slaveholding mistress, Mrs. Auld was singularly deficient; nature, which fits nobody for such an office, had done less for her than any lady I had known. It was no easy matter to induce her to think and to feel that the curly-headed boy, who stood by her side, and even leaned on her lap; who was loved by little Tommy, and who loved little Tommy in turn; sustained to her only the relation of a chattel. I was *more* than that, and she felt me to be more than that. I could talk and sing; I could laugh and weep; I could reason and remember; I could love and hate. I was human, and she, dear lady, knew and felt me to be so. How could she, then, treat me as a brute, without a mighty struggle with all the noble powers of her own soul. That struggle came, and the will and power of the husband was victorious. Her noble soul was overthrown; but, he that overthrew it did not, himself, escape the consequences. He, not less than the other parties, was injured in his domestic peace by the fall.

5   When I went into their family, it was the abode of happiness and contentment. The mistress of the house was a model of affection and tenderness. Her fervent piety and watchful uprightness made it impossible to see her without thinking and feeling— *"that woman is a Christian."* There was no sorrow nor suffering for which she had not a tear, and there was no innocent joy for which she did not a smile. She had bread for the hungry, clothes for the naked, and comfort for every mourner that came within her reach. Slavery soon proved its ability to divest her of these excellent qualities, and her home of its early happiness. Conscience cannot stand much violence. Once thoroughly broken down, *who* is he that can repair the damage? It may be broken toward the slave, on Sunday, and toward the master on Monday. It cannot endure such shocks. It must stand entire, or it does not stand at all. If my condition waxed bad, that of the family waxed not better. The first step, in the wrong direction, was the violence done to nature and to conscience, in arresting the benevolence that would have enlightened my young mind. In ceasing to instruct me, she must begin to justify herself *to* herself; and, once consenting to

take sides in such a debate, she was riveted to her position. One needs very little knowledge of moral philosophy, to see *where* my mistress now landed. She finally became even more violent in her opposition to my learning to read, than was her husband himself. She was not satisfied with simply doing as *well* as her husband had commanded her, but seemed resolved to better his instruction. Nothing appeared to make my poor mistress—after her turning toward the downward path—more angry, than seeing me, seated in some nook or corner, quietly reading a book or a newspaper. I have had her rush at me, with the utmost fury, and snatch from my hand such newspaper or book, with something of the wrath and consternation which a traitor might be supposed to feel on being discovered in a plot by some dangerous spy.

6   Mrs. Auld was an apt woman, and the advice of her husband, and her own experience, soon demonstrated, to her entire satisfaction, that education and slavery are incompatible with each other. When this conviction was thoroughly established, I was most narrowly watched in all my movements. If I remained in a separate room from the family for any considerable length of time, I was sure to be suspected of having a book, and was at once called upon to give an account of myself. All this, however, was entirely *too late*. The first, and never to be retraced, step had been taken. In teaching me the alphabet, in the days of her simplicity and kindness, my mistress had given me the *"inch,"* and now, no ordinary precaution could prevent me from taking the *"ell."*

7   Seized with a determination to learn to read, at any cost, I hit upon many expedients to accomplish the desired end. The plea which I mainly adopted, and the one by which I was most successful, was that of using my young white playmates, with whom I met in the street, as teachers. I used to carry, almost constantly, a copy of Webster's spelling book in my pocket; and, when sent on errands, or when play time was allowed me, I would step, with my young friends, aside, and take a lesson in spelling. I generally paid my *tuition fee* to the boys, with bread, which I also carried in my pocket. For a single biscuit, any of my hungry little comrades would give me a lesson more valuable to me than bread. Not every one, however, demanded this consideration, for there were those who took pleasure in teaching me, whenever I had a chance to be taught by them. I am strongly tempted to give the names of two or three of those little boys, as a slight testimonial of the gratitude and affection I bear them, but prudence forbids; not that it would injure me, but it might, possibly, embarrass them; for it is almost an unpardonable offense to do any thing, directly or indirectly, to promote a slave's freedom, in a slave state. It is enough to say, of my warm-hearted little play fellows, that they lived on Philpot street, very near Durgin & Bailey's shipyard.

8   Although slavery was a delicate subject, and very cautiously talked about among grown up people in Maryland, I frequently talked about it—and that very freely—with the white boys. I would, sometimes, say to them, while seated on a curb stone or a cellar door, "I wish I could be free, as you will be when you get to be men." "You will be free, you know, as

soon as you are twenty-one, and can go where you like, but I am a slave for life. Have I not as good a right to be free as you have?" Words like these, I observed, always troubled them; and I had no small satisfaction in wringing from the boys, occasionally, that fresh and bitter condemnation of slavery, that springs from nature, unseared and unperverted. Of all consciences let me have those to deal with which have not been bewildered by the cares of life. I do not remember ever to have met with a *boy*, while I was in slavery, who defended the slave system; but I have often had boys to console me, with the hope that something would yet occur, by which I might be made free. Over and over again, they have told me, that "they believed *I* had as good a right to be free as *they* had;" and that "they did not believe God ever made any one to be a slave." The reader will easily see, that such little conversations with my play fellows, had no tendency to weaken my love of liberty, nor to render me contented with my condition as a slave.

9   When I was about thirteen years old, and had succeeded in learning to read, every increase of knowledge, especially respecting the FREE STATES, added something to the almost intolerable burden of the thought—"I AM A SLAVE FOR LIFE." To my bondage I saw no end. It was a terrible reality, and I shall never be able to tell how sadly that thought chafed my young spirit. Fortunately, or unfortunately, about this time in my life, I had made enough money to buy what was then a very popular school book, viz: the *Columbian Orator.* I bought this addition to my library, of Mr. Knight, on Thames street, Fell's Point, Baltimore, and paid him fifty cents for it. I was first led to buy this book, by hearing some little boys say they were going to learn some little pieces out of it for the Exhibition. This volume was, indeed, a rich treasure, and every opportunity afforded me, for a time, was spent in diligently perusing it. Among much other interesting matter, that which I had perused and reperused with unflagging satisfaction, was a short dialogue between a master and his slave. The slave is represented as having been recaptured, in a second attempt to run away; and the master opens the dialogue with an upbraiding speech, charging the slave with ingratitude, and demanding to know what he has to say in his own defense. Thus upbraided, and thus called upon to reply, the slave rejoins, that he knows how little anything that he can say will avail, seeing that he is completely in the hands of his owner; and with noble resolution, calmly says, "I submit to my fate." Touched by the slave's answer, the master insists upon his further speaking, and recapitulates the many acts of kindness which he has performed toward the slave, and tells him he is permitted to speak for himself. Thus invited to the debate, the quondam slave made a spirited defense of himself, and thereafter the whole argument, for and against slavery, was brought out. The master was vanquished at every turn in the argument; and seeing himself to be thus vanquished, he generously and meekly emancipates the slave, with his best wishes for his prosperity. It is scarcely necessary to say, that a dialogue, with such an origin, and such an ending—read when the fact of my being a slave was a constant burden of grief—powerfully affected me;

and I could not help feeling that the day might come, when the well-directed answers made by the slave to the master, in this instance, would find their counterpart in myself.

10   This, however, was not all the fanaticism which I found in this *Columbian Orator.* I met there one of Sheridan's mighty speeches, on the subject of Catholic Emancipation, Lord Chatham's speech on the American war, and speeches by the great William Pitt and by Fox. These were all choice documents to me, and I read them, over and over again, with an interest that was ever increasing, because it was ever gaining in intelligence; for the more I read them, the better I understood them. The reading of these speeches added much to my limited stock of language, and enabled me to give tongue to many interesting thoughts, which had frequently flashed through my soul, and died away for want of utterance. The mighty power and heart-searching directness of truth, penetrating even the heart of a slaveholder, compelling him to yield up his earthly interests to the claims of eternal justice, were finely illustrated in the dialogue, just referred to; and from the speeches of Sheridan, I got a bold and powerful denunciation of oppression, and a most brilliant vindication of the rights of man. Here was, indeed, a noble acquisition. If I ever wavered under the consideration, that the Almighty, in some way, ordained slavery, and willed my enslavement for his own glory, I wavered no longer. I had now penetrated the secret of all slavery and oppression, and had ascertained their true foundation to be in the pride, the power and the avarice of man. The dialogue and the speeches were all redolent of the principles of liberty, and poured floods of light on the nature and character of slavery. With a book of this kind in my hand, my own human nature, and the facts of my experience, to help me, I was equal to a contest with the religious advocates of slavery, whether among the whites or among the colored people, for blindness, in this matter, is not confined to the former. I have met many religious colored people, at the south, who are under the delusion that God requires them to submit to slavery, and to wear their chains with meekness and humility. I could entertain no such nonsense as this; and I almost lost my patience when I found any colored man weak enough to believe such stuff. Nevertheless, the increase of knowledge was attended with bitter, as well as sweet results. The more I read, the more I was led to abhor and detest slavery, and my enslavers. "Slaveholders," thought I, "are only a band of successful robbers, who left their homes and went into Africa for the purpose of stealing and reducing my people to slavery." I loathed them as the meanest and the most wicked of men. As I read, behold! the very discontent so graphically predicted by Master Hugh, had already come upon me. I was no longer the light-hearted, gleesome boy, full of mirth and play, as when I landed first at Baltimore. Knowledge had come; light had penetrated the moral dungeon where I dwelt; and, behold! there lay the bloody whip, for my back, and here was the iron chain; and my good, *kind master,* he was the author of my situation. The revelation haunted me, stung me, and made me gloomy and miserable. As I writhed under the

sting and torment of this knowledge, I almost envied my fellow slaves their stupid contentment. This knowledge opened my eyes to the horrible pit, and revealed the teeth of the frightful dragon that was ready to pounce upon me, but it opened no way for my escape. I have often wished myself a beast, or a bird—anything, rather than a slave. I was wretched and gloomy, beyond my ability to describe. I was too thoughtful to be happy. It was this everlasting thinking which distressed and tormented me; and yet there was no getting rid of the subject of my thoughts. All nature was redolent of it. Once awakened by the silver trump of knowledge, my spirit was roused to eternal wakefulness. Liberty! the inestimable birthright of every man, had, for me, converted every object into an asserter of this great right. It was heard in every sound, and beheld in every object. It was ever present, to torment me with a sense of my wretched condition. The more beautiful and charming were the smiles of nature, the more horrible and desolate was my condition. I saw nothing without seeing it, and I heard nothing without hearing it. I do not exaggerate, when I say, that it looked from every star, smiled in every calm, breathed in every wind, and moved in every storm.

11   I have no doubt that my state of mind had something to do with the change in the treatment adopted, by my once kind mistress toward me. I can easily believe, that my leaden, downcast, and discontented look, was very offensive to her. Poor lady! She did not know my trouble, and I dared not tell her. Could I have freely made her acquainted with the real state of my mind, and given her the reasons therefore, it might have been well for both of us. Her abuse of me fell upon me like the blows of the false prophet upon his ass; she did not know that an *angel* stood in the way; and—such is the relation of master and slave—I could not tell her. Nature had made us *friends;* slavery made us *enemies.* My interests were in a direction opposite to hers, and we both had our private thoughts and plans. She aimed to keep me ignorant; and I resolved to know, although knowledge only increased my discontent. My feelings were not the result of any marked cruelty in the treatment I received; they sprung from the consideration of my being a slave at all. It was *slavery*—not its mere *incidents*—that I hated. I had been cheated. I saw through the attempt to keep me in ignorance; I saw that slaveholders would have gladly made me believe that they were merely acting under the authority of God, in making a slave of me, and in making slaves of others; and I treated them as robbers and deceivers. The feeding and clothing me well, could not atone for taking my liberty from me. The smiles of my mistress could not remove the deep sorrow that dwelt in my young bosom. Indeed, these, in time, came only to deepen my sorrow. She had changed; and the reader will see that I had changed, too. We were both victims to the same overshadowing evil—*she,* as mistress, *I,* as slave. I will not censure her harshly; she cannot censure me, for she knows I speak but the truth, and have acted in my opposition to slavery, just as she herself would have acted, in a reverse of circumstances.

Questions for Discussion

1. Explain the significance of his mistress's teaching Douglass to read and write. Contrast her attitude with that of her husband, Mr. Auld. How does his opposition affect Douglas?

2. Describe the process by which Douglass learned the "direct pathway from slavery to freedom." How was Mr. Auld's lecture an abolitionist's lecture?

3. Using your answer to the above question, show how owning a slave affects Mrs. Auld.

4. What clever devices does Douglas employ in order to continue to learn?

5. Why aren't the white boys who teach Douglass believers in slavery?

6. Douglass says that he discovered the secret of slavery and oppression: "the pride, the power and the avarice of man." Explain why you agree or disagree.

7. What part did Douglass's understanding of the word "Liberty" play in his quest to read and write?

Suggestions for Exploration and Writing

1. Write an essay explaining one of the following statements by Douglass:

   "Knowledge unfits a child to be a slave."

   "Nature has done almost nothing to prepare men and women to be either slaves or slaveholders."

   "Nature had made us *friends;* slavery made us *enemies.*"

2. Douglass says that "rigid training, long persisted in" prepares "men and women to be either slaves or slaveholders." Do you agree? Explain your response in an essay.

3. Compare Douglass's opinions of slavery with those of Harriet Jacobs in the previous unit.

4. After reading Douglass and Jacobs, write an essay on the ways in which owning other people dehumanizes the owners.

Chinua Achebe (b. 1930)

Chinua Achebe, a Nigerian novelist and man of letters who writes in English, is among the most highly respected and influential contemporary African authors. Achebe's early novels, Things Fall Apart *(1959),* No Longer at Ease *(1962), and* Arrow of Gold *(1964), explore the conflict between traditional tribal customs and the European values introduced by colonists. His later novels,* A Man of the People *(1964) and* Anthills of the Savannah *(1988), expose the corruption and*

conflicts in postcolonial Nigerian politics. Morning Yet on Creation
Day *(1975), from which the following essay comes, is a collection of
essays on the search for a genuinely Nigerian voice in letters.*

AFRICA AND HER WRITERS (1975)

1   Some time ago, in a very testy mood, I began a lecture with these
words: *Art for art's sake is just another piece of deodorized dog shit.* Today, and
particularly in these sublime and hallowed precincts,[1] I should be quite
prepared to modify my language if not my opinion. In other words I will
still insist that art is, and was always, in the service of man. Our ancestors
created their myths and legends and told their stories for a human purpose (including, no doubt, the excitation of wonder and pure delight);
they made their sculptures in wood and terra cotta, stone and bronze to
serve the needs of their times. Their artists lived and moved and had their
being in society and created their works for the good of that society.

2   I have just used the word *good,* which no decent man uses in polite society these days, and must hasten to explain. By *good* I do not mean moral
uplift, although—why not?—that would be part of it; I mean *good* in the
sense in which God at the end of each day's work of putting the world
together saw that what He had made was good. Then, and only then, did
He count it a day's job. *Good* in that sense does not mean pretty.

3   In the beginning art was good and useful; it always had its airy and magical qualities, of course; but even the magic was often intended to minister to a basic human need, to serve a down-to-earth necessity, as when the
cavemen drew pictures on the rock of animals they hoped to kill in their
next hunt!

4   But somewhere in the history of European civilization the idea that art
should be accountable to no one, and needed to justify itself to nobody
except itself, began to emerge. In the end it became a minor god and its
devotees became priests urging all who are desirous to approach its altar
to banish entirely from their hearts and minds such doubts and questions
as *What use is this to me?* as the ultimate irreverence and profanation.
Words like *use, purpose, value* are beneath the divine concerns of this Art,
and so are we, the vulgarians craving the message and the morality. This
Art exists independently of us, of all mankind. Man and his world may
indeed pass away but not a jot from the laws of this Art.

5   Do I exaggerate? Perhaps a little, but not too much, I think. True,
Edgar Allan Poe's famous lecture, "The Poetic Principle," may not now
be the gospel it was to earlier generations, but the romantic idea of "the
poem written solely for the poem's sake" still exerts a curious fascination
on all kinds of people. I remember my surprise a few years ago at a conference of African writers when some obscure Rhodesian poet announced
solemnly that a good poem writes itself. I very rarely wish writers ill, but

---

[1]Eliot House, Harvard University.

that day I would have been happy if Shango had silenced that one with a nicely aimed thunderbolt and given his ghost the eternal joy of watching new poems surface onto his earthly notebook (or whatever he scribbled his verses on).

6   Strangely enough (or perhaps not so strangely—perhaps we should rather say, appropriately) there is from the same European mainspring another stream flowing down the slopes on the other side of the hill, watering a different soil and sustaining a different way of life. There, on these other slopes, a poet is not a poet until the Writers' Union tells him so. Between these two peoples, an acrimonious argument rages. Each side hurls invective over the hill into the other camp. *Monstrous philistines! Corrupt, decadent!* So loud and bitter does the recrimination become that it is often difficult to believe that these two peoples actually live on two slopes of the same hill.

7   Once upon a time (according to my own adaptation of a favorite Yoruba story), two farmers were working their farms on either side of a road. As they worked they made friendly conversation across the road. Then Eshu, god of fate and lover of confusion, decided to upset the state of peace between them. A god with a sharp and nimble imagination, he took his decision as quickly as lightning. He rubbed one side of his body with white chalk and the other side with charcoal and walked *up* the road with considerable flourish between the farmers. As soon as he passed beyond earshot the two men jumped from their work at the same time. And one said: "Did you notice that extraordinary white man who has just gone up the road?" In the same breath the other asked: "Did you see that incredible black man I have just seen?" In no time at all the friendly questions turned into a violent argument and quarrel, and finally into a fight. As they fought they screamed: *He was white! He was black!* After they had belabored themselves to their heart's content they went back to their farms and resumed their work in gloomy and hostile silence. But no sooner had they settled down than Eshu returned and passed with even greater flourish between them *down* the road. Immediately the two men sprang up again. And one said: "I am sorry, my good friend. You were right; the fellow is white." And in the same breath the other farmer was saying: "I do apologize for my blindness. The man is indeed black, just as you said." And in no time again the two were quarreling and then fighting. As they fought this time, they shouted: *I was wrong! No, I was wrong!*

8   The recrimination between capitalist and communist aesthetics in our time is, of course, comparable to the first act of the farmers' drama—the fight for the exclusive claim on righteousness and truth. Perhaps Eshu will return one day and pass again between them down the road and inaugurate the second act—the fight for self-abasement, for a monopoly on guilt.

9   As African writers emerge onto the world stage, they come under pressure to declare their stand. Now, I am not one for opposing an idea or a proposition simply on the grounds that it is "un-African"—a common enough ploy of obscurantist self-interest; thus a modern leader anxious

to continue unchallenged his business of transforming public wealth into a dynastic fortune will often tell you that socialism (which, quite rightly, scares the daylights out of him) is un-African. We are not talking about *his* concern for Africanness. But there seems to me to be a genuine need for African writers to pause momentarily and consider whether anything in traditional African aesthetics will fit their contemporary condition.

10   Let me give one example from Nigeria. Among the Owerri Igbo there was a colorful ceremony called *mbari*, a profound affirmation of the people's belief in the indivisibility of art and society. Mbari was performed at the behest of the Earth goddess, Ala, the most powerful deity in the Igbo pantheon, for she was not only the owner of the soil but also controller of morality and creativity, artistic and biological. Every so many years Ala would instruct the community through her priest to prepare a festival of images in her honor. That night the priest would travel through the town, knocking on many doors to announce to the various households whom of their members Ala had chosen for the great work. These chosen men and women then moved into seclusion in a forest clearing, and under the instruction and guidance of master artists and craftsmen, began to build a house of images. The work might take a year or even two, but as long as it lasted the workers were deemed to be hallowed and were protected from undue contact from, and distraction by, the larger community.

11   The finished temple was architecturally simple—two side walls and a back wall under a high thatched roof. Steps ran the full width of the temple, ascending backward and upward almost to the roof. But in spite of the simplicity of its structure, mbari was often a miracle of artistic achievement—a breathtaking concourse of images in bright, primary colors. Since the enterprise was in honor of Ala, most of the work was done in her own materials—simple molded earth. But the execution turned this simple material into finished images of startling power and diversity. The goddess had a central seat, usually with a child on her knee—a telling juxtaposition of formidable (even, implacable) power and gentleness. Then there were other divinities; there were men, women, beasts, and birds, real or imaginary. Indeed, the total life of the community was reflected—scenes of religious duty, of day-to-day tasks and diversions, and even of village scandal. The work completed, the village declared a feast and a holiday to honor the goddess of creativity and her children, the makers of images.

12   This brief and inadequate description can give no idea of the impact of mbari. Even the early Christian missionaries who were shocked by the frankness of some of the portrayals couldn't quite take their eyes off! But all I want to do is to point out one or two of the aesthetic ideas underlying mbari. First, the making of art is not the exclusive concern of a particular caste or secret society. Those young men and women whom the goddess chose for the re-enactment of creation were not "artists." They were ordinary members of society. Next time around, the choice would fall on other people. Of course, mere nomination would not turn every

man into an artist—not even divine appointment could guarantee it. The discipline, instruction, and guidance of a master artist would be necessary. But not even a conjunction of those two conditions would insure infallibly the emergence of a new, exciting sculptor or painter. But mbari was not looking for that. It was looking for, and saying, something else: *There is no rigid barrier between makers of culture and its consumers. Art belongs to all and is a "function" of society.* When Senghor insists with such obvious conviction that every man is a poet, he is responding, I think, to this holistic concern of our traditional societies.

13   All this will, I dare say, sound like abominable heresy in the ears of mystique lovers. For their sake and their comfort, let me hasten to add that the idea of mbari does not deny the place or importance of the master with unusual talent and professional experience. Indeed it highlights such gift and competence by bringing them into play on the seminal potentialities of the community. Again, mbari does not deny the need for the creative artist to go apart from time to time so as to commune with himself, to look inwardly into his own soul. For when the festival is over, the villagers return to their normal lives again, and the master artists to their work and contemplation. But they can never after this experience, this creative communal enterprise, become strangers again to one another. And by logical and physical extension the greater community, which comes to the unveiling of the art and then receives its makers again into its normal life, becomes a beneficiary—indeed an active partaker—of this experience.

14   If one believes, as many seem to do in some so-called advanced cultures, that the hallmark of a true artist is the ability to ignore society (and paradoxically demand at the same time its attention and homage), then one must find the ruling concerns of mbari somewhat undramatic. Certainly no artist reared within the mbari culture could aspire to humiliate his community by hanging his canvas upside down in an exhibition and, withdrawing to a corner, watching viewers extol its many fine and hidden points with much nodding of the head and outpouring of sophisticated jargon. Could a more appalling relationship be imagined? And the artist who so blatantly dramatizes it has more to answer for than all those pathetic courtiers lost in admiration of the emperor's new clothes, desperately hiding in breathless garrulity the blankness of their vision. *They* are only victims of an irresponsible monarch's capriciousness. And quite rightly, it is not they but the emperor himself who suffers the ultimate humiliation.

15   There is, of course, a deep political implication to all this. The Igbo society from which the example of mbari was taken is notorious for its unbridled republicanism. A society that upholds and extols an opposing political system is likely to take a different cultural viewpoint. For example, the European aesthetic, which many African writers are accepting so uncritically, developed in a rigid oligarchical culture in which kings and their nobilities in the past cultivated a taste different from the common appetite. And since they monopolized the resources of the realm, they

were able to buy over the artists in the society through diverse bribes, inducements, and patronage to minister to this taste. Thus over many generations a real differentiation occurred between aristocratic culture and the common culture. The latter, having no resources to develop itself, went into stagnation. Of course, there is such a thing as poetic justice, and in the fullness of time the high culture, living so long in rarefied reaches of the upper atmosphere, became sick. Somehow it sensed that unless it made contact again with the ground it would surely die. So it descended to the earthy, stagnant pool of the common culture and began to fish out between delicate beaks such healing tidbits as four-letter words.

16   Where does the African writer come in, in all this? Quite frankly he is confused. Sometimes—in a spasmodic seizure of confidence—he feels called upon to save Europe and the West by giving them Africa's peculiar gifts of healing, irrigating (in the words of Senghor) the Cartesian rationalism of Europe with black sensitivity through the gift of emotion. In his poem *Prayer to Masks* we are those very children called to sacrifice their lives like the poor man his last garment,

> So that hereafter we may cry "hear" at the rebirth of the
>   world being the leaven that the white flour needs.
> For who else would teach rhythm to the world that has
>   died of machines and cannons?
>   For who else should ejaculate the cry of joy that arouses
>   the dead and the wise in a new dawn?
> Say who else could return the memory of life to men with
>   a torn hope?

17   And in his famous poem *New York* he tells that amazing metropolis what it must do to be saved.

> New York! I say to you: New York let black blood flow
>   into your blood
> That it may rub the rust from your steel joints, like an oil
>   of life
> That it may give to your bridges the bend of buttocks and
>   the suppleness of creepers.

18   The trouble is that personally I am not so sure of things to be able to claim for Africa such a messianic mission in the world. In the first place we would be hard put to it "in our present condition of health" (to use a common Nigerian cliché) to save anybody. In the second place the world may not wish to be saved, even if Africa had the power to.

19   In talking about the world here we really mean Europe and the West. But we have all got into the bad habit of regarding that slice of the globe as the whole thing. That an African writer can so easily slip into this error is a tribute to its hold upon the contemporary imagination. For those of Europe and the West, such a habit if not entirely excusable is at least understandable. It can even be amusing in a harmless way, as when, for

example, a game between Cincinnati and Minnesota is called the World Series. But it ceases to be funny when it consigns other continents and peoples into a kind of limbo; and it begins to border on the grotesque when these continents and peoples come to accept this view of the world and of themselves.

20 Senghor's solicitude for the health and happiness of Europe may indeed have a ring of quixotic adventure about it, but at least it seems to be rooted in a positive awareness of self. Not so some of the more recent—and quite bizarre—fashions in African literature; for example, the near-pathological eagerness to contract the sicknesses of Europe in the horribly mistaken belief that our claim to sophistication is improved thereby. I am talking, of course, about the *human-condition* syndrome. Presumably European art and literature have every good reason for going into a phase of despair. But ours does not. The worst we can afford at present is disappointment. Perhaps when we too have overreached ourselves in technical achievement without spiritual growth, we shall be entitled to despair. Or, who knows? We may even learn from the history of others and avoid that particular fate. But whether we shall learn or not, there seems to me no sense whatever in rushing out now, so prematurely, to an assignation with a cruel destiny that will not be stirring from her place for a long time yet.

21 There is a brilliant Ghanaian novelist, Ayi Kwei Armah, who seems to me to be in grave danger of squandering his enormous talent and energy in pursuit of the *human condition*. In an impressive first novel, *The Beautiful Ones Are Not Yet Born,* he gives us a striking parable of corruption in Ghana society and of one man who refuses to be contaminated by this filth.

22 It is a well-written book. Armah's command of language and imagery is of a very high order indeed. But it is a sick book. Sick, not with the sickness of Ghana, but with the sickness of the *human condition*. The hero, pale and passive and nameless—a creation in the best manner of existentialist writing—wanders through the story in an anguished half-sleep, neck-deep in despair and human excrement of which we see rather a lot in the book. Did I say he *refused* to be corrupted? He did not do anything as positive as refusing. He reminded me very strongly of that man and woman in a Jean-Paul Sartre novel who sit in anguished gloom in a restaurant and then in a sudden access of nihilistic energy seize table knives and stab their hands right through to the wood—to prove some very obscure point to each other. Except that Armah's hero would be quite incapable of suffering any seizure.

23 Ultimately the novel failed to convince me. And this was because Armah insists that this story is happening in Ghana and not in some modern, existentialist no-man's-land. He throws in quite a few realistic ingredients like Kwame Nkrumah to prove it. And that is a mistake. Just as the hero is nameless, so should everything else be; and Armah might have gotten away with a modern, "universal" story. Why did he not opt simply for that easy choice? I don't know. But I am going to be superstitious and say that Africa probably seized hold of his subconscious and insinuated there this deadly

obligation—deadly, that is, to universalistic pretentions—to use his considerable talents in the service of a particular people and a particular place. Could it be that under this pressure Armah attempts to tell what Europe would call a modern story and Africa a moral fable, at the same time; to relate the fashions of European literature to the men and women of Ghana? He tried very hard. But his Ghana is unrecognizable. This aura of cosmic sorrow and despair is as foreign and unusable as those monstrous machines Nkrumah was said to have imported from Eastern European countries. Said, that is, by critics like Armah.

24   True, Ghana was sick. And what country is not? But everybody has his own brand of ailment. Ayi Kwei Armah imposes so much foreign metaphor on the sickness of Ghana that it ceases to be true. And finally, the suggestion (albeit existentially tentative) of the hero's personal justification without faith nor works is grossly inadequate in a society where even a lunatic walking stark naked through the highways of Accra has an extended family somewhere suffering vicarious shame.

25   Armah is clearly an alienated writer, a modern writer complete with all the symptoms. Unfortunately Ghana is not a modern existentialist country. It is just a Western African state struggling to become a nation. So there is enormous distance between Armah and Ghana. There is something scornful, cold and remote about Armah's obsession with the filth of Ghana:

> Left-hand fingers in their careless journey from a hasty anus sliding all the way up the banister as their owners made the return trip from the lavatory downstairs to the office above. Right-hand fingers still dripping with the after-piss and the stale sweat from fat crotches. The callused palms of messengers after they had blown their clogged noses reaching for a convenient place to leave the well-rubbed moisture. Afternoon hands not entirely licked clean of palm soup and remnants of *kenkey.* . . .

26   You have to go to certain European writers on Africa to find something of the same attitude and icy distance:

> Fada is the ordinary native town of the Western Sudan. It has no beauty, convenience or health. It is a dwelling place at one stage from the rabbit warren and the badger burrow; and not so cleanly kept as the latter. It is . . . built on its own rubbish heaps, without charm even of antiquity. Its squalor and its stinks are all new. . . . All its mud walls are eaten as if by small-pox. . . . Its people would not know the change if time jumped back fifty thousand years. They live like mice or rats in a palace floor; all the magnificence and variety of the arts, the learning and the battles of civilization go on over their heads and they do not even imagine them.

27   That is from Joyce Cary's famous novel, *Mister Johnson,* "the best novel ever written about Africa" according to *Time* magazine. Joyce Cary was an alien writing about Africa; Ayi Kwei Armah is the alienated native. It seems that to achieve the modern alienated stance an African writer will end up writing like some white District Officer.

28   There are African writers who are prepared to say they are not African writers but just writers. It is a sentiment guaranteed to win applause in

Western circles. But it is a statement of defeat. A man is never more defeated than when he is running away from himself. When Pablo Neruda received the Nobel Prize for Literature in 1971, he said:

> I belong to all the people of Latin America, a little of whose soul I have tried to interpret.

29   I wonder what an African writer would have said. Perhaps "I belong to the universe, all of whose soul I have successfully interpreted."

30   I know the source of our problem, of course. *Anxiety.* Africa has had such a fate in the world that the very adjective *African* can still call up hideous fears of rejection. Better then to cut all links with this homeland, this liability, and become in one giant leap the universal man. Indeed, I understand the anxiety. But running away from myself seems to me a very inadequate way of dealing with an anxiety. And if writers should opt for such escapism, who is to meet the challenge?

31   Sometimes this problem appears in almost comical forms. A young Nigerian poet living and teaching in New York sent me in Nigeria a poem for the literary magazine I edit. It was a good poem but in one of his lines he used a plural Italian word as if it were a singular. And there was no reason I could see for invoking poetic license. So I made the slightest alteration imaginable in the verb to correct this needless error. The bright, young poet, instead of thanking me, wrote an angry and devastating letter in which he accused me of being a grammarian. I didn't mind that, really; it was a new kind of accusation. But in his final crushing statement he contrasted the linguistic conservatism of those who live in the outposts of the empire with the imaginative freedom of the dwellers of the metropolis.

32   At first I thought of replying but in the end decided it was a waste of my time. If I had replied, I would have agreed with him about our respective locations, but would have gone on to remind him that the outposts had always borne the historic role of defending the empire from the constant threat of the barbarian hordes; and so needed always to be awake and alert, unlike the easygoing, soft-living metropolis.

33   But jokes apart, this incident is really a neat parable of the predicament of the African writer in search of universality. He has been misled into thinking that the metropolis belongs to him. Well, not yet. For him there is still the inescapable grammar of values to straighten out, the confused vocabulary of fledgling polities. Ease and carelessness in our circumstance will only cause a total breakdown of communications.

34   But you might say: What does it really matter? A man could have the wrongest ideas and yet write good poems and good novels, while another with impeccable notions writes terrible books. This may be true. Certainly those who will write bad books will probably write bad books whatever ideas they may hold. It is the good, or the potentially good, writer who should interest us. And for him I will sooner risk good ideas than bad. I don't believe he will come to much harm by asking himself a few pointed questions.

35   The late Christopher Okigbo was perhaps a good example of an artist who sometimes had, and expressed, confusing ideas while producing immaculate poetry. He was, in the view of many, Africa's finest poet of our time. For while other poets wrote good poems, Okigbo conjured up for us an amazing, haunting poetic firmament of a wild and violent beauty. Well, Christopher Okigbo once said that he wrote his poems only for other poets: thus putting himself not just beyond the African pale but in a position that would have shocked the great English Romantic poet who defined himself as a man writing for men. On another occasion Okigbo said: "There is no African literature. There is good writing and bad writing—that's all." But quite quickly we are led to suspect that this was all bluff. For when Okigbo was asked why he turned to poetry, he said:

> The turning point came in 1958 when I found myself wanting to know myself better, and I had to turn and look at myself from inside. . . . And when I talk of looking inward to myself, I mean turning inward to examine myselves. This, of course, takes account of ancestors. . . . Because I do not exist apart from my ancestors.

36   And then, as though to spell it out clearly that ancestors does not mean some general psychological or genetic principle, Okigbo tells us specifically that he is the reincarnation of his maternal grandfather, a priest in the shrine of the Earth goddess. In fact, poetry becomes for him an anguished journey back from alienation to resumption of ritual and priestly functions. His voice becomes the voice of the sunbird of Igbo mythology, mysterious and ominous.

37   But it was not a simple choice or an easy return journey for Okigbo to make, for he never underrated his indebtedness to the rest of the world. He brought into his poetry all the heirlooms of his multiple heritage; he ranged with ease through Rome and Greece and Babylon, through the rites of Judaism and Catholicism, through European and Bengali literatures, through modern music and painting. But at least one perceptive Nigerian critic has argued that Okigbo's true voice only came to him in his last sequence of poems, *Path of Thunder*, when he had finally and decisively opted for an African inspiration. This opinion may be contested, though I think it has substantial merit. The trouble is that Okigbo is such a bewitching poet, able to cast such a powerful spell that, whatever he cares to say or sing, we stand breathless at the sheer beauty and grace of his sound and imagery. Yet there is that undeniable fire in his last poems which was something new. It was as though the goddess he sought in his poetic journey through so many alien landscapes, and ultimately found at home, had given him this new thunder. Unfortunately, when he was killed in 1967 he left us only that little, tantalizing hint of the new self he had found. But perhaps he will be reincarnated in other poets and sing for us again like his sunbird whose imperishable song survived the ravages of the eagles.

Questions for Discussion

1. Achebe says, "Our ancestors created their myths and legends and told their stories for a human purpose." What does Achebe consider to be the "human purpose" of art? What do you consider to be the "human purpose" of art?

2. Why does Achebe say that "no decent man uses [the word *good*] in polite society"? Judging from the rest of the essay, what is the **tone** of his statement?

3. What kinds of **images** does mbari include and what do they symbolize? What purposes for art does mbari suggest? What point does Achebe make through the example of mbari?

4. Achebe calls mbari a "reenactment of creation." What does he mean?

5. Is Achebe being fair when he argues that "the European aesthetic [. . .] developed in a rigid oligarchical culture"? Explain.

Suggestions for Exploration and Writing

1. Write an essay about a local equivalent of mbari in your hometown, a kind of art which is unique to your community, which expresses your community's values, and in which a substantial part of your community participates. Think of art in broad terms: a style of play, a local game, a festival, or a community picnic or parade.

2. Analyze the degree to which other works in this anthology exemplify or contradict Achebe's theories about art.

3. In an essay, discuss a person, like one Achebe mentions, who used art to humiliate you as if you were vulgar and unworthy.

Paul Theroux (b. 1941)

An adventurer, inveterate traveler, and prolific writer of sardonic travel essays and satiric novels set in the developing world, Paul Theroux graduated from the University of Massachusetts in 1963, a year after his arrest for leading a very early anti–Vietnam War rally. After graduating, he served briefly in the Peace Corps. Theroux has taught at universities in Malawi, Uganda, Singapore, and Virginia. His more than forty books include such novels as Waldo *(1967),* Fong and the Indians *(1968), and* Girls at Play *(1969), all three set in Africa;* Saint Jack *(1972), set in Singapore;* Kowloon Tong *(1997), set in Hong Kong; American Book Award nominee* Mosquito Coast *(1982), about an American family who move to Honduras; and two apparently quasi-autobiographical novels,* My Secret History *(1989) and* My Other Life *(1997). He has also published several volumes of travel essays, including* The Great Railway Bazaar: By Train through Asia

(1975), The Old Patagonian Express: By Train through the Americas *(1979)*, Sunrise with Seamonsters; Travels and Discoveries 1964–1984 *(1985)*, The Pillars of Hercules *(1995)*, *and* Fresh Air Fiend: Travel Writings 1985–2000 *(2001)*.

DISCOVERING DINGLE   (1976)

1   The nearest thing to writing a novel is traveling in a strange country. Travel is a creative act—not simply loafing and inviting your soul, but feeding the imagination, accounting for each fresh wonder, memorizing and moving on. The discoveries the traveler makes in broad daylight—the curious problems of the eye he solves—resemble those that thrill and sustain a novelist in his solitude. It is fatal to know too much at the outset: boredom comes as quickly to the traveler who knows his route as to the novelist who is overcertain of his plot. And the best landscapes, apparently dense or featureless, hold surprises if they are studied patiently, in the kind of discomfort one can savor afterward. Only a fool blames his bad vacation on the rain.

2   A strange country—but how strange? One where the sun bursts through the clouds at ten in the evening and makes a sunset as full and promising as dawn. An island which on close inspection appears to be composed entirely of rabbit droppings. Gloomy gypsies camped in hilarious clutter. People who greet you with "Nice day" in a pelting storm. Miles of fuchsia hedges, seven feet tall, with purple hanging blossoms like Chinese lanterns. Ancient perfect castles that are not inhabited; hovels that are. And dangers: hills and beach-cliffs so steep you either hug them or fall off. Stone altars that were last visited by Druids, storms that break and pass in minutes, and a local language that sounds like Russian being whispered and so incomprehensible that the attentive traveler feels, in the words of a native writer, "like a dog listening to music."

3   It sounds as distant and bizarre as The Land Where the Jumblies Live, and yet it is the part of Europe that is closest in miles to America, the thirty mile sausage of land on the southwest coast of Ireland that is known as the Dingle Peninsula. Beyond it is Boston and New York, where many of its people have fled. The land is not particularly fertile. Fishing is dangerous and difficult. Food is expensive; and if the Irish Government did not offer financial inducements to the natives they would probably shrink inland, like the people of Great Blasket Island who simply dropped everything and went ashore to the Dingle, deserting their huts and fields and leaving them to the rabbits and the ravens.

4   It is easy for the casual traveler to prettify the place with romantic hyperbole, to see in Dingle's hard weather and exhausted ground the Celtic Twilight, and in its stubborn hopeful people a version of Irishness that is to be cherished. That is the patronage of pity—the metropolitan's contempt for the peasant. The Irish coast, so enchanting for the man with the camera, is murder for the fisherman. For five of the eight days I was there the fishing boats remained anchored in Dingle Harbor, because it

was too wild to set sail. The dead seagulls, splayed out like old-fangled ladies' hats below Clogher Head, testify to the furious winds; and never have I seen so many sheep skulls bleaching on hillsides, so many cracked bones beneath bushes.

5 Farming is done in the most clumsily primitive way, with horses and donkeys, wagons and blunt plows. The methods are traditional by necessity—modernity is expensive, gas costs more than Guinness. The stereotype of the Irishman is a person who spends every night at the local pub, jigging and swilling; in the villages of this peninsula only Sunday night is festive and the rest are observed with tea and early supper.

6 "I don't blame anyone for leaving here," said a farmer in Dunquin. "There's nothing for young people. There's no work, and it's getting worse."

7 After the talk of the high deeds of Finn MacCool and the fairies and leprechauns, the conversation turns to the price of spare parts, the cost of grain, the value of the Irish pound which has sunk below the British one. Such an atmosphere of isolation is intensified and circumscribed by the language—there are many who speak only Gaelic. Such remoteness breeds political indifference. There is little talk of the guerrilla war in Northern Ireland, and the few people I tried to draw on the subject said simply that Ulster should become part of Eire.

8 Further east, in Cork and Killarney, I saw graffiti reading BRITS OUT or UP THE IRA. It is not only the shortage of walls or the cost of spray cans that keep the Irish in Dingle from scrawling slogans. I cannot remember any people so quickly hospitable or easier to meet. Passers-by nod in greeting, children wave at cars: it is all friendliness. At almost three thousand feet the shepherd salutes the climbers and then marches on with his dogs yapping ahead of him.

9 Either the people leave and go far—every Irishman I met had a relative in America—or they never stir at all. "I've lived here my whole life," said an old man in Curraheen on Tralee Bay; and he meant it—he had always sat in that chair and known that house and that tree and that pasture. But his friend hesitated. "Well, yes," this one said, "not here exactly. After I got married I moved further down the road." It is the outsider who sees Dingle whole; the Irish there live in solitary villages. And people who have only the vaguest notion of Dublin or London, and who have never left Ballydavid or Inch, show an intimate knowledge of American cities, Boston, Springfield, Newark or San Diego. The old lady in Dunquin, sister of the famous "Kruger" Kavanagh—his bar remains, a friendly ramshackle place with a dark side of bacon suspended over one bar and selling peat bricks, ice cream, shampoo and corn flakes along with the Guinness and the rum—that old lady considered Ventry (her new homestead, four miles away) another world, and yet she used her stern charm on me to recommend a certain bar on Cape Cod.

10 I did not find, in the whole peninsula, an inspired meal or a great hotel; nor can the peninsula be recommended for its weather. We had two days of rain, two of mist, one almost tropical, and one which was all

three, rain in the morning, mist in the afternoon, and sun that appeared in the evening and didn't sink until eleven at night—this was June. "Soft evening," says the fisherman; but that is only a habitual greeting—it might be raining like hell. In general, the sky is overcast, occasionally the weather is unspeakable: no one should go to that part of Ireland in search of sunny days. The bars, two or three to a village, are musty with rising damp and woodworm, and the pictures of President Kennedy—sometimes on yellowing newsprint, sometimes picked out daintily in needle-point on framed tea-towels—do little to relieve the gloom. The English habit of giving bars fanciful names, like The Frog and Nightgown or The White Hart, is virtually unknown in Ireland. I did not see a bar in any village that was not called simply Mahoney's, or Crowley's, or Foley's or O'Flaherty's: a bar is a room, a keg, an Irish name over the door, and perhaps a cat asleep on the sandwiches.

11   The roads are empty but narrow, and one—the three miles across the Conair Pass—is, in low cloud, one of the most dangerous I have ever seen, bringing a lump to my throat that I had not tasted since traversing the Khyber. The landscape is utterly bleak, and sometimes there is no sound but the wind beating the gorse bushes or the cries of gulls which—shrill and frantic—mimic something tragic, like a busload of schoolgirls careering off a cliff. The day we arrived my wife and I went for a walk, down the meadow to the sea. It was gray. We walked fifty feet. It rained. The wind tore at the outcrops of rock. We started back, slipping on seaweed, and now we could no longer see the top of the road, where we had begun the walk. It was cold; both of us were wet, feebly congratulating ourselves that we had remembered to buy rubber boots in Killarney.

12   Then Anne hunched and said, "It's bloody cold. Let's make this a one-night stand."

13   But we waited. It rained the next day. And the next. The third was misty, but after so much rain the mist gave us the illusion of good weather: there was some promise in the shifting clouds. But, really, the weather had ceased to matter. It was too cold to swim and neither of us had imagined sunbathing in Ireland. We had started to discover the place on foot, in a high wind, fortified by stout and a picnic lunch of crab's claws (a dollar a pound) and cheese and soda bread. Pausing, we had begun to travel.

14   There is no detailed guidebook for these parts. Two choices are open: to buy Sheet 20 of the Ordnance Survey Map of Ireland, or climb Mount Brandon and look down. We did both, and it was odd how, standing in mist among ecclesiastical-looking cairns (the mountain was a place of pilgrimage for early Christian monks seeking the intercession of St Brendan the Navigator), we looked down and saw that Smerwick and Ballyferriter were enjoying a day of sunshine, Brandon Head was rainy, and Mount Eagle was in cloud. Climbing west of Dingle is deceptive, a succession of false summits, each windier than the last; but from the heights of Brandon the whole peninsula is spread out like a topographical map, path and road, cove and headland. Down there was the Gallarus Oratory, like a

perfect boathouse in stone to which no one risks assigning a date (but probably 9th Cent.), and at a greater distance Great Blasket Island and the smaller ones with longer names around it. The views all over the peninsula are dramatic and unlikely, as anyone who has seen *Ryan's Daughter* knows—that bad dazzling movie was made in and around the fishing hamlet of Dunquin. The coastal cliffs are genuinely frightening, the coves echoic with waves that hit the black rocks and rise—foaming, perpendicular—at the fleeing gannets; and the long Slieve Mish Mountains and every valley—thirty miles of them—are, most weirdly, without trees.

15   We had spotted Mount Eagle. The following day we wandered from the sandy, and briefly sunny, beach at Ventry, through tiny farms to the dark sloping lake that is banked like a sink a thousand feet up the slope—more bones, more rabbits, and a mountain wall strafed by screeching gulls. We had begun to enjoy the wind and rough weather, and after a few days of it saw Dingle Town as too busy, exaggerated, almost large, without much interest, and full of those fairly grim Irish shops which display in the front window a can of beans, a fan belt, a pair of boots, two chocolate bars, yesterday's newspaper and a row of plastic crucifixes standing on fly-blown cookie boxes. And in one window—that of a shoe store—two bottles of "Guaranteed Pure Altar Wine"—the guarantee was lettered neatly on the label: "Certified by the Cardinal Archbishop of Lisbon and Approved by his Lordship the Most Reverend Dr Eamonn Casey, Bishop of Kerry."

16   But no one mentions religion. The only indication I had of the faith was the valediction of a lady in a bar in Ballyferriter, who shouted, "God Bless ye!" when I emptied my pint of Guinness.

17   On the rainiest day we climbed down into the cove at Coumeenoole, where—because of its unusual shape, like a ruined cathedral—there was no rain. I sent the children off for driftwood and at the mouth of a dry cave built a fire. It is the bumpkin who sees travel in terms of dancing girls and candlelight dinners on the terrace; the city-slicker's triumphant holiday is finding the right mountain-top or building a fire in the rain or recognizing the wildflowers in Dingle: foxglove, heather, bluebells.

18   And it is the city-slicker's conceit to look for untrodden ground, the five miles of unpeopled beach at Stradbally Strand, the flat magnificence of Inch Strand, or the most distant frontier of Ireland, the island off Dunquin called Great Blasket.

19   Each day, she and her sister-islands looked different. We had seen them from the cliffside of Slea Head, and on that day they had the appearance of sea monsters—high backed creatures making for the open sea. Like all off-shore islands, seen from the mainland, their aspect changed with the light: they were lizard-like, then muscular, turned from gray to green, acquired highlights that might have been huts. At dawn they seemed small, but they grew all day into huge and fairly fierce-seeming mountains in the water, diminishing at dusk into pink beasts and finally only hindquarters disappearing in the mist. Some days they were not there at all; on other days they looked linked to the peninsula.

20   It became our ambition to visit them. We waited for a clear day, and it came—bright and cloudless. But the boat looked frail, a rubber dinghy with an outboard motor. The children were eager; I looked at the high waves that lay between us and Great Blasket and implored the boatman for reassurance. He said he had never overturned—but he was young. On an impulse I agreed and under a half-hour later we arrived at the fore-shore on the east of the main island, soaking wet from the spray.

21   No ruin in Ireland prepared us for the ruins on Great Blasket. After many years of cozy habitation—described with good humor by Maurice O'Sullivan in *Twenty Years A-Growing* (1933)—the villagers were removed to the mainland in 1953. They could no longer support themselves: they surrendered their island to the sneaping wind. And their houses, none of them large, fell down. Where there had been parlors and kitchens and vegetable gardens and fowl-coops there was now bright green moss. The grass and moss and wildflowers combine to create a cemetery effect in the derelict village, the crumbled hut walls like old gravemarkers.

22   I think I have never seen an eerier or more beautiful island. Just beyond the village which has no name is a long sandy beach called White Strand, which is without a footprint; that day it shimmered like any in Bali. After our picnic we climbed to Sorrowful Cliff and discovered that the island which looked only steep from the shore was in fact precipitous. "Sure, it's a wonderful place to commit suicide," a man told me in Dun-quin. A narrow path was cut into the slope on which we walked single file—a few feet to the right and straight down were gulls and the dull sparkle of the Atlantic. We were on the windward side, heading for Fatal Cliff; and for hundreds of feet straight up rabbits were defying gravity on the steepness. The island hill becomes such a sudden ridge and so sharp that when we got to the top of it and took a step we were in complete silence: no wind, no gulls, no surf, only a green-blue vista of the coast of Kerry, Valencia Island and the soft headlands. Here on the lee side the heather was three feet thick and easy as a mattress. I lay down, and within minutes my youngest child was asleep on his stomach, his face on a cush-ion of fragrant heather. And the rest of the family had wandered singly to other parts of the silent island, so that when I sat up I could see them prowling alone, in detached discovery, trying—because we could not pos-sess this strangeness—to remember it.

Questions for Discussion

1. Theroux maintains that "travel is a creative act" like "writing a novel." In what ways is travel creative?

2. What does Theroux mean by "Only a fool blames his bad vacation on the rain"? He seems to revel in the bad weather on the Dingle Penin-sula. Why?

3. What American poet is Theroux referring to with the phrase "not simply loafing and inviting your soul"?

4. Theroux says, "the best landscapes [. . .] hold surprises if they are studied patiently." What surprises does he find in the Dingle Peninsula? What does he find strange about the place?

5. According to Theroux, the Dingle Peninsula is rainy, bleak, cold, treeless, and windy. Its food and hotels are far from good, its shops "grim." Why, then, does he appear to find the place fascinating and wonderful?

6. Explain what Theroux means when he says that calling the Irish people of the Dingle Peninsula "stubborn hopeful people [. . .] is the patronage of pity—the metropolitan's contempt for the peasant."

7. How would you explain Dingle's inhabitants' knowing more about some American cities than about Dublin or London?

8. Instead of making Dingle a "one-night stand," as suggested by Anne, Theroux's wife, they stay and discover Dingle. What do they discover? What effect do these things have on the Theroux family?

9. Look up the word *sneap*, and explain why Theroux's use of the word to describe the wind on Great Blasket is so appropriate.

10. What particular details stand out as exemplifying the essence of Dingle?

Suggestions for Exploration and Writing

1. Write a contrast essay developing Theroux's statement that what is "enchanting to the man with the camera [. . .] is murder for the fisherman."

2. Write an essay about a place you have visited that, like Dingle, is beautiful or wonderful in a strange and forbidding way.

3. Describe a vacation that for you would best fit Theroux's description of "detached discovery, trying—because we could not possess that strangeness—to remember it."

4. Describe a typical day in the town of Dingle.

5. Write a contrast between what a tourist might want on vacation and what he or she would get in Dingle.

Sandra Cisneros (b. 1954)

Sandra Cisneros was born in Chicago and received her BA in 1976 from Loyola University and her MFA from the University of Iowa in 1978. She has worked in the public school system and at several universities across the country. Cisneros has written novels, poems, essays, and short stories. The novel The House on Mango Street *(1983) won the Columbus Foundation's American Book Award in 1985.* Woman Hollering Creek and Other Stories *(1991) won several awards including the Los Angeles Times Best Book of Fiction for*

1991. Her books of poetry, Bad Boys (1980), My Wicked, Wicked Ways (1987), *and* Loose Woman (1994), *have also won critical acclaim. Cisneros gives voice to working-class Latinos in America while trying to establish her own voice. Currently she lives in San Antonio where she has just finished her latest novel,* Caramelo *(2002). The essay included here was originally given as a lecture at Indiana University in 1986.*

An Offering to the Power of Language   (1986)

1   "Mi'ja, it's me. Call me when you wake up." It was a message left on my phone machine from a friend. But when I heard that word "mi'ja," a pain squeezed my heart. My father was the only one who ever called me this. Because his death is so recent, the word overwhelmed me and filled me with grief.

2   With my father's death, the thread that links me to my other self, to my other language, was severed. Spanish binds me to my ancestors, but especially to my father, a Mexican national by birth who became a U.S. citizen by serving in World War II. My mother, who is Mexican American, learned her Spanish through this man, as I did. Forever after, every word spoken in that language is linked indelibly to him.

3   I continue to analyze and reflect on the power a word has to produce such an effect on me. As always, I am fascinated by how those of us caught between worlds are held under the spell of words spoken in the language of our childhood. After a loved one dies, your senses become oversensitized. Maybe that's why I sometimes smell my father's cologne in a room when no one else does. And why words once taken for granted suddenly take on new meanings.

4   "Mi'ja" (MEE-ha) from "mi hija" (me EE-ha). The words translate as "my daughter." Daughter, my daughter, daughter of mine, they're all stiff and clumsy, and have nothing of the intimacy and warmth of the word "mi'ja." "Daughter of my heart," maybe. Perhaps a more accurate translation of "mi'ja" is, I love you.

5   When I wish to address a child, lover or one of my many small pets, I use Spanish, a language filled with affection and familiarity. I can only liken it to the fried-tortilla smell of my mother's house or the way my brothers' hair smells like Alberto VO5 when I hug them. It just about makes me want to cry.

6   The language of our *antepasados,* those who came before us, connects us to our center, to who we are and directs us to our life work. Some of us have been lost, cut off from the essential wisdom and power. Sometimes, our parents or grandparents were so harmed by a society that treated them ill for speaking their native language that they thought they could save us from that hate by teaching us to speak only English. Those of us, then, live like captives, lost from our culture, ungrounded, forever wandering like ghosts with a thorn in the heart.

7   When my father was sick, I watched him dissolve before my eyes. Each day the cancer that was eating him changed his face, as if he was crumbling from within and turning into a sugar skull, the kind placed on altars for Day of the Dead. Because I'm a light sleeper, my job was to sleep on the couch and be the night watch. Father always woke several times in the night choking on his own bile. I would rush to hold a kidney-shaped bowl under his lips, wait for him to finish throwing up, the body exhausted beyond belief. When he was through, I rinsed a towel with cold water and washed his face. —*Ya estoy cansado de vivir*, my father would gasp.—*Si, yo se*, I know. But the body takes its time dying. I have reasoned, since then, that the purpose of illness is to let go. For the living to let the dying go, and for the dying to let go of this life and travel to where they must.

8   Whenever anyone discusses death, they talk about the inevitable loss, but no one ever mentions the inevitable gain. How when you lose a loved one, you suddenly have a spirit ally, an energy on the other side that is with you always, that is with you just by calling their name. I know my father watches over me in a much more thorough way than he ever could when he was alive. When he was living, I had to telephone long distance to check up on him and, if he wasn't watching one of his endless tele-novelas, he'd talk to me. Now I simply summon him in my thoughts. Papa. Instantly, I feel his presence surround and calm me.

9   I know this sounds like a lot of hokey new-age stuff, but really it's old age, so ancient and wonderful and filled with such wisdom that we have had to relearn it because our miseducation has taught us to name it "superstition." I have had to rediscover the spirituality of my ancestors, because my own mother was a cynic. So it came back to me a generation later, learned but not forgotten in some memory in my cells, in my DNA, in the palm of my hand that is made up of the same blood of my ancestors, in the transcripts I read from the great Mazatec visionary Maria Sabina Garcia of Oaxaca.

10   Sometimes a word can be translated into more than a meaning. In it is the translation of a world view, a way of looking at things and, yes, even a way of accepting what others might not perceive as beautiful. "Urraca," for example, instead of "grackle." Two ways of looking at a black bird. One sings, the other cackles. Or, "tocayola," your name-twin, and, therefore, your friend. Or, the beautiful "estrenar," which means to wear something for the first time. There is no word in English for the thrill and pride of wearing something new.

11   Spanish gives me a way of looking at myself and at the world in a new way. For those of us living between worlds, our job in the universe is to help others see with more than their eyes during this period of chaotic transition. Our work as bicultural citizens is to help others become visionary, to help us all examine our dilemmas in multiple ways and arrive at creative solutions; otherwise, we all will perish.

12   What does a skeleton mean to you? Satan worship? Heavy-metal music? Halloween? Or maybe it means—Death, you are a part of my life, and I recognize you, include you in mine, I even thumb my nose at you. Next Saturday, on the Day of the Dead, I honor and remember my *antepasados*, those who have died and gone on before me.

13   I think of those two brave women in Amarillo who lost their jobs for speaking Spanish, and I wonder at the fear in their employer. Did he think they were talking about him? What an egocentric! Doesn't he understand that speaking another language is another way of seeing, a way of being at home with one another, of saying to your listener, I know you, I honor you, you are my sister, my brother, my mother, my father, my family. If he learns Spanish, or any other language, he would be admitting I love and respect you, and I love to address you in the language of those you love.

14   This Day of the Dead I will make an offering, *una ofrenda,* to honor my father's life and to honor all immigrants everywhere who come to a new country filled with great hope and fear, dragging their beloved homeland with them in their language. My father appears to me now in the things that are most alive, that speak to me or attempt to speak to me through their beauty, tenderness and love. A bowl of oranges on my kitchen table. The sharp scent of a can filled with campaxiuchil, marigold flowers for Day of the Dead. The opening notes of an Agustin Lara bolero named "Farolito." The night sky filled with moist stars. *Mi'ja,* they call out to me, and my heart floods with joy.

Questions for Discussion

1. How is Cisneros "caught between worlds"? What advantages does her knowledge of two languages and cultures give here? What obligations?

2. What evidence in the essay reveals Cisneros' love of her original language and culture?

3. Interview someone whose native language is not the same as yours and together make a list of words that do not have exact equivalents in the languages. What do the languages lose because of these gaps? What is the effect on attempts to communicate exactly?

Suggestions for Exploration and Writing

1. Cisneros says, "Our work as bicultural citizens is to help others become visionary, to help us all examine our dilemmas in multiple ways and arrive at creative solutions, otherwise, we all will perish." In an essay explain how knowledge of more than one language adds to one's depth and breadth of perception.

2. In an essay, discuss several words that evoke powerful feelings in you.

3. Use the list that you prepared in question 3 above to write an essay on the difficulties of exact communication.

FICTION

Mark Twain (1835–1910)

Mark Twain is the pseudonym adopted by Samuel Langhorne Clemens. Twain grew up on the banks of the Mississippi River in Hannibal, Missouri, a locale which forms the backdrop for two of his finest novels, The Adventures of Tom Sawyer *(1876), and* The Adventures of Huckleberry Finn *(1885). By the time he published his first story at the age of thirty, Twain had already worked as a printer's apprentice, a riverboat pilot on the Mississippi River, and a reporter on the wild frontier in the 1860s in Nevada and California. In addition to* Tom Sawyer *and* Huckleberry Finn, *his books include* Innocents Abroad *(1869), a hilarious account of Americans in Europe;* Roughing It *(1872), comic nonfiction about his work as a reporter in the American West; and such cynical but thought-provoking later fiction as* "The Man That Corrupted Hadleyburg" *(1900) and* The Mysterious Stranger, *published posthumously in 1916.*

A FABLE   (1909)

1   Once upon a time an artist who had painted a small and very beautiful picture placed it so that he could see it in the mirror. He said, "This doubles the distance and softens it, and it is twice as lovely as it was before."

2   The animals out in the woods heard of this through the housecat, who was greatly admired by them because he was so learned, and so refined and civilized, and so polite and high-bred, and could tell them so much which they didn't know before, and were not certain about afterward. They were much excited about this new piece of gossip, and they asked questions, so as to get at a full understanding of it. They asked what a picture was, and the cat explained.

3   "It is a flat thing," he said; "wonderfully flat, marvelously flat, enchantingly flat and elegant. And, oh, so beautiful!"

4   That excited them almost to a frenzy, and they said they would give the world to see it. Then the bear asked:

5   "What is it that makes it so beautiful?"

6   "It is the looks of it," said the cat.

7   This filled them with admiration and uncertainty, and they were more excited than ever. Then the cow asked:

8   "What is a mirror?"

9   "It is a hole in the wall," said the cat. "You look in it, and there you see the picture, and it is so dainty and charming and ethereal and inspiring in its unimaginable beauty that your head turns round and round, and you almost swoon with ecstasy."

10   The ass had not said anything as yet; he now began to throw doubts. He said there had never been anything as beautiful as this before, and

probably wasn't now. He said that when it took a whole basketful of sesquipedalian adjectives to whoop up a thing of beauty, it was time for suspicion.

11   It was easy to see that these doubts were having an effect upon the animals, so the cat went off offended. The subject was dropped for a couple of days, but in the meantime curiosity was taking a fresh start, and there was a revival of interest perceptible. Then the animals assailed the ass for spoiling what could possibly have been a pleasure to them, on a mere suspicion that the picture was not beautiful, without any evidence that such was the case. The ass was not troubled; he was calm, and said there was one way to find out who was in the right, himself or the cat: he would go and look in that hole, and come back and tell what he found there. The animals felt relieved and grateful, and asked him to go at once—which he did.

12   But he did not know where he ought to stand; and so, through error, he stood between the picture and the mirror. The result was that the picture had no chance, and didn't show up. He returned home and said:

13   "The cat lied. There was nothing in that hole but an ass. There wasn't a sign of a flat thing visible. It was a handsome ass, and friendly, but just an ass, and nothing more."

14   The elephant asked:

15   "Did you see it good and clear? Were you close to it?"

16   "I saw it good and clear, O Hathi, King of Beasts. I was so close that I touched noses with it."

17   "This is very strange," said the elephant; "the cat was always truthful before—as far as we could make out. Let another witness try. Go, Baloo, look in the hole, and come and report."

18   So the bear went. When he came back, he said:

19   "Both the cat and the ass have lied; there was nothing in the hole but a bear."

20   Great was the surprise and puzzlement of the animals. Each was now anxious to make the test himself and get at the straight truth. The elephant sent them one at a time.

21   First, the cow. She found nothing in the hole but a cow.

22   The tiger found nothing in it but a tiger.

23   The lion found nothing in it but a lion.

24   The leopard found nothing in it but a leopard.

25   The camel found a camel, and nothing more.

26   Then Hathi was wroth, and said he would have the truth, if he had to go and fetch it himself. When he returned, he abused his whole subjectry for liars, and was in an unappeasable fury with the moral and mental blindness of the cat. He said that anybody but a near-sighted fool could see that there was nothing in the hole but an elephant.

MORAL, BY THE CAT

27   You can find in a text whatever you bring, if you will stand between it and the mirror of your imagination. You may not see your ears, but they will be there.

Questions for Discussion

1. Why does the artist position the picture across from the mirror?
2. Why do the other animals believe the cat to be "learned," refined," and "high-bred"?
3. Why does the cat refer to the mirror as "a hole in the wall"?
4. Why does the ass not believe the cat? What does he see in the mirror? Is it significant that he is the first to question the cat?
5. To what degree do you agree with Twain's suggestion that we see ourselves in a work of art?
6. What does Twain mean by "You may not see your ears, but they will be there"?

Suggestions for Exploration and Writing

1. Twain says that "you can find in a text whatever you bring, if you will stand between it and the mirror of your imagination." In an essay, explain how you found meaning in a text because of your own personal experience.
2. Write your own fable about how to appreciate a work of art.

Ray Bradbury (b. 1920)

One of America's most prolific writers of science fiction and fantasy, Ray Bradbury was born in Waukegan, Illinois, but has spent most of his life in Los Angeles, California. His novels and short stories have won numerous awards, including the Nebula, O. Henry Memorial, Prometheus, Benjamin Franklin, and Aviation-Space Writers and World Fantasy Lifetime Achievement Awards. His works have often been adapted for television and film. The most notable adaptations include The Martian Chronicles, *a 1980 miniseries;* Fahrenheit 451 *(1966), adapted from the 1953 novel;* The Illustrated Man *(1969);* It Came from Outer Space *(1953) and* It Came from Outer Space II *(1996);* Quest *(1983); and* Something Wicked This Way Comes *(1983), from the 1962 novel.*

THERE WILL COME SOFT RAINS (1950)

1   In the living room the voice-clock sang, *Tick-tock, seven o'clock, time to get up, time to get up, seven o'clock!* as if it were afraid that nobody would. The morning house lay empty. The clock ticked on, repeating and repeating its sounds into the emptiness. *Seven-nine, breakfast time, seven-nine!*

2   In the kitchen the breakfast stove gave a hissing sigh and ejected from its warm interior eight pieces of perfectly browned toast, eight eggs sunnyside up, sixteen slices of bacon, two coffees, and two cool glasses of milk.

3   "Today is August 4, 2026," said a second voice from the kitchen ceiling, "in the city of Allendale, California." It repeated the date three times

for memory's sake. "Today is Mr. Featherstone's birthday. Today is the anniversary of Tilita's marriage. Insurance is payable, as are the water, gas, and light bills."

4   Somewhere in the walls, relays clicked, memory tapes glided under electric eyes.

5   *Eight-one, tick-tock, eight-one o'clock, off to school, off to work, run, run, eight-one!* But no doors slammed, no carpets took the soft tread of rubber heels. It was raining outside. The weather box on the front door sang quietly: "Rain, rain, go away; rubbers, raincoats for today . . ." And the rain tapped on the empty house, echoing.

6   Outside, the garage chimed and lifted its door to reveal the waiting car. After a long wait the door swung down again.

7   At eight-thirty the eggs were shriveled and the toast was like stone. An aluminum wedge scraped them into the sink, where hot water whirled them down a metal throat which digested and flushed them away to the distant sea. The dirty dishes were dropped into a hot washer and emerged twinkling dry.

8   *Nine-fifteen,* sang the clock, *time to clean.*

9   Out of warrens in the wall, tiny robot mice darted. The rooms were acrawl with the small cleaning animals, all rubber and metal. They thudded against chairs, whirling their mustached runners, kneading the rug nap, sucking gently at hidden dust. Then, like mysterious invaders, they popped into their burrows. Their pink electric eyes faded. The house was clean.

10   *Ten o'clock.* The sun came out from behind the rain. The house stood alone in a city of rubble and ashes. This was the one house left standing. At night the ruined city gave off a radioactive glow which could be seen for miles.

11   *Ten-fifteen.* The garden sprinklers whirled up in golden founts, filling the soft morning air with scatterings of brightness. The water pelted windowpanes, running down the charred west side where the house had been burned evenly free of its white paint. The entire west face of the house was black, save for five places. Here the silhouette in paint of a man mowing a lawn. Here, as in a photograph, a woman bent to pick flowers. Still farther over, their images burned on wood in one titanic instant, a small boy, hands flung into the air; higher up, the image of a thrown ball, and opposite him a girl, hands raised to catch a ball which never came down.

12   The five spots of paint—the man, the woman, the children, the ball—remained. The rest was a thin charcoaled layer.

13   The gentle sprinkler rain filled the garden with falling light.

14   Until this day, how well the house had kept its peace. How carefully it had inquired, "Who goes there? What's the password?" and, getting no answer from lonely foxes and whining cats, it had shut up its windows and drawn shades in an old-maidenly preoccupation with self-protection which bordered on a mechanical paranoia.

15   It quivered at each sound, the house did. If a sparrow brushed a window, the shade snapped up. The bird, startled, flew off! No, not even a bird must touch the house!

16   The house was an altar with ten thousand attendants, big, small, servicing, attending, in choirs. But the gods had gone away, and the ritual of the religion continued senselessly, uselessly.

17   *Twelve noon.*

18   A dog whined, shivering, on the front porch.

19   The front door recognized the dog voice and opened. The dog, once huge and fleshy, but now gone to bone and covered with sores, moved in and through the house, tracking mud. Behind it whirred angry mice, angry at having to pick up mud, angry at inconvenience.

20   For not a leaf fragment blew under the door but what the wall panels flipped open and the copper scrap rats flashed swiftly out. The offending dust, hair, or paper, seized in miniature steel jaws, was raced back to the burrows. There, down tubes which fed into the cellar, it was dropped into the sighing vent of an incinerator which sat like evil Baal in a dark corner.

21   The dog ran upstairs, hysterically yelping to each door, at last realizing, as the house realized, that only silence was here.

22   It sniffed the air and scratched the kitchen door. Behind the door, the stove was making pancakes which filled the house with a rich baked odor and the scent of maple syrup.

23   The dog frothed at the mouth, lying at the door, sniffing, its eyes turned to fire. It ran wildly in circles, biting at its tail, spun in a frenzy, and died. It lay in the parlor for an hour.

24   *Two o'clock,* sang a voice.

25   Delicately sensing decay at last, the regiments of mice hummed out as softly as blown gray leaves in an electrical wind.

26   *Two-fifteen.*

27   The dog was gone.

28   In the cellar, the incinerator glowed suddenly and a whirl of sparks leaped up the chimney.

29   *Two thirty-five.*

30   Bridge tables sprouted from patio walls. Playing cards fluttered onto pads in a shower of pips. Martinis manifested on an oaken bench with egg-salad sandwiches. Music played.

31   But the tables were silent and the cards untouched.

32   At four o'clock the tables folded like great butterflies back through the paneled walls.

33   *Four-thirty.*

34   The nursery walls glowed.

35   Animals took shape: yellow giraffes, blue lions, pink antelopes, lilac panthers cavorting in crystal substance. The walls were glass. They looked out upon color and fantasy. Hidden films clocked through well-oiled

sprockets, and the walls lived. The nursery floor was woven to resemble a crisp, cereal meadow. Over this ran aluminum roaches and iron crickets, and in the hot still air butterflies of delicate red tissue wavered among the sharp aromas of animal spoors! There was the sound like a great matted yellow hive of bees within a dark bellows, the lazy bumble of a purring lion. And there was the patter of okapi feet and the murmur of a fresh jungle rain, like other hoofs, falling upon the summer-starched grass. Now the walls dissolved into distances of parched weed, mile on mile, and warm endless sky. The animals drew away into thorn brakes and water holes.

36   It was the children's hour.

37   *Five o'clock.* The bath filled with clear hot water.

38   *Six, seven, eight o'clock.* The dinner dishes manipulated like magic tricks, and in the study a *click*. In the metal stand opposite the hearth where a fire now blazed up warmly, a cigar popped out, half an inch of soft gray ash on it, smoking, waiting.

39   *Nine o'clock.* The beds warmed their hidden circuits, for nights were cool here.

40   *Nine-five.* A voice spoke from the study ceiling:

41   "Mrs. McClellan, which poem would you like this evening?"

42   The house was silent.

43   The voice said at last, "Since you express no preference, I shall select a poem at random." Quiet music rose to back the voice. "Sara Teasdale. As I recall, your favorite. . . .

> There will come soft rains and the smell of the ground,
> And swallows circling with their shimmering sound;
>
> And frogs in the pools singing at night,
> And wild plum trees in tremulous white;
>
> Robins will wear their feathery fire,
> Whistling their whims on a low fence-wire;
>
> And not one will know of the war, not one
> Will care at last when it is done.
>
> Not one would mind, neither bird nor tree,
> If mankind perished utterly;
>
> And Spring herself, when she woke at dawn
> Would scarcely know that we were gone."

44   The fire burned on the stone hearth and the cigar fell away into a mound of quiet ash on its tray. The empty chairs faced each other between the silent walls, and the music played.

45   At ten o'clock the house began to die.

46   The wind blew. A falling tree bough crashed through the kitchen window. Cleaning solvent, bottled, shattered over the stove. The room was ablaze in an instant!

47 "Fire!" screamed a voice. The house lights flashed, water pumps shot water from the ceilings. But the solvent spread on the linoleum, licking, eating, under the kitchen door, while the voices took it up in chorus: "Fire, fire, fire!"

48 The house tried to save itself. Doors sprang tightly shut, but the windows were broken by the heat and the wind blew and sucked upon the fire.

49 The house gave ground as the fire in ten billion angry sparks moved with flaming ease from room to room and then up the stairs. While scurrying water rats squeaked from the walls, pistoled their water, and ran for more. And the wall sprays let down showers of mechanical rain.

50 But too late. Somewhere, sighing, a pump shrugged to a stop. The quenching rain ceased. The reserve water supply which had filled baths and washed dishes for many quiet days was gone.

51 The fire crackled up the stairs. It fed upon Picassos and Matisses in the upper halls, like delicacies, baking off the oily flesh, tenderly crisping the canvases into black shavings.

52 Now the fire lay in beds, stood in windows, changed the colors of drapes!

53 And then, reinforcements.

54 From attic trapdoors, blind robot faces peered down with faucet mouths gushing green chemical.

55 The fire backed off, as even an elephant must at the sight of a dead snake. Now there were twenty snakes whipping over the floor, killing the fire with a clear cold venom of green froth.

56 But the fire was clever. It had sent flame outside the house, up through the attic to the pumps there. An explosion! The attic brain which directed the pumps was shattered into bronze shrapnel on the beams.

57 The fire rushed back into every closet and felt of the clothes hung there.

58 The house shuddered, oak bone on bone, its bared skeleton cringing from the heat, its wire, its nerves revealed as if a surgeon had torn the skin off to let the red veins and capillaries quiver in the scalded air. Help, help! Fire! Run, run! Heat snapped mirrors like the first brittle winter ice. And the voices wailed, Fire, fire, run, run, like a tragic nursery rhyme, a dozen voices, high, low, like children dying in a forest, alone, alone. And the voices fading as the wires popped their sheathings like hot chestnuts. One, two, three, four, five voices died.

59 In the nursery the jungle burned. Blue lions roared, purple giraffes bounded off. The panthers ran in circles, changing color, and ten million animals, running before the fire, vanished off toward a distant steaming river. . . .

60 Ten more voices died. In the last instant under the fire avalanche, other choruses, oblivious, could be heard announcing the time, playing music, cutting the lawn by remote-control mower, or setting an umbrella frantically out and in, the slamming and opening front door, a thousand things happening, like a clock shop when each clock strikes the hour insanely before or after the other, a scene of maniac confusion, yet unity; singing, screaming, a few last cleaning mice darting bravely out to carry

the horrid ashes away! And one voice, with sublime disregard for the situation, read poetry aloud in the fiery study, until all the film spools burned, until all the wires withered and the circuits cracked.

61   The fire burst the house and let it slam flat down, puffing out skirts of spark and smoke.

62   In the kitchen, an instant before the rain of fire and timber, the stove could be seen making breakfasts at a psychopathic rate, ten dozen eggs, six loaves of toast, twenty dozen bacon strips, which, eaten by fire, started the stove working again, hysterically hissing!

63   The crash. The attic smashing into kitchen and parlor. The parlor into cellar, cellar into sub-cellar. Deep freeze, armchair, film tapes, circuits, beds, and all like skeletons thrown in a cluttered mound deep under.

64   Smoke and silence. A great quantity of smoke.

65   Dawn showed faintly in the east. Among the ruins, one wall stood alone. Within the wall, a last voice said, over and over again and again, even as the sun rose to shine upon the heaped rubble and steam:

66   "Today is August 5, 2026, today is August 5, 2026, today is . . ."

Questions for Discussion

1. What early details suggest that this is a futuristic story about a technologically advanced civilization?

2. What does the author mean when he writes that "the gods had gone away, and the ritual of the religion continued senselessly, uselessly"?

3. What clues to the desolation and devastation does Bradbury give even before paragraph 10? What has caused the destruction?

4. What is the significance of the starving dog's death before the robots finish making the pancakes?

5. Explain the analogy in paragraph 16.

6. Using the silhouettes and the possessions within the house, describe the family that lived here.

7. What is the effect of the personification of the fire?

8. What is Bradbury suggesting may be a result of technological advances?

Suggestions for Exploration and Writing

1. After carefully rereading the story and Teasdale's poem, write an essay explaining why, in your opinion, Bradbury chose this poem's opening words as the title and included the poem in the story.

2. Make a list of mechanical devices or technological advances that have become like religions with rituals that are performed on a regular basis. Then choose one and explain how its rituals promote it to religious or, at least, cult status.

Woody Allen (b. 1935)

Born Allen Stewart Konigsberg, Woody Allen exhibited an early inter-
est in writing and at the age of seventeen joined NBC as a staff writer.
There he wrote for The Garry Moore Show *and Sid Caesar's* Your
Show of Shows. *His first screenplay,* What's New, Pussycat?
(1964), decided his future as a director. Since then he has written,
directed, and starred in many of his own films as an Academy
Award–winning filmmaker; he is one of the few directors with total
control over production. Many of Allen's films and stories are paro-
dies, science fiction, and spoofs of nineteenth-century Russian novels;
they often use wordplay, allusions, and juxtapositions of unusual ele-
ments. "The Kugelmass Episode," first published in the New Yorker,
won an O. Henry Award as one of the best stories of 1978.

THE KUGELMASS EPISODE (1977)

1   Kugelmass, a professor of humanities at City College, was unhappily
married for the second time. Daphne Kugelmass was an oaf. He also had
two dull sons by his first wife, Flo, and was up to his neck in alimony and
child support.

2   "Did I know it would turn out so badly?" Kugelmass whined to his analyst one day. "Daphne had promise. Who suspected she'd let herself go
and swell up like a beach ball? Plus she had a few bucks, which is not in
itself a healthy reason to marry a person, but it doesn't hurt, with the kind
of operating nut I have. You see my point?"

3   Kugelmass was bald and as hairy as a bear, but he had soul.

4   "I need to meet a new woman," he went on. "I need to have an affair.
I may not look the part, but I'm a man who needs romance. I need soft-
ness, I need flirtation. I'm not getting younger, so before it's too late I
want to make love in Venice, trade quips at '21,' and exchange coy glances
over red wine and candlelight. You see what I'm saying?"

5   Dr. Mandel shifted in his chair and said, "An affair will solve nothing.
You're so unrealistic. Your problems run much deeper."

6   "And also this affair must be discreet," Kugelmass continued. "I can't
afford a second divorce. Daphne would really sock it to me."

7   "Mr. Kugelmass—"

8   "But it can't be anyone at City College, because Daphne also works
there. Not that anyone on the faculty at C.C.N.Y. is any great shakes, but
some of those co-eds . . ."

9   "Mr. Kugelmass—"

10   "Help me. I had a dream last night. I was skipping through a meadow
holding a picnic basket and the basket was marked 'Options.' And then
I saw there was a hole in the basket."

11   "Mr. Kugelmass, the worst thing you could do is act out. You must simply express your feelings here, and together we'll analyze them. You have
been in treatment long enough to know there is no overnight cure. After
all, I'm an analyst, not a magician."

12   "Then perhaps what I need is a magician," Kugelmass said, rising from his chair. And with that he terminated his therapy.

13   A couple of weeks later, while Kugelmass and Daphne were moping around in their apartment one night like two pieces of old furniture, the phone rang.

14   "I'll get it," Kugelmass said. "Hello."

15   "Kugelmass?" a voice said. "Kugelmass, this is Persky."

16   "Who?"

17   "Persky. Or should I say The Great Persky?"

18   "Pardon me?"

19   "I hear you're looking all over town for a magician to bring a little exotica into your life? Yes or no?"

20   "Sh-h-h," Kugelmass whispered. "Don't hang up. Where are you calling from, Persky?"

21   Early the following afternoon, Kugelmass climbed three flights of stairs in a broken-down apartment house in the Bushwick section of Brooklyn. Peering through the darkness of the hall, he found the door he was looking for and pressed the bell. I'm going to regret this, he thought to himself.

22   Seconds later, he was greeted by a short, thin, waxy-looking man.

23   "*You're* Persky the Great?" Kugelmass said.

24   "The Great Persky. You want a tea?"

25   "No, I want romance. I want music. I want love and beauty."

26   "But not tea, eh? Amazing. O.K., sit down."

27   Persky went to the back room, and Kugelmass heard the sounds of boxes and furniture being moved around. Persky reappeared, pushing before him a large object on squeaky roller-skate wheels. He removed some old silk handkerchiefs that were lying on its top and blew away a bit of dust. It was a cheap-looking Chinese cabinet, badly lacquered.

28   "Persky," Kugelmass said, "what's your scam?"

29   "Pay attention," Persky said. "This is some beautiful effect. I developed it for a Knights of Pythias date last year, but the booking fell through. Get into the cabinet."

30   "Why, so you can stick it full of swords or something?"

31   "You see any swords?"

32   Kugelmass made a face and, grunting, climbed into the cabinet. He couldn't help noticing a couple of ugly rhinestones glued onto the raw plywood just in front of his face. "If this is a joke," he said.

33   "Some joke. Now, here's the point. If I throw any novel into this cabinet with you, shut the doors, and tap it three times, you will find yourself projected into that book."

34   Kugelmass made a grimace of disbelief.

35   "It's the emess," Persky said "My hand to God. Not just a novel, either. A short story, a play, a poem. You can meet any of the women created by the world's best writers. Whoever you dreamed of. You could carry on all you like with a real winner. Then when you've had enough you give a yell, and I'll see you're back here in a split second."

36   "Persky, are you some kind of outpatient?"

37   "I'm telling you it's on the level," Persky said.

38   Kugelmass remained skeptical. "What are you telling me—that this cheesy homemade box can take me on a ride like you're describing?"

39   "For a double sawbuck."

40   Kugelmass reached for his wallet. "I'll believe this when I see it," he said.

41   Persky tucked the bills in his pants pocket and turned toward his bookcase. "So who do you want to meet? Sister Carrie?[1] Hester Prynne?[2] Ophelia?[3] Maybe someone by Saul Bellow?[4] Hey, what about Temple Drake?[5] Although for a man your age she'd be a workout."

42   "French. I want to have an affair with a French lover."

43   "Nana?"[6]

44   "I don't want to have to pay for it."

45   "What about Natasha in *War and Peace?*"

46   "I said French. I know! What about Emma Bovary?[7] That sounds to me perfect."

47   "You got it Kugelmass. Give me a holler when you've had enough." Persky tossed in a paperback copy of Flaubert's novel.

48   "You sure this is safe?" Kugelmass asked as Persky began shutting the cabinet doors.

49   "Safe. Is anything safe in this crazy world?" Persky rapped three times on the cabinet and then flung open the doors.

50   Kugelmass was gone. At the same moment, he appeared in the bedroom of Charles and Emma Bovary's house at Yonville. Before him was a beautiful woman, standing alone with her back turned to him as she folded some linen. I can't believe this, thought Kugelmass, staring at the doctor's ravishing wife. This is uncanny. I'm here. It's her.

51   Emma turned in surprise. "Goodness, you startled me," she said. "Who are you?" She spoke in the same fine English translation as the paperback.

52   It's simply devastating, he thought. Then, realizing that it was he whom she had addressed, he said, "Excuse me. I'm Sidney Kugelmass. I'm from City College. A professor of humanities. C.C.N.Y.? Uptown. I—oh, boy!"

53   Emma Bovary smiled flirtatiously and said, "Would you like a drink? A glass of wine, perhaps?"

54   She is beautiful, Kugelmass thought. What a contrast with the troglodyte who shared his bed! He felt a sudden impulse to take this vision into his arms and tell her she was the kind of woman he had dreamed of all his life.

---

[1]Sister Carrie, a character in Theodore Dreiser's novel of the same name, becomes a prostitute.

[2]Hester Prynne, a character in Hawthorne's *The Scarlet Letter,* wears an "A" for adultery.

[3]Ophelia in Shakespeare's *Hamlet* is the young woman whom Hamlet loves.

[4]Saul Bellow is a contemporary American novelist.

[5]In William Faulkner's novel *Sanctuary,* Popeye rapes Temple Drake with a corncob.

[6]Nana is the sensuous heroine of Zola's *Nana.*

[7]Emma Bovary is the faithless wife in Flaubert's *Madame Bovary.*

55   "Yes, some wine," he said hoarsely. "White. No, red. No, white. Make it white."

56   "Charles is out for the day," Emma said, her voice full of playful implication.

57   After the wine, they went for a stroll in the lovely French countryside. "I've always dreamed that some mysterious stranger would appear and rescue me from the monotony of this crass rural existence," Emma said, clasping his hand. They passed a small church. "I love what you have on," she murmured. "I've never seen anything like it around here. It's so . . . so modern."

58   "It's called a leisure suit," he said romantically. "It was marked down." Suddenly he kissed her. For the next hour they reclined under a tree and whispered together and told each other deeply meaningful things with their eyes. Then Kugelmass sat up. He had just remembered he had to meet Daphne at Bloomingdale's. "I must go," he told her. "But don't worry, I'll be back."

59   "I hope so," Emma said.

60   He embraced her passionately, and the two walked back to the house. He held Emma's face cupped in his palms, kissed her again, and yelled, "O.K., Persky! I got to be at Bloomingdale's by three-thirty."

61   There was an audible pop, and Kugelmass was back in Brooklyn.

62   "So? Did I lie?" Persky asked triumphantly.

63   "Look, Persky, I'm right now late to meet the ball and chain at Lexington Avenue, but when can I go again? Tomorrow?"

64   "My pleasure. Just bring a twenty. And don't mention this to anybody."

65   "Yeah. I'm going to call Rupert Murdoch."[8]

66   Kugelmass hailed a cab and sped off to the city. His heart danced on point. I am in love, he thought, I am the possessor of a wonderful secret. What he didn't realize was that at this very moment students in various classrooms across the country were saying to their teachers, "Who is this character on page 100? A bald Jew is kissing Madame Bovary?" A teacher in Sioux Falls, South Dakota, sighed and thought, Jesus, these kids, with their pot and acid. What goes through their minds!

67   Daphne Kugelmass was in the bathroom-accessories department at Bloomingdale's when Kugelmass arrived breathlessly. "Where've you been?" she snapped. "It's four-thirty."

68   "I got held up in traffic," Kugelmass said.

69   Kugelmass visited Persky the next day, and in a few minutes was again passing magically to Yonville. Emma couldn't hide her excitement at seeing him. The two spent hours together, laughing and talking about their different backgrounds. Before Kugelmass left, they made love. "My God, I'm doing it with Madame Bovary!" Kugelmass whispered to himself. "Me, who failed freshman English."

70   As the months passed, Kugelmass saw Persky many times and developed a close and passionate relationship with Emma Bovary. "Make sure

[8]Rupert Murdoch is a wealthy Australian publisher and owner of several sensational tabloids.

and always get me into the book before page 120," Kugelmass said to the magician one day. "I always have to meet her before she hooks up with this Rodolphe character."

71   "Why?" Persky asked. "You can't beat his time?"

72   "Beat his time. He's landed gentry. Those guys have nothing better to do than flirt and ride horses. To me, he's one of those faces you see in the pages of *Women's Wear Daily*. With the Helmut Berger hairdo. But to her he's hot stuff."

73   "And her husband suspects nothing?"

74   "He's out of his depth. He's a lacklustre little paramedic who's thrown in his lot with a jitterbug. He's ready to go to sleep by ten, and she's putting on her dancing shoes. Oh, well . . . See you later."

75   And once again Kugelmass entered the cabinet and passed instantly to the Bovary estate at Yonville. "How you doing, cupcake?" he said to Emma.

76   "Oh, Kugelmass," Emma sighed. "What I have to put up with. Last night at dinner, Mr. Personality dropped off to sleep in the middle of the dessert course. I'm pouring my heart out about Maxim's and the ballet, and out of the blue I hear snoring."

77   "It's O.K., darling. I'm here now," Kugelmass said, embracing her. I've earned this, he thought, smelling Emma's French perfume and burying his nose in her hair. I've suffered enough. I've paid enough analysts. I've searched till I'm weary. She's young and nubile, and I'm here a few pages after Leon and just before Rodolphe. By showing up during the correct chapters, I've got the situation knocked.

78   Emma, to be sure, was just as happy as Kugelmass. She had been starved for excitement, and his tales of Broadway night life, of fast cars and Hollywood and TV stars, enthralled the young French beauty.

79   "Tell me again about O. J. Simpson," she implored that evening, as she and Kugelmass strolled past Abbé Bournisien's church.

80   "What can I say? The man is great. He sets all kinds of rushing records. Such moves. They can't touch him."

81   "And the Academy Awards?" Emma said wistfully. "I'd give anything to win one."

82   "First you've got to be nominated."

83   "I know. You explained it. But I'm convinced I can act. Of course, I'd want to take a class or two. With Strasberg maybe. Then if I had the right agent—"

84   "We'll see, we'll see. I'll speak to Persky."

85   That night, safely returned to Persky's flat, Kugelmass brought up the idea of having Emma visit him in the big city.

86   "Let me think about it," Persky said. "Maybe I could work it. Stranger things have happened." Of course, neither of them could think of one.

87   "Where the hell do you go all the time?" Daphne Kugelmass barked at her husband as he returned home late that evening. "You got a chippie stashed somewhere?"

88   "Yeah, sure, I'm just the type," Kugelmass said wearily. "I was with Leonard Popkin. We were discussing Socialist agriculture in Poland. You know Popkin. He's a freak on the subject."

89   "Well, you've been very odd lately," Daphne said. "Distant. Just don't forget about my father's birthday. On Saturday?"

90   "Oh, sure, sure," Kugelmass said, heading for the bathroom.

91   "My whole family will be there. We can see the twins. And Cousin Hamish. You should be more polite to Cousin Hamish—he likes you."

92   "Right, the twins," Kugelmass said, closing the bathroom door and shutting out the sound of his wife's voice. He leaned against it and took a deep breath. In a few hours, he told himself, he would be back in Yonville again, back with his beloved. And this time, if all went well, he would bring Emma back with him.

93   At three-fifteen the following afternoon, Persky worked his wizardry again. Kugelmass appeared before Emma, smiling and eager. The two spent a few hours at Yonville with Binet and then remounted the Bovary carriage. Following Persky's instructions, they held each other tightly, closed their eyes, and counted to ten. When they opened them, the carriage was just drawing up at the side door of the Plaza Hotel, where Kugelmass had optimistically reserved a suite earlier in the day.

94   "I love it! It's everything I dreamed it would be," Emma said as she swirled joyously around the bedroom, surveying the city from their window. "There's F.A.O. Schwarz. And there's Central Park, and the Sherry is which one? Oh, there—I see. It's too divine."

95   On the bed there were boxes from Halston and Saint Laurent. Emma unwrapped a package and held up a pair of black velvet pants against her perfect body.

96   "The slacks suit is by Ralph Lauren," Kugelmass said. "You'll look like a million bucks in it. Come on, sugar, give us a kiss."

97   "I've never been so happy!" Emma squealed as she stood before the mirror. "Let's go out on the town. I want to see *Chorus Line* and the Guggenheim and this Jack Nicholson character you always talk about. Are any of his flicks showing?"

98   "I cannot get my mind around this," a Stanford professor said. "First a strange character named Kugelmass, and now she's gone from the book. Well, I guess the mark of a classic is that you can reread it a thousand times and always find something new."

99   The lovers passed a blissful weekend. Kugelmass had told Daphne he would be away at a symposium in Boston and would return Monday. Savoring each moment, he and Emma went to the movies, had dinner in Chinatown, passed two hours at a discothèque, and went to bed with a TV movie. They slept till noon on Sunday, visited SoHo, and ogled celebrities at Elaine's. They had caviar and champagne in their suite on Sunday night and talked until dawn. That morning, in the cab taking them to Persky's apartment, Kugelmass thought, It was hectic, but worth it. I can't

bring her here too often, but now and then it will be a charming contrast with Yonville.

100 At Persky's, Emma climbed into the cabinet, arranged her new boxes of clothes neatly around her, and kissed Kugelmass fondly. "My place next time," she said with a wink. Persky rapped three times on the cabinet. Nothing happened.

101 "Hmmm," Persky said, scratching his head. He rapped again, but still no magic. "Something must be wrong," he mumbled.

102 "Persky, you're joking!" Kugelmass cried. "How can it not work?"

103 "Relax, relax. Are you still in the box, Emma?"

104 "Yes."

105 Persky rapped again—harder this time.

106 "I'm still here, Persky."

107 "I know, darling. Sit tight."

108 "Persky, we *have* to get her back," Kugelmass whispered. "I'm a married man, and I have a class in three hours. I'm not prepared for anything more than a cautious affair at this point."

109 "I can't understand it," Persky muttered. "It's such a reliable little trick."

110 But he could do nothing. "It's going to take a little while," he said to Kugelmass. "I'm going to have to strip it down. I'll call you later."

111 Kugelmass bundled Emma into a cab and took her back to the Plaza. He barely made it to his class on time. He was on the phone all day, to Persky and to his mistress. The magician told him it might be several days before he got to the bottom of the trouble.

112 "How was the symposium?" Daphne asked him that night.

113 "Fine, fine," he said, lighting the filter end of a cigarette.

114 "What's wrong? You're as tense as a cat."

115 "Me? Ha, that's a laugh. I'm as calm as a summer night. I'm just going to take a walk." He eased out the door, hailed a cab, and flew to the Plaza.

116 "This is no good," Emma said. "Charles will miss me."

117 "Bear with me, sugar," Kugelmass said. He was pale and sweaty. He kissed her again, raced to the elevators, yelled at Persky over a pay phone in the Plaza lobby, and just made it home before midnight.

118 "According to Popkin, barley prices in Kraków have not been this stable since 1971," he said to Daphne, and smiled wanly as he climbed into bed.

119 The whole week went by like that.

120 On Friday night, Kugelmass told Daphne there was another symposium he had to catch, this one in Syracuse. He hurried back to the Plaza, but the second weekend there was nothing like the first. "Get me back into the novel or marry me," Emma told Kugelmass. "Meanwhile, I want to get a job or go to class, because watching TV all day is the pits."

121 "Fine. We can use the money," Kugelmass said. "You consume twice your weight in room service."

122   "I met an Off Broadway producer in Central Park yesterday, and he said I might be right for a project he's doing," Emma said.

123   "Who is this clown?" Kugelmass asked.

124   "He's not a clown. He's sensitive and kind and cute. His name's Jeff Something-or-Other, and he's up for a Tony."

125   Later that afternoon, Kugelmass showed up at Persky's drunk.

126   "Relax," Persky told him. "You'll get a coronary."

127   "Relax. The man says relax. I've got a fictional character stashed in a hotel room, and I think my wife is having me tailed by a private shamus."

128   "O.K., O.K. We know there's a problem." Persky crawled under the cabinet and started banging on something with a large wrench.

129   "I'm like a wild animal." Kugelmass went on. "I'm sneaking around town, and Emma and I have had it up to here with each other. Not to mention a hotel tab that reads like the defense budget."

130   "So what should I do? This is the world of magic," Persky said. "It's all nuance."

131   "Nuance, my foot. I'm pouring Dom Pérignon and black eggs into this little mouse, plus her wardrobe, plus she's enrolled at the Neighborhood Playhouse and suddenly needs professional photos. Also, Persky, Professor Fivish Kopkind, who teaches Comp Lit and who has always been jealous of me, has identified me as the sporadically appearing character in the Flaubert book. He's threatened to go to Daphne. I see ruin and alimony; jail. For adultery with Madame Bovary, my wife will reduce me to beggary."

132   "What do you want me to say? I'm working on it night and day. As far as your personal anxiety goes, that I can't help you with. I'm a magician, not an analyst."

133   By Sunday afternoon, Emma had locked herself in the bathroom and refused to respond to Kugelmass's entreaties. Kugelmass stared out the window at the Wollman Rink and contemplated suicide. Too bad this is a low floor, he thought, or I'd do it right now. Maybe if I ran away to Europe and started life over. . . . Maybe I could sell the *International Herald Tribune,* like those young girls used to.

134   The phone rang. Kugelmass lifted it to his ear mechanically.

135   "Bring her over," Persky said. "I think I got the bugs out of it."

136   Kugelmass's heart leaped. "You're serious?" he said. "You got it licked?"

137   "It was something in the transmission. Go figure."

138   "Persky, you're a genius. We'll be there in a minute. Less than a minute."

139   Again the lovers hurried to the magician's apartment, and again Emma Bovary climbed into the cabinet with her boxes. This time there was no kiss. Persky shut the doors, took a deep breath, and tapped the box three times. There was the reassuring popping noise, and when Persky peered inside, the box was empty. Madame Bovary was back in her novel. Kugelmass heaved a great sigh of relief and pumped the magician's hand.

140   "It's over," he said. "I learned my lesson. I'll never cheat again, I swear it." He pumped Persky's hand again and made a mental note to send him a necktie.

141   Three weeks later, at the end of a beautiful spring afternoon, Persky answered his doorbell. It was Kugelmass, with a sheepish expression on his face.

142   "O.K., Kugelmass," the magician said. "Where to this time?"

143   "It's just this once," Kugelmass said. "The weather is so lovely, and I'm not getting any younger. Listen, you've read *Portnoy's Complaint*?[9] Remember The Monkey?"[10]

144   "The price is now twenty-five dollars, because the cost of living is up, but I'll start you off with one freebie, due to all the trouble I caused you."

145   "You're good people," Kugelmass said, combing his few remaining hairs as he climbed into the cabinet again. "This'll work all right?"

146   "I hope. But I haven't tried it much since all that unpleasantness."

147   "Sex and romance," Kugelmass said from inside the box. "What we go through for a pretty face."

148   Persky tossed in a copy of *Portnoy's Complaint* and rapped three times on the box. This time, instead of a popping noise there was a dull explosion, followed by a series of crackling noises and a shower of sparks. Persky leaped back, was seized by a heart attack, and dropped dead. The cabinet burst into flames, and eventually the entire house burned down.

149   Kugelmass, unaware of this catastrophe, had his own problems. He had not been thrust into *Portnoy's Complaint,* or into any other novel, for that matter. He had been projected into an old textbook, *Remedial Spanish,* and was running for his life over a barren, rocky terrain as the word *tener* ("to have")—a large and hairy irregular verb—raced after him on its spindly legs.

[9]*Portnoy's Complaint* is a novel by Philip Roth which, when it was first published, was a favorite of undergraduates because of its sexual explicitness.
[10]The Monkey is a sexually athletic young woman in *Portnoy's Complaint.*

Questions for Discussion

1. Why does Kugelmass want to have a love affair?

2. Kugelmass is given the option of meeting and loving any woman in any work of literature. If you were given the option of so choosing any man or woman, whom would you choose? Why?

3. Why does Persky mention as options such characters as Hester Prynne, Ophelia, Temple Drake, or Nana? How do these allusions add depth to the humor of the story?

4. What relationship between life and art does this story suggest? In what ways does it give new meaning to the term "escapist literature"?

Suggestions for Exploration and Writing

1. If you have read *Madame Bovary,* choose a scene before the entry of Rodolphe and rewrite it, adding Kugelmass. If you have not read

Madame Bovary, write an imagined scene set in either France or New York City from the point of view of Emma Bovary as she is seen in Allen's story.

2. At the end of Allen's story, Kugelmass becomes a character with "few remaining hairs" being chased by "a large and hairy irregular verb" in a remedial Spanish book. Compare his situation to becoming a character in a Stephen King novel or a similar work.

3. In a comic narrative, imagine yourself or a friend transported to a story or play in this anthology.

4. Cast yourself as a character in a recent movie and explain your reasons for selecting that character.

Mark Bourne (b. 1961)

Mark Bourne has published short stories in national magazines and original anthologies such as the Full Spectrum 5, *where "What Dreams Are Made On" appeared. His first fiction collection,* Mars Dust & Magic Shows, *appeared in 2001. A master's degree in theater led directly to a career in the astronomy field, where he has written and produced work for multimedia planetariums, videos, and science museum exhibits. He lives in Portland, Oregon.*

WHAT DREAMS ARE MADE ON   (1995)

Our revels now are ended. These our actors
(As I foretold you) were all spirits and
Are melted into air, into thin air,
And like the baseless fabric of this vision
The cloud-capp'd towers, the gorgeous palaces
The solemn temples, the great globe itself
Yea, all that it inherit, shall dissolve
And, like this insubstantial pageant faded
Leave not a rack behind. We are such stuff
As dreams are made on; and our little life
Is rounded with a sleep.

—*THE TEMPEST*

1   Golden flecks of sunlight shimmered off the shaft of piss streaming down from the highest balcony of the Globe Theater. It curved in the breeze toward Sally, speckling the middle balcony rail before her. Mayhap a gust of summer wind would blow it into the face of that perfumed matron, the one who sneered *"Whore"* when Sally squeezed past her earlier. But no—the stream plummeted past and hit the dirt below in a steady pish, as if shushing the raucous din of the playgoers around her.

2   And the low murmur of the voices within her.

3   They were back again, gathering in her head like an audience attending the theatre. They came more oft now. Did spirits work this way—whispering in daylight, then tormenting her dreams by night?

4   Fah! Spirits? Demons? Foolishness and fairy tales.

5   Yet they murmured inside her, haunting her more than ever before. *Everyone* believed in demons. King James even wrote about them, before he wrote the Bible.

6   Sally scratched between her legs through her coarse skirt, and in her pate airy voices gasped, sounding both shocked and delighted at her touch.

7   Across the yard, Libby and Mary sold oranges and themselves for a few shillings and a flea-infested bed for the night. Poor Mary's skin displayed the poxes oft included in the trade. Beneath her eyes, a filthy rag covered the hole where her nose had been. Sally thanked God *she* never suffered that way. *Viruses. Bacteria.* The language of the dreams had become her own. *Germs. Poor hygiene.* What God could spill out such poxes, yet leave her smooth and untouched?

8   Keening wails of sorrow sounded in her head. Or faint laughter. As usual, they were distant and unclear.

9   In the yard below, groundlings were enjoying the play they paid a penny to see, a low comedy about a rich old cuckold whose young wife was enjoyed by the young men of London society. Sally cheered the boy playing the wife, and stood on her toes to see him better. His legs, strong from dance and swordplay, carried him with nimble grace across the broad stage. At thirteen years, he already stood taller than older actors. Jack deserved better parts. The other King's Men said so. Even William had said so, before he returned to the quiet life of Stratford. This must be how a mother felt. Pride in her child's success. And in her own. Sally smiled at the boy's acrobatic antics. Vast arenas smiled inside her. Like a crowd at the Coliseum.

10   The Roman Coliseum had been airier than these new English theatres. She had seen it in her dreams, along with other places marvelously strange and foreign. Such as the dream of eating raspberry coldness in a glass tower as tall as the clouds. The man with the eyes lived in that one. He held her tenderly, as no other man did, and she laughed with him in the dream places. Dreams only half remembered after waking, fading like ghosts caught in churchyards at dawn.

11   The voices murmured louder. Or was it playgoers applauding? Sally looked into the crowd. Her eyes were drawn to a seat near the gallery rail.

12   The man sat there, staring up at her. Cheers and whistles blew between her ears.

13   Clothed in the finery of an Earl or a Duke, he watched her with eyes dark and bright, not rheumy and weak like other men's. Eyes she knew. Mayhap just a former customer? Wealthy men favored her. Yet that face was misplaced above the lacy ruff and dark doublet etched with gold. Eyes from a dream. Many dreams.

14   A thought flickered inside her like a candle flame, bright and hot. The stranger meant something. The end. Of what? Of everything. Sally was to

die. The thought pierced her soul and pulled through it like a thread. Fear surged into her blood.

15 She ran to the stairs that led to the street.

16 Vast crowds rose to their feet in a thunderstorm of applause. As always, they were nowhere close by.

17 Damp grass pressed up against the back of Sally's neck. The stars seemed to cool the night air. Just beyond her bare feet, starlight skipped across the black mirror of the Thames. She gazed into the arch of the Milky Way, which rose from the City shadows and curved behind her into Saint George's Field.

18 The voices were gone. For now.

19 The only sounds came from behind her, from the inn adjoining the Globe. Raucous laughter and men's tavern tales echoed among nearby homes. Framed in the bright rectangle of the alehouse door, moving shadows strutted and gestured to the rafters. The ritualistic end of another playhouse run.

20 Footsteps crunched on the path from the inn. Sally turned. A silhouetted figure approached her. Dim light glimmered off fair hair. The figure began running toward her, then leapt high into the air, somersaulted onto the grass nearby, and fell to its back, laughing.

21 Sally smiled. "You're going to do yourself an injury one day."

22 "Nay." Jack crawled over and sat beside her. "What are you doing?"

23 "Watching stars. Listening to old players. Why aren't you with them?"

24 "I'm not an old player."

25 His voice had deepened so much. She laid her hand lightly on his back.

26 He drew nearer, looked down into her face. "What troubles you?"

27 "Why do you ask?"

28 He turned to the river, as if the wet starlight would respond for him. "Your sleep is troubled more and more. I hear you through the wall. Your dreams. They vex you."

29 "Mayhap I am not alone at such times."

30 He looked hurt. "I know the different sounds. You know that."

31 "I'm sorry." Jack was not stupid. She closed her eyes. "I see the dreams more clearly in recent nights. But they are merely dreams." Could he hear the doubt in her voice?

32 "Dreams," he said, "where you live in fantastical lands, or in ages that be only in the histories. If they are mere dreams, why do you awaken many nights speaking aloud, or shouting. Once even crying?"

33 She stared overhead into the thick spray of stars. Her arm followed the Milky Way. "See that river in the heavens? To the Egyptians, that is Nut, Goddess of Night, whose long body arcs forever over the earth. Folk in other days lived wondrous strange lives."

34 "Mistress Coxham said we all lived in the history times, being born other babes ere being now, in England. Said we all live forever. She said."

35   "Mistress Coxham was a mad old crone. She said the devil bit her bum and the morning cock told prophecies."

36   "They said she was a witch and hanged her."

37   "They were mad, also, in their fashion. There are no witches. No demons. No spirits, sprites, or elfin folk." She tousled his hair. "And no Puck, I'm sorry to say."

38   Jack looked at her as though she were denying the existence of the Thames itself. "You were bewitched once, when you first to London came. Possessed by demons who stole your remembrances. So you said."

39   "'Twas hard drink eating my wits, so I said. Sack and wine fighting for the pleasure of driving me mad. It passed." Last night, she had awakened to the fading vapors of fine wine and raspberry.

40   Her earliest memories began just two summers ago, when she woke alongside a Southwark road with a flaming pain in her skull. She must have been sick and drunk and left for dead. Beaten, too, if the lump on her pate was any witness. She rubbed the back of her skull, where her hair hid a pebble-sized mound of raised flesh.

41   In London, she found work as a maidservant to a printer named Colesly. Jack had been Colesly's 'prentice, making pamphlets and setting books. Jack would read them and recite them for Sally when Colesly was asleep. The boy boasted that he was always excellent with books. He was only ten when Sally found him. And better learned, he proclaimed, than any Oxford dunghead.

42   She had seen the scars on Jack's back and the bruises on his face, and had heard him scream with Colesly's beatings in the work room. Then Colesly came for her. Made her do things. He laughed when he told her what he got from the boy. That's when she took Jack out into the night and they lived wherever shelter could be found. Sally turned to whoring. Jack took to the playhouse. All the same in most folks' eyes. They each found success in their craft, and earned enough to rent rooms at the inn next to the Globe, alongside the finest playhouse in London.

43   A silhouette crossed the open alehouse door. Sonorous, rhythmic words drifted on the air. Prospero, from *The Tempest*. William's farewell to his illusions and craft. Jack mouthed the words along with the shadow-actor. The boy stretched out in the grass and wove a long ribbon of Sally's raven hair between his fingers. "Lord Shakespeare himself asked me to be in that play." Sadness tinted his voice.

44   "I remember."

45   He grinned as he thumped his chest. "I was the first and best Miranda *The Tempest* will e'er see. I'll be the best player in the King's Men. And the best poet, too. He said so."

46   "Modesty once was a virtue."

47   "Only among the virtuous." He rolled onto his back, put his head against hers and clasped her hand. She held it tight and stillness hung between them. His voice had grown so deep this year. His words shoved away the silence. "You tell me of places strange and fanciful, with flying

fire-drakes that bear magical people, of paintings that move and speak, and of lands where colored suns shine and there is no night. I remember them. They become my plays."

48   "They are but dreams," she said.

49   "Mama told me such stories. Legends and travelers' tales about lands across the seas. I hear her in you."

50   "You speak of your mother rarely, Jack. Why do so now?"

51   "I never gave her thanks. Now seems a good time."

52   Not yet old enough for a man, nor young enough for a boy, she thought, recalling a line from *Twelfth Night*. Across the river, tiny fires flickered through London's far shop windows. A boatman shouted in the distance.

53   Jack brought her hand to his chest. "You are a faerie queen spirited away and placed sleeping by the road to save a woeful orphan from a villain, so he can become the greatest player-poet in the world." He brushed his hand along the starry arch overhead. "In all worlds. We shall move hearts in enchanted lands and make elf kings laugh and weep. And no man nor devil will split us one from the other." *Please, God, let him not grow too quickly.*

54   Jack tugged her hand and stood. "Come."

55   She sat up. "To?"

56   "The inn. Richard has a surprise."

57   "What manner of surprise?"

58   "I know not. He wants us all to come."

59   "Promise to stay away from sack and beer? And upstairs to bed ere midnight?"

60   He frowned. "Aye, Sally."

61   She rose. Cool sand squeezed between her toes.

62   "Sally."

63   "Yes, love."

64   "Do I play parts in your dreams?"

65   She said nothing. From the Thames, the boatman's bell echoed against dark dwellings.

66   The voices returned when she approached the alehouse. Louder, closer than before. She fell back against the doorframe and closed her eyes. The inn sounds shrank away, leaving her surrounded by an invisible throng. They entered her from behind her eyes and sounded delighted to return to this place.

67   *Go away!*

68   Anticipation boiled beneath the buzzing murmurs. Whispers that might carry affection, admiration, or the musky thrill an audience breathes out at public executions.

69   "Sally." Someone was shaking her shoulders. *"Sally."* She opened her eyes to Jack's face. She was startled by the fear etched into it. "Sally, are you ailing?"

70   She stepped into the shadows; the wall was cool against her back. She found a bright star overhead and focused on it. After a moment, she stood straight and met Jack's worried gaze.

71 "I'm well. The heat of a long day."

72 He studied her with wary scrutiny.

73 She took his hand. "Come. Does Richard not have a surprise?" He returned her smile, but it wavered as she pulled him into the tavern.

74 Lanterns tossed dirty light around the room, threw restless shadows on the walls. The air was heavy with the pleasant reek of malmsey and beer. Men sat at tables with bottles and mugs; some played games, others traded bawdy tales. Francis, the innkeeper, wrapped Sally's hand around a cool mug. He winked at her, then cocked his head toward a growing din at the other end of the room. Burly Richard Burbage stood on a table, extemporizing a devastating parody of a rival company. An audience was building around him, punctuating his performance with laughter and applause. As soon as he saw Sally and Jack, he grinned and clapped for attention.

75 "Sally-o, our Sally-o!" he sang. "A good woman among such rowdy men." A ragged cheer rose from the crowd, and Sally somehow found herself in front of the group. Richard pouted like a boy caught pulling the rose petals. "Please forgive our bawdy ways and give us all a kiss to dream on." He placed a hand to his middle and bent at the waist, as though performing at Court. The other men laughed good-naturedly and greeted her warmly before moving into loose knots of drinking and boasting.

76 Richard leapt from the table and took Sally by the shoulders. "'Tis good to see thee, Lady. You have not graced our company much of late."

77 She kissed his cheek. "I'm sorry, Richard. I haven't felt much like company lately."

78 He recreated Jack's worried look. "Your speech has been strange, Lady. Methought it must be tainted by the wealthy foreigners you entertain. And you have been troubled. Is there anything you would tell friend Richard?"

79 "Jack says you have a surprise." She stepped away and felt Richard's gaze as she moved to Jack's side.

80 Richard climbed back onto the table. He clapped again. The room went silent. Someone handed him a stack of pages.

81 "Friends, Romans, countrymen. Shut your ale holes. A message—" He held out a page. "—delivered me this day from our most honored poet (and wealthiest stocksharer) now living in familial lethargy in Stratford. He sends greetings—" His eyes brightened during the perfectly-timed dramatic pause. "—which you may receive on the morrow when he arrives here for the first performance of our play."

82 Astonishment sang out from the crowd. Since returning to Stratford, Will had not made a trip back to London. But he would be here for the premiere of his play registered in the Office of Revels as *The Famous History of the Life of King Henry the Eighth.*

83 Sally rubbed the base of her skull. Something about that play vexed her, but she couldn't say what. It surely wasn't one of Will's finest. A lantern flame snared her attention, and the hubbub of the actors faded. She searched for patterns in the fire, shapes and faces that danced away as quickly as they formed.

84   *Henry the Eighth* had been one of the many masques and entertainments commissioned to adorn the nuptials of King James' daughter to Frederick V, Elector Palatine, that February last. Sally remembered Will, tired and sick, sitting in this room on a raw December night, grumping about his collaborator, John Fletcher. Will called her "Sally-o" as he spoke of Anne and his quiet life near the Avon. He regaled her once again with stories of life in the theatre, of friends he had loved and outlived. He spoke of a dark lady, and brushed a mottled hand through his Sally-o's night-black hair. Sally kept him from drinking too much, then walked arm in arm with him through the snow to Richard's house.

85   The voices had been unusually clamorous that night.

86   A week before the royal wedding, William canceled the performance. Fletcher had insulted him before the company and refused to rewrite his portions of the script to William's desires. *Henry the Eighth* was removed from the roster and the scripts kept in careful storage.

87   Two weeks ago, the King's Men decided to bring to the stage Will's unperformed history play.

88   Richard was holding a page over his head as if it were a victory flag. "Gentlemen. Lady. Dear William arrives on the morn. Yet seeing our play is simple pretense. He is returning to us to take as his sole pupil and protégé one of our illustrious players. Come hither, Jack."

89   The boy let out a yelp and pushed through the men. Arms reached out to pat his back while a chorus of congratulations washed over him. Richard handed down the page. Jack grabbed it and read hungrily. Love and pride swelled within Sally. Jack was born to greatness, and would surely make his mark upon this earth under William's care and guidance. He was destined for nothing less.

90   Richard sat on the table and put an arm around the boy. "'Tis a grand honor, lad. I have trod the boards for well nigh thirty years, and the likes of you has never blessed us with such skill. You have gold in your veins, boy, and now the most perfect teacher shall help you mine it."

91   He handed Jack a thick manuscript. The title *Masque of the Planets* dominated the front page in Jack's careful penmanship. "He says this play is but the first jewel in your crown. Best of luck, lad, and a long life in our noble profession."

92   Mugs and bottles were raised. Someone began a boisterous song. Others joined in with singing, instruments, or dancing. Jack was on Richard's shoulders, waving like a king on a balcony.

93   Someone was watching her. She felt it.

94   Sally turned and peered through the doorway. The blackness beyond thickened and hardened, then stepped into the lantern light. The man from the dreams stood against the backcloth of night.

95   Voices behind her eyes gasped. Sally clasped her hands to her mouth, trapping the scream in her throat. Dream images burst through her head. Part of herself felt removed, distant, detached—in the scene, but now also among an unseen audience. Faintly, she heard Jack shouting, "Sally! This be your celebration too!"

96   The music ceased.

97   Sally slid doll-like to the floor. She heard her voice saying "No" and "Not again." She pissed herself and stared at the doorway. He watched her, as he had that afternoon at the Globe. His eyes were exactly the color of twilight. A creature, gray and hairless, squatted on his shoulder, flapping black batlike wings. Its face was twisted and almost human.

98   In her head, phantoms stood up and cheered.

99   The stranger moved toward Sally. Jack stepped between them, shaking. "I charge thee," he said. "Lay not a hand to this good lady. I knew demons plagued her, and I shall fight thee at Hell's throne."

100   The stranger reached out to Jack, in a pleading gesture. "Please. I can help her. It's not supposed to be like this." He took a step.

101   Jack glanced from the stranger to the actors, holding his stance. The winged thing raised its talons and shrieked. Jack ran to the players.

102   The man knelt beside her. He wrapped her in his cloak and cradled her tenderly. She felt her body go slack as he lifted her and carried her toward the stairs, shouting orders as he moved. His voice was as clear and dark as his eyes. "There's a trunk in the yard. Leave it outside her room. She's in good care. Everything will be as it's always been." He carried her up the steps. Jack's sobs cut the air.

103   Warm water flowed into her brain, which hummed with the incoming tide of a thousand thousand ghosts. It was the last thing Sally heard before she lost consciousness.

104   She awoke smelling beans and roast chicken. Her first thought was *I'm hungry.*

105   The window shutters were open, letting in a moist breeze. The full moon cast the only light into the room. It took her a moment to realize that the bed beneath her was not straw and dirty linen. It was supple and warm and molded itself to her body as she moved. It cushioned her head and bathed her in flowing comfort that searched her body for places to soothe. She pushed herself up onto one elbow and peered over the side of the bed. It was floating above the floor. She thought it odd that she wasn't surprised by that, and placed her head back on the pillow. Warmth flowed around her and she gave in to sleep. Her first dream was of raspberry ice cream.

106   When she opened her eyes again, the moon was higher and dulled by clouds. A lantern flickered on the floor, revealing a plateful of chicken, beans, and bread on the bed with her. A pot of water stood beside it. She sat up and devoured the meal.

107   "Have a napkin."

108   She turned. The man sat on a jeweled trunk against the door. He tossed her a soft towel. His face was warm, friendly, and familiar. Somehow, he looked older than he should.

109   "Your innkeeper friend keeps a fine larder," he said. "I left him a tip where he'll find it tomorrow. Everyone's finally gone home. They really care about you."

110　She realized then that she was naked and had been given a thorough sponge bath. Her dress hung on the lantern hook. She felt hollow inside, carved out. But not empty. Someone else was there, and they blended like merging flames.

111　"I tried contacting you at the play." His voice soothed her. "Your conditioning should have dissolved then. I don't understand why you ran."

112　When she did not respond, he looked disappointed. "You heard our audience when we made eye contact. They had no idea when or where I would show up. You should've seen the nielsen lines."

113　Memories flowed and congealed like cooling wax. Her room looked so dirty now, and the light was too dim. Despite the bath, she could smell her own sour sweat. A thick, hot costume seemed to drop from her shoulders, and she felt the part of her named Sally slide away, submerged and hidden. With the others.

114　She reached out. "Alexandros."

115　She pulled him close and hugged him tight. He returned the embrace, and she realized how sore and tired she was. She looked into his face and gently touched it with her fingertips. She wanted to speak, but words jumbled in her mind. She took his hands into hers.

116　Relief smoothed away the lines in his face, which set into that famous soft smile. "The leading man always returns in the final act." His fingers moved through her hair. "I've missed you. Two years is a long time in any century." His hand brushed her cheek, and she leaned into it, an automatic response. "How do you feel?"

117　As if I were just poured into a used body. "Same as always, only more so. It hasn't all come back to me yet." She rubbed the back of her head, where a—what was the thing called?—mnemosyne wove its microthin web into her brain. "My link?"

118　"Switched off. For now. So's mine, though I'll be the Network's virtual body until you're rested up. Welcome back, Selene."

119　"That's not my name."

120　"You'll feel that way for a while. This was a long run. Sally was a beautifully fleshed-out character. A lot of you in her."

121　"She *was* me. Is." Her head itched inside, and her skin was cool and damp, as if from a fever breaking.

122　He walked to the window and looked out over the river into the dark skyline of King James' London. "They're always you." He leaned through the window for a better view, then sharply pulled his hands away from the grimy ledge. "Full recall should take an hour or so." He had told her similar things on other occasions. She shivered and pulled a thick blanket around her. It snuggled comfortingly against her skin.

123　He turned and flashed the smile that thrilled millions of fans who were—how many centuries up the Channel? "You're now the model for all Total Immersion actors. The Network has a fat paychip waiting for you when we get back. But we'll have a day together in merry old England first. In the meantime, think about what you'd like your next role to be."

124   Something black and ugly moved in her soul—

125   At the far end of the Network's Time Channel, skindivers were awaiting their next episode. She was their eyes and ears. Their flesh. Their soul, too, when her thoughts and feelings rode the waves up the Channel. They paid well to join her in her skin.

126   —Then he was behind her, massaging her shoulders, finding all the right places. His hands moved down her back. She let the blanket fall away.

127   "Sally was so good," he said, "we gave you more episodes than the Caesar's Rome series. You've soloed to higher ratings than any of our series together. Marketing the recordings offworld has already put another fortune in our account. Told you I'd make you a star." She could hear his self-satisfied grin.

128   He lightly scraped his fingernails across her neck, the way she always liked. "I knew you'd end up at the Globe. You and Burbage kept the 'will-they-or-won't-they' fans tuned in. And The Man himself, Willy the Shakes. Who'd have guessed you'd get so cozy with your idol? The kid's a hit. He's been compared to the young Mozart." He eyed her with mock suspicion. "I'm glad he's not a few years older."

129   "Voices," she said. "I heard voices."

130   He twirled an upraised hand with a showman's flourish. "The smell of the horseshit, the roar of the crowd! You gave them Sally, your audience gave you their feedback. At your request, you'll remember."

131   "It was awful," she said. The link in her skull was an iron weight. Its tendrils snaked through her brain like rusty wires.

132   "You never really thought so. Deep down you knew it was normal. You, my dear, thrive on applause." He moved around to her front, his fingers combing through her hair.

133   "Hey," he said. "I'm up for applause too. The Network finally promoted me to Producer. That's why I didn't write myself into the series until yesterday."

134   No, she thought. That's not true. Something dark and smoky swirled in her memory. It dissolved when she grasped for it.

135   He cupped her chin and delicately tilted her head up. "I've learned to appreciate the biz side of showbiz," he said. He kissed her lightly on the lips, then smiled. "Congratulations. We're a hit." The face behind the smile stiffened. "Not bad for your first performance without your partner." His expression was unfamiliar, hard and uncomfortable on what should have been a gentle, sincere face.

136   The floating bed wriggled as Alexandros sat beside her. "You really scared me this evening," he said. "Recall should've been further along when you saw me. You were supposed to at least greet me as an old friend. Remember?" His voice was low while she watched the lantern's flame sculpt tiny images. "Remember the last time I helped you drop character? New York City, 1987?"

137   He stood and moved to the trunk, pulled it to the center of the room. When he touched its padlock, the lid opened, flooding the room with

electric blue brilliance. Alexandros pressed a jade bauble on the lid. The blue light changed to green. His shadow was huge on the wall as he reached into the trunk and withdrew an ice cream cone. It was half-eaten and began dripping only after he handed it to Sally.

138   "Another memento from another end of the world. You always need a souvenir, don't you? Taste it."

139   Raspberry. She held it like it might explode.

140   He forced a small laugh. "I never knew you liked raspberry until Sarah started craving it."

141   Sarah. As usual, she and Alex had been lovers in that series. Audiences loved when art imitated life. Her character had become a successful Broadway actress. He was the shining new executive in a Wall Street firm. Mr. and Mrs. Alex MacMillan, brought to you live from the 20th Century only on Network Time Channel 1! The finest reality a skindiver could buy; authentic historical drama—seeing, feeling, and smelling the bad ol' days before the world got too good to be interesting. The historians got their bread. The rest got their circuses.

142   When it came time to cancel that series, Alex dropped character first; the Network had no trouble dissolving his conditioning. But Sarah wouldn't die so easily. Selene remembered the screaming wail of the evac sirens.

143   "There we were in Central Park," he was saying, "With umpty-thousand scared shitless extras running in all directions just before the nukes blew." The nexus was open near the Alice in Wonderland statues. "You dropped character just in time." Just in time to step into the nexus and watch Manhattan go up in a rain of warheads that the "extras" believed came from Moscow.

144   "You never did let go of that ice cream. You almost clung to Sarah too long. The psi-shock of that one would've put half the 'divers into abuse treatment wards."

145   That series had played for over a year before the Network wrote in its smashing climax and then pulled the plug, erasing all insertions and alterations made to truetime—the bombs, the deaths, the artificial existence of Sarah and Alex MacMillan. As always, history neatly, tidily, irrevocably set itself right again. But the Network's temporary rewrites had done their job. When Selene and Alexandros returned up the Channel, they were greeted by adoring fans as well as a grateful—and wealthier—Network.

146   She had made friends there, in New York, 1987.

147   She felt the tears slide down her face, and was both angry and relieved by them. Alex held and rocked her, combing her hair with his fingers. "Hey. What's wrong? We got out. No one got hurt. Not in the end, anyway."

148   She broke his grasp and threw the ice cream hard. It struck the wall and spread across the dirt like an opening wound. She balled her fists and pounded him hard, harder, not hard enough. He dropped to the floor.

149   *"They were not extras,"* she shouted. "Not just characters. It wasn't make-believe. They were—they are—real people." She pointed out the window at London. Or New York, or Rome, Athens, San Francisco, or Pompeii.

150   He rubbed his ribs. "What the fuck are you talking about? We pulled the plug, didn't we? History snapped back to truetime. Just like always."

151   She remembered. Just like after the 'gods' wiped out Athens; after the nanoviruses mutated a Coliseum audience before killing them; after Comet Halley dropped into downtown 1910.

152   Alexandros stood, inspecting his costume for dust. "You should see what the gang in Creative Control have planned for Tokyo at the height of the monster movie craze." He picked her blanket from the floor and dusted it carefully before wrapping it around her shoulders. "I've never seen this in you before."

153   She didn't look up.

154   "It's still just acting, Sel."

155   But this time he was the one who had monitored her and made sure the skindivers knew when an episode was beginning. Alexandros had kept them tuned in and living Sally along with her. Had he been linked into her while she was in bed with other men, riding her flesh with the 'divers? Why not? That's showbiz!

156   What about life back home? Had he kept up his brilliant work on stages before vast audiences? He seemed so thrilled about his new life in the Network, and spoke as though trying to convince her of its value. Or, perhaps, convince himself.

157   She suddenly knew why Alex had inserted himself into this series at this time. She hugged the blanket tight. "It's time to end," she said flatly. "What happens now?"

158   The lantern's flame jiggled in a breeze, and his shadow stretched and twitched on the wall. "Ah. That is the question. The Channel's been open for two years. It's at full stretch and threatening to snap. We have just enough time for the double finale tomorrow."

159   "And what's that?"

160   He was like a child sharing a dirty secret. "Oh, you know. June 29, 1613. The Globe Theater goes up in flames during the first performance of *Henry the Eighth*."

161   "What?"

162   "This inn, too. Foosh! It's in truetime. The cannons caught the roof on fire. Ha! Two centuries before the *1812 Overture*. Fortunately, nobody got hurt."

163   Her brow tightened. "Then what's the other finale?"

164   "Guess. What's this culture's big bogeyman? Plague? Been done. Famine? Boring. God's wrathful vengeance? The Greeks did it better. Space aliens? Already played at Tharsis Mars Base."

165   *"Alex. Stop it."*

166   He sucked a breath, seeing that he had gone too far. He did something to the side of the trunk. The luminescence burned a harsh red. The gray-skinned creature with bat wings climbed out onto the brim. A twisted goblin joined it, baring yellow fangs in a hideous face. Then a bloated froglike creature with wasp wings flew out and lit on the upturned lid. It clapped four webbed hands and unrolled its tongue to its knees. A tongue of fire

shot from the gaping mouth, churning the air like a blowtorch. Other things with wings and horns and twisted human features clambered out and stood around the trunk. Many were clad in moss and leaves. The tallest stood as high as Selene's shoulders.

167   Alex bounced on his toes. "Isn't the props department wonderful?"

168   Monstrosities gibbered around her. Demons from a Boschian vision. Goblins and bogles used to frighten children at bedtime. Creatures from rural myths and ghost stories. The dark side of religion and faerie lore she had lived among for two long years. Fires glowed within their glassy eyes.

169   "They're obscene."

170   "They're state of the art. And these are just the small ones. They can be directed through our links." He extended an arm toward a drooling thing that unfolded its wings and flew to his sleeve. It coughed a bright orange flame.

171   "Or voice commands provide that certain Satanic flavor that so impresses the natives." He pressed a red gem on the trunk's lock. "Specter of Death!" He smirked at his over-dramatic voice. "Arise and obey my commands!"

172   A shroud-draped skeleton gripping a bloody scythe drifted up and filled the space from trunk to ceiling. The air smelled of earthworms and spoiled meat. Flames glowed behind the bone-gray eye sockets. Fingerbones clacked like bamboo, then raised the dripping, crescent blade over Selene's head. The skull turned toward her, unhinging its jaw in an impossible grin.

173   "Hold," Alex said. The apparition froze. "Press the ruby and they're fully voice-controlled. They'll obey direct commands. Try it, but be careful. Their programming tends toward the literal."

174   "No." She turned away from him and grabbed her dress. It smelled rank. Her words came hard and fast as she put it on. "You can't just rewrite people's lives for cheap thrills or to sell more commercial time. They exist—flesh and blood real live human beings like you and me." She thought of Jack. He was here, at the Globe, because of Sally. Sally had saved him. "No. That's wrong," she said. "We stopped being real a long time ago."

175   "You always did get too wrapped up in your characters."

176   "I like who I am here."

177   "You're a whore."

178   "Wasn't I always? Aren't you?"

179   For a beat, his face was hard and still. Then he continued: "People love you at our end. Millions of them on a hundred worlds!"

180   "You mean they love how well I fuck people they consider unreal, fictional." In each of their series together, their characters found reasons to break up their relationship with painful, stabbing words. It was a point the "true" Alex and Selene managed to ignore when out of character. She knew what hurt him. "That includes you, too."

181   A glacial chill came from his eyes. The caring, sensitive Alex she had known—that Sarah and Sharri and Simone and the others within her had known—was absent. The Producer, cool and reserved and superior.

182   "You always claimed," he said, "that you became an actor to change people. Ever since our first stage together." *A Midsummer Night's Dream* within the Great Orion Nebula. Titania with newborn stars at her feet. Alex's magnificent Oberon. "Now you're a solo Network success, and the standard for future Total Immersion projects. Now you can play on any stage you want. We have offers coming in from the finest performing companies in human space. That's all waiting for you back home."

183   A breeze brought in the smell of the shit pit outside her window. She had never noticed it before.

184   "Don't throw it away," he said. "After we raise some Shakespearean hell, we'll pull the plug and go home. Then the past two years will have never happened here."

185   She stepped toward the door. "They happened to me. I'll remember."

186   "Sally's a character! Just like Sarah and the others. What makes this series so goddamned special?" He was shouting when she slammed the door behind her.

187   She leaned against the hallway wall. Jack's room. Sally should go to him, be with him.

188   Too bad she wasn't here.

189   Selene ran down the stairs and into the newly arrived rain.

190   She walked until well past dawn, through filthy streets that were at once warmly familiar and strangely new. The town bustled with wagon wheels and shouting vendors. Farmers were already in the fields as sunlight turned the eastern clouds the color of dirty water. Her fingers brushed buildings as she passed them, memorizing the textures of wood and brick and loam. She sat on a low garden wall and listened for patterns in the rain as it struck the flowers. She focused her concentration, and a small glowing circle appeared in her field of vision. She ran her eyes across the garden. The icon remained in her view, always in the upper right corner. An empty circle. Good. The Network wasn't broadcasting her senses yet. Watching roses wasn't thrilling enough. She relaxed her concentration and the image vanished. Raindrops tapped her head and trickled down her back.

191   She wondered where the Channel nexus was focused, and was answered by another glowing glyph. The trunk. Of course. Alex had a colorful sense of theatrics. It was their pathway to home. Before he arrived, her link could have shown her the nexus as a glowing oval hole hovering above the inn, invisible to anyone not equipped with a bump in the skull and wires in the brain. But Sally had known nothing of Time Channels or neuralinks or skindivers.

192   Sally. A new persona could never be fully predicted. Which was part of the drama of Total Immersion. Language, social customs, mores. Synthesized memories of a life you never lived. All dumped into the brain before the Network dropped you unconscious in a new world and time. The rest came from within.

193   Selene had become a popular prostitute in the Sophocles' Greece series. And in Victoria's England. Her Caesar's Rome character nauseated her when she remembered it. Each of those women had been herself.

194   Alexandros had shared those other lives with her. In truetime, each was the other's partner, lover, friend, and teacher. He had nurtured her talent, helped it grow. Without him, she would not now be sitting on a garden wall down the road from Shakespeare's Globe.

195   What if the Channel collapsed before she returned through it? What if Alexandros returned alone, pulling the plug behind him? The universe strictly forbade return trips. Would she continue to live here in the history she helped shape, with truetime permanently and irrevocably altered? Or would she exist in a new truetime split off from the one she knew? Or else be edited out of existence entirely, along with Sally and her entire life here? The Network never told. The Network kept its secrets.

196   After those early series, certain critics accused them of slumming, of selling themselves for the latest trend. They were right. Each series had been tailored to the tastes of subscribers who paid to have life lived for them.

197   This time, though, the Network added a new plot twist. Sally began life with no predetermined memories, no history, alone on a dirt road with an entire identity to create. She had seen to that. Alex had stayed behind. She had a part in that, too.

198   Playing solo for the first time, she discovered a strong, content, fully-rounded character. Or had it been the other way around? The heart of acting beat with self-discovery. Exploration of the soul. Total Immersion had offered that, and her real stage work would now be even stronger than before.

199   Any stage she wanted. She could travel the stars again and hear applause on a hundred worlds. She had earned it. How could she toss that away? And for what? Watching others chewed away by disease. Shitting and pissing in pots or ditches. Stepping over the dead and dying in the streets.

200   Blossoms nodded and raindrops made muddy craters in the earth. The sound of water against dirt conjured a memory. Jack clutching her hand while they lay in the sandy grass by the river. The things he said. His boyish laughter. That so-adult confidence in his own immense talent. That was so long ago. A lifetime.

201   After a few hours, the drizzle stopped. She returned to Bankside, where clouds hung over the Globe like a low shroud. She looked up at the theatre's thatched roof and wooden walls, wondering how much rain was needed to prevent a fire. Useless thoughts. The blaze had happened. Would happen.

202   Selene climbed onto the stage, enjoying the odor of fresh paint. She admired the underside of the effects hut jutting out high above the stage and supported by two tall columns. Its gilded underside provided a ceiling painted to portray the heavens. To Sally, the hut had looked like a cottage held aloft above the players. To Selene, here was Hamlet's brave o'erhanging firmament, this majestical roof fretted with golden fire.

203   A square hole slid open in the ceiling. A round face poked down. The stagehand cupped his hands around his mouth and called down, asking if she had seen his assistant. When she said no, he cursed skillfully and thanked Sally, then vanished behind the panel sliding back into its piece of the sky.

204   In the tiring room, Richard and the others were exercising their bodies and throats, changing into costumes, and rehearsing bits of scenes. Robert, Augustine, Nick, and young Nathan. Kemp, Sly, Heminges, Condell. Friends she had known, it seemed, all her life. She saw them through Sally's eyes and heart. She was warm and at home here.

205   I will remember you.

206   They approached her. Through a false beard, Richard's face mirrored their distress.

207   "Lady. How fares you? That stranger, with that beast—"

208   She shushed him with a finger to his lips. She took his hands, looked around at all the others.

209   "I am well. Just stricken with an ague that has passed. That gentleman is an old friend, a traveler newly returned from the Indies. He studies the strange beasts of the isles. His pet was but a harmless Indian ape." Everyone knew the accounts of bizarre creatures in exotic new lands on the other side of the world. She looked into the thickly lined face of her friend. For the last time? She stroked his big arms. "I am well. Truly." Richard looked doubtful. Time to change the subject. "Where's Jack?" she said.

210   "The lad was late to this morn's practice. Said he dreamt about his performance, that this day would see his finest ever, though I know he wishes not to play women after today." Richard laughed and wrapped a big arm around Sally's shoulders. "Jack's a strong lad of stout mettle. Do not concern yourself."

211   He pulled her away from the others, then lowered his voice to a hoarse whisper. "The boy is troubled. He spoke of that . . . gentleman. A devil from your dreams, he said, come to take you to—" He sighed. "I understand not all he spoke. He left the playhouse soon after."

212   She squeezed his hands. "I shall speak with him." How would Sally say goodbye to Jack?

213   "William is at my home," Richard said. "He asks for you. He wishes to see his Sally-o, said he would search for you at the inn."

214   William Shakespeare is asking for me. Selene searched within herself for the simple calm pleasure Sally would have found in the news. "Thank you, Richard. I miss him."

215   He kissed her forehead. "Now, get thee gone, woman." He let go a kingly bellow. "Before King Henry relieves you of your pretty head!" The players laughed, and she gave each a hug or a kiss, saving the longest for Richard.

216   The inn's front room was empty save for mugs and bottles from the night before. She found a sack of coins tied to the innkeeper's apron. Alex had been generous.

217   Upstairs, she knocked on Jack's door, then called his name. No answer. She pushed the door open.

218   On the wall over his bed, a crude painting hung by a string from a nail in the wood. It was a brightly colored depiction of Sally and Jack. He had painted it shortly after they moved to these rooms. They were holding hands and smiling child-drawing smiles. She tapped the frame and watched their painting-selves sway back and forth on the string.

219   She heard a creak through the wall. That floorboard near her bed. Alex must be just waking. She was on her way to the door when she saw thick bundles of vellum stacked beside Jack's bed. Jack's plays. *Masque of the Planets* already had revisions inked into the margins. She gently turned the pages. Not strictly a comedy, romance, or tragedy, but a weaving of all three, *Masque* was based on stories she had told him, imaginative fables conjured from her dreams. Memories of a life hidden within Sally for two long years. She recognized the grace and style of words nurtured by long study of Will's work. Jack displayed insights and wit that belied his youth, and his imagination laced the tightly woven fabric of his characters and story-lines. There were passages here that could make other playwrights reach for a quill, such as those lesser talents who loitered at the Globe ready to borrow a catchy phrase or two. *Masque*'s main character was a stern but loving queen of a wondrous kingdom—a beautiful, wise woman named Serena, stolen away from her world by a handsome sorcerer with dark eyes.

220   She thought of the printshop and Colesly, of what Sally had done for Jack.

221   She placed the manuscript back where she found it and left the room.

222   In her chamber, the trunk was still there, but Alex was gone. A new dress hung on the lantern hook. It was richly detailed and bright with color. A *lady's* dress, the type worn by the wife of a powerful man.

223   On her bed lay a parchment scrolled in a red ribbon. When she touched it, the ribbon unfurled, the paper unrolled, and Alex's voice read his handwriting for her.

224   "Sel. Out seeing the sights. I hear there's bearbaiting down the street and cockfights at noon. Then to hit the City for a public execution. Hangings and pressings today. Now that's entertainment." The parchment laughed Alex's laugh.

225   "The final episode will begin before the play does, today at two o'clock. We'll remote the props to the playhouse just after the cannons fire. Then we'll be back here and down the rabbit hole before the inn goes up. This'll be our biggest audience yet, and we'll both be broadcasting for dual-P.O.V. I'm glad we're a team again. Sorry about last night. Hope you like the dress. It's more you, don't you think? Put it on and join me. Contact me when you're ready. Switch the trunk from voice-to link-control so we won't have to come back here until we pull the plug. Loving you. As always. Alex."

226   The recording rolled itself up and the ribbon wriggled back into a tidy bow.

227   She turned to the trunk. "Open."

228   The lid raised with the simulated creak of rusty hinges and red light spilled into the room. Within the trunk, a uniform bloody glow hid any sense of depth or perspective, like a bottomless well from a Puritan's hell-fire fantasies. A data screen blinked on within the upturned lid.

229   The voice programming was simple and flexible. "My personal storage," Selene said. The red glow turned to jade green. She reached in and lifted out a rough parchment adorned with flowing Greek text. It announced a new drama, *Oedipus Tyrannos*, to be performed at the amphitheatre that afternoon. Alex had given it to her at a fountain near the theatre, where they had made love before their character conditioning faded. The huge holographic Zeus had been impressive, hurling lightning wrath from the hovering Channel nexus. She had teledirected the Hera image herself.

230   A jeweled lace garter from Victoria's London, given to her by a dashing West End actor named Alex. They dined with Shaw and Oscar Wilde and Ellen Terry, then dropped character in time to watch Wells' three-legged Martian war machines spewing smoky black poison and streaming infernos into the streets. The Network spared no expense before it canceled that series.

231   A holobubble bearing the Tharsis Base insignia threw out colored light that coalesced into Alex and Sharri, a honeymoon couple newly arrived from Earth. They laughed and hugged and told each other sweet things. It was recorded the night of the group festivities that had left them both tired and sore and blissfully content. And had provided the second highest ratings in Network history. The highest came the following night, when "alien berserkers" slit open the pressure domes and liquefied the survivors in their lifesuits.

232   Souvenirs from alternative histories the Network had created and the universe had erased. She placed them back into the trunk. A few words returned its glow to red.

233   "Come out."

234   Obedient obscenities climbed, flew, floated, and slithered out of the trunk. They stood, perched, or hovered around her like hideous dolls waiting to be wound up. The first wave.

235   "Hold," she said. The pandoran menagerie halted. She looked at the gray winged thing that had been perched on Alex's shoulder.

236   "Fly."

237   It launched itself and flapped around the room in complex patterns. It screeched and reached out long arms tipped with scalpel-like talons.

238   "Stop."

239   It fluttered to the floor.

240   This first wave of props was to be controlled by her and Alex's neuralink commands. But the vocal-command mode was equally well programmed.

241   "Burn yourself."

242   Perhaps a hesitation crossed its rubbery face. Then its eyes glowed fiercely red. It turned its face downward and belched a blowtorch into its chest. The device was soon a stinking puddle smoking on the floor.

243   She felt a cool satisfaction.

244   The data screen indicated a second wave waiting deeper within the trunk's stygian light. Pre-programmed and self-controlled, they would stream from the trunk like an army from Hell, with no guidance from her or Alex. But the second wave would come alive only after the first wave was released.

245   She ordered them back into the trunk, and soon they were swallowed by the red glare.

246   "Close."

247   The trunk sealed in the light.

248   She heard noises beyond the wall. Jack's room. She closed the door silently behind her.

249   This time, Jack answered her knock.

250   "Sally!" He pulled her into the room. "The demon took you away. You—"

251   "Shhh." She hugged him, stroked his hair. "It's all right. I'm here." He clutched her elbows as if to assure himself she was indeed still flesh and blood.

252   She found the firmly maternal voice she used whenever Jack needed one. "What did I tell you about demons?"

253   He turned his eyes downward. "You said there be no demons or faerie folk. You said."

254   "'Tis truth. Now, let's hear no more about it."

255   He sat on the bed. She told him the same lies about Alex and the creature she had told the others. Jack nodded, his face set in a mask of concentrated scrutiny. "Aye, Sally," he said, but his eyes did not blink while he looked at her.

256   "Is something wrong, Jack?"

257   Jack seemed to wake from a spell. He turned away from her and fumbled with his pages. "Lord Shake—William wishes to live in London again, and you and I with him. His true family is here, he says. He will teach me verse and drama, and you can nurse his sickness and give him good company, he says."

258   Will needs me. Sally.

259   Jack hugged Will's letter against his chest. "He wishes me to help revise his new play. Called *Celestine*, from a tale I devised from your dreams. He will bring it here to me. Is that not grand news?"

260   A mixture of emotions swirled within her. The part of her that was Sally was delighted and honored. Will's guidance was exactly what Jack needed. It would be good for both, giving the elder poet the purpose and affection that Stratford and Anne could not, and providing the younger with a nurturer of his talent.

261   Today, June 29, 1613.

262   April 26, 1616. Less than three years left for Will, in the history that did not contain his Sally-o. She could change that.

263   "So you must stay, and none must take you away," Jack was saying.

264   He avoided her quizzical look by glancing down at his manuscript.

265   He was leafing through pages when he spoke again. "Mortals that speak to faeries must die." The *non sequitur* shook her. Jack shrugged and flipped a page. "William remembers that from country tales when he was young. Only faerie folk speak to faerie folk. I have gotten this wrong in my play, where magic folk and men travel to the planets together to save the magical queen." He looked at her with inquisitive interest, quill in hand. "Do spirits obey those not of magical birth?"

266   "If you like. 'Tis your play." She wanted desperately to change the subject.

267   Jack scribbled in a margin, then awkwardly put his papers together, moving his gangly arms and hands with nervous display. The back of one hand brushed against her breast, slowing just enough to follow its curve and find the nipple. It was no accident.

268   She stood. "I must meet someone, Jack. I'll see you at the play, mm?"

269   "Is't that man?"

270   "Yes, Jack."

271   He shifted his position, placing his hands in his lap.

272   "Sally—" His erection pushed beneath his clothing, and he squirmed, looking ashamed.

273   She was embarrassed for him, and cast her eyes around the room. Just leave and talk about this later. It was, after all, perfectly normal, right?

274   The nail above his bed held no painting. It protruded over a gap between two wallboards. Scratches in the surrounding wood showed where the hole had been enlarged. Jack made a soft, pained sound when Selene stepped to the wall and peered through the hole.

275   The view revealed most of her room, including the trunk. Most prominent, though, was her bed, well lit by sunlight from the window. At night, moonlight shone there.

276   She spun around. "How long has this been here?"

277   He looked at his hands folded in his lap.

278   An angry flame flared within her, licking her insides.

279   "How dare you! How long have you been watching—"

280   Something black and cancerous in her soul burst open like a pustule. She felt sticky inside, ugly, used. . . .

281   Jack was crying, saying he was sorry and he loved her and never again—

282   She slapped him, hard, fast, without thought. His head snapped to the side, an angry red print across his cheek. His sobs sliced into her, cutting her like knives. Selene saw what was laid open within.

283   Jack had simply watched her with the eyes of a boy trapped in the churning onslaught of adolescence. Millions of others had done far more. The largest audiences of her career. They needed her, she had told herself. It was good to be needed.

284　But beneath the well-played roles, winding like a stream through the subconscious caverns where Sally and the others lived, was disgust for everyone who rode her flesh and soul. She had dammed that stream from the beginning, patching the cracks with every new character.

285　Sally was different. Sally was stronger than Selene had ever been, freer than Sarah, Sharri, Simone and the others. Sally struck out with Selene's hand, driven by rage that had grown malignant. Jack was not the intended target; still, the blow shattered the ugliness, struck it away like shards from a sculptor's blade.

286　She felt dizzy, released from a locked box she never knew existed.

287　What had Jack become in the truetime where Sally did not exist? Had he even survived this far, to explore and discover who he could become? The future had never known of him. But Sally had changed everything.

288　Jack's face was red and wet. He sucked air with sharp breaths, staring at her with confusion and pain. She held and rocked him, wiped his tears. Before long, he was asleep. She kissed him, then closed the door quietly behind her as she left.

289　From now on, she was writing her own script. And rewriting one other. William said the purpose of acting was to hold a mirror up to nature. For the first time since her Network contract began, Selene liked what stared back at her through the looking-glass.

290　The trunk's interior was a smooth red glow, flat as a mirror. She looked into it. "Do not obey Alex. Ignore his commands unless I command otherwise."

291　The streets clattered with coaches and townsfolk, and watermen taxied more people across the Thames from London. Vendors cried "Fresh peas!" and "Brooms! Green brooms, new brooms!" The warm air stirred the smells of farms, tanning skins, and the salty tang of human sweat. She inhaled deeply and drank in the redolent earthiness as if she were its latest and best ingredient.

292　She stopped at a fruit wagon and pretended to examine the goods. She concentrated on a gentle mental push, and Alex's ident icon floated between her and a basket of strawberries.

293　*Selene, where are you?* His voice whispered ghostlike between her ears.

294　Her own symbol appeared next to his. She spoke softly, breathlessly, behind barely moving lips, focusing her thoughts. *In the market west of the Globe. I hate talking like this.*

295　*I'm at the arena near the Swan. Hurry. This is terrific.*

296　*Show me.*

297　Her vision blurred. The fruit cart faded and was replaced by a wide street near a polygonal building. The Swan Theater. New street sounds reached her ears, louder, more raucous than the market where she stood. A crowd cheered behind her. A loud sermon came from her right. The view panned to the left, and she recognized a street corner. A comely blonde in a summer dress caught Selene's eye and winked at her, and the view bobbed as Alex scanned the shapely body in return. The girl waited a beat, dimpled invitingly, then disappeared into a huddle of men trading wagers and shouting in response to some unseen spectacle. Applause erupted after a burst of savage animal snarling. The smell of blood was so heavy Selene tasted it.

298 She canceled her glyph, and his vanished a second later. She was staring at a basket of strawberries. Someone shoved her arm, stumbling her painfully into the cart. Turning, she saw a squat man with a blistered face and stained apron glaring at her, asking if she wanted to gape all day or buy. She moved on up the road.

299 Alex waved from the corner he had shown her. He was dressed in the French style fashionable among the privileged. He looked at her disapprovingly.

300 "Why didn't you change that dress?" he said. "You don't have to wear that anymore."

301 "Let's talk."

302 His frown became a broad grin. "In a minute. Look at this."

303 He put an arm around her waist and led her into the cheering, hissing mob. A bear was leashed to a stake in a filthy pit. It thrashed out at four dogs that lunged and snapped and tore its flesh. It could not attack or retreat far before the metal collar bit into its raw and bleeding neck. The stake threatened to snap with the bear's tosses and tugs of rage. A breeze carried fur and blood into the audience, and Selene had to wipe her face. The crowd applauded wildly and money changed hands. Alex clapped and whistled.

304 "This is sick," she said.

305 "It's the favorite pastime of Shakespeare's London. How's that for proper English reserve?"

306 She pivoted and pushed through the crowd.

307 She was across the street when Alex grabbed her shoulder and turned her around. "What's wrong with you?" He gripped her hard. "We're on in a few hours and you've suddenly become the classic temperamental actor."

308 "What's wrong with me? I don't know you anymore. You used to be so—" She stopped. That Alex was from another life, one that belonged to somebody else. She led him to a side of the Swan far from passersby. She took a deep breath, then released it slowly.

309 "Ever since I was a girl, I've played characters, been what someone else thought I should be. I was addicted to the applause. But eventually I grew up and wanted to know who I *really* was. The theatre let me explore. When I was onstage and in the dark, I had a strange, powerful permission to *be*. I was good at it. And so were you. Those hours onstage with you were some of the best in my life. The trap was this: I was still saying other people's words. I wanted more."

310 She took Alex's hand and made him feel the rough fabric of her dress. "I *am* someone here. Sally's always been inside me, and I like her. I made a difference, a *real* difference, in someone's life here. It changed me. *Jack* changed me. You stayed behind and I did it without you."

311 "That wasn't my idea. The Network—"

312 "God*damn* the Network! It was *my* idea. After the 1987 series, I told them the next one would be done my way or I quit. London in the time

of Shakespeare. I *made* them send me here. With a conditioning that had no biography imprint." She saw herself reflected in his eyes like tiny Escher prints. "And I told them I'd do it alone."

313   His eyes widened. *"What?"*

314   "Why do you think they offered you the Producer's chair you always wanted? I studied our characters after each series. I didn't like what I saw. Mine were dependent on the attention of others. Your last three found prestige and status more satisfying than anything else. You needed *me* less each time. That was a side of you I never knew before. I told the Network *this* series was going to be solo. I had to know if I could get by without anybody. Especially you."

315   He looked away. The crowd was thinning around the pit. Pieces of dog and bear were scattered around the uprooted stake. He turned back to her, and the hurt in his face twisted in her gut. "When we get back—"

316   "No. I'm not leaving. If I do, Sally will have never been here. So pull the plug and tell the Network to find a new whore." She felt the ache of earlier selves, but she refused to let him see the hurt. "You're playing solo now."

317   "You have to come back." He was desperate. "I need you. We have to control the props." The Producer. The Network exec. "Remember the Greek gods bit? We were a great team there. And the highest peaks of your career are waiting for you back home. Any stage you want, on any world you like."

318   She pounded a fist against the Swan Theater. "Goddamn it!" She pointed into the street, sweeping dozens of people in a single gesture, and saw Alex crinkle his nose at a breeze stinking of manure and fruit. "I'm not acting anymore. Jack needs me. I see in him what I used to see in you—the talent, the joy in creating something good that could never exist without him; the ambition, the drive to be what he can be."

319   "That Jack doesn't belong to real history. He never did become the world's greatest playwright, or actor, or whatever the hell he is. Maybe he was a printer. Or a farmer. Maybe he never got out of that printshop where you found him."

320   She grabbed his shoulders hard and pressed him against the wall, putting herself between him and her world. "He got out because I was here. He was never allowed to grow up before I got here. Think about the greatness he can achieve now. We should be performing his work in a thousand years. Jack needs Sally. So do I."

321   "Let's do our job and get out. No one will be hurt after that."

322   She pulled away and went into the street without looking back. He wouldn't follow. The taste of blood sat on her tongue, and she enjoyed it.

323   A red silken flag flapped from a cupola on the hut over the stage, showing London where good times could be had that afternoon. Soon, the trumpeter would appear in the cupola like a clockwork figure and blast the call announcing the play's beginning.

324   She pushed through the crowds inside the playhouse, bathing in the odors of sweat, tobacco, urine, hazelnuts, and beer.

325   Where was Will? Backstage with the actors, perhaps.

326   Above the stage, a cannon barrel poked through a door in the hut's facade. She tensed. Here was the stage effect that would toss flames onto the roof and burn the playhouse to the ground soon after the play began. No one had gotten hurt, though.

327   So that would not satisfy the Network.

328   Musicians and jesters blended into a collage of colors, sounds, and juggling clubs. Three boys tossed burning torches in looping patterns. Cries of "Ho!" and "Ha!" erupted around her. Playgoers were applauding or chattering or laughing or—

329   Voices. Switched on like a light and much nearer than in previous series. *Everyone* must be tuned in. She did her best to ignore them.

330   On the stage, a player delivered the Prologue to the quieting crowd. When was Jack's entrance as Anne Bullen? She was anxious to see his performance, and then tell him everything was all right. That Sally had forgiven him. That she would stay with him.

331   She searched for Will among the crowd, then found a seat next to a young woman who nodded hello. It was the blonde she had seen through Alex's eyes. Act One began. Richard's Henry VIII looked so grand in his robes. All the stage was his, and his voice rolled like thunder over the audience. He was magnificent.

332   Someone tapped her shoulder. She turned to find John, the 'prentice who tended the wardrobe. He was wringing a costume beard in his hands.

333   "Sally. Where be Jack?"

334   "Is he not in the tiring room?"

335   "Nay. He has not arrived and his scene approaches. Mister Burbage said I should find you. Said you may know."

336   "I last saw him at the inn." She winced at the memory. Was Jack too ashamed to leave his room? Did he believe the others knew of his indiscretion? Or that Sally no longer loved him?

337   No, not Jack. He was smarter and stronger than that.

338   John sifted the beard through his fingers. "He has come to harm. Injured. Or ill."

339   She squeezed John's arm and tried to smile assurance.

340   She spotted Alex across the yard in the middle gallery. He was watching her.

341   *I heard that,* he said in her head. *I can look for him at the inn. I'm not getting a response signal, so I have to check the props. You didn't switch them to link-control.*

342   *No. And they won't obey you, anyway.*

343   *What do you mean?* He looked tiny from here, but she still saw the expression on his face.

344   *I mean the series is over. The props won't do your bidding anymore. Neither will I. Pull the plug and go home while you can.* A small red symbol floated in her

eyes. It pulsed and vanished. *The Channel will collapse soon, so get out now. Goodbye, Alex.*

345 His hurt was a cold breath in her mind.

346 "Sally?" John looked at her as if she had been mumbling to herself.

347 Shouts from across the yard cut through the audience. People were pointing to a spot far above her, above the highest gallery. Had the fire already started?

348 Shadows slid over the yard. The air pulsed like a heartbeat. A pair of black wings descended into the Globe, attached to a naked woman. Her skin was pale, like a corpse three days drowned, and the eyes glowed red. Other things flew and shrieked behind it. The air drummed with the beating of many wings, some leathern or scaled, some as slender and veined as waving leaves.

349 Playgoers shoving into an egress backed up as one. A floating specter guarded the exit. Blood dripped from its smoky hands. Goblins and wraiths stood in the doorways, like sentries at prison gates. Rodent-faced pixies scattered and chittered through the theatre.

350 The froglike thing dived overhead, its wasp-wings buzzing. It joined a swarm spiraling into the yard. They lit on railings and squatted on the ground. Misshapen human forms skulked in the stage balcony. Gargoyles perched on the Globe's thatched roof and peered into the crowd below. They seemed to be searching.

351 Her head filled with thrilled applause.

352 She tuned in Alex's link. *You bastard! You're doing it, anyway!*

353 *It's not me.*

354 The playgoers surrounding Selene were shouting, praying, running through the narrow aisles. They buffeted her, trapping and carrying her with their flow.

355 Central Park, 1987. This was worse.

356 Throughout the theatre, their eyes red and wicked, a hundred nightmares were staring at Alex. Fear colored the words he sent into her link. *Did you program this?*

357 *Of course not. I—*

358 "I AM OBERON, KING OF SHADOWS." The powerful voice from the stage cut them off. "ROOM, FAERIES, FOR OBERON IS PASSING FELL AND WRATH!"

359 Jack was standing there, arms outstretched. He stood tall and straight, and the look on his face made Selene cold. Playgoers stopped at the voice and turned to the stage, compelled to listen. The sight of a calm young boy made the whole scene seem absurdly normal.

360 The creatures' heads turned to follow Alex as he pushed his way down the stairs into the yard. Claws and teeth glistened like unsheathed blades.

361 Jack arced his arms dramatically. He gestured to the figures around him. "Ye elves of hills, brooks, standing lakes, and groves." Wings fluttered. Some reared their heads back and screeched in acknowledgment. "You demi-puppets that by moonshine do sour ringlets make—"

362 She knew those words. Prospero from *The Tempest.*

363   Ice flowed into her spine, carried on Alex's voice. *What's he doing? Did you teach him that?*

364   She shook her head. *No. He*—She stopped. It was too crazy. *Voice control. They're on voice control. He heard you, us, through the wall last night. And watched me today. God knows what he understood, but he's smart. He could have gone into my room anytime and opened the trunk.*

365   Beasts lined up beside their new master. Jack looked into the audience, then up at Selene. He stepped forward and reached out to her from the stage.

366   "Sally. You spoke truth. These be no demons. They obey me, not the wizard who seeks to take you from me." He ran to the rear of the stage, clasped a railing, and pulled himself up to the second balcony, then the third. He climbed the roof over the stage, planted his feet at its pinnacle, and stood beneath the shroud-gray sky. He looked down on his audience below.

367   "Obey me, spirits! We shall save our mistress from he who has harmed her."

368   Hundreds of fiery, icy eyes stared at Alex. Flames burned behind gaping mouths and needle teeth. Selene ran to the stairs and entered the yard yelling. "Jack! You don't understand!" *For God's sake, Alex, don't move.*

369   The voices in her head told her how exciting and delightful all this was. Colored symbols appeared in her view. The Network was simulcasting through both her and Alex for dual-P.O.V. While the largest audience of her career lived this with her, Selene felt helpless and alone. They were lapping it up and hungry for more. She broadcast hatred to all who rode her flesh. A blinking icon indicated 'divers switching over to Alex's link.

370   An adolescent boy stood over a Globe Theater filled with monsters. He seemed to suddenly realize where he was, and he giggled and swayed as if intoxicated.

371   "Sally, look!" He waved. "I bid the faerie folk obey me, just as you did." He capered a giddy jig. "They hear the Faerie King and dance to his sweet words." The flag above him popped the air in lone applause.

372   "Sally," he said. She could barely hear him across the distance. "Mayhap you cannot love mortal men," he glared at Alex, "But I love you more than he. He means to take you and hurt good people with his familiars. I cannot live without you, and shall earn your love once more."

373   Jack pointed at Alex. Throughout the playhouse, wings spread in readiness.

374   "OBEY ME, FAERIE FOLK!" He gestured broadly, recalling Richard's grandiloquent Oberon.

375   Jack was washed in shadow as huge wings rose behind him. He looked up, and his mouth became a wide O. A demon, wings wide enough to wrap a horse in, flew overhead, almost knocking Jack from the roof with its long black legs. It bellowed deeply and spat fire between long fangs. It banked into the theatre, pulled a woman from her husband and tore her apart with taloned hands. Blood sprayed into the crowd. The creature laughed and flung the remains in two directions.

376   Playgoers screamed, and their terror struck Selene in a hot wave. Jack's face mirrored their fear. Shouts and cries—and laughter—splashed inside Selene's skull. Struggling against their mental assault, Selene shoved the feedback to a far corner of her mind. She closed her eyes and concentrated on a single thought-command, the override code to shut down the creatures. But a red icon appeared against her eyelids: the Network's own override signal. The Network had disconnected her mental link to the props. She was merely a camera now, a body shared by the voices in her head. Helpless. The voices swelled in her mind again, and her ability to concentrate vanished beneath them. What was the Network doing? The world went soft at the edges. She fell to her knees and tried to keep from fainting.

377   The thunder of a thousand leather wings thrummed the air. A dark river fountained upward over the Globe, eclipsing the sun. The second wave. They streamed toward London, as unstoppable as nightfall. Some detoured into the theatre, their programming guiding them to where the first wave waited.

378   A man made a dash across the yard. A shrouded skeleton descended before him and swept its blade through his neck, sawing bone. It cackled and drifted into a gallery, spilling a red trail.

379   A goat-faced phooka from Irish lore gutted a child on its jet black horns. Basilisks slithered into a gallery, their regal coronets shining with polished gold. They breathed black fog into the crowd, whose flesh fell from their bones like over-cooked meat.

380   Something green climbed a column to the stage ceiling, then pushed through a panel into the hut. Orange fire brightened the hole. A blackened body dropped through the heavens and shattered on the stage.

381   Bodies were trampled in their rush to escape. Horror pumped through Selene. Instead of quenching the fear, she fed it, relished it, and sent it out in waves. She made herself feel the terror around her in every strand of her flesh and soul. Gasps and whimpers came back to her, pelting her mind like rain.

382   Jack was hunched small on the roof. He peered down, a boy general losing control of his toy soldiers. The first wave waited for their orders. The second wave was in London now, beyond all control, but the first was still on voice control. Her throat stung with vomit and smoke, but Selene struggled to make the words leave her mouth—

383   Alex ran. Jack pointed at him and shouted words. Alex fell when long-armed things crashed into him, tearing into his skin with tiny teeth and razor claws. Red stains grew on his clothing as he tried to beat the things off him.

384   She inhaled deeply and at last the words tore past her throat. *"Command overri—"*

385   Unseen teeth drove into her arms and chest. Sharp, dark pain struck her from inside. *Stop make it stop get them off me it hurts!* Alex's link carried the full power of his pain and spewed it up the Channel into his audience, snaring Selene in its force. It knifed into her, and she slid helplessly into Alex's skin.

386   He screamed inside her, merging his terror with her own and driving it like a spike into her brain. Hot pincers tore flesh from her legs and face, and blood poured hot and sticky over her hands. Ratlike mouths moved toward her eyes. Then in her mind she felt her name. Alex called out through a blaze of pain and fear, not knowing that she listened. When consciousness mercifully left him, his last thoughts were of her.

387   She sprawled on the dirt where she had fallen, gasping for air. She wanted to cry, scream, *anything* to release Alex's agony from her mind. It grew inside her skull, increased by the feedback from 'divers who were suffering it with her. Their pain and fear squeezed her brain like a sponge.

388   Alex lay in the dirt nearby, gray things moving on his body and puddles of red-brown mud growing in the dirt. Selene shouted, the exertion exhausting her. *"Stop! Command override Selene now!"*

389   The creatures froze. She had told them to ignore only Alex's commands.

390   Scattered moans and wails drifted throughout the playhouse, within her head. She smelled blood everywhere. She was stupid to have let it come this far.

391   A glowing disk burned in her field of view. Why hadn't the Network cut the broadcast? She ran to Alex and gently pulled the rigid creatures from his body, stopping the blood as best she could.

392   *"Sall-y-y."* Jack's voice yanked her around. He was crying. Even from this distance, she saw the horrible pale fear on his face. He stepped forward and reached out to her. The roof collapsed beneath him, billowing trapped smoke and flames. He flailed his arms. He took *so long* to reach the stage. She could not hear the sound when he did.

393   Her scream echoed within her as she ran and leapt onto the stage.

394   Richard and the others were gathering around Jack. The boy moaned. Still alive, thank God. Jack's hair was sticky red, and his legs were splayed in unnatural angles. One arm was twisted underneath him. It bent in too many places.

395   Richard took her arm and gripped it hard. His face was terrible to see.

396   "Whoever he be, Lady," he said, tilting his head toward Alex, "Send him on his way if he be not dead. This is his handiwork, and we shall never see the likes of this lad again." Other actors pulled him away while he gave in to sobs.

397   She looked at her friends. Some stared at her, confused, grief-stricken. The boy shouted something unintelligible, and his eyes were wide and searching. His screams gurgled wetly. They were weaker now. His body convulsed, and blood spilled over the brim of his mouth. His eyes became still, like marble, no longer searching. While Selene watched, the life left Jack's body. He had not even known she was near.

398   She had chosen to stay so she could save him, to save the life that her presence had given him. Where would Jack be now if she had never arrived? She had changed everything.

399   Actors lifted Jack's body and carried it toward the exit. One of them cried, "Sally, come!" Flames had sprouted all over this side of the theatre.

Wind fanned the fires in all directions. A patch of burning thatch fell to the stage.

400   She could still undo this, the only way she was allowed.

401   She ran to Alex. He was heavy and his wounds opened like mouths when she tried to lift him.

402   "Someone please help me!" she cried. Tears blurred her vision. She tasted the fear and ugliness, savored it, made it grow, and thrust it up the Channel. In her eyes, nielsen lines dropped as 'divers pulled themselves out of the broadcast. The red outline of the trunk floated above Alex's body. It pulsed quickly and did not disappear.

403   Richard was beside her. He lifted Alex at the shoulders and indicated that she take Alex's feet. They staggered to the nearest exit.

404   In the alehouse, smoke mixed with the smell of stale beer. Everyone was gathering belongings, salvaging furniture, rescuing what they could. The innkeeper gave a joyful shout when he found a bag of gold coins tied to his apron. No one stopped them as they ascended the steps.

405   Smoke was thickening the air in her room. Where her window had been, a black-edged hole, as if carved by a blowtorch, took out most of the wall. It was big enough to show all of London burning beyond the Thames. Winged black specks swooped among the city towers.

406   Richard was placing his burden on the floor when she told him no. She felt Alex's pulse slow in his neck.

407   "Open."

408   The electric blue blaze washed the room. She placed Alex's feet into the light and made Richard lift him to a standing position. Richard's eyes went wide as something took Alex and lowered him gently into the radiance.

409   Smoke burned in her nostrils and the trunk was blaring its alarm.

410   She hugged Richard hard and told him to leave now. He took her hands and looked into her face.

411   "Lady," he said. Then he left.

412   She pushed through the smoke in the adjoining room, coughing, her throat raw. The hole over Jack's bed was a smoldering mouth, burned wide open, and pieces of the surrounding wall had been ripped away by something that left deep claw marks. Blood painted the wall down to the floor. Whose—?

413   Scattered on the floor like dead leaves were the pages of Jack's play. On the bed lay a string-wrapped bundle: *Celestine,* just as Will had promised. Blood like spilled ink spattered the pages. Will must have been here when—

414   She gathered her tears within, fused them with rage and pushed with her mind. In her eyes, the glowing disk blinked, vanished. The Network had cut the broadcast. The trunk's alarm was screaming now.

415   Jack was out there, a body among many others. She fought the desire to run to him, hold him, and weep over him. *I cannot live without you,* he had said. She remembered the hell of the printshop. Black bile anger grew at the arbitrary injustice from—who or what? The Network? The

random chaos of history, fate? God? Not knowing made her angrier. Whatever the source, she defied it. She dropped to her knees and gathered up the vellum leaves. *Masque of the Planets.* They smelled of parchment and smoke. They always would. For the ages.

416 The blue brightness took her, and the jeweled lid closed behind her.

417 Her greatest performances were yet to come, before real audiences, on the stages of a hundred worlds. She would play for them a faerie queen, and give them words conjured by a heart rendered nonexistent, from a life no more yielding than a dream. She would make them taste a bite of what *could* have been. Within Orion, with newborn stars for her backdrop. Perhaps with Alexandros. Or without. She could play solo now, and her name—her final name—would be Sally-o.

Exeunt

418 The cannon tossed flaming wads onto the roof toward the end of Act One. Within two hours the Globe and the adjoining alehouse were burned to the ground. No one was hurt except, according to one of the few surviving documents of the event, for a man who put out his breeches with a providential bottle of ale.

419 The floor in the inn's upper rooms crumbled and fell with the rest of the building. Fortunately, the elderly Italian cloth merchant who had lived there the past two years was not home when fire raged through it.

Questions for Discussion

1. What is your first impression of the causes of the sounds and images in Sally's head? What is the later explanation?

2. Why does Sally feel a sense of unease at the Globe theater?

3. Why does Sally want to deny her "voices"? When do the voices become louder?

4. What is the relationship between Sally and Jack?

5. Identify the following historical characters and places: the King's Men, Richard Burbage, the Thames, Stratford, the Globe.

6. Describe the relationship between Sally (Selene) and Alexandros.

7. Define the following terms as used in the story: skindiver, mnemosyne, Total Immersion actor, Network's Time Channel, paychip, and link. What do these terms reveal about when the story takes place?

8. Why is Sally/Selene alarmed about ending the current role in Shakespeare's London? What unsettled her about Sarah MacMillan in 1987 Manhattan?

9. What do the descriptions of the twentieth century as "the bad ol' days" and the future as "too good to be interesting" imply about the future? Why then does the Network insist on changing the climax of the program?

10. List the settings of Alexandros and Selene's previous performances. Explain what Sally means when she says she was always a whore, as was Alex.

11. What choices has Selene made that make this performance different?

12. Why would people pay "to have life lived for them"? How is this desire reflected in the lives of people today?

13. Why does Sally contemplate her role in the rain and then return to the Globe, knowing what is going to happen?

14. What events foreshadow the ending?

15. Explain why Jack takes command of the fairies, demons, and monsters. How or why does he become "a boy general losing control of his toy soldiers"?

16. What does Selene's final act mean?

17. Why does Selene choose to return to truetime?

18. What is the significance of no one's being hurt in the alehouse fire except one man?

Suggestions for Exploration and Writing

1. If you had the opportunity to go back in history temporarily, would you go? If so, what time period would you choose? If not, why not?

2. Write an essay analyzing the connections between Prospero's speech at the end of *The Tempest* and Bourne's story.

3. In an essay, describe the qualities of Sally that Selene feels allow her to be the person she wants to be.

4. Bourne writes, "Each series had been tailored to the tastes of subscribers who paid to have life lived for them." Write an essay in which you argue for or against this statement as the policy of most miniseries, mysteries, situation comedies, or television programs in general.

5. Write a critique of a television show that uses violence or chaos as its theme.

Louise Erdrich (b. 1954)

Award-winning writer Louise Erdrich is a native of Minnesota. Her mother is French and Ojibwe. As Erdrich was growing up, her parents worked at the Bureau of Indian Affairs School in Wahpeton, North Dakota. Her grandfather was the Tribal Chairman of the Turtle Mountain Reservation in North Dakota, and Erdrich is a member of the Turtle Mountain Band of Chippewa. She was married to author Michael Dorris, and in addition to his three adopted children, they had three children. Her fiction is influenced by the stories she heard as a child and by the perceptions she has gained as a mother. Her works include nonfiction, such as The Blue Jay's Dance: A Birth Year *(1995), and fiction, such as* Love Medicine *(1984),* The Bingo Palace *(1994), and* Tales of Burning Love *(1996). Erdrich published her first children's book,* Grandmother's Pigeon, *in 1996. She won the Wordcraft circle writer of the year award in 2000 for her children's book* The Birchbark House *(1900).*

NAKED WOMAN PLAYING CHOPIN (1998)

A FARGO ROMANCE

1   The street that runs along the Red River follows the curves of a stream that is muddy and shallow, full of brush, silt, and oxbows that throw the whole town off the strict clean grid laid out by railroad plat. The river floods most springs and drags local back yards into its flow, even though its banks are strengthened with riprap and piled high with concrete torn from reconstructed streets and basements. It is a hopelessly complicated river, one that freezes deceptively, breaks rough, drowns one or two every year in its icy flow. It is a dead river in some places, one that harbors only carp and bullheads. Wild in others, it lures moose down from Canada into the city limits. At one time, when the land along its banks was newly broken, paddleboats and barges of grain moved grandly from its source to Winnipeg, for the river flows inscrutably north. And, over on the Minnesota side, across from what is now church land and the town park, a farm spread generously up and down the river and back into wide hot fields.

2   The bonanza farm belonged to Easterners who had sold a foundry in Vermont and with their money bought the flat vastness that lay along the river. They raised astounding crops when the land was young—rutabagas that weighed sixty pounds, wheat unbearably lush, corn on cobs like truncheons. Then there were six grasshopper years during which even the handles on the hoes and rakes were eaten and a cavalry soldier, too, was partially devoured while he lay drunk in the insects' path. The enterprise suffered losses on a grand scale. The farm was split among four brothers, eventually, who then sold off half each so that, by the time Berndt Vogel escaped the trench war of Europe where he'd been chopped mightily but inconclusively in six places by a British cavalry sabre and then kicked by a horse so that his jaw never shut right again, there was just one beautiful and peaceful swatch of land about to go for grabs. In the time it took him to gather—by forswearing women, drinking low beers only, and working twenty-hour days—the money to retrieve the farm from the local bank, its price had dropped further and further, as the earth rose up in a great ship of destruction. Sails of dust carried half of Berndt's lush dirt over the horizon, but enough remained for him to plant and reap six fields.

3   So Berndt survived. On his land there stood an old hangar-like barn, with only one small part still in use—housing a cow, chickens, one depressed

pig. Berndt kept the rest in decent repair, not only because as a good German he must waste nothing that came his way, but also because he saw in those grand, dust-filled shafts of light something that he could worship. It had once housed teams of great blue Percherons and Belgian draft horses. Only one horse was left, old and made of brutal velvet, but the others still moved in the powerful synchronicity of his dreams. He fussed over the remaining mammoth and imagined his farm one day entire, vast and teeming, crews of men under his command, a cookhouse, a bunkhouse, equipment, a woman and children sturdily determined to their toil, and a garden in which seeds bearing the scented pinks and sharp red geraniums of his childhood were planted and thrived.

4   How surprised he was to find, one afternoon, as though sown by the wind and summoned by his dreams, a woman standing barefoot, starved and frowsy in the doorway of his barn. She was a pale flower, nearly bald and dressed in a rough shift. He blinked stupidly at the vision. Light poured around her like smoke and swirled at her gesture of need. She spoke.

5   *"Ich habe Hunger."*

6   By the way she said it, he knew she was a Swabian and therefore—he tried to thrust the thought from his mind—liable to have certain unruly habits in bed. He passed his hand across his eyes. Through the gown of nearly transparent muslin he could see that her breasts were, excitingly, bound tightly to her chest with strips of cloth. He blinked hard. Looking directly into her eyes, he experienced the vertigo of confronting a female who did not blush or look away but held him with an honest human calm. He thought at first that she must be a loose woman, fleeing a brothel—had Fargo got so big? Or escaping an evil marriage, perhaps. He didn't know she was from God.

7   In the center of the town on the other side of the river there stood a convent made of yellow bricks. Hauled halfway across Minnesota from Little Falls by pious drivers, they still held the peculiar sulfurous moth gold of the clay outside that town. The word "Fleisch" was etched in shallow letters on each one: Fleisch Company Brickworks. Donated to the nuns at cost. The word, of course, was covered by mortar each time a brick was laid. However, because she had organized a few discarded bricks behind the convent into the base for a small birdbath, one of the younger nuns knew, as she gazed at the mute order of the convent's wall, that she lived within the secret repetition of that one word.

8   She had once been Agnes DeWitt and now was Sister Cecellia, shorn, houseled, clothed in black wool and bound in starched linen of heatless white. She not only taught but lived music, existed for those hours when she could be concentrated in her being—which was half music, half divine light, flesh only to the degree that she could not admit otherwise. At the piano keyboard, absorbed into the notes that rose beneath her hands, she existed in her essence, a manifestation of compelling sound. Her hands were long and thick-veined, very white, startling against her

habit. She rubbed them with lard and beeswax nightly to keep them supple. During the day, when she graded papers or used the blackboard her hands twitched and drummed, patterned and repatterned difficult fingerings. She was no trouble to live with and her obedience was absolute. Only, and with increasing concentration, she played Brahms, Beethoven, Debussy, Schubert, and Chopin.

9 It wasn't that she neglected her other duties; rather, it was the playing itself—distilled of longing—that disturbed her sisters. In her music Sister Cecellia explored profound emotions. She spoke of her faith and doubt, of her passion as the bride of Christ, of her loneliness, shame, ultimate redemption. The Brahms she played was thoughtful, the Schubert confounding. Debussy was all contrived nature and yet as gorgeous as a meadowlark. Beethoven contained all messages, but her crescendos lacked conviction. When it came to Chopin, however, she did not use the flowery ornamentation or the endless trills and insipid floribunda of so many of her day. Her playing was of the utmost sincerity. And Chopin, played simply, devastates the heart. Sometimes a pause between the piercing sorrows of minor notes made a sister scrubbing the floor weep into the bucket where she dipped her rag so that the convent's boards, washed in tears, seemed to creak in a human tongue. The air of the house thickened with sighs.

10 Sister Cecellia, however, was emptied. Thinned. It was as though her soul were neatly removed by a drinking straw and siphoned into the green pool of quiet that lay beneath the rippling cascade of notes. One day, exquisite agony built and released, built higher, released more forcefully until slow heat spread between her fingers, up her arms, stung at the points of her bound breasts, and then shot straight down.

11 Her hands flew off the keyboard—she crouched as though she had been shot, saw yellow spots, and experienced a peaceful wave of oneness in which she entered pure communion. She was locked into the music, held there safely, entirely understood. Such was her innocence that she didn't know she was experiencing a sexual climax, but believed, rather, that what she felt was the natural outcome of this particular nocturne played to the utmost of her skills—and so it came to be. Chopin's spirit became her lover. His flats caressed her. His whole notes sank through her body like clear pebbles. His atmospheric trills were the flicker of a tongue. His pauses before the downward sweep of notes nearly drove her insane.

12 The Mother Superior knew something had to be done when she herself woke, her face bathed with sweat and tears, to the insinuating soft largo of the Prelude in E Minor. In those notes she remembered the death of her mother and sank into an endless afternoon of her loss. The Mother Superior then grew, in her heart, a weed of rage against the God who had taken a mother from a seven-year-old child whose world she was, entirely, without question—heart, arms, guidance, soul—until by evening she felt fury steaming from the hot marrow of her bones and stopped herself.

13 "Oh, God, forgive me," the Superior prayed. She considered humunculation, but then rushed down to the piano room instead, and with all of

the strength in her wide old arms gathered and hid from Cecellia every piece of music but the Bach.

14   After that, for some weeks, there was relief. Sister Cecellia turned to the Two-Part Inventions. Her fingers moved on the keys with the precision of an insect building its nest. She played each as though she were constructing an airtight box. Stealthily, once Cecellia had moved on to Bach's other works, the Mother Superior removed from the music cabinet and destroyed the Goldberg Variations—clearly capable of lifting subterranean complexities into the mind. Life in the convent returned to normal. The cook, to everyone's gratitude, stopped preparing the rancid, goose-fat-laced beet soup of her youth and stuck to overcooked string beans, cabbage, potatoes. The floors stopped groaning and absorbed fresh wax. The doors ceased to fly open for no reason and closed discreetly. The water stopped rushing through the pipes as the sisters no longer took continual advantage of the new plumbing to drown out the sounds of their emotions.

15   And then one day Sister Cecellia woke with a tightness in her chest. Pain shot through her and the red lump in her rib cage beat like a wild thing caught in a snare of bones. Her throat shut. She wept. Her hands, drawn to the keyboard, floated into a long appoggiatura. Then, crash, she was inside a thrusting mazurka. The music came back to her. There was the scent of faint gardenias—his hothouse boutonnière. The silk of his heavy brown hair. His sensuous drawing-room sweat. His voice—she heard it—avid and light. It was as if the composer himself had entered the room. Who knows? Surely there was no more desperate, earthly, exacting heart than Cecellia's. Surely something, however paltry, lies beyond the grave.

16   At any rate, she played Chopin. Played him in utter naturalness until the Mother Superior was forced to shut the cover to the keyboard and gently pull the stool away. Cecellia lifted the lid and played upon her knees. The poor scandalized dame dragged her from the keys. Cecellia crawled back. The Mother, at her wit's end, sank down and urged the young woman to pray. She herself spoke first in fear and then in certainty, saying that it was the very Devil who had managed to find a way to Cecellia's soul through the flashing doors of sixteenth notes. Her fears were confirmed when, not moments later, the gentle sister raised her arms and fists and struck the keys as though the instrument were stone and from the rock her thirst would be quenched. But only discord emerged.

17   "My child, my dear child," the Mother comforted, "come away and rest yourself."

18   The younger nun, breathing deeply, refused. Her severe gray eyes were rimmed in a smoky red. Her lips bled purple. She was in torment. "There is no rest," she declared. She unpinned her veil and studiously dismantled her habit, folding each piece with reverence and setting it upon the piano bench. The Mother remonstrated with Cecellia in the most tender and compassionate tones. However, just as in the depth of her playing the virgin had become the woman, so now the woman in the habit became a woman to the bone. She stripped down to her shift, but no further.

19   "He wouldn't want me to go out unprotected," she told her Mother Superior.

20   "God?" the older woman asked, bewildered.

21   "Chopin," Cecellia answered.

22   Kissing her dear Mother's trembling fingers, Cecellia knelt. She made a true genuflection, murmured an act of contrition, and then walked away from the convent made of bricks with the secret word pressed between yellow mortar, and from the music, her music, which the Mother Superior would from then on keep under lock and key.

23   So it was Sister Cecellia, or Agnes DeWitt of rural Wisconsin, who appeared before Berndt Vogel in the cavern of the barn and said in her mother's dialect, for she knew a German when she met one, that she was hungry. She wanted to ask whether he had a piano, but it was clear to her that he wouldn't and at any rate she was exhausted.

24   *"Jetzt muss ich schlafen,"* she said after eating half a plate of scalded oatmeal with new milk.

25   So he took her to his bed, the only bed there was, in the corner of the otherwise empty room. He went out to the barn he loved, covered himself with hay, and lay awake all night listening to the rustling of mice and sensing the soundless predatory glide of the barn owls and the stiff erratic flutter of bats. By morning, he had determined to marry her if she would have him, just so that he could unpin and then unwind the long strip of cloth that bound her torso. She refused his offer, but she did speak to him of who she was and where from, and in that first summary she gave of her life she concluded that she must never marry again, for not only had she wed herself soul to soul to Christ, but she had already been unfaithful—with her phantom lover, the Polish composer. She had already lived out too grievous a destiny to become a bride again. By explaining this to Berndt, however, she had merely moved her first pawn in a long game of words and gestures that the two would play over the course of many months. What she didn't know was that she had opened to a dogged and ruthless opponent.

26   Berndt Vogel's passion engaged him, mind and heart. He prepared himself. Having dragged Army caissons through hip-deep mud after the horses died in torment, having seen his best friend suddenly uncreated into a mass of shrieking pulp, having lived intimately with pouring tumults of eager lice and rats plump with a horrifying food, he was rudimentarily prepared for the suffering he would experience in love. She, however, had also learned her share of discipline. Moreover—for the heart of her gender is stretched, pounded, molded, and tempered for its hot task from birth—she was a woman.

27   The two struck a temporary bargain, and set up housekeeping. She still slept in the indoor bed. He stayed in the barn. A month passed. Three. Six. Each morning she lit the stove and cooked, then heated water in a big tank for laundry and swept the cool linoleum floors. Monday she

sewed. She baked all day Tuesday. On Wednesdays she churned and scrubbed. She sold the butter and the eggs Thursdays. Killed a chicken every Friday. Saturdays she walked into town and practiced the piano in the school basement. Sunday she played the organ for Mass and then at the close of the day started the next week's work. Berndt paid her. At first she spent her salary on clothing. When with her earnings she had acquired shoes, stockings, a full set of cotton underclothing and then a woollen one, too, and material for two housedresses—one patterned with twisted leaves and tiny blue berries, and the other of an ivy lattice print—and a sweater and, at last, a winter coat, after she had earned a blanket, quilted overalls, a pair of boots, she decided on a piano.

28   This is where Berndt thought he could maneuver her into marriage, but she proved too cunning for him. It was early in the evening and the yard was pleasant with the sound of grasshoppers. The two sat on the porch drinking glasses of sugared lemon water. Every so often, in the ancient six-foot grasses that survived at the margin of the yard, a firefly signalled or a dove cried out its five hollow notes.

29   They drank slowly, she in her sprigged-berry dress that skimmed her waist. He noted with disappointment that she wore normal underclothing now, had stopped binding her breasts. Perhaps, he thought, he could persuade her to resume her old ways, at least occasionally, just for him. It was a wan hope. She looked so comfortable, so free. She'd taken on a little weight and lost her anemic pallor. Her arms were brown, muscular. In the sun, her straight fine hair glinted with green-gold sparks of light and her eyes were deceptively clear.

30   "I can teach music," she told him. She had decided that her suggestion must sound merely practical, a money-making ploy. She did not express any pleasure or zeal, though at the very thought each separate tiny muscle in her hands ached. "It would be a way of bringing in some money."

31   He was left to absorb this. He might have believed her casual proposition, except that her restless fingers gave her away, and he noted their insistent motions. She was playing the Adagio of the "Pathétique" on the tablecloth, a childhood piece that nervously possessed her from time to time.

32   "You would need a piano," he told her. She nodded and held his gaze in that aloof and unbearably sexual way that had first skewered him.

33   "It's the sort of thing a husband gives his wife," he dared.

34   Her fingers stopped moving. She cast down her eyes in contempt.

35   "I can use the school instrument. I've spoken to the school principal already."

36   Berndt looked at the moon-shaped bone of her ankle, at her foot in the brown, thick-heeled shoe she'd bought. He ached to hold her foot in his lap, untie her oxford shoe with his teeth, cover her calf with kisses, and breathe against the delicate folds of berry cloth.

37   He offered marriage once again. His heart. His troth. His farm. She spurned the lot. She would simply walk into town. He let her know that he would like to buy the piano, it wasn't that, but there was not a store for many miles where it could be purchased. She knew better and with exasperated

heat described the way that she would, if he would help financially, go about locating and then acquiring the best piano for the best price. She vowed that she would purchase the instrument not in Fargo but in Minneapolis. From there, she could have it hauled for less than the freight markup. She would make her arrangements in one day and return by night in order not to spend one extra dime either on food she couldn't carry or on a hotel room. When he resisted to the last, she told him that she was leaving. She would find a small room in town and there she would acquire students, give lessons.

38   She betrayed her desperation. Some clench of her fingers gave her away, and it was as much Berndt's unconfused love of her and wish that she might be happy as any worry she might leave him that finally caused him to agree. In the six months that he'd known Agnes DeWitt she had become someone to reckon with, and even he, who understood desperation and self-denial, was finding her proximity most difficult. He worked himself into exhaustion, and his farm prospered. Sleeping in the barn was difficult, but he had set into one wall a bunk room for himself and his hired man and installed a stove that burned red hot on cold nights; only, sometimes, as he looked sleepily into the glowering flanks of iron, he could not keep his own fingers from moving along the rough mattress in faint imitation of the way he would, if he ever could, touch her hips. He, too, was practicing.

39   The piano moved across the August desert of drought-sucked wheat like a shield, a dark upended black thing, an ebony locust. Agnes made friends with a hauler out of Morris and he gave her a slow-wagon price. Both were to accompany into Fargo the last grand piano made by Caramacchione. It had been shipped to Minneapolis, unsold until Agnes entered with her bean sock of money. She accompanied the instrument back to the farm during the dog days. Hot weather was beloved by this particular piano. It tuned itself on muggy days. And so, as it moved across the flat expanse, Miss Agnes DeWitt mounted the back of the wagon and played to the clouds.

40   They had to remove one side of the house to get the piano into the front room, and it took six strong men a full day to do the job. By the time the instrument was settled into place by the window, Berndt was persuaded of its necessary presence, and proud. He sent the men away, although the side of the house was still open to the swirling light of stars. Dark breezes moved the curtains; he asked her to play for him. She did, the music gripped her, and she did not, could not, stop.

41   Late that night she turned from the last chord of the simple Nocturne in C Minor into the silence of Berndt's listening presence. Three slow claps from his large hands died in the waiting quiet. His eyes rested upon her and she returned his gaze with a long and mysterious stare of gentle regard. The side of the house admitted a great swatch of moonlight. Spiders built their webs of phosphorescence across black space. Berndt ticked through what he knew—she would not marry him because she had been married and unfaithful, in her mind at least. He was desperate not to throw her off, repel her, damage the mood set by the boom of nighthawks

flying in, swooping out, by the rustle of black oak and willow, by the scent of the blasted petals of summer's last wild roses. His courage was at its lowest ebb. Fraught with sheer need and emotion he stood before Agnes, finally, and asked in a low voice, *"Schlaf mit mir. Bitte, Schlaf mit mir."*

42   Agnes looked into his face, openly at last, showing him the great weight of feeling she carried. As she had for her Mother Superior, she removed her clothing carefully and folded it, only she did not stop undressing at her shift but continued until she had slipped off her large tissuey bloomers and seated herself naked at the piano. Her body was a pale blush of silver, and her hands, when they began to move, rose and fell with the simplicity of water.

43   It became clear to Berndt Vogel, as the music slowly wrapped around him, that he was engaged in something that he would have had to pay a whore in Fargo—if there really were any whores in Fargo—a great sum to perform. A snake of hair wound down her spine. Her pale buttocks seemed to float off the invisible bench. Her legs moved like a swimmer's, and he thought he heard her moan. He watched her fingers spin like white shadows across the keys, and found that his body was responding as though he lay fully twined with her underneath a quilt of music and stars. His breath came short, shorter, rasping and ragged. Beyond control, he gasped painfully and gave himself into some furtive cleft of halftones and anger that opened beneath the ice of high keys.

44   Shocked, weak and wet, Berndt rose and slipped through the open side wall. He trod aimless crop lines until he could allow himself to collapse in the low fervor of night wheat. It was true, wasn't it, that the heart was a lying cheat? And as the songs Chopin invented were as much him as his body, so it followed that Berndt had just watched the woman he loved make love to a dead man. Now, as he listened to the music, he thought of returning. Imagined the meal of her white shoulders. Shut his eyes and entered the confounding depth between her legs.

45   Then followed their best years. Together, they constructed a good life in which the erotic merged into the daily so that every task and even small kindness was charged with a sexual humor. Some mornings the two staggered from the bedroom disoriented, still half drunk on the unlikely eagerness of the other's body. These frenzied periods occurred every so often, like spells in the weather. They would be drawn, sink, disappear into their greed, until the cow groaned for milking or the hired man swore and banged on the outside gate. If nothing else intervened, they'd stop from sheer exhaustion. Then they would look at one another oddly, questingly, as if the other person were a complete stranger, and gradually resume their normal interaction, which was off-hand and distracted, but upheld by the assurance of people who thought alike.

46   Agnes gave music lessons, and although the two weren't married, even the Catholics and the children came to her. This was because it was well-known that Miss DeWitt's first commitment had been to Christ. It was understandable that she would have no other marriage. Although she did not take the Holy Eucharist on her tongue, she was there at church each

Sunday morning, faithful and devout, to play the organ. There, she, of course, played Bach, with a purity of intent purged of any subterranean feeling, strictly, and for God.

47   So when the river began to rise one spring, Berndt had already gone where life was deepest many times, and he did not particularly fear the rain. But what began as a sheer mist became an even sprinkle and then developed into a slow, pounding shower that lasted three days, then four, then on the fifth day, when it should have tapered off, increased.

48   The river boiled along swiftly, a gray soup still contained, just barely, within its high banks. On day six the rain stopped, or seemed to. The storm had moved upstream. All day while the sun shone pleasantly the river heaved itself up, tore into its flow new trees and boulders, created tip-ups, washouts, areas of singing turbulence, and crawled, like an infant, toward the farm. Berndt rushed around uneasily, pitching hay into the high loft, throwing chickens up after the hay, wishing he could throw the horse up as well, and the house, and—because Agnes wrung her hands—the piano. But the piano was earth-anchored and well-tuned by the rainy air, so, instead of worrying, Agnes practiced.

49   Once the river started to move, it gained confidence. It had no problem with fences or gates, wispy windbreaks, ditches. It simply levelled or attained the level of whatever stood in its path. Water jumped up the lawn and collected behind the sacks of sand that Berndt had desperately filled and laid. The river tugged itself up the porch and into the house from one side. From the other side it undermined an already weak foundation that had temporarily shored up the same wall once removed to make way for the piano. The river tore against the house and then, like a child tipping out a piece of candy from a box, it surged underneath and rocked the floor, and the piano crashed through the weakened wall.

50   It landed in the swift current of the yard, Agnes with it. Berndt saw only the white treble clef of her dress as she spun away, clutching the curved lid. It bobbed along the flower beds first, and then, as muscular new eddies caught it, touched down on the shifting lanes of Berndt's wheat fields, and farther, until the revolving instrument and the woman on it reached the original river and plunged in. They were carried not more than a hundred feet before the piano lost momentum and sank. As it went down, Agnes thought at first of crawling into its box, nestling for safety among the cold, dead strings. But, as she struggled with the hinged cover, she lost her grip and was swept north. She should have drowned, but there was a snag of rope, a tree, two men in a fishing skiff risking themselves to save a valuable birding dog. They pulled Agnes out and dumped her in the bottom of the boat, impatient to get the dog. She gagged, coughed, and passed out in a roil of feet and fishing tackle.

51   When she came to, she was back in the convent, which was on high ground and open to care for victims of the flood. Berndt was not among the rescued. When the river went down and the heat rose, he

was found snagged in a tip-up of roots, tethered to his great blue steaming horse. As Agnes recovered her strength, did she dream of him? Think of him entering her and her receiving him? Long for the curve of his hand on her breast? Yes and no. She thought again of music. Chopin. Berndt. Chopin.

52   He had written a will, in which he declared her his common-law wife and left to her the farm and all upon it. There, she raised Rosecomb Bantams, Dominikers, Reds. She bought another piano and played with an isolated intensity that absorbed her spirit.

53   A year or so after Berndt's death, her students noticed that she would stop in the middle of a lesson and smile out the window as though welcoming a long-expected visitor. One day the neighbor children went to pick up the usual order of eggs and were most struck to see the white-and-black-flecked Dominikers flapping up in alarm around Miss DeWitt as she stood magnificent upon the green grass.

54   Tall, slender, legs slightly bowed, breasts jutting a bit to either side, and the flare of hair flicking up the center of her—naked. She looked at the children with remote kindness. Asked, "How many dozen?" Walked off to gather the eggs.

55   That episode made the gossip-table rounds. People put it off to Berndt's death and a relapse of nerves. She lost only a Lutheran student or two. She continued playing the organ for Mass, and at home, in the black, black nights, Chopin. And if she was asked, by an innocent pupil too young to understand the meaning of discretion, why she sometimes didn't wear clothes, Miss DeWitt would answer that she removed her clothing when she played the music of a particular bare-souled composer. She would nod meditatively and say in her firmest manner that when one enters into such music, one should be naked. And then she would touch the keys.

Questions for Discussion

1. Explain how the description of the river at the beginning helps to define the story and foreshadow what happens.

2. Why does Agnes's playing Chopin disturb the other sisters in the convent?

3. What is the Mother Superior's role in the story? What does she hope to accomplish by hiding the music and dragging Sister Cecellia away from the piano? Why did she then keep the music under lock and key after Sister Cecellia left?

4. Why does Agnes refuse to marry Berndt? What do marriage and Berndt mean to her? Why then does she agree to sleep with him?

5. Explain Erdrich's description of Agnes's relationship to music: "She not only taught but lived music, existed for those hours when she could be concentrated in her being—which was half music, half divine light, flesh only to the degree that she could not admit otherwise."

6. How can music speak "of her faith and doubt, of her passion as the bride of Christ, of her loneliness, shame, ultimate redemption"?

7. Explain why, even though Agnes has not agreed to marry him, Berndt agrees to sleep in the barn and to remove one wall so that Agnes can get her piano into the house.

8. Explain how music can be for Agnes both a religious and a sexual experience.

Suggestion for Exploration and Writing

1. As Mother Superior did, many authority figures try to change what they feel is inappropriate behavior by forbidding it. Does this method work? In an essay, analyze why or why not.

POETRY

John Keats (1795–1821)

John Keats was, along with William Wordsworth, Samuel Taylor Coleridge, Lord Byron, and Percy Bysshe Shelley, one of the leading poets of the Romantic period in England. Nearly all of his greatest poems were written in one year, 1818–1819, and published in Lamia, Isabella, and Other Poems *(1820). Keats's poetry celebrates beauty in rich, lush images; his magnificent collected letters, a work of art in their own right, gained increasing attention in the twentieth century. Keats was stricken with tuberculosis and died at the age of twenty-five.*

ODE ON A GRECIAN URN   (1819)

I

Thou still unravish'd bride of quietness,
　　Thou foster-child of silence and slow time,
Sylvan historian, who canst thus express
　　A flowery tale more sweetly than our rhyme:
5　What leaf-fring'd legend haunts about thy shape
　　　Of deities or mortals, or of both,
　　　　In Tempe or the dales of Arcady?
　　What men or gods are these? What maidens loth?
What mad pursuit? What struggle to escape?
10　　　What pipes and timbrels? What wild ecstasy?

II

Heard melodies are sweet, but those unheard
　Are sweeter; therefore, ye soft pipes, play on;
Not to the sensual ear, but, more endear'd,
　Pipe to the spirit ditties of no tone:
15　Fair youth, beneath the trees, thou canst not leave
　　Thy song, nor ever can those trees be bare;
　　　Bold Lover, never, never canst thou kiss,
Though winning near the goal—yet, do not grieve;
　　She cannot fade, though thou hast not thy bliss,
20　　　For ever wilt thou love, and she be fair!

III

Ah, happy, happy boughs! that cannot shed
　Your leaves, nor ever bid the Spring adieu;
And, happy melodist, unwearied,
　For ever piping songs for ever new;
25　More happy love! more happy, happy love!
　　For ever warm and still to be enjoy'd,
　　　For ever panting, and for ever young;
All breathing human passion far above,
　　That leaves a heart high-sorrowful and cloy'd,
30　　　A burning forehead, and a parching tongue.

IV

Who are these coming to the sacrifice?
　To what green altar, O mysterious priest,
Lead'st thou that heifer lowing at the skies,
　And all her silken flanks with garlands drest?
35　What little town by river or sea shore,
　　Or mountain-built with peaceful citadel,
　　　Is emptied of this folk, this pious morn?
And, little town, thy streets for evermore
　　Will silent be; and not a soul to tell
40　　　Why thou art desolate, can e'er return.

V

O Attic shape! Fair attitude! with brede
　Of marble men and maidens overwrought,
With forest branches and the trodden weed;
　Thou, silent form, dost tease us out of thought
45　As doth eternity: Cold Pastoral!

When old age shall this generation waste,
   Thou shalt remain, in midst of other woe
Than ours, a friend to man, to whom thou say'st,
   'Beauty is truth, truth beauty,'—that is all
50   Ye know on earth, and all ye need to know.

Questions for Discussion

1. Keats begins by addressing an urn or vase. What does he mean when
   he calls the urn a "still unravish'd bride of quietness," a "foster-child
   of silence and slow time," and a "Sylvan historian"?

2. How can "unheard" melodies be "sweeter" than "heard" ones?

3. At the beginning of the second stanza, Keats addresses the "pipes,"
   and midway through the second stanza, he addresses lovers. In the
   third stanza, Keats addresses "happy boughs" and in the fourth a
   priest. Where did he find the pipes, the lovers, the boughs, and the
   priest? What do they all have in common?

4. How can the speaker say to the lovers, "For ever wilt thou love, and
   she be fair"?

Suggestion for Exploration and Writing

1. Supporting your answer with references to your own experience,
   argue for or against the statement: "'Beauty is truth, truth beauty.'"

Robert Browning (1812–1889)

*A brief biography of Robert Browning precedes "Porphyria's Lover" in
the Men and Women section.*

Caliban upon Setebos   (1864)

"Thou thoughtest that I was altogether such a one as thyself."

(David, Psalms 50.21)

[Will sprawl, now that the heat of day is best,
Flat on his belly in the pit's much mire,
With elbows wide, fists clenched to prop his chin.
And, while he kicks both feet in the cool slush,
5   And feels about his spine small eft-things course,
Run in and out each arm, and make him laugh;
And while above his head a pompion-plant,
Coating the cave-top as a brow its eye,

Creeps down to touch and tickle hair and beard,
10   And now a flower drops with a bee inside,
And now a fruit to snap at, catch and crunch,—
He looks out o'er yon sea which sunbeams cross
And recross till they weave a spider-web
(Meshes of fire, some great fish breaks at times)
15   And talks to his own self, howe'er he please,
Touching that other, whom his dam called God.
Because to talk about Him, vexes—ha,
Could He but know! and time to vex is now,
When talk is safer than in winter-time.
20   Moreover Prosper and Miranda sleep
In confidence he drudges at their task,
And it is good to cheat the pair, and gibe,
Letting the rank tongue blossom into speech.][1]

Setebos, Setebos, and Setebos!
25   Thinketh, He dwelleth i' the cold o' the moon.

Thinketh He made it, with the sun to match,
But not the stars; the stars came otherwise;
Only made clouds, winds, meteors, such as that:
Also this isle, what lives and grows thereon,
30   And snaky sea which rounds and ends the same.

Thinketh, it came of being ill at ease:
He hated that He cannot change His cold,
Nor cure its ache. Hath spied an icy fish
That longed to 'scape the rock-stream where she lived,
35   And thaw herself within the lukewarm brine
O' the lazy sea her stream thrusts far amid,
A crystal spike 'twixt two warm walls of wave;
Only, she ever sickened, found repulse
At the other kind of water, not her life,
40   (Green-dense and dim-delicious, bred o' the sun)
Flounced back from bliss she was not born to breathe,
And in her old bounds buried her despair,
Hating and living warmth alike: so He.

Thinketh, He made thereat the sun, this isle,
45   Trees and the fowls here, beast and creeping thing.
Yon otter, sleek-wet, black, lithe as a leech;
Yon auk, one fire-eye in a ball of foam,
That floats and feeds; a certain badger brown
He hath watched hunt with that slant white-wedge eye

---

[1]The bracketed lines at the beginning and end are Caliban's thoughts. The rest of the poem is spoken aloud.

50   By moonlight; and the pie with the long tongue
      That pricks deep into oak warts for a worm,
      And says a plain word when she finds her prize,
      But will not eat the ants; the ants themselves
      That build a wall of seeds and settled stalks
55   About their hole—He made all these and more,
      Made all we see, and us, in spite: how else?
      He could not, Himself, make a second self
      To be His mate; as well have made Himself:
      He would not make what He mislikes or slights,
60   An eyesore to Him, or not worth His pains:
      But did, in envy, listlessness or sport,
      Make what Himself would fain, in a manner, be—
      Weaker in most points, stronger in a few,
      Worthy, and yet mere playthings all the while,
65   Things He admires and mocks too,—that is it.
      Because, so brave, so better though they be,
      It nothing skills if He begin to plague.
      Look, now, I melt a gourd-fruit into mash,
      Add honeycomb and pods, I have perceived,
70   Which bite like finches when they bill and kiss,—
      Then, when froth rises bladdery, drink up all,
      Quick, quick, till maggots scamper through my brain;
      Last, throw me on my back i' the seeded thyme,
      And wanton, wishing I were born a bird.
75   Put case, unable to be what I wish,
      I yet could make a live bird out of clay:
      Would not I take clay, pinch my Caliban
      Able to fly?—for, there, see, he hath wings,
      And great comb like the hoopoe's to admire,
80   And there, a sting to do his foes offence,
      There, and I will that he begin to live,
      Fly to yon rock-top, nip me off the horns
      Of grigs high up that make the merry din,
      Saucy through their veined wings, and mind me not.
85   In which feat, if his leg snapped, brittle clay,
      And he lay stupid-like,—why, I should laugh;
      And if he, spying me, should fall to weep,
      Beseech me to be good, repair his wrong,
      Bid his poor leg smart less or grow again,—
90   Well, as the chance were, this might take or else
      Not take my fancy: I might hear his cry,
      And give the mankin three sound legs for one,
      Or pluck the other off, leave him like an egg
      And lessoned he was mine and merely clay.

95   Were this no pleasure, lying in the thyme,
      Drinking the mash, with brain become alive,
      Making and marring clay at will? So He.

      Thinketh, such shows nor right nor wrong in Him,
      Nor kind, nor cruel: He is strong and Lord.
100   Am strong myself compared to yonder crabs
      That march now from the mountain to the sea;
      Let twenty pass, and stone the twenty-first,
      Loving not, hating not, just choosing so.
      Say, the first straggler that boasts purple spots
105   Shall join the file, one pincer twisted off;
      Say, this bruised fellow shall receive a worm,
      And two worms he whose nippers end in red;
      As it likes me each time, I do: so He.

      Well then, supposeth He is good i' the main,
110   Placable if His mind and ways were guessed,
      But rougher than His handiwork, be sure!
      Oh, He hath made things worthier than Himself,
      And envieth that, so helped, such things do more
      Than He who made them! What consoles but this?
115   That they, unless through Him, do nought at all,
      And must submit: what other use in things?
      Hath cut a pipe of pithless elder-joint
      That, blown through, gives exact the scream o' the jay
      When from her wing you twitch the feathers blue:
120   Sound this, and little birds that hate the jay
      Flock within stone's throw, glad their foe is hurt:
      Put case such pipe could prattle and boast forsooth
      "I catch the birds, I am the crafty thing,
      I make the cry my maker cannot make
125   With his great round mouth; he must blow through mine!"
      Would not I smash it with my foot? So He.

      But wherefore rough, why cold and ill at ease?
      Aha, that is a question! Ask, for that,
      What knows,—the something over Setebos
130   That made Him, or He, may be, found and fought,
      Worsted, drove off and did to nothing, perchance.
      There may be something quiet o'er His head,
      Out of His reach, that feels nor joy nor grief,
      Since both derive from weakness in some way.
135   I joy because the quails come; would not joy
      Could I bring quails here when I have a mind:
      This Quiet, all it hath a mind to, doth.
      Esteemeth stars the outposts of its couch,
      But never spends much thought nor care that way.

140　It may look up, work up,—the worse for those
　　It works on! Careth but for Setebos
　　The many-handed as a cuttle-fish,
　　Who, making Himself feared through what He does,
　　Looks up, first, and perceives he cannot soar
145　To what is quiet and hath happy life;
　　Next looks down here, and out of very spite
　　Makes this a bauble-world to ape yon real,
　　These good things to match those as hips do grapes.
　　'Tis solace making baubles, ay, and sport.
150　Himself peeped late, eyed Prosper at his books
　　Careless and lofty, lord now of the isle:
　　Vexed, stitched a book of broad leaves, arrow-shaped,
　　Wrote thereon, he knows what, prodigious words;
　　Has peeled a wand and called it by a name;
155　Weareth at whiles for an enchanter's robe
　　The eyed skin of a supple oncelot;
　　And hath an ounce sleeker than youngling mole,
　　A four-legged serpent he makes cower and couch,
　　Now snarl, now hold its breath and mind his eye,
160　And saith she is Miranda and my wife:
　　Keeps for his Ariel a tall pouch-bill crane
　　He bids go wade for fish and straight disgorge;
　　Also a sea-beast, lumpish, which he snared,
　　Blinded the eyes of, and brought somewhat tame,
165　And split its toe-webs, and now pens the drudge
　　In a hole o' the rock and calls him Caliban;
　　A bitter heart that bides its time and bites.
　　Plays thus at being Prosper in a way,
　　Taketh his mirth with make-believes; so He.
170　His dam held that the Quiet made all things
　　Which Setebos vexed only: holds not so.
　　Who made them weak, meant weakness He might vex.
　　Had He meant other, while His hand was in,
　　Why not make horny eyes no thorn could prick,
175　Or plate my scalp with bone against the snow,
　　Or overscale my flesh 'neath joint and joint
　　Like an orc's armour? Ay,—so spoil His sport!
　　He is the One now: only He doth all.

　　Saith, He may like, perchance, what profits Him.
180　Ay, himself loves what does him good; but why?
　　Gets good no otherwise. This blinded beast
　　Loves whoso places flesh-meat on his nose,
　　But, had he eyes, would want no help, but hate
　　Or love, just as it liked him: He hath eyes.
185　Also it pleaseth Setebos to work,

Use all His hands, and exercise much craft,
By no means for the love of what is worked.
Tasteth, himself, no finer good i' the world
When all goes right, in this safe summer-time,
190   And he wants little, hungers, aches not much,
Than trying what to do with wit and strength.
Falls to make something: piled yon pile of turfs,
And squared and stuck there squares of soft white chalk,
And, with a fish-tooth, scratched a moon on each,
195   And set up endwise certain spikes of tree,
And crowned the whole with a sloth's skull a-top,
Found dead i' the woods, too hard for one to kill.
No use at all i' the work, for work's sole sake;
Shall some day knock it down again: so He.

200   Saith He is terrible: watch His feats in proof!
One hurricane will spoil six good months' hope.
He hath a spite against me, that I know,
Just as He favours Prosper, who knows why?
So it is, all the same, as well I find.
205   Wove wattles half the winter, fenced them firm
With stone and stake to stop she-tortoises
Crawling to lay their eggs here: well, one wave,
Feeling the foot of Him upon its neck,
Gaped as a snake does, lolled out its large tongue,
210   And licked the whole labour flat: so much for spite.
Saw a ball flame down late (yonder it lies)
Where, half an hour before, I slept i' the shade:
Often they scatter sparkles: there is force!
Dug up a newt He may have envied once
215   And turned to stone, shut up Inside a stone.
Please Him and hinder this?—What Prosper does?
Aha, if He would tell me how! Not He!
There is the sport: discover how or die!
All need not die, for of the things o' the isle
220   Some flee afar, some dive, some run up trees;
Those at His mercy,—why, they please Him most
When . . . when . . . well, never try the same way twice!
Repeat what act has pleased, He may grow wroth.
You must not know His ways, and play Him off,
225   Sure of the issue. Doth the like himself:
Spareth a squirrel that it nothing fears
But steals the nut from underneath my thumb,
And when I threat, bites stoutly in defence:
Spareth an urchin that contrariwise,
230   Curls up into a ball, pretending death

For fright at my approach: the two ways please.
But what would move my choler more than this,
That either creature counted on its life
To-morrow and next day and all days to come,
235   Saying, forsooth, in the inmost of its heart,
"Because he did so yesterday with me,
And otherwise with such another brute,
So must he do henceforth and always."—Ay?
Would teach the reasoning couple what "must" means!
240   Doth as he likes, or wherefore Lord? So He.

Conceiveth all things will continue thus,
And we shall have to live in fear of Him
So long as He lives, keeps His strength: no change,
If He have done His best, make no new world
245   To please Him more, so leave off watching this,—
If He surprise not even the Quiet's self
Some strange day,—or, suppose, grow into it
As grubs grow butterflies: else, here are we,
And there is He, and nowhere help at all.

250   Believeth with the life, the pain shall stop.
His dam held different, that after death
He both plagued enemies and feasted friends:
Idly! He doth His worst in this our life,
Giving just respite lest we die through pain,
255   Saving last pain for worst,—with which, an end.
Meanwhile, the best way to escape His ire
Is, not to seem too happy. Sees, himself,
Yonder two flies, with purple films and pink,
Bask on the pompion-bell above: kills both.
260   Sees two black painful beetles roll their ball
On head and tail as if to save their lives:
Moves them the stick away they strive to clear.

Even so, would have Him misconceive, suppose
This Caliban strives hard and ails no less,
265   And always, above all else, envies Him;
Wherefore he mainly dances on dark nights,
Moans in the sun, gets under holes to laugh,
And never speaks his mind save housed as now:
Outside, groans, curses. If He caught me here,
270   O'erheard this speech, and asked "What chucklest at?"
Would, to appease Him, cut a finger off,
Or of my three kid yearlings burn the best,
Or let the toothsome apples rot on tree,
Or push my tame beast for the orc to taste:

275 While myself lit a fire, and made a song
And sung it, "*What I hate, be consecrate*
To celebrate Thee and Thy state, no mate
For Thee; what see for envy in poor me?"
Hoping the while, since evils sometimes mend,
280 Warts rub away and sores are cured with slime,
That some strange day, will either the Quiet catch
And conquer Setebos, or likelier He
Decrepit may doze, doze, as good as die.

[What, what? A curtain o'er the world at once!
285 Crickets stop hissing: not a bird—or, yes,
There scuds His raven that has told Him all!
It was fool's play, this prattling! Ha! The wind
Shoulders the pillared dust, death's house o' the move,
And fast invading fires begin! White blaze—
290 A tree's head snaps—and there, there, there, there, there,
His thunder follows! Fool to gibe at Him!
Lo! Lieth flat and loveth Setebos!
Maketh his teeth meet through his upper lip,
Will let those quails fly, will not eat this month
295 One little mess of whelks, so he may 'scape!]

Questions for Discussion

1. What do Caliban's opening thoughts reveal about him and his attitudes toward Prospero and Miranda?
2. According to Caliban, what were Setebos's reason for creating the island?
3. What does he believe to be Setebos's limitations?
4. What standards does Caliban use in deciding what Setebos is like? Why does he continually add, "So He"?
5. Interpret Caliban's conclusion in lines 98 through 108.
6. Does Caliban believe Setebos to be the supreme or only creator? What lines support your answer?
7. Explain Caliban's description of himself as "A bitter heart that bides its time and bites."
8. Why, according to Caliban, did Setebos make other creatures vulnerable?
9. What lines support a belief that Caliban believes that Setebos is capricious?
10. Explain Caliban's theories about the afterlife.
11. What does Caliban believe is "the best way to escape [Setebos's] ire"? What are the best ways to appease Setebos?

Suggestions for Exploration and Writing

1. Write a description of Setebos as perceived by Caliban. Alternatively, write a comparison of Setebos as perceived by Caliban and what you believe a supreme being is or should be.

2. Explain in an essay how Browning, in this poem, reverses the concept that God made man in his own image.

3. Examine the character Caliban in *The Tempest* and explain which of his physical and moral characteristics Browning has adopted in his poem and what he has added.

Archibald MacLeish (1892–1982)

*Archibald MacLeish was an American scholar, teacher, poet, essayist, critic, and playwright. He served for five years (1939–1944) as Librarian of Congress. Primarily known for his short poems, MacLeish also received a Pulitzer Prize for J.B., a verse dramatization of the biblical story of Job. Though MacLeish was not one of the first **Imagists**, his "Ars Poetica" is often mentioned as one of the best examples of Imagist writing.*

ARS POETICA   (1926)

A poem should be palpable and mute
As a globed fruit,

Dumb
As old medallions to the thumb,

5   Silent as the sleeve-worn stone
Of casement ledges where the moss has grown—

A poem should be wordless
As the flight of birds.

A poem should be motionless in time
10   As the moon climbs,

Leaving, as the moon releases
Twig by twig the night-entangled trees,

Leaving, as the moon behind the winter leaves,
Memory by memory the mind—
15   A poem should be motionless in time
As the moon climbs.

A poem should be equal to:
Not true.

For all the history of grief
20   An empty doorway and a maple leaf.

For love
The leaning grasses and two lights above the sea—

A poem should not mean
But be.

Questions for Discussion

1. Explain each of the three statements that MacLeish makes about poetry.

2. What pictures do the **similes** and **metaphors** provide? In what ways do these devices communicate, even more clearly than expository writing can, a definition of poetry?

Suggestion for Exploration and Writing

1. Both Reed and MacLeish use poetic form to give their definitions of poetry. In a **comparison-contrast** essay, examine these definitions of poetry. If possible, explain the poets' selection of the poetic form for their definitions.

W. H. Auden (1907–1973)

A brief biography of W. H. Auden precedes "The Unknown Citizen" in the Freedom and Responsibility Unit.

MUSÉE DES BEAUX ARTS   (1940)

About suffering they were never wrong,
The Old Masters: how well they understood
Its human position; how it takes place
While someone else is eating or opening a window or just walking
5   dully along;
How, when the aged are reverently, passionately waiting
For the miraculous birth, there always must be
Children who did not specially want it to happen, skating
On a pond at the edge of the wood:
10   They never forgot
That even the dreadful martyrdom must run its course
Anyhow in a corner, some untidy spot
Where the dogs go on with their doggy life and the torturer's horse
Scratches its innocent behind on a tree.
15   In Brueghel's *Icarus*, for instance: how everything turns away
Quite leisurely from the disaster; the ploughman may
Have heard the splash, the forsaken cry,
But for him it was not an important failure; the sun shone

As it had to on the white legs disappearing into the green
20   Water; and the expensive delicate ship that must have seen
Something amazing, a boy falling out of the sky,
Had somewhere to get to and sailed calmly on.

Questions for Discussion

1. What is "the miraculous birth"?

2. What can the "Old Masters" reveal about suffering?

3. Find a reproduction of Brueghel's *The Fall of Icarus*. The background of this painting depicts the fall of Icarus after he has disregarded the advice of his father, Daedalus, and flown too close to the sun, melting the wax that held his wings together. Explain how the painting supports Auden's claim about the "Old Masters."

Suggestion for Exploration and Writing

1. Write an essay describing a work of art that you admire, explaining what special meaning it has for you.

Lawrence Ferlinghetti (b. 1919)

*Lawrence Ferlinghetti is an American poet, novelist, and playwright who was an important member of the **Beat** movement. He opened the first paperback bookstore in the United States, a shop that became a center for jazz performances and poetry readings. Many of his poems use irony and sarcasm to protest the status quo. Ferlinghetti believes that poetry can improve society.*

CONSTANTLY RISKING ABSURDITY   (1958)

Constantly risking absurdity
                        and death
whenever he performs
                        above the heads
5   of his audience
the poet like an acrobat
            climbs on rime
                        to a high wire of his own making
and balancing on eyebeams
10   above a sea of faces
            paces his way
                        to the other side of day
    performing entrechats
                        and sleight-of-foot tricks

15 and other high theatrics
     and all without mistaking
   any thing
     for what it may not be
  For he's the super realist
20   who must perforce perceive
   taut truth
     before the taking of each stance or step
  in his supposed advance
    toward that still higher perch
25 where Beauty stands and waits
     with gravity
      to start her death-defying leap
And he
  a little charleychaplin man
30   who may or may not catch
   her fair eternal form
     spreadeagled in the empty air
  of existence

Questions for Discussion

1. In one long sentence Ferlinghetti compares the poet to the high-wire acrobat. In what ways are they alike? Why do they both take risks?

2. What effect does the reading aloud of "must perforce perceive / taut truth" have on the speed of the poem? How is this speed relevant to that of a tightrope walker?

3. Why is a poet a "super realist"?

4. Explain the use of "charleychaplin." Describe the image conveyed by this **allusion.**

5. What effect does the arrangement of the lines have on the meaning of the poem?

Suggestions for Exploration and Writing

1. In an **expository** essay, describe the skills and talents which you think make a person a poet.

2. Write an essay agreeing or disagreeing with this statement: The profession of poet is costly for the person who chooses it.

Countee Cullen (1903–1948)

A brief biography of Countee Cullen precedes "Incident" in the Grief and Loss Unit.

Yet Do I Marvel (1925)

I doubt not God is good, well-meaning, kind,
And did he stoop to quibble could tell why
The little buried mole continues blind,
Why flesh that mirrors him must some day die,
5　Make plain the reason tortured Tantalus
Is baited with the fickle fruit, declare
If merely brute caprice dooms Sisyphus
To struggle up a never-ending stair.

Inscrutable His ways are and immune
10　To catechism by a mind too strewn
With petty cares to slightly understand
What awful brain compels His awful hand;
Yet do I marvel at this curious thing:
To make a poet black, and bid him sing!

Questions for Discussion

1. What acts of God puzzle the narrator?
2. To Cullen, what is the most "inscrutable" and "curious" of all of God's creations? Explain why.
3. Research the myths of Tantalus and Sisyphus and explain the last four lines of the octave.
4. What limitations does Cullen suggest the human brain has?
5. Explain the double meaning of the word *awful* in line 12.
6. Taking into consideration the time in which the poet lived, explain the last two lines.

Suggestions for Exploration and Writing

1. In an essay, explain what you think is the most curious or inscrutable event of the last two years.
2. How does Cullen use the traditional form of the English sonnet to present his question rather than to answer it?
3. Compare Cullen's view of God to Caliban's view of Setebos.

Audre Lorde (1934–1992)

Born to Granadian parents, Audre Lorde attended school and lived most of her life in New York. Inarticulate as a small child, she spoke in rhythm or in poetry form to express herself. Lorde wrote about subjects that lead to confrontation. As a feminist poet, she portrays strong African American women who challenge the status quo.

THE ART OF RESPONSE (1986)

The first answer was incorrect
the second was
sorry   the third trimmed its toenails
on the Vatican steps
5   the fourth went mad
the fifth
nursed a grudge until it bore twins
that drank poisoned grape juice in Jonestown
the sixth   wrote a book about it
10   the seventh
argued a case before the Supreme Court
against taxation on Girl Scout Cookies
the eighth held a news conference
while four Black babies
15   and one other   picketed New York City
for a hospital bed to die in
the ninth and tenth swore
Revenge on the Opposition
and the eleventh dug their graves
20   next to Eternal Truth
the twelfth
processed funds from a Third World country
that provides doctors for Central Harlem
the thirteenth
25   refused
the fourteenth sold cocaine and shamrocks
near a toilet in the Big Apple circus
the fifteenth
changed the question.

Questions for Discussion

1. How does Lorde build the "art" of answering a question? What is the significance of the fifteenth's response?

2. Why isn't the question to which all are responding ever given?

3. Select one response and discuss its humor or its deeper implications.

Suggestions for Exploration and Writing

1. Write an essay explaining what you think the question is and why. Or explain what the question is and what the fifteenth person's change is.

2. Explain how responding to essay questions on an exam can be an art form.

Ishmael Reed (b. 1938)

*Ishmael Reed is a controversial American poet and novelist. A savage **satirist**, Reed attacks what he believes to be a dying Western cultural tradition as incompatible with African and Asian traditions. His poems sometimes take the form of rituals designed to separate readers and African American poets from the influence of the dominant culture.*

BEWARE : DO NOT READ THIS POEM   (1972)

tonite   ,   thriller was
abt an ol woman   ,   so vain she
surrounded herself w/
   many mirrors

5 it got so bad that finally she
locked herself indoors & her
whole life became the
   mirrors

one day the villagers broke
10 into her house   ,   but she was too
swift for them   .   she disappeared
   into a mirror

each tenant who bought the house
after that   ,   lost a loved one to
15   the ol woman in the mirror   :
   first a little girl
   then a young woman
   then the young woman/s husband

the hunger of this poem is legendary
20 it has taken in many victims
back off from this poem
it has drawn in yr feet
back off from this poem
it has drawn in yr legs
25 back off from this poem
it is a greedy mirror
you are into this poem   .   from
   the waist down
nobody can hear you can they   ?
30 this poem has had you up to here
   belch
this poem aint got no manners
you cant call out frm this poem
relax now & go w/this poem
35 move & roll on to this poem

do not resist this poem
this poem has yr eyes
this poem has his head
this poem has his arms
40   this poem has his fingers
this poem has his fingertips

this poem is the reader & the
reader this poem
statistic   :   the us bureau of missing persons reports
45   that in 1968 over 100,000 people disappeared
leaving no solid clues
nor trace   only
a space   in the lives of their friends

Questions for Discussion

1. Reed attacks the common conception of poetry as pretty, nice, and innocuous. What claims does this poem make for the power of art?
2. What does this poem imply about the subjects of art?

Suggestions for Exploration and Writing

1. In what sense(s) might a work of art or a culture consume one?
2. What is the point of the statistic at the end of the poem?

Fred Chappell (b. 1936)

Fred Chappell spent his childhood in the Appalachian Mountains of Canton, North Carolina, where he learned to shape his poems in many forms and to tell a story with humor and a serious moral thread. A graduate of Duke University, Chappell has taught at the University of North Carolina at Greensboro for many years. His books of poetry include The World Between the Eyes *(1971),* Source *(1985), and* Spring Garden *(1995). His novels include* I Am One of You Forever *(1985) and* Brighten the Corner Where You Are *(1989). In addition to the Bollingen Prize in Poetry, Chappell has won the Ingersoll Foundation's T. S. Eliot Prize.*

THE GARDEN   (1989)

The garden is a book about the gardener.

His thoughts, set down in vivid greenery,
The white light and the gold light nourish.
Firm sentences of grapevine, boxwood paragraphs,
5   End-stops of peonies and chrysanthemums,
Cut drowsy shadows from the afternoon.

Out of their hiding places the humid twilight
Lures the stars. The perfumes of the grass
Draw like cool curtains across the mind
10   And what the mind is certain it is certain of.

So that the twilight fragrances are clearly audible,
The garden stroking the senses with slow roses.
Bats ramble overhead, tacking from star
To early star as if putting in at ports of call.
15   And then the Chinese lantern is lit as it was in childhood,
As central in that place as an island lighthouse.

The gardener is a book about his garden.
He walks among these leaves as easy as morning
Come to scatter its robins and tender noises.
20   As the plants inhale the morning and its cool light,
The book is open once again that was never shut.
What now we do not know we shall never know.

Questions for Discussion

1. Explain the appropriateness of the metaphors "sentences of grape-vine," "boxwood paragraphs," and "end-stops of peonies and chrysanthemums."

2. Explain the meaning of the last two lines.

3. In what ways is a garden a work of art?

Suggestions for Exploration and Writing

1. In the first line, Chappell says that "The garden is a book about the gardener." Then in the first line of the last stanza he says, "The gardener is a book about his garden." Write an essay clarifying these metaphors.

2. In an essay, explain what a garden might reveal about its gardener.

Seamus Heaney (b. 1939)

Seamus Heaney was born in County Derry in Northern Ireland, where his father was a farmer and cattle dealer; this locale has been influential in his writing. He has described his move away from the farm as a removal from "the earth of farm labour to the heaven of education." At St. Columb's College and Queen's University, Belfast, he learned Latin, Irish, and Anglo-Saxon, languages that have influenced his poetry. In addition to poetry, Heaney writes incisive literary criticism. He has taught at several universities, including the University of California at Berkeley, Carysfort College, and Harvard University. In 1995, Heaney was awarded the Nobel Prize in Literature.

DIGGING   (1966)

Between my finger and my thumb
The squat pen rests; snug as a gun.

Under my window, a clean rasping sound
When the spade sinks into gravelly ground:
5   My father, digging. I look down

Till his straining rump among the flowerbeds
Bends low, comes up twenty years away
Stooping in rhythm through potato drills
Where he was digging.

10   The coarse boot nestled on the lug, the shaft
Against the inside knee was levered firmly.
He rooted out tall tops, buried the bright edge deep
To scatter new potatoes that we picked
Loving their cool hardness in our hands.

15   By God, the old man could handle a spade.
Just like his old man.

My grandfather cut more turf in a day
Than any other man on Toner's bog.
Once I carried him milk in a bottle
20   Corked sloppily with paper. He straightened up
To drink it, then fell to right away
Nicking and slicing neatly, heaving sods
Over his shoulder, going down and down
For the good turf. Digging.

25   The cold smell of potato mould, the squelch and slap
Of soggy peat, the curt cuts of an edge
Through living roots awaken in my head.
But I've no spade to follow men like them.

Between my finger and my thumb
30   The squat pen rests.
I'll dig with it.

Questions for Discussion

1. The speaker describes his father's and his grandfather's digging. What are they digging for? What is the speaker's attitude
   toward them?

2. Explain the speaker's metaphorical parallel of the shovel and the pen.

3. What is the narrator digging for?

Suggestion for Exploration and Writing

1. Compare this poem to Ferlinghetti's description of the poet.

Billy Collins (b. 1941)

A brief biography of Billy Collins precedes "Forgetfulness" in the Grief and Loss Unit.

INTRODUCTION TO POETRY   (1988)

I ask them to take a poem
and hold it up to the light
like a color slide

or press an ear against its hive.
5   I say drop a mouse into a poem
and watch him probe his way out,

or walk inside the poem's room
and feel the walls for a light switch.

I want them to waterski
10   across the surface of a poem
waving at the author's name on the shore.

But all they want to do
is tie the poem to a chair with rope
and torture a confession out of it.

15   They begin beating it with a hose
to find out what it really means.

Questions for Discussion

1. What method of teaching is Collins satirizing?

2. Explain each of the metaphors for how to read a poem.

3. What contrast is Collins making between different ways of reading a poem? How would he like people to regard a poem? How do "they" regard a poem?

Suggestion for Exploration and Writing

1. Compare this poem with Ishmael Reed's directions about what not to do with a poem.

POEM

(1988)

Some poems name their subjects.
The titles are *On* this or *On* that,
or they hang like small marquees
indicating what is playing inside:
5   "Celibacy," "Ostriches at Dusk."

Other poems fall into it as they go along.
You trip over a word while carrying
a tray of vocabulary out to the pool
only to discover that broken glass
10   is a good topic.

Still others have no subject
other than themselves to gnaw on.
The fly lands on the swatter.
The movie runs backwards
15   and catches fire in the projector.
This species apes us well
by talking only about itself.

Such is often the case with poems
afflicted by the same plain title
20   as this one:
a sign by the road announcing a bump.

Questions for Discussion

1. What does Collins mean by "You trip over a word while carrying / a tray of vocabulary"?

2. What does Collins mean by "broken glass is a good subject"?

3. What is Collins implying about "us" in the last two lines of the third stanza?

4. Explain Collins's concluding metaphor: "a sign by the road announcing a bump."

Suggestions for Exploration and Writing

1. Either alone or in groups, prepare a "tray of vocabulary" and try to trip your classmates with these words.

2. Compare this definition of poetry to those by Ishmael Reed and Archibald MacLeish.

Gregory Djanikian (b. 1949)

Gregory Djanikian's poetry has been published in many of the most prestigious poetry journals, such as Poetry *and* Iowa

Review. *His books of poetry include* The Man in the Middle *(1984),* Falling Deeply into America *(1989), and* About Distance *(1995). He presently teaches creative writing at the University of Pennsylvania.*

HOW I LEARNED ENGLISH   (1988)

It was in an empty lot
Ringed by elms and fir and honeysuckle.
Bill Corson was pitching in his buckskin jacket,
Chuck Keller, fat even as a boy, was on first,
His t-shirt riding up over his gut,
Ron O'Neill, Jim, Dennis, were talking it up
In the field, a blue sky above them
Tipped with cirrus.
                    And there I was,
Just off the plane and plopped in the middle
Of Williamsport, Pa., and a neighborhood game,
Unnatural and without any moves,
My notions of baseball and America
Growing fuzzier each time I whiffed.

So it was not impossible that I,
Banished to the outfield and daydreaming
Of water, or a hotel in the mountains,
Would suddenly find myself in the path
Of a ball stung by Joe Barone.
I watched it closing in
Clean and untouched, transfixed
By its easy arc before it hit
My forehead with a thud.
                    I fell back,
Dazed, clutching my brow,
Groaning, "Oh my shin, oh my shin,"
And everybody peeled away from me
And dropped from laughter, and there we were,
All of us writhing on the ground for one reason
Or another.
            Someone said "shin" again,
There was a wild stamping of hands on the ground,
A kicking of feet, and the fit
Of laughter overtook me too,
And that was important, as important
As Joe Barone asking me how I was
Through his tears, picking me up
And dusting me off with hands like swatters,
And though my head felt heavy,

40   I played on till dusk
       Missing flies and pop-ups and grounders
       And calling out in desperation things like
       "Yours" and "take it," but doing all right,
       Tugging at my cap in just the right way,
45   Crouching low, my feet set,
       "Hum baby" sweetly on my lips.

Questions for Discussion

1. How does the poem develop its title?
2. What language difficulties are most apparent in the poem?
3. In what sense(s) might baseball be regarded as a kind of language? How might learning to play baseball teach an immigrant American English?
4. In what ways is the game of baseball an important part of American culture? What does it reveal about Americans as a people?
5. Why do the narrator's teammates laugh when he is hit in the forehead by a baseball? Why does Joe Barone cry?

Suggestion for Exploration and Writing

1. If English is not your native language, write an essay about an incident that caused you to learn new words or recount a story about a humorous mistake you made while learning the language.

Victor Hernández Cruz (b. 1949)

A brief biography of Victor Hernández Cruz precedes "Problems with Hurricanes" in the Grief and Loss Unit.

TODAY IS A DAY OF GREAT JOY   (1989)

       when they stop poems
       in the mail & clap
       their hands & dance to
       them

5   when women become pregnant
       by the side of poems
       the strongest sounds making
       the river go along

       it is a great day

10   as poems fall down to
       movie crowds in restaurants
       in bars

when poems start to
knock down walls to
15   choke politicians
when poems scream &
begin to break the air

that is the time of
true poets that is
20   the time of greatness

a true poet aiming
poems & watching things
fall to the ground

it is a great day

Questions for Discussion

1. What kinds of poems do people sing and dance to?
2. What kinds of poems knock down walls? What kind of walls?
3. Choose a clause beginning with *when* or *as* and explain the joy of that idea.
4. Cruz describes "a true poet aiming / poems & watching things / fall to the ground." What does he mean? At whom is he aiming poems? What does Cruz imply is the purpose of poems?

Suggestions for Exploration and Writing

1. Cruz describes the ability of literature and of poems in particular to create or destroy. Using any of the poems in this anthology, write an essay on the power of poetry to (1) create, (2) destroy, (3) communicate, or (4) reveal.
2. Using one of the four functions listed in 1, above, write an essay explaining how this function applies to drama, fiction, or the essay.
3. In Russia and in Ireland, poetry and the poet are revered. Is the same homage paid to poets in America? Why or why not?
4. Write an essay in which you explain each of the metaphors Cruz uses to portray the unique power and joy of poetry.

Alberto Ríos (b. 1952)

Ríos, a highly respected modern Hispanic American writer, was born in Nogales, Arizona, to an English mother and a Mexican American father. He has received the Walt Whitman Award of the Academy of American Poets (1981), the Western States Book Award (1984), the Pushcart Prize IX (1989), and the Mountain Plains Library Author of the Year Award (1991). Ríos has published both poetry and fiction: Whispering to Fool the Wind *(1981) and* The Iguana Killer *(1984).*

THE VIETNAM WALL   (1985)

I
Have seen it
And I like it: The magic,
The way like cutting onions
5   It brings water out of nowhere.
Invisible from one side, a scar
Into the skin of the ground
From the other, a black winding
Appendix line.
10   A dig.
    An archaeologist can explain.
The walk is slow at first
Easy, a little black marble wall
Of a dollhouse,
15   A smoothness, a shine
The boys in the street want to give.
One name. And then more
Names, long lines, lines of names until
They are the shape of the U.N. building
20   Taller than I am: I have walked
Into a grave.
And everything I expect has been taken away, like that, quick:
    The names are not alphabetized.
    They are in the order of dying,
25   An alphabet of—somewhere—screaming.
I start to walk out. I almost leave
But stop to look up names of friends,
My own name. There is somebody
Severiano Ríos.
30   Little kids do not make the same noise
Here, junior high school boys don't run
Or hold each other in headlocks.
No rules, something just persists
Like pinching on St. Patrick's Day
35   Every year for no green.
    No one knows why.
Flowers are forced
Into the cracks
Between sections.
40   Men have cried
At this wall.
I have
Seen them.

Questions for Discussion

1. Why is the wall "a scar / Into the skin of the ground"?
2. In what ways is the Vietnam Wall a grave that the speaker has walked into? Why *into?*
3. In what ways have his expectations been overwhelmed by reality?
4. Why does he stop to look up his own name?
5. What do his references to "little kids" or "junior high school boys" have to do with the monument to the Vietnam War?
6. What is the "something" that "just persists"?

Suggestions for Exploration and Writing

1. Explain how art (without language) can sometimes speak louder than language.
2. Have you ever visited a monument? If so, write your reaction to that monument as an art form.

Li-Young Lee (b. 1957)

A brief biography of Li-Young Lee precedes "The Gift" in the Family Unit.

PERSIMMONS   (1986)

In sixth grade Mrs. Walker
slapped the back of my head
and made me stand in the corner
for not knowing the difference
5 between *persimmon* and *precision.*
How to choose

persimmons. This is precision.
Ripe ones are soft and brown-spotted.
Sniff the bottoms. The sweet one
10 will be fragrant. How to eat:
put the knife away, lay down newspaper.
Peel the skin tenderly, not to tear the meat.
Chew the skin, suck it,
and swallow. Now, eat
15 the meat of the fruit,

so sweet,
all of it, to the heart.

Donna undresses, her stomach is white.
In the yard, dewy and shivering
20   with crickets, we lie naked,
face-up, face-down.
I teach her Chinese.
Crickets: *chiu chiu.* Dew: I've forgotten.

Naked: I've forgotten.
25   *Ni, wo:*   you and me.
I part her legs,
remember to tell her
she is beautiful as the moon.

Other words
30   that got me into trouble were
fight and *fright, wren* and *yarn.*
Fight was what I did when I was frightened,
fright was what I felt when I was fighting.
Wrens are small, plain birds,
35   yarn is what one knits with.
Wrens are soft as yarn.
My mother made birds out of yarn.
I loved to watch her tie the stuff;
a bird, a rabbit, a wee man.

40   Mrs. Walker brought a persimmon to class
and cut it up
so everyone could taste
a *Chinese apple.* Knowing
it wasn't ripe or sweet, I didn't eat
45   but watched the other faces.

My mother said every persimmon has a sun
inside, something golden, glowing,
warm as my face.

Once, in the cellar, I found two wrapped in newspaper,
50   forgotten and not yet ripe.
I took them and set both on my bedroom windowsill,
where each morning a cardinal
sang, *The sun, the sun.*

Finally understanding
55   he was going blind,
my father sat up all one night
waiting for a song, a ghost.
I gave him the persimmons,

60 swelled, heavy as sadness,
and sweet as love.

This year, in the muddy lighting
of my parents' cellar, I rummage, looking
for something I lost.
My father sits on the tired, wooden stairs,
65 black cane between his knees,
hand over hand, gripping the handle.

He's so happy that I've come home.
I ask how his eyes are, a stupid question.

All gone, he answers.
70 Under some blankets, I find a box.
inside the box I find three scrolls.
I sit beside him and untie
three paintings by my father:
Hibiscus leaf and a white flower.
75 Two cats preening.
Two persimmons, so full they want to drop from the cloth.

He raises both hands to touch the cloth,
asks, *Which is this?*

This is persimmons, Father.

80 *Oh, the feel of the wolftail on the silk,*
the strength, the tense
precision in the wrist.
I painted them hundreds of times
eyes closed. These I painted blind.
85 *Some things never leave a person:*
scent of the hair of one you love,
the texture of persimmons,
in your palm, the ripe weight.

Questions for Discussion

1. What does the word *persimmon* mean to the speaker? What associations does it bring to mind? How is it related to the word *precision*?

2. How does the erotic episode with Donna relate in the narrator's mind to persimmons?

3. How sensitive is the speaker to the subtle meanings of and relationships between words? How sensitive is the teacher to them?

4. What languages besides English and Chinese are represented in this poem?

5. What have the father's painting and his blindness to do with the rest of the poem?

Suggestions for Exploration and Writing

1. This poem implicitly asks what is meant by the word *meaning*. When a word is used, it may refer to an object, action, or idea; or it may refer to a whole series of associations it symbolizes. In an analysis of Lee's poem, contrast the speaker's sense of the symbolic richness of language with the teacher's insistence that words correctly signify one's meaning.

2. In an essay, discuss in detail the rich private and personal associations brought to mind by a particular concrete noun.

DRAMA

William Shakespeare (b. 1939)

A brief biography of William Shakespeare precedes Othello *in the Grief and Loss Unit.*

> *Shakespeare's final play,* The Tempest, *is neither tragedy nor comedy, but a strange genre-defying mix. Sometimes called a tragi-comedy, sometimes a romance, the play takes as one of its dominant themes the power of art to transform the world, both physically and morally. The setting itself, an exotic and, to the European mind, remote island, has no real counterpart but is Shakespeare's own creation. Ruling the island through the arts of magic acquired through years of study, Prospero uses his powers to create moral tests for a group of European nobles shipwrecked on his island.*
> *As in most comedies, the play ends happily with an impending marriage and the freeing of Prospero's servants, Caliban and Ariel. Unlike most comedies, however, it could not be said of* The Tempest *that the society it depicts has been restored to stability. The primary source of order in the play is Prospero, whose magical powers have brought events to a point of moral order and stability. But clearly this point is merely one point on a continuum, for Prospero has renounced those powers of art that have transformed his world and given him control of it. Most of the main characters, including Prospero himself, will be leaving Prospero's magic island to return to Europe, a "brave new world" to Miranda, but a world Prospero, who responds to Miranda, "'Tis new to thee," knows all too well to be the old corrupt world from which he had escaped years before.*
> *Prospero's famous farewell to his magical arts has often been interpreted as Shakespeare's personal farewell to the stage:*

> Our revels now are ended. These our actors,
> As I foretold you, were all spirits and
> Are melted into air, into thin air;
> And, like the baseless fabric of this vision,
> The cloud-capped towers, the gorgeous palaces
> The solemn temples, the great globe itself,
> Yea, all which it inherit, shall dissolve,

And, like this insubstantial pageant faded,
Leave not a rack behind. We are such stuff
As dreams are made on, and our little life
Is rounded with a sleep

THE TEMPEST (1611)

Names of the Actors

ALONSO:	King of Naples
SEBASTIAN:	his brother
PROSPERO:	the right Duke of Milan
ANTONIO:	his brother, the usurping Duke of Milan
FERDINAND:	son to the King of Naples
ADRIAN AND FRANCISCO:	Lords
CALIBAN:	a savage and deformed slave
TRINCULO:	a jester
STEPHANO:	a drunken butler
MASTER OF A SHIP	
BOATSWAIN	
MARINERS	
MIRANDA:	daughter to Prospero
ARIEL:	an airy spirit
IRIS, CERES, JUNO, NYMPHS, REAPERS:	[presented by] spirits

[Other Spirits attending on Prospero]

The Scene

An uninhabited island

1.1

A tempestuous noise of thunder and lightning heard.
Enter a Shipmaster and a Boatswain.

MASTER: Boatswain!

BOATSWAIN: Here, Master. What cheer?

3 MASTER: Good, speak to the mariners. Fall to 't yarely,
or we run ourselves aground. Bestir, bestir!
Exit.

Enter Mariners.

BOATSWAIN: Heigh, my hearts! Cheerly, cheerly,
my hearts! Yare, yare! Take in the topsail.
7 Tend to the Master's whistle.—Blow till thou
8 burst thy wind, if room enough!

Enter Alonso, Sebastian, Antonio, Ferdinand, Gonzalo, and others.

1.1 **Location: On board ship, off the island's coast.**
3 **Good** i.e., it's good you've come, or, my good fellow.   **yarely** nimbly
7 **Tend** attend.   **Blow** (Addressed to the wind.)
8 **if room enough** as long as we have sea room enough

ALONSO: Good Boatswain, have care. Where's the Master?
10   Play the men.
BOATSWAIN: I pray now, keep below.
ANTONIO: Where is the Master, Boatswain?
BOATSWAIN: Do you not hear him? You mar our labor.
14   Keep your cabins! You do assist the storm.
15 GONZALO: Nay, good, be patient.
BOATSWAIN: When the sea is. Hence! What cares these
17   roarers for the name of king? To cabin! Silence!
Trouble us not.
GONZALO: Good, yet remember whom thou hast
aboard.
BOATSWAIN: None that I more love than myself. You are
a councillor; if you can command these elements to
23   silence and work the peace of the present, we will
24   not hand a rope more. Use your authority. If you
cannot, give thanks you have lived so long and make
yourself ready in your cabin for the mischance of the
27   hour, if it so hap.—Cheerly, good hearts!—Out of
our way, I say.
Exit.

GONZALO: I have great comfort from this fellow.
Methinks he hath no drowning mark upon him; his
31   complexion is perfect gallows. Stand fast, good Fate,
to his hanging! Make the rope of his destiny our
33   cable, for our own doth little advantage. If he be not
34   born to be hanged, our case is miserable.
Exeunt [courtiers].

Enter Boatswain.

BOATSWAIN: Down with the topmast! Yare! Lower,
36   lower! Bring her to try wi' the main course.

---

10 Play the men act like men (?) ply, urge the men to exert themselves (?)
14 Keep remain in
15 good good fellow
17 roarers waves or winds, or both; spoken to as though they were "bullies" or "blusterers"
23 work [. . .] present bring calm to our present circumstances
24 hand handle
27 hap happen
31 complexion [. . .] gallows appearance shows he was born to be hanged (and therefore, according to the proverb, in no danger of drowning)
33 our [. . .] advantage our own cable is of little benefit
34 case is miserable circumstances are desperate
36 Bring [. . .] course sail her close to the wind by means of the mainsail

38 *(A cry within.)* A plague upon this howling! They are
louder than the weather or our office.

Enter Sebastian, Antonio, and Gonzalo.

39 Yet again? What do you here? Shall we give o'er and
drown? Have you a mind to sink?

SEBASTIAN: A pox o' your throat, you bawling, blasphemous, incharitable dog!

BOATSWAIN: Work you, then.

ANTONIO: Hang, cur! Hang, you whoreson, insolent
noisemaker! We are less afraid to be drowned than
thou art.

47 GONZALO: I'll warrant him for drowning, though the
ship were no stronger than a nutshell and as

49 leaky as an unstanched wench.

50 BOATSWAIN: Lay her ahold, ahold! Set her two courses.
Off to sea again! Lay her off!

Enter Mariners, wet.

MARINERS: All lost! To prayers, to prayers! All lost!

[*The Mariners run about in confusion, exiting at random.*]

53 BOATSWAIN: What, must our mouths be cold?

GONZALO: The King and Prince at prayers! Let's assist them,
For our case is as theirs.

SEBASTIAN: I am out of patience.

57 ANTONIO: We are merely cheated of our lives by drunkards.

58 This wide-chapped rascal! Would thou mightst lie drowning

59 The washing of ten tides!

GONZALO: He'll be hanged yet,
Though every drop of water swear against it

62 And gape at wid'st to glut him.
(A confused noise within:)   "Mercy on us!"—

---

38 our office i.e., the noise we make at our work
39 give o'er give up
47 warrant him for drowning guarantee that he will never be drowned
49 unstanched insatiable, loose, unrestrained (suggesting also "incontinent" and "menstrual")
50 ahold ahull, close to the wind.   **courses** sails, i.e., foresail as well as mainsail, set in an attempt to get the ship back out into open water
53 must [. . .] cold i.e., must we drown in the cold sea, or, let us heat up our mouths with liquor
57 merely utterly
58 wide-chapped with mouth wide open
57–59 lie [. . .] tides (Pirates were hanged on the shore and left until three tides had come in.)
62 at wid'st wide open.   **glut** swallow

64   "We split, we split!"—"Farewell my wife and children!"—
       "Farewell, brother!"—"We split, we split, we split!"

[*Exit Boatswain.*]

ANTONIO: Let's all sink wi' the King.
SEBASTIAN: Let's take leave of him.
       Exit [*with Antonio*].

GONZALO: Now would I give a thousand furlongs of sea
69   for an acre of barren ground: long heath, brown furze,
70   anything. The wills above be done! But I would fain
       die a dry death.
       Exit.

                              1.2

Enter Prospero [in his magic cloak] and Miranda.

1   MIRANDA: If by your art, my dearest father, you have
2   Put the wild waters in this roar, allay them.
       The sky, it seems, would pour down stinking pitch,
4   But that the sea, mounting to th' welkin's cheek,
       Dashes the fire out. O, I have suffered
6   With those that I saw suffer! A brave vessel,
       Who had, no doubt, some noble creature in her,
       Dashed all to pieces. O, the cry did knock
       Against my very heart! Poor souls, they perished.
       Had I been any god of power, I would
11   Have sunk the sea within the earth or ere
       It should the good ship so have swallowed and
13   The freighting souls within her.
14   PROSPERO: Be collected.
15   No more amazement. Tell your piteous heart
       There's no harm done.

64 **split** break apart
69 **heath** heather.   **furze** gorse, a weed growing on wasteland
70 **fain** rather
1.2 **Location: The island, near Prospero's cell.** On the Elizabethan stage, this cell
is implicitly at hand throughout the play, although in some scenes the convention of
flexible distance allows us to imagine characters in other parts of the island.
1 **art** magic
2 **allay** pacify
4 **welkin's cheek** sky's face
6 **brave** gallant, splendid
11 **or ere** before
13 **freighting** forming the cargo.
14 **collected** calm, composed
15 **amazement** consternation.   **piteous** pitying

MIRANDA: O, woe the day!
PROSPERO: No harm.
19   I have done nothing but in care of thee,
        Of thee, my dear one, thee, my daughter, who
        Art ignorant of what thou art, naught knowing
22   Of whence I am, nor that I am more better
23   Than Prospero, master of a full poor cell,
        And thy no greater father.
MIRANDA: More to know
26   Did never meddle with my thoughts.
PROSPERO: 'Tis time
        I should inform thee farther. Lend thy hand
        And pluck my magic garment from me. So,
        [*laying down his magic cloak and staff*]
        Lie there, my art.—Wipe thou thine eyes. Have comfort.
31   The direful spectacle of the wreck, which touched
32   The very virtue of compassion in thee,
33   I have with such provision in mine art
        So safely ordered that there is no soul—
35   No, not so much perdition as an hair
36   Betid to any creature in the vessel
37   Which thou heard'st cry, which thou saw'st sink. Sit down,
        For thou must now know farther.
MIRANDA [*sitting*]:   You have often
        Begun to tell me what I am, but stopped
41   And left me to a bootless inquisition,
        Concluding, "Stay, not yet."
PROSPERO: The hour's now come;
        The very minute bids thee ope thine ear.
        Obey, and be attentive. Canst thou remember
        A time before we came unto this cell?
        I do not think thou canst, for then thou wast not
48   Out three years old.
MIRANDA: Certainly, sir, I can.

19 **but** except
22 **more better** of higher rank
23 **full** very
26 **meddle** mingle
31 **wreck** shipwreck
32 **virtue** essence
33 **provision** foresight
35 **perdition** loss
36 **Betid** happened
37 **Which** whom
41 **bootless inquisition** profitless inquiry
48 **Out** fully

PROSPERO: By what? By any other house or person?
   Of anything the image, tell me, that
   Hath kept with thy remembrance.
MIRANDA: 'Tis far off,
54   And rather like a dream than an assurance
   That my remembrance warrants. Had I not
   Four or five women once that tended me?
PROSPERO: Thou hadst, and more, Miranda. But how is it
   That this lives in thy mind? What seest thou else
59   In the dark backward and abysm of time?
60   If thou rememberest aught ere thou cam'st here,
   How thou cam'st here thou mayst.
MIRANDA: But that I do not.
PROSPERO: Twelve year since, Miranda, twelve year since,
   Thy father was the Duke of Milan and
   A prince of power.
MIRANDA: Sir, are not you my father?
67 PROSPERO: Thy mother was a piece of virtue, and
   She said thou wast my daughter; and thy father
   Was Duke of Milan, and his only heir
70   And princess no worse issued.
MIRANDA: O the heavens!
   What foul play had we, that we came from thence?
   Or blessèd was 't we did?
PROSPERO: Both, both, my girl!
   By foul play, as thou sayst, were we heaved thence,
76   But blessedly holp hither.
MIRANDA: O, my heart bleeds
78   To think o' the teen that I have turned you to,
79   Which is from my remembrance! Please you, farther.
PROSPERO: My brother and thy uncle, called Antonio—
   I pray thee mark me—that a brother should
82   Be so perfidious!—he whom next thyself
   Of all the world I loved, and to him put
84   The manage of my state, as at that time
85   Through all the seigniories it was the first,

54–55 assurance [. . .] warrants certainty that my memory guarantees
59 backward [. . .] time abyss of the past
60 aught anything
67 piece masterpiece, exemplar
70 no worse issued no less nobly born, descended
76 holp helped
78 teen [. . .] to trouble I've caused you to remember or put you to
79 from out of
82 next next to
84 manage management, administration
85 seigniories i.e., city-states of northern Italy

86   And Prospero the prime duke, being so reputed
      In dignity, and for the liberal arts
      Without a parallel; those being all my study,
      The government I cast upon my brother
90   And to my state grew stranger, being transported
      And rapt in secret studies. Thy false uncle—
      Dost thou attend me?
MIRANDA: Sir, most heedfully.
94 PROSPERO: Being once perfected how to grant suits,
      How to deny them, who t' advance and who
96   To trash for overtopping, new created
97   The creatures that were mine, I say, or changed 'em,
98   Or else new formed 'em; having both the key
      Of officer and office, set all hearts i' the state
100   To what tune pleased his ear, that now he was
      The ivy which had hid my princely trunk
102   And sucked my verdure out on 't. Thou attend'st not.
MIRANDA: O, good sir, I do.
PROSPERO: I pray thee, mark me.
      I, thus neglecting worldly ends, all dedicated
106   To closeness and the bettering of my mind
107   With that which, but by being so retired,
108   O'erprized all popular rate, in my false brother
      Awaked an evil nature; and my trust,
110   Like a good parent, did beget of him
      A falsehood in its contrary as great
      As my trust was, which had indeed no limit,
113   A confidence sans bound. He being thus lorded

86 **prime** first in rank and importance
90 **to [. . .] stranger** i.e., withdrew from my responsibilities as duke.   **transported**
carried away
94 **perfected** grown skillful
96 **trash** check a hound by tying a cord or weight to its neck.   **overtopping** running
too far ahead of the pack; surmounting, exceeding one's authority
97 **creatures** dependents
97–98 **or changed [. . .] formed 'em** i.e., either changed their loyalties and duties
or else created new ones
98 **key** (1) key for unlocking (2) tool for tuning stringed instruments
100 **that** so that
102 **verdure** vitality.   **on 't** of it
106 **closeness** retirement, seclusion
107–08 **but [. . .] rate** i.e., were it not that its private nature caused me to neglect
my public responsibilities, had a value far beyond what public opinion could appreciate, or, simply because it was done in such seclusion, had a value not appreciated by
popular opinion
110 **good parent** (Alludes to the proverb that good parents often bear bad children;
see also line 139.)   **of** in
113 **sans** without.   **lorded** raised to lordship, with power and wealth

Not only with what my revenue yielded
115   But what my power might else exact, like one
116   Who, having into truth by telling of it,
Made such a sinner of his memory
118   To credit his own lie, he did believe
119   He was indeed the Duke, out o' the substitution
120   And executing th' outward face of royalty
With all prerogative. Hence his ambition growing—
Dost thou hear?
MIRANDA: Your tale, sir, would cure deafness.
124   PROSPERO: To have no screen between this part he played
125   And him he played it for, he needs will be
126   Absolute Milan. Me, poor man, my library
127   Was dukedom large enough. Of temporal royalties
128   He thinks me now incapable; confederates—
129   So dry he was for sway—wi' the King of Naples
130   To give him annual tribute, do him homage,
131   Subject his coronet to his crown, and bend
132   The dukedom yet unbowed—alas, poor Milan!—
To most ignoble stooping.
MIRANDA: O the heavens!
135   PROSPERO: Mark his condition and th' event, then tell me
If this might be a brother.
MIRANDA: I should sin
138   To think but nobly of my grandmother.
Good wombs have borne bad sons.

---

115 else otherwise, additionally
116–118 Who [. . .] lie i.e., who, by repeatedly telling the lie (that he was indeed Duke of Milan), made his memory such a confirmed sinner against truth that he began to believe his own lie. **into** unto, against. **To** so as to
119 out o' as a result of
120 And [. . .] royalty and (as a result of) his carrying out all the visible functions of royalty
124–125 To have [. . .] it for to have no separation or barrier between his role and himself. (Antonio wanted to act in his own person, not as substitute.)
125 needs will be insisted on becoming
126 Absolute Milan unconditional Duke of Milan
127 temporal royalties practical prerogatives and responsibilities of a sovereign
128 confederates conspires, allies himself
129 dry thirsty. **sway** power
130 him i.e., the King of Naples
131 his [. . .] his Antonio's [. . .] the King of Naples's. **bend** make bow down
132 yet hitherto
135 condition pact. **event** outcome
138 but other than

PROSPERO: Now the condition.
    This King of Naples, being an enemy
142   To me inveterate, hearkens my brother's suit,
143   Which was that he, in lieu o' the premises
    Of homage and I know not how much tribute,
145   Should presently extirpate me and mine
    Out of the dukedom and confer fair Milan,
    With all the honors, on my brother. Whereon,
    A treacherous army levied, one midnight
    Fated to th' purpose did Antonio open
    The gates of Milan, and, i' the dead of darkness,
151   The ministers for the purpose hurried thence
    Me and thy crying self.
MIRANDA: Alack, for pity!
    I, not remembering how I cried out then,
155   Will cry it o'er again. It is a hint
156   That wrings mine eyes to 't.
PROSPERO: Hear a little further,
    And then I'll bring thee to the present business
    Which now's upon 's, without the which this story
160   Were most impertinent.
MIRANDA: Wherefore did they not
    That hour destroy us?
163 PROSPERO: Well demanded, wench.
    My tale provokes that question. Dear, they durst not,
165   So dear the love my people bore me, nor set
166   A mark so bloody on the business, but
167   With colors fairer painted their foul ends.
168   In few, they hurried us aboard a bark,
    Bore us some leagues to sea, where they prepared
170   A rotten carcass of a butt, not rigged,

---

142 hearkens listens to
143 he the King of Naples.   **in [. . .] premises** in return for the stipulation
145 presently extirpate at once remove
151 ministers [. . .] purpose agents employed to do this.   **thence** from there
155 hint occasion
156 wrings (1) constrains (2) wrings tears from
160 impertinent irrelevant.   **Wherefore** why
163 demanded asked.   **wench** (Here a term of endearment.)
165–166 set [. . .] bloody i.e., make obvious their murderous intent. (From the practice of marking with the blood of the prey those who have participated in a successful hunt.)
167 fairer apparently more attractive
168 few few words.   **bark** ship
170 butt cask, tub

171 Nor tackle, sail, nor mast; the very rats
172 Instinctively have quit it. There they hoist us,
 To cry to th' sea that roared to us, to sigh
 To th' winds whose pity, sighing back again,
175 Did us but loving wrong.

MIRANDA: Alack, what trouble
 Was I then to you!

PROSPERO: O, a cherubin
 Thou wast that did preserve me. Thou didst smile,
 Infusèd with a fortitude from heaven,
181 When I have decked the sea with drops full salt,
182 Under my burden groaned, which raised in me
183 An undergoing stomach, to bear up
 Against what should ensue.

MIRANDA: How came we ashore?

PROSPERO: By Providence divine.
 Some food we had, and some fresh water, that
 A noble Neapolitan, Gonzalo,
 Out of his charity, who being then appointed
 Master of this design, did give us, with
191 Rich garments, linens, stuffs, and necessaries,
192 Which since have steaded much. So, of his gentleness,
 Knowing I loved my books, he furnished me
 From mine own library with volumes that
 I prize above my dukedom.

196 MIRANDA: Would I might
197 But ever see that man!

PROSPERO: Now I arise.

      [He puts on his magic cloak.]

199 Sit still, and hear the last of our sea sorrow.
 Here in this island we arrived; and here
201 Have I, thy schoolmaster, made thee more profit

---

171 Nor tackle neither rigging
172 quit abandoned
175 Did [. . .] wrong (i.e., the winds pitied Prospero and Miranda, though of necessity they blew them from shore)
181 decked covered (with salt tears); adorned
182 which i.e., the smile
183 undergoing stomach courage to go on
191 stuffs supplies
192 steaded much been of much use. **So, of** similarly, out of
196 Would I wish
197 But ever i.e., someday
199 sea sorrow sorrowful adventure at sea
201 more profit profit more

202   Than other princess' can, that have more time
203   For vainer hours and tutors not so careful.
    MIRANDA: Heavens thank you for 't! And now, I pray you, sir—
    For still 'tis beating in my mind—your reason
    For raising this sea storm?
    PROSPERO: Know thus far forth:
    By accident most strange, bountiful Fortune,
209   Now my dear lady, hath mine enemies
    Brought to this shore; and by my prescience
211   I find my zenith doth depend upon
212   A most auspicious star, whose influence
213   If now I court not, but omit, my fortunes
    Will ever after droop. Here cease more questions.
215   Thou art inclined to sleep. 'Tis a good dullness,
216   And give it way. I know thou canst not choose.
                         [*Miranda sleeps.*]
217   Come away, servant, come! I am ready now.
    Approach, my Ariel, come.

    Enter Ariel.

    ARIEL: All hail, great master, grave sir, hail! I come
    To answer thy best pleasure; be 't to fly,
    To swim, to dive into the fire, to ride
222   On the curled clouds, to thy strong bidding task
223   Ariel and all his quality.
    PROSPERO: Hast thou, spirit,
225   Performed to point the tempest that I bade thee?
    ARIEL: To every article.
227   I boarded the King's ship. Now on the beak,
228   Now in the waist, the deck, in every cabin,

---

202 princess' princesses. (Or the word may be *princes,* referring to royal children both male and female.)
203 vainer more foolishly spent
209 my dear lady (Refers to Fortune, not Miranda.)
211 zenith height of fortune. (Astrological term.)
212 influence astrological power
213 omit ignore
215 dullness drowsiness
216 give it way let it happen (i.e., don't fight it)
217 Come away come
222 task make demands upon
223 quality (1) fellow spirits (2) abilities
225 to point to the smallest detail
227 beak prow
228 waist midships.   **deck** poop deck at the stern

229   I flamed amazement. Sometimes I'd divide
      And burn in many places; on the topmast,
231   The yards, and bowsprit would I flame distinctly,
      Then meet and join. Jove's lightning, the precursors
      O' the dreadful thunderclaps, more momentary
234   And sight-outrunning were not. The fire and cracks
235   Of sulfurous roaring the most mighty Neptune
      Seem to besiege and make his bold waves tremble,
      Yea, his dread trident shake.
PROSPERO: My brave spirit!
239   Who was so firm, so constant, that this coil
      Would not infect his reason?
ARIEL: Not a soul
242   But felt a fever of the mad and played
      Some tricks of desperation. All but mariners
      Plunged in the foaming brine and quit the vessel,
      Then all afire with me. The King's son, Ferdinand,
246   With hair up-staring—then like reeds, not hair—
      Was the first man that leapt; cried, "Hell is empty,
      And all the devils are here!"
PROSPERO: Why, that's my spirit!
      But was not this nigh shore?
ARIEL: Close by, my master.
PROSPERO: But are they, Ariel, safe?
ARIEL: Not a hair perished.
254   On their sustaining garments not a blemish,
255   But fresher than before; and, as thou bad'st me,
256   In troops I have dispersed them 'bout the isle.
      The King's son have I landed by himself,
258   Whom I left cooling of the air with sighs
259   In an odd angle of the isle, and sitting,
260   His arms in this sad knot.   [*He folds his arms.*]

229 flamed amazement struck terror in the guise of fire, i.e., Saint Elmo's fire
231 distinctly in different places
234 sight-outrunning swifter than sight.   **were not** could not have been
235 Neptune Roman god of the sea
239 coil tumult
242 of the mad i.e., such as madmen feel
246 up-staring standing on end
254 sustaining garments garments that buoyed them up in the sea
255 bad'st ordered
256 troops groups
258 cooling of cooling
259 angle corner
260 sad knot (Folded arms are indicative of melancholy.)

PROSPERO: Of the King's ship,
The mariners, say how thou hast disposed,
And all the rest o' the fleet.
ARIEL: Safely in harbor
265 Is the King's ship; in the deep nook, where once
266 Thou called'st me up at midnight to fetch dew
267 From the still-vexed Bermudas, there she's hid;
The mariners all under hatches stowed,
269 Who, with a charm joined to their suffered labor,
I have left asleep. And for the rest o' the fleet,
Which I dispersed, they all have met again
272 And are upon the Mediterranean float
Bound sadly home for Naples,
Supposing that they saw the King's ship wrecked
And his great person perish.
PROSPERO: Ariel, thy charge
Exactly is performed. But there's more work.
What is the time o' the day?
279 ARIEL: Past the mid season.
280 PROSPERO: At least two glasses. The time twixt six and now
Must by us both be spent most preciously.
282 ARIEL: Is there more toil? Since thou dost give me pains,
283 Let me remember thee what thou hast promised,
Which is not yet performed me.
PROSPERO: How now? Moody?
What is 't thou canst demand?
ARIEL: My liberty.
PROSPERO: Before the time be out? No more!
ARIEL: I prithee,
Remember I have done thee worthy service,
Told thee no lies, made thee no mistakings, served
Without or grudge or grumblings. Thou did promise
293 To bate me a full year.
PROSPERO: Dost thou forget
From what a torment I did free thee?
ARIEL: No.

265 **nook** bay
266 **dew** (Collected at midnight for magical purposes; compare with line 324.)
267 **still-vexed Bermudas** ever stormy Bermudas. The Folio text reads "Bermoothes."
269 **with [. . .] labor** by means of a spell added to all the labor they have undergone
272 **float** sea
279 **mid season** noon
280 **glasses** hourglasses
282 **pains** labors
283 **remember** remind
293 **bate** remit, deduct

PROSPERO: Thou dost, and think'st it much to tread the ooze
Of the salt deep,
To run upon the sharp wind of the north,
300   To do me business in the veins o' the earth
301   When it is baked with frost.
ARIEL: I do not, sir.
PROSPERO: Thou liest, malignant thing! Hast thou forgot
304   The foul witch Sycorax, who with age and envy
305   Was grown into a hoop? Hast thou forgot her?
ARIEL: No, sir.
PROSPERO: Thou hast. Where was she born? Speak. Tell me.
308 ARIEL: Sir, in Argier.
PROSPERO: O, was she so? I must
Once in a month recount what thou hast been,
Which thou forgett'st. This damned witch Sycorax,
For mischiefs manifold and sorceries terrible
To enter human hearing, from Argier,
314   Thou know'st, was banished. For one thing she did
They would not take her life. Is not this true?
ARIEL: Ay, sir.
317 PROSPERO: This blue-eyed hag was hither brought with child
And here was left by the sailors. Thou, my slave,
As thou report'st thyself, was then her servant;
320   And, for thou wast a spirit too delicate
To act her earthy and abhorred commands,
322   Refusing her grand hests, she did confine thee,
By help of her more potent ministers
And in her most unmitigable rage,
Into a cloven pine, within which rift
Imprisoned thou didst painfully remain
A dozen years; within which space she died
And left thee there, where thou didst vent thy groans
329   As fast as mill wheels strike. Then was this island—

---

300 do me do for me.   **veins** veins of minerals, or, underground streams, thought to be analogous to the veins of the human body
301 baked hardened
304 envy malice
305 grown into a hoop i.e., so bent over with age as to resemble a hoop
308 Argier Algiers
314 one [. . .] did (Perhaps a reference to her pregnancy, for which her life would be spared.)
317 blue-eyed with dark circles under the eyes or with blue eyelids, implying pregnancy.
with child pregnant
320 for because
322 hests commands
329 as mill wheels strike as the blades of a mill wheel strike the water

330   Save for the son that she did litter here,
331   A freckled whelp, hag-born—not honored with
       A human shape.
333   ARIEL: Yes, Caliban her son.
334   PROSPERO: Dull thing, I say so: he, that Caliban
       Whom now I keep in service. Thou best know'st
       What torment I did find thee in. Thy groans
       Did make wolves howl, and penetrate the breasts
       Of ever-angry bears. It was a torment
       To lay upon the damned, which Sycorax
       Could not again undo. It was mine art,
341   When I arrived and heard thee, that made gape
       The pine and let thee out.
       ARIEL: I thank thee, master.
       PROSPERO: If thou more murmur'st, I will rend an oak
345   And peg thee in his knotty entrails till
       Thou hast howled away twelve winters.
       ARIEL: Pardon, master.
348   I will be correspondent to command
349   And do my spriting gently.
       PROSPERO: Do so, and after two days
       I will discharge thee.
       ARIEL: That's my noble master!
       What shall I do? Say what? What shall I do?
       PROSPERO: Go make thyself like a nymph o' the sea. Be subject
       To no sight but thine and mine, invisible
       To every eyeball else. Go take this shape
       And hither come in 't. Go, hence with diligence!

       Exit [*Ariel*].

       Awake, dear heart, awake! Thou hast slept well.
       Awake!
       MIRANDA: The strangeness of your story put
361   Heaviness in me.

---

330 Save except.   **litter** give birth to
331 whelp offspring. (Used of animals.)   **hag-born** born of a female demon
333 Yes [. . .] **son** (Ariel is probably concurring with Prospero's comments about a
"freckled whelp," not contradicting the point about "A human shape.")
334 Dull [. . .] **so** i.e., exactly, that's what I said, you dullard
341 gape open wide
345 his its
348 correspondent responsive, submissive
349 spriting duties as a spirit.   **gently** willingly, ungrudgingly
361 Heaviness drowsiness

PROSPERO: Shake it off. Come on,
    We'll visit Caliban, my slave, who never
    Yields us kind answer.
MIRANDA: 'Tis a villain, sir,
    I do not love to look on.
PROSPERO: But, as 'tis,
368   We cannot miss him. He does make our fire,
369   Fetch in our wood, and serves in offices
    That profit us.—What ho! Slave! Caliban!
    Thou earth, thou! Speak.
CALIBAN (*within*):   There's wood enough within.
PROSPERO: Come forth, I say! There's other business for thee.
374   Come, thou tortoise! When?

    Enter Ariel like a water nymph.

375   Fine apparition! My quaint Ariel,
    Hark in thine ear.   [*He whispers.*]
ARIEL: My lord, it shall be done.
    Exit.

378   PROSPERO: Thou poisonous slave, got by the devil himself
379   Upon thy wicked dam, come forth!

    Enter Caliban.

380   CALIBAN: As wicked dew as e'er my mother brushed
381   With raven's feather from unwholesome fen
382   Drop on you both! A southwest blow on ye
    And blister you all o'er!
PROSPERO: For this, be sure, tonight thou shalt have cramps,
385   Side-stitches that shall pen thy breath up. Urchins
386   Shall forth at vast of night that they may work
    All exercise on thee. Thou shalt be pinched
388   As thick as honeycomb, each pinch more stinging
389   Than bees that made 'em.

---

368 miss do without
369 offices functions, duties
374 When (An exclamation of impatience.)
375 quaint ingenious
378 got begotten, sired
379 dam mother. (Used of animals.)
380 wicked mischievous, harmful
381 fen marsh, bog
382 southwest i.e., wind thought to bring disease
385 Urchins hedgehogs; here, suggesting goblins in the guise of hedgehogs
386 vast lengthy, desolate time. (Malignant spirits were thought to be restricted to the hours of darkness.)
388 As thick as honeycomb i.e., all over, with as many pinches as a honeycomb has cells
389 'em i.e., the honeycomb

CALIBAN: I must eat my dinner.
This island's mine, by Sycorax my mother,
Which thou tak'st from me. When thou cam'st first,
Thou strok'st me and made much of me, wouldst give me
Water with berries in 't, and teach me how
395   To name the bigger light, and how the less,
That burn by day and night. And then I loved thee
And showed thee all the qualities o' th' isle,
The fresh springs, brine pits, barren place and fertile.
399   Cursed be I that did so! All the charms
Of Sycorax, toads, beetles, bats, light on you!
For I am all the subjects that you have,
402   Which first was mine own king; and here you sty me
In this hard rock, whiles you do keep from me
The rest o' th' island.
PROSPERO: Thou most lying slave,
406   Whom stripes may move, not kindness! I have used thee,
407   Filth as thou art, with humane care, and lodged thee
In mine own cell, till thou didst seek to violate
The honor of my child.
CALIBAN: Oho, Oho! Would 't had been done!
411   Thou didst prevent me; I had peopled else
This isle with Calibans.
413 MIRANDA: Abhorrèd slave,
414   Which any print of goodness wilt not take,
Being capable of all ill! I pitied thee,
Took pains to make thee speak, taught thee each hour
One thing or other. When thou didst not, savage,
Know thine own meaning, but wouldst gabble like
419   A thing most brutish, I endowed thy purposes
420   With words that made them known. But thy vile race,
Though thou didst learn, had that in 't which good natures
Could not abide to be with; therefore wast thou
Deservedly confined into this rock,
Who hadst deserved more than a prison.

---

395 the bigger [. . .] less i.e., the sun and the moon. (See Genesis 1.16: "God then made two great lights: the greater light to rule the day, and the less light to rule the night.")
399 charms spells
402 sty confine as in a sty
406 stripes lashes
407 humane (Not distinguished as a word from *human.*)
411 peopled else otherwise populated
413–424 Abhorrèd [. . .] prison (Sometimes assigned by editors to Prospero.)
414 print imprint, impression
419 purposes meanings, desires
420 race natural disposition; species, nature

CALIBAN: You taught me language, and my profit on 't

426   Is I know how to curse. The red plague rid you

427   For learning me your language!

428 PROSPERO: Hagseed, hence!

429   Fetch us in fuel, and be quick, thou'rt best,

430   To answer other business. Shrugg'st thou, malice?

      If thou neglect'st or dost unwillingly

432   What I command, I'll rack thee with old cramps,

433   Fill all thy bones with aches, make thee roar

      That beasts shall tremble at thy din.

CALIBAN: No, pray thee.

      [*Aside.*] I must obey. His art is of such power

437   It would control my dam's god, Setebos,

      And make a vassal of him.

439 PROSPERO: So, slave, hence!

Exit Caliban.

Enter Ferdinand; and Ariel, invisible, playing and singing.
[Ferdinand does not see Prospero and Miranda.]

Ariel's Song.

ARIEL:

      Come unto these yellow sands,

         And then take hands;

442   Curtsied when you have, and kissed

443   The wild waves whist;

444   Foot it featly here and there,

445   And, sweet sprites, bear

446   The burden. Hark, hark!

447   *Burden, dispersedly* [*within*]. Bow-wow.

---

426 red plague plague characterized by red sores and evacuation of blood.   **rid** destroy
427 learning teaching.
428 Hagseed offspring of a female demon
429 thou'rt best you'd be well advised
430 answer other business perform other tasks
432 old such as old people suffer, or, plenty of
433 aches (Pronounced "aitches.")
437 Setebos (A god of the Patagonians, named in Robert Eden's *History of Travel*, 1577.)
439 s.d. Ariel, invisible (Ariel wears a garment that by convention indicates he is invisible to the other characters.)
442 Curtsied [. . .] have when you have curtsied
442–443 kissed [. . .] whist kissed the waves into silence, or, kissed while the waves are being hushed
444 Foot it featly dance nimbly
445 sprites spirits
446 burden refrain, undersong
447 s.d. dispersedly i.e., from all directions, not in unison

The watchdogs bark.

[*Burden, dispersedly within.*] Bow-wow.

Hark, hark! I hear

The strain of strutting chanticleer

Cry Cock-a-diddle-dow.

FERDINAND: Where should this music be? I' th' air or th' earth?

454 It sounds no more; and sure it waits upon
455 Some god o' th' island. Sitting on a bank,
Weeping again the King my father's wreck,
This music crept by me upon the waters,
458 Allaying both their fury and my passion
459 With its sweet air. Thence I have followed it,
Or it hath drawn me rather. But 'tis gone.
No, it begins again.

Ariel's Song.

ARIEL:

Full fathom five thy father lies.

Of his bones are coral made.

Those are pearls that were his eyes.

Nothing of him that doth fade

But doth suffer a sea change

Into something rich and strange.

468 Sea nymphs hourly ring his knell.

Burden [*within*]. Ding dong.

Hark, now I hear them, ding dong bell.

471 FERDINAND: The ditty does remember my drowned father.
This is no mortal business, nor no sound
473 That the earth owes. I hear it now above me.
474 PROSPERO [*to Miranda*]: The fringèd curtains of thine eye advance
And say what thou seest yond.

MIRANDA: What is 't? A spirit?

Lord, how it looks about! Believe me, sir,
478 It carries a brave form. But 'tis a spirit.

PROSPERO:

No, wench, it eats and sleeps and hath such senses

As we have, such. This gallant which thou seest

---

454 waits upon serves, attends
455 bank sandbank
458 passion grief
459 Thence i.e., from the bank on which I sat
468 knell announcement of a death by the tolling of a bell
471 remember commemorate
473 owes owns
474 advance raise
478 brave excellent

481   Was in the wreck; and, but he's something stained
482   With grief, that's beauty's canker, thou mightst call him
      A goodly person. He hath lost his fellows
      And strays about to find 'em.
MIRANDA: I might call him
      A thing divine, for nothing natural
      I ever saw so noble.
488 PROSPERO [*aside*]:   It goes on, I see,
      As my soul prompts it.—Spirit, fine spirit, I'll free thee
      Within two days for this.
     FERDINAND [*seeing Miranda*]: Most sure, the goddess
492   On whom these airs attend!—Vouchsafe my prayer
493   May know if you remain upon this island,
      And that you will some good instruction give
495   How I may bear me here. My prime request,
496   Which I do last pronounce, is—O you wonder!—
497   If you be maid or no?
MIRANDA: No wonder, sir,
      But certainly a maid.
FERDINAND: My language? Heavens!
501   I am the best of them that speak this speech,
      Were I but where 'tis spoken.
     PROSPERO [*coming forward*]:   How? The best?
      What wert thou if the King of Naples heard thee?
505 FERDINAND: A single thing, as I am now, that wonders
506   To hear thee speak of Naples. He does hear me,
507   And that he does I weep. Myself am Naples,
508   Who with mine eyes, never since at ebb, beheld
      The King my father wrecked.
MIRANDA: Alack, for mercy!

---

481 but except that.   **something stained** somewhat disfigured
482 canker cankerworm (feeding on buds and leaves)
488 It goes on i.e., my plan works
492 airs songs.   **Vouchsafe** grant
493 May know i.e., that I may know.   **remain** dwell
495 bear me conduct myself.   **prime** chief
496 wonder (Miranda's name means "to be wondered at.")
497 maid or no i.e., a human maiden as opposed to a goddess or married woman
501 best i.e., in birth
505 single (1) solitary, being at once King of Naples and myself (2) feeble
506, 507 Naples the King of Naples
506 He does hear me i.e., the King of Naples does hear my words, for I am King of Naples
507 And [. . .] weep i.e., and I weep at this reminder that my father is seemingly dead, leaving me heir
508 at ebb i.e., dry, not weeping

FERDINAND: Yes, faith, and all his lords, the Duke of Milan
512   And his brave son being twain.
PROSPERO [*aside*]:   The Duke of Milan
514   And his more braver daughter could control thee,
    If now 'twere fit to do 't. At the first sight
516   They have changed eyes.—Delicate Ariel,
    I'll set thee free for this. [*To Ferdinand.*] A word, good sir.
518   I fear you have done yourself some wrong. A word!
MIRANDA [*aside*]: Why speaks my father so ungently? This
    Is the third man that e'er I saw, the first
    That e'er I sighed for. Pity move my father
    To be inclined my way!
FERDINAND: O, if a virgin,
    And your affection not gone forth, I'll make you
    The Queen of Naples.
PROSPERO: Soft, sir! One word more.
527   [*Aside.*] They are both in either's pow'rs; but this swift business
528   I must uneasy make, lest too light winning
529   Make the prize light. [*To Ferdinand.*] One word
        more: I charge thee
531   That thou attend me. Thou dost here usurp
532   The name thou ow'st not, and hast put thyself
    Upon this island as a spy, to win it
534   From me, the lord on 't.
FERDINAND: No, as I am a man.
MIRANDA: There's nothing ill can dwell in such a temple.
    If the ill spirit have so fair a house,
538   Good things will strive to dwell with 't.
PROSPERO: Follow me.—
    Speak not you for him; he's a traitor.—Come,
    I'll manacle thy neck and feet together.
    Seawater shalt thou drink; thy food shall be
    The fresh-brook mussels, withered roots, and husks
    Wherein the acorn cradled. Follow.

512 **son** (The only reference in the play to a son of Antonio.)
514 **more braver** more splendid.   **control** refute
516 **changed eyes** exchanged amorous glances
518 **done** [. . .] **wrong** i.e., spoken falsely
527 **both in either's** each in the other's
528 **uneasy** difficult
528–29 **light** [. . .] **light** easy . . . cheap
531 **attend** follow, obey
532 **ow'st** ownest
534 **on 't** of it
538 **strive** [. . .] **with 't** i.e., expel the evil and occupy the *temple*, the body

FERDINAND: No!
546   I will resist such entertainment till
547   Mine enemy has more power.
                              He draws, and is charmed from moving.
MIRANDA: O dear father,
549   Make not too rash a trial of him, for
550   He's gentle, and not fearful.
PROSPERO: What, I say,
552   My foot my tutor?—Put thy sword up, traitor,
       Who mak'st a show but dar'st not strike, thy conscience
554   Is so possessed with guilt. Come, from thy ward,
       For I can here disarm thee with this stick
       And make thy weapon drop. [*He brandishes his staff.*]
MIRANDA [*trying to hinder him*]: Beseech you, father!
PROSPERO: Hence! Hang not on my garments.
MIRANDA: Sir, have pity!
560   I'll be his surety.
PROSPERO: Silence! One word more
       Shall make me chide thee, if not hate thee. What,
       An advocate for an impostor? Hush!
       Thou think'st there is no more such shapes as he,
       Having seen but him and Caliban. Foolish wench,
566   To the most of men this is a Caliban,
       And they to him are angels.
MIRANDA: My affections
       Are then most humble; I have no ambition
       To see a goodlier man.
PROSPERO [*to Ferdinand*]: Come on, obey.
572   Thy nerves are in their infancy again
       And have no vigor in them.
FERDINAND: So they are.
575   My spirits, as in a dream, are all bound up.
       My father's loss, the weakness which I feel,
       The wreck of all my friends, nor this man's threats

546 entertainment treatment
547 s.d. charmed magically prevented
549 rash harsh
550 gentle wellborn.   **fearful** frightening, dangerous, or perhaps, cowardly
552 foot subordinate. (Miranda, the foot, presumes to instruct Prospero, the head.)
554 ward defensive posture (in fencing)
560 surety guarantee
566 To compared to
572 nerves sinews
575 spirits vital powers

578 To whom I am subdued, are but light to me,
    Might I but through my prison once a day
580 Behold this maid. All corners else o' th' earth
    Let liberty make use of; space enough
    Have I in such a prison.
PROSPERO [*aside*]:   It works. [*To Ferdinand.*] Come on.—
    Thou hast done well, fine Ariel! [*To Ferdinand.*]
    Follow me.
586 [*To Ariel.*] Hark what thou else shalt do me.
MIRANDA [*to Ferdinand*]:   Be of comfort.
    My father's of a better nature, sir,
589 Than he appears by speech. This is unwonted
    Which now came from him.
PROSPERO [*to Ariel*]:   Thou shalt be as free
592 As mountain winds; but then exactly do
    All points of my command.
ARIEL: To th' syllable.
PROSPERO [*to Ferdinand*]:
    Come, follow. [*To Miranda.*] Speak not for him.

Exeunt.

2.1

Enter Alonso, Sebastian, Antonio, Gonzalo, Adrian,
Francisco, and others.

GONZALO [*to Alonso*]: Beseech you, sir, be merry. You have cause,
    So have we all, of joy, for our escape
3   Is much beyond our loss. Our hint of woe
    Is common; every day some sailor's wife,
5   The masters of some merchant, and the merchant,
    Have just our theme of woe. But for the miracle,
    I mean our preservation, few in millions
    Can speak like us. Then wisely, good sir, weigh
9   Our sorrow with our comfort.

---

578 light unimportant
580 corners else other corners, regions
586 me for me
589 unwonted unusual
592 then until then, or, if that is to be so
2.1 Location: Another part of the island.
3 hint occasion
5 masters [. . .] the merchant officers of some merchant vessel and the merchant
himself, the owner
9 with against

ALONSO: Prithee, peace.
SEBASTIAN [*aside to Antonio*]: He receives comfort like
12   cold porridge.
13   ANTONIO [*aside to Sebastian*]: The visitor will not give
14   him o'er so.
SEBASTIAN: Look, he's winding up the watch of his wit;
      by and by it will strike.
GONZALO [*to Alonso*]: Sir—
18   SEBASTIAN [*aside to Antonio*]: One. Tell.
19   GONZALO: When every grief is entertained that's
20   offered, comes to th' entertainer—
21   SEBASTIAN: A dollar.
GONZALO: Dolor comes to him, indeed. You have
      spoken truer than you purposed.
SEBASTIAN: You have taken it wiselier than I meant
      you should.
GONZALO [*to Alonso*]: Therefore, my lord—
ANTONIO: Fie, what a spendthrift is he of his tongue!
28   ALONSO [*to Gonzalo*]: I prithee, spare.
GONZALO: Well, I have done. But yet—
SEBASTIAN [*aside to Antonio*]: He will be talking.
31   ANTONIO [*aside to Sebastian*]: Which, of he or Adrian,
32   for a good wager, first begins to crow?
33   SEBASTIAN: The old cock.
34   ANTONIO: The cockerel.
SEBASTIAN: Done. The wager?
36   ANTONIO: A laughter.

---

12 porridge (punningly suggested by *peace*, i.e., "peas" or "pease," a common ingredient
of porridge)
13 visitor one taking nourishment and comfort to the sick, as Gonzalo is doing.
13–14 give him o'er abandon him
18 Tell keep count
19–20 When [. . .] entertainer when every sorrow that presents itself is accepted without
resistance, there comes to the recipient
21 dollar widely circulated coin, the German thaler and the Spanish piece of eight.
(Sebastian puns on *entertainer* in the sense of innkeeper; to Gonzalo, *dollar* suggests
"dolor," grief.)
28 spare forbear, cease
31–32 Which . . . crow which of the two, Gonzalo or Adrian, do you bet will speak (crow)
first?
33 old cock i.e., Gonzalo
34 cockerel i.e., Adrian
36 laughter (1) burst of laughter (2) sitting of eggs. (When Adrian, the *cockerel*, begins to
speak two lines later, Sebastian loses the bet. The Folio speech prefixes in lines 39–40 are
here reversed so that Antonio enjoys his laugh as the prize for winning, as in the proverb
"He who laughs last laughs best" or "He laughs that wins." The Folio assignment can work
in the theater, however, if Sebastian pays for losing with a sardonic laugh of concession.)

37 SEBASTIAN: A match!
38 ADRIAN: Though this island seem to be desert—
ANTONIO: Ha, ha, ha!
40 SEBASTIAN: So, you're paid.
ADRIAN: Uninhabitable and almost inaccessible—
SEBASTIAN: Yet—
ADRIAN: Yet—
44 ANTONIO: He could not miss 't.
45 ADRIAN: It must needs be of subtle, tender, and
46 delicate temperance.
47 ANTONIO: Temperance was a delicate wench.
48 SEBASTIAN: Ay, and a subtle, as he most learnedly
49 delivered.
ADRIAN: The air breathes upon us here most sweetly.
SEBASTIAN: As if it had lungs, and rotten ones.
ANTONIO: Or as 'twere perfumed by a fen.
GONZALO: Here is everything advantageous to life.
54 ANTONIO: True, save means to live.
SEBASTIAN: Of that there's none, or little.
56 GONZALO: How lush and lusty the grass looks!
How green!
58 ANTONIO: The ground indeed is tawny.
59 SEBASTIAN: With an eye of green in 't.
ANTONIO: He misses not much.
61 SEBASTIAN: No. He doth but mistake the truth totally.
GONZALO: But the rarity of it is—which is indeed
almost beyond credit—

37 A match a bargain; agreed
38 desert uninhabited
40 you're paid i.e., you've had your laugh
44 miss 't (1) avoid saying "Yet" (2) miss the island
45 must needs be has to be
46 temperance mildness of climate
47 Temperance a girl's name.   **delicate** (Here it means "given to pleasure, voluptuous"; in line 46, "pleasant." Antonio is evidently suggesting that *tender, and delicate temperance* sounds like a Puritan phrase, which Antonio then mocks by applying the words to a woman rather than an island. He began this bawdy comparison with a double entendre on *inaccessible*, line 41.)
48 subtle (Here it means "tricky, sexually crafty"; in line 45, "delicate.")
49 delivered uttered. (Sebastian joins Antonio in baiting the Puritans with his use of the pious cant phrase *learnedly delivered*.)
54 save except
56 lusty healthy
58 tawny dull brown, yellowish
59 eye tinge, or spot (perhaps with reference to Gonzalo's eye or judgment)
61 but merely

64   SEBASTIAN: As many vouched rarities are.

GONZALO: That our garments, being, as they were,
drenched in the sea, hold notwithstanding their
freshness and glosses, being rather new-dyed than
stained with salt water.

69   ANTONIO: If but one of his pockets could speak, would
it not say he lies?

71   SEBASTIAN: Ay, or very falsely pocket up his report.

GONZALO: Methinks our garments are now as fresh as
when we put them on first in Afric, at the marriage of
the King's fair daughter Claribel to the King of Tunis.

SEBASTIAN: 'Twas a sweet marriage, and we prosper well
in our return.

ADRIAN: Tunis was never graced before with such a
78   paragon to their queen.

GONZALO: Not since widow Dido's time.

ANTONIO [*aside to Sebastian*]: Widow? A pox o' that!
How came that "widow" in? Widow Dido!

SEBASTIAN: What if he had said "widower Aeneas" too?
83   Good Lord, how you take it!

ADRIAN [*to Gonzalo*]: "Widow Dido" said you? You make
85   me study of that. She was of Carthage, not of Tunis.

GONZALO: This Tunis, sir, was Carthage.

ADRIAN: Carthage?

GONZALO: I assure you, Carthage.

89   ANTONIO: His word is more than the miraculous harp.

SEBASTIAN: He hath raised the wall, and houses too.

ANTONIO: What impossible matter will he make easy
next?

SEBASTIAN: I think he will carry this island home in his
pocket and give it his son for an apple.

---

64 vouched rarities allegedly real though strange sights
69 pockets i.e., because they are muddy
71 pocket up i.e., conceal, suppress; often used in the sense of "receive unprotestingly,
fail to respond to a challenge."   **his report** (Sebastian's jest is that the evidence of
Gonzalo's soggy and sea-stained pockets would confute Gonzalo's speech and his reputation for truth telling.)
78 to for
79 widow Dido Queen of Carthage, deserted by Aeneas. (She was, in fact, a widow when
Aeneas, a widower, met her, but Antonio may be amused at Gonzalo's prudish use of the
term "widow" to describe a woman deserted by her lover.)
83 take understand, respond to, interpret
85 study of think about
89 miraculous harp (Alludes to Amphion's harp, with which he raised the walls of
Thebes; Gonzalo has exceeded that deed by re-creating ancient Carthage—*wall and
houses*—mistakenly on the site of modern-day Tunis. Some Renaissance commentators
believed, like Gonzalo, that the two sites were near each other.)

94 ANTONIO: And, sowing the kernels of it in the sea,
      bring forth more islands.
96 GONZALO: Ay.
97 ANTONIO: Why, in good time.
98 GONZALO [*to Alonso*]: Sir, we were talking that our
      garments seem now as fresh as when we were at
      Tunis at the marriage of your daughter, who is now
      queen.
102 ANTONIO: And the rarest that e'er came there.
103 SEBASTIAN: Bate, I beseech you, widow Dido.
      ANTONIO: O, widow Dido? Ay, widow Dido.
105 GONZALO: Is not, sir, my doublet as fresh as the first
106   day I wore it? I mean, in a sort.
107 ANTONIO: That "sort" was well fished for.
      GONZALO: When I wore it at your daughter's marriage.
      ALONSO: You cram these words into mine ears against
110   The stomach of my sense. Would I had never
111   Married my daughter there! For, coming thence,
112   My son is lost and, in my rate, she too,
      Who is so far from Italy removed
      I ne'er again shall see her. O thou mine heir
      Of Naples and of Milan, what strange fish
      Hath made his meal on thee?
      FRANCISCO: Sir, he may live.
118   I saw him beat the surges under him
      And ride upon their backs. He trod the water,
      Whose enmity he flung aside, and breasted
      The surge most swoll'n that met him. His bold head
      'Bove the contentious waves he kept, and oared
123   Himself with his good arms in lusty stroke

94 kernels seeds
96 Ay (Gonzalo may be reasserting his point about Carthage, or he may be responding ironically to Antonio, who, in turn, answers sarcastically.)
97 in good time (An expression of ironical acquiescence or amazement, i.e., "sure, right away.")
98 talking saying
102 rarest most remarkable, beautiful
103 Bate abate, except, leave out. (Sebastian says sardonically, surely you should allow widow Dido to be an exception.)
105 doublet close-fitting jacket
106 in a sort in a way
107 sort (Antonio plays on the idea of drawing lots and on "fishing" for something to say.)
110 The stomach [. . .] sense my appetite for hearing them
111 Married given in marriage
112 rate estimation, opinion
118 surges waves
123 lusty vigorous

124 To th' shore, that o'er his wave-worn basis bowed,
125 As stooping to relieve him. I not doubt
      He came alive to land.
ALONSO: No, no, he's gone.
SEBASTIAN [*to Alonso*]: Sir, you may thank yourself for this great loss,
129 That would not bless our Europe with your daughter,
130 But rather loose her to an African,
131 Where she at least is banished from your eye,
132 Who hath cause to wet the grief on 't.
ALONSO: Prithee, peace.
134 SEBASTIAN: You were kneeled to and importuned otherwise
135 By all of us, and the fair soul herself
      Weighed between loathness and obedience at
137 Which end o' the beam should bow. We have lost your son,
      I fear, forever. Milan and Naples have
139 More widows in them of this business' making
      Than we bring men to comfort them.
      The fault's your own.
142 ALONSO: So is the dear'st o' the loss.
GONZALO: My lord Sebastian,
      The truth you speak doth lack some gentleness
145 And time to speak it in. You rub the sore
146 When you should bring the plaster.
SEBASTIAN: Very well.
148 ANTONIO: And most chirurgeonly.

124 that [. . .] bowed i.e., that projected out over the base of the cliff that had
been eroded by the surf, thus seeming to bend down toward the sea.   **his** its.
125 As as if
129 That you who
130 rather would rather.   **loose** (1) release, let loose (2) lose
131 is banished from your eye is not constantly before your eye to serve as a reproachful
reminder of what you have done
132 Who [. . .] on 't i.e., your eye, which has good reason to weep because of this, or,
Claribel, who has good reason to weep for it
134 importuned urged, implored
135–137 the fair [. . .] bow Claribel herself was poised uncertainly between unwillingness
to marry and obedience to her father as to which end of the scales should sink, which
should prevail
139 of [. . .] making on account of this marriage and subsequent shipwreck
142 dear'st heaviest, most costly
145 time appropriate time
146 plaster (A medical application.)
148 chirurgeonly like a skilled surgeon. (Antonio mocks Gonzalo's medical analogy of a
plaster applied curatively to a wound.)

GONZALO [*to Alonso*]: It is foul weather in us all, good sir,
  When you are cloudy.
151 SEBASTIAN [*to Antonio*]:   Fowl weather?
ANTONIO [*to Sebastian*]:   Very foul.
153 GONZALO: Had I plantation of this isle, my lord—
ANTONIO [*to Sebastian*]: He'd sow 't with nettle seed.
155 SEBASTIAN: Or docks, or mallows.
157 GONZALO: And were the king on 't, what would I do?
SEBASTIAN: Scape being drunk for want of wine.
158 GONZALO: I' the commonwealth I would by contraries
159 Execute all things; for no kind of traffic
   Would I admit; no name of magistrate;
161 Letters should not be known; riches, poverty,
162 And use of service, none; contract, succession,
163 Bourn, bound of land, tilth, vineyard, none;
164 No use of metal, corn, or wine, or oil;
   No occupation; all men idle, all,
   And women too, but innocent and pure;
   No sovereignty—
SEBASTIAN: Yet he would be king on 't.
ANTONIO: The latter end of his commonwealth
   forgets the beginning.
GONZALO: All things in common nature should produce
   Without sweat or endeavor. Treason, felony,
173 Sword, pike, knife, gun, or need of any engine
   Would I not have; but nature should bring forth,
175 Of its own kind, all foison, all abundance,
   To feed my innocent people.
SEBASTIAN: No marrying 'mong his subjects?
ANTONIO: None, man, all idle—whores and knaves.

---

151 Fowl (with a pun on *foul*, returning to the imagery of lines 31–36)
153 plantation colonization (with subsequent wordplay on the literal meaning, "planting")
155 docks, mallows (Weeds used as antidotes for nettle stings.)
157 Scape escape. **want** lack. (Sebastian jokes sarcastically that this hypothetical ruler would be saved from dissipation only by the barrenness of the island.)
158 by contraries by what is directly opposite to usual custom
159 traffic trade
161 Letters learning
162 use of service custom of employing servants. **succession** holding of property by right of inheritance
163 Bourn [. . .] tilth boundaries, property limits, tillage of soil
164 corn grain
173 pike lance. **engine** instrument of warfare
175 foison plenty

GONZALO: I would with such perfection govern, sir,
180   T' excel the Golden Age.
181 SEBASTIAN: 'Save His Majesty!
ANTONIO: Long live Gonzalo!
GONZALO: And—do you mark me, sir?
ALONSO: Prithee, no more. Thou dost talk nothing to me.
GONZALO: I do well believe Your Highness, and did it
186   to minister occasion to these gentlemen, who are of
187   such sensible and nimble lungs that they always use
        to laugh at nothing.
ANTONIO: 'Twas you we laughed at.
GONZALO: Who in this kind of merry fooling am nothing
        to you; so you may continue, and laugh at nothing still.
ANTONIO: What a blow was there given!
193 SEBASTIAN: An it had not fallen flat-long.
194 GONZALO: You are gentlemen of brave mettle; you
195   would lift the moon out of her sphere if she would
        continue in it five weeks without changing.

Enter Ariel [invisible] playing solemn music.

197 SEBASTIAN: We would so, and then go a-batfowling.
ANTONIO: Nay, good my lord, be not angry.
199 GONZALO: No, I warrant you, I will not adventure
200   my discretion so weakly. Will you laugh me asleep?
201   For I am very heavy.
202 ANTONIO: Go sleep, and hear us.

[All sleep except Alonso, Sebastian, and Antonio.]

ALONSO: What, all so soon asleep? I wish mine eyes
204   Would, with themselves, shut up my thoughts. I find
        They are inclined to do so.

---

180 the Golden Age the age, according to Hesiod, when Cronus, or Saturn, ruled the world; an age of innocence and abundance.
181 'Save God save
186 minister occasion furnish opportunity.
187 sensible sensitive.   **use** are accustomed
193 An if.   **flat-long** with the flat of the sword, i.e., ineffectually. (Compare with "fallen flat.")
194 mettle temperament, courage. (The sense of *metal*, indistinguishable as a form from *mettle*, continues the metaphor of the sword.)
195 sphere orbit. (Literally, one of the concentric zones occupied by planets in Ptolemaic astronomy.)
197 a-batfowling hunting birds at night with lantern and *bat*, or "stick"; also, gulling a simpleton. (Gonzalo is the simpleton, or fowl, and Sebastian will use the moon as his lantern.)
199–200 adventure [. . .] weakly risk my reputation for discretion for so trivial a cause (by getting angry at these sarcastic fellows)
201 heavy sleepy
202 Go [. . .] us i.e., get ready for sleep, and we'll do our part by laughing
204 Would [. . .] thoughts would shut off my melancholy brooding when they close themselves in sleep

SEBASTIAN: Please you, sir,
207   Do not omit the heavy offer of it.
       It seldom visits sorrow; when it doth,
       It is a comforter.
ANTONIO: We two, my lord,
       Will guard your person while you take your rest,
       And watch your safety.
ALONSO: Thank you. Wondrous heavy.
       [*Alonso sleeps. Exit Ariel.*]

SEBASTIAN: What a strange drowsiness possesses them!
ANTONIO: It is the quality o' the climate.
SEBASTIAN: Why
       Doth it not then our eyelids sink? I find not
       Myself disposed to sleep.
ANTONIO: Nor I. My spirits are nimble.
220   They fell together all, as by consent;
       They dropped, as by a thunderstroke. What might,
       Worthy Sebastian, O, what might—? No more.
       And yet methinks I see it in thy face,
224   What thou shouldst be. Th' occasion speaks thee, and
       My strong imagination sees a crown
       Dropping upon thy head.
SEBASTIAN: What, art thou waking?
ANTONIO: Do you not hear me speak?
SEBASTIAN: I do, and surely
230   It is a sleepy language, and thou speak'st
       Out of thy sleep. What is it thou didst say?
       This is a strange repose, to be asleep
       With eyes wide open—standing, speaking, moving—
       And yet so fast asleep.
ANTONIO: Noble Sebastian,
236   Thou lett'st thy fortune sleep—die, rather; wink'st
       Whiles thou art waking.
238 SEBASTIAN: Thou dost snore distinctly;
       There's meaning in thy snores.
ANTONIO: I am more serious than my custom. You
241   Must be so too if heed me, which to do
242   Trebles thee o'er.

207 omit neglect. **heavy** drowsy
220 They the sleepers. **consent** common agreement
224 occasion speaks thee opportunity of the moment calls upon you, i.e., proclaims you
       usurper of Alonso's crown
230 sleepy dreamlike, fantastic
236 wink'st (you) shut your eyes
238 distinctly articulately
241 if heed if you heed
242 Trebles thee o'er makes you three times as great and rich. **standing water** water that
neither ebbs nor flows, at a standstill

SEBASTIAN: Well, I am standing water.

ANTONIO: I'll teach you how to flow.

245 SEBASTIAN: Do so. To ebb

246   Hereditary sloth instructs me.

ANTONIO: O,

248   If you but knew how you the purpose cherish

249   Whiles thus you mock it! How, in stripping it,

250   You more invest it! Ebbing men, indeed,

251   Most often do so near the bottom run

   By their own fear or sloth.

SEBASTIAN: Prithee, say on.

254   The setting of thine eye and cheek proclaim

255   A matter from thee, and a birth indeed

256   Which throes thee much to yield.

ANTONIO: Thus, sir:

258   Although this lord of weak remembrance, this

   Who shall be of as little memory

260   When he is earthed, hath here almost persuaded—

261   For he's a spirit of persuasion, only

262   Professes to persuade—the King his son's alive,

   'Tis as impossible that he's undrowned

   As he that sleeps here swims.

SEBASTIAN: I have no hope

   That he's undrowned.

ANTONIO: O, out of that "no hope"

268   What great hope have you! No hope that way is

   Another way so high a hope that even

---

245 ebb recede, decline

246 Hereditary sloth natural laziness and the position of younger brother, one who cannot inherit

248–49 If [. . .] mock it if you only knew how much you really enhance the value of ambition even while your words mock your purpose

249–50 How [. . .] invest it i.e., how the more you speak flippantly of ambition, the more you, in effect, affirm it. **invest** clothe. (Antonio's paradox is that, by skeptically stripping away illusions, Sebastian can see the essence of a situation and the opportunity it presents or that, by disclaiming and deriding his purpose, Sebastian shows how valuable it really is.)

251 the bottom i.e., on which unadventurous men may go aground and miss the tide of fortune

254 setting set expression (of earnestness)

255 matter matter of importance

256 throes causes pain, as in giving birth. **yield** give forth, speak about

258 this lord i.e., Gonzalo. **remembrance** (1) power of remembering (2) being remembered after his death

260 earthed buried

261–62 only [. . .] persuade whose whole function (as a privy councillor) is to persuade

268 that way i.e., in regard to Ferdinand's being saved

270   Ambition cannot pierce a wink beyond,
271   But doubt discovery there. Will you grant with me
       That Ferdinand is drowned?
SEBASTIAN: He's gone.
ANTONIO: Then tell me,
       Who's the next heir of Naples?
SEBASTIAN: Claribel.
ANTONIO: She that is Queen of Tunis; she that dwells
278   Ten leagues beyond man's life; she that from Naples
279   Can have no note, unless the sun were post—
       The Man i' the Moon's too slow—till newborn chins
281   Be rough and razorable; she that from whom
282   We all were sea-swallowed, though some cast again,
       And by that destiny to perform an act
       Whereof what's past is prologue, what to come
285   In yours and my discharge.
SEBASTIAN: What stuff is this? How say you?
       'Tis true my brother's daughter's Queen of Tunis,
       So is she heir of Naples, twixt which regions
       There is some space.
290 ANTONIO: A space whose every cubit
       Seems to cry out, "How shall that Claribel
292   Measure us back to Naples? Keep in Tunis,
293   And let Sebastian wake." Say this were death
       That now hath seized them, why, they were no worse
295   Than now they are. There be that can rule Naples
296   As well as he that sleeps, lords that can prate
       As amply and unnecessarily
298   As this Gonzalo. I myself could make
299   A chough of as deep chat. O, that you bore
       The mind that I do! What a sleep were this
       For your advancement! Do you understand me?

270–71 Ambition . . . there ambition itself cannot see any further than that hope
(of the crown), is unsure of finding anything to achieve beyond it or even there
270 wink glimpse
278 Ten [. . .] life i.e., further than the journey of a lifetime
279 note news, intimation.   **post** messenger
281 razorable ready for shaving.   **from** on our voyage from
282 cast were disgorged (with a pun on *casting* of parts for a play)
285 discharge performance
290 cubit ancient measure of length of about twenty inches
292 Measure us i.e., traverse the cubits, find her way.   **Keep** stay. (Addressed to Claribel.)
293 wake i.e., to his good fortune
295 There be there are those
296 prate speak foolishly
298–99 I [. . .] chat I could teach a jackdaw to talk as wisely, or, be such a garrulous
talker myself

SEBASTIAN: Methinks I do.

303 ANTONIO: And how does your content
304   Tender your own good fortune?

SEBASTIAN: I remember
   You did supplant your brother Prospero.

ANTONIO: True.
   And look how well my garments sit upon me,
309   Much feater than before. My brother's servants
   Were then my fellows. Now they are my men.

SEBASTIAN: But, for your conscience?

312 ANTONIO: Ay, sir, where lies that? If 'twere a kibe,
313   'Twould put me to my slipper; but I feel not
   This deity in my bosom. Twenty consciences
315   That stand twixt me and Milan, candied be they
316   And melt ere they molest! Here lies your brother,
   No better than the earth he lies upon,
   If he were that which now he's like—that's dead,
   Whom I, with this obedient steel, three inches of it,
320   Can lay to bed forever; whiles you, doing thus,
321   To the perpetual wink for aye might put
   This ancient morsel, this Sir Prudence, who
323   Should not upbraid our course. For all the rest,
324   They'll take suggestion as a cat laps milk;
325   They'll tell the clock to any business that
   We say befits the hour.

SEBASTIAN: Thy case, dear friend,
   Shall be my precedent. As thou gott'st Milan,
   I'll come by Naples. Draw thy sword. One stroke
330   Shall free thee from the tribute which thou payest,
   And I the king shall love thee.

---

303 content desire, inclination
304 Tender regard, look after
309 feater more becomingly, fittingly
312 kibe chilblain, here a sore on the heel
313 put me to oblige me to wear
315 Milan the dukedom of Milan.   **candied** frozen, congealed in crystalline form.
   be they may they be
316 molest interfere
320 thus similarly. (The actor makes a stabbing gesture.)
321 wink sleep, closing of eyes.   **aye** ever
323 Should not would not then be able to
324 take suggestion respond to prompting
325 tell the clock i.e., agree, answer appropriately, chime
330 tribute (See 1.2.130–144.)

ANTONIO: Draw together;
And when I rear my hand, do you the like
334   To fall it on Gonzalo.   [*They draw.*]
SEBASTIAN: O, but one word.
                                          [*They talk apart.*]

Enter Ariel [*invisible*], *with music and song.*

ARIEL [*to Gonzalo*]: My master through his art foresees the danger
That you, his friend, are in, and sends me forth—
For else his project dies—to keep them living.

Sings in Gonzalo's ear.
          While you here do snoring lie,
          Open-eyed conspiracy
341   His time doth take.
          If of life you keep a care,
          Shake off slumber, and beware.
          Awake, awake!
345   ANTONIO: Then let us both be sudden.
GONZALO [*waking*]: Now, good angels preserve the King!

[*The others wake.*]

ALONSO: Why, how now, ho, awake? Why are you drawn?
Wherefore this ghastly looking?
GONZALO: What's the matter?
350   SEBASTIAN: Whiles we stood here securing your repose,
Even now, we heard a hollow burst of bellowing
Like bulls, or rather lions. Did 't not wake you?
It struck mine ear most terribly.
ALONSO: I heard nothing.
ANTONIO: O, 'twas a din to fright a monster's ear,
To make an earthquake! Sure it was the roar
Of a whole herd of lions.
ALONSO: Heard you this, Gonzalo?
GONZALO: Upon mine honor, sir, I heard a humming,
And that a strange one too, which did awake me.
361   I shaked you, sir, and cried. As mine eyes opened,
I saw their weapons drawn. There was a noise,
363   That's verily. 'Tis best we stand upon our guard,
Or that we quit this place. Let's draw our weapons.
ALONSO: Lead off this ground, and let's make further search

334 **fall it** let it fall
341 **time** opportunity
345 **sudden** quick
350 **securing** standing guard over
361 **cried** called out
363 **verily** true

For my poor son.
GONZALO: Heavens keep him from these beasts!
For he is, sure, i' th' island.
ALONSO: Lead away.
ARIEL [*aside*]: Prospero my lord shall know what I have done.
So, King, go safely on to seek thy son.

Exeunt [separately].

2.2

Enter Caliban with a burden of wood. A noise of thunder heard.

CALIBAN: All the infections that the sun sucks up
2   From bogs, fens, flats, on Prosper fall, and make him
3   By inchmeal a disease! His spirits hear me,
4   And yet I needs must curse. But they'll nor pinch,
5   Fright me with urchin shows, pitch me i' the mire,
6   Nor lead me, like a firebrand, in the dark
Out of my way, unless he bid 'em. But
For every trifle are they set upon me,
9   Sometimes like apes, that mow and chatter at me
And after bite me; then like hedgehogs, which
Lie tumbling in my barefoot way and mount
Their pricks at my footfall. Sometimes am I
13   All wound with adders, who with cloven tongues
Do hiss me into madness.

Enter Trinculo.

                          Lo, now, lo!
Here comes a spirit of his, and to torment me
For bringing wood in slowly. I'll fall flat.
18   Perchance he will not mind me.   [*He lies down.*]

2.2 Location: **Another part of the island.**
2 flats swamps
3 By inchmeal inch by inch
4 needs must have to.   **nor** neither
5 urchin shows elvish apparitions shaped like hedgehogs
6 like a firebrand they in the guise of a will-o'-the-wisp
9 mow make faces
13 wound with entwined by
18 mind notice

¹⁹ TRINCULO: Here's neither bush nor shrub to bear off
any weather at all. And another storm brewing; I hear
it sing i' the wind. Yond same black cloud, yond huge
²² one, looks like a foul bombard that would shed his
liquor. If it should thunder as it did before, I know
not where to hide my head. Yond same cloud cannot
choose but fall by pailfuls. [*Seeing Caliban.*] What have
we here, a man or a fish? Dead or alive? A fish, he
smells like a fish; a very ancient and fishlike smell; a
²⁸ kind of not-of-the-newest Poor John. A strange fish!
Were I in England now, as once I was, and had but
³⁰ this fish painted, not a holiday fool there but would
give a piece of silver. There would this monster make
³² a man. Any strange beast there makes a man. When
³³ they will not give a doit to relieve a lame beggar, they
will lay out ten to see a dead Indian. Legged like a
³⁵ man, and his fins like arms! Warm, o' my troth! I do
³⁶ now let loose my opinion, hold it no longer: this is no
³⁷ fish, but an islander, that hath lately suffered by a
thunderbolt. [*Thunder.*] Alas, the storm is come
³⁹ again! My best way is to creep under his gaberdine.
There is no other shelter hereabout. Misery acquaints
⁴¹ a man with strange bedfellows. I will here shroud till
⁴² the dregs of the storm be past.
[*He creeps under Caliban's garment.*]

Enter Stephano, singing, [a bottle in his hand].

STEPHANO:
"I shall no more to sea, to sea,
Here shall I die ashore—"
This is a very scurvy tune to sing at a man's funeral.
Well, here's my comfort.   *Drinks.*

19 bear off keep off
22 foul bombard dirty leather jug.   **his** its
28 Poor John salted fish, type of poor fare
30 painted i.e., painted on a sign set up outside a booth or tent at a fair
31–32 make a man (1) make one's fortune (2) be indistinguishable from an Englishman
33 doit small coin
35 o' my troth by my faith
36 hold it hold it in
37 suffered i.e., died
39 gaberdine cloak, loose upper garment
41 shroud take shelter.
42 dregs i.e., last remains (as in a *bombard* or jug, line 22)

(Sings.)

47   "The master, the swabber, the boatswain, and I,
           The gunner and his mate,
        Loved Mall, Meg, and Marian, and Margery,
           But none of us cared for Kate.
51   For she had a tongue with a tang,
              Would cry to a sailor, 'Go hang!'
           She loved not the savor of tar nor of pitch,
54   Yet a tailor might scratch her where'er she did itch.
             Then to sea, boys, and let her go hang!"
This is a scurvy tune too. But here's my comfort.

Drinks.

57 CALIBAN: Do not torment me! O!
58 STEPHANO: What's the matter? Have we devils here?
59   Do you put tricks upon 's with savages and men of Ind, ha?
    I have not scaped drowning to be afeard now of your
61   four legs. For it hath been said, "As proper a man
62   as ever went on four legs cannot make him give ground";
    and it shall be said so again while Stephano breathes
64   at' nostrils.
    CALIBAN: This spirit torments me! O!
    STEPHANO: This is some monster of the isle with four
67   legs, who hath got, as I take it, an ague. Where the devil
68   should he learn our language? I will give him some
69   relief, if it be but for that. If I can recover him and keep
    him tame and get to Naples with him, he's a present
71   for any emperor that ever trod on neat's leather.
    CALIBAN: Do not torment me, prithee. I'll bring my
    wood home faster.
74 STEPHANO: He's in his fit now and does not talk after
75   the wisest. He shall taste of my bottle. If he have never

---

47 swabber crew member whose job is to wash the decks
51 tang sting
54 tailor [. . .] itch (A dig at tailors for their supposed effeminacy and a bawdy suggestion of satisfying a sexual craving.)
57 Do [. . .] me (Caliban assumes that one of Prospero's spirits has come to punish him.)
58 What's the matter what's going on here?
59 put tricks upon 's trick us with conjuring shows.   **Ind** India
61 proper handsome.
62 four legs (The conventional phrase would supply *two legs*, but the creature Stephano thinks he sees has four.)
64 at' at the
67 ague fever. (Probably both Caliban and Trinculo are quaking; see lines 57 and 81.)
68 should he learn could he have learned
69 for that i.e., for knowing our language.   **recover** restore
71 neat's leather cowhide
74–75 after the wisest in the wisest fashion

76   drunk wine afore, it will go near to remove his fit. If I
77   can recover him and keep him tame, I will not take
78   too much for him. He shall pay for him that hath him,
and that soundly.
CALIBAN: Thou dost me yet but little hurt; thou wilt
81   anon, I know it by thy trembling. Now Prosper works
upon thee.
STEPHANO: Come on your ways. Open your mouth. Here
84   is that which will give language to you, cat. Open your
85   mouth. This will shake your shaking, I can tell you,
and that soundly. [*Giving Caliban a drink.*] You cannot
87   tell who's your friend. Open your chaps again.
TRINCULO: I should know that voice. It should be—but
he is drowned, and these are devils. O, defend me!
90   STEPHANO: Four legs and two voices—a most delicate
monster! His forward voice now is to speak well of his
92   friend; his backward voice is to utter foul speeches
93   and to detract. If all the wine in my bottle will recover
94   him, I will help his ague. Come. [*Giving a drink.*]
Amen! I will pour some in thy other mouth.
TRINCULO: Stephano!
STEPHANO: Doth thy other mouth call me? Mercy,
97   mercy! This is a devil, and no monster. I will leave
him. I have no long spoon.
99   TRINCULO: Stephano! If thou beest Stephano, touch me
and speak to me, for I am Trinculo—be not afeard—
thy good friend Trinculo.
STEPHANO: If thou beest Trinculo, come forth. I'll pull
thee by the lesser legs. If any be Trinculo's legs, these
are they. [*Pulling him out.*] Thou art very Trinculo

---

76 afore before.   **go near to** be in a fair way to.
77 recover restore
77–78 I will [. . .] much i.e., no sum can be too much
78 He shall [. . .] hath him i.e., anyone who wants him will have to pay dearly for him.
78 hath possesses, receives
81 anon presently
84–85 cat [. . .] mouth (Allusion to the proverb "Good liquor will make a cat speak.")
87 chaps jaws
90 delicate ingenious
92 backward voice (Trinculo and Caliban are facing in opposite directions. Stephano supposes the monster to have a rear end that can emit *foul speeches* or foul-smelling wind at the monster's *other mouth,* line 97.)
93–94 If [. . .] him even if it takes all the wine in my bottle to cure him
94 help cure
97 call me i.e., call me by name, know supernaturally who I am
99 long spoon (Allusion to the proverb "He that sups with the devil has need of a long spoon.")

106   indeed! How cam'st thou to be the siege of this
107   mooncalf? Can he vent Trinculos?
TRINCULO: I took him to be killed with a thunderstroke.
    But art thou not drowned, Stephano? I hope now thou
110   art not drowned. Is the storm overblown? I hid me
    under the dead mooncalf's gaberdine for fear of the
    storm. And art thou living, Stephano? O Stephano,
    two Neapolitans scaped!   [*He capers with Stephano.*]
STEPHANO: Prithee, do not turn me about. My stomach
115   is not constant.
116   CALIBAN: These be fine things, an if they be not spirits.
117   That's a brave god, and bears celestial liquor.
    I will kneel to him.
STEPHANO: How didst thou scape? How cam'st thou
    hither? Swear by this bottle how thou cam'st hither.
121   I escaped upon a butt of sack which the sailors heaved
122   o'erboard—by this bottle, which I made of the bark
123   of a tree with mine own hands since I was cast ashore.
CALIBAN [*kneeling*]: I'll swear upon that bottle to be thy
    true subject, for the liquor is not earthly.
STEPHANO: Here. Swear then how thou escapedst.
TRINCULO: Swum ashore, man, like a duck. I can swim like
    a duck, I'll be sworn.
129   STEPHANO: Here, kiss the book. Though thou canst swim
    like a duck, thou art made like a goose.
    [*Giving him a drink.*]

TRINCULO: O Stephano, hast any more of this?
STEPHANO: The whole butt, man. My cellar is in a rock
    by the seaside, where my wine is hid.—How now,
    mooncalf? How does thine ague?
CALIBAN: Hast thou not dropped from heaven?
STEPHANO: Out o' the moon, I do assure thee. I was the
137   Man i' the Moon when time was.

---

106 siege excrement
107 mooncalf monstrous or misshapen creature (whose deformity is caused by the
malignant influence of the moon).   **vent** excrete, defecate
110 overblown blown over
115 not constant unsteady
116 an if if
117 brave fine, magnificent.   **bears** he carries
121 butt of sack barrel of Canary wine
122 by this bottle i.e., I swear by this bottle
123 since after
129 book i.e., bottle (but with ironic reference to the practice of kissing the Bible in
swearing an oath; see *I'll be sworn* in line 128)
137 when time was once upon a time

CALIBAN: I have seen thee in her, and I do adore thee.

139   My mistress showed me thee, and thy dog, and thy bush.

STEPHANO: Come, swear to that. Kiss the book. I will
    furnish it anon with new contents. Swear.
    [*Giving him a drink.*]

142 TRINCULO: By this good light, this is a very shallow
    monster! I afeard of him? A very weak monster!
    The Man i' the Moon? A most poor credulous monster!

145   Well drawn, monster, in good sooth!

CALIBAN [*to Stephano*]: I'll show thee every fertile inch o' th' island,
    And I will kiss thy foot. I prithee, be my god.

TRINCULO: By this light, a most perfidious and drunken

149   monster! When 's god's asleep, he'll rob his bottle.

CALIBAN: I'll kiss thy foot. I'll swear myself thy subject.

STEPHANO: Come on then. Down, and swear.

    [*Caliban kneels.*]

TRINCULO: I shall laugh myself to death at this puppy-
    headed monster. A most scurvy monster! I could find
    in my heart to beat him—

STEPHANO: Come, kiss.

156 TRINCULO: But that the poor monster's in drink. An
    abominable monster!

CALIBAN: I'll show thee the best springs. I'll pluck thee berries.
    I'll fish for thee and get thee wood enough.
    A plague upon the tyrant that I serve!
    I'll bear him no more sticks, but follow thee,
    Thou wondrous man.

TRINCULO: A most ridiculous monster, to make a
    wonder of a poor drunkard!

165 CALIBAN: I prithee, let me bring thee where crabs grow,

166   And I with my long nails will dig thee pignuts,
    Show thee a jay's nest, and instruct thee how

---

139 dog [. . .] bush (The Man in the Moon was popularly imagined to have with him a dog and a bush of thorn.)
142 By [. . .] light by God's light, by this good light from heaven
145 Well drawn well pulled (on the bottle).   **in good sooth** truly, indeed
149 When [. . .] bottle i.e., Caliban wouldn't even stop at robbing his god of his bottle if he could catch him asleep
156 in drink drunk
165 crabs crab apples, or perhaps crabs
166 pignuts earthnuts, edible tuberous roots

168 To snare the nimble marmoset. I'll bring thee
To clustering filberts, and sometimes I'll get thee
170 Young scamels from the rock. Wilt thou go with me?
STEPHANO: I prithee now, lead the way without any
more talking.—Trinculo, the King and all our com-
173 pany else being drowned, we will inherit here.—
Here, bear my bottle.—Fellow Trinculo, we'll fill him
by and by again.
CALIBAN *(sings drunkenly):*
Farewell, master, farewell, farewell!
TRINCULO: A howling monster; a drunken monster!
CALIBAN:
No more dams I'll make for fish,
179 Nor fetch in firing
At requiring,
181 Nor scrape trenchering, nor wash dish.
'Ban, 'Ban, Ca–Caliban
183 Has a new master. Get a new man!
184 Freedom, high-day! High-day, freedom! Freedom,
high-day, freedom!
STEPHANO: O brave monster! Lead the way.

Exeunt.

3.1

Enter Ferdinand, bearing a log.

1 FERDINAND: There be some sports are painful, and their labor
2 Delight in them sets off. Some kinds of baseness
3 Are nobly undergone, and most poor matters
4 Point to rich ends. This my mean task

168 marmoset small monkey
170 scamels (Possibly *seamews*, mentioned in a contemporary account, or shellfish, or perhaps from *squamelle*, "furnished with little scales." Contemporary French and Italian travel accounts report that the natives of Patagonia in South America ate small fish described as *fort scameux* and *squame.*)
173 else in addition, besides ourselves   **inherit** take possession
179 firing firewood
181 trenchering trenchers, wooden plates
183 Get a new man (Addressed to Prospero.)
184 high-day holiday
3.1 Location: Before Prospero's cell.
1–2 There [. . .] sets off some pastimes are laborious, but the pleasure we get from them compensates for the effort. (Pleasure is *set off* by labor as a jewel is set off by its foil.)
2 baseness menial activity
3 undergone undertaken.   **most poor** poorest
4 mean lowly

5   Would be as heavy to me as odious, but
6   The mistress which I serve quickens what's dead
    And makes my labors pleasures. O, she is
    Ten times more gentle than her father's crabbed,
    And he's composed of harshness. I must remove
    Some thousands of these logs and pile them up,
11   Upon a sore injunction. My sweet mistress
    Weeps when she sees me work and says such baseness
13   Had never like executor. I forget;
    But these sweet thoughts do even refresh my labors,
15   Most busy lest when I do it.

Enter Miranda; and Prospero [at a distance, unseen].

MIRANDA: Alas now, pray you,
    Work not so hard. I would the lightning had
18   Burnt up those logs that you are enjoined to pile!
19   Pray, set it down and rest you. When this burns,
20   'Twill weep for having wearied you. My father
    Is hard at study. Pray now, rest yourself.
22   He's safe for these three hours.
FERDINAND: O most dear mistress,
24   The sun will set before I shall discharge
    What I must strive to do.
MIRANDA: If you'll sit down,
    I'll bear your logs the while. Pray, give me that.
    I'll carry it to the pile.
FERDINAND: No, precious creature,
    I had rather crack my sinews, break my back,
    Than you should such dishonor undergo
    While I sit lazy by.
MIRANDA: It would become me
    As well as it does you; and I should do it
    With much more ease, for my good will is to it,
    And yours it is against.

5 but were it not that
6 quickens gives life to
11 sore injunction severe command
13 Had [. . .] **executor** i.e., was never before undertaken by so noble a being.
I forget i.e., I forget that I'm supposed to be working, or, I forget my happiness, oppressed by my labor
15 Most [. . .] **it** i.e., busy at my labor but with my mind on other things (?) (The line may be in need of emendation.)
18 enjoined commanded
19 this i.e., the log
20 weep i.e., exude resin
22 these the next
24 discharge complete

PROSPERO [*aside*]:   Poor worm, thou art infected!
38   This visitation shows it.
MIRANDA: You look wearily.
FERDINAND: No, noble mistress, 'tis fresh morning with me
41   When you are by at night. I do beseech you—
Chiefly that I might set it in my prayers—
What is your name?
MIRANDA: Miranda.—O my father,
45   I have broke your hest to say so.
46 FERDINAND: Admired Miranda!
Indeed the top of admiration, worth
What's dearest to the world! Full many a lady
48   I have eyed with best regard, and many a time
49   The harmony of their tongues hath into bondage
Brought my too diligent ear. For several virtues
51   Have I liked several women, never any
With so full soul but some defect in her
Did quarrel with the noblest grace she owed
54   And put it to the foil. But you, O you,
55   So perfect and so peerless, are created
Of every creature's best!
57 MIRANDA: I do not know
One of my sex; no woman's face remember,
Save, from my glass, mine own. Nor have I seen
More that I may call men than you, good friend,
And my dear father. How features are abroad
62   I am skilless of; but, by my modesty,
63   The jewel in my dower, I would not wish
Any companion in the world but you;
Nor can imagination form a shape,
Besides yourself, to like of. But I prattle
67   Something too wildly, and my father's precepts
68   I therein do forget.

38 visitation (1) Miranda's visit to Ferdinand (2) visitation of the plague, i.e., infection of love
41 by nearby
45 hest command
46 Admired Miranda (Her name means "to be admired or wondered at.")
48 dearest most treasured
49 best regard thoughtful and approving attention
51 diligent attentive.   **several** various (also in line 52)
54 owed owned
55 put [. . .] foil (1) overthrew it (as in wrestling) (2) served as a *foil*, or "contrast," to set it off
57 Of out of
62 How [. . .] abroad what people look like in other places
63 skilless ignorant.   **modesty** virginity
67 like of be pleased with, be fond of
68 Something somewhat

70 FERDINAND: I am in my condition
    A prince, Miranda; I do think, a king—
72   I would, not so!—and would no more endure
73   This wooden slavery than to suffer
74   The flesh-fly blow my mouth. Hear my soul speak:
    The very instant that I saw you did
    My heart fly to your service, there resides
    To make me slave to it, and for your sake
    Am I this patient log-man.
  MIRANDA: Do you love me?
  FERDINAND: O heaven, O earth, bear witness to this sound,
81   And crown what I profess with kind event
82   If I speak true! If hollowly, invert
83   What best is boded me to mischief! I
84   Beyond all limit of what else i' the world
    Do love, prize, honor you.
  MIRANDA [*weeping*]:   I am a fool
    To weep at what I am glad of.
  PROSPERO [*aside*]:   Fair encounter
    Of two most rare affections! Heavens rain grace
    On that which breeds between 'em!
  FERDINAND: Wherefore weep you?
  MIRANDA: At mine unworthiness, that dare not offer
    What I desire to give, and much less take
94   What I shall die to want. But this is trifling,
    And all the more it seeks to hide itself
96   The bigger bulk it shows. Hence, bashful cunning,
    And prompt me, plain and holy innocence!
    I am your wife, if you will marry me;
99   If not, I'll die your maid. To be your fellow
    You may deny me, but I'll be your servant
101   Whether you will or no.

70 condition rank
72 would wish (it were)
73 wooden slavery being compelled to carry wood
74 flesh-fly insect that deposits its eggs in dead flesh.   **blow** befoul with fly eggs
81 kind event favorable outcome
82 hollowly insincerely, falsely.   **invert** turn
83 boded in store for.   **mischief** harm
84 what whatever
94 die (Probably with an unconscious sexual meaning that underlies all of lines 92–96.)
to want through lacking
96 bashful cunning coyness
99 maid handmaiden, servant.   **fellow** mate, equal
101 will desire it.

102 FERDINAND: My mistress, dearest,
      And I thus humble ever.
      MIRANDA: My husband, then?
105 FERDINAND: Ay, with a heart as willing
      As bondage e'er of freedom. Here's my hand.
      MIRANDA [*clasping his hand*]: And mine, with my heart in 't. And
      now farewell
      Till half an hour hence.
109 FERDINAND: A thousand thousand!

      Exeunt [Ferdinand and Miranda, separately].

      PROSPERO: So glad of this as they I cannot be,
111   Who are surprised with all; but my rejoicing
      At nothing can be more. I'll to my book,
      For yet ere suppertime must I perform
114   Much business appertaining.

      Exit.

                          3.2

      Enter Caliban, Stephano, and Trinculo.

1 STEPHANO: Tell not me. When the butt is out, we will
2   drink water, not a drop before. Therefore bear up and
3   board 'em. Servant monster, drink to me.
4 TRINCULO: Servant monster? The folly of this island! They
      say there's but five upon this isle. We are three of them;
6   if th' other two be brained like us, the state totters.
      STEPHANO: Drink, servant monster, when I bid thee.
8   Thy eyes are almost set in thy head.   [*Giving a drink.*]
9 TRINCULO: Where should they be set else? He were a
10   brave monster indeed if they were set in his tail.

---

102 **My mistress** i.e., the woman I adore and serve (not an illicit sexual partner)
105 **willing** desirous
109 **A thousand thousand** i.e., a thousand thousand farewells
111 **with all** by everything that has happened, or, *withal*, "with it"
114 **appertaining** related to this
3.2 Location: Another part of the island.
1 **out** empty
2–3 **bear** [. . .] **'em** (Stephano uses the terminology of maneuvering at sea and boarding
a vessel under attack as a way of urging an assault on the liquor supply.)
4 **folly of** i.e., stupidity found on
6 **be brained** are endowed with intelligence
8 **set** fixed in a drunken stare, or, sunk, like the sun
9 **set** placed
10 **brave** fine, splendid

STEPHANO: My man-monster hath drowned his tongue
    in sack. For my part, the sea cannot drown me. I
13   swam, ere I could recover the shore, five and thirty
14   leagues off and on. By this light, thou shalt be my lieu-
15   tenant, monster, or my standard.
16 TRINCULO: Your lieutenant, if you list; he's no standard.
17 STEPHANO: We'll not run, Monsieur Monster.
18 TRINCULO: Nor go neither, but you'll lie like dogs and
    yet say nothing neither.
STEPHANO: Mooncalf, speak once in thy life, if thou
    beest a good mooncalf.
CALIBAN: How does thy honor? Let me lick thy shoe.
    I'll not serve him. He is not valiant.
TRINCULO: Thou liest, most ignorant monster, I am
25   in case to jostle a constable. Why, thou debauched fish,
    thou, was there ever man a coward that hath drunk so
27   much sack as I today? Wilt thou tell a monstrous lie,
    being but half a fish and half a monster?
CALIBAN: Lo, how he mocks me! Wilt thou let him, my lord?
TRINCULO: "Lord," quoth he? That a monster should be
31   such a natural!
CALIBAN: Lo, lo, again! Bite him to death, I prithee.
STEPHANO: Trinculo, keep a good tongue in your head.
34   If you prove a mutineer—the next tree! The poor
    monster's my subject, and he shall not suffer indignity.
CALIBAN: I thank my noble lord. Wilt thou be pleased
    To hearken once again to the suit I made to thee?
38 STEPHANO: Marry, will I. Kneel and repeat it. I will
    stand, and so shall Trinculo.   [*Caliban kneels.*]

39   *Enter Ariel, invisible.*

---

13 recover gain, reach
14 leagues units of distance, each equaling about three miles. **off and on** intermittently.
By this light (An oath: by the light of the sun.)
15 standard standard-bearer, ensign (as distinguished from *lieutenant,* lines 15–16)
16 list prefer. **no standard** i.e., not able to stand up
17 run (1) retreat (2) urinate (taking Trinculo's *standard,* line 16, in the old sense of "conduit")
18 go walk. **lie** (1) tell lies (2) lie prostrate (3) excrete
25 in case [. . .] **constable** i.e., in fit condition, made valiant by drink, to taunt or challenge the police. **debauched** (1) seduced away from proper service and allegiance (2) depraved
27 sack Spanish white wine
31 natural (1) idiot (2) natural as opposed to unnatural, monsterlike
34 the next tree i.e., you'll hang
38 Marry i.e., indeed. (Originally an oath, "by the Virgin Mary.")
39 s.d. invisible i.e., wearing a garment to connote invisibility, as at 1.2.439

CALIBAN: As I told thee before, I am subject to a tyrant,
    A sorcerer, that by his cunning hath
    Cheated me of the island.
ARIEL [*mimicking Trinculo*]: Thou liest.
CALIBAN: Thou liest, thou jesting monkey, thou!
    I would my valiant master would destroy thee.
    I do not lie.
STEPHANO: Trinculo, if you trouble him any more in 's
48   tale, by this hand, I will supplant some of your teeth.
TRINCULO: Why, I said nothing.
STEPHANO: Mum, then, and no more.—Proceed.
CALIBAN: I say by sorcery he got this isle;
    From me he got it. If thy greatness will
    Revenge it on him—for I know thou dar'st,
54   But this thing dare not—
STEPHANO: That's most certain.
CALIBAN: Thou shalt be lord of it, and I'll serve thee.
57 STEPHANO: How now shall this be compassed? Canst
    thou bring me to the party?
CALIBAN: Yea, yea, my lord. I'll yield him thee asleep,
    Where thou mayst knock a nail into his head.
ARIEL: Thou liest; thou canst not.
62 CALIBAN: What a pied ninny's this! Thou scurvy patch!—
    I do beseech thy greatness, give him blows
    And take his bottle from him. When that's gone
    He shall drink naught but brine, for I'll not show him
66   Where the quick freshes are.
STEPHANO: Trinculo, run into no further danger. Interrupt
68   the monster one word further and, by this hand, I'll
69   turn my mercy out o' doors and make a stockfish of thee.
70 TRINCULO: Why, what did I? I did nothing. I'll go farther
    off.
STEPHANO: Didst thou not say he lied?
ARIEL: Thou liest.
STEPHANO: Do I so? Take thou that. [*He beats Trinculo.*]
74   As you like this, give me the lie another time.

48 supplant uproot, displace
54 this thing i.e., Trinculo
57 compassed achieved
62 pied ninny fool in motley. **patch** fool
66 quick freshes running springs
68 one word further i.e., one more time
69 turn [. . .] doors i.e., forget about being merciful. **stockfish** dried cod beaten before cooking
70 off away
74 give me the lie call me a liar to my face

TRINCULO: I did not give the lie. Out o' your wits and
    hearing too? A pox o' your bottle! This can sack
77   and drinking do. A murrain on your monster, and the
    devil take your fingers!
CALIBAN: Ha, ha, ha!
STEPHANO: Now, forward with your tale. [*To Trinculo.*]
    Prithee, stand further off.
CALIBAN: Beat him enough. After a little time
    I'll beat him too.
STEPHANO: Stand farther.—Come, proceed.
CALIBAN: Why, as I told thee, 'tis a custom with him
    I' th' afternoon to sleep. There thou mayst brain him,
    Having first seized his books; or with a log
88   Batter his skull, or paunch him with a stake,
89   Or cut his weasand with thy knife. Remember
    First to possess his books, for without them
91   He's but a sot, as I am, nor hath not
    One spirit to command. They all do hate him
    As rootedly as I. Burn but his books.
94   He has brave utensils—for so he calls them—
95   Which, when he has a house, he'll deck withal.
    And that most deeply to consider is
    The beauty of his daughter. He himself
    Calls her a nonpareil. I never saw a woman
    But only Sycorax my dam and she;
    But she as far surpasseth Sycorax
    As great'st does least.
102 STEPHANO: Is it so brave a lass?
103 CALIBAN: Ay, lord. She will become thy bed, I warrant,
    And bring thee forth brave brood.
STEPHANO: Monster, I will kill this man. His daughter
    and I will be king and queen—save Our Graces!—
    and Trinculo and thyself shall be viceroys. Dost thou
    like the plot, Trinculo?
TRINCULO: Excellent.
STEPHANO: Give me thy hand. I am sorry I beat thee;
    but, while thou liv'st, keep a good tongue in thy head.

---

77 murrain plague (Literally, a cattle disease.)
88 paunch stab in the belly
89 weasand windpipe
91 sot fool
94 brave utensils fine furnishings
95 deck withal furnish it with
102 brave splendid, attractive
103 become suit (sexually)

CALIBAN: Within this half hour will he be asleep.
Wilt thou destroy him then?
STEPHANO: Ay, on mine honor.
ARIEL [*aside*]: This will I tell my master.
CALIBAN: Thou mak'st me merry; I am full of pleasure.
117   Let us be jocund. Will you troll the catch
118   You taught me but whilere?
119 STEPHANO: At thy request, monster, I will do reason,
120   any reason.—Come on, Trinculo, let us sing.   *Sings.*
121   "Flout 'em and scout 'em
And scout 'em and flout 'em!
Thought is free."
124 CALIBAN: That's not the tune.

Ariel plays the tune on a tabor and pipe.

STEPHANO: What is this same?
TRINCULO: This is the tune of our catch, played by the
127   picture of Nobody.
STEPHANO: If thou beest a man, show thyself in thy
129   likeness. If thou beest a devil, take 't as thou list.
TRINCULO: O, forgive me my sins!
131 STEPHANO: He that dies pays all debts. I defy thee.
Mercy upon us!
CALIBAN: Art thou afeard?
STEPHANO: No, monster, not I.
CALIBAN: Be not afeard. The isle is full of noises,
Sounds, and sweet airs, that give delight and hurt not.
Sometimes a thousand twangling instruments
Will hum about mine ears, and sometimes voices
That, if I then had waked after long sleep,
Will make me sleep again; and then, in dreaming,
The clouds methought would open and show riches
Ready to drop upon me, that when I waked
143   I cried to dream again.

---

117 jocund jovial, merry.   **troll the catch** sing the round
118 but whilere only a short time ago
119–120 reason, any reason anything reasonable
121 Flout scoff at.   **scout** deride
124 s.d. tabor small drum
127 picture of Nobody (Refers to a familiar figure with head, arms, and legs but no trunk.)
129 take 't [. . .] list i.e., take my defiance as you please, as best you can
131 He [. . .] debts i.e., if I have to die, at least that will be the end of all my woes and obligations
143 to dream desirous of dreaming

STEPHANO: This will prove a brave kingdom to me,
    where I shall have my music for nothing.
CALIBAN: When Prospero is destroyed.
147 STEPHANO: That shall be by and by. I remember the story.
TRINCULO: The sound is going away. Let's follow it, and
    after do our work.
STEPHANO: Lead, monster; we'll follow. I would I could
151   see this taborer! He lays it on.
TRINCULO: Wilt come? I'll follow, Stephano.

    Exeunt [following Ariel's music].

3.3

Enter Alonso, Sebastian, Antonio, Gonzalo, Adrian,
Francisco, etc.

1 GONZALO: By 'r lakin, I can go no further, sir.
    My old bones aches. Here's a maze trod indeed
3   Through forthrights and meanders! By your patience,
4   I needs must rest me.
ALONSO: Old lord, I cannot blame thee,
6   Who am myself attached with weariness,
7   To th' dulling of my spirits. Sit down and rest.
    Even here I will put off my hope, and keep it
9   No longer for my flatterer. He is drowned
    Whom thus we stray to find, and the sea mocks
11   Our frustrate search on land. Well, let him go.
                    [Alonso and Gonzalo sit.]
12 ANTONIO *[aside to Sebastian]*: I am right glad that he's so
    out of hope.
13   Do not, for one repulse, forgo the purpose
    That you resolved t' effect.
SEBASTIAN *[to Antonio]*:   The next advantage
16   Will we take throughly.

---

147 **by and by** very soon
151 **lays it on** i.e., plays the drum vigorously
3.3 Location: Another part of the island.
1 **By 'r lakin** by our Ladykin, by our Lady
3 **forthrights and meanders** paths straight and crooked
4 **needs must** have to
6 **attached** seized
7 **To [. . .] spirits** to the point of being dull-spirited
9 **for** as
11 **frustrate** frustrated
12 **right** very
13 **for** because of
16 **throughly** thoroughly

ANTONIO [*to Sebastian*]:   Let it be tonight,
18   For, now they are oppressed with travel, they
19   Will not, nor cannot, use such vigilance
       As when they are fresh.
21   SEBASTIAN [*to Antonio*]:   I say tonight. No more.

   Solemn and strange music; and Prospero on the top, invisible.

ALONSO: What harmony is this? My good friends, hark!
GONZALO: Marvelous sweet music!

   Enter several strange shapes, bringing in a banquet,
   and dance about it with gentle actions of salutations;
   and, inviting the King, etc., to eat, they depart.

24   ALONSO: Give us kind keepers, heavens! What were these?
25   SEBASTIAN: A living drollery. Now I will believe
       That there are unicorns; that in Arabia
27   There is one tree, the phoenix' throne, one phoenix
       At this hour reigning there.
     ANTONIO.   I'll believe both;
30   And what does else want credit, come to me
       And I'll be sworn 'tis true. Travelers ne'er did lie,
       Though fools at home condemn 'em.
     GONZALO: If in Naples
       I should report this now, would they believe me
       If I should say I saw such islanders?
36   For, certes, these are people of the island,
37   Who, though they are of monstrous shape, yet note,
       Their manners are more gentle, kind, than of
       Our human generation you shall find
       Many, nay, almost any.
     PROSPERO [*aside*]:   Honest lord,
       Thou hast said well, for some of you there present
       Are worse than devils.

---

18 **now** now that.   **travel** (Spelled *trauaile* in the Folio and carrying the sense of labor as
well as traveling.)
19 **use** apply
21 **s.d. on the top** at some high point of the tiring-house or the theater, on a third level
above the gallery
24 **kind keepers** guardian angels
25 **living** with live actors.   **drollery** comic entertainment, caricature, puppet show
27 **phoenix** mythical bird consumed to ashes every five hundred to six hundred years,
only to be renewed into another cycle
30 **want credit** lack credence
36 **certes** certainly
37 **monstrous** unnatural

44 ALONSO: I cannot too much muse
Such shapes, such gesture, and such sound, expressing—
46 Although they want the use of tongue—a kind
Of excellent dumb discourse.
48 PROSPERO [*aside*]:   Praise in departing.
FRANCISCO. They vanished strangely.
SEBASTIAN: No matter, since
51 They have left their viands behind, for we have stomachs.
Will 't please you taste of what is here?
ALONSO: Not I.
GONZALO: Faith, sir, you need not fear. When we were boys,
55 Who would believe that there were mountaineers
56 Dewlapped like bulls, whose throats had hanging at 'em
57 Wallets of flesh? Or that there were such men
58 Whose heads stood in their breasts? Which now we find
59 Each putter-out of five for one will bring us
60 Good warrant of.
61 ALONSO: I will stand to and feed,
62 Although my last—no matter, since I feel
63 The best is past. Brother, my lord the Duke,
64 Stand to, and do as we.   [*They approach the table.*]

*Thunder and lightning. Enter Ariel, like a harpy,
claps his wings upon the table, and with a quaint device
the banquet vanishes.*

65 ARIEL: You are three men of sin, whom Destiny—
That hath to instrument this lower world
And what is in 't—the never-surfeited sea
68 Hath caused to belch up you, and on this island

44 muse wonder at
46 want lack
48 Praise in departing i.e., save your praise until the end of the performance. (Proverbial.)
51 viands provisions.   **stomachs** appetites
55 mountaineers mountain dwellers
56 Dewlapped having a dewlap, or fold of skin hanging from the neck, like cattle
57 Wallets pendent folds of skin, wattles
58 in their breasts (i.e., like the Anthropophagi described in *Othello*, 1.3.158)
59 putter-out [. . .] **one** one who invests money or gambles on the risks of travel on the condition that the traveler who returns safely is to receive five times the amount deposited; hence, any traveler
60 Good warrant assurance
61 stand to fall to; take the risk
62 Although my last even if this were to be my last meal
63 best best part of life
64 s.d. harpy a fabulous monster with a woman's face and breasts and a vulture's body, supposed to be a minister of divine vengeance.   **quaint device** ingenious stage contrivance.   **the banquet vanishes** i.e., the food vanishes; the table remains until line 95
65–68 whom [. . .] **up you** you whom Destiny, controller of the sublunary world as its instrument, has caused the ever hungry sea to belch up

Where man doth not inhabit, you 'mongst men
Being most unfit to live. I have made you mad;
71 And even with suchlike valor men hang and drown
72 Their proper selves.

[*Alonso, Sebastian, and Antonio draw their swords.*]

You fools! I and my fellows
Are ministers of Fate. The elements
75 Of whom your swords are tempered may as well
76 Wound the loud winds, or with bemocked-at stabs
77 Kill the still-closing waters, as diminish
78 One dowl that's in my plume. My fellow ministers
79 Are like invulnerable. If you could hurt,
80 Your swords are now too massy for your strengths
And will not be uplifted. But remember—
For that's my business to you—that you three
From Milan did supplant good Prospero;
84 Exposed unto the sea, which hath requit it,
Him and his innocent child; for which foul deed
The powers, delaying, not forgetting, have
Incensed the seas and shores, yea, all the creatures,
Against your peace. Thee of thy son, Alonso,
They have bereft; and do pronounce by me
90 Ling'ring perdition, worse than any death
Can be at once, shall step by step attend
92 You and your ways; whose wraths to guard you from—
93 Which here, in this most desolate isle, else falls
94 Upon your heads—is nothing but heart's sorrow
95 And a clear life ensuing.

He vanishes in thunder; then, to soft music, enter
the shapes again, and dance, with mocks and mows,
and carrying out the table.

71 **suchlike valor** i.e., the reckless valor derived from madness
72 **proper** own
75 **whom** which.   **tempered** composed and hardened
76 **bemocked-at** scorned
77 **still-closing** always closing again when parted
78 **dowl** soft, fine feather
79 **like** likewise, similarly.   **If** even if
80 **massy** heavy
84 **requit** requited, avenged
90 **perdition** ruin, destruction
92 **whose** (Refers to the heavenly powers.)
93 **else** otherwise
94 **is nothing** there is no way
95 **clear** unspotted, innocent.   **s.d. mocks and mows** mocking gestures and grimaces

96 PROSPERO: Bravely the figure of this harpy hast thou
97   Performed, my Ariel; a grace it had devouring.
98   Of my instruction hast thou nothing bated
99   In what thou hadst to say. So, with good life
100   And observation strange, my meaner ministers
101   Their several kinds have done. My high charms work,
    And these mine enemies are all knit up
103   In their distractions. They now are in my power;
    And in these fits I leave them, while I visit
    Young Ferdinand, whom they suppose is drowned,
    And his and mine loved darling.

    [*Exit above.*]

107 GONZALO: I' the name of something holy, sir, why stand you
    In this strange stare?
109 ALONSO: O, it is monstrous, monstrous!
110   Methought the billows spoke and told me of it;
    The winds did sing it to me, and the thunder,
    That deep and dreadful organ pipe, pronounced
113   The name of Prosper; it did bass my trespass.
114   Therefor my son i' th' ooze is bedded; and
115   I'll seek him deeper than e'er plummet sounded,
    And with him there lie mudded.

    Exit.

SEBASTIAN: But one fiend at a time,
118   I'll fight their legions o'er.
ANTONIO: I'll be thy second.

    Exeunt [Sebastian and Antonio].

96 Bravely finely, dashingly
97 a grace [. . .] devouring i.e., you gracefully caused the banquet to disappear as if you had consumed it (with puns on *grace,* meaning "gracefulness" and "a blessing on the meal," and on *devouring,* meaning "a literal eating" and "an all-consuming or ravishing grace")
98 bated abated, omitted
99 So in the same fashion.   **good life** faithful reproduction
100 observation strange exceptional attention to detail.   **meaner** i.e., subordinate to Ariel
101 several kinds individual parts
103 distractions trancelike state
107 why (Gonzalo was not addressed in Ariel's speech to the *three men of sin,* line 65, and is not, as they are, in a maddened state; see lines 120–122.)
109 it i.e., my sin (also in line 110)
110 billows waves
113 bass my trespass proclaim my trespass like a bass note in music
114 Therefor in consequence of that
115 plummet a lead weight attached to a line for testing depth.   **sounded** probed, tested the depth of
118 o'er one after another

120   GONZALO: All three of them are desperate. Their great guilt,
     Like poison given to work a great time after,
122   Now 'gins to bite the spirits. I do beseech you,
     That are of suppler joints, follow them swiftly
124   And hinder them from what this ecstasy
     May now provoke them to.
    ADRIAN: Follow, I pray you.

Exeunt omnes.

4.1

Enter Prospero, Ferdinand, and Miranda.

PROSPERO: If I have too austerely punished you,
     Your compensation makes amends, for I
3   Have given you here a third of mine own life,
     Or that for which I live; who once again
5   I tender to thy hand. All thy vexations
     Were but my trials of thy love, and thou
7   Hast strangely stood the test. Here, afore heaven,
     I ratify this my rich gift. O Ferdinand,
9   Do not smile at me that I boast her off,
     For thou shalt find she will outstrip all praise
11   And make it halt behind her.
    FERDINAND: I do believe it
13   Against an oracle.
    PROSPERO: Then, as my gift and thine own acquisition
     Worthily purchased, take my daughter. But
     If thou dost break her virgin-knot before
17   All sanctimonious ceremonies may
     With full and holy rite be ministered,
19   No sweet aspersion shall the heavens let fall

---

120 desperate despairing and reckless
122 bite the spirits sap their vital powers through anguish
124 ecstasy mad frenzy
4.1 Location: Before Prospero's cell.
3 a third i.e., Miranda, into whose education Prospero has put a third of his life (?)
or who represents a large part of what he cares about, along with his dukedom and
his learned study (?)
5 tender offer
7 strangely extraordinarily
9 boast her off i.e., praise her so, or, perhaps an error for "boast of her"; the Folio reads
"boast her of"
11 halt limp
13 Against an oracle even if an oracle should declare otherwise
17 sanctimonious sacred
19 aspersion dew, shower

To make this contract grow; but barren hate,
Sour-eyed disdain, and discord shall bestrew
22 The union of your bed with weeds so loathly
That you shall hate it both. Therefore take heed,
24 As Hymen's lamps shall light you.

FERDINAND: As I hope
26 For quiet days, fair issue, and long life,
With such love as 'tis now, the murkiest den,
28 The most opportune place, the strong'st suggestion
29 Our worser genius can, shall never melt
30 Mine honor into lust, to take away
31 The edge of that day's celebration
32 When I shall think or Phoebus' steeds are foundered
Or Night kept chained below.

PROSPERO: Fairly spoke.
Sit then and talk with her. She is thine own.
[*Ferdinand and Miranda sit and talk together.*]
36 What, Ariel! My industrious servant, Ariel!

Enter Ariel.

ARIEL: What would my potent master? Here I am.
38 PROSPERO: Thou and thy meaner fellows your last service
Did worthily perform, and I must use you
40 In such another trick. Go bring the rabble,
O'er whom I give thee power, here to this place.
Incite them to quick motion, for I must
Bestow upon the eyes of this young couple
44 Some vanity of mine art. It is my promise,
And they expect it from me.
46 ARIEL: Presently?

22 weeds (in place of the flowers customarily strewn on the marriage bed)
24 As [. . .] you i.e., as you long for happiness and concord in your marriage. (Hymen was the Greek and Roman god of marriage; his symbolic torches, the wedding torches, were supposed to burn brightly for a happy marriage and smokily for a troubled one.)
26 issue offspring
28 suggestion temptation
29 worser genius evil genius, or, evil attendant spirit.   **can** is capable of
30 to so as to
31 edge keen enjoyment, sexual ardor
32 or either.   **foundered** broken down, made lame. (Ferdinand will wait impatiently for the bridal night.)
36 What now then
38 meaner fellows subordinates
40 trick device.   **rabble** band, i.e., the *meaner fellows* of line 38
44 vanity (1) illusion (2) trifle (3) desire for admiration, conceit
46 Presently immediately

47   PROSPERO: Ay, with a twink.
      ARIEL: Before you can say "Come" and "Go,"
            And breathe twice, and cry "So, so,"
            Each one, tripping on his toe,
51   Will be here with mop and mow.
            Do you love me, master? No?
      PROSPERO: Dearly, my delicate Ariel. Do not approach
            Till thou dost hear me call.
55   ARIEL: Well; I conceive.
          Exit.

56   PROSPERO: Look thou be true; do not give dalliance
            Too much the rein. The strongest oaths are straw
            To the fire i' the blood. Be more abstemious,
59   Or else good night your vow!
      FERDINAND: I warrant you, sir,
61   The white cold virgin snow upon my heart
62   Abates the ardor of my liver.
      PROSPERO: Well.
64   Now come, my Ariel! Bring a corollary,
65   Rather than want a spirit. Appear, and pertly!—
66   No tongue! All eyes! Be silent.   *Soft music.*

      Enter Iris.

67   IRIS: Ceres, most bounteous lady, thy rich leas
68   Of wheat, rye, barley, vetches, oats, and peas;
69   Thy turfy mountains, where live nibbling sheep,
70   And flat meads thatched with stover, them to keep;
71   Thy banks with pionèd and twillèd brims,

47 with a twink in the twinkling of an eye
51 mop and mow gestures and grimaces
55 conceive understand
56 true true to your promise
59 good night i.e., say good-bye to.   **warrant** guarantee
61 The white [. . .] heart i.e., the ideal of chastity and consciousness of Miranda's chaste innocence enshrined in my heart
62 liver (as the presumed seat of the passions)
64 corollary surplus, extra supply
65 want lack.   **pertly** briskly
66 No tongue all the beholders are to be silent (lest the spirits vanish).   **s.d. Iris** goddess of the rainbow and Juno's messenger
67 Ceres goddess of the generative power of nature.   **leas** meadows
68 vetches plants for forage, fodder
70 meads meadows.   **stover** winter fodder for cattle
71 pionèd and twillèd undercut by the swift current and protected by roots and branches that tangle to form a barricade

72 Which spongy April at thy hest betrims
73 To make cold nymphs chaste crowns; and thy broom groves,
74 Whose shadow the dismissèd bachelor loves,
75 Being lass-lorn; thy poll-clipped vineyard;
76 And thy sea marge, sterile and rocky hard,
77 Where thou thyself dost air: the queen o' the sky,
78 Whose watery arch and messenger am I,
79 Bids thee leave these, and with her sovereign grace,

Juno descends [slowly in her car].

Here on this grass plot, in this very place,
81 To come and sport. Her peacocks fly amain.
82 Approach, rich Ceres, her to entertain.

Enter Ceres.

CERES: Hail, many-colored messenger, that ne'er
Dost disobey the wife of Jupiter,
85 Who with thy saffron wings upon my flowers
Diffusest honeydrops, refreshing showers,
87 And with each end of thy blue bow dost crown
88 My bosky acres and my unshrubbed down,
89 Rich scarf to my proud earth. Why hath thy queen
Summoned me hither to this short-grassed green?
IRIS: A contract of true love to celebrate,
92 And some donation freely to estate
On the blest lovers.
CERES: Tell me, heavenly bow,
95 If Venus or her son, as thou dost know,
Do now attend the Queen? Since they did plot

72 **spongy** wet.   **hest** command
73 **broom groves** clumps of broom, gorse, yellow-flowered shrub
74 **dismissèd bachelor** rejected male lover
75 **poll-clipped** pruned, lopped at the top, or *pole-clipped,* "hedged in with poles"
76 **sea marge** shore
77 **thou [. . .] air** you take the air, go for walks.   **queen o' the sky** i.e., Juno
78 **watery arch** rainbow
79 **s.d. Juno descends** i.e., starts her descent from the "heavens" above the stage (?)
81 **peacocks** birds sacred to Juno and used to pull her chariot.   **amain** with full speed
82 **entertain** receive
85 **saffron** yellow
87 **bow** i.e., rainbow
88 **bosky** wooded.   **unshrubbed down** open upland
89 **scarf** (The rainbow is like a colored silk band adorning the earth.)
92 **estate** bestow
95 **son** i.e., Cupid.   **as** as far as

97   The means that dusky Dis my daughter got,
98   Her and her blind boy's scandaled company
      I have forsworn.
100   IRIS: Of her society
101   Be not afraid. I met her deity
102   Cutting the clouds towards Paphos, and her son
103   Dove-drawn with her. Here thought they to have done
104   Some wanton charm upon this man and maid,
      Whose vows are that no bed-right shall be paid
      Till Hymen's torch be lighted; but in vain.
107   Mars's hot minion is returned again;
108   Her waspish-headed son has broke his arrows,
109   Swears he will shoot no more, but play with sparrows
110   And be a boy right out.

      [*Juno alights.*]

111   CERES: Highest Queen of state,
112   Great Juno, comes; I know her by her gait.
113   JUNO: How does my bounteous sister? Go with me
      To bless this twain, that they may prosperous be,
115   And honored in their issue.   *They sing:*
      JUNO: Honor, riches, marriage blessing,
               Long continuance, and increasing,
118   Hourly joys be still upon you!
               Juno sings her blessings on you.
120   CERES: Earth's increase, foison plenty,
121   Barns and garners never empty,
               Vines with clustering bunches growing,
               Plants with goodly burden bowing;

---

97 that whereby.   **dusky** dark.   **Dis** [. . .] **got** (Pluto, or *Dis,* god of the infernal regions, carried off Proserpina, daughter of Ceres, to be his bride in Hades.)
98 her i.e., Venus's.   **scandaled** scandalous
100 society company
101 her deity i.e., Her Highness
102 Paphos place on the island of Cyprus, sacred to Venus
103 Dove-drawn (Venus's chariot was drawn by doves.)   **done** placed
104 wanton charm lustful spell
107 Mars's hot minion i.e., Venus, the beloved of Mars.   **returned** i.e., returned to Paphos
108 waspish-headed hotheaded, peevish
109 sparrows (Supposed lustful, and sacred to Venus.)
110 right out outright
111 Highest [. . .] **state** most majestic Queen
112 gait i.e., majestic bearing
113 sister i.e., fellow goddess (?)
115 issue offspring
118 still always
120 foison plenty plentiful harvest
121 garners granaries

Spring come to you at the farthest
125 In the very end of harvest!
Scarcity and want shall shun you;
Ceres' blessing so is on you.
FERDINAND: This is a most majestic vision, and
129 Harmonious charmingly. May I be bold
To think these spirits?
PROSPERO: Spirits, which by mine art
I have from their confines called to enact
My present fancies.
FERDINAND: Let me live here ever!
135 So rare a wondered father and a wife
Makes this place Paradise.

Juno and Ceres whisper, and send Iris on employment.

PROSPERO: Sweet now, silence!
Juno and Ceres whisper seriously;
There's something else to do. Hush and be mute,
Or else our spell is marred.
141 IRIS [*calling offstage*]: You nymphs, called naiads, of the
windring brooks,
142 With your sedged crowns and ever-harmless looks,
143 Leave your crisp channels, and on this green land
Answer your summons; Juno does command.
145 Come, temperate nymphs, and help to celebrate
A contract of true love. Be not too late.

Enter certain nymphs.

147 You sunburned sicklemen, of August weary,
148 Come hither from the furrow and be merry.
Make holiday; your rye-straw hats put on,
150 And these fresh nymphs encounter every one
151 In country footing.

*Enter certain reapers, properly habited. They join with the nymphs in a graceful
dance, towards the end whereof Prospero starts suddenly, and speaks; after
which, to a strange, hollow, and confused noise, they heavily vanish.*

---

125 In [. . .] harvest i.e., with no winter in between
129 charmingly enchantingly
135 wondered wonder-performing, wondrous
141 naiads nymphs of springs, rivers, or lakes.   **windring** wandering, winding (?)
142 sedged made of reeds.   **ever-harmless** ever innocent
143 crisp curled, rippled
145 temperate chaste
147 sicklemen harvesters, field workers who cut down grain and grass.   **of August weary**
i.e., weary of the hard work of the harvest
148 furrow i.e., plowed fields
150 encounter join
151 country footing country dancing.   **s.d. properly** suitably.   **heavily** slowly, dejectedly

PROSPERO [*aside*]: I had forgot that foul conspiracy
    Of the beast Caliban and his confederates
    Against my life. The minute of their plot
155   Is almost come. [*To the Spirits.*] Well done! Avoid; no more!
FERDINAND [*to Miranda*]: This is strange. Your father's in some passion
157   That works him strongly.
MIRANDA: Never till this day
    Saw I him touched with anger so distempered.
160 PROSPERO: You do look, my son, in a moved sort,
    As if you were dismayed. Be cheerful, sir.
162   Our revels now are ended. These our actors,
    As I foretold you, were all spirits and
    Are melted into air, into thin air;
165   And, like the baseless fabric of this vision,
    The cloud-capped towers, the gorgeous palaces,
167   The solemn temples, the great globe itself,
168   Yea, all which it inherit, shall dissolve,
    And, like this insubstantial pageant faded,
170   Leave not a rack behind. We are such stuff
171   As dreams are made on, and our little life
172   Is rounded with a sleep. Sir, I am vexed.
    Bear with my weakness. My old brain is troubled.
174   Be not disturbed with my infirmity.
175   If you be pleased, retire into my cell
    And there repose. A turn or two I'll walk
177   To still my beating mind.
FERDINAND, MIRANDA: We wish your peace.

Exeunt [Ferdinand and Miranda].

179 PROSPERO: Come with a thought! I thank thee, Ariel. Come.

Enter Ariel.

155 **Avoid** withdraw
157 **works** affects, agitates
160 **moved sort** troubled state, condition
162 **revels** entertainment, pageant
165 **baseless fabric** unsubstantial theatrical edifice or contrivance
167 **great globe** (With a glance at the Globe Theatre.)
168 **which it inherit** who subsequently occupy it
170 **rack** wisp of cloud
171 **on** of
172 **rounded** surrounded (before birth and after death), or crowned, rounded off
174 **with** by
175 **retire** withdraw, go
177 **beating** agitated
179 **with a thought** i.e., on the instant, or, summoned by my thought, no sooner
thought of than here

180 ARIEL: Thy thoughts I cleave to. What's thy pleasure?
PROSPERO: Spirit,
    We must prepare to meet with Caliban.
183 ARIEL: Ay, my commander. When I presented Ceres,
    I thought to have told thee of it, but I feared
    Lest I might anger thee.
PROSPERO: Say again, where didst thou leave these varlets?
ARIEL: I told you, sir, they were red-hot with drinking;
    So full of valor that they smote the air
    For breathing in their faces, beat the ground
190   For kissing of their feet; yet always bending
    Towards their project. Then I beat my tabor,
192   At which, like unbacked colts, they pricked their ears,
193   Advanced their eyelids, lifted up their noses
194   As they smelt music. So I charmed their ears
195   That calflike they my lowing followed through
196   Toothed briers, sharp furzes, pricking gorse, and thorns,
    Which entered their frail shins. At last I left them
198   I' the filthy-mantled pool beyond your cell,
    There dancing up to the chins, that the foul lake
200   O'erstunk their feet.
PROSPERO: This was well done, my bird.
    Thy shape invisible retain thou still.
203   The trumpery in my house, go bring it hither,
204   For stale to catch these thieves.
ARIEL: I go, I go.   *Exit.*
PROSPERO: A devil, a born devil, on whose nature
    Nurture can never stick; on whom my pains,
    Humanely taken, all, all lost, quite lost!
    And as with age his body uglier grows,
210   So his mind cankers. I will plague them all,
    Even to roaring.

---

180 cleave cling, adhere
183 presented acted the part of, or, introduced
190 bending aiming
192 unbacked unbroken, unridden
193 Advanced lifted up
194 As as if
195 lowing mooing
196 furzes, gorse prickly shrubs
198 filthy-mantled covered with a slimy coating
200 O'erstunk smelled worse than, or, caused to stink terribly
203 trumpery cheap goods, the *glistering apparel* mentioned in the following stage direction
204 stale (1) decoy (2) out-of-fashion garments (with possible further suggestions of "horse piss," as in line 218, and "steal," pronounced like *stale*). *For stale* could also mean "fit for a prostitute."
210 cankers festers, grows malignant

Enter Ariel, loaden with glistering apparel, etc.

212   Come, hang them on this line.

[*Ariel hangs up the showy finery; Prospero and Ariel remain, invisible.*] *Enter Caliban, Stephano, and Trinculo, all wet.*

CALIBAN: Pray you, tread softly, that the blind mole may
Not hear a foot fall. We now are near his cell.
STEPHANO: Monster, your fairy, which you say is a
harmless fairy, has done little better than played
217   the jack with us.
TRINCULO: Monster, I do smell all horse piss, at which
my nose is in great indignation.
STEPHANO: So is mine. Do you hear, monster? If I
should take a displeasure against you, look you—
TRINCULO: Thou wert but a lost monster.
CALIBAN: Good my lord, give me thy favor still.
Be patient, for the prize I'll bring thee to
225   Shall hoodwink this mischance. Therefore speak softly.
All's hushed as midnight yet.
TRINCULO: Ay, but to lose our bottles in the pool—
STEPHANO: There is not only disgrace and dishonor in
that, monster, but an infinite loss.
TRINCULO: That's more to me than my wetting. Yet this
is your harmless fairy, monster!
232   STEPHANO: I will fetch off my bottle, though I be o'er
233   ears for my labor.
CALIBAN: Prithee, my king, be quiet. Seest thou here,
This is the mouth o' the cell. No noise, and enter.
Do that good mischief which may make this island
Thine own forever, and I thy Caliban
For aye thy footlicker.
STEPHANO: Give me thy hand. I do begin to have bloody thoughts.
240   TRINCULO [*seeing the finery*]. O King Stephano! O peer!
O worthy Stephano! Look what a wardrobe here
is for thee!

---

212 line lime tree or linden.   **s.d. Prospero and Ariel remain** (The staging is uncertain.
They may instead exit here and return with the spirits at line 274.)
217 jack (1) knave (2) will-o'-the-wisp
225 hoodwink this mischance (Misfortune is to be prevented from doing further harm by
being hooded like a hawk and also put out of remembrance.)
232–233 o'er ears i.e., totally submerged and perhaps drowned
240 King [. . .] peer (Alludes to the old ballad beginning, "King Stephen was a worthy
peer.")

CALIBAN: Let it alone, thou fool, it is but trash.

TRINCULO: Oho, monster! We know what belongs to a

245 frippery. O King Stephano! [*He puts on a gown.*]

246 STEPHANO: Put off that gown, Trinculo. By this hand,
I'll have that gown.

TRINCULO: Thy Grace shall have it.

249 CALIBAN: The dropsy drown this fool! What do you mean

250 To dote thus on such luggage? Let 't alone
And do the murder first. If he awake,

252 From toe to crown he'll fill our skins with pinches,
Make us strange stuff.

254 STEPHANO: Be you quiet, monster.—Mistress line, is not

255 this my jerkin? [*He takes it down.*] Now is the jerkin

256 under the line. Now, jerkin, you are like to lose your

257 hair and prove a bald jerkin.

258 TRINCULO: Do, do! We steal by line and level, an 't like
Your Grace.

STEPHANO: I thank thee for that jest. Here's a garment
for 't. [*He gives a garment.*] Wit shall not go unrewarded
while I am king of this country. "Steal by line and

263 level" is an excellent pass of pate. There's another
garment for 't.

265 TRINCULO: Monster, come, put some lime upon your
fingers, and away with the rest.

CALIBAN: I will have none on 't. We shall lose our time,

268 And all be turned to barnacles, or to apes

269 With foreheads villainous low.

245 **frippery** place where cast-off clothes are sold
246 **Put off** put down, or, take off
249 **dropsy** disease characterized by the accumulation of fluid in the connective tissue of the body
250 **luggage** cumbersome trash
252 **crown** head
254 **Mistress line** (Addressed to the linden or lime tree upon which, at line 212, Ariel hung the *glistering apparel.*)
255 **jerkin** jacket made of leather
256 **under the line** under the lime tree (with punning sense of being south of the equinoctial line or equator; sailors on long voyages to the southern regions were popularly supposed to lose their hair from scurvy or other diseases. Stephano also quibbles bawdily on losing hair through syphilis, and in *Mistress* and *jerkin.*)   **like** likely.
257 **bald** (1) hairless, napless (2) meager
258 **Do, do** i.e., bravo. (Said in response to the jesting or to the taking of the jerkin, or both.)   **by line and level** i.e., by means of plumb line and carpenter's level, methodically (with pun on *line*, "lime tree," line 256, and *steal*, pronounced like *stale*, i.e., prostitute, continuing Stephano's bawdy quibble).   **an 't like** if it please
263 **pass of pate** sally of wit. (The metaphor is from fencing.)
265 **lime** birdlime, sticky substance (to give Caliban sticky fingers)
268 **barnacles** barnacle geese, formerly supposed to be hatched from barnacles attached to trees or to rotting timber; here, evidently used, like *apes,* as types of simpletons
269 **villainous** miserably

270 STEPHANO: Monster, lay to your fingers. Help to bear
271   this away where my hogshead of wine is, or I'll turn
272   you out of my kingdom. Go to, carry this.
    TRINCULO: And this.
    STEPHANO: Ay, and this.
            [*They load Caliban with more and more garments.*]

    A noise of hunters heard. Enter divers spirits, in shape of dogs
    and hounds, hunting them about, Prospero and Ariel setting
    them on.

    PROSPERO: Hey, Mountain, hey!
    ARIEL: Silver! There it goes, Silver!
    PROSPERO: Fury, Fury! There, Tyrant, there! Hark! Hark!
         [*Caliban, Stephano, and Trinculo are driven out.*]
    Go, charge my goblins that they grind their joints
279   With dry convulsions, shorten up their sinews
280   With agèd cramps, and more pinch-spotted make them
281   Than pard or cat o' mountain.
    ARIEL: Hark, they roar!
283   PROSPERO: Let them be hunted soundly. At this hour
    Lies at my mercy all mine enemies.
    Shortly shall all my labors end, and thou
286   Shalt have the air at freedom. For a little
    Follow, and do me service.

    Exeunt.

5.1

    Enter Prospero in his magic robes, [with his staff,] and Ariel.

    PROSPERO: Now does my project gather to a head.
2   My charms crack not, my spirits obey, and Time
3   Goes upright with his carriage. How's the day?

---

270 lay to start using.   **this** i.e., the *glistering apparel.*
271 hogshead large cask
272 Go to (An expression of exhortation or remonstrance.)
279 dry associated with age, arthritic (?)   **convulsions** cramps
280 agèd characteristic of old age
281 pard panther or leopard.   **cat o' mountain** wildcat
283 soundly thoroughly (and suggesting the sounds of the hunt)
286 little little while longer
5.1 Location: Before Prospero's cell.
2 crack collapse, fail. (The metaphor is probably alchemical, as in *project* and *gather to a head,* line 1.)
3 his carriage its burden. (Time is no longer heavily burdened and so can go *upright,* "standing straight and unimpeded.")

4 ARIEL: On the sixth hour, at which time, my lord,
    You said our work should cease.
PROSPERO: I did say so,
    When first I raised the tempest. Say, my spirit,
    How fares the King and 's followers?
ARIEL: Confined together
    In the same fashion as you gave in charge,
    Just as you left them; all prisoners, sir,
12   In the line grove which weather-fends your cell.
13   They cannot budge till your release. The King,
14   His brother, and yours abide all three distracted,
    And the remainder mourning over them,
    Brim full of sorrow and dismay; but chiefly
    Him that you termed, sir, the good old lord, Gonzalo.
    His tears runs down his beard like winter's drops
19   From eaves of reeds. Your charm so strongly works 'em
20   That if you now beheld them your affections
    Would become tender.
PROSPERO: Dost thou think so, spirit?
23 ARIEL: Mine would, sir, were I human.
PROSPERO: And mine shall.
25   Hast thou, which art but air, a touch, a feeling
    Of their afflictions, and shall not myself,
27   One of their kind, that relish all as sharply
28   Passion as they, be kindlier moved than thou art?
    Though with their high wrongs I am struck to the quick,
    Yet with my nobler reason 'gainst my fury
31   Do I take part. The rarer action is
    In virtue than in vengeance. They being penitent,
    The sole drift of my purpose doth extend
    Not a frown further. Go release them, Ariel.
    My charms I'll break, their senses I'll restore,
    And they shall be themselves.
ARIEL: I'll fetch them, sir.
                          Exit.

---

4 On approaching
12 line grove grove of lime trees. **weather-fends** protects from the weather
13 your release you release them
14 distracted out of their wits
19 eaves of reeds thatched roofs
20 affections disposition, feelings
23 human (Spelled *humane* in the Folio and encompassing both senses.)
25 touch sense, apprehension
27–28 that [. . .] they I who experience human passions as acutely as they
28 kindlier (1) more sympathetically (2) more naturally, humanly
31 rarer nobler

[Prospero traces a charmed circle with his staff.]

38 PROSPERO: Ye elves of hills, brooks, standing lakes, and groves,
    And ye that on the sands with printless foot
    Do chase the ebbing Neptune, and do fly him
41   When he comes back; you demi-puppets that
42   By moonshine do the green sour ringlets make,
    Whereof the ewe not bites; and you whose pastime
44   Is to make midnight mushrooms, that rejoice
45   To hear the solemn curfew; by whose aid,
46   Weak masters though ye be, I have bedimmed
    The noontide sun, called forth the mutinous winds,
48   And twixt the green sea and the azured vault
49   Set roaring war; to the dread rattling thunder
50   Have I given fire, and rifted Jove's stout oak
51   With his own bolt; the strong-based promontory
52   Have I made shake, and by the spurs plucked up
    The pine and cedar; graves at my command
    Have waked their sleepers, oped, and let 'em forth
55   By my so potent art. But this rough magic
56   I here abjure, and when I have required
    Some heavenly music—which even now I do—
58   To work mine end upon their senses that
59   This airy charm is for, I'll break my staff,
    Bury it certain fathoms in the earth,
    And deeper than did ever plummet sound
    I'll drown my book.   *Solemn music.*

Here enters Ariel before; then Alonso, with a frantic gesture,
attended by Gonzalo; Sebastian and Antonio in like

38–55 Ye [. . .] art (This famous passage is an embellished paraphrase of Golding's translation of Ovid's *Metamorphoses*, 7.197–219.)
41 demi-puppets puppets of half size, i.e., elves and fairies
42 green sour ringlets fairy rings, circles in grass (actually produced by mushrooms)
44 midnight mushrooms mushrooms appearing overnight
45 curfew evening bell, usually rung at nine o'clock, ushering in the time when spirits are abroad
46 Weak masters i.e., subordinate spirits, as in 4.1.38 (?)
48 the azured vault i.e., the sky
49–50 to [. . .] fire I have discharged the dread rattling thunderbolt
50 rifted riven, split.   **oak** a tree that was sacred to Jove
51 bolt lightning bolt
52 spurs roots
55 rough violent
56 required requested
58 their senses that the senses of those whom
59 airy charm i.e., music

manner, attended by Adrian and Francisco. They all enter
the circle which Prospero had made, and there stand
charmed; which Prospero observing, speaks:

63 [*To Alonso.*] A solemn air, and the best comforter
64 To an unsettled fancy, cure thy brains,
65 Now useless, boiled within thy skull!
     [*To Sebastian and Antonio.*] There stand,
     For you are spell-stopped.—
     Holy Gonzalo, honorable man,
69 Mine eyes, e'en sociable to the show of thine,
70 Fall fellowly drops. [*Aside.*] The charm dissolves apace,
     And as the morning steals upon the night,
     Melting the darkness, so their rising senses
73 Begin to chase the ignorant fumes that mantle
74 Their clearer reason.—O good Gonzalo,
     My true preserver, and a loyal sir
76 To him thou follow'st! I will pay thy graces
77 Home both in word and deed.—Most cruelly
     Didst thou, Alonso, use me and my daughter.
79 Thy brother was a furtherer in the act.—
80 Thou art pinched for 't now, Sebastian. [*To Antonio.*] Flesh and blood,
     You, brother mine, that entertained ambition,
82 Expelled remorse and nature, whom, with Sebastian,
     Whose inward pinches therefore are most strong,
     Would here have killed your king, I do forgive thee,
     Unnatural though thou art.—Their understanding
     Begins to swell, and the approaching tide
87 Will shortly fill the reasonable shore
     That now lies foul and muddy. Not one of them
     That yet looks on me, or would know me.—Ariel,
     Fetch me the hat and rapier in my cell.

     [*Ariel goes to the cell and returns immediately.*]

63 **air** song.   **and** i.e., which is
64 **fancy** imagination
65 **boiled** i.e., extremely agitated
69 **sociable** sympathetic.   **show** appearance
70 **Fall** let fall
73 **ignorant fumes** fumes that render them incapable of comprehension.   **mantle** envelop
74 **clearer** growing clearer
76 **pay thy graces** requite your favors and virtues
77 **Home** fully
79 **furtherer** accomplice
80 **pinched** punished, afflicted
82 **remorse** pity.   **nature** natural feeling.   **whom** i.e., who
87 **reasonable shore** shores of reason, i.e., minds. (Their reason returns, like the incoming tide.)

91   I will discase me and myself present
92   As I was sometime Milan. Quickly, spirit!
     Thou shalt ere long be free.

Ariel sings and helps to attire him.

ARIEL:
           Where the bee sucks, there suck I.
96   In a cowslip's bell I lie;
           There I couch when owls do cry.
           On the bat's back I do fly
98   After summer merrily.
           Merrily, merrily shall I live now
           Under the blossom that hangs on the bough.
PROSPERO: Why, that's my dainty Ariel! I shall miss thee,
102 But yet thou shalt have freedom. So, so, so.
     To the King's ship, invisible as thou art!
     There shalt thou find the mariners asleep
     Under the hatches. The Master and the Boatswain
     Being awake, enforce them to this place,
107 And presently, I prithee.
ARIEL: I drink the air before me and return
109 Or ere your pulse twice beat.

     Exit.

GONZALO: All torment, trouble, wonder, and amazement
     Inhabits here. Some heavenly power guide us
112 Out of this fearful country!
PROSPERO: Behold, sir King,
     The wrongèd Duke of Milan, Prospero.
     For more assurance that a living prince
     Does now speak to thee, I embrace thy body;
     And to thee and thy company I bid
     A hearty welcome.   [*Embracing him.*]
ALONSO: Whe'er thou be'st he or no,
120 Or some enchanted trifle to abuse me,

---

91 discase disrobe
92 As [. . .] Milan in my former appearance as Duke of Milan
96 couch lie
98 After i.e., pursuing
102 So, so, so (Expresses approval of Ariel's help as valet.)
107 presently immediately
109 Or ere before
112 fearful frightening
120 trifle trick of magic.   **abuse** deceive

121 As late I have been, I not know. Thy pulse
Beats as of flesh and blood; and, since I saw thee,
Th' affliction of my mind amends, with which
124 I fear a madness held me. This must crave—
125 An if this be at all—a most strange story.
126 Thy dukedom I resign, and do entreat
127 Thou pardon me my wrongs. But how should Prospero
Be living, and be here?
PROSPERO [*to Gonzalo*]:   First, noble friend,
130 Let me embrace thine age, whose honor cannot
Be measured or confined.   [*Embracing him.*]
GONZALO: Whether this be
Or be not, I'll not swear.
PROSPERO: You do yet taste
135 Some subtleties o' th' isle, that will not let you
Believe things certain. Welcome, my friends all!
[*Aside to Sebastian and Antonio.*]
137 But you, my brace of lords, were I so minded,
I here could pluck His Highness' frown upon you
139 And justify you traitors. At this time
I will tell no tales.
SEBASTIAN: The devil speaks in him.
PROSPERO: No.
[*To Antonio.*] For you, most wicked sir, whom to call brother
Would even infect my mouth, I do forgive
Thy rankest fault—all of them; and require
146 My dukedom of thee, which perforce I know
Thou must restore.
ALONSO: If thou be'st Prospero,
Give us particulars of thy preservation,
150 How thou hast met us here, whom three hours since

---

121 **late** lately
124 **crave** require
125 **An [. . .] all** if this is actually happening. **story** i.e., explanation
126 **Thy [. . .] resign** (Alonso made arrangement with Antonio at the time of Prospero's
banishment for Milan to pay tribute to Naples; see 1.2.130–47.)
127 **wrongs** wrongdoings
130 **thine age** your venerable self
135 **subtleties** illusions, magical powers (playing on the idea of "pastries, concoctions")
137 **brace** pair
139 **justify you** prove you to be
146 **perforce** necessarily
150 **whom** i.e., who

Were wrecked upon this shore; where I have lost—
How sharp the point of this remembrance is!—
My dear son Ferdinand.

154 PROSPERO: I am woe for 't, sir.

ALONSO: Irreparable is the loss, and Patience
Says it is past her cure.

PROSPERO: I rather think

158 You have not sought her help, of whose soft grace

159 For the like loss I have her sovereign aid
And rest myself content.

ALONSO: You the like loss?

162 PROSPERO: As great to me as late, and supportable

163 To make the dear loss, have I means much weaker
Than you may call to comfort you; for I
Have lost my daughter.

ALONSO: A daughter?
O heavens, that they were living both in Naples,

168 The king and queen there! That they were, I wish

169 Myself were mudded in that oozy bed
Where my son lies. When did you lose your daughter?

PROSPERO: In this last tempest. I perceive these lords

172 At this encounter do so much admire

173 That they devour their reason and scarce think
Their eyes do offices of truth, their words

175 Are natural breath. But, howsoever you have
Been jostled from your senses, know for certain
That I am Prospero and that very duke

178 Which was thrust forth of Milan, who most strangely
Upon this shore, where you were wrecked, was landed
To be the lord on 't. No more yet of this,

181 For 'tis a chronicle of day by day,
Not a relation for a breakfast nor

154 woe sorry
158 of [. . .] grace by whose mercy
159 sovereign efficacious
162 late recent
162–163 supportable [. . .] have I to make the deeply felt loss bearable, I have
168 That so that
169 mudded buried in the mud
172 admire wonder
173 devour their reason i.e., are openmouthed, dumbfounded
173–175 scarce [. . .] breath scarcely believe that their eyes inform them accurately as to what they see or that their words are naturally spoken
178 of from
181 of day by day requiring days to tell

Befitting this first meeting. Welcome, sir.
This cell's my court. Here have I few attendants,
185 And subjects none abroad. Pray you, look in.
My dukedom since you have given me again,
187 I will requite you with as good a thing,
At least bring forth a wonder to content ye
189 As much as me my dukedom.

Here Prospero discovers Ferdinand and Miranda,
playing at chess.

190 MIRANDA: Sweet lord, you play me false.
FERDINAND: No, my dearest love,
I would not for the world.
193 MIRANDA: Yes, for a score of kingdoms you should wrangle,
194 And I would call it fair play.
ALONSO: If this prove
196 A vision of the island, one dear son
Shall I twice lose.
SEBASTIAN: A most high miracle!
FERDINAND [*approaching his father*]: Though the seas threaten,
they are merciful;
I have cursed them without cause. [*He kneels.*]
ALONSO: Now all the blessings
202 Of a glad father compass thee about!
Arise, and say how thou cam'st here. [*Ferdinand rises.*]
MIRANDA: O, wonder!
How many goodly creatures are there here!
206 How beauteous mankind is! O brave new world
That has such people in 't!
PROSPERO: 'Tis new to thee.
ALONSO: What is this maid with whom thou wast at play?
210 Your eld'st acquaintance cannot be three hours.

---

185 abroad away from here, anywhere else
187 requite repay
189 s.d. discovers i.e., by opening a curtain, presumably rearstage
190 play me false i.e., press your advantage
193–194 Yes [. . .] play i.e., yes, even if we were playing for twenty kingdoms, something less than the whole world, you would still press your advantage against me, and I would lovingly let you do it as though it were fair play, or, if you were to play not just for stakes but literally for kingdoms, my complaint would be out of order in that your "wrangling" would be proper
196 vision illusion
202 compass encompass, embrace
206 brave splendid, gorgeously appareled, handsome
210 eld'st longest

Is she the goddess that hath severed us,
And brought us thus together?

FERDINAND: Sir, she is mortal;
But by immortal Providence she's mine.
I chose her when I could not ask my father
For his advice, nor thought I had one. She
Is daughter to this famous Duke of Milan,
Of whom so often I have heard renown,
But never saw before; of whom I have
Received a second life; and second father
This lady makes him to me.

ALONSO: I am hers.
But O, how oddly will it sound that I
Must ask my child forgiveness!

PROSPERO: There, sir, stop.
Let us not burden our remembrances with
227   A heaviness that's gone.

GONZALO: I have inly wept,
Or should have spoke ere this. Look down, you gods,
And on this couple drop a blessèd crown!
231   For it is you that have chalked forth the way
Which brought us hither.

ALONSO: I say amen, Gonzalo!
234   GONZALO: Was Milan thrust from Milan, that his issue
Should become kings of Naples? O, rejoice
Beyond a common joy, and set it down
With gold on lasting pillars: In one voyage
Did Claribel her husband find at Tunis,
And Ferdinand, her brother, found a wife
Where he himself was lost; Prospero his dukedom
241   In a poor isle; and all of us ourselves
242   When no man was his own.

ALONSO [*to Ferdinand and Miranda*]: Give me your hands.
244   Let grief and sorrow still embrace his heart
245   That doth not wish you joy!

227 **heaviness** sadness. **inly** inwardly
231 **chalked** [. . .] **way** marked as with a piece of chalk the pathway
234 **Was Milan** was the Duke of Milan
241–42 **all** [. . .] **own** all of us have found ourselves and our sanity when we all had lost our senses
244 **still** always. **his** that person's
245 **That** who

GONZALO: Be it so! Amen!

*Enter Ariel, with the Master and Boatswain
amazedly following.*

O, look, sir, look, sir! Here is more of us.
I prophesied, if a gallows were on land,
249 This fellow could not drown.—Now, blasphemy,
250 That swear'st grace o'erboard, not an oath on shore?
Hast thou no mouth by land? What is the news?
BOATSWAIN: The best news is that we have safely found
Our King and company; the next, our ship—
254 Which, but three glasses since, we gave out split—
255 Is tight and yare and bravely rigged as when
We first put out to sea.
ARIEL [*aside to Prospero*]: Sir, all this service
Have I done since I went.
259 PROSPERO [*aside to Ariel*]: My tricksy spirit!
260 ALONSO: These are not natural events; they strengthen
From strange to stranger. Say, how came you hither?
BOATSWAIN: If I did think, sir, I were well awake,
263 I'd strive to tell you. We were dead of sleep,
And—how we know not—all clapped under hatches,
265 Where but even now, with strange and several noises
Of roaring, shrieking, howling, jingling chains,
And more diversity of sounds, all horrible,
We were awaked; straightway at liberty;
Where we, in all her trim, freshly beheld
Our royal, good, and gallant ship, our Master
271 Cap'ring to eye her. On a trice, so please you,
272 Even in a dream, were we divided from them
273 And were brought moping hither.

---

249 **blasphemy** i.e., blasphemer
250 **That swear'st grace o'erboard** i.e., you who banish heavenly grace from the ship by
your blasphemies.   **not an oath** aren't you going to swear an oath
254 **glasses** i.e., hours.   **gave out** reported, professed to be
255 **yare** ready.   **bravely** splendidly
259 **tricksy** ingenious, sportive
260 **strengthen** increase
263 **dead of sleep** deep in sleep
265 **several** diverse
271 **Cap'ring to eye** dancing for joy to see.   **On a trice** in an instant
272 **them** i.e., the other crew members
273 **moping** in a daze

ARIEL [*aside to Prospero*]:   Was 't well done?

PROSPERO [*aside to Ariel*]: Bravely, my diligence. Thou shalt be free.

ALONSO: This is as strange a maze as e'er men trod,

  And there is in this business more than nature

278 Was ever conduct of. Some oracle

  Must rectify our knowledge.

PROSPERO: Sir, my liege,

281 Do not infest your mind with beating on

282 The strangeness of this business. At picked leisure,

283 Which shall be shortly, single I'll resolve you,

284 Which to you shall seem probable, of every

285 These happened accidents; till when, be cheerful

286 And think of each thing well. [*Aside to Ariel.*] Come hither, spirit.

  Set Caliban and his companions free.

  Untie the spell. [*Exit Ariel.*] How fares my gracious sir?

  There are yet missing of your company

290 Some few odd lads that you remember not.

Enter Ariel, driving in Caliban, Stephano, and Trinculo,
in their stolen apparel.

291 STEPHANO: Every man shift for all the rest, and let no

  man take care for himself; for all is but fortune.

293 Coragio, bully monster, coragio!

294 TRINCULO: If these be true spies which I wear in my

  head, here's a goodly sight.

296 CALIBAN: O Setebos, these be brave spirits indeed!

297 How fine my master is! I am afraid

  He will chastise me.

SEBASTIAN: Ha, ha!

  What things are these, my lord Antonio?

278 **conduct** guide
281 **infest** harass, disturb.   **beating on** worrying about
282 **picked** chosen, convenient
283 **single** privately, by my own human powers.   **resolve** satisfy, explain to
284 **probable** plausible
284–285 **of every These** about every one of these
285 **accidents** occurrences
286 **well** favorably
290 **odd** unaccounted for
291 **shift** provide.   **for all the rest** (Stephano drunkenly gets wrong the saying "Every man for himself.")
293 **Coragio** courage.   **bully monster** gallant monster. (Ironical.)
294 **true spies** accurate observers (i.e., sharp eyes)
296 **brave** handsome
297 **fine** splendidly attired

Will money buy 'em?

ANTONIO: Very like. One of them

Is a plain fish, and no doubt marketable.

304 PROSPERO: Mark but the badges of these men, my lords,

305   Then say if they be true. This misshapen knave,

His mother was a witch, and one so strong

That could control the moon, make flows and ebbs,

308   And deal in her command without her power.

These three have robbed me, and this demidevil—

310   For he's a bastard one—had plotted with them

To take my life. Two of these fellows you

312   Must know and own. This thing of darkness I

Acknowledge mine.

CALIBAN: I shall be pinched to death.

ALONSO: Is not this Stephano, my drunken butler?

SEBASTIAN: He is drunk now. Where had he wine?

317 ALONSO: And Trinculo is reeling ripe. Where should they

318   Find this grand liquor that hath gilded 'em?

319   [*To Trinculo.*] How cam'st thou in this pickle?

TRINCULO: I have been in such a pickle since I saw you

last that, I fear me, will never out of my bones.

322   I shall not fear flyblowing.

SEBASTIAN: Why, how now, Stephano?

STEPHANO: O, touch me not! I am not Stephano, but a cramp.

325 PROSPERO: You'd be king o' the isle, sirrah?

326 STEPHANO: I should have been a sore one, then.

ALONSO [*pointing to Caliban*]: This is a strange thing as e'er I looked on.

PROSPERO: He is as disproportioned in his manners

As in his shape.—Go, sirrah, to my cell.

Take with you your companions. As you look

331   To have my pardon, trim it handsomely.

---

304 badges emblems of cloth or silver worn by retainers to indicate whom they serve.
(Prospero refers here to the stolen clothes as emblems of their villainy.)
305 true honest
308 deal [. . .] power wield the moon's power, either without her authority or beyond
her influence, or, even though to do so was beyond Sycorax's own power
310 bastard counterfeit
312 own recognize, admit as belonging to you
317 reeling ripe stumblingly drunk
318 gilded (1) flushed, made drunk (2) covered with gilt (suggesting the horse urine)
319 pickle (1) fix, predicament (2) pickling brine (in this case, horse urine)
322 flyblowing i.e., being fouled by fly eggs (from which he is saved by being pickled)
325 sirrah (Standard form of address to an inferior, here expressing reprimand.)
326 sore (1) tyrannical (2) sorry, inept (3) wracked by pain
331 trim prepare, decorate

CALIBAN: Ay, that I will; and I'll be wise hereafter
333   And seek for grace. What a thrice-double ass
    Was I to take this drunkard for a god
    And worship this dull fool!
PROSPERO: Go to. Away!
ALONSO: Hence, and bestow your luggage where you found it.
SEBASTIAN: Or stole it, rather.

    [*Exeunt Caliban, Stephano, and Trinculo.*]

PROSPERO: Sir, I invite Your Highness and your train
    To my poor cell, where you shall take your rest
341   For this one night; which, part of it, I'll waste
    With such discourse as, I not doubt, shall make it
    Go quick away: the story of my life,
344   And the particular accidents gone by
    Since I came to this isle. And in the morn
    I'll bring you to your ship, and so to Naples,
    Where I have hope to see the nuptial
    Of these our dear-belovèd solemnized;
349   And thence retire me to my Milan, where
    Every third thought shall be my grave.
ALONSO: I long
    To hear the story of your life, which must
353   Take the ear strangely.
354 PROSPERO: I'll deliver all;
    And promise you calm seas, auspicious gales,
356   And sail so expeditious that shall catch
357   Your royal fleet far off. [*Aside to Ariel.*] My Ariel, chick,
    That is thy charge. Then to the elements
359   Be free, and fare thou well!—Please you, draw near.

    Exeunt omnes [*except Prospero*].

333 grace pardon, favor
341 waste spend
344 accidents occurrences
349 retire me return
353 Take take effect upon, enchant
354 deliver declare, relate
356–57 catch [. . .] far off enable you to catch up with the main part of your royal fleet,
now afar off en route to Naples (see 1.2.272–73)
359 draw near i.e., enter my cell

Epilogue S*poken by Prospero.*

Now my charms are all o'erthrown,
And what strength I have 's mine own,
Which is most faint. Now, 'tis true,
I must be here confined by you
Or sent to Naples. Let me not,
Since I have my dukedom got
And pardoned the deceiver, dwell
In this bare island by your spell,
9   But release me from my bands
10   With the help of your good hands.
11   Gentle breath of yours my sails
Must fill, or else my project fails,
13   Which was to please. Now I want
14   Spirits to enforce, art to enchant,
And my ending is despair,
16   Unless I be relieved by prayer,
17   Which pierces so that it assaults
18   Mercy itself, and frees all faults.
19   As you from crimes would pardoned be,
20   Let your indulgence set me free.   *Exit.*

Epilogue.
9 bands bonds
10 hands i.e., applause (the noise of which would break the spell of silence)
11 Gentle breath favorable breeze (produced by hands clapping or favorable comment)
13 want lack
14 enforce control
16 prayer i.e., Prospero's petition to the audience
17 assaults rightfully gains the attention of
18 frees obtains forgiveness for
19 crimes sins
20 indulgence (1) humoring, lenient approval (2) remission of punishment for sin

Questions for Discussion

Act 1

1. Explain Prospero's claim to Miranda: "I have done nothing but in care of thee."

2. Why does Prospero say that their coming to this island is both "foul play" and "Blessed"?

3. Explain the situation by which Prospero lost his dukedom and arrived on the island.

4. How has Ariel aided Prospero? What is his promised reward?

5. Explain Caliban's origins and the way he lost favor with Prospero. What human qualities does he represent?

Act 2

1. Why do Sebastian and Antonio mock Gonzalo? What does their behavior reveal about them?

2. What crime does Antonio propose to Sebastian? How does it parallel Antonio's crime?

3. What is Caliban's opinion of Trinculo and Stephano?

Act 3

1. What lies does Caliban tell about Prospero? For what purpose?

2. What is Prospero trying to accomplish by using his magic to create the banquet and then having Ariel forbid the men to eat?

Act 4

1. What is the purpose of the presentation of Iris, Ceres, and Juno? What do these goddesses represent?

2. Examine the famous speech of Prospero in 4.1.162–72. In what ways does it apply both to the scene Prospero has just created and to the end of Shakespeare's career?

Act 5

1. What does Prospero's speech to Ariel in 5.1.24–36 reveal about his character?

2. Explain Prospero's reasons for abjuring his magic, breaking his staff, and drowning his book.

3. What are Caliban's claims in 332–33? Is he sincere? What future would you predict for him?

4. Why is the freeing of Ariel both a happy occasion and a sad one?

Suggestions for Exploration and Writing

1. Miranda exclaims, "O brave new world / That has such people in 't." In an essay, explain what you might exclaim upon seeing today's human beings for the first time and why you would choose that exclamation.

2. Reread the passages that use puns, sarcasm, and other forms of humor. Then write an essay classifying these and showing what they add to the play. Alternatively, write an essay showing how Shakespeare uses the cruel humor of some characters to reveal their true personalities.

3. In an essay, give your theories about why Prospero forgives those who have wronged him and who benefits most from his forgiveness.

4. Explain which of Prospero's speeches have led to the assumption that this play was Shakespeare's farewell to the stage and why they might lead to this conclusion.

Casebook
on Joyce Carol Oates

WRITING ABOUT ILLUSION AND REALITY

Focusing on the dreams and imaginings of young girls that render them
both hopeful and vulnerable, this casebook will allow you to explore in
discussion and writing two complementary yet quite different stories by
Joyce Carol Oates. The critical essays that follow should suggest ways of
reading Oates's stories as well as some possible comparisons to Flannery
O'Connor, two of whose works are featured in another casebook in the
Quest unit, the final unit in this textbook.

Joyce Carol Oates (b. 1938)

*Joyce Carol Oates, a highly skilled and extraordinarily productive American
writer of poems, criticism, and fiction, is best known for her more than twenty
darkly violent novels. From* Them *(1969), which won a National Book
Award, to* Beasts *(2002), Oates's novels represent an unusually large body
of distinguished achievement. Born a Roman Catholic in Lockport, New York,
Oates depicts a world devoid of saving grace. A realistic writer whose characters speak a colloquial dialogue full of allusions to popular culture, Oates
explores the surrealistic, nightmarish encounters that haunt the empty, lost
souls she creates.*

WHERE ARE YOU GOING, WHERE HAVE YOU BEEN?   (1970)
FOR BOB DYLAN

1   Her name was Connie. She was fifteen and she had a quick nervous giggling habit of craning her neck to glance into mirrors, or checking other people's faces to make sure her own was all right. Her mother, who noticed everything and knew everything and who hadn't much reason any longer to look at her own face, always scolded Connie about it. "Stop gawking at yourself, who are you? You think you're so pretty?" she would say. Connie would raise her eyebrows at these familiar complaints and look right through her mother, into a shadowy vision of herself as she was right at that moment: she knew she was pretty and that was everything. Her mother had been pretty once too, if you could believe those old snapshots in the album, but now her looks were gone and that was why she was always after Connie.

2   "Why don't you keep your room clean like your sister? How've you got your hair fixed—what the hell stinks? Hair spray? You don't see your sister using that junk."

3   Her sister June was twenty-four and still lived at home. She was a secretary in the high school Connie attended, and if that wasn't bad enough—with her in the same building—she was so plain and chunky and steady that Connie had to hear her praised all the time by her mother and her mother's sisters. June did this, June did that, she saved money and helped clean the house and cooked and Connie couldn't do a thing, her mind was all filled with trashy daydreams. Their father was away at work most of the time and when he came home he wanted supper and he read the newspaper at supper and after supper he went to bed. He didn't bother talking much to them, but around his bent head Connie's mother kept picking at her until Connie wished her mother was dead and she herself was dead and it was all over. "She makes me want to throw up sometimes," she complained to her friends. She had a high, breathless, amused voice which made everything she said sound a little forced, whether it was sincere or not.

4   There was one good thing: June went places with girl friends of hers, girls who were just as plain and steady as she, and so when Connie wanted to do that her mother had no objections. The father of Connie's best girl friend drove the girls the three miles to town and left them off at a shopping plaza, so that they could walk through the stores or go to a movie, and when he came to pick them up again at eleven he never bothered to ask what they had done.

5   They must have been familiar sights, walking around that shopping plaza in their shorts and flat ballerina slippers that always scuffed the sidewalk, with charm bracelets jingling on their thin wrists; they would lean together to whisper and laugh secretly if someone passed by who amused or interested them. Connie had long dark blond hair that drew anyone's eye to it, and she wore part of it pulled up on her head and puffed out

and the rest of it she let fall down her back. She wore a pull-over jersey blouse that looked one way when she was at home and another way when she was away from home. Everything about her had two sides to it, one for home and one for anywhere that was not home: her walk that could be childlike and bobbing, or languid enough to make anyone think she was hearing music in her head, her mouth which was pale and smirking most of the time, but bright and pink on these evenings out, her laugh which was cynical and drawling at home—"Ha, ha, very funny"—but high-pitched and nervous anywhere else, like the jingling of the charms on her bracelet.

6   Sometimes they did go shopping or to a movie, but sometimes they went across the highway, ducking fast across the busy road, to a drive-in restaurant where older kids hung out. The restaurant was shaped like a big bottle, though squatter than a real bottle, and on its cap was a revolving figure of a grinning boy who held a hamburger aloft. One night in mid-summer they ran across, breathless with daring, and right away someone leaned out a car window and invited them over, but it was just a boy from high school they didn't like. It made them feel good to be able to ignore him. They went up through the maze of parked and cruising cars to the bright-lit, fly-infested restaurant, their faces pleased and expectant as if they were entering a sacred building that loomed out of the night to give them what haven and what blessing they yearned for. They sat at the counter and crossed their legs at the ankles, their thin shoulders rigid with excitement, and listened to the music that made everything so good: the music was always in the background like music at a church service, it was something to depend upon.

7   A boy named Eddie came in to talk with them. He sat backwards on his stool, turning himself jerkily around in semi-circles and then stopping and turning again, and after a while he asked Connie if she would like something to eat. She said she did and so she tapped her friend's arm on her way out—her friend pulled her face up into a brave droll look—and Connie said she would meet her at eleven, across the way. "I just hate to leave her like that," Connie said earnestly, but the boy said that she wouldn't be alone for long. So they went out to his car and on the way Connie couldn't help but let her eyes wander over the windshields and faces all around her, her face gleaming with a joy that had nothing to do with Eddie or even this place; it might have been the music. She drew her shoulders up and sucked in her breath with the pure pleasure of being alive, and just at that moment she happened to glance at a face just a few feet from hers. It was a boy with shaggy black hair, in a convertible jalopy painted gold. He stared at her and then his lips widened into a grin. Connie slit her eyes at him and turned away, but she couldn't help glancing back and there he was still watching her. He wagged a finger and laughed and said, "Gonna get you, baby," and Connie turned away again without Eddie noticing anything.

8   She spent three hours with him, at the restaurant where they ate hamburgers and drank Cokes in wax cups that were always sweating, and then down an alley a mile or so away, and when he left her off at five to eleven

only the movie house was still open at the plaza. Her girl friend was there, talking with a boy. When Connie came up the two girls smiled at each other and Connie said, "How was the movie?" and the girl said, "*You* should know." They rode off with the girl's father, sleepy and pleased, and Connie couldn't help but look at the darkened shopping plaza with its big empty parking lot and its signs that were faded and ghostly now, and over at the drive-in restaurant where cars were still circling tirelessly. She couldn't hear the music at this distance.

9   Next morning June asked her how the movie was and Connie said, "So-so."

10   She and that girl and occasionally another girl went out several times a week that way, and the rest of the time Connie spent around the house—it was summer vacation—getting in her mother's way and thinking, dreaming, about the boys she met. But all the boys fell back and dissolved into a single face that was not even a face, but an idea, a feeling, mixed up with the urgent insistent pounding of the music and the humid night air of July. Connie's mother kept dragging her back to the daylight by finding things for her to do or saying, suddenly, "What's this about the Pettinger girl?"

11   And Connie would say nervously, "Oh, her. That dope." She always drew thick clear lines between herself and such girls, and her mother was simple and kindly enough to believe her. Her mother was so simple, Connie thought, that it was maybe cruel to fool her so much. Her mother went scuffling around the house in old bedroom slippers and complained over the telephone to one sister about the other, then the other called up and the two of them complained about the third one. If June's name was mentioned her mother's tone was approving, and if Connie's name was mentioned it was disapproving. This did not really mean she disliked Connie and actually Connie thought that her mother preferred her to June because she was prettier, but the two of them kept up a pretense of exasperation, a sense that they were tugging and struggling over something of little value to either of them. Sometimes, over coffee, they were almost friends, but something would come up—some vexation that was like a fly buzzing suddenly around their heads—and their faces went hard with contempt.

12   One Sunday Connie got up at eleven—none of them bothered with church—and washed her hair so that it could dry all day long, in the sun. Her parents and sister were going to a barbecue at an aunt's house and Connie said no, she wasn't interested, rolling her eyes to let her mother know just what she thought of it. "Stay home alone then," her mother said sharply. Connie sat out back in a lawn chair and watched them drive away, her father quiet and bald, hunched around so that he could back the car out, her mother with a look that was still angry and not at all softened through the windshield, and in the back seat poor old June all dressed up as if she didn't know what a barbecue was, with all the running yelling kids and the flies. Connie sat with her eyes closed in the sun, dreaming

and dazed with the warmth about her as if this were a kind of love, the caresses of love, and her mind slipped over onto thoughts of the boy she had been with the night before and how nice he had been, how sweet it always was, not the way someone like June would suppose but sweet, gentle, the way it was in movies and promised in songs; and when she opened her eyes she hardly knew where she was, the back yard ran off into weeds and a fence-line of trees and behind it the sky was perfectly blue and still. The asbestos "ranch house" that was now three years old startled her—it looked small. She shook her head as if to get awake.

13   It was too hot. She went inside the house and turned on the radio to drown out the quiet. She sat on the edge of her bed, barefoot, and listened for an hour and a half to a program called XYZ Sunday Jamboree, record after record of hard, fast, shrieking songs she sang along with, interspersed by exclamations from "Bobby King": "An' look here you girls at Napoleon's—Son and Charley want you to pay real close attention to this song coming up!"

14   And Connie paid close attention herself, bathed in a glow of slow-pulsed joy that seemed to rise mysteriously out of the music itself and lay languidly about the airless little room, breathed in and breathed out with each gentle rise and fall of her chest.

15   After a while she heard a car coming up the drive. She sat up at once, startled, because it couldn't be her father so soon. The gravel kept crunching all the way in from the road—the driveway was long—and Connie ran to the window. It was a car she didn't know. It was an open jalopy, painted a bright gold that caught the sunlight opaquely. Her heart began to pound and her fingers snatched at her hair, checking it, and she whispered "Christ. Christ," wondering how bad she looked. The car came to a stop at the side door and the horn sounded four short taps as if this were a signal Connie knew.

16   She went into the kitchen and approached the door slowly, then hung out the screen door, her bare toes curling down off the step. There were two boys in the car and now she recognized the driver: he had shaggy, shabby black hair that looked crazy as a wig and he was grinning at her.

17   "I ain't late, am I?" he said.

18   "Who the hell do you think you are?" Connie said.

19   "Toldja I'd be out, didn't I?"

20   "I don't even know who you are."

21   She spoke sullenly, careful to show no interest or pleasure, and he spoke in a fast bright monotone. Connie looked past him to the other boy, taking her time. He had fair brown hair, with a lock that fell onto his forehead. His sideburns gave him a fierce, embarrassed look, but so far he hadn't even bothered to glance at her. Both boys wore sunglasses. The driver's glasses were metallic and mirrored everything in miniature.

22   "You wanta come for a ride?" he said.

23   Connie smirked and let her hair fall loose over one shoulder.

24   "Don'tcha like my car? New paint job," he said. "Hey."

25   "What?"

26   "You're cute."

27   She pretended to fidget, chasing flies away from the door.

28   "Don'tcha believe me, or what?" he said.

29   "Look, I don't even know who you are," Connie said in disgust.

30   "Hey, Ellie's got a radio, see. Mine's broke down." He lifted his friend's
arm and showed her the little transistor the boy was holding, and now
Connie began to hear the music. It was the same program that was playing inside the house.

31   "Bobby King?" she said.

32   "I listen to him all the time. I think he's great."

33   "He's kind of great," Connie said reluctantly.

34   "Listen, that guy's *great*. He knows where the action is."

35   Connie blushed a little, because the glasses made it impossible for
her to see just what this boy was looking at. She couldn't decide if she
liked him or if he was just a jerk, and so she dawdled in the doorway and
wouldn't come down or go back inside. She said "What's all that stuff
painted on your car?"

36   "Can'tcha read it?" He opened the door very carefully, as if he was
afraid it might fall off. He slid out just as carefully, planting his feet firmly
on the ground, the tiny metallic world in his glasses slowing down like
gelatine hardening and in the midst of it Connie's bright green blouse.
"This here is my name, to begin with," he said. ARNOLD FRIEND was
written in tarlike black letters on the side, with a drawing of a round grinning face that reminded Connie of a pumpkin, except it wore sunglasses.
"I wanta introduce myself, I'm Arnold Friend and that's my real name
and I'm gonna be your friend, honey, and inside the car's Ellie Oscar, he's
kinda shy." Ellie brought his transistor radio up to his shoulder and balanced it there. "Now these numbers are a secret code, honey," Arnold
Friend explained. He read off the numbers 33, 19, 17 and raised his eyebrows at her to see what she thought of that, but she didn't think much
of it. The left rear fender had been smashed and around it was written,
on the gleaming gold background: DONE BY CRAZY WOMAN DRIVER.
Connie had to laugh at that. Arnold Friend was pleased at her laughter
and looked up at her. "Around the other side's a lot more—you wanta
come and see them?"

37   "No."

38   "Why not?"

39   "Why should I?"

40   "Don'tcha wanta see what's on the car? Don'tcha wanta go for a ride?"

41   "I don't know."

42   "Why not?"

43   "I got things to do."

44   "Like what?"

45   "Things."

46   He laughed as if she had said something funny. He slapped his thighs. He was standing in a strange way, leaning back against the car as if he were balancing himself. He wasn't tall, only an inch or so taller than she would be if she came down to him. Connie liked the way he was dressed, which was the way all of them dressed: tight faded jeans stuffed into black, scuffed boots, a belt that pulled his waist in and showed how lean he was, and a white pull-over shirt that was a little soiled and showed the hard small muscles of his arms and shoulders. He looked as if he probably did hard work, lifting and carrying things. Even his neck looked muscular. And his face was a familiar face, somehow: the jaw and chin and cheeks slightly darkened, because he hadn't shaved for a day or two, and the nose long and hawk-like, sniffing as if she were a treat he was going to gobble up and it was all a joke.

47   "Connie, you ain't telling the truth. This is your day set aside for a ride with me and you know it," he said, still laughing. The way he straightened and recovered from his fit of laughing showed that it had been all fake.

48   "How do you know what my name is?" she said suspiciously.

49   "It's Connie."

50   "Maybe and maybe not."

51   "I know my Connie," he said, wagging his finger. Now she remembered him even better, back at the restaurant, and her cheeks warmed at the thought of how she sucked in her breath just at the moment she passed him—how she must have looked to him. And he had remembered her. "Ellie and I come out here especially for you," he said. "Ellie can sit in back. How about it?"

52   "Where?"

53   "Where what?"

54   "Where're we going?"

55   He looked at her. He took off the sunglasses and she saw how pale the skin around his eyes was, like holes that were not in shadow but instead in light. His eyes were chips of broken glass that catch the light in an amiable way. He smiled. It was as if the idea of going for a ride somewhere, to some place, was a new idea to him.

56   "Just for a ride, Connie sweetheart."

57   "I never said my name was Connie," she said.

58   "But I know what it is. I know your name and all about you, lots of things," Arnold Friend said. He had not moved yet but stood still leaning back against the side of his jalopy. "I took a special interest in you, such a pretty girl, and found out all about you like I know your parents and sister are gone somewheres and I know where and how long they're going to be gone, and I know who you were with last night, and your best girl friend's name is Betty. Right?"

59   He spoke in a simple lilting voice, exactly as if he were reciting the words to a song. His smile assured her that everything was fine. In the car, Ellie turned up the volume on his radio and did not bother to look around at them.

60   "Ellie can sit in the back seat," Arnold Friend said. He indicated his friend with a casual jerk of his chin, as if Ellie did not count and she should not bother with him.

61   "How'd you find out all that stuff?" Connie said.

62   "Listen: Betty Schultz and Tony Fitch and Jimmy Pettinger and Nancy Pettinger," he said, in a chant. "Raymond Stanley and Bob Hutter—"

63   "Do you know all those kids?"

64   "I know everybody."

65   "Look, you're kidding. You're not from around here."

66   "Sure."

67   "But—how come we never saw you before?"

68   "Sure you saw me before," he said. He looked down at his boots, as if he were a little offended. "You just don't remember."

69   "I guess I'd remember you," Connie said.

70   "Yeah?" He looked up at this, beaming. He was pleased. He began to mark time with the music from Ellie's radio, tapping his fists lightly together. Connie looked away from his smile to the car, which was painted so bright it almost hurt her eyes to look at it. She looked at that name, ARNOLD FRIEND. And up at the front fender was an expression that was familiar—MAN THE FLYING SAUCERS. It was an expression kids had used the year before, but didn't use this year. She looked at it for a while as if the words meant something to her that she did not yet know.

71   "What're you thinking about? Huh?" Arnold Friend demanded. "Not worried about your hair blowing around in the car, are you?"

72   "No."

73   "Think I maybe can't drive good?"

74   "How do I know?"

75   "You're a hard girl to handle. How come?" he said. "Don't you know I'm your friend? Didn't you see me put my sign in the air when you walked by?"

76   "What sign?"

77   "My sign." And he drew an X in the air, leaning out toward her. They were maybe ten feet apart. After his hand fell back to his side the X was still in the air, almost visible. Connie let the screen door close and stood perfectly still inside it, listening to the music from her radio and the boy's blend together. She stared at Arnold Friend. He stood there so stiffly relaxed, pretending to be relaxed, with one hand idly on the door handle as if he were keeping himself up that way and had no intention of ever moving again. She recognized most things about him, the tight jeans that showed his thighs and buttocks and the greasy leather boots and the tight shirt, and even that slippery friendly smile of his, that sleepy dreamy smile that all the boys used to get across ideas they didn't want to put into words. She recognized all this and also the singsong way he talked, slightly mocking, kidding, but serious and a little melancholy, and she recognized the way he tapped one fist against the other in homage to the perpetual music behind him. But all these things did not come together.

78   She said suddenly, "Hey, how old are you?"

79   His smile faded. She could see then that he wasn't a kid, he was much older—thirty, maybe more. At this knowledge her heart began to pound faster.

80   "That's a crazy thing to ask. Can'tcha see I'm your own age?"

81   "Like hell you are."

82   "Or maybe a couple years older, I'm eighteen."

83   "Eighteen?" she said doubtfully.

84   He grinned to reassure her and lines appeared at the corners of his mouth. His teeth were big and white. He grinned so broadly his eyes became slits and she saw how thick the lashes were, thick and black as if painted with a black tarlike material. Then he seemed to become embarrassed, abruptly, and looked over his shoulder at Ellie. "*Him,* he's crazy," he said. "Ain't he a riot, he's a nut, a real character." Ellie was still listening to the music. His sunglasses told nothing about what he was thinking. He wore a bright orange shirt unbuttoned halfway to show his chest, which was a pale, bluish chest and not muscular like Arnold Friend's. His shirt collar was turned up all around and the very tips of the collar pointed out past his chin as if they were protecting him. He was pressing the transistor radio up against his ear and sat there in a kind of daze, right in the sun.

85   "He's kinda strange," Connie said.

86   "Hey, she says you're kinda strange! Kinda strange!" Arnold Friend cried. He pounded on the car to get Ellie's attention. Ellie turned for the first time and Connie saw with shock that he wasn't a kid either—he had a fair, hairless face, cheeks reddened slightly as if the veins grew too close to the surface of his skin, the face of a forty-year-old baby. Connie felt a wave of dizziness rise in her at this sight and she stared at him as if waiting for something to change the shock of the moment, make it all right again. Ellie's lips kept shaping words, mumbling along, with the words blasting in his ear.

87   "Maybe you two better go away," Connie said faintly.

88   "What? How come?" Arnold Friend cried. "We come out here to take you for a ride. It's Sunday." He had the voice of the man on the radio now. It was the same voice, Connie thought. "Don'tcha know it's Sunday all day and honey, no matter who you were with last night today you're with Arnold Friend and don't you forget it!—Maybe you better step out here," he said, and this last was in a different voice. It was a little flatter, as if the heat was finally getting to him.

89   "No. I got things to do."

90   "Hey."

91   "You two better leave."

92   "We ain't leaving until you come with us."

93   "Like hell I am—"

94   "Connie, don't fool around with me. I mean, I mean, don't fool *around,*" he said, shaking his head. He laughed incredulously. He placed

his sunglasses on top of his head, carefully, as if he were indeed wearing a wig, and brought the stems down behind his ears. Connie stared at him, another wave of dizziness and fear rising in her so that for a moment he wasn't even in focus but was just a blur, standing there against his gold car, and she had the idea that he had driven up the driveway all right but had come from nowhere before that and belonged nowhere and that everything about him and even about the music that was so familiar to her was only half real.

95   "If my father comes and sees you—"

96   "He ain't coming. He's at the barbecue."

97   "How do you know that?"

98   "Aunt Tillie's. Right now they're—uh—they're drinking. Sitting around," he said vaguely, squinting as if he were staring all the way to town and over to Aunt Tillie's backyard. Then the vision seemed to get clear and he nodded energetically. "Yeah. Sitting around. There's your sister in a blue dress, huh? And high heels, the poor sad bitch—nothing like you, sweetheart! And your mother's helping some fat woman with the corn, they're cleaning the corn—husking the corn—"

99   "What fat woman?" Connie cried.

100   "How do I know what fat woman. I don't know every goddam fat woman in the world!" Arnold Friend laughed.

101   "Oh, that's Mrs. Hornby. . . . Who invited her?" Connie said. She felt a little light-headed. Her breath was coming quickly.

102   "She's too fat. I don't like them fat. I like them the way you are, honey," he said, smiling sleepily at her. They stared at each other for awhile, through the screen door. He said softly, "Now what you're going to do is this: you're going to come out that door. You're going to sit up front with me and Ellie's going to sit in the back, the hell with Ellie, right? This isn't Ellie's date. You're my date. I'm your lover, honey."

103   "What? You're crazy—"

104   "Yes, I'm your lover. You don't know what that is but you will," he said. "I know that too. I know all about you. But look: it's real nice and you couldn't ask for nobody better than me, or more polite. I always keep my word. I'll tell you how it is, I'm always nice at first, the first time. I'll hold you so tight you won't think you have to try to get away or pretend anything because you'll know you can't. And I'll come inside you where it's all secret and you'll give in to me and you'll love me—"

105   "Shut up! You're crazy!" Connie said. She backed away from the door. She put her hands against her ears as if she'd heard something terrible, something not meant for her. "People don't talk like that, you're crazy," she muttered. Her heart was almost too big now for her chest and its pumping made sweat break out all over her. She looked out to see Arnold Friend pause and then take a step toward the porch lurching. He almost fell. But, like a clever drunken man, he managed to catch his balance. He wobbled in his high boots and grabbed hold of one of the porch posts.

106   "Honey?" he said. "You still listening?"

107   "Get the hell out of here!"

108   "Be nice, honey. Listen."

109   "I'm going to call the police—"

110   He wobbled again and out of the side of his mouth came a fast spat curse, an aside not meant for her to hear. But even this "Christ!" sounded forced. Then he began to smile again. She watched this smile come, awkward as if he were smiling from inside a mask. His whole face was a mask, she thought wildly, tanned down onto his throat but then running out as if he had plastered make-up on his face but had forgotten about his throat.

111   "Honey—? Listen, here's how it is. I always tell the truth and I promise you this: I ain't coming in that house after you."

112   "You better not! I'm going to call the police if you—if you don't—"

113   "Honey," he said, talking right through her voice, "honey, I'm not coming in there but you are coming out here. You know why?"

114   She was panting. The kitchen looked like a place she had never seen before, some room she had run inside but which wasn't good enough, wasn't going to help her. The kitchen window had never had a curtain, after three years, and there were dishes in the sink for her to do—probably—and if you ran your hand across the table you'd probably feel something sticky there.

115   "You listening, honey? Hey?"

116   "—going to call the police—"

117   "Soon as you touch the phone I don't need to keep my promise and can come inside. You won't want that."

118   She rushed forward and tried to lock the door. Her fingers were shaking. "But why lock it," Arnold Friend said gently, talking right into her face. "It's just a screen door. It's just nothing." One of his boots was at a strange angle, as if his foot wasn't in it. It pointed out to the left, bent at the ankle. "I mean, anybody can break through a screen door and glass and wood and iron or anything else if he needs to, anybody at all and specially Arnold Friend. If the place got lit up with a fire honey you'd come running out into my arms, right into my arms and safe at home—like you knew I was your lover and'd stopped fooling around. I don't mind a nice shy girl but I don't like no fooling around." Part of those words were spoken with a slight rhythmic lilt, and Connie somehow recognized them—the echo of a song from last year, about a girl rushing into her boy friend's arms and coming home again—

119   Connie stood barefoot on the linoleum floor, staring at him. "What do you want?" she whispered.

120   "I want you," he said.

121   "What?"

122   "Seen you that night and thought, that's the one, yes sir. I never needed to look any more."

123   "But my father's coming back. He's coming to get me. I had to wash my hair first—" She spoke in a dry, rapid voice, hardly raising it for him to hear.

124   "No, your daddy is not coming and yes, you had to wash your hair and you washed it for me. It's nice and shining and all for me, I thank you, sweetheart," he said, with a mock bow, but again he almost lost his balance. He had to bend and adjust his boots. Evidently his feet did not go all the way down; the boots must have been stuffed with something so that he would seem taller. Connie stared out at him and behind him Ellie in the car, who seemed to be looking off toward Connie's right, into nothing. This Ellie said, pulling the words out of the air one after another as if he were just discovering them, "You want me to pull out the phone?"

125   "Shut your mouth and keep it shut," Arnold Friend said, his face red from bending over or maybe from embarrassment because Connie had seen his boots. "This ain't none of your business."

126   "What—what are you doing? What do you want?" Connie said. "If I call the police they'll get you, they'll arrest you—"

127   "Promise was not to come in unless you touch that phone, and I'll keep that promise," he said. He resumed his erect position and tried to force his shoulders back. He sounded like a hero in a movie, declaring something important. He spoke too loudly and it was as if he were speaking to someone behind Connie. "I ain't made plans for coming in that house where I don't belong but just for you to come out to me, the way you should. Don't you know who I am?"

128   "You're crazy," she whispered. She backed away from the door but did not want to go into another part of the house, as if this would give him permission to come through the door. "What do you . . . You're crazy, you . . ."

129   "Huh? What're you saying, honey?"

130   Her eyes darted everywhere in the kitchen. She could not remember what it was, this room.

131   "This is how it is, honey: you come out and we'll drive away, have a nice ride. But if you don't come out we're gonna wait till your people come home and then they're all going to get it."

132   "You want that telephone pulled out?" Ellie said. He held the radio away from his ear and grimaced, as if without the radio the air was too much for him.

133   "I toldja shut up, Ellie," Arnold Friend said, "you're deaf, get a hearing aid, right? Fix yourself up. This little girl's no trouble and's gonna be nice to me, so Ellie keep to yourself, this ain't your date—right? Don't hem in on me. Don't hog. Don't crush. Don't bird dog. Don't trail me," he said in a rapid meaningless voice, as if he were running through all the expressions he'd learned but was no longer sure which one of them was in style, then rushing on to new ones, making them up with his eyes closed, "Don't crawl under my fence, don't squeeze in my chipmunk hole, don't sniff my glue, suck my popsicle, keep your own greasy fingers on yourself!" He shaded his eyes and peered in at Connie, who was backed against the kitchen table. "Don't mind him honey he's just a creep. He's

a dope. Right? I'm the boy for you and like I said you come out here nice like a lady and give me your hand, and nobody else gets hurt, I mean, your nice old bald-headed daddy and your mummy and your sister in her high heels. Because listen: why bring them in this?"

134   "Leave me alone," Connie whispered.

135   "Hey, you know that old woman down the road, the one with the chickens and stuff—you know her?"

136   "She's dead!"

137   "Dead? What? You know her?" Arnold Friend said.

138   "She's dead—"

139   "Don't you like her?"

140   "She's dead—she's—she isn't here any more—"

141   "But don't you like her, I mean, you got something against her? Some grudge or something?" Then his voice dipped as if he were conscious of a rudeness. He touched the sunglasses perched on top of his head as if to make sure they were still there. "Now you be a good girl."

142   "What are you going to do?"

143   "Just two things, or maybe three," Arnold Friend said. "But I promise it won't last long and you'll like me that way you get to like people you're close to. You will. It's all over for you here, so come on out. You don't want your people in any trouble, do you?"

144   She turned and bumped against a chair or something, hurting her leg, but she ran into the back room and picked up the telephone. Something roared in her ear, a tiny roaring, and she was so sick with fear that she could do nothing but listen to it—the telephone was clammy and very heavy and her fingers groped down to the dial but were too weak to touch it. She began to scream into the phone, into the roaring. She cried out, she cried for her mother, she felt her breath start jerking back and forth in her lungs as if it were something Arnold Friend were stabbing her with again and again with no tenderness. A noisy sorrowful wailing rose all about her and she was locked inside it the way she was locked inside the house.

145   After a while she could hear again. She was sitting on the floor with her wet back against the wall.

146   Arnold Friend was saying from the door, "That's a good girl. Put the phone back."

147   She kicked the phone away from her.

148   "No, honey. Pick it up. Put it back right."

149   She picked it up and put it back. The dial tone stopped.

150   "That's a good girl. Now come outside."

151   She was hollow with what had been fear, but what was now just an emptiness. All that screaming had blasted it out of her. She sat, one leg cramped under her, and deep inside her brain was something like a pinpoint of light that kept going and would not let her relax. She thought, I'm not going to see my mother again. She thought, I'm not going to sleep in my bed again. Her bright green blouse was all wet.

152   Arnold Friend said, in a gentle-loud voice that was like a stage voice, "The place where you came from ain't there any more, and where you had in mind to go is cancelled out. This place you are now—inside your daddy's house—is nothing but a cardboard box I can knock down any time. You know that and always did know it. You hear me?"

153   She thought, I have got to think. I have to know what to do.

154   "We'll go out to a nice field, out in the country here where it smells so nice and it's sunny," Arnold Friend said. "I'll have my arms around you so you won't need to try to get away and I'll show you what love is like, what it does. The hell with this house! It looks solid all right," he said. He ran a fingernail down the screen and the noise did not make Connie shiver, as it would have the day before. "Now put your hand on your heart, honey. Feel that? That feels solid too but we know better, be nice to me, be sweet like you can because what else is there for a girl like you but to be sweet and pretty and give in?—and get away before her people come back?"

155   She felt her pounding heart. Her hand seemed to enclose it. She thought for the first time in her life that it was nothing that was hers, that belonged to her, but just a pounding, living thing inside this body that wasn't really hers either.

156   "You don't want them to get hurt," Arnold Friend went on. "Now get up, honey. Get up all by yourself."

157   She stood up.

158   "Now turn this way. That's right. Come over here to me—Ellie, put that away, didn't I tell you? You dope. You miserable creepy dope," Arnold said. His words were not angry but only part of an incantation. The incantation was kindly. "Now come out through the kitchen to me honey and let's see a smile, try it, you're a brave sweet little girl and now they're eating corn and hotdogs cooked to bursting over an outdoor fire, and they don't know one thing about you and never did and honey you're better than them because not a one of them would have done this for you."

159   Connie felt the linoleum under her feet; it was cool. She brushed her hair back out of her eyes. Arnold Friend let go of the post tentatively and opened his arms for her, his elbows pointing in toward each other and his wrists limp, to show that this was an embarrassed embrace and a little mocking, he didn't want to make her self-conscious.

160   She put out her hand against the screen. She watched herself push the door slowly open as if she were safe back somewhere in the other doorway, watching this body and this head of long hair moving out into the sunlight where Arnold Friend waited.

161   "My sweet little blue-eyed girl," he said, in a half-sung sigh that had nothing to do with her brown eyes but was taken up just the same by the vast sunlit reaches of the land behind him and on all sides of him, so much land that Connie had never seen before and did not recognize except to know that she was going to it.

Questions for Discussion

1. How does Connie feel about her mother's constant nagging? How does Connie react?

2. What is most important to Connie? Why?

3. Why does Arnold Friend fake laughter and pretend to be a teenager even though he must know Connie will see through his charade? What attracts Connie to Arnold and Ellie? What frightens her?

4. How does Arnold know so much about Connie? How does Arnold convince Connie that she is powerless before him?

5. What will happen to Connie?

VALENTINE (1999)

1   In upstate New York in those years there were snowstorms so wild and fierce they could change the world, within a few hours, to a place you wouldn't know. First came the heavy black thunderheads over Lake Erie, then the wind hammering overhead like a freight train, then the snowflakes erupting, flying, swirling like crazed atoms. If there'd been a sun it was extinguished, gone. Night and day were reversed, the fallen snow emitted such a radium-glare.

2   I was fifteen years old living in the Red Rock section of Buffalo with an aunt, an older sister of my mother's, and her husband who was retired from the New York Central Railroad with a disability pension. My own family was what you'd called "dispersed"—we were all alive, seven of us, I believed we were all alive, but we did not live together in the same house any longer. In fact, the house, an old rented farmhouse twenty miles north of Buffalo, was gone. Burned to the ground.

3   Valentine's Day 1959, the snowstorm began in midafternoon and already by 5 P.M. the power lines were down in Buffalo. Hurriedly we lit kerosene lamps whose wicks smoked and stank as they emitted a begrudging light. We had a flashlight, of course, and candles. In extra layers of clothes we saw our breaths steam as we ate our cold supper on plates like ice. I cleaned up the kitchen as best I could without hot water, for that was always my task, among numerous others, and I said "Goodnight, Aunt Esther" to my aunt who frowned at me seeing someone not me in my place who filled her heart with sisterly sorrow and I said "Goodnight, Uncle Herman" to the man designated as my uncle, who was no blood-kin of mine, a stranger with damp eyes always drifting onto me and a mouth like a smirking scar burn. "Goodnight" they murmured as if resenting the very breath expelled for my sake. *Goodnight don't run on the stairs don't drop the candle and set the house on fire.*

4   Upstairs was a partly finished attic narrow as a tunnel with a habitable space at one end—my "room." The ceiling was covered in strips of peeling

insulation and so steep-slanted I could stand up only in the center. The floorboards were splintery and bare except for a small shag rug, a discard of my aunt's, laid down by my bed. The bed was another discard of my aunt's, a sofa of some mud-brown prickly fabric that pierced sheets laid upon it like whiskers sprouting through skin. But this was *a bed of my own* and I had not ever had *a bed of my own* before. Nor had I ever had *a room of my own, a door to shut against others* even if, like the attic door, it could not be locked.

5   By midnight the storm had blown itself out and the alley below had vanished in undulating dunes of snow. Everywhere snow! Glittering like mica in the moonlight! And the moon—a glowing battered-human face in a sky strangely starless, black as a well. The largest snowdrift I'd ever seen, shaped like a right-angled triangle, slanted up from the ground to the roof close outside my window. My aunt and her husband had gone to bed downstairs hours ago and the thought came to me unbidden *I can run away, no one would miss me.*

6   Along Huron Street, which my aunt's house fronted, came a snowplow, red light flashing atop its cab; otherwise there were few vehicles and these were slow-moving with groping headlights, like wounded beasts. Yet even as I watched there came a curiously shaped small vehicle to park at the mouth of the alley; and the driver, a long-legged man in a hooded jacket, climbed out. To my amazement he stomped through the snow into the alley to stand peering up toward my window, his breath steaming. Who? Who was this? *Mr. Lacey, my algebra teacher?*

7   For Valentine's Day that morning I had brought eight homemade valentines to school made of stiff red construction paper edged with paper lace, in envelopes decorated with red-ink hearts; the valentine TO MR. LACEY was my masterpiece, the largest and most ingeniously designed, interlocking hearts fashioned with a ruler and compass to resemble geometrical figures in three dimensions. HAPPY VALEN-TINE'S DAY I had neatly printed in black ink. Of course I had not signed any of the valentines and had secretly slipped them into the lockers of certain girls and boys and Mr. Lacey's onto his desk after class. I had instructed myself not to be disappointed when I received no valentines in return, not a single valentine in return, and I was not disappointed when at the end of the school day I went home without a single one: *I was not.*

8   Mr. Lacey seemed to have recognized me in the window where I stood staring, my outspread fingers on the glass bracketing my white astonished face, for he'd begun climbing the enormous snowdrift that lifted to the roof! How assured, how matter-of-fact, as if this were the most natural thing in the world. I was too surprised to be alarmed, or even embarrassed—my teacher would see me in a cast-off sweater of my brother's that was many sizes too large for me and splotched with oil stains, he would see my shabby little room that wasn't really a room, just part of an unfinished

attic. He would know I was the one who'd left the valentine TO MR. LACEY on his desk in stealth not daring to sign my name. *He would know who I was, how desperate for love.*

9   Once on the roof, which was steep, Mr. Lacey made his way to my window cautiously. The shingles were covered in snow, icy patches beneath. There was a rumor that Mr. Lacey was a skier, and a skater, though his lanky body did not seem the body of an athlete and in class sometimes he seemed distracted in the midst of speaking or inscribing an equation on the blackboard; as if there were thoughts more crucial to him than tenth-grade algebra at Thomas E. Dewey High School which was one of the poorest schools in the city. But now his footing was sure as a mountain goat's, his movements agile and unerring. He crouched outside my window tugging to lift it—*Erin? Make haste!*

10   I was helping to open the window which was locked in ice. It had not been opened for weeks. Already it seemed I'd pulled on my wool slacks and wound around my neck the silver muffler threaded with crimson yarn my mother had given me two or three Christmases ago. I had no coat or jacket in my room and dared not risk going downstairs to the front closet. I was very excited, fumbling, biting my lower lip, and when at last the window lurched upward the freezing air rushed in like a slap in the face. Mr. Lacey's words seemed to reverberate in my ears *Make haste, make haste!—not a moment to waste!* It was his teasing-chiding classroom manner that nonetheless meant business. Without hesitating, he grabbed both my hands—I saw that I was wearing the white angora mittens my grandmother had knitted for me long ago, which I'd believed had been lost in the fire—and hauled me through the window.

11   Mr. Lacey led me to the edge of the roof, to the snowdrift, seeking out his footprints where he knew the snow to be fairly firm, and carefully he pulled me in his wake so that I seemed to be descending a strange kind of staircase. The snow was so fresh-fallen it lifted like powder at the slightest touch or breath, glittering even more fiercely close up, as if the individual snowflakes, of such geometrical beauty and precision, contained minute sparks of flame. *Er-in, Er-in, now your courage must begin* I seemed to hear and suddenly we were on the ground and there was Mr. Lacey's Volkswagen at the mouth of the alley, headlights burning like cat's eyes and tusks of exhaust curling up behind. How many times covertly I'd tracked with my eyes that ugly-funny car shaped like a sardine can, its black chassis speckled with rust, as Mr. Lacey drove into the teachers' parking lot each morning between 8:25 A.M. and 8:35 A.M. How many times I'd turned quickly aside in terror that Mr. Lacey would see *me.* Now I stood confused at the mouth of the alley, for Huron Street and all of the city I could see was so changed, the air so terribly cold like a knifeblade in my lungs; I looked back at the darkened house wondering if my aunt might wake and discover me gone, and what then would happen?—as Mr. Lacey urged *Come, Erin, hurry! She won't even know you're gone* unless he said

She won't ever know you're gone. Was it true? Not long ago in algebra class I'd printed in the margin of my textbook

MR.
L.
IS
AL
WA
YS
RI
GH
T!

which I'd showed Linda Bewley across the aisle, one of the popular tenth-grade girls, a B+ student and very pretty and popular, and Linda frowned trying to decipher the words which were meant to evoke Mr. Lacey's pole-lean frame, but she never did get it and turned away from me annoyed.

12   Yet it was so: Julius Lacey was always always right.

13   Suddenly I was in the cramped little car and Mr. Lacey was behind the wheel driving north on icy Huron Street. *Where are we going?* I didn't dare ask. When my grades in Mr. Lacey's class were less than 100 percent I was filled with anxiety that turned my fingers and toes to ice for even if I'd answered nearly all the questions on a test correctly *how could I know I could answer the next question? solve the next problem? and the next?* A nervous passion drove me to comprehend not just the imme-diate problem but the principle behind it, for behind everything there was an elusive and tyrannical principle of which Mr. Lacey was the sole custodian; and I could not know if he liked me or was bemused by me or merely tolerated me or was in fact disappointed in me as a student who should have been earning perfect scores at all times. He was twenty-six or -seven years old, the youngest teacher at the school, whom many students feared and hated, and a small group of us feared and admired. His severe, angular face registered frequent dissatisfaction as if to indicate *Well, I'm waiting! Waiting to be impressed! Give me one good reason to be impressed!*

14   Never had I seen the city streets so deserted. Mr. Lacey drove no more than twenty miles an hour passing stores whose fronts were obliterated by snow like waves frozen at their crests and through intersections where no traffic lights burned to guide us and our only light was the Volkswagen's headlights and the glowering moon large in the sky as a fat navel orange held at arm's length. We passed Carthage Street that hadn't yet been plowed—a vast river of snow six feet high. We passed Templeau Street where a city bus had been abandoned in the intersection, humped with snow like a forlorn creature of the Great Plains. We passed Sturgeon Street where broken electrical wires writhed and crackled in the snow like snakes crazed with pain. We passed Childress Street where a water main had burst and an arc of water had frozen glistening in a graceful curve at

least fifteen feet high at its crest. At Ontario Avenue Mr. Lacey turned right, the Volkswagen went into a delirious skid, Mr. Lacey put out his arm to keep me from pitching forward—*Erin, take care!* But I was safe. And on we drove.

15   Ontario Avenue, usually so crowded with traffic, was deserted as the surface of the moon. A snowplow had forged a single lane down the center. On all sides were unfamiliar shapes of familiar objects engulfed in snow and ice—parking meters? mailboxes? abandoned cars? Humanoid figures frozen in awkward, surprised postures—hunched in doorways, frozen in midstride on the sidewalk? *Look! Look at the frozen people!* I cried in a raw loud girl's voice that so frequently embarrassed me when Mr. Lacey called upon me unexpectedly in algebra class; but Mr. Lacey shrugged saying *Just snowmen, Erin—don't give them a second glance.* But I couldn't help staring at these statue-figures for I had an uneasy sense of being stared at by them in turn, through chinks in the hard-crusted snow of their heads. And I seemed to hear their faint despairing cries *Help! help us!*—but Mr. Lacey did not slacken his speed.

16   (Yet: who could have made so many "snowmen," so quickly after the storm? Children? Playing so late at night? And where were these children now?)

17   Mysteriously Mr. Lacey said *There are many survivors, Erin. In all epochs, just enough survivors.* I wanted to ask should we pray for them? pressing my hands in the angora mittens against my mouth to keep them from crying, for I knew how hopeless prayer was in such circumstances, God only helps those who don't require His help.

18   Were we headed for the lakefront?—we crossed a swaying bridge high above railroad tracks, and almost immediately after that another swaying bridge high above an ice-locked canal. We passed factories shut down by the snowstorm with smokestacks so tall their rims were lost in mist. We were on South Main Street now passing darkened shuttered businesses, warehouses, a slaughterhouse; windowless brick buildings against whose walls snow had been driven as if sandblasted in eerie, almost legible patterns.

These were messages, I was sure!—yet I could not read them.

19   Out of the corner of my eye I watched Mr. Lacey as he drove. We were close together in the cramped car; yet at the same time I seemed to be watching us from a distance. At school there were boys who were fearful of Mr. Lacey yet, behind his back, sneered at him muttering what they'd like to do with him, slash his car tires, beat him up, and I felt a thrill of satisfaction *If you could see Mr. Lacey now!* for he was navigating the Volkswagen so capably along the treacherous street, past snowy hulks of vehicles abandoned by the wayside. He'd shoved back the hood of his wool

jacket—how handsome he looked! Where by day he often squinted behind his glasses, by night he seemed fully at ease. His hair was long and quill-like and of the subdued brown hue of a deer's winter coat; his eyes, so far as I could see, had a luminous coppery sheen. I recalled how at the high school Mr. Lacey was regarded with doubt and unease by the other teachers, many of whom were old enough to be his parents; he was considered arrogant because he didn't have an education degree from a state teachers' college, like the others, but a master's degree in math from the University of Buffalo where he was a part-time Ph.D. student. *Maybe I will reap where I haven't had any luck sowing* he'd once remarked to the class, standing chalk in hand at the blackboard which was covered in calculations. And this remark too had passed over our heads.

20   Now Mr. Lacey was saying as if bemused *Here, Erin—the edge. We'll go no farther in this direction.* For we were at the shore of Lake Erie—a frozen lake drifted in snow so far as the eye could see. (Yet I seemed to know how beneath the ice the water was agitated as if boiling, sinuous and black as tar.) Strewn along the beach were massive ice-boulders that glinted coldly in the moonlight. Even by day at this edge of the lake you could see only an edge of the Canadian shore, the farther western shore was lost in distance. I was in terror that Mr. Lacey out of some whim would abandon me here, for never could I have made my way back to my aunt's house in such cold.

21   But already Mr. Lacey was turning the car around, already we were driving inland, a faint tinkling music seemed to draw us, and within minutes we were in a wooded area I knew to be Delaware Park—though I'd never been there before. I had heard my classmates speak of skating parties here and had yearned to be invited to join them as I had yearned to be invited to visit the homes of certain girls, without success. *Hang on! Hang on!* Mr. Lacey said, for the Volkswagen was speeding like a sleigh on curving lanes into the interior of a deep evergreen forest. And suddenly—we were at a large oval skating rink above which strings of starry lights glittered like Christmas bulbs, where dozens, hundreds of elegantly dressed skaters circled the ice as if there had never been any snowstorm, or any snowstorm that mattered to *them.* Clearly these were privileged people, for electric power had been restored for their use and burned brilliantly, wastefully on all sides. *Oh Mr. Lacey I've never seen anything so beautiful* I said, biting my lip to keep from crying. It was a magical, wondrous place—the Delaware Park Skating Rink! Skaters on ice smooth as glass—skating round and round to gay, amplified music like that of a merry-go-round. Many of the skaters were in brightly colored clothes, handsome sweaters, fur hats, fur muffs; beautiful dogs of no breed known to me trotted alongside their masters and mistresses, pink tongues lolling in contentment. There were angel-faced girls in skaters' costumes, snug little pearl-buttoned velvet jackets and flouncy skirts to midthigh, gauzy knit stockings and kidskin boot-skates with blades that flashed like sterling silver—my heart yearned to see such skates for I'd learned to skate on rusted old skates formerly belonging to my older sis-

ters, on a creek near our farmhouse, in truth I had never really learned to skate, not as these skaters were skating, so without visible effort, strife, or anxiety. Entire families were skating—mothers and fathers hand in hand with small children, and older children, and white-haired elders who must have been grandparents!—and the family dog trotting along with that look of dogs laughing. There were attractive young people in groups, and couples with their arms around each other's waist, and solitary men and boys who swiftly threaded their way through the crowd unerring as undersea creatures perfectly adapted to their element. Never would I have dared join these skaters except Mr. Lacey insisted. Even as I feebly protested *Oh but I can't, Mr. Lacey—I don't know how to skate* he was pulling me to the skate rental where he secured a pair of skates for each of us; and suddenly there I was stumbling and swaying in the presence of real skaters, my ankles weak as water and my face blotched with embarrassment, oh what a spectacle—but Mr. Lacey had closed his fingers firmly around mine and held me upright, refused to allow me to fall. *Do as I do! Of course you can skate! Follow me!* So I had no choice but to follow, like an unwieldy lake barge hauled by a tugboat.

22   How loud the happy tinkling music was out on the ice, far louder than it had seemed on shore, as the lights too were brighter, nearly blinding. *Oh! Oh!* I panted in Mr. Lacey's wake, terrified of slipping and falling; breaking a wrist, an arm, a leg; terrified of falling in the paths of swift skaters whose blades flashed sharp and cruel as butcher knives. Everywhere was a harsh hissing sound of blades slicing the surface of the ice, a sound you couldn't hear on shore. I would be cut to ribbons if I fell! All my effort was required simply to stay out of the skaters' paths as they flew by, with no more awareness of me than if I were a passing shadow; the only skaters who noticed me were children, girls as well as boys, already expert skaters as young as nine or ten who glanced at me with smiles of bemusement, or disdain. *Out! out of our way! you don't belong here on our ice!* But I was stubborn too, I persevered, and after two or three times around the rink I was still upright and able to skate without Mr. Lacey's continuous vigilance, my head high and my arms extended for balance. My heart beat in giddy elation and pride. I was skating! At last! Mr. Lacey dashed off to the center of the ice where more practiced skaters performed, executing rapid circles, figure eights, dancerlike and acrobatic turns, his skate blades flashing, and a number of onlookers applauded, as I applauded, faltering but regaining my balance, skating on. I was not graceful—not by any stretch of the imagination—and I guessed I must have looked a sight, in an old baggy oil-stained sweater and rumpled wool slacks, my kinky-snarly red-brown hair in my eyes—but I wasn't quite so clumsy any longer, my ankles were getting stronger and the strokes of my skate-blades more assured, sweeping. How happy I was! How proud! I was beginning to be warm, almost feverish inside my clothes.

23   Restless as a wayward comet a blinding spotlight moved about the rink singling out skaters, among them Mr. Lacey as he spun at the very center

of the rink, an unlikely, storklike figure to be so graceful on the ice; for some reason then the spotlight abruptly shifted—to me! I was so caught by surprise I nearly tipped, and fell—I heard applause, laughter—saw faces at the edge of the rink grinning at me. Were they teasing, or sincere? Kindly, or cruel? I wanted to believe they were kindly for the rink was such a happy place but I couldn't be sure as I teetered past, arms flailing to keep my balance. I couldn't be certain but I seemed to see some of my high school classmates among the spectators; and some of my teachers; and others, adults, a caseworker from the Erie County family services department, staring at me disapprovingly. The spotlight was tormenting me: rushing at me, then falling away; allowing me to skate desperately onward, then seeking me out again swift and pitiless as a cheetah in pursuit of prey. The harshly tinkling music ended in a burst of static as if a radio had been turned violently up, then off. A sudden vicious wind rushed thin and sharp as a razor across the ice. My hair whipped in the wind, my ears were turning to ice. My fingers in the tight angora mittens were turning to ice, too. Most of the skaters had gone home, I saw to my disappointment, the better-dressed, better-mannered skaters, all the families, and the only dogs that remained were wild-eyed mongrels with bristling hackles and stumpy tails. Mr. Lacey and I skated hastily to a deserted snowswept section of the rink to avoid these dogs, and were pursued by the damned spotlight; here the ice was rippled and striated and difficult to skate on. An arm flashed at the edge of the rink, I saw a jeering white face, and an ice-packed snowball came flying to strike Mr. Lacey between his shoulder blades and shatter in pieces to the ground. Furious, his face reddening, Mr. Lacey whirled in a crouch—*Who did that? Which of you?* He spoke with his classroom authority but he wasn't in his classroom now and the boys only mocked him more insolently. They chanted something that sounded like *Lac-ey! Lac-ey! Ass-y! Assy-Asshole!* Another snowball struck him on the side of the head, sending his glasses flying and skittering along the ice. I shouted for them to *stop! stop!* and a snowball came careening past my head, another struck my arm, hard. Mr. Lacey shook his fist daring to move toward our attackers but this only unleashed a barrage of snowballs; several struck him with such force he was knocked down, a starburst of red at his mouth. Without his glasses Mr. Lacey looked young as a boy himself, dazed and helpless. On my hands and knees I crawled across the ice to retrieve his glasses, thank God there was only a hairline crack on one of the lenses. I was trembling with anger, sobbing. I was sure I recognized some of the boys, boys in my algebra class, but I didn't know their names. I crouched over Mr. Lacey asking was he all right? was he all right? seeing that he was stunned, pressing a handkerchief against his bleeding mouth. It was one of his white cotton handkerchiefs he'd take out of a pocket in class, shake ceremoniously open, and use to polish his glasses. The boys trotted away jeering and laughing. Mr. Lacey and I were alone, the only skaters remaining on the rink. Even the mongrel dogs had departed.

24   It was very cold now. Earlier that day there'd been a warning—temperatures in the Lake Erie–Lake Ontario region would drop as low that night, counting the windchill factor, as –30 degrees Fahrenheit. The wind stirred snake-skeins of powdery snow as if the blizzard might be returning. Above the rink most of the lightbulbs had burnt out or had been shattered by the rising wind. The fresh-fallen snow that had been so purely white was now trampled and littered; dogs had urinated on it; strewn about were cigarette butts, candy wrappers, lost boots, mittens, a wool knit cap. My pretty handknit muffler lay on the ground stiffened with filth—one of the jeering boys must have taken it from me when I was distracted. I bit my lip to keep from crying, the muffler had been ruined and I refused to pick it up. Subdued, silent, Mr. Lacey and I hunted our boots amid the litter, and left our skates behind in a slovenly mound, and limped back to the Volkswagen that was the only vehicle remaining in the snowswept parking lot. Mr. Lacey swore seeing the front windshield had been cracked like a spider's web, very much as the left lens of his glasses had been cracked. Ironically he said *Now you know, Erin, where the Delaware Park Skating Rink is.*

25   The bright battered-face moon had sunk nearly to the treeline, about to be sucked into blankest night.

26   In the Bison City Diner adjacent to the Greyhound bus station on Eighth Street, Mr. Lacey and I sat across a booth from each other, and Mr. Lacey gave our order to a brassy-haired waitress in a terse mutter—*two coffees, please.* Stern and frowning to discourage the woman from inquiring after his reddened face and swollen, still bleeding mouth. And then he excused himself to use the men's room. My bladder was aching, I had to use the rest room too, but would have been too shy to slip out of the booth if Mr. Lacey hadn't gone first.

27   It was 3:20 A.M. So late! The electricity had been restored in parts of Buffalo, evidently—driving back from the park we saw streetlights burning, traffic lights again operating. Still, most of the streets were deserted; choked with snow. The only other vehicles were snowplows and trucks spewing salt on the streets. Some state maintenance workers were in the Bison Diner, which was a twenty-four-hour diner, seated at the counter, talking and laughing loudly together and flirting with the waitress who knew them. When Mr. Lacey and I came into the brightly lit room, blinking, no doubt somewhat dazed-looking, the men glanced at us curiously but made no remarks. At least, none that we could hear. Mr. Lacey touched my arm and gestured with his head for me to follow him to a booth in the farthest corner of the diner—as if it was the most natural thing in the world, Mr. Lacey and me, sliding into that very booth.

28   In the clouded mirror in the women's room I saw my face strangely flushed, eyes shining like glass. This was a face not exactly known to me; more like my older sister Janice's, yet not Janice's, either. I cupped cold water into my hands and lowered my face to the sink grateful for the

water's coolness for my skin was feverish and prickling. My hair was matted as if someone had used an eggbeater on it and my sweater, my brother's discard, was more soiled than I'd known, unless some of the stains were blood—for maybe I'd gotten Mr. Lacey's blood on me out on the ice. *Er-in Don-egal* I whispered aloud in awe, amazement. In wonder. Yes, in pride! I was fifteen years old.

29   Inspired, I searched through my pockets for my tube of raspberry lipstick, and eagerly dabbed fresh color on my mouth. The effect was instantaneous. *Barbaric!* I heard Mr. Lacey's droll voice for so he'd once alluded to female "makeup" in our class *painting faces like savages with a belief in magic.* But he'd only been joking.

30   I did believe in magic, I guess. I had to believe in something!

31   When I returned to the booth in a glow of self-consciousness there was Mr. Lacey with his face freshly washed too, and his lank hair dampened and combed. His part was on the left side of his head, and wavery. He squinted up at me—his face pinched in a quick frowning smile signaling he'd noticed the lipstick, but certainly wouldn't comment on it. Pushed a menu in my direction—*Order anything you wish, Erin, you must be starving* and I picked up the menu to read it, for in fact I was light-headed with hunger, but the print was blurry as if under water and to my alarm I could not decipher a word. In regret I shook my head no, no thank you. *No, Erin? Nothing?* Mr. Lacey asked, surprised. Elsewhere in the diner a jukebox was playing a sentimental song—"Are You Lonesome Tonight?" At the counter, amid clouds of cigarette smoke, the workmen and the brassy-haired waitress erupted in laughter.

32   It seemed that Mr. Lacey had left his bloody handkerchief in the car and, annoyed and embarrassed, was dabbing at his mouth with a wadded paper towel from the men's room. His upper lip was swollen as if a bee had stung it and one of his front teeth was loose in its socket and still leaked blood. Almost inaudibly he whispered *Damn. Damn. Damn.* His coppery-brown eye through the cracked left lens of his glasses was just perceptibly magnified and seemed to be staring at me with unusual intensity. I shrank before the man's gaze for I feared he blamed me as the source of his humiliation and pain. In truth, I *was* to blame; these things would never have happened to Julius Lacey except for me.

33   Yet when Mr. Lacey spoke it was with surprising kindness. Asking *Are you sure you want nothing to eat, Erin? Nothing, nothing—at all?*

34   I could have devoured a hamburger half raw, and a plate of greasy french fries heaped with ketchup, but there I was shaking my head *no, no thank you Mr. Lacey.*

35   Why?—I was stricken with self-consciousness, embarrassment. To eat in the presence of this man! The intimacy would have been paralyzing, like stripping myself naked before him.

36   Indeed it was awkward enough when the waitress brought us our coffee, which was black, hotly steaming in thick mugs. Once or twice in my life I'd tried to drink coffee, for everyone seemed to drink it, and the taste

was repulsive to me, so bitter! But now I lifted the mug to my lips and sipped timidly at the steaming hot liquid black as motor oil. Seeing that Mr. Lacey disdained to add dairy cream or sugar to his coffee, I did not add any to my own. I was already nervous and almost at once my heart gave odd erratic beats and my pulse quickened.

37   One of my lifetime addictions, to this bitterly black steaming-hot liquid, would begin at this hour, in such innocence.

38   Mr. Lacey was saying with an air of reluctance, finality *In every equation there is always an x-factor, and in every x-factor there is the possibility, if not the probability, of tragic misunderstanding.* Out of his jacket pocket he'd taken, to my horror, a folded sheet of paper—red construction paper!—and was smoothing it out on the tabletop. I stared, I was speechless with chagrin. *You must not offer yourself in such a fashion, not even in secret, anonymously* Mr. Lacey said with a teacher's chiding frown. *The valentine heart is the female genitals, you will be misinterpreted.*

39   There was a roaring in my ears confused with music from the jukebox. The bitter black coffee scalded my throat and began to race along my veins. Words choked me *I'm sorry. I don't know what that is. Don't know what you're speaking of. Leave me alone, I hate you!* But I could not speak, just sat there shrinking to make myself as small as possible in Mr. Lacey's eyes staring with a pretense of blank dumb ignorance at the elaborate geometrical valentine TO MR. LACEY I had made with such hope the other night in the secrecy of my room, knowing I should not commit such an audacious act yet knowing, with an almost unbearable excitement, like one bringing a lighted match to flammable material, that I was going to do it.

40   Resentfully I said *I guess you know about me, my family. I guess there aren't any secrets.*

41   Mr. Lacey said *Yes, Erin. There are no secrets. But it's our prerogative not to speak of them if we choose.* Carefully he was refolding the valentine to return to his pocket, which I interpreted as a gesture of forgiveness. He said *There is nothing to be ashamed of, Erin. In you, or in your family.*

42   Sarcastically I said *There isn't?*

43   Mr. Lacey said *The individuals who are your mother and father came together out of all the universe to produce you. That's how you came into being, there was no other way.*

44   I couldn't speak, I was struck dumb. Wanting to protest, to laugh but could not. Hot tears ran down my cheeks.

45   Mr. Lacey persisted, gravely *And you love them, Erin. Much more than you love me.*

46   Mutely I shook my head *no.*

47   Mr. Lacey said, with his air of completing an algebra problem on the blackboard, in a tone of absolute finality *Yes. And we'll never speak of it again after tonight. In fact, of any of this*—making an airy magician's gesture that encompassed not just the Bison Diner but the city of Buffalo, the very night—*ever again.*

48   And so it was, we never did speak of it again. Our adventure that night following Valentine's Day 1959, ever again.

49   Next Monday at school, and all the days, and months, to come, Mr. Lacey and I maintained our secret. My heart burned with a knowledge I could not speak! But I was quieter, less nervous in class than I'd ever been; as if, overnight, I'd matured by years. Mr. Lacey behaved exactly, I think, as he'd always behaved toward me; no one could ever have guessed, in any wild flight of imagination, the bond between us. My grades hovered below 100 percent, for Mr. Lacey was surely one to wish to retain the power of giving tests no student could complete to perfection. With a wink he said *Humility goeth in place of a fall, Erin.* And in September when I returned for eleventh grade, Julius Lacey who might have been expected to teach solid geometry to my class was gone: returned to graduate school, we were told. Vanished forever from our lives.

50   All this was far in the future! That night, I could not have foreseen any of it. Nor how, over thirty years later, on the eve of Valentine's Day I would remove from its hiding place at the bottom of a bureau drawer a blood-stained man's handkerchief initialed *JNL,* fine white cotton yellowed with time, and smooth its wrinkles with the edge of my hand, and lift it to my face like Veronica her veil.

51   By the time Mr. Lacey and I left the Bison Diner the light there had become blinding and the jukebox music almost deafening. My head would echo for days *lonely? lonely? lonely?* Mr. Lacey drove us hurriedly south on Huron Street passing close beneath factory smokestacks rimmed at their tops with bluish-orange flame, spewing clouds of gray smoke that, upon impact with the freezing wind off Lake Erie, coalesced into fine gritty particles and fell back to earth like hail. These particles drummed on the roof, windshield, and hood of the Volkswagen, bouncing and ricocheting off, denting the metal. *God damn* Mr. Lacey swore softly *will You never cease!*

52   Abruptly then we were home. At my aunt's shabby woodframe bungalow at 3998 Huron Street, Buffalo, New York, that might have been any one of dozens, hundreds, even thousands of similar woodframe one-and-a-half-story bungalows in working-class neighborhoods of the city. The moon had vanished as if it had never been and the sky was depthless as a black paper cutout, but a streetlamp illuminated the mouth of the snowed-in alley and the great snowdrift in the shape of a right-angled triangle lifting to the roof below my window. *What did I promise, Erin?—no one knows you were ever gone* Mr. Lacey's words seemed to reverberate in my head without his speaking aloud. With relief I saw that the downstairs windows of the house were all darkened but there was a faint flickering light up in my room—the candle still burning, after all these hours. Gripping my hand tightly, Mr. Lacey led me up the snowdrift as up a treacherous stairs, fitting his boots to the footprints he'd originally made, and I followed suit, desperate not to slip and fall. *Safe at home, safe at home!* Mr.

Lacey's words sounded close in my ears, unless it was *Safe alone, safe alone!* I heard. Oh! the window was frozen shut again! so the two of us tugged, tugged, tugged, Mr. Lacey with good-humored patience until finally ice shattered, the window lurched up to a height of perhaps twelve inches. I'd begun to cry, a sorry spectacle, and my eyelashes had frozen within seconds in the bitter cold so Mr. Lacey laughed kissing my left eye, and then my right eye, and the lashes were thawed, and I heard *Goodbye, Erin!* as I climbed back through the window.

Questions for Discussion

1. What kind of relationships have characterized Erin's home life? How well does she get along with her aunt and her aunt's husband?

2. How does Erin relate to her classmates? Why is she *"desperate for love"?*

3. What do the students and other teachers think of Mr. Lacey? How do they treat him? Why?

4. Erin says of Mr. Lacey, "behind everything there was an elusive and tyrannical principle of which Mr. Lacey was the sole custodian." What does she mean? Why is Erin attracted to Mr. Lacey? What do she and Mr. Lacey have in common?

5. What does Mr. Lacey know about Erin that you would not expect him to know?

6. Did Erin's evening with Mr. Lacey actually happen? Or was it a dream? What details in the story suggest that it might actually have happened? What details suggest it was a dream?

7. What does Erin learn from her evening with Mr. Lacey? How does she mature as a result of her experience?

8. What precisely is Mr. Lacey's role in Erin's life? What about him is good? What about him is evil?

"DON'T YOU KNOW WHO I AM?" THE GROTESQUE IN OATES'S "WHERE ARE YOU GOING, WHERE HAVE YOU BEEN?"

JOYCE M. WEGS[1]

Joyce Carol Oates's ability to absorb and then to transmit in her fiction the terror which is often a part of living in America today has been frequently noted and admired. For instance, Walter Sullivan praises her skill by noting that "horror resides in the transformation of what we know best, the intimate and comfortable details of our lives made suddenly threatening."[2]

[1]Reprinted with permission from *Journal of Narrative Technique* 5 (1975), 66–72.

[2]Walter Sullivan, "The Artificial Demon: Joyce Carol Oates and the Dimensions of the Real," *The Hollins Critic,* 9, No. 4 (Dec., 1972), 2.

Although he does not identify it as such, Sullivan's comment aptly describes a classic instance of a grotesque intrusion; a familiar world suddenly appears alien. Oates frequently evokes the grotesque in her fiction, drawing upon both its tranditional or demonic and its contemporary or psychological manifestations.[3] In the prize-winning short story, "Where Are You Going, Where Have You Been?", Oates utilizes the grotesque in many of its forms to achieve a highly skillful integration of the multiple levels of the story and, in so doing, to suggest a transcendent reality which reaches beyond surface realism to evoke the simultaneous mystery and reality of the contradictions of the human heart. Full of puzzling and perverse longings, the heart persists in mixing lust and love, life and death, good and evil. Oates's teenage protagonist, Connie, discovers that her dream love-god also wears the face of lust, evil and death.

Centering the narrative on the world of popular teenage music and culture, Oates depicts the tawdry world of drive-in restaurants and shopping plazas blaring with music with a careful eye for authentic surface detail. However, her use of popular music as a thematic referent is typical also of her frequent illumination of the illusions and grotesquely false values which may arise from excessive devotion to such aspects of popular culture as rock music, movies, and romance magazines. In all of her fiction as in this story, she frequently employs a debased religious imagery to suggest the gods which modern society has substituted for conventional religion. Oates delineates the moral poverty of Connie, her fifteen-year-old protagonist, by imaging a typical evening Connie spends at a drive-in restaurant as a grotesquely parodied religious pilgrimage. Left by her friend's father to stroll at the shopping center or go to a movie, Connie and her girlfriend immediately cross the highway to the restaurant frequented by older teenagers. A grotesque parody of a church, the building is bottle-shaped and has a grinning boy holding a hamburger aloft on top of it. Unconscious of any ludicrousness, Connie and her friend enter it as if going into a "sacred building"[4] which will give them "what haven and blessing they yearned for." (31) It is the music which is "always in the background, like music at a church service" (31) that has invested this "bright-lit, fly-infested" (31) place with such significance. Indeed, throughout the story the music is given an almost mystical character, for it evokes in Connie a mysterious pleasure, a "glow of slow-pulsed joy that seemed to rise mysteriously out of the music itself." (33)

Although the story undoubtedly has a moral dimension,[5] Oates does not take a judgmental attitude toward Connie. In fact, much of the terror

[3]Joyce Markert Wegs, "The Grotesque in Some American Novels of the Nineteen-Sixties: Ken Kesey, Joyce Carol Oates, Sylvia Plath," Diss., University of Illinois, 1973.

[4]Joyce Carol Oates, "Where Are You Going, Where Have You Been?" *The Wheel of Love* (1970; rpt. Greenwich, Conn: Fawcett, 1972), p. 31. All subsequent references to the story appear within parentheses in the text.

[5]See Walter Sullivan, "Where Have All the Flowers Gone?: The Short Story in Search of Itself," *Sewanee Review,* 78, No. 3 (Summer, 1970), 537.

of the story comes from the recognition that there must be thousands of Connies. By carefully including telltale phrases, Oates demonstrates in an understated fashion why Connies exist. Connie's parents, who seem quite typical, have disqualified themselves as moral guides for her. At first reading, the reader may believe Connie's mother to be concerned about her daughter's habits, views, and friends; but basically their arguments are little more than a "pretense of exasperation, a sense that they [. . . are] tugging and struggling over something of little value to either of them." (32). Connie herself is uncertain of her mother's motives for constantly picking at her; she alternates between a view that her mother's harping proceeds from jealousy of Connie's good looks now that her own have faded (29) and a feeling that her mother really prefers her over her plain older sister June because she is prettier. (32) In other words, to Connie and her mother, real value lies in beauty. Connie's father plays a small role in her life, but by paralleling repeated phrases, Oates suggests that this is precisely the problem. Because he does not "bother talking much" (30) to his family, he can hardly ask the crucial parental questions, "Where are you going?" or "Where have you been?" The moral indifference of the entire adult society is underscored by Oates's parallel description of the father of Connie's friend, who also "never [. . . bothers] to ask" what they did when he picks up the pair at the end of one of their evenings out. Similarly, on Sunday morning, "none of them bothered with church," (33) not even that supposed paragon, June.

Since her elders do not bother about her, Connie is left defenseless against the temptations represented by Arnold Friend. A repeated key phrase emphasizes her helplessness. As she walks through the parking lot of the restaurant with Eddie, she can not "help but" (31) look about happily, full of joy in a life characterized by casual pickups and constant music. When she sees Arnold in a nearby car, she looks away, but her instinctive flirtatiousness triumphs and she can not "help but" (31) look back. Later, like Lot's wife leaving Sodom and Gomorrah, she cannot "help but look back" (32) at the plaza and drive-in as her friend's father drives them home. In Connie's case, the consequences of the actions she cannot seem to help are less biblically swift to occur and can not be simply labeled divine retribution.

Since music is Connie's religion, its values are hers also. Oates does not include the lyrics to any popular songs here, for any observer of contemporary America could surely discern the obvious link between Connie's high esteem for romantic love and youthful beauty and the lyrics of scores of hit tunes. The superficiality of Connie's values becomes terrifyingly apparent when Arnold Friend, the external embodiment of the teenage ideal celebrated in popular songs, appears at Connie's home in the country one Sunday afternoon when she is home alone, listening to music and drying her hair. It is no accident that Arnold's clothes, car, speech, and taste in music reflect current teenage chic almost exactly, for they constitute part of a careful disguise intended to reflect Arnold's self-image as an accomplished youthful lover.

Suspense mounts in the story as the reader realizes along with Connie that Arnold is not a teenager and is really thirty or more. Each part of his disguise is gradually revealed to be grotesquely distorted in some way. His shaggy black hair, "crazy as a wig," (34) is evidently really a wig. The mask-like appearance of his face has been created by applying a thick coat of makeup; however, he has carelessly omitted his throat. (41) Even his eye-lashes appear to be made-up, but with some tarlike material. In his cloth-ing, his disguise appears more successful, for Connie approves of the way he dresses, as "all of them dressed." (36) in tight jeans, boots, and pullover. When he walks, however, Connie realizes that the runty Arnold, conscious that the ideal teenage dream lover is tall, has stuffed his boots; the result is, however, that he can hardly walk and staggers ludicrously. Attempting to bow, he almost falls. Similarly, the gold jalopy covered with teenage slang phrases seems authentic until Connie notices that one of them is no longer in vogue. Even his speech is not his own, for it recalls lines borrowed from disc jockeys, teenage slang, and lines from popular songs. Arnold's strange companion, Ellie Oscar, is just as grotesque as Arnold. Almost totally absorbed in listening to music and interrupting this activity only to offer threatening assistance to Arnold, Ellie is no youth either; he has the "face of a forty-year-old baby." (39) Although Arnold has worked out his disguise with great care, he soon loses all subtlety in letting Connie know of his evil intentions; he is not simply crazy but a criminal with plans to rape and probably to murder Connie.

However, Arnold is far more than a grotesque portrait of a psycho-pathic killer masquerading as a teenager; he also has all the traditional sinister traits of that arch-deceiver and source of grotesque terror, the devil. As is usual with Satan, he is in disguise; the distortions in his appear-ance and behavior suggest not only that his identity is faked but also hint at his real self. Equating Arnold and Satan is not simply a gratuitous con-nection designed to exploit traditional demonic terror, for the early pages of the story explicitly prepare for this linking by portraying popular music and its values as Connie's perverted version of religion. When Arnold comes up the drive, her first glance makes Connie believe that a teenage boy with his jalopy, the central figure of her religion, has arrived; there-fore, she murmurs "Christ, Christ" (34) as she wonders about how her newly-washed hair looks. When the car—a parodied golden chariot?—stops, a horn sounds "as if this were a signal Connie knew." (34) On one level, the horn honks to announce the "second coming" of Arnold, a demonic Day of Judgment. Although Connie never specifically recognizes Arnold as Satan, her first comment to him both hints at his infernal ori-gins and faithfully reproduces teenage idiom: "Who the *hell* do you think you are?" (emphasis mine, 34) When he introduces himself, his name too hints at his identity, for "friend" is uncomfortably close to "fiend"; his ini-tials could well stand for Arch Fiend. The frightened Connie sees Arnold as "only half real"; (39) he "had driven up her driveway all right but had come from nowhere before that and belonged nowhere." (39) Especially supernatural is his mysterious knowledge about her, her family, and her friends. At one point, he even seems to be able to see all the way to the barbecue which Connie's family is attending and to get a clear vision of what all the guests are doing. Typical of his ambiguous roles is his hint that he had something to do with the death of the old woman who lived down the road. It is never clear whether Arnold has killed her, has simply heard of her death, or knows about it in his devil role of having come to take her away to hell. Although Arnold has come to take Connie away, in his traditional role as evil spirit, he may not cross a threshold uninvited; he repeatedly mentions that he is not going to come in after Connie, and he never does. Instead, he lures Connie out to him. Part of his success may be attributed to his black magic in having put his sign on her—X for victim. (37–38) Because the devil is not a mortal being, existing as he does in all ages, it is not surprising that he slips in remembering what slang terms are in vogue. Similarly, his foolish attempt at a bow may result from a mixup in temporal concepts of the ideal lover. In addition, his clumsy bow may be due to the fact that it must be difficult to manipulate boots if one has cloven feet!

Although Oates attempts to explain the existence of Connie, she makes no similar effort to explain the existence of Arnold, for that would constitute an answer to the timeless and insoluble problem of evil in the world. As this story shows, Oates would agree with Pope Paul VI's recent commentary on the "terrible reality" of evil in the world, but she would not, I feel sure, endorse his view of this evil as being literally embodied in a specific being. Pope Paul describes evil as "not merely a lack of something, but an effective agent, a living spiritual being, perverted and perverting. A terrible reality. Mysterious and frightening."[6] Oates's description of her own views on religion is in terms strikingly similar to the language used by Pope Paul. To her, religion is a "kind of psychological manifestation of deep powers, deep imaginative, mysterious powers, which are always with us, and what has in the past been called supernatural I would prefer simply to call natural. However, though these things are natural, they are still inaccessible and cannot be understood, cannot be controlled."[7] Thus, although Arnold is clearly a symbolic Satan, he also functions on a psychological level.

On this level, Arnold Friend is the incarnation of Connie's unconscious erotic desires and dreams, but in uncontrollable nightmare form. When she first sees Arnold in the drive-in, she instinctively senses his sinister attraction, for she cannot "help glancing back" (31) at him. Her "trashy daydreams" (30) are largely filled with blurred recollections of the caresses of the many boys she has dated. That her dreams are a kind of generalized sexual desire—although Connie does not consciously

    [6]Andrew M. Greeley, "The Devil, You Say," *The New York Times Magazine*, 4 Feb., 1973, p. 26, quotes an address by Pope Paul on 15 Nov., 1972, as reported in the Vatican newspaper.

    [7]Linda Kuehl, "An Interview with Joyce Carol Oates," *Commonweal*, 91 (5 Dec., 1969), 308.

identify them as such—is made evident by Oates's description of Connie's summer dreams: "But all the boys fell back and dissolved into a single face that was not even a face but an idea, a feeling, mixed up with the urgent insistent pounding of the music and the humid night air of July." (32) What is frightening about Arnold is that he voices and makes explicit her own sexual desires; teenage boys more usually project their similar message with "that sleepy dreamy smile that all the boys used to get across ideas they didn't want to put into words." (38) Connie's reaction to his bluntness is one of horror: "People don't talk like that, you're crazy." (40)

Connie's fear drives her into a grotesque separation of mind from body in which her unconscious self takes over and betrays her. Terror-stricken, she cannot even make her weak fingers dial the police; she can only scream into the phone. In the same way that she is Arnold's prisoner, locked inside the house he alternately threatens to knock down or burn down, she is also a prisoner of her own body: "A noisy sorrowful wailing rose all about her and she was locked inside it the way she was locked inside this house." (44) Finally, her conscious mind rejects any connection with her body and its impulses; her heart seems "nothing that was hers" "but just a pounding, living thing inside this body that wasn't really hers either." (45) In a sense, her body with its puzzling desires "decides" to go with Arnold although her rational self is terrified of him: "She watched herself push the door slowly open as if she were back safe somewhere in the other doorway, watching this body and this head of long hair moving out into the sunlight where Arnold Friend waited." (45)

Oates encourages the reader to look for multiple levels in this story and to consider Arnold and Connie at more than face value by her repeated emphasis on the question of identity. The opening of the story introduces the concept to which both Connie and her mother seem to subscribe—being pretty means being someone. In fact, her mother's acid questions as she sees Connie at her favorite activity of mirror-gazing— "Who are you? You think you're so pretty?" (29)—also introduce the converse of this idea, namely, that those who lack physical beauty have no identity. As does almost everything in the story, everything about Connie has "two sides to it." (30) However, Connie's nature, one for at home and one for "anywhere that was not home," (30) is simple in comparison to that of Arnold. Connie's puzzled questions at first query what role Arnold thinks he is playing: "Who the hell do you think you are?" (34) Then she realizes that he sees himself all too literally as the man of her dreams, and she becomes more concerned about knowing his real identity. By the time that Arnold asks, "Don't you know who I am?" (42) Connie realizes that it is no longer a simple question of whether he is a "jerk" (35) or someone worth her attention but of just how crazy he is. By the end she knows him to be a murderer, for she realizes that she will never see her family again. (44) However, only the reader sees Arnold's Satan identity. Connie's gradual realization of Arnold's identity brings with it a recognition of the actual significance of physical beauty: Arnold is indeed someone to be concerned about, even if he is no handsome youth. At the conclusion Connie has lost all identity except that of victim, for Arnold's half-sung sigh about her blue eyes ignores the reality of her brown ones. In Arnold's view, Connie's personal identity is totally unimportant.

Dedicated to contemporary balladeer Bob Dylan, this story in a sense represents Oates's updated prose version of a ballad in which a demon lover carries away his helpless victim. By adding modern psychological insights, she succeeds in revealing the complex nature of the victim of a grotesque intrusion by an alien force; on one level, the victim actually welcomes and invites this demonic visitation. Like Bob Dylan, she grafts onto the ballad tradition a moral commentary which explores but does not solve the problems of the evils of our contemporary society; an analagous Dylan ballad is his "It's a Hard Rain's a Gonna' Fall." Even the title records not only the ritual parental questions but also suggests that there is a moral connection between the two questions: where Connie goes is related to where she has been. Oates does not judge Connie in making this link, however; Connie is clearly not in complete control over where she has been. The forces of her society, her family, and her self combine to make her fate inescapable.

THE PIED PIPER OF TUCSON: HE CRUISED IN A GOLDEN CAR, LOOKING FOR THE ACTION

DON MOSER[1]

Hey, c'mon babe, follow me.
I'm the Pied Piper, follow me.
I'm the Pied Piper.
And I'll show you where it's at

—POPULAR SONG, TUCSON, WINTER 1965

At dusk in Tucson, as the stark, yellow-flared mountains begin to blur against the sky, the golden car slowly cruises Speedway. Smoothly it rolls down the long, divided avenue, past the supermarkets, the gas stations and the motels; past the twist joints, the sprawling drive-in restaurants. The car slows for an intersection, stops, then pulls away again. The exhaust mutters against the pavement as the young man driving takes the machine swiftly, expertly through the gears. A car pulls even with him; the teenage girls in the front seat laugh, wave and call his name. The young man glances toward the rearview mirror, turned always so that he can look at his own reflection, and he appraises himself.

The face is his own creation: the hair dyed a raven black, the skin darkened to a deep tan with pancake make-up, the lips whitened, the whole

[1] *Life*, March 4, 1966.

effect heightened by a mole he has painted on one cheek. But the deep-set blue eyes are all his own. Beautiful eyes, the girls say.

Approaching the Hi-Ho, the teenagers' nightclub, he backs off on the accelerator, then slowly cruises on past Johnie's Drive-in. There the cars are beginning to orbit and accumulate in the parking lot—neat sharp cars with deep-throated mufflers and Maltese-cross decals on the windows. But it's early yet. Not much going on. The driver shifts up again through the gears, and the golden car slides away along the glitter and gimcrack of Speedway. Smitty keeps looking for the action.

Whether the juries in the two trials decide that Charles Howard Schmid Jr. did or did not brutally murder Alleen Rowe, Gretchen Fritz, and Wendy Fritz has from the beginning seemed of almost secondary importance to the people of Tucson. They are not indifferent. But what disturbs them far beyond the question of Smitty's guilt or innocence are the revelations about Tucson itself that have followed on the disclosure of the crimes. Starting with the bizarre circumstances of the killings and on through the ugly fragments of the plot—which in turn hint at other murders as yet undiscovered, at teenage sex, blackmail, even connections with the *Cosa Nostra*—they have had to view their city in a new and unpleasant light. The fact is that Charles Schmid—who cannot be dismissed as a freak, an aberrant of no consequence—had for years functioned successfully as a member, even a leader of the yeastiest stratum of Tucson's teenage society.

As a high school student Smitty had been, as classmates remember, an outsider—but not that far outside. He was small but he was a fine athlete, and in his last year—1960—he was a state gymnastics champion. His grades were poor, but he was in no trouble to speak of until his senior year, when he was suspended for stealing tools from a welding class.

But Smitty never really left the school. After his suspension he hung around waiting to pick up kids in a succession of sharp cars which he drove fast and well. He haunted all the teenage hangouts along Speedway, including the bowling alleys and the public swimming pool—and he put on spectacular diving exhibitions for girls far younger than he.

At the time of his arrest last November, Charles Schmid was twenty-three years old. He wore face make-up and dyed his hair. He habitually stuffed three or four inches of old rags and tin cans into the bottoms of his high-topped boots to make himself taller than his five-foot-three and stumbled about so awkwardly while walking that some people thought he had wooden feet. He pursed his lips and let his eyelids droop in order to emulate his idol, Elvis Presley. He bragged to girls he knew a hundred ways to make love, that he ran dope, that he was a Hell's Angel. He talked about being a rough customer in a fight (he was, though he was rarely in one), and he always carried in his pocket tiny bottles of salt and pepper, which he said he used to blind his opponents. He liked to use highfalutin language and had a favorite saying, "I can manifest my neurotical emotions, emancipate an epicureal instinct, and elaborate on my heterosexual tendencies."

He occasionally shocked even those who thought they knew him well. A friend says he once saw Smitty tie a string to a tail of his pet cat, swing it around his head and beat it bloody against a wall. Then he turned calmly and asked, "You feel compassion—why?"

Yet even while Smitty tried to create an exalted, heroic image of himself, he had worked on a pitiable one. "He thrived on feeling sorry for himself," recalls a friend, "and making others feel sorry for him." At various times Smitty told intimates that he had leukemia and didn't have long to live. He claimed that he was adopted, that his real name was Angel Rodriguez, that his father was a "bean" (local slang for Mexican, an inferior race in Smitty's view), and that his mother was a famous lawyer who would have nothing to do with him.

He had a nice car. He had plenty of money from his parents, who ran a nursing home, and he was always glad to spend it on anyone who'd listen to him. He had a pad of his own where he threw parties and he had impeccable manners. He was always willing to help a friend and he would send flowers to girls who were ill. He was older and more mature than most of his friends. He knew where the action was, and if he wore makeup—well, at least he was *different.*

Some of the older kids—those who worked, who had something else to do—thought Smitty was a creep. But to the youngsters—to the bored and the lonely, to the dropout and the delinquent, to the young girls with beehive hairdos and tight pants they didn't quite fill out, and to the boys with acne and no jobs—to these people, Smitty was a kind of folk hero. Nutty maybe, but at least more dramatic, more theatrical, more *interesting* than anyone else in their lives; a semi-ludicrous, sexy-eyed pied-piper who, stumbling along in his rag-stuffed boots, led them up and down Speedway.

On the evening of May 31, 1964, Alleen Rowe prepared to go to bed early. She had to be in class by six a.m. and she had an examination the next day. Alleen was a pretty girl of fifteen, a better-than-average student who talked about going to college and becoming an oceanographer. She was also a sensitive child—given to reading romantic novels and taking long walks in the desert at night. Recently she had been going through a period of adolescent melancholia, often talking with her mother, a nurse, about death. She would, she hoped, be some day reincarnated as a cat.

On this evening, dressed in a black bathing suit and thongs, her usual costume around the house, she had watched the Beatles on TV and had tried to teach her mother to dance the Frug. Then she took her bath, washed her hair, and came out to kiss her mother good night. Norma

Rowe, an attractive, womanly divorcée, was somehow moved by the girl's clean fragrance and said, "You smell so good—are you wearing perfume?"

"No, Mom," the girl answered, laughing, "it's just me."

A little later Mrs. Rowe looked in on her daughter, found her apparently sleeping peacefully, and then left for her job as a night nurse in a Tucson hospital. She had no premonition of danger, but she had lately been concerned about Alleen's friendship with a neighbor girl named Mary French.

Mary and Alleen had been spending a good deal of time together, smoking and giggling and talking girl talk in the Rowe backyard. Norma Rowe did not approve. She particularly did not approve of Mary French's friends, a tall, gangling boy of nineteen named John Saunders and another named Charles Schmid. She had seen Smitty racing up and down the street in his car and once, when he came to call on Alleen and found her not at home, he had looked at Norma so menacingly with his "pinpoint eyes" that she had been frightened.

Her daughter, on the other hand, seemed to have mixed feelings about Smitty. "He's creepy," she once told her mother, "he just makes me crawl. But he can be nice when he wants to."

At any rate, later that night—according to Mary French's sworn testimony—three friends arrived at Alleen Rowe's house: Smitty, Mary French, and Saunders. Smitty had frequently talked with Mary French about killing the Rowe girl by hitting her over the head with a rock. Mary French tapped on Alleen's window and asked her to come out and drink beer with them. Wearing a shift over her bathing suit, she came willingly enough.

Schmid's two accomplices were strange and pitiable creatures. Each of them was afraid of Smitty, yet each was drawn to him. As a baby, John Saunders had been so afflicted with allergies that scabs encrusted his entire body. To keep him from scratching himself his parents had tied his hands and feet to the crib each night, and when eventually he was cured he was so conditioned that he could not go to sleep without being bound hand and foot.

Later, a scrawny boy with poor eyesight ("Just a skinny little body with a big head on it"), he was taunted and bullied by larger children; in turn he bullied those who were smaller. He also suffered badly from asthma and he had few friends. In high school he was a poor student and constantly in minor trouble.

Mary French, nineteen, was—to put it straight—a frump. Her face, which might have been pretty, seemed somehow lumpy, her body shapeless. She was not dull but she was always a poor student, and she finally had simply stopped going to high school. She was, a friend remembers, "fantastically in love with Smitty. She just sat home and waited while he went out with other girls."

Now, with Smitty at the wheel, the four teen-agers headed for the desert, which begins out Golf Links Road. It is spooky country, dry and empty, the yellow sand clotted with cholla and mesquite and stunted, strangely green palo verde trees, and the great humanoid saguaro that hulk against the sky. Out there at night you can hear the yip and ki-yi of coyotes, the piercing screams of wild creatures—cats, perhaps.

According to Mary French, they got out of the car and walked down into a wash, where they sat on the sand and talked for a while, the four of them. Schmid and Mary then started back to the car. Before they got there, they heard a cry and Schmid turned back toward the wash. Mary went on to the car and sat in it alone. After forty-five minutes, Saunders appeared and said Smitty wanted her to come back down. She refused, and Saunders went away. Five or ten minutes later, Smitty showed up. "He got into the car," says Mary, "and he said, 'We killed her. I love you very much.' He kissed me. He was breathing real hard and seemed excited." Then Schmid got a shovel from the trunk of the car and they returned to the wash. "She was lying on her back and there was blood on her face and head," Mary French testified. Then the three of them dug a shallow grave and put the body in it and covered it up. Afterwards, they wiped Schmid's car clean of Alleen's fingerprints.

More than a year passed. Norma Rowe had reported her daughter missing and the police searched for her—after a fashion. At Mrs. Rowe's insistence they picked up Schmid, but they had no reason to hold him. The police, in fact, assumed that Alleen was just one more of Tucson's runaways.

Norma Rowe, however, had become convinced that Alleen had been killed by Schmid, although she left her kitchen light on every night in case Alleen did come home. She badgered the police and she badgered the sheriff until the authorities began to dismiss her as a crank. She began to imagine a high-level conspiracy against her. She wrote the state attorney general, the FBI, the U.S. Department of Health, Education and Welfare. She even contacted a New Jersey mystic, who said she could see Alleen's body out in the desert under a big tree.

Ultimately Norma Rowe started her own investigation, questioning Alleen's friends, poking around, dictating her findings to a tape recorder; she even tailed Smitty at night, following him in her car, scared stiff that he might spot her.

Schmid, during this time, acquired a little house of his own. There he held frequent parties, where people sat around amid his stacks of *Playboy* magazines, playing Elvis Presley records and drinking beer.

He read Jules Feiffer's novel, *Harry, the Rat with Women,* and said that his ambition was to be like Harry and have a girl commit suicide over him. Once, according to a friend, he went to see a minister, who gave him a Bible and told him to read the first three chapters of John. Instead Schmid tore the pages out and burned them in the street. "Religion is a farce," he announced. He started an upholstery business with some friends, called himself "founder and president," but then failed to put up the money he promised and the venture was short-lived.

He decided he liked blondes best, and took to dyeing the hair of various teenage girls he went around with. He went out and bought two imitation diamonds for about $13 apiece and then engaged himself, on the same day, both to Mary French and to a fifteen-year-old girl named Kathy Morath. His plan, he confided to a friend, was to put each of the girls to work and have them deposit their salaries in a bank account held jointly with him. Mary French did indeed go to work in the convalescent home Smitty's parents operated. When their bank account was fat enough, Smitty withdrew the money and bought a tape recorder.

By this time Smitty also had a girl from a higher social stratum than he usually was involved with. She was Gretchen Fritz, daughter of a prominent Tucson heart surgeon. Gretchen was a pretty, thin, nervous girl of seventeen with a knack for trouble. A teacher described her as "erratic, subversive, a psychopathic liar."

At the horsy private school she attended for a time she was a misfit. She not only didn't care about horses, but she shocked her classmates by telling them they were foolish for going out with boys without getting paid for it. Once she even committed the unpardonable social sin of turning up at a formal dance party accompanied by boys wearing what was described as beatnik dress. She cut classes, she was suspected of stealing and when, in the summer before her senior year, she got into trouble with juvenile authorities for her role in an attempted theft at a liquor store, the headmaster suggested she not return and then recommended she get psychiatric treatment.

Charles Schmid saw Gretchen for the first time at a public swimming pool in the summer of 1964. He met her by the simple expedient of following her home, knocking on the door and, when she answered, saying, "Don't I know you?" They talked for an hour. Thus began a fierce and stormy relationship. A good deal of what authorities know of the development of this relationship comes from the statements of a spindly scarecrow of a young man who wears pipestem trousers and Beatle boots: Richard Bruns. At the time Smitty was becoming involved with Gretchen, Bruns was eighteen years old. He had served two terms in the reformatory at Fort Grant. He had been in and out of trouble all his life, had never fit in anywhere. Yet, although he never went beyond the tenth grade in school and his credibility on many counts is suspect, he is clearly intelligent and even sensitive. He was, for a time, Smitty's closest friend and confidant, and he is today one of the mainstays of the state's case against Smitty. His story:

"He and Gretchen were always fighting," says Bruns. "She didn't want him to drink or go out with the guys or go out with other girls. She wanted him to stay home, call her on the phone, be punctual. First she would get suspicious of him, then he'd get suspicious of her. They were made for each other."

Their mutual jealousy led to sharp and continual arguments. Once she infuriated him by throwing a bottle of shoe polish on his car. Another time she was driving past Smitty's house and saw him there with some other girls. She jumped out of her car and began screaming. Smitty took off into the house, out the back, and climbed a tree in his backyard.

His feelings for her were an odd mixture of hate and adoration. He said he was madly in love with her, but he called her a whore. She would let Smitty in her bedroom window at night. Yet he wrote an anonymous letter to the Tucson Health Department accusing her of having venereal disease and spreading it about town. But Smitty also went to enormous lengths to impress Gretchen, once shooting holes through the windows of his car and telling her that thugs, from whom he was protecting her, had fired at him. So Bruns described the relationship.

On the evening of August 16, 1965, Gretchen Fritz left the house with her little sister Wendy, a friendly, lively thirteen-year-old, to go to a drive-in movie. Neither girl ever came home again. Gretchen's father, like Aleen Rowe's mother, felt sure that Charles Schmid had something to do with his daughters' disappearance, and eventually he hired Bill Heilig, a private detective, to handle the case. One of Heilig's men soon found Gretchen's red compact car parked behind a motel, but the police continued to assume that the girls had joined the ranks of Tucson's runaways.

About a week after Gretchen disappeared, Bruns was at Smitty's home. "We were sitting in the living room," Bruns recalls. "He was sitting on the sofa and I was in the chair by the window and we got on the subject of Gretchen. He said, 'You know I killed her?' I said I didn't, and he said, 'You know where?' I said no. He said, 'I did it here in the living room. First I killed Gretchen, then Wendy was still going *"huh, huh, huh,"* so I [. . . here Bruns showed how Smitty made a garroting gesture.] Then I took the bodies and put them in the trunk of the car. I put the bodies in the most obvious place I could think of because I just didn't care any more. Then I ditched the car and wiped it clean."

Bruns was not particularly upset by Smitty's story. Months before, Smitty had told him of the murder of Aleen Rowe, and nothing had come of that. So he was not certain Smitty was telling the truth about the Fritz girls. Besides, Bruns detested Gretchen himself. But what happened next, still according to Bruns's story, did shake him up.

One night not long after, a couple of tough-looking characters, wearing sharp suits and smoking cigars, came by with Smitty and picked up Bruns. Smitty said they were Mafia, and that someone had hired them to look for Gretchen. Smitty and Bruns were taken to an apartment where several men were present whom Smitty later claimed to have recognized as local *Cosa Nostra* figures.

They wanted to know what had happened to the girls. They made no threats, but the message, Bruns remembers, came across loud and clear. These were no street-corner punks: these were the real boys. In spite of the intimidating company, Schmid lost none of his insouciance. He said he didn't know where Gretchen was, but if she turned up hurt he wanted these men to help him get whoever was responsible. He added that he thought she might have gone to California.

By the time Smitty and Bruns got back to Smitty's house, they were both a little shaky. Later that night, says Bruns, Smitty did the most unlikely thing imaginable: he called the FBI. First he tried the Tucson office and couldn't raise anyone. Then he called Phoenix and couldn't get an agent there either. Finally he put in a person-to-person call to J. Edgar Hoover in Washington. He didn't get Hoover, of course, but he got someone and told him that the Mafia was harassing him over the disappearance of a girl. The FBI promised to have someone in touch with him soon.

Bruns was scared and said so. It occurred to him now that if Smitty really had killed the Fritz girls and left their bodies in an obvious place, they were in very bad trouble indeed—with the Mafia on one hand and the FBI on the other. "Let's go bury them," Bruns said.

"Smitty stole the keys to his old man's station wagon," says Bruns, "and then we got a flat shovel—the only one we could find. We went to Johnie's and got a hamburger, and then we drove out to the old drinking spot [in the desert]—that's what Smitty meant when he said the most obvious place. It's where we used to drink beer and make out with girls.

"So we parked the car and got the shovel and walked down there, and we couldn't find anything. Then Smitty said, 'Wait, I smell something.' We went in opposite directions looking, and then I heard Smitty say, 'Come here.' I found him kneeling over Gretchen. There was a white rag tied around her legs. Her blouse was pulled up and she was wearing a white bra and Capris.

"Then he said, 'Wendy's up this way.' I sat there for a minute. Then I followed Smitty to where Wendy was. He'd had the decency to cover her—except for one leg, which was sticking up out of the ground.

"We tried to dig with the flat shovel. We each took turns. He'd dig for a while and then I'd dig for a while, but the ground was hard and we couldn't get anywhere with that flat shovel. We dug for twenty minutes and finally Smitty said we'd better do something because it's going to get light. So he grabbed the rag that was around Gretchen's legs and dragged her down in the wash. It made a noise like dragging a hollow shell. It stunk like hell. Then Smitty said wipe off her shoes, there might be fingerprints, so I wiped them off with my handkerchief and threw it away.

"We went back to Wendy. Her leg was sticking up with a shoe on it. He said take off her tennis shoe and throw it over there. I did, I threw it. Then he said, 'Now you're in this as deep as I am.'" By then, the sisters had been missing for about two weeks.

Early next morning Smitty did see the FBI. Nevertheless—here Bruns's story grows even wilder—that same day Smitty left for California, accompanied by a couple of Mafia types, to look for Gretchen Fritz. While there, he was picked up by the San Diego police on a complaint that he was impersonating an FBI officer. He was detained briefly, released and then returned to Tucson.

But now, it seemed to Richard Bruns, Smitty began acting very strangely. He startled Bruns by saying, "I've killed—not three times, but four. Now it's your turn, Richie." He went berserk in his little house, smashing his fist through a wall, slamming doors, then rushing out into the backyard in nothing but his undershorts, when he ran through the night screaming, "God is going to punish me!" He also decided, suddenly, to get married— to a fifteen-year-old girl who was a stranger to most of his friends.

Bruns went to Ohio to stay with his grandmother and to try to get a job. It was hopeless. He couldn't sleep at night, and if he did doze off he had his old nightmare again.

One night he blurted out the whole story to his grandmother in their kitchen. She thought he had had too many beers and didn't believe him. "I hear beer does strange things to a person," she said comfortingly. At her words Bruns exploded, knocked over a chair and shouted, "The one time in my life when I need advice what do I get?" A few minutes later he was on the phone to the Tucson police.

Things happened swiftly. At Bruns's frantic insistence, the police picked up Kathy Morath and put her in protective custody. They went into the desert and discovered—precisely as Bruns had described them—the grisly, skeletal remains of Gretchen and Wendy Fritz. They started the machinery that resulted in the arrest a week later of John Saunders and Mary French. They found Charles Schmid working in the yard of his little house, his face layered with make-up, his nose covered by a patch of adhesive plaster which he had worn for five months, boasting that his nose was broken in a fight, and his boots packed full of old rags and tin cans. He put up no resistance.

John Saunders and Mary French confessed immediately to their roles in the slaying of Alleen Rowe and were quickly sentenced, Mary French to four to five years, Saunders to life. When Smitty goes on trial for this crime, on March 15, they will be principal witnesses against him.

Meanwhile Richie Bruns, the perpetual misfit, waits apprehensively for the end of the Fritz trial, desperately afraid that Schmid will go free. "If he does," Bruns says glumly, "I'll be the first one he'll kill."

As for Charles Schmid, he has adjusted well to his period of waiting. He is polite and agreeable with all, though at the preliminary hearings he glared menacingly at Richie Bruns. Dressed tastefully, tie neatly knotted, hair carefully combed, his face scrubbed clean of make-up, he is a short, compact, darkly handsome young man with a wide, engaging smile and those deepset eyes.

O'Connor's Mrs. May and Oates's Connie;
An Unlikely Pair of Religious Initiates[1]

Nancy Bishop Dessommes

When Joyce Carol Oates was asked in a 1969 interview whether she was like Flannery O'Connor, she responded,

> I don't know. I used to think that I was influenced by O'Connor. I don't know that I am really. She is so religious, and her works have to be seen as religious works with this other rather creepy dimension in the background, whereas in my writing there is only the natural world. (Kuehl 307)

A few weeks later, Oates was to publish a collection of stories (eventually titled *The Wheel of Love*) on the theme of love, including the much-debated, often anthologized "Where Are You Going, Where Have You Been?" Perhaps this story stands out from the others in the collection because of its uncharacteristic "other rather creepy dimension in the background." Critics cannot seem to decide whether Connie, the 15-year-old protagonist of the story, has had a dream, seen the devil, or simply been seduced and possibly murdered by a psychotic intruder. But one thing is certain. The story is fraught with religious overtones and nightmarish imagery, and it is doubtful that "only the natural world" is presented. Joyce Carol Oates's respect for Flannery O'Connor's work is well known, and despite Oates's claim to the contrary, "Where Are You Going, Where Have You Been?" is very much like O'Connor's short stories, most notably "Greenleaf." Readers of O'Connor will recognize in Connie the shortcomings of such popular O'Connor figures as Mrs. Turpin, Hulga, and Julian. As in most of O'Connor's stories, the central character is self-centered, complacent, haughty, and essentially, though unwittingly, devoid of true moral conscience. But Connie and her story have the most in common with Mrs. May, the selfish widow of "Greenleaf." Both women are forced, in a moment of self-realization, to recognize the divine presence in the world; they must, if only for an instant, come to terms with moral responsibility and concern for affairs other than those of the self.

The plots of the two stories seem to have little in common; however, both are initiations of a woman who, in response to an intruder—a male sexual figure—is forced to see herself and the world as she never has before. Whereas O'Connor emphasizes the exposition of her story, concentrating on the events that lead up to Mrs. May's being gored by the Greenleafs' bull, Oates sustains the suspense of Connie's meeting with her abductor, suggesting that Arnold Friend's violation of Connie's mind and body, while seductively gradual, is nonetheless as violent as Mrs. May's death.

In Oates's story, Connie has chosen to stay home alone, having declined the offer to accompany her parents and older sister, June, on

[1] *Studies in Short Fiction* 31.3 (Summer 1994) 430–33, online, Galileo, Academic Search Premier, Galileo 24 January 2002 <http://chostvgw21.epnet.com>.

a family barbecue at her aunt's house. While she is drying her freshly washed hair in the sun, tuned in to a popular teen music station, a stranger, accompanied by a companion, drives into her driveway, claiming he has come to pick her up for a date. Connie has a vague recollection of having seen the stranger peripherally—and having snubbed him—the night before at the local drive in hamburger joint. As the stranger, who identifies himself as Arnold Friend and his silent companion as Ellie Oscar, continues to pressure Connie into getting into his car, an old jalopy painted gold, Connie gradually realizes to her horror that the visitor is actually much older than he wants to appear. Connie becomes more and more frightened as Arnold Friend makes sexual suggestions and intimations that he is about to seize control of her mind. He has an uncanny knowledge of Connie's family and personal life and suggests that he may have murdered one of Connie's neighbors. After making a veiled threat to hurt Connie's family upon their return, Arnold manages to convince her to come out of the house and join him. She then crosses over into the other world of adulthood; into "the vast sunlit reaches of the land [. . .] so much land that Connie had never seen before and did not recognize except to know that she was going to it" (Oates 54). What actually happens to Connie from that point is not shown, but to most readers there is little doubt that she will be raped and possibly killed by this gentleman caller who has come to show her what "love" is: "Yes, I'm your lover. You don't know what that is, but you will" (47).

"Greenleaf" is a similar story. Mrs. May, a widow and dairy farmer by necessity, is forced to deal with an intruder on her property, the scrub bull of her tenant family, the Greenleafs. Mrs. May, who struggles to keep her business in order, becomes unhinged at the threatening presence of a Greenleaf bull on her property, one that she feels is sure to breed with her superior dairy cows and "ruin the breeding schedule" (O'Connor 28). After unsuccessful attempts to get Mr. Greenleaf to retrieve the bull, Mrs. May drives him to the pasture and orders him to shoot the animal. During the quarter of an hour or so that Mr. Greenleaf pursues the bull through woods, Mrs. May becomes impatient and blows the horn, apparently exciting the bull, who then emerges from the trees, charges her, and finally "burie[s] his head in her lap, like a wild tormented lover" (52). Mr. Greenleaf arrives, running for the first time in the story, and executes the beast with four shots from the rifle. "She did not hear the shots but she felt the quake in the huge body as it sank, pulling her forward on its head, so that she seemed, when Mr. Greenleaf reached her, to be bent over whispering some last discovery into the animal's ear" (53).

Though on the surface the carefree teenaged Connie and the frustrated middle-aged Mrs. May seem to have little in common, they are strikingly similar in character and share many of the same problems. Both live in an egoistic world psychologically separated from family and spiritually isolated from religion. Typically teenaged, Connie thinks of little beyond maintaining her own good looks, impressing boys, and living for the excitement of the moment. Her greatest challenge in life is to escape parental supervision long enough to sneak across the highway from the mall, where she is supposed to be seeing a movie with a friend, to the forbidden zone: "Sometimes they went across the highway, ducking fast across the busy road, to a drive-in restaurant where older kids hung out" (36). Unlike her dull and obedient sister June, Connie thrives on risk. On her trips across the highway, she is so "breathless with daring" (36) it is no wonder that she dismisses her family as tedious; like most teens, she prefers peer approval to parental and depends on it for her identity: "She had a quick nervous giggling habit of craning her neck to glance into mirrors, or checking other people's faces to make sure her own was all right" (34). Understandably, Connie prefers the hangout to her homelife, which is characterized by antagonism and indifference. Her mother is a source of aggravation, nagging at Connie to "Stop gawking at yourself, who are you? You think you're so pretty?" (34). Her father and June barely exist to Connie. As Joyce M. Wegs points out, "Connie's parents, who seem quite typical, have disqualified themselves as moral guides for her." Wegs continues, "Because [Connie's father] does not 'bother talking much' (30) to his family, he can hardly ask the crucial parental questions, 'Where are you going?' or 'Where have you been?'" (Wegs 88).

Though Connie's self-absorption can be excused as normal, her lack of religious training nonetheless creates a serious deficiency in her ability to be aware of the potential for evil in the world. In Connie's family "none of them bothered with church" (38) and the only reference Connie makes to a deity occurs during her panic over being caught without enough warning to prepare her face and hair for company: "Her heart began to pound and her fingers snatched at her hair, checking it, and she whispered 'Christ. Christ,' wondering how bad she looked" (40). It is clear from Oates's use of imagery that Connie has replaced traditional religion with the false religion of secularism. The drive-in restaurant, steepled with "a revolving figure of a grinning boy who held a hamburger aloft" (36), stands in grotesque tribute to a belief in the superficial world of self-indulgence that "give[s . . . Connie and her friends] what haven and what blessing they yearned for" (36). It is little wonder that Connie, unprepared for dealing with evil realities of the adult world, succumbs to the pressure of the satanic Arnold Friend. A young woman whose thoughts about sexual love are "of the boy she had been with the night before and about how nice he had been, how sweet it always was [. . .] sweet, gentle, the way it was in movies and promised in songs" (39) is set up for a fall. As Connie is soon to learn, she only thinks she is in control of the boys, of her love life; a few moments with Arnold Friend, however, and Connie is under his control: "She watched herself push the door slowly open as if she were safe back somewhere in the other doorway, watching this body and this head of long hair moving out into the sunlight where Arnold Friend waited" (54).

Similarly, Mrs. May thinks she is in control of her domain; her family and farm, however, are in decay. Mrs. May is really controlled by Mr. Greenleaf, who takes advantage of her from the first, when he responds to her notice for a farmhand: "I seen your ad and I will come have 2 boys" (34). As Mr. Greenleaf soon reveals, he has cleverly failed to mention his wife and five daughters, who are apparently part of the package. Soon the farm is populated with three generations of Greenleafs.

Just as Connie cannot look to her parents for protection from the likes of Arnold Friend, Mrs. May cannot depend on her family to help ward off the invasion of the Greenleafs. Her relationship to her sons is at least as antagonistic as Connie's is with her parents. Mrs. May's two older, still unmarried sons—Scofield, an insurance "policy man," and Wesley, an "intellectual"—offer their mother no help on the farm, only ridicule. Aware of her airs of superiority and fear of a Greenleaf takeover, they tease her without mercy: "Scofield would yodel and say, 'Why Mamma, I'm not going to marry until you're dead and gone and then I'm going to marry me some nice fat girl that can take over this place [. . .] some nice lady like Mrs. Greenleaf'" (29). Mrs. May's greatest fear is that her farm will degenerate to Greenleaf level, though her family structure is already in the same state as her semi-collapsed farmhouse.

Mrs. May, like Connie, doesn't bother much with religion, but her substitute for faith is her attachment to her good name and the defense of her property. God comes last. In Mrs. May's world God is a cliché: "I thank God for that!" she exclaims in response to Mr. Greenleaf's observation that "all boys ain't alike." But Mr. Greenleaf offers a penetrating and sincere reply: "'I thank gawd for ever thang,' he drawled" (41). Mrs. May tolerates the Greenleaf variety of religion, but she herself has put religion away, compartmentalizing it into its proper place: in a building to serve as a warehouse of nice girls for her boys to meet and a place to contain Jesus' name. "She thought the word, Jesus, should be kept inside the church building like other words inside the bedroom. She was a good Christian woman with a large respect for religion, though she did not, of course, believe any of it was true" (31). David Eggenschwiler, in *The Christian Humanism of Flannery O'Connor*, classifies Mrs. May as a Kierkegaardian Philistine figure: "Mrs. May is one of those characters who exalt intellectuality or common sense and deny their passions, their animality, and the power of the irrational" (52). No one better embodies the power of the irrational than Mrs. Greenleaf, whose rites of healing include rolling in the dirt and swaying on all fours over the news clippings of movie stars' divorces. Mrs. May, who finds Mrs. Greenleaf's behavior abhorrent, considers herself an expert on what Jesus would want; "'Jesus,' she said, drawing herself back, 'would be ashamed of you'"

(31). But it is the Greenleaf spirit of surrender to the religious realm of existence that is embodied in the powerful yet humble scrub bull that visits Mrs. May at night "like some patient god come down to woo her" (24). And it is, of course, the bull that is victorious and helps Mrs. May discover, too late, her error.

The most intriguing similarity between the stories is the authors' use of the nightmarish, sexually alarming, male intruder who appears unexpectedly to disturb the comfortable universe the female character has built. Both females are threatened by the grotesque embodiment of spiritual reality and are conquered by that force in a cataclysmic vision at the end of the story. Interestingly, both intruders are anticipated, if not experienced, in a dream. Although the question of whether Arnold Friend is a vision, a "daymare," or a literal abductor has been thoroughly argued, a close reading does reveal that Connie's experience has all the earmarks of a nightmare, one that has been triggered by the shaggy-haired boy in the gold car whom she had seen at the drive-in.[2] Critics who have argued that Arnold Friend is real (and those who have argued the dream theory) have overlooked one detail from the drive-in scene: the car itself, "a convertible jalopy painted gold" (37). Oates makes no mention of the dented bumper, strange slogans, or cartoonish pictures that Connie notices right away when the car is parked in her driveway. The reader would think that such an unusual sight at the local teen hangout would be sure to draw a comment, if not a crowd. But only Connie—not even the group she is walking with—notices the boy who speaks only to her: "Gonna get you, baby" (37). During Connie's imaginary encounter with Friend, the details about the car—especially the sexist comment "DONE BY CRAZY WOMAN DRIVER" written around the smashed fender—take on psychological significance, as does the character of Friend himself.

Connie's vision expresses the anxiety typical of dreams: the search for self-identity, fear of the future, and suppressed sexual desire. Larry Rubin concludes that "the episode with Arnold Friend, then, may be viewed as the vehicle for fulfillment of Connie's deep-rooted desire for ultimate sexual gratification, a fearsome business which, for the uninitiated female, may involve destruction of the person" (59). Greg Johnson sees the dream strictly as feminist allegory: "The story describes the beginning of a young and sexually attractive girl's enslavement within a conventional, male-dominated sexual relationship.[. . . It] is a cautionary tale, suggesting that young women are 'going' exactly where their mothers and grandmothers have already 'been': into sexual bondage at the hands of a male Friend'"

---

[2]Larry Rubin argues convincingly that Connie has fallen asleep in the sun and has had a dream about a composite figure that symbolizes her fear of the adult world. He discusses the references to sleep that frame the Arnold Friend episode and the nightmare quality of her inability to control the situation.

(102–03). Connie cannot help but feel an attraction to this composite of all the boys she has met, the embodiment of all the urges her parents would have her resist. Still, Connie fears that Friend will enter the house where she stands just inside the screen door and take her on his own terms, for she knows instinctively that he is evil. As Joyce Wegs points out, "Although Arnold has come to take Connie away, in his traditional role as evil spirit, he may not cross a threshold uninvited; he repeatedly mentions that he is not going to come in after Connie, and he never does. Instead, he lures Connie out to him" (90). Connie, like Mrs. May, has not thought much about her own vulnerability and what lies past her immediate concerns of daily living, nor does she expect to meet up with an exaggerated picture of the spiritual dimension of life that she has heretofore not recognized. Just as Arnold Friend appears as a representation of all Connie's desires and fears, the menacing scrub bull that has been stalking Mrs. May has also entered her dreams, wherein its presence suggests the same moral and sexual uncertainties that Connie feels. In the blur between sleep and wake, Mrs. May imagines the bull dominating her space the way Arnold Friend invades Connie's house: "[it] had eaten everything from the beginning of the fence line up to the house and now was eating the house and calmly with the same steady rhythm would continue through the house, eating her and the boys, and then on, eating everything but the Greenleafs" (25). Awakened by the steady chewing sound, she peeks through the blinds and spies the bull "chewing calmly like an uncouth country suitor" (25). Like Arnold Friend, the bull is in no hurry to possess her; he waits like a "patient god" to make his move. He has his territory marked from outside her bedroom window just as Arnold Friend marks Connie with an "X" in the air soon after his arrival. In both stories, with the first appearance of the intruder, the conflict is defined as a struggle for power over the female's body as well as her property. Suzanne Paulson points to Mr. Greenleaf as the real threat to Mrs. May's security—even her sexual security: "Mr. Greenleaf appears to represent male potency: his phallic nature is emphasized in the figure of his sons' bull, which he allows to run loose in Mrs. May's herd—his way of asserting power over his female employer and of establishing his own territory" (40). The bull is an obvious symbol of male sexual aggression, and Mrs. May, who believes that certain "other words [should be kept] inside the bedroom," has likely denied her own sexuality since becoming a widow and assuming the traditional male role of caretaker. It is little wonder that such sexual repression would surface in a dream as an image of fear.

On the spiritual level, the bull is more closely associated with Mrs. Greenleaf, whom Mrs. May describes as "large and loose," yet for all her dirtiness and uncouthness, she is Mrs. May's moral superior. Since Mrs. May is unpracticed at praying for suffering souls and screaming out to Jesus, she feels threatened by these ritual performances she happens upon in the woods, and she attaches to them the same fear she feels toward the bull: "She felt as if some violent unleashed force had broken out of the ground and was charging toward her" (30–31). What Mrs. May senses in this scene is, of course, a foreshadowing of the disaster to come, one that will prove to be her "moment of grace." According to Suzanne Paulson,

> Depicting the worst in human nature is for O'Connor an act of faith, a repetition of God's intention to shock us into "grace." What some readers see as cynical and distorted views of human life, O'Connor sees as honest representations—however exaggerated and symbolic—of human suffering and sin repressed by the community in order to assuage the guilt of individual members. (86)

Connie's bizarre experience with Arnold Friend could likewise be interpreted as a "cynical and distorted view of human life." But in a more significant reading of the story, Connie's grueling Sunday afternoon appointment with evil symbolizes her coming to terms with the internal and external struggles evident in her life, as well as those of countless young women like her. Like Mrs. May, Connie has been blindsided by a force buried in the mundane that was too obvious for her to recognize. And this force bears the face of evil. David Eggenschwiler speaks of O'Connor's use of the bull as a symbol of evil in "Greenleaf":

> [Mrs. May] even experiences revelation through a demonic form: she becomes aware of God through a symbolic, Dionysian immolation of her self, which is not to say that such immolation is a Christian ideal any more than being pierced by a bull is an ideal form of sexual behavior. Such patterns of reaction also help to explain why Miss O'Connor so often uses satanic instruments to enlighten her characters: she is not only showing that God moves in mysterious ways and brings good out of evil; she is also exploring the psychological and religious view that demonic characters experience God's mercy through demonic structures that oppose or caricature their own forms of idolatry. (64)

The same could be said of Oates and her story. While it is difficult to view Mrs. May or Connie as demonic characters, they are both idolaters of sorts, and both are in need of God's mercy and grace.

At the outcome of each character's ordeal is a moral insight, or revelation, one that elevates the ordinary woman to the state of religious hero. Mrs. May dies getting only a glimpse of the "last discovery" that has come too late for her to act on, but Connie actually becomes a savior to her family. Connie, who has only resented her parents and sister before, cries out for her mother in the end; and in a final act of heroism, surrenders herself to Arnold Friend, who has just reminded her that he plans to harm her family upon their return should she refuse to come out to him. "You don't want them to get hurt" (53), he says, and immediately she stands up to leave with him. She receives her "moment of grace" in classic O'Connor style: by having it violently thrust upon her. Unlike other O'Connor protagonists, she is not hit in the head with a book, forced to watch her mother collapse and die on the sidewalk, or even taken in and mentally raped by a deranged Bible salesman. Instead, like the lonely widow, she endures sexual intimidation by a stranger and is at once destroyed and, ironically, saved by the force that conquers her.

Works Cited

Eggenschwiler, David. *The Christian Humanism of Flannery O'Connor.* Detroit: Wayne State UP, 1972.

Johnson, Greg. *Understanding Joyce Carol Oates.* Columbia: U of South Carolina P, 1987.

Kuehl, Linda. "An Interview with Joyce Carol Oates." *Commonweal* 91 (1969): 307–10.

Oates. Joyce Carol. "Where Are You Going, Where Have You Been?" *The Wheel of Love.* New York: Vanguard, 1970, 34–54.

O'Connor, Flannery. "Greenleaf." *Everything That Rises Must Converge.* New York: Farrar, 1965, 24–53.

Paulson, Suzanne Morrow. *Flannery O'Connor: A Study of the Short Fiction.* Boston: Twayne, 1988.

Rubin, Larry. "Oates's 'Where Are You Going, Where Have You Been?'" *Explicator* 42.4 (1984): 57–59.

Wegs, Joyce M. "'Don't You Know Who I Am?': The Grotesque in Oates's 'Where Are You Going, Where Have You Been?'" *Journal of Narrative Technique* 5 (1975): 66–72. Rpt. in *Critical Essays on Joyce Carol Oates.* Ed. Linda W. Wagner. Boston: Hall, 1979, 87–92.

Escape from Reality?

Kimberly Prevett

1   In much of her work, Joyce Carol Oates depicts American life with a violent and mysterious focus. According to her biography in the Encarta Online Encyclopedia,

> Gothic elements, emphasizing the mysterious and horrifying aspects of life, also appear frequently in Oates's writing. For example, violence, often male and sexual, consistently plays a prominent role in the lives of her characters. ("Oates, J.C.")

2   The short stories "Where Are You Going, Where Have You Been?" and "Valentine" by Joyce Carol Oates both feature as the

main character an adolescent girl facing a turning point in her life. In addition to the characterization of Connie in "Where Are You Going, Where Have You Been?" and Erin in "Valentine," the stories have several other parallels. Although physically living in the same house, Connie is very disconnected from her family; Erin is separated physically from her immediate family and lives with her aunt and uncle. Each girl's desire to escape a less than perfect family leads her to dream-like encounters with an older man who has the power to control her thoughts and actions.

3   According to Dessommes, Connie is a typical teenager who "thinks of little beyond maintaining her own good looks, impressing boys, and living for the excitement of the moment" (1266). Her story occurs during summer vacation; and Connie wears shorts, goes barefoot, and spends time "getting in her mother's way and thinking, dreaming about the boys she met" (Oates, "Where" 1226). Connie struggles to find her identity; "Everything about her had two sides to it, one for home and one for anywhere that was not home" ("Where" 1225).

4   Erin's story takes places during a winter snowstorm, and she bundles herself up in hand-me-down sweaters, wool pants, muffler, and gloves, afraid her teacher will see who she is, "how desperate for love" (Oates, "Valentine" 1239). Erin makes homemade Valentines, sends them anonymously, and convinces herself that she is not disappointed when she receives none. She "Yearned to be invited to visit the homes of certain girls, without success" ("Valentine" 1242). She is obsessed with making good grades and says, "When my grades in Mr. Lacey's class were less than 100 percent I was filled with anxiety that turned my fingers and toes to ice [. . .]" ("Valentine" 1240).

5   Connie works to separate herself from her family, often escaping by going "across the highway, ducking fast across the busy road, to a drive-in restaurant where the older kids hung out" ("Where" 1255). According to Wegs, Connie's parents have disqualified themselves as moral guides for her. Her mother picks at her about inconsequential things, and her father does not "'bother talking much'" (1251). Wegs also includes Connie's friend's father among the morally indifferent adult society because he "'never [. . . bothers] to ask'" (1251). This lack of a moral compass leaves Connie unprepared to deal with the evil that comes her way.

6   It is not clearly evident what has happened to separate Erin from the other members of her family; however, when the story begins, she is alone with her indifferent Aunt Ester and an uncle, "who was no blood kin of [hers]" ("Valentine" 1237). Oates highlights Erin's sense of isolation when she writes, "'Goodnight' they murmured as if resenting the very breath expelled for my sake" ("Valentine"1237). She feels that she could run away and no one would miss her. When Erin's teacher says, "<u>Come, Erin, hurry! She won't even know you're gone</u>" Erin thinks he might have said, "<u>She won't ever know you're gone</u>" ("Valentine" 1239-40).

7   A vaguely familiar stranger, who identifies himself as Arnold Friend, comes to take Connie away. Even though she is the more outgoing and adventuresome of the two girls, she fights against leaving with him. Her early suspicion turns quickly to fear as he makes sexual comments and as she begins to see through his disguise. Arnold threatens to harm her family when he says, "[. . . .] give me you hand and nobody else gets hurt [. . . .] why bring them in this?" ("Where" 1235). With fear for her family

as a driving factor, she goes along with him to a fate that is unclear but certainly not positive.

8   Someone she feels she knows well lures Erin from her home. Unlike Connie, Erin goes willingly on a strange dream-like journey with her math teacher, Mr. Lacey. He is the object of her secret affection and the recipient of one of her homemade valentines. She is very embarrassed when he says, "You must not offer yourself in such a fashion, not even in secret [. . . .] The valentine heart is the female genitals, you will be misinterpreted" ("Valentine" 1247). However, at the end of the evening when she is returned safely to her home, she thinks that he may be saying "Safe alone, safe alone" ("Valentine" 1249). She does not know at the time that "[. . .] over thirty years later [. . .] I would remove from its hiding place [. . .] a bloodstained man's handkerchief initialed, JNL" ("Valentine" 1248).

9   The dream-like effect of Erin's adventure and the implied violent ending of Connie's encounter are consistent with Joyce Carol Oates's view of America as a place of violence where young women are faced with mystery and horror. In "Valentine" and "Where Are You Going? Where Have You Been?" Joyce Carol Oates uses older men who prey upon the minds of the young girls. In their respective realities, they are offered an escape, although it may not be the one they had originally wished for.

Works Cited

Dessommes, Nancy Bishop. "O'Connor's Mrs. May and Oates's Connie: An Unlikely Pair of Religious Initiates." <u>Studies in Short Fiction</u> 31.3 (Summer 1994): 433-40. Henderson, Day, and Waller. 1264-71.

Henderson, Gloria, Bill Day and Sandra Waller, eds. <u>Literature and Ourselves</u>. 4th ed. New York: Longman, 2003.

Oates, Joyce Carol. "Where Are You Going, Where Have You Been." The Wheel of Love and Other Stories. N.p.: John Hawkins, 1970. Henderson, Day, and Waller. 1224-36.

- - -. "Valentine." The Collector of Hearts: New Tales of the Grotesque. New York: Plume, 1998. 211-27. Henderson, Day, and Waller. 1237-49.

"Oates, J.C." Microsoft™ Encarta Online Encyclopedia 2001. 6 Feb. 2002 <http://www.encarta.MSN.com>.

Wegs, Joyce M. "'Don't You Know Who I Am?' The Grotesque in Oates's 'Where Are You Going Where Have You Been?'" Critical Essays on Joyce Carol Oates. Ed. Linda W. Wagner. Boston: G. K. Hall & Co., 1979. Henderson, Day, and Waller. 1249-55.

Suggestions for Exploration and Writing

1. In an essay, discuss in detail how you would have responded either to Friend or to Lacey or to both.

2. Rewrite one of the stories so that Connie encounters Mr. Lacey or Erin encounters Arnold Friend.

3. In a researched essay, discuss Oates's use in "Where Are You Going, Where Have You Been?" of Don Moser's article "The Pied Piper of Tucson." How does Oates change the original story? What effects does she create through these clearly deliberate changes?

4. Using Nancy Dessommes's essay as well as other sources, write a detailed essay analyzing Arnold Friend and the Misfit (see Flannery O'Connor's "A Good Man Is Hard to Find" in the Quest unit) as embodiments of evil.

5. Using some of the essays in this casebook, analyze Oates's stories as dreams. As dreams, what do the stories reveal about the hearts and minds of the dreamers?

6. The two stories together might be seen as suggesting the difficulty of distinguishing good from evil. In a researched essay, discuss that difficulty by discussing in detail the similarities between Lacey, who appears to be good, and Friend, who appears to be evil. How are you able to determine that one is good and one is evil?

7. Each of the two stories might be read as a journey into self-discovery. Using research, write an essay discussing what Connie and Erin learn about themselves.

Imagination and Discovery: Suggestions for Writing

1. The introduction to this unit claims that because it balances both inner experience and outer experience, both the human imagination and the world it discovers, art raises profound questions about the nature of truth, the essence of reality. Select one or more of the works in this unit and write an essay that illustrates how art can raise questions about truth or reality.

2. In the Freedom and Responsibility unit, Tim O'Brien's narrator in "How to Tell a True War Story" insists that the truth of art does not depend on factual accuracy. Use at least two of the works in this unit to support the claim that art, through imagination, sometimes reveals truth that transcends fact.

3. Select two or more works in this unit to illustrate that imagination can lead to discovery—of self, of others, or of truth.

4. Write an analysis applying Prospero's famous speech in 4.1.162–172 to any other work in this unit.

5. Illustrate the ways in which Shakespeare's *The Tempest* influences the content of either Bourne's "What Dreams Are Made On" or Browning's "Caliban upon Setebos."

6. Using any three works in this unit, explain the relationship of creator (writer, artist, reader, etc.) to creation.

7. In what ways does a work of art belong to everyone? Explain, using examples from any section of this book.

8. Language, whether in works of literature or in life, is meant to communicate. Using one or more of the works, examine the problems that arise when communication fails.

9. Select one or more of the works in this unit to discuss emotional involvement in works of art.

Imagination and Discovery: Writing about Film

1. One of the purposes of art is to provoke our imaginations so that we see the ordinary world in a new way. As an exercise in creating visual poetry, take an ordinary event from your daily life (getting out of bed, fixing coffee, putting on makeup, playing basketball), and plan a brief screenplay of the event that will freight it with unexpected emotional values—make it seem beautiful, silly, disturbing, or surprising. You will want to write out an outline or draw up a storyboard (a series of cartoonlike drawings) for a sequence of shots and supply a sound track. For your shots, think about what the camera will see (foreground and background), from what angle, and for how long and what movements the camera will make. Then think about how one

shot will cut into another and how the image of the first shot will relate to the next. Also consider what you want the action to sound like. Do you want to supply inappropriate sounds for actions? Do you want the action to happen in time to specific music?

2. American audiences tend to avoid foreign films because they feel that subtitles interfere with the experience of viewing the movie. In fact, after a few minutes, our minds adjust to reading and watching quite easily, and many foreign films offer us a window into very different cultural dreams. Watch a well-made foreign film and reflect on what it does in terms of event, character, theme, or visual style that an American film wouldn't do. What is new or fresh about the characters, the style of filmmaking, or the construction of the story? Some titles you may find interesting include *City of Lost Children; Red Fireworks, Green Fireworks; Fanny and Alexander; Swept Away; The Horseman on the Roof; Shanghai Triad; Belle Epoque; Eat, Drink, Man, Woman; Yojimbo;* and *Crouching Tiger, Hidden Dragon.*

Quest

George Tooker, "In the Summerhouse," (detail) 1958. Smithsonian American Art Museum, Washington, D.C.

A wareness that humanity cannot "live by bread alone" (Matthew 4:4) predates Christ by thousands of years. The theme of the quest, which ultimately reveals humanity in a search for meaning, for a truth beyond the purely physical, is older than written literature. It finds expression in ancient religions and myths, in the Babylonian epic of *Gilgamesh,* and in the great oral epics of Homer, particularly *The Odyssey.* A recurring theme in art, mythology, and religion is the human need and resulting search for a defining direction, order, and meaning. In a sense, the quest, the search for an ultimate truth, might be seen as one defining characteristic of humanity.

The quest for truth begins not in certainty but in doubt, in questioning. Renowned physicist Stephen Hawking begins and ends his book *A Brief History of Time* by asking questions about the origin of the universe, questions whose answer Hawking, gifted scientist that he is, does not presume to know. Ozzie, in Philip Roth's "The Conversion of the Jews," is so tormented by his elders' refusal to take seriously his very sincere questions that he ends up casting doubt on all they have believed in. Plato's quest for truth—his philosophy—begins, proceeds, and ends with question after question. The wisdom of Jesus's "Sermon on the Mount" arises out of his questioning of received wisdom, his refusal to accept the status quo. Blake raises without answering the question whether the God who made the Lamb could make the Tyger.

Anguished questioning torments even writers and characters of profound faith. Faith seems not to end the quest but to begin it anew. Hopkins's "God's Grandeur," though written in praise of God and though ending in a strongly affirmative sestet, nevertheless reveals in its second quatrain grave doubts about our capacity to know God. The woman in Fred Chappell's "An Old Woman Reading the Book of Job" reads Job repeatedly to try to understand "A God who suffers the suffering of man." Flannery O'Connor, a devout Catholic, sees modern men and women as so immersed in the world as to be wholly unaware of their own inadequacy. For O'Connor, only the inexplicable and often violent grace of God can give a person some sense of order and meaning. O'Connor's quest cannot even begin without grace.

The quest for truth may sometimes be quite costly. In Roth's "The Conversion of the Jews," Ozzie's persistent questioning antagonizes both his rabbi and his mother, and Socrates's insistence on questioning received wisdom led to his being condemned to death. Because he regards his quest as too costly, Prufrock, the narrator of T. S. Eliot's "The Love Song of J. Alfred

Prufrock," is unable even to ask his most superficial question. We see in him the predicament of many people today, unable to believe in God or any ultimate truth, thoroughly disoriented, searching in spite of themselves for truth and direction in a world that apparently offers neither.

Despite the difficulty of the quest, the search for a truth that transcends the merely physical world continues. Plato's philosopher finds his way out of the cave. Ozzie, in spite of the odds, continues to try to understand. Writers as different as the Old Testament psalmist, William Butler Yeats, and Gerard Manley Hopkins offer us a vision of what we might attain, of a transcendent existence beyond the ravages of pain and age.

As the persistent questioning of Socrates, the endless searching of Alfred, Lord Tennyson's Ulysses, and the eloquent frozen action of John Keats's Grecian urn make clear, often the joy, meaning, and order we seek are in the quest itself. Even one of the most devout of medieval mystics, the monk Brother Lawrence, saw his vocation not as resting in God but as constantly *practicing* God's presence. Like Tennyson's Ulysses, we feel compelled to search: "to strive, to seek, to find, and not to yield."

Writing about Quest

The theme of the quest—whether for knowledge of self, knowledge of the nature of humanity, or knowledge of God—is perhaps the richest source of writing topics. Many works tell of more than one quest, and each genre in this unit offers you a wide variety of subjects. You might select the work that appeals to you most and let that work determine your subject and the type of essay you will write, or you might decide that you would prefer to write about one quest and then select one or more works that illustrate that quest. For example, if you wanted to write about the search for knowledge of self, you might select James Joyce's "Araby," an initiation story. If your professor allows you to use works from other units that include the quest theme, you might write about Katherine Anne Porter's "The Grave," another story about self-discovery. If you prefer to write about poetry, you might write an essay classifying the types of sterility and loneliness portrayed in "The Love Song of J. Alfred Prufrock." In drama, Carson McCullers's *Member of the Wedding* offers you an opportunity to write about a lonely girl searching for a sense of belonging as Frankie seeks "the we of me."

If you choose to write about the quest for the nature of humanity, you will find that it is often inextricably intertwined with the other two types of quests. For example, you might write an essay about Tennyson's poem showing how Ulysses, in setting goals for himself, challenges his men to share in his quest. Another essay about the nature of humanity might explain how Hazel in Toni Cade Bambara's "Raymond's Run," while enjoying the talent that gives her personal satisfaction, learns a new admiration for and understanding of her brother.

The quest for a satisfactory relationship with God permeates great literature, and this unit offers a wide variety of works on this subject. You might, for example, write about the ironic point of view in Arthur C. Clarke's "The Star," which tells of a moral crisis faced by a Jesuit priest, or compare the ways in which Philip Roth and Bernard Malamud create humor in stories about characters who seek to understand the complex role of religion in their lives. The stories in the Flannery O'Connor casebook offer startling accounts of women who are shocked into a recognition of their own nature and their relationship to God. The questions at the end of the casebook suggest a variety of types of essays and subjects. You might, for example, write a character sketch of the Misfit, the grandmother, or Mrs. May. You might write a cause-and-effect essay on the Misfit as a violent agent of change, or you might interpret the symbolism in either of the stories.

When Quimby Melton was asked to write an essay using the O'Connor casebook, he was already familiar with Flannery O'Connor's fiction, having previously read several of her stories; however, he selected a story he had not read before: "Greenleaf." After reading the story carefully, he thought about the symbolism, themes, and characterization. Then he read the critical essays and constructed his thesis statement based on his interpretation of the story and on his decision about what would make a workable topic. The thesis that he chose allowed him to use his previous knowledge about O'Connor's religious beliefs and about the American South as he discussed the symbols in the story and the ways in which they clarify and vivify the theme. Once he had selected his subject, Quimby wrote the whole essay in one night. His professor suggested a few minor changes, but the essay required little revision. Quimby's essay is included at the end of the O'Connor casebook.

ESSAYS

Plato (c. 429–347 BC)

*The philosopher and teacher Plato was a high-born Athenian who studied under Socrates and taught Aristotle. Plato founded a school in the grove sacred to the hero Academus and called it the Academy. The Republic, Plato's plan for a utopia, includes the most famous of all allegories, the **allegory** of the cave, which delineates his philosophical view of reality. Plato customarily wrote in **dialogues**, often using Socrates as a character. Because of its emphasis on the transcendent, Plato's philosophy influenced many later religions, including Christianity and Islam.*

ALLEGORY OF THE CAVE[1]   (FOURTH CENTURY BC)

1   And now, I said, let me show in a figure how far our nature is enlightened or unenlightened:—Behold! human beings living in an underground den, which has a mouth open towards the light and reaching all along the den; here they have been from their childhood, and have their legs and necks chained so that they cannot move, and can only see before them, being prevented by the chains from turning round their heads. Above and behind them a fire is blazing at a distance, and between the fire and the prisoners there is a raised way; and you will see, if you look, a low wall built along the way, like the screen which marionette players have in front of them, over which they show the puppets.

2   I see.

3   And do you see, I said, men passing along the wall carrying all sorts of vessels, and statues and figures of animals made of wood and stone and various materials, which appear over the wall? Some of them are talking, others silent.

4   You have shown me a strange image, and they are strange prisoners.

5   Like ourselves, I replied; and they see only their own shadows, or the shadows of one another, which the fire throws on the opposite wall of the cave?

6   True, he said; how could they see anything but the shadows if they were never allowed to move their heads?

7   And of the objects which are being carried in like manner they would only see the shadows?

8   Yes, he said.

9   And if they were able to converse with one another, would they not suppose that they were naming what was actually before them?

[1]From Plato's *The Republic,* translated by Benjamin Jowett.

10   Very true.

11   And suppose further that the prison had an echo which came from the other side, would they not be sure to fancy when one of the passers-by spoke that the voice which they heard came from the passing shadow?

12   No question, he replied.

13   To them, I said, the truth would be literally nothing but the shadows of the images.

14   That is certain.

15   And now look again, and see what will naturally follow if the prisoners are released and disabused of their error. At first, when any of them is liberated and compelled suddenly to stand up and turn his neck round and walk and look towards the light, he will suffer sharp pains; the glare will distress him, and he will be unable to see the realities of which in his former state he had seen the shadows; and then conceive some one saying to him, that what he saw before was an illusion, but that now, when he is approaching nearer to being and his eye is turned towards more real existence, he has a clearer vision,—what will be his reply? And you may further imagine that his instructor is pointing to the objects as they pass and requiring him to name them,—will he not be perplexed? Will he not fancy that the shadows which he formerly saw are truer than the objects which are now shown to him?

16   Far truer.

17   And if he is compelled to look straight at the light, will he not have a pain in his eyes which will make him turn away to take refuge in the objects of vision which he can see, and which he will conceive to be in reality clearer than the things which are now being shown to him?

18   True, he said.

19   And suppose once more, that he is reluctantly dragged up a steep and rugged ascent, and held fast until he is forced into the presence of the sun himself, is he not likely to be pained and irritated? When he approaches the light his eyes will be dazzled, and he will not be able to see anything at all of what are now called realities.

20   Not all in a moment, he said.

21   He will require to grow accustomed to the sight of the upper world. And first he will see the shadows best, next the reflections of men and other objects in the water, and then the objects themselves; then he will gaze upon the light of the moon and the stars and the spangled heaven; and he will see the sky and the stars by night better than the sun or the light of the sun by day?

22   Certainly.

23   Last of all he will be able to see the sun, and not mere reflections of him in the water, but he will see him in his own proper place, and not in another; and he will contemplate him as he is.

24   Certainly.

25   He will then proceed to argue that this is he who gives the season and the years, and is the guardian of all that is in the visible world, and in a

certain way the cause of all things which he and his fellows have been accustomed to behold?

26   Clearly, he said, he would first see the sun and then reason about him.

27   And when he remembered his old habitation, and the wisdom of the den and his fellow-prisoners, do you not suppose that he would felicitate himself on the change, and pity them?

28   Certainly, he would.

29   And if they were in the habit of conferring honours among themselves on those who were quickest to observe the passing shadows and to remark which of them went before, and which followed after, and which were together; and who were therefore best able to draw conclusions as to the future, do you think that he would care for such honours and glories, or envy the possessors of them? Would he not say with Homer,

"Better to be the poor servant of a poor master,"

and to endure anything, rather than think as they do and live after their manner?

30   Yes, he said, I think that he would rather suffer anything than entertain these false notions and live in this miserable manner.

31   Imagine once more, I said, such an one coming suddenly out of the sun to be replaced in his old situation; would he not be certain to have his eyes full of darkness?

32   To be sure, he said.

33   And if there were a contest, and he had to compete in measuring the shadows with the prisoners who had never moved out of the den, while his sight was still weak, and before his eyes had become steady (and the time which would be needed to acquire this new habit of sight might be very considerable), would he not be ridiculous? Men would say of him that up he went and down he came without his eyes; and that it was better not even to think of ascending; and if any one tried to loose another and lead him up to the light, let them only catch the offender, and they would put him to death.

34   No question, he said.

35   This entire allegory, I said, you may now append, dear Glaucon, to the previous argument; the prison-house is the world of sight, the light of the fire is the sun, and you will not misapprehend me if you interpret the journey upwards to be the ascent of the soul into the intellectual world according to my poor belief, which, at your desire, I have expressed—whether rightly or wrongly God knows. But, whether true or false, my opinion is that in the world of knowledge the idea of good appears last of all, and is seen only with an effort; and, when seen, is also inferred to be the universal author of all things beautiful and right, parent of light and of the lord of light in this visible world, and the immediate source of reason and truth in the intellectual; and that this is the power upon which he who would act rationally either in public or private life must have his eye fixed.

36   I agree, he said, as far as I am able to understand you.

37   Moreover, I said, you must not wonder that those who attain to this beatific vision are unwilling to descend to human affairs; for their souls are ever hastening into the upper world where they desire to dwell; which desire of theirs is very natural, if our allegory may be trusted.

38   Yes, very natural.

39   And is there anything surprising in one who passes from divine contemplations to the evil state of man, misbehaving himself in a ridiculous manner; if, while his eyes are blinking and before he has become accustomed to the surrounding darkness, he is compelled to fight in courts of law, or in other places, about the images or the shadows of images of justice, and is endeavouring to meet the conceptions of those who have never yet seen absolute justice?

40   Anything but surprising, he replied.

41   Any one who has common sense will remember that the bewilderments of the eyes are of two kinds, and arise from two causes, either from coming out of the light or from going into the light, which is true of the mind's eye, quite as much as of the bodily eye; and he who remembers this when he sees any one whose vision is perplexed and weak, will not be too ready to laugh; he will first ask whether that soul of man has come out of the brighter life, and is unable to see because unaccustomed to the dark, or having turned from darkness to the day is dazzled by excess of light. And he will count the one happy in his condition and state of being, and he will pity the other; or, if he have a mind to laugh at the soul which comes from below into the light, there will be more reason in this than in the laugh which greets him who returns from above out of the light into the den.

42   That, he said, is a very just distinction.

43   But then, if I am right, certain professors of education must be wrong when they say that they can put a knowledge into the soul which was not there before, like sight into blind eyes.

44   They undoubtedly say this, he replied.

45   Whereas, our argument shows that the power and capacity of learning exists in the soul already; and that just as the eye was unable to turn from darkness to light without the whole body, so too the instrument of knowledge can only by the movement of the whole soul be turned from the world of becoming into that of being, and learn by degrees to endure the sight of being, and of the brightest and best of being, or in other words, of the good.

46   Very true.

47   And must there not be some art which will effect conversion in the easiest and quickest manner; not implanting the faculty of sight, for that exists already, but has been turned in the wrong direction, and is looking away from the truth?

48   Yes, he said, such an art may be presumed.

49   And whereas the other so-called virtues of the soul seem to be akin to bodily qualities, for even when they are not originally innate they can be

implanted later by habit and exercise, the virtue of wisdom more than anything else contains a divine element which always remains, and by this conversion is rendered useful and profitable; or, on the other hand, hurtful and useless. Did you never observe the narrow intelligence flashing from the keen eye of a clever rogue—how eager he is, how clearly his paltry soul sees the way to his end; he is the reverse of blind, but his keen eyesight is forced into the service of evil, and he is mischievous in proportion to his cleverness?

50   Very true, he said.

51   But what if there had been a circumcision of such natures in the days of their youth; and they had been severed from those sensual pleasures, such as eating and drinking, which, like leaden weights, were attached to them at their birth, and which drag them down and turn the vision of their souls upon the things that were below—if, I say, they had been released from these impediments and turned in the opposite direction, the very same faculty in them would have seen the truth as keenly as they see what their eyes are turned to now.

52   Very likely.

53   Yes, I said; and there is another thing which is likely, or rather a necessary inference from what has preceded, that neither the uneducated and uninformed of the truth, nor yet those who never make an end of their education, will be able ministers of State; not the former, because they have no single aim of duty which is the rule of all their actions, private as well as public; nor the latter, because they will not act at all except upon compulsion, fancying that they are already dwelling apart in the Islands of the Blest.

54   Very true, he replied.

55   Then, I said, the business of us who are the founders of the State will be to compel the best minds to attain that knowledge which we have already shown to be the greatest of all—they must continue to ascend until they arrive at the good; but when they have ascended and seen enough we must not allow them to do as they do now.

56   What do you mean?

57   I mean that they remain in the upper world: but this must not be allowed; they must be made to descend again among the prisoners in the den, and partake of their labours and honours, whether they are worth having or not.

58   But is not this unjust? he said; ought we to give them a worse life, when they might have a better?

59   You have again forgotten, my friend, I said, the intention of the legislator, who did not aim at making any one class in the State happy above the rest; the happiness was to be in the whole State, and he held the citizens together by persuasion and necessity, making them benefactors of the State, and therefore benefactors of one another; to this end he created them, not to please themselves, but to be his instruments in binding up the State.

60 True, he said, I had forgotten.

61 Observe, Glaucon, that there will be no injustice in compelling our philosophers to have a care and providence of others; we shall explain to them that in other States, men of their class are not obliged to share in the toils of politics: and this is reasonable, for they grow up at their own sweet will, and the government would rather not have them. Being self-taught, they cannot be expected to show any gratitude for a culture which they have never received. But we have brought you into the world to be rulers of the hive, kings of yourselves and of the other citizens, and have educated you far better and more perfectly than they have been educated, and you are better able to share in the double duty. Wherefore each of you, when his turn comes, must go down to the general underground abode, and get the habit of seeing in the dark. When you have acquired the habit, you will see ten thousand times better than the inhabitants of the den, and you will know what the several images are, and what they represent, because you have seen the beautiful and just and good in their truth. And thus our State which is also yours will be a reality, and not a dream only, and will be administered in a spirit unlike that of other States, in which men fight with one another about shadows only and are distracted in the struggle for power, which in their eyes is a great good. Whereas the truth is that the State in which the rulers are most reluctant to govern is always the best and most quietly governed, and the State in which they are most eager, the worst.

62 Quite true, he replied.

63 And will our pupils, when they hear this, refuse to take their turn at the toils of State, when they are allowed to spend the greater part of their time with one another in the heavenly light?

64 Impossible, he answered; for they are just men, and the commands which we impose upon them are just; there can be no doubt that every one will take office as a stern necessity, and not after the fashion of our present rulers of State.

65 Yes, my friend, I said; and there lies the point. You must contrive for your future rulers another and a better life than that of a ruler, and then you may have a well ordered State; for only in the State which offers this, will they rule who are truly rich, not in silver and gold, but in virtue and wisdom, which are the true blessings of life. Whereas if they go to the administration of public affairs, poor and hungering after their own private advantage, thinking that hence they are to snatch the chief good, order there can never be; for they will be fighting about office, and the civil and domestic broils which thus arise will be the ruin of the rulers themselves and of the whole State.

66 Most true, he replied.

67 And the only life which looks down upon the life of political ambition is that of true philosophy. Do you know of any other?

68 Indeed, I do not, he said.

69 And those who govern ought not to be lovers of the task? For, if they are, there will be rival lovers, and they will fight.

70   No question.

71   Who then are those whom we shall compel to be guardians? Surely they will be the men who are wisest about affairs of State, and by whom the State is best administered, and who at the same time have other honours and another and a better life than that of politics?

72   They are the men, and I will choose them, he replied.

73   And now shall we consider in what way such guardians will be produced, and how they are to be brought from darkness to light,—as some are said to have ascended from the world below to the gods?

74   By all means, he replied.

Questions for Discussion

1. Why does Socrates, the first-person **narrator** of this dialogue, ask questions rather than make statements?

2. An **allegory** is a story in which concrete elements signify specific things or ideas other than themselves. Explain the significance of the following elements in Plato's allegory: the cave, the sun, the men in the cave, the one man who escapes, his first reaction to the sun's light, and his subsequent actions and their results.

3. Why, according to Socrates, do those who attain knowledge of "the idea of the good" have difficulty concentrating on ordinary human affairs? Can you cite examples of highly educated people who lack common sense? How does Plato's allegory explain this lack?

4. According to Socrates, how valid is the justice of most societies?

5. What difficulty in finding ideal rulers does Socrates see?

6. What does the allegory of the cave suggest about most human intelligence?

Suggestions for Exploration and Writing

1. Apply Socrates's allegory to contemporary politics. First assess the quality of the United States's political leaders; then explain, based on the cave allegory, the reasons for their quality or lack thereof.

2. Argue for or against the following statement: "The State in which the rulers are most reluctant to govern is always the best and most quietly governed, and the State in which they are most eager, the worst."

V. S. Naipaul (b. 1932)

Born in Trinidad to parents of Indian descent, V. S. Naipaul was educated at University College, Oxford, and began his long and distinguished writing career in 1954 in London. His ten novels, which have won numerous awards, include The Mystic Masseur *(1957);*

Miguel Street (1959); A House for Mr. Biswas (1961); In a Free State (1971), which won the Booker Award; Guerrillas (1975); A Bend in the River (1979); and A Way in the World (1971). He has also written ten books of nonfiction about the extensive traveling he has done since 1960. Two of his travel books, Among the Believers: An Islamic Journey *(1981) and* Beyond Belief: Islamic Excursions among the Converted Believers *(1998), from which the essay "Loss" included here is taken, record his travels among followers of Islam in Iran, Pakistan, Indonesia, and Malaysia.*

Loss (1998)

1   For most of the Muslims of the subcontinent[1] the partition of 1947[2] had been like a great victory, "like God," as a man had said to me in Lahore in 1979. Now every day in the newspapers there were stories of the killings in the great port city of Karachi. That was where many of the Muslim migrants from India, townspeople, middle-class or lower middle-class, had gone after partition. Nearly half a century later the descendants of these people, feeling themselves strangers still, unrepresented, cheated, without power, had taken up arms against the state, in a merciless guerrilla war.

2   In Iqbal's[3] convert's scheme Islam should have been identity enough for everybody. But the people of Sindh (the province where Karachi was) didn't like seeing their land, half empty and half desert though it was, overrun by better educated and more ambitious strangers. The land of Sindh was ancient, and always slightly apart. The people had their own history and language and feudal reverences. They had set up political barriers, some overt, some hidden, against the strangers from India, the *mohajirs.* And in Pakistan the *mohajirs* had nowhere else to go.

3   Partition, once a cause for joy, had become like a wound for some of these mohajirs. For some the memories of those days still lived.

4   Salman, a journalist, was born in 1952. He was tormented by, and endlessly sought to reconstruct, the events of four days in 1947 in the town of Jalandhar, now in Indian Punjab. At some point in those four days, between the fourteenth and eighteenth of August, 1947, the absolute beginning of independence for both India and Pakistan, his grandmother

---

[1]subcontinent: the Indian subcontinent, including India, Pakistan, and Bangladesh.

[2]partition of 1947: In 1947, Britain, by the Indian Independence Act, granted independence to India. Simultaneously, in response to pressure by the Muslim League, the Act established a separate nation, Pakistan, in majority-Muslim parts of northern India. At the time of this partition, there was much violence between Hindus and Muslims. Partition also created a serious refugee crisis, as millions of Hindus left Pakistan for predominantly Hindu India and millions of Muslims left India for predominantly Muslim Pakistan.

[3]Iqbal: Mohammed Iqbal, an Islamic poet living in pre-partition India, who in 1930 gave an impassioned address to the Muslim League advocating a separate all-Muslim state on the Indian subcontinent.

was murdered in her house in Jalandhar, with others of the family. On the fourteenth she was alive, protected by Hindu neighbors. On the eighteenth Salman's mother's father, who had been hiding somewhere else, went to the house, a middle-class Indian courtyard house, and found it empty, with blood spattered on the walls but with no corpses.

5   Salman's grandfather ran away. He must have been about fifty at that time. He managed to get on a train going to what had become Pakistan—just a short run away, along lines that until four days before had been open and busy. The train was attacked on the way. He arrived in Lahore buried under dead bodies. He was one of the few survivors.

6   Salman got to know the story when he was fifteen. Until that time he had lived with the idea of the Hindu and the Sikh as the ultimate evil. But when he heard this story he felt no anger. The story was too terrible for anger. It didn't matter then who had done the killing.

7   The blood on the walls of a house he didn't know (Salman had not been to Jalandhar or India) and could only imagine, the absence of bodies: the details, or the blankness of detail, from a time before he was born, worked on Salman, became the background to his life in Pakistan. He could spend minutes wondering, when the story came back to him, how the people in the house had actually met death. Had they been cut to pieces? Had they—dreadful thought—been abused?

8   There were other stories of that time which he got from an uncle: of the uncle (and no doubt others) hiding behind oil drums and taunting the Hindu and Sikh rioters, who didn't want India to be broken up:

But kay rahé ga Hindustan!
Bun kay rahé ga Pakistan!
Divided Hindustan will be!
Pakistan will be founded!

In the 1960s these stories, of death and riot, began to rankle with Salman. "I would think we had lost so much for this country, and this is what we are doing to it now."

9   But there had been a long serene period in the new country. The family had lost everything in Jalandhar, but Salman's father, a civil engineer, was working for the government—he was in Baluchistan at the time of the riots in Jalandhar—and so there was money every month. In 1952, the year of Salman's birth, his father left the government to set up on his own. For ten years and more his practice flourished. He brought up his family in a religious way. All the rituals were honored, and there were Koranic recitations. Salman as a child knew many prayers by heart. Religion was part of the serenity of his childhood.

10   In 1965, when he was thirteen, Salman became aware of another kind of Islam. This was at the time of the short, inconclusive war with India. "There were songs exhorting mujahids to go to war and promising them paradise, heaven. Mobs of people from the city of Lahore, armed only with clubs, set out to fight the holy war against the infidel Hindu. They had

to be turned back. They had been charged up by the mullah. The interesting thing was that the mullah was not leading those people. He was sitting safe in his mosque."

11   In this way Salman was introduced to the idea of *jihad,* holy war. It was a special Muslim idea. He explained it like this: "In Christianity Christ died for all Christians. He can ensure heaven for them. In Islam Mohammed can only make a submission in your favor for being a follower of his. It is only Allah who makes the final decision on the merit won by good deeds. Nothing is greater, so far as goodness goes, than jihad in the name of Allah." Jihad was not meant metaphorically. "The word of the Koran is taken very literally. It is blasphemous even to think of it as an allegory. The Koran lays great store by jihad. It is one of the sayings of Mohammed—not in the Koran, it's one of the traditions—'If you see an un-Islamic practice you stop it by force. If you do not possess the power to stop it, you condemn it verbally. If not that also, then you condemn it in your heart.' As far back as I remember I have known this. I think this tradition gives the Muslim license to act violently."

12   In 1965 he saw for the first time the idea given a public, mob expression. And though he saw people then doing "silly things," he understood both their need to win merit as followers of Mohammed, and also their fear of hell.

13   "Endless whipping with fiery flames, and fire beyond imagination. Having to drink pus. It's very graphic in the traditions. In the Koran there's just mention of the fires and the endlessness of punishment."

14   In 1968, when he was sixteen, and in his first year at Government Science College, Lahore, Salman found himself part of just such a mob. There was a review in *Time* or *Newsweek* of a book called *The Warrior Prophet.* Two or three copies of the magazine with the review had somehow got to the college and were passed around. No one had seen the book, but the boys decided to take out a procession to protest about it. It was during a break; the boys were sitting outside. There was no particular leader. The boys were all as religiously well trained as Salman. The idea of the public protest simply came to them, and they became a mob. Salman went along with them, though he remembered very clearly, all the way through, that he hadn't found anything obnoxious about Islam or the Prophet in the review. The weather was good. It was winter, the best season in Lahore, and they shouted slogans against the United States and broke up a couple of minibuses.

15   The mullah who in 1965 had charged up his congregation, and sent them off to the front to fight with sticks, had stayed behind quite safe in his mosque. It wasn't his business to fight. His business was to charge people up, to remind them as graphically and passionately as he could of the rewards of jihad and the horrors of hell.

16   He was like the mullah I heard about (from someone else) who had been drafted in, with other mullahs, to campaign against Mr. Bhutto in 1977. This mullah was short and fat, in no way personable, and known to be unreliable. But that didn't matter; he was a wonderful preacher, with

a powerful voice. There was a curfew at the time, but it was relaxed (as it had to be) for the Friday prayers. The people who went to the mullah's mosque found themselves listening to more than prayers. They heard stories, from Islamic history, of heroism and martyrdom, in the mullah's famous voice and wonderful declamatory style. He asked them to be worthy of the past, to take up jihad, and not to ignore the forces of evil around them. "Say to the enemy, 'You test your arrows on us, and we shall test our breast against your arrows.'" It sounded like poetry, and authoritative for that reason, though no one could place it. The actual words didn't mean anything, but they drove people wild; and at the end of those Friday prayers poor Mr. Bhutto's curfew had been rendered harmless. The congregation went away full of religious hate, determined to earn a little more merit in heaven by sending Mr. Bhutto to hell.

17   That the mullah was unreliable, and not a moral man in any recognizable way, was not important. He was not offering himself as a guide. It was his business as a mullah to keep the converted people on their toes, and when there was need to charge them up, to fix their minds on hell and heaven, and to tell them that when the time came only Allah would be their judge. This was an aspect of the religious state—the state created for converts alone, where religion was not a matter of private conscience—that the poet Iqbal had never considered: that such a state could always be manipulated, easy to undermine, full of simple roguery.

18   There was something else that Iqbal had never considered: that in the new state the nature of history would alter, and with that altering of the historical sense, the intellectual life of the country would inevitably be diminished. The mullahs would always hold the ring, would limit inquiry. All the history of the ancient land would cease to matter. In the school history books, or the school "civics" books, the history of Pakistan would become only an aspect of the history of Islam. The Muslim invaders, and especially the Arabs, would become the heroes of the Pakistan story. The local people would be hardly there, in their own land, or would be there only as ciphers swept aside by the agents of the faith.

19   It is a dreadful mangling of history. It is a convert's view; that is all that can be said for it. History has become a kind of neurosis. Too much has to be ignored or angled; there is too much fantasy. This fantasy isn't in the books alone; it affects people's lives.

20   Salman, talking of this neurosis, said, "Islam doesn't show on my face. We have nearly all, subcontinental Muslims, invented Arab ancestors for ourselves. Most of us are sayeds, descendants of Mohammed through his daughter Fatima and cousin and son-in-law Ali. There are others—like my family—who have invented a man called Salim al-Rai. And yet others who have invented a man called Qutub Shah. Everybody has got an ancestor who came from Arabia or Central Asia. I am convinced my ancestors would have been medium to low-caste Hindus, and despite their conversion they would not have been in the mainstream of Muslims. If you read Ibn Battuta and earlier travelers you can sense the condescending

attitude of the Arab travelers to the converts. They would give the Arab name of someone, and then say, 'But he's an Indian.'

21   "This invention of Arab ancestry soon became complete. It had been adopted by all families. If you hear people talking you would believe that this great and wonderful land was nothing but wild jungle, that no human beings lived here. All of this was magnified at the time of partition, this sense of not belonging to the land, but belonging to the religion. Only one people in Pakistan have reverence for their land, and that's the Sindhis."

22   This was what lay all around Salman's serene childhood. These fantasies and illusions, which to some extent were also his when he was a child, were to become his subject when he became a writer. They took time to discover; they needed the adult eye; they required him to stand a little outside himself.

23   But even while he was still an adolescent Salman began to have intimations of being somewhat apart. Just a few months after he had gone along with that schoolboy demonstration about *The Warrior Prophet* (feeling all the time that it was unjustified), and in that little afternoon jihad had helped to break up a couple of minibuses, something happened that unsettled him.

24   It was Ramadan, the fasting month. He had been told, and he believed, that if he stayed up praying on one particular night during the last ten days of Ramadan, he would be cleansed of all his sins; he would become a new man. They told him he would feel lighter; that was impressed on him. That year the big night was the night of the twenty-seventh. He and his brother and his sister and the rest of the family stayed up praying. In the morning he didn't feel any different. He had been looking forward to a great feeling of lightness. He was disappointed. But he didn't have the courage to tell anyone in the family.

25   His disappointment, and the worry about it, might have been greater at this particular time because, after a decade and a half of success, his father's civil engineering business had begun to fail. The actual work was holding up, but Salman's father had begun to make a series of misjudgments about people. Salman was still at school; his father's business troubles would have worried him.

26   Two or three years later—Salman's father's business going down all the time—there was another incident, this time at the end of Ramadan. Id is the great festival at the end of Ramadan, and the Id prayers are always in a congregation. Salman's father had taken the car to go to the mosque he always went to, and Salman and his brother were going on foot to look for a mosque in the neighborhood. Salman said to his brother, "What a waste of time."

27   The brother said, "Especially when you don't even believe in it."

28   Salman said, "What? You too?"

29   The brother said, "Our elder sister doesn't believe either. Don't you know?"

30   Salman had a high regard for his brother's intellect. The worry he had felt about losing his faith dropped away. He didn't feel he was letting down the people who had died in the riots in Jalandhar in 1947.

31   All three children of the family had lost religion. But, as his business had gone down, Salman's father had grown more devout and more intolerant. One of the festivals the family had celebrated when Salman was a child was the Basant, or Spring Festival. Now Salman's father banned it as un-Islamic, something from the Hindu and pagan past. There were great quarrels with his daughter when she came from Karachi, where she lived. She was not as quiet as Salman and his brother. She spoke her mind, and the arguments could become quite heated. One day, when Salman's father's brother was also present, Salman's father said, "Let her be. She's an apostate. Don't get into these arguments with her." And he walked away in anger. The house would have been full of strains.

32   Salman's father wanted Salman to be an engineer. But Salman's mathematics were bad, and just before his twentieth birthday he joined the army. He had developed an interest in guns. He had no religious faith now, but he was the complete Pakistani soldier. He was passionate about going to war with India, though there had been the Bangladesh defeat just the year before.

33   "It was in my mind that we—or I, personally—had to get even for the murder of my grandparents and my two aunts. It must have been with me always, but this was a very cold feeling. Like a seasoned murderer going in for his hundredth kill. I wasn't excited or emotional about it. It was just something I had to do. I didn't talk about my grandparents, but I was very vocal about going back to war with India. This was with my army companions. Not at home."

34   After two or three years this feeling left him. He also fell out of love with the army. He couldn't find people to talk to, and he was rebuked for talking about books and trying to impress. Three years later he was able to leave the army. He joined a multinational company in Karachi. The job came through an army friend whose uncle was the number two in the company.

35   So Salman went to Karachi, the mohajir city. Life was not easy. He lived in the beginning as a paying guest in a family; after that there was a shabby little rented room with a kitchen. He moved up the ladder slowly. He had a friend in the company. One day when they were talking Salman mentioned the *Reader's Digest*. The friend laughed. Salman said he wanted to learn. The friend was pleased; he began to guide Salman, and Salman looked back on this as the start of his education.

36   After five years he married, and then, like his father, he gave up the security of his job and became self-employed. He did so at a bad time. Karachi had grown and grown since independence; it had received immigrants from India and from all parts of Pakistan; and now the Sindhi-Punjabi-mohajir tensions were about to turn nasty.

37   In January 1987, less than four years after he had married, Salman and his wife lost all their money. A friend had told them that at their stage in

life they should be thinking of the future and making some investments. They had put their money in different investment companies; they had been careful, as they thought, to spread the risks; but one day all the companies just vanished. The friend had persuaded them to invest in a company run by missionary mullahs. These mullahs were not militant; they wanted only to make Muslims good, to bring strayers back into the fold, and to win fresh converts. The friend said to Salman and his wife, "You may not have faith, but this is the only company that's truly reliable." That was where most of Salman's money and his wife's money went.

38   This tragedy was matched by the tragedy of the streets. "Things were getting bad in Karachi and Sindh during this time. Between 1987 and 1989 this terrible thing began to happen in Karachi. A solitary pedestrian at night would be approached from behind by a motorcyclist and stabbed in the back. There must have been fifty or a hundred-odd cases. They would happen once every week or so. Just an isolated incident somewhere. I do not recall reading anywhere that any one stabber had been apprehended. I was getting more and more upset about it.

39   "In July 1987 this incident happened. I had to drive my wife to the airport at two in the morning. On the way back I ran out of petrol. I knew there wasn't enough when I started, but I thought I would buy at one of the many points. This was a city that never really slept. But every single petrol station was closed for fear of armed robberies. I took my wife to the airport. My petrol was now very low. On the way back, about two kilometers from home, the car stopped. It would have been just after two in the morning. So I parked the car and started walking.

40   "I have never felt such a raging fear—it was surging inside me. I still very distinctly remember looking at the walls at the side of the road to see which one was easier to jump over, and escape, in case I was attacked. And then I heard this motorcyclist coming up from far behind. *Put-put-put.* I was utterly and completely terrified. And in this scramble of thoughts the only thing I remember was this desire to escape, to go over a wall. I don't know what kept me there. And the *put-put-put* came nearer. I looked back. He was a lone rider. The attackers were always two. So I knew he wasn't one. But still the fear was real. I stopped walking. And he came *put-put-put.* He said, 'What are you doing on the street at this time? Don't you know it's dangerous?' I told him. He asked where I was going. When I told him he said, 'Get on, I will drive you home.' He was an Urdu-speaking man. I laughed and asked him, 'You said it's dangerous. What are you doing on the street?' He said, 'I'm on the way to the Indian consulate, to be first in line for the visa.' Just after two in the morning. That is what people had to do. He must have had relations in India. He was going visiting. He wasn't getting away from the danger."

41   Salman and his wife had been playing with the idea of leaving Karachi and going back to Lahore. This experience decided him. Later that morning he telephoned his wife and said, "We really have to get away."

42   "It wasn't really fear. Fear for my own life. It was the sorrow of living in an unjust, cruel society. Everything was collapsing. It's as though those poor people who died in Jalandhar died in vain. Why should my aunts and grandparents have to pay with their lives—for nothing? There was no bitterness. Just a sense of the unfairness in it all."

43   About six months after the motorcycle incident, people who were suffering in Karachi, like Salman, organized a peace rally. There were about five hundred at the rally. They were people who had lost hope. It was wintertime, very lovely and pleasant in Karachi. The people in the rally smiled and nodded at one another. Many had tears in their eyes.

44   "There was an immense feeling of brotherhood, of belonging. No slogans. It was just a walk for peace in Karachi. And all along I had this lump in my throat and I thought I would break out crying. Everybody knew that we were all partners in this grief, for whatever was happening to that city. Everybody used to have this feeling for that city. It never went to sleep. And people used to say—the Punjabis and the Pathans—that it was a kind-hearted city, especially good to its poorer inhabitants."

45   That year, in the first week of September, there was a massacre of some three hundred people in the city of Hyderabad, the second city of Sindh. Unidentified gunmen opened up, and in ten or fifteen minutes killed those three hundred. It was part of the mohajir war. Sometimes the mohajirs did the killing, sometimes the army. Salman met some friends that day. They said to him, "You look sick. Has someone died?" He said, "No, no. No one's died."

46   On that day Salman and his wife decided to leave Karachi. It took them three months to wind up their affairs.

47   It wasn't easy for Salman to make a living. The restricted intellectual needs of the country offered him few openings as a writer, didn't encourage him to grow. He was poorly rewarded for what he did.

48   He had become a kind of wanderer. He found solace now in wilderness. The country at least offered him that; there were great tracts of desert and mountain where a man might feel no one had been before.

49   He carried the old torment with him: the first four days of independence in 1947, from the fourteenth of August to the eighteenth, and the empty courtyard house in Jalandhar with blood on the walls.

50   He had not been to India, and he was beginning to think he should go there. There was a journey he wished to make. He wanted the journey to start on the eleventh of August, and he wanted it to start in the Himalayan hill station of Solan. From Solan on the eleventh of August, 1947, his aunt (who was to be murdered within a week) had written to her husband that it was getting very dangerous in Solan; he was to come at once and take her back to Jalandhar. He went and brought her down in the train. He said later (he was one of the survivors) that the hatred and tension in the railway coach was something they could feel. But they got without trouble to the house in Jalandhar on the fourteenth of August.

51   That was the journey Salman wanted to do again one year, within those dates, if he could get an Indian visa. "To mark the beginning of this thing."

Questions for Discussion

1. What explanation does Salman give for *jihad*, or Islamic holy war? How, according to Salman, do some Muslims justify violence?
2. Where did Salman and the people of his country get their names? Why?
3. What, according to Salman, has happened to the culture of Pakistan?
4. What leads to Salman's loss of faith?
5. Who is to blame for the violence in Sindhi and Jalandhar? Can blame be easily attributed to any single group?

Suggestions for Exploration and Writing

1. According to Salman, *jihad* refers to literal violence. Write a paper based on the Islamic concept of *jihad*, considering all of its meanings. Consider using a translation of the Koran as one of your sources, but be aware that few Muslims consider their holy book translatable from the Arabic.
2. Pakistan was established as a religious state. Discuss the reasons for its failure to achieve the ideal harmony its founders envisioned.
3. Discuss in detail the failure of another community based on an ideal—perhaps a church or a club.

Stephen Hawking (b. 1942)

Though he has been bound to a wheelchair by Lou Gehrig's disease since he was twenty-six, Stephen Hawking is a brilliant and gifted cosmologist and theoretical physicist. A graduate of Cambridge University, he has taught on the faculty there since 1973. Since 1979 he has held the position of Lucasian Professor of Physics, a post once held by Isaac Newton. Among his many publications on physics is A Brief History of Time *(1988), a book of theoretical physics written for nonscientists.*

CONCLUSION TO *A BRIEF HISTORY OF TIME* (1988)

1   We find ourselves in a bewildering world. We want to make sense of what we see around us and to ask: What is the nature of the universe? What is our place in it and where did it and we come from? Why is it the way it is?

2   To try to answer these questions we adopt some "world picture." Just as an infinite tower of tortoises supporting the flat earth is such a picture, so is the theory of superstrings. Both are theories of the universe, though the latter is much more mathematical and precise than the former. Both

theories lack observational evidence: no one has ever seen a giant tortoise with the earth on its back, but then, no one has seen a superstring either. However, the tortoise theory fails to be a good scientific theory because it predicts that people should be able to fall off the edge of the world. This has not been found to agree with experience, unless that turns out to be the explanation for the people who are supposed to have disappeared in the Bermuda Triangle!

3   The earliest theoretical attempts to describe and explain the universe involved the idea that events and natural phenomena were controlled by spirits with human emotions who acted in a very humanlike and unpredictable manner. These spirits inhabited natural objects, like rivers and mountains, including celestial bodies, like the sun and moon. They had to be placated and their favors sought in order to ensure the fertility of the soil and the rotation of the seasons. Gradually, however, it must have been noticed that there were certain regularities: the sun always rose in the east and set in the west, whether or not a sacrifice had been made to the sun god. Further, the sun, the moon, and the planets followed precise paths across the sky that could be predicted in advance with considerable accuracy. The sun and the moon might still be gods, but they were gods who obeyed strict laws, apparently without any exceptions, if one discounts stories like that of the sun stopping for Joshua.

4   At first, these regularities and laws were obvious only in astronomy and a few other situations. However, as civilization developed, and particularly in the last 300 years, more and more regularities and laws were discovered. The success of these laws led Laplace at the beginning of the nineteenth century to postulate scientific determinism, that is, he suggested that there would be a set of laws that would determine the evolution of the universe precisely, given its configuration at one time.

5   Laplace's determinism was incomplete in two ways. It did not say how the laws should be chosen and it did not specify the initial configuration of the universe. These were left to God. God would choose how the universe began and what laws it obeyed, but he would not intervene in the universe once it had started. In effect, God was confined to the areas that nineteenth-century science did not understand.

6   We now know that Laplace's hopes of determinism cannot be realized, at least in the terms he had in mind. The uncertainty principle of quantum mechanics implies that certain pairs of quantities, such as the position and velocity of a particle, cannot both be predicted with complete accuracy.

7   Quantum mechanics deals with this situation via a class of quantum theories in which particles don't have well-defined positions and velocities but are represented by a wave. These quantum theories are deterministic in the sense that they give laws for the evolution of the wave with time. Thus if one knows the wave at one time, one can calculate it at any other time. The unpredictable, random element comes in only when we

try to interpret the wave in terms of the positions and velocities of particles. But maybe that is our mistake: maybe there are no particle positions and velocities, but only waves. It is just that we try to fit the waves to our preconceived ideas of positions and velocities. The resulting mismatch is the cause of the apparent unpredictability.

8   In effect, we have redefined the task of science to be the discovery of laws that will enable us to predict events up to the limits set by the uncertainty principle. The question remains, however: How or why were the laws and the initial state of the universe chosen?

9   In this book I have given special prominence to the laws that govern gravity, because it is gravity that shapes the large-scale structure of the universe, even though it is the weakest of the four categories of forces. The laws of gravity were incompatible with the view held until quite recently that the universe is unchanging in time: the fact that gravity is always attractive implies that the universe must be either expanding or contracting. According to the general theory of relativity, there must have been a state of infinite density in the past, the big bang, which would have been an effective beginning of time. Similarly, if the whole universe recollapsed, there must be another state of infinite density in the future, the big crunch, which would be an end of time. Even if the whole universe did not recollapse, there would be singularities in any localized regions that collapsed to form black holes. These singularities would be an end of time for anyone who fell into the black hole. At the big bang and other singularities, all the laws would have broken down, so God would still have had complete freedom to choose what happened and how the universe began.

10   When we combine quantum mechanics with general relativity, there seems to be a new possibility that did not arise before: that space and time together might form a finite, four-dimensional space without singularities or boundaries, like the surface of the earth but with more dimensions. It seems that this idea could explain many of the observed features of the universe, such as its large-scale uniformity and also the smaller-scale departures from homogeneity, like galaxies, stars, and even human beings. It could even account for the arrow of time that we observe. But if the universe is completely self-contained, with no singularities or boundaries, and completely described by a unified theory, that has profound implications for the role of God as Creator.

11   Einstein once asked the question: "How much choice did God have in constructing the universe?" If the no boundary proposal is correct, he had no freedom at all to choose initial conditions. He would, of course, still have had the freedom to choose the laws that the universe obeyed. This, however, may not really have been all that much of a choice; there may well be only one, or a small number, of complete unified theories, such as the heterotic string theory, that are self-consistent and allow the existence of structures as complicated as human beings who can investigate the laws of the universe and ask about the nature of God.

12   Even if there is only one possible unified theory, it is just a set of rules and equations. What is it that breathes fire into the equations and makes a universe for them to describe? The usual approach of science of constructing a mathematical model cannot answer the questions of why there should be a universe for the model to describe. Why does the universe go to all the bother of existing? Is the unified theory so compelling that it brings about its own existence? Or does it need a creator, and, if so, does he have any other effect on the universe? And who created him?

13   Up to now, most scientists have been too occupied with the development of new theories that describe *what* the universe is to ask the question *why*. On the other hand, the people whose business it is to ask *why*, the philosophers, have not been able to keep up with the advance of scientific theories. In the eighteenth century, philosophers considered the whole of human knowledge, including science, to be their field and discussed questions such as: Did the universe have a beginning? However, in the nineteenth and twentieth centuries, science became too technical and mathematical for the philosophers, or anyone else except a few specialists. Philosophers reduced the scope of their inquiries so much that Wittgenstein, the most famous philosopher of this century, said, "The sole remaining task for philosophy is the analysis of language." What a comedown from the great tradition of philosophy from Aristotle to Kant!

14   However, if we do discover a complete theory, it should in time be understandable in broad principle by everyone, not just a few scientists. Then we shall all, philosophers, scientists, and just ordinary people, be able to take part in the discussion of the question of why it is that we and the universe exist. If we find the answer to that, it would be the ultimate triumph of human reason—for then we would know the mind of God.

Questions for Discussion

1. What does the phrase "world picture" mean?

2. Explain why you think there can or cannot be anomalies—exceptions to natural law—that might also be called miracles.

3. Hawking summarizes Laplace's determinism: "God would choose how the universe began and what laws it obeyed, but he would not intervene in the universe once it had started." Do you agree? Why or why not?

4. To what degree does Hawking provide answers to the questions he raises? Can his questions ultimately be answered? How?

5. Hawking asks, "Is the unified theory so compelling that it brings about its own existence? Or does it need a creator, and if so, does he have any other effect on the universe?" What are your answers to these questions? On what do you base your answers?

Mike Rose (b. 1944)

Mike Rose, the child of immigrant parents, grew up in Los Angeles. His parents' quest for an excellent education for their son and the accidental misplacement of Mike Rose in the school system led him to devote his career to researching, describing, and improving education. Rose has a PhD in education from UCLA and is presently a professor at the UCLA Graduate School of Education and Information Studies. His 1989 book, Lives on the Boundary: The Struggles and Achievements of America's Underprepared, *describes some of the problems in education; his 1995 book,* Possible Lives: The Promise of Public Education in America, *presents his vision of the almost limitless possibilities for public education. The essay that follows is from* Lives on the Boundary.

I JUST WANNA BE AVERAGE (1989)

1   Budding manhood. Only adults talk about adolescence budding. Kids have no choice but to talk in extremes; they're being wrenched and buffeted, rabbit-punched from inside by systemic thugs. Nothing sweet and pastoral here. Kids become ridiculous and touching at one and the same time: passionate about the trivial, fixed before the mirror, yet traversing one of the most important rites of passage in their lives—liminal people, silly and profoundly human. Given my own expertise, I fantasized about concocting the fail-safe aphrodisiac that would bring Marianne Bilpusch, the cloakroom monitor, rushing into my arms or about commanding a squadron of bosomy, linguistically mysterious astronauts like Zsa Zsa Gabor. My parents used to say that their son would have the best education they could afford. Maybe I would be a doctor. There was a public school in our neighborhood and several Catholic schools to the west. They had heard that quality schooling meant private, Catholic schooling, so they somehow got the money together to send me to Our Lady of Mercy, fifteen or so miles southwest of Ninety-first and Vermont. So much for my fantasies. Most Catholic secondary schools then were separated by gender.

2   It took two buses to get to Our Lady of Mercy. The first started deep in South Los Angeles and caught me at midpoint. The second drifted through neighborhoods with trees, parks, big lawns, and lots of flowers. The rides were long but were livened up by a group of South L.A. veterans whose parents also thought that Hope had set up shop in the west end of the county. There was Christy Biggars, who, at sixteen, was dealing and was, according to rumor, a pimp as well. There were Bill Cobb and Johnny Gonzales, grease-pencil artists extraordinaire, who left Nembutal-enhanced swirls of "Cobb" and "Johnny" on the corrugated walls of the bus. And then there was Tyrrell Wilson. Tyrrell was the coolest kid I knew. He ran the dozens like a metric halfback, laid down a rap that outrhymed and outpointed Cobb, whose rap was good but not great—the curse of a moderately soulful kid trapped in white skin. But it was Cobb who would sneak a radio onto the bus, and thus underwrote his patter

with Little Richard, Fats Domino, Chuck Berry, the Coasters, and Ernie K. Doe's mother-in-law, an awful woman who was "sent from down below." And so it was that Christy and Cobb and Johnny G. and Tyrrell and I and assorted others picked up along the way passed our days in the back of the bus, a funny mix brought together by geography and parental desire.

3   Entrance to school brings with it forms and releases and assessments. Mercy relied on a series of tests, mostly the Stanford-Binet, for placement, and somehow the results of my tests got confused with those of another student named Rose. The other Rose apparently didn't do very well, for I was placed in the vocational track, a euphemism for the bottom level. Neither I nor my parents realized what this meant. We had no sense that Business Math, Typing, and English–Level D were dead ends. The current spate of reports on the schools criticizes parents for not involving themselves in the education of their children. But how would someone like Tommy Rose, with his two years of Italian schooling, know what to ask? And what sort of pressure could an exhausted waitress apply? The error went undetected, and I remained in the vocational track for two years. What a place.

4   My homeroom was supervised by Brother Dill, a troubled and unstable man who also taught freshman English. When his class drifted away from him, which was often, his voice would rise in paranoid accusations, and occasionally he would lose control and shake or smack us. I hadn't been there two months when one of his brisk, face-turning slaps had my glasses sliding down the aisle. Physical education was also pretty harsh. Our teacher was a stubby ex-lineman who had played old-time pro ball in the Midwest. He routinely had us grabbing our ankles to receive his stinging paddle across our butts. He did that, he said, to make men of us. "Rose," he bellowed on our first encounter; me standing geeky in line in my baggy shorts. "'Rose'? What the hell kind of name is that?"

5   "Italian, sir," I squeaked.

6   "Italian! Ho. Rose, do you know the sound a bag of shit makes when it hits the wall?"

7   "No, sir."

8   "Wop!"

9   Sophomore English was taught by Mr. Mitropetros. He was a large, bejeweled man who managed the parking lot at the Shrine Auditorium. He would crow and preen and list for us the stars he'd brushed against. We'd ask questions and glance knowingly and snicker, and all that fueled the poor guy to brag some more. Parking cars was his night job. He had little training in English, so his lesson plan for his day work had us reading the district's required text, *Julius Caesar,* aloud for the semester. We'd finish the play way before the twenty weeks was up, so he'd have us switch parts again and again and start again: Dave Snyder, the fastest guy at Mercy, muscling through Caesar to the breathless squeals of Calpurnia, as interpreted by Steve Fusco, a surfer who owned the school's most envied paneled wagon. Week ten and Dave and Steve would take on new

roles, as would we all, and render a water-logged Cassius and a Brutus that are beyond my powers of description.

10   Spanish I—taken in the second year—fell into the hands of a new recruit. Mr. Montez was a tiny man, slight, five foot six at the most, soft-spoken and delicate. Spanish was a particularly rowdy class, and Mr. Montez was as prepared for it as a doily maker at a hammer throw. He would tap his pencil to a room in which Steve Fusco was propelling spitballs from his heavy lips, in which Mike Dweetz was taunting Billy Hawk, a half-Indian, half-Spanish, reed-thin, quietly explosive boy. The vocational track at Our Lady of Mercy mixed kids traveling in from South L.A. with South Bay surfers and a few Slavs and Chicanos from the harbors of San Pedro. This was a dangerous miscellany: surfers and hodads and South-Central blacks all ablaze to the metronomic tapping of Hector Montez's pencil.

11   One day Billy lost it. Out of the corner of my eye I saw him strike out with his right arm and catch Dweetz across the neck. Quick as a spasm, Dweetz was out of his seat, scattering desks, cracking Billy on the side of the head, right behind the eye. Snyder and Fusco and others broke it up, but the room felt hot and close and naked. Mr. Montez's tenuous authority was finally ripped to shreds, and I think everyone felt a little strange about that. The charade was over, and when it came down to it, I don't think any of the kids really wanted it to end this way. They had pushed and pushed and bullied their way into a freedom that both scared and embarrassed them.

12   Students will float to the mark you set. I and the others in the vocational classes were bobbing in pretty shallow water. Vocational education has aimed at increasing the economic opportunities of students who do not do well in our schools. Some serious programs succeed in doing that, and through exceptional teachers—like Mr. Gross in *Horace's Compromise*—students learn to develop hypotheses and troubleshoot, reason through a problem, and communicate effectively—the true job skills. The vocational track, however, is most often a place for those who are just not making it, a dumping ground for the disaffected. There were a few teachers who worked hard at education; young Brother Slattery, for example, combined a stern voice with weekly quizzes to try to pass along to us a skeletal outline of world history. But mostly the teachers had no idea of how to engage the imaginations of us kids who were scuttling along at the bottom of the pond.

13   And the teachers would have needed some inventiveness, for none of us was groomed for the classroom. It wasn't just that I didn't know things—didn't know how to simplify algebraic fractions, couldn't identify different kinds of clauses, bungled Spanish translations—but that I had developed various faulty and inadequate ways of doing algebra and making sense of Spanish. Worse yet, the years of defensive tuning out in elementary school had given me a way to escape quickly while seeming at least half alert. During my time in Voc. Ed., I developed further into a

mediocre student and a somnambulant problem solver, and that affected the subjects I did have the wherewithal to handle: I detested Shakespeare; I got bored with history. My attention flitted here and there. I fooled around in class and read my books indifferently—the intellectual equivalent of playing with your food. I did what I had to do to get by, and I did it with half a mind.

14 But I did learn things about people and eventually came into my own socially. I liked the guys in Voc. Ed. . . .

15 The tragedy is that you have to twist the knife in your own gray matter to make this defense work. You'll have to shut down, have to reject intellectual stimuli or diffuse them with sarcasm, have to cultivate stupidity, have to convert boredom from a malady into a way of confronting the world. Keep your vocabulary simple, act stoned when you're not or act more stoned than you are, flaunt ignorance, materialize your dreams. It is a powerful and effective defense—it neutralizes the insult and the frustration of being a vocational kid and, when perfected, it drives teachers up the wall, a delightful secondary effect. But like all strong magic, it exacts a price.

16 My own deliverance from the Voc. Ed. world began with sophomore biology. Every student, college prep to vocational, had to take biology, and unlike the other courses, the same person taught all sections. When teaching the vocational group, Brother Clint probably slowed down a bit or omitted a little of the fundamental biochemistry, but he used the same book and more or less the same syllabus across the board. If one class got tough, he could get tougher. He was young and powerful and very handsome, and looks and physical strength were high currency. No one gave him any trouble.

17 I was pretty bad at the dissecting table, but the lectures and the textbook were interesting: plastic overlays that, with each turned page, peeled away skin, then veins and muscle, then organs, down to the very bones that Brother Clint, pointer in hand, would tap out on our hanging skeleton. Dave Snyder was in big trouble, for the study of life—versus the living of it—was sticking in his craw. We worked out a code for our multiple-choice exams. He'd poke me in the back: once for the answer under *A,* twice for *B,* and so on; and when he'd hit the right one, I'd look up to the ceiling as though I were lost in thought. Poke: cytoplasm. Poke, poke: methane. Poke, poke, poke: William Harvey. Poke, poke, poke, poke: islets of Langerhans. This didn't work out perfectly, but Dave passed the course, and I mastered the dreamy look of a guy on a record jacket. And something else happened. Brother Clint puzzled over this Voc. Ed. kid who was racking up 98s and 99s on his tests. He checked the school's records and discovered the error. He recommended that I begin my junior year in the College Prep program. According to all I've read since, such a shift, as one report put it, is virtually impossible. Kids at that level rarely cross tracks. The telling thing is how chancy both my placement into and exit from Voc.

Ed. was; neither I nor my parents had anything to do with it. I lived in one world during spring semester, and when I came back to school in the fall, I was living in another.

18   Switching to College Prep was a mixed blessing. I was an erratic student. I was undisciplined. And I hadn't caught onto the rules of the game: Why work hard in a class that didn't grab my fancy? I was also hopelessly behind in math. Chemistry was hard; toying with my chemistry set years before hadn't prepared me for the chemist's equations. Fortunately, the priest who taught both chemistry and second-year algebra was also the school's athletic director. Membership on the track team covered me; I knew I wouldn't get lower than a C. U.S. history was taught pretty well, and I did okay. But civics was taken over by a football coach who had trouble reading the textbook aloud—and reading aloud was the centerpiece of his pedagogy. College Prep at Mercy was certainly an improvement over the vocational program—at least it carried some status—but the social science curriculum was weak, and the mathematics and physical sciences were simply beyond me. I had a miserable quantitative background and ended up copying some assignments and finessing the rest as best I could. Let me try to explain how it feels to see again and again material you should once have learned but didn't.

19   You are given a problem. It requires you to simplify algebraic fractions or to multiply expressions containing square roots. You know this is pretty basic material because you've seen it for years. Once a teacher took some time with you, and you learned how to carry out these operations. Simple versions, anyway. But that was a year or two or more in the past, and these are more complex versions, and now you're not sure. And this, you keep telling yourself, is ninth- or even eighth-grade stuff.

20   Next it's a word problem. This is also old hat. The basic elements are as familiar as story characters: trains speeding so many miles per hour or shadows of buildings angling so many degrees. Maybe you know enough, have sat through enough explanations, to be able to begin setting up the problem: "If one train is going this fast . . ." or "This shadow is really one line of a triangle. . . ." Then: "Let's see . . ." "How did Jones do this?" "Hmmmm." "No." "No, that won't work." Your attention wavers. You wonder about other things: a football game, a dance, that cute new checker at the market. You try to focus on the problem again. You scribble on paper for a while, but the tension wins out and your attention flits elsewhere. You crumple the paper and begin daydreaming to ease the frustration.

21   The particulars will vary, but in essence this is what a number of students go through, especially those in so-called remedial classes. They open their textbooks and see once again the familiar and impenetrable formulas and diagrams and terms that have stumped them for years. There is no excitement here. *No* excitement. Regardless of what the teacher says, this is not a new challenge. There is, rather, embarrassment and frustration and, not surprisingly, some anger in being reminded once again of long-standing inadequacies. No wonder so many students finally attribute their difficulties to something inborn, organic: "That part of my

brain just doesn't work." Given the troubling histories many of these students have, it's miraculous that any of them can lift the shroud of hopelessness sufficiently to make deliverance from these classes possible.

22   Through this entire period, my father's health was deteriorating with cruel momentum. His arteriosclerosis progressed to the point where a simple nick on his shin wouldn't heal. Eventually it ulcerated and widened. Lou Minton would come by daily to change the dressing. We tried renting an oscillating bed—which we placed in the front room—to force blood through the constricted arteries in my father's legs. The bed hummed through the night, moving in place to ward off the inevitable. The ulcer continued to spread, and the doctors finally had to amputate. My grandfather had lost his leg in a stockyard accident. Now my father too was crippled. His convalescence was slow but steady, and the doctors placed him in the Santa Monica Rehabilitation Center, a sun-bleached building that opened out onto the warm spray of the Pacific. The place gave him some strength and some color and some training in walking with an artificial leg. He did pretty well for a year or so until he slipped and broke his hip. He was confined to a wheelchair after that, and the confinement contributed to the diminishing of his body and spirit.

23   I am holding a picture of him. He is sitting in his wheelchair and smiling at the camera. The smile appears forced, unsteady, seems to quaver, though it is frozen in silver nitrate. He is in his mid-sixties and looks eighty. Late in my junior year, he had a stroke and never came out of the resulting coma. After that, I would see him only in dreams, and to this day that is how I join him. Sometimes the dreams are sad and grisly and primal: my father lying in a bed soaked with his suppuration, holding me, rocking me. But sometimes the dreams bring him back to me healthy: him talking to me on an empty street, or buying some pictures to decorate our old house, or transformed somehow into someone strong and adept with tools and the physical.

24   Jack MacFarland couldn't have come into my life at a better time. My father was dead, and I had logged up too many years of scholastic indifference. Mr. MacFarland had a master's degree from Columbia and decided, at twenty-six, to find a little school and teach his heart out. He never took any credentialing courses, couldn't bear to, he said, so he had to find employment in a private system. He ended up at Our Lady of Mercy teaching five sections of senior English. He was a beatnik who was born too late. His teeth were stained, he tucked his sorry tie in between the third and fourth buttons of his shirt, and his pants were chronically wrinkled. At first, we couldn't believe this guy, thought he slept in his car. But within no time, he had us so startled with work that we didn't much worry about where he slept or if he slept at all. We wrote three or four essays a month. We read a book every two to three weeks, starting with the *Iliad* and ending up with Hemingway. He gave us a quiz on the reading every other day. He brought a prep school curriculum to Mercy High.

25   MacFarland's lectures were crafted, and as he delivered them he would pace the room jiggling a piece of chalk in his cupped hand, using it to scribble on the board the names of all the writers and philosophers and plays and novels he was weaving into his discussion. He asked questions often, raised everything from Zeno's paradox to the repeated last line of Frost's "Stopping by Woods on a Snowy Evening." He slowly and carefully built up our knowledge of Western intellectual history—with facts, with connections, with speculations. We learned about Greek philosophy, about Dante, the Elizabethan world view, the Age of Reason, existentialism. He analyzed poems with us, had us reading sections from John Ciardi's *How Does a Poem Mean?* making a potentially difficult book accessible with his own explanations. We gave oral reports on poems Ciardi didn't cover. We imitated the styles of Conrad, Hemingway, and *Time* magazine. We wrote and talked, wrote and talked. The man immersed us in language.

26   Even MacFarland's barbs were literary. If Jim Fitzsimmons, hung over and irritable, tried to smart-ass him, he'd rejoin with a flourish that would spark the indomitable Skip Madison—who'd lost his front teeth in a hapless tackle—to flick his tongue through the gap and opine, "good chop," drawing out the single "o" in stinging indictment. Jack MacFarland, this tobacco-stained intellectual, brandished linguistic weapons of a kind I hadn't encountered before. Here was this *egghead,* for God's sake, keeping some pretty difficult people in line. And from what I heard, Mike Dweetz and Steve Fusco and all the notorious Voc. Ed. crowd settled down as well when MacFarland took the podium. Though a lot of guys groused in the schoolyard, it just seemed that giving trouble to this particular teacher was a silly thing to do. Tomfoolery, not to mention assault, had no place in the world he was trying to create for us, and instinctively everyone knew that. If nothing else, we all recognized MacFarland's considerable intelligence and respected the hours he put into his work. It came to this: The troublemaker would look foolish rather than daring. Even Jim Fitzsimmons was reading *On the Road* and turning his incipient alcoholism to literary ends.

27   There were some lives that were already beyond Jack MacFarland's ministrations, but mine was not. I started reading again as I hadn't since elementary school. I would go into our gloomy little bedroom or sit at the dinner table while, on the television, Danny McShane was paralyzing Mr. Moto with the atomic drop, and work slowly back through *Heart of Darkness,* trying to catch the words in Conrad's sentences. I certainly was not MacFarland's best student; most of the other guys in College Prep, even my fellow slackers, had better backgrounds than I did. But I worked very hard, for MacFarland had hooked me. He tapped my old interest in reading and creating stories. He gave me a way to feel special by using my mind. And he provided a role model that wasn't shaped on physical prowess alone, and something inside me that I wasn't quite aware of responded to that. Jack MacFarland established a literacy club, to borrow a phrase of Frank Smith's, and invited me—invited all of us—to join.

28   There's been a good deal of research and speculation suggesting that the acknowledgment of school performance with extrinsic rewards—smiling faces, stars, numbers, grades—diminishes the intrinsic satisfaction children experience by engaging in reading or writing or problem solving. While it's certainly true that we've created an educational system that encourages our best and brightest to become cynical grade collectors and, in general, have developed an obsession with evaluation and assessment, I must tell you that venal though it may have been, I loved getting good grades from MacFarland. I now know how subjective grades can be, but then they came tucked in the back of essays like bits of scientific data, some sort of spectroscopic readout that said, objectively and publicly, that I had made something of value. I suppose I'd been mediocre for too long and enjoyed a public redefinition. And I suppose the workings of my mind, such as they were, had been private for too long. My linguistic play moved into the world; like the intergalactic stories I told years before on Frank's berry-splattered truck bed, these papers with their circled, red B-pluses and A-minuses linked my mind to something outside it. I carried them around like a club emblem.

29   One day in the December of my senior year, Mr. MacFarland asked me where I was going to go to college. I hadn't thought much about it. Many of the students I teach today spent their last year in high school with a physics text in one hand and the Stanford catalog in the other, but I wasn't even aware of what "entrance requirements" were. My folks would say that they wanted me to go to college and be a doctor, but I don't know how seriously I ever took that; it seemed a sweet thing to say, a bit of supportive family chatter, like telling a gangly daughter she's graceful. The reality of higher education wasn't in my scheme of things: No one in the family had gone to college; only two of my uncles had completed high school. I figured I'd get a night job and go to the local junior college because I knew that Snyder and Company were going there to play ball. But I hadn't even prepared for that. When I finally said, "I don't know," MacFarland looked down at me—I was seated in his office—and said, "Listen, you can write."

30   My grades stank. I had A's in biology and a handful of B's in a few English and social science classes. All the rest were C's—or worse. MacFarland said I would do well in his class and laid down the law about doing well in the others. Still, the record for my first three years wouldn't have been acceptable to any four-year school. To nobody's surprise, I was turned down flat by USC and UCLA. But Jack MacFarland was on the case. He had received his bachelor's degree from Loyola University, so he made calls to old professors and talked to somebody in admissions and wrote me a strong letter. Loyola finally accepted me as a probationary student. I would be on trial for the first year, and if I did okay, I would be granted regular status. MacFarland also intervened to get me a loan, for I could never have afforded a private college without it. Four more years of religion classes and four more years of boys at one school, girls at another. But at least I was going to college. Amazing.

31   In my last semester of high school, I elected a special English course fashioned by Mr. MacFarland, and it was through this elective that there arose at Mercy a fledgling literati. Art Mitz, the editor of the school newspaper and a very smart guy, was the kingpin. He was joined by me and by Mark Dever, a quiet boy who wrote beautifully and who would die before he was forty. MacFarland occasionally invited us to his apartment, and those visits became the high point of our apprenticeship: We'd clamp on our training wheels and drive to his salon.

32   He lived in a cramped and cluttered place near the airport, tucked away in the kind of building that architectural critic Reyner Banham calls a *dingbat*. Books were all over: stacked, piled, tossed, and crated, underlined and dog eared, well worn and new. Cigarette ashes crusted with coffee in saucers or spilled over the sides of motel ashtrays. The little bedroom had, along two of its walls, bricks and boards loaded with notes, magazines, and oversized books. The kitchen joined the living room, and there was a stack of German newspapers under the sink. I had never seen anything like it: a great flophouse of language furnished by City Lights and Café le Metro. I read every title. I flipped through paperbacks and scanned jackets and memorized names: Gogol, *Finnegan's Wake*, Djuna Barnes, Jackson Pollock, *A Coney Island of the Mind*, F. O. Matthiessen's *American Renaissance*, all sorts of Freud, *Troubled Sleep*, Man Ray, *The Education of Henry Adams*, Richard Wright, *Film as Art*, William Butler Yeats, Marguerite Duras, *Redburn, A Season in Hell, Kapital*. On the cover of Alain-Fournier's *The Wanderer* was an Edward Gorey drawing of a young man on a road winding into dark trees. By the hotplate sat a strange Kafka novel called *Amerika*, in which an adolescent hero crosses the Atlantic to find the Nature Theater of Oklahoma. Art and Mark would be talking about a movie or the school newspaper, and I would be consuming my English teacher's library. It was heady stuff. I felt like a Pop Warner athlete on steroids.

33   Art, Mark, and I would buy stogies and triangulate from MacFarland's apartment to the Cinema, which now shows X-rated films but was then L.A.'s premiere art theater, and then to the musty Cherokee Bookstore in Hollywood to hobnob with beatnik homosexuals—smoking, drinking bourbon and coffee, and trying out awkward phrases we'd gleaned from our mentor's bookshelves. I was happy and precocious and a little scared as well, for Hollywood Boulevard was thick with a kind of decadence that was foreign to the South Side. After the Cherokee, we would head back to the security of MacFarland's apartment, slaphappy with hipness.

34   Let me be the first to admit that there was a good deal of adolescent passion in this embrace of the avant-garde: self-absorption, sexually charged pedantry, an elevation of the odd and abandoned. Still it was a time during which I absorbed an awful lot of information: long lists of titles, images from expressionist paintings, new wave shibboleths, snippets of philosophy, and names that read like Steve Fusco's misspellings—Goethe, Nietzsche, Kierkegaard. Now this is hardly the stuff

of deep understanding. But it was an introduction, a phrase book, a Baedeker to a vocabulary of ideas, and it felt good at the time to know all these words. With hindsight I realize how layered and important that knowledge was.

35   It enabled me to do things in the world. I could browse bohemian bookstores in far-off, mysterious Hollywood; I could go to the Cinema and see events through the lenses of European directors; and, most of all, I could share an evening, talk that talk, with Jack MacFarland, the man I most admired at the time. Knowledge was becoming a bonding agent. Within a year or two, the persona of the disaffected hipster would prove too cynical, too alienated to last. But for a time it was new and exciting: It provided a critical perspective on society, and it allowed me to act as though I were living beyond the limiting boundaries of South Vermont.

Questions for Discussion

1. Does Rose's explanation of why he and others might remain in the wrong school track have validity? Why or why not?

2. Rose says: "The vocational track [. . .] is most often a place for those who are just not making it, a dumping ground for the disaffected." Do you agree or disagree? Give reasons for your position.

3. What does Rose mean by "years of defensive tuning out in elementary school"? What means of escape do students use during class? Why?

4. What kinds of students did Rose admire? Why? Were they good role models? Why or why not?

5. In what ways was Rose's transition to a "college prep" curriculum a "mixed blessing"?

6. What characteristics earned Jack MacFarland the respect and admiration of his students? How did he challenge them?

7. What role did his father's illnesses, coma, and eventual death play in Rose's life?

Suggestions for Exploration and Writing

1. Rose says, "Students will float to the mark you [teachers] set." What does he mean? Do you agree? Explain your answer in an essay.

2. Write an essay about a teacher who made a difference in your education.

3. Explain how each of the following teachers would hurt an average or below-average student's quest for an education: Brother Dill, Mitropetros, and Montez. What negative qualities that would hinder education do they possess?

FICTION

James Joyce (1882–1941)

One of the most famous, influential, and controversial writers of the twentieth century, James Joyce was born in Dublin in 1882. Joyce excelled at the Irish Catholic schools where he was educated, and his experiences at these schools were a major influence on his later work, especially on his first novel, Portrait of the Artist As a Young Man *(1916). Joyce spent most of his life in Trieste, Rome, and Paris. Both his novels and his short stories are justly ranked as works that, though unique, were major influences on later writers. His collection of stories in* Dubliners, *ending with* "The Dead," *appeared in 1914. The American magazine* Little Review *began publication of Joyce's novel* Ulysses *in 1920, but the courts stopped publication when the publishers were convicted of obscenity; it was finally published in 1922.* Finnegans Wake, *his last novel, was published in 1939, three years before his death.*

ARABY   (1914)

1   North Richmond Street, being blind, was a quiet street except at the hour when the Christian Brothers' School set the boys free. An uninhabited house of two stories stood at the blind end, detached from its neighbors in a square ground. The other houses of the street, conscious of decent lives within them, gazed at one another with brown imperturbable faces.

2   The former tenant of our house, a priest, had died in the back drawing room. Air, musty from having been long enclosed, hung in all the rooms, and the waste room behind the kitchen was littered with old useless papers. Among these I found a few paper-covered books, the pages of which were curled and damp: *The Abbot,* by Walter Scott, *The Devout Communicant,* and *The Memoirs of Vidocq.* I liked the last best because its leaves were yellow. The wild garden behind the house contained a central apple tree and a few straggling brushes under one of which I found the late tenant's rusty bicycle pump. He had been a very charitable priest; in his will he had left all his money to institutions and the furniture of his house to his sister.

3   When the short days of winter came dusk fell before we had well eaten our dinners. When we met in the street the houses had grown somber. The space of sky above us was the color of ever-changing violet and towards it the lamps of the street lifted their feeble lanterns. The cold air stung us and we played till our bodies glowed. Our shouts echoed in the silent street. The career of our play brought us through the dark muddy lanes behind the houses where we ran the gauntlet of the rough tribes from the cottages, to the back doors of the dark odorous stables where a coachman smoothed and combed the horse or shook music from the buckled harness. When we returned to the street, light from the kitchen windows had filled the areas. If my uncle was seen turning the corner we hid in the shadow until we had seen him safely housed. Or if Mangan's

sister came out on the doorstep to call her brother in to his tea we watched her from our shadow peer up and down the street. We waited to see whether she would remain or go in and, if she remained, we left our shadow and walked up to Mangan's steps resignedly. She was waiting for us, her figure defined by the light from the half-opened door. Her brother always teased her before he obeyed and I stood by the railings looking at her. Her dress swung as she moved her body and the soft rope of her hair tossed from side to side.

4   Every morning I lay on the floor in the front parlor watching her door. The blind was pulled down to within an inch of the sash so that I could not be seen. When she came out on the doorstep my heart leaped. I ran to the hall, seized my books and followed her. I kept her brown figure always in my eye and, when we came near the point at which our ways diverged, I quickened my pace and passed her. This happened morning after morning. I had never spoken to her, except for a few casual words, and yet her name was like a summons to all my foolish blood.

5   Her image accompanied me even in places the most hostile to romance. On Saturday evenings when my aunt went marketing I had to go to carry some of the parcels. We walked through the flaring streets, jostled by drunken men and bargaining women, amid the curses of laborers, the shrill litanies of shop boys who stood on guard by the barrels of pigs' cheeks, the nasal chanting of street singers, who sang a *come-all-you* about O'Donovan Rossa, or a ballad about the troubles in our native land. These noises converged in a single sensation of life for me: I imagined that I bore my chalice safely through a throng of foes. Her name sprang to my lips at moments in strange prayers and praises which I myself did not understand. My eyes were often full of tears (I could not tell why) and at times a flood from my heart seemed to pour itself out into my bosom. I thought little of the future. I did not know whether I would ever speak to her or not or, if I spoke to her, how I could tell her of my confused adoration. But my body was like a harp and her words and gestures were like fingers running upon the wires.

6   One evening I went into the back drawing room in which the priest had died. It was a dark rainy evening and there was no sound in the house. Through one of the broken panes I heard the rain impinge upon the earth, the fine incessant needles of water playing in the sodden beds. Some distant lamp or lighted window gleamed below me. I was thankful that I could see so little. All my senses seemed to desire to veil themselves and, feeling that I was about to slip from them, I pressed the palms of my hands together until they trembled, murmuring: *"O love! O love!"* many times.

7   At last she spoke to me. When she addressed the first words to me I was so confused that I did not know what to answer. She asked me was I going to *Araby.* I forgot whether I answered yes or no. It would be a splendid bazaar, she said; she would love to go.

8   "And why can't you?" I asked.

9   While she spoke she turned a silver bracelet round and round her wrist. She could not go, she said, because there would be a retreat that week in her convent. Her brother and two other boys were fighting for their caps and I was alone at the railings. She held one of the spikes, bowing her head towards me. The light from the lamp opposite our door caught the white curve of her neck, lit up her hair that rested there and, falling, lit up the hand upon the railing. It fell over one side of her dress and caught the white border of a petticoat, just visible as she stood at ease.

10   "It's well for you," she said.

11   "If I go," I said, "I will bring you something."

12   What innumerable follies laid waste my waking and sleeping thoughts after that evening! I wished to annihilate the tedious intervening days. I chafed against the work of school. At night in my bedroom and by day in the classroom her image came between me and the page I strove to read. The syllables of the word *Araby* were called to me through the silence in which my soul luxuriated and cast an Eastern enchantment over me. I asked for leave to go to the bazaar on Saturday night. My aunt was surprised and hoped it was not some Freemason affair. I answered few questions in class. I watched my master's face pass from amiability to sternness; he hoped I was not beginning to idle. I could not call my wandering thoughts together. I had hardly any patience with the serious work of life which, now that it stood between me and my desire, seemed to me child's play, ugly monotonous child's play.

13   On Saturday morning I reminded my uncle that I wished to go to the bazaar in the evening. He was fussing at the hall stand, looking for the hat brush, and answered me curtly:

14   "Yes, boy, I know."

15   As he was in the hall I could not go into the front parlor and lie at the window. I left the house in bad humor and walked slowly towards the school. The air was pitilessly raw and already my heart misgave me.

16   When I came home to dinner my uncle had not yet been home. Still it was early. I sat staring at the clock for some time and, when its ticking began to irritate me, I left the room. I mounted the staircase and gained the upper part of the house. The high cold empty gloomy rooms liberated me and I went from room to room singing. From the front window I saw my companions playing below in the street. Their cries reached me weakened and indistinct and, leaning my forehead against the cool glass, I looked over at the dark house where she lived. I may have stood there for an hour, seeing nothing but the brown-clad figure cast by my imagination, touched discreetly by the lamplight at the curved neck, at the hand upon the railings and at the border below the dress.

17   When I came downstairs again I found Mrs. Mercer sitting at the fire. She was an old garrulous woman, a pawnbroker's widow, who collected used stamps for some pious purpose. I had to endure the gossip of the tea table. The meal was prolonged beyond an hour and still my uncle did

not come. Mrs. Mercer stood up to go; she was sorry she couldn't wait any longer, but it was after eight o'clock and she did not like to be out late, as the night air was bad for her. When she had gone I began to walk up and down the room, clenching my fists. My aunt said:

18   "I'm afraid you may put off your bazaar for this night of Our Lord."

19   At nine o'clock I heard my uncle's latchkey in the hall door. I heard him talking to himself and heard the hall stand rocking when it had received the weight of his overcoat. I could interpret these signs. When he was midway through his dinner I asked him to give me the money to go to the bazaar. He had forgotten.

20   "The people are in bed and after their first sleep now," he said.

21   I did not smile. My aunt said to him energetically:

22   "Can't you give him the money and let him go? You've kept him late enough as it is."

23   My uncle said he was very sorry he had forgotten. He said he believed in the old saying: "All work and no play makes Jack a dull boy." He asked me where I was going and, when I had told him a second time he asked me did I know *The Arab's Farewell to His Steed*. When I left the kitchen he was about to recite the opening lines of the piece to my aunt.

24   I held a florin tightly in my hand as I strode down Buckingham Street towards the station. The sight of the streets thronged with buyers and glaring with gas recalled to me the purpose of my journey. I took my seat in a third-class carriage of a deserted train. After an intolerable delay the train moved out of the station slowly. It crept onward among ruinous houses and over the twinkling river. At Westland Row Station a crowd of people pressed to the carriage doors; but the porters moved them back, saying that it was a special train for the bazaar. I remained alone in the bare carriage. In a few minutes the train drew up beside an improvised wooden platform. I passed out on to the road and saw by the lighted dial of a clock that it was ten minutes to ten. In front of me was a large building which displayed the magical name.

25   I could not find any sixpenny entrance and, fearing that the bazaar would be closed, I passed in quickly through a turnstile, handing a shilling to a weary-looking man. I found myself in a big hall girdled at half its height by a gallery. Nearly all the stalls were closed and the greater part of the hall was in darkness. I recognized a silence like that which pervades a church after a service. I walked into the center of the bazaar timidly. A few people were gathered about the stalls which were still open. Before a curtain, over which the words *Café Chantant* were written in colored lamps, two men were counting money on a salver. I listened to the fall of the coins.

26   Remembering with difficulty why I had come I went over to one of the stalls and examined porcelain vases and flowered tea sets. At the door of the stall a young lady was talking and laughing with two young gentlemen. I remarked their English accents and listened vaguely to their conversation.

27   "O, I never said such a thing!"

28   "O, but you did!"

29 "O, but I didn't!"

30 "Didn't she say that?"

31 "Yes, I heard her."

32 "O, there's a . . . fib!"

33 Observing me, the young lady came over and asked me did I wish to buy anything. The tone of her voice was not encouraging; she seemed to have spoken to me out of a sense of duty. I looked humbly at the great jars that stood like eastern guards at either side of the dark entrance to the stall and murmured:

34 "No, thank you."

35 The young lady changed the position of one of the vases and went back to the two young men. They began to talk of the same subject. Once or twice the young lady glanced at me over her shoulder.

36 I lingered before her stall, though I knew my stay was useless, to make my interest in her wares seem the more real. Then I turned away slowly and walked down the middle of the bazaar. I allowed the two pennies to fall against the sixpence in my pocket. I heard a voice call from one end of the gallery that the light was out. The upper part of the hall was now completely dark.

37 Gazing up into the darkness I saw myself as a creature driven and derided by vanity; and my eyes burned with anguish and anger.

Questions for Discussion

1. Who is the narrator? What are his feelings toward Mangan's sister?

2. How does the description of the neighborhood set the tone and prepare for the conclusion?

3. What do the many references to the church and religion suggest about the boy's attitude and his sense of mission?

4. What does Araby at first symbolize for the narrator? How does this symbol change?

5. What details at the bazaar reveal the difference between the way the narrator sees Araby and the way those who are holding the bazaar see it?

6. Explain the last sentence of the story. Why does this simple disappointment seem so devastating to the narrator?

Suggestions for Exploration and Writing

1. Write an essay describing one of your experiences in which your expectations were far higher than the reality.

2. Examine the feelings of the narrator for Mangan's sister and write an essay explaining whether his feelings and his subsequent actions are or are not typical of a boy or girl who has become infatuated for the first time.

3. In an essay, analyze the ways in which the narrator changes as the story progresses.

Bernard Malamud (1914–1986)

One of America's foremost writers from the 1950s through the 1980s, Malamud in his fiction treats his fellow Jews as exemplars of all people who find a way to endure with dignity through pain and anguish. As in "Angel Levine," his fiction often reveals the humor in the ordinary and even painful, the miraculous in the mundane. Malamud won a Pulitzer Prize for the novel The Fixer *(1966) and National Book Awards for* The Fixer *and* The Magic Barrel *(1958), the collection of stories from which "Angel Levine" is taken.*

ANGEL LEVINE   (1958)

1   Manischevitz, a tailor, in his fifty-first year suffered many reverses and indignities. Previously a man of comfortable means, he overnight lost all he had, when his establishment caught fire and, after a metal container of cleaning fluid exploded, burned to the ground. Although Manischevitz was insured against fire, damage suits by two customers who had been hurt in the flames deprived him of every penny he had collected. At almost the same time, his son, of much promise, was killed in the war, and his daughter, without so much as a word of warning, married a lout and disappeared with him as off the face of the earth. Thereafter Manischevitz was victimized by excruciating backaches and found himself unable to work even as a presser—the only kind of work available to him—for more than an hour or two daily, because beyond that the pain from standing became maddening. His Fanny, a good wife and mother, who had taken in washing and sewing, began before his eyes to waste away. Suffering shortness of breath, she at last became seriously ill and took to her bed. The doctor, a former customer of Manischevitz, who out of pity treated them, at first had difficulty diagnosing her ailment but later put it down as hardening of the arteries at an advanced stage. He took Manischevitz aside, prescribed complete rest for her, and in whispers gave him to know there was little hope.

2   Throughout his trials Manischevitz had remained somewhat stoic, almost unbelieving that all this had descended upon his head, as if it were happening, let us say, to an acquaintance or some distant relative; it was in sheer quantity of woe incomprehensible. It was also ridiculous, unjust, and because he had always been a religious man, it was in a way an affront to God. Manischevitz believed this in all his suffering. When his burden had grown too crushingly heavy to be borne he prayed in his chair with shut hollow eyes: "My dear God, sweetheart, did I deserve that this should happen to me?" Then recognizing the worthlessness of it, he put aside the complaint and prayed humbly for assistance: "Give Fanny back her health, and to me for myself that I shouldn't feel pain in every step. Help now or tomorrow is too late. This I don't have to tell you." And Manischevitz wept.

3   Manischevitz's flat, which he had moved into after the disastrous fire, was a meager one, furnished with a few sticks of chairs, a table, and bed,

in one of the poorer sections of the city. There were three rooms: a small, poorly-papered living room; an apology for a kitchen, with a wooden ice-box; and the comparatively large bedroom where Fanny lay in a sagging secondhand bed, gasping for breath. The bedroom was the warmest room of the house and it was here, after his outburst to God, that Manischevitz, by the light of two small bulbs overhead, sat reading his Jewish newspaper. He was not truly reading, because his thoughts were everywhere; however the print offered a convenient resting place for his eyes, and a word or two, when he permitted himself to comprehend them, had the momentary effect of helping him forget his troubles. After a short while he discovered, to his surprise, that he was actively scanning the news, searching for an item of great interest to him. Exactly what he thought he would read he couldn't say—until he realized, with some astonishment, that he was expecting to discover something about himself. Manischevitz put his paper down and looked up with the distinct impression that someone had entered the apartment, though he could not remember having heard the sound of the door opening. He looked around: the room was very still, Fanny sleeping, for once, quietly. Half-frightened, he watched her until he was satisfied she wasn't dead; then, still disturbed by the thought of an unannounced visitor, he stumbled into the living room and there had the shock of his life, for at the table sat a Negro reading a newspaper he had folded up to fit into one hand.

4   "What do you want here?" Manischevitz asked in fright.

5   The Negro put down the paper and glanced up with a gentle expression. "Good evening." He seemed not to be sure of himself, as if he had got into the wrong house. He was a large man, bonily built, with a heavy head covered by a hard derby, which he made no attempt to remove. His eyes seemed sad, but his lips, above which he wore a slight mustache, sought to smile; he was not otherwise prepossessing. The cuffs of his sleeves, Manischevitz noted, were frayed to the lining and the dark suit was badly fitted. He had very large feet. Recovering from his fright, Manischevitz guessed he had left the door open and was being visited by a case worker from the Welfare Department—some came at night—for he had recently applied for relief. Therefore he lowered himself into a chair opposite the Negro, trying, before the man's uncertain smile, to feel comfortable. The former tailor sat stiffly but patiently at the table, waiting for the investigator to take out his pad and pencil and begin asking questions; but before long he became convinced the man intended to do nothing of the sort.

6   "Who are you?" Manischevitz at last asked uneasily.

7   "If I may, insofar as one is able to, identify myself, I bear the name of Alexander Levine."

8   In spite of all his troubles Manischevitz felt a smile growing on his lips. "You said Levine?" he politely inquired.

9   The Negro nodded. "That is exactly right."

10   Carrying the jest farther, Manischevitz asked, "You are maybe Jewish?"

11   "All my life I was, willingly."

12   The tailor hesitated. He had heard of black Jews but had never met one. It gave an unusual sensation.

13   Recognizing in afterthought something odd about the tense of Levine's remark, he said doubtfully, "You ain't Jewish anymore?"

14   Levine at this point removed his hat, revealing a very white part in his black hair, but quickly replaced it. He replied, "I have recently been disincarnated into an angel. As such, I offer you my humble assistance, if to offer is within my province and ability—in the best sense." He lowered his eyes in apology. "Which calls for added explanation: I am what I am granted to be, and at present the completion is in the future."

15   "What kind of angel is this?" Manischevitz gravely asked.

16   "A bona fide angel of God, within prescribed limitations," answered Levine, "not to be confused with the members of any particular sect, order, or organization here on earth operating under a similar name."

17   Manischevitz was thoroughly disturbed. He had been expecting something but not this. What sort of mockery was it—provided Levine was an angel—of a faithful servant who had from childhood lived in the synagogues, always concerned with the word of God?

18   To test Levine he asked, "Then where are your wings?"

19   The Negro blushed as well as he was able. Manischevitz understood this from his changed expression. "Under certain circumstances we lose privileges and prerogatives upon returning to earth, no matter for what purpose, or endeavoring to assist whosoever."

20   "So tell me," Manischevitz said triumphantly, "how did you get here?"

21   "I was transmitted."

22   Still troubled, the tailor said, "If you are a Jew, say the blessing for bread."

23   Levine recited it in sonorous Hebrew.

24   Although moved by the familiar words Manischevitz still felt doubt that he was dealing with an angel.

25   "If you are an angel," he demanded somewhat angrily, "give me the proof."

26   Levine wet his lips. "Frankly, I cannot perform either miracles or near miracles, due to the fact that I am in a condition of probation. How long that will persist or even consist, I admit, depends on the outcome."

27   Manischevitz racked his brains for some means of causing Levine positively to reveal his true identity, when the Negro spoke again:

28   "It was given me to understand that both your wife and you require assistance of a salubrious nature?"

29   The tailor could not rid himself of the feeling that he was the butt of a jokester. Is this what a Jewish angel looks like? he asked himself. This I am not convinced.

30   He asked a last question. "So if God sends to me an angel, why a black? Why not a white that there are so many of them?"

31   "It was my turn to go next," Levine explained.

32   Manischevitz could not be persuaded. "I think you are a faker."

33   Levine slowly rose. His eyes showed disappointment and worry. "Mr. Manischevitz," he said tonelessly, "if you should desire me to be of assistance to you any time in the near future, or possibly before, I can be found"—he glanced at his fingernails—"in Harlem."

34   He was by then gone.

35   The next day Manischevitz felt some relief from his backache and was able to work four hours at pressing. The day after, he put in six hours; and the third day four again. Fanny sat up a little and asked for some halvah to suck. But on the fourth day the stabbing, breaking ache afflicted his back, and Fanny again lay supine, breathing with blue-lipped difficulty.

36   Manischevitz was profoundly disappointed at the return of his active pain and suffering. He had hoped for a longer interval of easement, long enough to have some thought other than of himself and his troubles. Day by day, hour by hour, minute after minute, he lived in pain, pain his only memory, questioning the necessity of it, inveighing against it, also, though with affection, against God. Why *so much*, Gottenyu? If He wanted to teach His servant a lesson for some reason, some cause—the nature of His nature—to teach him, say, for reasons of his weakness, his pride, perhaps, during his years of prosperity, his frequent neglect of God—to give him a little lesson, why then any of the tragedies that had happened to him, any *one* would have sufficed to chasten him. But *all together*—the loss of both his children, his means of livelihood, Fanny's health and his—that was too much to ask one frail-boned man to endure. Who, after all, was Manischevitz that he had been given so much to suffer? A tailor. Certainly not a man of talent. Upon him suffering was largely wasted. It went nowhere, into nothing: into more suffering. His pain did not earn him bread, nor fill the cracks in the wall, nor lift, in the middle of the night, the kitchen table; only lay upon him, sleepless, so sharply oppressively that he could many times have cried out yet not heard himself through this thickness of misery.

37   In this mood he gave no thought to Mr. Alexander Levine, but at moments when the pain waivered, slightly diminishing, he sometimes wondered if he had been mistaken to dismiss him. A black Jew and angel to boot—very hard to believe, but suppose he *had* been sent to succor him, and he, Manischevitz, was in his blindness too blind to comprehend? It was this thought that put him on the knife-point of agony.

38   Therefore the tailor, after much self-questioning and continuing doubt, decided he would seek the self-styled angel in Harlem. Of course he had great difficulty, because he had not asked for specific directions, and movement was tedious to him. The subway took him to 116th Street, and from there he wandered in the dark world. It was vast and its lights lit nothing. Everywhere were shadows, often moving. Manischevitz hobbled along with the aid of a cane, and not knowing where to seek in the blackened tenement buildings, looked fruitlessly through store windows. In the stores he saw people and *everybody* was black. It was an

amazing thing to observe. When he was too tired, too unhappy to go farther, Manischevitz stopped in front of a tailor's store. Out of familiarity
with the appearance of it, with some sadness he entered. The tailor, an
old skinny Negro with a mop of woolly gray hair, was sitting cross-legged
on his workbench, sewing a pair of full-dress pants that had a razor slit all
the way down the seat.

39   "You'll excuse me, please, gentleman," said Manischevitz, admiring the
tailor's deft, thimbled fingerwork, "but you know maybe somebody by
the name Alexander Levine?"

40   The tailor, who Manischevitz thought, seemed a little antagonistic to
him, scratched his scalp.

41   "Cain't say I ever heared dat name."

42   "Alex-ander Lev-ine," Manischevitz repeated it.

43   The man shook his head. "Cain't say I heared."

44   About to depart, Manischevitz remembered to say: "He is an angel,
maybe."

45   "Oh *him*," said the tailor clucking. "He hang out in dat honky tonk
down here a ways." He pointed with his skinny finger and returned to the
pants.

46   Manischevitz crossed the street against a red light and was almost run
down by a taxi. On the block after the next, the sixth store from the corner was a cabaret, and the name in sparkling lights was Bella's. Ashamed
to go in, Manischevitz gazed through the neon-lit window, and when the
dancing couples had parted and drifted away, he discovered at a table on
the side, towards the rear, Levine.

47   He was sitting alone, a cigarette butt hanging from the corner of his
mouth, playing solitaire with a dirty pack of cards, and Manischevitz felt
a touch of pity for him, for Levine had deteriorated in appearance. His
derby was dented and had a gray smudge on the side. His ill-fitting suit
was shabbier, as if he had been sleeping in it. His shoes and trouser cuffs
were muddy, and his face was covered with an impenetrable stubble the
color of licorice. Manischevitz, though deeply disappointed, was about to
enter, when a big-breasted Negress in a purple evening gown appeared
before Levine's table, and with much laughter through many white teeth,
broke into a vigorous shimmy. Levine looked straight at Manischevitz with
a haunted expression, but the tailor was too paralyzed to move or
acknowledge it. As Bella's gyrations continued, Levine rose, his eyes lit in
excitement. She embraced him with vigor, both his hands clasped around
her big restless buttocks and they tangoed together across the floor,
loudly applauded by the noisy customers. She seemed to have lifted
Levine off his feet and his large shoes hung limp as they danced. They
slid past the windows where Manischevitz, white-faced, stood staring in.
Levine winked slyly and the tailor left for home.

48   Fanny lay at death's door. Through shrunken lips she muttered concerning her childhood, the sorrows of the marriage bed, and loss of her

children, yet wept to live. Manischevitz tried not to listen, but even without ears he would have heard. It was not a gift. The doctor panted up the stairs, a broad but bland, unshaven man (it was Sunday) and soon shook his head. A day at most, or two. He left at once, not without pity, to spare himself Manischevitz's multiplied sorrow; the man who never stopped hurting. He would someday get him into a public home.

49   Manischevitz visited a synagogue and there spoke to God, but God had absented himself. The tailor searched his heart and found no hope. When she died he would live dead. He considered taking his life although he knew he wouldn't. Yet it was something to consider. Considering, you existed. He railed against God—Can you love a rock, a broom, an emptiness? Baring his chest, he smote the naked bones, cursing himself for having believed.

50   Asleep in a chair that afternoon, he dreamed of Levine. He was standing before a faded mirror, preening small decaying opalescent wings. "This means," mumbled Manischevitz, as he broke out of sleep, "that it is possible he could be an angel." Begging a neighbor lady to look in on Fanny and occasionally wet her lips with a few drops of water, he drew on his thin coat, gripped his walking stick, exchanged some pennies for a subway token, and rode to Harlem. He knew this act was the last desperate one of his woe: to go without belief, seeking a black magician to restore his wife to invalidism. Yet if there was no choice, he did at least what was chosen.

51   He hobbled to Bella's but the place had changed hands. It was now, as he breathed, a synagogue in a store. In the front, towards him, were several rows of empty wooden benches. In the rear stood the Ark, its portals of rough wood covered with rainbows of sequins; under it a long table on which lay the sacred scroll unrolled, illuminated by the dim light from a bulb on a chain overhead. Around the table, as if frozen to it and the scroll, which they all touched with their fingers, sat four Negroes wearing skullcaps. Now as they read the Holy Word, Manischevitz could, through the plate glass window, hear the singsong chant of their voices. One of them was old, with a gray beard. One was bubble-eyed. One was humpbacked. The fourth was a boy, no older than thirteen. Their heads moved in rhythmic swaying. Touched by this sight from his childhood and youth, Manischevitz entered and stood silent in the rear.

52   "Neshoma," said bubble eyes, pointing to the word with a stubby finger. "Now what dat mean?"

53   "That's the word that means soul," said the boy. He wore glasses.

54   "Let's git on wid de commentary," said the old man.

55   "Ain't necessary," said the humpback. "Souls is immaterial substance. That's all. The soul is derived in that manner. The immateriality is derived from the substance, and they both, causally an' otherwise, derived from the soul. There can be no higher."

56   "That's the highest."

57   "Over de top."

58   "Wait a minute," said bubble eyes. "I don't see what is dat immaterial substance. How come de one gits hitched up to de odder?" He addressed the humpback.

59   "Ask me something hard. Because it is substanceless immateriality. It couldn't be closer together, like all the parts of the body under one skin—closer."

60   "Hear now," said the old man.

61   "All you done is switched de words."

62   "It's the primum mobile, the substanceless substance from which comes all things that were incepted in the idea—you, me and everything and body else."

63   "Now how did all dat happen? Make it sound simple."

64   "It de speerit," said the old man. "On de face of de water moved de speerit. An' dat was good. It say so in de Book. From de speerit ariz de man."

65   "But now listen here. How come it become substance if it all de time a spirit?"

66   "God alone done dat."

67   "Holy! Holy! Praise His Name."

68   "But has dis spirit got some kind of a shade or color?" asked bubble eyes, deadpan.

69   "Man of course not. A spirit is a spirit."

70   "Then how come we is colored?" he said with a triumphant glare.

71   "Ain't got nothing to do wid dat."

72   "I still like to know."

73   "God put the spirit in all things," answered the boy. "He put it in the green leaves and the yellow flowers. He put it with the gold in the fishes and the blue in the sky. That's how come it came to us."

74   "Amen."

75   "Praise Lawd and utter loud His speechless name."

76   "Blow de bugle till it bust the sky."

77   They fell silent, intent upon the next word. Manischevitz approached them.

78   "You'll excuse me," he said. "I am looking for Alexander Levine. You know him maybe?"

79   "That's the angel," said the boy.

80   "Oh, *him*," snuffed bubble eyes.

81   "You'll find him at Bella's. It's the establishment right across the street," the humpback said.

82   Manischevitz said he was sorry that he could not stay, thanked them, and limped across the street. It was already night. The city was dark and he could barely find his way.

83   But Bella's was bursting with the blues. Through the window Manischevitz recognized the dancing crowd and among them sought Levine. He was sitting loose-lipped at Bella's side table. They were tippling from an almost empty whiskey fifth. Levine had shed his old clothes, wore a

shiny new checkered suit, pearl-gray derby, cigar, and big, two-tone button shoes. To the tailor's dismay, a drunken look had settled upon his formerly dignified face. He leaned toward Bella, tickled her ear lobe with his pinky, while whispering words that sent her into gales of raucous laughter. She fondled his knee.

84   Manischevitz, girding himself, pushed open the door and was not welcomed.

85   "This place reserved."

86   "Beat it, pale puss."

87   "Exit, Yankel, Semitic trash."

88   But he moved towards the table where Levine sat, the crowd breaking before him as he hobbled forward.

89   "Mr. Levine," he spoke in a trembly voice. "Is here Manischevitz."

90   Levine glared blearily. "Speak yo' piece, son."

91   Manischevitz shuddered. His back plagued him. Cold tremors tormented his crooked legs. He looked around, everybody was all ears.

92   "You'll excuse me. I would like to talk to you in a private place."

93   "Speak, Ah is a private pusson."

94   Bella laughed piercingly. "Stop it, boy, you killin' me."

95   Manischevitz, no end disturbed, considered fleeing but Levine addressed him:

96   "Kindly state the pu'pose of yo' communication with yo's truly."

97   The tailor wet cracked lips. "You are Jewish. This I am sure."

98   Levine rose, nostrils flaring. "Anythin' else yo' got to say?"

99   Manischevitz's tongue lay like stone.

100   "Speak now or fo'ever hold off."

101   Tears blinded the tailor's eyes. Was ever man so tried? Should he say he believed a half-drunken Negro to be an angel?

102   The silence slowly petrified.

103   Manischevitz was recalling scenes of his youth as a wheel in his mind whirred: believe, do not, yes, no, yes, no. The pointer pointed to yes, to between yes and no, to no, no it was yes. He sighed. It moved but one had still to make a choice.

104   "I think you are an angel from God." He said it in a broken voice, thinking, If you said it it was said. If you believed it you must say it. If you believed, you believed.

105   The hush broke. Everybody talked but the music began and they went on dancing. Bella, grown bored, picked up the cards and dealt herself a hand.

106   Levine burst into tears. "How you have humiliated me."

107   Manischevitz apologized.

108   "Wait'll I freshen up." Levine went to the men's room and returned in his old clothes.

109   No one said goodbye as they left.

110   They rode to the flat via subway. As they walked up the stairs Manischevitz pointed with his cane at his door.

111   "That's all been taken care of," Levine said. "You best go in while I take off."

112   Disappointed that it was so soon over but torn by curiosity, Manischevitz followed the angel up three flights to the roof. When he got there the door was already padlocked.

113   Luckily he could see through a small broken window. He heard an odd noise, as though of a whirring of wings, and when he strained for a wider view, could have sworn he saw a dark figure borne aloft on a pair of magnificent black wings.

114   A feather drifted down. Manischevitz gasped as it turned white, but it was only snowing.

115   He rushed downstairs. In the flat Fanny wielded a dust mop under the bed and then upon the cobwebs on the wall.

116   "A wonderful thing, Fanny," Manischevitz said. "Believe me, there are Jews everywhere."

Questions for Discussion

1. How does an understanding of the story of Job in the Bible enrich your understanding of Manischevitz's story?

2. Why does Manischevitz not believe that Levine is a Jewish angel? Why do you suppose Malamud chose to portray Levine in a way that is so surprising to Manischevitz?

3. Although "Angel Levine" is a story about a man's intense suffering, it is nevertheless humorous. What details add humor to the story without reducing its pathos?

Suggestions for Exploration and Writing

1. Write a character sketch of either Manischevitz or Levine.

2. In an essay, compare the two forms of prejudice portrayed in this story.

3. Write an essay comparing Manischevitz's experience with that of the grandmother in Flannery O'Connor's "A Good Man Is Hard to Find."

Arthur C. Clarke (b. 1917)

Arthur C. Clarke, a British physicist and mathematician, writes fiction and nonfiction. His works, selling in the millions, have been translated into dozens of languages. A 1945 paper published in Wireless World *helped to set the stage for modern telecommunications. Clarke is, however, probably best known for the screenplay for Stanley Kubrick's 2001:* A Space Odyssey, *based on Clarke's short story "Sentinel of Eternity." "The Star," published in 1955, won a Hugo award for excellence in science fiction.*

The Star

(1955)

1 It is three thousand light years to the Vatican. Once, I believed that space could have no power over faith, just as I believed that the heavens declared the glory of God's handiwork. Now I have seen that handiwork, and my faith is sorely troubled. I stare at the crucifix that hangs on the cabin wall above the Mark VI Computer, and for the first time in my life I wonder if it is no more than an empty symbol.

2 I have told no one yet, but the truth cannot be concealed. The facts are there for all to read, recorded on the countless miles of magnetic tape and the thousands of photographs we are carrying back to Earth. Other scientists can interpret them as easily as I can, and I am not one who would condone that tampering with the truth which often gave my order a bad name in the olden days.

3 The crew are already sufficiently depressed: I wonder how they will take this ultimate irony. Few of them have any religious faith, yet they will not relish using this final weapon in their campaign against me—that private, good-natured, but fundamentally serious, war which lasted all the way from Earth. It amused them to have a Jesuit as chief astrophysicist: Dr. Chandler, for instance, could never get over it (why are medical men such notorious atheists?). Sometimes he would meet me on the observation deck, where the lights are always low so that the stars shine with undiminished glory. He would come up to me in the gloom and stand staring out of the great oval port, while the heavens crawled slowly around us as the ship turned end over end with the residual spin we had never bothered to correct.

4 "Well, Father," he would say at last, "it goes on forever and forever, and perhaps *Something* made it. But how you can believe that Something has a special interest in us and our miserable little world—that just beats me." Then the argument would start, while the stars and nebulae would swing around us in silent, endless arcs beyond the flawlessly clear plastic of the observation port.

5 It was, I think, the apparent incongruity of my position that caused most amusement to the crew. In vain I would point to my three papers in the *Astrophysical Journal,* my five in the *Monthly Notices of the Royal Astronomical Society.* I would remind them that my order has long been famous for its scientific works. We may be few now, but ever since the eighteenth century we have made contributions to astronomy and geophysics out of all proportion to our numbers. Will my report on the Phoenix Nebula end our thousand years of history? It will end, I fear, much more than that.

6 I do not know who gave the nebula its name, which seems to me a very bad one. If it contains a prophecy, it is one that cannot be verified for several billion years. Even the word nebula is misleading: this is a far smaller object than those stupendous clouds of mist—the stuff of unborn stars—that are scattered throughout the length of the Milky Way. On the cosmic scale, indeed, the Phoenix Nebula is a tiny thing—a tenuous shell of gas surrounding a single star.

7   Or what is left of a star . . .

8   The Rubens engraving of Loyola seems to mock me as it hangs there above the spectrophotometer tracings. What would *you*, Father, have made of this knowledge that has come into my keeping, so far from the little world that was all the universe you knew? Would your faith have risen to the challenge, as mine has failed to do?

9   You gaze into the distance, Father, but I have traveled a distance beyond any that you could have imagined when you founded our order a thousand years ago. No other survey ship has been so far from Earth: we are at the very frontiers of the explored universe. We set out to reach the Phoenix Nebula, we succeeded, and we are homeward bound with our burden of knowledge. I wish I could lift that burden from my shoulders, but I call to you in vain across the centuries and the light-years that lie between us.

10   On the book you are holding the words are plain to read. AD MAJOREM DEI GLORIAM, the message runs, but it is a message I can no longer believe. Would you still believe it, if you could see what we have found?

11   We knew, of course, what the Phoenix Nebula was. Every year, in our galaxy alone, more than a hundred stars explode, blazing for a few hours or days with thousands of times their normal brilliance before they sink back into death and obscurity. Such are the ordinary novae—the commonplace disasters of the universe. I have recorded the spectrograms and light curves of dozens since I started working at the Lunar Observatory.

12   But three or four times in every thousand years occurs something beside which even a nova pales into total insignificance.

13   When a star becomes a *supernova*, it may for a little while outshine all the massed suns of the galaxy. The Chinese astronomers watched this happen in A.D. 1054, not knowing what it was they saw. Five centuries later, in 1572, a supernova blazed in Cassiopeia so brilliantly that it was visible in the daylight sky. There have been three more in the thousand years that have passed since then.

14   Our mission was to visit the remnants of such a catastrophe, to reconstruct the events that led up to it, and, if possible, to learn its cause. We came slowly in through the concentric shells of gas that had been blasted out six thousand years before, yet were expanding still. They were immensely hot, radiating even now with a fierce violet light, but were far too tenuous to do us any damage. When the star had exploded, its outer layers had been driven upward with such speed that they had escaped completely from its gravitational field. Now they formed a hollow shell large enough to engulf a thousand solar systems, and at its center burned the tiny, fantastic object which the star had now become—a White Dwarf, smaller than the Earth, yet weighing a million times as much.

15   The glowing gas shells were all around us, banishing the normal night of interstellar space. We were flying into the center of a cosmic bomb that had detonated millennia ago and whose incandescent fragments were still hurling apart. The immense scale of the explosion, and the fact that the debris already covered a volume of space many billions of miles across, robbed the scene of any visible movement. It would take decades before

the unaided eye could detect any motion in these tortured wisps and eddies of gas, yet the sense of turbulent expansion was overwhelming.

16　We had checked our primary drive hours before, and were drifting slowly toward the fierce little star ahead. Once it had been a sun like our own, but it had squandered in a few hours the energy that should have kept it shining for a million years. Now it was a shrunken miser, hoarding its resources as if trying to make amends for its prodigal youth.

17　No one seriously expected to find planets. If there had been any before the explosion, they would have been boiled into puffs of vapor, and their substance lost in the greater wreckage of the star itself. But we made the automatic search, as we always do when approaching an unknown sun, and presently we found a single small world circling the star at an immense distance. It must have been the Pluto of this vanished solar system, orbiting on the frontiers of the night. Too far from the central sun ever to have known life, its remoteness had saved it from the fate of all its lost companions.

18　The passing fires had seared its rocks and burned away the mantle of frozen gas that must have covered it in the days before the disaster. We landed, and we found the Vault.

19　Its builders had made sure that we should. The monolithic marker that stood above the entrance was now a fused stump, but even the first long-range photographs told us that here was the work of intelligence. A little later we detected the continent-wide pattern of radio-activity that had been buried in the rock. Even if the pylon above the Vault had been destroyed, this would have remained, an immovable and all but eternal beacon calling to the stars. Our ship fell toward this gigantic bull's-eye like an arrow into its target.

20　The pylon must have been a mile high when it was built, but now it looked like a candle that had melted down into a puddle of wax. It took us a week to drill through the fused rock, since we did not have the proper tools for a task like this. We were astronomers, not archaeologists, but we could improvise. Our original purpose was forgotten: this lonely monument, reared with such labor at the greatest possible distance from the doomed sun, could have only one meaning. A civilization that knew it was about to die had made its last bid for immortality.

21　It will take us generations to examine all the treasures that were placed in the Vault. They had plenty of time to prepare, for their sun must have given its first warnings many years before the final detonation. Everything that they wished to preserve, all the fruit of their genius, they brought here to this distant world in the days before the end, hoping that some other race would find it and that they would not be utterly forgotten. Would we have done as well, or would we have been too lost in our own misery to give thought to a future we could never see or share?

22　If only they had had a little more time! They could travel freely enough between the planets of their own sun, but they had not yet learned to cross the interstellar gulfs, and the nearest solar system was a hundred light-years away. Yet even had they possessed the secret of the Transfinite

Drive, no more than a few millions could have been saved. Perhaps it was better thus.

23   Even if they had not been so disturbingly human as their sculpture shows, we could not have helped admiring them and grieving for their fate. They left thousands of visual records and the machines for projecting them, together with elaborate pictorial instructions from which it will not be difficult to learn their written language. We have examined many of these records, and brought to life for the first time in six thousand years the warmth and beauty of a civilization that in many ways must have been superior to our own. Perhaps they only showed us the best, and one can hardly blame them. But their words were very lovely, and their cities were built with a grace that matches anything of man's. We have watched them at work and play, and listened to their musical speech sounding across the centuries. One scene is still before my eyes—a group of children on a beach of strange blue sand, playing in the waves as children play on Earth. Curious whiplike trees line the shore, and some very large animal is wading in the shadows yet attracting no attention at all.

24   And sinking into the sea, still warm and friendly and life-giving, is the sun that will soon turn traitor and obliterate all this innocent happiness.

25   Perhaps if we had not been so far from home and so vulnerable to loneliness, we should not have been so deeply moved. Many of us had seen the ruins of ancient civilizations on other worlds, but they had never affected us so profoundly. This tragedy was unique. It is one thing for a race to fail and die, as nations and cultures have done on Earth. But to be destroyed so completely in the full flower of its achievement, leaving no survivors—how could that be reconciled with the mercy of God?

26   My colleagues have asked me that, and I have given what answers I can. Perhaps you could have done better, Father Loyola, but I have found nothing in the *Exercitia Spiritualia* that helps me here. They were not an evil people: I do not know what gods they worshiped, if indeed they worshiped any. But I have looked back at them across the centuries, and have watched while the loveliness they used their last strength to preserve was brought forth again into the light of their shrunken sun. They could have taught us much: why were they destroyed?

27   I know the answers that my colleagues will give when they get back to Earth. They will say that the universe has no purpose and no plan, that since a hundred suns explode every year in our galaxy, at this very moment some race is dying in the depths of space. Whether that race has done good or evil during its lifetime will make no difference in the end: there is no divine justice, for there is no God.

28   Yet, of course, what we have seen proves nothing of the sort. Anyone who argues thus is being swayed by emotion, not logic. God has no need to justify His actions to man. He who built the universe can destroy it when He chooses. It is arrogance—it is perilously near blasphemy—for us to say what He may or may not do.

29   This I could have accepted, hard though it is to look upon whole worlds and peoples thrown into the furnace. But there comes a point

when even the deepest faith must falter, and now, as I look at the calculations lying before me, I know I have reached that point at last.

30   We could not tell, before we reached the nebula, how long ago the explosion took place. Now, from the astronomical evidence and the record in the rocks of that one surviving planet, I have been able to date it very exactly. I know in what year the light of this colossal conflagration reached our Earth. I know how brilliantly the supernova whose corpse now dwindles behind our speeding ship once shone in terrestrial skies. I know how it must have blazed low in the east before sunrise, like a beacon in that oriental dawn.

31   There can be no reasonable doubt: the ancient mystery is solved at last. Yet, oh God, there were so many stars you could have used. What was the need to give these people to the fire, that the symbol of their passing might shine above Bethlehem?

Questions for Discussion

1. What is the **point of view** in "The Star"? Why is it crucial to the **irony** of the ending?

2. Is this Jesuit priest an exacting scientist? Why does he face a spiritual crisis? Explain his statement at the beginning of the story: "Once, I believed that space could have no power over faith, just as I believed that the heavens declared the glory of God's handiwork. Now I have seen that handiwork, and my faith is sorely troubled."

3. What is the priest's answer to skeptics who argue that "the universe has no purpose and no plan" and that "there is no God"? Is the priest comfortable with his answer?

Suggestions for Exploration and Writing

1. Analyze in an essay how Clark's use of a Jesuit priest as narrator is vital to the irony in the story.

2. Compare the priest's religious dilemma with the quandary faced by Ozzie in Roth's "The Conversion of the Jews."

Philip Roth (b. 1933)

Born in Newark, New Jersey, Philip Roth is a contemporary American novelist, short story writer, and man of letters. Goodbye, Columbus *(1955), his first book, is a collection of short stories including "The Conversion of the Jews." Roth frequently takes as his subject the urban Jews among whom he grew up. His novels, often comic, include the hilarious* Portnoy's Complaint *(1969), about a Jewish man afflicted with an insatiable sexual desire for gentile women;* Letting Go *(1962);* The Great American Novel *(1973); and the Zuckerman trilogy:* Zuckerman Bound *(1985),* The Counterlife *(1988), and* Deception *(1990); and* American Pastoral *(1997), for which he won the Pulitzer Prize in 1998.*

THE CONVERSION OF THE JEWS   (1955)

1   "You're a real one for opening your mouth in the first place," Itzie said. "What do you open your mouth all the time for?"

2   "I didn't bring it up, Itz, I didn't," Ozzie said.

3   "What do you care about Jesus Christ for anyway?"

4   "I didn't bring up Jesus Christ. He did. I didn't even know what he was talking about. Jesus is historical, he kept saying. Jesus is historical." Ozzie mimicked the monumental voice of Rabbi Binder.

5   "Jesus was a person that lived like you and me," Ozzie continued. "that's what Binder said—"

6   "Yeah? . . . so what! What do I give two cents whether he lived or not. And what do you gotta open your mouth!" Itzie Lieberman favored closed-mouthedness, especially when it came to Ozzie Freedman's questions. Mrs. Freedman had to see Rabbi Binder twice before about Ozzie's questions and this Wednesday at four-thirty would be the third time. Itzie preferred to keep *his* mother in the kitchen; he settled for behind-the-back subtleties such as gestures, faces, snarls and other less delicate barnyard noises.

7   "He was a real person, Jesus, but he wasn't like God, and we don't believe he is God." Slowly, Ozzie was explaining Rabbi Binder's position to Itzie, who had been absent from Hebrew School the previous afternoon.

8   "The Catholics," Itzie said helpfully, "they believe in Jesus Christ, that he's God." Itzie Lieberman used "the Catholics" in its broadest sense—to include the Protestants.

9   Ozzie received Itzie's remark with a tiny head bob, as though it were a footnote, and went on. "His mother was Mary, and his father probably was Joseph," Ozzie said. "But the New Testament says his real father was God."

10   "His *real* father?"

11   "Yeah," Ozzie said, "that's the big thing, his father's supposed to be God."

12   "Bull."

13   "That's what Rabbi Binder says, that it's impossible—"

14   "Sure it's impossible. That stuff's all bull. To have a baby you gotta get laid," Itzie theologized. "Mary hadda get laid."

15   "That's what Binder says: 'the only way a woman can have a baby is to have intercourse with a man.'"

16   "He said *that,* Ozz?" For a moment it appeared that Itzie had put the theological question aside. "He said that, intercourse?" A little curled smile shaped itself in the lower half of Itzie's face like a pink mustache. "What you guys do, Ozz, you laugh or something?"

17   "I raised my hand."

18   "Yeah? Whatja say?"

19   "That's when I asked the question."

20   Itzie's face lit up. "Whatja ask about—intercourse?"

21   "No, I asked the question about God, how if He could create the heaven and earth in six days, and make all the animals and the fish and the light in six days—the light especially, that's what always gets me, that He could make the light. Making fish and animals, that's pretty good—"

22   "That's damn good." Itzie's appreciation was honest but unimaginative: it was as though God had just pitched a one-hitter.

23   "But making light . . . I mean when you think about it, it's really something," Ozzie said. "Anyway, I asked Binder if He could make all that in six days, and He could *pick* the six days he wanted right out of nowhere, why couldn't He let a woman have a baby without having intercourse."

24   "You said intercourse, Ozz, to Binder?"

25   "Yeah."

26   "Right in class?"

27   "Yeah."

28   Itzie smacked the side of his head.

29   "I mean, no kidding around," Ozzie said, "that'd really be nothing. After all that other stuff, that'd practically be nothing."

30   Itzie considered a moment. "What'd Binder say?"

31   "He started all over again explaining how Jesus was historical and how he lived like you and me but he wasn't God. So I said I under*stood* that. What I wanted to know was different."

32   What Ozzie wanted to know was always different. The first time he had wanted to know how Rabbi Binder could call the Jews "The Chosen People" if the Declaration of Independence claimed all men to be created equal. Rabbi Binder tried to distinguish for him between political equality and spiritual legitimacy, but what Ozzie wanted to know, he insisted vehemently, was different. That was the first time his mother had to come.

33   Then there was the plane crash. Fifty-eight people had been killed in a plane crash at La Guardia. In studying a casualty list in the newspaper his mother had discovered among the list of those dead eight Jewish names (his grandmother had nine but she counted Miller as a Jewish name); because of the eight she said the plane crash was "a tragedy." During free-discussion time on Wednesday Ozzie had brought to Rabbi Binder's attention this matter of "some of his relations" always picking out the Jewish names. Rabbi Binder had begun to explain cultural unity and some other things when Ozzie stood up at his seat and said that what he wanted to know was different. Rabbi Binder insisted that he sit down and it was then that Ozzie shouted that he wished all fifty-eight were Jews. That was the second time his mother came.

34   "And he kept explaining about Jesus being historical, and so I kept asking him. No kidding, Itz, he was trying to make me look stupid."

35   "So what he finally do?"

36   "Finally he starts screaming that I was deliberately simple-minded and a wise guy, and that my mother had to come, and this was the last time. And that I'd never get bar-mitzvahed if he could help it. Then, Itz, then

he starts talking in that voice like a statue, real slow and deep, and he says that I better think over what I said about the Lord. He told me to go to his office and think it over." Ozzie leaned his body towards Itzie.

37   "Itz, I thought it over for a solid hour, and now I'm convinced God could do it."

38   Ozzie had planned to confess his latest transgression to his mother as soon as she came home from work. But it was a Friday night in November and already dark, and when Mrs. Freedman came through the door she tossed off her coat, kissed Ozzie quickly on the face, and went to the kitchen table to light the three yellow candles, two for the Sabbath and one for Ozzie's father.

39   When his mother lit the candles she would move her two arms slowly towards her, dragging them through the air, as though persuading people whose minds were half made up. And her eyes would get glassy with tears. Even when his father was alive Ozzie remembered that her eyes had gotten glassy, so it didn't have anything to do with his dying. It had something to do with lighting the candles.

40   As she touched the flaming match to the unlit wick of a Sabbath candle, the phone rang, and Ozzie, standing only a foot from it, plucked it off the receiver and held it muffled to his chest. When his mother lit candles Ozzie felt there should be no noise; even breathing, if you could manage it, should be softened. Ozzie pressed the phone to his breast and watched his mother dragging whatever she was dragging, and he felt his own eyes get glassy. His mother was a round, tired, gray-haired penguin of a woman whose gray skin had begun to feel the tug of gravity and the weight of her own history. Even when she was dressed up she didn't look like a chosen person. But when she lit candles she looked like something better; like a woman who knew momentarily that God could do anything.

41   After a few mysterious minutes she was finished. Ozzie hung up the phone and walked to the kitchen table where she was beginning to lay the two places for the four-course Sabbath meal. He told her that she would have to see Rabbi Binder next Wednesday at four-thirty, and then he told her why. For the first time in their life together she hit Ozzie across the face with her hand.

42   All through the chopped liver and chicken soup part of the dinner Ozzie cried; he didn't have any appetite for the rest.

43   On Wednesday, in the largest of the three basement classrooms of the synagogue, Rabbi Marvin Binder, a tall, handsome, broad-shouldered man of thirty with thick strong-fibered black hair, removed his watch from his pocket and saw that it was four o'clock. At the rear of the room Yakov Blotnik, the seventy-one-year-old custodian, slowly polished the large window, mumbling to himself, unaware that it was four o'clock or six o'clock, Monday or Wednesday. To most of the students Yakov Blotnik's mumbling, along with his brown curly beard, scythe nose, and two heel-trailing black cats, made of him an object of wonder, a foreigner, a relic,

towards whom they were alternately fearful and disrespectful. To Ozzie the mumbling had always seemed a monotonous, curious prayer; what made it curious was that old Blotnik had been mumbling so steadily for so many years, Ozzie suspected he had memorized the prayers and forgotten all about God.

44 "It is now free-discussion time," Rabbi Binder said. "Feel free to talk about any Jewish matter at all—religion, family, politics, sports—"

45 There was silence. It was a gusty, clouded November afternoon and it did not seem as though there ever was or could be a thing called baseball. So nobody this week said a word about that hero from the past, Hank Greenberg—which limited free discussion considerably.

46 And the soul-battering Ozzie Freedman had just received from Rabbi Binder had imposed its limitation. When it was Ozzie's turn to read aloud from the Hebrew book the rabbi had asked him petulantly why he didn't read more rapidly. He was showing no progress. Ozzie said he could read faster but that if he did he was sure not to understand what he was reading. Nevertheless, at the rabbi's repeated suggestion Ozzie tried, and showed a great talent, but in the midst of a long passage he stopped short and said he didn't understand a word he was reading, and started in again at a drag-footed pace. Then came the soul-battering.

47 Consequently when free-discussion time rolled around none of the students felt too free. The rabbi's invitation was answered only by the mumbling of feeble old Blotnik.

48 "Isn't there anything at all you would like to discuss?" Rabbi Binder asked again, looking at his watch. "No questions or comments?"

49 There was a small grumble from the third row. The rabbi requested that Ozzie rise and give the rest of the class the advantage of his thought.

50 Ozzie rose. "I forget it now," he said, and sat down in his place.

51 Rabbi Binder advanced a seat towards Ozzie and poised himself on the edge of the desk. It was Itzie's desk and the rabbi's frame only a dagger's-length away from his face snapped him to sitting attention.

52 "Stand up again, Oscar," Rabbi Binder said calmly, "and try to assemble your thoughts."

53 Ozzie stood up. All his classmates turned in their seats and watched as he gave an unconvincing scratch to his forehead.

54 "I can't assemble any," he announced and plunked himself down.

55 "Stand up!" Rabbi Binder advanced from Itzie's desk to the one directly in front of Ozzie; when the rabbinical back was turned Itzie gave it five-fingers off the tip of his nose, causing a small titter in the room. Rabbi Binder was too absorbed in squelching Ozzie's nonsense once and for all to bother with titters. "Stand up, Oscar. What's your question about?"

56 Ozzie pulled a word out of the air. It was the handiest word. "Religion."

57 "Oh, now you remember."

58 "Yes."

59 "What is it?"

60 Trapped, Ozzie blurted the first thing that came to him. "Why can't He make anything He wants to make!"

61   As Rabbi Binder prepared an answer, a final answer, Itzie, ten feet behind him, raised one finger on his left hand, gestured it meaningfully towards the rabbi's back, and brought the house down.

62   Binder twisted quickly to see what had happened and in the midst of the commotion Ozzie shouted into the rabbi's back what he couldn't have shouted to his face. It was a loud, toneless sound that had the timbre of something stored inside for about six days.

63   "You don't know! You don't know anything about God!"

64   The rabbi spun back towards Ozzie. "What?"

65   "You don't know—you don't—"

66   "Apologize, Oscar, apologize!" It was a threat.

67   "You don't—"

68   Rabbi Binder's hand flicked out at Ozzie's cheek. Perhaps it had only been meant to clamp the boy's mouth shut, but Ozzie ducked and the palm caught him squarely on the nose.

69   The blood came in a short, red spurt on to Ozzie's shirt front.

70   The next moment was all confusion. Ozzie screamed, "You bastard, you bastard!" and broke for the classroom door. Rabbi Binder lurched a step backwards, as though his own blood had started flowing violently in the opposite direction, then gave a clumsy lurch forward and bolted out the door after Ozzie. The class followed after the rabbi's huge blue-suited back, and before old Blotnik could turn from his window, the room was empty and everyone was headed full speed up the three flights leading to the roof.

71   If one should compare the light of day to the life of man: sunrise to birth; sunset—the dropping down over the edge—to death; then as Ozzie Freedman wiggled through the trapdoor of the synagogue roof, his feet kicking backwards bronco-style at Rabbi Binder's outstretched arms—at that moment the day was fifty years old. As a rule, fifty or fifty-five reflects accurately the age of late afternoons in November, for it is that month, during those hours, that one's awareness of light seems no longer a matter of seeing, but of hearing: light begins clicking away. In fact, as Ozzie locked shut the trapdoor in the rabbi's face, the sharp click of the bolt into the lock might momentarily have been mistaken for the sound of the heavier gray that had just throbbed through the sky.

72   With all his weight Ozzie kneeled on the locked door; any instant he was certain that Rabbi Binder's shoulder would fling it open, splintering the wood into shrapnel and catapulting his body into the sky. But the door did not move and below him he heard only the rumble of feet, first loud then dim, like thunder rolling away.

73   A question shot through his brain. "Can this be *me?*" For a thirteen-year-old who had just labeled his religious leader a bastard, twice, it was not an improper question. Louder and louder the question came to him—"Is it me? It is me?"—until he discovered himself no longer kneeling, but racing crazily towards the edge of the roof, his eyes crying, his throat screaming, and his arms flying everywhichway as though not his own.

74 "Is it me? Is it me Me Me Me Me! It has to be me—but is it!"

75 It is the question a thief must ask himself the night he jimmies open his first window, and it is said to be the question with which bridegrooms quiz themselves before the altar.

76 In the few wild seconds it took Ozzie's body to propel him to the edge of the roof, his self-examination began to grow fuzzy. Gazing down at the street, he became confused as to the problem beneath the question: was it, is-it-me-who-called-Binder-a-bastard? or, is-it-me-prancing-around-on-the-roof? However, the scene below settled all, for there is an instant in any action when whether it is you or somebody else is academic. The thief crams the money in his pockets and scoots out the window. The bridegroom signs the hotel register for two. And the boy on the roof finds a streetful of people gaping at him, necks stretched backwards, faces up, as though he were the ceiling of the Hayden Planetarium. Suddenly you know it's you.

77 "Oscar! Oscar Freedman!" A voice rose from the center of the crowd, a voice that, could it have been seen, would have looked like the writing on scroll. "Oscar Freedman, get down from there. Immediately!" Rabbi Binder was pointing one arm stiffly up at him; and at the end of that arm, one finger aimed menacingly. It was the attitude of a dictator, but one—the eyes confessed all—whose personal valet had spit neatly in his face.

78 Ozzie didn't answer. Only for a blink's length did he look towards Rabbi Binder. Instead his eyes began to fit together the world beneath him, to sort out people from places, friends from enemies, participants from spectators. In little jagged starlike clusters his friends stood around Rabbi Binder, who was still pointing. The topmost point on a star compounded not of angels but of five adolescent boys was Itzie. What a world it was, with those stars below, Rabbi Binder below . . . Ozzie, who a moment earlier hadn't been able to control his own body, started to feel the meaning of the word control: he felt Peace and he felt Power.

79 "Oscar Freedman, I'll give you three to come down."

80 Few dictators give their subjects three to do anything; but, as always, Rabbi Binder only looked dictatorial.

81 "Are you ready, Oscar?"

82 Ozzie nodded his head yes, although he had no intention in the world—the lower one or the celestial one he'd just entered—of coming down even if Rabbi Binder should give him a million.

83 "All right then," said Rabbi Binder. He ran a hand through his black Samson hair as though it were the gesture prescribed for uttering the first digit. Then, with his other hand cutting a circle out of the small piece of sky around him, he spoke. "One!"

84 There was no thunder. On the contrary, at that moment, as though "one" was the cue for which he had been waiting, the world's least thunderous person appeared on the synagogue steps. He did not so much come out the synagogue door as lean out, onto the darkening air. He clutched at the doorknob with one hand and looked up at the roof.

85   "Oy!"

86   Yakov Blotnik's old mind hobbled slowly, as if on crutches, and though he couldn't decide precisely what the boy was doing on the roof, he knew it wasn't good—that is, it wasn't-good-for-the-Jews. For Yakov Blotnik life had fractionated itself simply: things were either good-for-the-Jews or no-good-for-the-Jews.

87   He smacked his free hand to his in-sucked cheek, gently. "Oy, Gut!" And then quickly as he was able, he jacked down his head and surveyed the street. There was Rabbi Binder (like a man at an auction with only three dollars in his pocket, he had just delivered a shakey "Two!"), there were the students, and that was all. So far it-wasn't-so-bad-for-the-Jews. But the boy had to come down immediately, before anybody saw. The problem: how to get the boy off the roof?

88   Anybody who has ever had a cat on the roof knows how to get him down. You call the fire department. Or first you call the operator and you ask her for the fire department. And the next thing there is great jamming of brakes and clanging of bells and shouting of instructions. And then the cat is off the roof. You do the same thing to get a boy off the roof.

89   That is, you do the same thing if you are Yakov Blotnik and you once had a cat on the roof.

90   When the engines, all four of them, arrived, Rabbi Binder had four times given Ozzie the count of three. The big hook-and-ladder swung around the corner and one of the firemen leaped from it, plunging head-long towards the yellow fire hydrant in front of the synagogue. With a huge wrench he began to unscrew the top nozzle. Rabbi Binder raced over to him and pulled at his shoulder.

91   "There's no fire . . ."

92   The fireman mumbled back over his shoulder and, heatedly, continued working at the nozzle.

93   "But there's no fire, there's no fire . . ." Binder shouted. When the fireman mumbled again, the rabbi grasped his face with both his hands and pointed it up at the roof.

94   To Ozzie it looked as though Rabbi Binder was trying to tug the fireman's head out of his body, like a cork from a bottle. He had to giggle at the picture they made: it was a family portrait—rabbi in black skullcap, fireman in red fire hat, and the little yellow hydrant squatting beside like a kid brother, bareheaded. From the edge of the roof Ozzie waved at the portrait, a one-handed, flapping, mocking wave; in doing it his right foot slipped from under him. Rabbi Binder covered his eyes with his hands.

95   Firemen work fast. Before Ozzie had even regained his balance, a big, round, yellowed net was being held on the synagogue lawn. The firemen who held it looked up at Ozzie with stern, feelingless faces.

96   One of the firemen turned his head towards Rabbi Binder. "What, is the kid nuts or something?"

97   Rabbi Binder unpeeled his hands from his eyes, slowly, painfully, as if they were tape. Then he checked: nothing on the sidewalk, no dents in the net.

98   "Is he gonna jump, or what?" the fireman shouted.

99   In a voice not at all like a statue, Rabbi Binder finally answered. "Yes, Yes, I think so . . . He's been threatening to . . ."

100   Threatening to? Why, the reason he was on the roof, Ozzie remembered, was to get away; he hadn't even thought about jumping. He had just run to get away, and the truth was that he hadn't really headed for the roof as much as he'd been chased there.

101   "What's his name, the kid?"

102   "Freedman," Rabbi Binder answered. "Oscar Freedman."

103   The fireman looked up at Ozzie. "What is it with you, Oscar? You gonna jump, or what?"

104   Oscar did not answer. Frankly, the question had just arisen.

105   "Look, Oscar, if you're gonna jump, jump—and if you're not gonna jump, don't jump. But don't waste our time, willya?"

106   Ozzie looked at the fireman and then at Rabbi Binder. He wanted to see Rabbi Binder cover his eyes one more time.

107   "I'm going to jump."

108   And then he scampered around the edge of the roof to the corner, where there was no net below, and he flapped his arms at his sides, swishing the air and smacking his palms to his trousers on the down-beat. He began screaming like some kind of engine, "Wheeeee . . . wheeeeee," and leaning way out over the edge with the upper half of his body. The firemen whipped around to cover the ground with the net. Rabbi Binder mumbled a few words to Somebody and covered his eyes. Everything happened quickly, jerkily, as in a silent movie. The crowd, which had arrived with the fire engines, gave out a long, Fourth-of-July fireworks oooh-aahhh. In the excitement no one had paid the crowd much heed, except, of course, Yakov Blotnik, who swung from the door-knob counting heads. "Fier und tsvansik . . . finf und tsvantsik . . . Oy, Gut!" It wasn't like this with the cat.

109   Rabbi Binder peeked through his fingers, checked the sidewalk and net. Empty. But there was Ozzie racing to the other corner. The firemen raced with him but were unable to keep up. Whenever Ozzie wanted to he might jump and splatter himself upon the sidewalk, and by the time the firemen scooted to the spot all they could do with their net would be to cover the mess.

110   "Wheeeee . . . wheeeee . . ."

111   "Hey, Oscar," the winded fireman yelled, "What the hell is this, a game or something?"

112   "Wheeeee . . . wheeeee . . ."

113   "Hey, Oscar—"

114   But he was off now to the other corner, flapping his wings fiercely. Rabbi Binder couldn't take it any longer—the fire engines from nowhere,

the screaming suicidal boy, the net. He fell to his knees, exhausted, and with his hands curled together in front of his chest like a little dome, he pleaded, "Oscar, stop it, Oscar. Don't jump, Oscar. Please come down . . . Please don't jump."

115   And further back in the crowd a single voice, a single young voice, shouted a lone word to the boy on the roof.

116   "Jump!"

117   It was Itzie. Ozzie momentarily stopped flapping.

118   "Go ahead, Ozz—jump!" Itzie broke off his point of the star and courageously, with the inspiration not of a wise-guy but of a disciple, stood alone. "Jump, Ozz, jump!"

119   Still on his knees, his hands still curled, Rabbi Binder twisted his body back. He looked at Itzie, then, agonizingly, back to Ozzie.

120   "OSCAR, DON'T JUMP! PLEASE, DON'T JUMP . . . please please . . ."

121   "Jump!" This time it wasn't Itzie but another point of the star. By the time Mrs. Freedman arrived to keep her four-thirty appointment with Rabbi Binder, the whole little upside down heaven was shouting and pleading for Ozzie to jump, and Rabbi Binder no longer was pleading with him not to jump, but was crying into the dome of his hands.

122   Understandably Mrs. Freeman couldn't figure out what her son was doing on the roof. So she asked. "Ozzie, my Ozzie, what are you doing? My Ozzie, what is it?"

123   Ozzie stopped wheeeeeing and slowed his arms down to a cruising flap, the kind birds use in soft winds, but he did not answer. He stood against the low, clouded, darkening sky—light clicked down swiftly now, as on a small gear—flapping softly and gazing down at the small bundle of woman who was his mother.

124   "What are you doing, Ozzie?" She turned towards the kneeling Rabbi Binder and rushed so close that only a paper-thickness of dusk lay between her stomach and his shoulders.

125   "What is my baby doing?"

126   Rabbi Binder gaped up at her but he too was mute. All that moved was the dome of his hands; it shook back and forth like a weak pulse.

127   "Rabbi, get him down! He'll kill himself. Get him down, my only baby . . ."

128   "I can't," Rabbi Binder said, "I can't . . ." and he turned his handsome head towards the crowd of boys behind him. "It's them. Listen to them."

129   And for the first time Mrs. Freedman saw the crowd of boys, and she heard what they were yelling.

130   "He's doing it for them. He won't listen to me. It's them." Rabbi Binder spoke like one in a trance.

131   "For them?"

132   "Yes."

133   "Why for them?"

134   "They want him to . . ."

135   Mrs. Freeman raised her two arms upward as though she were conducting the sky. "For them he's doing it!" And then in a gesture older than pyramids, older than prophets and floods, her arms came slapping down to her sides. "A martyr I have. Look!" She tilted her head to the roof, Ozzie was still flapping softly. "My martyr."

136   "Oscar, come down, *please*," Rabbi Binder groaned.

137   In a startlingly even voice Mrs. Freedman called to the boy on the roof. "Ozzie, come down, Ozzie. Don't be a martyr, my baby."

138   As though it were a litany, Rabbi Binder repeated her words. "Don't be a martyr, my baby. Don't be a martyr."

139   "Gawhead, Ozz—*be* a Martin!" It was Itzie. "Be a Martin, be a Martin," and all the voices joined in singing for Martindom, whatever *it* was. "Be a Martin, be a Martin . . ."

140   Somehow when you're on a roof the darker it gets the less you can hear. All Ozzie knew was that two groups wanted two new things: his friends were spirited and musical about what they wanted; his mother and the rabbi were even-toned, chanting, about what they didn't want. The rabbi's voice was without tears now and so was his mother's.

141   The big net stared up at Ozzie like a sightless eye. The big, clouded sky pushed down. From beneath it looked like a gray corrugated board. Suddenly, looking up into that unsympathetic sky, Ozzie realized all the strangeness of what these people, his friends, were asking: they wanted him to jump, to kill himself; they were singing about it now—it made them happy. And there was an even greater strangeness: Rabbi Binder was on his knees, trembling. If there was a question to be asked now it was not "Is it me?" but rather "Is it us? . . . Is it us?"

142   Being on the roof, it turned out, was a serious thing. If he jumped would the singing become dancing? Would it? What would jumping stop? Yearningly, Ozzie wished he could rip open the sky, plunge his hands through, and pull our the sun; and on the sun, like a coin, would be stamped JUMP or DON'T JUMP.

143   Ozzie's knees rocked and sagged a little under him as though they were setting him for a dive. His arms tightened, stiffened, froze, from shoulders to fingernails. He felt as if each part of his body were going to vote as to whether he should kill himself or not—and each part as though it were independent of *him*.

144   The light took an unexpected click down and the new darkness, like a gag, hushed the friends singing for this and the mother and rabbi chanting for that.

145   Ozzie stopped counting votes, and in a curiously high voice, like one who wasn't prepared for speech, he spoke.

146   "Mamma?"

147   "Yes, Oscar."

148   "Mamma, get down on your knees, like Rabbi Binder."

149   "Oscar—"

150   "Get down on your knees," he said, "or I'll jump."

151   Ozzie heard a whimper, then a quick rustling, and when he looked down where his mother had stood he saw the top of a head and beneath that a circle of dress. She was kneeling beside Rabbi Binder.

152   He spoke again. "Everybody kneel." There was the sound of everybody kneeling.

153   Ozzie looked around. With one hand he pointed towards the synagogue entrance. "Make *him* kneel."

154   There was a noise, not of kneeling, but of body-and-cloth stretching. Ozzie could hear Rabbi Binder saying in a gruff whisper, ". . . or he'll *kill* himself," and when next he looked there was Yakov Blotnik off the doorknob and for the first time in his life upon his knees in the Gentile posture of prayer.

155   As for the firemen—it is not as difficult as one might imagine to hold a net taut while you are kneeling.

156   Ozzie looked around again; and then he called to Rabbi Binder.

157   "Rabbi?"

158   "Yes, Oscar."

159   "Rabbi Binder, do you believe in God."

160   "Yes."

161   "Do you believe God can do Anything?" Ozzie leaned his head out into the darkness. "Anything?"

162   "Oscar, I think—"

163   "Tell me you believe God can do Anything."

164   There was a second's hesitation. Then: "God can do Anything."

165   "Tell me you believe God can make a child without intercourse."

166   "He can."

167   "Tell me!"

168   "God," Rabbi Binder admitted, "can make a child without intercourse."

169   "Mamma, you tell me."

170   "God can make a child without intercourse," his mother said.

171   "Make *him* tell me." There was no doubt who *him* was.

172   In a few moments Ozzie heard an old comical voice say something to the increasing darkness about God.

173   Next, Ozzie made everybody say it. And then he made them all say they believed in Jesus Christ—first one at a time, then all together.

174   When the catechizing was through it was the beginning of evening. From the street it sounded as if the boy on the roof might have sighed.

175   "Ozzie?" A woman's voice dared to speak. "You'll come down now?"

176   There was no answer, but the woman waited, and when a voice finally did speak it was thin and crying, and exhausted as that of an old man who has just finished pulling the bells.

177   "Mamma, don't you see—you shouldn't hit me. He shouldn't hit me. You shouldn't hit me about God, Mamma. You should never hit anybody about God—"

178   "Ozzie, please come down now."

179   "Promise me, promise me you'll never hit anybody about God."

180   He had asked only his mother, but for some reason everyone kneeling in the street promised he would never hit anybody about God.

181   Once again there was silence.

182   "I can come down now, Mamma," the boy on the roof finally said. He turned his head both ways as though checking the traffic lights. "Now I can come down . . ."

183   And he did, right into the center of the yellow net that glowed in the evening's edge like an overgrown halo.

Questions for Discussion

1. How do Itzie's interests contrast to Ozzie's? What do these contrasts suggest about their levels of thinking?

2. Why do adults have difficulty with Ozzie's questions? Is Ozzie, as Rabbi Binder maintains, "deliberately simple-minded"? Are Ozzie's questions intended to be irreverent? Are they valid questions?

3. How effectively does Ozzie's mother handle his questions? How effectively does Rabbi Binder handle them?

4. Why does Ozzie run to the roof? Does he have any serious intention of jumping? Why do Itzie and Ozzie's other friends shout for him to jump?

5. Why does Ozzie make the rabbi, his mother, and all his friends kneel and declare their belief in Jesus Christ? Given their religious beliefs, what does such a declaration mean?

6. Discuss the **irony** of the title.

Suggestions for Exploration and Writing

1. Ozzie's asking his rabbi, his mother, and his friends to declare their belief in Jesus is an extreme action. In effect, he is requiring them to repudiate their faith. Analyze the causes of Ozzie's extreme action.

2. Attack or defend this statement: Efforts to stifle a child's quest for truth result in rebellion.

3. Ozzie calls Rabbi Binder a "bastard" twice. Write a character analysis of Rabbi Binder, explaining why Ozzie sees him in this negative way.

Toni Cade Bambara (1939–1995)

Toni Cade adopted the name Bambara from a name she found in a sketchbook in her great grandmother's trunk. This renaming of herself, with an emphasis on personal history, demonstrates her fascination with the myths, music, and history of African Americans. After receiving a bachelor of arts degree in theater art and English from Queens College and studying at Commedia del'Arte in Milan, Italy, Bambara taught at several colleges throughout the Northeast. She settled in Atlanta and taught at Spelman College. Many of her works skillfully portray adolescents coming to grips with their environment and show the politics and cultural activities of the urban community.

RAYMOND'S RUN (1960)

1   I don't have much work to do around the house like some girls. My mother does that. And I don't have to earn my pocket money by hustling; George runs errands for the big boys and sells Christmas cards. And anything else that's got to get done, my father does. All I have to do in life is mind my brother Raymond, which is enough.

2   Sometimes I slip and say my little brother Raymond. But as any fool can see he's much bigger and he's older too. But a lot of people call him my little brother cause he needs looking after cause he's not quite right. And a lot of smart mouths got lots to say about that too, especially when George was minding him. But now, if anybody has anything to say to Raymond, anything to say about his big head, they have to come by me. And I don't play the dozens or believe in standing around with somebody in my face doing a lot of talking. I much rather just knock you down and take my chances even if I am a little girl with skinny arms and a squeaky voice, which is how I got the name Squeaky. And if things get too rough, I run. And as anybody can tell you, I'm the fastest thing on two feet.

3   There is no track meet that I don't win the first-place medal. I used to win the twenty-yard dash when I was a little kid in kindergarten. Nowadays, it's the fifty-yard dash. And tomorrow I'm subject to run the quarter-meter relay all by myself and come in first, second, and third. The big kids call me Mercury cause I'm the swiftest thing in the neighborhood. Everybody knows that—except two people who know better, my father and me. He can beat me to Amsterdam Avenue with me having a two-fire-hydrant head start and him running with his hands in his pockets and whistling. But that's private information. Cause can you imagine some thirty-five-year-old man stuffing himself into PAL shorts to race little kids? So as far as everyone's concerned, I'm the fastest and that goes for Gretchen, too, who has put out the tale that she is going to win the first-place medal this year. Ridiculous. In the second place, she's got short legs. In the third place, she's got freckles. In the first place, no one can beat me and that's all there is to it.

4   I'm standing on the corner admiring the weather and about to take a stroll down Broadway so I can practice my breathing exercises, and I've got Raymond walking on the inside close to the buildings, cause he's subject to fits of fantasy and starts thinking he's a circus performer and that the curb is a tightrope strung high in the air. And sometimes after a rain he likes to step down off his tightrope right into the gutter and slosh around getting his shoes and cuffs wet. Then I get hit when I get home. Or sometimes if you don't watch him he'll dash across traffic to the island in the middle of Broadway and give the pigeons a fit. Then I have to go

behind him apologizing to all the old people sitting around trying to get some sun and getting all upset with the pigeons fluttering around them, scattering their newspapers and upsetting the wax paper lunches in their laps. So I keep Raymond on the inside of me, and he plays like he's driving a stage-coach which is O.K. by me so long as he doesn't run me over or interrupt my breathing exercises, which I have to do on account of I'm serious about my running, and I don't care who knows it.

5   Now some people like to act like things come easy to them, won't let on that they practice. Not me. I'll high-prance down 34th Street like a rodeo pony to keep my knees strong even if it does get my mother uptight so that she walks ahead like she's not with me, don't know me, is all by herself on a shopping trip, and I am somebody else's crazy child. Now you take Cynthia Procter for instance. She's just the opposite. If there's a test tomorrow, she'll say something like, "Oh, I guess I'll play handball this afternoon and watch television tonight," just to let you know she ain't thinking about the test. Or like last week when she won the spelling bee for the millionth time, "A good thing you got 'receive,' Squeaky, cause I would have got it wrong. I completely forgot about the spelling bee." And she'll clutch the lace on her blouse like it was a narrow escape. Oh, brother. But of course when I pass her house on my early morning trots around the block, she is practicing the scales on the piano over and over and over and over. Then in music class she always lets herself get bumped around so she falls accidently on purpose onto the piano stool and is so surprised to find herself sitting there that she decides just for fun to try out the ole keys. And what do you know— Chopin's waltzes just spring out of her fingertips and she's the most surprised thing in the world. A regular prodigy. I could kill people like that. I stay up all night studying the words for the spelling bee. And you can see me any time of day practicing running. I never walk if I can trot, and shame on Raymond if he can't keep up. But of course he does, cause if he hangs back someone's liable to walk up to him and get smart, or take his allowance from him, or ask him where he got that great big pumpkin head. People are so stupid sometimes.

6   So I'm strolling down Broadway breathing out and breathing in on counts of seven, which is my lucky number, and here comes Gretchen and her sidekicks: Mary Louise, who used to be a friend of mine when she first moved to Harlem from Baltimore and got beat up by everybody till I took up for her on account of her mother and my mother used to sing in the same choir when they were young girls, but people ain't grateful, so now she hangs out with the new girl Gretchen and talks about me like a dog; and Rosie, who is as fat as I am skinny and has a big mouth where Raymond is concerned and is too stupid to know that there is not a big deal of difference between herself and Raymond and that she can't afford to throw stones. So they are steady coming up Broadway and I see right away that it's going to be one of those Dodge City scenes cause the street ain't that big and they're close to the buildings just as we are. First I think

I'll step into the candy store and look over the new comics and let them pass. But that's chicken and I've got a reputation to consider. So then I think I'll just walk straight on through them or even over them if necessary. But as they get to me, they slow down. I'm ready to fight, cause like I said I don't feature a whole lot of chitchat, I much prefer to just knock you down right from the jump and save everybody a lotta precious time.

7   "You signing up for the May Day races?" smiles Mary Louise, only it's not a smile at all. A dumb question like that doesn't deserve an answer. Besides, there's just me and Gretchen standing there really, so no use wasting my breath talking to shadows.

8   "I don't think you're going to win this time," says Rosie, trying to signify with her hands on her hips all salty, completely forgetting that I have whupped her behind many times for less salt than that.

9   "I always win cause I'm the best," I say straight at Gretchen who is, as far as I'm concerned, the only one talking in this ventriloquist-dummy routine. Gretchen smiles, but it's not a smile, and I'm thinking that girls never really smile at each other because they don't know how and don't want to know how and there's probably no one to teach us how, cause grownup girls don't know either. Then they all look at Raymond who has just brought his mule team to a standstill. And they're about to see what trouble they can get into through him.

10   "What grade you in now, Raymond?"

11   "You got anything to say to my brother, you say it to me, Mary Louise Williams of Raggedy Town, Baltimore."

12   "What are you, his mother?" sasses Rosie.

13   "That's right, Fatso. And the next word out of anybody and I'll be *their* mother too." So they just stand there and Gretchen shifts from one leg to the other and so do they. Then Gretchen puts her hands on her hips and is about to say something with her freckle-face self but doesn't. Then she walks around me looking me up and down but keeps walking up Broadway, and her sidekicks follow her. So me and Raymond smile at each other and he says "Giddyap" to his team and I continue with my breathing exercises, strolling down Broadway toward the ice man on 145th with not a care in the world cause I am Miss Quicksilver herself.

14   I take my time getting to the park on May Day because the track meet is the last thing on the program. The biggest thing on the program is the Maypole dancing, which I can do without, thank you, even if my mother thinks it's a shame I don't take part and act like a girl for a change. You'd think my mother'd be grateful not to have to make me a white organdy dress with a big satin sash and buy me new white baby-doll shoes that can't be taken out of the box till the big day. You'd think she'd be glad her daughter ain't out there prancing around a Maypole getting the new clothes all dirty and sweaty and trying to act like a fairy or a flower or whatever you're supposed to be when you should be trying to be yourself, whatever that is, which is, as far as I am concerned, a poor black girl who really can't afford to buy shoes and a new dress you only wear once a lifetime cause it won't fit next year.

15   I was once a strawberry in a Hansel and Gretel pageant when I was in nursery school and didn't have no better sense than to dance on tiptoe with my arms in a circle over my head doing umbrella steps and being a perfect fool just so my mother and father could come dressed up and clap. You'd think they'd know better than to encourage that kind of nonsense. I am not a strawberry. I do not dance on my toes. I run. That is what I am all about. So I always come late to the May Day program, just in time to get my number pinned on and lay in the grass till they announce the fifty-yard dash.

16   I put Raymond in the little swings, which is a tight squeeze this year and will be impossible next year. Then I look around for Mr. Pearson, who pins the numbers on. I'm really looking for Gretchen if you want to know the truth, but she's not around. The park is jam-packed. Parents in hats and corsages and breast-pocket handkerchiefs peeking up. Kids in white dresses and light blue suits. The parkees unfolding chairs and chasing the rowdy kids from Lenox as if they had no right to be there. The big guys with their caps on backwards, leaning against the fence swirling the basketballs on the tips of their fingers, waiting for all these crazy people to clear out the park so they can play. Most of the kids in my class are carrying bass drums and glockenspiels and flutes. You'd think they'd put in a few bongos or something for real like that.

17   Then here comes Mr. Pearson with his clipboard and his cards and pencils and whistles and safety pins and fifty million other things he's always dropping all over the place with his clumsy self. He sticks out in a crowd because he's on stilts. We used to call him Jack and the Beanstalk to get him mad. But I'm the only one that can outrun him and get away, and I'm too grown for that silliness now.

18   "Well, Squeaky," he says, checking my name off the list and handing me number seven and two pins. And I'm thinking he's got no right to call me Squeaky, if I can't call him Beanstalk.

19   "Hazel Elizabeth Deborah Parker," I correct him and tell him to write it down on his board.

20   "Well, Hazel Elizabeth Deborah Parker, going to give someone else a break this year?" I squint at him real hard to see if he is seriously thinking I should lose the race on purpose just to give someone else a break. "Only six girls running this time," he continues, shaking his head sadly like it's my fault all of New York didn't turn out in sneakers. "That new girl should give you a run for your money." He looks around the park for Gretchen like a periscope in a submarine movie. "Wouldn't it be a nice gesture if you were . . . to ahhh . . ."

21   I give him such a look he couldn't finish putting that idea into words. Grownups got a lot of nerve sometimes. I pin number seven to myself and stomp away, I'm so burnt. And I go straight for the track and stretch out on the grass while the band winds up with "Oh, the Monkey Wrapped His Tail Around the Flagpole," which my teacher calls by some other name. The man on the loudspeaker is calling everyone over to the track and I'm on my back looking at the sky, trying to pretend I'm in the country, but I can't

because even grass in the city feels hard as sidewalk, and there's just no pretending you are anywhere but in a "concrete jungle" as my grandfather says.

22   The twenty-yard dash takes all of two minutes cause most of the little kids don't know no better than to run off the track or run the wrong way or run smack into the fence and fall down and cry. One little kid, though, has got the good sense to run straight for the white ribbon up ahead so he wins. Then the second-graders line up for the thirty-yard dash and I don't even bother to turn my head to watch cause Raphael Perez always wins. He wins before he even begins by psyching the runners, telling them they're going to trip on their shoelaces and fall on their faces or lose their shorts or something, which he doesn't really have to do since he is very fast, almost as fast as I am. After that is the forty-yard dash which I used to run when I was in first grade. Raymond is hollering from the swings cause he knows I'm about to do my thing cause the man on the loudspeaker has just announced the fifty-yard dash, although he might just as well be giving a recipe for angel food cake cause you can hardly make out what he's saying for the static. I get up and slip off my sweat pants and then I see Gretchen standing at the starting line, kicking her legs out like a pro. Then as I get into place I see that ole Raymond is on the line on the other side of the fence, bending down with his fingers on the ground just like he knew what he was doing. I was going to yell at him but then I didn't. It burns up your energy to holler.

23   Every time, just before I take off in a race, I always feel like I'm in a dream, the kind of dream you have when you're sick with fever and feel all hot and weightless. I dream I'm flying over a sandy beach in the early morning sun, kissing the leaves of the trees as I fly by. And there's always the smell of apples, just like in the country when I was little and used to think I was a choo-choo train, running through the fields of corn and chugging up the hill to the orchard. And all the time I'm dreaming this, I get lighter and lighter until I'm flying over the beach again, getting blown through the sky like a feather that weighs nothing at all. But once I spread my fingers in the dirt and crouch over the Get on Your Mark, the dream goes and I am solid again and am telling myself, Squeaky you must win, you must win, you are the fastest thing in the world, you can even beat your father up Amsterdam if you really try. And then I feel my weight coming back just behind my knees then down to my feet then into the earth and the pistol shot explodes in my blood and I am off and weightless again, flying past the other runners, my arms pumping up and down and the whole world is quiet except for the crunch as I zoom over the gravel of the track. I glance to my left and there is no one. To the right, a blurred Gretchen, who's got her chin jutting out as if it would win the race all by itself. And on the other side of the fence is Raymond with his arms down to his side and the palms tucked up behind him, running in his very own style, and it's the first time I ever saw that and I almost stop to watch my brother Raymond on his first run. But the white ribbon is bouncing toward me and I tear past it, racing into the distance till my feet with a mind of their own start digging up footfuls of dirt and brake me short. Then all

the kids standing on the side pile on me, banging me on the back and slapping my head with their May Day programs, for I have won again and everybody on 151st Street can walk tall for another year.

24   "In first place . . ." the man on the loudspeaker is clear as a bell now, but then he pauses and the loudspeaker starts to whine. Then static. And I lean down to catch my breath and here comes Gretchen walking back, for she's overshot the finish line too, huffing and puffing with her hands on her hips taking it slow, breathing in steady time like a real pro and I sort of like her a little for the first time. "In first place . . ." and then three or four voices get all mixed up on the loudspeaker and I dig my sneaker into the grass and stare at Gretchen who's staring back, we both wondering just who did win. I can hear old Beanstalk arguing with the man on the loudspeaker and then a few others running their mouths about what the stopwatches say. Then I hear Raymond yanking at the fence to call me and I wave to shush him, but he keeps rattling the fence like a gorilla in a cage like in them gorilla movies, but then like a dancer or something he starts climbing hand over hand and remembering how he looked running with his arms down to his side and with the wind pulling his mouth back and his teeth showing and all, it occurred to me that Raymond would make a very fine runner. Doesn't he always keep up with me on my trots? And he surely knows how to breathe in counts of seven cause he's always doing it at the dinner table, which drives my brother George up the wall. And I'm smiling to beat the band cause if I've lost this race, or if me and Gretchen tied, or even if I've won, I can always retire as a runner and begin a whole new career as a coach with Raymond as my champion. After all, with a little more study I can beat Cynthia and her phony self at the spelling bee. And if I bugged my mother, I could get piano lessons and become a star. And I have a big rep as the baddest thing around. And I've got a roomful of ribbons and medals and awards. But what has Raymond got to call his own?

25   So I stand there with my new plans, laughing out loud by this time as Raymond jumps down from the fence and runs over with his teeth showing and his arms down to the side, which no one before him has quite mastered as a running style. And by the time he comes over I'm jumping up and down so glad to see him—my brother Raymond, a great runner in the family tradition. But of course everyone thinks I'm jumping up and down because the men on the loudspeaker have finally gotten themselves together and compared notes and are announcing "In first place— Miss Hazel Elizabeth Deborah Parker." (Dig that.) "In second place—Miss Gretchen P. Lewis." And I look at Gretchen wondering what the "P" stands for. And I smile. Cause she's good, no doubt about it. Maybe she'd like to help me coach Raymond; she obviously is serious about running, as any fool can see. And she nods to congratulate me and then she smiles. And I smile. We stand there with this big smile of respect between us. It's about as real a smile as girls can do for each other, considering we don't practice real smiling every day, you know, cause maybe we too busy being flowers or fairies or strawberries instead of something honest and worthy of respect . . . you know . . . like being people.

Questions for Discussion

1. Why is the **first person point of view** effective here?
2. What is the relationship between Hazel and her brother Raymond? Describe the relationship between Hazel and her father and that between Hazel and her mother.
3. Is Hazel bragging or just being honest about her area of expertise, running? Why is practicing important to her?
4. What bothers Hazel about Cynthia Porter? Why?
5. Why does Hazel want Mr. Pearson, who pins on the numbers at the race, to call her Hazel Elizabeth Deborah Parker? What is their relationship? Does Pearson really want Hazel to let Gretchen win the race?
6. Describe the dream Hazel has. Why is it important?

Suggestions for Exploration and Writing

1. Looking at Raymond after the race, Hazel has an **epiphany** or awakening. Hazel asks, "But what has Raymond got to call his own?" Discuss Hazel's new aspirations for Raymond, Gretchen, and herself.
2. At various times Bambara emphasizes a genuine smile or a sarcastic smile or the absence of a smile. Reread the last sentence of the story, and write an essay that discusses "real smiling" and the meaning of that last sentence.

Margaret Atwood (b. 1939)

Canadian writer Margaret Atwood is recognized as an outstanding poet, novelist, and short story writer. Since 1964, she has published numerous highly acclaimed books of poetry. Her novels, often described as feminist, include The Handmaid's Tale *(1985), a novel set in the future, which was subsequently produced as a movie. As a story writer who is often compared to Chekhov, Atwood creates complex, believable characters. In addition, she is a literary critic; her* Survival: A Thematic Guide to Canadian Literature *(1972) was an astonishing, if controversial, success. Atwood's major themes include loneliness, love, and the individual's quest for identity. Her mastery of and love of language are clearly exhibited in her stories and in her novels, such as* The Robber Bride *(1993) and* The Blind Assassin, *the winner of the 2000 Booker Prize. Atwood's fascination with stories about the future is illustrated in "Homelanding."*

HOMELANDING (1990)

1   1. Where should I begin? After all, you have never been there; or if you have, you may not have understood the significance of what you saw, or thought you saw. A window is a window, but there is looking out and

looking in. The native you glimpsed, disappearing behind the curtain, or into the bushes, or down the manhole in the mainstreet—my people are shy—may have been only your reflection in the glass. My country specializes in such illusions.

2   2. Let me propose myself as typical. I walk upright on two legs, and have in addition two arms, with ten appendages, that is to say, five at the end of each. On the top of my head, but not on the front, there is an odd growth, like a species of seaweed. Some think this is a kind of fur, others consider it modified feathers, evolved perhaps from scales like those of lizards. It serves no functional purpose and is probably decorative.

3   My eyes are situated in my head, which also possesses two small holes for the entrance and exit of air, the invisible fluid we swim in, and one larger hole, equipped with bony protuberances called teeth, by means of which I destroy and assimilate certain parts of my surroundings and change them into myself. This is called eating. The things I eat include roots, berries, nuts, fruits, leaves, and the muscle tissues of various animals and fish. Sometimes I eat their brains and glands as well. I do not as a rule eat insects, grubs, eyeballs or the snouts of pigs, though these are eaten with relish in other countries.

4   3. Some of my people have a pointed but boneless external appendage, in the front, below the navel or midpoint. Others do not. Debate about whether the possession of such a thing is an advantage or disadvantage is still going on. If this item is lacking, and in its place there is a pocket or inner cavern in which fresh members of our community are grown, it is considered impolite to mention it openly to strangers. I tell you this because it is the breach of etiquette most commonly made by tourists.

5   In some of our more private gatherings, the absence of cavern or prong is politely overlooked, like club feet or blindness. But sometimes a prong and a cavern will collaborate in a dance, or illusion, using mirrors and water, which is always absorbing for the performers but frequently grotesque for the observers. I notice that you have similar customs.

6   Whole conventions and a great deal of time have recently been devoted to discussions of this state of affairs. The prong people tell the cavern people that the latter are not people at all and are in reality more akin to dogs or potatoes, and the cavern people abuse the prong people for their obsession with images of poking, thrusting, probing and stabbing. Any long object with a hole at the end, out of which various projectiles can be shot, delights them.

7   I myself—I am a cavern person—find it a relief not to have to worry about climbing over barbed wire fences or getting caught in zippers.

8   But that is enough about our bodily form.

9   4. As for the country itself, let me begin with the sunsets, which are long and red, resonant, splendid and melancholy, symphonic you might almost say; as opposed to the short boring sunsets of other countries, no more interesting than a lightswitch. We pride ourselves on our sunsets. "Come and see the sunset," we say to one another. This causes everyone to rush outdoors or over to the window.

10   Our country is large in extent, small in population, which accounts for our fear of large empty spaces, and also our need for them. Much of it is covered in water, which accounts for our interest in reflections, sudden vanishings, the dissolution of one thing into another. Much of it however is rock, which accounts for our belief in Fate.

11   In summer we lie about in the blazing sun, almost naked, covering our skins with fat and attempting to turn red. But when the sun is low in the sky and faint, even at noon, the water we are so fond of changes to something hard and white and cold and covers up the ground. Then we cocoon ourselves, become lethargic, and spend much of our time hiding in crevices. Our mouths shrink and we say little.

12   Before this happens, the leaves on many of our trees turn blood red or lurid yellow, much brighter and more exotic than the interminable green of jungles. We find this change beautiful. "Come and see the leaves," we say, and jump into our moving vehicles and drive up and down past the forests of sanguinary trees, pressing our eyes to the glass.

13   We are a nation of metamorphs.

14   Anything red compels us.

15   5. Sometimes we lie still and do not move. If air is still going in and out of our breathing holes, this is called sleep. If not, it is called death. When a person has achieved death a kind of picnic is held, with music, flowers and food. The person so honoured, if in one piece, and not, for instance, in shreds or falling apart, as they do if exploded or a long time drowned, is dressed in becoming clothes and lowered into a hole in the ground, or else burnt up.

16   These customs are among the most difficult to explain to strangers. Some of our visitors, especially the young ones, have never heard of death and are bewildered. They think that death is simply one more of our illusions, our mirror tricks; they cannot understand why, with so much food and music, the people are sad.

17   But you will understand. You too must have death among you. I can see it in your eyes.

18   6. I can see it in your eyes. If it weren't for this I would have stopped trying long ago, to communicate with you in this halfway language which is so difficult for both of us, which exhausts the throat and fills the mouth with sand; if it weren't for this I would have gone away, gone back. It's this knowledge of death, which we share, where we overlap. Death is our common ground. Together, on it, we can walk forward.

19   By now you must have guessed: I come from another planet. But I will never say to you, *Take me to your leaders*. Even I—unused to your ways though I am—would never make that mistake. We ourselves have such beings among us, made of cogs, pieces of paper, small disks of shiny metal, scraps of coloured cloth. I do not need to encounter more of them.

20   Instead I will say, take me to your trees. Take me to your breakfasts, your sunsets, your bad dreams, your shoes, your nouns. Take me to your fingers; take me to your deaths.

21   These are worth it. These are what I have come for.

Questions for Exploration

1. Who is the narrator? Describe her physical appearance.

2. To whom is the narrator describing her country? Where do you believe she is from?

3. Which of her descriptions are humorous? Why?

4. Why has the narrator chosen these people to try to communicate with?

5. Explain why she would "never say [. . .], *Take me to your leaders.*" To whom or what would she ask to be taken? Why?

Suggestions for Exploration and Writing

1. Write an essay or story explaining your country or culture to a being from another planet.

2. In an essay, explain the narrator's quest.

3. Using Atwood's style, write an essay about a holiday as told to someone who considers you an alien. Discuss in your essay any customs and rituals associated with the holiday.

POTRY

Psalm 8, traditionally attributed to David, is one of the 150 poems that make up the book of Psalms in the Old Testament. Often described as a lyrical echo of the first book of Genesis, this psalm celebrates God's creations.

PSALM 8   (ELEVENTH–TENTH CENTURY BC)

1 To the chief Musician upon Gittith, A Psalm of David.
O Lord our Lord, how excellent *is* thy name in all the earth! who hast set thy glory above the heavens.
2 Out of the mouth of babes and sucklings hast thou ordained strength because of thine enemies, that thou mightest still the enemy and the avenger.
3 When I consider thy heavens, the work of thy fingers, the moon and the stars, which thou hast ordained;
4 What is man, that thou art mindful of him? and the son of man, that thou visitest him?
5 For thou hast made him a little lower than the angels, and hast crowned him with glory and honour.

6 Thou madest him to have dominion over the works of thy hands;
thou hast put all *things* under his feet:
7 All sheep and oxen, yea, and the beasts of the field;
8 The fowl of the air, and the fish of the sea, *and whatsoever* passeth
through the paths of the seas.
9 O Lord our Lord, how excellent *is* thy name in all the earth!

Questions for Discussion

1. In what order does the psalmist perceive the wonders of God?

2. What prompts the psalmist's questions? What is the **tone** in the psalm?

3. What vision of humanity and its purpose does the psalmist present?
How well has humanity fulfilled that purpose?

John Donne (1572–1631)

*A brief biography of John Donne precedes "A Valediction: Forbidding
Mourning" in the Men and Women Unit.*

HOLY SONNET 14 (CA. 1610)

Batter my heart, three person'd God; for, you
As yet but knocke, breathe, shine, and seeke to mend;
That I may rise, and stand, o'erthrow mee, and bend
Your force, to breake, blowe, burn and make me new.
5   I, like an usurpt towne, to another due,
Labour to admit You, but Oh, to no end;
Reason Your viceroy in mee, mee should defend
But is captiv'd, and proves weake or untrue,
Yet dearely I love You, and would be lov'd faine,
10 But am betroth'd unto Your enemie,
Divorce mee, untie, or breake that knot againe,
Take mee to You, imprison mee, for I
Except You enthrall mee, never shall be free,
Nor ever chaste, except You ravish mee.

Questions for Discussion

1. What does the strong verb "batter" suggest? What is the speaker asking God to do in this anguished and unorthodox prayer? Why?

2. The first four lines of the **sonnet** are dominated by strong action verbs. What is the effect of these verbs? What is the effect of the **alliterative** *b*s in these lines?

3. Explain the extended **simile** developed in the second quatrain.

4. Explain the **paradoxes** in the last two lines.

Suggestion for Exploration and Writing

1. In an analysis, show how **imagery,** sound, **diction,** and **syntax** develop the **tone** of Donne's "Batter My Heart."

John Milton (1608–1674)

John Milton, educated at Cambridge and a master of Greek, Latin, Italian, and Hebrew, isolated himself after graduation from college to read the great books. After writing several controversial pamphlets, including Areopagitica *(1644), an argument for freedom of the press, he served as foreign secretary under Oliver Cromwell, Puritan Lord Protector of England from 1653 to 1658. Milton's* Paradise Lost *(1667), based on the Genesis account of humanity's fall, is regarded as the greatest* **epic** *poem written in English. Both* Paradise Lost *and* Paradise Regained *(1671) were written during Milton's last years, when he was blind and embittered.*

SONNET 16 (1655)

When I consider how my light is spent,
   Ere half my days, in this dark world and wide,
   And that one talent which is death to hide,
   Lodged with me useless, though my soul more bent
5 To serve therewith my Maker, and present
   My true account, lest he returning chide,
   Doth God exact day-labour, light denied,
   I fondly ask; but Patience to prevent
That murmur, soon replies, "God doth not need
10   Either man's work or his own gifts, who best
   Bear his mild yoke, they serve him þest. His state
Is kingly. Thousands at his bidding speed
   And post o'er land and ocean without rest:
   They also serve who only stand and wait."

Questions for Discussion

1. To what does Milton refer when he speaks of "that one talent which is death to hide / Lodged with me useless [. . .]"? Who gave Milton the talent to which he refers?

2. Milton asks, "Doth God exact day-labour, light denied?" What does he imply?

3. Patience says that man is not going to be judged on his "work" or "gifts." On what is man going to be judged?

4. Explain the last line of the poem.

Suggestions for Exploration and Writing

1. Milton speaks of presenting the "true account" of his life and actions to God. If you had to present the true account of yourself to God or to someone else in authority, what would it be? Why?

2. In an essay, discuss whether you agree with the last line of Milton's poem.

William Blake (1757–1827)

A brief biography of William Blake precedes "London" in the Freedom and Responsibility Unit.

THE LAMB   (1789)

Little Lamb, who made thee?
Dost thou know who made thee?
Gave thee life & bid thee feed,
By the stream & o'er the mead;
⁵ Gave thee clothing of delight,
Softest clothing wooly bright;
Gave thee such a tender voice,
Making all the vales rejoice!
　　Little Lamb I'll tell thee,
¹⁰ 　　Little Lamb I'll tell thee!
He is callèd by thy name,
For he calls himself a Lamb:
He is meek & he is mild,
He became a little child:
¹⁵ I a child & thou a lamb,
We are callèd by his name.
　　Little Lamb God bless thee.
　　Little Lamb God bless thee.

Questions for Discussion

1. How would you describe the **diction** of this poem? Who is the speaker? Why does Blake use the archaic terms *thee* and *thou?*

2. How does the speaker feel about the Lamb? How do sound, **imagery, and diction** develop the **tone?**

3. What particular qualities of the Lamb appeal to the speaker? What does the Lamb **symbolize?**

4. What do the lines "For he calls himself a Lamb," "He became a little child," and "We are callèd by his name" mean?

THE TYGER   (1974)

Tyger! Tyger! burning bright
In the forests of the night,
What immortal hand or eye
Could frame thy fearful symmetry?

5   In what distant deeps or skies
Burnt the fire of thine eyes?
On what wings dare he aspire?
What the hand, dare seize the fire?

And what shoulder, & what art,
10   Could twist the sinews of thy heart?
And when thy heart began to beat,
What dread hand? & what dread feet?

What the hammer? what the chain?
In what furnace was thy brain?
15   What the anvil? what dread grasp
Dare its deadly terrors clasp?

When the stars threw down their spears,
And water'd heaven with their tears,
Did he smile his work to see?
20   Did he who made the Lamb make thee?

Tyger! Tyger! burning bright
In the forests of the night,
What immortal hand or eye
Dare frame thy fearful symmetry?

Questions for Discussion

1. What qualities of the tiger are suggested by the phrase "fearful symmetry"?

2. What is Blake alluding to in the lines "When the stars threw down their spears / And water'd heaven with their tears"?

3. Can the question "Did he who made the Lamb make thee?" be answered? If so, how? If not, why not?

4. What does the tiger symbolize?

Suggestion for Exploration and Writing

1. In an essay, analyze "The Lamb" and "The Tyger" as representing two contrasting but complementary visions of God and of the created world.

William Wordsworth (1770-1850)

A brief biography of William Wordsworth precedes "The World is Too Much with Us" in the Freedom and Responsibility Unit.

MY HEART LEAPS UP (1807)

My heart leaps up when I behold
  A Rainbow in the sky:
So was it when my life began;
So is it now I am a Man;
So be it when I shall grow old,
  Or let me die!
The Child is Father of the Man;
And I could wish my days to be
Bound each to each by natural piety.

5

Questions for Discussion

1. What very familiar figure of speech does the poet use in the first line? What does it suggest about his feeling for nature? Why would he rather die than lose the capacity for this feeling?

2. What does the **paradox** "The Child is Father of the Man" mean?

3. What does the speaker mean by "natural piety"?

Suggestion for Exploration and Writing

1. In an essay, explain what things in life make your "heart leap up."

Alfred, Lord Tennyson (1809-1892)

Tennyson succeeded Wordsworth as English Poet Laureate. Tennyson's early poems were not acclaimed; however, after the death of a friend caused him to write an extended elegy, In Memoriam (1853), and Queen Victoria named him a Lord, Tennyson became one of the most popular poets of his day. Among his works are Maud, and Other Poems (1855) and Idylls of the King (1859), an extended poem about King Arthur.

ULYSSES (1833)

It little profits that an idle king,
By this still hearth, among these barren crags,
Match'd with an aged wife, I mete and dole
Unequal laws unto a savage race,

5   That hoard, and sleep, and feed, and know not me.
     I cannot rest from travel: I will drink
     Life to the lees: all times I have enjoy'd
     Greatly, have suffer'd greatly, both with those
     That loved me, and alone; on shore, and when
10   Thro' scudding drifts the rainy Hyades
     Vext the dim sea: I am become a name;
     For always roaming with a hungry heart
     Much have I seen and known; cities of men
     And manners, climates, councils, governments,
15   Myself not least, but honour'd of them all;
     And drunk delight of battle with my peers,
     Far on the ringing plains of windy Troy.
     I am a part of all that I have met;
     Yet all experience is an arch wherethro'
20   Gleams that untravell'd world, whose margin fades
     For ever and for ever when I move.
     How dull it is to pause, to make an end,
     To rust unburnish'd, not to shine in use!
     As tho' to breathe were life. Life piled on life
25   Were all too little, and of one to me
     Little remains: but every hour is saved
     From that eternal silence, something more,
     A bringer of new things; and vile it were
     For some three suns to store and hoard myself,
30   And this gray spirit yearning in desire
     To follow knowledge like a sinking star,
     Beyond the utmost bound of human thought.
     This is my son, mine own Telemachus,
     To whom I leave the sceptre and the isle—
35   Well-loved of me, discerning to fulfil
     This labour, by slow prudence to make mild
     A rugged people, and thro' soft degrees
     Subdue them to the useful and the good.
     Most blameless is he, centred in the sphere
40   Of common duties, decent not to fail
     In offices of tenderness, and pay
     Meet adoration to my household gods
     When I am gone. He works his work, I mine.
     There lies the port; the vessel puffs her sail:
45   There gloom the dark broad seas. My mariners,
     Souls that have toil'd, and wrought, and thought with me—
     That ever with a frolic welcome took
     The thunder and the sunshine, and opposed
     Free hearts, free foreheads—you and I are old;

50 Old age hath yet his honour and his toil;
    Death closes all: but something ere the end,
    Some work of noble note, may yet be done,
    Not unbecoming men that strove with Gods.
    The lights begin to twinkle from the rocks:
55 The long day wanes: the slow moon climbs: the deep
    Moans round with many voices. Come, my friends,
    'Tis not too late to seek a newer world.
    Push off, and sitting well in order smite *hit*
    The sounding furrows; for my purpose holds
60 To sail beyond the sunset, and the baths
    Of all the western stars, until I die.
    It may be that the gulfs will wash us down:
    It may be we shall touch the Happy Isles,
    And see the great Achilles, whom we knew.
65 Tho' much is taken, much abides; and tho'
    We are not now that strength which in old days
    Moved earth and heaven; that which we are, we are;
    One equal temper of heroic hearts,
    Made weak by time and fate, but strong in will
70 To strive, to seek, to find, and not to yield. *Con!*

Learn Nothing

Questions for Discussion

1. Why does Ulysses say that he "will drink / Life to the lees"? Why does he still crave the "untravel'd world"?

2. Ulysses says he has "enjoyed greatly" and "suffered greatly." Why is the word *greatly* important?

3. Why is Telemachus Ulysses's ideal heir?

Suggestions for Exploration and Writing

1. Write an essay about someone who has the same characteristics and the same yearnings as Ulysses.

2. "Do Not Go Gentle into That Good Night" by Dylan Thomas has a similar message. Compare the poems' themes.

3. Are you a Ulysses or a Telemachus? Discuss.

Gerard Manley Hopkins (1844–1889)

Born into a High Anglican family in England, Gerard Manley Hopkins in 1866 converted to Catholicism. Two years later, he entered the Jesuit order and in 1877 was ordained a Jesuit priest. His sometimes anguished poems, which were not published until

*1918, reveal a man of strong faith sometimes racked by doubts about the adequacy of his devotion and service. Hopkins developed an experimental metrical system he called **sprung rhythm**, basing his lines on the number of accents rather than the number of syllables.*

GOD'S GRANDEUR (1877)

The world is charged with the grandeur of God.
  It will flame out, like shining from shook foil;
  It gathers to a greatness, like the ooze of oil
Crushed. Why do men then now not reck his rod?
5 Generations have trod, have trod, have trod;
  And all is seared with trade; bleared, smeared with toil;
  And wears man's smudge and shares man's smell: the soil
Is bare now, nor can foot feel, being shod.

And for all this, nature is never spent:
10 There lives the dearest freshness deep down things;
And though the last lights off the black West went
  Oh, morning, at the brown brink eastward, springs—
Because the Holy Ghost over the bent
  World broods with warm breast and with ah! bright wings.

Questions for Discussion

1. What is the effect of the word *charged* in the first line?

2. What **images** does Hopkins use to characterize the grandeur of God? Where does this grandeur appear?

3. What is the effect of the repetition in line 5?

4. What is Hopkins's answer to the question in line 4? Compare his answer to Wordsworth's lament in "The World Is Too Much with Us."

5. What is the effect of the final image?

Suggestion for Exploration and Writing

1. Hopkins's poem celebrates the grandeur and freshness of God's creation, sensitizing readers to even the apparently dull and ordinary. Compare Hopkins's sense of divine imminence with Annie Dillard's in "Heaven and Earth in Jest."

William Butler Yeats (1865–1939)

A brief biography of William Butler Yeats precedes "A Prayer for My Daughter" in the Family Unit.

SAILING TO BYZANTIUM   1927

I

That is no country for old men. The young
In one another's arms, birds in the trees
—Those dying generations—at their song,
The salmon-falls, the mackerel-crowded seas,
5   Fish, flesh, or fowl, commend all summer long
Whatever is begotten, born, and dies.
Caught in that sensual music all neglect
Monuments of unageing intellect.

II

An aged man is but a paltry thing,
10   A tattered coat upon a stick, unless
Soul clap its hands and sing, and louder sing
For every tatter in its mortal dress,
Nor is there singing school but studying
Monuments of its own magnificence;
15   And therefore I have sailed the seas and come
To the holy city of Byzantium.

III

O sages standing in God's holy fire
As in the gold mosaic of a wall,
Come from the holy fire, perne in a gyre,
20   And be the singing-masters of my soul.
Consume my heart away; sick with desire
And fastened to a dying animal
It knows not what it is; and gather me
Into the artifice of eternity.

IV

25   Once out of nature I shall never take
My bodily form from any natural thing,
But such a form as Grecian goldsmiths make
Of hammered gold and gold enamelling
To keep a drowsy Emperor awake;
30   Or set upon a golden bough to sing
To lords and ladies of Byzantium
Of what is past, or passing, or to come.

Questions for Discussion

1. What place is the speaker describing in the first stanza? Why is it "no country for old men"? What **images** define this world?

2. What does the "artifice of eternity" suggest about Yeats's conception of life after death?

3. Why would Yeats want to be resurrected as a golden bird?

4. At the beginning of the poem Yeats refers to "[w]hatever is begotten, born, and dies." At the end he imagines himself a golden bird singing of "what is past, or passing, or to come." How do these three-part phrases define the difference between the speaker in his original country and the speaker in Byzantium?

Suggestions for Exploration and Writing

1. Yeats says in *A Vision* that Byzantium represented for him a culture so unified in its religious, cultural, and practical life that an artist spoke for and was heard by the whole people. Read Book V, section IV of *A Vision*, research Byzantium, and write a paper on why Byzantium meant so much to Yeats that he would prefer to spend eternity there.

2. How does the bird **symbolize** a means of transcending the physical world?

T. S. Eliot (1888–1965)

Eliot, born an American and the grandson of a Unitarian minister, changed his nationality and his religion, becoming a British citizen and a devout Anglican. Eliot's early poems, like "The Love Song of J. Alfred Prufrock" and "The Hollow Men," expressed the disenchantment and disillusionment of many people in the early twentieth century. The Waste Land (1922) is considered by many critics to be the ultimate expression of the modern condition. Eliot's conversion to the Anglican faith, however, changed his outlook completely; and his later works such as "Ash Wednesday" and The Four Quartets (1934–1944) depict human beings' search for a sustaining faith. An ardent admirer of Dante, Eliot learned medieval Italian in order to read The Divine Comedy in its original form. The quotation with which Eliot begins "The Love Song of J. Alfred Prufrock" is a statement of Guido da Montefeltro, a sinner in Dante's Inferno, who says that he would not tell Dante his story if he thought that there was any chance that Dante would return to earth to repeat it.

THE LOVE SONG OF J. ALFRED PRUFROCK (1917)

S'io credessi che mia risposta fosse
A persona che mai tornasse al mondo,
Questa fiamma staria senza più scosse.
Ma perciocchè giammai di questo fondo
Non tornò vivo alcum, s'i' odo il vero,
Senza tema d'infamia ti rispondo.

Let us go then, you and I,
When the evening is spread out against the sky
Like a patient etherized upon a table;
Let us go, through certain half-deserted streets,
5   The muttering retreats
Of restless nights in one-night cheap hotels
And sawdust restaurants with oyster-shells:
Streets that follow like a tedious argument
Of insidious intent
10 To lead you to an overwhelming question . . .

Oh, do not ask, "What is it?"
Let us go and make our visit.

In the room the women come and go
Talking of Michelangelo.
15   The yellow fog that rubs its back upon the window panes,
The yellow smoke that rubs its muzzle on the window panes,
Licked its tongue into the corners of the evening,
Lingered upon the pools that stand in drains,
Let fall upon its back the soot that falls from chimneys,
20 Slipped by the terrace, made a sudden leap,
And seeing that it was a soft October night,
Curled once about the house, and fell asleep.

And indeed there will be time
For the yellow smoke that slides along the street,
25 Rubbing its back upon the window panes;
There will be time, there will be time
To prepare a face to meet the faces that you meet;
There will be time to murder and create,
And time for all the works and days of hands
30 That lift and drop a question on your plate:
Time for you and time for me,
And time yet for a hundred indecisions,
And for a hundred visions and revisions,
Before the taking of a toast and tea.

35 In the room the women come and go
Talking of Michelangelo.

And indeed there will be time
To wonder, "Do I dare?" and, "Do I dare?"—
Time to turn back and descend the stair,
40   With a bald spot in the middle of my hair—
(They will say: "How his hair is growing thin!")
My morning coat, my collar mounting firmly to the chin,
My necktie rich and modest, but asserted by a simple pin—
(They will say: "But how his arms and legs are thin!")
45   Do I dare
Disturb the universe?
In a minute there is time
For decisions and revisions which a minute will reverse.

For I have known them already, known them all:
50   Have known the evenings, mornings, afternoons,
I have measured out my life with coffee spoons;
I know the voices dying with a dying fall
Beneath the music from a farther room.
        So how should I presume?

55   And I have known the eyes already, known them all—
The eyes that fix you in a formulated phrase,
And when I am formulated, sprawling on a pin,
When I am pinned and wriggling on the wall,
Then how should I begin
60   To spit out all the butt-ends of my days and ways?
        And how should I presume?

And I have known the arms already, known them all—
Arms that are braceleted and white and bare
(But in the lamplight, downed with light brown hair!)
65   Is it perfume from a dress
        That makes me so digress?
Arms that lie along a table, or wrap about a shawl.
        And should I then presume?
        And how should I begin?

70   Shall I say, I have gone at dusk through narrow streets,
And watched the smoke that rises from the pipes
Of lonely men in shirtsleeves, leaning out of windows?. . .
I should have been a pair of ragged claws
Scuttling across the floors of silent seas.

75   And the afternoon, the evening, sleeps so peacefully!
Smoothed by long fingers,
Asleep . . . tired . . . or it malingers,
Stretched on the floor, here beside you and me.
Should I, after tea and cakes and ices,
80   Have the strength to force the moment to its crisis?

But though I have wept and fasted, wept and prayed,
Though I have seen my head (grown slightly bald) brought
    in upon a platter,
I am no prophet—and here's no great matter;
I have seen the moment of my greatness flicker,
85 And I have seen the eternal Footman hold my coat, and snicker,
    And in short, I was afraid.

    And would it have been worth it, after all,
After the cups, the marmalade, the tea,
Among the porcelain, among some talk of you and me,
90 Would it have been worth while
To have bitten off the matter with a smile,
To have squeezed the universe into a ball
To roll it toward some overwhelming question,
To say: "I am Lazarus, come from the dead,
95 Come back to tell you all, I shall tell you all"—
If one, settling a pillow by her head,
    Should say: "That is not what I meant at all;
      That is not it, at all."

    And would it have been worth it, after all,
100 Would it have been worth while,
After the sunsets and the dooryards and the sprinkled streets,
After the novels, after the teacups, after the skirts that trail
    along the floor—
And this, and so much more?—
It is impossible to say just what I mean!
105 But as if a magic lantern threw the nerves in patterns on a screen:
Would it have been worth while
If one, settling a pillow or throwing off a shawl,
And turning toward the window, should say: "That is not it at all,
    That is not what I meant, at all."

110   No! I am not Prince Hamlet, nor was meant to be;
Am an attendant lord, one that will do
To swell a progress, start a scene or two,
Advise the prince: withal, an easy tool,
Deferential, glad to be of use,
115 Politic, cautious, and meticulous;
Full of high sentence, but a bit obtuse;
At times, indeed, almost ridiculous—
Almost, at times, the Fool.

I grow old . . . I grow old . . .
120 I shall wear the bottoms of my trousers rolled.

Shall I part my hair behind? Do I dare to eat a peach?
I shall wear white flannel trousers, and walk upon the beach.
I have heard the mermaids singing, each to each.
I do not think that they will sing to me.

125   I have seen them riding seaward on the waves,
Combing the white hair of the waves blown back
When the wind blows the water white and black.
We have lingered in the chambers of the sea
By seagirls wreathed with seaweed red and brown,
130   Till human voices wake us, and we drown.

Questions for Discussion

1. What does Eliot suggest about Prufrock by beginning the poem with a quotation from Dante's *Inferno*?

2. Explain the effect of the description in the opening ten lines. What does this description tell you about Prufrock's world?

3. Why must Prufrock "prepare a face to meet the faces that you meet"? How is this similar to Eleanor Rigby's "wearing the face / that she keeps in a jar by the door"?

4. Explain the following line: "I have measured out my life with coffee spoons."

5. Why does Prufrock say that he "should have been a pair of ragged claws / Scuttling across the floors of silent seas"? Do you think he could have been more fulfilled as a crab? Why or why not?

6. Explain the pathos of Prufrock's saying, "I have heard the mermaids singing, each to each. / I do not think that they will sing to me." Why is his opinion of himself more pathetic because he has "heard the mermaids" sing?

7. From what do "human voices wake us," and why, then, do "we drown"?

8. What is Prufrock afraid to ask? Why is he afraid to ask it?

Suggestions for Exploration and Writing

1. Write an essay using the following thesis statement: J. Alfred Prufrock is the perfect example of the indecisiveness and insecurity of many people in the modern world.

2. In his poem, Eliot alludes to Andrew Marvell's "To His Coy Mistress," thereby inviting comparison between Marvell's speaker and Prufrock. Write an essay in which you contrast these two speakers.

Langston Hughes (1902–1967)

A brief biography of Langston Hughes is included in the casebook in the Men and Women Unit.

HARLEM   (1951)

What happens to a dream deferred?

Does it dry up
like a raisin in the sun?
Or fester like a sore—
5   And then run?
Does it stink like rotten meat?
Or crust and sugar over—
like a syrupy sweet?

Maybe it just sags
10   like a heavy load.

Or does it explode?

Questions for Discussion

1. What does Hughes mean by "a dream deferred"? Why would a dream be deferred?

2. Hughes uses several strong verbs in describing what could happen to a "dream deferred": the dream could "dry up," "fester," "run," "stink," "crust and sugar over," "sag," or "explode." What is your response to these verbs?

3. Why does Hughes never identify the kind of dream he has in mind?

Suggestion for Exploration and Writing

1. If you, or a friend or relative, have had an unfulfilled or postponed dream, describe the experience and its results.

James Wright (1927–1980)

Wright, born in Martins Ferry, Ohio, graduated from Kenyon College and was a Fulbright scholar in Vienna. While studying and teaching at the University of Washington, he published his first collection of poetry, The Green Wall *(1957), followed by* Saint Judas *(1959). In 1963, he published* The Branch Shall Not Break, *noteworthy for its free verse and surrealistic poems. His collections of poems also include* Gather at the River *(1967);* Collected Poems *(1971), for which he won the Pulitzer Prize;* Two Citizens *(1973);* Moments of an Italian Summer *(his prose poems); and* This Journey *(1980), published shortly before he died.*

SMALL FROGS KILLED ON THE HIGHWAY   (1971)

Still,
I would leap too
Into the light,
If I had the chance.
5   It is everything, the wet green stalk of the field
On the other side of the road.
They crouch there, too, faltering in terror
And take strange wing. Many
Of the dead never moved, but many
10   Of the dead are alive forever in the split second
Auto headlights more sudden
Than their drivers know.
The drivers burrow backward into dank pools
Where nothing begets
15   Nothing.

Across the road, tadpoles are dancing
On the quarter thumbnail
Of the moon. They can't see,
Not yet.

Questions for Discussion

1. What is the significance of beginning the poem with "Still," as though continuing a conversation?

2. Why do the frogs leap to get to the other side of the road knowing that they will probably die? Why does the speaker say that leaping into the light is "everything"? Who or what do the frogs represent?

3. How are some of the dead frogs "alive forever in the split second / Auto headlights"? What is on the other side of the highway? What is the frog's real quest?

4. Why are the tadpoles dancing on the other side? What don't they "see, / Not yet"?

Suggestions for Exploration and Writing

1. Using the poem as a guide, write an essay that parallels this poem about frogs with the actions of some humans.

2. Wright often wrote in his later poems about the disenfranchised, the social outcast, and social injustice. Write an essay in which you analyze this poem from one of these three perspectives.

N. Scott Momaday (b. 1934)

*N. Scott Momaday, a Kiowa, studied at the University of New Mexico
and received his doctorate from Stanford University in 1963. His first
novel,* House Made of Dawn *(1968), won a Pulitzer Prize and brought
him accolades for bringing prestige to Native American writers. The Way
to Rainy Mountain (1969) describes the oral histories and migration
stories of his ancestors as imagined by his grandmother. His second novel,*
The Ancient Child *(1989), is a story about a spiritual journey.*

CARRIERS OF THE DREAM WHEEL   (1992)

This is the Wheel of Dreams
Which is carried on their voices,
By means of which their voices turn
And center upon being.
5   It encircles the First World,
This powerful wheel.
They shape their songs upon the wheel
And spin the names of the earth and sky,
The aboriginal names.
10   They are old men, or men
Who are old in their voices,
And they carry the wheel among the camps,
Saying: Come, come,
Let us tell the old stories,
15   Let us sing the sacred songs.

Questions for Discussion

1. Explain what Momaday means when he says that the "Wheel of
   dreams" is "carried on their voices"?

2. In Kiowa cosmology, the wheel suggests the continuing cycle of oral
   tales and songs. What are all of the uses of the wheel? Why are these
   uses and dreams important to the Kiowa?

3. Explain the imagery of the wheel.

Suggestion for Exploration and Writing

1. In an essay, explain why the telling of old stories is important to your
   or to any culture.

Fred Chappell (b. 1936)

*A brief biography of Fred Chappell precedes "The Garden" in the
Imagination and Discovery Unit.*

FOREVER MOUNTAIN (1985)
J. T. Chappell (1912–1978)

Now a lofty smoke has cleansed my vision.

I see my father has gone to climb
Lightly the Pisgah slope, taking the time
He's got a world of, making spry headway
5   In the fresh green mornings, stretching out
Noontimes in the groves of beech and maple.
He has cut a walking stick of second-growth hickory
And through the amber afternoon he measures
Its shadow and his own shadow on a sunny rock.
10   Not marking the hour, but observing
The quality of light come over him.
He is alone, except what voices out of time
Swarm to his head like bees to the bee-tree crown,
The voices of former life as indistinct as heat.

15   By the clear trout pool he builds his fire at twilight,
And in the night a granary of stars
Rises in the water and spreads from edge to edge.
He sleeps, to dream the tossing dream
Of the horses of pine trees, their shoulders
20   Twisting like silk ribbon in the breeze.

He rises glad and early and goes his way,
Taking by plateaus the mountain that possesses him.

My vision blurs blue with distance,
I see no more.
25   Forever Mountain has become a cloud
That light turns gold, that wind dislimns.

      This is continually a prayer.

Questions for Discussion

1. Why does Chappell's narrator use the image of the mountain to discuss his father's death?

2. Discuss the sight imagery in the poem. Consider such lines as "My vision blurs blue with distance, / I see no more" and "Now a lofty smoke has cleansed my vision."

3. What does Chappell mean by *"This is continually a prayer"*?

Suggestions for Exploration and Writing

1. Compare the father's quest with the son's quest.

2. Write an essay explaining how one of your quests in life has been influenced by the quest of one or both of your parents.

AN OLD MOUNTAIN WOMAN
READING THE BOOK OF JOB   (1989)

The veiny wrist, the knobby finger joints,
The scar-creased palm, the thumb she lifts to wet
And lift the corner of the memoried page,
Turning once more through Job's bewilderment:
5   What histories are written into her hand . . .

Aforetime she was as a tabret, but now
They change the night to day, the light is short,
The world delivered to ungodly shadow.
The darkness of her hand darkens the page.
10   She straightens her bifocals in which the words,
Reflected, jitter, then come to rest like moths.
It is November. The woodstove shifts its log
And grumbles. The night is longer than her fire.

She moves her lips to read but does not speak.
15   What is there to answer to the terrible words,
To these sharp final words that engrave the fate
Of an old man hammered to bronze. She sees the man
As if he stood before her, thrown by the storm
Of time to be her husband, her dead husband.
20   She knows the man as man, his house and fields
Up Jarvis Creek going down in sawbriar,
The doctor bills chewing the farm like locusts.
Bleak Job scourged ceaseless in the starless night,
Her husband whom lean ravishment made holy:
25   The whirlwind-savage hand of God forecloses
The mortgage; the fields are auctioned clod by clod,
The skies are auctioned cloud by pallid cloud.

The Book of Job draws all its shadow over
Her thumbed-limp Bible. Saint Paul does not escape,
30   Jesus Himself does not shine clear of Job,
The darkness of that blindly punished lament.
Shall any teach God knowledge?—But if He knows,
And still permits . . .

                   There is a weeping madness
35   In thoughts she tries so tiredly to push away.
Her trust lies down in dirt like a fractured tower.

Everything shall be restored, the Book
Tells her. But why should it be taken away?
Or given at the start? Her husband Charles,
40   The man she knows as Job, mild unto death,
She doubts shall be restored. The Book of Job
Distills to salt in the tear that seals her eye.

Let her then go out on Ember Mountain,
And cry out in his stead and say those words
45   She shall imagine for him, picturing
Herself there in the dark, in pitiless wind,
Raising her old fist to dare the lightning
And gates of wrath, herself alone in wind,
Saying the words that God's wind lacerates.
50   Let it be her stricken, blasted, shriveled
Like a candlewick and not the man
Her husband, whom the Lord like a hunting lion
Has carried off, her Job who suffered silence
As he went down never to rise again.

55   That silence does not yield. Her vision tears;
She never shall curse God, she never shall
Climb Ember Mountain again, nor ever weep.

But now she feels a throb in this old house
In which she sits alone, nursing her fire,
60   Her fear. A tremor as of someone walking
Another room, the kitchen or cold bedroom.
Someone unfamiliar is walking there,
Someone no kin to her, maybe no friend,
Who comes to bring her tidings the dead have risen
65   And all the wholeness of the earth restored.
She holds her breath; the phantom goes away.

She shuts the book of Job. She will not suffer
A God Who suffers the suffering of man,
Who sends the fatherless their broken arms,
70   Who sends away the widows empty of faith.
Tonight's no night for the heartless bedside prayer.

Questions for Discussion

1. To whom does "they" refer in the second stanza?

2. Why does the woman choose Job to read? How does she apply the story of Job to her life?

3. What does Chappell mean when he says, "She knows the man as man, his house and fields"?

4. Explain the line: *"Shall any teach God knowledge?"*

5. Explain why the woman wants to push away her thoughts. What is her "trust" and why does it lie in "dirt"? Explain what her questions mean.

6. Would it have helped the old woman to go out on Ember Mountain to shout the words her husband did not? Defend your answer.

7. Explain the last line of the poem in terms of tomorrow night.

8. What is the woman's quest?

Suggestion for Exploration and Writing

1. Write about an experience in which you questioned God's role in something that happened. How did you resolve your questioning?

Joseph Brodsky (1940–1996)

Joseph Brodsky was a native of Leningrad but moved to the United States in 1972 when he was exiled by the Soviet Union. Known primarily as a poet, he also wrote plays and essays. Brodsky received the Nobel Prize for Literature in 1987; as a tribute to his works, he was appointed Poet Laureate of the United States in 1992.

DECEMBER 24, 1971   (1972)

For V.S.

TRANSLATED BY ALAN MYERS WITH THE AUTHOR

When it's Christmas we're all of us magi.
At the grocers' all slipping and pushing.
Where a tin of halvah, coffee-flavored,
is the cause of a human assault-wave
5   by a crowd heavy-laden with parcels:
each one his own king, his own camel.

Nylon bags, carrier bags, paper cones,
caps and neckties all twisted up sideways.
Reek of vodka and resin and cod,
10   orange mandarins, cinnamon, apples.
Floods of faces, no sign of a pathway
toward Bethlehem, shut off by blizzard.

And the bearers of moderate gifts
leap on buses and jam all the doorways,
15   disappear into courtyards that gape,
though they know that there's nothing inside there:
not a beast, not a crib, nor yet her,
round whose head gleams a nimbus of gold.

Emptiness. But the mere thought of that
20   brings forth lights as if out of nowhere.
Herod reigns but the stronger he is,
the more sure, the more certain the wonder.
In the constancy of this relation
is the basic mechanics of Christmas.

25   That's what they celebrate everywhere,
for its coming push tables together.
No demand for a star for a while,
but a sort of good will touched with grace
can be seen in all men from afar,
30   and the shepherds have kindled their fires.

Snow is falling: not smoking but sounding
chimney pots on the roof, every face like a stain.
Herod drinks. Every wife hides her child.
He who comes is a mystery: features
35   are not known beforehand, men's hearts may
not be quick to distinguish the stranger.

But when drafts through the doorway disperse
the thick mist of the hours of darkness
and a shape in a shawl stands revealed,
40   both a newborn and Spirit that's Holy
in your self you discover; you stare
skyward, and it's right there:
                                    a star.

Questions for Discussion

1. Who are the "magi" referred to in the first line? What does Brodsky mean by "When it's Christmas we're all of us magi"?

2. How do the people in the first two stanzas differ from the magi of the Christmas story in Matthew 2?

3. What does the author mean by "Floods of faces, no sign of a pathway / toward Bethlehem, shut off by blizzard"?

4. Explain why Brodsky says that December 24 is "Emptiness."

5. Whom does Brodsky refer to in the lines "her, / round whose head gleams a nimbus of gold"?

6. Who was Herod? What does Brodsky mean by "Herod reigns but the stronger he is, / the more sure, the more certain the wonder"? What does Herod symbolize in this context?

7. What or whom does the speaker encounter in the last stanza? Does the last stanza contradict or enhance the message of the other six?

Suggestions for Exploration and Writing

1. Explain the third line of the fifth stanza—"No demand for a star for a while"—in relation to the last three lines: "you stare / skyward, and it's right there: / a star."

2. Write an essay about what you seek just before Christmas, on Christmas Day, or during an annual event celebrated by your family or in your culture.

Judith Ortiz Cofer (b. 1952)

A brief biography of Judith Ortiz Cofer precedes "Anniversary" in the Men and Women Unit.

LATIN WOMEN PRAY   (1987)

Latin women pray
In incense sweet churches
They pray in Spanish to an Anglo God
With a Jewish heritage.
5   And this Great White Father
Imperturbable in his marble pedestal
Looks down upon his brown daughters
Votive candles shining like lust
In his all seeing eyes
10   Unmoved by their persistent prayers.

Yet year after year
Before his image they kneel
Margarita Josefina Maria and Isabel
All fervently hoping
15   That if not omnipotent
At least he be bilingual

Questions for Discussion

1. What is Cofer's purpose in referring to God as an Anglo, Jewish "Great White Father"? How is this description related to the line "Looks down upon his brown daughters"?

2. Why does Cofer say that this God is "Unmoved by their persistent prayers"?

3. What is the Latin women's hope? Does the humor distract from the seriousness of their hope?

Suggestion for Exploration and Writing

1. In an essay, examine the assumptions of the women about the race, language, sex, and power of God.

Cathy Song (b. 1955)

Song, who was born of Chinese parents in Hawaii, has written extensively about the pull of her Chinese roots against her American status. Song's book Picture Bride *was the winner of the Yale Younger Poets Award in 1982. "Heaven" comes from her collection* Frameless Windows, Squares of Light *(1988). Much of her work is autobiographical.*

HEAVEN   (1988)

He thinks when we die we'll go to China.
Think of it—a Chinese heaven
where, except for his blond hair,
the part that belongs to his father,
5   everyone will look like him.
China, that blue flower on the map,
bluer than the sea
his hand must span like a bridge
to reach it.
10   An octave away.

I've never seen it.
It's as if I can't sing that far.
But look—
on the map, this black dot.
15   Here is where we live,
on the pancake plains
just east of the Rockies,
on the other side of the clouds.
A mile above the sea,
20   the air is so thin, you can starve on it.
No bamboo trees
but the alpine equivalent,
reedy aspen with light, fluttering leaves.
Did a boy in Guangzhou[1] dream of this
25   as his last stop?

I've heard the trains at night
whistling past our yards,
what we've come to own,
the broken fences, the whiny dog, the rattletrap cars.
30   It's still the wild west,
mean and grubby,
the shootouts and fistfights in the back alley.
With my son the dreamer
and my daughter, who is too young to walk,
35   I've sat in this spot

---

[1]Or Canton, seaport city in southeastern China.

and wondered why here?
Why in this short life,
this town, this creek they call a river?

He had never planned to stay,
40   the boy who helped to build
the railroads for a dollar a day.
He had always meant to go back.
When did he finally know
that each mile of track led him further away,
45   that he would die in his sleep,
dispossessed,
having seen Gold Mountain,
the icy wind tunneling through it,
these landlocked, makeshift ghost towns?

50   It must be in the blood,
this notion of returning.
It skipped two generations, lay fallow,
the garden an unmarked grave.
On a spring sweater day
55   it's as if we remember him.
I call to the children.
We can see the mountains
shimmering blue above the air.
If you look really hard
60   says my son the dreamer,
leaning out from the laundry's rigging,
the work shirts fluttering like sails,
you can see all the way to heaven.

Questions for Discussion

1. Who is the speaker? What is her attitude toward her son's yearning for China?

2. Why is it important to the son that "everyone will look like him" in heaven?

3. Explain why the speaker says that the "notion of returning [to China] / [. . .] skipped two generations"? Why did the grandfather come to America? Is his quest diminished by the knowledge that he died "dispossessed"?

4. Explain the significance of the last line.

5. Explain how China can be "An octave away."

6. What image begins and ends the poem? Why?

Suggestions for Exploration and Writing

1. Examine the language used in the poem. Discuss how the unique phrasing contributes to your understanding of the poem.

2. Our views of heaven and God are influenced by our own culture and race. The son in "Heaven" thinks that everyone should look like him. Judith Ortiz Cofer in "Latin Women Pray" hopes that God is bilingual. Write an essay or a poem giving your description of what heaven is like.

LOST SISTER   (1983)

1

In China,
even the peasants
named their first daughters
Jade—
5 the stone that in the far fields
could moisten the dry season,
could make men move mountains
for the healing green of the inner hills
glistening like slices of winter melon.

10 And the daughters were grateful:
they never left home.
To move freely was a luxury
stolen from them at birth.
Instead, they gathered patience,
15 learning to walk in shoes
the size of teacups,
without breaking—
the arc of their movements
as dormant as the rooted willow.
20 as redundant as the farmyard hens.
But they traveled far
in surviving,
learning to stretch the family rice,
to quiet the demons,
25 the noisy stomachs

2

There is a sister
across the ocean,
who relinquished her name,
diluting jade green
30 with the blue of the Pacific.
Rising with a tide of locusts,

she swarmed with others
to inundate another shore.
In America,
35   there are many roads
and women can stride along with men.

But in another wilderness,
the possibilities,
the loneliness,
40   can strangulate like jungle vines.
The meager provisions and sentiments
of once belonging—
fermented roots, Mah-Jongg[1] tiles and firecrackers—
set but a flimsy household
45   in a forest of nightless cities.
A giant snake rattles above,
spewing black clouds into your kitchen.
Dough-faced landlords
slip in and out of your keyholes,
50   making claims you don't understand,
tapping into your communication systems
of laundry lines and restaurant chains.

You find you need China:
your one fragile identification,
55   a jade link
handcuffed to your wrist.
You remember your mother
who walked for centuries,
footless—
60   and like her,
you have left no footprints,
but only because
there is an ocean in between,
the unremitting space of your rebellion.

[1]An Oriental game.

Questions for Exploration and Writing

1. Why does Song say that moving freely in China is a "luxury / stolen
   from them at birth"?

2. In part 1, the Chinese sister is "grateful" and a survivor. What is she
   grateful for? What does she survive?

3. In part 2, why is the American sister compared to one of the many
   locusts?

4. What are some of the differences between the two sisters' lives?

5. What is the "flimsy household / in a forest of nightless cities"? Are one sister's living conditions better than those of the sister left behind in the China fields?

6. How has the American sister diluted her "jade green / with the blue of the Pacific"?

7. Who is the *you* referred to in the last verse? Why does Song say that *you* "need China"?

8. Why does neither the American sister nor her mother leave footprints?

Suggestions for Exploration and Writing

1. Write an essay in which you explain who is the lost sister—the one left behind in China or the one who lives in America. Support your answer by using references from the poem.

2. Using the images from the poem, write an essay comparing the sister who stayed at home with the sister who came to America.

3. If you live in a country other than your native land, describe the things that you miss the most about your home.

4. Write an essay comparing the tones of these two poems by Song.

DRAMA

Carson McCullers (1917–1967)

A brief biography of Carson McCullers precedes "A Domestic Dilemma" in the Family Unit.

THE MEMBER OF THE WEDDING (1946)

List of Characters

BERENICE SADIE BROWN

FRANKIE ADDAMS

JOHN HENRY WEST

JARVIS

JANICE

MR. ADDAMS

MRS. WEST

HELEN FLETCHER

DORIS

SIS LAURA

T.T. WILLIAMS

HONEY CAMDEN BROWN

BARNEY MACKEAN

Time: August, 1945

Place: A small Southern town

ACT ONE: *A late afternoon in August*

ACT TWO: *Afternoon of the next day*

ACT THREE
Scene One: *The wedding day—afternoon of the next day*
                    following Act Two
Scene Two: *4 A.M. the following morning*
Scene Three: *Late afternoon, in the following November*

ACT 1

A part of a Southern back yard and kitchen. At stage left there is a scupper-
nong arbor. A sheet, used as a stage curtain, hangs raggedly at one side of the
arbor. There is an elm tree in the yard. The kitchen has in the center a table
with chairs. The walls are drawn with child drawings. There is a stove to the
right and a small coal heating stove with coal scuttle in rear center of kitchen.
The kitchen opens on the left into the yard. At the interior right a door leads
to a small inner room. A door at the left leads into the front hall. The lights
go on dimly, with a dream-like effect, gradually revealing the family in the
yard and Berenice Sadie Brown in the kitchen. Berenice, the cook, is a stout,
motherly Negro woman with an air of great capability and devoted protection.
She is about forty-five years old. She has a quiet, flat face and one of her eyes
is made of blue glass. Sometimes, when her socket bothers her, she dispenses
with the false eye and wears a black patch. When we first see her she is wear-
ing the patch and is dressed in a simple print work dress and apron.

   Frankie, a gangling girl of twelve with blonde hair cut like a boy's, is
wearing shorts and a sombrero and is standing in the arbor gazing ador-
ingly at her brother Jarvis and his fiancée Janice. She is a dreamy, restless
girl, and periods of energetic activity alternate with a rapt attention to her
inward world of fantasy. She is thin and awkward and very much aware of
being too tall. Jarvis, a good-looking boy of twenty-one, wearing an army
uniform, stands by Janice. He is awkward when he first appears because this
is his betrothal visit. Janice, a young, pretty, fresh-looking girl of eighteen or
nineteen is charming, but rather ordinary, with brown hair done up in a
small knot. She is dressed in her best clothes and is anxious to be liked by her
new family. Mr. Addams, Frankie's father, is a deliberate and absent-minded
man of about forty-five. A widower of many years, he has become set in his
habits. He is dressed conservatively, and there is about him an old-fashioned
look and manner. John Henry, Frankie's small cousin, aged seven, picks
and eats any scuppernongs he can reach. He is a delicate, active boy and
wears gold-rimmed spectacles which give him an oddly judicious look. He is
blond and sunburned and when we first see him he is wearing a sun-suit
and is barefooted.

(Berenice Sadie Brown is busy in the kitchen.)

JARVIS: Seems to me like this old arbor has shrunk. I remember when I was a child it used to seem absolutely enormous. When I was Frankie's age, I had a vine swing here. Remember, Papa?

FRANKIE: It don't seem so absolutely enormous to me, because I am so tall.

JARVIS: I never saw a human grow so fast in all my life. I think maybe we ought to tie a brick to your head.

FRANKIE *(hunching down in obvious distress)*: Oh, Jarvis! Don't.

JANICE: Don't tease your little sister. I don't think Frankie is too tall. She probably won't grow much more. I had the biggest portion of my
10   growth by the time I was thirteen.

FRANKIE: But I'm just twelve. When I think of all the growing years ahead of me, I get scared.

(Janice goes to Frankie and puts her arms around her comfortingly. Frankie stands rigid, embarrassed and blissful.)

JANICE: I wouldn't worry.

(Berenice comes from the kitchen with a tray of drinks. Frankie rushes eagerly to help her serve them.)

FRANKIE: Let me help.

BERENICE: Them two drinks is lemonade for you and John Henry. The others got liquor in them.

FRANKIE: Janice, come sit on the arbor seat. Jarvis, you sit down too.

(Jarvis and Janice sit close together on the wicker bench in the arbor. Frankie hands the drinks around, then perches on the ground before Janice and Jarvis and stares adoringly at them.)

FRANKIE: It was such a surprise when Jarvis wrote home you are going to be married.

20 JANICE: I hope it wasn't a bad surprise.

FRANKIE: Oh, Heavens no! *(with great feeling)* As a matter of fact . . . *(She strokes Janice's shoes tenderly and Jarvis' army boot.)* If only you knew how I feel.

MR. ADDAMS: Frankie's been bending my ears ever since your letter came, Jarvis. Going on about weddings, brides, grooms, etc.

JANICE: It's lovely that we can be married at Jarvis' home.

MR. ADDAMS: That's the way to feel, Janice. Marriage is a sacred institution.

FRANKIE: Oh, it will be beautiful.

JARVIS: Pretty soon we'd better be shoving off for Winter Hill. I have to
30   be back in barracks tonight.

FRANKIE: Winter Hill is such a lovely, cold name. It reminds me of ice and snow.

JANICE: You know it's just a hundred miles away, darling.

JARVIS: Ice and snow indeed! Yesterday the temperature on the parade ground reached 102.

(Frankie takes a palmetto fan from the table and fans first Janice, then Jarvis.)

JANICE: That feels so good, darling. Thanks.

FRANKIE: I wrote you so many letters, Jarvis, and you never, never would answer me. When you were stationed in Alaska, I wanted so much to hear about Alaska. I sent you so many boxes of home-made candy,
40   but you never answered me.

JARVIS: Oh, Frankie. You know how it is . . .

FRANKIE *(sipping her drink)*: You know this lemonade tastes funny. Kind of sharp and hot. I believe I got the drinks mixed up.

JARVIS: I was thinking my drink tasted mighty sissy. Just plain lemonade—no liquor at all.

(Frankie and Jarvis exchange their drinks. Jarvis sips his.)

JARVIS: This is better.

FRANKIE: I drank a lot. I wonder if I'm drunk. It makes me feel like I had four legs instead of two. I think I'm drunk. *(She gets up and begins to stagger around in imitation of drunkenness.)* See! I'm drunk! Look,
50   Papa, how drunk I am! *(Suddenly she turns a hand spring; then there is a blare of music from the club house gramophone off to the right.)*

JANICE: Where does the music come from? It sounds so close.

FRANKIE: It is. Right over there. They have club meetings and parties with boys on Friday nights. I watch them here from the yard.

JANICE: It must be nice having your club house so near.

FRANKIE: I'm not a member now. But they are holding an election this afternoon, and maybe I'll be elected.

JOHN HENRY: Here comes Mama.

(Mrs. West, John Henry's mother, crosses the yard from the right. She is a vivacious, blonde woman of about thirty-three. She is dressed in sleazy, rather dowdy summer clothes.)

MR. ADDAMS: Hello, Pet. Just in time to meet our new family member.

MRS. WEST: I saw you out here from the window.

60   JARVIS *(rising, with Janice)*: Hi, Aunt Pet. How is Uncle Eustace?

MRS. WEST: He's at the office.

JANICE *(offering her hand with the engagement ring on it)*: Look, Aunt Pet. May I call you Aunt Pet?

MRS. WEST *(hugging her)*: Of course, Janice. What a gorgeous ring!

JANICE: Jarvis just gave it to me this morning. He wanted to consult his father and get it from his store, naturally.

MRS. WEST: How lovely.

MR. ADDAMS: A quarter carat—not too flashy but a good stone.

MRS. WEST *(to Berenice, who is gathering up the empty glasses)*: Berenice,
70   what have you and Frankie been doing to my John Henry? He sticks over here in your kitchen morning, noon and night.

BERENICE: We enjoys him and Candy seems to like it over here.

MRS. WEST: What on earth do you do to him?

BERENICE: We just talks and passes the time of day. Occasionally plays cards.

MRS. WEST: Well, if he gets in your way just shoo him home.

BERENICE: Candy don't bother nobody.

JOHN HENRY (*walking around barefooted in the arbor*): These grapes are so squelchy when I step on them.

80 MRS. WEST: Run home, darling, and wash your feet and put on your sandals.

JOHN HENRY: I like to squelch on the grapes.

(*Berenice goes back to the kitchen.*)

JANICE: That looks like a stage curtain. Jarvis told me how you used to write plays and act in them out here in the arbor. What kind of shows do you have?

FRANKIE: Oh, crook shows and cowboy shows. This summer I've had some cold shows—about Esquimos and explorers—on account of the hot weather.

JANICE: Do you ever have romances?

90 FRANKIE: Naw . . . (*with bravado*) I had crook shows for the most part. You see I never believed in love until now. (*Her look lingers on Janice and Jarvis. She hugs Janice and Jarvis, bending over them from back of the bench.*)

MRS. WEST: Frankie and this little friend of hers gave a performance of "The Vagabond King" out here last spring.

(*John Henry spreads out his arms and imitates the heroine of the play from memory, singing in his high childish voice.*)

JOHN HENRY: Never hope to bind me. Never hope to know. (*speaking*) Frankie was the king-boy. I sold the tickets.

MRS. WEST: Yes, I have always said that Frankie has talent.

FRANKIE: Aw, I'm afraid I don't have much talent.

JOHN HENRY: Frankie can laugh and kill people good. She can die, too.

FRANKIE (*with some pride*): Yeah, I guess I die all right.

100 MR. ADDAMS: Frankie rounds up John Henry and those smaller children, but by the time she dresses them in the costumes, they're worn out and won't act in the show.

JARVIS (*looking at his watch*): Well, it's time we shove off for Winter Hill— Frankie's land of icebergs and snow—where the temperature goes up to 102.

(*Jarvis takes Janice's hand. He gets up and gazes fondly around the yard and the arbor. He pulls her up and stands with his arm around her, gazing around him at the arbor and yard.*)

JARVIS: It carries me back—this smell of mashed grapes and dust. I remember all the endless summer afternoons of my childhood. It does carry me back.

FRANKIE: Me too. It carries me back, too.

MR. ADDAMS (*putting one arm around Janice and shaking Jarvis' hand*):
110   Merciful Heavens! It seems I have two Methuselahs in my family!
Does it carry you back to your childhood too, John Henry?

JOHN HENRY: Yes, Uncle Royal.

MR. ADDAMS: Son, this visit was a real pleasure. Janice, I'm mighty
pleased to see my boy has such lucky judgment in choosing a wife.

FRANKIE: I hate to think you have to go. I'm just now realizing you're here.

JARVIS: We'll be back in two days. The wedding is Sunday.

(*The family move around the house toward the street. John Henry enters the
kitchen through the back door. There are the sounds of "good-byes" from
the front yard.*)

JOHN HENRY: Frankie was drunk. She drank a liquor drink.

BERENICE: She just made out like she was drunk—pretended.

JOHN HENRY: She said, "Look, Papa, how drunk I am," and she couldn't
120   walk.

FRANKIE'S VOICE: Good-bye, Jarvis. Good-bye, Janice.

JARVIS' VOICE: See you Sunday.

MR. ADDAMS' VOICE: Drive carefully, son. Good-bye, Janice.

JANICE'S VOICE: Good-bye and thanks, Mr. Addams. Good-bye, Frankie
darling.

ALL THE VOICES: Good-bye! Good-bye!

JOHN HENRY: They are going now to Winter Hill.

(*There is the sound of the front door opening, then of steps in the hall.
Frankie enters through the hall.*)

FRANKIE: Oh, I can't understand it! The way it all just suddenly happened.

BERENICE: Happened? Happened?

130   FRANKIE: I have never been so puzzled.

BERENICE: Puzzled about what?

FRANKIE: The whole thing. They are so beautiful.

BERENICE (*after a pause*): I believe the sun done fried your brains.

JOHN HENRY (*whispering*): Me too.

BERENICE: Look here at me. You jealous.

FRANKIE: Jealous?

BERENICE: Jealous because your brother's going to be married.

FRANKIE (*slowly*): No. I just never saw any two people like them. When
they walked in the house today it was so queer.

140   BERENICE: You jealous. Go and behold yourself in the mirror. I can see
from the color of your eyes.

(*Frankie goes to the mirror and stares. She draws up her left shoulder,
shakes her head, and turns away.*)

FRANKIE (*with feeling*): Oh! They were the two prettiest people I ever saw.
I just can't understand how it happened.

BERENICE: Whatever ails you?—actin' so queer.

FRANKIE: I don't know. I bet they have a good time every minute of the day.

JOHN HENRY: Less us have a good time.

FRANKIE: Us have a good time? Us? *(She rises and walks around the table.)*

BERENICE: Come on. Less have a game of three-handed bridge.

(They sit down to the table, shuffle the cards, deal, and play a game.)

150 FRANKIE: Oregon, Alaska, Winter Hill, the wedding. It's all so queer.

BERENICE: I can't bid, never have a hand these days.

FRANKIE: A spade.

JOHN HENRY: I want to bid spades. That's what I was going to bid.

FRANKIE: Well, that's your tough luck. I bid them first.

JOHN HENRY: Oh, you fool jackass! It's not fair!

BERENICE: Hush quarreling, you two. *(She looks at both their hands.)* To tell the truth, I don't think either of you got such a grand hand to fight over the bid about. Where is the cards? I haven't had no kind of a hand all week.

160 FRANKIE: I don't give a durn about it. It is immaterial with me. *(There is a long pause. She sits with her head propped on her hand, her legs wound around each other.)* Let's talk about them—and the wedding.

BERENICE: What you want to talk about?

FRANKIE: My heart feels them going away—going farther and farther away—while I am stuck here by myself.

BERENICE: You ain't here by yourself. By the way, where's your Pa?

FRANKIE: He went to the store. I think about them, but I remembered them more as a feeling than as a picture.

BERENICE: A feeling?

FRANKIE: They were the two prettiest people I ever saw. Yet it was like I
170 couldn't see all of them I wanted to see. My brains couldn't gather together quick enough to take it all in. And then they were gone.

BERENICE: Well, stop commenting about it. You don't have your mind on the game.

FRANKIE *(playing her cards, followed by John Henry)*: Spades are trumps and you got a spade. I have some of my mind on the game.

(John Henry puts his donkey necklace in his mouth and looks away.)

FRANKIE: Go on, cheater.

BERENICE: Make haste.

JOHN HENRY: I can't. It's a king. The only spade I got is a king, and I don't want to play my king under Frankie's ace. And I'm not going
180 to do it either.

FRANKIE *(throwing her cards down on the table)*: See, Berenice, he cheats!

BERENICE: Play your king, John Henry. You have to follow the rules of the game.

JOHN HENRY: My king. It isn't fair.

FRANKIE: Even with this trick, I can't win.

BERENICE: Where is the cards? For three days I haven't had a decent hand. I'm beginning to suspicion something. Come on less us count these old cards.

FRANKIE: We've worn these old cards out. If you would eat these old
190   cards, they would taste like a combination of all the dinners of this summer together with a sweaty-handed, nasty taste. Why, the jacks and the queens are missing.

BERENICE: John Henry, how come you do a thing like that? So that's why you asked for the scissors and stole off quiet behind the arbor. Now Candy, how come you took our playing cards and cut out the pictures?

JOHN HENRY: Because I wanted them. They're cute.

FRANKIE: See? He's nothing but a child. It's hopeless. Hopeless!

BERENICE: Maybe so.

FRANKIE: We'll just have to put him out of the game. He's entirely too
200   young.

(John Henry whimpers.)

BERENICE: Well, we can't put Candy out of the game. We gotta have a third to play. Besides, by the last count he owes me close to three million dollars.

FRANKIE: Oh, I am sick unto death. *(She sweeps the cards from the table, then gets up and begins walking around the kitchen. John Henry leaves the table and picks up a large blonde doll on the chair in the corner.)* I wish they'd taken me with them to Winter Hill this afternoon. I wish tomorrow was Sunday instead of Saturday.

BERENICE: Sunday will come.

FRANKIE: I doubt it. I wish I was going somewhere for good. I wish I had a
210   hundred dollars and could just light out and never see this town again.

BERENICE: It seems like you wish for a lot of things.

FRANKIE: I wish I was somebody else except me.

JOHN HENRY *(holding the doll)*: You serious when you gave me the doll a while ago?

FRANKIE: It gives me a pain just to think about them.

BERENICE: It is a known truth that gray-eyed peoples are jealous.

(There are sounds of children playing in the neighboring yard.)

JOHN HENRY: Let's go out and play with the children.

FRANKIE: I don't want to.

JOHN HENRY: There's a big crowd, and they sound like they having a
220   mighty good time. Less go.

FRANKIE: You got ears. You heard me.

JOHN HENRY: I think maybe I better go home.

FRANKIE: Why, you said you were going to spend the night. You just can't eat dinner and then go off in the afternoon like that.

JOHN HENRY: I know it.

BERENICE: Candy, Lamb, you can go home if you want to.

JOHN HENRY: But less go out, Frankie. They sound like they having a lot of fun.

FRANKIE: No, they're not. Just a crowd of ugly, silly children. Running
230   and hollering and running and hollering. Nothing to it.

JOHN HENRY: Less go!

FRANKIE: Well, then I'll entertain you. What do you want to do? Would you like for me to read to you out of The Book of Knowledge, or would you rather do something else?

JOHN HENRY: I rather do something else. *(He goes to the back door, and looks into the yard. Several young girls of thirteen or fourteen, dressed in clean print frocks, file slowly across the back yard.)* Look. Those big girls.

FRANKIE: *(running out into the yard)*: Hey, there. I'm mighty glad to see you. Come on in.

HELEN: We can't. We were just passing through to notify our new member.

240   FRANKIE *(overjoyed)*: Am I the new member?

DORIS: No, you're not the one the club elected.

FRANKIE: Not elected?

HELEN: Every ballot was unanimous for Mary Littlejohn.

FRANKIE: Mary Littlejohn! You mean that girl who just moved in next door? That pasty fat girl with those tacky pigtails? The one who plays the piano all day long?

DORIS: Yes. The club unanimously elected Mary.

FRANKIE: Why, she's not even cute.

HELEN: She is too; and, furthermore, she's talented.

250   FRANKIE: I think it's sissy to sit around the house all day playing classical music.

DORIS: Why, Mary is training for a concert career.

FRANKIE: Well, I wish to Jesus she would train somewhere else.

DORIS: You don't have enough sense to appreciate a talented girl like Mary.

FRANKIE: What are you doing in my yard? You're never to set foot on my Papa's property again. *(Frankie shakes Helen.)* Son-of-a-bitches. I could shoot you with my Papa's pistol.

JOHN HENRY *(shaking his fists)*: Son-of-a-bitches.

260   FRANKIE: Why didn't you elect me? *(She goes back into the house.)* Why can't I be a member?

JOHN HENRY: Maybe they'll change their mind and invite you.

BERENICE: I wouldn't pay them no mind. All my life I've been wantin' things that I ain't been gettin'. Anyhow those club girls is fully two years older than you.

FRANKIE: I think they have been spreading it all over town that I smell bad. When I had those boils and had to use that black bitter-smelling ointment, old Helen Fletcher asked me what was that funny smell I had. Oh, I could shoot every one of them with a pistol.

(Frankie sits with her head on the table. John Henry approaches and pats the back of Frankie's neck.)

270 JOHN HENRY: I don't think you smell so bad. You smell sweet, like a hundred flowers.

FRANKIE: The son-of-a-bitches. And there was something else. They were telling nasty lies about married people. When I think of Aunt Pet and Uncle Eustace! And my own father! The nasty lies! I don't know what kind of fool they take me for.

BERENICE: That's what I tell you. They too old for you.

(John Henry raises his head, expands his nostrils and sniffs at himself. Then Frankie goes into the interior bedroom and returns with a bottle of perfume.)

FRANKIE: Boy! I bet I use more perfume than anybody else in town. Want some on you, John Henry? You want some, Berenice? *(She sprinkles perfume.)*

JOHN HENRY: Like a thousand flowers.

280 BERENICE: Frankie, the whole idea of a club is that there are members who are included and the non-members who are not included. Now what you ought to do is to round you up a club of your own. And you could be the president yourself. *(There is a pause.)*

FRANKIE: Who would I get?

BERENICE: Why, those little children you hear playing in the neighborhood.

FRANKIE: I don't want to be the president of all those little young left-over people.

BERENICE: Well, then enjoy your misery. That perfume smells so strong it kind of makes me sick.

(John Henry plays with the doll at the kitchen table and Frankie watches.)

290 FRANKIE: Look here at me, John Henry. Take off those glasses. *(John Henry takes off his glasses.)* I bet you don't need those glasses. *(She points to the coal scuttle.)* What is this?

JOHN HENRY: The coal scuttle.

FRANKIE *(taking a shell from the kitchen shelf)*: And this?

JOHN HENRY: The shell we got at Saint Peter's Bay last summer.

FRANKIE: What is that little thing crawling around on the floor?

JOHN HENRY: Where?

FRANKIE: That little thing crawling around near your feet.

JOHN HENRY: Oh. *(He squats down.)* Why, it's an ant. How did that get in

300 here?

FRANKIE: If I were you I'd just throw those glasses away. You can see good as anybody.

BERENICE: Now quit picking with John Henry.

FRANKIE: They don't look becoming. *(John Henry wipes his glasses and puts them back on.)* He can suit himself. I was only telling him for his own good. *(She walks restlessly around the kitchen.)* I bet Janice and Jarvis are members of a lot of clubs. In fact, the army is kind of like a club.

(John Henry searches through Berenice's pocketbook.)

BERENICE: Don't root through my pocketbook like that, Candy. Ain't a
wise policy to search folks' pocketbooks. They might think you trying
310   to steal their money.
JOHN HENRY: I'm looking for your new glass eye. Here it is. *(He hands
Berenice the glass eye.)* You got two nickels and a dime.

(Berenice takes off her patch, turns away and inserts the glass eye.)

BERENICE: I ain't used to it yet. The socket bothers me. Maybe it don't fit
properly.
JOHN HENRY: The blue glass eye looks very cute.
FRANKIE: I don't see why you had to get that eye. It has a wrong
expression—let alone being blue.
BERENICE: Ain't anybody ask your judgment, wise-mouth.
JOHN HENRY: Which one of your eyes do you see out of the best?
320   BERENICE: The left eye, of course. The glass eye don't do me no seeing
good at all.
JOHN HENRY: I like the glass eye better. It is so bright and shiny—a real
pretty eye. Frankie, you serious when you gave me this doll a while ago?
FRANKIE: Janice and Jarvis. It gives me this pain just to think about them.
BERENICE: It is a known truth that gray-eyed people are jealous.
FRANKIE: I told you I wasn't jealous. I couldn't be jealous of one of them
without being jealous of them both. I 'sociate the two of them
together. Somehow they're just so different from us.
BERENICE: Well, I were jealous when my foster-brother, Honey, married
330   Clorina. I sent a warning I could tear the ears off her head. But you see
I didn't. Clorina's got ears just like anybody else. And now I love her.
FRANKIE *(stopping her walking suddenly)*: J.A.—Janice and Jarvis. Isn't that
the strangest thing?
BERENICE: What?
FRANKIE: J.A.—Both their names begin with "J.A."
BERENICE: And? What about it?
FRANKIE *(walking around the kitchen table)*: If only my name was Jane.
Jane or Jasmine.
BERENICE: I don't follow your frame of mind.
340   FRANKIE: Jarvis and Janice and Jasmine. See?
BERENICE: No. I don't see.
FRANKIE: I wonder if it's against the law to change your name. Or add to it.
BERENICE: Naturally. It's against the law.
FRANKIE *(impetuously)*: Well, I don't care. F. Jasmine Addams.
JOHN HENRY *(approaching with the doll)*: You serious when you give me
this? *(He pulls up the doll's dress and pats her.)* I will name her Belle.
FRANKIE: I don't know what went on in Jarvis' mind when he brought
me that doll. Imagine bringing me a doll! I had counted on Jarvis
bringing me something from Alaska.
350   BERENICE: Your face when you unwrapped that package was a study.

FRANKIE: John Henry, quit pickin' at the doll's eyes. It makes me so nervous. You hear me! *(He sits the doll up.)* In fact, take the doll somewhere out of my sight.

JOHN HENRY: Her name is Lily Belle.

(John Henry goes out and props the doll up on the back steps. There is the sound of an unseen Negro singing from the neighboring yard.)

FRANKIE *(going to the mirror)*: The big mistake I made was to get this close crew cut. For the wedding, I ought to have long brunette hair. Don't you think so?

BERENICE: I don't see how come brunette hair is necessary. But I warned you about getting your head shaved off like that before you did it. But nothing would do but you shave it like that.

FRANKIE *(stepping back from the mirror and slumping her shoulders)*: Oh, I am so worried about being so tall. I'm twelve and five-sixth years old and already five feet five and three-fourths inches tall. If I keep on growing like this until I'm twenty-one, I figure I will be nearly ten feet tall.

JOHN HENRY *(re-entering the kitchen)*: Lily Belle is taking a nap on the back steps. Don't talk so loud, Frankie.

FRANKIE *(after a pause)*: I doubt if they ever get married or go to a wedding. Those freaks.

BERENICE: Freaks. What freaks you talking about?

FRANKIE: At the fair. The ones we saw there last October.

JOHN HENRY: Oh, the freaks at the fair! *(He holds out an imaginary skirt and begins to skip around the room with one finger resting on the top of his head.)* Oh, she was the cutest little girl I ever saw. I never saw anything so cute in my whole life. Did you, Frankie?

FRANKIE: No. I don't think she was cute.

BERENICE: Who is that he's talking about?

FRANKIE: That little old pin-head at the fair. A head no bigger than an orange. With the hair shaved off and a big pink bow at the top. Bow was bigger than the head.

JOHN HENRY: Shoo! She was too cute.

BERENICE: That little old squeezed-looking midget in them little trick evening clothes. And that giant with the hang-jaw face and them huge loose hands. And that morphidite! Half man—half woman. With that tiger skin on one side and that spangled skirt on the other.

JOHN HENRY: But that little-headed girl was cute.

FRANKIE: And that wild colored man they said came from a savage island and ate those real live rats. Do you think they make a very big salary?

BERENICE: How would I know? In fact, all them freak folks down at the fair every October just gives me the creeps.

FRANKIE *(after a pause, and slowly)*: Do I give you the creeps?

BERENICE: You?

FRANKIE: Do you think I will grow into a freak?

BERENICE: You? Why certainly not, I trust Jesus!

FRANKIE *(going over to the mirror, and looking at herself)*: Well, do you think I will be pretty?

BERENICE: Maybe. If you file down them horns a inch or two.

FRANKIE *(turning to face Berenice, and shuffling one bare foot on the floor)*: Seriously.

BERENICE: Seriously, I think when you fill out you will do very well. If you behave.

400 FRANKIE: But by Sunday, I want to do something to improve myself before the wedding.

BERENICE: Get clean for a change. Scrub your elbows and fix yourself nice. You will do very well.

JOHN HENRY: You will be all right if you file down them horns.

FRANKIE *(raising her right shoulder and turning from the mirror)*: I don't know what to do. I just wish I would die.

BERENICE: Well, die then!

JOHN HENRY: Die.

FRANKIE *(suddenly exasperated)*: Go home! *(There is a pause.)* You heard
410 me! *(She makes a face at him and threatens him with the fly swatter. They run twice around the table.)* Go home! I'm sick and tired of you, you little midget.

(John Henry goes out, taking the doll with him.)

BERENICE: Now what makes you act like that? You are too mean to live.

FRANKIE: I know it. *(She takes a carving knife from the table drawer.)* Something about John Henry just gets on my nerves these days. *(She puts her left ankle over her right knee and begins to pick with the knife at a splinter in her foot.)* I've got a splinter in my foot.

BERENICE: That knife ain't the proper thing for a splinter.

FRANKIE: It seems to me that before this summer I used always to have such a good time. Remember this spring when Evelyn Owen and me
420 used to dress up in costumes and go down town and shop at the five-and-dime? And how every Friday night we'd spend the night with each other either at her house or here? And then Evelyn Owen had to go and move away to Florida. And now she won't even write to me.

BERENICE: Honey, you are not crying, is you? Don't that hurt you none?

FRANKIE: It would hurt anybody else except me. And how the wisteria in town was so blue and pretty in April but somehow it was so pretty it made me sad. And how Evelyn and me put on that show the Glee Club did at the High School Auditorium? *(She raises her head and beats time with the knife and her fist on the table, singing loudly with sudden energy.)* Sons of toil and danger! Will you serve a stranger! And bow
430 down to Burgundy! *(Berenice joins in on "Burgundy." Frankie pauses, then begins to pick her foot again, humming the tune sadly.)*

BERENICE: That was a nice show you children copied in the arbor. You will meet another girl friend you like as well as Evelyn Owen. Or maybe Mr. Owen will move back into town. *(There is a pause.)* Frankie, what you need is a needle.

FRANKIE: I don't care anything about my old feet. *(She stomps her foot on the floor and lays down the knife on the table.)* It was just so queer the way it happened this afternoon. The minute I laid eyes on the pair of them I had this funny feeling. *(She goes over and picks up a saucer of milk near the cat-hole in back of the door and pours the milk in the sink.)* How old were you, Berenice, when you married your first husband?

440   BERENICE: I were thirteen years old.

FRANKIE: What made you get married so young for?

BERENICE: Because I wanted to.

FRANKIE: You never loved any of your four husbands but Ludie.

BERENICE: Ludie Maxwell Freeman was my only true husband. The other ones were just scraps.

FRANKIE: Did you marry with a veil every time?

BERENICE: Three times with a veil.

FRANKIE *(pouring milk into the saucer and returning the saucer to the cat-hole)*: If only I just knew where he is gone. Ps, ps, ps . . . Charles, Charles.

BERENICE: Quit worrying yourself about that old alley cat. He's gone off

450   to hunt a friend.

FRANKIE: To hunt a friend?

BERENICE: Why certainly. He roamed off to find himself a lady friend.

FRANKIE: Well, why don't he bring his friend home with him? He ought to know I would be only too glad to have a whole family of cats.

BERENICE: You done seen the last of that old alley cat.

FRANKIE *(crossing the room)*: I ought to notify the police force. They will find Charles.

BERENICE: I wouldn't do that.

FRANKIE *(at the telephone)*: I want the police force, please . . . Police

460   force? . . . I am notifying you about my cat . . . Cat! He's lost. He is almost pure Persian.

BERENICE: As Persian as I is.

FRANKIE: But with short hair. A lovely color of gray with a little white spot on his throat. He answers to the name of Charles, but if he don't answer to that, he might come if you call "Charlina." . . . My name is Miss F. Jasmine Addams and the address is 124 Grove Street.

BERENICE *(giggling as Frankie re-enters)*: Gal, they going to send around here and tie you up and drag you off to Milledgeville. Just picture them fat blue police chasing tomcats around alleys and hollering,

470   "Oh Charles! Oh come here, Charlina!" Merciful Heavens.

FRANKIE: Aw, shut up!

(Outside a voice is heard calling in a drawn-out chant, the words almost indistinguishable: "Lot of okra, peas, fresh butter beans . . . ")

BERENICE: The trouble with you is that you don't have no sense of humor no more.

FRANKIE *(disconsolately)*: Maybe I'd be better off in jail.

(The chanting voice continues and an ancient Negro woman, dressed in a clean print dress with several petticoats, the ruffle of one of which shows, crosses the yard. She stops and leans on a gnarled stick.)

FRANKIE: Here comes the old vegetable lady.

BERENICE: Sis Laura is getting mighty feeble to peddle this hot weather.

FRANKIE: She is about ninety. Other old folks lose their faculties, but she found some faculty. She reads futures, too.

BERENICE: Hi, Sis Laura. How is your folks getting on?

480   SIS LAURA: We ain't much, and I feels my age these days. Want any peas today? *(She shuffles across the yard.)*

BERENICE: I'm sorry, I still have some left over from yesterday. Good-bye, Sis Laura.

SIS LAURA: Good-bye. *(She goes off behind the house to the right, continuing her chant.)*

(When the old woman is gone Frankie begins walking around the kitchen.)

FRANKIE: I expect Janice and Jarvis are almost to Winter Hill by now.

BERENICE: Sit down. You make me nervous.

FRANKIE: Jarvis talked about Granny. He remembers her very good. But when I try to remember Granny, it is like her face is changing—like a face seen under water. Jarvis remembers Mother too, and I don't

490   remember her at all.

BERENICE: Naturally! Your mother died the day that you were born.

FRANKIE *(standing with one foot on the seat of the chair, leaning over the chair back and laughing)*: Did you hear what Jarvis said?

BERENICE: What?

FRANKIE *(after laughing more)*: They were talking about whether to vote for C. P. MacDonald. And Jarvis said, "Why I wouldn't vote for that scoundrel if he was running to be dogcatcher." I never heard anything so witty in my life. *(There is a silence during which Berenice watches Frankie, but does not smile.)* And you know what Janice remarked. When Jarvis mentioned about how much I've grown, she said she

500   didn't think I looked so terribly big. She said she got the major portion of her growth before she was thirteen. She said I was the right height and had acting talent and ought to go to Hollywood. She did, Berenice.

BERENICE: O.K. All right! She did!

FRANKIE: She said she thought I was a lovely size and would probably not grow any taller. She said all fashion models and movie stars . . .

BERENICE: She did not. I heard her from the window. She only remarked that you probably had already got your growth. But she didn't go on and on like that or mention Hollywood.

510   FRANKIE: She said to me . . .

BERENICE: She said to you! This is a serious fault with you, Frankie. Somebody just makes a loose remark and then you cozen it in your mind until nobody would recognize it. Your Aunt Pet happened to mention to Clorina that you had sweet manners and Clorina passed it on to you. For what it was worth. Then next thing I know you are going all around and bragging how Mrs. West thought you had the finest manners in town and ought to go to Hollywood, and I don't know what-all you didn't say. And that is a serious fault.

FRANKIE: Aw, quit preaching at me.

520 BERENICE: I ain't preaching. It's the solemn truth and you know it.

FRANKIE: I admit it a little. (*She sits down at the table and puts her forehead on the palms of her hands. There is a pause, and then she speaks softly.*) What I need to know is this. Do you think I made a good impression?

BERENICE: Impression?

FRANKIE: Yes.

BERENICE: Well, how would I know?

FRANKIE: I mean, how did I act? What did I do?

BERENICE: Why, you didn't do anything to speak of.

FRANKIE: Nothing?

BERENICE: No. You just watched the pair of them like they was ghosts.

530 Then, when they talked about the wedding, them ears of yours stiffened out the size of cabbage leaves . . .

FRANKIE (*raising her hand to her ear*): They didn't!

BERENICE: They did.

FRANKIE: Some day you going to look down and find that big fat tongue of yours pulled out by the roots and laying there before you on the table.

BERENICE: Quit talking so rude.

FRANKIE (*after a pause*): I'm so scared I didn't make a good impression.

BERENICE: What of it? I got a date with T. T. and he's supposed to pick me up here. I wish him and Honey would come on. You make

540 me nervous.

(*Frankie sits miserably, her shoulders hunched. Then with a sudden gesture she bangs her forehead on the table. Her fists are clenched and she is sobbing.*)

BERENICE: Come on. Don't act like that.

FRANKIE (*her voice muffled*): They were so pretty. They must have such a good time. And they went away and left me.

BERENICE: Sit up. Behave yourself.

FRANKIE: They came and went away, and left me with this feeling.

BERENICE: Hosee! I bet I know something. (*She begins tapping with her heel: one, two, three—bang! After a pause, in which the rhythm is established, she begins singing.*) Frankie's got a crush! Frankie's got a crush! Frankie's got a crush on the *wedding!*

FRANKIE: Quit!

550 BERENICE: Frankie's got a crush! Frankie's got a crush!

FRANKIE: You better quit! (*She rises suddenly and snatches up the carving knife.*)

BERENICE: You lay down that knife.

FRANKIE: Make me. (*She bends the blade slowly.*)

BERENICE: Lay it down, *Devil. (There is a silence.)* Just throw it! You just!

(After a pause Frankie aims the knife carefully at the closed door leading to the bedroom and throws it. The knife does not stick in the wall.)

FRANKIE: I used to be the best knife thrower in this town.

BERENICE: Frances Addams, you goin' to try that stunt once too often.

FRANKIE: I warned you to quit pickin' with me.

BERENICE: You are not fit to live in a house.

FRANKIE: I won't be living in this one much longer; I'm going to run away from home.

BERENICE: And a good riddance to a big old bag of rubbage.

FRANKIE: You wait and see. I'm leaving town.

BERENICE: And where do you think you are going?

FRANKIE *(gazing around the walls)*: I don't know.

BERENICE: You're going crazy. That's where you going.

FRANKIE: No. *(solemnly)* This coming Sunday after the wedding, I'm leaving town. And I swear to Jesus by my two eyes I'm never coming back here any more.

BERENICE *(going to Frankie and pushing her damp bangs back from her forehead)*: Sugar? You serious?

FRANKIE *(exasperated)*: Of course! Do you think I would stand here and say that swear and tell a story? Sometimes, Berenice, I think it takes you longer to realize a fact than it does anybody who ever lived.

BERENICE: But you say you don't know where you going. You going, but you don't know where. That don't make no sense to me.

FRANKIE *(after a long pause in which she again gazes around the walls of the room)*: I feel just exactly like somebody has peeled all the skin off me. I wish I had some good cold peach ice cream. *(Berenice takes her by the shoulders.)*

(During the last speech, T. T. Williams and Honey Camden Brown have been approaching through the back yard. T. T. is a large and pompous-looking Negro man of about fifty. He is dressed like a church deacon, in a black suit with a red emblem in the lapel. His manner is timid and over-polite. Honey is a slender, limber Negro boy of about twenty. He is quite light in color and he wears loud-colored, snappy clothes. He is brusque and there is about him an odd mixture of hostility and playfulness. He is very high-strung and volatile. They are trailed by John Henry. John Henry is dressed for afternoon in a clean white linen suit, white shoes and socks. Honey carries a horn. They cross the back yard and knock at the back door. Honey holds his hand to his head.)

FRANKIE: But every word I told you was the solemn truth. I'm leaving here after the wedding.

BERENICE *(taking her hands from Frankie's shoulders and answering the door)*: Hello, Honey and T. T. I didn't hear you coming.

T. T.: You and Frankie too busy discussing something. Well, your foster-brother, Honey, got into a ruckus standing on the sidewalk in front of the Blue Moon Café. Police cracked him on the haid.

BERENICE *(turning on the kitchen light)*: What! *(She examines Honey's head.)* Why, it's a welt the size of a small egg.

HONEY: Times like this I feel like I got to bust loose or die.

BERENICE: What were you doing?

HONEY: Nothing. I was just passing along the street minding my own business when this drunk soldier came out of the Blue Moon Café and ran into me. I looked at him and he gave me a push. I pushed
590   him back and he raised a ruckus. This white M.P. came up and slammed me with his stick.

T. T.: It was one of those accidents can happen to any colored person.

JOHN HENRY *(reaching for the horn)*: Toot some on your horn, Honey.

FRANKIE: Please blow.

HONEY *(to John Henry, who has taken the horn)*: Now, don't bother my horn, Butch.

JOHN HENRY: I want to toot it some.

(John Henry takes the horn, tries to blow it, but only succeeds in slobbering in it. He holds the horn away from his mouth and sings: "Too-ty-toot, too-ty-toot." Honey snatches the horn away from him and puts it on the sewing table.)

HONEY: I told you not to touch my horn. You got it full of slobber inside and out. It's ruined! *(He loses his temper, grabs John Henry by the shoulders and shakes him hard.)*

600   BERENICE *(slapping Honey)*: Satan! Don't you dare touch that little boy! I'm going to stomp out your brains!

HONEY: You ain't mad because John Henry is a little boy. It's because he's a white boy. John Henry knows he needs a good shake. Don't you, Butch?

BERENICE: Ornery—no good!

(Honey lifts John Henry and swings him, then reaches in his pocket and brings out some coins.)

HONEY: John Henry, which would you rather have—the nigger money or the white money?

JOHN HENRY: I rather have the dime. *(He takes it.)* Much obliged. *(He goes out and crosses the yard to his house.)*

BERENICE: You troubled and beat down and try to take it out on a little
610   boy. You and Frankie just alike. The club girls don't elect her and she turns on John Henry too. When folks are lonesome and left out, they turn so mean. T. T., do you wish a small little quickie before we start?

T. T. *(looking at Frankie and pointing toward her)*: Frankie ain't no tattle-tale. Is you? *(Berenice pours a drink for T. T.)*

FRANKIE *(disdaining his question)*: That sure is a cute suit you got on, Honey. Today I heard somebody speak of you as Lightfoot Brown. I think that's such a grand nickname. It's on account of your travel-ling—to Harlem, and all the different places where you have run away, and your dancing. Lightfoot! I wish somebody would call me
620   Lightfoot Addams.

BERENICE: It would suit me better if Honey Camden had brick feets. As it is, he keeps me so anxious-worried. C'mon, Honey and T. T. Let's go! *(Honey and T. T. go out.)*

FRANKIE: I'll go out into the yard.

(Frankie, feeling excluded, goes out into the yard. Throughout the act the light in the yard has been darkening steadily. Now the light in the kitchen is throwing a yellow rectangle in the yard.)

BERENICE: Now Frankie, you forget all that foolishness we were discussing. And if Mr. Addams don't come home by good dark, you go over to the Wests'. Go play with John Henry.

HONEY AND T. T. *(from outside)*: So long!

FRANKIE: So long, you all. Since when have I been scared of the dark?

630   I'll invite John Henry to spend the night with me.

BERENICE: I thought you were sick and tired of him.

FRANKIE: I am.

BERENICE *(kissing Frankie)*: Good night, Sugar!

FRANKIE: Seems like everybody goes off and leaves me. *(She walks towards the Wests' yard, calling, with cupped hands.)* John Henry. John Henry.

JOHN HENRY'S VOICE: What do you want, Frankie?

FRANKIE: Come over and spend the night with me.

JOHN HENRY'S VOICE: I can't.

FRANKIE: Why?

640 JOHN HENRY: Just because.

FRANKIE: Because why? *(John Henry does not answer.)* I thought maybe me and you could put up my Indian tepee and sleep out here in the yard. And have a good time. *(There is still no answer.)* Sure enough. Why don't you stay and spend the night?

JOHN HENRY *(quite loudly)*: Because, Frankie. I don't want to.

FRANKIE *(angrily)*: Fool Jackass! Suit yourself! I only asked you because you looked so ugly and so lonesome.

JOHN HENRY *(skipping toward the arbor)*: Why, I'm not a bit lonesome.

FRANKIE *(looking at the house)*: I wonder when that Papa of mine is

650   coming home. He always comes home by dark. I don't want to go into that empty, ugly house all by myself.

JOHN HENRY: Me neither.

FRANKIE *(standing with outstretched arms, and looking around her)*: I think something is wrong. It is too quiet. I have a peculiar warning in my bones. I bet you a hundred dollars it's going to storm.

JOHN HENRY: I don't want to spend the night with you.

FRANKIE: A terrible, terrible dog-day storm. Or maybe even a cyclone.

JOHN HENRY: Huh.

FRANKIE: I bet Jarvis and Janice are now at Winter Hill. I see them just

660   plain as I see you. Plainer. Something is wrong. It is too quiet.

(A clear horn begins to play a blues tune in the distance.)

JOHN HENRY: Frankie?

FRANKIE: Hush! It sounds like Honey.

(The horn music becomes jazzy and spangling, then the first blues tune is repeated. Suddenly, while still unfinished, the music stops. Frankie waits tensely.)

FRANKIE: He has stopped to bang the spit out of his horn. In a second he will finish. *(after a wait)* Please, Honey, go on finish!

JOHN HENRY *(softly)*: He done quit now.

FRANKIE *(moving restlessly)*: I told Berenice that I was leavin' town for good and she did not believe me. Sometimes I honestly think she is the biggest fool that ever drew breath. You try to impress something on a big fool like that, and it's just like talking to a
670   block of cement. I kept on telling and telling and telling her. I told her I had to leave this town for good because it is inevitable. Inevitable.

(Mr. Addams enters the kitchen from the house, calling: "Frankie, Frankie.")

MR. ADDAMS *(calling from the kitchen door)*: Frankie, Frankie.

FRANKIE: Yes, Papa.

MR. ADDAMS *(opening the back door)*: You had supper?

FRANKIE: I'm not hungry.

MR. ADDAMS: Was a little later than I intended, fixing a timepiece for a railroad man. *(He goes back through the kitchen and into the hall, calling: "Don't leave the yard!")*

JOHN HENRY: You want me to get the weekend bag?

680   FRANKIE: Don't bother me, John Henry. I'm thinking.

JOHN HENRY: What you thinking about?

FRANKIE: About the wedding. About my brother and the bride. Everything's been so sudden today. I never believed before about the fact that the earth turns at the rate of about a thousand miles a day. I didn't understand why it was that if you jumped up in the air you wouldn't land in Selma or Fairview or somewhere else instead of the same back yard. But now it seems to me I feel the world going around very fast. *(Frankie begins turning around in circles with arms outstretched. John Henry copies her. They both turn.)* I feel it turning and
690   it makes me dizzy.

JOHN HENRY: I'll stay and spend the night with you.

FRANKIE *(suddenly stopping her turning)*: No. I just now thought of something.

JOHN HENRY: You just a little while ago was begging me.

FRANKIE: I know where I'm going.

(There are sounds of children playing in the distance.)

JOHN HENRY: Let's go play with the children, Frankie.

FRANKIE: I tell you I know where I'm going. It's like I've known it all my life. Tomorrow I will tell everybody.

JOHN HENRY: Where?

700 FRANKIE *(dreamily)*: After the wedding I'm going with them to Winter Hill. I'm going off with them after the wedding.

JOHN HENRY: You serious?

FRANKIE: Shush, just now I realized something. The trouble with me is that for a long time I have been just an "I" person. All other people can say "we." When Berenice says "we" she means her lodge and church and colored people. Soldiers can say "we" and mean the army. All people belong to a "we" except me.

JOHN HENRY: What are we going to do?

FRANKIE: Not to belong to a "we" makes you too lonesome. Until this
710 afternoon I didn't have a "we," but now after seeing Janice and Jarvis I suddenly realize something.

JOHN HENRY: What?

FRANKIE: I know that the bride and my brother are the "we" of me. So I'm going with them, and joining with the wedding. This coming Sunday when my brother and the bride leave this town, I'm going with the two of them to Winter Hill. And after that to whatever place that they will ever go. *(There is a pause.)* I love the two of them so much and we belong to be together. I love the two of them so much because they are the *we* of me.

(The curtain falls.)

ACT 2

The scene is the same: the kitchen of the Addams home. Berenice is cooking. John Henry sits on the stool, blowing soap bubbles with a spool. It is the afternoon of the next day.

(The front door slams and Frankie enters from the hall.)

720 BERENICE: I been phoning all over town trying to locate you. Where on earth have you been?

FRANKIE: Everywhere. All over town.

BERENICE: I been so worried I got a good mind to be seriously mad with you. Your Papa came home to dinner today. He was mad when you didn't show up. He's taking a nap now in his room.

FRANKIE: I walked up and down Main Street and stopped in almost every store. Bought my wedding dress and silver shoes. Went around by the mills. Went all over the complete town and talked to nearly everybody in it.

730 BERENICE: What for, pray tell me?

FRANKIE: I was telling everybody about the wedding and my plans.
(She takes off her dress and remains barefooted in her slip.)

BERENICE: You mean just people on the street? *(She is creaming butter and sugar for cookies.)*

FRANKIE: Everybody. Storekeepers. The monkey and monkey-man. A soldier. Everybody. And you know the soldier wanted to join with

me and asked me for a date this evening. I wonder what you do
on dates.

BERENICE: Frankie, I honestly believe you have turned crazy on us. Walking all over town and telling total strangers this big tale. You know in
your soul this mania of yours is pure foolishness.

740 FRANKIE: Please call me F. Jasmine. I don't wish to have to remind you
any more. Everything good of mine has got to be washed and ironed
so I can pack them in the suitcase. *(She brings in a suitcase and opens
it.)* Everybody in town believes that I'm going. All except Papa. He's
stubborn as an old mule. No use arguing with people like that.

BERENICE: Me and Mr. Addams has some sense.

FRANKIE: Papa was bent over working on a watch when I went by the
store. I asked him could I buy the wedding clothes and he said
charge them at MacDougals. But he wouldn't listen to any of my
plans. Just sat there with his nose to the grindstone and answered

750 with—kind of grunts. He never listens to what I say. *(There is a pause.)*
Sometimes I wonder if Papa loves me or not.

BERENICE: Course he loves you. He is just a busy widowman—set in
his ways.

FRANKIE: Now I wonder if I can find some tissue paper to line this suitcase.

BERENICE: Truly, Frankie, what makes you think they want you taggin'
along with them? Two is company and three is a crowd. And that's the
main thing about a wedding. Two is company and three is a crowd.

FRANKIE: You wait and see.

BERENICE: Remember back to the time of the flood. Remember Noah

760 and the Ark.

FRANKIE: And what has that got to do with it?

BERENICE: Remember the way he admitted them creatures.

FRANKIE: Oh, shut up your big old mouth!

BERENICE: Two by two. He admitted them creatures two by two.

FRANKIE *(after a pause)*: That's all right. But you wait and see. They will
take me.

BERENICE: And if they don't?

FRANKIE *(turning suddenly from washing her hands at the sink)*: If they don't,
I will kill myself.

770 BERENICE: Kill yourself, how?

FRANKIE: I will shoot myself in the side of the head with the pistol that
Papa keeps under his handkerchiefs with Mother's picture in the
bureau drawer.

BERENICE: You heard what Mr. Addams said about playing with that
pistol. I'll just put this cookie dough in the icebox. Set the table
and your dinner is ready. Set John Henry a plate and one for me.
*(Berenice puts the dough in the icebox. Frankie hurriedly sets the table.
Berenice takes dishes from the stove and ties a napkin around John Henry's
neck.)* I have heard of many a peculiar thing. I have knew men to fall
in love with girls so ugly that you wonder if their eyes is straight.

JOHN HENRY: Who?

780   BERENICE: I have knew women to love veritable satans and thank Jesus
when they put their split hooves over the threshold. I have knew boys
to take it into their heads to fall in love with other boys. You know
Lily Mae Jenkins?

FRANKIE: I'm not sure. I know a lot of people.

BERENICE: Well, you either know him or you don't know him. He prisses
around in a girl's blouse with one arm akimbo. Now this Lily Mae
Jenkins fell in love with a man name Juney Jones. A man, mind you.
And Lily Mae turned into a girl. He changed his nature and his sex
and turned into a girl.

790   FRANKIE: What?

BERENICE: He did. To all intents and purposes. *(Berenice is sitting in the
center chair at the table. She says grace.)* Lord, make us thankful for what
we are about to receive to nourish our bodies. Amen.

FRANKIE: It's funny I can't think who you are talking about. I used to
think I knew so many people.

BERENICE: Well, you don't need to know Lily Mae Jenkins. You can live
without knowing him.

FRANKIE: Anyway, I don't believe you.

BERENICE: I ain't arguing with you. What was we speaking about?

800   FRANKIE: About peculiar things.

BERENICE: Oh, yes. As I was just now telling you I have seen many a
peculiar thing in my day. But one thing I never knew and never
heard tell about. No, siree. I never in all my days heard of anybody
falling in love with a wedding. *(There is a pause.)* And thinking it all
over I have come to a conclusion.

JOHN HENRY: How? How did that boy change into a girl? Did he kiss his
elbow? *(He tries to kiss his elbow.)*

BERENICE: It was just one of them things, Candy Lamb. Yep, I have come
to the conclusion that what you ought to be thinking about is a beau.

810   A nice little white boy beau.

FRANKIE: I don't want any beau. What would I do with one? Do you
mean something like a soldier who would maybe take me to the
Idle Hour?

BERENICE: Who's talking about soldiers? I'm talking about a nice little
white boy beau your own age. How 'bout that little old Barney
next door?

FRANKIE: Barney MacKean! That nasty Barney!

BERENICE: Certainly! You could make out with him until somebody better
comes along. He would do.

820   FRANKIE: You are the biggest crazy in this town.

BERENICE: The crazy calls the sane the crazy.

*(Barney MacKean, a boy of twelve, shirtless and wearing shorts, and
Helen Fletcher, a girl of twelve or fourteen, cross the yard from the left, go
through the arbor and out on the right. Frankie and John Henry watch
them from the window.)*

FRANKIE: Yonder's Barney now with Helen Fletcher. They are going to the alley behind the Wests' garage. They do something bad back there. I don't know what it is.

BERENICE: If you don't know what it is, how come you know it is bad?

FRANKIE: I just know it. I think maybe they look at each other and peepee or something. They don't let anybody watch them.

JOHN HENRY: I watched them once.

FRANKIE: What do they do?

830 JOHN HENRY: I saw. They don't peepee.

FRANKIE: Then what do they do?

JOHN HENRY: I don't know what it was. But I watched them. How many of them did you catch, Berenice? Them beaus?

BERENICE: How many? Candy Lamb, how many hairs is in this plait? You're talking to Miss Berenice Sadie Brown.

FRANKIE: I think you ought to quit worrying about beaus and be content with T. T. I bet you are forty years old.

BERENICE: Wise-mouth. How do you know so much? I got as much right as anybody else to continue to have a good time as long as I can.

840 And as far as that goes, I'm not so old as some peoples would try and make out. I ain't changed life yet.

JOHN HENRY: Did they all treat you to the picture show, them beaus?

BERENICE: To the show, or one thing or another. Wipe off your mouth.

(There is the sound of piano tuning.)

JOHN HENRY: The piano tuning man.

BERENICE: Ye Gods, I seriously believe this will be the last straw.

JOHN HENRY: Me too.

FRANKIE: It makes me sad. And jittery too. *(She walks around the room.)* They tell me that when they want to punish the crazy people in Milledgeville, they tie them up and make them listen to piano tuning. *(She puts the empty coal scuttle on her head and walks around the table.)*

850 BERENICE: We could turn on the radio and drown him out.

FRANKIE: I don't want the radio on. *(She goes into the interior room and takes off her dress, speaking from inside.)* But I advise you to keep the radio on after I leave. Some day you will very likely hear us speak over the radio.

BERENICE: Speak about what, pray tell me?

FRANKIE: I don't know exactly what about. But probably some eye witness account about something. We will be asked to speak.

BERENICE: I don't follow you. What are we going to eye witness? And who will ask us to speak?

JOHN HENRY *(excitedly)*: What, Frankie? Who is speaking on the radio?

860 FRANKIE: When I said *we*, you thought I meant you and me and John Henry West. To speak over the world radio. I have never heard of anything so funny since I was born.

JOHN HENRY *(climbing up to kneel on the seat of the chair)*: Who? What?

FRANKIE: Ha! Ha! Ho! Ho! Ho! Ho!

(Frankie goes around punching things with her fist, and shadow boxing. Berenice raises her right hand for peace. Then suddenly they all stop. Frankie goes to the window, and John Henry hurries there also and stands on tiptoe with his hands on the sill. Berenice turns her head to see what has happened. The piano is still. Three young girls in clean dresses are passing before the arbor. Frankie watches them silently at the window.)

JOHN HENRY *(softly)*: The club of girls.

FRANKIE: What do you son-of-a-bitches mean crossing my yard? How many times must I tell you not to set foot on my Papa's property?

BERENICE: Just ignore them and make like you don't see them pass.

FRANKIE: Don't mention those crooks to me.

(T. T. and Honey approach by way of the back yard. Honey is whistling a blues tune.)

870 BERENICE: Why don't you show me the new dress? I'm anxious to see what you selected. *(Frankie goes into the interior room. T. T. knocks on the door. He and Honey enter.)* Why T. T. what you doing around here this time of day?

T. T.: Good afternoon, Miss Berenice. I'm here on a sad mission.

BERENICE *(startled)*: What's wrong?

T. T.: It's about Sis Laura Thompson. She suddenly had a stroke and died.

BERENICE: What! Why she was by here just yesterday. We just ate her peas. They in my stomach right now, and her lyin' dead on the cooling board this minute. The Lord works in strange ways.

880 T. T.: Passed away at dawn this morning.

FRANKIE *(putting her head in the doorway)*: Who is it that's dead?

BERENICE: Sis Laura, Sugar. That old vegetable lady.

FRANKIE *(unseen, from the interior room)*: Just to think—she passed by yesterday.

T. T.: Miss Berenice, I'm going around to take up a donation for the funeral. The policy people say Sis Laura's claim has lapsed.

BERENICE: Well, here's fifty cents. The poor old soul.

T. T.: She was brisk as a chipmunk to the last. The Lord had appointed the time for her. I hope I go that way.

890 FRANKIE *(from the interior room)*: I've got something to show you all. Shut your eyes and don't open them until I tell you. *(She enters the room dressed in an orange satin evening dress with silver shoes and stockings.)* These are the wedding clothes. *(Berenice, T. T. and John Henry stare.)*

JOHN HENRY: Oh, how pretty!

FRANKIE: Now tell me your honest opinion. *(There is a pause.)* What's the matter? Don't you like it, Berenice?

BERENICE: No. It don't do.

FRANKIE: What do you mean? It don't do.

BERENICE: Exactly that. It just don't do. *(She shakes her head while Frankie looks at the dress.)*

FRANKIE: But I don't see what you mean. What is wrong?

900 BERENICE: Well, if you don't see it I can't explain it to you. Look there at your head, to begin with. *(Frankie goes to the mirror.)* You had all your hair shaved off like a convict and now you tie this ribbon around this head without any hair. Just looks peculiar.

FRANKIE: But I'm going to wash and try to stretch my hair tonight.

BERENICE: Stretch your hair! How you going to stretch your hair? And look at them elbows. Here you got on a grown woman's evening dress. And that brown crust on your elbows. The two things just don't mix. *(Frankie, embarrassed, covers her elbows with her hands. Berenice is still shaking her head.)* Take it back down to the store.

910 T. T.: The dress is too growny looking.

FRANKIE: But I can't take it back. It's bargain basement.

BERENICE: Very well then. Come here. Let me see what I can do.

FRANKIE *(going to Berenice, who works with the dress)*: I think you're just not accustomed to seeing anybody dressed up.

BERENICE: I'm not accustomed to seein' a human Christmas tree in August.

JOHN HENRY: Frankie's dress looks like a Christmas tree.

FRANKIE: Two-faced Judas! You just now said it was pretty. Old double-faced Judas! *(The sounds of piano tuning are heard again.)* Oh, that piano tuner!

920 BERENICE: Step back a little now.

FRANKIE *(looking in the mirror)*: Don't you honestly think it's pretty? Give me your candy opinion.

BERENICE: I never knew anybody so unreasonable! You ask me my candy opinion, I give you my candy opinion. You ask me again, and I give it to you again. But what you want is not my honest opinion, but my good opinion of something I know is wrong.

FRANKIE: I only want to look pretty.

BERENICE: Pretty is as pretty does. Ain't that right, T. T.? You will look well enough for anybody's wedding. Excepting your own.

(Mr. Addams enters through the hall door.)

930 MR. ADDAMS: Hello, everybody. *(to Frankie)* I don't want you roaming around the streets all morning and not coming home at dinner time. Looks like I'll have to tie you up in the back yard.

FRANKIE: I had business to tend to. Papa, look!

MR. ADDAMS: What is it, Miss Picklepriss?

FRANKIE: Sometimes I think you have turned stone blind. You never even noticed my new dress.

MR. ADDAMS: I thought it was a show costume.

FRANKIE: Show costume! Papa, why is it you don't ever notice what I have on or pay any serious mind to me? You just walk around like a
940 mule with blinders on, not seeing or caring.

MR. ADDAMS: Never mind that now. *(to T. T. and Honey)* I need some help down at my store. My porter failed me again. I wonder if you or Honey could help me next week.

T. T.: I will if I can, sir, Mr. Addams. What days would be convenient for you, sir?

MR. ADDAMS: Say Wednesday afternoon.

T. T.: Now, Mr. Addams, that's one afternoon I promised to work for Mr. Finny, sir. I can't promise anything, Mr. Addams. But if Mr. Finny change his mind about needing me, I'll work for you, sir.

950 MR. ADDAMS: How about you, Honey?

HONEY *(shortly)*: I ain't got the time.

MR. ADDAMS: I'll be so glad when the war is over and you biggety, worthless niggers get back to work. And, furthermore, you *sir* me! Hear me?

HONEY *(reluctantly)*: Yes,—sir.

MR. ADDAMS: I better go back to the store now and get my nose down to the grindstone. You stay home, Frankie. *(He goes out through the hall door.)*

JOHN HENRY: Uncle Royal called Honey a nigger. Is Honey a nigger?

BERENICE: Be quiet now, John Henry. *(to Honey)* Honey, I got a good mind to shake you till you spit. Not saying *sir* to Mr. Addams, and acting so

960 impudent.

HONEY: T. T. said sir enough for a whole crowd of niggers. But for folks that calls me nigger, I got a real good nigger razor. *(He takes a razor from his pocket. Frankie and John Henry crowd close to look. When John Henry touches the razor Honey says:)* Don't touch it, Butch, it's sharp. Liable to hurt yourself.

BERENICE: Put up that razor, Satan! I worry myself sick over you. You going to die before your appointed span.

JOHN HENRY: Why is Honey a nigger?

BERENICE: Jesus knows.

HONEY: I'm so tensed up. My nerves been scraped with a razor.

970 Berenice, loan me a dollar.

BERENICE: I ain't handing you no dollar, worthless, to get high on them reefer cigarettes.

HONEY: Gimme, Berenice, I'm so tensed up and miserable. The nigger hole. I'm sick of smothering in the nigger hole. I can't stand it no more.

(Relenting, Berenice gets her pocketbook from the shelf, opens it, and takes out some change.)

BERENICE: Here's thirty cents. You can buy two beers.

HONEY: Well, thankful for tiny, infinitesimal favors. I better be dancing off now.

T. T.: Same here. I still have to make a good deal of donation visits this

980 afternoon. *(Honey and T. T. go to the door.)*

BERENICE: So long, T. T. I'm counting on you for tomorrow and you too, Honey.

FRANKIE and JOHN HENRY: So long.

T. T.: Good-bye, you all. Good-bye. *(He goes out, crossing the yard.)*

BERENICE: Poor ole Sis Laura. I certainly hope that when my time comes I will have kept up my policy. I dread to think the church would ever have to bury me. When I die.

JOHN HENRY: Are you going to die, Berenice?

BERENICE: Why, Candy, everybody has to die.

990 JOHN HENRY: Everybody? Are you going to die, Frankie?

FRANKIE: I doubt it. I honestly don't think I'll ever die.

JOHN HENRY: What is "die"?

FRANKIE: It must be terrible to be nothing but black, black, black.

BERENICE: Yes, baby.

FRANKIE: How many dead people do you know? I know six dead people in all. I'm not counting my mother. There's William Boyd who was killed in Italy. I knew him by sight and name. An' that man who climbed poles for the telephone company. An' Lou Baker. The porter at Finny's place who was murdered in the alley back of Papa's store.
1000 Somebody drew a razor on him and the alley people said that his cut throat shivered like a mouth and spoke ghost words to the sun.

JOHN HENRY: Ludie Maxwell Freeman is dead.

FRANKIE: I didn't count Ludie; it wouldn't be fair. Because he died just before I was born. *(to Berenice)* Do you think very frequently about Ludie?

BERENICE: You know I do. I think about the five years when me and Ludie was together, and about all the bad times I seen since. Sometimes I almost wish I had never knew Ludie at all. It leaves you too lonesome afterward. When you walk home in the evening
1010 on the way from work, it makes a little lonesome quinch come in you. And you take up with too many sorry men to try to get over the feeling.

FRANKIE: But T. T. is not sorry.

BERENICE: I wasn't referring to T. T. He is a fine upstanding colored gentleman, who has walked in a state of grace all his life.

FRANKIE: When are you going to marry with him?

BERENICE: I ain't going to marry with him.

FRANKIE: But you were just now saying . . .

BERENICE: I was saying how sincerely I respect T. T. and sincerely regard
1020 T. T. *(There is a pause.)* But he don't make me shiver none.

FRANKIE: Listen, Berenice, I have something queer to tell you. It's something that happened when I was walking around town today. Now I don't exactly know how to explain what I mean.

BERENICE: What is it?

FRANKIE *(now and then pulling her bangs or lower lip)*: I was walking along and I passed two stores with a alley in between. The sun was frying hot. And just as I passed this alley, I caught a *glimpse* of something in the corner of my left eye. A dark double shape. And this glimpse brought to my mind—so sudden and clear—my brother and the
1030 bride that I just stood there and couldn't hardly bear to look and see what it was. It was like they were there in that alley, although I knew

that they are in Winter Hill almost a hundred miles away. *(There is a pause.)* Then I turn slowly and look. And you know what was there? *(There is a pause.)* It was just two colored boys. That was all. But it gave me such a queer feeling.

(Berenice has been listening attentively. She stares at Frankie, then draws a package of cigarettes from her bosom and lights one.)

BERENICE: Listen at me! Can you see through these bones in my forehead? *(She points to her forehead.)* Have you, Frankie Addams, been reading my mind? *(There is a pause.)* That's the most remarkable thing I ever heard of.

1040 FRANKIE: What I mean is that . . .

BERENICE: I know what you mean. You mean right here in the corner of your eye. *(She points to her eye.)* You suddenly catch something there. And this cold shiver run all the way down you. And you whirl around. And you stand there facing Jesus knows what. But not Ludie, not who you want. And for a minute you feel like you been dropped down a well.

FRANKIE: Yes. That is it. *(Frankie reaches for a cigarette and lights it, coughing a bit.)*

BERENICE: Well, that is mighty remarkable. This is a thing been happening to me all my life. Yet just now is the first time I ever heard it put

1050 into words. *(There is a pause.)* Yes, that is the way it is when you are in love. A thing known and not spoken.

FRANKIE *(patting her foot)*: Yet I always maintained I never believed in love. I didn't admit it and never put any of it in my shows.

JOHN HENRY: I never believed in love.

BERENICE: Now I will tell you something. And it is to be a warning to you. You hear me, John Henry. You hear me, Frankie.

JOHN HENRY: Yes. *(He points his forefinger.)* Frankie is smoking.

BERENICE *(squaring her shoulders)*: Now I am here to tell you I was happy. There was no human woman in all the world more happy than I was

1060 in them days. And that includes everybody. You listening to me, John Henry? It includes all queens and millionaires and first ladies of the land. And I mean it includes people of all color. You hear me, Frankie? No human woman in all the world was happier than Berenice Sadie Brown.

FRANKIE: The five years you were married to Ludie.

BERENICE: From that autumn morning when I first met him on the road in front of Campbell's Filling Station until the very night he died, November, the year 1933.

FRANKIE: The very year and the very month I was born.

1070 BERENICE: The coldest November I ever seen. Every morning there was frost and puddles were crusted with ice. The sunshine was pale yellow like it is in winter time. Sounds carried far away, and I remember a hound dog that used to howl toward sundown. And everything I seen come to me as a kind of sign.

FRANKIE: I think it is a kind of sign I was born the same year and the same month he died.

BERENICE: And it was a Thursday towards six o'clock. About this time of day. Only November. I remember I went to the passage and opened the front door. Dark was coming on; the old hound was howling far away. And I go back in the room and lay down on Ludie's bed. I lay myself down over Ludie with my arms spread out and my face on his face. And I pray that the Lord would contage my strength to him. And I ask the Lord let it be anybody, but not let it be Ludie. And I lay there and pray for a long time. Until night.

JOHN HENRY: How? *(in a higher, wailing voice)* How, Berenice?

BERENICE: That night he died. I tell you he died. Ludie! Ludie Freeman! Ludie Maxwell Freeman died! *(She hums.)*

FRANKIE *(after a pause)*: It seems to me I feel sadder about Ludie than any other dead person. Although I never knew him. I know I ought to cry sometimes about my mother, or anyhow Granny. But it looks like I can't. But Ludie—maybe it was because I was born so soon after Ludie died. But you were starting out to tell some kind of a warning.

BERENICE *(looking puzzled for a moment)*: Warning? Oh, yes! I was going to tell you how this thing we was talking about applies to me. *(As Berenice begins to talk Frankie goes to a shelf above the refrigerator and brings back a fig bar to the table.)* It was the April of the following year that I went one Sunday to the church where the congregation was strange to me. I had my forehead down on the top of the pew in front of me, and my eyes were open—not peeping around in secret, mind you, but just open. When suddenly this shiver ran all the way through me. I had caught sight of something from the corner of my eye. And I looked slowly to the left. There on the pew, just six inches from my eyes, was this *thumb*.

FRANKIE: What thumb?

BERENICE: Now I have to tell you. There was only one small portion of Ludie Freeman which was not pretty. Every other part about him was handsome and pretty as anyone would wish. All except this right thumb. This one thumb had a mashed, chewed appearance that was not pretty. You understand?

FRANKIE: You mean you suddenly saw Ludie's thumb when you were praying?

BERENICE: I mean I seen *this* thumb. And as I knelt there just staring at this thumb, I begun to pray in earnest. I prayed out loud! Lord, manifest! Lord, manifest!

FRANKIE: And did He—manifest?

BERENICE: Manifest, my foot! *(spitting)* You know who that thumb belonged to?

FRANKIE: Who?

BERENICE: Why, Jamie Beale. That big old no-good Jamie Beale. It was the first time I ever laid eyes on him.

1120 FRANKIE: Is that why you married him? Because he had a mashed thumb like Ludie's?

BERENICE: Lord only knows. I don't. I guess I felt drawn to him on account of that thumb. And then one thing led to another. First thing I know I had married him.

FRANKIE: Well, I think that was silly. To marry him just because of that thumb.

BERENICE: I'm not trying to dispute with you. I'm just telling you what actually happened. And the very same thing occurred in the case of Henry Johnson.

1130 FRANKIE: You mean to sit there and tell me Henry Johnson had one of those mashed thumbs too?

BERENICE: No. It was not the thumb this time. It was the coat. *(Frankie and John Henry look at each other in amazement. After a pause Berenice continues.)* Now when Ludie died, them policy people cheated me out of fifty dollars so I pawned everything I could lay hands on, and I sold my coat and Ludie's coat. Because I couldn't let Ludie be put away cheap.

FRANKIE: Oh! Then you mean Henry Johnson bought Ludie's coat and you married him because of it?

BERENICE: Not exactly. I was walking down the street one evening when I suddenly seen this shape appear before me. Now the shape of this

1140 boy ahead of me was so similar to Ludie through the shoulders and the back of the head that I almost dropped dead there on the sidewalk. I followed and run behind him. It was Henry Johnson. Since he lived in the country and didn't come into town, he had chanced to buy Ludie's coat and from the back view it looked like he was Ludie's ghost or Ludie's twin. But how I married him I don't exactly know, for, to begin with, it was clear that he did not have his share of sense. But you let a boy hang around and you get fond of him. Anyway, that's how I married Henry Johnson.

FRANKIE: He was the one went crazy on you. Had eatin' dreams and

1150 swallowed the corner of the sheet. *(There is a pause.)* But I don't understand the point of what you was telling. I don't see how that about Jamie Beale and Henry Johnson applies to me.

BERENICE: Why, it applies to everybody and it is a warning.

FRANKIE: But how?

BERENICE: Why, Frankie, don't you see what I was doing? I loved Ludie and he was the first man I loved. Therefore I had to go and copy myself forever afterward. What I did was to marry off little pieces of Ludie whenever I come across them. It was just my misfortune they all turned out to be the wrong pieces. My intention was to repeat me

1160 and Ludie. Now don't you see?

FRANKIE: I see what you're driving at. But I don't see how it is a warning applied to me.

BERENICE: You don't! Then I'll tell you. *(Frankie does not nod or answer. The piano tuner plays an arpeggio.)* You and that wedding tomorrow.

That is what I am warning about. I can see right through them two
gray eyes of yours like they was glass. And what I see is the saddest
piece of foolishness I ever knew.

JOHN HENRY: *(in a low voice)*: Gray eyes is glass.

(Frankie tenses her brows and looks steadily at Berenice.)

BERENICE: I see what you have in mind. Don't think I don't. You see
1170   something unheard of tomorrow, and you right in the center. You
think you going to march to the preacher right in between your
brother and the bride. You think you going to break into that wedding, and then Jesus knows what else.

FRANKIE: No. I don't see myself walking to the preacher with them.

BERENICE: I see through them eyes. Don't argue with me.

JOHN HENRY *(repeating softly)*: Gray eyes is glass.

BERENICE: But what I'm warning is this. If you start out falling in love
with some unheard-of thing like that, what is going to happen to
you? If you take a mania like this, it won't be the last time and of that
1180   you can be sure. So what will become of you? Will you be trying to
break into weddings the rest of your days?

FRANKIE: It makes me sick to listen to people who don't have any sense.

(She sticks her fingers in her ears and hums.)

BERENICE: You just settin' yourself this fancy trap to catch yourself in
trouble. And you know it.

FRANKIE: They will take me. You wait and see.

BERENICE: Well, I been trying to reason seriously. But I see it is no use.

FRANKIE: You are just jealous. You are just trying to deprive me of all the
pleasure of leaving town.

BERENICE: I am just trying to head this off. But I still see it is no use.

1190   JOHN HENRY: Gray eyes is glass.

(The piano is played to the seventh note of the scale and this is repeated.)

FRANKIE *(singing)*: Do, ray, mee, fa, sol, la, tee, do. Tee. Tee. It could
drive you wild. *(She crosses to the screen door and slams it.)* You didn't say
anything about Willis Rhodes. Did he have a mashed thumb or a
coat or something? *(She returns to the table and sits down.)*

BERENICE: Lord, now that really was something.

FRANKIE: I only know he stole your furniture and was so terrible you had
to call the Law on him.

BERENICE: Well, imagine this! Imagine a cold bitter January night.
And me laying all by myself in the big parlor bed. Alone in the house
1200   because everybody else had gone for the Saturday night. Me, mind
you, who hates to sleep in a big empty bed all by myself at any time.
Past twelve o'clock on this cold, bitter January night. Can you remember winter time, John Henry? *(John Henry nods.)* Imagine! Suddenly
there comes a sloughing sound and a tap, tap, tap. So Miss Me . . .

*(She laughs uproariously and stops suddenly, putting her hand over
her mouth.)*

FRANKIE: What? *(leaning closer across the table and looking intently at Berenice)* What happened?

(Berenice looks from one to the other, shaking her head slowly. Then she speaks in a changed voice.)

BERENICE: Why, I wish you would look yonder. I wish you would look.
(Frankie glances quickly behind her, then turns back to Berenice.)
FRANKIE: What? What happened?
BERENICE: Look at them two little pitchers and them four big ears.
1210 *(Berenice gets up suddenly from the table.)* Come on, chillin, less us roll out the dough for the cookies tomorrow. *(Berenice clears the table and begins washing dishes at the sink.)*
FRANKIE: If it's anything I mortally despise, it's a person who starts out to tell something and works up people's interest, and then stops.
BERENICE *(still laughing)*: I admit it. And I am sorry. But it was just one of them things I suddenly realized I couldn't tell you and John Henry.

(John Henry skips up to the sink.)

JOHN HENRY *(singing)*: Cookies! Cookies! Cookies!
FRANKIE: You could have sent him out of the room and told me. But don't think I care a particle about what happened. I just wish Willis Rhodes had come in about that time and slit your throat. *(She goes out into the hall.)*
1220 BERENICE *(still chuckling)*: That is a ugly way to talk. You ought to be ashamed. Here, John Henry, I'll give you a scrap of dough to make a cookie man.

(Berenice gives John Henry some dough. He climbs up on a chair and begins to work with it. Frankie enters with the evening newspaper. She stands in the doorway, then puts the newspaper on the table.)

FRANKIE: I see in the paper where we dropped a new bomb—the biggest one dropped yet. They call it a atom bomb. I intend to take two baths tonight. One long soaking bath and scrub with a brush. I'm going to try to scrape this crust off my elbows. Then let out the dirty water and take a second bath.
BERENICE: Hooray, that's a good idea. I will be glad to see you clean.
JOHN HENRY: I will take two baths.

(Berenice has picked up the paper and is sitting in a chair against the pale white light of the window. She holds the newspaper open before her and her head is twisted down to one side as she strains to see what is printed there.)

1230 FRANKIE: Why is it against the law to change your name?
BERENICE: What is that on your neck? I thought it was a head you carried on that neck. Just think. Suppose I would suddenly up and call myself Mrs. Eleanor Roosevelt. And you would begin naming yourself Joe Louis. And John Henry here tried to pawn himself off as Henry Ford.

FRANKIE: Don't talk childish; that is not the kind of changing I mean.
I mean from a name that doesn't suit you to a name you prefer.
Like I changed from Frankie to F. Jasmine.

BERENICE: But it would be a confusion. Suppose we all suddenly change
1240   to entirely different names. Nobody would ever know who anybody
was talking about. The whole world would go crazy.

FRANKIE: I don't see what that has to do with it.

BERENICE: Because things accumulate around your name. You have a
name and one thing after another happens to you and things have
accumulated around the name.

FRANKIE: But what has accumulated around my old name? *(Berenice does
not reply.)* Nothing! See! My name just didn't mean anything. Nothing
ever happened to me.

BERENICE: But it will. Things will happen.

1250   FRANKIE: What?

BERENICE: You pin me down like that and I can't tell you truthfully.
If I could, I wouldn't be sitting here in this kitchen right now, but
making a fine living on Wall Street as a wizard. All I can say is that
things will happen. Just what, I don't know.

FRANKIE: Until yesterday, nothing ever happened to me.

*(John Henry crosses to the door and puts on Berenice's hat and shoes, takes
her pocketbook and walks around the table twice.)*

BERENICE: John Henry, take off my hat and my shoes and put up my
pocketbook. Thank you very much. *(John Henry does so.)*

FRANKIE: Listen, Berenice. Doesn't it strike you as strange that I am I
and you are you? Like when you are walking down a street and you
1260   meet somebody. And you are you. And he is him. Yet when you look
at each other, the eyes make a connection. Then you go off one way.
And he goes off another way. You go off into different parts of town,
and maybe you never see each other again. Not in your whole life.
Do you see what I mean?

BERENICE: Not exactly.

FRANKIE: That's not what I meant to say anyway. There are all these
people here in town I don't even know by sight or name. And we
pass alongside each other and don't have any connection. And they
don't know me and I don't know them. And now I'm leaving town
1270   and there are all these people I will never know.

BERENICE: But who do you want to know?

FRANKIE: Everybody. Everybody in the world.

BERENICE: Why, I wish you would listen to that. How about people like
Willis Rhodes? How about them Germans? How about them Japanese?

(Frankie knocks her head against the door jamb and looks up at the ceiling.)

FRANKIE: That's not what I mean. That's not what I'm talking about.

BERENICE: Well, what *is* you talking about?

(A child's voice is heard outside, calling: "Batter up! Batter up!")

JOHN HENRY *(in a low voice)*: Less play out, Frankie.

FRANKIE: No. You go. *(after a pause)* This is what I mean.

(Berenice waits, and when Frankie does not speak again, says:)

BERENICE: What on earth is wrong with you?

FRANKIE *(after a long pause, then suddenly, with hysteria)*:

1280   Boyoman! Manoboy! When we leave Winter Hill we're going to more places than you ever thought about or even knew existed. Just where we will go first I don't know, and it don't matter. Because after we go to that place we're going on to another. Alaska, China, Iceland, South America. Travelling on trains. Letting her rip on motorcycles. Flying around all over the world in airplanes. Here today and gone tomorrow. All over the world. It's the damn truth. Boyoman!
(She runs around the table.)

BERENICE: Frankie!

FRANKIE: And talking of things happening. Things will happen so fast we won't hardly have time to realize them. Captain Jarvis Addams

1290   wins highest medals and is decorated by the President. Miss F. Jasmine Addams breaks all records. Mrs. Janice Addams elected Miss United Nations in beauty contest. One thing after another happening so fast we don't hardly notice them.

BERENICE: Hold still, fool.

FRANKIE *(her excitement growing more and more intense)*: And we will meet them. Everybody. We will just walk up to people and know them right away. We will be walking down a dark road and see a lighted house and knock on the door and strangers will rush to meet us and say: "Come in! Come in!" We will know decorated aviators and New

1300   York people and movie stars. We will have thousands and thousands of friends. And we will belong to so many clubs that we can't even keep track of all of them. We will be members of the whole world. Boyoman! Manoboy!

(Frankie has been running round and round the table in wild excitement and when she passes the next time Berenice catches her slip so quickly that she is caught up with a jerk.)

BERENICE: *Is* you gone raving wild? *(She pulls Frankie closer and puts her arm around her waist.)* Sit here in my lap and rest a minute. *(Frankie sits in Berenice's lap. John Henry comes close and jealously pinches Frankie.)* Leave Frankie alone. She ain't bothered you.

JOHN HENRY: I'm sick.

BERENICE: Now no, you ain't. Be quiet and don't grudge your cousin a little bit love.

1310 JOHN HENRY *(hitting Frankie)*: Old mean bossy Frankie.

BERENICE: What she doing so mean right now? She just laying here wore out. *(They continue sitting. Frankie is relaxed now.)*

FRANKIE: Today I went to the Blue Moon—this place that all the soldiers
are so fond of and I met a soldier—a red-headed boy.

BERENICE: What is all this talk about the Blue Moon and soldiers?

FRANKIE: Berenice, you treat me like a child. When I see all these
soldiers milling around town I always wonder where they came
from and where they are going.

BERENICE: They were born and they going to die.

1320 FRANKIE: There are so many things about the world I do not understand.

BERENICE: If you did understand you would be God. Didn't you know that?

FRANKIE: Maybe so. *(She stares and stretches herself on Berenice's lap, her long
legs sprawled out beneath the kitchen table.)* Anyway, after the wedding I
won't have to worry about things any more.

BERENICE: You don't have to now. Nobody requires you to solve the riddles
of the world.

FRANKIE *(looking at newspaper)*: The paper says this new atom bomb is
worth twenty thousand tons of T.N.T.

BERENICE: Twenty thousand tons? And there ain't but two tons of coal in
1330 the coal house—all that coal.

FRANKIE: The paper says the bomb is a very important science discovery.

BERENICE: The figures these days have got too high for me. Read in the
paper about ten million peoples killed. I can't crowd that many peoples in my mind's eye.

JOHN HENRY: Berenice, is the glass eye your mind's eye?

*(John Henry has climbed up on the back rungs of Berenice's chair and has been
hugging her head. He is now holding her ears.)*

BERENICE: Don't yank my head back like that, Candy. Me and Frankie
ain't going to float up through the ceiling and leave you.

FRANKIE: I wonder if you have ever thought about this? Here we are—
right now. This very minute. Now. But while we're talking right
1340 now, this minute is passing. And it will never come again. Never in
all the world. When it is gone, it is gone. No power on earth could
bring it back again.

JOHN HENRY *(beginning to sing)*: I sing because I'm happy,

I sing because I'm free,
For His eye is on the sparrow,
And I know He watches me.

BERENICE *(singing)*: Why should I feel discouraged?
Why should the shadows come?
Why should my heart be lonely,
1350 Away from heaven and home?
For Jesus is my portion,
My constant friend is He,
For His eye is on the sparrow,

And I know He watches me,
So, I sing because I'm happy.

(John Henry and Frankie join on the last three lines.)

I sing because I'm happy,
I sing because I'm free,
For His eye is on the sparrow,
And I know He watches . . .

1360 BERENICE: Frankie, you got the sharpest set of human bones I ever felt.

(The curtain falls.)

ACT 3

SCENE 1

The scene is the same: the kitchen. It is the day of the wedding. When the curtain rises Berenice, in her apron, and T. T. Williams in a white coat have just finished preparations for the wedding refreshments. Berenice has been watching the ceremony through the half-open door leading into the hall. There are sounds of congratulations offstage, the wedding ceremony having just finished.

BERENICE *(to T. T. Williams)*: Can't see much from this door. But I can see Frankie. And her face is a study. And John Henry's chewing away at the bubble gum that Jarvis bought him. Well, sounds like it's all over. They crowding in now to kiss the bride. We better take this cloth off the sandwiches. Frankie said she would help you serve.

T. T.: From the way she's been acting, I don't think we can count much on her.

BERENICE: I wish Honey was here. I'm so worried about him since what you told me. It's going to storm. It's a mercy they didn't decide to
1370   have the wedding in the back yard like they first planned.

T. T.: I thought I'd better not minch the matter. Honey was in a bad way when I saw him this morning.

BERENICE: Honey Camden don't have too large a share of judgment as it is, but when he gets high on them reefers, he's got no more judgment than a four-year-old child. Remember that time he swung at the police and nearly got his eyes beat out?

T. T.: Not to mention six months on the road.

BERENICE: I haven't been so anxious in all my life. I've got two people scouring Sugarville to find him. *(in a fervent voice)* God, you took Ludie
1380   but please watch over my Honey Camden. He's all the family I got.

T. T.: And Frankie behaving this way about the wedding. Poor little critter.

BERENICE: And the sorry part is that she's perfectly serious about all this foolishness. *(Frankie enters the kitchen through the hall door.)* Is it all over? *(T. T. crosses to the icebox with sandwiches.)*

FRANKIE: Yes. And it was such a pretty wedding I wanted to cry.

BERENICE: You told them yet?

FRANKIE: About my plans—no, I haven't yet told them.

(John Henry comes in and goes out.)

BERENICE: Well, you better hurry up and do it, for they going to leave the house right after the refreshments.

FRANKIE: Oh, I know it. But something just seems to happen to my throat; every time I tried to tell them, different words came out.

BERENICE: What words?

FRANKIE: I asked Janice how come she didn't marry with a veil. *(with feeling)* Oh, I'm so embarrassed. Here I am all dressed up in this tacky evening dress. Oh, why didn't I listen to you! I'm so ashamed.

(T. T. goes out with a platter of sandwiches.)

BERENICE: Don't take everything so strenuous like.

FRANKIE: I'm going in there and tell them now! *(She goes.)*

JOHN HENRY *(coming out of the interior bedroom, carrying several costumes)*: Frankie sure gave me a lot of presents when she was packing the suitcase. Berenice, she gave me all the beautiful show costumes.

BERENICE: Don't set so much store by all those presents. Come tomorrow morning and she'll be demanding them back again.

JOHN HENRY: And she even gave me the shell from the Bay. *(He puts the shell to his ear and listens.)*

BERENICE: I wonder what's going on up there. *(She goes to the door and opens it and looks through.)*

T. T. *(returning to the kitchen)*: They all complimenting the wedding cake. And drinking the wine punch.

BERENICE: What's Frankie doing? When she left the kitchen a minute ago she was going to tell them. I wonder how they'll take this total surprise. I have a feeling like you get just before a big thunder storm.

(Frankie enters, holding a punch cup.)

BERENICE: You told them yet?

FRANKIE: There are all the family around and I can't seem to tell them. I wish I had written it down on the typewriter beforehand. I try to tell them and the words just—die.

BERENICE: The words just die because the very idea is so silly.

FRANKIE: I love the two of them so much. Janice put her arms around me and said she had always wanted a little sister. And she kissed me. She asked me again what grade I was in in school. That's the third time she's asked me. In fact, that's the main question I've been asked at the wedding.

(John Henry comes in, wearing a fairy costume, and goes out. Berenice notices Frankie's punch and takes it from her.)

FRANKIE: And Jarvis was out in the street seeing about this car he borrowed for the wedding. And I followed him out and tried to tell him. But while I was trying to reach the point, he suddenly grabbed me by the elbows and lifted me up and sort of swung me. He said: "Frankie, the lankie, the alaga fankie, the tee-legged, toe-legged, bow-legged Frankie." And he gave me a dollar bill.

BERENICE: That's nice.

FRANKIE: I just don't know what to do. I have to tell them and yet I don't know how to.

BERENICE: Maybe when they're settled, they will invite you to come and visit with them.

FRANKIE: Oh no! I'm going *with* them.

(Frankie goes back into the house. There are louder sounds of voices from the interior. John Henry comes in again.)

1430 JOHN HENRY: The bride and the groom are leaving. Uncle Royal is taking their suitcases out to the car.

(Frankie runs to the interior room and returns with her suitcase. She kisses Berenice.)

FRANKIE: Good-bye, Berenice. Good-bye, John Henry. *(She stands a moment and looks around the kitchen.)* Farewell, old ugly kitchen. *(She runs out.)*

(There are sounds of good-byes as the wedding party and the family guests move out of the house to the side-walk. The voices get fainter in the distance. Then, from the front sidewalk there is the sound of disturbance. Frankie's voice is heard, diminished by distance, although she is speaking loudly.)

FRANKIE'S VOICE: That's what I am telling you. *(Indistinct protesting voices are heard.)*

MR. ADDAMS' VOICE *(indistinctly)*: Now be reasonable, Frankie.

FRANKIE'S VOICE *(screaming)*: I have to go. Take me! Take me!

JOHN HENRY *(entering excitedly)*: Frankie is in the wedding car and they can't get her out. *(He runs out but soon returns.)* Uncle Royal and my Daddy are having to haul and drag old Frankie. She's holding onto
1440 the steering wheel.

MR. ADDAMS' VOICE: You march right along here. What in the world has come into you? *(He comes into the kitchen with Frankie who is sobbing.)* I never heard of such an exhibition in my life. Berenice, you take charge of her.

(Frankie flings herself on the kitchen chair and sobs with her head in her arms on the kitchen table.)

JOHN HENRY: They put old Frankie out of the wedding. They hauled her out of the wedding car.

MR. ADDAMS *(clearing his throat)*: That's sufficient, John Henry. Leave Frankie alone. *(He puts a caressing hand on Frankie's head.)* What makes you want to leave your old papa like this? You've got Janice
1450 and Jarvis all upset on their wedding day.

FRANKIE: I love them so!

BERENICE *(looking down the hall)*: Here they come. Now please be reasonable, Sugar.

(The bride and groom come in. Frankie keeps her face buried in her arms and does not look up. The bride wears a blue suit with a white flower corsage pinned at the shoulder.)

JARVIS: Frankie, we came to tell you good-bye. I'm sorry you're taking it like this.

JANICE: Darling, when we are settled we want you to come for a nice visit with us. But we don't yet have any place to live. *(She goes to Frankie and caresses her head. Frankie jerks.)* Won't you tell us good-bye now?

1460   FRANKIE *(with passion)*: We! When you say *we*, you only mean you and Jarvis. And I am not included. *(She buries her head in her arms again and sobs.)*

JANICE: Please, darling, don't make us unhappy on our wedding day. You know we love you.

FRANKIE: See! *We*—when you say we, I am not included. It's not fair.

JANICE: When you come visit us you must write beautiful plays, and we'll all act in them. Come, Frankie, don't hide your sweet face from us. Sit up. *(Frankie raises her head slowly and stares with a look of wonder and misery.)* Good-bye, Frankie, darling.

JARVIS: So long, now, kiddo.

(They go out and Frankie still stares at them as they go down the hall. She rises, crosses towards the door and falls on her knees.)

1470   FRANKIE: Take me! Take me!

(Berenice puts Frankie back on her chair.)

JOHN HENRY: They put Frankie out of the wedding. They hauled her out of the wedding car.

BERENICE: Don't tease your cousin, John Henry.

FRANKIE: It was a frame-up all around.

BERENICE: Well, don't bother no more about it. It's over now. Now cheer up.

FRANKIE: I wish the whole world would die.

BERENICE: School will begin now in only three more weeks and you'll find another bosom friend like Evelyn Owen you so wild about.

1480   JOHN HENRY *(seated below the sewing machine)*: I'm sick, Berenice. My head hurts.

BERENICE: No you're not. Be quiet, I don't have the patience to fool with you.

FRANKIE *(hugging her hunched shoulders)*: Oh, my heart feels so cheap!

BERENICE: Soon as you get started in school and have a chance to make these here friends, I think it would be a good idea to have a party.

FRANKIE: Those baby promises rasp on my nerves.

BERENICE: You could call up the society editor of the *Evening Journal* and have the party written up in the paper. And that would make the fourth time your name has been published in the paper.

FRANKIE *(with a trace of interest)*: When my bike ran into that automobile, the paper called me Fankie Addams, F-A-N-K-I-E. *(She puts her head down again.)*

JOHN HENRY: Frankie, don't cry. This evening we can put up the teepee and have a good time.

FRANKIE: Oh, hush up your mouth.

BERENICE: Listen to me. Tell me what you would like and I will try to do it if it is in my power.

FRANKIE: All I wish in the world, is for no human being ever to speak to me as long as I live.

BERENICE: Bawl, then, misery.

(Mr. Addams enters the kitchen, carrying Frankie's suitcase, which he sets in the middle of the kitchen floor. He cracks his finger joints. Frankie stares at him resentfully, then fastens her gaze on the suitcase.)

MR. ADDAMS: Well, it looks like the show is over and the monkey's dead.

FRANKIE: You think it's over, but it's not.

MR. ADDAMS: You want to come down and help me at the store tomorrow? Or polish some silver with the shammy rag? You can even play with those old watch springs.

FRANKIE *(still looking at her suitcase)*: That's my suitcase I packed. If you think it's all over, that only shows how little you know. *(T. T. comes in.)* If I can't go with the bride and my brother as I was meant to leave this town, I'm going anyway. Somehow, anyhow, I'm leaving town. *(Frankie raises up in her chair.)* I can't stand this existence—this kitchen—this town—any longer! I will hop a train and go to New York. Or hitch rides to Hollywood, and get a job there. If worse comes to worse, I can act in comedies. *(She rises.)* Or I could dress up like a boy and join the Merchant Marines and run away to sea. Somehow, anyhow, I'm running away.

BERENICE: Now quiet down—

FRANKIE *(grabbing the suitcase and running into the hall)*: Please, Papa, don't try to capture me.

(Outside the wind starts to blow.)

JOHN HENRY *(from the doorway)*: Uncle Royal, Frankie's got your pistol in her suitcase.

(There is the sound of running footsteps and of the screen door slamming.)

BERENICE: Run catch her.

(T. T. and Mr. Addams rush into the hall, followed by John Henry.)

MR. ADDAMS' VOICE: Frankie! Frankie! Frankie!

(Berenice is left alone in the kitchen. Outside the wind is higher and the hall door is blown shut. There is a rumble of thunder, then a loud clap. Thunder and flashes of lightning continue. Berenice is seated in her chair, when John Henry comes in.)

JOHN HENRY: Uncle Royal is going with my Daddy, and they are chasing her in our car. *(There is a thunder clap.)* The thunder scares me, Berenice.

BERENICE *(taking him in her lap)*: Ain't nothing going to hurt you.

JOHN HENRY: You think they're going to catch her?

BERENICE *(putting her hand to her head)*: Certainly. They'll be bringing her home directly. I've got such a headache. Maybe my eye socket and all these troubles.

1530

JOHN HENRY *(with his arms around Berenice)*: I've got a headache, too. I'm sick, Berenice.

BERENICE: No you ain't. Run along, Candy. I ain't got the patience to fool with you now.

(Suddenly the lights go out in the kitchen, plunging it in gloom. The sound of wind and storm continues and the yard is a dark storm-green.)

JOHN HENRY: Berenice!

BERENICE: Ain't nothing. Just the lights went out.

JOHN HENRY: I'm scared.

BERENICE: Stand still, I'll just light a candle. *(muttering)* I always keep one around, for such like emergencies. *(She opens a drawer.)*

1540

JOHN HENRY: What makes the lights go out so scarey like this?

BERENICE: Just one of them things, Candy.

JOHN HENRY: I'm scared. Where's Honey?

BERENICE: Jesus knows. I'm scared, too. With Honey snow-crazy and loose like this—and Frankie run off with a suitcase and her Papa's pistol. I feel like every nerve been picked out of me.

JOHN HENRY *(holding out his seashell and stroking Berenice)*: You want to listen to the ocean?

(The curtain falls.)

SCENE 2

The scene is the same. There are still signs in the kitchen of the wedding: punch glasses and the punch bowl on the drainboard. It is four o'clock in the morning. As the curtain rises, Berenice and Mr. Addams are alone in the kitchen. There is a crepuscular glow in the yard.

MR. ADDAMS: I never was a believer in corporal punishment. Never spanked Frankie in my life, but when I lay my hands on her . . .

1550

BERENICE: She'll show up soon—but I know how you feel. What with worrying about Honey Camden, John Henry's sickness and Frankie, I've never lived through such a anxious night. *(She looks through the window. It is dawning now.)*

MR. ADDAMS: I'd better go and find out the last news of John Henry, poor baby. *(He goes through the hall door.)*

(Frankie comes into the yard and crosses to the arbor. She looks exhausted and almost beaten. Berenice has seen her from the window, rushes into the yard and grabs her by the shoulders and shakes her.)

BERENICE: Frankie Addams, you ought to be skinned alive. I been so worried.

FRANKIE: I've been so worried too.

BERENICE: Where have you been this night? Tell me everything.

FRANKIE: I will, but quit shaking me.

1560 BERENICE: Now tell me the A and the Z of this.

FRANKIE: When I was running around the dark scary streets, I begun to realize that my plans for Hollywood and the Merchant Marines were child plans that would not work. I hid in the alley behind Papa's store, and it was dark and I was scared. I opened the suitcase and took out Papa's pistol. *(She sits down on her suitcase.)* I vowed I was going to shoot myself. I said I was going to count three and on three pull the trigger. I counted one—two—but I didn't count three— because at the last minute, I changed my mind.

BERENICE: You march right along with me. You going to bed.

1570 FRANKIE: Oh, Honey Camden!

(Honey Camden Brown, who has been hiding behind the arbor, has suddenly appeared.)

BERENICE: Oh, Honey, Honey. *(They embrace.)*

HONEY: Shush, don't make any noise; the law is after me.

BERENICE *(in a whisper)*: Tell me.

HONEY: Mr. Wilson wouldn't serve me so I drew a razor on him.

BERENICE: You kill him?

HONEY: Didn't have no time to find out. I been runnin' all night.

FRANKIE: Lightfoot, if you drew a razor on a white man, you'd better not let them catch you.

BERENICE: Here's six dolla's. If you can get to Fork Falls and then to
1580 Atlanta. But be careful slippin' through the white folks' section. They'll be combing the county looking for you.

HONEY *(with passion)*: Don't cry, Berenice.

BERENICE: Already I feel that rope.

HONEY: Don't you dare cry. I know now all my days have been leading up to this minute. No more "boy this—boy that" —no bowing, no scraping. For the first time, I'm free and it makes me happy. *(He begins to laugh hysterically.)*

BERENICE: When they catch you, they'll string you up.

HONEY *(beside himself, brutally)*: Let them hang me—I don't care. I tell you I'm glad. I tell you I'm happy. *(He goes out behind the arbor.)*

1590 FRANKIE *(calling after him)*: Honey, remember you are Lightfoot. Nothing can stop you if you want to run away.

(Mrs. West, John Henry's mother, comes into the yard.)

MRS. WEST: What was all that racket? John Henry is critically ill. He's got
to have perfect quiet.

FRANKIE: John Henry's sick, Aunt Pet?

MRS. WEST: The doctors say he has meningitis. He must have perfect quiet.

BERENICE: I haven't had time to tell you yet. John Henry took sick sudden
last night. Yesterday afternoon when I complained of my head, he
said he had a headache too and thinking he copies me I said, "Run
along, I don't have the patience to fool with you." Looks like a judgment on me. There won't be no more noise, Mrs. West.

MRS. WEST: Make sure of that. *(She goes away.)*

FRANKIE *(putting her arm around Berenice)*: Oh, Berenice, what can we do?

BERENICE *(stroking Frankie's head)*: Ain't nothing we can do but wait.

FRANKIE: The wedding—Honey—John Henry—so much has happened
that my brain can't hardly gather it in. Now for the first time I realize
that the world is certainly—a sudden place.

BERENICE: Sometimes sudden, but when you are waiting, like this, it
seems so slow.

(The curtain falls.)

SCENE 3

*The scene is the same: the kitchen and arbor. It is months later, a November
day, about sunset.*

*The arbor is brittle and withered. The elm tree is bare except for a few
ragged leaves. The yard is tidy and the lemonade stand and sheet stage curtain are now missing. The kitchen is neat and bare and the furniture has
been removed. Berenice, wearing a fox fur, is sitting in a chair with an old
suitcase and doll at her feet. Frankie enters.*

FRANKIE: Oh, I am just mad about these Old Masters.

BERENICE: Humph!

FRANKIE: The house seems so hollow. Now that the furniture is packed.
It gives me a creepy feeling in the front. That's why I came back
here.

BERENICE: Is that the only reason why you came back here?

FRANKIE: Oh, Berenice, you know. I wish you hadn't given quit notice
just because Papa and I are moving into a new house with Uncle
Eustace and Aunt Pet out in Limewood.

BERENICE: I respect and admire Mrs. West but I'd never get used to
working for her.

FRANKIE: Mary is just beginning this Rachmaninoff Concerto. She may
play it for her debut when she is eighteen years old. Mary playing the
piano and the whole orchestra playing at one and the same time,
mind you. Awfully hard.

BERENICE: Ma-ry Littlejohn.

FRANKIE: I don't know why you always have to speak her name in a tinged voice like that.

BERENICE: Have I ever said anything against her? All I said was that she is too lumpy and marshmallow white and it makes me nervous to see her just setting there sucking them pigtails.

1630 FRANKIE: Braids. Furthermore, it is no use our discussing a certain party. You could never possibly understand it. It's just not in you.

(Berenice looks at her sadly, with faded stillness, then pats and strokes the fox fur.)

BERENICE: Be that as it may. Less us not fuss and quarrel this last afternoon.

FRANKIE: I don't want to fuss either. Anyway, this is not our last afternoon. I will come and see you often.

BERENICE: No, you won't, baby. You'll have other things to do. Your road is already strange to me.

(Frankie goes to Berenice, pats her on the shoulder, then takes her fox fur and examines it.)

FRANKIE: You still have the fox fur that Ludie gave you. Somehow this little fur looks so sad—so thin and with a sad little fox-wise face.

BERENICE *(taking the fur back and continuing to stroke it)*: Got every reason
1640 to be sad. With what has happened in these two last months. I just don't know what I have done to deserve it. *(She sits, the fur in her lap, bent over with her forearms on her knees and her hands limply dangling.)* Honey gone and John Henry, my little boy gone.

FRANKIE: You did all you could. You got poor Honey's body and gave him a Christian funeral and nursed John Henry.

BERENICE: It's the way Honey died and the fact that John Henry had to suffer so. Little soul!

FRANKIE: It's peculiar—the way it all happened so fast. First Honey caught and hanging himself in the jail. Then later in that same week, John Henry died and then I met Mary. As the irony of fate
1650 would have it, we first got to know each other in front of the lipstick and cosmetics counter at Woolworth's. And it was the week of the fair.

BERENICE: The most beautiful September I ever seen. Countless white and yellow butterflies flying around them autumn flowers—Honey dead and John Henry suffering like he did and daisies, golden weather, butterflies—such strange death weather.

FRANKIE: I never believed John Henry would die. *(There is a long pause. She looks out the window.)* Don't it seem quiet to you in here? *(There is another, longer pause.)* When I was a little child I believed that out
1660 under the arbor at night there would come three ghosts and one of the ghosts wore a silver ring. *(whispering)* Occasionally when it gets so quiet like this I have a strange feeling. It's like John Henry is hovering somewhere in this kitchen—solemn looking and ghost-grey.

A BOY'S VOICE *(from the neighboring yard)*: Frankie, Frankie.

FRANKIE *(calling to the boy)*: Yes, Barney. *(to Berenice)* Clock stopped. *(She shakes the clock.)*

THE BOY'S VOICE: Is Mary there?

FRANKIE *(to Berenice)*: It's Barney MacKean. *(to the boy, in a sweet voice)* Not yet. I'm meeting her at five. Come on in, Barney, won't you?

BARNEY: Just a minute.

1670   FRANKIE *(to Berenice)*: Barney puts me in mind of a Greek god.

BERENICE: What? Barney puts you in mind of a what?

FRANKIE: Of a Greek god. Mary remarked that Barney reminded her of a Greek god.

BERENICE: It looks like I can't understand a thing you say no more.

FRANKIE: You know, those old-timey Greeks worship those Greek gods.

BERENICE: But what has that got to do with Barney MacKean?

FRANKIE: On account of the figure.

(Barney MacKean, a boy of thirteen, wearing a football suit, bright sweater and cleated shoes, runs up the back steps into the kitchen.)

BERENICE: Hi, Greek god Barney. This afternoon I saw your initials chalked down on the front sidewalk. M.L. loves B.M.

1680   BARNEY: If I could find out who wrote it, I would rub it out with their faces. Did you do it, Frankie?

FRANKIE *(drawing herself up with sudden dignity)*: I wouldn't do a kid thing like that. I even resent you asking me. *(She repeats the phrase to herself in a pleased undertone.)* Resent you asking me.

BARNEY: Mary can't stand me anyhow.

FRANKIE: Yes she can stand you. I am her most intimate friend. I ought to know. As a matter of fact she's told me several lovely compliments about you. Mary and I are riding on the moving van to our new house. Would you like to go?

1690   BARNEY: Sure.

FRANKIE: O.K. You will have to ride back with the furniture 'cause Mary and I are riding on the front seat with the driver. We had a letter from Jarvis and Janice this afternoon. Jarvis is with the Occupation Forces in Germany and they took a vacation trip to Luxembourg. *(She repeats in a pleased voice:)* Luxembourg. Berenice, don't you think that's a lovely name?

BERENICE: It's kind of a pretty name, but it reminds me of soapy water.

FRANKIE: Mary and I will most likely pass through Luxembourg when we—are going around the world together.

(Frankie goes out followed by Barney and Berenice sits in the kitchen alone and motionless. She picks up the doll, looks at it and hums the first two lines of "I Sing Because I'm Happy." In the next house the piano is heard again, as the curtain falls.)

Questions for Discussion

Act I

1. Identify the time and place in which the play takes place.

2. Frankie says, "I wish I was somebody else except me." Is this statement typical of a girl her age? Explain.

3. Why does Frankie want to belong to the club of older girls? What is her attitude when they select someone else? What does Frankie mean when she says, "I don't want to be the president of all those little young left-over people"?

4. Why does Frankie want to change her name to F. Jasmine?

5. Explain the symbolism of the blues tune that stops in the middle and, in Act 2, the unfinished scales.

6. Explain what Frankie means when she says, "All people belong to a 'we' except me." What does she decide is "the we of me"?

Act 2

1. Why has Frankie wandered all over town telling everyone about the wedding and saying that she is leaving town? Why did the soldier ask her for a date?

2. Throughout the play, Frankie and Berenice discuss various aspects of sex. How does McCullers let us know how much (or how little) Frankie understands about sex?

3. Explain Berenice's statement that she has tried to "marry off little pieces of Lutie" ever since he died. Why will she not marry T. T.?

4. Why, throughout the play, when John Henry says that he is sick, does no one believe him?

Act 3

1. How does McCullers prepare her audience for Frankie's behavior at the wedding and immediately after the wedding?

2. What does Frankie mean when she says, "The world is [. . .] a sudden place"? Contrast this statement with Berenice's opinion that "when you are waiting [. . .] it seems so slow."

3. The last scene takes place several months after the rest of the play. In those few months what dramatic changes have taken place? How has Frankie changed? How is she the same?

Suggestions for Exploration and Writing

1. The three deaths in the play emphasize the fragility of life, yet each one is very different. In an essay, classify and discuss the three types of death in the play.

2. Discuss the way in which McCullers uses music to reinforce the themes of loneliness and incompleteness. How does her inclusion of the song "His Eye Is on the Sparrow" affect these themes?

3. Throughout the play, Frankie seeks a sense of belonging and knowledge of her own identity. Write an essay on Frankie's search for identity and the ways in which she changes as she learns about herself.

4. When Frankie thinks that she will be a member of the wedding, she says that she and the bride and groom will be "members of the whole world." To what extent was that statement true at the time of the play? To what extent is it true now?

Casebook
on Flannery O'Connor

WRITING ABOUT FAITH

The final casebook in this text combines several quests seen in other works in this unit: the quest for religion, the quest for knowledge of oneself, and the quest for ways in which to understand one's relationships with others. Though Flannery O'Connor writes from the point of view of a woman who grew up in the South and of a devout Catholic, the questions her very unusual characters seek to answer are universal. O'Connor's comments in her essay "The Fiction Writer and His Country" will help you to gain insight into her own views about writing, and the essays by literary scholars will help you as you write your own essays about the stories.

Flannery O'Connor (1925–1964)

*Flannery O'Connor was a devout Catholic who, in the short time that she lived, wrote two novels and many short stories that vividly portray the incompleteness of human beings without religion. Except for her graduate study at the University of Iowa, O'Connor spent most of her life in Milledgeville, Georgia, where she observed the people and the land that would become the basis for most of her works. Because her characters are far from ordinary and because their fates are often disastrous, O'Connor is frequently described as a Southern **Gothic** writer. Her characters range from unbelievers, like Mrs. May in "Greenleaf" and the grandmother in "A Good Man Is Hard to Find" who, in spite of their superficiality and self-centeredness, believe themselves to be good Christians, to committed if unorthodox Christians, like Mrs. Greenleaf. O'Connor's stories tell of events that cause arrogant and imperceptive people to see more clearly into reality and to begin their quest for truth.*

A Good Man Is Hard to Find   (1953)

1   The grandmother didn't want to go to Florida. She wanted to visit some of her connections in east Tennessee and she was seizing at every chance to change Bailey's mind. Bailey was the son she lived with, her only boy. He was sitting on the edge of his chair at the table, bent over the orange sports section of the *Journal*. "Now look here, Bailey," she said, "see here, read this," and she stood with one hand on her thin hip and the other rattling the newspaper at his bald head. "Here this fellow that calls himself The Misfit is aloose from the Federal Pen and headed toward Florida and you read here what it says he did to these people. Just you read it. I wouldn't take my children in any direction with a criminal like that aloose in it. I couldn't answer to my conscience if I did."

2   Bailey didn't look up from his reading so she wheeled around then and faced the children's mother, a young woman in slacks, whose face was as broad and innocent as a cabbage and was tied around with a green headkerchief that had two points on the top like rabbit's ears. She was sitting on the sofa, feeding the baby his apricots out of a jar. "The children have been to Florida before," the old lady said. "You all ought to take them somewhere else for a change so they would see different parts of the world and be broad. They never have been to east Tennessee."

3   The children's mother didn't seem to hear her but the eight-year-old boy, John Wesley, a stocky child with glasses, said, "If you don't want to go to Florida, why dontcha stay at home?" He and the little girl, June Star, were reading the funny papers on the floor.

4   "She wouldn't stay at home to be queen for a day," June Star said without raising her yellow head.

5   "Yes and what would you do if this fellow, The Misfit, caught you?" the grandmother said.

6   "I'd smack his face," John Wesley said.

7   "She wouldn't stay at home for a million bucks," June Star said "Afraid she'd miss something. She has to go everywhere we go."

8   "All right, Miss," the grandmother said. "Just remember that the next time you want me to curl your hair."

9   June Star said her hair was naturally curly.

10   The next morning the grandmother was the first one in the car, ready to go. She had her big black valise that looked like the head of a hippopotamus in one corner, and underneath it she was hiding a basket with Pity Sing, the cat, in it. She didn't intend for the cat to be left alone in the house for three days because he would miss her too much and she was afraid he might brush against one of the gas burners and accidentally asphyxiate himself. Her son, Bailey, didn't like to arrive at a motel with a cat.

11   She sat in the middle of the back seat with John Wesley and June Star on either side of her. Bailey and the children's mother and the baby sat in front and they left Atlanta at eight forty-five with the mileage on the

car at 55890. The grandmother wrote this down because she thought it would be interesting to say how many miles they had been when they got back. It took them twenty minutes to reach the outskirts of the city.

12   The old lady settled herself comfortably, removing her white cotton gloves and putting them up with her purse on the shelf in front of the back window. The children's mother still had on slacks and still had her hair tied up in a green kerchief, but the grandmother had on a navy blue straw sailor hat with a bunch of white violets on the brim and a navy blue dress with a small white dot in the print. Her collars and cuffs were white organdy trimmed with lace and at her neckline she had pinned a purple spray of cloth violets containing a sachet. In case of an accident, anyone seeing her dead on the highway would know at once that she was a lady.

13   She said she thought it was going to be a good day for driving, neither too hot nor too cold, and she cautioned Bailey that the speed limit was fifty-five miles an hour and that the patrolmen hid themselves behind billboards and small clumps of trees and sped out after you before you had a chance to slow down. She pointed out interesting details of the scenery: Stone Mountain; the blue granite that in some places came up to both sides of the highway; the brilliant red clay banks slightly streaked with purple; and the various crops that made rows of green lacework on the ground. The trees were full of silver-white sunlight and the meanest of them sparkled. The children were reading comic magazines and their mother had gone back to sleep.

14   "Let's go through Georgia fast so we won't have to look at it much," John Wesley said.

15   "If I were a little boy," said the grandmother, "I wouldn't talk about my native state that way. Tennessee has the mountains and Georgia has the hills."

16   "Tennessee is just a hillbilly dumping ground," John Wesley said, "and Georgia is a lousy state too."

17   "You said it," June Star said.

18   "In my time," said the grandmother, folding her thin veined fingers, "children were more respectful of their native states and their parents and everything else. People did right then. Oh look at the cute little pickaninny!" she said and pointed to a Negro child standing in the door of a shack. "Wouldn't that make a picture, now?" she asked and they all turned and looked at the little Negro out of the back window. He waved.

19   "He didn't have any britches on," June Star said.

20   "He probably didn't have any," the grandmother explained. "Little niggers in the country don't have things like we do. If I could paint, I'd paint that picture," she said.

21   The children exchanged comic books.

22   The grandmother offered to hold the baby and the children's mother passed him over the front seat to her. She set him on her knee and bounced him and told him about the things they were passing. She rolled

her eyes and screwed up her mouth and stuck her leathery thin face into his smooth bland one. Occasionally he gave her a faraway smile. They passed a large cotton field with five or six graves fenced in the middle of it, like a small island. "Look at the graveyard!" the grandmother said, pointing it out. "That was the old family burying ground. That belonged to the plantation."

23   "Where's the plantation?" John Wesley asked.

24   "Gone With the Wind," said the grandmother. "Ha. Ha."

25   When the children finished all the comic books they had brought, they opened the lunch and ate it. The grandmother ate a peanut butter sandwich and an olive and would not let the children throw the box and the paper napkins out the window. When there was nothing else to do they played a game by choosing a cloud and making the other two guess what shape it suggested. John Wesley took one the shape of a cow and June Star guessed a cow and John Wesley said, no, an automobile, and June Star said he didn't play fair, and they began to slap each other over the grandmother.

26   The grandmother said she would tell them a story if they would keep quiet. When she told a story, she rolled her eyes and waved her head and was very dramatic. She said once when she was a maiden lady she had been courted by a Mr. Edgar Atkins Teagarden from Jasper, Georgia. She said he was a very good-looking man and a gentleman and that he brought her a watermelon every Saturday afternoon with his initials cut in it, E. A. T. Well, one Saturday, she said, Mr. Teagarden brought the watermelon and there was nobody at home and he left it on the front porch and returned in his buggy to Jasper, but she never got the watermelon, she said, because a nigger boy ate it when he saw the initials, E. A. T.! This story tickled John Wesley's funny bone and he giggled and giggled but June Star didn't think it was any good. She said she wouldn't marry a man that just brought her a watermelon on Saturday. The grandmother said she would have done well to marry Mr. Teagarden because he was a gentlemen and had bought Coca-Cola stock when it first came out and that he had died only a few years ago, a very wealthy man.

27   They stopped at The Tower for barbecued sandwiches. The Tower was a part stucco and part wood filling station and dance hall set in a clearing outside of Timothy. A fat man named Red Sammy Butts ran it and there were signs stuck here and there on the building and for miles up and down the highway saying, TRY RED SAMMY'S FAMOUS BARBECUE. NONE LIKE FAMOUS RED SAMMY'S! RED SAM! THE FAT BOY WITH THE HAPPY LAUGH. A VETERAN! RED SAMMY'S YOUR MAN!

28   Red Sammy was lying on the bare ground outside The Tower with his head under a truck while a gray monkey about a foot high, chained to a small chinaberry tree, chattered nearby. The monkey sprang back into the tree and got on the highest limb as soon as he saw the children jump out of the car and run toward him.

29   Inside, The Tower was a long dark room with a counter at one end and tables at the other and dancing space in the middle. They all sat down at

a board table next to the nickelodeon and Red Sam's wife, a tall burnt-brown woman with hair and eyes lighter than her skin, came and took their order. The children's mother put a dime in the machine and played "The Tennessee Waltz," and the grandmother said that tune always made her want to dance. She asked Bailey if he would like to dance but he only glared at her. He didn't have a naturally sunny disposition like she did and trips made him nervous. The grandmother's brown eyes were very bright. She swayed her head from side to side and pretended she was dancing in her chair. June Star said play something she could tap to so the children's mother put in another dime and played a fast number and June Star stepped out onto the dance floor and did her tap routine.

30   "Ain't she cute?" Red Sam's wife said, leaning over the counter. "Would you like to come be my little girl?"

31   "No I certainly wouldn't," June Star said. "I wouldn't live in a broken-down place like this for a million bucks!" and she ran back to the table.

32   "Ain't she cute?" the woman repeated, stretching her mouth politely.

33   "Aren't you ashamed?" hissed the grandmother.

34   Red Sam came in and told his wife to quit lounging on the counter and hurry up with these people's order. His khaki trousers reached just to his hip bones and his stomach hung over them like a sack of meal swaying under his shirt. He came over and sat down at a table nearby and let out a combination sigh and yodel. "You can't win," he said. "You can't win," and he wiped his sweating red face off with a gray hand-kerchief. "These days you don't know who to trust," he said. "Ain't that the truth?"

35   "People are certainly not nice like they used to be," said the grandmother.

36   "Two fellers come in here last week," Red Sammy said, "driving a Chrysler. It was a old beat-up car but it was a good one and these boys looked all right to me. Said they worked at the mill and you know I let them fellers charge the gas they bought? Now why did I do that?"

37   "Because you're a good man!" the grandmother said at once.

38   "Yes'm, I suppose so," Red Sam said as if he were struck with this answer.

39   His wife brought the orders, carrying the five plates all at once with-out a tray, two in each hand and one balanced on her arm. "It isn't a soul in this green world of God's that you can trust," she said. "And I don't count nobody out of that, not nobody," she repeated, looking at Red Sammy.

40   "Did you read about that criminal, The Misfit, that's escaped?" asked the grandmother.

41   "I wouldn't be a bit surprised if he didn't attack this place right here," said the woman. "If he hears about it being here, I wouldn't be none sur-prised to see him. If he hears it's two cent in the cash register, I wouldn't be a tall surprised if he . . . "

42   "That'll do," Red Sam said. "Go bring these people their Co'-Colas," and the woman went off to get the rest of the order.

43   "A good man is hard to find," Red Sammy said. "Everything is getting terrible. I remember the day you could go off and leave your screen door unlatched. Not no more."

44   He and the grandmother discussed better times. The old lady said that in her opinion Europe was entirely to blame for the way things were now. She said the way Europe acted you would think we were made of money and Red Sam said it was no use talking about it, she was exactly right. The children ran outside into the white sunlight and looked at the monkey in the lacy chinaberry tree. He was busy catching fleas on himself and biting each one carefully between his teeth as if it were a delicacy.

45   They drove off again into the hot afternoon. The grandmother took cat naps and woke up every five minutes with her own snoring. Outside of Toombsboro she woke up and recalled an old plantation that she had visited in this neighborhood once when she was a young lady. She said the house had six white columns across the front and that there was an avenue of oaks leading up to it and two little wooden trellis arbors on either side in front where you sat down with your suitor after a stroll in the garden. She recalled exactly which road to turn off to get to it. She knew that Bailey would not be willing to lose any time looking at an old house, but the more she talked about it, the more she wanted to see it once again and find out if the little twin arbors were still standing. "There was a secret panel in this house," she said craftily, not telling the truth but wishing that she were, "and the story went that all the family silver was hidden in it when Sherman came through but it was never found . . . "

46   "Hey!" John Wesley said. "Let's go see it! We'll find it! We'll poke all the woodwork and find it! Who lives there? Where do you turn off at? Hey, Pop, can't we turn off there?"

47   "We never have seen a house with a secret panel!" June Star shrieked. "Let's go to the house with the secret panel! Hey Pop, can't we go see the house with the secret panel!"

48   "It's not far from here, I know," the grandmother said. "It wouldn't take over twenty minutes."

49   Bailey was looking straight ahead. His jaw was as rigid as a horseshoe. "No," he said.

50   The children began to yell and scream that they wanted to see the house with the secret panel. John Wesley kicked the back of the front seat and June Star hung over her mother's shoulder and whined desperately into her ear that they never had any fun even on their vacation, that they could never do what THEY wanted to do. The baby began to scream and John Wesley kicked the back of the seat so hard that his father could feel the blows in his kidney.

51   "All right!" he shouted and drew the car to a stop at the side of the road. "Will you all shut up? Will you all just shut up for one second? If you don't shut up, we won't go anywhere."

52   "It would be very educational for them," the grandmother murmured.

53   "All right," Bailey said, "but get this: this is the only time we're going to stop for anything like this. This is the one and only time."

54   "The dirt road that you have to turn down is about a mile back," the grandmother directed. "I marked it when we passed."

55   "A dirt road," Bailey groaned.

56   After they had turned around and were headed toward the dirt road, the grandmother recalled other points about the house, the beautiful glass over the front doorway and the candle-lamp in the hall. John Wesley said that the secret panel was probably in the fireplace.

57   "You can't go inside this house," Bailey said. "You don't know who lives there."

58   "While you all talk to the people in front, I'll run around behind and get in a window," John Wesley suggested.

59   "We'll all stay in the car," his mother said.

60   They turned onto the dirt road and the car raced roughly along in a swirl of pink dust. The grandmother recalled the times when there were no paved roads and thirty miles was a day's journey. The dirt road was hilly and there were sudden washes in it and sharp curves on dangerous embankments. All at once they would be on a hill, looking down over the blue tops of trees for miles around, then the next minute, they would be in a red depression with the dust-coated trees looking down on them.

61   "This place had better turn up in a minute," Bailey said, "or I'm going to turn around."

62   The road looked as if no one had traveled on it for months.

63   "It's not much farther," the grandmother said and just as she said it, a horrible thought came to her. The thought was so embarrassing that she turned red in the face and her eyes dilated and her feet jumped up, upsetting her valise in the corner. The instant the valise moved, the newspaper top she had over the basket under it rose with a snarl and Pity Sing, the cat, sprang onto Bailey's shoulder.

64   The children were thrown to the floor and their mother, catching the baby, was thrown out the door onto the ground; the old lady was thrown into the front seat. The car turned over once and landed right-side-up in a gulch off the side of the road. Bailey remained in the driver's seat with the cat—gray-striped with a broad white face and an orange nose—clinging to his neck like a caterpillar.

65   As soon as the children saw they could move their arms and legs, they scrambled out of the car, shouting, "We've had an ACCIDENT!" The grandmother was curled up under the dashboard, hoping she was injured so that Bailey's wrath would not come down on her all at once. The horrible thought she had had before the accident was that the house she had remembered so vividly was not in Georgia but in Tennessee.

66   Bailey removed the cat from his neck with both hands and flung it out the window against the side of a pine tree. Then he got out of the car and started looking for the children's mother. She was sitting against the side of the red gutted ditch, holding the screaming baby, but she only had a

cut down her face and a broken shoulder. "We've had an ACCIDENT!" the children screamed in a frenzy of delight.

67   "But nobody's killed," June Star said with disappointment as the grandmother limped out of the car, her hat still pinned to her head but the broken front brim standing up at a jaunty angle and the violet spray hanging off the side. They all sat down in the ditch, except the children, to recover from the shock. They were all shaking.

68   "Maybe a car will come along," said the children's mother hoarsely.

69   "I believe I have injured an organ," said the grandmother, pressing her side, but no one answered her. Bailey's teeth were clattering. He had on a yellow sport shirt with bright blue parrots designed in it and his face was as yellow as the shirt. The grandmother decided that she would not mention that the house was in Tennessee.

70   The road was about ten feet above and they could see only the tops of the trees on the other side of it. Behind the ditch they were sitting in there were more woods, tall and dark and deep. In a few minutes they saw a car some distance away on top of a hill, coming slowly as if the occupants were watching them. The grandmother stood up and waved both her arms dramatically to attract their attention. The car continued to come on slowly, disappeared around a bend and appeared again, moving even slower, on top of the hill they had gone over. It was a big black battered hearse-like automobile. There were three men in it.

71   It came to a stop just over them and for some minutes, the driver looked down with a steady expressionless gaze to where they were sitting, and didn't speak. Then he turned his head and muttered something to the other two and they got out. One was a fat boy in black trousers and a red sweat shirt with a silver stallion embossed on the front of it. He moved around on the right side of them and stood staring, his mouth partly open in a kind of loose grin. The other had on khaki pants and a blue striped coat and a gray hat pulled down very low, hiding most of his face. He came around slowly on the left side. Neither spoke.

72   The driver got out of the car and stood by the side of it, looking down at them. He was an older man than the other two. His hair was just beginning to gray and he wore silver-rimmed spectacles that gave him a scholarly look. He had a long creased face and didn't have on any shirt or undershirt. He had on blue jeans that were too tight for him and was holding a black hat and a gun. The two boys also had guns.

73   "We've had an ACCIDENT!" the children screamed.

74   The grandmother had the peculiar feeling that the bespectacled man was someone she knew. His face was as familiar to her as if she had known him all her life but she could not recall who he was. He moved away from the car and began to come down the embankment, placing his feet carefully so that he wouldn't slip. He had on tan and white shoes and no socks, and his ankles were red and thin. "Good afternoon," he said. "I see you all had you a little spill."

75   "We turned over twice!" said the grandmother.

76   "Oncet," he corrected. "We seen it happen. Try their car and see will it run, Hiram," he said quietly to the boy with the gray hat.

77   "What you got that gun for?" John Wesley asked. "Whatcha gonna do with that gun?"

78   "Lady," the man said to the children's mother, "would you mind calling them children to sit down by you? Children make me nervous. I want all you all to sit down right together there where you're at."

79   "What are you telling US what to do for?" June Star asked.

80   Behind them the line of woods gaped like a dark open mouth. "Come here," said their mother.

81   "Look here now," Bailey began suddenly, "we're in a predicament! We're in . . . "

82   The grandmother shrieked. She scrambled to her feet and stood staring. "You're The Misfit!" she said. "I recognized you at once!"

83   "Yes'm," the man said, smiling slightly as if he were pleased in spite of himself to be known, "but it would have been better for all of you, lady, if you hadn't of reckernized me."

84   Bailey turned his head sharply and said something to his mother that shocked even the children. The old lady began to cry and The Misfit reddened.

85   "Lady," he said, "don't you get upset. Sometimes a man says things he don't mean. I don't reckon he meant to talk to you thataway."

86   "You wouldn't shoot a lady, would you?" the grandmother said and removed a clean handkerchief from her cuff and began to slap at her eyes with it.

87   The Misfit pointed the toe of his shoe into the ground and made a little hole and then covered it up again. "I would hate to have to," he said.

88   "Listen," the grandmother almost screamed, "I know you're a good man. You don't look a bit like you have common blood. I know you must come from nice people!"

89   "Yes ma'am," he said, "finest people in the world." When he smiled he showed a row of strong white teeth. "God never made a finer woman than my mother and my daddy's heart was pure gold," he said. The boy with the red sweat shirt had come around behind them and was standing with his gun at his hip. The Misfit squatted down on the ground. "Watch them children, Bobby Lee," he said. "You know they make me nervous." He looked at the six of them huddled together in front of him and he seemed to be embarrassed as if he couldn't think of anything to say. "Ain't a cloud in the sky," he remarked, looking up at it. "Don't see no sun but don't see no cloud neither."

90   "Yes, it's a beautiful day," said the grandmother. "Listen," she said, "you shouldn't call yourself The Misfit because I know you're a good man at heart. I can just look at you and tell."

91   "Hush!" Bailey yelled. "Hush! Everybody shut up and let me handle this!" He was squatting in the position of a runner about to sprint forward but he didn't move.

92   "I pre-chate that, lady," the Misfit said and drew a little circle in the ground with the butt of his gun.

93   "It'll take a half a hour to fix this here car," Hiram called, looking over the raised hood of it.

94   "Well, first you and Bobby Lee get him and that little boy to step over yonder with you," The Misfit said, pointing to Bailey and John Wesley. "The boys want to ast you something," he said to Bailey. "Would you mind stepping back in them woods there with them?"

95   "Listen," Bailey began, "we're in a terrible predicament! Nobody realizes what this is," and his voice cracked. His eyes were as blue and intense as the parrots in his shift and he remained perfectly still.

96   The grandmother reached up to adjust her hat brim as if she were going to the woods with him but it came off in her hand. She stood staring at it and after a second she let it fall on the ground. Hiram pulled Bailey up by the arm as if he were assisting an old man. John Wesley caught hold of his father's hand and Bobby Lee followed. They went off toward the woods and just as they reached the dark edge, Bailey turned and supporting himself against a gray naked pine trunk, he shouted, "I'll be back in a minute, Mamma, wait on me!"

97   "Come back this instant!" his mother shrilled but they all disappeared into the woods.

98   "Bailey Boy!" the grandmother called in a tragic voice but she found she was looking at The Misfit squatting on the ground in front of her. "I just know you're a good man," she said desperately. "You're not a bit common!"

99   "Nome, I ain't a good man," The Misfit said after a second as if he had considered her statement carefully, "but I ain't the worst in the world neither. My daddy said I was a different breed of dog from my brothers and sisters. 'You know,' Daddy said, 'it's some that can live their whole life out without asking about it and it's others has to know why it is, and this boy is one of the latters. He's going to be into everything!'" He put on his black hat and looked up suddenly and then away deep into the woods as if he were embarrassed again. "I'm sorry I don't have on a shirt before you ladies," he said, hunching his shoulders slightly. "We buried our clothes that we had on when we escaped and we're just making do until we can get better. We borrowed these from some folks we met," he explained.

100   "That's perfectly all right," the grandmother said. "Maybe Bailey has an extra shirt in his suitcase."

101   "I'll look and see terrectly," The Misfit said.

102   "Where are they taking him?" the children's mother screamed.

103   "Daddy was a card himself," The Misfit said. "You couldn't put any thing over on him. He never got in trouble with the Authorities though. Just had the knack of handling them."

104   "You could be honest too if you'd only try," said the grandmother. "Think how wonderful it would be to settle down and live a comfortable life and not have to think about somebody chasing you all the time."

105   The Misfit kept scratching in the ground with the butt of his gun as if he were thinking about it. "Yes'm, somebody is always after you," he murmured.

106   The grandmother noticed how thin his shoulder blades were just behind his hat because she was standing up looking down on him. "Do you ever pray?" she asked.

107   He shook his head. All she saw was the black hat wiggle between his shoulder blades. "Nome," he said.

108   There was a pistol shot from the woods, followed closely by another. Then silence. The old lady's head jerked around. She could hear the wind move through the tree tops like a long satisfied insuck of breath. "Bailey Boy!" she called.

109   "I was a gospel singer for a while," The Misfit said. "I been most everything. Been in the arm service, both land and sea, at home and abroad, been twict married, been an undertaker, been with the railroads, plowed Mother Earth, been in a tornado, seen a man burnt alive oncet," and he looked up at the children's mother and the little girl who were sitting close together, their faces white and their eyes glassy; "I even seen a woman flogged," he said.

110   "Pray, pray," the grandmother began, "pray, pray . . . "

111   "I never was a bad boy that I remember of," The Misfit said in an almost dreamy voice, "But somewheres along the line I done something wrong and got sent to the penitentiary. I was buried alive," and he looked up and held her attention to him by a steady stare.

112   "That's when you should have started to pray," she said. "What did you do to get sent up to the penitentiary that first time?"

113   "Turn to the right, it was a wall," The Misfit said, looking up again at the cloudless sky. "Turn to the left, it was a wall. Look up it was a ceiling, look down it was a floor. I forget what I done, lady. I set there and set there, trying to remember what it was I done and I ain't recalled it to this day. Oncet in a while, I would think it was coming to me, but it never come."

114   "Maybe they put you in by mistake," the old lady said vaguely.

115   "Nome," he said. "It wasn't no mistake. They had the papers on me."

116   "You must have stolen something," she said.

117   The Misfit sneered slightly. "Nobody had nothing I wanted," he said. "It was a head-doctor at the penitentiary said what I had done was kill my daddy but I known that for a lie. My daddy died in nineteen ought nineteen of the epidemic flu and I never had a thing to do with it. He was buried in the Mount Hopewell Baptist churchyard and you can go there and see for yourself."

118   "If you would pray," the old lady said, "Jesus would help you."

119   "That's right," The Misfit said.

120   "Well then, why don't you pray?" she asked trembling with delight suddenly.

121   "I don't want no hep," he said. "I'm doing all right by myself."

122   Bobby Lee and Hiram came ambling back from the woods. Bobby Lee was dragging a yellow shirt with bright blue parrots in it.

123 "Thow me that shirt, Bobby Lee," The Misfit said. The shirt came flying at him and landed on his shoulder and he put it on. The grandmother couldn't name what the shirt reminded her of. "No, lady," The Misfit said while he was buttoning it up, "I found out the crime don't matter. You can do one thing or you can do another, kill a man or take a tire off his car, because sooner or later you're going to forget what it was you done and just be punished for it."

124 The children's mother had begun to make heaving noises as if she couldn't get her breath. "Lady," he asked, "would you and that little girl like to step off yonder with Bobby Lee and Hiram and join your husband?"

125 "Yes, thank you," the mother said faintly. Her left arm dangled helplessly and she was holding the baby, who had gone to sleep, in the other. "Hep that lady up, Hiram," The Misfit said as she struggled to climb out of the ditch, "and Bobby Lee, you hold onto that little girl's hand."

126 "I don't want to hold hands with him," June Star said. "He reminds me of a pig."

127 The fat boy blushed and laughed and caught her by the arm and pulled her off into the woods after Hiram and her mother.

128 Alone with The Misfit, the grandmother found that she had lost her voice. There was not a cloud in the sky nor any sun. There was nothing around her but woods. She wanted to tell him that he must pray. She opened and closed her mouth several times before anything came out. Finally she found herself saying, "Jesus, Jesus," meaning, Jesus will help you, but the way she was saying it, it sounded as if she might be cursing.

129 "Yes'm," The Misfit said as if he agreed. "Jesus thown everything off balance. It was the same case with Him as with me except He hadn't committed any crime and they could prove I had committed one because they had the papers on me. Of course," he said, "they never shown me my papers. That's why I sign myself now. I said long ago, you get you a signature and sign everything you do and keep a copy of it. Then you'll know what you done and you can hold up the crime to the punishment and see do they match and in the end you'll have something to prove you ain't been treated right. I call myself The Misfit," he said, "because I can't make what all I done wrong fit what all I gone through in punishment."

130 There was a piercing scream from the woods, followed closely by a pistol report. "Does it seem right to you, lady, that one is punished a heap and another ain't punished at all?"

131 "Jesus!" the old lady cried. "You've got good blood! I know you wouldn't shoot a lady! I know you come from nice people! Pray! Jesus, you ought not to shoot a lady. I'll give you all the money I've got!"

132 "Lady," The Misfit said, looking beyond her far into the woods, "there never was a body that give the undertaker a tip."

133 There were two more pistol reports and the grandmother raised her head like a parched old turkey hen crying for water and called "Bailey Boy, Bailey Boy!" as if her heart would break.

134 "Jesus was the only One that ever raised the dead," The Misfit continued, "and He shouldn't have done it. He thown everything off balance.

If He did what He said, then it's nothing for you to do but thow away everything and follow Him, and if He didn't, then it's nothing for you to do but enjoy the few minutes you got left the best way you can—by killing somebody or burning down his house or doing some other meanness to him. No pleasure but meanness," he said and his voice had become almost a snarl.

135   "Maybe He didn't raise the dead," the old lady mumbled, not knowing what she was saying and feeling so dizzy that she sank down in the ditch with her legs twisted under her.

136   "I wasn't there so I can't say He didn't," The Misfit said. "I wisht I had of been there," he said, hitting the ground with his fist. "It ain't right I wasn't there because if I had of been there I would of known. Listen lady," he said in a high voice, "if I had of been there I would of known and I wouldn't be like I am now." His voice seemed about to crack and the grandmother's head cleared for an instant. She saw the man's face twisted close to her own as if he were going to cry and she murmured, "Why you're one of my babies. You're one of my own children!" she reached out and touched him on the shoulder. The Misfit sprang back as if a snake had bitten him and shot her three times through the chest. Then he put his gun down on the ground and took off his glasses and began to clean them.

137   Hiram and Bobby Lee returned from the woods and stood over the ditch, looking down at the grandmother who half sat and half lay in a puddle of blood with her legs crossed under her like a child's and her face smiling up at the cloudless sky.

138   Without his glasses, The Misfit's eyes were red-rimmed and pale and defenseless-looking. "Take her off and thow her where you thown the others," he said picking up the cat that was rubbing itself against his leg.

139   "She was a talker, wasn't she?" Bobby Lee said, sliding down the ditch with a yodel.

140   "She would of been a good woman," The Misfit said, "if it had been somebody there to shoot her every minute of her life."

141   "Some fun!" Bobby Lee said.

142   "Shut up, Bobby Lee," The Misfit said. "It's no real pleasure in life."

Questions for Discussion

1. How is the end of the story **foreshadowed** in the events that precede it?

2. What is the purpose of the incident at Red Sammy's? What do this incident and the story about Mr. Teagarden reveal about the grandmother?

3. Why does the grandmother tell Red Sammy and the Misfit that they are good men? Does she believe what she says? On what does the grandmother base her moral judgments of people? What does she mean when she says that the Misfit is "not a bit common"?

4. Discuss the **symbolism** of the hearse, the woods, and the sky without a sun.

5. Why does the Misfit call himself by that name? What does he resent about Jesus? He says, "If He did what He said, then it's nothing for you to do but thow away everything and follow Him." Does the Misfit's assessment of Christianity here accord with Jesus's gospel?

6. Why does the grandmother say to the Misfit, "Why you're one of my babies. You're one of my own children"? Why does he kill her when she touches him?

7. Explain the Misfit's statement that the grandmother "would of been a good woman [. . .] if it had been somebody there to shoot her every minute of her life." Explain why you do or do not agree with him.

8. If you knew nothing about his past and had not read the end of the story, how would you judge the Misfit upon meeting him? Does he seem a bloodthirsty killer? How does his treatment of the family compare to the family's treatment of each other? How do you explain the Misfit's murderousness?

GREENLEAF (1956)

1   Mrs. May's bedroom window was low and faced on the east and the bull, silvered in the moonlight, stood under it, his head raised as if he listened—like some patient god come down to woo her—for a stir inside the room. The window was dark and the sound of her breathing too light to be carried outside. Clouds crossing the moon blackened him and in the dark he began to tear at the hedge. Presently they passed and he appeared again in the same spot, chewing steadily, with a hedge-wreath that he had ripped loose for himself caught in the tips of his horns. When the moon drifted into retirement again, there was nothing to mark his place but the sound of steady chewing. Then abruptly a pink glow filled the window. Bars of light slid across him as the venetian blind was slit. He took a step backward and lowered his head as if to show the wreath across his horns.

2   For almost a minute there was no sound from inside, then as he raised his crowned head again, a woman's voice, guttural as if addressed to a dog, said, "Get away from here, Sir!" and in a second muttered, "Some nigger's scrub bull."

3   The animal pawed the ground and Mrs. May, standing bent forward behind the blind, closed it quickly lest the light make him charge into the shrubbery. For a second she waited, still bent forward, her nightgown hanging loosely from her narrow shoulders. Green rubber curlers sprouted neatly over her forehead and her face beneath them was smooth as concrete with an egg-white paste that drew the wrinkles out while she slept.

4   She had been conscious in her sleep of a steady rhythmic chewing as if something were eating one wall of the house. She had been aware that whatever it was had been eating as long as she had had the place and had eaten everything from the beginning of her fence line up to

the house and now was eating the house and calmly with the same steady rhythm would continue through the house, eating her and the boys, and then on, eating everything but the Greenleafs, on and on, eating everything until nothing was left but the Greenleafs on a little island all their own in the middle of what had been her place. When the munching reached her elbow, she jumped up and found herself, fully awake, standing in the middle of her room. She identified the sound at once: a cow was tearing at the shrubbery under her window. Mr. Greenleaf had left the lane gate open and she didn't doubt that the entire herd was on her lawn. She turned on the dim pink table lamp and then went to the window and slit the blind. The bull, gaunt and long-legged, was standing about four feet from her, chewing calmly like an uncouth country suitor.

5   For fifteen years, she thought as she squinted at him fiercely, she had been having shiftless people's hogs root up her oats, their mules wallow on her lawn, their scrub bulls breed her cows. If this one was not put up now, he would be over the fence, ruining her herd before morning—and Mr. Greenleaf was soundly sleeping a half mile down the road in the tenant house. There was no way to get him unless she dressed and got in her car and rode down there and woke him up. He would come but his expression, his whole figure, his every pause, would say: "Hit looks to me like one or both of them boys would not make their maw ride out in the middle of the night thisaway. If hit was my boys, they would have got thet bull up theirself."

6   The bull lowered his head and shook it and the wreath slipped down to the base of his horns where it looked like a menacing prickly crown. She had closed the blind then; in a few seconds she heard him move off heavily.

7   Mr. Greenleaf would say, "If hit was my boys they would never have allowed their maw to go after hired help in the middle of the night. They would have did it theirself."

8   Weighing it, she decided not to bother Mr. Greenleaf. She returned to bed thinking that if the Greenleaf boys had risen in the world it was because she had given their father employment when no one else would have him. She had had Mr. Greenleaf fifteen years but no one else would have had him five minutes. Just the way he approached an object was enough to tell anybody with eyes what kind of a worker he was. He walked with a high-shouldered creep and he never appeared to come directly forward. He walked on the perimeter of some invisible circle and if you wanted to look him in the face, you had to move and get in front of him. She had not fired him because she had always doubted she could do better. He was too shiftless to go out and look for another job; he didn't have the initiative to steal, and after she had told him three or four times to do a thing, he did it; but he never told her about a sick cow until it was too late to call the veterinarian and if her barn had caught on fire, he would have called his wife to see the flames before he began to put them out. And of the wife, she didn't even like to think. Beside the wife, Mr. Greenleaf was an aristocrat.

9   "If it had been my boys," he would have said, "they would have cut off their right arm before they would have allowed their maw to . . . "

10   "If your boys had any pride, Mr. Greenleaf," she would like to say to him some day, "there are many things that they would not *allow* their mother to do."

11   The next morning as soon as Mr. Greenleaf came to the back door, she told him there was a stray bull on the place and that she wanted him penned up at once.

12   "Done already been here three days," he said, addressing his right foot which he held forward, turned slightly as if he were trying to look at the sole. He was standing at the bottom of the three back steps while she leaned out the kitchen door, a small woman with pale near-sighted eyes and grey hair that rose on top like the crest of some disturbed bird.

13   "Three days!" she said in the restrained screech that had become habitual with her.

14   Mr. Greenleaf, looking into the distance over the near pasture, removed a package of cigarets from his shirt pocket and let one fall into his hand. He put the package back and stood for a while looking at the cigaret. "I put him in the bull pen but he torn out of there," he said presently. "I didn't see him none after that." He bent over the cigaret and lit it and then turned his head briefly in her direction. The upper part of his face sloped gradually into the lower which was long and narrow, shaped like a rough chalice. He had deep-set fox-colored eyes shadowed under a grey felt hat that he wore slanted forward following the line of his nose. His build was insignificant.

15   "Mr. Greenleaf," she said, "get that bull up this morning before you do anything else. You know he'll ruin the breeding schedule. Get him up and keep him up and the next time there's a stray bull on this place, tell me at once. Do you understand?"

16   "Where you want him put at?" Mr. Greenleaf asked.

17   "I don't care where you put him," she said. "You are supposed to have some sense. Put him where he can't get out. Whose bull is he?"

18   For a moment Mr. Greenleaf seemed to hesitate between silence and speech. He studied the air to the left of him. "He must be somebody's bull," he said after a while.

19   "Yes, he must!" she said and shut the door with a precise little slam.

20   She went into the dining room where the two boys were eating breakfast and sat down on the edge of her chair at the head of the table. She never ate breakfast but she sat with them to see that they had what they wanted. "Honestly!" she said, and began to tell about the bull, aping Mr. Greenleaf saying, "It must be *somebody's* bull."

21   Wesley continued to read the newspaper folded beside his plate but Scofield interrupted his eating from time to time to look at her and laugh. The two boys never had the same reaction to anything. They were as different, she said, as night and day. The only thing they did have in

common was that neither of them cared what happened on the place. Scofield was a business type and Wesley was an intellectual.

22   Wesley, the younger child, had had rheumatic fever when he was seven and Mrs. May thought that this was what had caused him to be an intellectual. Scofield, who had never had a day's sickness in his life, was an insurance salesman. She would not have minded his selling insurance if he had sold a nicer kind but he sold the kind that only Negroes buy. He was what Negroes call a "policy man." He said there was more money in nigger-insurance than any other kind, and before company, he was very loud about it. He would shout, "Mamma don't like to hear me say it but I'm the best nigger-insurance salesman in this county!"

23   Scofield was thirty-six and he had a broad pleasant smiling face but he was not married. "Yes," Mrs. May would say, "and if you sold decent insurance, some *nice* girl would be willing to marry you. What nice girl wants to marry a nigger-insurance man? You'll wake up some day and it'll be too late."

24   And at this Scofield would yodel and say, "Why Mamma, I'm not going to marry until you're dead and gone and then I'm going to marry me some nice fat farm girl that can take over this place!" And once he had added, "—some nice lady like Mrs. Greenleaf." When he had said this, Mrs. May had risen from her chair, her back stiff as a rake handle, and had gone to her room. There she had sat down on the edge of her bed for some time with her small face drawn. Finally she had whispered, "I work and slave, I struggle and sweat to keep this place for them and soon as I'm dead, they'll marry trash and bring it in here and ruin everything. They'll marry trash and ruin everything I've done," and she had made up her mind at that moment to change her will. The next day she had gone to her lawyer and had had the property entailed so that if they married, they could not leave it to their wives.

25   The idea that one of them might marry a woman even remotely like Mrs. Greenleaf was enough to make her ill. She had put up with Mr. Greenleaf for fifteen years, but the only way she had endured his wife had been by keeping entirely out of her sight. Mrs. Greenleaf was large and loose. The yard around her house looked like a dump and her five girls were always filthy; even the youngest one dipped snuff. Instead of making a garden or washing their clothes, her preoccupation was what she called "prayer healing."

26   Every day she cut all the morbid stories out of the newspaper—the accounts of women who had been raped and criminals who had escaped and children who had been burned and of train wrecks and plane crashes and the divorces of movie stars. She took these to the woods and dug a hole and buried them and then she fell on the ground over them and mumbled and groaned for an hour or so, moving her huge arms back and forth under her and out again and finally just lying down flat and, Mrs. May suspected, going to sleep in the dirt.

27   She had not found out about this until the Greenleafs had been with her a few months. One morning she had been out to inspect a field that she had wanted planted in rye but that had come up in clover because Mr. Greenleaf had used the wrong seeds in the grain drill. She was returning through a wooded path that separated two pastures, muttering to herself and hitting the ground methodically with a long stick she carried in case she saw a snake. "Mr. Greenleaf," she was saying in a low voice, "I cannot afford to pay for your mistakes. I am a poor woman and this place is all I have. I have two boys to educate. I cannot . . . "

28   Out of nowhere a guttural agonized voice groaned, "Jesus! Jesus!" In a second it came again with a terrible urgency. "Jesus! Jesus!"

29   Mrs. May stopped still, one hand lifted to her throat. The sound was so piercing that she felt as if some violent unleashed force had broken out of the ground and was charging toward her. Her second thought was more reasonable: somebody had been hurt on the place and would sue her for everything she had. She had no insurance. She rushed forward and turning a bend in the path, she saw Mrs. Greenleaf sprawled on her hands and knees off the side of the road, her head down.

30   "Mrs. Greenleaf!" she shrilled, "what's happened?"

31   Mrs. Greenleaf raised her head. Her face was a patchwork of dirt and tears and her small eyes, the color of two field peas, were red-rimmed and swollen, but her expression was as composed as a bulldog's. She swayed back and forth on her hands and knees and groaned. "Jesus, Jesus."

32   Mrs. May winced. She thought the word, Jesus, should be kept inside the church building like other words inside the bedroom. She was a good Christian woman with a large respect for religion, though she did not, of course, believe any of it was true. "What is the matter with you?" she asked sharply.

33   "You broken my healing," Mrs. Greenleaf said, waving her aside. "I can't talk to you until I finish."

34   Mrs. May stood, bent forward, her mouth open and her stick raised off the ground as if she were not sure what she wanted to strike with it.

35   "Oh Jesus, stab me in the heart!" Mrs. Greenleaf shrieked. "Jesus, stab me in the heart!" and she fell back flat in the dirt, a huge human mound, her legs and arms spread out as if she were trying to wrap them around the earth.

36   Mrs. May felt as furious and helpless as if she had been insulted by a child. "Jesus," she said, drawing herself back, "would be *ashamed* of you. He would tell you to get up from there this instant and go wash your children's clothes!" and she had turned and walked off as fast as she could.

37   Whenever she thought of how the Greenleaf boys had advanced in the world, she had only to think of Mrs. Greenleaf sprawled obscenely on the ground, and say to herself, "Well, no matter how far they *go,* they *came* from that."

38   She would like to have been able to put in her will that when she died, Wesley and Scofield were not to continue to employ Mr. Greenleaf. She was capable of handling Mr. Greenleaf; they were not. Mr. Greenleaf had

pointed out to her once that her boys didn't know hay from silage. She had pointed out to him that they had other talents, that Scofield was a successful business man and Wesley a successful intellectual. Mr. Greenleaf did not comment, but he never lost an opportunity of letting her see, by his expression or some simple gesture, that he held the two of them in infinite contempt. As scrub-human as the Greenleafs were, he never hesitated to let her know that in any like circumstance in which his own boys might have been involved, they—O. T. and E. T. Greenleaf—would have acted to better advantage.

39   The Greenleaf boys were two or three years younger than the May boys. They were twins and you never knew when you spoke to one of them whether you were speaking to O. T. or E. T., and they never had the politeness to enlighten you. They were long-legged and raw-boned and red-skinned, with bright grasping fox-colored eyes like their father's. Mr. Greenleaf's pride in them began with the fact that they were twins. He acted, Mrs. May said, as if this were something smart they had thought of themselves. They were energetic and hard-working and she would admit to anyone that they had come a long way—and that the Second World War was responsible for it.

40   They had both joined the service and, disguised in their uniforms, they could not be told from other people's children. You could tell, of course, when they opened their mouths but they did that seldom. The smartest thing they had done was to get sent overseas and there to marry French wives. They hadn't married French trash either. They had married nice girls who naturally couldn't tell that they murdered the king's English or that the Greenleafs were who they were.

41   Wesley's heart condition had not permitted him to serve his country but Scofield had been in the army for two years. He had not cared for it and at the end of his military service, he was only a Private First Class. The Greenleaf boys were both some kind of sergeants, and Mr. Greenleaf, in those days, had never lost an opportunity of referring to them by their rank. They had both managed to get wounded and now they both had pensions. Further, as soon as they were released from the army, they took advantage of all the benefits and went to the school of agriculture at the university—the taxpayers meanwhile supporting their French wives. The two of them were living now about two miles down the highway on a piece of land that the government had helped them to buy and in a brick duplex bungalow that the government had helped them to build and pay for. If the war had made anyone, Mrs. May said, it had made the Greenleaf boys. They each had three little children apiece, who spoke Greenleaf English and French, and who, on account of their mothers' background, would be sent to the convent school and brought up with manners. "And in twenty years," Mrs. May asked Scofield and Wesley, "do you know what those people will be?

42   "*Society,*" she said blackly.

43   She had spent fifteen years coping with Mr. Greenleaf and, by now, handling him had become second nature with her. His disposition on any particular day was as much a factor in what she could and couldn't do as

the weather was, and she had learned to read his face the way real country people read the sunrise and sunset.

44   She was a country woman only by persuasion. The late Mr. May, a business man, had bought the place when land was down, and when he died it was all he had to leave her. The boys had not been happy to move to the country to a broken-down farm, but there was nothing else for her to do. She had the timber on the place cut and with the proceeds had set herself up in the dairy business after Mr. Greenleaf had answered her ad. "i seen yor add and i will come have 2 boys," was all his letter said, but he arrived the next day in a pieced-together truck, his wife and five daughters sitting on the floor in back, himself and the two boys in the cab.

45   Over the years they had been on her place, Mr. and Mrs. Greenleaf had aged hardly at all. They had no worries, no responsibilities. They lived like the lilies of the field, off the fat that she struggled to put into the land. When she was dead and gone from overwork and worry, the Greenleafs, healthy and thriving, would be just ready to begin draining Scofield and Wesley.

46   Wesley said the reason Mrs. Greenleaf had not aged was because she released all her emotions in prayer healing. "You ought to start praying, Sweetheart," he had said in the voice that, poor boy, he could not help making deliberately nasty.

47   Scofield only exasperated her beyond endurance but Wesley caused her real anxiety. He was thin and nervous and bald and being an intellectual was a terrible strain on his disposition. She doubted if he would marry until she died but she was certain that then the wrong woman would get him. Nice girls didn't like Scofield but Wesley didn't like nice girls. He didn't like anything. He drove twenty miles every day to the university where he taught and twenty miles back every night, but he said he hated the twenty-mile drive and he hated the second-rate university and he hated the morons who attended it. He hated the country and he hated the life he lived; he hated living with his mother and his idiot brother and he hated hearing about the damn dairy and the damn help and the damn broken machinery. But in spite of all he said, he never made any move to leave. He talked about Paris and Rome but he never went even to Atlanta.

48   "You'd go to those places and you'd get sick," Mrs. May would say. "Who in Paris is going to see that you get a salt-free diet? And do you think if you married one of those odd numbers you take out that *she* would cook a salt-free diet for you? No indeed, she would not!" When she took this line, Wesley would turn himself roughly around in his chair and ignore her. Once when she had kept it up too long, he had snarled, "Well, why don't you do something practical, Woman? Why don't you pray for me like Mrs. Greenleaf would?"

49   "I don't like to hear you boys make jokes about religion," she had said. "If you would go to church, you would meet some nice girls."

50   But it was impossible to tell them anything. When she looked at the two of them now, sitting on either side of the table, neither one caring the least if a stray bull ruined her herd—which was their herd, their future—when she looked at the two of them, one hunched over a paper

and the other teetering back in his chair, grinning at her like an idiot, she wanted to jump up and beat her fist on the table and shout, "You'll find out one of these days, you'll find out what *Reality* is when it's too late!"

51   "Mamma," Scofield said, "don't you get excited now but I'll tell you whose bull that is." He was looking at her wickedly. He let his chair drop forward and he got up. Then with his shoulders bent and his hands held up to cover his head, he tiptoed to the door. He backed into the hall and pulled the door almost to so that it hid all of him but his face. "You want to know, Sugarpie?" he asked.

52   Mrs. May sat looking at him coldly.

53   "That's O. T. and E. T.'s bull," he said. "I collected from their nigger yesterday and he told me they were missing it," and he showed her an exaggerated expanse of teeth and disappeared silently.

54   Wesley looked up and laughed.

55   Mrs. May turned her head forward again, her expression unaltered. "I am the only *adult* on this place," she said. She leaned across the table and pulled the paper from the side of his plate. "Do you see how it's going to be when I die and you boys have to handle him?" she began. "Do you see why he didn't know whose bull that was? Because it was theirs. Do you see what I have to put up with? Do you see that if I hadn't kept my foot on his neck all these years, you boys might be milking cows every morning at four o'clock?"

56   Wesley pulled the paper back toward his plate and staring at her full in the face, he murmured, "I wouldn't milk a cow to save your soul from hell."

57   "I know you wouldn't," she said in a brittle voice. She sat back and began rapidly turning her knife over at the side of her plate. "O. T. and E. T. are fine boys," she said. "They ought to have been my sons." The thought of this was so horrible that her vision of Wesley was blurred at once by a wall of tears. All she saw was his dark shape, rising quickly from the table. "And you two," she cried, "you two should have belonged to that woman!"

58   He was heading for the door.

59   "When I die," she said in a thin voice, "I don't know what's going to become of you."

60   "You're always yapping about when-you-die," he growled as he rushed out, "but you look pretty healthy to me."

61   For some time she sat where she was, looking straight ahead through the window across the room into a scene of indistinct greys and greens. She stretched her face and her neck muscles and drew in a long breath but the scene in front of her flowed together anyway into a watery grey mass. "They needn't think I'm going to die any time soon," she muttered, and some more defiant voice in her added: I'll die when I get good and ready.

62   She wiped her eyes with the table napkin and got up and went to the window and gazed at the scene in front of her. The cows were grazing on two pale green pastures across the road and behind them, fencing them in, was a black wall of trees with a sharp sawtooth edge that held off the indifferent sky. The pastures were enough to calm her. When she looked

out any window in her house, she saw the reflection of her own character. Her city friends said she was the most remarkable woman they knew, to go, practically penniless and with no experience, out to a rundown farm and make a success of it. "Everything is against you," she would say, "the weather is against you and the dirt is against you and the help is against you. They're all in league against you. There's nothing for it but an iron hand!"

63   "Look at Mamma's iron hand!" Scofield would yell and grab her arm and hold it up so that her delicate blue-veined little hand would dangle from her wrist like the head of a broken lily. The company always laughed.

64   The sun, moving over the black and white grazing cows, was just a little brighter than the rest of the sky. Looking down, she saw a darker shape that might have been its shadow cast at an angle, moving among them. She uttered a sharp cry and turned and marched out of the house.

65   Mr. Greenleaf was in the trench silo, filling a wheelbarrow. She stood on the edge and looked down at him. "I told you to get up that bull. Now he's in with the milk herd."

66   "You can't do two thangs at oncet," Mr. Greenleaf remarked.

67   "I told you to do that first."

68   He wheeled the barrow out of the open end of the trench toward the barn and she followed close behind him. "And you needn't think, Mr. Greenleaf," she said, "that I don't know exactly whose bull that is or why you haven't been in any hurry to notify me he was here. I might as well feed O. T. and E. T.'s bull as long as I'm going to have him here ruining my herd."

69   Mr. Greenleaf paused with the wheelbarrow and looked behind him. "Is that them boys' bull?" he asked in an incredulous tone.

70   She did not say a word. She merely looked away with her mouth taut.

71   "They told me their bull was out but I never known that was him," he said.

72   "I want that bull put up now," she said, "and I'm going to drive over to O. T. and E. T.'s and tell them they'll have to come get him today. I ought to charge for the time he's been here—then it wouldn't happen again."

73   "They didn't pay but seventy-five dollars for him," Mr. Greenleaf offered.

74   "I wouldn't have had him as a gift," she said.

75   "They was just going to beef him," Mr. Greenleaf went on, "but he got loose and run his head into their pickup truck. He don't like cars and trucks. They had a time getting his horn out the fender and when they finally got him loose, he took off and they was too tired to run after him—but I never known that was him there."

76   "It wouldn't have paid you to know, Mr. Greenleaf," she said. "But you know now. Get a horse and get him."

77   In a half hour, from her front window she saw the bull, squirrel-colored, with jutting hips and long light horns, ambling down the dirt road that ran in front of the house. Mr. Greenleaf was behind him on the horse. "That's a Greenleaf bull if I ever saw one," she muttered. She went out on the porch and called, "Put him where he can't get out."

78   "He likes to bust loose," Mr. Greenleaf said, looking with approval at the bull's rump. "This gentleman is a sport."

79   "If those boys don't come for him, he's going to be a dead sport," she said. "I'm just warning you."

80   He heard her but he didn't answer.

81   "That's the awfullest looking bull I ever saw," she called but he was too far down the road to hear.

82   It was mid-morning when she turned into O. T. and E. T.'s driveway. The house, a new red-brick, low-to-the-ground building that looked like a warehouse with windows, was on top of a treeless hill. The sun was beating down directly on the white roof of it. It was the kind of house that everybody built now and nothing marked it as belonging to the Greenleafs except three dogs, part hound and part spitz, that rushed out from behind it as soon as she stopped her car. She reminded herself that you could always tell the class of people by the class of dog, and honked her horn. While she sat waiting for someone to come, she continued to study the house. All the windows were down and she wondered if the government could have air-conditioned the thing. No one came and she honked again. Presently a door opened and several children appeared in it and stood looking at her, making no move to come forward. She recognized this as a true Greenleaf trait—they could hang in a door, looking at you for hours.

83   "Can't one of you children come here?" she called.

84   After a minute they all began to move forward, slowly. They had on overalls and were barefooted but they were not as dirty as she might have expected. There were two or three that looked distinctly like Greenleafs; the others not so much so. The smallest child was a girl with untidy black hair. They stopped about six feet from the automobile and stood looking at her.

85   "You're mighty pretty," Mrs. May said, addressing herself to the smallest girl.

86   There was no answer. They appeared to share one dispassionate expression between them.

87   "Where's your Mamma?" she asked.

88   There was no answer to this for some time. Then one of them said something in French. Mrs. May did not speak French.

89   "Where's your daddy?" she asked.

90   After a while, one of the boys said, "He ain't hyar neither."

91   "Ahhhh," Mrs. May said as if something had been proven. "Where's the colored man?"

92   She waited and decided no one was going to answer. "The cat has six little tongues," she said. "How would you like to come home with me and let me teach you how to talk?" She laughed and her laugh died on the silent air. She felt as if she were on trial for her life, facing a jury of Greenleafs. "I'll go down and see if I can find the colored man," she said.

93   "You can go if you want to," one of the boys said.

94   "Well, thank you," she murmured and drove off.

95   The barn was down the lane from the house. She had not seen it before but Mr. Greenleaf had described it in detail for it had been built according to the latest specifications. It was a milking parlor arrangement where the cows are milked from below. The milk ran in pipes from the machines to the milk house and was never carried in no bucket, Mr. Greenleaf said, by no human hand. "When you gonter get you one?" he had asked.

96   "Mr. Greenleaf," she had said, "I have to do for myself. I am not assisted hand and foot by the government. It would cost me $20,000 to install a milking parlor. I barely make ends meet as it is."

97   "My boys done it," Mr. Greenleaf had murmured, and then—"but all boys ain't alike."

98   "No indeed!" she had said. "I thank God for that!"

99   "I thank Gawd for ever-thang," Mr. Greenleaf had drawled.

100   You might as well, she had thought in the fierce silence that followed; you've never done anything for yourself.

101   She stopped by the side of the barn and honked but no one appeared. For several minutes she sat in the car, observing the various machines parked around, wondering how many of them were paid for. They had a forage harvester and a rotary hay baler. She had those too. She decided that since no one was here, she would get out and have a look at the milking parlor and see if they kept it clean.

102   She opened the milking room door and stuck her head in and for the first second she felt as if she were going to lose her breath. The spotless white concrete room was filled with sunlight that came from a row of windows head-high along both walls. The metal stanchions gleamed ferociously and she had to squint to be able to look at all. She drew her head out the room quickly and closed the door and leaned against it, frowning. The light outside was not so bright but she was conscious that the sun was directly on top of her head, like a silver bullet ready to drop into her brain.

103   A Negro carrying a yellow calf-feed bucket appeared from around the corner of the machine shed and came toward her. He was a light yellow boy dressed in the cast-off army clothes of the Greenleaf twins. He stopped at a respectable distance and set the bucket on the ground.

104   "Where's Mr. O. T. and Mr. E. T.?" she asked.

105   "Mist O. T. he in town, Mist E. T. he off yonder in the field," the Negro said, pointing first to the left and then to the right as if he were naming the position of two planets.

106   "Can you remember a message?" she asked, looking as if she thought this doubtful.

107   "I'll remember it if I don't forget it," he said with a touch of sullenness.

108   "Well, I'll write it down then," she said. She got in her car and took a stub of pencil from her pocket book and began to write on the back of an empty envelope. The Negro came and stood at the window. "I'm Mrs. May," she said as she wrote. "Their bull is on my place and I want him off *today*. You can tell them I'm furious about it."

109   "That bull lef here Sareday," the Negro said, "and none of us ain't seen him since. We ain't knowed where he was."

110   "Well, you know now," she said, "and you can tell Mr. O. T. and Mr. E. T. that if they don't come get him today, I'm going to have their daddy shoot him the first thing in the morning. I can't have that bull ruining my herd." She handed him the note.

111   "If I knows Mist O. T. and Mist E. T.," he said, taking it, "they goin to say you go ahead on and shoot him. He done busted up one of our trucks already and we be glad to see the last of him."

112   She pulled her head back and gave him a look from slightly bleared eyes. "Do they expect me to take my time and my worker to shoot their bull?" she asked. "They don't want him so they just let him loose and expect somebody else to kill him? He's eating my oats and ruining my herd and I'm expected to shoot him too?"

113   "I speck you is," he said softly. "He done busted up . . ."

114   She gave him a very sharp look and said, "Well, I'm not surprised. That's just the way some people are," and after a second she asked, "Which is boss, Mr. O. T. or Mr. E. T.?" She had always suspected that they fought between themselves secretly.

115   "They never quarls," the boy said. "They like one man in two skins."

116   "Hmp. I expect you just never heard them quarrel."

117   "Nor nobody else heard them neither," he said, looking away as if this insolence were addressed to some one else.

118   "Well," she said, "I haven't put up with their father for fifteen years not to know a few things about Greenleafs."

119   The Negro looked at her suddenly with a gleam of recognition. "Is you my policy man's mother?" he asked.

120   "I don't know who your policy man is," she said sharply. "You give them that note and tell them if they don't come for that bull today, they'll be making their father shoot it tomorrow," and she drove off.

121   She stayed at home all afternoon waiting for the Greenleaf twins to come for the bull. They did not come. I might as well be working for them, she thought furiously. They are simply going to use me to the limit. At the supper table, she went over it again for the boys' benefit because she wanted them to see exactly what O. T. and E. T. would do. "They don't want that bull," she said, "—pass the butter—so they simply turn him loose and let somebody else worry about getting rid of him for them. How do you like that? I'm the victim. I've always been the victim."

122   "Pass the butter to the victim," Wesley said. He was in a worse humor than usual because he had had a flat tire on the way home from the university.

123   Scofield handed her the butter and said, "Why Mamma, ain't you ashamed to shoot an old bull that ain't done nothing but give you a little scrub strain in your herd? I declare," he said, "with the Mamma I got it's a wonder I turned out to be such a nice boy!"

124   "You ain't her boy, Son," Wesley said.

125   She eased back in her chair, her fingertips on the edge of the table.

126   "All I know is," Scofield said, "I done mighty well to be as nice as I am seeing what I come from."

127   When they teased her they spoke Greenleaf English but Wesley made his own particular tone come through it like a knife edge. "Well lemme tell you one thang, Brother," he said, leaning over the table, "that if you had half a mind you would already know."

128   "What's that, Brother?" Scofield asked, his broad face grinning into the thin constricted one across from him.

129   "That is," Wesley said, "that neither you nor me is her boy . . . ," but he stopped abruptly as she gave a kind of hoarse wheeze like an old horse lashed unexpectedly. She reared up and ran from the room.

130   "Oh, for God's sake," Wesley growled. "What did you start her off for?"

131   "I never started her off," Scofield said. "You started her off."

132   "Hah."

133   "She's not as young as she used to be and she can't take it."

134   "She can only give it out," Wesley said. "I'm the one that takes it."

135   His brother's pleasant face had changed so that an ugly family resemblance showed between them. "Nobody feels sorry for a lousy bastard like you," he said and grabbed across the table for the other's shirtfront.

136   From her room she heard a crash of dishes and she rushed back through the kitchen into the dining room. The hall door was open and Scofield was going out of it. Wesley was lying like a large bug on his back with the edge of the over-turned table cutting him across the middle and broken dishes scattered on top of him. She pulled the table off him and caught his arm to help him rise but he scrambled up and pushed her off with a furious charge of energy and flung himself out of the door after his brother.

137   She would have collapsed but a knock on the back door stiffened her and she swung around. Across the kitchen and back porch, she could see Mr. Greenleaf peering eagerly through the screenwire. All her resources returned in full strength as if she had only needed to be challenged by the devil himself to regain them. "I heard a thump," he called, "and I thought the plastering might have fell on you."

138   If he had been wanted someone would have had to go on a horse to find him. She crossed the kitchen and the porch and stood inside the screen and said, "No, nothing happened but the table turned over. One of the legs was weak," and without pausing, "the boys didn't come for the bull so tomorrow you'll have to shoot him."

139   The sky was crossed with thin red and purple bars and behind them the sun was moving down slowly as if it were descending a ladder. Mr. Greenleaf squatted down on the step, his back to her, the top of his hat on a level with her feet. "Tomorrow I'll drive him home for you," he said.

140   "Oh no, Mr. Greenleaf," she said in a mocking voice, "you drive him home tomorrow and next week he'll be back here. I know better than that." Then in a mournful tone, she said, "I'm surprised at O. T. and E. T. to treat me this way. I thought they'd have more gratitude. Those boys spent some mighty happy days on this place, didn't they, Mr. Greenleaf?"

141   Mr. Greenleaf didn't say anything.

142   "I think they did," she said. "I think they did. But they've forgotten all the nice little things I did for them now. If I recall, they wore my

boys' old clothes and played with my boys' old toys and hunted with my boys' old guns. They swam in my pond and shot my birds and fished in my stream and I never forgot their birthday and Christmas seemed to roll around very often if I remember it right. And do they think of any of those things now?" she asked. "NOOOOO," she said.

143   For a few seconds she looked at the disappearing sun and Mr. Greenleaf examined the palms of his hands. Presently as if it had just occurred to her, she asked, "Do you know the real reason they didn't come for that bull?"

144   "Naw I don't," Mr. Greenleaf said in a surly voice.

145   "They didn't come because I'm a woman," she said. "You can get away with anything when you're dealing with a woman. If there were a man running this place . . . "

146   Quick as a snake striking Mr. Greenleaf said, "You got two boys. They know you got two men on the place."

147   The sun had disappeared behind the tree line. She looked down at the dark crafty face, upturned now, and at the wary eyes, bright under the shadow of the hatbrim. She waited long enough for him to see that she was hurt and then she said, "Some people learn gratitude too late, Mr. Greenleaf, and some never learn it at all," and she turned and left him sitting on the steps.

148   Half the night in her sleep she heard a sound as if some large stone were grinding a hole on the outside wall of her brain. She was walking on the inside, over a succession of beautiful rolling hills, planting her stick in front of each step. She became aware after a time that the noise was the sun trying to burn through the tree line and she stopped to watch, safe in the knowledge that it couldn't, that it had to sink the way it always did outside of her property. When she first stopped it was a swollen red ball, but as she stood watching it began to narrow and pale until it looked like a bullet. Then suddenly it burst through the tree line and raced down the hill toward her. She woke up with her hand over her mouth and the same noise, diminished but distinct, in her ear. It was the bull munching under her window. Mr. Greenleaf had let him out.

149   She got up and made her way to the window in the dark and looked out through the slit blind, but the bull had moved away from the hedge and at first she didn't see him. Then she saw a heavy form some distance away, paused as if observing her. This is the last night I am going to put up with this, she said, and watched until the iron shadow moved away in the darkness.

150   The next morning she waited until exactly eleven o'clock. Then she got in her car and drove to the barn. Mr. Greenleaf was cleaning milk cans. He had seven of them standing up outside the milk room to get the sun. She had been telling him to do this for two weeks. "All right, Mr. Greenleaf," she said, "go get your gun. We're going to shoot that bull."

151   "I thought you wanted theseyer cans . . . "

152   "Go get your gun, Mr. Greenleaf," she said. Her voice and face were expressionless.

153   "That gentleman torn out of there last night," he murmured in a tone of regret and bent again to the can he had his arm in.

154   "Go get your gun, Mr. Greenleaf," she said in the same triumphant toneless voice. "The bull is in the pasture with the dry cows. I saw him from my upstairs window. I'm going to drive you up to the field and you can run him into the empty pasture and shoot him there."

155   He detached himself from the can slowly. "Ain't nobody ever ast me to shoot my boys' own bull!" he said in a high rasping voice. He removed a rag from his back pocket and began to wipe his hands violently, then his nose.

156   She turned as if she had not heard this and said, "I'll wait for you in the car. Go get your gun."

157   She sat in the car and watched him stalk off toward the harness room where he kept a gun. After he had entered the room, there was a crash as if he had kicked something out of his way. Presently he emerged again with the gun, circled behind the car, opened the door violently and threw himself onto the seat beside her. He held the gun between his knees and looked straight ahead. He'd like to shoot me instead of the bull, she thought, and turned her face away so that he could not see her smile.

158   The morning was dry and clear. She drove through the woods for a quarter of a mile and then out into the open where there were fields on either side of the narrow road. The exhilaration of carrying her point had sharpened her senses. Birds were screaming everywhere, the grass was almost too bright to look at, the sky was an even piercing blue. "Spring is here!" she said gaily. Mr. Greenleaf lifted one muscle somewhere near his mouth as if he found this the most asinine remark ever made. When she stopped at the second pasture gate, he flung himself out of the car door and slammed it behind him. Then he opened the gate and she drove through. He closed it and flung himself back in, silently, and she drove around the rim of the pasture until she spotted the bull, almost in the center of it, grazing peacefully among the cows.

159   "The gentleman is waiting on you," she said and gave Mr. Greenleaf's furious profile a sly look. "Run him into that next pasture and when you get him in, I'll drive in behind you and shut the gate myself."

160   He flung himself out again, this time deliberately leaving the car door open so that she had to lean across the seat and close it. She sat smiling as she watched him make his way across the pasture toward the opposite gate. He seemed to throw himself forward at each step and then pull back as if he were calling on some power to witness that he was being forced. "Well," she said aloud as if he were still in the car, "it's your own boys who are making you do this, Mr. Greenleaf." O. T. and E. T. were probably splitting their sides laughing at him now. She could hear their identical nasal voices saying, "Made Daddy shoot our bull for us. Daddy don't know no better than to think that's a fine bull he's shooting. Gonna kill Daddy to shoot that bull!"

161   "If those boys cared a thing about you, Mr. Greenleaf," she said, "they would have come for that bull. I'm surprised at them."

162   He was circling around to open the gate first. The bull, dark among the spotted cows, had not moved. He kept his head down, eating constantly. Mr. Greenleaf opened the gate and then began circling back to approach him from the rear. When he was about ten feet behind him, he flapped his arms at his sides. The bull lifted his head indolently and then lowered it again and continued to eat. Mr. Greenleaf stooped again and picked up something and threw it at him with a vicious swing. She decided it was a sharp rock for the bull leapt and then began to gallop until he disappeared over the rim of the hill. Mr. Greenleaf followed at his leisure.

163   "You needn't think you're going to lose him!" she cried and started the car straight across the pasture. She had to drive slowly over the terraces and when she reached the gate, Mr. Greenleaf and the bull were nowhere in sight. This pasture was smaller than the last, a green arena, encircled almost entirely by woods. She got out and closed the gate and stood looking for some sign of Mr. Greenleaf but he had disappeared completely. She knew at once that his plan was to lose the bull in the woods. Eventually, she would see him emerge somewhere from the circle of trees and come limping toward her and when he finally reached her, he would say, "If you can find that gentleman in them woods, you're better than me."

164   She was going to say, "Mr. Greenleaf, if I have to walk into those woods with you and stay all afternoon, we are going to find that bull and shoot him. You are going to shoot him if I have to pull the trigger for you." When he saw she meant business he would return and shoot the bull quickly himself.

165   She got back into the car and drove to the center of the pasture where he would not have so far to walk to reach her when he came out of the woods. At this moment she could picture him sitting on a stump, marking lines in the ground with a stick. She decided she would wait exactly ten minutes by her watch. Then she would begin to honk. She got out of the car and walked around a little and then sat down on the front bumper to wait and rest. She was very tired and she lay her head back against the hood and closed her eyes. She did not understand why she should be so tired when it was only mid-morning. Through her closed eyes, she could feel the sun, red-hot overhead. She opened her eyes slightly but the white light forced her to close them again.

166   For some time she lay back against the hood, wondering drowsily why she was so tired. With her eyes closed, she didn't think of time as divided into days and nights but into past and future. She decided she was tired because she had been working continuously for fifteen years. She decided she had every right to be tired, and to rest for a few minutes before she began working again. Before any kind of judgement seat, she would be able to say: I've worked, I have not wallowed. At this very instant while she was recalling a life-time of work, Mr. Greenleaf was loitering in the woods and Mrs. Greenleaf was probably flat on the ground, asleep over her holeful of clippings. The woman had got worse over the years and Mrs. May

believed that now she was actually demented. "I'm afraid your wife has let religion warp her," she said once tactfully to Mr. Greenleaf. "Everything in moderation, you know."

167   "She cured a man once that half his gut was eat out with worms," Mr. Greenleaf said, and she had turned away, half-sickened. Poor souls, she thought now, so simple. For a few seconds she dozed.

168   When she sat up and looked at her watch, more than ten minutes had passed. She had not heard any shot. A new thought occurred to her: suppose Mr. Greenleaf had aroused the bull chunking stones at him and the animal had turned on him and run him up against a tree and gored him? The irony of it deepened: O. T. and E. T. would then get a shyster lawyer and sue her. It would be the fitting end to her fifteen years with the Greenleafs. She thought of it almost with pleasure as if she had hit on the perfect ending for a story she was telling her friends. Then she dropped it, for Mr. Greenleaf had a gun with him and she had no insurance.

169   She decided to honk. She got up and reached inside the car window and gave three sustained honks and two or three shorter ones to let him know she was getting impatient. Then she went back and sat down on the bumper again.

170   In a few minutes something emerged from the tree line, a black heavy shadow that tossed its head several times and then bounded forward. After a second she saw it was the bull. He was crossing the pasture toward her at a slow gallop, a gay almost rocking gait as if he were overjoyed to find her again. She looked beyond him to see if Mr. Greenleaf was coming out of the woods too but he was not. "Here he is, Mr. Greenleaf!" she called and looked on the other side of the pasture to see if he could be coming out there but he was not in sight. She looked back and saw that the bull, his head lowered, was racing toward her. She remained perfectly still, not in fright, but in a freezing unbelief. She stared at the violent black streak bounding toward her as if she had no sense of distance, as if she could not decide at once what his intention was, and the bull had buried his head in her lap, like a wild tormented lover, before her expression changed. One of his horns sank until it pierced her heart and the other curved around her side and held her in an unbreakable grip. She continued to stare straight ahead but the entire scene in front of her had changed—the tree line was a dark wound in a world that was nothing but sky—and she had the look of a person whose sight has been suddenly restored but who finds the light unbearable.

171   Mr. Greenleaf was running toward her from the side with his gun raised and she saw him coming though she was not looking in his direction. She saw him approaching on the outside of some invisible circle, the tree line gaping behind him and nothing under his feet. He shot the bull four times through the eye. She did not hear the shots but she felt the quake in the huge body as it sank, pulling her forward on its head, so that she seemed, when Mr. Greenleaf reached her, to be bent over whispering some last discovery into the animal's ear.

Questions for Discussion

1. What does Mrs. May's comment about Mr. Greenleaf that "he didn't have the initiative to steal" reveal about her?

2. Who does Mrs. May feel is responsible for any success the Greenleaf boys have had? Why?

3. Why does Mrs. May get so angry and frustrated at Mr. Greenleaf? Why can she not stand Mrs. Greenleaf?

4. What does Mrs. May mean when she refers to the Greenleafs as "scrub-humans"?

5. In the confrontations between Mrs. May and Mr. Greenleaf, who wins? How?

6. Describe the relationship between Mrs. May and her sons. Why do they not appreciate her financial support and advice?

7. Mrs. May says to Mrs. Greenleaf: "Jesus . . . would be ashamed of you. He would tell you to get up from there this instant and go wash your children's clothes!" How do you suppose Jesus would have responded to Mrs. Greenleaf? to Mrs. May? On what do you base your answer?

8. How does Mrs. Greenleaf's prayer to Jesus as she lies on the ground foreshadow the end of the story?

9. The narrator says of Mrs. May, "She felt as if she were on trial for her life, facing a jury of Greenleafs." How does this observation define Mrs. May's relationship to the Greenleafs?

10. Mrs. May says of religion, "Everything in moderation." Would O'Connor agree? Do you agree?

11. When the bull gores Mrs. May, the narrator says, "she had the look of a person whose sight has been suddenly restored but who finds the light unbearable." Explain this passage.

THE FICTION WRITER AND HIS COUNTRY   (1957)

1 [. . .] I am no disbeliever in spiritual purpose and no vague believer. I see from the standpoint of Christian orthodoxy. This means that for me the meaning of life is centered in our Redemption by Christ and what I see in the world I see in its relation to that. I don't think that this is a position that can be taken halfway or one that is particularly easy in these times to make transparent in fiction.

2   Some may blame preoccupation with the grotesque on the fact that here we have a Southern writer and that this is just the type of imagination that Southern life fosters. I have written several stories which did not seem to me to have any grotesque characters in them at all, but which have immediately been labeled grotesque by non-Southern readers. I find it hard to believe that what is observable behavior in one section can be entirely without parallel in another. At least, of late,

Southern writers have had the opportunity of pointing out that none of us invented Elvis Presley and that that youth is himself probably less an occasion for concern than his popularity, which is not restricted to the Southern part of the country. The problem may well become one of finding something that is *not* grotesque and of deciding what standards we would use in looking.

3   My own feeling is that writers who see by the light of their Christian faith will have, in these times, the sharpest eyes for the grotesque, for the perverse, and for the unacceptable. In some cases, these writers may be unconsciously infected with the Manichean spirit of the times and suffer the much-discussed disjunction between sensibility and belief, but I think that more often the reason for this attention to the perverse is the difference between their beliefs and the beliefs of their audience. Redemption is meaningless unless there is cause for it in the actual life we live, and for the last few centuries there has been operating in our culture the secular belief that there is no such cause.

4   The novelist with Christian concerns will find in modern life distortions which are repugnant to him, and his problem will be to make these appear as distortions to an audience which is used to seeing them as natural; and he may well be forced to take ever more violent means to get his vision across to this hostile audience. When you can assume that your audience holds the same beliefs you do, you can relax a little and use more normal means of talking to it; when you have to assume that it does not, then you have to make your vision apparent by shock— to the hard of hearing you shout, and for the almost-blind you draw large and startling figures.

5   Unless we are willing to accept our artists as they are, the answer to the question, "Who speaks for America today?" will have to be: the advertising agencies. They are entirely capable of showing us our unparalleled prosperity and our almost classless society, and no one has ever accused them of not being affirmative. Where the artist is still trusted, he will not be looked to for assurance. Those who believe that art proceeds from a healthy, and not from a diseased, faculty of the mind will take what he shows them as a revelation, not of what we ought to be but of what we are at a given time and under given circumstances; that is, as a limited revelation but revelation nevertheless.

6   When we talk about the writer's country we are liable to forget that no matter what particular country it is, it is inside as well as outside him. Art requires a delicate adjustment of the outer and inner worlds in such a way that, without changing their nature, they can be seen through each other. To know oneself is to know one's region. It is also to know the world, and it is also, paradoxically, a form of exile from that world. The writer's value is lost, both to himself and to his country, as soon as he ceases to see that country as a part of himself, and to know oneself is, above all, to know what one lacks. It is to measure oneself against Truth, and not the other

way around. The first product of self-knowledge is humility, and this is not a virtue conspicuous in any national character.

7   St. Cyril of Jerusalem, in instructing catechumens, wrote: "The dragon sits by the side of the road, watching those who pass. Beware lest he devour you. We go to the Father of Souls, but it is necessary to pass by the dragon." No matter what form the dragon may take, it is of this mysterious passage past him, or into his jaws, that stories of any depth will always be concerned to tell, and this being the case, it requires considerable courage at any time, in any country, not to turn away from the storyteller.

Questions for Discussion

1. List and explain O'Connor's statements about the **grotesque.**

2. According to O'Connor, what is the duty of the Christian novelist?

3. Explain O'Connor's metaphor of the dragon and the passage.

THE SEARCH FOR REDEMPTION: FLANNERY O'CONNOR'S FICTION[1]
BY FREDERICK J. HOFFMAN

The first impression one has of Flannery O'Connor's work is of its extraordinary lucidity; given, that is, what she expects to communicate, she does communicate it with most remarkable clarity and ease. Of course, one needs to know just what it is; she is concerned with the problem of how a writer, "by indirections, finds directions out." She has a reputation for obscurity, for not giving the expected turn to the reader, for not rewarding him for his having taken the trouble to read her.

The best statement she has given of her purpose and method is a talk she gave at the College of Saint Teresa (Winona, Minnesota) in the fall of 1960. Responding to a critic's suggestion that she is probably not a "Catholic novelist" because she doesn't write on "Catholic subjects," she said:

> The Catholic novelist in the South is forced to follow the spirit into strange places and to recognize it in many forms not totally congenial to him. But the fact that the South is the Bible Belt increases rather than decreases his sympathy for what he sees. His interest will in all likelihood go immediately to those aspects of Southern life where the religious feeling is most intense and where its outward forms are farthest from the Catholic.[2]

Her major subjects are the struggle for redemption, the search for Jesus, and the meaning of "prophecy": all of these in an intensely evangelical Protestant South, where the need for Christ is expressed without shyness

[1]From *The Added Dimension: The Art and Mind of Flannery O'Connor,* ed. Melvin J. Friedman and Lewis A. Lawson (New York: Fordham University Press, 1977), 32–48.
[2]Flannery O'Connor, "The Role of the Catholic Novelist," *Greyfriar* [Siena Studies in Literature], VII (1964), 8.

and where "prophecy" is intimately related to the ways in which men are daily challenged to define themselves.[3] The literary problem raised by this peculiarity of "place" (though it may be located elsewhere as well, as a "need for ceremony," or a desperate desire to "ritualize" life) is neatly described by Miss O'Connor: she must, she says, define in unnaturally emphatic terms what would not otherwise be accepted, or what might be misunderstood. The sentiment (or some emotional reaction) will get in the way. "There is something in us," she said, in the same talk, "as storytellers and as listeners to stories, that demands the redemptive act, that demands that what falls at least be offered the chance to be restored."[4] But the rituals of any church are not comprehended by a large enough majority of readers; therefore,

> When I write a novel in which the central action is a baptism, I know that for the larger percentage of my readers, baptism is a meaningless rite: therefore I have to imbue this action with an awe and terror which will suggest its awful mystery.[5]

Miss O'Connor writes about intensely religious acts and dilemmas in a time when people are much divided on the question of what actually determines a "religious act." Definitions are not easy, and, frequently, what is being done with the utmost seriousness seems terribly naive, or simple-minded, to the reader. She must, therefore, force the statement of it into a pattern of "grotesque" action, which reminds one somewhat of Franz Kafka,[6] at least in its violation of normal expectations.

We have the phenomenon of a Catholic writer describing a Protestant, an evangelical, world, to a group of readers who need to be forced or shocked and/or amused into accepting the validity of religious states. The spirit of evil abounds, and the premonition of disaster is almost invariably confirmed. Partly, this is because the scene is itself grotesquely exaggerated (though eminently plausible at the same time); partly it is because Christian sensibilities have been, not so much blunted as rendered bland

[3]See Sister M. Bernetta Quinn, "View from a Rock: The Fiction of Flannery O'Connor and J. F. Powers," *Critique*, II (Fall, 1958), 19–27: "The center of all Catholic fiction is the Redemption. However mean or miserable or degraded human life may seem to the natural gaze, it must never be forgotten that God considered it valuable enough to send His only Son that He might reclaim it" (21). See *A Handbook of Christian Theology* (New York: Meridian Books, 1958), p. 296: "Thus the God who ransoms, redeems, and delivers Israel out of her bondage is the God who, in Christ, pays the price which restores sinful mankind to freedom and new life. In this act of redemption two interrelated theological emphases are dominant: God's *love* by which He takes the initiative, and man's sin which occasions the situation from which God redeems him."

[4]"The Role of the Catholic Novelist," pp. 10–11.

[5]*Ibid.*, p. 11.

[6]See Melvin J. Friedman, in *Recent American Fiction*, edited by Joseph J. Waldmeir (Boston: Houghton Mifflin, 1963), p. 241. Friedman also cites Nathanael West, as does John Hawkes, "Flannery O'Connor's Devil," *Sewanee Review*, LXX (Summer, 1962), 396. Hawkes mentions an interesting conjunction of influences on himself: "it was Melville's granddaughter [Eleanor Melville Metcalf], a lady I was privileged to know in Cambridge, Massachusetts, who first urged me to read the fiction of Flannery O'Connor, and—further—[. . .] this experience occurred just at the time I had discovered the short novels of Nathanael West."

and over-simple. The contrast of the fumbling grandmother and The Misfit, in Miss O'Connor's most famous story, "A Good Man Is Hard to Find," is a case in point. The grandmother is fully aware of the expected terror, but she cannot react "violently" to it. She must therefore use commonplaces to meet a most uncommon situation:

> "If you would pray," the old lady said, "Jesus would help you."
> "That's right," The Misfit said.
> "Well then, why don't you pray?" she asked trembling with delight suddenly.
> "I don't want no hep," he said. "I'm doing all right by myself."

Another truth about Miss O'Connor's fiction is its preoccupation with the Christ figure, a use of Him that is scarcely equalled by her contemporaries. The Misfit offers an apparently strange but actually a not uncommon observation:

> "Jesus was the only One that ever raised the dead, [. . .] and He shouldn't have done it. He thown everything off balance. If He did what He said, then it's nothing for you to do but thow away everything and follow Him, and if He didn't, then it's nothing for you to do but enjoy the few minutes you got left the best you can—by killing somebody or burning down his house or doing some other meanness to him. No pleasure but meanness," he said and his voice became almost a snarl.

One of Paul Tillich's most effective statements has to do with the relationship of man to Jesus Christ, in volume two of his most impressive *Systematic Theology*. "Jesus Christ," he says, "combines the individual name with the title, 'the Christ,'" and "Jesus as the Christ is both a historical fact and a subject of believing reception."[7] Perhaps more important, and in line with his attempt to review theology in existentialist terms, Tillich says: "Son of God becomes the title of the one in whom the essential unity of God and man has appeared under the conditions of existence. The essentially universal becomes existentially unique."[8]

As all of us know, the crucifixion was historically a defeat for the messianic cause, whose followers wanted Jesus literally to triumph over the Romans and to restore the Jews to power. But it was also, and most importantly, the source of grace; or, as Tillich puts it, "'Christ' became an individual with supernatural powers who, through a voluntary sacrifice, made it possible for God to save those who believe in him."[9] It

---

[7] *Systematic Theology* (Chicago: University of Chicago Press, 1951), vol. II, p. 98. It is interesting that many of Miss O'Connor's characters want to "see a sign": that is, they want Christ's divinity manifested directly. The Misfit is such a one; Hazel Motes of *Wise Blood* struggles against a Christian mission on the grounds that Christ as God has never revealed Himself; Mr. Head and his grandson have a remarkable experience of illumination, when they see the plaster statue of a Negro (in "The Artificial Nigger"); and the young Tarwater of *The Violent Bear It Away* has a "voice" (variously called "stranger," "friend," and "mentor") who tries to deny Jesus because there has been no "sign" of Him.

[8] *Ibid*, p. 110.

[9] *Ibid*, p. 111.

is this latter figure whom Miss O'Connor's heroes spend so much energy and time denying; many of them also are on the way to accepting Him.

In almost all of Miss O'Connor's fiction, the central crisis involves a confrontation with Jesus, "the Christ." In the manner of Southern Protestantism, these encounters are quite colloquial and intimate. The "Jesus" on the lips of her characters is someone who hovers very near; with Him, her personalities frequently carry on a personal dialogue. The belief, or the disbelief, in Him is almost immediate. He is "Jesus" made almost entirely human and often limited in theological function. Man often "takes over" from Him, or threatens to do so. The so-called "grotesques" of Flannery O'Connor's fiction are most frequently individual souls, imbued with religious sentiments of various kinds, functioning in the role of the surrogate Christ or challenging Him to prove Himself. Not only for literary strategy, but because such manifestations *are* surreal, Miss O'Connor makes these acts weird demonstrations of human conduct: "irrational" in the sense of their taking issue with a rational view of events. [. . .]

The figure of Jesus haunts almost all of her characters. They are, half the time, violently opposed to Him (or, in His image, opposed to some elder who has tried to force His necessity upon them), because they cannot see beyond themselves to a transcendent existence. Hazel Motes and Tarwater are both haunted by the rank and stinking corporeality of their elders, whom they have seen dead and—in dream or in reality—been obliged to bury.

These experiences serve to make them resist the compunctions of grace, and turn away from the prospects of redemption. But the alternative is singularly uninviting. Hazel Motes has no success preaching the new church "without Christ," and Tarwater finds his uncle either pathetic or farcical. They react violently at the turn of their journeys: Motes blinds himself in a mixture of the desire for penitence and the will to prove his courage; Tarwater has recourse both to water and fire, from mixed motives of defiance and fear.

This clarity of vision comes in part from Miss O'Connor's having herself had a satisfactory explanation of these religious drives, and therefore being in a position to portray the violent acts of those who possess the drives but are unable to define goals or direct energies toward them. The grotesqueries of her fiction are in effect a consequence of her seeing what she calls "the Manichean spirit of the times," in which the religious metaphors retain their power but cannot be precisely delineated by persons driven by the necessities they see in them. Violence, in this setting, assumes a religious meaning; it is, in effect, the sparks caused by the clash of religious desire and disbelief.

The novelist with Christian concerns will find in modern life distortions which are repugnant to him, and his problem will be to make these appear as distortions to an audience which is used to seeing them as natural; and he may well be forced to take ever more violent means to get his vision across to his hostile audience.[10]

The matter becomes extremely delicate, in the light of her other observations: for example, that "Art requires a delicate adjustment of the outer and inner worlds in such a way that, without changing their nature, they can be seen through each other."[11] This remark suggests that the religious metaphors are, above all, psychological realities; that these are dramatized in the desperate struggles her characters have, at one time against but finally in the mood of accepting the Christian demands and rewards. When Miss O'Connor makes the following summary of her vision, therefore, she is simply defining the ultimate goals of her characters, whether they have been represented or not in the act of achieving them.

> I see from the standpoint of Christian orthodoxy. This means that for me the meaning of life is centered in our Redemption by Christ and that what I see in the world I see in its relation to that. I don't think that this is a position that can be taken halfway or one that is particularly easy in these times to make transparent in fiction.[12]

[10]"The Fiction Writer and His Country," in *The Living Novel, a Symposium,* edited by Granville Hicks (New York: Macmillan, 1957), pp. 162–63.

[11]*Ibid,* p. 163.

[12]*Ibid,* p. 162.

VIOLENCE AND THE GROTESQUE[1]

BY GILBERT H. MULLER

Miss O'Connor's technical strategy in the application of violence is to show precisely how the destructive impulse brings the horror of man's grotesque state home to him. Because this kind of violence is religiously motivated, it differs considerably from those gratuitous forms of violence in fiction which are used to exploit current tastes. The violence in Miss O'Connor's fiction is real, yet it has a metaphysical dimension arising from man's loss of theological identity. If in terms of effect this violence partakes of exaggeration, sensationalism, and shock, it nevertheless raises problems which treat the moral and religious order of the universe. The author was quick to distinguish violence in the pure grotesque from its presence in other adulterated forms. She objected to the attempts of some critics to place her within the School of Southern Degeneracy, and she asserted that every time she was associated with this gothic beast she "felt like Br'er Rabbit stuck on the tarbaby."[2] She was emphatic in denying that she utilized violence as a gothic contrivance, remarking that gothicism was a degeneracy which was rarely recognized as such. Fictional assessment of violence in ethical and theological terms is one quality which sets

[1]From *Nightmares and Visions: Flannery O'Connor and the Catholic Grotesque* (Athens: University of Georgia Press, 1972), pp. 72–98.

[2]"Some Aspects of the Grotesque in Southern Fiction," in *Mystery and Manners,* ed. Sally and Robert Fitzgerald (New York: Farrar, Strauss & Giroux, 1969), p. 38.

the grotesque apart from a gothic aesthetic, since the violence implicit in gothic fiction has little moral foundation: it exists to satisfy itself, and does not serve as a meaningful vision. Conversely, when violence appears in the grotesque, as in the hecatomb which frames "A Good Man is Hard to Find," it is used to suggest the lack of any framework of order in the universe; it reinforces the grotesque by working *against* the ideals of social and moral order to create an alienated perspective.[. . .]

Acts of violence in Miss O'Connor's fiction illuminate a world of continual spiritual warfare. The Misfit in "A Good Man Is Hard to Find" kills people not because he enjoys murder, but because like Meursault in *L'Etranger* he is powerless to control his impulses when faced with the indifference of the universe. His act of violence is not totally irrational because its manifestation points toward the spiritual disorder of the world. The Misfit therefore is not presented merely as a pathological murderer, but as a crazed latter-day anchorite, wielding a gun instead of a gnarled club. Still he is without grace, and he complicates the grotesque situation of the Bailey family as well as of himself by ignoring the cardinal commandment—"Thou shalt not kill." Slaughter is a part of the natural process, and modern war demonstrates that it is a part of the human process as well. Yet from a Catholic perspective the injunction placed upon man not to kill is a radical one—and one which must be obeyed. In human and theological terms to kill is to lapse into evil.

Ultimately violence in Flannery O'Connor's fiction forces the reader to confront the problem of evil and to seek alternatives to it. Because Miss O'Connor uses violence to shock her characters (and readers), it becomes the most singular expression of sin within her grotesque landscape. Time and again in her stories violence intrudes suddenly upon the familiar and seemingly secure world and turns the landscape into a secular hell. Thus the slow pastoral seduction planned by Hulga in "Good Country People" is disrupted by Manley Pointer's outrages against her body and spirit. Similarly Julian's world in "Everything That Rises Must Converge" suddenly becomes chaotic when violence ruins what previously had been an innocuous, albeit distasteful, bus trip. Obviously violence of this type occupies a crucial position in making the world seem strange, terrifying, and deprived of grace. As Frederick J. Hoffman remarks in what is perhaps the finest book on violence in contemporary literature: "Surprise is an indispensable element of the fact of violence in modern life. A carefully plotted pattern of expected events has always been needed to sustain a customary existence. A sudden break in the routine challenges the fullest energy of man's power of adjustment. Suddenness is a quality of violence. It is a sign of force breaking through the design established to contain it."[3] [. . .]

The violent figure frequently becomes an extension of the world which he inhabits. His spiritual desolation is reflected in the very landscape through which he moves, for in this landscape images of violence and disorder prevail. Flannery O'Connor pays strict attention to scene, to landscape

---

[3] *The Mortal No: Death and the Modern Imagination* (Princeton: Princeton Univ. Press, 1964), p. 292.

in disarray, because by being a reflection of the interior self of the character, it assumes a complicity, despite its supposedly inanimate nature, in the bizarre disjunctiveness of the universe. The potentially violent and hostile landscape is a mark of Miss O'Connor's fiction and serves as a vivid image of a worldly Inferno. And of course with the author, a violent landscape is almost by extension a grotesque landscape. In other words the reductive power of violence unleashes essentially grotesque currents of feeling. In "A Good Man Is Hard to Find," for instance, the deranged mind of the Misfit, and the secular impulses of a family preordained to destruction, find an objective correlative in images of a distorted and inimical wasteland. The twisted setting in the story mirrors spiritual and moral decay, and the peaceful rhythms usually associated with a family trip are continually undercut by the images of destruction which are juxtaposed against it. Cotton fields with small islands of graves, the dirt road with "sudden washes in it and sharp curves on dangerous embankments," the line of woods which gapes "like a dark open mouth" create a landscape which is menacing and alien. Even the diner which the family stops at for lunch is a precarious structure, lacking any solidarity or harmony, and is presided over by a sadistic monkey which bites fleas between its teeth with delight. Here, and in other stories such as "A Circle in the Fire" (1954) and "A View of the Woods" (1957), the environment impinges upon characters and is potentially violent: physical description consistently works in opposition to people's desire for harmony and order, and it also affords a premonition of disaster.

Flannery O'Connor's technique of description is terse and severe, tending always toward the impressionistic, in which landscape is distilled into primary images which render a picture of a violent physical world. Miss O'Connor, a watercolorist of considerable talent, concentrates upon line and color to evoke locale swiftly; considering the premium which she placed upon the stark outlines of her fiction, any profusion of description would work against her overall narrative intentions, and thus she relied upon the synthetic method of drawing objects in the physical world together to achieve a concentrated effect. Whether describing the countryside or the metropolis, the author is carefully selective and austere, building up a pattern of imagery and frequently counterpointing these images in order to create a charged atmosphere and to make a thematic statement.

The landscapes depicted in Flannery O'Connor's fiction seem to intensify man's propensity for physical, psychological, and spiritual violence. In a world deprived of meaning, in a world which is ruthless and cruel, the only consolation which her characters have is an ability to exploit others through violence. Arson, rape, mutilation, suicide, and murder are some of the extremes of violent behavior that appear in O'Connor's fiction, and what is curious about these manifestations is that characters such as Rufus, Shiftlet, and the Bible salesman actually take pleasure in wanton acts of destruction. This pleasure in violence, a phenomenon which preoccupies many behavioral scientists and such philosophers as Karl Jaspers, deprives men of being, although the malefactors believe mistakenly that it serves to define their lives. As such, violence becomes a manifestation of the demonic, understood in the medieval sense of the word, as a force which obliterates identity and damns human beings. Even the Misfit, with his debased logic, comprehends a world without meaning, and in such a world, where it is impossible to attach one's loyalties to any overriding ethical or theological position, the only pleasure and consolation for the lack of meaning must come from amoral acts of violence. Unlike the Hemingway protagonist, who attempts to channel violence into such acceptable institutions as war, hunting, and the bullfight, the characters in O'Connor's fiction rarely seek social justification for their destructive acts. If any justification is required, it exists in the universe itself, in a fallen and grotesque world where a perverse Creator forces man to attest to his damnation every moment of his life.

At the root of violence in Miss O'Connor's fiction lies this concept of the depraved and potentially lethal world, in which the destiny of man is seemingly imposed upon him by a vaguely apprehended source. W. M. Frohock in *The Novel of Violence in America* cogently explains the dilemma which faces the violent protagonist: "The hero finds himself in a predicament such that the only possible exit is through infliction of harm on some other human. In the infliction of harm he also finds the way to his own destruction. But still he accepts the way of violence because life, as he sees it, is like that: violence is man's fate." Life—in the existential sense of the word—is like that, even at the most mundane level. [. . .]

The entire strategy of violence in Flannery O'Connor's stories of the grotesque is to reveal how complicity in destruction carries men away from God, away from that center of mystery which she was constantly trying to define and which Catholics term grace. This is why violent death is the one act of paramount importance in O'Connor's fiction: it serves to define evil in society. The feud violence which exists in "Greenleaf," for example, is clearly delineated not only in terms of class hatreds but also in terms of good and evil. The pervasive aura of violence in this story reveals the corruption of the will and the need of grace. This kind of violence is a form of spiritual punishment, and in "Revelation," "The Lame Shall Enter First," and many other of her tales it is admonitory. Mrs. May obviously disdains the low origins and primitive ways of the Greenleafs as well as their newly acquired success. With their fox-colored eyes and dark crafty faces they seem to be cast in the mold of Faulkner's tenacious Snopes clan. Yet the Greenleafs, as their name implies, are in basic harmony with nature. More importantly Mrs. Greenleaf embraces a variety of worship which is reminiscent of early mystery religions based on vegetation and on earth. Her mortification and ecstasy, which are appalling to Mrs. May, are ways of experiencing the spiritual through nature; moreover, Mrs. Greenleaf thinks in terms of a primitive salvation for mankind. Mrs. May's failure to understand the rituals which Mrs. Greenleaf enacts before her eyes signifies the modern failure to integrate religious mystery with culture. It also explains why Mrs. May's destiny of necessity must be violent, because hers is the fate of the individual who is estranged from the basic forces of the community and from grace.

Another indication of evil in "Greenleaf" is the alienation which exists among the members of the May family. Estrangement within the family is of course one of the most common forms of sublimated violence and overt feuding in Flannery O'Connor's fiction. In "Greenleaf" Mrs. May's two sons loathe their mother and hate each other as well. Wesley, the younger of the brothers, bears spiritual kinship to Hulga, Asbury, and other effete intellectuals who are encountered frequently in Miss O'Connor's stories. He is sickly, sardonic, ill-natured, and rude—a vacuous academician consumed by a brutal sense of determinism. Scofield is much coarser than his brother; patterned after Jason Compson, he displays a marked degeneracy in his manners. Both brothers are perversely preoccupied with their mother's death, and this act suggests how individuals can consciously choose to perform or to wish acts of evil. [. . .]

The ultimate battle is against evil—and against the devil incarnated in concrete forms—in the figure of a Bible salesman, an old man with a peppermint cane, or a friendly figure in a panama hat. In this situation violence becomes a mark of faith. As the noted historian Jacques Ellul has written: "The whole meaning of the violence of love is contained in Paul's word that evil is to be overcome with good (Romans 12:17–21). This is a generalization of the Sermon on the Mount. And it is important for us to understand that this sermon shows what the violence of love is. Paul says, 'Do not let yourself be overcome by evil.' This then is the fight—and not only spiritual, for Paul and the whole Bible are very realistic and see that evil is constantly incarnated."[4]

The violence of love is synonymous with faith, and only this sort of violence is effectual in face of the grotesque. Characters like Thomas in "The Comforts of Home" and Hulga in "Good Country People" fail to recognize the true battle. But others accept it reluctantly, undergo violence and suffering, and rage successfully against the absurd. All O'Connor's protagonists are denied basic needs. A few perceive the grotesque nature of the world; they demand recognition of their own worthiness in this world, sense the futility and frustration arising from this need, and consequently embrace what seemingly is the most lucid course of action—violence. In short, whether we are speaking of the Misfit or of Francis Marion Tarwater, this kind of antagonist revolts against an unsatisfactory state of affairs. He indulges in violence because he wants to see if faith can survive. Flannery O'Connor considers all her characters—and the society they compose—as ruled by this harsh geometry of religion. Against the potential framework of religious order she sets violence and disorder, and then she

---

[4]*Violence: Reflections from a Christian Perspective* (New York: Seabury, 1969), pp. 172–73. I am indebted to Mr. Ellul for his concept of love as a spiritual force and also for his cogent explanation of the incarnation of spiritual forms. The latter, of course, is standard Catholic doctrine. Miss O'Connor, for instance, in referring to Christ rather than the devil, states: "Christ didn't redeem us by a direct intellectual act, but became incarnate in human form, and he speaks to us now through the mediation of a visible Church. All this may seem a long way from the subject of fiction, but it is not, for the main concern of the fiction writer is with mystery as it is incarnated in human life" (*Mystery and Manners*, p. 176).

tries to resolve the ambiguity by forcing her characters into those varieties of extreme situation which test the limits of the grotesque.

The extreme situation reveals the paradoxical nature of violence in O'Connor's fiction. Young Bevel's drowning in "The River," for instance, permits him a unique salvation, as does the drowning of Bishop in *The Violent Bear It Away*. Guizac's crucifixion in "The Displaced Person" is also his sacrifice for a depraved culture. The Misfit's murders reveal the horror of a world without Christ. The flagellation of O. E. Parker, the physical assaults of Manley Pointer, the depravities of Rufus Johnson are all examples of violence operating from the shifting and highly ambiguous perspective, for we see in these stories that the infliction of pain and suffering leads to purification and self-knowledge, either for the victimizer or the victim, or for that curious figure, like the Misfit and Shiftlet, Tarwater and Hazel Motes, who is both victim and victimizer, who initiates violence only to discover that it rebounds upon him.[. . .]

Revelation of the true kingdom—or, as Miss O'Connor called it, the true country—is a primary concern in her fiction, and it is for this reason that she utilized motifs of violence to get at the incongruous nature of reality and to reveal the vitality of the grotesque as technique and vision. In a paragraph that has become a classic statement on the value of the grotesque one can see how the concept of violence fits into Flannery O'Connor's vision:

> The novelist with Christian concerns will find in modern life distortions which are repugnant to him, and his problem will be to make these appear as distortions to an audience which is used to seeing them as natural; and he may well be forced to take ever more violent means to get his vision across to this hostile audience. When you assume that your audience holds the same beliefs you do, you can relax a little and use more normal ways of talking to it; when you have to assume that it does not, then you have to make your vision apparent by shock—to the hard of hearing you shout, and for the almost-blind you draw large and startling figures.[5]

The world of the grotesque, whether we are talking about O'Connor and Faulkner, Thomas Pynchon and James Purdy, or Vladimir Nabokov and Jorge Borges, is a world of distortions—in character and landscape and also in spirit. Demonic and violent acts therefore are a means whereby we can fix the precise limits of meaning in this alien and mysterious world. At the same time violence becomes a source of hope whereby man can transcend his grotesque condition. As Miss O'Connor has written in reference to "A Good Man Is Hard to Find":

> We hear many complaints about the prevalence of violence in modern fiction, and it is always assumed that this violence is a bad thing and meant to be an end in itself. With the serious writer, violence is never an end in itself. It is the extreme situation that best reveals what we are essentially, and I believe these are times when writers are most interested in what we are essentially, than in the tenor of our daily lives. Violence is a force which can be used for good or evil, and among the things taken by it is the kingdom

of heaven. But regardless of what can be taken by it, the man in the violent situation reveals those qualities least dispensable in his personality, those qualities which are all he will have to take into eternity with him; and since the characters in this story are all on the verge of eternity, it is appropriate to think of what they take with them.[6]

In the broadest sense, to reflect on the grotesque is to reflect upon violence: essentially the modern condition reveals that violence creates a perilous balance between the horrifying and the ludicrous. Flannery O'Connor knew that the grotesque, by descending into the claustral world of violence, of the incongruous and irrational, contains within itself the germ whereby a transcendent order can be discovered: in an ambiguous world you look for absolutes, and when you face the unknown you invariably recognize spiritual mystery. Violence speaks to us about our experience of such a world by revealing the human need for something beyond a purely secular vision.

[6]Ibid., pp. 113–14.

Understanding Flannery O'Connor: Greenleaf[1]

by Margaret Earley Whitt

"Greenleaf" is the earliest story of the collection [*Everything That Rises Must Converge*] and her first top-award recipient for the O. Henry. It was published first in the summer 1956 issue of the *Kenyon Review,* appearing a year after the publication of *A Good Man Is Hard to Find.* The story was also included in *The Best American Short Stories of 1957.* "Greenleaf" joins three earlier stories in featuring a lone woman who seeks to protect her farm property and to control the people who live on it. Mrs. May has hired some "good country people" to assist in working the land, whose irritating ways irk the stubborn landowner. "Greenleaf" is O'Connor's last story that features a hard-working farm-owning woman who has problems of control with both the hired help and her children. As a transition story, it is the first of four stories that O'Connor writes about a single mother struggling with an adult still-at-home son.

All of the single threads of the story line—Mrs. May's struggling dynamics with her sons, their constant comparisons to the more successful Greenleaf boys, the striking contrast of Mrs. May's and Mrs. Greenleaf's responses to religion—converge in the momentary dilemma of this story: the scrub bull that has come to court Mrs. May and to invade her property and her herd of cows. This bull has connections with the myth in which Zeus disguises himself as a white bull and carries off Europa to Crete,[2] as well as biblical connections to the holy hunt of the unicorn, where the

[1]From *Understanding Flannery O'Connor* (Columbia: University of South Carolina Press, 1995). 121–26.

[2]See John C. Shields, "Flannery O'Connor's 'Greenleaf' and the Myth of Europa and the Bull" *Studies in Short Fiction* 18 (1981): 421–31.

courting animal becomes a symbolic Christ figure that pierces Mrs. May through the heart with a deeper understanding of Christian reality.[3] Before the bull and Mrs. May have a final and fatal meeting, O'Connor makes clear the limited perspective with which Mrs. May views the world.

Mrs. May, "a small woman with pale near-sighted eyes and grey hair that [rises] on top like the crest of some disturbed bird" (503), has sole responsibility for the success of her farm. Her two adult sons—thirty-six-year-old Scofield, the "nigger-insurance salesman" (504), and Wesley, the younger intellectual—have one thing in common, "neither of them care[s] what happen[s] on the place" (504). Both sons verbally abuse their mother at every opportunity. Scofield suggests that she can easily be replaced by some "nice fat farm girl" wife that he will choose upon her death (505). Wesley, who causes her "real anxiety" (509), "wouldn't milk a cow to save [her] soul from hell" (510). As a final blow in this daily barrage, he also strips his mother of parenthood; to Scofield, he taunts: "Neither you nor me is her boy" (517). Mrs. May, on the other hand, remains foremost a Southern mother. She feels a duty to her sons and takes whatever treatment they offer. Although she does not eat breakfast with them, she sits "with them to see that they [have] what they wanted" (504). She makes sure that Wesley maintains his salt-free diet. Mrs. May's downfall, however, is that she constantly reminds her sons how great her own sacrifice has been, and she stands at the ready with plenty of good advice about how they could improve their lives. For example, if Scofield would sell "decent insurance, some *nice* girl would be willing to marry [him]. What nice girl wants to marry a nigger-insurance man?" (505). Mrs. May does not hear her racist comments. Her simplistic worldview extends to every aspect of her life and beyond: "I'll die when I get good and ready" (511).

Mrs. May's relationship with her sons is complicated by the success of her hired people's twin sons, a few years younger than her own. Mr. Greenleaf, her employee for fifteen years, is always quick to point out what his sons would do by comparison. Because of the rigid class structure that so permeated the South of O'Connor's day, the upper-class landowning Mrs. May has to endure the comeuppance from a lower class that refuses to adhere to old rules: "As scrub-human as the Greenleafs were, [Mr. Greenleaf] never hesitated to let her know that in any like circumstance in which his own boys might have been involved—O. T. and E. T. Greenleaf—would have acted to better advantage" (507). Mrs. May is prepared to credit anything outside and beyond the boys with their elevated place in the world: the war that sent them to Europe, where they could "disguise" themselves in uniform (507), court and marry French women who do not realize they are "murder[ing] the king's English" (508), and "manage" to get wounded and receive a pension (508). She takes credit as well for her contribution to their rise and wants to hold it over them

---

[3]See Kristen Meek, "Flannery O'Connor's 'Greenleaf' and the Holy Hunt for the Unicorn" *Flannery O'Connor Bulletin* 19 (1990): 30–37.

when she discovers the scrub bull on her property belongs to O. T. and E. T. She reminds Mr. Greenleaf, with a repetition of the first person possessive pronoun, that his boys "wore my boys' old clothes and played with my boys' old toys and hunted with my boys' old guns"; further, for Mrs. May, those twins had access to "my pond [. . .], my birds [. . .], my stream" (518). Mrs. May is without subtlety or nuance; her only deficiency is that she is a woman: "You can get away with anything when you're dealing with a woman. If there were a man running this place" (519). She tolerates her own sons' fighting: "Nobody feels sorry for a lousy bastard like you" (517), shouts one to the other before the dishes crash, the table is overturned, and the boys are grabbing each other's shirtfronts. Because her own boys fight, Mrs. May is sure the Greenleafs do, but according to their hired help, "they never quarls. [. . .] They like one man in two skins" (516). Mrs. May and her sons are denied the superiority she feels is the privilege of her class.

Mrs. May carries her superficial thinking into matters of religion as well. She has reduced religion to attending church, a "proper" place for her boys to "meet some nice girls" (510). Mrs. Greenleaf, by contrast, takes religion to the "preoccupation" of "prayer healing" (505). By clipping appropriate stories from the paper—rape, burned children, escaped criminals, train wrecks, plane crashes, and movie star divorces—burying them in the ground, and praying over them, she is in direct communication with the healing power of her Jesus: "Oh Jesus, stab me in the heart!" (506). Mrs. May is shocked at her first encounter with Mrs. Greenleaf's ritual, for her Jesus is a practical man. She knows that Jesus would be "*ashamed*" of Mrs. Greenleaf and tell her to "get up from there this instant and go wash [her] children's clothes!" (507). Mrs. Greenleaf, with her backwoods fundamentalist perspective, values the mystery of Jesus as deity, accepting his power to right the wrongs of the day. Mrs. May understands the language of the Christian religion where it fits in society, and how she might work it to her advantage, but "she [does] not, of course, believe any of it [is] true" (506).

Into the melee of these relationships comes the bull, an "uncouth country suitor" (502). The May boys have the advantage over their mother as Scofield knows it is the Greenleaf boys' bull. The Greenleaf boys have no intention of reclaiming the bull and are willing to let Mrs. May assume the responsibility of having their father kill it. As O'Connor closes in on the activity of the killing scene, she advances the bull to symbol. From the opening scene with his Christlike hedge wreath "caught in the tips of his horns" (501), his presumptuous invasion of her property, until the end when he picks up the pace of his wooing, no longer the "patient god" (501), the bull, as an image of Christ, crosses at a "slow gallop" and then, suddenly, is "racing toward her" (523). Until this point in the story, Mrs. May has set her own schedule and controlled her world, but now the bull changes everything. Mrs. May moves from "freezing unbelief" (523), not just her response to the bull's charge but her response to religion's role in her life, to "the look of a person whose sight has been suddenly restored but who finds the light unbearable" (523). O'Connor uses repetition of language and image to draw the parallel between Mrs. May's response to the earlier scene of Mrs. Greenleaf in her prayer healing and the charging bull. With Mrs. Greenleaf, Mrs. May stops still: "The sound was so piercing that she felt as if some violent unleashed force had broken out of the ground and was charging toward her" (506). Facing the bull, Mrs. May remains perfectly still: "She stared at the violent black streak bounding toward her as if she had no sense of distance" until his horn "sank until it pierced her heart" (523). Mrs. Greenleaf's figurative chant for Jesus to stab her in the heart takes on a literal action as the bull stabs Mrs. May through her heart. O'Connor has set up the scene of the "last discovery" of Mrs. May, as she whispers "into the animal's ear" (524), to be the beginning of understanding her own limitations. O'Connor suggests that Mrs. May reaches the Teilhardian Omega Point of God in the "unbearable" light.

Works Cited

Meek, Kristen. "Flannery O'Connor's 'Greenleaf' and the Holy Hunt of the Unicorn." *Flannery O'Connor Bulletin* 19 (1990): 30–37. Makes a biblical connection with the events of the story.

Shields, John C. "Flannery O'Connor's 'Greenleaf' and the Myth of Europa and the Bull." *Studies in Short Fiction* 18 (1981): 421–31. A detailed study of how myth's portrayal of the union of sky and earth informs a reading of this story.

Greenleaf's Destructive Bull and Paean to the Common Man

Quimby Melton IV

1   Beyond a field of common travail lies a structure of human social interaction which divides worker and owner. Though both work the field, though both love and bleed in the common field, one owns and one does not. Taken with the linguistic, financial, familial-historic, and general physical appearances that divide human society, this owner versus worker relationship seems quite unjust. The relationship between the owner/worker and his quasi-serf employee is nowhere better seen than in the rural, post-reconstruction American South. This "rigid class structure that so [permeates] the South of O'Connor's day" (Whitt 1470) serves as a

perfect canvas for the story "Greenleaf," which exists as a song of praise for the worker and the injustice he and his family face from the higher social strata: a stratification upon which O'Connor seemingly frowns throughout the story as she lauds the common man. O'Connor is not content, however, simply to frown upon this injustice; rather, through the use of the bull as both symbolic and manifest character of Greenleaf, she destroys those who would denounce the common man.

2   O'Connor uses the Greenleafs as her embodiment of the common man, i.e., the common laborer. She fixes the social standing of her characters early in the story as Mrs. May is awakened by a bull, crowned by a wreath of greenery, chewing on a bush directly outside her bedroom window. She immediately curses her worker, Mr. Greenleaf, for "[leaving] the lane gate open" (O'Connor 1441) as if all problems on her farm are Mr. Greenleaf's fault. However, directly before this curse, O'Connor has defended the Greenleafs by establishing their safety in the strange dream Mrs. May is having. In this apocalyptic dream, the bull is eating Mrs. May's entire surroundings. Her whole world, as it is in this dream, is in danger of being consumed by this bull. "[E]verything from the beginning of [Mrs. May's] fence line up to the house" has been eaten by the bull; and now, "with the same steady rhythm" (1440-41), the bull is threatening the house, Mrs. May, and her two sons. The bull, a continued symbol of destruction throughout the story, both threatens and threatens to destroy Mrs. May's world much like the Apocalyptic Dragoons of the Christian faith: a faith "she [does] not, of course, believe [. . .] [is] true" (1444). The Greenleafs, symbols of the simple faithful as well as of the common worker, will be safe from the apocalyptic bull's destruction "on a little island all their own in the middle of what [was Mrs. May's] place" (1441). By placing the bull as a

symbol of apocalyptic destruction, O'Connor establishes the saved
and the damned: the "salt-of-the-earth" (Matthew 5:13) Greenleafs
will be saved while the hypocritical and judgmental Mays will be
consumed.

3   O'Connor also praises the simple faith of the common laborer.
The Greenleafs will be saved from the apocalypse because their
earthly religion is a living, active one built on the pillars of prayer,
practice, and faith. Mrs. Greenleaf buries the evil she sees in the
daily paper not to overlook the negativity but to give to God of the
problems of the world. Like Donne's cry, "Batter my heart, three
person'd God," Mrs Greenleaf cries to God to "stab [her] in the heart"
(1444) as she prays over the buried newspaper clippings. Mr.
Greenleaf also shows his religious faith when he softly mentions to
Mrs. May, "I thank Gawd for ever-thang" (1450). The Greenleafs are
not ashamed of their faith and do not believe, as Mrs. May does,
that Jesus, "should be kept inside the church building" (1444). Mrs.
May respects religion but is "shocked at [. . .] Mrs. Greenleaf's
ritual [. . .] and understands [. . .] where [the Christian religion]
fits in society and how she might work it to her advantage" (Whitt
1471); but she does not understand the spiritual fervor of the
Greenleafs. Even O. T. and E. T. Greenleaf's children will be "sent to
a convent school and brought up with manners" (1445) by the
religious faithful. Ironically, through hard work, sacrifice, and the
final honing of religious education, the common worker Greenleafs
will have achieved in two generations the status of "society," which
Mrs. May has lost in one.

4   O'Connor praises the unity of the Greenleafs and uses the
symbols of unity versus disunity to further separate the class of
worker and owner/worker. The Greenleafs are unified as a family
unit. They have peace not strife; Mrs. May notices that "over the
years [the Greenleafs] had been on her place, [they] had aged hardly

at all." The Greenleafs have "no worries, no responsibilities" and live "like the lilies of the field" (1446). The Greenleaf boys, O. T. and E. T., are "fine boys" (1447), according to Mrs. May; according to O. T. and E. T.'s hired hand, they never quarrel as if they are "one man in two skins" (1451). Unity pervades the Greenleafs in religion, brotherhood, and peace. The May boys, however, are "as different . . . as night and day" (1442) and there is constant strife in the May family. The boys fight with their mother and are dissatisfied with life; as a culmination of the strife, Scofield and Wesley physically assault one another at the dinner table. Through the great corpus of evidence O'Connor supplies, it is obvious that the unity and simple wants and needs as well as faith of the Greenleafs afford their happiness. O'Connor praises them for this by showing the alternative to their happiness through the form of the Mays and their disunity and resulting strife.

5   Between the families, there is also strife, not unity. Mrs. May does not like the Greenleafs, and Mr. Greenleaf is quite sardonic in his unspoken way towards his boss. The bull as destroyer furthers the separation of the families. Because of the bull, Mrs. May judges and dislikes the Greenleafs even more, and Mr. Greenleaf further despises his boss. The bull sweeps in and destroys the already fragile relationship that exists between owner/worker and worker, thus pushing reconciliation further from their grasp. The bull also creates the final destruction as he destroys the person and life of Mrs. May. Mrs. May, by the end of the story, has created for herself a grand inferiority to the Greenleafs. She feels she is neither appreciated for her work nor any longer in control of her farm. By commanding the destruction of the bull, Mrs. May feels that she will reassert her authority and destroy the bull before he both symbolically and literally destroys her. Ultimately, the bull is reasserted as destroyer and true authority, for he takes the life of

Mrs. May and teaches her the truth of life and religion. The bull is enrobed in a Christ-like persona as he stabs Mrs. May's heart in a final revelation of Mrs. Greenleaf's prayer. She who supposed she would "die when [she got] good and ready" (1447) is taught a lesson on the fragility of life by a pesky, charging bull with an aversion to automobiles. The light she sees is radiant because of the religious and mortal lessons Mrs. May has learned about truth and the mutability of life.

6   In the final moments of life, Mrs. May realizes the truth and inherent goodness of the Greenleaf way of life. She forgets her petty worries and injuries and, for an instant, is human. In the moment of death, she is neither rich nor poor, neither simple nor educated. Mrs. May transcends the temporal aspects of life and is shown the truth of life: all are human and equally susceptible to death and resurrection. Ultimately both bull and Mrs. May are destroyed by the common man in the form of Mr. Greenleaf in a final cry of victory and praise for the worker over the oppressive elite. Victory, at the end of "Greenleaf," belongs to the Greenleafs: O'Connor's final affirmation of the superiority of the common man.

Works Cited

Henderson, Gloria Mason, Bill Day, and Sandra Stevenson Waller, eds. <u>Literature and Ourselves.</u> 4th ed. New York: Longman, 2003.

O'Connor, Flannery. "Greenleaf." <u>The Complete Stories.</u> New York: The Noonday Press, 1998. 311-34. Henderson, Day, and Waller. 1440-56.

Whitt, Margaret Earley. <u>Understanding Flannery O'Connor.</u> Columbia: University of South Carolina Press, 1995. 121-26. Henderson, Day, and Waller. 1469-72.

Suggestions for Exploration, Research, and Writing

1. In a documented essay, show how the grandmother is responsible for the deaths of her family members in "A Good Man Is Hard to Find."

2. In "Greenleaf," what are some of the things that the bull, appearing at the beginning and the ending of the story, might symbolize?

3. Write an essay comparing Mrs. May's sons with E.T. and O.T.

4. What are the standards Mrs. May uses to classify people?

5. In a character analysis, illustrate how Mrs. May's jealousy, rage, self-pity, and obsession with control define her character.

6. In an essay, discuss the symbolism of the names in the O'Connor stories.

7. Using the critical essays and at least two characters from the O'Connor stories, discuss what the characters substitute for a belief in God.

8. Compare Mrs. May to the grandmother. How might Flannery O'Connor regard them?

9. O'Connor is especially skillful at using irony to portray the problems faced by people who lack a sincere belief in God. Using the critical essays in this casebook and O'Connor's essay, discuss her use of irony in "A Good Man Is Hard to Find" and/or "Greenleaf."

10. Each of the protagonists in the O'Connor stories reaches a point where she realizes her personal inadequacy and helplessness. O'Connor might say that each experiences divine grace. After reading O'Connor's stories and the critical essays in this casebook, write a researched paper analyzing the nature of divine grace as manifested in O'Connor's fiction.

11. O'Connor has a good eye for the humorously grotesque, seemingly irrelevant details that realistically characterize people. Carefully examine her use of such detail in the stories, and explain how her grotesque descriptions of people express her religious vision.

12. His father said of the Misfit, "'It's some that can live their whole life without asking about it, and its others has to know why it is, and this boy is one of the latters.'" Compare this Misfit to one or more other questioning misfits such as Mrs. May or Ozzie Freedman.

13. The Misfit and the bull are violent agents of change in O'Connor's protagonists' lives. Discuss what each appears to represent in O'Connor's Christian vision.

14. What attitudes toward Christianity do the characters exemplify? Which of the characters are most clearly followers of Christ?

Quest: Suggestions for Writing

1. Several characters in this section think they have all the answers they need about the meaning and purpose of their lives. In an essay, show how these characters are made to see that they, like others, are pilgrims or seekers, that their lives must be a continual quest for meaning.

2. Taking into consideration that the goals of the quest can be defined in a number of ways, choose two selections from this unit and show how they define two different aspects of the quest.

3. Using at least two of the works in this unit, discuss one quest or several quests that seem to be universal.

4. The individual's search for his or her own identity is a major theme in literature. Using two stories and/or the play from this section, write a documented essay on this theme.

5. Write an essay on one of the following topics: quests of the modern individual, religion and the quest, my quest, or my search for identity.

Quest: Writing about Film

1. Action-adventure movies are among the most popular for today's audiences. In these movies, often a single character overcomes unbelievable odds to accomplish a task or quest. Compare the characters and events in a popular action-adventure movie to the characters and events in one of the short stories in this unit. How do they differ in their portrayals of quest?

2. *The Lord of the Rings* is a marvelous film about a mythical quest. The heroes of the film—Frodo, Gandalf, and Strider—are based on ancient models; and they differ from contemporary heroes like Neo, Trinity, and Morpheus in *The Matrix*, although both sets of characters face foes of superhuman capabilities. Compare characters from *The Lord of the Rings* with the heroes of a quest film in a modern setting. Consider their emotional ranges, their abilities, the characters' independence or dependence, and their understanding of themselves. If you have read *The Lord of the Rings*, compare one of the characters as portrayed in the books with the same character in the film.

Appendix A

CRITICAL APPROACHES
TO LITERATURE

In the twentieth century, literary theorists have developed a variety of approaches to literature that are more narrowly defined than the three general approaches described in our introduction—text-oriented, author-oriented, and reader-oriented approaches. These critical approaches to literature often overlap and frequently have more than one name. Some of the most important are **formalism (or New Criticism), biographical criticism, historical criticism, sociological criticism, psychological criticism, archetypal (or mythic) criticism, gender criticism, deconstructionist criticism,** and **cultural studies criticism.**

Formalism

Formalism, or **New Criticism,** describes the work of literature as the sum of its parts. **Formalism** developed in part as a reaction to what its proponents saw as an excessive emphasis on autobiographical, historical, and sociological criticism. Formalists reject analysis of a work of literature that is based on whether or not the author achieved his or her goals, labeling this form of analysis the "intentional fallacy" because it is based on what is unknowable and irrelevant. Similarly, they reject reader-response criticism as irrelevant and overly subjective, labeling it the "affective fallacy." Instead, formalism focuses on a close reading, or **explication,** of the literary work itself.

    Formalism also emphasizes an examination of the words and patterns within the work, especially as they are used as **images** and **symbols.** Formalists often examine the ways in which **irony** and **paradox** are used to develop **theme.** For example, a **formalist** approach might consider the ways in which the words, images, symbols, paradoxes, and irony effectively create the tone in Edwin Arlington Robinson's "Richard Cory" or might examine Flannery O'Connor's use of dialogue between the Misfit and the grandmother in "A Good Man Is Hard to Find" to reveal the shallowness of the grandmother's definition of goodness and the emptiness of both characters' lives without divine grace. Furthermore, **formalism** recognizes the differences in **genres** and may examine whether a work fulfills the expectations for its genre.

Biographical Criticism

Other critics examine influences outside the literary works in order to analyze and interpret the works. **Biographical criticism** focuses on how the author's life has influenced the work. Biographical critics believe that a reader who is familiar with details about the author's family, education, career, or religion may know which clues to look for in interpreting a work or may have added insight into the meaning of that work. For example, knowing that Ursula K. Le Guin's father was an anthropologist may aid the reader in understanding the moral implications of the worlds she creates in her novels and in "The Ones Who Walk Away from Omelas." Similarly, knowing about the differences between Alice Walker's background and her mother's life may help the reader to understand how members of the same family can have such differing lifestyles and views of heritage in "Everyday Use."

Historical Criticism

Historical criticism reminds readers that authors are influenced by the cultural milieus in which they live and that their works reflect these milieus. Historical critics contend that the reader who knows details about the specific time, place, and events depicted in a work can read it with greater understanding. For example, a historical critic might examine the history of sharecropping in the post–Civil War South in order to elucidate meaning in Arna Bontemps's "A Summer Tragedy." Historical critics also examine the ways in which interpretations may have changed over the life of the work.

Sociological Criticism

Sociological criticism begins by examining the cultures and beliefs of the time during which a work of literature was created. Believing that art imitates life, sociological critics point out that both the artist and the work of art are directly influenced by the artist's values, belief systems, roles, mores, and demographics. Sociological critics may consider the way in which the work reflects its society. For example, these critics might compare the drug culture as it existed within the musical community in Harlem during the 1930s and 1940s with James Baldwin's description in "Sonny's Blues" or might compare the concept of a "fit mother" in the second half of the twentieth century in the United States with Madison Smartt Bell's portrayal of the mother in "Customs of the Country"—a story that suggests a sociological approach even in its title. Because sociological critics believe that an author's knowledge of and concern for his or her audience invariably affect that author's work, they also assess information about that audience.

One sociological approach, **Marxist criticism,** takes an exclusively political point of view in interpreting literature. Marxist critics believe that every work of literature, whether intentionally or unintentionally, promotes or espouses a political ideology. Thus, a Marxist critic might examine Arna Bontemps's "A Summer Tragedy" to demonstrate the unfortunate consequences of the capitalist exploitation of labor. For the Marxist critic, the ideal work of art will make readers aware of the class struggle so as to encourage them to side with the proletariat.

Psychological Criticism

Psychological criticism is based mainly on the theories of Freud and his followers. Freud himself began the psychological examination into the nature of creativity, describing it as an escape into fantasy that can provide insights for both the author and the reader. Freud's theory that a work of literature is an expression of the author's unconscious desires is the basis for much psychological criticism; a good example is the critical discussion of Charlotte Perkins Gilman's portrayal of a mental breakdown in "The Yellow Wallpaper."

Another psychological approach suggested by Freud's work focuses on using psychoanalytic techniques to interpret fictional characters. For example, a critic interpreting Shakespeare's tragedy *Othello* might use Freud's concept of the id, ego, and superego to explain Iago's vengeful and destructive actions. A psychological critic might study the reasons for the interactions between the migrant workers in Eric Skipper's "The Runt."

Archetypal Criticism

Another approach, which grew partially out of psychological theory, is **archetypal**, or **mythic**, **criticism**. In his theory of the "collective unconscious," Swiss psychologist Carl Jung asserted that all humans unconsciously share in the total experience of the human race. Jung also suggested that this collective unconscious reveals itself in the form of "archetypes," universal symbols or images that occur repeatedly in creative human history. These recurring archetypes often take the form of opposites, such as light and dark or heaven and hell. An example of the light–dark dichotomy is found in the imagery in James Baldwin's "Sonny's Blues." A few archetypal figures include the hero; the villain; the woman as earth mother, platonic ideal, or temptress; and the scapegoat, of which Ursula K. Le Guin's "The Ones Who Walk Away from Omelas" presents an excellent example.

Jung's theory of archetypes reinforces Sir James George Frazer's earlier work, published in *The Golden Bough*, the first anthropological study of myth and ritual. Through his studies, Frazer found that cultures with no common history and no physical contact have similar mythic explanations for their experiences and for the natural phenomena that puzzle them. For example, almost all cultures believe in a destruction myth, the most frequent describing the destruction of humanity by flood. The death–rebirth myth, which follows the cycle of the seasons and the life cycle, is the most universal of archetypes. Other archetypal **motifs** include the quest, the initiation, and the journey. The final thematic section of *Literature and Ourselves* includes examples of the quest. The Jesuit priest in Arthur C. Clarke's "The Star" seeks to reconcile his religious faith with his newly acquired knowledge, and Ozzie in Philip Roth's "The Conversion of the Jews" searches for intelligent answers to his religious questions, not condescension and violence. The initiation rite is illustrated by Miranda's growing awareness of her femininity and her mortality in Katherine Anne Porter's "The Grave." Because the archetypal or mythic approach examines recurring universal figures and motifs, it offers an effective way to compare literature over the centuries.

Gender Criticism

Gender criticism explores the effects of gender roles, attitudes, and dynamics on writers, works, and audiences. Feminist critics in particular believe that literature previously has been written primarily by men for men, and they see one of the roles of their criticism as including women writers and the "woman's point of view." These critics have also focused attention on previously neglected works by women authors, including Zora Neale Hurston and Charlotte Perkins Gilman. Virginia Woolf pointed out difficulties faced by women writers who had not been allowed to reach their creative potential; her essay "Professions for Women" tells of the Victorian woman's struggles with the "Angel in the House." Feminist critics also attempt to expose hidden sexual biases in literary works and to help readers identify and question stereotypes of women. Feminist criticism of Emily Dickinson has revealed previously overlooked meanings in many of the poems. Almost all of the works in the Men and Women thematic unit could be subjects of gender criticism. For example, Kate Chopin's story describes a situation faced by a woman who lives alone in a world dominated by men, and the poems of Edna St. Vincent Millay and Janice Mirikitani illustrate some of the new freedoms of women.

Gender criticism has, however, not been exclusively feminist criticism. In response to feminist criticism, other critics have begun to examine the impact of male authorship, the masculine point of view, and male stereotypes on literature. David Osborne in "Beyond the Cult of Fatherhood" examines the expanding roles of modern men, and Bobbie Ann Mason's "Shiloh" portrays a situation in which the roles of husband and wife seem to be reversed. Gender criticism can shed new light on older works or influence new authors.

Deconstructionist Criticism

Like the formalists, the **deconstructionists** begin with a close reading of the text; however, the deconstructionists believe that textual explication is not enough. These critics believe that accurate readings of a work entail a distrust of both the language and the author. Such a reading may result in a discovery that the work has no organic unity and indeed no distinct boundaries. The deconstructionist critic views the work and the author with great skepticism and unravels the text in order to uncover hidden truths that even the author may not be aware of. For example, a deconstructionist critic might contend that the attitudes of other characters toward Othello reveal a racism beyond that directly stated in Shakespeare's play and perhaps beyond anything that Shakespeare himself had imagined. Deconstructionists attempt to expose the inability of the text to achieve closure or to reveal "objective" truth. In other words, deconstructionists claim that the work cannot validate itself.

Cultural Studies Criticism

Cultural studies applies the methods of literary criticism to previously overlooked or undervalued areas of our common everyday culture. Cultural studies "reads," or critically analyzes, more than just literary texts; cultural studies critics examine both textual and nontextual subjects from beyond the scope of the literary canon. Semiotics (the science of signs) allows cultural critics to "read" common objects as texts in order to investigate the underlying meanings and assumptions that guide our day-to-day existence. For example, wearing blue jeans to the mall is now considered acceptable, whereas wearing blue jeans to church might be seen as disrespectful. Blue jeans still convey some of the rebel reputation they possessed during the 1950s, when blue-jean-wearing teenagers were often viewed as juvenile delinquents. The negative connotations have faded sufficiently so that blue jeans are common casual wear, yet enough of the old interpretation remains that few would find them acceptable in more formal situations. The people frowning at the teenagers wearing blue jeans in church are, in a way, performing a semiotic analysis of their clothing and reading them as disrespectful. Cultural studies critics are interested in how the underlying meanings of common objects and practices are created and conveyed. From fast food to fashion trends, from punk rock to hip-hop, from television commercials to romance novels, cultural studies calls into question the dividing lines between "high" and "low" art and literature while investigating the assumptions that shape our attitudes and behaviors.

When applied to literary texts, cultural studies analysis seeks to clarify the contexts in which any literary work is composed and understood. A critic analyzing Joyce Carol Oates's "Where Are You Going, Where Have You Been?" from a cultural studies perspective might investigate aspects of 1960s youth culture such as rock'n'roll, fashion, and teen slang in order to gain a deeper perspective of the character of Connie. A critic might utilize lyrics from rock songs of the time to illustrate the nature of the "glow of slow pulsed joy" that Connie feels when she listens to the music. Many popular songs of the period resonate with sexual double entendres, and Connie herself is beginning to explore a newfound sexuality as part of her defiance of parental authority. Further, a cultural studies critic might interpret Arnold Friend, with his promise of sexual violence coupled with an awkward use of teen slang and mock-worship of rock'n'roll, as a representation of Connie's own insecurities and fears regarding her disavowal of her family's values and behaviors. In sum, a cultural studies critic is willing to go outside the boundaries of the text in order to explore the contexts in which a literary work is conveyed or portrayed.

Appendix B

WRITING ABOUT FILM:
THE MATRIX AND *THE SCARLET*
LETTER AS CASE STUDIES

BY PATRICK MCCORD

In critical writing about film narratives (movies), we can use most of the same analytic methods we use to write about literature: character, setting, plot, theme, and, although it's trickier, point of view. However, because film is narrated in photographic and sound images and not in words, we need to use different vocabulary and analytic devices for discussing the sound and light information a film presents. Before outlining these techniques, however, we should first briefly examine the principal differences between the way we experience film and literary narrative and how those differences can affect our thinking.

There are five main differences between audiovisual narratives—movies—and literary narratives—novels and short stories. If you think about film and literature, most of these differences are obvious, but because we often *don't* think about how media create images and ideas, we need to bring them to mind.

1. Literary narratives are written in *words* that are, for the most part, *abstract* or *arbitrary* signs that convey *only* symbolic meaning. Films, on the other hand, are recorded or constructed *sound and light images* that convey meaning by *concrete* or *motivated* signs; they are images taken from the real world that *also* have symbolic associations. A *symbol* is a signal that carries connotations.

2. Literary narratives are organized using only *the single information track of language* to signify meaning. Because words are powerful signifiers that carry rich connotations, the single track of writing can stimulate us to imagine whole story-worlds (the fictional world of the narrative). In contrast, audiovisual narratives use *several information tracks* to create actual perceptions that represent the film's story-world. Although our minds tend to unify our experience of the separate tracks just as we unify our sense-perceptions in real life, it will help your critical analysis to sort them out. There are five information tracks in a movie:

   a. the *dialogue track* of the characters speaking the words of the screenplay

   b. the *photography track*, which shows the characters and events (this track may also include special visual effects or computer-generated images)

   c. the *music soundtrack*—any musical score that accompanies the images of action

    d. the *situation soundtrack*—any incidental noises that occur during the action such as a door closing, a car crash, or a pistol shot (these sounds are usually manufactured in a special sound studio)

    e. sometimes, on the photography track, *written words are shown* either in the story or, as in the case of titles or cards, outside the world of the story but commenting on the story

3. In reading and interpreting literary narratives, you must expend your own energy to translate the word-symbols into your own imagined perceptions and concepts that will then make up the story. But films are self-propelled; they unspool before us with the ease of dreaming. And because we enter their story-worlds using the same perceptual abilities we use in daily life, everyone gets the same perceptual story information although—and here's the rub—not everyone will make the same associative meanings out of the image- and sound-symbols.

4. Written stories are ancient forms of communication, while film is comparatively modern. Indeed, the latest methods of film production make even films as recent as the 1980s seem a bit dated, while experimental fictional styles of the 1980s still seem challenging today.

5. Literature is generally the language of a single writer, working with a few friends and editors, but vast teams of artisans are organized by a director and production team in order to record or construct the sounds and images of a film; usually hundreds but sometimes thousands of people work on a single film.

What Do Differences Mean?

We need to recognize that these differences do affect the way we think—or don't think—about the denotations and connotations of film and literature. Here are some of the problems embedded in the different signal systems and their effects on us.

    Because literary narratives *already* make us think abstractly as we translate word-symbols to imaginary images, we have a tendency to consider literature as naturally the more abstract, connotative, and important medium. Because of its symbolic delivery system, literature seems to *require* a certain amount of analytic interpretation. Moreover, because of the use of a single track of words, we may think the author is speaking directly to us as we read. Finally, because literature requires a bit of an effort and is associated with "old" stuff, young people can get impatient with the translating words into imaginary worlds when it's so easy to simply switch on the TV or go to the cinema to see a prefabricated story-world.

    In contrast, because movies are easy and fun to watch, we have a tendency to think that they don't affect our abstract or connotative understanding of the world. Because everyone gets the same information at the same pace in a movie, we may think that the meanings are "obvious" and that there's really nothing to analyze or interpret. Finally, because films seem so contemporary and are often consciously constructed to make money, it's easy to dismiss them as mere "entertainment."

    If you have had any of these considerations, reflect on the following: like movies, most "great literature" was popular and was often profitable "entertainment" when it was written. Even today, millions of "literary" novels are sold every year, and because the books are popular, many are made into movies. Although the words of a story and images of a movie are perceived by different parts of the brain, *when we analyze stories—whether cinematic or literary—we mobilize the same parts of the brain,* so, when it comes to understanding why we have thoughts and feelings about literature and movies, we work with similar mental tools. Yes, words may *seem* more challenging to decipher or interpret, but if you learn to concentrate as if you were reading when watching a movie, you'll discover you can "read" the connotative implications in the images on the silver screen in much the same way as you can a printed page. In fact, this appendix is designed to help you "read" in this way. Finally, just as every word in a short story or novel was carefully chosen by a writer, every image in a film was carefully created by teams of artists and their assistants. Movies have a distinct design; they are not "natural" or accidental creations but fabulously complicated works of art. The best "reading" of a film will account for as many details as possible.

A final point: we think of ourselves, of our lives, in narrative terms—you are the main character in *The Story of [Your Name]'s Life.* It is a fascinating and epic tale with many events, settings, and characters seen from your first-person point of view as well as from a third-person point of view when you recall the past or imagine the future. But stop to consider how you learned to think this way. The ways that we conceptualize our lives as stories are learned from and determined by other stories—models—by which we gauge ourselves, learn appropriate behavior, and derive our values. Therefore, it is important to be conscious of the potential meanings of our "entertainments," whether literary or cinematic, because these stories can profoundly affect our own stories. In fact, sometimes the analytic or interpretive methods we use in analyzing these narratives can be useful in considering our own behaviors as we make decisions about what we want and who we are.

Tools for Film Analysis: "Reading" a Movie

When we *read* a story, we focus on the single information track of the writing: What do the words mean? How are they organized? What do they sound like? What images do they conjure? How do they it work as an artistic system? We need to be able to *perform similar focused operations* with the many tracks of film, but you can see right away that all those information tracks make "reading" a film seem like a confusing project. However, reading a film is easier than it looks if you know how to organize cinematic images into bits of information in the same way you organize your reading of a poem into verses, images, and rhymes.

We can think of how film is "written" in three phases: what the camera does; how the film stock is then edited (cut and spliced together); and how design details—the *mise en scène*—supplied by lights, sets, props, costumes, and actors create meaning.

Camera

Although there may seem to be a lot of terminology to describe camera work and editing, with a very little practice, you'll notice a basic logic to it. In order to better understand it, turn the sound off as you watch a movie or TV. You'll be able to focus better on what the camera, the editors, the actors, and designers are doing, and you'll notice how—in a well-made film—sound usually isn't necessary to tell the story.

Shot, Sequence, Scene

Just as the *word* is the basic element of written language, the *shot* is the basic cinematic element. A shot is just what the camera sees in one "look" or one continuous film exposure. Shots can be quite brief, or they can last a long time. When you examine a shot, notice how all the details of the visual and audio tracks work together to create an image-message; then consider how that shot relates to the movie as a whole. Shots are linked together by *cuts* (so called because the film stock is cut with scissors or a razor and spliced together by editors to make the final version of the movie out of thousands of shots).

The first shot of Neo (Keanu Reeves) in *The Matrix* (Andy and Larry Wachowski, 1999) shows him lying face down by his computer screen, which is showing newspaper articles about Morpheus; this shot then cuts to another angle on Neo and his computer. As we watch, the screen writes out, "Wake up, Neo [. . .]" and in the next shot, he does. Denotatively, the shots simply show us that Neo has fallen asleep at his computer and that it might have a mind of its own; connotatively, however, this first shot sequence sets up the movie's main themes. It foreshadows the basic conflict of the film—man versus computer—and it also suggests that Neo is "asleep" to the workings of the Matrix and that in the course of the movie he will have an "awakening."

Just as words are organized into larger structures like sentences, paragraphs, and scenes or chapters, shots are organized into *sequences* and *scenes*. When you write about film, you will want to refer to specific shots, sequences, or scenes to focus your analytic attention.

A *sequence* is a series of linked shots that show one continuous action or conversation; a *scene*—as it is in drama—is all action at one physical location.

We see two sequences of shots in the first scene at Neo's apartment. One sequence shows him waking up by his computer—an *action sequence*—and the other sequence shows his conversation at the door when he decides—like Alice—to follow the white rabbit—a *dialog sequence*.

Usually, we see just one or two main sequences within a single scene, but sometimes an action sequence will cover several scenic locations.

The first *sequence* in the film follows Trinity from her cell phone conversation in the Heart o' the City Hotel through her fight with the cops. However, this sequence is *cross-cut* with another sequence that shows the arrival of the Agents in the street below and their progress through the building. Eventually, both sequences come together in the chase sequence over the rooftops and to the phone booth; this action covers several scenic locations.

Scenes (and sometimes sequences) are constructed to focus on a few basic narrative events. Generally speaking, we recognize seven kinds of narrative events making up the plot of any narrative. Recognizing the narrative purpose of a particular scene will help you to focus on how the plot works and to make comparisons between texts.

1. Introduction of setting and characters
2. Explanation of state of affairs
3. Initiating event that changes in the state of affairs
4. Emotional response or statement of a goal by the main character in reaction to initiating event
5. Complicating actions
6. Conflict and outcome
7. Reactions to outcome

Depending on the complexity of a plot, you can see that these chains of events repeat themselves in and out of sequence throughout a story, although we'll tend to see more of 1, 2, and 3 in the early going when we need to get *exposition,* or background information, and more of 4, 5, 6, and 7 as we come to know our characters and settings and the action is driving toward conclusion.

You can see how Trinity's and Neo's first scenes at the hotel and apartment are *introducing* us to their characters. When they meet, their scene at the club explains a *state of affairs,* and Neo's scene with his boss at the office continues to explain his state of affairs. However, the delivery of the cell phone is an *initiating event* that changes the state of affairs and gives Neo a chance to make choices. Similarly, at the end of the film, when the Agents capture Morpheus, this scene also acts as an initiating event that causes Neo and Trinity to *respond* by deciding to rescue him. Their shoot out in the lobby begins a series of *complicating actions* leading to the martial arts *conflict* between Neo and Agent Smith. Now, interestingly, the *outcome* of that conflict is that Neo dies; however, Trinity's emotional response then initiates a new change of affairs that sets up Neo's final conflict in which he sees the Matrix and defeats Agent Smith.

Framing

Once you notice shots, sequences, scenes, and events, you need to look for the way the camera *frames* images to create emphasis or stimulate emotional response. As a general rule, important plot information is at the center 40 percent of the frame in a *T*-shaped area called the *T-bar;* however, details outside the *T*-bar often give hints about how we should feel about characters or setting.

Shots frame the action in roughly three distances:

Close-up is usually used to show a face that nearly fills the frame, with the background out of focus. Close-ups create a sense of intimacy or intensity. Sometimes close-ups on an object or gesture focus us on a particular possibility, action, or motif.

Medium shot is a shot of a character or characters from the knees or waist up in a specific setting. Medium shots generally show how characters relate to each other or to a specific context.

Long shot shows the whole character usually doing something, and it emphasizes the character's activity (running, riding a horse, fighting).

We usually also describe a shot by the number of characters in the frame. In the scene where Neo meets Morpheus, we first see a long shot of Morpheus that jump-cuts to a medium close-up that then zooms in to a full close-up; this is followed by a medium two-shot of Neo and Trinity as they walk into a medium three-shot of Neo, Morpheus, and Trinity. When Neo meets the other guerilla-hackers on board the submarine, we see a group long-shot that zooms into a two-shot of Neo and Morpheus.

In addition, we occasionally see three other framing distances that create specific effects.

Extreme close-ups are when a facial or body part or a particular object completely fills the frame. They give a sense of extreme intimacy or urgency, like the extreme close-up of the ringing phone just before Trinity sprints to the phone booth to get taken out of the Matrix.

Extreme long shots show a small character or characters in a larger setting; they tend to emphasize the character's relationship to the larger physical surroundings.

Panoramic shots show vast landscapes and may or may not include characters, but they emphasize the power and/or beauty of the physical setting.

For the most part, a particular shot framing maintains focus on an object in the *T*-bar; however, when a shot moves focus from one part of the frame to another, it is *racking focus.*

In the scene when the cops bust Trinity in the hotel, we see a shot that focuses first on a close-up of a cop's handcuffs in the left *foreground,* which then racks focus to a medium shot of Trinity, hands on her head and apparently defenseless in the right *background.* The effect of the rack focus, however, seems to emphasize and energize Trinity, and it leads into the fight sequence.

Angles

Usually, the camera is situated to make the viewer feel at the same eye level as characters in the frame; however, when the camera is *angled* for a shot, it can have an effect on how we feel.

Angle up: The camera is looking up at a character so that the character seems above us; therefore, we may respect or fear the character.

Angle down: Looking down on a character can imply pity, disdain, or vulnerability.

A *ceiling shot* or *shot from above* is from a very high point above the characters and is often used to suggest that characters believe they are alone, are in an intimate circumstance, or are being threatened.

One of the first shots of Neo is a ceiling shot that shows him asleep and surrounded by electronic clutter; it suggests his loneliness and reliance on gadgets for companionship and entertainment.

A *point-of-view shot* shows us exactly what a character would see; we are seeing (and usually hearing) from the character's point of view. Point-of-view shots are used to get us aligned with a particular character and thereby feeling closer to her/him emotionally; they are sometimes used for humor.

When Neo opens the door on his friends, we see them from his point of view and then see him from theirs. The friends, shown in a group, are well dressed and fashionably late; they appear social and hip. Neo, from their point of view, is peering out from a chained slit and seems isolated and suspicious.

Camera Movement

Within a particular shot, the camera may make several kinds of framing movements to create an effect or render an emotional quality.

A *zoom in* causes the image in frame to grow larger, while a *zoom out* is when the image shrinks.

The first time we see Morpheus, the camera *angles up* on him in a *medium close-up,* making him seem imposing and possibly dangerous. In addition, the lens slowly zooms in on him while we hear a thunderclap on the sound track; this camera work and sound design make him seem impressive and powerful.

When the camera swivels horizontally to follow action, it is *panning;* when the camera moves vertically it is *tilting;* when the camera itself is moving to follow action, it is *tracking,* or *dollying.* When the camera seems to float above ground level, it is usually a *crane shot,* but it may also be a *helicopter shot* if the camera point of view actually flies.

As you learn to notice camera movement, you'll recognize that the effects of certain moves depend, in part, on context.

Editing

The shots that make up a sequence are carefully planned and spliced together so that we don't notice the cutting and experience the film with the seamless continuity of a dream. This method of editing is called *continuity editing*. To disguise their cuts, editors *cut on dialog* or *cut on action*.

Dialog cutting alternates shots from speaker to speaker, pretty much as we would shift our visual focus from speaker to speaker while watching a play.

Action cutting gives emphasis to motions or activities; if a door closes or a character throws a punch, chances are it signals a cut. You can watch Morpheus's and Neo's martial arts sparring scene for the way the cutting emphasizes certain moves. You may have noticed that music videos are often choreographed so that cutting occurs on *both* action of the image track and dialog (the lyrics) of the sound track.

Editors can chose various ways to hide or to emphasize the cuts in order to create different senses of transition or *different relationships between shots*.

Straight cuts—when one shot is joined directly to the next—are the most common method for linking shots.

Match cuts are made to match shapes or movements between shots to suggest continuity or contrast, depending on the images. Watch action sequences for the way that characters' movements—running or fighting—are cut to make a logical flow from shot to shot. In dialog sequences, *eyelines* match from one shot to the next, so the viewer feels a consistent relationship to characters (most of the time, eyes appear at exactly one-quarter of the way down from the top of the frame regardless of close-up, medium, or long).

Cross-cutting is when one scene is cut into another scene that is happening at the same time (see above; the Agents arrive while Trinity is fighting the cops).

Jump cuts break a continuous action into a series of shots. Jump cuts can create a jittery mood or convey a sense of tension or threat. Many of the fight scenes employ jump cuts as well as *slow motion*.

Fade in is when the screen starts black and then lightens to reveal the shot image; a *fade out* goes from the shot to black. Fades are usually at the beginning or end of a scene, and they stretch out time in a way that feels contemplative.

A *lap dissolve* fades out of one shot as the next image fades in. Dissolves are also used to begin or end scenes, and they tend to emphasize the relationship between the two situations or to show the passage of time.

The Matrix begins with a computer-screen sequence that is a clever series of dissolves creating the impression that the viewer is being taken inside the computer screen (much as Alice went through the looking glass).

A *cutaway* is a straight cut or a dissolve that goes from a shot of a character to show what the character is thinking.

A *wipe* is when the image from the next shot seems to wipe the image of the previous shot off the screen. (While there aren't any wipes in *The Matrix*, *Home Improvement* is a television show that often used creative wipes.)

In dialog sequences, the shots alternate between speakers in a *shot/reverse shot* relationship. The scene is shot with the camera positioned just behind the shoulder of one character, then it's reshot from the *reverse position* behind the other conversing character, and then the two shots are cut together with straight cuts. Shot/reverse shot style includes the viewer in the conversation as an intimate eavesdropper.

The length of individual shots within a sequence gives it a *pace*. Dialog scenes tend to have longer shots and therefore a slower pace than action scenes. Sequences are paced to create emotional effects or *tones*.

In the scene when Neo and Trinity meet at the club, their sequence is paced slowly with cuts on dialog to give it a romantic tone as we focus on their body language. When, at the end of the movie, they have the shootout in the lobby on their way to rescue Morpheus, the cutting is rapid, creating a tone of anxiety that adds to a sense of danger and conflict.

Mise en Scène. The Design within the Frame

Once you know how to look for camera work, you are ready to mine the richest vein of cinematic meaning, the details of what the camera sees and how they work with the script to create profound impressions of meaning. *Mise en scène* (French for "staging an action") is the technical term for the way design elements are organized in a particular frame. Why French? Because French critics were the first to regard movies as an art form, and their work is historically basic to how we think about film art. *Mise en scène* includes those design elements that film shares with theater: acting, lighting, setting, costume, and properties (portable items like guns, handbags, laptop computers, and rolling pins).

By noticing the details of *mise en scène*—or you can call it *frame design*—we begin to notice how every detail of a film is chosen for thematic effect. Indeed, most directors plan their shooting by making *storyboards* in the *preproduction* phase, before filming begins. Storyboards are drawings of every shot arranged in comic book fashion to plot out camera work, continuity, possible edits, and the various design elements. Once the director has the boards, he or she meets with the film's design captains to make sure that all the elements will work together to match an overall "vision" of the story-world and that the various fabrications and purchases will be made on time for the shooting schedule. Before shooting can begin, the director or designers make sure that sets and costumes are colored properly; that car crashes and explosion can be safely staged; that supplies, medical personnel, food, and money are available; and that all the elements are constructed so that props, lights, and microphones can be placed properly. Most important, however, is that the director plan every element of the film so that the tiny specifics of design work together to make a consistent artistic statement.

The longest process in preproduction is usually casting. Actors are often selected for their star power, true, but even a star must be believable as a particular kind of character. We may think that people are just who they are, but in fact, people—their appearances and personalities—carry symbolic information. While Keanu Reeves may be denotatively a nice-looking young man, that doesn't give him neutral significance. His image also has many connotative associations attached to it: he is lithe and in good physical condition, possibly an athlete; he is a white-skinned American male and therefore culturally knowledgeable about white American male behaviors; he has appeared as other characters in other movies that audiences will know; and in American culture, he is considered attractive. The Wachowskis considered all of these traits and connotations when they chose Reeves to play Neo. The same is true of all the characters.

Keanu Reeves is a good cast for Neo, not only because he is handsome and athletic but also, as the Oracle (Gloria Foster) says, because he can seem "not too bright." This gives him a childlike quality that is good for an innocent savior figure who is "reborn" twice during the film. Casting Morpheus as a complicated black man (Laurence Fishburne) and completing the central trinity with a tough, smart woman (Carrie-Anne Moss) creates a multicultural, post-feminist power base for the film. Add to this African American Dozer (Anthony Rae Parker); Tank (Marcus Chong), who is African/Asian/Hispanic American; South Asian American Apoch (Julian Arahanga); and Switch (Belinda McClory), who is a pale blonde and possibly lesbian, and you have a range of types that generally imply a cross-section of American culture.

Film acting takes an actor's natural looks and abilities and layers other levels of meaning onto them. Because nothing is random or accidental in a film, when making a critical analysis, consider how an actor's gestures, emotions, costumes, and props have all been designed to create a specific impression of who that character is, what he or she wants or needs, and what strengths or weaknesses he or she may have.

Hugo Weaving has a natural drawl in his voice when he speaks, but in *The Matrix*, as Agent Smith, he chooses to emphasize this tendency to make himself more machinelike.

Lighting is another aspect of the film image that is easy to think is just "natural." Yet lighting can create mood and atmosphere; it can make a character seem beautiful or diseased or indecisive, or when working with other design aspects, it can help create contrasting worlds.

When characters are aboard *The Nebuchadnezzar*—in the real world—they are dressed in tattered clothing, they eat gruel, and the story-world is lit to appear bluish and cool. However, when characters are in the Matrix, they wear designer fashions, carry designer firearms and designer cell phones, and dine on steaks and fine wine—yet here, the story world is lit to appear yellow and warm, although with a noticeable greenish glow. These design elements, heightened by the lighting design, draw our attention to the contrast between the world of the Matrix and reality; and, in the process, they emphasize the theme of values: what is important in life, materialistic illusions or honest realities? Do we want to make our own choices and relationships, or do we want them to be plotted for us by media and advertising interests?

What to Look For in Design Elements

As you consider how *mise en scène* works with the script to create meaning, you will want to ask yourself three key questions to help your analysis:

1. How do details in the frame or in the script contribute to meanings? Neo keeps his contraband software in a hollowed-out book, *Simulacra and Simulations,* by Jean Baudrillard. Baudrillard wrote that simulacra are media-created experiences we mistake for "real." The use of the book serves to underscore the thematic problem of identifying reality, and it suggests that Neo is not only surrounded with computers and technology but also has thought about what it all means and about technology's effects on people.

2. How can various design or script elements be linked to form a system or systems of meaning? In the scene when his friends arrive to buy the software, we notice that Neo's apartment number is 101. This numeral

is not an accident; it signals several associative networks of meaning central to the film's main themes. It refers to the basic binary code used in computer programming and sets up the theme of Human versus Computer. In addition, it connects Neo with the number 1, suggesting to us that he will, eventually, be "the one" who—like the biblical Jesus—saves humanity. Even his name, "Neo," is an anagram of "one." Moreover, "neo" is Latin for "new," suggesting that Neo is the new man, "the one" to save humankind from machine domination. This theme is picked up by the dialog with his friends in the same scene. When Neo hands Choi (Marc Gray) the contraband software, Choi exclaims, "Hallelujah. You're my savior, man. My own personal Jesus Christ!" This scene subtly foreshadows the ending in which Neo dies but is then resurrected via Trinity's kiss, and then he goes on to vanquish the smoothly satanic Agent Smith.

3. How do the elements change over the course of the film? When we first meet Neo, he is a mess; he lives in a sloppy apartment, seems indecisive and confused, wears geeky clothing, works in a sterile office at a job he hates, and doesn't even have a girlfriend. By the end of the film, he is a martial arts master decked out in leather clothing with a similarly attired mate, and he seems to be the master of a complex and visually interesting world. This dramatic change—which is central to the movie's thematic meanings—is created, to a large degree, by acting and design elements.

Writing

When writing about film, you will need to marshal all these skills to make an exact point about the movie you're analyzing. In the sections above, some of the points made might be used in essays with the following theses:

1. *The Matrix* is a high-tech religious story in which Neo appears, very much like Jesus, to save mankind from evil illusions.

2. On the surface, *The Matrix* is a science-fiction action movie, but on a deeper level, it is an inquiry into values as the world becomes increasingly computer- and media-dependent. The film asks these questions: What is real? What is valuable?

3. Neo's adventures in *The Matrix* are much like Alice's in Wonderland and through the looking glass; both characters start out unformed and childish, yet through various strange and challenging experiences they come to a deeper understanding of themselves and the world.

The Scarlet Letter: Thoughts about Film and Literary Adaptation

Many films are adapted from literary works, and there are two ways to think about such films. The first way is to consider the film as a lesser form and, as such, it should slavishly attempt to provide accurate illustrations of the literary work's characters, settings, events, and imagery. This is certainly the viewpoint we usually hear in book-to-movie discussions. But, given that readers' viewpoints generate slightly different imaginings about a written text because words mean slightly different things to different readers and given that a book takes many hours of personal concentration to read while a movie unspools before our eyes in an effortless hundred minutes or so, this critical position seems doomed to a level of dissatisfaction. No matter how good a movie is, it will have to change the plot or leave out scenes or characters. Did you ever meet anyone who had read the book and then seen the movie who liked the movie better?

On the other hand, if you consider that film and literature are different yet *equally important* narrative forms, you may wish to consider that the film is not supposed to be merely an illustration of the reading experience but that it may present *another version* of similar events, characters, and settings that may have contrasting thematic value. This critical approach can free you from rigid expectations or illustrative needs; instead, you can enjoy the inevitable differences between the narratives. Indeed, some of the fun of reading and watching comes from noticing possible differences and considering what purposes they serve; after all, the film makers are narrative artists in their own right: they have made their design choices for a reason. In fact, the literary text and the film text are in a kind of conversation with each other.

Here's a case in point: When Roland Joffe made *The Scarlet Letter* (1995) starring Demi Moore and, as the opening credits warned, "Freely adapted from the novel by Nathaniel Hawthorne," many critics dismissed it as "dumb" because the movie text dared to change the story and even reversed Hawthorne's famous ending in which Hester accepts wearing the scarlet *A* as her role in the village. Because the film narrative violated the events and settings depicted in the Great Novel and possibly because Demi Moore was then the most powerful woman in Hollywood who had, nevertheless, appeared pregnant and nude on the cover of the August 1991 issue of *Vanity Fair,* reviewers accused it of being historically inaccurate and of appropriating Hawthorne for "feminist purposes." Because they were operating out of a sense of prejudice based on the classic novel's supposed superiority to the popular film, these reviewers embarrassed themselves with their misogyny and by making many claims that proved to be simply wrong.

What these critics failed to notice was that their own sense of history was based *not* on actual Puritan history but on what they recalled of the Hawthorne novel, and while Hawthorne was a pretty good amateur historian, his version betrays cultural inaccuracies influenced by his own Victorian morals while the movie's depiction of the Bay Puritans was in many marked ways *more* accurate historically. In this regard, the film, despite its own cultural biases, was able to improve on the novel.

As far as the claim of a feminist hijacking went, these critics again revealed their ignorance because Hawthorne's novel created similar sensation when it was published in 1850. Then, the male critics panned the book the way film critics panned the movie. The Victorians thought the way the novel presented Hester was dangerous, radical, and even "French" because of the way it so directly portrayed a woman's oppression. However, the female readers of the day, recognizing the terrible truth of Hester's story in their own lives, purchased the book in such numbers that it became a fixture of the American literary canon. A more astute viewer sees that the film was simply a continuation of the novel's project to portray a powerful, sensual, and imaginative woman trapped in a grim social context; but, by changing Hawthorne's depressing ending, the film was appealing to a postfeminist twentieth-century

audience in a way that Hawthorne's Victorian audience could never understand. But isn't this still in the spirit of the great book? By choosing to portray Hester in this way, Demi Moore was liberating the literary legend, just as
she portrayed controversial characters that are liberated from conventional
roles in *G.I. Jane* (1997) and *Indecent Proposal* (1993).

Artists who dare to do inventive work often offend established critics. Had
the film critics not been prejudiced by their preconceptions, they would not
have exposed their poor understanding of both American history and the
novel's historical force, and they might have enjoyed a beautifully pho-
tographed, historically grounded, and playfully feminist retelling of Hester
Prynne's story.

Technical Hints for Writing about Film

When writing your essay, the first time you mention a film, name the director and offer the year of release in parentheses after the title; thereafter, when
you want to make a claim about the film, attribute your perception to the film
itself, *not* to the director's intention (unless you have talked to the director
about what was intended). Always refer to the characters by their character
names and, after the first mention, give the actor's name in parentheses (you
may take notes during the credits or find most cast lists on the Internet; a
handy site is <http://us.imdb.com>, the Internet Movie Database).

> Andy and Larry Wachowski's film <u>The Matrix</u> (1999)
> depicts Neo (Keanu Reeves) as a Sci-Fi Jesus-the-Son fig-
> ure in a cyberworld trinity with a God-the-Father figure
> Morpheus (Laurence Fishburne) and a Holy Spirit figure—
> who else?—Trinity (Carrie-Anne Moss).

On your Works Cited page, the following is the correct MLA style for citing
a movie.

Note: you should double-space lines and double-space after every period.
You can usually find the information for the Works Cited entry as well as
many complete screenplays on the Internet.

<u>The Matrix.</u> Dir. Andy and Larry Wachowski. Perf. Keanu Reeves,
Laurence Fishburne, Carrie-Anne Moss, Joe Pantoliano, and
Hugo Weaving. Warner Brothers, 1999.

Appendix C

DOCUMENTING A RESEARCH PAPER: MLA STYLE SHEET

When assigned a research paper, ask your instructor what documentation system you should use in your paper. Several excellent style sheets are available, some designed for particular disciplines. Two of the most often used for papers in the humanities are *The MLA [Modern Language Association] Handbook for Writers of Research Papers* and *The Chicago Manual of Style*. In this text, the *MLA Handbook* will be the basis for documentation in the sample essays. The MLA form is briefly summarized in this section. You might want to consult the *MLA Handbook* for further information and examples.

Documentation of Quotations, Paraphrases, and Summaries

Unless the information is common knowledge, you *must* document any information borrowed from other sources, whether quoted, paraphrased, or summarized. **Paraphrasing** is retelling the original material *in your own words;* if your paraphrase includes any of the original wording, those words must be put in quotation marks. In paraphrasing, be careful not to alter the author's tone or meaning. A paraphrase differs from a summary primarily in length: a paraphrase is about the same length as the original source, but a summary is a concise overview. Because paraphrases and summaries are based on ideas that are not your own, you must document them even though you are not quoting the author directly. Failure to do so is **plagiarism,** the academic equivalent of stealing. Any material quoted must be put in quotation marks and documented. Use quotations judiciously, and avoid back-to-back quotations. Most teachers prefer that no more than one-fifth of your paper be in quotation marks. To prevent your paper from becoming a string of quotations, you should develop the technique of blending paraphrase with short quotations.

Parenthetical Citations

You should always introduce your quotations, making sure that they connect with your sentences grammatically. One method of introducing quotations is simply to mention the speaker or writer:

> Prufrock repeats, "In the room the women come and go / Talking of Michelangelo" (Eliot 35-36).

You may also use a whole sentence followed by a colon to introduce a quotation:

> Munro uses several vivid examples of foreshadowing:
> "Cynthia was somebody dead, and an American, and a girl" (125).

If the material quoted is already in quotation marks, put a single quotation inside the double quotation marks:

> Munro (129) delays revealing Meg's fate: "the lifeguard
> [. . .] was pointing toward the deep end of the pool, saying, 'What's that?'"

As these examples show, the *MLA Handbook* requires parenthetical citation immediately following a quotation, paraphrase, or summary. The citations correspond to titles listed on the Works Cited page at the end of the paper. After a paraphrase, the documentation precedes the punctuation, if any punctuation is appropriate at that point in the sentence. After quotations, the parenthetical documentation usually follows quotation marks and precedes terminal punctuation. If the final punctuation is a question mark or an exclamation point, the parenthetical documentation may be included earlier in the sentence:

> The grandmother (O'Connor 367) asks, "You wouldn't shoot a lady, would you?"

Your parenthetical citation must give the reader (1) enough information to locate the complete bibliographical information on the Works Cited page and (2) the exact page where the cited material appears in the source. If the Works Cited page lists only one source by an author and the author's name has not already been mentioned in the sentence, your citation will consist of the author's last name and the page number. If the author's name has been given in the sentence, you need give only the page number. Notice that no comma appears before the page number. In paraphrases, an effective technique is to introduce the borrowed material with the author's name and to add the page number at the end of the borrowed material. This method lets the reader know exactly where the paraphrase begins. The following examples illustrate correct documentation where a paraphrase or quotation is introduced with the author's name:

> In Gilman's "The Yellow Wallpaper," the narrator implies that, although her husband loves her, he wants to tell her exactly what to do (253).

> Didion says, "Marriage is the classic betrayal" (167).

If the Works Cited page includes two or more works by the same author, your parenthetical citation must include a title. Long titles may be shortened. In the following examples, the full title is "A Good Man Is Hard to Find."

> O'Connor describes the Misfit: "He was an older man than the other two. His hair was just beginning to gray and he wore silver-rimmed spectacles that gave him a scholarly look" ("A Good Man" 146).

> The grandmother says, "If you would pray, [. . .] Jesus would help you" (O'Connor, "A Good Man" 150).

If you want to use information that is already quoted, you should first try to find the original source. If you cannot find the original, however, you may use the material by giving credit to both sources, as in the following example:

> James Russell Lowell decided to omit Thoreau's last sentence in <u>The Maine Woods</u>, which says, "It [the pine tree] is as immortal as I am, and perchance will go to as high a heaven, there to tower above me still" (qtd. in Matthews 251).

The complete bibliographical material on the Works Cited page would be listed under Matthews, not under Thoreau.

If your source has two or three authors, all last names are listed in the parenthetical citation; if there are more than three authors, the first author is listed followed by "et al.," meaning "and others."

> According to the article, "The group has a suspicious history" (McGee et al. 29).

If the source has no author, use its title. Thus, the citation should be as follows: ("Wife Is Not Convicted of Murder" 20).

If the work referred to has more than one volume, the volume number must be included: (Graves 1: 256).

If several works provide the same information that is being paraphrased, the documentation should give credit to all: (Graves 1: 256; Campbell 112; Hamilton 29). If more than three authors give the same information and it is not considered general knowledge, content notes are effective (see below).

Long Quotations and Poetry

If your quotation is long, over four lines, you must indent it on the left. The indentation indicates that the information is quoted. Therefore, quotation marks are not needed unless the material quoted was already in quotation marks, as in the second example below. Note that in an indented quotation final punctuation precedes the parenthetical citation.

> Capote's narrator says,
>
>> This is our last Christmas together.
>>
>> Life separates us. Those who Know Best decide
>> that I belong in a military school. [. . .] I have a new
>> home too. But it doesn't count. Home is where my
>> friend is, and there I never go. (48–49)
>
> Ozzie recounts to his friend Itzie the rabbi's extreme
> reaction:
>
>> "Finally, he starts screaming that I was deliberately
>> simple-minded and a wise guy, and that my mother
>> had to come, and this was the last time. And that
>> I'd never get bar-mitzvahed if he could help it."
>> (Roth 456)

Quotation marks are necessary here because the passage is quoted in the source.

When you are quoting poetry, if you cite one or two lines, include the quotation in the text, using a slash to show where the line ended:

> In "A Prayer for My Daughter," Yeats wishes, "And
> may her bridegroom bring her to a house / Where all's
> accustomed" (74-75).

If you quote more than two lines of poetry, indent the quotation and set the lines as the poet does:

> Yeats prays that his daughter have beauty but know
>
> how to value it:
>
> > May she be granted beauty and yet not
> >
> > Beauty to make a stranger's eye distraught,
> >
> > Or hers before a looking glass. (17-19)

Notice that citations to poetry list line rather than page numbers.

You must reproduce quotations *exactly* unless you indicate that changes have been made. Changes may be indicated by using ellipses or brackets.

If you omit something from a quotation, let the reader know by using ellipses, three spaced dots. If you omit a whole sentence, use four dots (three ellipses and a period). If you omit a line or more of poetry, include an entire line of spaced dots. Most teachers prefer that if you quote only a few words and make them a grammatical part of your sentence, you omit the ellipses. Note that the new MLA form requires that, when you add ellipses, you put them in brackets in order to differentiate them from ellipses included in the original source.

> Greiner describes Frost's "An Old Man's Winter Night" as
>
> "nothing if not a poem of despair, and [. . .] a companion
>
> piece [. . .] to T. S. Eliot's equally fine 'Gerontion'" (231).

> Frost, in his poem "Out, Out—," personifies the saw,
>
> saying,
>
> > [. . .] At the word, the saw,
> >
> > As if to prove saws knew what supper meant,
> >
> > Leaped out at the boy's hand, [. . .]
> >
> > [. . . . . .]
> >
> > Neither refused the meeting. (13-17)

> Gerber believes that Frost's "Home Burial" is "modern
>
> in theme" (229).

Brackets are used to add information inside a quotation for clarification or grammatical correctness or to indicate that the original material contains an error:

> When Kugelmass visits Persky the Great, Persky
>
> "[removes] some old silk handkerchiefs that were lying
>
> on [the cabinet's] top" (Allen 341).

The Latin word *sic* is used to indicate an error in a quotation:

> The reporter accused the senator of "having forgotten
> his principals [sic]" (Johnson A1).

Works Cited Page

On the Works Cited page, list alphabetically *all* sources for your paper.

Books
Basic citations for books include the following information if it is available or applicable: author, title, editor, edition, place, publisher, publication date, and volume. Examples of some book citations follow:

Book with One Author

Keillor, Garrison. <u>Happy to Be Here: Stories and Comic Pieces</u>.
New York: Atheneum, 1982.

Two or More Works by the Same Author

O'Connor, Flannery. <u>The Violent Bear It Away</u>. New York: Farrar,
Straus & Cudahy, 1960.

- - -.<u>Wise Blood</u>. 2nd ed. New York: Farrar, Straus & Cudahy,
1962.

Work with Two Authors or Editors

Andrew, Malcolm, and Ronald Waldron, eds. <u>The Poems of the
Pearl Manuscript: Pearl, Cleanness, Patience, Sir Gawain and
the Green Knight</u>. Berkeley: U of California P, 1979.

Work with More Than Three Authors

Tucker, Susan Martin, et al. <u>Patient Care Standards: Nursing
Process, Diagnosis, and Outcome</u>. 5th ed. St. Louis: Mosby–
Year Book, 1992.

Work with Both Author and Editor

Webster, John. <u>The White Devil</u>. Ed. John Russell Brown. Oxford:
Manchester UP, 1968.

Work with a Translator

Mann, Thomas. The Magic Mountain. Trans. H. T. Lowe-Porter.

New York: Knopf, 1953.

An Introduction or Preface

Woollcott, Alexander. Introduction. The Complete Works of Lewis

Carroll. New York: Modern Library, n.d.

Notice the use of n.d. when the book does not include a publication date.
Similarly, n.p. means no place or no publisher is given in the book.

Article or Story Printed as a Part of a Book

Hemingway, Ernest. "The Snows of Kilimanjaro." The Short Stories

of Ernest Hemingway. New York: Scribner's, 1966. 52-77.

Poem, Story, or Article Reprinted in a Book

Kenny, Maurice. "Wild Strawberry." Dancing Back Strong the

Nation. Fredonia, NY: White Pine Press, 1981. Rpt. in Harper's

Anthology of 20th Century Native American Poetry. Ed. Duane

Niatum. New York: Harper and Row, 1988. 37-38.

Notice that when a work is published or reprinted as a part of a book,
as illustrated in the two entries above, specific pages are given.

Work of Several Volumes

Bullough, Geoffrey, ed. Narrative and Dramatic Sources of

Shakespeare. 8 vols. London: Routledge and Kegan Paul,

1966-1975.

One Volume of a Multiple Volume Set

Bullough, Geoffrey, ed. The Comedies: 1597-1603. London:

Routledge and Kegan Paul, 1968. Vol. 3 of Narrative and

Dramatic Sources of Shakespeare. 8 vols. 1966-1975.

Periodicals

Basic citations for periodicals include the following information: author, article title, periodical name, series number or name, volume number (for a scholarly journal), publication date, and page numbers.

Article in a Scholarly Journal

Licala, Elizabeth. "Charles Clough's Dreampix." Art in America 80

(July 1992): 94-97.

Article from a Monthly Magazine

Barrett, Michael J. "The Case for More School Days." Atlantic

Monthly Nov. 1990: 78, 80-81.

Article in a Weekly Magazine

McCallister, J. F. O. "The Other Player." Time 10 Aug. 1992: 30.

Article from a Journal Found on Microfilm

Marston, Jane. "Epistemology and the Solipsistic Consciousness

in Flannery O'Connor's 'Greenleaf.'" Microfilm. Studies in Short

Fiction 21 (Fall 1984): 375-82.

Newspaper Article

Mydans, Seth. "In an Assault on Tradition, More Schools Last All

Year." New York Times 18 Aug. 1991: A1, A22.

CD-ROM
If you are documenting material that you found in full text form on a CD-ROM, use an entry like the following, taken from the Government Reporter section of SIRS, on your works cited page.

Grant, Agnes, and LaVina Gillespie. "Using Literature by

American Indians and Alaska Natives in Secondary Schools."

ERIC Digest Sept. 1992: n.p. SIRS Government Reporter.

CD-ROM. Social Issues Resources Series. May 1996.

Electronic Sources
A wealth of material is also available on the Internet, from indexes to full text articles, accessible through the World Wide Web. In addition to the materials available through search engines, you may be able to access materials from other libraries such as the Library of Congress or the British Library, from any branch of the federal government, or from current news sources such as CNN. To document sources that have previously been published but that you found through a web source, first follow the directions

for documenting the book or article. Then add the following information, when it is available or pertinent:

1. Name of the database or professional site, underlined, or name of the personal site
2. Name of the editor, if available
3. Version number, if given
4. Date of the posting of the electronic publication
5. Name of the sponsor of the webpage (university or institution, for example)
6. Date on which the material was found during research
7. Electronic address of the source in angle brackets

Scholarly Database

Seamus Heaney. Ed. Paul Jones. April 1997. University

of North Carolina. 29 June 1998 〈http://sunsite.unc.edu/

dykki/poetry/heaney/〉.

Short Work Within a Scholarly Project

Heaney, Seamus. "Bogland." Seamus Heaney. Ed. Paul Jones.

April 1997. University of North Carolina. 29 June 1998

〈http://sunsite.unc.edu/ipa/heaney/bogland.html〉.

Personal or Professional Site

Atwood, Margaret. "Spotty-Handed Villainesses." O. W. Toad, Ltd.,

1994. 12 April 1998 〈http://www.io.org-toadaly/vlness.htm〉.

Nunes, Mark. Online Theory. 29 June 1998 〈http://www.dc.

peachnet.edu/~mnunes/theory.html〉.

Book

Austen, Jane. Pride and Prejudice. cit 1813. Ed. R. W. Chapman.

23 Aug. 1998. Wiretap 〈ftp://wiretap.area.com/Library/

Classic/pride.ja〉.

Article in a Scholarly Journal

Churchill, Mary Faggan. "Alice Walker and Zora Neale Hurston:

The Common Bond." MELUS 22.3 (Fall 1997). 29 June 1998

〈callisto.gsu.edu:4000/QUERY:fel+1:Chkscreen+11:bad+html/〉.

Bilger, Audrey. "Goblin Laughter: Violent Comedy and the

    Condition of Women in Fanney Burney and Jane Austen."

    <u>Women's Studies</u> 24.4 (1995): n.pag. 14 Feb. 1998

    ⟨http://www.cognito.com/0003/articles/00016736/16736229.htm⟩.

Unsigned Article in a Newspaper or on a Newswire

"Pathfinder Mission Reshaped Knowledge About Mars."

    <u>CNNinteractive</u> 29 June 1998. 29 June 1998 ⟨http://cnn.com.

    TECH/space/9806/29/pathfinder.whatwelearned/⟩.

Article in a Magazine

VanBiema, David. "In Search of Moses." <u>Time</u> 14 Dec. 1998.

    16 Dec. 1998. ⟨http://cgi.pathfinder.com/time/magazine/1998/

    dom/981214/cover1.htm⟩.

E-mail (Electronic mail)

Sample, Maxine. "Re: African Writers." E-mail to Sandra Waller.

    1 July 1998.

Other Sources
There are many other sources of information, including computer software, television and radio programs, recordings, performances, works of art, letters, interviews, and films. Consult the *MLA Handbook* for complete details. Representative samples are shown here:

Personal Interview

Lindbergh, Marsha. Personal interview. 25 June 1992.

Film

<u>Bram Stoker's Dracula</u>. Dir. Francis Ford Coppola. Columbia, 1992.

Videotape

<u>Barnburning</u>. Dir. Peter Werner. Prod. Calvin Scaggs. American

    Short Story Series. Videocassette. Monterey Home Video. 1980.

Works from One Book
If you are using several works from one book—for example, if you are writing a documented essay using one of the casebooks in this textbook—you have a

choice of two forms for the Works Cited page. You may give the complete information about the textbook in each entry, or you may include one complete entry for the textbook and list only the editor or editors and page numbers at the end of each additional entry. The first form would look like this:

Works Cited

Melton, Quimby, IV. "Greenleaf's Destructive Bull and Paean to the Common Man." Literature and Ourselves. 4th ed. Ed. Gloria Mason Henderson, Bill Day, and Sandra Stevenson Waller. New York: Longman, 2003. 1472-76.

Muller, Gilbert H. "Violence and the Grotesque." Nightmares and Visions: Flannery O'Conner and the Catholic Grotesque. Athens: U of Georgia P., 1972. Rpt. in Literature and Ourselves. 4th ed. Ed. Gloria Mason Henderson, Bill Day, and Sandra Stevenson Waller. New York: Longman, 2003. 1463-69.

O'Connor, Flannery. "Greenleaf." The Complete Stories. New York: Noonday Press, 1998. 311-34. Rpt. in Literature and Ourselves. 4th ed. Ed. Gloria Mason Henderson, Bill Day, and Sandra Stevenson Waller. New York: Longman, 2003. 1440-56.

The same Works Cited page using the second form would look like this:

Works Cited

Henderson, Gloria Mason, Bill Day, and Sandra Stevenson Waller, eds. Literature and Ourselves. 4th ed. New York: Longman, 2003.

Melton, Quimby, IV. "Greenleaf's Destructive Bull and Paean to the Common Man." Henderson, Day, and Waller. 1472-76.

Muller, Gilbert H. "Violence and the Grotesque." Nightmares and Visions: Flannery O'Conner and the Catholic Grotesque. Athens: U of Georgia P., 1972. Henderson, Day, and Waller. 1463-69.

O'Connor, Flannery. "Greenleaf." The Complete Stories. New York: Noonday Press, 1998. 311-34. Henderson, Day, and Waller. 1440-56.

Content Notes
You may use content notes to add information that you would like the reader
to know but that would interfere with the flow or organization of your paper.
Content notes do not, as a rule, give documentation, but if you are citing so
many sources that listing them in the text would be awkward, you could list
them in content notes instead. Also, if the content note itself includes a quotation, give the citation and list the source in the Works Cited page. Include
the notes on a separate page before the Works Cited page. Indicate notes in
the text with consecutive numbers one-half space above the line, like this:[1]
On the Content Notes page, indent the first line of each note and precede it
with a raised number corresponding to the number in the text.
    Some examples of content notes follow:

Acknowledgments

[1]The author would like to thank Maxine Sample for

lending her essential materials on Alice Walker.

Comparison

[2]Cf. Carlos Baker's comment on Hemingway's return

(121-22).

Note: Baker must be listed on the Works Cited page. (The abbreviation
"cf." means "compare.")

[3]Similar opinions are expressed by Marcus (123-27),

Johnston (14-19), and Wilcox (211-21).

Exceptions to Prevailing Point of View

[4]Wilson disagrees with this interpretation (198-203).

Glossary

Allegory A work in which concrete elements such as characters, objects, or incidents represent abstract qualities. This form of writing is often used to teach religious principles or ethical behavior or to espouse political agendas. Allegories were very popular in the Middle Ages. The play *Everyman* and Dante's *Divine Comedy* are examples. A more modern allegory is George Orwell's *Animal Farm*.

Alliteration Repetition at close intervals of consonant sounds in phrases or lines of poetry: for example, "*b*end / Your force to *b*reake, *b*low, *b*urn, and *m*ake *m*e new."

Allusion An indirect reference to literature, a historical event, a famous person or character, or a work of art.

Anagnorisis In tragedy, the point at which a character reaches recognition, discovery, or self-awareness, the change from ignorance to knowledge.

Analogy Comparison of things otherwise thought to be dissimilar; point-by-point comparison.

Analysis Examination of a subject by separating it or breaking it down into parts.

Anaphora Rhetorical device that repeats a word, phrase, or clause at the beginning of consecutive sentences. For an example, see Elizabeth Barrett Browning's Sonnet 43, lines 7–9.

Antagonist An opposing force or character; that element which opposes or clashes with the main character or protagonist.

Apostrophe An address to a real or fictional person or thing.

Archetypal or **mythic criticism** Criticism that focuses on universal figures, symbols, images, and motifs; similar mythic explanations and experiences are used to compare literature of different eras.

Archetype A prototype (situation, character, or action) or model from which all others or similar types are patterned; anything that appears repeatedly in literature, such as a legend, quest, or situation.

Aside A dramatic device in which a character delivers a short speech or remark to the audience. This remark usually reveals the speaker's emotions or thoughts; the assumption is that no one except the audience can hear the remark.

Assonance Repetition at close intervals of similar vowel sounds in phrases or in lines of poetry: for example, "I love thee to the d*e*pth, and br*ea*dth and height / My soul can r*ea*ch, when f*ee*ling [....]"

Beat movement A movement that climaxed in 1956 in San Francisco and New York City and whose members, disgusted by the crass commercialism of society, dropped out, invented their own vocabulary, and experimented with illegal drugs. Beat movement members included writers such as Jack Kerouac, Lawrence Ferlinghetti, Allen Ginsberg, and Norman Mailer.

Biographical criticism Criticism that focuses on the way in which the author's family life, education, religion, career, and/or nationality influence the work; analyzing beyond the work itself for evidence of personal influences.

Blank verse Unrhymed poetry in iambic pentameter (ten syllables with the stress on every second syllable).

Blocking Grouping and arranging action and characters on stage.

Caesura A natural, strong pause within a line of poetry.

Character A person in a work; the personality traits or qualities of that person.

Characterization Development and presentation of the personality of a character, usually through actions, speech, reputation, appearance, and the author's attitude toward this person.

Classification Organization according to a methodical division into groups or clusters; the system of grouping or arranging.

Cliché Expression, idea, or saying that loses its effectiveness through overuse; a platitude; a trite remark.

Climax The moment of greatest excitement, interest, or tension before the resolution of a play or narrative; a turning point.

Comedy A literary work, usually a play, that ends happily and that often includes humor and laughter.

Complication A plot stage in which a **conflict** appears; a part of the rising action of the narrative.

Conflict The opposition between protagonist and antagonist in a play or narrative; the opposition between the protagonist and another force, either within him- or herself or without, e.g. between the person and the environment, the person and society, or the person and the cosmic.

Connotation Suggestive, implied, or emotional meaning of a word or phrase.

Consonance Repetition of consonant sounds in a line of verse either at the beginning of or within the words.

Couplet A pair of consecutive rhymed lines in verse. A **closed couplet** has two self-contained, rhymed lines that express a complete thought. An **open couplet** contains two rhymed lines that do not form a complete thought. A **heroic couplet** consists of a closed couplet in iambic pentameter.

Crisis A turning point or crucial moment in literature when the protagonist has to make a decision or resolve friction; **crisis** and **climax** may arrive at the same time or at entirely different times.

Cultural studies criticism Criticism that examines both textual and nontextual subjects beyond the scope of the usual literary canon.

Deconstructionist criticism Deconstructionists contend that the author and the text cannot be trusted to reveal objective reality. Therefore, this criticism insists that the work must be completely unraveled through close reading of the text to reveal hidden meanings, or the lack thereof, beyond what the author intended or what the work implies.

Denotation The dictionary, literal, or exact meaning of a word.

Denouement A French term meaning resolution or settlement of loose ends; the untangling of the plot.

Dialect Speech or speech patterns of a particular region, occupational or social group, or culture. Dialect is usually perceived as deviating from "standard" speech.

Dialogue Conversation between at least two characters.

Diction An author's choice and arrangement of words and phrases.

Dramatic foil In drama, a character who sets off or intensifies the qualities of another character through a marked contrast.

Dramatic irony Marked difference in knowledge between the audience and a character in the play. The audience understands the meaning of certain words or events that the character does not understand. The most famous example of **dramatic irony** appears in Sophocles's *Oedipus the King*.

Dramatic monologue Poem spoken by one person but addressed to one or more listeners, revealing the speaker's character.

Dynamic Term used to refer to a character who undergoes a change in personality or behavior by the end of the literary work.

Elegy Lyric poem meditating on or celebrating a death.

Enjambment The running on of one line of poetry to the next line without end punctuation.

Epic A long narrative poem written in a dignified style on a majestic theme, relating the exploits of a national hero.

Epigram A short, witty poem or saying that makes a satirical point.

Epiphany In literature, a sudden manifestation or revelation of meaning; an instinctive perception of reality.

Epistolary Suitable to letters; poetry or fiction composed as a series of letters.

Exposition The beginning or opening of a play or a story; the introduction of characters, conflicts, and other information important to the reader.

Fable A short narrative that usually teaches a moral; a short story with an uplifting message. Fables often use animals to make a point.

Fiction An imaginative narrative such as a short story or novel.

Figure of speech Language not taken literally; image conveyed through nonliteral language, such as with a **metaphor** or **simile.**

First-person point of view Narration using *I* or *we*. See **unreliable narrator.**

Flashback A break in the chronological presentation of a story to return to the past or to an earlier episode.

Flat character A character who is not fully developed; the character is often one-dimensional.

Foil A character who, through sharply defined opposing traits, emphasizes the characteristics of another; a foil is usually a minor character.

Foot In poetry, a unit of stressed and unstressed syllables or heavy and light stresses. The metrical patterns include the following: *Anapest:* two unstressed syllables followed by one stressed syllable. *Dactyl:* a stressed syllable followed by two unstressed syllables. *Iamb:* an unstressed syllable followed by a stressed syllable. *Trochee:* a stressed syllable followed by an unstressed syllable. *Spondee:* two stressed syllables.

Foreshadowing Hints or clues that help to predict a later event.

Formalism or **new criticism** Criticism that repudiates reader response, author's intention, or biographical analysis. Formalism focuses on a close reading of the work with emphasis on how the parts work to create the whole: irony, paradox, theme, images, and symbols.

Gender criticism Literary analysis based on the differences between female and male perspectives in writing and reading literature; this criticism considers gender biases and stereotypes in literary works.

Genre Literary type or kind of literature; the four kinds are fiction, drama, poetry, and nonfiction. Genres can be further subdivided, such as nonfiction into the essay or the autobiography, and fiction into the novel or the short story.

Gothic A literary style using a mysterious environment and mood to set the stage for terror and mystery.

Grotesque A bizarre, distorted, or incongruous approach to a subject, often including violence.

Hamartia The Greek term for the hero's flaw in character or for an error in judgment leading to the hero's downfall.

Historical criticism Criticism that studies the influences of the author's cultural milieu on the work or examines the ways in which interpretations may have changed over the history of the work.

Hyperbole Figurative language that uses exaggeration for effect: for example, "It's raining cats and dogs."

Image, imagery A mental or visual impression that employs an appeal to one of the five senses.

Imagists Poets and other artists belonging to a movement that rebelled against Romanticism in the early 1900s. These artists focused on free verse (unrhymed verse without a metrical pattern) and imagery.

Initiation story A narrative in which a character undergoes some ordeal that leads to maturity.

Irony Contradiction; discrepancy or contrast between what is implied and what is real. **Verbal irony** is the use of words to impart double or opposite meanings. **Situational irony** relates to an event that turns out contrary to what is expected. See also **dramatic irony.**

Lyric A short poem expressing the emotions of the writer or singer. In the past, a **lyric** was usually accompanied by the lyre, a musical instrument.

Marxist criticism See **sociological criticism.**

Metaphor Figure of speech that uses an implied comparison between two distinctly different things; one term is defined in relationship to another term: for example, life is a cabaret.

Metaphysical poets A group of seventeenth-century English poets (especially John Donne and Robert Herrick) whose works are characterized by incredible and subtle imagery.

Meter The rhythm or beat of verse; a measured pattern of stressed and unstressed syllables. See also **foot.**

Metonymy Figurative language that uses a closely associated attribute to represent the thing itself. For example, the White House often symbolizes the president of the United States.

Minimalism The use of as few words as possible to convey meaning accurately; in art, as few strokes as possible; the bare minimum.

Monologue A long speech by a person or character to the audience, to a character not present, or to him- or herself.

Motivation The reason a character behaves, talks, or becomes what he or she is; the driving force or forces behind a character's actions.

Mystery A narrative whose plot involves the solution of a puzzle or crime and usually creates suspense.

Mythic criticism See **archetypal criticism.**

Narration A story, fictional or nonfictional; the process of telling a story.

Narrator The teller of a story or novel.

New criticism See **formalism.**

Nonfiction novel A novel that deals with real rather than fictional characters or situations.

Novel A long fictional prose work with a complex plot.

Objective point of view The simple reporting of observable events; similar to unbiased newspaper reporting.

Octave An eight-line stanza or the first eight lines of a sonnet.

Ode A long lyrical poem addressing or exalting a person or object using a distinguished style and elaborate format.

Omniscient point of view Literally all-knowing point of view whereby the author can recall the thoughts and actions of all characters and can be in several places at one time.

Onomatopoeia The use of words that sound like the actions they name; for example, splash or buzz.

Oxymoron A figure of speech that joins two words with contradictory meaning; for example, a heavy lightness or a thunderous silence.

Parable A short story that illustrates a moral or religious lesson.

Paradox A seemingly contradictory or unbelievable statement that, upon reflection, reveals a truth.

Paraphrase Restatement in the writer's or speaker's own words.

Parody A satirical or humorous imitation of another work; a literary work that imitates the style of another work; ridiculing something through imitation.

Personification Figurative language giving an inanimate object, animal, or abstraction human characteristics; for example, the jungle swallowed him.

Plot The sequence of events in a narrative. Elements of plot include conflict, complication, climax, and resolution.

Poem An arrangement of written or spoken words in lines with or without rhyme or meter and typically using figurative language.

Point of view The perspective from which a story is narrated.

Premise An assertion serving as the basis for an argument.

Props, property Furniture or other movable articles in a play. Props do not include costumes, curtains, or background.

Protagonist The main or central character in fiction or drama.

Psychological criticism Based mainly on the theories of Freud, psychological criticism asserts that a literary work is an expression of the author's unconscious yearnings and that psychoanalytic techniques can be used to interpret fictional characters.

Pun Rhetorical device humorously using a word or words with different meanings but with similar sounds; sometimes referred to as a play on words.

Quatrain A four-line stanza of poetry.

Quintet A five-line stanza of poetry.

Resolution See **denouement.**

Rhetorical question A question that does not require an answer; a question that is asked for effect or to make a point.

Rhyme In poetry, the repetition of sounds at the ends of lines or within lines.

Rhythm Pattern of stressed and unstressed sounds in poetry.

Round character A character who is fully developed; a multidimensional character.

Satire A literary work that ridicules some aspect of society or some human folly or vice.

Satirist A person who writes satires.

Sestet A six-line stanza or the last six lines of a Petrarchan sonnet, which rhyme *cde, cde.*

Set The scenery and properties on the stage.

Setting The time, place, and physical and cultural environment of a story, play, or poem.

Simile Figure of speech that compares two distinctly different things using the words *as* or *like.*

Sociological criticism Criticism that considers the way in which a work reflects society's values, roles, beliefs, mores, and demographics or the way in which a critic can assess information about the audience that the author is writing for. One type of sociological approach is **Marxist criticism,** which maintains that works of literature are politically motivated, whether intentionally or unintentionally, and makes the reader aware of the class struggle through literature.

Soliloquy A stylistic technique in which a character voices thoughts aloud to the audience.

Sonnet A fourteen-line poem in iambic pentameter.

Speaker The person who speaks a poem.

Sprung rhythm A highly irregular metrical pattern developed by English poet Gerard Manley Hopkins. A metrical foot may consist either of a single stressed syllable or of a stressed syllable followed by one or more unstressed syllables; for example, "Oh, morning at the brown brink eastward springs—"

Stage directions Instructions given by the playwright to the stage manager, director, actors, and all others involved in the production of a play.

Static A term used to refer to a stereotypical, simplified character who fails to grow or change in personality or behavior by the end of the work.

Stereotype A fixed or traditional conception of a person, group, or idea held by a number of people without allowing for individuality.

Style The manner in which the author expresses himself or herself. Style includes imagery, symbolism, diction, and sentence structure—the language the author uses.

Symbol An object, person, or action that suggests something else, usually a feeling or abstract quality.

Symbolism The use of symbols in a literary work.

Synaesthesia Concurrent responses to senses; blending of two or more senses, as in "green-black smear of smell" or "a sweet cold silver noise."

Synecdoche A figure of speech in which the whole stands for a part (e.g., army for a soldier) or a part stands for the whole (e.g., wheels for a car).

Syntax Sentence structure and word order; planned arrangement of words to show relationships.

Terza rima A stanza form utilizing three-line units (tercets) with interlocking rhymes; *aba, bcb, cdc, ded,* and so forth.

Theater of the absurd Drama movement of the mid-twentieth century that used absurd, *inconsistent,* often meaningless situations and conversations expressing existentialism or isolation.

Theme Major ideas, moral precepts, or abstract principles underlying a work. The main idea expressed in a work of literature.

Thesis The central idea of an essay, usually expressed in one sentence in the introduction and then developed in the body paragraphs.

Third-person limited Narration of a story in the third person strictly limited to the thoughts and perceptions of a single character.

Tone The attitude of author, speaker, and/or narrator toward the subject or situation of a literary work; for example, ironic, nonchalant, humorous, melancholy, objective, or sarcastic.

Tragedy A play (or other work) showing the protagonist in an internal or external struggle that eventually leads to his downfall or ruin; a work in which the protagonist goes from happiness to misery.

Tragic hero or **heroine** Protagonist in a tragedy who, according to Aristotle, must be basically good but flawed, must be aristocratic, must be believable, and must behave consistently. Modern tragic heroes and heroines do not always fit Aristotle's definition; in particular, they are often working-class people.

Unreliable narrator The teller of a story whose narration is biased or limited.

Villanelle A nineteen-line poem made up of five tercets and one quatrain and rhyming *aba, aba, aba, aba, aba, abaa.* The first line is repeated in lines 6, 12, and 18; the third line is repeated in lines 9, 15, and 19.

Acknowledgments

Men and Women

Essays

Fiction

Poetry

"Two Bodies" by Octavio Paz, from *Selected Poems*, copyright © 1973 by Octavio Paz and Muriel Rukeyser. Reprinted by permission of New Directions Publishing Corp.

"Living in Sin" from *Collected Early Poems: 1950–1970* by Adrienne Rich. Copyright © 1993, 1955 by Adrienne Rich. Used by permission of W.W. Norton & Company, Inc.

"Barbie Doll" from *Circles on the Water* by Marge Piercy. Copyright © 1982 by Marge Piercy. Reprinted by permission of Alfred A. Knopf, a division of Random House, Inc.

"Breaking Tradition" from *Shedding Silence*, copyright © 1987 by Janice Mirikitani. Reprinted by permission of Celestial Arts, P.O. Box 7123, Berkeley, CA 94707.

"Anniversary" from *The Latin Deli: Prose and Poetry* by Judith Ortiz Cofer. Copyright © 1993 by Judith Ortiz Cofer. Reprinted by permission of The University of Georgia Press.

"Courtship" from *Thomas and Beulah* (Carnegie-Mellon University Press, Pittsburgh). Copyright © 1986 by Rita Dove. Reprinted by permission of the author.

"Courtship, Diligence" from *Thomas and Beulah* (Carnegie-Mellon University Press, Pittsburgh). Copyright © 1986 by Rita Dove. Reprinted by permission of the author.

Drama

"A Doll's House," from *Ghosts and Other Plays* by Henrik Ibsen, translated by Michael Meyer. Copyright © 1966 by Michael Meyer. Reprinted by permission of Harold Ober Associates, Incorporated. CAUTION: This play is fully protected in whole, in part, or in any form under the copyright laws of the United States of America, the British Empire including the Dominion of Canada, and all other countries of the Copyright Union, and is subject to royalty. All rights, including motion picture, radio, television, recitation, and public reading, are strictly reserved. For professional and amateur rights all inquiries should be addressed to the Author's Agent: Robert A. Freedman Dramatic Agency Inc., 1501 Broadway, New York, NY 10036.

Casebook on Three Poets: Emily Dickinson, Robert Frost, and Langston Hughes

Emily Dickinson

Poems 106 "The Daisy follows soft the Sun—", 199, "I'm wife—I've finished that—", 284, "The Drop, that wrestles in the Sea—", 339, "I tend my flowers for thee—", and 732 "She rose to His Requirement—dropt" Reprinted by permission of the publishers and the Trustees of Amherst College from *The Poems of Emily Dickinson*, Thomas H. Johnson, ed., Cambridge, Mass.: The Belknap Press of Harvard University Press, Copyright © 1951, 1955, 1979 by the President and Fellows of Harvard College.

"Subverting the Cult of Domesticity: Emily Dickinson's Critique of Women's Work" by Gertrude Reif Hughes. Reprinted from *Legacy*, volume 3, number 1 (spring 1986) by permission of the University of Nebraska Press. Copyright © 1986 by the University of Nebraska Press.

"The Invisible Lady: Emily Dickinson and the Female Experience" by Joanne Dobson. Reprinted from *Legacy*, volume 3, number 1 (spring 1986) by permission of the University of Nebraska Press. Copyright © 1986 by the University of Nebraska Press.

"Writing Doubly: Emily Dickinson and the Female Experience" by Suzanne Juhasz. Reprinted from *Legacy*, volume 3, number 1 (spring 1986) by permission of the University of Nebraska Press. Copyright © 1986 by the University of Nebraska Press.

"Oh, Vision of Language: Dickinson's Poems of Love and Death" by Margaret Homans. Reprinted from *Feminist Critics Read Emily Dickinson* by Suzanne Juhasz. Copyright © 1983 by Indiana University Press.

Robert Frost

"Home Burial" by Robert Frost from *The Poetry of Robert Frost*, edited by Edward Connery Lathem, copyright © 1936, 1956 by Robert Frost, copyright © 1964 by Lesley Frost Ballantine, copyright 1928, 1969 by Henry Holt and Company, Inc. Reprinted by permission of Henry Holt and Company, LLC.

"The Death of the Hired Man" by Robert Frost from *The Poetry of Robert Frost*, edited by Edward Connery Lathem, copyright © 1936, 1956 by Robert Frost, copyright © 1964 by Lesley Frost Ballantine, copyright 1928, 1969 by Henry Holt and Company, Inc. Reprinted by permission of Henry Holt and Company, LLC.

"The Silken Tent" from *The Poetry of Robert Frost* edited by Edward Connery Lathem. Copyright 1942 by Robert Frost, © 1970 by Lesley Frost Ballantine, © 1969 by Henry Holt and Company. Reprinted by permission of Henry Holt and Company, LLC.

"Talking about Poems with Robert Frost" by William G. O'Donnell from *The Massachusetts Review*, copyright © 1998, The Massachusetts Review, Inc.

From *Toward Robert Frost: The Reader and the Poet* by Judith Oster, copyright © 1991. Reprinted by permission of The University of Georgia Press.

Langston Hughes

"Mother to Son," "A Song to a Negro Wash-Woman," "Jazzonia," "The Weary Blues," and "I, Too" from *Collected Poems* by Langston Hughes. Copyright © 1994 by the Estate of Langston Hughes. Reprinted by permission of Alfred A. Knopf, a Division of Random House, Inc.

"The 'Crystal Stair' Within" from *The Art and Imagination of Langston Hughes* by R. Baxter Miller, Copyright © 1989. Reprinted by permission of The University Press of Kentucky.

"Langston Hughes: Poetry, Blues, and Gospel—Somewhere to Stand" by Steven C. Tracy from *Langston Hughes—The Man, His Art, and His Continuing Influence*, edited by C. James Trotman, copyright © 1995. Reprinted by permission of C. James Trotman.

"The Harlem of Langston Hughes' Poetry" by Arthur P. Davis from *Critical Essays on Langston Hughes* by Edward J. Mullen, copyright 1986. Reprinted by permission of The Gale Group.

"Transcendent Women, Earthbound Men" by Brittney Victor. Reprinted by permission of the author.

Grief and Loss

Essays

"Yom Kippur: The Day Without Forgiveness" from *Legends of Our Time* by Elie Wiesel, (New York: Schocken Books, 1982.) Copyright © 1982 by Elie Wiesel. Reprinted by permission of Georges Borchardt, Inc., for the author.

"Heaven and Earth in Jest," from *Pilgrim at Tinker Creek* by Annie Dillard. Copyright © 1974 by Annie Dillard. Reprinted by permission of HarperCollins Publishers.

"The Road to Alexandra" from *Kaffir Boy* by Mark Mathabane. Copyright © 1986 by Mark Mathabane. Reprinted with the permission of Scribner, a division of Simon & Schuster Adult Publishing Group.

Reprinted from Lee Stringer, *Grand Central Winter*, pp. 13–33, 1998. Published by Seven Stories Press by permission of the publisher.

Fiction

"Winter Dreams" from *All the Sad Young Men* by F. Scott Fitzgerald. Reprinted with the permission of Scribner, an imprint of Simon & Schuster Adult Publishing Group.

"The Grave" from *The Leaning Tower and Other Stories*, copyright 1944 and renewed 1972 by Katherine Anne Porter, reprinted by permission of Harcourt, Inc.

"A Rose for Emily from *The Collected Stories of William Faulkner* by William Faulkner. Copyright © 1930 and renewed 1958 by William Faulkner. Reprinted by permission of Random House, Inc.

"A Summer Tragedy," from *The Old South and Other Stories* by Arna Bontemps. Copyright © 1933 by Arna Bontemps, renewed © 1961. Reprinted by permission of Harold Ober Associates Incorporated.

"The Stolen Party" by Liliana Heker from *Other Fires: Short Fiction by Latin American Women* by Albert Manguel. Copyright © 1985 by Alberto Manguel. Reprinted by permission of Clarkson Potter Publishers, a division of Random House, Inc.

"Customs of the Country" © 1988 by Madison Bell, from the collection titled *Barking Man and Other Stories* (Ticknor and Fields, 1990). Used by permission of the Author. First published in Harper's Magazine.

"The Runt" by Eric Skipper from the *Roanoke Review*, Volume XXVI, Number 2, Winter 2001. Reprinted by permission.

Poetry

"In Flanders Fields" by John McCrae from *Welcome to Flanders Fields* by Daniel G. Dancocks, 1988.

"Design" by Robert Frost from *The Poetry of Robert Frost*, edited by Edward Connery Lathem, copyright © 1936, 1956 by Robert Frost, copyright © 1964 by Lesley Frost Ballantine, copyright 1928, 1969 by Henry Holt and Company, Inc. Reprinted by permission of Henry Holt and Company, LLC.

"Once by the Pacific" by Robert Frost from *The Poetry of Robert Frost*, edited by Edward Connery Lathem, copyright © 1936, 1956 by Robert Frost, copyright © 1964 by Lesley Frost Ballantine, copyright 1928, 1969 by Henry Holt and Company, Inc. Reprinted by permission of Henry Holt and Company, LLC.

"Buffalo Bill's Defunct" from *Complete Poems: 1904–1962* by e. e. cummings, edited by George J. Firmage. Copyright 1923, 1951, © 1991 by the Trustees for the e.e. cummings Trust. Copyright © 1976 by George James Firmage. Used by permission of Liveright Publishing Corporation.

"anyone lived in a pretty how town" from *Complete Poems: 1904–1962* by e. e. cummings, edited by George J. Firmage. Copyright 1940, © 1968, 1991 by the Trustees for the e.e. cummings Trust. Copyright © 1976 by George James Firmage. Used by permission of Liveright Publishing Corporation.

"If We Must Die," from *Selected Poems of Claude McKay* (Harcourt Brace, 1981), by Claude McKay. Reprinted by permission of Archives of Claude McKay, Carl Cowl, Administrator.

"Dulce et Decorum Est" by Wilfred Owen. Wilfred Owen: *Collected Poems of Wilfred Owen*. Copyright © 1963 by Chatto & Windus, Ltd. Reprinted by permission of New Directions Publishing Corporation.

"Drama for Winter Night (Fifth Avenue)" from *Collected Poems* by Langston Hughes. Copyright © 1994 by the Estate of Langston Hughes. Reprinted by permission of Alfred A. Knopf, a division of Random House, Inc.

"Incident" from *Color* by Countee Cullen. Copyright © 1925 by Harper & Brothers; copyright renewed 1953 by Ida M. Cullen. Reprinted by permission of GRM Associates, Inc., Agents for the Estate of Ida. M. Cullen.

"Naming of Parts" and "Judging Distances" from *A Map of Verona* by Henry Reed. Reprinted by permission of Oxford University Press.

"Do Not Go Gentle into that Good Night," from *Dylan Thomas: Poems of Dylan Thomas* by Dylan Thomas. Copyright 1945 by The Trustees for the Estate of Dylan Thomas. Reprinted by permission of New Directions Publishing Corporation and David Higham Associates Limited.

"Our Ancestors' Short Lives" from *View With A Grain of Sand*, copyright © 1993 by Wislawa Szymborska, English translation by Stanislaw Baranczak and Clare Cavanagh copyright © 1995 by Harcourt, Inc., reprinted by permission of the publisher.

"The Young Wife" from *The Arkansas Testament* by Derek Walcott. Copyright © 1987 by Derek Walcott. Reprinted by permission of Farrar, Straus and Giroux, LLC.

"University Hospital, Boston" from *American Primitive* by Mary Oliver. Copyright © 1978, 1979, 1980, 1981, 1982, 1983 by Mary Oliver. By permission of Little, Brown and Company (Inc.).

"How to Eat Crow on a Cold Sunday Morning" by Angela de Hoyas from *Woman, Woman*. Copyright © 1985 by Arte Publico Press. Reprinted by permission of Arte Publico Press-University of Houston, 1985.

"Forgetfulness" from *Questions About Angels*, by Billy Collins, © 1991. Reprinted by permission of the University of Pittsburgh Press.

"On the Subway" from *The Gold Cell* by Sharon Olds. Copyright © 1987 by Sharon Olds. Reprinted by permission of Alfred A. Knopf, Inc.

"Pantoun for Chinese Women" by Shirley Geok-lin Lim from *Monsoon History*, Skoob Pacifica, 1994.

"Problems with Hurricanes" by Victor Hernández Cruz from *Rhythm, Content & Flavor*. Copyright © 1989 by Arte Publico Press. Reprinted by permission of Arte Publico Press-University of Houston, 1985.

"Try to Praise the Mutilated World" by Adam Zagajewski. Reprinted by permission of Farrar, Straus and Giroux, LLC.

Drama

"Othello, the Moor of Venice," from *The Complete Works of Shakespeare*, Fourth Edition, edited by David Bevington. Copyright © 1992 by HarperCollins Publishers, Inc. Published by HarperCollins College Publishers.

Casebook on Amy Tan

"Young Girl's Wish" by Amy Tan. Copyright © 1995 by Amy Tan. First appeared in *The New Yorker*.

"Immortal Heart" by Amy Tan. Copyright © 2000/2001 by Amy Tan. First appeared in *The New Yorker*. Reprinted with permission of the author and the Sandra Dijkstra Literary Agency.

"The Hundred Secret Senses" and "Amy Tan and Asian American Literature" from *Amy Tan, A Critical Companion* by E.D. Huntley. Reproduced with permission of Greenwood Publishing Group, Inc., Westport, CT.

"Chinese American Women, Language, and Moving Subjectivity" by Victoria Chen from *Modern Critical Views, Amy Tan*, edited by Harold Bloom.

"Man Must Die" by Gael Fowler. Reprinted by permission of the author.

Freedom and Responsibility

Essays

"The Slave Who Dared to Feel Like a Man" by Harriet Jacobs from *Incidents in the Life of a Slave Girl, Written by Herself*, by Harriet A. Jacobs, with an introduction by Jean Fagan Yellin, pp. 17–26 Cambridge, Mass.: Harvard University Press, Copyright © 1987, 2000 by the President and Fellows of Harvard College.

"Letter from Birmingham City Jail," from *Why We Can't Wait* by Martin Luther King, Jr. Copyright © 1963, 1964 by Martin Luther King, Jr. Reprinted by permission of HarperCollins Publishers.

"The Trial" from *Open Letters, Selected Writings 1965–1990* by Vaclav Havel.

Fiction

"The Man Who Was Almost a Man" from *Eight Men* by Richard Wright. Copyright 1940 © 1961 by Richard Wright. Copyright renewed 1989 by Ellen Wright. Reprinted by permission of HarperCollins Publishers, Inc.

"As Simple As That" from *Holding Wonder* by Zenna Henderson.

"Frustration" from *Gold, The Final Science Fiction Collection* by Isaac Asimov.

"Harrison Bergeron" by Kurt Vonnegut, from *Welcome to the Monkey House* by Kurt Vonnegut, Jr. Copyright © 1961 by Kurt Vonnegut, Jr. Used by permission of Delacorte Press/Seymour Lawrence, a division of Random House, Inc.

"The Ones Who Walk Away From Omelas," from *The Wind's Twelve Quarters* by Ursula K. Le Guin. Copyright © 1973 by Ursula K. Le Guin; first appeared in *New Dimensions 3*. Reprinted by permission of the author and the author's agent, Virginia Kidd.

"A & P" from *Pigeon Feathers and Other Stories* by John Updike. Copyright © 1962 by John Updike. Reprinted by permission of Alfred A. Knopf, a division of Random House, Inc.

Imagination and Discovery

"Introduction to Poetry" and "Poem" from *The Apple that Astonished Paris* by Billy Collins. Copyright 1988 by Billy Collins. Reprinted by permission of The University of Arkansas Press.

"How I Learned English" by Gregory Djanikian from *Falling Deeply Into America*. Copyright © 1989 by Gregory Djanikian. Reprinted by permission of Carnegie Mellon University Press.

"today is a day of great joy" by Victor Hernández Cruz from *Rhythm, Content & Flavor*. Reprinted by permission of Arte Publico Press-University of Houston.

"The Vietnam Wall" by Alberto Rios from *Currents from the Dancing River: Contemporary Latino Fiction, Nonfiction, and Poetry*. Published originally in *The Lime Orchard Woman*. Copyright © 1988 by Alberto Ríos. Reprinted by permission of the author.

"Persimmons" from *Rose, Poems by Li-Young Lee*. Copyright © 1986 by Li-Young Lee. Reprinted by permission of BOA Editions, Ltd.

Drama

"The Tempest" by William Shakespeare from *The Complete Works of Shakespeare*, Fourth Edition, edited by David Bevington. Reprinted by permission of Pearson Education, Inc.

Casebook on Joyce Carol Oates

"Where Are You Going, Where Have You Been?" by Joyce Carol Oates from *The Wheel of Love and Other Stories*. Copyright © 1970 by Joyce Carol Oates. Reprinted by permission of John Hawkins & Associates, Inc.

"Valentine" from *The Collector of Hearts* by Joyce Carol Oates, copyright © 1998 by Joyce Carol Oates. Used by permission of Viking Penguin, a division of Penguin Putnam Inc.

"Don't You Know Who I Am?" The Grotesque in Oates's "Where Are You Going, Where Have You Been?" by Joyce M. Wegs from *Critical Essays on Joyce Carol Oates* by Linda W. Wagner-Martin.

"The Pied Piper of Tucson: He Cruised in a Gold Car, Looking for the Action" by Don Moser from *Life*, March 4, 1966. © 1966 Time Inc. Reprinted by permission.

"O'Connor's Mrs. May and Oates's Connie: An Unlikely Pair of Religious Initiates" by Nancy Bishop Dessommes from *Studies in Short Fiction*, Summer 1994, Vol. 31, Issue 3.

"Escape from Reality?" by Kimberly Prevett. Reprinted by permission of the author.

Quest

Essays

"Loss" from *Beyond Belief: Islamic Excursions Among the Converted Peoples* by V.S. Naipaul.

From *A Brief History of Time* by Stephen W. Hawking. Copyright © 1988 by Stephen W. Hawking. Interior illustrations copyright © 1988 by Ron Miller. Used by permission of Bantam Books, a division of Random House, Inc.

Abridgment of "I Just Wanna Be Average" from *Lives on the Boundary: The Struggles and Achievements of America's Underprepared* by Mike Rose. Copyright © 1989 by Mike Rose. Reprinted with the permission of The Free Press, a division of Simon & Schuster Adult Publishing Group.

Fiction

"Araby" from *Dubliners* by James Joyce, copyright 1916 by B.W. Heubsch. Definitive text copyright © 1967 by the Estate of James Joyce. Used by permission of Viking Penguin, a division of Penguin Putnam Inc.

"Angel Levine" from *The Magic Barrel* by Bernard Malamud. Copyright © 1950, 1958, renewed 1977, 1986 by Bernard Malamud. Reprinted by permission of Farrar, Straus and Giroux, LLC.

Poetry

Drama

Casebook on Flannery O'Connor

"The Search for Redemption: Flannery O'Connor's Fiction" by Frederick J. Hoffman from *The Added Dimension: The Art and Mind of Flannery O'Connor*, ed. Melvin J. Friedman and Lewis A. Lawson (New York: Fordham University Press, 1966), pages 32–36 and 45–46. Copyright © 1966, 2977 by Fordham University Press. Reprinted by permission of the publisher.

"Violence and the Grotesque" by Gilbert H. Muller from *Nightmares and Visions: Flannery O'Connor and the Catholic Grotesque* by Gilbert H. Muller. Copyright © 1972 by the University of Georgia Press. Reprinted by permission of the University of Georgia Press.

From *Understanding Flannery O'Connor*, by Margaret Earley Whitt, copyright © 1995. Reprinted by permission of the University of South Carolina Press.

"Greenleaf's Destructive Bull and Paean to the Common Man" by Quimby Melton IV. Reprinted by permission of the author.

Photo Credits

Page 168: AP/Wide World Photos

Page 252: © Art Resource, NY

Page 425: © Topham/The Image Works

Page 444: Howard Sochurek/TimePix

Page 470: Robert Kelley/ TimePix

Page 496: © Francis G. Mayer/CORBIS

Page 752: © Topham/The Image Works

Page 816: © Scala/Art Resource, NY

Page 962: © Miriam Berkley Photography

Page 1024: © The Museum of Modern Art/Licensed by SCALA/Art Resource, NY

Page 1223: AP/Wide World Photos

Page 1278: © Smithsonian American Art Museum, Washington DC/Art Resource, NY

Page 1427: © Joe McTyre Photography

Index